Encyclopedia of American Communes, 1663–1963

Encyclopedia of
American
Communes,
1663–1963

Foster Stockwell

McFarland & Company, Inc., Publishers
Jefferson, North Carolina, and London

British Library Cataloguing-in-Publication data are available

Library of Congress Cataloguing-in-Publication Data

Stockwell, Foster.
    Encyclopedia of American communes, 1663–1963 / Foster
Stockwell.
      p. cm.
    Includes bibliographical references and index.
    ISBN 0-7864-0455-8 (library binding : 50# acid-free paper)∞
    1. Collective settlements — United States — Encyclopedias.
I. Title.
HX653.S65   1998
335'.973'03 — dc21   97-44083
                                                  CIP

Manufactured in the United States of America

McFarland & Company, Inc., Publishers
  Box 611, Jefferson, North Carolina 28640

Contents

About the Encyclopedia

This encyclopedia is arranged alphabetically by commune name. Those who would like to follow the pattern of commune building in a chronological fashion should look at the listing of all the communes by date order in Appendix 1.

For many of the entries there is at least one bibliographical reference to point an interested reader toward a more extensive source of information. The full citation for each of these references can be found in the bibliography at the end of this book. Also recommended, for those who wish to push further, is the bibliography of American communes compiled by Timothy Miller (see bibliography). That book does not cover all of the 516 communes listed herein, but it provides an exhaustive list of citations for the ones it does include.

In many of the entries in this book there are names of other communes listed in bold type. It is suggested that the reader turn to entries so marked for further information about the aims of the particular type of commune or because the entry being pointed to may contain bibliographical information not included with the first entry so as to avoid duplication.

Introduction

Most experimental communities were known as "communist and socialist settlements" before 1840. By 1860, the designation had changed to "communitarian," and around 1920, "intentional community" came into vogue. But since 1960, all such attempts at forming models to effect change have been known as "communes." Of course, other names have been used — cooperatives, affinity groups, expanded families, experimental communities, utopian experiments, collectives, or just colonies. But whatever such experiments were called, they all were in the utopian tradition that has ever been part of the American heritage.

Utopianism is imbedded in the American dream of the "land of opportunity," in concepts of the "New World experiment," and in what Marxists criticize as "American exceptionalism." And it is in the United States that most of the world's communes have been established, even though men and women for thousands of years have made plans for utopias. An American continent filled with comparatively inexpensive and unspoiled land encouraged such social experimentation. Communitarians who failed in one place could usually find land and opportunity elsewhere. The frontier beckoned to them and strengthened their illusions about the feasibility of their projects.

It was a communitarian view that was expressed by President James Madison in 1834 to the English visitor Harriet Martineau when he said that the American Republic is "useful in proving things before held impossible." And it was again a communitarian view that President Franklin D. Roosevelt expressed a century later in speaking with his secretary of labor, Frances Perkins. Roosevelt told her that "The beauty of our state-federal system is that people can experiment. If it has fatal consequences in one place, it has little effect upon the rest of the country. If a new, apparently fanatical, program works well, it will be copied. If it doesn't, you won't hear of it again."

This desire to experiment by setting up a communal venture is founded

3

on the ideal of societal perfection, and for that reason, communes are much more than just the dreamy schemes of a handful of society dropouts. Illusive as that ideal may be, utopianism has ever been a potential force in the civilizing process. Utopianism motivates ethical understandings. It presents models for social planning. It gives hope for renewed life — a more just and fulfilled life — even though utopia is forever becoming and can never be an accomplished fact.

A basic belief in the establishment of all communal experiments is that it is possible to reshape the future by deliberately laying foundations in the present. The proponent establishes a new community as a lever to pry society loose from its ancient abuses. He or she imagines the growth of a new society through the continual reduplication of the successful elements of the experimental community. For the most part, the proponent worries little about whether political and economic forces at work in established society will permit such contemplated changes. All that the communitarian considers necessary is to present a plan for social salvation, begin to experiment with it on a small scale, interest the general public in its development, and then watch it grow among the population.

516 Communal Experiments

If we take the period of three hundred years starting from 1663 with America's first commune (Swanendael) and ending in 1963 with the founding of the anarchist Tolstoy Farm, we count a total of 516 different communal experiments. The year 1963 is a good place to stop because shortly thereafter came the period of lifestyle experimentation in the mid and late 1960s that produced hundreds of attempts at communal living each year. Some of the earliest communes still exist; others have left interesting remnants for the curious investigator. The records of still others can be found only in old books, magazines, and newspapers.

Since 1684, when the Labidists set up the Bohemia Manor commune in Maryland, there has been at least one active communal experiment functioning at all times in the United States. We are speaking here only of communal settlements founded by groups of people who were attempting to establish a new social pattern based on a vision of an ideal society, people who withdrew from the community at large to embody that vision in an experiment form. We are not including experiments that through cooperative effort sought to transform society without withdrawing from it: consumers' and self-help cooperatives, factory profit-sharing leagues, and urban cooperative housing projects. Also excluded are those groups that withdrew from society for religious, health, or psychological reasons, but reduplicated the economic patterns of existing society, such as Amish villages and ethnic enclaves.

Figure 1. Religious vs. Secular Purposes Among the 516 American Communes

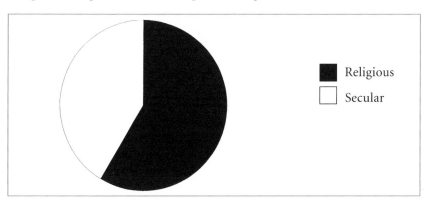

Furthermore, projects that were organized in North America for emigration elsewhere, such as Kerista, which finally settled in South America, and the Zionist training camps that sent people to Israel, are omitted from this list, as are enterprises that were projected with much fanfare but never actually began. The most famous of those were a planned colony named "Paradise," sponsored by Gustav Priber about 1736, and the so-called "Pantisocracy" in America that writers Samuel Taylor Coleridge, Robert Southy, and others worked on in 1794.

Many of the 516 communes described in this book lasted no more than a year or two. Yet the general impression that all communes are basically unstable and can survive but a few months is belied by statistics. Harmony, near Pittsburgh, lasted a hundred years, from the time of the Louisiana Purchase to the launching of the first airplane by the Wright brothers at Kitty Hawk. Ephrata in Philadelphia, formed a year before Benjamin Franklin published his first edition of the *Poor Richard's Almanac*, lasted 202 years. And the Shaker colony at Sabathday Lake, Maine, still today has a handful of members. It was established when the city of Chicago was just a trading post and fort surrounded by Indians.

The records show that these 516 communes were started in every part of the United States: from Mist, Oregon, to Estero, Florida; from Gorham, Maine, to San Diego, California; and even in Wilcox County, Alaska. They were set up, in fact, in every state except Hawaii, Idaho, Oklahoma, Rhode Island, and Wyoming. And the recent burst of communal activity has filled even these five gaps.

Not only were communes started everywhere, but their history reflects the historical movement of the country as a whole. Every major social movement that affected the lives of most Americans also rocked the communes. Each religious revival, for example, produced new members for the many communitarian experiments, despite the fact that most of these revivals

Figure 2. Number of American Communes
Functioning Within 20-Year Time Periods

Period	Number of Communes
1951-1963	████████████████████████ (~120)
1931-1950	█████████████████████████ (~122)
1911-1930	████████████████████ (~98)
1891-1910	██████████████████████ (~107)
1871-1890	████████████████████████████ (~140)
1851-1870	████████████████ (~80)
1831-1850	███████████████████████ (~113)
1811-1830	██████████ (~48)
1791-1810	███████ (~33)
1771-1790	███ (~17)
1751-1770	██ (~13)
1731-1750	█ (~7)
1711-1730	(~3)
1691-1710	(~3)
1663-1690	(~2)

```
     0    20   40   60   80  100  120  140
```

emphasized individual religious experience rather than collective doctrines in theology.

The same was true of every economic crisis. Each brought converts to communalism. The panic and depression of 1837 provided recruits for the many Fourierist communities. The 1857, 1893, and 1907 panics provided converts for many other communes. Again and again the individual histories of these settlements, particularly those that lasted more than a decade, report the sudden influx of unemployed people in times of crisis.

After the Great Depression of 1929, the federal government itself became involved in promoting and sponsoring communitarian-like settlements in order to deal with the problems of unemployment. The 145 cooperative farms and communities sanctioned by the government were clearly established in support of communitarian ideals. And they were finally closed, after the economy improved, because of strong opposition on the part of advocates of "individualism" and "free enterprise." A list of those government experiments can be found at the end of this book.

For the most part, communalists themselves have failed to realize how many experiments have existed other than a few that somewhat resembled their own. Some commune advocates did compile lists of the ones they knew about, but even the longest of these are woefully short. The best known of such lists were gathered by W.A. Hinds, Ralph Albertson, F.A. Bushee, Alexander Kent, Henrik Infield, and Otohiko Okugawa (whose listing is published in Robert S. Fogarty's *Dictionary*). Some of these lists are flawed by the fact that they include the same communes twice under different names. Others give a separate number to a single commune every time it moved to a different location. Furthermore, some of the lists include settlements that are not generally considered communes because they had no cooperative economic base, such as the several Salvation Army settlements, Thomas Hughes' Rugby colony of Englishmen, and the theosophist community called Krotona.

A Question of Names

Historians and sociologists often classify the communes as either religious or secular, but this distinction is hardly clear. No single theological principle united all the religious ones, and no single belief motivated all the secular ones. Both the religious and secular communes had common social origins in the revolt of discontented groups from the pressures and dislocations of existing society. And both had in their remote background common ideological roots in the ancient doctrine of natural law and the Manichaean view of the demonic nature of private property.

Classifications that distinguish between the foreign language–speaking experiments — German, French, Swedish, and Yiddish — and those established by English-speaking citizens also lead nowhere. The United States was built by a diverse group of people who came from many countries and many different cultures. The immigrants who were permitted to do so usually held firmly to their native customs and language, refusing to assimilate until the first and even second generations perished. The immigrants who settled in communes were able to preserve their traditions, language, and dress more easily than those who moved into the city ghettos.

Other commune classifications — urban vs. rural, uniformity vs. diversity, charismatic vs. acephalous — make note of obvious distinctions but tell little of why the lifestyles adopted by the communalists were meaningful to the participants. And differences in the basic aims of the communalists are quite indistinct under such classifications.

Communes should properly be examined on the basis of their stated purposes, even when they fail to reach their goal. The task can be fascinating. It gives insights into the universal human needs that particular communes did meet with some success, and other human needs with which they never dealt. Indeed it is tragic that most would-be communalists today fail to study the record and programs of the early American communes. For those who are ignorant of the past are doomed to repeat its errors.

Figure 3. Number of Communes in Each State Between 1663 and 1963

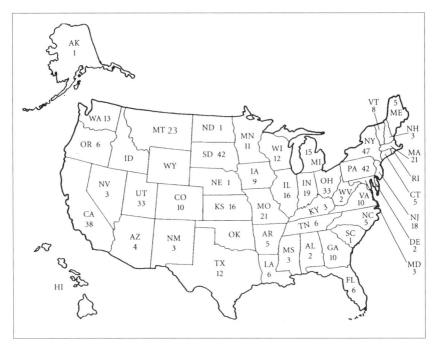

The Detractors

Reformers who do not withdraw from society and who continue to work through established legislative channels have always viewed commune builders with amusement, and revolutionaries have held them in contempt. Marx and his coworker, Friedrich Engels, writing from a revolutionary perspective, labeled all communitarians as "muddle-headed utopians" who depend on "man's good nature" rather than on any "scientific" understanding of how history develops. Yet before Marx and Engels fully solidified their own theories, they had looked with great interest on some of the American communal experiments.

Engels, in December 1884, wrote an article for *New Moral World*, a British journal espousing socialism. In that article he cited the American communes to show that "communism, the social life and work based on the common possession of goods, is, that is to say, not only possible but has actually been realized…, and with the best result." He described thirteen of the American experiments, including two Shaker communities, the Rappite experiment called Harmony, and Brook Farm.

In later years Marx and Engels refused to discuss questions of this sort because they then believed that political science can only describe social changes, not give utopian pictures of what society will look like when it changes. They regarded themselves as analysts of the disintegration of capitalist society, not gurus of the future. They argued that history will resolve such questions when the time of communism has come. Yet Marx, in formulating his motto "From each according to his abilities, to each according to his needs," was expressing the very essence of utopianism, although he failed to recognize this.

Commune organizers have often said that their experiments were really more scientific than the most sophisticated theories of the "scientific" Marxists. After all, what can be more in the spirit of science than the testing of hypotheses in a small way before an attempt is made to apply them on a large scale. Aldous Huxley put it well in *Adonis and the Alphabet* when he wrote, "For anyone who is interested in human beings and their so largely unrealized potentialities, even the silliest experiment has value if only in demonstrating what ought not to be done."

Societal Pressures

Communalists are often charged with being un–American because they are so critical of existing society and because they decide to withdraw from it. This view conveniently fits into a reduced ideology that defines whatever is not understood as basically evil. From such a perspective, commune members are seen as despotic and hopelessly regimented, while the greater part of American society is considered to be democratic and individualistic. Communalists are seen as extreme, while the members of orthodox society are moderate. Communalists are considered to be alien; the orthodox are "ordinary people." Communalists are sinful; the orthodox, virtuous.

At its simplest level, this hostility against communes grows from a fear of those who are different. Some of the communalists, in emigrating to America to set up their experiments, rigidly retained their European languages, customs, and dress. They were subsequently reviled by the more established English-speaking members of American society because they refused to assimilate into the "melting-pot culture." The Hutterites in communes of South Dakota, who have retained their German dialect for daily conversation, still today are shunned as foreigners by neighboring farmers despite the fact that all living Hutterites were either born in the United States or in Canada.

This kind of outside hostility has destroyed some communes. Yet in many cases it has strengthened the members' resolve to succeed. Opposition usually challenges a group to get more clarity on its purposes. It gives their aims some meaning and importance, and increases their self-esteem. As Ralph Turner and Lewis Killiam put it in *Collective Behavior*, persecution "heightens the symbolic intensity of a group's values."

In theory, the isolation that most communalists seek to achieve for their experiments should be some protection against outside hostility. But complete isolation is never really possible, particularly in the modern world. At every turn, members of a commune find themselves having to touch and interact with broader society. Their property is subject to taxes; their buildings and health are subject to civil inspectors. Clothing and other items must frequently be purchased from department stores and mail order companies. The use of trucks and cars requires contact with gas station attendants and repair shops.

The designers of America's early commune experiments were also bound by conventional thought patterns and moral disciplines to a much greater extent than they usually realized. No matter how wild and various their experiments, no community model was ever totally new. The members and organizers could withdraw from some of their nation's more obvious institutions and expressions, but, because these cultural attitudes and mores were a part of their heritage, they inevitably selected and modified from the culture they ostensibly rejected. And this has always been the case with utopian planning. Plato, in designing his *Republic*, could not escape a structured hierarchy of priests, warriors, and servants, and Thomas More could not conceive of his *Utopia* without slaves and war. Thus each communal plan is a reservoir of ideas partly rooted in the past and partly budding forth from new crossing and mutations.

No social order, of course, can be better than the human beings who take part in it. And though every communitarian seeks to combine freedom with welfare, justice with order, power with prosperity, truth with beauty, scientific truth with moral good, and technical proficiency with practical wisdom, such plans fail in the realization because of natural inadequacies in human potential. As the anthropologist John W. Bennett once put it, "A commune is not a heaven on earth; it is the human on earth."

Commune leadership structures may effectively assign farming, clean-up, and other duties, but it takes individual determination to get the job done to the satisfaction of everyone — determination that overcomes self-interest. Where one or two members fail to fulfill their obligations, the other members' enthusiasm for doing their own share soon wanes.

Despite human failings, however, close observers of these experiments throughout the nineteenth century and into the early twentieth century generally agree that life in the most successful of the communes was greatly superior to life in the non-communal, acquisitive world. The participants were freed from poverty, the dependence on changing attitudes of employers, and the erratic behavior of the "free" economy. The members were healthy and had an astounding record of longevity. Their children were often well instructed, and the women usually enjoyed equal rights with men.

There are advocates of individualism who say that a commune, by its very nature, destroys individual initiative and curbs creativity. But working together with others does not mean that the individual necessarily sublimates his or her initiative. This myth is belied by the many creative contributions made by individual communitarians in art, music, literature, architecture, furniture design, invention, and farming while living in a commune.

Those who say that creativity is destroyed by collectivism have been brainwashed into thinking that creativity is some kind of inner-directed process dependent only on self-satisfaction. What they forget is that the satisfaction can be outer-directed and come from creation on behalf of the group rather than only on behalf of the self. Corporateness actually lets individual creativity loose; it does not stifle it. If there is nowhere to market individual creativity, as is so often the case in an individualistic and profit-oriented society, then that creativity is simply a figment of one's imagination.

THE ENCYCLOPEDIA

Adam-ondi-Ahman (1838), four miles north of Gallatin, Missouri, was a Mormon United Order commune established by Lyman Wight and later named by Joseph Smith, Jr., the founder of the Mormon religion. Smith said the name meant "Adam's Consecrated Land."

Wight, a veteran of the War of 1812, had been one of the 17 original members of the first Mormon commune, Ridgon's **Kirtland** in Ohio. He was also one of the most colorful characters in early Mormon history. He was described by a contemporary as a rough, uneducated man who was nicknamed "the Wild Ram of the Mountains." After his conversion to Mormonism, Wight quickly caught its missionary spirit and he went out to preach the new faith in the fishing districts of Ohio and then Missouri. During the day he fished with the men, and at night he conducted revival meetings in the school houses, standing on a stove barefoot, with short sleeves and trouser legs rolled up. Wight baptized 100 of these fishing families within a few weeks after he left Kirtland. Many of them later joined his Missouri community. Its location was on the great bend of the Grand River where Wight also began a ferry service to take people across the river. It is estimated that 900 people eventually settled at Adam-ondi-Ahman, including many who had to flee from the **Zion** commune. The members built nearly 200 homes at Adam-ondi-Ahman. Some also lived in covered wagons while awaiting the construction of more houses.

Here, as at the other Mormon communes in Missouri, non–Mormon neighbors formed a mob that attacked the commune members with rocks, clubs, and knives when they went into Gallatin at election time to vote in opposition to slavery. The Mormons retaliated by returning and capturing the town, burning and sacking a warehouse there and a tailor shop. When the governor of Missouri called out the army to force the Mormons to leave his state, all of the members of Adam-ondi-Ahman migrated to **Nauvoo** in Illinois, where the Mormons from **Far West** and elsewhere were now gathering.

A dilapidated log cabin, said to be the home of Wight, still stands on the side of a hill at the site, although all the other homes were burned to the ground. Wight later established another Mormon commune, **Zodiac**, in Texas.

Adonai Shomo (1861–1897), started at Athol, Masachusetts, was a Christian communist community, its name signifying "the Lord, the Spirit, is there." The commune was led by Frederick Howland, a Quaker who had become a Second Adventist. The 30 members were known to their neighbors as Fullerites since the land for their commune was contributed by Leonard Fuller, one of the members. They based their advocacy of communism of goods on the teachings of the early Christian church, and they celebrated the Sabbath on Saturday, as the seventh day of the week, rather than on Sunday.

Since Howland believed himself to be immortal, his death in 1864 came as a great shock to the community. A man named Cook then assumed leadership, and shortly thereafter the members moved ten miles south to the town of Petersham. Here Cook was imprisoned for unexplained "revolting practices." From 1865 on the leader was Asa F. Richards. The members owned 840 acres at Petersham and had a number of large buildings in which they lived and worked. The commune closed with Richards' death, and the property was sold to satisfy creditors. Books with sections that focus on Adonai Shomo are Hinds' *American Communities* and Wooster's *Communities of the Past and Present*.

Alcuin Community (1941), at Sugargrove, Pennsylvania, was a Catholic Worker farm (see **Maryfarm** on Staten Island) established by John and Mary Thornton of New York City. It had about 15 members.

Alfred (1793–1932), at Alfred, Maine, about 30 miles southwest of Portland, was a Shaker settlement (see **Watervliet**) that grew to a membership of 200. Benjamin Barnes, a Shaker convert, gave the initial land for this commune. More land was purchased over the years until the size of Alfred's holdings reached 11,000 acres.

Besides dwellings, the commune had a barn measuring 144 x 45 feet, saw mill, grist mill, tannery, school, and small library. The members manufactured and sold garden seeds, brooms, hair sieves, dry measures, baskets, and fans. Elder John Barnes and Sister Sarah Kendal were the first leaders. These two were also appointed to head the **Sabbathday Lake Village** Shaker commune, which is also in Maine and not too far away. It was established a year later than was Alfred.

When Alfred was closed, the remaining 15 members moved to Sabbathday Lake Village. Henry Green, John B. Vance, and Harriet Coolbroth were the leaders of Alfred at that time. The land and buildings were then sold for a Roman Catholic teachers school.

Allen's Camp (1876–1882), at what is now Joseph City, Arizona, was a Mormon communal settlement of over 200 members that followed the United Order structure in use at **Orderville**.

The members tried to dam the Little Colorado River for irrigation purposes. They worked at this project for 960 days and spent $5,000 on it, but they finally disbanded the commune when they failed at the task.

Alphadelphia Phalanx (1844–1848), on the Kalamazoo River near Galesburg, Kalamazoo County, Michigan, was a Fourierist commune (see **Social Reform Unity**) established by Dr. H. R. Schetterly of Ann Arbor and other people from various cities in Michigan. More than 1,300 people applied for membership, but the commune could only accommodate 200. Most of these were farmers, though there were also some construction workers, shoemakers, tailors, blacksmiths, and printers.

They had 2,814 acres of land, 927 of which were already under cultivation before they occupied the land. The members erected a two-story wooden phalanxtry building (523 feet long), as well as a saw mill, machine shop, some other shops, and a large furnace. They also established a part-time school and published two newspapers, the *Tocsin* and the *Primitive Expounder*. The latter was a semi-monthly edited by Rev. James Billings and R. Thornton. The members subscribed to some 70 newspapers and magazines on an exchange basis.

The exact cause of this commune's breakup is not known, but some assume it was because of poor management. The property later became Kalamazoo County's house and farm.

Altruist Community (1894–1895), at a place named Gibsonville after the wealthy Detroit citizen who donated the property in Genesee County, Michigan, was a farming commune set up for needy people in Detroit. C. W. Gibson, along with his brothers, established a stock company to promote the project, and he purchased 450 acres of land for it. He hoped to populate the commune with 50 of the poorest families in Detroit, families to be selected by the poor commissioners of that city.

The participants were to be given their housing, clothing, and all the necessary tools needed to provide a living. The entire proceeds from the farm and other labor were to go into a communal treasury that would keep the commune solvent. Gibson also expected them to live together in a hotel that he was going to construct on the property. In all, he spent $50,000 on the project before the first members moved there.

In January 1895 there were 160 members living in 40 houses at the Altruist community. They had set up a broom factory as well as a basket industry. Both a laundry and a creamery were planned but never constructed. According to Gibson, this was "to be one of the largest and most prosperous altruist communities in the country" within a few years. However, it did not last longer than one year.

Altruist Community (1901–1907), at Sulphur Springs, Missouri, about 23 miles south of St. Louis, was the last of six communal settlements established by Alcander Longley (see **Fourier Phalanx**). It had about ten members who owned 40 acres of land. They lived in a log house that was on the property when they occupied it and in a six-room frame house that they rented. They held all property in common. Here is where Longley's magazine, *The Altruist*, was printed. There are no remnants of the commune, and the town of Sulphur Springs, once noted as a fine spa, has also almost disappeared.

Altruria (1894–1896), seven miles north of Santa Rosa, California, was a Christian Socialist community deriving its name from William Dean Howells' utopian novel, *A Traveler from Altruria*. This novel tells of a man who comes to New England from a utopian country known as Altruria. He stops at an exclusive resort hotel where he astounds the guests by assisting the hotel employees in their tasks and by asking the guests embarrassing questions about American society. The story ends with a description of the ideal society in his utopian country.

The leader of Altruria commune was Unitarian Minister Edward Biron Payne (1845–1923), and most of the members came from Payne's congregation in Berkeley, California. They included bricklayers, carpenters, weavers, bakers, and at least one university professor. Throughout the existence of this commune, Payne continued to commute between Santa Rosa and Berkeley so that he could run both his church and the community.

The perhaps 40 members added seven cottages to the three houses and grist mill that were on 185 acres of land they purchased for the project. It was in a hilly and densely wooded area. They created vegetable and fruit gardens, raised cattle and poultry, and constructed an apiary. They also made furniture and carpets for sale, and they published a weekly paper, the *Altrurian*. But they never completed the construction of a hotel that they started to build, a hotel that was intended to contain their dining hall, offices, and library.

Much of the life at Altruria was festive. They held socials, song recitals, picnics, and Christmas parties. Their rule was that members should do whatever job they wished and work only as long as they wished. Members were paid in colony checks that they could redeem for goods at the community store. They also had a school for the children that was under the direction of Miss Whittier, who came from Pasadena.

Much of the financial support for the project came from sustaining Altrurian clubs in various California cities. But, by the summer of 1895, their financial problems became so great that they decided to send most of the members elsewhere to find better land for a more productive Altrurian community. One group moved to a new site at Cloverdale (see **Cloverdale Altruria**), and another moved to a place within the town of Santa Rosa (see **Santa Rosa Altruria**). The 14 members who remained at the original site closed this project by June 1896. A book with a section that focuses on Altruria is Hine's *California's Utopian Communities*.

Amana (1843–1932), first located at Ebenezer, New York, and then at Amana, Iowa, was founded by a group of pietists from Germany who were known as True Inspirationists. They believed that God spoke through men and women chosen as "instruments" and "messengers." They were persecuted in Germany because they refused all service in the armed forces, kept their children out of government-run schools, and forbade all oaths of allegiance to the state. They came to the United States under the leadership of Christian Metz (1793–1867), who, like their other leaders, went through a period of intense trembling and shaking before delivering any of his prophetic statements.

Metz had been a carpenter before he became the leader of the True Inspirationists. In 1842, he had a revelation that all the scattered congregations of True Inspirationists in Germany should be gathered together for a great migration to the New World. He sailed for New York, with four other followers, in September. There they purchased a 5,000 acre Seneca Indian reservation at the price of $10 per acre. Much of this land now lies within the city of Buffalo. The pietists were fortunate in having several members of considerable wealth who contributed large sums to the common stock so that Metz was able to make the purchase. Three hundred fifty True Inspirationists arrived in America in 1843 to start the commune, and more followed the next year.

Metz eventually acquired 25,000 acres of fertile land and timbered hills in Iowa, and the commune was moved there in 1855. In time they established seven separate villages on the Iowa property, naming the first one Amana. The others were West Amana, South Amana, High Amana, East Amana, Middle Amana, and Homestead. When the colonists first got to Iowa, their membership was about 800. By 1878 the membership reached its highest point, 1,600.

Metz, speaking as the messenger of the Lord, proclaimed that all should dwell in a state of complete and total economic communism. The constitution they subsequently wrote provided that every bit of property, with the exception of clothing and household goods, should be held in common.

At first several families lived in each dwelling. But this practice was discontinued shortly after they settled in Iowa, and each family then erected their own home of brick, stone, and wood. Most of the Amanaites were farmers, although there were also a few carpenters, draftsmen, bakers, brew masters, butchers, and sausage makers.

By 1878, in addition to many large farms, the members owned four saw

Amana, as it was seen in 1900 (Amana Heritage Society of Amana, Iowa).

mills, two grist mills, a tannery, a print shop, and two woolen mills. They also had hundreds of horses, more than a thousand head of cattle, and between two and three thousand sheep and swine. They became famous for their printed cloth, yarns, flannels, and other woolen goods. They also made furniture from their extensive walnut trees.

Their food was ample but plain; dress was simple and drab. They ate in groups of 30 to 50, women and men at separate tables. However, the women worked beside the men in the fields. While committed to a simple life, they did use tobacco heavily, drank freely of their own beer and wine, and took pride in flower growing. Singing was promoted, though musical instruments were outlawed. Men were not permitted to marry until after age 24. Life was regulated by supervisors and trustees elected by the whole membership, including all widows and unmarried women past 30 years of age, though women did not hold elective office.

Their children were kept in school from the age of 6 to 13. They learned both English and German, and here both boys and girls were taught to knit. Most reading was limited to the Bible or "inspired" writings of their leaders. They did, however, subscribe to some journals and newspapers from the outside world that were circulated from one member to another. They also printed their own religious books, many of which were records of their own history. They did not allow pictures as tending toward idol worship, and all card games were forbidden. Because the members were pacifists, they hired substitutes to fill their military quota during the Civil War.

After Christian Metz died, his place as the spiritual leader was taken by Barbara Heynemann, who had been an illiterate servant in Germany before she joined the group. She lived into her 80s.

The commune prospered until the 1920s when they first began to accumulate debts. In 1929 their surplus was all gone and the Great Depression sent prices for their products tumbling. By 1931 the community was $500,000 in debt. A committee of 47 members was then established to plan for the future of the colony. On its recommendations, they transformed their communist economy into a producing and marketing cooperative, essentially ending the communal phase of their life in 1932. After this, religious authority was confined to the church, and the communal aspects of the work and dining hall were abandoned.

The Amana villages still stand and are occupied by former members. A lucrative air-conditioning and refrigeration business that they started during World War II made the town of Amana prosper more than ever before. The refrigerator plant was sold in 1950 and moved away from the town. Among the buildings to be seen in the Amana colonies today are many two-story, gabled houses built by the residents, as well as their church and their stores. At the village of Amana, the oldest, a visitor will find the home of Christian Metz as well as a still-operating furniture shop, woolen mill, and bakery, all dating from the communal period. At Middle Amana there is another woolen mill and a printing shop, and at West Amana there is a flour mill that still employs the old mill stones for grinding grain. Books with sections that focus on Amana are Calverton's *Where Angels Dared to Tread*, Hinds' *American Communities*, and Nordhoff's *The Communistic Societies of the United States*.

American Settlers Co-operative Association (1898–1899), at Duke (now Ruskin), Georgia, was a commune of 35 farmers from Ohio and Indiana. The group had been assembled at Dayton, Ohio, and their motto was "each for all and all for each." They had 760 acres of land on which they constructed more than 50 houses before they decided to merge with the **Ruskin Commonwealth**, which moved from Tennessee to join them.

Amity (1959–1964), first at Seattle, Washington, and then near Littleton, Colorado, was a modern attempt to form a Perfectionist-type commune (see **Putney Corporation**) in which there was the practice of mutual criticism, every adult member was considered married to all the others, and all property was owned communally. Amity at one point had 24 members, most of whom had been students at the University of Washington. Those wishing to join the commune were given a four-month trial before they were accepted into full membership.

Unlike the earlier Perfectionist communes — notably **Oneida**— where all the income came from projects within the community, the Amity members worked in professional jobs outside the commune in order to earn living expenses for the project. But like Oneida, they received a great deal of criticism from outsiders because of their marriage practices. In 1963 the remaining eleven members (five men, four women, and two children) moved the commune to the location near Littleton, Colorado, but there they still believed themselves under such hostile pressure from public opinion that they refused to give their address to any non-members.

Anaheim (1857–1860), California, began as a cooperative effort of 50 German artisans from San Francisco. They called their experiment Anaheim as a combination of the German word for home and part of the name of the South Ana River where their 1,165 acres were located. The group purchased the land from Don Juan Pacifico Ontiveros, the original Mexican grantee, and they sent one of their members, George Hansen, to divide the property into 20-acre lots.

Hansen also planned 50 house lots, installed water systems, and set out trees, vines, and windbreaks with the help of Mexican labor before the rest of the colonists arrived. He erected a fence of 40,000 willow posts around the entire colony to protect it from roving cattle and other livestock. The willow posts took root and formed a living wall around the area. The grapes he planted prospered and brought the cooperative owners a relatively quick return on their investment.

The settlers included two or three carpenters, four blacksmiths, a brewer, an engraver, three watchmakers, a shoemaker, a bookbinder, a miller, a hatter, a poet, and a musician. Their plan was to farm the land cooperatively under the supervision of a general manager. But, shortly after they settled on the property, they decided to abandon the cooperative nature of their experiment.

The first house, built by George Hansen when he arrived in 1857, is still standing, although it has since been moved from its original location on North Los Angeles Street to 414 West Street. It is now maintained as a museum of relics of pioneer days. There is also a marker 600 yards to the southwest of Highway 1 and Bay Boulevard that commemorates Anaheim Landing, a port that the colonists constructed to service their community. Books with sections that focus on Anaheim are Cleland's *From Wilderness to Empire: A History of California* and Hine's *California's Utopian Communities.*

Ananda Ashram (1923–present), at La Crescenta, California, north of Los Angeles, is a monastic community set up by Swami Paramananda (1883–1940), founder of the Vedanta Society. He came to the United States from India to be an assistant to a swami in New York City. However, he soon moved to Boston and gathered his own band of disciples, calling the group the Boston Vedanta Society. The word "vedanta" comes from the joining of two Sanskrit words to mean "the end of wisdom."

He visited California in 1916 and returned there in 1923 to purchase a 140 acre estate in the La Crescenta Valley, a secluded location of great scenic beauty. Here at this ashram, or religious retreat, his followers live a communal life, place themselves completely under the Swami's tutelage, and hope to purify themselves through work and meditation.

One house was already on the property when it was purchased. This became the first residence. The members then built a row of cabins, a large two-story guest house, and a temple that seats more than 100 persons and has a manual organ to provide music. The temple was designed to blend into the landscape. The membership here has never been larger than 20, most of them upper-middle-class American women.

In 1929 Paramananda returned to Boston and established the **Cohasset Ashram**, and in the late 1960s other ashrams were set up in other parts of the United States by his followers. The Vedanta movement now claims 125,000 members, though this is undoubtedly an exaggeration. There are perhaps 1,200 followers in the movement today. They are now led by Gayatri Devi, Paramananda's niece from India. A book with a section that focuses on the Ananda Ashram is Veysey's *The Communal Experience*.

Ancora Community (1878), at Ancora, New Jersey, was a communal settlement of no more than ten members led by Samuel Fowler.

Aptos Farm (1943), at Aptos near the Montgomery Bay in Santa Cruz County, California, was a Catholic Worker farm (see **Maryfarm** on Staten Island) that may have had as many as 15 members.

Arden (1900–present), at Arden, Delaware, is a single-tax community (see **Fairhope**) that was started by sculptor and pacifist George Frank Stephens and architect William L. Price. They selected Delaware for their enclave because this state had a large number of single-tax advocates who conducted a third-party campaign in the 1900s that gained a great deal of publicity for the movement. Soap manufacturer Joseph Fels provided the money to purchase the land for this commune.

From the beginning Arden was a community that attracted many artists. It is only about 20 miles from Philadelphia, so members can work there and maintain homes in the Arden community. By 1909 every lot of the 163 acres of land was taken and a large number

of additional applications for membership were on file. Many of the members lived in tents until they could build cabins or homes of their own.

Members leased their land for $22 an acre and paid $3 to become members of the Arden Club, which runs the social and cultural affairs of the community. The business affairs are conducted by elected trustees and a committee of five civic aids. Members also gather in a monthly town meeting.

In the spring of 1910, author Upton Sinclair (see **Helicon Home**) moved to Arden from Fairhope and remained there for one and a half years. He reported in his autobiography that some of the members included George Brown, an anarchist shoemaker; Hal Ware, son of Communist leader Ella Reeve Bloor and later organizer of the first American tractor brigade to the Soviet Union; Donald Stephens, son of the sculptor and also active in the tractor-aid plan; and Scott Nearing, then a professor at the University of Pennsylvania and later a noted author of books on questions and models of socialism.

The community declined somewhat during the 1929 depression and following the death of Stephens in 1935, but has since enlarged to as many as 1,000 members. Fiske Warren, a Boston paper manufacturer, provided funds for the purchase of additional acres of land to enlarge the size of the community. Their Craftsman's Guild, which maintains a craft shop to foster weaving, woodcarving, and pottery, is quite famous. In recent years some of the members have included landscape painter Leander Leitner, sculptor Marcus Aurelius Renzetti, and artist-writer Rose Santee. A book with a section that focuses on Arden is Sinclair's *The Autobiography of Upton Sinclair*.

Arkansas Community (1883), near what is now Brinkley, Arkansas, was a Jewish agricultural commune of 150 members. Some of them came from **Sicily Island**, the Jewish agricultural settlement in Louisiana that had been destroyed by a flood. The Arkansas Community was started on such worthless agricultural land that heat and rains, as well as malaria and yellow fever, quickly killed the colony, forcing the members to disband.

Army of Industry (1914–1918), west of Auburn, California, was a Christian Socialist commune established by Gerald Geraldson, who had briefly been a member of **Kaweah**. It was located on a hundred-acre fruit farm that Geraldson inherited from his father. The members — 40 at the commune's height — changed the packing plant into a communal dining hall and the nine other buildings on the property into their living and working quarters.

Geraldson held that private property is an outgrowth of Original Sin, and therefore no member was permitted to own any kind of property. The colony provided all the basic needs for its members. But there was little screening of applicants, and so the membership included many drifters and ne'er-do-wells with prison records. The orchard did poorly and the community steadily lost money. Finally Geraldson and other more stable members had to take jobs in the city to help finance the project. After the commune collapsed, Geraldson moved to New York City and opened a settlement house on the East Side, called Brotherhood House. A book with a section that focuses on the Army of Industry is Hine's *California's Utopian Communities*.

Askov (1906–1916), in Pine County, Minnesota, began as a cooperative community established by the Danish People's Society on 20,000 acres of cutover and burned-over land. At the time it included the townsite of Partridge as well as a logging camp, abandoned store, log house, and post office. In time the members built houses, a church, and a school where classes were conducted in both English and Danish.

The farming settlement followed a cooperative system developed in Denmark, in which each member contributed to the project in direct proportion to the number of cows that the person owned, yet each member had only one vote in community affairs. Their creamery and Danish folk school were justly famous. When the cooperative nature of the enterprise ended, there were about 1,000 members. The town still has several consumer cooperative enterprises, and its buildings reflect the heritage of the communal background. A book with a section that focuses on Askov is *One Hundred Years in Pine County*.

Association of Brotherly Cooperation
see **Joyful**

Atherton Stewardship Community (1929–1932), at Atherton, Missouri, was a Mormon cooperative farm established by members of the Reorganized Church of the Latter Day Saints, with headquarters in Independence, Missouri. This branch of Mormonism was started by some of the Mormons who did not go to Utah with Bringham Young, including members of the Joseph Smith family who remained at **Nauvoo** after most of the others left.

Approximately 60 people from the Reorganized Church of the Latter Day Saints set up the Atherton Stewardship

Community on 2,500 acres of church-owned land. The location is about 15 miles from Independence. They built homes, a lumber yard, and chicken barns, and they divided their farming profits equally. D. R. Hughes was elected to be the general manager and Otho Clark became the secretary-treasurer. J. A. Koehler, who later became a bishop of the church, gave the project his spiritual leadership. But the members found it difficult to sell their produce during the Great Depression, and so they finally had to disband the commune. An article with information that focuses on the Atherton Stewardship Community is *Story of the Atherton Adventure*, written by members of the Reorganized Church of Latter Day Saints.

Aurora (1855–1881), first in the Willapa Hills area of southwestern Washington and then at Aurora, Oregon, was a commune established by Dr. William Keil, the founder of the **Bethel** commune. His purpose was to establish a new home for the German-speaking members of Bethel, a home that would be in such a sparsely populated part of the country that they would not be influenced by the lures of the individualistic society that surrounded their Missouri location. Keil named the commune in honor of his favorite daughter, and the town has retained its name ever since.

Keil called this a Christian communist community, which is the same term as he used for Bethel. As he put it in describing Aurora, "No man owns anything individually but every man owns everything as a full partner and with an equal voice in its use and its increase and the profits accruing from it…we are one family. 'From every man according to his capacity, to every man according to his needs' is the rule that runs through our law of love."

After sending an investigation team to the Washington Territory, Keil traveled there with 80 members of Bethel to set up the new commune. He took the body of his 19-year-old son, Willie, with him. The young man had died shortly before the entourage set out on their six-month journey. Keil poured a chemical preservative into the casket to keep the body intact during the time that it took to reach their destination, and he finally buried the lad at their new home.

But half a year after they started the commune in the Willapa Hills, they decided to move south because the land they had selected in Washington was not good for growing crops. They were able to secure 23,000 acres in Oregon, and by the spring of 1857, they had built many houses, opened a hotel and drugstore, and planted orchards and vineyards there. Within the community the members used no money, everyone obtaining what supplies they needed from the common supply.

In time they also set up schools, a saw mill, a tan yard, a grist and saw mill, workshops for a cabinet maker, a blacksmith, a wagon maker, a shoemaker, a carpenter, a tailor, and tin smiths, as well as looms for weaving wool, carding machinery, and drying houses for fruit. They also had two excellent musical bands that traveled as far as Portland to perform. The fruit they produced was considered the best in the state of Oregon, and the spool beds, oak chests, and woven-bottom chairs they made are collector's items today.

As the years went by, more and more members arrived from Bethel until the total membership at Aurora grew to 1,000. Many of these were young men from Bethel who fled to the Oregon community to avoid the draft when the Civil War began. In refusing to participate in the war, they were following Keil's pacifist teachings. Bethel, however, did not disband as Keil had expected it would after Aurora was on a firm footing, but continued to operate until several years after Keil's death.

One of the new members at Aurora was Professor Christopher W. Wolff, who arrived in 1863. He was a graduate of the University of Göttingen, and he had studied with most of the leading socialist theorists in Europe, including Cabet (see **Icaria**), Babeuf, Fourier (see **Social Reform Unity**), Proudhon, and even Karl Marx. He was one of the few intellectuals to join Aurora, and he came with a considerable collection of books. Thus Aurora acquired a library, something that they never had at Bethel and something for which the rest of the members had little desire. Because of his knowledge of European socialism, Wolff proved a great help to Keil in formulating economic designs for the community.

But after Keil died in 1877, the communal nature of Aurora became less appealing to the membership and their numbers began to decline. Both Aurora and the now-tiny Bethel were disbanded in 1881. Some of the farm houses and buildings that were once part of the Aurora commune are still standing. Books with sections that focus on Aurora are Calverton's *Where Angels Dared to Tread*, Hinds' *American Communities*, and Nordhoff's *The Communistic Societies of the United States*.

Ayers (1945–present), near Lewiston, Montana, is a Hutterite Brüderhof (see **Bon Homme**). They had 55 members in 1964 and were then led by John Stahl.

Baring Street Fellowship (1960–1963), in Philadelphia, Pennsylvania, was a pacifist community of 11 Quakers and Mennonites who were fraternally related to **Reba Place** in Evanston, Illinois. They lived in a single house at 3619 Baring Street, and the members worked at outside jobs. They were led by Lewis Benson.

Bass Lake Farm (1941–1946), near Minneapolis, Minnesota, was a cooperative experiment for pacifists under the leadership of the Rev. Elliot Marston. The location was then on the outskirts of the city but the land is now within the city limits. Some of the ten members were interned in conscientious objector camps during World War II. Besides crops, the members raised cattle and chickens on their 80 acres. The only trained farmer among them was Rev. Marston. The project was disbanded after his death. Some of the members then joined the **Celo Community**. A book with a section that focuses on the Bass Lake Farm is Infield's *Utopia and Experiment*.

Bayard Lane Homestead Community (1937–1964), at Suffern, New York, was established by Ralph Borsodi (1881–1977), a leading advocate of the modern homesteading movement. He envisioned small plots of land, grouped into an intentional community, as the best means of alleviating most of the world's ills.

Borsodi, trained as an economist, was working as an advertising and marketing consultant in New York City when he took a job in 1932 as a consultant to the Council of Social Agencies in Dayton, Ohio. Armed with a government grant of $50,000 he established the Dayton Homesteads in 1933, one of the first projects in the federal government's program to establish farming cooperatives as a means of alleviating unemployment during the depression. After President Roosevelt federalized all such projects in June 1934, Borsodi sued the government for breach of contract. In response, the government let his project continue under local direction. But Borsodi soon quit in disgust over what he considered bureaucratic red tape. He then moved back to New York.

His homestead movement began with the founding of the Bayard Lane and along with it an educational research center called the School of Living. The community eventually encompassed 16 families, or about 45 people. He hoped, through the success of Bayard Lane, to widely promote his ideas about intentional homesteading. He also wrote several books to set forth his views, the most popular being *Education for Living*. Borsodi's approach to homestead farming was to utilize machinery in order to eliminate drudgery, yet to reintroduce domestic crafts (weaving, canning, etc.) wherever they seemed practical.

At the Bayard Lane Homestead Community and the several other communities established by his followers, Borsodi set up a cooperative credit plan, a cooperative buying plan, and a cooperative wage system for work done for the entire community, such as home building. Here he also began to call his movement the Green Revolution Movement. Yet his bitterness against government intervention caused him to become increasingly more anarchistic in his outlook and social ideas.

Borsodi's School of Living closed in 1945. It was later reopened by Mildred Loomis, who had worked closely with Borsodi, and is now located at her home in Brookville, Ohio.

Beadle County Colony (1905–1936), also known as the Lake Byron Colony, was a Hutterite Brüderhof (see **Bon Homme**) located near Lake Byron in Beadle County, South Dakota. The approximately 100 members had come originally from Canada when a Hutterite commune there divided. But the land was too poor for farming at this location so in 1922 they moved the commune onto the lands adjacent to the **Wolf Creek** Brüderhof near Freeman, South Dakota. Then in 1936 they moved back to Canada, where the commune still exists in Alberta.

Beaver Creek *see* **Watervliet in Ohio**

Beersheba (1882–1888), on Pawnee Creek near present-day Kalvesta, Hodgeman County, Kansas, was a Jewish agricultural commune (see **Sicily Island**) of about 60 members, established through the efforts of people in Cincinnati. They lived in dugout shelters and worshipped at a sod synagogue. After a little more than a year of existence, there was a dispute within the community that resulted in the managers selling their farm implements and animals. This led to great hardships for those who decided to try to keep the project going. The men of the commune had to go to Dodge City, Garden City, and other nearby towns to find employment, while their wives and children remained at the commune trying to farm the land.

Belle Terre (1925), about two miles from Point Jefferson, New York, was an anarchist community that lasted only a few months. It was formed by five members from the **Mohegan Colony**, who departed from there with George S. Seldes because they considered Mohegan too rigidly controlled by power groups, which Seldes labeled Communist.

Bellview (1875–1877), probably in Iron County, Utah, was a Mormon commune of the **St. George** United Order type. It had perhaps 50 members and closed after the death of the Mormon leader, Brigham Young.

Bellville (1917–1947), in Nansemond County, Virginia, was a communal settlement that served as headquarters for the Church of God and Saints of Christ, popularly known as the "Black Jews." The commune was established by Bishop William H. Plummer, although the initial purchase of the land in 1902 was made by the founder of this denomination, William S. Crowdy.

Crowdy had been employed on the Santa Fe Railroad as a cook until the latter part of 1896 when he claimed to have received a vision from God calling him to lead his people to the true religion and giving him prophetic endowment. Crowdy then left his home in Guthrie, Oklahoma, and went to Lawrence, Kansas, where he began to organize his church. He appointed himself the first bishop, and in 1900, moved the headquarters to Philadelphia, Pennsylvania. The headquarters was moved to Bellville in 1917.

The Church of God and Saints of Christ teaches that black people are descendants of the "lost tribes of Israel," and that Jews were originally black, but changed the color of their skins through a process of mixing with white people. The members observe the rites of both the Old and New Testaments so that they have elaborate ceremonies around foot washing, circumcision, baptism, the holy kiss, sacrifices, et cetera. They further observe the Jewish calendar and celebrate Passover, and they follow the Old Testament precedent of observing the Sabbatic year in which they allow the land to lay fallow and plant no crops. The church also strongly advocates temperance.

The commune maintained a home for aged widows and orphans and the Bellville Industrial School, which had classes up to a junior high school level. They also cultivated about a thousand acres of land, operated several small industries, and maintained a commissary. An elder supervised these enterprises in which the members were assigned to work. Weekly rations and clothing were passed out to the members through the commissary.

At the time this community ceased to operate as a commune, it had around 130 members, though there may have been as many as 300 members earlier. The denomination also has churches in Washington, D.C., Philadelphia, New York City, and in the West Indies. In 1959 their membership was listed at 40,000. Some church members went to Israel one year and claimed the right to live there, but they were not welcomed with enthusiasm and eventually returned to America. A book with a section that focuses on Bellville is Clark's *The Small Sects in America.*

Bennett Co-operative Colony (1873–1877), two miles north of Long Lane in Dallas County, Missouri, was established by William H. Bennett. He had been a member of the **Friendship Community**, but left there because of dissatisfaction with Alcander Longley's leadership. Little more is known about this commune except that it probably disbanded as prosperity returned to the area following the depression of 1873. Perhaps there were as many as ten members. Bennett later organized the **Home Employment Co-operative**

Company at or near the same location.

Berlin Community (1865–1866), at Berlin Heights, Ohio, was an 18-member commune of freethinkers, some of whom were probably members of the earlier **Point Hope** commune that was established nearby. This commune was also called the Christian Republic. One of the leaders was James Towner (1823–1913), who later joined **Oneida** and caused some problems in that commune by his opposition to its founder. Another member of the Berlin Community was John S. Patterson, who moved his publication, the *Social Revolutionist*, here from the disbanded **Rising Star Community**.

Humorist Charles F. Browne, writing under the name of "Artemus Ward," penned a highly-derogatory story about the atheists, spiritualists, and followers of a variety of church doctrines that formed the membership of this Berlin Community.

Bermudian Settlement (1752–1760), in York County, Pennsylvania, was founded by Seventh-day Baptists under the leadership of Johann Jacob Kimmel. It was located on the Bermudian Creek between the present county line and where the creek empties into the Conawago River. This is about 20 miles west of Harrisburg.

Kimmel and his colleague, Johann Heinrich Lohman, had been merchants in Germany before they came with their wives to America to join the Seventh-day Baptist commune at **Ephrata**. They had been able to convince a group of friends to emigrate with them in 1749 and the entire group entered Ephrata. But Kimmel eventually had disagreements with the leadership at Ephrata and left with some of his group to set up another Seventh-day commune in York County. In time the membership at the Bermudian Settlement reached about 30. The settlement suffered from occasional Indian attacks, but survived and did well economically.

Kimmel's wife died in 1753 and so he returned to Ephrata. His colleague Lohman was then assigned by the leadership of the Seventh-day Baptist movement to take his place at the Bermudian Settlement. George Adam Martin was assigned to assist him. But after Lohman and his wife died within three days of each other, the colony quickly declined. A book with a section that focuses on the Bermudian Settlement is Sachse's *The German Sectarians of Pennsylvania, 1708–1800: A Critical and Legendary History of the Ephrata Cloister and the Dunkers.*

Bethany Fellowship (1945–present), first at Minneapolis and then at nearby Bloomington, Minnesota, is a fundamentalist Christian commune of about 100 members. All of them came from the Independent Bethany Church in Minneapolis, and the initial purpose of the five families that started this commune was to demonstrate to others in the congregation that Christian commitment meant a return to the communal lifestyle of the first-century Christians, as described in the Book of Acts. They sold their homes and moved into a 30-room house, pooling all resources earned from outside employment to support their experiment and to provide funds for some foreign missionaries.

In 1947 they moved to Bloomington, where they have a missionary training and Bible institute, a factory for producing small electrical items, a printing plant, and a number of buildings for

Bethel, Missouri, as Keil's commune was seen in 1875 (Corner House Publishers).

housing. Their monthly magazine is *The Message of the Cross*. No money is paid in salaries to the fellowship members, many of whom teach at their training institute, and any surplus funds they raise are put into the missionary work.

Bethel (1844–1881), now a town in Shelby County, Missouri, was founded by Dr. William Keil (1812–1877), a Prussian merchant-tailor and mystic who advocated Christian communism. In 1855 there were 650 members, most of whom were of German or Pennsylvania Dutch origin.

Keil had come to the United States in 1835 and within two years had been converted to Methodism. He studied to become a licensed Methodist preacher with a congregation of German-speaking people. But then he became convinced that true Christians must live as communists and resigned from the Methodist church, denouncing all creeds and declaring that he would call himself nothing other than "Christian" from then on.

He decided to devote his life to creating a Christian community that he would call Bethel. Keil purchased land in Missouri for this commune and encouraged members of his former congregation to join him there. He sent supporters throughout West Virginia, Ohio, Kentucky, Indiana, and Iowa to spread his doctrines and to encourage German and Dutch-speaking people to join Bethel.

At its height, the Bethelites owned about 4,000 acres of good farming land, a saw mill, a grist mill, a tannery, a drug store, a general store, a distillery, a woolen factory, and shops for blacksmiths, coopers, tinners, shoemakers, tailors, hatters, and weavers. Their homes were constructed of brick, and they operated a hotel, a school, and a church. They also had a tract of land that they called Nineveh in the adjoining county of Adair.

Under Keil's leadership there were six trustees chosen by the members. These trustees acted as foremen and determined what work needed to be done. Each family lived in their own home and had a small garden plot, but they purchased their clothes and most of their staples from the common store.

The community supported a band that provided entertainment for the many festivals they held in which, it is said, everyone participated with gaiety and enthusiasm. The members used tobacco and liquor, though in moderation. They had no library, and for the most part, the only book anyone in this community read was the Bible. When members wanted to quit the commune, they were given an amount of money equal to what they had originally contributed to the common treasury, and sometimes a little extra to help them get started elsewhere in the outside world.

Although the members were faithful to Keil's wishes and maintained their communal lifestyle without complaint, he realized that the lures and pressures of the individualistic outside world were so strong in Missouri that these would eventually bring the downfall of the Bethel community. He therefore decided to move the members to the more sparsely-populated Washington or Oregon Territory where such enticements could not affect them. Keil sent a small delegation to that area to investigate conditions there. They came back with a favorable report. He then led 80 members in 1855 from Bethel to their new home in the Willapa Hills area of southwestern Washington. But the land there proved too poor for growing crops and so they soon moved south to a place in Oregon that he called **Aurora**. Many of the members of Bethel moved to the new Oregon commune, but some remained in Missouri and kept the Bethel commune functioning until four years after Keil's death.

Several of the original Bethel buildings are also still standing, including a half-timbered tannery. The hotel and Keil's home are open to visitors. Books with sections that focus on Bethel are Calverton's *Where Angels Dared to Tread*, Hinds' *American Communities*, and Nordhoff's *The Communistic Societies of the United States*.

Bethlehem (1741–1844), at Bethlehem, Pennsylvania, was a Moravian General Economy community founded by 17 Moravians under the leadership of Peter Boehler (1712–1775), one of the most influential persons in the early history of the American Moravian Church. The commune, started on 4,100 acres of land, proved quite successful and reached a membership of 1,622 persons by 1840. Its motto was "we pray together, we labor together, we suffer together, we rejoice together." The town was given the name "Bethlehem" by Bishop Spangenberg (see **Savannah**), who assumed the duties of general superintendent of this community in 1744. He was replaced in 1747 by Bishop John Nitschmann (1696–1772).

Their first dwelling house was a log cabin that they built. But many more buildings soon went up as other Moravians came from Europe to join the enterprise. By 1742 they had many houses, a grist mill, saw mills, oil mill, corn mill, fulling mill, a now-famous pottery, a tannery, a dying manufactory, a brewery, a tavern, a general store, and an apothecary. The large forge they constructed later became the basis of the present-day Bethlehem Steel Corporation. The land was good and yielded timber and stone for all their buildings; grain, fruit, and vegetables for all their food; and flax for all their clothing. Whereas under the Herrnhut system, used in the Moravian communes of Europe, each member was permitted to retain most of their earnings and their room and board was paid for, under the General Economy, used at Bethlehem, all earnings became part of the general church fund.

Like all the successful Moravian settlements, there was a Brethren's House for unmarried men, a Sisters' House for unmarried women, and a Widow's House. Two superintendents were assigned to each of these houses — one to look after the temporal and the other the religious affairs of the inhabitants. Religious services for all in the commune were held every evening at the church.

Eventually the Bethlehem property included the Indian villages of Nisky, Friedenshuetten (Tents of Peace), and Gnadenhuetten (Tents of Grace), located on an added tract of land that the members purchased for this purpose. Gnadenhuetten was subjected to a terrible Indian massacre in 1755, brought about by a mob of farmers and villagers who lived nearby and hated both Indians and Moravians. As a result, the members of Bethlehem constructed the new town named Nain to house the Indian refugees and others from the less protected Indian settlements nearby. The Moravians conducted religious services in these towns in the Mohican and Delaware languages.

The American Revolution in 1776 brought much public resentment against the Bethlehem community because its members refused to take up arms. Yet the willingness of the Moravians to nurse the sick and wounded redeemed them in their neighbors' eyes. Bishop Ettwein, at that time the leader of the Bethlehem congregation, was a personal friend of General Washington. Ettwein turned the Brethren's house into an army hospital for Continental troops. After 1815 this building was used for a girl's school — the Moravian College and

Seminary for Females — first established in 1742 and the first girl's school in America.

Bethlehem was probably the most musical of the Moravian communes, though all of them were known for the use of instrumental music as an accompaniment during work hours. The members proceeded to the harvest field to the sound of music. Trumpeters led them to work on their buildings, and they had frequent musical processions to celebrate the completion of any project. At least one member, John Antes, was an accomplished composer, and Hayden's *The Creation* got its first American performance at Bethlehem, as did his *Seasons*, *Song of the Bell*, *Seven Sleepers*, and *Paradise and the Peri*. The Bethlehem members also published certain scores by Bach, which they obtained from people in the European Moravian communities, before such works were printed in Europe.

As the economic life of the community prospered, the necessity for every member to engage fully in the labor of the community became less urgent, and so disagreements began to develop among them over the fact that some worked hard while others could be lazy. Also, as early as 1759, there was a demand for more family privacy, and as a result some of the buildings were turned into family apartment houses. When Nathaniel Seidel and Frederick von Marschall were put in charge of Bethlehem, they began to dissolve the General Economy system and reformulate the community under the Herrnhut system used in Europe. By 1762 this process was completed.

The work rules now included the following: everyone was required to support the public interests of the community; the congregation was to care for those who could not provide for themselves; no marriage was to be contracted without the knowledge of the elders and parents; no one was to lend or borrow money or start a new trade without first consulting a committee; and whoever built a house had no right to sell it without consulting the same committee. The community as a whole maintained ownership of the property, and gained profits from the various mills, stores, and other industries. However, member families could now own their own homes and household properties.

By 1884 Bethelehem had become so prosperous that the members decided to disband their communal structures. The town was incorporated into a borough in 1845, and it has since rapidly increased in size and population. Though some of the Moravian buildings can still be seen and visited, the city of Bethlehem now has few indications of this once-thriving commune. Books that have sections that focus on Bethlehem are Sessler's *Communal Pietism Among Early American Moravians* and Martin's *Historical Sketch of Bethlehem in Pennsylvania.*

Bethlehem-Yehuda (1882–1885), on the line between Davison and Aurora counties in South Dakota, was a Jewish agricultural commune (see **Sicily Island**). It was composed of 32 unmarried Russian men who called themselves the Sons of Freedom and, unlike most of the other Jewish would-be farmers, refused financial help from any of the American Jewish philanthropies. Their 165 acres of land were located near the **Crémieux** agricultural community.

In their constitution for Bethlehem-Yehuda, they stated that they intended to be a model for other such groups in proving "that Jews, like other groups, are capable of becoming agri-

culturalists." The members maintained their Russian heritage by gathering in the evenings for discussion and entertainment, all conducted in the Russian language. They also published a Russian-language newspaper. But their crops soon failed and many of the members left for New York City in discouragement. Finally the commune was liquidated when there were only a few members left.

Bettina (1847–1848), on the north bank of the Llano River where Elm Creek flows into it, about a mile from Castell, Texas, was a commune of 33 male students who came from the German universities of Giessen and Heidelberg. They based their economy on total communism, and started their experiment by constructing a temporary, reed-covered shed to live in. It was 40 by 20 feet in size. Later they replaced this with an adobe structure.

In 1848 they raised 200 bushels of corn. But they abandoned their project that summer because of conflicts within the group. Their leaders were Dr. Ferdinand von Herff and Gustav Schleicker. Dr. Herff returned to Germany, but the others remained in Texas. Five of them helped establish another German-speaking commune in that state — **Tusculum**. Schleicker was later elected to the Texas House of Representatives and Senate, and, in 1874, to the U.S. House of Representatives. A book with a section that focuses on Bettina is Biesele's *The History of the German Settlements in Texas, 1831–1861.*

Beula *see* **Watervliet in Ohio**.

Bhoodan Center (1960–1972), near Oakhurst, California, was a Quaker-oriented commune and center for research on communal living. It was organized in

1960 under the leadership of Charles Davis, and it never had more than 15 members. *Bhoodan* is a Hindu term for "sharing of land." The group also called itself the Manahar Cooperative Fellowship, the Hindu word *manahar* meaning "harmony of man and nature." A book with a section that focuses on the Bhoodan Center is Roberts' *The New Communes: Coming Together in America.*

Big Stone Brüderhof (1958–present), near Graceville, Minnesota, is a Hutterite commune (see **Bon Homme**). In 1964, there were 108 members and the commune was led by Samuel Hofer.

Birch Creek (1947–present), near Valier, Montana, is a Hutterite Brüderhof (see **Bon Homme**) that had 79 members in 1964. Its minister was Jacob Waldner.

Bishop Hill (1846–1862), in Henry County, Illinois, was a commune of Swedish immigrants led by Erik Janson (1808–1850). Most of the members were farmers from the region of Helsingland in Sweden, and they were pietists and separatists from the Lutheran state church. Janson, their chief preacher, had clairvoyant tendencies and thought of himself as a reincarnation of Christ. He taught that the Bible alone should be used for religious services, although he wrote hymns and developed a catechism for the community. He also mobilized his followers for public burnings of the orthodox Lutheran hymn books and catechisms. Janson was frequently arrested by Swedish officials because of his beliefs and actions. One of his primary teachings was that all Christians should practice community of property because that was the state of the early Christian church.

In 1845 Janson sent one of his followers, Olaf Olson, to the United States to look for a place where the group might live together, free from religious persecution. Olson found the location in Illinois and the 800 members then settled there in 1846, the wealthier ones paying for the land and all the travel expenses.

During their first year in Illinois the members of the Bishop Hill commune suffered great privation, having to live in caves that they hollowed from a gorge near the South Edwards Creek that ran through their property. They had to use a cloth tent for their church that first year. But, in time, they prospered. By 1859 they owned 12,000 acres of good farmland, were out of debt, and were raising some of the finest cattle in the state. They now had a brick church, a kitchen and dining hall for their communal meals, brick houses for each family, a bakery, a dye house, a weaving factory, a laundry, tailor and shoemaker shops, wagon and harness shops, a blacksmith shop, and even a hotel.

Everyone, both male and female, worked together in teams, some for a maximum of 18 hours a day. The members were able to add to the commune's income by working together in such teams to build bridges and roadbeds for the Chicago, Burlington, and Quincy Railroad line. Contemporary reports show that their life centered around church services, was relatively happy, and reflected many aspects of their Swedish background. Some of their history and lifestyle are depicted in a collection of paintings completed by the primitive artist Olaf Krans (1838–1916). These show the commune members at work in groups on a variety of projects, and include individual portraits of the leading members. The paintings are now on display at the Bishop Hill

Bishop Hill's Colony Church that now serves as museum for the Swedish commune (photo by author).

Historic Site, maintained by the Illinois State Historical Society.

In 1850 Janson was shot and killed in the Henry County courthouse by John Root, a man on trial for forcibly abducting Janson's niece from Bishop Hill. For a few days after Janson's death, his followers fully expected him to rise again, but as he did not move they finally buried him. Janson's wife and the commune business manager, Jonas Olson, then assumed leadership and made no changes in the daily routine that Janson had established. In 1861 the community raised a company of soldiers to fight on the Union side in the Civil War. One of the members of this group later graduated with honors from West Point. The commune continued to prosper, and the membership grew to 1,100 before the participants decided to abandon their communal economy. This happened after one of their number, Nils Heden, visited several Shaker communes and returned to Bishop Hill to advocate the system of celibacy in force among the Shakers. Debate over the value of celibacy to the Christian lifestyle expanded into disagreements over religious doctrines and finally to charges of financial mismanagement. In a surprisingly short time the members agreed to divide their communal property equally and to convert to other religions — some to Methodism and others to Seventh-day Adventism.

Many of the remains of Bishop Hill's commune can be seen today. These include their church, their bakery and brewery building, their school house, their cheese factory, many of their homes, and the cemetery with Janson's grave. Books with sections that focus on Bishop Hill are Calverton's *Where Angels Dared to Tread*, Holloway's *Heavens on Earth*, and Nordhoff's *The Communistic Societies of the United States*.

Bloomfield Union Association (1844–1847), also known as the Union Association and as the North Bloomfield Association, was a Fourierist commune (see **Social Reform Unity**) located on the west side of Honeoye Creek near the village of North Bloomfield, New York. The phalanx had about 500 members and 750 acres of land.

The phalanxtry building they constructed is still standing. They also built a cider mill, a saw mill, a grist mill, and a broom handle factory. One of the leaders was Edwin A. Stillman, a civil engineer who had just a few months earlier been a member of Noyes' **Putney Corporation**, a Perfectionist commune. After he left the Perfectionists, Stillman became an ardent convert of Fourierism and remained with the Bloomfield Union Association until it ended.

Blue Spring (1826–1827), about eight miles southwest of Bloomington, Indiana, was an Owenite community (see **New Harmony**) that started with 18 families but soon added nine more to grow to a total membership of about 75 persons, several of whom were teachers and ministers from Monroe County, Indiana. They owned 80 acres of land near the large spring from which the community derived its name.

The members drafted a constitution on April 10, 1826, acquired more land, and erected 24 cabins to live in. They enclosed their cabins within a stockade to protect themselves from Indians. They also built a schoolhouse, granary, and two stores. Two of the leaders were John Givens and Dudley C. Smith.

It is not known why this commune closed or what happened to the members. Their site is now marked by a Church of Christ sanctuary called Harmony. It stands about one mile northeast of Blue Spring.

Blumengard (1950–present), north of Wecota, South Dakota, is a Brüderhof (see **Bon Homme**) established by a group of Hutterites who came from Manitoba, Canada. They had 102 members in 1964 and Jacob Hofer was their leader.

Bohemia Manor (1684–1727), in Cecil County, Maryland (about three miles south of Chesapeake City), was a communal settlement of perhaps 100 members established by Jasper Dankaerts (1639–1702) and Peter Sluyter (1645–1722). They were Labadists, persons who advocated the teachings of the Frenchman Jean de Labadie. Some sources say that the community was first set up in New York, but this is a mistake. Dankaerts and Sluyter may have considered New York, but they wisely decided to go to Maryland where there was more religious toleration at the time. New York was ruled by Governor Andros, a Catholic who was openly hostile to all Labadists.

The founder of the Labadist movement, Jean de Labadie (1610–1674), was a Jesuit priest who, under the ever widening influence of the Reformation, broke with the Catholic Church and began to preach his own somewhat mystical theology throughout France. He gathered many followers and fortunately was protected from prosecution by Cardinal Richelieu. But when the Cardinal died in 1642, Labadie was attacked by church authorities and then arrested because of his writings and teachings. He was sentenced to life imprisonment, a sentence later changed to expulsion from France. He then preached in Geneva and Utrecht, and numbered among his followers Anna

Maria van Schruman, famed as one of the most learned women of her day.

Labadie eventually established a communal settlement near Amsterdam, Holland. This was moved after his death to castle grounds near Weiwert, Holland. A short-lived colony of Labadists was also established in Surinam in 1680. But many of the Labadists were convinced that the best place for setting up one of their communes would be in America. They raised money to send Dankaerts and Sluyter there in search of the right place to establish a new home.

The record of the American travels of these two emissaries is recorded in the *Journal of Jasper Dankaerts*, a book that still has merit as a human narrative about the persons and social conditions then prevailing in Boston, New York, New Jersey, Delaware, and Maryland. One particularly interesting section tells of the visit of these two to Harvard College, where they found the students meeting for classes in an upstairs "smoke-filled" and "tavern-like" room. The college had only 20 students at that time. In Maryland, Dankaerts and Sluyter were able to convert Ephraim Herman, a man who owned a very large tract of land in that area. Herman sold them 3,750 acres for the commune.

Most of the members at Bohemia Manor came from Holland, although there were a few from New Amsterdam (New York). The Labadists were close in their beliefs to those of the Quakers, particularly in relation to the doctrine of being guided by the spirit rather than by Biblical injunctions. Their prayers were always silent ones, and they dressed in the most simple fashion. The entire community ate together at separate tables — one for men and one for women — though each family lived in their own dwelling with doors unlocked to symbolize the communal nature of the settlement. Marriage was regarded as holy, and children were considered to belong to the Lord rather than to their parents. Thus they were raised by the community as a whole. Converts to the Labadist faith were required to separate from non–Labadist wives or husbands when they joined the settlement.

The labor in the community was equally divided among all the members. They raised tobacco, corn, flax, hemp, and cattle. On the whole, their food, clothing, and houses, though ordinary and simple, were equal to or superior to those of the individualist farmers who lived on the land adjacent to theirs.

As early as 1688, a proposal was made that they divide the community property among the members, each of whom would give up a fourth of their investment as a result. However, it was not until 1698 that this was done. Most of the members then abandoned the communal system, although a few tried to maintain their common lifestyle for a while afterward. By 1727 the colony, or its remains, was extinct. The community in Holland also divided its estates about 1698, and dwindled after 1703 until the last "speaker" died in 1732 and the Labadist society dissolved.

At the time of the division of the Bohemia Manor land, Sluyter, who was the designated head of the colony, reserved the best of it for himself. His behavior in later years was reportedly quite inconsistent with the principles of the Labadist society. He dealt in slaves, and was said to have treated many of them with extreme cruelty. When he died, he was a wealthy man. Books that have sections that focus on Bohemia Manor are Calverton's *Where Angels Dared to Tread* and James' *The Labadist Colony in Maryland*.

One of the original chalk-stone dwellings at Bon Homme as it stands today (drawing by Lois Will).

Bohemian Cooperative Farming Company (1913–1916), one mile west of Mayland, Tennessee, was a cooperative project for about 40 people from Bohemia. They had 5,300 acres of land that was completely covered with woods so that it had to be cleared for farming. In time they cleared and cultivated four fields of 30 acres each. Their principal crops were corn and potatoes. They also raised grapes, apples, pears, and mulberries.

The members worked seven days a week and observed only two holidays, Christmas and New Year. All the land was held in common, and they had a common treasury, a common storehouse, and 12 homes. Each home included a stable for horses. They sent their children to public school.

Dissension over the leadership caused the community to split into two camps in 1914, and a pitched battle between them ended in the severe wounding of one member. Law officers had to be called, and the president, a man named Heiser, left the commune under their protective custody. The last two families, the Sedvaks and the Heins, departed from this commune in 1916, and the land then reverted to the Nashville Trust Company because of nonpayment on the mortgage. A book with a section that focuses on the Bohemian Cooperative Farming Company is Miller's *Some Tennessee Utopias.*

Bon Homme (1874–present), at Bon Homme, South Dakota, was the first of many Hutterite communes, or Brüderhofs, established in the United States. Michael Waldner, a blacksmith, was the leader of the agricultural group at the time, and the members came from Moravia by way of several hundred years' exile in Russia. They had been forced to flee there in 1595 because of persecution. The pacifist beliefs of the Hutterites eventually led to their harassment and persecution in Russia and they were once more forced to migrate, this time to the United States. It is said that they were assured by President Grant that their pacifism would not cause trouble because "America would never fight in another war."

The Hutterites trace their decision to adopt a communal lifestyle to a particular event in 1528 when they stopped for rest and worship while fleeing through Moravia. Their leader read them the passage in Acts where the Christians held all things in common, and then he placed his cloak in front of his colleagues so that the members could put their money and other worldly possessions on top of it. From that moment on they have always shared equally. They developed the structures for their communities while in Russia, structures that have maintained Hutterite culture through 450 years of persecution, hardship, and prosperity.

As a community the Hutterites are closely knit. They believe it is sinful to marry outside their religion and so three family names now constitute nearly half of the present-day membership, and different leaders of various Hutterite communes can have the same first and last names, which causes some confusion in gathering statistics about them. Their cardinal principles are communal ownership of all property, pacifism, simple living, and adult baptism. Jewelry, art, and such creature comforts as overstuffed chairs are regarded as tools of the devil, as are radios, television sets, and movies. However they do have one telephone in each of their communes and they do read daily newspapers.

The uniformity of architecture in their buildings and the neat, unpaved walks between their homes is a visual testimony to the orderly existence of these communitarians. Time is measured out as discreetly as space.

There is an accepted activity for every moment of the day, each day of the week, and each season of the year.

They appear to hold onto the past tenaciously in everything except farming. Here they use modern trucks, tractors, and other equipment with great success. The Hutterites are among the most prosperous farmers in the states of South Dakota and Montana, where most of the Brüderhofs in the United States are located. They seem, in fact, to have discovered the secret of using technology without letting it dominate their lives and destroy their tranquillity.

Men and boys wear gray-black jackets and trousers, black felt hats in summer and fur ones in winter. The women and girls wear long black dresses. They cover their heads with shawls. After they marry, the men grow beards. The average Hutterite colony has at least four or five apartment buildings for family living quarters. Many of these are constructed of chalk-stone; some are also frame structures. Each family is allotted two to five rooms, depending on the number of children. There are community outhouses and showers, and one dining room serves the whole community. Each colony has many barns and workshops.

The women divide up the household duties and the men do the farm work. Hutterites disapprove of the use of firearms and tobacco, and physical punishment is generally unknown among them. All important decisions are made by a democratic majority, called together for a business meeting by the Brüderhof minister, who is elected to that post.

Children are given a grammar-school education, though formal education beyond the primary grades is not encouraged. However each child is required to attend a religious school in the commune from age 3 until baptism, usually at about age 20. They permit no instrumental music, and the only art they have is their needlework and crafts. The children do have their own games and the young people engage in group singing. Their main diversion is that of visiting neighboring Hutterite colonies and conversing among themselves. Much of the communication within each Brüderhof takes place in German, even though most of the members now speak English.

When the Bon Homme commune grew to a size of between 130 and 150 as a result of natural population growth within the community and Hutterites from Russia joining them, they divided the membership in half and set up a second commune. This policy has since been followed by all other Brüderhofs in the United States and Canada, so that the number of Hutterite communes increases as their population increases. In this way the communities are always kept somewhere close to 100 members. They believe that a large community places too much strain on the land and the established social structures. Whenever they decide to divide this way, land is purchased somewhere else for the new Brüderhof. The communes thus established are not satellites of the old ones, but separate communities in themselves, with separate leadership elected from within the new Brüderhof.

As in Russia, the Hutterite communes in the United States have suffered their share of persecution, particularly during wartime. The Hutterites were harassed almost beyond endurance during the period of irrational patriotism of the First World War. They were criticized at the beginning of the war for being unpatriotic, both because of their pacifism and because of their continued use of the "language of our enemy"—Germany.

Their churches were painted yellow by vigilante groups, who captured individual Hutterites and forced them to kiss the American flag. At one Hutterite colony the cattle were run off by hostile townspeople to be sold, the profit used to purchase Liberty Bonds in support of the war effort.

Added to such harassments, the Hutterites had to face the problems of conscription into the army. Their leaders sent a desperate appeal to President Woodrow Wilson on behalf of the young men at their colonies, outlining the Hutterite beliefs and pleading that the youth not be forced into the army against their religious convictions. But, beginning in the fall of 1917, young Hutterites were drafted and virtually dragged away to the army camps where they were put into special conscientious-objector barracks.

The extensive ridicule, and in some cases actual torture, inflicted on the Hutterite conscientious objectors by their army guards has been fully documented. Four Hutterites — Jacob Wipf and Jacob, David, and Michael Hofer — died as a result of the treatment they received after their induction. Even after the war, a group of anti–Hutterites raided one of the Hutterite communities and took their grape wine under the guise of the Prohibition Law. These raiders then assembled at the county seat and drank it.

The situation became so intolerable that most Hutterites migrated to Canada. But in 1935 some returned to farm their deserted lands in South Dakota. Today most neighbors leave them in peace. But as recently as 1949, State Congressman J. W. Dawson of Spink County, South Dakota, organized 75 farmers "to resist further expansion of the Hutterites." Dawson called them "Russians living an un–American existence," and said that they reaped huge profits from the state's land but gave nothing for the defense of their country. He further argued that their colonies destroyed "the existence of family-type farms." Fortunately for the Hutterites, Dawson's campaign dissolved after he lost the next election.

But despite such problems, the Hutterites do not share in the widespread symptoms of alienation and futility found in much of broader American society. In fact they are conspicuous for their lack of identity problems. Psychologists Joseph Eaton and Robert Weil, who have made a study of the mental health of Hutterites, found that in many respects they demonstrate fewer symptoms of neuroses than do most other Americans.

When the first members of the Bon Homme colony came to the United States, they purchased about 2,500 acres for this colony under the Homestead Act at a cost of $25,000. Their first crop season was a good one, and they were able to keep out the locusts that destroyed the crops of many other South Dakota farmers that year. They also maintained herds of geese, flocks of pigeons, a large herd of sheep, many cattle, and fruit trees. Their main product, however, was flour that they stored in a tall flour mill.

During World War I, when hostility against the Hutterites reached its greatest extent, neighbors put broken glass in this flour mill in order to be able to accuse the Hutterites of sabotaging the war effort. The Bon Homme community, however, was not intimidated by these groundless accusations. They remained in South Dakota and never moved to Canada, as did the other colonies that experienced such hostility.

In 1964 Bon Homme had 108 members. Their minister was Jacob Waldner. In the same year there were a total of 4,210 Hutterites in the whole United States and 10,497 in Canada for a total of 14,707 in both countries. Throughout the United States they had set up 57 separate Brüderhofs by 1963. And more have been established since that date. Books with sections that focus on Bon Homme are Conkin's *Two Paths to Utopia: The Hutterites and the Llano Colony* and Peters' *All Things in Common: The Hutteran Way of Life.*

Broad River (1756–1783), in Craven County, South Carolina, was a Seventh-day Baptist community organized by Israel Seymour, a former sailor, pirate captain, Indian fighter, and leader of the **Nantmel** Seventh-day Baptist commune. The exact location of this settlement is unknown, though it was in the Parish of St. Mark at some point along the 85-mile stretch of the Broad River north of present-day Columbia, South Carolina.

Seymour had moved to this area to be near some of the settlers recently arrived from Chester County, Pennsylvania, the location of his Nantmel community. Possibly some of them had even been members of Nantmel. Earlier Seymour had departed from Chester County totally despised by the other members of the Seventh-day Baptist denomination because of his irresponsible behavior. He had joined the army in South Carolina and, during a battle with the Indians, almost lost his life. He now vowed, therefore, to mend his ways.

Seymour told the people from Pennsylvania about his experiences and his new-found faith, and being a rather charismatic figure, they decided to accept him as their pastor. Within a

Brook Farm residence building, today used as Lutheran orphanage (photo by author).

short time he had organized them into an Ephrata-style commune, although Seymour decided to abandon Ephrata's celibacy rule. He married the daughter of Victor Nally, one of the members of his Broad River commune, and had three children.

The membership at Broad River eventually reached more than 40 persons and the experiment lasted for more than 25 years. Some of the members were John Dumckly, Joshua Edwards, Benjamin Gregory, Eli Harris, and Thomas Owen. In 1783 they sent a letter to **Ephrata**, signed by Seymour and all the other members, telling of their success and suggesting further contact with that Seventh-day Baptist center. But the Ephrata Brothers and Sisters declined to answer and the Broad River settlement has left no other records.

Brocton Community *see* **Brotherhood of the New Life.**

Brook Farm (1841–1847), at West Roxbury, Massachusetts, now within the city limits of Boston, began as a product of the transcendentalist movement and a showplace for Christian socialism. The commune was founded by George Ripley, had more than 120 members at its highest point, and was widely regarded as an intellectual center. After four years of existence, the members changed its purpose into that of a Fourierist community.

The transcendentalist movement of the 1830s developed in New England as a reaction against the mechanical materialism and rationalism of much eighteenth century philosophy. Most of the inspiration for this movement came from Unitarian ministers, people like William Ellery Channing, who believed that the spirit had gone out of the churches and that religion needed a new vision. The proponents claimed that the invisible spirit is the true reality, and held that each person is an extension of a universal spirit, or "over-soul," that speaks through them in a unique and creative way. They defended the right of each individual to follow the dictates of his or her own conscience, rather than established religious authority. Probably the most outstanding spokesman for transcendentalism was the essayist and philosopher Ralph Waldo Emerson.

The founder of Brook Farm, George Ripley (1802–1880), was one of Unitarianism's most promising ministers. He bought the 22-acre property for the experiment in 1840. It contained a farm house and a large barn. With his wife, sister, and 15 other people, including novelist Nathaniel Hawthorne and journalist Charles Dana, he moved there in April 1841. They agreed that labor could offset the price of board, and decided that each member should work 60 hours a week from May to October and 48 from November to April. Members who did not work were charged $4 a week for their rent, fuel, light, and laundry. Each member was allowed one vote in all matters relating to the disposition of community funds.

In time, the amount of property was extended to include 208 acres, and the members made substantial additions to the original house, purchased or built three others, and constructed a workshop and a greenhouse. Later, during their Fourierist period, they partially completed a huge phalanxtry building. Besides the chores of farming and housekeeping, members engaged in carpentry, shoemaking, printing, and the manufacturing of small items such as lamps and coffee pots.

The most notable achievement of Brook Farm was its school that anticipated many developments of progressive education, a school that Harvard College recommended as a suitable place for young men who needed special instruction and temporary seclusion because of difficulties in college. The curriculum included Latin, German, Greek, moral philosophy, mathematics, botany, English classics, music, art, and other advanced courses. They also had a three-year course in theoretical and practical agriculture, and they encouraged the arts of music and drawing. Each student was expected to devote an hour or two each day to some kind of manual labor. A measure of their success in education can be seen in the strong attacks that were directed against them by a few now-forgotten college professors who called them "miseducators" and "destroyers of the young."

George P. Bradford, a member of Brook Farm and part of its teaching staff, later said this was the only school in New England at that time that offered "a varied culture — intellectual, moral and practical." The program was roughly based on the theories and practices of the great Swiss educational pioneer, J. H. Pestalozzi. The Brook Farmers attempted to make everyone a teacher of what he or she knew, and everyone a learner of what he or she did not know. An infant school, for those under 6 years of age, was also set up, as well as a primary school.

Enjoyment was as seriously pursued at Brook Farm as any other activity. There were boating parties, picnics, dances, lectures, and long walks. Literary societies and reading clubs flourished, and impromptu plays and charades offered much amusement. Frequently the members hiked to Boston to hear good music, a journey of nine miles. There was also a constant stream of visitors to the farm. During the first year alone, over 4,000 people came to see how the experiment was progressing. Among these visitors were such distinguished personalities as Henry James, Ralph Waldo Emerson, William Channing, Horace Greeley, Margaret Fuller, and Henry David Thoreau, apparently the only visitor disappointed with the place. Thoreau later wrote, "I'd rather keep bachelor's hall in hell than go to board in heaven if that place is heaven."

In its short career, Brook Farm brought into association with itself, directly through membership or indirectly through visitors, the most outstanding of New England's literary and philosophic talent. One member, George William Curtis, later became a noted writer. Another, Isaac Thomas Hecker, was instrumental in forming the Roman Catholic Paulist Order. And still another, John Orvis, became a noted champion of workers' rights and proponent of business and labor cooperatives.

On May 3, 1845, the members of Brook Farm reorganized into a Fourierist commune (see **Social Reform Unity**) and renamed it Brook Farm Phalanx. At that point the headquarters of Fourierism moved to Brook Farm from New York City, and the magazine of Fourierism, the *Phalanx*, was changed in name to the *Harbinger*, to be published here. This magazine soon became one of the outstanding periodicals for recording the intellectual events of that day. It included among its contributors James Russell Lowell, John Greenlief Whittier, and Henry James, as well as other leading writers. National conventions of the Fourierists were now also held at Brook Farm. One of these was dedicated, in Channing's words, to "a united contemplation of the wonderful progress...of the great truths of Social Science discovered by Charles Fourier."

But on March 3, 1846, their nearly-completed phalanxtry building burned to the ground, a disaster from which Brook Farm never recovered. The community disbanded in 1847. On April 13, 1849, the farm was sold at auction. Ripley's original farm house is now the Martin Luther Orphans' Home, operated by the Evangelical Lutheran Church. The site is on the west side of Baker Street in Boston, north of its intersection with the Veterans of Foreign Wars Parkway, formerly called the Brook Farm Parkway.

Emerson spoke often of Brook Farm, and though he never supported it, wrote the following verdict on the venture:

> Brook Farm existed six or seven years, when the society broke up and the farm was sold, and all parties came out with a loss; some had spent on it the accumulations of years. At the moment all regarded it as a failure; but I do not think that all so regard it now, but probably as an important chapter in their experience, which has been of life-long value. What knowledge has it not afforded them! What personal power which the studies of character have given; what accumulated culture many members owe to it; what mutual pleasure they took of each other! A close union like that of a ship's cabin, of persons in various conditions; clergymen, young collegians, merchants, mechanics, farmers' sons and daughters, with men of rare opportunities and culture.

Nathaniel Hawthorne, who left Brook Farm in great disillusionment, wrote about it in a thinly disguised satire titled *The Blithedale Romance* (1852). Here he recounts with some venom how some commune members were permitted to spend their time reading poetry while others had to tend the cows. The book rightly contrasts the aims of the professional reformers who organized the commune with their actual accomplishments. But Hawthorne's bitterness over the actions of those he describes so overshadows the work that the plot of the novel becomes vague and the conversations labored. In the end, the book fails both as a romance and as a satirical comment on commune life. Books with sections that focus on Brook Farm are Madison's *Critics and Crusaders* and Swift's *Brook Farm, Its Members, Scholars and Visitors.*

Brooklyn Perfectionists (1849–1855), at Brooklyn, New York, was a commune that developed out of the teachings of John Humphrey Noyes (see **Putney Corporation**). There were only about ten members and they were closely related to the parent commune, **Oneida**, to which they moved when they closed this community. The Brooklyn Perfectionists did much of the early printing for the Perfectionist movement. They also manufactured suitcases and other types of traveling bags.

Brotherhood (1847), in the southeastern corner of Clermont County, Ohio, was a ten-member community established on the abandoned land of the **Clermont Phalanx**. It was organized by John O. Wattles, who had been a member of that commune as well as the **Prairie Home Community**. He called himself a Christian communist and his stated purpose was "to secure education, elevation, purity, and unity of the human family" through agricultural and industrial labor. He later established one other commune, the **Grand Prairie Harmonial Association**, near Lafayette, Indiana. The Brotherhood closed after floods destroyed the homes of the ten members.

Brotherhood Community (1953–1960), near Springville, Pennsylvania, was a pacifist community of about ten members that was organized by the Rev. Richard and Elena Fichter. They organized the community following Rev. Fichter's dismissal as a pastor of the Springville Methodist Church because of his refusal to pay income taxes to a government that he believed allocated much of its money for the military establishment. The commune members owned 92 acres of land that they operated as a dairy farm. They also engaged in peace walks, picketing of missile bases, and other kinds of demonstrations for disarmament.

Brotherhood of the New Age *see* **Southern Co-operative Association of Apalachicola.**

Brotherhood of the New Life (1861–1881), first at Wassiac, then Amenia, and finally Brocton, New York, was a spiritualist community led by Thomas Lake Harris (1823–1906). He was a Universalist minister and poet who had earlier pastored two churches in New York City. It is said that one of his sermons led directly to the founding of the New York Juvenile Asylum. Harris left the first church in 1848 after he became interested in spiritualism, and he then organized an Independent Christian Congregation called the Church of the Good Shepherd. Publisher Horace Greeley was one of its members. But Harris, in 1850, departed from that congregation to join the **Mountain Cove** spiritualist commune in West Virginia for a brief period. He also began publication of a monthly magazine, *The Herald of Light*, and he went to England to lecture widely on spiritualism.

The commune he founded with a handful of followers at Wassiac was often referred to as "The Use" by its members, after the idea that all members surrendered themselves to divine use or purpose. They had two particularly distinctive practices: "open breathing," a method of respiration by which the Divine breath was supposed to enter the body; and "celibate marriage," a system in which all members were said to live in spiritual union with a "heavenly counterpart."

By the time this community moved to Brocton, they owned 1,600 acres of land and their membership had grown to 75, including several American women of high social position and some people from England and Japan. Two of these were Lawrence Oliphant (1829–1888) and his mother, who contributed large sums of money to the project. Oliphant even gave up his seat in the English House of Lords in order to move to this American commune. Another member who gave a sizable fortune to Harris was Jane Lee Waring, a rich American. The members engaged in agriculture and wine making, and even for a short time ran a hotel and restaurant in the nearby village. The commune was sometimes also called Salem-on-Erie and, by those less friendly, the Brocton Community.

Harris strongly opposed the use of private property for individual ends and, increasingly with the years, became involved in socialist politics. By 1861 he was attending many labor meetings and writing songs for these gatherings. In an issue of *The New Republic* that year, he wrote an article that laid out his theological foundations for socialism. He complained that most other socialists were faulty in their thinking because they did not base their ideas on religion. He wrote of Christ as the "Socialist of all Socialists."

In 1873 Harris quarreled with Oliphant and left the Brotherhood of the New Life, taking some of its members with him. They moved to Califor-

nia where Harris set up the **Fountain Grove** spiritualist commune. Oliphant continued to run the Wassiac settlement until 1881 when he sold the property and departed. The few remaining members at the Brotherhood of the New Life then moved to California to rejoin Harris. Books with sections that focus on the Brotherhood of the New Life are Hinds' *American Communities*, Hine's *California's Utopian Communities*, and Noyes' *History of American Socialisms*.

Brown House (1962–1963), 101 Sixth Avenue in San Francisco, California, was formed as a cooperative community for 12 persons by Leo F. Koch. He was a former professor of biology at the University of Illinois who was fired in the 1950s for his advocacy of more liberal sexual relations between students. The members were all active in the peace movement. Most were unemployed. According to Koch, "We bought out needed food supplies wholesale and enjoyed each other's company enough to provide quite a saving in cost of entertainment." The residence has since been torn down to be replaced by a modern apartment building.

Bryn Gweld (1940–present), at Southampton, in Bucks County, Pennsylvania, is a homestead community established by followers of Ralph Borsodi (see **Bayard Lane Homestead Community**). It had 124 members in 1959, including a contractor, engineer, lawyer, editor, stained glass artist, tool designer, social worker, and school teacher.

The community encompasses 240 acres, 80 of which are held in common. Each member is expected to give a day's work each month to common community labor, although each member family is expected to finance and build their own home. All community business is handled at meetings of the entire adult membership.

Buffalo Colony (1907–1918), in Beadle County, South Dakota, was a Hutterite Brüderhof (see **Bon Homme**) of about 100 members founded by people from the **Tripp** Brüderhof. They moved to a second location in the same county in 1913, and were then known as the **James Valley Colony**. In 1918 they moved to Manitoba, Canada, where they still exist.

Bunkerville (1875–1882), about three miles south of Mesquite, Nevada, was a Mormon commune that adopted the United Order system in use at **Orderville** so that the members might build an irrigation system to bring water from a river below to their fields high above on a plateau of land. The community had perhaps 200 members.

Bureau County Phalanx see **Lamoille Agricultural and Mechanical Association**

Burley Colony see **Cooperative Brotherhood**

Burning Bush (1913–1919), one mile southeast of Bullard, Texas, was established by a group of Methodists who had left their church to form the evangelical Metropolitan Church Association that had its headquarters in Waukesha, Wisconsin. They gathered small groups of followers in Virginia, West Virginia, Louisiana, and Texas, and then purchased the 1,520-acre site for this commune. It was also known as the Metropolitan Institute of Texas.

The 375 members held all their goods in common, drew from a common storehouse, and ate at a common table, although they lived in separate houses. They had a church, saw mill, and cannery. At one point they tried to drill an oil well on the property, but it came up dry. They believed that it was possible, after gaining a "second blessing," to live without sin, to speak in tongues, and to cure illness by faith alone. They forbade the use of liquor and tobacco. Neighbors often called them "holy jumpers" because of the enthusiasm with which they worshipped.

The commune disbanded shortly after World War I because the group's financial backer, Duke Farson, lost his bond business in Chicago. The land was then seized for debts and sold at auction on April 15, 1919.

Calavaros County Community (1887), in Calavaros County, California, was a Jewish cooperative farm (see **Sicily Island**) of perhaps ten members. Its exact location cannot be verified and little else is known about it.

Cambridge Perfectionists (1849–1855), at Cambridge, Vermont, was a commune of about ten followers of the teachings of John Humphrey Noyes (see **Putney Corporation**). They were organized into a commune by some Perfectionists from the **Oneida** community.

Camphill Village (1955–present), at Copake, New York, is a Christian community established to care for mentally retarded adults. It was modeled on a similar community in Scotland that was started in 1939 by Dr. Karl Koenig, a Viennese pediatrician. Among the founders of this New York commune were Helmut and Gerda von Jeetze. There are 220 members, of whom half are mentally handicapped. They work on farms and in craft shops, where they manufacture enameled copper ware, woodwork, woven goods, and batik.

Shakers in worship (Crown House Publishers).

The community includes custom-built homes, farm buildings, and a large meeting hall. The rehabilitation program is supported by private donations, corporate grants, government benefits received by the handicapped residents, and money received from the farm products and craft items that the residents make.

The program at Camphill is based on the Curative Education methods developed by Rudolph Steiner. At the heart of this philosophy is the conviction that all human beings, handicapped or not, must be allowed to develop their spiritual potential fully and take their rightful place in society. Training in useful skills, nondenominational spiritual support, cultural activities and recreation is available to all the handicapped villagers who participate and contribute to the community along with their nonhandicapped coworkers and their families.

As Helmut von Jeetze puts it, "The handicapped person is actually a homeless person. There has to be someone who will create a place the handicapped will consider home." Five other Camphill settlements of this type have been established in Minnesota and Pennsylvania, but all at a later date than the communities included in this book. A book with a section that focuses on Camphill Village is Fairfield's *Communes U.S.A.: A Personal Tour.*

Canterbury (1792–1992), New Hampshire, 12 miles north of Concord, was a Shaker commune (see **Watervliet**) that was once the center for Shaker music. The initial 100 acres for the community was donated by Benjamin Whitcher and Henry Clough, both converts to Shakerism. Later purchases increased the size of this property until it encompassed 3,000 acres. Although the land was rather poor for farming, it did include some timber and a sheep farm. The first leaders were Job Bishop and Hannah Goodrich.

In the early years, the members of Canterbury manufactured spinning wheels, sieves, dry measures, mortars, brooms, whips, and scythe handles. But the invention of a crude washing machine at the **Mount Lebanon** Shaker commune, which was later improved and patented at Canterbury, led them to drop some of these lines and turn to making large washing machines and mangles for hotels and public institutions. They also manufactured wood stoves, wove woolen cloth, knit wool socks, had a herb and dairy industry, and sold stock and hay. One of their most popular and widely advertised products was Corbett's Shaker Syrup and Sarsaparilla. This was initially formulated by Tom Corbett, a member who also built a static electric machine in 1810 that had its charge drawn off into a Leyden jar. It is said to have been the first therapeutic electric machine made in the United States.

The community reached its peak of prosperity under David Parker, who became a leader at age 19. He was known as one of the most honorable business men in the state, and was called upon to defend the Shakers before the state legislature and to defend their pacifist position before Congress. During his administration the commune grew in membership to 300, assembled into three "families."

Because much of the land at Canterbury was on top of a high plateau, the members constructed eight ponds, or reservoirs, and water was transported by aqueduct to all the households below. Mills were built next to these ponds. The community also had a steam laundry, tannery, infirmary, and library of 400 volumes. They built their meeting house in 1792, main dwelling of 56 rooms in 1793, schoolhouse in 1823, and a barn that was large enough to hold 100 cows in 1858.

Canterbury became the center of musical knowledge for Shakerism around 1870. It provided music teachers for many of their other Shaker communes, and on their printing press were printed many Shaker hymn books. In 1852 Elder Henry Clay Blinn (1824–1905) collected and published a book of Shaker hymns and anthems. Some years later the community hired Professor Davis of Concord, New Hampshire, to come to the settlement and give them singing lessons.

Elder Arthur Bruce, a gifted musician with a fine baritone voice, organized the Shaker Ladies Quartet that gave concerts in many towns throughout New England. Eldress Dorothy Durgin, one of the best Shaker hymn writers, composed over 30 hymns at Canterbury. It is also here that the most famous of Shaker hymns, "Simple Gifts," was probably written. Eventually the members even developed an orchestra of two violins, a coronet, a cello, two saxophones, a drum, cymbals, a pipe organ, and a piano.

Canterbury had three remaining members living communally on the property in 1982, but the last one died ten years later, so the commune no longer exists and the site has now been turned into a Shaker museum.

Canterbury (1957), at Canterbury, New Hampshire, was established by eight members of the **Macedonia Cooperative** after it disbanded. One of the members, Louis Gosho, was killed in a construction accident, and the community came to an end soon after. His wife then joined the **May Valley Cooperative Community**.

Canton Phalanx (1845), a few miles from Canton, Illinois, was a commune organized by members of the First New Jerusalem Swedenborgian Church of Canton. They had become convinced that the teachings of the Fourierists regarding the establishment of communes (see **Social Reform Unity**) were correct, and they had decided to start their own phalanx. In the spring of 1845 all the members of the church (perhaps 45 persons) moved to a farm owned by John F. Randolph, a leader of the church and president of the Illinois Association of Swedenborgians.

Randolph's property covered three to four hundred acres. It included a large mill that the members turned into their phalanx building. To this they attached a series of clapboard shanties in order to enlarge it so that they could all live within the one structure. The additions made the whole building look so strange that it was nicknamed "The Bird." The members also used several cabins on the land for workshops and living quarters, as well as Randolph's home.

Randolph died in the early part of the summer. The Canton Phalanx was disbanded in the fall. The breakup of this commune signaled the end of the Swedenborgian Church in Canton. A book with a section that focuses on the Canton Phalanx is Bestor's *American Phalanxes, the Fourierist Phase of Socialism in the United States.*

Cape May Farm (1943), at Cape May, New Jersey, was a Catholic Worker farm (see **Maryfarm** on Staten Island) of perhaps 15 members. It lasted only a few months before it closed.

Carp Lake (1882), at Carp Lake, Michigan, near the Straits of Mackinac, was an agricultural commune of about 30 Russian Jews (see **Sicily Island**). They knew little about farming and did not have enough capital to keep the project alive for more than a few months.

Cedar Vale Benevolent and Educational Society (1875–1877), at Cedar Vale, Kansas, was formed by Alexander Malikov and 14 other Russian revolutionaries who had originally come to the United States to join the **Investigating Community**, but found such differences with that group that they formed their own commune nearby. The members had all participated in the revolutionary movement in Russia and now rejected violence in favor of a spiritual regeneration aimed at bringing about personal perfection. They acquired 160 acres of land about four miles from the Investigating Community, and they practiced a combination of Quakerism and socialism.

But the Russians had difficulty maintaining their commune life because of personality conflicts and so they invited William Frey of the Investigating Community to join them. They thought his experience in leading other communes would prove of value. Frey did so, which effectively led to the closing of the Investigating Community. But within two years this Cedar Vale commune also closed. Some of the Russians were homesick and had decided to return to Russia, Malikov among them. One couple joined the Shakers, and Frey moved to New York City to work toward the reform of the world.

Celesta (1862–1864), four miles west of Laporte, Pennsylvania, was a Second-Adventist commune founded by Peter Armstrong (1800–1892) and his wife. Armstrong had prospered enough as a peddler in Philadelphia to purchase the 2,500 acres of land for the community, which he divided into 360 lots arranged somewhat like the street plan for Philadelphia. He issued an appeal for settlers through his publication called the *Day Star of Zion and Banner of Life of Philadelphia and Celesta.*

The members awaited the second coming of Christ in 1863. They held that a total of 144,000 people were to be gathered to await this event. Their membership, however, never grew to more than 20, although Armstrong's paper had a circulation of 3,000. The members erected four houses, two barns, a saw mill, and some smaller buildings. They also cleared 100 acres to begin farming.

When the second coming did not occur as Armstrong had predicted, hardships and dissatisfaction among the members forced the abandonment of their project. Armstrong then deeded the land to "Almighty God," and it was taken over by the county for unpaid taxes. Books with sections that focus on Celesta are Fogarty's *All Things New* and Wooster's *Communities of the Past and Present.*

Celo Community (1937–present), about six miles from Micaville, North Carolina, and near Mt. Celo, is a commune that was started by Quakers under the leadership of Arthur E. Morgan. Morgan had previously been president of Antioch College and then chairman of the Tennessee Valley Authority.

The commune has 1,200 acres of land and has had more than 90 members at one time. They claim there are presently about 20 families on a waiting list of applicants. Each participating family owns their own home. The membership is no longer exclusively Quaker in religious preference. They have a health clinic for members and people from the surrounding area, a pharmaceutical manufacturing plant, a woodworking shop, a cooperative store, a camp for 7–12-year-old girls and boys, a highly-accredited boarding school for grades seven to nine, and a printing plant.

Celo members take part in many activities in the wider community, including a community arts council and music program, a prison ministry, Meals on Wheels, the Western North Carolina Alliance, and other such projects. In 1982 the Celo Community was cited nationally for its activity in solar housing. One of its members, Wendell Thomas, was designated posthumously as "Solar Pioneer of the Year" for his work in that field. A book with a section that focuses on Celo is Infield's *Cooperative Communities at Work.*

Charles Mix Brüderhof (1949–present), also called the Platte Brüderhof, is a Hutterite colony (see **Bon Homme**) near Academy in Charles Mix County, South Dakota. In 1964 it had 76 members and was led by Joseph Waldner.

Chatham Colony Association (1923–1969), at Chatham, New Jersey, was a cooperative community of Jewish artists that may have had as many as 55 members at one time.

Cheat River (1751–1758), in Preston County, West Virginia, was a Seventh-day Baptist commune given this name because of its location. The site, on the eastern bank of the river, was three miles east of Kingwood, in an area now called Dunkards Hollow. It was formed by the Eckerlin brothers — Gabriel, Samuel, and Israel — who had been asked to depart from the main Seventh-day Baptist commune, **Ephrata**, because their shrewd business activities were said to be causing an attitude of selfishness among the members there. The Eckerlin brothers also established a Seventh-day Baptist commune in Virginia (see **Mahanaim**).

The eight members of Cheat River at first tried to establish their settlement at a place about ten miles below Morgantown, West Virginia. But the Delaware Indians, with whom they were friendly, urged them to move in order to avoid contact with the Iroquois Indians, then on the warpath.

At Cheat River they erected a mill, built cabins, planted grain, made maple sugar, and kept a string of 28 horses. In 1758, the settlement was attacked and destroyed by the Iroquois, led by a Catholic priest from Pennsylvania. According to one authority this is the only known case of religious persecution by the Roman Catholic clergy of provincial Pennsylvania. Four commune members were killed, three captured, and Samuel Eckerlin alone escaped because he was away on a trading trip at the time. He later joined the **Shenandoah** commune.

Cheltenham (1858–1864), now within the city limits of St. Louis, Missouri, was an Icarian commune (see **Icaria**) formed by 18 or more followers of Étienne Cabet. They were among a group of 180, including Cabet, who had left **Icarian Nauvoo** in 1856 over a dispute regarding Cabet's plans to move that commune to Iowa. Though their leader died soon after they reached St. Louis, this handful of his most devoted followers went ahead with plans to establish a new Icarian commune, this one called Cheltenham. When it closed five years later, the members went to Corning, Iowa, where some of the others who had departed from Nauvoo with Cabet had already established the second **Icaria**.

Chesterfield (1892–1901), near Chesterfield, Connecticut, was a cooperative Jewish farm (see **Sicily Island**) organized by Hayyim Pankin, who had only recently come to the United States from Russia. It had approximately 75 members, most of whom also came from Russia. They decided to run their commune as a dairy farm. They were assisted by funds from the Baron de Hirsch Fund, and they built a steam-operated creamery and a synagogue in 1897.

Sometime after 1901 they ceased to function as a cooperative community, though most of the participants continued to live in the area as private dairy farmers. The town of Chesterfield today is the center for the New England Hebrew Farmers Society, the cultural and religious organization of Jewish tobacco, potato, and produce farmers.

Chicago-Colorado Colony (1871–1873), at Longmont, Colorado, was a cooperative venture based on the constitution and model of **Union Colony** of Greeley. Most of the 400 members came from Illinois, though some were residents of Colorado. Each family paid a membership fee of $155. The president was Robert Collyer, a well-known Unitarian minister from Chicago. C. N. Pratt, who had originally proposed the idea for this commune, became secretary. They named their town Longmont because Longs Peak dominated the skyline there. Within three months they had erected 50 buildings. They dissolved the cooperative nature of the project after a few years, according to plan. A book with a section that focuses on the Chicago-Colorado Colony is Willard's *The Union Colony of Greeley, Colorado, 1869–1871*.

Children's Land *see* **Shalam**

Christ the Worker Farm (1941–1945), near Oxford, Pennsylvania, was a Catholic Worker farm (see **Maryfarm** on Staten Island) that had about 20 members. Among them were Paul Toner, Dave Mason, and Dick Aherne. They had to close this commune because it was too expensive to maintain.

Christian Commonwealth (1896–1900), near Columbus, Georgia, was a Christian socialist commune founded by the Rev. Ralph Albertson (1866–1926), who had been a member of the **Willard Cooperative Colony**, and George Howard Gibson. They purchased land that had once been a plantation, and their membership eventually grew to 300. Fully ten percent of those who joined the commune were later asked to resign because their attitude toward cooperative living was not considered "of the best."

The commune had a school that taught college courses, including music, drawing, and languages. They also planted 35 acres of peaches, plums, pears, prunes, cherries, figs, apricots, pecans, and grapes. They had a sawmill, a shingle machine, a number of dwellings, a steam laundry, a general kitchen/dining room/library building, and a printing house where they published their magazine, *The Social Gospel*.

The members eventually found that the costs of publishing the magazine were too much of a drain on the community, and they decided to move it to Jamestown, New York, where it continued publication. But its removal from the commune caused disagreements that prompted many members to leave. After the community disbanded, some of the ex-members moved to Elgin, Illinois, and began publishing another magazine, *Social Ideals*.

Christian Commonwealth Colony of Louisiana (1931–1933), three miles from Newllano, Louisiana, was founded in 1931 by Christian socialist and former Methodist missionary Dr. Samuel Irwin. It had about eight members, a two-story log house, a cabin, and a barn. A planned orphanage and school were never completed. The members worked at various trades to finance the project and opened the buildings for church retreats. Irwin acted as a minister for weddings and funerals at the nearby **Newllano** commune. After his wife died in 1932, he moved away and the commune closed the next year. The house and cabins are still standing. A book with a section that focuses on the Christian Commonwealth Colony of Louisiana is Conkin's *Two Paths to Utopia: The Hutterites and the Llano Colony*.

Christian Corporation (1896–1897), near Lincoln, Nebraska, was organized by George Howard Gibson, an advocate of the Protestant Social Gospel movement. He had previously published a temperance paper, the *Rising Tide*, in Omaha, Nebraska, and then worked for the Farmer's Alliance as editor of the *Alliance-Independent*. Gibson chartered the Christian Corporation in April 1985, after purchasing a 480-acre site near Lincoln. He claimed 99 supporters for the project, but there were probably no more than 30 members. When Ralph Albertson of the **Willard Cooperative Colony** approached him about forming a new commune in Georgia, Gibson decided to abandon this Christian Corporation project and take his members to the **Christian Commonwealth**.

Christian Faith and Life Community (1952–1961), at Austin, Texas, was the first of two communes led by Joseph

Wesley Matthews, a former professor of theology at the Perkins School of Theology in Austin. The other was the **Ecumenical Institute** of Chicago. The Christian Faith and Life Community had about 20 members, mostly students at the University of Texas. Here Matthews began to create and test his unique program for training clergy and lay persons in the structures and ideals of 20th century theology. The methods were later perfected at the Ecumenical Institute. The community closed when Matthews was asked by the Church Federation of Greater Chicago to move to Evanston, Illinois, and head the newly-formed Ecumenical Institute. Matthews took some of the members of this commune with him to staff the new body. These included Joe Pierce, Joe Slicker, and Gene Marshall. A book with a section that focuses on the Christian Faith and Life Community is Clark's *Manpower for Mission.*

Christian Republic *see* **Berlin Community**

Christian Social Association (1899–1904), at Madison, Wisconsin, was a cooperative community of 48 people that closed because of the withdrawal of most of its members.

Church of Hope (1957–1965), in Chicago, Illinois, was a community established by Church of the Brethren minister Julius Belser in one of the poorest sections of the city. Their purpose was to set up a communal congregation of God's people in an urban ghetto. The membership reached 12, but they were forced to close after an urban renewal program marked their building for destruction. Because this commune was located at 1237 South Peoria Street, it was also called the Peoria Street Fellowship. When it closed, the members joined **Reba Place** in Evanston, Illinois.

Cincinnati Phalanx *see* **Clermont Phalanx**

Clarion Colony (1911–1916), west of Gunnison in Sanpete County, Utah, was a Jewish farm commune (see **Sicily Island**) founded by the Jewish Agricultural and Colonial Association and headed by Rabbi Isaac Landman of Philadelphia. The approximately 75 members came mostly from the slums of New York and Philadelphia, where most of them had been garment workers. There was also one carpenter, one plumber, one painter, and a furrier. They had the backing of the National Farm School at Doyelston, Pennsylvania, and the bonds for their colonization fund were held by Jacob H. Schiff, Julius Rosenwald, the Mormon church, and the governor of Utah. The members, however, abandoned the experiment following an unsuccessful fund raising trip in the East by one of their number, Simon Bamberger. Benjamin Brown, who later organized the **Sunrise Cooperative Farms**, was a member of this commune. A book that focuses on the Clarion Colony is Goldberg's *Back to the Soil.*

Clark Brüderhof (1955–present), near Raymond, South Dakota, is a Hutterite community (see **Bon Homme**) that had 88 members in 1964 and was led by Fred Waldner.

Clarkson Association (1843–1845), at what is now the village of North Hamlin, New York, was a Fourierist commune that was also known at various times as the Western New York Industrial Association, the Clarkson Domain, and the Port Richmond Phalanx. It was the first Fourierist community established after **Social Reform Unity**.

The 420 members owned 1,460 acres, erected living quarters, a flour mill, two saw mills, a machine shop, farm buildings, and barns. Besides cultivating the land, they raised oxen, pigs, guinea fowls, chickens, ducks, geese, and bees. Among the leading members were Thomas Pond, Samuel Porter, Hiram Carmichael, Jonathan Greig, and Dr. Edward Theller. The latter was an Irish Catholic who had been captured during the Canadian rebellion of 1837, when he commanded a schooner in an expedition against the government there. He later escaped from the citadel at Quebec, came to America, and authored a two-volume book on his part in the rebellion.

One modern authority on this commune (historian A. E. Bestor) has suggested that it failed because the water power from the creek that flowed through the property was inadequate for the running of their mills. However Jonathan Greig said after the commune closed, "The beginning and ending of our troubles was … we were without the pale and protection of law, for want of incorporation. Consequently we could do no business, could not buy or sell land or other property, could not sue or be sued, could neither make ourselves responsible, nor compel others to become so; and as the majority of us were never able to adopt the dreamy abstractions of non-resistance and no-law, we were unable to live and prosper in that kingdom of smoke 'above the world.'"

Clarkson Domain *see* **Social Reform Unity**

Clermont Phalanx (1844–1846), originally named the Cincinnati Phalanx, was located on the lowlands of the Ohio River, near the present villages of Rural and Utopia in Clermont County, Ohio. It was a Fourierist community (see **Social Reform Unity**) organized in Cincinnati, Ohio, and there were about 120 members, including Alcander Longley, who had earlier been a member of the Fourierist **North American Phalanx** in New Jersey, and John O. Wattles, who came from the **Prairie Home Community** in Ohio. Wade Loofburrow, a man of some wealth, was the president, and George Sampson was the secretary. They owned 1,140 acres of land.

When the members occupied the land, they found three log cabins already there. They erected a saw-and-grist mill, two farm buildings, and several temporary buildings. They also built a three-story brick phalanxtry, 80 by 30 feet, for the members to live in. They planted 30 acres of wheat and 1,000 fruit trees of various kinds.

When the experiment ended, the members agreed to only sell their land to persons who might use it to promote other communitarian settlements. Two such experiments were thereafter set up on the abandoned land. These were Wattles' **The Brotherhood** and Warren's **Utopia**.

The fact that the Clermont Phalanx failed did not dampen the enthusiasm of the Cincinnati advocates for Fourier's ideas. In 1848 about 25 of them moved to Indiana with Alcander Longley to establish the **Fourier Phalanx**.

Clover Leaf Brüderhof (1963–present), near Carthage, South Dakota, is a Hutterite commune (see **Bon Homme**) with perhaps 100 members.

Cloverdale Altruria (1895–1896), west of Cloverdale, California, was established by 16 Christian Socialists from the financially-troubled colony of **Altruria**. They had an 80-acre farm that was purchased for them by James Aitken.

Coal Creek (1825–1832), near Stone Bluff, Indiana, was established by 13 Christian rationalists under the leadership of William Ludlow. He and James M. Dorsey had earlier developed elaborate plans for a communitarian society that they called the Rational Brethren of Oxford, but these never materialized. For Coal Creek they hoped to purchase 1,000 acres of land. It is not known how much property the Coal Creek commune actually covered after it was started, and Dorsey abandoned the project to join Robert Owen's **New Harmony** commune before Coal Creek was initiated.

However, Ludlow finally gathered 12 other people to start Coal Creek. He had written to Thomas Jefferson on July 30, 1824, to gain the president's support for the project. Jefferson responded on September 6, with hopes for its success. He said, "A society of seventy families, the number you name, may very possibly be governed as a single family, subsisting on their common industry, and holding all things in common. Some regulators of the family you still must have, and it remains to be seen at what point of your increasing population your simple regulations will cease to be sufficient to preserve order, peace and justice. The experiment is interesting; I shall not live to see its issue but I wish it success equal to your hopes and to yourself and society, prosperity and happiness."

In the latter part of 1825, Ludlow visited and lectured at New Harmony, returning to Coal Creek in 1826. Then, in 1830, he withdrew from the community and joined New Harmony. The other members of Coal Creek agreed to pay him back what he had already put into the common fund, but Ludlow did not believe this was enough and went to court over the matter. A settlement was reached on May 3, 1832, and the commune died shortly thereafter. One of the members, Isaac Romine, founded the **First Community of Man's Free Brotherhood** near Covington, Indiana, the following year. A book with a section that focuses on Coal Creek is Bestor's *Backwoods Utopias: The Sectarian and Owenite Phases of Communitarian Socialism in America, 1663–1828.*

Cohasset Ashram (1929–present), at Cohasset, Massachusetts, was established by Swami Paramananda, the founder of the Vedanta Society (see **Ananda Ashram**). The 20-acre site is in a secluded and wooded area southeast of Boston. There have never been more than about 20 members living here, most of them women. They live communally and follow a highly regulated pattern of living.

Colchester Farm (1944–1946), at Colchester, Vermont, was a Catholic Worker farm (see **Maryfarm** on Staten Island) established by Norman and Donald Langlois. It had about 15 members who raised food for the movement's Burlington, Vermont, House of Hospitality.

Colony of Equality (1843–1846), also known as Hunt's Colony and Spring Lake, was an Owenite commune located at Spring Lake in Waukesha County, Wisconsin. The 31 people from England, led by Thomas Hunt, wanted to set up a commune patterned after the ideas of Robert Owen (see **New Harmony**). They included a bookbinder, plasterer, butcher, wood turner, tailor, and glover.

They purchased 160 acres with funds contributed by various cooperative societies in England, including the Utilitarian Association of United Interests, the Utilitarian Co-operative Emigration Society, and the Democratic Society. None of the members, however, were farmers and so they did poorly at agriculture. They elected a butcher named Johnson as their farmer-in-chief. When the group disbanded, they divided everything equally. It is said that they lost about one-third of their investment.

Colorado Cooperative Company (1894–1901), at Pinon, now Nucla, Colorado, was a commune that was founded by E. L. Gallatin. It had about 100 members who made their living by farming and cutting timber. They published a weekly newspaper, *The Altrurian*, and had a harness shop, sawmill, blacksmith shop, dairy, drug store, and boarding house. Members were paid for their work in food supplies, shelter, and water rights at the rate of 20 cents an hour. Their major project — the building of a ditch from the San Miguel River to their land 300 feet above the river — was not completed until 1910, after they had abandoned the cooperative nature of their enterprise. They voted to do this and to discontinue the newspaper on January 15, 1901. Books with sections that focus on the Colorado Cooperative Company are Hinds' *American Communities* and Wooster's *Communities of the Past and Present*.

Columbia Cooperative Colony *see* **Nehalem Valley Cooperative Colony**

Columbian Phalanx (1845), on the Muskingum River, seven miles above Zanesville, Ohio, was a Fourierist settlement (see **Social Reform Unity**) of 128 members. Most of the members came from a Fourierist support group known as the Beverly Association of Morgan County, Ohio. Their cultivated land included 137 acres of wheat, 13 acres of rye, 150 acres of corn, 100 acres of oats, 15 acres of potatoes, 4 acres of beans, 40 acres of pumpkins, and 1 acre of sweet potatoes, as well as land planted in cabbages, turnips, buckwheat, flax, and other garden plants.

Commonwealth College (1923–1940), which was founded at Newllano, Louisiana, moved to Mena, Arkansas, in 1924, and then to Mill Creek Bluff, 11 miles from Mena, in 1925. It was established by economist William E. Zeuch as a cooperative community and training center for those entering the labor movement and other vocations related to economic and social reform. His plan was to keep the college operating by having the students work in a communal way at productive labor while attending the school.

Zeuch initially reached an agreement with the colonists at the **Newllano** commune to use 40 acres of their land for this project. Only one college building was constructed before a struggle for control of both the Newllano commune and Commonwealth College erupted between Zeuch and George Pickett, the head of Newllano. Zeuch departed, taking Commonwealth College to Mena, Arkansas. He rented buildings in Mena for the school and then he purchased 320 acres on Mill Creek Bluff, where the students lived in tents until they were able to construct some frame buildings. Eventually they put up 25 of these: two men's dormitories, two women's dormitories, cottages for the teachers and married students, a library, an administration building, a store, a root cellar, a barn, and a small laboratory building.

At its height, in the early part of 1932, there were about 90 residents at Commonwealth, including students, faculty, and maintenance crew. They came from all parts of the United States and a few even came from Cuba, Germany, England, and China. All residents were required to participate in the education process. Even teachers were expected to take classes from other teachers. No one received any pay for maintenance work or the harvesting of commune garden crops. Though the students paid $60 a semester to attend the school, this income never covered the costs of running it. Throughout Commonwealth's history, about $10,000 had to be raised every year in grants and donations from interested persons, labor organizations, and other groups to keep the school operating.

Under the direction of Zeuch, the curriculum was so broad that it included courses by almost anyone who wanted to teach, including Swedenborgians and diet faddists. Zeuch was more inter-ested in developing an individual's personality than in directing the individual into some specific area of training. When Zeuch took a leave of absence in 1931, the other members never asked him to come back. Instead, they appointed Lucian Koch director.

Koch put the school's emphasis primarily on labor union education, and for its remaining years, Commonwealth was then viewed as a non-partisan labor college. The teachers were young, dedicated, and generally excellent. They included a Montana minister, an Arkansas schoolteacher, a Louisiana journalist, and several leaders from the labor movement, including for brief periods organizers of such stature as Victor Reuther of the United Auto Workers. Many of the graduates of Commonwealth College became labor professionals. Some went on to complete degrees as medical doctors, lawyers, social workers, teachers, and anthropologists. One student even became the governor of Arkansas. This was Orville

Faculty cottages at Commonwealth College in the late 1930s (drawing by Lois Will).

Faubus, a liberal at the time and the son of a socialist leader in Arkansas. However, by the time he became governor, Faubus had turned into a racist who tried to prevent the integration of the public schools in Little Rock.

Kooch resigned in September 1935 to take a post with the government's National Recovery Administration (NRA). He was replaced by Richard Whitten, a New Orleans socialist, and then by the Rev. Claude C. Williams, an Arkansas Presbyterian who had a national reputation for leadership in the cause of labor and civil rights. Under Williams' direction, Commonwealth turned its attention to the South and attempted to recruit much of its student body from the South. The college, however, existing in an all-white county of Arkansas, never did admit black members, though there were a number of black visitors much to the disgust of neighboring farmers.

After a printing press was brought to the community, the *Commonwealth College Fortnightly*, previously mimeographed, was published in printed form. Its name was changed to *The Commoner* in May 1938. The printing press also turned out the *Windsor Quarterly*, one of the little magazines of the era, and the community became an exchange or clearinghouse for most of the other little magazines published during that period.

For the most part, the neighboring farmers were surprisingly friendly to Commonwealth. They came to trade at the community store and attended the school square dances. The fact that the Commonwealth students and faculty took an interest in their relief problems partly accounted for this. Also, the school nurse established a health care program that extended beyond the community to the surrounding farmers.

The Commonwealth leadership, however, was constantly harassed by state officials. In 1935 a bill was introduced into the state legislature aimed at outlawing the school. In response, Commonwealth organized a national committee to successfully defeat this bill. Among the committee participants were such well-known persons as Jane Addams, H. L. Mencken, Alexander Meiklejohn, Mrs. Edward Bellamy, and Methodist Bishop Francis J. McConnell.

The Ku Klux Klan also circulated a pamphlet attacking the school. And the Rev. Luther D. Summers, a Baptist preacher from Hot Springs, Arkansas, moved to Mena to recruit a following on the basis of weekly sermons against this "den of free love and nudism." Ironically, when Commonwealth finally closed in July 1940, Rev. Summers bought the school library, one of the most extensive and well-catalogued collections of labor material in the country. He then publicly burned all the books and pamphlets.

Visitors to the commune site in 1974 reported that a few of the buildings were still standing, but by now they are probably torn down. Books with sections that focus on Commonwealth College are Conkin's *Two Paths to Utopia: The Hutterites and the Llano Colony* and Koch's *Educational Commune: The Story of Commonwealth College.*

Commonwealth of Israel (1899–1902), at a place once called Adullam in Mason County, Texas, was a Baptist commune of 150 farmers and mechanics. They hoped that by their example all other Baptists would come to realize what it might be like to live in a Christian society. The members communally owned 900 acres of land and worked an eight-hour day. Their leaders were James D. Tracy and J. W. Fairchild. Although they disbanded in less than three years, many of the members later said they were generally satisfied with conditions in this community.

Communia (1847–1856), about seven miles south of Elkader in Clayton County, Iowa, was established by nine Germans and a Frenchman under the leadership of Joseph Venus. He was a blacksmith by trade and, like the others, had no practical farming experience. The commune grew to a membership of 70, all of them socialists and labor organizers and their families.

Each member contributed all their money to the general fund and they all shared whatever profits accrued from their 1,400 acres of land. They built three log houses, a blacksmith shop, a brick yard, and a lime kiln. They also owned some livestock.

Shortly after the commune was founded, they were joined by a group from the disbanded **New Helvetia**, as well by Heinrick Koch, a German watchmaker and radical from St. Louis, Missouri, who was the publisher of the *Vorwärts* and the *Antipaff*, both socialist periodicals. Koch had recently returned from the Mexican War, in which he led a German contingent and for which he later received a land grant from the government. After he sold this, he moved to Dubuque, Iowa, where he became a leading politician.

Also joining Communia was William Weitling (1808–1871), a tailor, radical pamphleteer, and organizer of workingmen's lodges in Europe and later in the United States. He published the periodical *Republik der Arbeiter* after he came to the United States in order to promote his socialist ideas. Weitling joined Communia in 1852 and became one of its administrators. He is today perhaps best remembered as the opponent of Karl Marx in a famous debate over the direction of the early communist movement that took place while Weitling was still in Europe.

Communia had a history of bitter quarrels and lawsuits, particularly between Weitling and the other colonists. When the project was disbanded in 1856, some of the remaining members moved to **Icaria**. Remnants of the buildings still stand. A book with a section that focuses on Communia is Wittke's *We Who Built America: The Saga of the Immigrant*.

Congregation of Saints (1843–1844), at Lexington, LaGrange County, Indiana, was a commune of about 50 members led by the Rev. Samuel Bradford, the pastor of a local church called The Community of Saints. The congregation of this church had been the major religious group in the area for many years, and the members of this church had been instrumental in raising funds to build a schoolhouse, one of the best in the county.

It is not known how much land the participants in the commune purchased for the project, but they stated that their intention was to own from two to six thousand acres. They divided their profits according to each member's labor, and stood for equal rights for women. When Rev. Bradford died in 1844, both his church and the commune also died. A book with a section that focuses on the Congregation of Saints is Rerick's *Counties of LaGrange and Noble, Indiana*.

Cooperative Brotherhood (1898–1912), at Burley, Washington, 14 miles northwest of Tacoma, was founded by members of Social Democracy of America, a political party allied with Eugene Debs' American Railway Union. At the time, this organization was replacing the Cooperative Commonwealth (see **Equality Colony**) as the body that did the most to promote socialist and cooperative values. The first convention of the Social Democracy of America produced a split in the membership between a majority committed to the idea of forming socialist colonies and a minority who wanted to focus the work on political action.

The Cooperative Brotherhood commune, which was also called the Burley Colony, had nearly 200 resident members at one point. There were also 1,227 non-resident members in 26 states and all the provinces of Canada. Non-resident members paid $120 in dues for ten years to support Social Democracy of America's program and to take advantage of the organization's liberal insurance program. Resident members paid nothing, though each head of family had to sign a contract agreeing to accept work assignments, obey rules and regulations, and help provide services as needed. The leaders of the commune included Cyrus Field Willard, J. S. Ingalls, J. B. Fowler, Wilfred P. Borland, and Jerome C. DeArmond. Willard was a friend of Edward Bellamy and had helped form, in 1888, the first Nationalist Club in America (see **Ruskin Commonwealth**).

Most of the resident members engaged in farming and logging. They had 300 acres of land, a saw and shingle mill, individual dwellings, a large hotel, large barn, schoolhouse, blacksmith shop, shoe shop, laundry, cigar factory, and a few other buildings. They also published a newspaper called the *Co-operator*, and talked of forming other such settlements in California and Oregon, but never did. Musical and literary programs were held regularly in the schoolhouse, and there were also occasional lectures given by outsiders.

The insurance program for non-resident members was unique among American communes. Under this agreement, any paid-up member who was "totally and permanently incapacitated either by sickness or accident for his usual vocation" was to be provided a home for his family at the Cooperative Brotherhood. Should the member die, his family would also be welcomed at the commune.

The commune came to an end after several of the stockholders petitioned the court to have the colony dissolved and to appoint a receiver. By that time most of the members had departed and so there was little resistance to this move among the few remaining members. The ill-kept gravesite on a slope above the village of Burley is a reminder of the commune that once stood there. A book with a section that focuses on the Cooperative Brotherhood is LeWarne's *Utopias on Puget Sound, 1885–1915*.

Cooperative Brotherhood of Winters Island (1893–1898) was established near the joining of the San Joaquin and Sacramento Rivers, east of San Francisco, California, by Erastus Kelsey, a leader of the Oakland Nationalist Club. He had been one of the many visitors at the **Kaweah Co-operative Commonwealth** commune and was so impressed with what he saw there that he approached Haskell, the founder of Kaweah, with a proposal to organize a similar community on Winters Island, which Kelsey owned. When Haskell showed no interest in supporting another commune, Kelsey turned to Mrs. Kate Lockwood Nevins, an organizer for the Farmer's Alliance in California and an active member of the Populist Party. She was enthusiastic about the idea and together they established the Winters Island commune.

The new settlement was established in July 1893, on the model used at Kaweah, with 100 members, the maximum number stipulated in their Articles of Incorporation. The island, however, suffered from floods each month, as ocean tides surged through the Golden Gate and up the Sacramento River. To prevent water damage, the Winters Island members began to build dikes surrounding their land. They met quarterly to elect directors and to allocate work on the farm, dikes, and the building of barns and houses. The island provided 636 acres of cultivable land, which they allotted to hay, summer vegetables, and a small orchard. Their most successful crop was onions.

Many of the members were skilled laborers who held jobs in surrounding towns and came to Winters Island to participate in the work of the commune only on weekends. A. J. Gregg, a carpenter, served as the first president and managed the community's business affairs until the settlement closed in 1898. In 1894 he ran for the post of lieutenant governor of California under the Populist Party banner, but he did not win.

The depression of the 1890s forced most of them to abandon this project because they could not meet the $5 a month membership assessment. (The membership entry fee was only $1.25.) By 1898 the commune was closed, though a few members continued to live on Winters Island. Mrs. Nevins remained there until 1930, at which time she was 75 years of age. A book with a section that focuses on the Cooperative Brotherhood of Winters Island is Hine's *California's Utopian Communities*.

Cooperative Industrial College (1899–1902), at Blairsville in Union County, Georgia, was organized by 24 former members of the **Ruskin Commonwealth**. They owned 240 acres of land, a farm building, a cotton gin, and some cattle. The leaders were two graduates, one from the University of Chicago and the other from a German military school.

Cooperative Subsistence Colony (1933–1934), on the Little Luckiamute River, 13 miles south of Dallas, Oregon, was patterned after **Newllano**. It had about 150 socialists as members, many of them skilled industrial workers from Oregon and California. They had a 1,120-acre tract of logged-off land that they purchased from the Oregon Western Timber Company, and lived in the reconstructed homes of a former logging town called Black Rock. The town had once been one of the busiest mill towns in the state but by 1933 was almost deserted. Each member contributed $250 or the equivalent in goods, to the project. They farmed, raised Angora rabbits, and manufactured furniture and other wood products for sale. The colony closed after less than a year, probably because their farming efforts were relatively unsuccessful.

Cotopaxi (1882–1885), at Cotopaxi, Colorado, was a Jewish agricultural commune (see **Sicily Island**) of 64 members. It was supported by the Hebrew Emigrant Aid Society of New York, and they had 1,780 acres of land. However, only about 100 acres were suitable for cultivation and water was scarce. As their farming failed, many of the members were forced to work for the nearby Saltiel mine and to cut railroad ties. A faded "Saltiel's" sign is all that now marks the community site.

Coxsackie *see* **Forrestville**

Crémieux (1882–1885), on the county line between Davison and Aurora counties in South Dakota, about 14 miles from Mt. Vernon, was a 200-member Jewish agricultural commune established by Herman Rosenthal from **Sicily Island** and Benoir Greenberg. They named it after Isaac Adolph Crémieux, the founder of the Paris-based Alliance Israélite Universelle that assisted them financially. Some of the members came from Sicily Island with Rosenthal. That commune had been destroyed by a massive flood earlier in the year.

At Crémieux, they planted oats, wheat, rye, barley, and flax. But during their second year, wheat bugs destroyed much of their crop. Thunderstorms damaged their crops in the third year, and soon afterward many of the members departed, some going to Iowa and others to Minnesota and New York. Greenberg and Rosenthal stayed until the end with a few remaining members. Then Greenberg opened a grocery store in South Dakota and Rosenthal moved to New York, where he took a job with the public library.

Cropperville (1939–1942), about 15 miles southwest of Poplar Bluff, Missouri, was a cooperative community that was started for about 500 dispossessed sharecroppers, most of whom were black. The sharecroppers had been forced from their homes and land after they made demands on the land owners for a living wage. They were led by Owen H. Whitfield, a black Baptist minister and organizer for the Southern Tenant Farmers Union. The sharecroppers encamped on U.S. Highway 61 for five days in rain, snow, and raw weather until the state police came and moved them off the highway.

A white sympathizer, Claude Fisher, then purchased a 92-acre tract of land for them, and the members began this experiment, which was also sometimes called the Lost Colony of Cropperville. Only about 25 acres of the land were tillable, as the region was low and swampy. The members received assistance from the Fellowship of Reconciliation, the American Friends Service Committee, the Negro Elks, the Congress of Industrial Organizations (CIO) office in St. Louis, Missouri, and the government's Farm Security Administration.

They were often harassed by surrounding white farmers, who resented the existence of these black communalists in their midst. Night after night, shots were fired into the community, and oaths were shouted at them from passing cars. The few white families who had joined the experiment at the beginning left shortly after it was established because of this harassment.

Since the residents of Cropperville represented a sizable voting block, both the Missouri Democrats and Republicans tried to curry their favor as election time drew near. The Democrats provided them with a smooth gravel road from the main highway, and the Republicans built them a 30 by 40 foot community building for their political rallies. This was soon turned into a schoolhouse and a church. The members disbanded around the end of 1942 because of the new jobs provided by war production, which relieved the economic pressures that originally led to the establishment of this community. A book with a section that focuses on Cropperville is Deem's *History of Butler County, Missouri*.

Cupertino (1916), near San Jose, California, was a colony of Little Landers (see **San Ysidro Little Landers**) who may have numbered as many as one hundred members.

Cutlerite Mormons (1913–1970), at Clitherall, Minnesota, was a commune that developed out of the teachings of Alpheus Cutler (1784–1864), a Mormon leader who disagreed with and departed from Brigham Young during the journey of Mormons from **Nauvoo** in Illinois to Utah. Cutler was a veteran of the War of 1812 and was converted to Mormonism in 1837. At **Kirtland**, Joseph Smith appointed him one of the seven elders of the church, and at Nauvoo he became the master stone mason for the construction of the temple there.

While traveling west with the main body of Mormons, Cutler reportedly saw two half-moons in the sky with their backs together. This he took as a sign directing him to withdraw from the others and form a new church. With a few followers, he then did so at Fisher Grove in Fremont County, Iowa, on September 19, 1853. The church is now known as the Church of Jesus Christ (Cutlerites). But Cutler's attempts to establish a communal settlement among his followers proved a failure. After he died, his successor, Chauncey Whiting, took the church members northward to Clitherall where Whiting also tried to set up a community with common ownership of goods, but this too failed and resulted in the loss of many followers.

However, Whiting's son, Isaac, succeeded in doing so in 1913. The members held all things in common, governed by common consent, took a pacifist position in regard to war, and did not support polygamy, as some of the Mormons did in Utah. For a time this commune operated two stores in Clitherall, but by 1960 only maintained

their church building (constructed in 1929). They had 180 members in 1915, and were down to only five by the late 1960s. A book with a section that focuses on the Cutlerite Mormons is Palmer's *The Cutlerite Settlement of Clitherall, Minnesota.*

Darby Plains (1822–1825) was a Shaker settlement (see **Watervliet**) about 25 miles northwest of Columbus, Ohio. It was started as a result of the conversion of Nathan Burlingame, the pastor for a group of New Light Baptists. There were about 40 members of this commune, and they selected the plantation of Samuel Rice for their site. They constructed their meeting house in 1823. However, the location was unhealthy and fever eventually forced them to close Darby Plains and move to the **Whitewater** Shaker commune.

Davis House *see* **Point Hope**

Dawn Valcour (1874–1875), on Valcour Island in Lake Champlain, New York, was a spiritualist and semi–Fourierist commune (see **Social Reform Unity**) established by John Wilcox of Chicago. He had acquired 800 acres of land, which included this island and a nursery on the Vermont side of the lake, from Orrin Shippman of Colchester, Vermont, in payment for a debt. Wilcox advertised for members to join his "Head Center of Advanced Spiritualism and Free Love" in *Woodhull and Claflin's Weekly* and some other magazines. In August, 1874, 12 individuals settled on the island to start the commune. Hannah White shared the leadership with Wilcox. Their plan was to build a phalanxtry building in which all the members could live, and to organize the life of the commune like that of a Fourierist phalanx. They would have a child-care center, work only three days a week at the same wage rate regardless of the job done, and make all decisions on the basis of voting, with everyone over the age of 15 eligible to vote. They opposed marriage because of "the cruelties perpetuated under the hell-begotten phase of the present marriage system."

The community closed after about a year partly because Shippman had deceived the members over the fact that he did not have clear title to the property. In November 1875, the remaining members departed for New York City. A book with a section that focuses on Dawn Valcour is Fogarty's *All Things New*.

Deerfield (1947–present), near Danvers, Montana, is a Hutterite Brüderhof (see **Bon Homme**). In 1964 it had 52 members and was led by Paul Stahl.

Delta Cooperative Farm (1936–1942), near Roundlake, Mississippi, was established to aid the plight of destitute sharecroppers. It was started by Sherwood Eddy, a leader of the Christian Student Volunteer Movement and of the YMCA. Eddy founded the community as an interracial cooperative farm after he had completed an investigation of the conditions of the sharecroppers who were evicted from their land for joining the Tenant Farmers' Union.

He had reported that the very first day of the investigation shocked him when he saw aspects of slavery, feudalism, and fascism in the attitudes of the landowners toward the evicted sharecroppers, both black and white. During this investigation Eddy was arrested, along with his co-investigators, by a local deputy sheriff in one Southern town. The apparent cause for the arrest was that they were visiting the homes of some of the black families.

Eddy raised $17,500 among Northern contributors for the purchase of 2,138 acres of land. He established a national board of trustees that included theologian Reinhold Niebuhr, Bishop William Scarlett, physiology professor William Amberson, and John Rust, the inventor of a mechanical cotton-picker.

By 1938 there were more than 100 members at the Delta Cooperative Farm. The whole community operated as two cooperatives — a producers' cooperative that managed the planting, cultivation, and building, and a consumers' cooperative that supervised the distribution of supplies and sale of products outside the community. They had 30 frame houses, a sawmill, a blacksmith shop, a school, a commissary, a hog farm, a poultry farm, and a vegetable garden. They raised cotton on the rest of the land. Every six months, the entire community elected its own interracial advisory board of five members.

The community suffered greatly from hostility on the part of surrounding farmers, who opposed the members' attitude of racial equality. Because of this hostility, many members departed in fear. Eddy eventually decided to establish a smaller community near Cruger, Mississippi (see **Providence Cooperative Farm**), and to gradually transfer the Delta Cooperative Farm members there. He closed the Delta project in 1942 and sold the land for $32,000 cash. A book with a section that focuses on the Delta Cooperative Farm is Eddy's *Eighty Adventurous Years*.

Dr. Abraham Brooke's Experiment (1843–1845), at Marlboro, Ohio, was started by Dr. Brooke after he left the **Marlboro Association** commune because the members there did not "practice communism with enough thoroughness." This communal experiment had only five or six members. After it disbanded, Dr. Brooke continued to live on the property with his family. Nothing is known about who the other members were or how the commune operated.

Dorrilites (1797–1798), at Leyden, Mass., were a group of 40 vegetarians who maintained communism of property and refused to use leather because animals had to be killed in order to get it. Their leader, Mr. Dorril, had been an English army officer under General Burgoyne. He resigned from office to begin preaching that he was a prophet of God.

Many of the members of this commune came from Guilford, Vermont, but there were others from "very respectable" families in Leyden and Barnardston, Massachusetts. They practiced strict vegetarianism, refusing even to wear clothes that had been produced from the skin of animals. They wore wool foot coverings instead of leather shoes, and a blacksmith who acted as the treasurer for the group made his bellows from cloth instead of leather.

The Dorrilites held open worship services each week, services at which they ate, sang, danced to violin music, and heard a sermon by Mr. Dorril. The Rev. Joseph Lathop of Springfield, Massachusetts, was their most vocal opponent. He vigorously attacked the Dorrilites from his pulpit, charging that they spent their Sabbath in labor and diversion.

The downfall of this commune came in 1798 after Dorril announced that he had a God-given power that made him immune from pain. A member of Lathop's congregation, Captain Ezekiel Foster, physically attacked Dorril during one of his open lectures, proceeding to beat him until he pleaded for

mercy and admitted that he had been hurt. It is said that Dorril also promised Foster, "upon penalty of his life, never to impose upon the people more." Thereafter the community disbanded. Books with sections that focus on the Dorrilites are Ludlum's *Social Ferment in Vermont, 1791–1850* and Thompson's *History of Vermont, Vol. II.*

Duncan Ranch (1963–present), near Twodot, Montana, is a Hutterite Brüderhof (see **Bon Homme**) with 81 members in 1964. Their minister is John Entz.

Eagle Creek (1808–1810), in Adams County, three miles from West Union, Ohio, was a Shaker commune (see **Watervliet**) that probably had no more than 25 members. Two years after Eagle Creek was founded, the members here joined with those at the **Red Banks** and **Straight Creek** Shaker communes to form **West Union**.

East Texas Cooperative Association *see* **Magnolia**

Economy *see* **Harmony**

Ecumenical Institute (1962–1981), first in Evanston and then in Chicago, Illinois, was a religious community established by theologian Joseph Wesley Matthews. He had been the leader of the **Christian Faith and Life Community** in Austin, Texas, when he was asked by the Church Federation of Greater Chicago to go to Evanston and head up the newly-established Ecumenical Institute, a training school established at the meeting of the World Council of Churches held in Evanston. Matthews agreed to do so, closed down his commune in Austin, and moved with some of the members to Evanston.

Soon he had turned the training school into a commune much like the one in Austin.

In 1964 the members of the Ecumenical Institute rented buildings of a closed Brethren seminary at 410 South Trumbull Street on Chicago's West Side and moved the commune there. Because the Chicago neighborhood was a part of Chicago's black ghetto, the school had difficulty attracting students to that location. However the institute members soon announced their intention to rebuild the spirit and structures of the ghetto area. They also planned to develop secular and religious training courses for church people throughout the United States and the world, and to begin a renewal movement within the Christian church as a whole.

Their communal and educational program proved highly successful. By 1968 there were 250 members living in the Chicago commune. Part of the membership worked at various occupations throughout the city to provide an income for the community and to finance educational courses that other members conducted in churches throughout the United States. The housing facilities were too small for the enlarged membership and their expanded program so they decided to establish communes in other cities that would coordinate their work through the central headquarters in Chicago.

By 1970 the membership in the Chicago and the other institute communes that they called "Religious Houses" stood at 1,300. They eventually moved their headquarters to the North Side of Chicago, a building at 4750 Sheridan Road, although they continued to maintain a small presence at the West Side location.

At least 60,000 persons had taken their basic theological course, Religious

Studies I, by 1968. This course used papers by modern theologians Paul Tillich, Rudolph Bultmann, Dietrich Bonhoeffer, and H. Richard Niebuhr to "demythologize" the Scriptures so they could be understood in terms of the modern world. The institute members saw the teacher's role as one of enabling dialogue between the student and the document being studied. The course was quite intensive and taught on weekends at the institute building and in all types of churches and other facilities across the continent. The Ecumenical Institute members also taught a series of advanced courses in both theology and culture.

Their reformation model for the ghetto community (called the 5th City model because 5th Avenue once formed the northern boundary of the project area) was designed to achieve comprehensiveness, the lack of which they viewed as the major failure of other attempts at community reorganization. A total of 625 specific social problems were identified by the commune members working with persons from the ghetto community, and 80 social agencies were projected to deal with these. The agencies included a health center, a credit union, an employment service, a legal-aid clinic, a housing rehabilitation corporation, a new shopping center, various schools, and other services.

The Ecumenical Institute also launched similar projects in depressed areas in several parts of the world during the 1970s. One was in Oombulgurri, Australia; one in Lapu-Lapu, the Philippines; one in Maliwada, India; one in London, England, and so on. An attempt by Matthews to get the World Council of Churches to adopt his program and outlook failed, and he began to turn his attention more and more to revitalizing the secular world rather than the religious community. The Religious Studies program was de-emphasized as the Ecumenical Institute began to turn its full attention to conducting secular courses and holding consultations, called town meetings, in communities throughout the United States. In 1974 they set up a secular structure called the Institute of Cultural Affairs to facilitate this process. By the end of 1975, they had conducted 4,276 such town meetings involving 228,000 individuals.

A number of members now left the commune because they believed it was turning away from its religious roots to embrace the secular structures of American business. Yet Matthews and others argued that the American business community, with interests and access to almost every part of the world, was a quite logical place from which to field the institute's global message of social renewal.

Matthews died in 1977, and the communal aspects of the institute began to disintegrate thereafter. Within a year the name of the organization had been changed to the Institute of Cultural Affairs and many of their religious houses had closed. Although the Chicago office remains open today and some of their community projects are still functioning under the leadership of former Ecumenical Institute members, all aspects of the Ecumenical Institute as a commune ended around 1981. A book with a section that focuses on the Ecumenical Institute is Clark's *Manpower for Mission*.

Elm Spring (1877–1918), on the James River, near Freeman, South Dakota, was a Hutterite Brüderhof (see **Bon Homme**) that was under the leadership of a high school teacher. They moved to Alberta, Canada, during World War I to avoid persecution directed against

them as pacifists. There were about 100 members at the time.

Emmaus (1740–1835), on the site of the present town by that name a few miles south of Allentown, Pennsylvania, was a Moravian General Economy community of about 100 members. All of them came there from the Moravian **Savannah** settlement in Georgia after that disbanded. The community was given its name by Bishop Augustus Gottlieb Spangenberg, one of the leading developers of Moravian communes in the United States. The members, like those at the other Moravian settlements, based their economy and lifestyle on the Herrnhut system used in the Moravian communities of Europe and at Savannah.

Enfield (1790–1917), Connecticut, located in Hartford County about 12 miles south of Springfield, Massachusetts, was a Shaker settlement (see **Watervliet**) that had as many as two hundred members in 1848. They owned 3,300 acres of land and had a lucrative garden-seed business, marketing their seeds prior to the Civil War primarily in the South. They also raised livestock and sold hay.

Enfield is credited with building the first one-horse buggy in the United States, and sowing the country's first manmade forest, planted by Elder Omar Pease in 1866. Their business of making lead pipe by hand ended with the mechanization of this industry elsewhere. Moses Johnson, a member of Enfield, built a number of the early churches for other Shaker communes.

After Enfield closed, the property was purchased by the state and it is now used for the rehabilitation of "trusty" prisoners as the Osborn State Prison Farm. Two Shaker buildings are preserved — the Old Brick Meeting House, constructed in 1792, and Meacham House, construction date unknown.

Enfield (1793–1923), New Hampshire, in the northern part of Grafton County, was a Shaker commune (see **Watervliet**) that had 330 members at its high point, divided into three "families." They owned 3,000 acres of land, some of it given to them by James Jewett, a well-to-do farmer.

Job Bishop and Hannah Goodrich were the first leaders of this community. The primary building here was a four-story high stone structure erected in 1840. At the time it was considered the most expensive building in the state, with the exception of the State House at Concord. Other Enfield buildings included three saw mills, a woolen mill, grist mill, fulling mill, spinning mill, tanning house, machine shop, carpenter's shop, blacksmith's shop, shoemaker's shop, infirmary, school, and laundry that was run by water power and had a centrifugal drier that was in use prior to 1875.

The members made and sold spinning wheels, rakes, ladders, pitchforks, scythe handles, looms, buckets and tubs, brooms, dry measures, linen, cotton and woolen goods, garden seeds, herbs, maple sugar, applesauce, patent medicines, and baked goods. The brimstone match was invented here, as was a folding pocket stereoscope.

Caleb Dyer, one of the trustees at Enfield, was a particularly able businessman, and he established a woolen company for the commune with offices in New York City. The venture collapsed, however, when a drunken man from outside the community shot Dyer, killing him on the spot. Other capable trustees included Samuel Barker and True W. Heath. One elder, Henry Cummings, caused a great scandal in this celibate community when he eloped with one of the female members.

Enfield had many visitors over the years who came to view the Shakers at work and worship, the most prominent being President James Monroe in 1817. When Enfield closed, the seven remaining members moved to the **Canterbury** Shaker commune. The commune's buildings and land were then sold to the Canadian Roman Catholic Brotherhood of La Salette.

Ephrata (1732–1934), at Ephrata, Pennsylvania, was a German Seventh-day Baptist community founded by Joseph Conrad Beissel (1690–1768). He named this commune after the ancient designation for the Biblical city of Bethlehem, and it had as many as 300 members at its highest point, around 1750.

The Seventh-day Baptists were one of the several groups that evolved from the Church of the Brethren (popularly known as Dunkards, Dunkers, or Tunkers, from the German word "to dip" because of their method of baptism). The first Church of the Brethren congregation began to worship in Germany in 1708, but by 1719 all the members of this denomination had moved to Pennsylvania to escape persecution. They first settled in the Germantown, Pennsylvania, area where Beissel, later to become the founder of the Seventh-day Baptists and the one who set up the Ephrata commune, also began his ministry.

Beissel, at the age of 27, had undergone a religious conversion through his contact with members of the Church of the Brethren. He did not, however, join that group but continued to work as a journeyman baker, a trade to which he had been apprenticed at an early age. His master was somewhat of a musician,

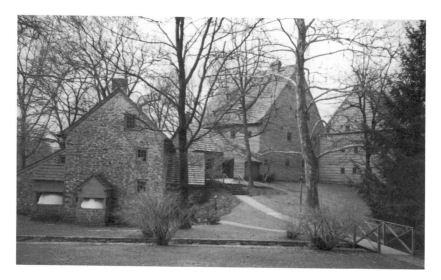

Ephrata cloisters as they appear today (courtesy of Ephrata Cloister, Pennsylvania Historical and Museum Collection).

and so besides teaching Beissel the trade, taught the boy to play a violin. Beissel was later to compose many hymns and other musical works after he came to America.

His support for the Brethren's cause and his own belief that celibacy was a requirement for anyone serving God, as well as his other radical views, led to Beissel's expulsion from several states in Germany. Finally he decided to emigrate to Pennsylvania where the Brethren were now living and join the communal experiment he had heard of called the **Women of the Wilderness**. Two friends, George Stiefel and Jacob Stuntz, agreed to go with him. But when the three arrived in Pennsylvania, they discovered that the Women of the Wilderness commune was already dispersed.

For a time Beissel lived with the Church of the Brethren members and worked with Peter Becker at Germantown, learning the weaver's trade. Becker was later to be designated head of the Church of the Brethren. In time, however, Beissel realized that if he were to live by his mystical and celibate beliefs, he would need to withdraw from the other members of the Brethren and become somewhat of a hermit.

In 1721, with his friend Stuntz, he erected a cabin on Mill Creek in Lancaster County, Pennsylvania. Their intention was to live only for the service of God. In this cabin they set up the first free school in the county, and here they taught the alphabet and catechism to youth from surrounding German farm families. They decided to keep the seventh day as their Sabbath, which was contrary to the practice of the Brethren. But in baptism and other religious matters they followed that church. In time, others came to live with them and share their somewhat solitary life, though some, like Stiefel, left in the midst of religious disagreements.

Eventually Beissel began to make plans to set up a Seventh-day Baptist settlement. He made a trip to the **Bo-**

hemia Manor commune in Maryland to learn about their problems and successes. The discussions held there with Peter Sluyter and others probably led to Beissel's decision to follow several of the Bohemia Manor practices when he established Ephrata, including the separation of sexes at meals and in other activities.

Beissel was ready to start Ephrata by 1732. He at first called the commune Economy, but soon after changed the name. With the help of those who were sharing his lifestyle, Beissel constructed a wooden building (now destroyed) on Mount Zion, a hill that rises above the Cocalico River, but by 1753 he moved the settlement to the meadow at the base of the hill, where the unique wooden cloisters of Ephrata still stand today.

Life in this commune demanded total celibacy if one were to serve Christ. Married couples could join, but they were pledged to refrain from sexual relations. The men, known as Solitary Brethren, were separated from the women, known as Sisters. Both lived in cells that were only four floorboards wide, two persons to a cell. Each cell had a small but high window. The beds were narrow, wooden ledges and the pillows were wooden blocks. The discomfort of these sleeping arrangements provided one of the ways in which members disciplined themselves for communion with God. By rule, all members slept for only two three-hour periods during the night. They rose to worship at midnight and then again at four in the morning before they began the day's work.

Another part of their discipline required that each member regularly give Beissel a written statement on their own "spiritual" condition. These confessionals were read aloud before the entire congregation.

Both men and women wore unattractive hoods, and the sisters were veiled. The men wore beards. Shoes, never worn in summer, were made of wood and hide. The buildings were constructed entirely of wood, without any nails or metal parts that might destroy their mystical nature.

At first Ephrata consisted of only one building in which both the Brethren and Sisters were housed. But this led to suspicion on the part of farmers and others living in the surrounding area and so separate housing was constructed. Eventually there were some married couples living in cottages around the center of the community who supported and participated in parts of the life at Ephrata. They received a sum from the common fund but were not considered members of the commune. Many were former Brethren and Sisters who had left the order and married.

The members operated a tannery, bake house, grist mill, saw mill, flaxseed oil mill, paper mill, fulling and bark mills, looms for weaving woolen and linen cloth, a bookbindery, and a famous printing press, the first in Pennsylvania outside of Philadelphia. On it was printed the earliest American edition of Bunyan's *Pilgrim's Progress* (in German) and a greater quantity of work of literary character than on any other press in the colonies. It was the first press in the Western world to print in both English and German typefaces. Their outstanding achievement was the *Martyrer Spiegel*, a 1,514-page story of the persecutions of the Mennonites in Europe. During the American Revolution this press printed the Continental money at a time when the British occupied Philadelphia.

Three brothers named Eckerling — Gabriel, Samuel, and Israel — were active in promoting the economic life of this commune and developing its various enterprises. They supervised the erection of a granary for the storage of rye and corn, and they built brick bake ovens for the making of bread that was given to needy settlers in the villages near Ephrata (probably the first organized assistance to the poor in the United States). But the three brothers were eventually expelled from the commune because Beissel came to view their activities as contributing to an attitude of selfishness among the members and a desire to abandon the communal lifestyle.

Some of the other known commune participants included Conrad Weiser, one-time elder of the Lutheran Church and an expert on Indian dialects and customs; Pastor Peter Miller (1710–1834), a scholarly theologian, linguist, and graduate of Heidelberg University; and the wife of Christopher Sauer, one of the best known publishers and printers in the American colonies. Miller, a friend of George Washington, translated the Declaration of Independence into seven languages. He took over the leadership of Ephrata after Beissel died. Mrs. Sauer eventually became the prioress of Ephrata.

Music was an important part of life at this commune. The members maintained a music school, and there were three women's and two men's choirs. The voice ranges of the members were developed by special training and special diets said to alter the vocal chords. Both men and women sang in falsetto voice. Beissel himself wrote over 1,000 hymns, of which 441 were published in 1747. The German author Thomas Mann, in his novel *Dr. Faustus* (1917), praised Beissel's system of harmony. Beissel was also the author of the first book of German poetry published in the United States, a book printed by Benjamin Franklin.

The community also had a school in which ornamental Gothic script and manuscript illumination were taught. The students included both commune members and outsiders.

Since the creed of Ephrata forbade members bearing arms, none of the commune participants took part in the American Revolution, but they did aid the sick and wounded of Washington's army after the Battle of Brandywine. And during the Revolution, Ephrata billeted 500 American soldiers. Of these about 200 died from wounds and smallpox. They were buried beside the graves of the Sisters who died caring for them. The commune must have also given some help to the British because later both the British government and the government of Pennsylvania offered compensation for their assistance during the war. Beissel refused on the grounds that this would be a temptation to worldliness.

Ephrata did not actually close until 1934, but by that time there were only a handful of residents. The closure coincided with the dissolution of the Seventh-day Baptist denomination. Ephrata's buildings are still standing. They are now maintained as a museum by the Pennsylvania Historical and Museum Commission. The narrow halls and tiny bedrooms give visitors some of the sense of the mystery that surrounded life there. Also visitors can see the remains of strange footprints on the ceiling of one of the rooms. These were treated with great reverence by the commune members who could give no reasonable explanation as to how the footprints got there in the first place. During summer months, visitors can see a pageant about the history of this religious community and hear a choir sing some of the music written there. Books with sections that focus on

Ephrata are Calverton's *Where Angels Dared to Tread* and Sachse's *The German Sectarians of Pennsylvania, 1708–1800: A Critical and Legendary History of the Ephrata Cloister and the Dunkers.*

Ephriam (1850–1853), at Green Bay, Wisconsin, was a Moravian settlement established by Nils Otto Tank, a wealthy Norwegian aristocrat, and A.M. Iverson, a theological student whom Tank persuaded to join him in the experiment.

Although other Moravian settlements had long since given up communal ownership of property, Tank, despite his wealth, believed that the principles of Christian communism were fundamental to the Moravian faith.

Tank purchased fertile land for the experiment at a cost of $1,500 and gathered a group of Moravian emigrants, then living in Milwaukee, Wisconsin, to join him there. Their pastor, the Rev. Fett, was among the 45 members. The site of this commune is known locally as Tanktown and it is entirely within the city of Green Bay.

The members decided to re-establish the Herrnhut system of organization used in the earlier Moravian communes (see **Bethlehem**). They laid out the dwelling lots and farms, and made plans for a church, schools, and parks. One of their most notable achievements was the establishment of a college in which Iverson taught religion and Tank taught history, languages, and science.

Prior to building their Moravian church, which is still standing at its original location, they worshiped in a small church on their property that had originally been constructed for an Indian mission. Tank himself lived in a home on the property that was built in 1776 by a fur trapper.

By the end of the first year dissen-sion arose among the members. Rev. Fett became skeptical of Tank's motives and began to suggest to Iverson that Tank only wanted to rule as a lord over the community. The conflict came to a head when Tank refused to give the residents title to the land they occupied, arguing that it was contrary to the principles of Christian communism as held by their faith. The group then fell apart. Some members went West, others to Sturgeon Bay, Wisconsin, and still others joined Iverson at a new commune, also called **Ephriam**, in Door County, Wisconsin. Years later Iverson was to state that his suspicions about Tank's motives were wholly unfounded.

Tank remained at his home, now the oldest dwelling in Wisconsin, until he died many years later. The house was recently moved to the Heritage State Park in Allouez, Wisconsin.

Ephriam (1853–1864), in Door County, Wisconsin, was a Moravian settlement started by A.M. Iverson, a theological scholar and pastor who departed from Tank's **Ephriam** colony at Green Bay with a group of dissatisfied members. At its height the community had about 40 participants, including some Norwegian fishermen in the area whom Iverson converted. The town on this site, named after the commune, is now a popular summer resort.

The members supported the community by farming and fishing. They also cut trees for fence posts, which they shipped to Chicago. Though some of the members continued to live on the property for many years, the community disbanded soon after Iverson left to take up a post as pastor of a Moravian church. His log cabin and the commune's Moravian church, built in 1857, are still standing. A book with a section that focuses on Ephriam is Holand's

First log cabin erected by commune members at Ephriam (photo by author).

Old Peninsula Days: Tales and Sketches of the Door County Peninsula.

Equality Colony (1897–1907), just east of Blanchard in Skagit County, Washington, was a project started by the Brotherhood of the Cooperative Commonwealth, a large socialist organization that was founded in 1895 and had its headquarters in Maine. The Commonwealth had three primary purposes: to educate the public in the principles of socialism, to unite all socialists in one organization, and to establish cooperative colonies and industries within a single state with the aim of eventually turning the whole state to socialism. It included among its membership labor-leader Eugene Debs, muckraking journalist Henry Demarest Lloyd, and socialist editor Julius A. Wayland (see **Ruskin Commonwealth**). After the Equality Colony was formed, much of the organization's energies turned to keeping it functioning, and

interest in other socialist aims declined. This eventually destroyed the Brotherhood.

The initial 280 acres of land for the Equality Colony were purchased by Ed Pelton, one of the leaders of the Brotherhood. He traveled from New England to the state of Washington to locate a site for this commune. The one he found occupied a wooded hillside on which there was a creek that flowed throughout the year. The members added more land later to bring the total up to 600 acres. Their first communal structures were built on the lower slope. Private homes were afterward constructed further up the hill.

Each family paid $160 to join, and the members came from many different parts of the United States. They grew to 300 at the high point of this commune, in 1898. Some of them included Norman Wallace Lermond from Maine, who was the founder of the Brotherhood of the Cooperative Commonwealth, and

Henry and Kate Halladay from Kansas. Henry was the president of Equality in its early years. There were also Mr. and Mrs. Carey Lewis and Kenneth McKensie from Washington state, W.H. Kaufman from Minnesota, and Charles H. Swigart from Ohio.

The members engaged in farming and fishing, had a saw and shingle mill, bakery, public kitchen, laundry, root house, store, and several fishing boats. They manufactured furniture from the commune's ready lumber supply and published a weekly, *Industrial Freedom.* There was also a magazine for children called *Young Socialist.* More than half of the members lived in two apartment houses that they built, though there were also a number of private homes. In 1898 they opened a school for the younger children. They entertained themselves by putting on plays and skits and holding dances and organized group singing in the evenings and on weekends.

Alexander Horr, an anarchist, arrived from New York in 1905 with some others. Under his influence, the name of the commune was changed to Freeland, its constitution was altered, and the members were organized into small competitive groups. Then, within a year, the commune closed. Some of the members later joined **Llano.** Books with sections that focus on the Equality Colony are Hinds' *American Communities* and LeWarne's *Utopias on Puget Sound, 1885–1915.*

Equity (1830–1832), located in Tuscarawas County, Ohio, was the first of three anarchist communes established by Josiah Warren (1798–1874). He was a musician and inventor who is credited with being the founder of American philosophical anarchism. He was even called "a remarkable American" by British philosopher John Stuart Mill, who often refrained from giving credit to persons on the other side of the Atlantic.

Warren moved from Boston, Massachusetts, to Cincinnati, Ohio, in order to teach music and work as an orchestra leader. In 1821, he invented and patented a lard-burning lamp, and then established a profitable lamp factory. But in 1825 he heard a lecture by Robert Owen that so inspired Warren, he sold the factory and moved his family to Owen's **New Harmony** commune. By 1827 Warren had returned to Cincinnati disgusted with Owen's theories but intent on experimenting with his own ideas for a structure in which all goods and services would be based solely on cost.

He began his experiment by setting up, on May 18, 1827, an Equity store at the corner of Fifth and Elm streets in Cincinnati. The operation was simple. All the buyer had to pay for, besides the initial cost price, was the time occupied by the salesman in transmitting the goods to the customer. No profit was to be charged on anything. The store and Warren's theories had many supporters, and when he closed the project two years later, it showed neither loss nor gain. In later years Warren opened several other stores of this type, one even in the village of New Harmony after Owen's experiment there had ended.

Warren was described by contemporaries as a short, thickset man with a large forehead. His work in music, mechanics, and social theory was quite original. His inventions included a speed printing press, a self-inking cylinder press, a process for making stereotype plates cheaply and easily, and a process by which sun-burnt bricks could be manufactured out of lime and gravel.

He also wrote and printed a monthly journal, "The Peaceful Revolutionist," which lasted but a year, and developed a unique form of musical notation.

Equity, his first commune, was established on 400 acres of land. It had 15 members. Warren took great pride in the fact that no meetings for legislation needed to take place in his commune. They had "no officers, no priests nor prophets," he said, and he argued that "Peace, harmony, ease, security, happiness, will be found only in individuality." The commune lasted until malaria and influenza forced its abandonment two years after it began. Books with sections that focus on Equity are Bailie's *Josiah Warren* and Calverton's *Where Angels Dared to Tread*.

EskDale (1942–1968), near Garrison, Utah, was a fundamentalist Christian community organized by the Order of Aaron and led by Chief High Priest M.L. Glendenning, who may have once been a Mormon. The members claimed they were organized by Moses in 1736 B.C., although no one had ever heard of them until they incorporated at Salt Lake City the year they formed the commune. Much of their literature was devoted to attacking Mormon beliefs and to prooftexting Bible references. For "theological reasons" they refused to give membership figures, but evidence from their tracts and letters suggests that they had about 50 members. At one time they conducted a school for all ages, but by 1960 they made their income by raising cattle, sheep, and poultry on their 7,000 acres of land.

Espanola (1960–present), near Espanola, Washington, is a Hutterite Brüderhof (see **Bon Homme**) that had 45 members in 1964. Paul Gross, the author of *The Hutterite Way* and a number of articles on the Hutterites, is the minister of this colony.

Esperanza (1877–1880), at Urbana, Kansas, was a commune of about ten idealists who published *The Star of Hope*, a monthly journal, and owned a hotel. The members supported the Socialist Labor Party and called for an eight-hour day.

Estero (1894–1965), Florida, about 16 miles south of Fort Myers, was established by Cyrus Reed Teed (see **Koresh Community**) and other members of the Koreshan movement as a center for Teed's new religion, the Church Triumphant. The land for the commune came from Gustav Dampkohler, a German immigrant Teed converted to the Koreshan philosophy while lecturing in Florida. This man turned 320 acres over to Teed. Later, the Koreshans added plots to this initial gift until there were 6,000 acres of good farming land for the commune.

The members, who reached a high of 200 in 1906, constructed a communal dining hall and kitchen with the second floor devoted to housing for women. They had a separate house for men, a house for the community officers, a dairy, a bake shop, schools for children, and a floating stage on which they produced dramas by the latest playwrights. They also had an art hall that is still standing. It contained works by a number of artists, including those of Teed's son, Douglas, a noted painter. They had a brass band, an orchestra, and published two magazines: *The Flaming Sword*, printed until 1949 when a fire destroyed their printing plant, and the *American Eagle*, a horticultural journal. The community specialized in raising citrus fruits and truck vegetables. In the early 1900s they produced some of the finest fruit grown in Florida.

The Koreshans, in 1906, formed their own political party, the Progressive Liberty Party, to unseat what they considered backward elements of the Lee County Democratic machine. Their antimachine campaigning so antagonized the town marshall at Fort Myers that he challenged Teed to a fistfight in which Teed was severely injured. He died many months later from this injury. Electrotherapeutic treatments by Gustav Faber, one of the members who used a therapeutic machine of his own design, could do nothing to save Teed's life.

But Teed had told his followers that he would rise from the dead, and so they gathered around his body to await the expected event. After two or three days the body showed signs of decay, and county health officers ordered it buried. Teed's body was then placed in a concrete tomb on Estero Island off the Florida coast. But a hurricane in 1921 swept the tomb away without Teed ever having returned to the living.

With Teed's death, Faber claimed leadership of the commune, as did Annie G. Ordway, Teed's highest ranking assistant. Faber won out and Ordway soon left Estero with a few followers. She set up the **Order of Theocracy** at Fort Myers in 1910. In 1949, a visitor reported that there were 12 remaining members, the oldest being 93 years of age. The community closed in 1965, and the land was then deeded to the state of Florida. Besides the art hall, there are several buildings of Estero that are still standing. Books with sections that focus on the Koresh Community are Carmer's *Dark Trees in the Wind*, Gardner's *Fads and Fallacies in the Name of Science* and Webber's *Escape to Utopia: The Communal Movement in America*.

Buildings of Cyrus Teed's Estero still stand, but are now deserted (drawing by Lois Will).

Evergreen Community (1958–present), also called the Norfolk Brüderhof and Deer Spring, is located at Norfolk, Connecticut. It is a community of the Society of Brothers (see **Woodcrest**). The commune has about 200 members.

Fairhope (1894–present), which is located in the Alabama resort town by the same name that grew up around it, is a community based on the single-tax principles of Henry George (1839–1897). George argued that land is a free gift of nature; that all persons have an equal right to use the land; and that it is unfair for a few to acquire great wealth by holding land that increases in value. He proposed to make any increase in the value of land ("the unearned increment") the source of all taxation. He further argued that such a tax was not only the most just of all taxes, but the only one apt "to stimulate industry, to open new opportunities to capital, and to increase the production of wealth." Some of the many followers of Henry George established cooperative communities — eight in the United States — based on his ideas of how the economic system should function. They called these enclaves.

Fairhope was the first of these single-tax enclaves. It was originally known as the Fairhope Industrial Association, but in 1904, the members changed its name to the Fairhope Single Tax Corporation. The founders included Ernest B. Gaston, a former advocate of Edward Bellamy's kind of socialism (see **Ruskin Commonwealth**) and a man who had tried unsuccessfully to set up a socialist commune in Louisiana; Joseph Fels, a millionaire soap manufacturer from Philadelphia who provided funds for the start of such communities both in the United States and Europe, and James Bellangee. The initiators launched a paper called the *Liberty Bell* to promote their enterprise, later changing the name of the paper to the *Courier*.

Anyone could join the settlement who had the approval of the executive council and who could pay the $100 entrance fee. There were soon many members, though only about ten actually lived on the land during the first year. At its height, in the early 1900s, the resident membership reached about 300. Included among these was novelist Upton Sinclair (see **Helicon Home**), who lived there with his family in 1909. There were 75 resident members in 1936, and there are perhaps 50 today. The community increased its land holdings from 132 acres in 1894 to 1,600 acres in 1936. Most of this land, however, is rather poor soil for farming.

Fairhope built a wharf in 1895 and operated it until it was destroyed in a storm in 1906. They also tried to establish a 14-mile railroad in 1912, but the project was never completed. Undoubtedly their most successful enterprise was a School of Organic Education, started in 1907 under the direction of Marietta Johnson. It still operates, though it has declined in size and program since her death in 1938.

Johnson taught that there is a distinction between training and growing. She held that when adults are training a child they dominate that child, while when they are concerned with the growing process of a child they act to provide the right conditions. She therefore set up her school to serve the interests of the child rather than to fit the child into the preconceived standards of the adult world. She postponed, for example, the teaching of reading, writing, and arithmetic until a child was 9 or 10 years old, and she also had no examinations or report cards. Educators John Dewey and Charles H. Henderson visited the school in its early days and praised Johnson's methods, some of which have since been incorporated into the principles of progressive education. A book with a section that focuses on Fairhope is Alyea's *Fairhope 1894– 1954.*

Falsington (1956), at Falsington, Pennsylvania, was a cooperative community of eight people active in the peace movement. It existed for only a few months. One member, David Gayle, was later active in the **Church of Hope** at Chicago. His sister joined **Woodcrest** near Rifton, New York.

Family *see* **Kirtland**

Far West (1837–1839) was a Mormon United Order commune (see **Kirtland**) located five miles from Kingston, Missouri. Its initial membership was composed of many of the Mormons who had to flee from **Zion**. Until the founder of this religion, Joseph Smith, Jr., and Sidney Rigden moved here from Ohio, along with most of the other members from Kirtland, Far West was led by Oliver Cowdery and Parley Pratt.

Smith, along with W.W. Phelps, John Whitmer and Brigham Young, made plans for building a magnificent city at this site, one with a 396-foot-wide square and four main streets that were each 100 feet wide, as well as others of narrower proportions. A temple location was selected and excavation begun. Many houses were constructed and various workshops established. Eventually the population at Far West grew to about 4,000 persons.

But friction developed between the members and their non–Mormon neighbors, both because of religious prejudice and the fact that the Mormons were opposed to slavery. Pro-slavery senti-

ments were strong in Missouri at that time. In the fall of 1838, a mob attacked the commune in what is known in Mormon history as "the massacre at Haun's Mill." About 20 members were killed, and Smith, Rigden, and some others were arrested. In 1839, the Mormons were ordered to leave Missouri by Governor Lillburn W. Boggs. Those who had been arrested later able to escape to Illinois, where they established **Nauvoo**.

After the Mormons left Far West, all the houses they built there were torn down. Today only a cornfield marks the site of this once prosperous community.

Farmington Brüderhof *see* **New Meadow Run**

Father Divine's Peace Mission (1915–1963) was established in Brooklyn, New York, by Father Divine (1877–1965). He was the grandson of slaves and his birthname was George Baker. As a young man he opened a mission in Savannah and took the title "Son of Righteousness," but the city authorities arrested him and sentenced him on a trumped-up charge to six months on the county chain gang. After he was released, he went to Charleston, South Carolina, and from there to Baltimore, Maryland, where he worked briefly as a gardener. In Baltimore he joined a religious group led by a "Father Joseph," and became one of his "messengers." Baker returned to Georgia to organize for Father Joseph, but was soon arrested again and tried for insanity. He was released on condition that he never return to Georgia.

Baker then moved to Brooklyn where, for a time, he worked with John Hickerson, who called himself Bishop St. John the Divine. When Baker was ready to establish his own movement, distinctly different from the other religious cults he had been associated with because of his intention to make it communal, he took the name Major Morgan J. Divine. He called the commune Father Divine's Peace Mission. Initially he had about 12 followers, including his "spiritual wife" (he advocated celibacy) who was known as "Mother Divine." Here he also first experimented with the use of a meal as the central worship symbol for his movement.

In 1919 he purchased a house at Sayville, Long Island, where he transferred his followers. They set up an employment agency and began to serve free meals to all who cared to come. Gradually visitors were attracted there; by 1931 they were arriving in great numbers. The residents of Sayville were annoyed by the gaiety and noise of the Peace Mission feasts, but more than that they objected to the large influx of black people from Harlem. The community leaders had Father Divine arrested on a disorderly conduct charge, fined him $500, and sentenced him to a year in jail. Four days later the judge on the case dropped dead of a heart attack and Divine said from his cell, "I hated to do it." His followers immediately recognized the happening as proof of Father Divine's divinity.

The headquarters was moved to Harlem where there would not be such harassment, and the movement grew steadily. Mission after mission was opened until, by the early 1940s, there were sections of this movement in 26 states, as well as in England, Canada, Switzerland, Panama, Hawaii, Australia, and the British West Indies. These missions, however, were not communal. Only the national headquarters in Harlem was, and here there may have been 2,000 members. Divine also opened many businesses, the profits of which went to the headquarters. These included restaurants, stores, garages, schools, meat markets, hotels, and homes for men and for women. Land was purchased at Kingston, New York, for a farm, and the same was true of land purchased near Atlantic City. The weekly newspaper of the movement was called *New Day*, it earlier having been named *The Spoken Word*.

Funds came from contributions by members and from visitors at the communion banquets. These were impressive affairs that included much singing, revival-type confessions and testimony, and a closing message by Father Divine himself. (When he could not be present, his message was read to the assembly.) The cost of the banquet was always modest, as was the cost of a meal at any of the movement's Peace Restaurants. In the 1940s the restaurant meals were either ten or fifteen cents. For $2 a week a member could get lodging at the million dollar resort hotel owned by the movement in Atlantic City. Contributions and other funds poured into the headquarters so lavishly that one week in 1949 alone Father Divine banked $500,000. At his death in 1965, the movement was estimated to control properties worth $10,000,000.

Father Divine's influence within Harlem was courted by both the city and national political machines. Eventually he launched his own Righteous Government Political Party with a platform that called for racial equality, censorship of the press, abolition of labor unions and life insurance, the substitution of the word "peace" for "hello" since the latter included the word "hell," and a means by which doctors must guarantee cures and be liable for the deaths of patients. Within his own movement he allowed no immorality, profanity, drinking, or smoking. Husbands and wives had to live separately, the children being cared for in the women's hotels.

Part of Father Divine's appeal came from the fact that the members believed him to be God and thus had a chance to participate with him in the joys of the Kingdom on Earth rather than having to wait for this privilege in the hereafter promised by other religious leaders.

He moved the headquarters to Philadelphia in 1942 because of legal difficulties in New York, and he made his last public appearance in 1963. After that he was bedridden with arteriosclerosis. The movement is now led by Sweet Angel, a white, blond, Canadian woman (born Edna Rose Ritchings) who had joined the movement before 1946 and replaced Mother Divine as Baker's "spiritual wife."

The communal aspects of Father Divine's Peace Mission ended two years before his death, although the sect still exists. Mother Divine lives in the Woodmont Estate on Spring Mill Road in Gladwyne (a suburb of Philadelphia), which is now their headquarters. This building is opened to the public on special days. A book with a section that focuses on Father Divine's Peace Mission is Braden's *Those Who Believe: A Study of Modern American Cults and Minority Religious Movements*.

Fellowship Farm (1907–1918), at Westwood, Massachusetts, was a cooperative community founded by Unitarian minister George Littlefield. Each member paid $2.50 a month for their acre of land, on which they could farm or start small industries. Littlefield made the down payment on 75 acres that contained a large house and a barn.

The approximately 40 members who eventually joined this commune included carpenters, cabinet makers, machinists, printers, and a violin maker.

They raised hens and apples. Three years after the project was started and running, Littlefield departed. He moved first to Missouri, where he joined others in setting up **Fruit Crest**, and then to California, where he helped to establish the **Los Angeles Fellowship Farm**. A book with a section that focuses on Fellowship Farm is Hine's *California's Utopian Communities*.

Fellowship Farm (1940–1945), near West Acton, Massachusetts, was established by the Boston branch of the Fellowship of Reconciliation, a well-known pacifist organization. The manager was Robert Brainard, and it had only four members living full-time at the commune, though more than a dozen persons from Boston and Cambridge joined them on weekends for farming. When the project was closed, their old farmhouse and farmland were sold to a private developer.

Fellowship Farm Cooperative (1912–1940), at North Stelton, New Jersey, was formed by about 75 German socialists, most of whom were Jewish. They raised the money to purchase their property through advertisements in the New York *Call*, a socialist newspaper. They also had the advice of the Rev. George Littlefield of **Fellowship Farm** at Westwood, Massachusetts, in starting their project.

The members established a cooperative garment factory, grocery store, and bus line, but their attempts at farming did not succeed, with the exception of a few members who raised poultry. Most members had to continue to commute to New York City each day to work.

Fernside *see* **Tyringham**

Ferrer Colony (1915–1950), at North Stelton, New Jersey, was an anarchist community, named for the Spanish educator Francisco Ferrer, who, in 1909, had been executed in Spain for treason. Ferrer had earlier created a large network of anticlerical private educational institutions throughout Spain, and he had developed some noted theories about how best to create a well-rounded learning program. His supporters in New York City organized the Francisco Ferrer Association in 1910 to study these theories. Some of them set up the Ferrer Modern School in 1915 to put Ferrer's ideas into practice. They located the school at North Stelton, a village close to New York City.

The commune, which was established next to this school and gave it support, was started by Harry Kelley (1871–1933), Joseph Cohen (1881–1953), and Leonard Abbott (1878–1953). Abbott later authored *Francisco Ferrer, His Life, Work, Martyrdom*. At one time there were as many as 300 members, including the children. They built a total of 80 houses, as well as other structures. Many of them worked at jobs in New York City to support the community, and both the school and the commune also received support from donations given by trade unions and private individuals.

Life at the Ferrer Colony was a mixture of work and pleasure. There were swimming parties in the afternoon and dancing and lectures in the evening. Many of the members took classes at the Ferrer Modern School, and there were endless discussions and arguments between the participants in the various anarchist factions and between the anarchists and the socialist and communist members. Eventually both Cohen and Kelley left because of disagreements over the leadership of the commune. Cohen then set up the **Sunrise Cooperative Farm** in Michigan. Kelley started

two other anarchist communes, the **Mohegan Colony** and **Mount Airy**. Some better-known members of the Ferrer Colony were the mother of folksinger Joan Baez; George S. Seldes, who later set up the **Belle Terre** anarchist commune, and Joseph Freeman, one of the founders of the Communist magazine *New Masses*.

The Ferrer Modern School over the years had many distinguished teachers and lecturers, none of whom were members of the commune. Among these were philosopher Will Durant, artist Rockwell Kent, writer Manuel Komroff, newspaperman Lincoln Stephens, and the well-known anarchist Emma Goldman. The school closed during the Second World War, but the commune continued until 1950. A book with a section that particularly focuses on the Ferrer Colony is Veysey's *The Communal Experience: Anarchist and Mystical Counter-Culture in America*.

First Community of Man's Free Brotherhood (1833–1835), near Covington, Indiana, was established by Isaac Romine. He had earlier been a member of the **Coal Creek** commune. There were perhaps ten members here. When this commune disbanded, most of the members moved to the **Grand Prairie Harmonial Association**.

Forest River (1950–present), near Fordville, North Dakota, is a Hutterite Brüderhof (see **Bon Homme**) that was formed out of the division of another Hutterite commune in Canada. The Forest River members experienced great difficulties when they decided to allow a community of refugees from Germany to join them. The refugees, members of the Society of Brothers, had been living in a Hutterite-like settlement in Paraguay. Some of them were invited to come to the United States and join the Forest River commune.

But disagreements soon erupted between the Hutterites and this group of would-be Hutterites from Paraguay. None of the other Hutterite communities in the United States would accept any of them, especially because the refugees wanted to establish a complex educational system at Forest River and open the commune to all interested visitors. Most of the Forest River Hutterites withdrew in protest and returned to their original colony in Canada.

The Society of Brothers members eventually proved to be such poor farmers that the Forest River commune soon declined. Eventually the people from Paraguay decided to move to a new community that other members of the Society of Brothers had established in Rifton, New York (see **Woodcrest**). They left, taking a number of the remaining Hutterites with them. Only four disgraced and bewildered Hutterite members stayed at Forest River. The other Hutterite communities banned these four from their fellowship until late in 1963, when they were granted re-admission and other members were sent to join them in rebuilding the Forest River Brüderhof. In 1964 the membership at Forest River stood at 51 and they were led by Andrew Hofer.

Forrestville (1826–1827), also known as Coxsackie, was an Owenite community located at Lapham's Mills, near Coxsackie, New York. It was modeled on the Owenite **New Harmony** commune, and settled around March 1826, when they printed their constitution. According to this document, "a Baptist, a Methodist, a Universalist, a Quaker, a Calvinist, a Deist, or any other ist, provided he or she is a genuine good moralist, are equally privileged and equally esteemed."

At the start there were 31 members in four families, but before the end of the year the membership had grown to over 60. The leading members were Dr. Samuel Underhill (later head of the **Kendel** Owenite commune), Nathaniel Underhill, John Newberry, William G. Macy, Jethro Macy, and Jacob Peterson, who had been a member of the **Franklin** Owenite commune. Other families, locally prominent, included the Quimbys, Dickensons, Fosdicks, and Weeks.

The commune had a total of 350 acres, two saw mills, one grist mill, a carding machine, and a tannery. They worked at wagon making, shoe making, blacksmithing, coopering, and agriculture. However, Forrestville closed after a year because of disagreements among the members. As one of them later wrote: "We wanted men and women who would work together for each other's good." The property was sold in October 1827. More than half of the members then made a hard winter's journey to Ohio and joined the **Kendel** Owenite community.

Forty-Eighters Colony (1850), in Washington County, Wisconsin, was a cooperative settlement established by perhaps ten intellectuals and revolutionaries who had participated in the 1848 uprisings in Germany and elsewhere. They had several hundred acres of land and built a crude dwelling in which they lived. Only one member was married and his wife acted as the commune's cook. This member was the composer Hans Balatka, a Moravian who later became the director of a music school in Chicago and conducted orchestras in Milwaukee, St. Louis, and Chicago. None of them, however, were farmers, and the experiment failed in less than a year. The best known member of this commune was Carl Schurz, who later

Barn of the old Fountain Grove commune can still be seen from Highway 101, near Santa Rosa, California (photo by author).

became a noted U.S. senator and secretary of the interior under President Rutherford B. Hayes. A book with a section that focuses on the Forty-Eighters Colony is Wittke's *We Who Built America: The Saga of the Immigrant.*

Fountain Grove (1875–1892), at Santa Rosa, California, was a spiritualist commune of 30 members organized by Thomas Lake Harris after he left the **Brotherhood of New Life** community in New York. Through two purchases, Harris acquired 1,200 acres for the settlement. He preferred to call it an experiment in Theo-Socialism rather than a commune.

The members for the first five years tried to establish a dairy, but then planted most of the land in grapes, which by 1886 produced 70,000 gallons of wine a year. They dined together in a large communal dining hall, joining hands for grace, and singing at the end of the meal. For many months Harris, who was a highly imaginative poet, provided them with a new poem each morning at breakfast. Their library was described in local newspapers in the 1880s as the largest in California.

Rumors of scandalous activities on the part of Harris led to the commune's downfall. One visitor, a Christian Scientist and suffragette, charged in an article she wrote that the members were held in virtual slavery by the autocrat Harris. To save the experiment, he departed in 1892 and returned to New York City. Though the others remained, Fountain Grove soon abandoned its communitarian nature.

A spiritualist to the last, Harris declared in 1894 that he had attained technical immortality through a complete spiritual union with his heavenly counterpart, who he referred to as the Lily Queen. He also repeatedly predicted the imminent end of the world.

In 1920 all the land became the property of Kanaye Nagasawa, a Japanese spiritualist and disciple of Harris, the only member still living there. Nagasawa managed the winery until his own death in 1934.

The community house burned in the early 1900s and Harris' mansion has been torn down, but other buildings remain, including the winery and some rather interesting barns. The Fountain Grove Winery near Freeway 101 stands today as a memorial to this commune. A book with a section that focuses on Fountain Grove is Hine's *California's Utopian Communities*.

Fountain of the World (1949–1967), at Canoga Park, north of Los Angeles, California, was established by Krishna Venta, a robed and barefooted spiritual leader who claimed to be the living Christ. His real name was Francis Pencovic and he had once worked as a boilermaker in San Francisco. The members numbered 140 in 1956, although they said that they represented thousands of followers.

The garments the members wore were quite colorful. Krishna Venta himself had robes of yellow; his students, robes of green. Members who could administer medicine wore blue, the ones taking responsibility for leadership, gray; and those who prepared meals, brown. Anyone wishing to join the commune was permitted to stay for a 90-day probationary period, and, if accepted, was required to give all material possessions to the community in return for one of the robes.

The members raised goats and poultry, though they themselves seldom ate meat. The women members went each day into Los Angeles to canvass door to door for donations of food and money. They often used the initials W.K.F.L. before the name of their community to stand for wisdom, knowledge, faith, and love.

Krishna Venta, who insisted that his followers adhere strictly to the Ten Commandments, was arrested several times during the years of the commune's existence, once for nonsupport of two children by his first wife, and other times for check forgery, sending threatening letters to President Roosevelt, panhandling, and gambling with the communal treasury.

He did have a knack for publicity, and news of the commune members often made the papers. The pictures of members barefooted and in their unique robes appeared when they took an active part in assisting at scenes of great tragedy in the area, such as when they directed traffic after a nearby plane crash in July 1949, and later when they helped at the site of an earthquake that did damage in Bakersfield and at the scene of a flood that damaged parts of Ventura. Krishna Venta even showed up in Washington, D.C., at the Army-McCarthy hearings of 1954, to tell a much amused press corps that "the three Joes" had caused most of the troubles in the world. He said he was referring to Joe McCarthy, Joe Stalin, and Tojo.

In 1956 Krishna Venta decided to set up another commune near Homer, Alaska (see **Fountain of the World in Alaska**). Some of the members then filed homestead claims and moved there. But in December 1958, the main building at Canoga Park was destroyed by an explosion that killed ten members, including Krishna Venta. His second wife, Mother Ruth, assumed the leadership. Police charged two ex-members with setting the explosion. A book with a section that focuses on the Fountain of the World is Mathison's *Faiths, Cults and Sects in America*.

Fountain of the World in Alaska (1956–1967), near Homer, Alaska, was a colony established by 120 followers of Krishna Venta in California (see **Fountain of the World**). The members filed homestead claims before they moved to Alaska to assure that they would have a place to live. The commune closed at about the same time as the California parent community disbanded.

Fourier Phalanx (1858), one mile south of Moore's Hill, Indiana, in Dearborn County, was a Fourierist community (see **Social Reform Unity**) of about 25 members from Cincinnati, Ohio. They were led by Alcander Longley (1832–1918), who had been a member of the **Clermont Phalanx** and the **North American Phalanx** some years earlier. The Fourier Phalanx lasted only about four months and there are no records of its other members, economy, or activities.

Longley was one of five sons of a Universalist minister in Cincinnati. With his brothers he started a printing firm in that city that specialized in publishing reformist literature. After hearing a speech by Albert Brisbane, the American advocate of Fourierism, Longley became a convert of that program for setting up Phalanx communities. He also began to edit and publish *The Phalansterian Record*, a monthly that was devoted to the ideas of Fourier. Longley was convinced that the failure of the two Fourierist communes with which he had been associated earlier was due to their inability to follow the principles elaborated by Fourier and Brisbane. He therefore decided to establish the Fourier Phalanx with some followers from Cincinnati. But, after this commune in Indiana also failed, Longley announced his disillusionment with Fourierism and his adoption of Christian communism as his goal.

He returned to Cincinnati to continue to work as a printer and then as a post office clerk. His brothers dissolved the printing firm in 1860. In 1867 Longley moved with his family (he was married three times) to the **Icaria** commune in Iowa, where he stayed only a few months. Then in January 1868, he moved his family to St. Louis, Missouri, and soon began publication of *The Communist*, which continued to appear until 1917 though its name was later changed to *The Altruist*. He also established five short-lived communes in various parts of Missouri — the **Reunion Community**, **Friendship Community**, **Relief**, **Mutual Aid Cooperative Association**, and **Altruist Community**. All of these closed because of lack of capital.

He was a strong advocate of equal rights for women, a member of the Socialist Labor Party in St. Louis, and the inventor of a phonetic system of musical notation in which the figures he used indicated the length of sound while the staff indicated the pitch.

Franklin (1826), also called the Haverstraw community, was an Owenite settlement (see **New Harmony**) near Haverstraw, New York. The 120-acre woodland site included two mansion houses as well as 12 to 14 out-buildings, a saw mill, and a rolling and splitting mill. There was also a stream that ran through the property.

The 80 members included George Huston (d. 1840), who had been imprisoned in England for atheistic writings; Henry A. Fay, a civil liberties lawyer; Abner Kneeland and Robert Jennings, both Universalist preachers; and Jacob Peterson, who later moved to the **Forrestville** commune and became a leader there. Others were cabinet makers, farmers, and tailors.

The group planned to support themselves through farming and to live rationally by avoiding "absurd and irrational systems of religion — and marriage combined with some of these irrational systems," but their beliefs angered the surrounding farmers. Also their neighbors found the costumes that the women adopted (pantalets on the legs and a gown that reached only to the knees) to be abhorrent.

One of the members, James M'Knight, left in disgust after he had been asked to work on Sunday. He wrote, "Ye who love the music of the stirring fife, ye who live to trip the 'light fantastic toe' and gamble away the hours which ought to be devoted to reflection and religious contemplation, go to the Franklin Community, there, undisturbed by thought, or religious melancholy, you may pass your evenings in threading the giddy mazes of the ball, and laugh at the stirrings of remorse, and the upbraidings of a guilty conscience."

A series of financial mistakes brought Franklin to a close after only five months. Some of the members then joined Forrestville. One later wrote, "We wanted men and women of skillful industry, sober and honest, with a knowledge of themselves, and a disposition to command and be commanded, and not men and women whose sole occupation was to parade and talk."

Fraternal Community, No. 1 *see* **Hopedale**

Free Acres (1909–present), about six miles southeast of Berkeley Heights, New Jersey, is a single-tax community (see **Fairhope**) that was established by philosophical anarchist Bolten Hall. It now has about 100 voting members, many of whom work in New York City. They are organized into a folk guild, dramatic guild, garden guild, arts and crafts guild, and many committees that meet at an eighteen-century community farmhouse. They hold discussion groups every Sunday afternoon.

The 80-acre commune with about 50 homes also has an artesian well to supply water, open air theater, swimming pool, and tennis court. The members pay $20 a year for one acre of land. Among the former residents were actor and movie star James Cagney and author MacKinlay Kantor. A book with a section that focuses on Free Acres is Huntington's *Enclaves of Single Tax or Economic Rent.*

Freedom Colony (1897–1905), four miles west of Fulton, Kansas, on the Little Osage River, was a commune organized by the General Labor Exchange of Missouri, which set up no other communes. There were 13 members, all of whom had to be active in the General Labor Exchange and could join only by unanimous agreement of the other members. Their 60 acres of land included a coal shaft and had an estimated value of $2,400. They worked at farming, coal mining, and lumber milling, and they published a newspaper called *Progressive Thought.*

Freedom Colony (1912), in the Willamette River Valley of Oregon, was a farming commune established by about 125 members of the Russian Molokan church. The Molokans are Christian pacifists who follow many of the ideas of the Russian author Leo Tolstoy. They worship in private homes rather than churches and believe that the "voice within" each person is an adequate religious guide. When they lived in Russia prior to coming to the United States they were terribly persecuted because of their beliefs. The group is closely allied to the better-known Dukhobors of Canada.

Although some Molokans still live in California and Oregon in non-communal relationships, none are willing to talk to strangers and so their historical record is quite blurred. It is known, however, that they set up seven farming communes between 1912 and 1924, none of which lasted more than a year or two. As unsuccessful as these experiments were economically, they did allow the Molokans to preserve their Russian traditions and religious convictions.

The Freedom Colony members had 1,000 acres of land, but this commune lasted only a few months because they were ill advised in the way they drew up legal papers for the purchase of the property. According to their deed, if any member defaulted in payment, the entire colony lost its land. Thus legal problems soon enveloped them and forced them to disband. An article with information that focuses on the Freedom Colony and the Molokans is Dunn's *American Molokans and Canadian Dukhobors: Economic Position and Ethnic Identity*, a paper presented at the 1973 International Congress of Anthropological and Ethnological Sciences.

Freeland *see* **Equality Colony**

Freeland Association (1900–1906), at Freeland, Washington, was a cooperative community of about 75 members organized by Seattle entrepreneur James Gleason and two other socialists, George Washington Daniels and Henry L. Stevens (a former member of the **Cooperative Brotherhood** in Washington). Some of the members came from the **Equality Colony**, where they had become dissatisfied with the leadership but wished to continue to live in a cooperative environment. They had two thousand acres, a cooperative store, a small steamboat, and other cooperative enterprises. The members divided their profits equally, and they elected their

board of trustees annually. After the cooperative nature of this enterprise ended, the commune left its name to the town that later developed at this location. A few old houses are the only remnants of the commune that can be seen today. Books with sections that focus on the Freeland Association are Hinds' *American Communities* and LeWarne's *Utopias on Puget Sound, 1885–1915*.

Friedens-Verein *see* **Peace Union Settlement**

Friedheim (1899–1900), located in Virginia, was a religious commune of 52 persons about which almost nothing is known. It is said that it failed because of human weaknesses. There may have been a connection between this community and **Lystra**, another religious commune in the state of Virginia that existed at about the same time, although this is unknown.

Friendly Association for Mutual Interests *see* **Kendal** and **Valley Forge**

Friendship Community (1872–1877), a few miles west of Buffalo, Missouri, was a commune of about 15 members organized by Alcander Longley (see **Fourier Phalanx**), who was an advocate of Christian communism. The members owned 500 acres of land on which they farmed, raised fruit, and bred stock. Part of this land was prairie and part of it was wooded. All property was held in common. The constitution provided that three-fourths of the membership had to vote for a candidate before he or she could be elected to office. It was at the Friendship Community that Longley began to publish *The Communist*, later changed in name to *The Altruist*. The community closed because of dissatisfaction among the members and insufficient capital to keep the project functioning properly. A book with a section that focuses on the Friendship Community is the *History of Laclede, Camden, Dallas, Webster, Wright, Texas, Pulaski, Phelps and Dent Counties, Missouri.*

Fruit Crest (1911–1912), at Independence, Missouri, was a commune established by several socialists, including Christian Balzac Hoffman and George Littlefield. Littlefield was a Unitarian minister who had earlier founded the **Fellowship Farm** at Westwood, Massachusetts, and assisted in the setting up of the **Fellowship Farm Cooperative** in New Jersey. The perhaps 30 members of Fruit Crest farmed the 35 acres of land that they purchased in 1911. They modeled their commune after Fellowship Farm.

Fruit Hills (1845–1848), on the Little Miami River in Warren County, Ohio, 26 miles from Cincinnati, was an anarchist community of about 25 members, organized by Orson S. Murray, who had formerly been a member of the **Prairie Home Community**, also in Ohio. The members of Fruit Hills owned 127 acres of land that included an orchard, some timber, a few old cabins, and three horses.

They took great pride in the fact that they had no creed, no constitution, no laws, and no government. Although Murray did not believe in any religion or god, one of the members, John White, was a spiritualist. The *Regenerator*, a weekly periodical devoted to communalism and under Murray's editorship, was published here, and the members practiced vegetarianism and cold water bathing. It is not known how the community functioned or why it closed.

Fruitlands (1843–1845), located about one mile from Harvard, Massachusetts, was a transcendentalist community (see **Brook Farm**) of 11 persons. Although it was small and a failure in every way, Fruitlands has attained a major place in history because its founder, the noted transcendentalist Amos Bronson Alcott (1790–1888), was the father of novelist Louisa May Alcott. At the time he established Fruitlands, he was already well-known as an author and educator.

Alcott had previously set up his own school in Boston to further his transcendentalist ideas, but his teachings were considered so liberal that attendance soon dropped by more than two-thirds. He had to sell his own library to pay for the debts. The school finally closed after he admitted a black girl, an act that caused most of the remaining parents to withdraw their children. For a short time afterwards Alcott tried farming, but did not do well because of his activities in the social movements of the day — anti-slavery, temperance, and vegetarianism.

In 1842 he visited England and returned with Henry Wright, Charles Lane, and William Lane, the latter's son. These three mystics, with Alcott, bought the hundred-acre tract of land near Harvard that would be suitable for their Fruitlands commune. The land included a farmhouse, barn, and some apple trees. The other members joined them within a few months. One of these was Isaac Hecker, who had come from the Brook Farm commune.

The members of Fruitlands practiced vegetarianism, planted mulberry trees to begin sericulture, and pulled their own plows because they did not wish to use the labor of animals. They also refused to use cotton because it was the product of slave labor, refused to use leather for which animals must be killed, and refused to use manure for fertilizer. They planted their crops late and carelessly. When harvest time came, all the men of the community were away attending a meeting. Mrs. Alcott and her daughters could rescue only a few of the crops before the rest were destroyed in a storm.

By winter, most members departed. The project was abandoned in January 1845. Charles Lane and his son, William, among the last to leave, joined the **Harvard** Shakers. Alcott would have also done so had his wife not prevented it. Louisa May Alcott later wrote of her experiences at the commune in a book called *Transcendental Wild Oats*.

The Fruitlands farmhouse still stands on the site. It has been turned into a museum of artifacts related to transcendentalism. Nearby is a Shaker museum. Books with sections that focus on Fruitlands are Calverton's *Where Angels Dared to Tread* and Holloway's *Heavens on Earth*.

German Colonization Company (1869–1871), in Custer County, Colorado, seven or eight miles south of Silver Cliff, was a cooperative community of German Americans from Chicago. The members were organized by Carl Wulsten, an editor of Chicago's *Stats Zeitung* and a Union Army veteran. His purpose was to ameliorate "the physical condition of the poorer class of Germans, who were condemned by a cruel fate to work in greasy, ill-ventilated, and nerve-destroying factories in the great city of Chicago."

The group of about 250 colonists gathered together in Chicago to adopt a constitution and elect officers on August 24, 1869. Each member contributed $250 to the project and agreed to accept the cooperative plan for a five-year term. At the end of that time the profits were to be divided equally. They sent Wulsten, Rudolph Jeske, and Theodore Heinlein to Colorado to select a site. These men chose land in a broad park-like mountain valley lying between the Wet Mountains and the Sangre de Cristo Range.

On February 8, 1870, the other members left Chicago to join them. They reached the meadows of Wet Mountains Valley in March and immediately began to prepare the land for farming. By September, signs of disintegration in the enthusiasm for the community were already appearing and many colonists departed. Apparently the leadership was poor and there was a general lack of familiarity with the type of farming that was needed in this mountain setting. Those who remained were not prepared for the severe winter. Only emergency supplies sent by Denver businessmen saved them from disaster. By the spring of 1871 the colony had come to an end. A book with a section that focuses on the German Colonization Company is Willard's *The Union Colony of Greeley, Colorado, 1869–1871*.

German Socialist Colony (1873–1878), located 45 miles north of Lynchburg, Virginia, was a commune of 83 socialists who purchased 264 acres of land for their experiment. They repaired and improved several buildings that were formerly used to house slaves and turned these into their living quarters. They tried with some success to cultivate the rather poor farmland and they mined the ochre deposits on their property to bring in an income. Eugene L. Fischer joined this commune after he left **Warm Springs Colony**.

Germania Company (1857–1879), at Germania, Marquette County, Wisconsin, was a cooperative community of about 40 Seventh-day Adventists from Groton, Massachusetts. Their hope was to effect a renewal of commitment within their denomination by establishing a more Christian community.

They had 1,200 acres of land, a large community house, flour mills, cooper shop, general store, harness and shoemaking shop, and wagon and blacksmith shop. The daily activities included prayer meetings every evening. The members were able to maintain their communal style of life until their leader, Benjamin Hall, died. Then they disbanded. State Senator C. E. Pierce was one of the children in this community. A book with a section that focuses on the Germania Company is Wooster's *Communities of the Past and Present.*

Gilead (1886), in Comanche County, Kansas, was a Jewish agricultural settlement (see **Sicily Island**) of about 50 persons who came from Romania. Their attempt at communal living lasted only a few months before they disbanded.

Gilpin's Point (1927–1940), near Preston, Maryland, was a single-tax community (see **Fairhope**) established on a plantation that had played a minor role in the American Revolution. The land covered 108 acres and had five dwellings when it was purchased. At least two more homes were constructed before the members decided to close the community. Frank Borland was the superintendent and there were perhaps 25 members. A book with a section that focuses on Gilpin's Point is Huntington's *Enclaves of Economic Rent for 1931.*

Glacier Brüderhof (1951–present) is a Hutterite commune (see **Bon Homme**) near the town of Cut Bank, Montana. In 1964 they had 132 members and Joseph Waldner was their minister.

Glendale (1874–1877), Utah, was a **St. George**–type Mormon United Order community for a few years. It had about 150 members.

Glendale (1949–present), five miles south of Frankfort, South Dakota, and near the James River, is a Hutterite Brüderhof (see **Bon Homme**). In 1964, it had 162 members and was led by John Waldner.

Glendale Molokan Colony (1916–1920), near Glendale, Arizona, was a Molokan farming commune (see **Freedom Colony**) of about 50 members. During World War I, 15 of them were arrested for refusing to register for the draft. Pacifist Ammon Hennacy, in his *The Book of Ammon*, tells of visiting these Molokans when they were in jail.

Glennis Cooperative Industrial Company (1894–1896), 17 miles south of Tacoma, Washington, on the Eatonville Road, was a commune inspired by the writings of Edward Bellamy (see **Ruskin Commonwealth**). It was established on 160 acres of homestead land that were provided by Oliver A. Verity, a carpenter and occasional politician. The commune had nearly 30 members, as well as a blacksmith shop, cigar factory, dairy, school, and post office. But there were constant debates and arguments among the members over restrictive by-laws that some of them wanted to impose on the others, by-laws that regulated aspects of life and others considered "personal matters." This, combined with the fact that some members were unwilling to do their share of the work, sapped the strength of the commune. Most of them departed, leaving only seven to continue the experiment. Three of these — Verity, George H. Allen, and B. Frank Odell — later established the **Mutual Home Association**.

Glenwood (1874–1880), Utah, was a Mormon United Order settlement of about 500 members based on the model at **St. George**. At this commune, as soon as a boy's voice fully changed, he was expected to do two things: select a vocation and choose his wife. Couples went to the temple in Glenwood to get married and, on their return, found a house had been built for them in their absence. Everyone in the community went to church on Sunday and to square dances that were held once a week on other days. The United Order was maintained here longer than at any of the other St. George–type communes.

Goose Pond (1844), at the foot of the Pocono Mountains in Pike County, Pennsylvania, was established by members of the One-Mention Society under the leadership of Mr. Hudson, a former member of the **One-Mention Community**. Since the members were all advocates of the ideas of Robert Owen, they hoped to successfully set up a commune much like his **New Harmony**.

The Goose Pond members were able to obtain the land that had recently been abandoned by the **Social Reform Unity** Fourierist commune and, with members from both the city branches of their organization and some from the One-Mention Community, this commune soon grew to 60 participants. But it was disbanded within a few months because of disagreements among the members and their lack of farming experience. This ended any further attempts to set up "villages of cooperation" on the Robert Owen model.

Gorham (1808–1819), at Gorham, Maine, about ten miles west of Portland, was a community of 52 Shakers (see **Watervliet**). When they decided to close this commune, the members all moved to the Shaker **Sabbathday Lake Village** commune.

Gorstville (1843–1850), near present-day Cross Plains, Dane County, Wisconsin, was established by the English Temperance and Emigration Society. The membership of 700, most of them from England, was led by Robert Gorst. An advertisement in an October 1844 copy of a Madison, Wisconsin, newspaper says that the agent for Gortsville was Charles Reeve.

Their extensive tract of land stretched from Dane County into Iowa County, and they assigned 80 acres to each household. Every family lived in the town they built and called Gorstville. They maintained their semi-communal structure until 1850, when they decided to abandon it and divide the property among themselves. No remnant of the town exists today. A book with a section that focuses on Gorstville is Keyes' *History of Dane County*.

Goshen Community (1825–1826), at Goshen Field, about three miles south of New Harmony, Indiana, was an Owenite commune started by former members of **New Harmony**. The perhaps ten participants had all been farmers in Posey County, Indiana, prior to joining the New Harmony commune, and most of them were Methodists. When a boatload of goods they produced at the commune sank on its way down the Mississippi River to New Orleans, they became so demoralized that they decided to give up their experiment and return to their original farms.

Gould Farm (1913–present), at Great Barrington, Massachusetts, is a cooperative farm that operates as a retreat for homeless and emotionally disturbed persons. It was established by William J. Gould. The members share in the common tasks and cost of maintenance according to their ability. Much support comes from outside sources.

At times Gould Farm had as many as 100 members of various races and creeds. Most of them have supported a pacifist position in regard to human conflict. They work in a dairy barn, pasteurizing plant, poultry barn, vegetable garden, and an occupational therapy studio. The property of 550 acres contains a heavily wooded recreation area. The director appointed in the 1960s was the Rev. Hampton E. Price, formerly a Baptist minister in Chicago. The community welcomes a limited number of visitors.

Gracevale (1948–present), in Lake County, South Dakota, is a Hutterite Brüderhof (see **Bon Homme**) that had 75 members in 1964 and was led by Samuel Hofer.

Grand Prairie Community (1845–1846), near Kramer in Warren County, Indiana, 25 miles west of Lafayette, was a Christian communist commune led by Gilbert F. Bailey. The approximately 25 members settled on 200 acres of farmland owned by Abram R. Crane, one of the members. Another was Thomas Evans. The land included eight acres of timber. Little else is known about this community.

Grand Prairie Harmonial Association (1853), at a place now called Kramer in the northern part of Warren County, Indiana, 25 miles west of Lafayette, was a community of about 50 people organized by John O. Wattles. He had previously started **The Brotherhood**, and before that had been a member of two other communes. The members erected three buildings on their 350 acres of land. The president of this commune was Charles High, the corresponding secretary was Edgar Ryan, the recording secretary was Alvin High, and the treasurer was Thomas Scott. It is not known why the commune disbanded. A book with a section that particularly focuses on the Grand Prairie Harmonial Association is Battle's *Counties of Warren, Benton, Jasper, and Newton, Indiana.*

Grander Age Colony (1894–1898), near Handsboro, Mississippi, between Gulfport and Biloxi, was a commune started by E.A. Cowell, publisher of the *Cooperative Age* at St. Paul, Minnesota, and S.W. Rose of Handsboro. There were approximately 15 members.

Groveland (1826–1895), also known as Sonyea, was a Shaker community (see **Watervliet**) first located at Sodas Point, New York, to the west of Rochester and on the banks of Lake Ontario. After the members sold their land to the **Sodas Bay Phalanx**, they moved to Groveland in Livingston County, 37 miles south of Rochester. There they had 1,670 acres of land and reached a maximum of 200 members, organized into two "families."

The leaders at the beginning were Calvin Green and Jeremiah Talcott, who came from the **Mount Lebanon** Shaker commune. The members raised cattle, sweet corn, apples, and broom corn. They owned a saw mill, grist mill, dairy, steam laundry, blacksmith shop, tailor shop, dress-making shop, school, and a 400-volume library.

However, this commune suffered

from a flood and a fire that burned seven of their buildings in one night. When they sold their property to the state of New York in 1895, the remaining members moved to the Watervliet Shaker settlement. The land is now used for an institution for epileptics, called the Craig Colony.

Halcyon *see* **Temple Home**

Halidon (1911–1940), at Cumberland Mills near Westbrook, Maine, was a single-tax community (see **Fairhope**) of about 50 members. Boston paper manufacturer Fiske Warren purchased the initial 173 acres of land for this commune and was one of its trustees, although he never lived in the community. His paper mill was located only about one mile from the community and about half the members worked in that mill. The members set up a cooperative store in 1919 and purchased more land to bring the size of the property to over 200 acres. The commune was closed after Warren died. A book with a section that focuses on Halidon is Huntington's *Enclaves of Single Tax or Economic Rent.*

Hancock (1790–1960), at Hancock, Massachusetts, in the Berkshire Mountains, about one mile from the New York State Line, was a Shaker community (see **Watervliet**) organized by Calvin Harlow and Sarah Harrison. At its height there were 300 members separated into six "families." Land for this commune was donated by Daniel Goodrich, the son of a deacon in the Baptist church. He joined the Shakers despite strong opposition from his father.

Still standing is Hancock's most interesting feature — a round two-story barn of stone that has a twelve-sided wooden story on top of this and a hexagonal bell tower above the whole structure. The roundness allowed one to drive a load of hay into the barn, go completely around the inside and out the door again, after unloading the hay into the center of the building. The barn was constructed in 1826. The site of this commune was turned into a Shaker museum after the last member departed in 1960.

Hand County Brüderhof (1949–present), 15 miles south of Miller, South Dakota, is a Hutterite commune (see **Bon Homme**) now occupying the land of the Milltown Hutterite colony that moved to Canada. The community is also sometimes called the Millerdale Colony, and in 1964 had 86 members. It was then led by John Waldner.

Harmonia (1852–1863), at Kiantone Springs, one mile south of Kiantone, New York, and almost on the Pennsylvania boundary line, was a spiritualist community of about 40 members. It was led by John Murray Spear (1804–1877), a former leader in the antislavery movement in Boston who had become a spiritualist after he was nearly killed by a mob of pro-slavery advocates. He was a close friend of the well-known abolitionist Wendell Phillips and of the poet Henry Longfellow, and, after he embraced spiritualism, he claimed to be conversant with the souls of all great leaders in history.

Spear chose this location for the commune because of its spring, the mud of which he said had "remarkable spiritual powers." The members built ten structures, none still standing, in which all the rooms were either oval or octagonal in shape, the "symbols of perfection." They also built a 35-room hotel for guests. But, to the amusement of surrounding farmers, much of their spare time was spent digging for a nonexistent treasure of gold that Spear envisioned to be lying inside a nearby hill.

In 1858 a national spiritualist convention was held at Harmonia, and in 1859 some of the members took a river expedition to New Orleans, Louisiana, to proclaim the imminent collapse of the United States. A book with a section that focuses on Harmonia is Doty's *The Historic Annals of Southwestern New York*.

Harmonia (1924), near Plainfield, New Jersey, was a cooperative Jewish farm community (see **Sicily Island**) that may have had only five members and lasted only a few months.

Harmonial Vegetarian Society (1860–1861), at Harmony Springs, now Sulphur Springs, Arkansas, was a community of 15 vegetarians who wished to practice communal living. According to their publication, *The Theocrat*, they considered their commune a theocracy.

They were doing relatively well in this experiment until the Civl War reached their area in 1861. A unit of Confederate troops occupied their buildings and evicted the members. Following the Battle of Pea Ridge in March 1862, the commune buildings were burned to the ground. An article that focuses on the Harmonial Vegetarian Society is Ford's "The Harmonial Vegetarian Society," in the *Arkansas Democrat*, February 5, 1961.

Harmony (1804–1903), a prosperous and long-lasting commune that was led by George Rapp, was first established at Harmony, Pennsylvania. Rapp then moved it to New Harmony, Indiana, and finally back to Pennsylvania again, to a place called Economy. The mem-

bers, who numbered more than 1,000 at their highest point, most of whom were German immigrants, shared all things in common, lived by a rule of celibacy, and accepted Rapp's leadership without question.

Rapp was born in 1757 at Iptingen in Würtemberg, Germany, the son of a farmer. As a boy he was an avid student of the Bible. But as he grew older, he became dissatisfied with the outlook of the churches and especially their seeming lack of concern for the poor. At age 30 he began to preach to a small congregation of friends in his own home. He ultimately became convinced that Christ would come again within his own lifetime. He remained so firmly convinced of this, in fact, that on the very day of his death at age 90 he said, "If I did not believe that the Lord intended me to present my people to Him on the last day, I would think I was dieing."

The clergy in Würtemberg, resenting the impact of Rapp's preaching and the growing number of his followers, began to persecute him and other Rappites. But the group continued to grow despite this. Within six years Rapp had gathered some 300 families into a separatist church. He decided, in 1803, that they should emigrate to the United States where they might worship freely in a communal environment. The members agreed and pooled their money to send him with his son and two others to purchase land for the experiment.

Rapp found 5,000 acres of wild countryside in the Valley of Connoquenessing about 25 miles north of Pittsburgh, Pennsylvania, which he purchased. An adopted son, Frederick, had remained behind in Germany to complete arrangements for transporting Rapp's followers, and in the summer of 1804 more than 700 of them came to the

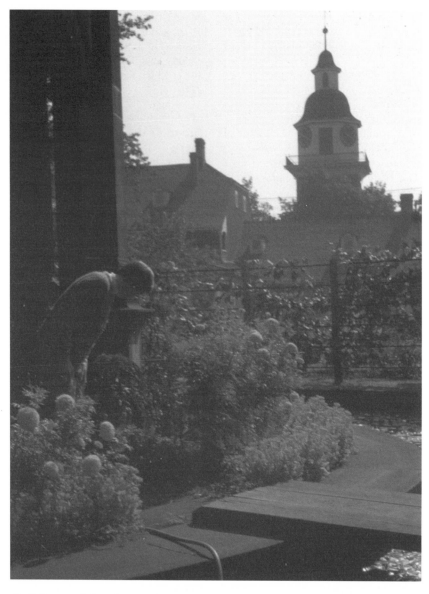

Buildings and church tower built by the Rappites at Harmony (photo by author).

United States. The ablest went immediately to the newly-purchased land to prepare dwellings, while the rest lived briefly in different parts of Maryland and Pennsylvania. There were about 750 men, women, and children when they all finally gathered at the Harmony settlement.

They put their possessions into a common fund, adopted a common style of dress and housing, and agreed to labor for the common good of the whole body. In the first year they erected between 40 and 50 log houses, planted extensive crops, and became almost totally self-sufficient.

Four years later, during a period of deep religious fervor, Rapp made the decision that they should adopt the celibate way of life. It was his belief that Adam contained both sexes within himself, and had it not been for the sin Eve committed, Adam would have given birth to children. Father Rapp argued that if men and women lived properly consecrated lives, they might someday return to this state, and each, within himself or herself, be able to bear children. After that, although husbands and wives continued to live together in the same houses at Harmony, they were expected to "abide" by the celibate rule. Over the years a few children were born to the members, but only a few. The parents were not banished or even punished, except by communal disapproval, which was likely hard enough to bear. At the same time that they agreed to the rule of celibacy, they also agreed to give up the use of tobacco in any form.

George Rapp represents one of the best examples of wise leadership among the American commune builders. His community thrived because of his charisma and his ability to gain cooperation among followers. Members of this community described Father Rapp as "a man before whom no evil could stand," and as a man who "knew everything — how to do it, what was the best way." After Rapp died one member said, "He was a *man*; he told us what to do, and how to be good," and another said, "When I met him in the street if I had a bad thought in my head, it flew away."

After a few years Rapp realized that the site in Pennsylvania was a poor choice because there was no waterway nearby for trade and communication and the land was not good for growing wine grapes. So, in 1814, he moved the commune to a more desirable place, 30,000 acres of land in Indiana's Wabash River Valley. The only remains of the community at Harmony, Pennsylvania, are a few buildings, the Rappite cemetery, and an old German clock tower said to be the oldest operating tower clock in the Western hemisphere.

At what is now called New Harmony, Indiana, the members increased in wealth. And there Rapp decided to destroy all records of what any single member had originally contributed to the enterprise so that they would live in complete equality. He purchased one of the first steam engines to be used in the New World and built a steamboat for their river trade. In state elections, Rapp cast the ballots for everyone in the commune, opposing in their name any introduction of slavery into the state.

The New Harmony commune barges loaded with wheat, corn, oats, butter, wax, horses, cattle, hogs, hides, furs, sugar, linen, cheese, flax, logs, shingles, chairs, shoes, yarns, apples, cider, geese, honey, bacon, eggs, and animal skins went up and down the Mississippi Valley in a brisk trade. The commune's brewery and distillery produced better beer and alcohol than almost any other in the area, and they now also began to produce fine cutlery. They set up outlet stores for their goods in Vincennes, Indiana, and St. Louis, Missouri. New members came from Germany to join them, and the commune thrived.

In 1824, Rapp moved the commune back to Pennsylvania, saying there was too much fever in the area. Some guessed, however, that Rapp did this because he realized that in order to hold the members together it would be wise to begin again at a new location. They were becoming too prosperous in Indiana to want to continue their communal lifestyle. He sold the Indiana land and buildings to British social reformer Robert Owen for his **New Harmony** commune. The Indiana site still contains a two-story community house that the Rappites built there, as well as a few smaller Rappite houses, the Rappite cemetery, and a widely-praised Rappite rose door.

Father Rapp picked as the new site a place only 15 miles from their first home, but on the banks of the Ohio River and also on the main stage road. The commune was renamed Economy, and it soon prospered just as the commune had in Indiana. The Duke of Saxe-Weimar, who visited Economy in 1826, reported that the factories and workshops were all warmed during the winter by means of pipes connected to a steam engine. He also remarked on the neatness of everything, and noted that they had a fine museum of costly paintings (one of which was "Christ Healing the Sick" by Benjamin West) and that they gave much attention to music.

Besides the goods they produced in their cotton mills, grist mill, and saw mill, the members now planted orchards and vineyards, and began the culture of silk. They maintained a large hotel and no visitors, even homeless transients, were turned away from it. Both the gardens around Rapp's house and a special maze made of bushes and paths were objects of pleasure for the visitors and members.

Rapp's Economy did face one serious threat to its existence. In 1831 a German adventurer who called himself Count Maximilian de Leon, but whose real name was Bernhard Müller (1787–1834), arrived with a few followers to spend the winter at the commune. In the spring, Count de Leon began to proclaim his own doctrines, those of noncelibate marriage and a more comfortable life. He proposed to replace Rapp in leadership and succeeded in causing a serious division among the members. A vote was taken as to who should lead Economy, and Count de Leon was able to capture 250 votes, while Father Rapp secured 500. It was therefore decided that the Count's followers should leave the commune within three months. They were given $5,000 on the agreement that they relinquish all further claims on the community.

The Count and his followers withdrew to Phillipsburg (now Monaca) a village ten miles from Economy on the other side of the river. They called their community **New Philadelphia** and, although de Leon set this commune up much like Rapp's, the Count was a poor organizer and soon squandered much of the money they had been given. Count de Leon and the others began to resent the settlement they had made, and prepared to march on Economy to reclaim that commune for themselves. They attacked the place on April 12, 1833. But, at the first sight of the invaders, Father Rapp took all the men into the woods, leaving the women on guard inside the buildings. As the Count's followers forced open doors, they were met with hot water, brooms, coals, kicks, and loud scoldings. They quickly scattered.

Father Rapp died on August 7, 1848, but the commune continued to function in the way he had designated that it should be operated. Leadership was now provided by two trustees and seven elders. The trustees were R.L.

Baker and J. Henrici, and after Baker's death, Jonathan Lenz. For many years Miss Gertrude Rapp, a granddaughter of the founder, was also a leading member of Economy.

Yet, as the years went by, the membership began to die out and the factories had to close. For a time, the trustees hired outside help, including 200 Chinese whom they reportedly treated well, to service these industries. The community was finally dissolved in 1903. The land was then purchased by the American Bridge Company, and much of it today is used by the Bethlehem Steel Corporation. Rapp's house, a church, several other houses, gardens, and a number of museum relics are on display in the two-block area set aside as a state museum.

Byron memorialized Harmony in a brief section of his epic poem *Don Juan*:

When Rapp the Harmonist embargoed marriage
In his harmonious settlement which flourishes
Strangely enough as yet without miscarriage,
Who call'd he 'Harmony' as state sans wedlock?
Now here I've got the preacher at a dead lock.

Because he either meant to sneer at harmony
Or marriage, by divorcing them thus oddly;
But whether reverend Rapp learn'd this in
                Germany
Or not, 'tis said his sect is rich and godly,
Pious and pure, beyond what I can term any
Of ours....
                (Canto XV)

Books with sections that focus on Harmony are Hinds' *American Communities*, Nordhoff's *The Communistic Societies of the United States*, and Young's *Angel in the Forest: A Fairy Tale of Two Utopias*.

Harrisburgh (1874–1877), near St. George, Utah, was a Mormon commune of about 50 people that copied the United Order model used at **St. George**. They dropped this economic system shortly after the death of Mormon leader Brigham Young.

Harvard (1793–1918), in the valley of the Nashua River, several miles from the present town of Harvard, Massachusetts, was a Shaker colony (see **Watervliet**) that once had 200 members organized into four "families." This commune encompassed 1,800 acres of land, some of which had been occupied earlier by the **Harvard New Lighters** commune.

Elezer Rand and Hannah Kendal were the first leaders of Harvard. The members marketed garden seeds, herbs, brooms, and crops of hay. Their herb business developed so rapidly that they had to construct a special herb house to handle it. Their stone barn was constructed so that it had entrances on three levels.

Sarah Babbit invented the first circular saw at Harvard and made the first cut nails from sheet metal instead of forging each nail singly. Two other notable members were Elijah Myrick, who developed such good relations with the nearby town of Harvard that he was chosen to serve as a member of the school board there, and Elder Augustus Grosvenor. The latter saddled the commune with a $25,000 debt when he built a 40-room home. Grosvenor was removed from his post for this mistake.

Bronson Alcott's **Fruitlands** commune was located near this Shaker settlement, and when Fruitlands closed, two members of that commune, Charles Lane and his son, joined the Shakers. Alcott might have joined them, too, had his wife not prevented it. For a time the Fruitlands property was even put under the care of the Harvard Shakers.

When Harvard closed, the remaining members moved to the **Mount Lebanon** Shaker community and sold the land to Fiske Warren, a single-tax enthusiast. Warren then set up his **Tahanto** commune on the property.

Only two of the Shaker buildings remain at the site — a brick tavern and the Shaker hospital. William Dean Howells lived in this tavern while writing *The Undiscovered Country*, a novel based on Shaker materials. One other building still stands, but it was moved from the Harvard site to the site of Fruitlands where it now serves as a Shaker museum.

Harvard New Lighters (1769–1781), which derived its name from the New Light revival movement that swept through the United States in the late 1700s and early 1800s, was led by a self-styled preacher called Reverend Shadrach Ireland. They established their commune in the fall of 1769 in a house they built near Harvard, Massachusetts.

The leader had experienced a radical conversion during a highly emotional revival meeting conducted by the well-known Methodist preacher George Whitfield. The results of the conversion of Ireland, a tall, red-haired man were hardly, however, what Whitfield might have anticipated or desired. Ireland suddenly came to the conclusion that he possessed several gifts of God — the ability to speak in tongues, to receive revelations from heaven, and to practice the laying on of hands. Although he was a woodcutter and maker of clay pipes in Charlestown, Massachusetts, he now left that trade and began to preach to his neighbors and friends. He prophesied that he would never die, and he denounced the Congregational Church, of which he was a member, for ignoring the problems of poverty and economic abuse. His attacks on the church so angered the people of Charlestown that finally they ran him out of the village as a heretic. Fleeing with him was Abigail Lougee, a young woman he called his "spiritual wife."

Ireland fled to Harvard where he was protected by two families named Willard and Cooper. He held religious meetings in their homes until he had gathered enough followers to start a communal settlement. The approximately 25 members erected a large, square house with a secret stairway leading from the cellar door to the cupola. The home is still standing.

When Ireland died in the summer of 1780, his followers watched over his body expecting him to revive. This did not happen, and they finally had to bury him because his body was beginning to decay. Abigail Lougee and most of the members departed in disappointment. But Abigail Cooper and a few others continued to maintain the commune in their square house until 1781, when Mother Ann Lee, founder of the Shaker movement, arrived in Harvard and convinced them to embrace Shakerism (see **Watervliet**). A book with a section that focuses on the Harvard New Lighters is Webber's *Escape to Utopia*.

Haverstraw *see* **Franklin**

Hays Socialists (1877), near Hays, Kansas, but known as Hays City at that time, was a commune of about 25 Danish and German socialists led by Louis Albert François Pio (1841–1894), Paul Geleff, and W.A. Hansen. Pio had been active in the socialist movement in Europe and had been jailed there for three years on a charge of "crimes against public authority." Afterward he edited a Danish socialist newspaper called the *Social-Demokraten*.

It was Pio's hope to create a community in which socialists could live and work free of bourgeois government interference. They chose Kansas, which Geleff had visited, because it offered good land where they could live in some isolation and thus cement their social relations. But immediately after they began the communal existence, arguments flared between the Danes and the Germans. Apparently the Germans had little confidence in the Danes' ability to understand political theory, and the women of both groups battled with one another over who should do what in the kitchen. The experiment lasted only six weeks before the members agreed to sell everything. Each person received a total of $30 from the proceeds. Pio remained in the United States, working first for the Florida Railroad company and then managing a pavilion at the Chicago World's Fair of 1893. Most of the others returned to Europe. Books with a section that focus on the Hays Socialists are Fogarty's *All Things New* and Wittke's *We Who Built America: The Saga of the Immigrant.*

Hayward Heath (1916), in Alameda County, California, was a community of approximately 100 advocates of the Little Land movement. For more information on this movement, see **San Ysidro Little Landers.**

Heaven City (1923–1963) was established by Albert J. Moore of Chicago on 130 acres of land near Harvard, Illinois. Through lectures and many pamphlets he preached a strange mixture of adventism and belief in reincarnation. He predicted that 1923 would experience the worst depression in history, that 1924 would be a year of universal labor strikes, that 1925 would produce a worldwide revolution, and that 1926 would have a great war in which three-fourths of the world's population would be wiped out. The "new dawn" would follow all these events.

The approximately 100 members waited in vain to see these happenings, but never lost faith in their leader. They lived separately as families in a single building, but could not own property or even insurance. They all worked on the farm, which had cows, horses, goats, and varous crops. The children were taught in the Froebel and Montessori educational systems.

The commune was moved to Mukwonago, Wisconsin, in 1932, and disbanded after Moore's death in 1963. One of the trustees, S.P. Talcott, turned their commune building into the Heaven City Hotel that is still operated by a few of the members who remained on the property. A book with a section that focuses on Heaven City is Wooster's *Communities of the Past and Present.*

Hebron (1874–1877), a short distance from Enterprise, Utah, was a Mormon United Order settlement of the **St. George** type. It had about 50 members and ceased to exist after the death of Mormon leader Brigham Young.

Hebron (1883), in southwestern Kansas, was a Jewish agricultural settlement (see **Sicily Island**) of about 175 people. Nothing more is known about it.

Helicon Home (1906–1907), on the heights behind the Palisades, overlooking Englewood, New Jersey, was organized by novelist Upton Sinclair (1878–1968) as a cooperative home and community. It occupied the nine-and-a-half acre site of a former boys' school called Helicon Hall, from which the commune got its name. Eventually there were 54 members, including novelists Sinclair Lewis, Alice MacGowan, Grace MacGowan Cook, and Edith Summers, as well as poet Alan Updegraff. Psychologist William James, educator John

Dewey, and sculptor Jo Davidson were regular visitors.

Sinclair was a socialist at the time and already well known as the author of *The Jungle*, a novel exposing the evil and unsanitary conditions in the Chicago meat-packing industry. He later ran unsuccessfully for both the office of president of the United States and for governor of California on the Socialist ticket.

In 1906 he wrote an article for the *Independent* magazine outlining his plans for a commune and inviting interested persons to correspond with him about it. Many did, and some of them joined. They were charged $3 to $9 a week to maintain their membership in the commune. The most successful aspect of Helicon Home was apparently the handling of their children. The members employed an outsider to give full-time care to their 14 children, with the mothers assisting her on a rotating and part-time basis. When their building burned to the ground on March 7, 1907, the communal experiment was disbanded. A book with a section that focuses on Helicon Home is Sinclair's *The Autobiography of Upton Sinclair*.

Hiawatha Village Association (1893–1896), in Schoolcraft County, Michigan, was a commune of socialists started by Abraham Byers of Manistique, Michigan. He was inspired to start the project after reading *The Product Sharing Village* by Walter Thomas Mills, a temperance lecturer and socialist educator who had amassed a fortune in real estate. Byers invited Mills to become president of Hiawatha, a post Mills readily accepted. Eventually there were 225 members. Most of them came from Chicago, Iowa, Michigan, and Texas, and many had been engaged in the labor movement.

Each family paid $100 to join the commune, which had 1,080 acres of hardwood land, 125 head of cattle, and 25 horses. They operated a saw mill, erected a number of dwellings, and published a newspaper called *The Industrial Christian* that promoted "product sharing for all." Members were paid for their labor in time credits that could be exchanged for goods at the commune's store. But they had difficulty finding a market for the products they produced and there was much dissension among the members over problems of equalizing the work. Mills withdrew in 1895, and all the others departed within a few months afterward. A book with a section that focuses on the Hiawatha Village Association is Fogarty's *All Things New*.

Hickory Hill (1953–1954), at Tappan, New York, was a community that seems to have left only its name. It was listed in two small directories of modern communities, but all attempts to correspond with the members or get information about it have failed. There might have been five members.

Highland Home *see* **Prairie Home Community**

Highlander Folk School (1932–1961), at Monteagle, Tennessee, was established by Myles Horton and Congregational minister Don West as a workers education school and community. It was roughly patterned on the Danish Folk School movement that Horton had studied in Europe. The school had the approval of many prominent national leaders, including educator John Dewey and Eleanor Roosevelt, even though it was not welcomed with any enthusiasm in the South.

During the first years, Horton

taught skills and crafts to local farmers who could no longer make a living off the land, but by the middle of the 1930s the school had become a labor training center where workers from all over the South could learn the techniques of organizing and running their own unions. In 1938 the commune and its school were racially integrated. Many Southerners, both white and black, had their first real experience of communication and sharing on the basis of equality in the educational workshops run at Highlander. This provoked much hostility on the part of surrounding farmers and townspeople who wanted to preserve the racial divisions that then existed throughout the South.

One of the Highlander graduates was Rosa Parks, the black woman who in 1955 refused to give up her seat in a Montgomery, Alabama, bus to a white man and was arrested for violating the state's segregation laws. The incident triggered the historic Montgomery bus boycott under the leadership of the Rev. Martin Luther King, Jr., and the launching of the civil rights movement of the 1960s.

Zylphia Horton, the first wife of the director, was music coordinator for Highlander until she died in 1956. She collected folk songs, labor songs, gospel songs, and spirituals and taught them to the students. She is credited with saving the old hymn *We Will Overcome*, and changing it with a new rhythm and new verses to the more grammatical and stunningly effective *We Shall Overcome*.

The commune was harassed by local and state authorities throughout its history. Newspapers and citizen's councils across the South attacked it in editorials and speeches, and the Ku Klux Klan frequently demonstrated against the commune. Governor Griffin of Georgia called it a "Communist training school."

Highlander was a center for the civil rights movement in the 1950s. In 1961, the state of Tennessee revoked the school's charter and confiscated its property, shortly after local racists burned their main educational building to the ground. The school continues today in Knoxville, Tennessee, although the commune was closed after its property was taken. There were probably never more than 30 permanent residents at the commune, even though thousands of students attended the school over the years. A book with a section that focuses on Highlander is Adams' *Unearthing Seeds of Fire: The Idea of Highlander*.

Hilldale (1963–present), near Havre, Montana, is a Hutterite Brüderhof (see **Bon Homme**) with 103 members in 1964 and Joseph Waldner as the leader.

Hillside (1951–present), near Sweet Grass, Montana, is a Hutterite Brüderhof (see **Bon Homme**) that had 91 members in 1964 and was led by Andreas Wurtz.

Hillside Brüderhof (1961–present), near Huron, South Dakota, is a Hutterite commune (see **Bon Homme**). It had 76 members in 1964 and was led by Michael Waldner.

Holden (1874–1877), Utah, was a United Order Mormon commune set up on the model used at **St. George** for a period of several years. It had about 200 members.

Holy City (1918–1954), five miles south of Los Gatos, California, was established by religious leader William E. Riker (1873–1969), who four times ran for governor of California on an openly racist platform. Riker had worked as a mechanic in San Francisco until he experienced a "divine revelation" that led him to found this colony. He claimed that his insights came from his nerves, and central to most of his doctrines was a white supremacist form of religion he called the Perfect Christian Divine Way.

He opposed the state Fair Employment Practices Commission and urged laws that would prevent Negroes and Asians from owning businesses in the state. Curiously enough, he was not anti–Semitic and included among his followers a Jewish disciple, David Aaron. Riker was also in and out of jail during much of his career as head of the commune. He was arrested on charges of reckless driving, breach of promise, evasion of taxes, fraud, sedition, and even murder, but was never convicted. During World War II he supported the Axis powers and was indicted for treason.

The 30 members of this settlement lived communally, separated by sex. They owned a grocery store, garage, restaurant, service station, mineral water concern, barber shop, radio station, and printing shop. The latter produced an almost endless collection of pamphlets and handbills that were distributed to visitors and at various places around the state. The print shop was managed by Stephan Rozum. They engaged in rudimentary farming on their 180 acres of land, though most of the colony's income came from the tourist trade. Because the community was next to the state highway that ran between the San Francisco Bay area and the beach resort of Santa Cruz, the members erected circus signs and provided various amusements to attract passersby.

After the highway was rerouted, the colony began to decline. Fire eventually destroyed their main building, called the Hall of Mystery. And a land development company took over their property in 1954, effectively ending the community, though Riker and a few followers continued to live in the now-dilapidated buildings. At age 93, to the surprise of everyone, Riker joined the Roman Catholic Church. He died in a state mental hospital. There are one or two tumble-down building remains still visible at the edge of the now little-used highway. The site of the destroyed main building is occupied by a commercial glass works plant. Books with sections that focus on Holy City are Hine's *California's Utopian Communities* and Kagan's *New World Utopias: A Photographic History of the Search for Community.*

Holy Family Farm (1947–1953), at Richland, Missouri, in the foothills of the Ozarks, was a ten-member Catholic Worker farm (see **Maryfarm** on Staten Island) that was established by Larry Heaney and Martin Paul, both of whom had earlier initiated **St. Isador's Farm** in Minnesota. They planted an orchard and strawberries, but never had a very successful crop. When Heaney died of pneumonia in April 1949, his wife took over the management of the commune.

Home (1877–1880), in Benzie County, Michigan, at a place once called Gilmore that is no longer on the state maps, was an independent communist settlement of 12 members. They owned 320 acres of land, and they had a printed constitution and bylaws that have since been lost.

Home Employment Co-operative Company (1894–1906), near Long Lane in Dallas County, Missouri, was the second commune established by William H. Bennett. His earlier one, the **Bennett Cooperative Colony**, had disbanded in 1877, and this one may have occupied the same land as the first. It covered 180 acres and included houses, a store, and a shingle mill. There were 20 members, all calling themselves socialists. Two of them besides Bennett had belonged to the earlier experiment. The cost of membership was $300. Each participant worked an eight-hour day, and before this commune closed, the members established a broom factory, a barber shop, and a blacksmith shop.

Hope (1774–1808), at Hope in Warren County, New Jersey, was a Moravian General Economy community of about 100 members, most of whom came from the **Bethlehem** Moravian community in Pennsylvania. They owned 1,000 acres of land on which they built houses, two mills, a brewery, distillery, tannery, public inn, and a church.

The refusal of any members to participate during the Revolutionary War resulted in their being labeled Tories by neighboring farmers. However the devoted care they gave to wounded soldiers of the Colonial army redeemed them in the eyes of their critics. This commune was disbanded after a smallpox epidemic killed most of the residents. Several of their buildings are still standing and there is a cemetery in Hope containing between 40 and 50 Moravian graves.

Hopedale (1842–1868), about one mile from Milford, Massachusetts, was a joint-stock commune organized by Universalist minister Adin Ballou (1803–1890). He was a prolific writer, an opponent of war, slavery, and intemperance, and he surrounded himself with like-minded people. In 1831, along with several other ministers, Ballou withdrew from the Universalists to form a new denomination.

The commune, at first called the Fraternal Community, No. 1, was established on 250 acres of land known as "the Dale," for which the members paid $4,000. They decided later to use this name Dala and preface it with the word "Hope." They signed a covenant that bound them to abstain from murder, hatred, unchastity, use of liquor, and participation in all military and civic activities, including voting in elections.

Over a period of years the members of Hopedale built homes, roads, machine shops, barns, a school, and a chapel. They also created an extensive library. In time, they increased their land holdings to 600 acres and their membership to 175. They published a magazine, *The Practical Christian*, which was edited by Ballou. In 1854 he also write a widely-distributed book called *Practical Christian Socialism* that he hoped would result in the organizing of other communities of this type. One was established for a short time in Minnesota by about 30 persons who came from Hopedale. It was called **Union Grove**.

Ballou was succeeded as president of Hopedale by Ebenezer D. Draper in 1852. Draper, with the cooperation of his brother George, soon made arrangements to purchase three-fourths of the property for himself and to dissolve the settlement. Members who disagreed with Draper's actions continued the community, much reduced in size, until 1868. Draper and his family prospered on their section of the land and eventually became wealthy manufacturers of textile machinery. Today this family owns substantial parts of the present town of Hopedale.

Ballou maintained to the end of

his life that the community failed for moral rather than financial reasons. He argued that the membership showed a lack of "whole-souled consecration" to their purpose. A statue of Ballou was erected in 1900 that stands in Hopedale. Books with sections that focus on Hopedale are Calverton's *Where Angels Dared to Tread* and Noyes' *History of American Socialisms.*

Hopewell (1851–1852), at what is now Hopeville, Iowa, was a Fourierist commune (see **Social Reform Unity**) of about 15 persons, all of whom came from Farmington, Iowa. Little else is known of this experiment.

House of David (1903–present), at Benton Harbor, Michigan, was established by Benjamin Franklin Purnell (1861–1927), who declared himself King and ruled the commune with his wife, Queen Mary. Purnell was born in Kentucky and made a living for a time as a broom salesman and wandering preacher. Then, in Detroit, Michigan, he joined a religious group headed by Michael Mills, a man who subsequently died in jail. Purnell assumed leadership of this group, claiming he was the "seventh messenger" sent to prepare for the "in-gathering of Israel." (The previous six messengers had all lived in England.) He called on his followers to sell their homes and farms and go with him to Benton Harbor, where he intended to set up a cooperative community. The original 130 acres of land were purchased with money given to King Benjamin by a carriage maker he converted.

In time, 900 members were living in this commune. They held King Benjamin to be supreme in all temporal and spiritual affairs and, as adventists, they saw signs that the end of the world was near at hand. They also believed that

King Benjamin had succeeded in conquering death and would never die. His death came as a surprise but did not diminish their faith in his teachings, and a remnant of King Benjamin's followers still maintain the community today.

The members are vegetarians, do not drink wine, and live communally. All the men wear long hair and beards. They have maintained at various times a resort hotel, five large resident buildings, some small industries, fruit farms, an amusement park, zoo, band, and a noted baseball team.

It is reported that as many as 200,000 visitors used to go to the park each season during its heyday. Writer Ring Lardner left this account of his visit there: "It sounds like a roadhouse," but "it was even better'n that. You couldn't get nothin' to drink, but they was plenty to see and hear — band concerts, male and female; movin' pitchers; a zoo; a bowlin' alley; and more funny-lookin' people than I ever seen at an amusement park before."

Some of the beliefs of this group led to fantastic interpretations of the Scriptures, and some of their writings are openly racist. In a pamphlet entitled "Where Did Cain Get His Wife?" one of the members explains that the snake in the story of Adam and Eve was not really a serpent at all but a black man specifically created by God to commit adultery with Eve. The offspring was Cain, who, being born in sin, took a wife from among "the black and evil people."

In 1923 a few of the members brought suit against King Benjamin for restoration of the property they had given to the House of David and for their wages. The investigation that followed resulted in one of the most sensational scandals ever to surround an

Two House of David Buildings, constructed in 1906, as they stand today (House of David, Benton Harbor, Michigan).

American religious sect. It was said that the members lived in dormitories and received poor food and clothing, while King Benjamin lived in a "palace" in wealthy style. There were also sordid tales of sexual initiation ceremonies in which the 62-year-old King seduced young girls of the colony. For a long time, King Benjamin eluded the police by hiding in the basement of one of the buildings, but they finally located him and took him to jail to await the court case. The charges and counter-charges preceeding the trial led to King Benjamin's death. He did not live long enough to learn that he had been acquitted of the charges.

A struggle for leadership of the commune then began with Harry T. Dewhirst, who had once been a judge in California, moving into power, much to the dismay of Queen Mary and Francis Thorpe, formerly King Benjamin's right-hand man. The membership split into factions. Queen Mary left the community and set up her own commune, the **Israelite City of David**, right next to the House of David.

Judge Dewhirst proved a good business manager and the House of David commune prospered. He allowed members to smoke, much to the dismay of the more orthodox followers of Queen Mary. In 1937 he built a cold storage plant to hold apples grown in the colony's fruit farms. He also constructed a cannery. Further, he added a miniature train to transport visitors around the park and zoo.

Dewhirst died in 1947 at the age of 66. An elected board now directs the spiritual and temporal affairs of the House of David and a branch colony in Sidney, Australia. The membership today is small, but they still operate a trailer camp for visitors, printing establishment, machine shops, and greenhouses. The miniature train no longer runs, the baseball team is gone, and there aren't even enough musicians to continue the band. But a visit to the House of David can still prove interesting. Books with sections that focus on the House of David are Mathison's *Faiths, Cults and Sects in America* and Quaife's *Lake Michigan*.

Hunt's Colony *see* **Colony of Equality**

Huron (1944–present), in Beadle County, South Dakota, is a Hutterite Brüderhof (see **Bon Homme**) that settled on the lands of the earlier Huron colony that moved to Canada. Jacob Wollman was the leader in 1964 and they had 95 members at that time.

Huron Colony (1906–present), first on Lake Byron, about 16 miles from Huron, South Dakota, then in Manitoba, Canada, and, since 1937, near Mitchell, South Dakota, is a Hutterite Brüderhof (see **Bon Homme**). It is now usually known as the Jamesville Colony, since it occupies the former lands of the first Jamesville Hutterite commune. In 1964, it had 95 members and was led by David Glanzer.

Icaria (1848), in Fannin County, Texas, was organized by the French socialist and utopian novelist Étienne Cabet (1788–1856), who purchased one million acres of land, sight unseen, for the project. The commune lasted only three months before it collapsed due to the poor state of the land and the spread of malaria among the 69 members, five of whom died in the attempt to establish this commune. Their only physician, Doctor Roviera, became insane.

Cabet was a lawyer, but he had lost his right to practice because of his defense of radicals and revolutionaries.

He took part in the July revolution of 1830, and then was appointed procureur-général of Corsica by Louis Phillipe. But his opposition to the administration of France soon caused him to lose his appointment. In 1831 he was elected to the French Chamber of Deputies where he joined the extreme radicals as an advocate for the rights of labor. But in 1883 his writings so antagonized the authorities that he had to flee to England, remaining in exile for five years.

On his return to France in 1839, Cabet published a utopian romance, *Voyage et Adventures de Lord William Carisdall en Ecarie*, which described an imaginary cooperative society. The book became an immediate best-seller. By 1847, it was reported that there were 400,000 adherents of the doctrines described in Cabet's Icarian romance.

Cabet then published an article projecting an Icarian community in the United States and several hundred people quickly responded with requests to be included among its members. The land he purchased in Texas lay along the Red River, but it was in widely-scattered, half-section tracts, hardly suitable for communal agriculture. However, the 69 members, meant to be an advance party, arrived there in June 1848, built some huts and tried to break the prairie before discouragement forced them to return to New Orleans where they met up with Cabet and the main body of 500 colonists. Five more members of this advance party died on the journey back to New Orleans. Cabet then realized that he would have to set up his Icarian experiment elsewhere, and decided to lease the almost deserted city of Nauvoo, Illinois, from the Mormons who had been forced out of the state. He took his Icarian followers there instead of to Texas (see **Icarian Nau-**

voo). A book with a section that focuses on Icaria is Hinds' *American Communities*.

Icaria (1860–1878), at Corning, Iowa, was a commune established by a group of French-speaking followers of Cabet (see **Icaria** in Texas) on a site that he had designated for the experiment before he died. Many of them had departed with Cabet from **Icarian Nauvoo** in Illinois during a dispute over the direction of that commune. They were, however, unable to start the Iowa experiment because they lacked funds to purchase the land until they were later joined by between 50 and 60 others who came from Icarian Nauvoo after it ceased to be a commune.

The members began this community with 4,000 acres of land and $20,000 in debts. At first they had to live in mud hovels, then in log cabins they built, and finally in nearly a dozen frame houses they also built. They constructed a large, central building that was used as a common dining room and assembly hall, a saw mill, a grist mill, and a blacksmith's shop. And they acquired 150 head of cattle, 600 head of sheep, 250 hogs, and 30 horses. Eventually the community grew to 83 members, including Don Ignatius Montaldo and Antoine Von Gauvain, who had come from Icarian Nauvoo. These two taught Greek, German, Latin, and French in the commune school that was set up for children under the age of 16. Two other members were Armand DeHay and Jules Leroux, who later started the **Icaria Speranza** commune in California.

Every Saturday night the commune members held a business meeting for all adults, and at each meeting elected the president for the coming week. Besides the president they elected a secretary, a treasurer, and four directors — one for agriculture, one for clothing, one for general industry, and the last for building. Although Sunday was designated a day of rest, they held no religious services. They had a library of at least 2,000 volumes, and the commune also published some excellent periodicals.

During the Civil War, most of the male members enlisted in the Union Army. At this time, because they could sell wool from their sheep at the inflated wartime prices, the commune began to release itself from its debts. They had earlier had to forfeit at least a fourth of their land to creditors.

From time to time there were violent disagreements among the commune members over political issues that were almost always sparked by events in Europe. The growth of Marxism there stirred the community, and for a time it looked as if this commune might become the center for the Marxist First International in the United States. Followers of Marx, who were exiles from France because of their participation in the Paris Commune of 1871, began to congregate there. In 1878 these newer members and the older ones split over the rules and management of the community. They resolved the problem by dividing into two separate communes, **New Icaria** and **Jeune Icarie**, each taking a different part of the property.

Several of the wooden buildings used by the commune still stand. Books with sections that focus on Icaria are Hinds' *American Communities* and Hine's *California's Utopian Communities*.

Icaria Speranza (1881–1886), located on a fertile tract of land on the banks of the Russian River, three miles south of Cloverdale, California, was established by Armand DeHay and Jules Leroux, two followers of Cabet (see **Icaria** in Texas). Both had been members of **Icaria** in Iowa, and DeHay had also briefly participated in **Jeune Icarie**. Leroux was not only a follower of Cabet but also of the French social thinker, Henri Saint-Simon.

They purchased the 885 acres of land for $15,000, and the membership in this commune eventually reached 55, including Emile Bée, an exile from France because of his revolutionary activities there. Bée later became the leader of a California section of the Socialist Labor Party.

The first thing the Icaria Speranze members built was a saw mill to be used as they cleared the property of trees. Then they built a number of small frame dwellings and a large, two-story clapboard homestead with broad porches in which they all ate together and had their social activities. They planted grape vines and 100 acres of wheat, as well as five acres in fruit trees. They also planned to raise cattle but never accomplished this.

In contrast to the six earlier Icarian communities, the members of this California commune elected committees rather than individual officers to direct their work. The four committees were a work committee, a home consumption committee, an education committee, and an accounts committee. The Board of Administrators was composed of two members from each of these committees. A General Assembly, composed of all adult members, met at least twice a year.

Many of the members expected to be enriched by the sale of their lands in Iowa that had been used for **Jeune Icarie**, but the courts in the state ruled otherwise. This loss apparently broke the spirit of these members, and soon after the court's ruling, Icaria Speranza

was dissolved. Some of the members later became well-to-do California ranchers. The main house and some outbuildings are still standing. A book with a section that focuses on Icaria Speranza is Hine's *California's Utopian Communities*.

Icarian Nauvoo (1849–1860) at Nauvoo, Illinois, was a 500-member commune established by Étienne Cabet (see **Icaria**) on property abandoned by the Mormons when they fled west. At this location there were many houses standing empty, the land was good, and the city seemed to Cabet an adequate solution as a temporary settlement until he could find a better location for his commune.

Most of the members came from France. Among them were Dedant, an authority on bee culture; Emile Vallet, a sociologist of note; A. Piquenard, afterward the architect of the capitol buildings of Iowa and Illinois; Don Ignatius Montaldo, a friend and companion of both the military hero Garibaldi and the novelist Chateaubriand; and Antoine Von Gauvain, a journalist who had been decorated with the Legion of Honor in France and was later the editor of a newspaper in New York City. There were also several musicians, two painters of wide reputation, a noted engineer, and a leading physician from Vienna.

The members of Icarian Nauvoo built a lucrative wine-making business that is still maintained by their descendants. There was complete freedom of religion at the community. There was also a theater with artists drawn from the membership, and a musical band of about 50 instruments. The members considered all the children the common property of the commune, and raised them together in public buildings. Boys

House built by Icarians Phelps and Esther Mix is now a museum at Nauvoo (courtesy of Icarian Living History Museum).

and girls attended separate schools. The boys' school house was constructed from the bricks of the Mormon temple that had been destroyed by an arsonist in 1848, shortly after the Mormons departed.

By 1853, Cabet had decided on an Iowa location for his community, where the members might begin from scratch building their own homes and breaking their own ground according to his grand design. He began to make preparations to move there, and he became an American citizen in 1854. But most of the others at Icarian Nauvoo did not agree with his plans since they found life relatively comfortable at the Nauvoo location. Much dissension arose over the matter, and the conflict eventually spilled over into the management of the Paris office of the Icarian movement. The situation became so intense that civil authorities had to intervene to confirm the election of three new directors who overruled Cabet and his supporters.

Cabet then withdrew to St. Louis with 180 supporters, where he died of a stroke within a week. He was buried there and, soon after this, some of the most devoted of these followers set up **Cheltenham** near St. Louis. The main body of Icarians remained at Icarian Nauvoo until it ceased to be communal. Then some of them left for the second **Icaria** that was eventually established in Iowa. The rest remained at Nauvoo.

Many of their buildings, most of which were originally erected by the Mormons, are still standing. Their boys' school was for many years used as a Catholic Parochial school. Books with sections that focus on Icarian Nauvoo are Hinds' *American Communities* and Nordhoff's *The Communistic Societies of the United States*.

Industrial Fraternity *see* **Point Hope**

Ink (1925), now a small town three miles north of Mena, Arkansas, was established as a site for **Commonwealth College** by four families from **Newllano** in Louisiana (perhaps ten people). The fact that the school later refused to move to this location left the members of this commune bitter against the college for many years afterwards. The initiators chose the name Ink when they were filling out forms for the establishment of a post office at the site. The blank on the form was designated "fill in ink," and so, with good humor, they did just that. The commune lasted but a few months, though one of the member families, the Gilberts, are still living at the site.

Integral Phalanx (1845–1846) was a Fourierist community (see **Social Reform Unity**) located first near Middletown, Ohio, and than at a place 14 miles southwest of Springfield, Illinois. The Ohio location included 900 acres of land owned by Abner Enoch that fronted on the south bank of the Miami River. It also included a large flour mill, saw mill, lath factory, and shingle cutter, all run by water power.

The leader of this commune was John S. Williams, who had come from Cincinnati, Ohio. Two issues of a semi-monthly paper, *Plowshare and Pruning-Hook*, were printed there. The publication was abandoned after the group moved to Illinois.

The members found the Ohio location unsuitable to their needs and so within ten months they left the area for Illinois, where they joined another Fourierist group, the Sangamon Association, that was planning to start their own phalanx but had not yet done so. The Sangamon group, however, had purchased 508 acres of land in Lomi township for their commune. The leader of the Sangamon group was Theophilus Sweet, a Campbellite preacher. The unit-

ing of the two groups brought the total membership of the Integral Phalanx to 120 persons. There were five or six buildings already on the Illinois property, and they erected a frame phalanx building. The commune may have lasted another ten months, but it then disbanded. There are no visible remnants.

Investigating Community (1875), at Cedar Vale, Kansas, was a commune formed by the split off of two families, the Freys and the Rights, from the **Progressive Community**. They were angry at the way that the members of that commune had abandoned their socialist ideals and turned to spiritualism and food fads. The two families were able to convince a few others from the Progressive Community to join them, and eventually there were about eight members of this new commune that advocated monogamy and communism. They took with them a third of the acreage formerly held by the Progressive Community. In the fall three people from Russia, led by Alexander Malikov, came to the Investigating Community to determine whether their group of 15 persons from Russia should join it or not. But there were disagreements between the members of the Investigating Community and Malikov, and so the group from Russia decided to form a commune of their own, called the **Cedar Vale Benevolent and Educational Society**. Frey later joined them and the Investigating Community closed.

Iowa Pioneer Phalanx (1844–1845), on the north bank of the Des Moines River about nine miles from Oskaloosa, Iowa, was a Fourierist experiment (see **Social Reform Unity**) organized at Watertown, New York. The river has changed course since the time the commune occupied 320 acres of land there, and so much of the site where the Iowa Pioneer Phalanx once stood is now under water.

All the original members came from New York State, and they settled on their land in April 1844. They constructed a phalanxtry building, or long house, and partitioned it so that there were two rooms for each family. They served seven meals each day, and organized their own drama and opera groups. More participants from New York came some months later to bring the total membership to 320. However, the group disbanded in May 1845, leaving only some graves and dilapidated buildings to mark the spot. These have since been swept away by the river.

Irenia (1696–1699), a short distance north of Germantown, Pennsylvania (now part of Philadelphia), was a pietist commune established by Henry Bernhard Köster. There was a tiny village nearby at the time called Plymouth (not to be confused with the present town of Plymouth, Pennsylvania). The members sometimes also called their settlement the True Church of Philadelphia or Brotherly Love. The name "Irenia" comes from the tabernacle they built in the center of their property.

Köster had formerly been a member of Kelpius' commune and came with him from Germany in 1694, but he left that settlement in 1696 after an argument with Kelpius (see **Women of the Wilderness**). Köster was well known in the Philadelphia region as a man who could preach in both German and English, as he had often done so on behalf of Kelpius' commune. Thus he soon was able to find a few followers willing to work with him in establishing the new commune, which he decided should be based on the Women of the Wilder-

ness model. The nine members who joined Köster were dissident Quakers led by William Davis. They pooled their money to purchase the land for the settlement.

Little is known of the life at Irenia, except that the members shared all things in common. They disbanded in 1699, after Köster left them to return to Europe in search of a publisher for a long, mystical dissertation he wrote in Latin while at Irenia. Köster never returned to America. A book with a section that focuses on Irenia is Sachse's *The German Pietists of Provincial Pennsylvania, 1694–1708*.

Israelite City of David (1930–present), at Benton Harbor, Michigan, was formed by 217 members of the **House of David** after they left that community in a dispute over its leadership. They were followers of Queen Mary, who had previously shared the responsibility for the House of David with King Benjamin, her recently-deceased husband.

Although the Israelite City of David was established directly adjacent to the other commune, the members of this community have steadfastly refused to recognize or associate in any way with the members of the House of David. They consider those remaining with the parent commune to be rebels against God, or "Danites." They built their own living quarters and have owned and managed, at various times, a downtown Benton Harbor hotel, a vegetarian restaurant, and several farms in the county. For a time they, like the members of the House of David, maintained their own baseball team and band.

Queen Mary died in 1953 at the age of 93. Until the end, she was still anticipating the resurrection of King Benjamin. Books with sections that focus on the Israelite City of David are

Quaife's *Lake Michigan* and Webber's *Escape to Utopia: The Communal Movement in America.*

Jackson Family (1846–1860), in Philadelphia, Pennsylvania, was a Shaker community composed of 13 black members led by Mother Rebecca Jackson. They had all been members of a Millerite church that invited the **Mount Lebanon** Shaker community to send missionaries to their city. Many of these Millerites converted to Shakerism and, along with Mother Jackson, joined the **Watervliet** Shaker commune in New York. But eventually Mother Jackson decided to return to Philadelphia and set up her own Shaker community. The members worked in people's homes as servants during and day and slept in their Shaker community at night. The Watervliet Shakers took a general interest in this group and helped to subsidize them.

James Valley Colony *see* **Buffalo Colony**

Jamesville (1886–1918), on the James River near Mitchell, South Dakota, was a Hutterite Brüderhof (see **Bon Homme**) that faced almost constant hostility from neighbors. Once their mill was burned down by a group of marauders and several times their dam that provided water power for the mill was destroyed. The Hutterites were finally forced to substitute a gas engine for water power to operate the mill. During World War I, patriots from nearby Mitchell drove off 100 of their steers and 1,000 sheep, which the raiders sold at half price for the purpose of buying Liberty Bonds. But the U.S. government refused to accept such tainted cash and it was later deposited in a bank in the name of the Jamesville Hutterites.

The 100 members of Jamesville finally moved to Alberta, Canada, where the commune still exists. The land was briefly used for one of the New Deal subsistence homesteads and then, in 1937, it became the property of the Hutterite **Huron Colony**.

Jasper Colony (1851–1853), in Lenox Township, Iowa County, Iowa, was a Swedenborgian settlement of about 20 members who came from the Eastern states and originally from Germany. They were led by the Rev. Herman D. Diekoener, a firm believer in Christian communism and a man who hoped the experiment would encourage other Swedenborgians to set up similar communities.

The members owned about 1,000 acres of land, and they built a long community house, a number of log residence houses, and a common kitchen and dining room. They made their own furniture, with the exception of a few pieces brought by some members from St. Louis, including the wooden benches that they used instead of chairs in the dining room. The community house was said to symbolize both the principle of collective life and the colonists' fear of surrounding Indians.

In the long run, their communal stance did not have much effect on the other Swedenborgian congregations in the United States or Europe, and they abandoned the project in the spring of 1853. According to one source, the richness of Iowa farming land kindled their desire for private property. One of the members, George Gurmeister, later organized a Swedenborgian church at Lenox. Another, Henry Burmeister, became a school teacher in the area. A book with a section that focuses on the Jasper Colony is Ransom's *Pioneer Recollections.*

Jefferson County Industrial Association (1843–1844), at Cold Creek, about two miles from Watertown, New York, was a Fourierist settlement (see **Social Reform Unity**) that may have had as many as 400 members. They owned 600 acres of land that was donated for the purpose by several farmers who joined the commune. They also maintained a shop in Watertown for the sale of their farm produce and manufactured goods (products unknown).

This community was organized by Alonzo M. Watson, who assumed the presidency of this phalanx. He was a lawyer and he helped to form a confederation of Fourierist phalanxes called the American Industrial Union. After the Jefferson County Industrial Association closed at the end of a year's time, Watson joined the **Sodus Bay Phalanx** and became its president. Then, when Sodus Bay closed, Watson opened a grocery store and hotel in Baltimore.

One of the members of the Jefferson County Industrial Association said that it came to an end because of bad management. According to this source, one of the farmers who donated land for the project lost almost everything he owned as a result of the commune's failure.

Jeffersonville (1827), Indiana, had an Owenite community for a short period of time in 1827. The commune was actually intended to be located some 30 miles north of Cincinnati, Ohio, on land purchased for that purpose from General Neville, an enthusiast for Robert Owen's concept of "villages of cooperation." The General had purchased his 2,500 acres some years before in the hope of starting a town that would be named after him. But the General had no success in attracting people to his development, so he agreed to sell the land to Owenites from **New Harmony** for $15,000.

A group of 80 persons started out from the New Harmony settlement to occupy the land near Cincinnati, but they never reached the site. Instead, they settled on a farm near Jeffersonville. Little is known of their community, and not long afterward the group broke up.

Jeune Icarie (1878–1886), at Corning, Iowa, was an Icarian commune (see **Icaria** in Texas) that was formed after the split-up of the **Icaria** commune at Corning. It was composed of the younger members of the old community, including Armand DeHay, and grew to a total of 75 before it was dissolved by the courts because of its debts. By that time, however, most of the members had already gone to California to participate in the last of the Icarian experiments, **Icaria Speranza**.

Johnson (1874–1877), about 13 miles east of Kanab, Utah, was a Mormon United Order commune patterned after the one at **St. George**. It had about 50 members and it was organized following a visit to this village by Brigham Young, who urged the people there to adopt the United Order plan. The members ceased their communal lifestyle after Young's death.

Joyful (1881–1884), near Bakersfield, California, was a six-member diet-reform community led by Sarah and Isaac B. Rumford, both of whom had previously been active in the temperance and women's rights movements. They said that they formed this commune in order to return to the early communal life of the Christians, and that before all else such a simple life required a revolution in eating habits.

The members ate no meat or cooked foods and followed what they called an Edenic Diet. They ate only one meal a day, and their typical meal consisted of grains eaten either dry or moistened with water or fruit juice, followed by grated apple, mashed almonds, and pounded raisins. Dessert was flour and water, flavored by strawberries or vanilla and frozen as an ice cream.

The commune members published a newspaper called the *Joyful News Cooperator*. They later changed the commune's name to the Association of Brotherly Cooperation. After they disbanded, the Rumfords continued to promote their Edenic Diet for many years thereafter throughout California. A book with a section that focuses on Joyful is Hine's *California's Utopian Communities*.

Kanab (1874–1877), Utah, was a Mormon United Order community, patterned after the one at **St. George**, that lasted for three years. It had over 500 members, and collapsed because of dissension over community affairs.

Kanara (1874–1877), at what is now Kanarraville, Utah, was a Mormon commune based on the United Order model in use at **St. George**. It had about 75 members.

Kane County Community (1877–1878), in Kane County, Illinois, was a cooperative venture of about 12 persons.

Kanosh (1874–1877), Utah, was a Mormon United Order commune for three years until the death of Mormon leader Brigham Young. It based its economy on the **St. George** model. There were about 250 members.

Kansas Cooperative Farm *see* **Prairie Home Colony**

Kaweah Co-operative Commonwealth (1885–1892), on the banks of the Kaweah River in eastern Tulare County, California (now part of the Sequoia National Park), was organized by San Francisco labor leaders Burnette G. Haskell (1857–1907) and James J. Martin. They based their experiment on principles expounded in Laurence Gronlund's book, *Co-operative Commonwealth* (published circa 1880). This popularization of Marxism was widely read and was hailed by American socialists of the time as "the first comprehensive work in English on Socialism." It was not popular in Europe, however, because it played down the role of the class struggle on which European socialists put their fundamental emphasis.

Haskell has been characterized by a labor historian as "one of the most erratic and brilliant geniuses in the history of the labor movement on the Pacific Coast." He studied law at the University of California and was a newspaper editor and lawyer for the Republican Party in California before he became involved in the trade union movement. He then organized the International Workingmen's Association in San Francisco, one of the more radical unions of that time and a body claiming ideals identical with the Marxist First International. He also worked unsuccessfully in 1883 to bring unity between the competing socialist and anarchist parties in the United States. Martin, who had been a close associate of Haskell in forming the branch of the International Workingmen's Association, became the secretary for Kaweah.

Haskell and Martin acquired land for the commune under both the Timberland Act and the Homestead Act. In October 1885, an initial group of 68 men gathered to form the commune. Eventually the mostly male resident membership grew to about 300. Many of them were skilled laborers and trade union representatives. Also included were Charles F. Keller, a native of Germany who had served in the Civil War and then ran a meat market in Eureka, California; George Patch, the former owner of a hay-press company in Kansas City; and a few artists, musicians, and men of letters. Some were dress-reform advocates, phonetic spelling fanatics, vegetarians, Swedenborgians, and advocates of various other fads of the time. Yet, as William Carey Jones of the University of California said after visiting the commune, "They are all, perhaps without exception, intelligent, thoughtful, earnest, readers of books and journals, alive to the great economic and social questions of the day."

Each member paid $500 to be a part of the community, $400 of which could be paid for in goods or labor. The commune members allowed for non-resident members as well, who paid fees for the privilege of voting on community matters. Though he lived in Boston, Gronlund himself joined Kaweah as a nonresident member and, in 1890, was elected general secretary of the commune.

In organizing their community, the members followed most of the bare structural suggestions found in Gronlund's book. Among these were the rules they used to choose their leadership. It was Gronlund's belief that all officers should be elected from below by the workers, but removal from office should be done only from above by responsible superiors. The members also adopted Gronlund's rather cumbersome organizational directives. Thus they composed themselves into three divisions, 13 departments, over 50 bureaus, and countless sections.

Their economy was organized on a time-check system with checks issued in denominations ranging from 10 to 20,000 minutes. The checks were the

Members of Kaweah gather for a picnic (University of California Library, Berkeley).

official medium of exchange at the colony. They could be redeemed for money: .05 for 10 minutes, $100 for 20,000 minutes. All work was considered of equal value, whether that of a blacksmith or that of a trustee. Health care was free and provided by a nonresident physician member who lived nearby.

At first the members lived in tents, but then built log cabins for themselves. They eventually also constructed a community center, a community store, a print shop, a blacksmith shop, a barn, and some sheds, none of which remain standing today. They engaged in the lumber industry and fashioned an 18-mile long road into the area. This road can still be seen today, although it is no longer used. It took the members four years to complete, and at one point attained a height of 8,000 feet on a steady grade of eight feet to the hundred. They organized a band and an orchestra, held literary and scientific classes, and sponsored lectures and readings. They named some of the larger redwood trees after socialist heroes. The one they called the Karl Marx tree — by far the largest — is the one now known to tourists as the General Sherman tree.

From the beginning the colonists faced hostility from government authorities. This, rather than internal problems, brought their community to an end. The title to the land was never clear since officials in Washington, somewhat confused by why so many individuals were applying for land in that area all at one time, suspected foul play and withdrew the area from entry subject to investigation. Then, on September 25, 1890, Congress established Sequoia National Park, forcing the members off the land by the end of 1892. There was also hostility from some of the California timber interests who opposed both the communal nature of this project and the economic competition that the settlers provided to their log-cutting businesses. After Kaweah disbanded, a similar commune was started in 1893 by a visitor who had been impressed by the cooperative spirit he saw at Kaweah (see **Cooperative Brotherhood of Winters Island**).

Today, there is a small post office still in use that is named Kaweah. It stands about three miles north of Three Rivers. Although this post office was constructed several years after the commune's demise, it was named for the project and stands on land once held by the commune.

Haskell later wrote somewhat bitterly about the disappearance of the project: "There is no bribe money in our pockets; and beaten and ragged as we are, we are not ashamed... And is there no remedy, then, for the evils that oppress the poor? And is there no surety that the day is coming when justice and right shall reign on earth? I do not know; but I believe, and I hope, and I trust." He later joined the Bellamy Nationalist movement (see **Ruskin Commonwealth**) and then the Populist movement that worked successfully to elect members to the U.S. Congress and state legislatures in the 1890s. A book with a section that focuses on the Kaweah Cooperative Commonwealth is Hine's *California's Utopian Communities*.

Kendal (1826–1829), also known as the Friendly Association for Mutual Interests, was located at a place now within the city limits of Massillon, Ohio. It was probably the most successful of all the Owenite experiments (see **New Harmony**) and, after the influx of some of the members from the disbanded **Forrestville** Owenite commune in 1827, the membership at Kendal reached 150.

The founders of this commune, a group of men from the two Ohio towns of Massillon and Canton, agreed to purchase 2,113 acres for their experiment from the estate of Thomas Rotch for $20,000. These men were, for the most part, substantial citizens in the area, and they decided to turn over their farms as the down payment. Rotch himself joined the commune along with them, and together they signed a "Bond of Social Compact" on May 29, 1826. Some of the others were Isaac Bowman, Richard Williams, Zacheus Stanton, Charles Griffin, Matthew Macy, and Micajah Macy.

Kendal members manufactured woolen goods, grew hops, and did general farming. They also organized a lyceum, had a library of several hundred volumes, and held frequent public debates. Robert Owen visited them to give several lectures at Kendal in July 1828.

When the people from Forrestville joined them, they decided to name Dr. Samuel Underhill (1796–1859), one of those in the Forrestville group, as the leader of Kendal. But by September and October 1828, some of the members began to leave, and on January 1, 1829, the remaining members appointed an agent "to make deeds of the Kendal Community land." On January 3 it was decided to "discontinue business as a Company."

John Harmon, one of the last members to depart, described the reasons for ending this experiment as follows: Kendal "progressed harmoniously and prosperously, so long as the members had their health and a hope of paying for their domain. But a summer-fever attacked us, and seven heads of families died, among whom were several of our own most valued and useful members.... So we were compelled to give up and disperse, losing what we had paid, which was about seven thousand dollars. But we formed friendships that were enduring, and the failure never for a moment weakened my faith in the value of Communism."

Kinder Lou (1894–1896), five miles west of Valdosta, Georgia, was an educational and socialist experiment modeled after **Ruskin Commonwealth**. It had a membership of about ten, including some who joined them when that commune moved to Tennessee.

King Ranch *see* **Lewiston Colony**

Kingdom of Heaven (1867–1881), between Mill Creek and Russel Creek, near Walla Walla, Washington, was a Mormon commune (see **Kirtland**) organized by William W. Davies (1833–1906). He was born in Wales and came to the United States where he converted to Mormonism. He settled at Willard, Utah, and soon became a follower of Joseph Morris, joining his **Zion** commune in Utah. After a company of militia from Salt Lake City destroyed Zion, Davies fled to Idaho and then to Montana. In 1865 he had a vision that he should found the Kingdom of Heaven. He then gathered 40 other Morrisites at a place he had selected in Washington.

More members came from San Francisco and Portland as a result of the missionary work that the members did, until the commune at its height numbered 70 members. They owned 480 acres of land that was registered in Davies' name, and they held all property in common. The members also accepted Davies as "the spirit of God," and his son, Arthur, as "God made manifest in the world." Locally the lad was known as the "Walla Walla Jesus." But the boy died of diphtheria in 1880 and that same year one of the members brought a lawsuit against the commune that forced the sale of its property. A book with a section that particularly focuses on the Kingdom of Heaven is Fogarty's *All Things New.*

Kingston (1875–1882), Utah, was a Mormon communal settlement designed on the United Order model in use at **Orderville**. It had about 100 members. When the Edmunds anti-polygamy act was passed by Congress, many of the Mormon leaders were forced into hiding and the Kingston commune came to an end.

Kingwood (1954–1956), at Kingwood, New Jersey, was a pacifist community of about 15 people led by Francis Hall. When this commune closed, the members decided to merge with the **Woodcrest** commune near Rifton, New York. Hall, however, departed because of disagreements with the Woodcrest members. He later became the director of a Quaker retreat center in New York State.

Kirkridge (1945–present), between Bangor and Stroudsburg, Pennsylvania, is a community established in 1945 by John Oliver Nelson, a professor of theology at Yale, as an interdenominational Christian retreat center. Here visiting ministers and lay persons can participate in corporate and silent contemplation for a few days at a time. The commune is modeled after the Iona community in Scotland, and there are only eight members in residence. They have a remodeled 135-year-old farm house, two modern houses, and cabins for visitors. There is also a hewn-stone, glass-enclosed retreat house from which participants can view more than 30 miles of mountain grandeur.

From the close of evening worship at 9:15 P.M. until the close of morning worship at 8:30 A.M., absolute silence is maintained by both the members and visitors. The eight permanent members also scrupulously tithe and abide by the rule of daily personal devotions. An article with information that focuses on Kirkridge is Savacool's "Kirkridge," *Church Management,* December 1949.

Kirtland (1830–1838), three-and-a-half miles from Kirtland, Ohio, began as a settlement of 17 persons practicing total community of goods. They at first called their commune the Family, but within a matter of weeks they were converted by Mormon missionaries and this settlement became the first of many Mormon communes. The leader was Sidney Rigdon (1793–1876), a Disciples of Christ minister who reportedly once heard Robert Owen give a speech about the value of building "villages of cooperation" (see **New Harmony**). Although Rigdon disagreed with many of Owen's ideas, they did plant an image of communalism in his mind and led him to establish this commune. Eventually Rigdon was to become the most outstanding leader of early Mormonism next to Joseph Smith, Jr. (1805–1844), the founder of the Mormon religion.

Historians generally agree that Smith's impetus to start a new church came directly from the series of revivals that were sweeping across the United States in the opening years of the second quarter of the nineteenth century. It was also in the midst of such revivalistic fervor that the Mormons were able to build their membership and to erect their various communes.

Smith was born in Palmyra, New York. As a teenager he claimed that he had a vision in which he saw God and Jesus Christ. They told him to join no

Massive stone temple, built by Mormon communalists at Kirtland (drawings by Lois Will).

church but, in later visions, authorized him to set up the Church of Jesus Christ. On September 21, 1823, an angel, Moroni, appeared in yet another vision to tell Smith that a record of the history of the ancient inhabitants of the United States had been written by a person named Mormon, and that this history was engraved on plates of gold buried in Cumorah Hill, only four miles from Palmyra. Smith reportedly dug up these golden tablets and from them translated the *Book of Mormon*, which became the church's Bible.

Smith continued to have revelations throughout his life, which are the basis for most of the original Mormon doctrines. One of these revelations, which came to him during conflicts with pro-slavery forces in Missouri, later led to open racism on the part of the Utah

Mormons after the leader died. Smith himself, however, always took an anti-slavery position and even authorized the naming of a black priest while he was living at **Nauvoo** in Illinois.

On April 6, 1830, Smith and five others founded their church at Fayette, New York. That same year Oliver Cowdery, Parley Pratt, and some other Mormons were sent westward by Smith to preach the new gospel to the Indians. They stayed for two weeks at Kirtland, Ohio, where they met and converted Rigdon and the 16 other persons in his communal settlement. Rigdon and his group enthusiastically helped the visiting Mormons conduct revival meetings in the area. Within a few weeks they had 127 converts to the new religion. Smith then moved with others in his church to Kirtland, while Cowdery and Pratt moved on to Missouri where they established **Zion**. Lyman Wight, one of Rigdon's original 16 members, also went out from Kirtland to preach among the fishing families along the Ohio River. He set up the **Adam-ondi-Ahman** commune in Missouri.

In talks with Smith, Rigdon was able to convince the church leader that all the Mormon religious centers should be structured as communes. It was after this that Smith then had the revelation of a "more perfect law of the Lord," sometimes called the "Law of Consecration," the "Order of Enoch," the "Order of Stewardships," or the "United Order." This law made it a rule of the church that "every man may receive according as he stands in need." Yet, at the same time, each member of the church was appointed "a steward over his own property, or that which he has received." Smith's model was not the kind of pure communism that Rigdon had instituted for the Family, but it was a modified economic system that put control of all property within each church commune in the hands of its leader or bishop of the church. It should be noted that there was probably one other influence on Smith that led to his acceptance of communal structures — that of his uncle, Jason Mack. Mack had established a religious commune in New Brunswick, Canada, said to have contained 30 families.

The "more perfect law" worked in this way. A convert turned over to his church bishop all his own land and other possessions, with a deed that made the bishop the legal owner. The bishop then returned to the convert any goods and property that he might need for the support of his family. Thus rich and poor might begin life anew on the same economic level, at least in theory, the poor having been awarded some of the goods previously owned by the rich. Each member could subsequently develop this church-owned land as he wished, only having to turn over his surplus to the Bishop once a year. The surplus was kept in the Bishop's storehouse for church purposes and relief of the poor.

In reality, the plan seldom worked for long. Problems often arose concerning transfer of property, and there were also difficulties in the collection of the surplus and in the division of land. Yet several times in the history of the Mormon church (and of groups that broke away from the main body but retained their beliefs) there have been movements to revive the United Order. These were conducted with revivalistic fervor comparable to that displayed when Smith and Rigdon preached among the Mormons. And the United Order has remained the ideal for church members, even though tithing is now the basic symbol of church loyalty.

The commune near Kirtland grew to a membership of about 3,000 persons and expanded its land ownership into the village of Kirtland itself before it collapsed in 1838 due to financial mismanagement. The members, besides constructing many homes and buildings that have since been destroyed, began several industries and built a massive stone temple that is still standing on a hill above the village. It took three years to build, covers a 59 by 79 foot area, and cost $40,000. The rectangular architecture is interesting in that it combines Gothic, Grecian, Venetian, Georgian, and Egyptian architectural motifs in a somewhat harmonious way. The temple has two stories and an attic. Books with sections that focus on Kirtland are Evans' *Joseph Smith, An American Prophet* and O'Dea's *The Mormons*.

Koinonia (1942–1993), at Americus, Georgia, is a pacifist farm commune established by Clarence Jordan (1912–1969) and Martin England, two ministers from the Southern Baptist Theological Seminary at Louisville, Kentucky. The name comes from the Greek word for fellowship. The members speak of themselves as a pacifist group, and many of the earliest ones were conscientious objectors during World War II. However the record of this commune has been more one of involvement in the field of race relations than in opposition to war.

Starting with 440 acres, the Koinonia members have increased their holdings to 1,400 acres. They have raised peanuts, pecans, corn, cotton, cattle, hogs, goats, and poultry. They are, in fact, credited with introducing poultry production into Sumpter County, Georgia, and their hams are famous throughout the United States. The members share all things in common and live in complete racial equality. They numbered 67 in 1957 (52 white and 15 black).

Overt hostility from neighbors against Koinonia because of their interracial policy began as early as 1950. But after the U.S. Supreme Court ruled against segregation in all schools, this community became a prime target for Southern segregationists. Members were beaten and arrested without cause when they traveled on roads away from the community property. They were shot at from passing cars as they worked in the fields, and their pecan-processing plant and roadside fruit stand (with cold-storage equipment) were dynamited. One of their houses was strafed by a submachine gun.

In the spring of 1958, a total of 297 fruit and nut trees were cut down by vandals. The members of Koinonia were also refused loans by the local bank and had to buy all their clothing by mail order because local stores conducted a

Sunday afternoon worship service at Koinonia (photo by Betty Jones).

boycott against them. This boycott by the local merchants lasted for 13 years.

The pressure became so intense, with visits from robed Ku Klux Klan delegations demanding that the colony disband, that finally the Koinonia leaders sent a plea to President Dwight D. Eisenhower requesting protection. The government turned their plea over to Georgia Governor Marvin Griffin, who, instead of protecting them, instituted a county grand jury investigation against the commune. The jury indicted the leadership of Koinonia for subversion, saying that the members practiced "peonage" on "guileless Negroes," that the farm amassed huge profits on which they paid no taxes, and that the members burned their own buildings and persecuted themselves to gain sympathy.

Now that integration has been reluctantly accepted throughout the county, such pressures on the commune have abated. The members are continuing in their policy of racial equality and religious pacifism, and they welcome interested visitors to come and see how well their policy is working.

In the late 1980s and early 1990s the residents of Koinonia began selling plots of their land to poor farmers in the area for whatever price the farmers could pay, in the hope that this would enable the farmers to find new hope and security in their lives. The Koinonia members also participated with the plot-purchasers in building their homes through the program known as Habitat for Humanity. They closed the commune in 1993, with some of the members then forming Jubilee Partners, an organization to further the Habitat for Humanity program.

Before he died, Clarence Jordan wrote several "Cotton Patch" versions of New Testament scriptures to bring the message of the Bible home to the people of Georgia and elsewhere. In the introduction to the first of these books he wrote, "We want to be participants in the faith, not merely spectators."

Called "colloquial translations with a Southern accent," Jordan, in these Cotton Patch books, emphasizes the humanity of Christ. His text depicts Jesus as wrapped in a blanket and laid in an apple box at his birth; killed by lynchers; and when he came out of the vault on Easter morning, came to his disciples and said, "Howdy." A book with a section that focuses on Koinonia is Hedgepath's *The Alternative: Communal Life in New America.*

Koresh Community (1880–1882), at Moravia, New York, was the first of three communal settlements set up by Cyrus Reed Teed (1839–1908), who was the founder of the Koreshan movement that claimed 5,000 followers in 1905. He called himself Koresh after the Hebrew form of his name, and devoted his life to disseminating his theory of the universe, which he named "the cellular cosmogony." His central idea was that the surface of the earth is concave, rather than convex, and that humanity lives on the inside of a hollow ball 8,000 miles in diameter. Thus the sun, moon, and stars are all inside the sphere, and a direct route to China should be straight up into the sky rather than down through the earth.

Teed considered the stars to be merely reflections of the planets that he believed were actually seven mercury disks. The sun, he said, is half light and half dark; its rotation causing the phenomenon of rising and setting. He made elaborate preparations to measure the curvature of the Earth with an instrument he called the Koreshan Geodetic Staff and in this way prove that the world is really concave. According to Teed, this cellular theory, which had come to him in a midnight revelation, was necessary to any understanding of God, humanity, immortality, and social relations. He later added elements of reincarnation and alchemy to his beliefs, and he claimed to have discovered the "philosopher's stone."

This commune, the smallest of the three he established, had only about five members. They turned over all their possessions to the community and practiced celibacy. After the commune closed, Teed moved to Chicago and started **Koreshan**. Books with sections that focus on the Koresh Community are Carmer's *Dark Trees in the Wind* and Gardner's *Fads and Fallacies in the Name of Science*.

Koreshan (1885–1903), first in New York City, where it was located in a flat at 135th Street near Eighth Avenue, and then in Chicago, was a commune established by Cyrus Reed Teed after his **Koresh Community** failed. The membership in New York was only six, but in Chicago they grew to 126. Teed moved there in 1886 after a lecture he gave in that city met with great success. It was here that Teed added the belief in reincarnation to his teachings, possibly because of the influence of several Hindu groups that were prominent at the Chicago World's Columbian Exposition of 1893.

In Chicago, the commune occupied a rambling mansion on Cottage Grove Avenue in an area of the city called Washington Heights. The members called their building Beth-Ophra. They had a printing plant that employed 40 to 50 persons and printed their newspaper, *The Guiding Star*, as well as many jobs not related to the Koreshan movement. Eventually they occupied three other buildings in the city. Teed was away from the commune much of the time, speaking before groups of followers and curiosity seekers in San Francisco, Denver, Baltimore, Portland, and elsewhere. In 1894 he reportedly collected $60,000 from these speaking engagements. But eventually he decided to close this project and start another at **Estero**, Florida. Many of the members moved there with him. Books with sections that focus on Koreshan are Carmer's *Dark Trees in the Wind* and Gardner's *Fads and Fallacies in the Name of Science*.

Koreshan Unity (1890–1891), in San Francisco, California, was a commune established by Cyrus Teed (see **Koreshan**) after a successful lecture tour in that city. The commune was located on Noe Street, and here the printing of Koreshan books and pamphlets began. The members also had a store that they called the Bureau of Equitable Commerce. When Koreshan was moved to Chicago, the approximately 15 members of this commune joined them there.

Kristeen Community (1845–1846), on the Wabash and Erie Canal, about 35 miles from Peru, Indiana, was a commune established by Charles Mowland and others who had been members of the **Prairie Home Community**. The approximately 30 members owned 376 acres of land by the edge of the Tippecanoe River. They engaged in the timber and lumber trades. Orson S. Murray and John O. Wattles, both of whom had participated in Prairie Home, were listed as trustees of this community, although they were not members.

LaGrange Phalanx (1843–1846), near Mongo, LaGrange County, Indiana, was a Fourierist project (see **Social Reform**

Unity) located on 1,045 acres of land. They had a two-story phalanx house, or phalanxtry, that measured 210 by 24 feet in circumference. It had a front veranda on both stories. The dining room, 40 by 20 feet, was on the ground floor and their schoolroom was directly above this. Each family had a living room and two bedrooms within this phalanx house.

Altogether there were 120 members, most of them were farmers who came from Indiana and Michigan. They were led by W.S. Prentiss and William Anderson, who acted as secretaries for the commune. Other leading members were Benjamin Jones, Harvey Olmstead, William Seaburn, and Ephriam Seeley. Jones owned about half of the land and apparently caused much dissatisfaction by making financial decisions on the basis of his economic power, even though he was not an elected leader.

Besides the phalanx house, they had three barns, some outhouses, and a blacksmith shop. The community disbanded sometime after June 1846.

Lake Byron Colony *see* **Beadle County Colony**

Lamoille Agricultural and Mechanical Association (1843–1844), also known as the Bureau County Phalanx, was a Fourierist community (see **Social Reform Unity**) of about 25 members located at LaMoille, Illinois, a town some 90 miles west of Chicago. Its president was Timothy Edwards, and the secretary was Samuel Edwards. Other individuals named in its charter were John Kendall, Justin H. Olds, and Elisha Fassett. This commune attempted to operate like a full-sized Fourierist phalanx, but could only continue for a little less than a year.

Lasker (1885–1888), near Ford, Kansas, was a Jewish agricultural commune (see **Sicily Island**) of about 30 members. It was established by the Montifiore Agricultural Aid Society of New York City and was named after Edward Lasker, a statesman in New York. The members owned only nine square miles of land on which they harvested a modest crop. Their water supply was 15 miles distant. They lived in six sod houses that they built themselves. Drought ruined their second year's planting and they finally disbanded in the third year.

Leeds (1874–1877), Utah, was a Mormon United Order commune of about 75 members for several years. They based their model on **St. George**.

Leeser (1883), in Finney County, Kansas, was a Jewish agricultural commune (see **Sicily Island**) of about 20 members. It lasted for only a few months, and little else is known about it.

Leraysville Phalanx (1844), near what is now LeRaysville, in Bradford County, Pennsylvania, was a Fourierist commune (see **Social Reform Unity**) that began operation on 600 acres of land owned by George M. Brink. There were about 40 members, and they were led by the Rev. Lemuel C. Boulding, the pastor of a Swedenborgian church that was on the property. Boulding was also the publisher of a newspaper called *The North American Phalanx*, which was printed at the Leraysville Phalanx for a few months and was published elsewhere until 1847, after the commune closed. The agent for the Leraysville Phalanx was Solomon Brown.

Lewiston Colony (1912–present), near Lewiston, Montana, is a Hutterite Brü-

Original Community House at Lititz, now used as a parsonage, is attached to the church sanctuary, built in 1787 (photo by Pastor Adin A. Ward).

derhof (see **Bon Homme**) established by 60 people from the **Wolf Creek** Brüderhof. In 1920 they moved to Alberta, Canada, but returned to their Montana lands in 1935. After that they were known as the King Ranch. In 1964, there were 50 members and their leader was Elias Walter.

Liberty Cooperative Association (1896–1897), at Hustburg in Benton County, Tennessee, was a commune that had a primary school. There were only a few members, perhaps ten at most, and it lasted for a little more than a year.

Lititz (1754–1844), about 8 miles north of Lancaster, Pennsylvania, was founded by Moravians on 500 acres of land donated to them by George Klein for the purpose of setting up a community. The commune was operated under the General Economy model used at **Bethlehem**, and it was considered to be one of the best functioning of the General Economy communes in the United States. It had about 100 members. In 1765 the members of Lititz began to manufacture organs and pianos, and in 1794 they established Linden Hall Junior College, one of the oldest girl's schools in America.

Llano del Rio (1914–1918), 45 miles north of Los Angeles, California, in the Antelope Valley, was a socialist colony established by a noted Los Angeles lawyer, Job Harriman (1861–1925). He had been active in the Nationalist movement (see **Ruskin Commonwealth**) and had run unsuccessfully for election as governor of California on the Socialist Labor Party ticket in 1898, as vice-president of the United States along with Eugene V. Debs on the Socialist Party ticket in 1900, and as mayor of Los Angeles on the American Socialist Party ticket in 1911.

His first-hand knowledge of communes came from his position as president of Altruria Subcouncil Number Five, an organization that promoted and gave support to the **Altruria** commune near Santa Rosa, California.

Starting with only five members, a team of horses, five pigs, and a cow, the Llano colony grew to 150 members by 1915, and 1,100 members by 1917. Together they owned about 9,000 acres in the Antelope Valley. They purchased this land from the Mescal Water and Land Company, a noncommunal temperance society development. Harriman also purchased the *Western Comrade*, a socialist journal that he used to widely publicize the Llano project. It was Harriman's belief that the economic system of capitalism would not disappear until "the industries from which it draws its subsistence should have first been transformed into cooperative enterprises." He argued that capitalism would lose its supporters if socialism showed greater economic efficiency in such a demonstration project as Llano.

At its height, Llano had industries of all kinds. These included a laundry, cannery, shoe shop, garage, blacksmith shop, dairy, machine shop, planing mill, rug works, paint shop, lime kiln, cabinet shop, flour mill, sawmill, brickyard, bakery, fish hatchery, barber shop, printing plant, and commissary. There was also a hotel; one of the largest rabbitries in the United States; an apiary; hundreds of horses, cows, chickens, turkeys, goats, and hogs; steam tractors; orchards; and many acres of alfalfa.

Members were paid $4 a day in wages, provided with all supplies at cost, promised two week vacations each year, and permitted to keep their personal property, including automobiles. They lived in adobe homes and ate in a large dining hall. A colony kindergarten was operated by Prudence Stokes Brown, who had studied under Dr. Maria Montessori in Italy.

The members had hobby clubs and organized athletic teams. Their big holiday of the year was the world socialist holiday, May Day, which was also the founding day for the commune. Guests everywhere were invited to Llano for this annual celebration. The members displayed industrial products, held a parade and track meet, served a large dinner, and ended with a big dance.

But, as early as 1915, the California Commissioner of Corporations began to give the colonists trouble. (Harriman had incorporated the project as the Llano del Rio Company of California.) The commissioner investigated Llano and reported that he found waste in the colony's water supply and profiteering in its cooperative store. Legal pressures to close the commune were soon instigated. Harriman, to circumvent these pressures, purchased some land in Nevada and chartered a new corporation in that state that bought all the property of the California corporation. The tactic saved the commune.

Yet Harriman realized it would never be perfectly secure from legal maneuvering in this California location and that it should be moved to a less vulnerable site. He therefore secretly purchased land from the Gulf Lumber Company in Louisiana in 1917 and publicized the start of a second colony near Leesville, Louisiana (see **Newllano**). He fully intended to liquidate the California project, but not until the other one was firmly grounded. The California commune continued as a fruit farm with a decreased membership until 1918. In the end, only a small part of the Llano membership made the journey to Louisiana.

Today a small post office called Llano, on Highway 138 in Antelope Valley, preserves the commune's name. There also are a few ruins, notably the stone pillars and chimneys of the colony's hotel, along the highway about a half mile west of this post office. Books with sections that focus on Llano del Rio are Conkin's *Two Paths to Utopia: The Hutterites and the Llano Colony* and Hine's *California's Utopian Colonies.*

Lopez Island Community (1911–1920), at Lopez in San Juan County, Washington, was established by Thomas Gourley, a fundamentalist preacher from the town of Ballard, Washington. With 175 followers he settled on Lopez Island, where they all lived in tents until they obtained enough lumber to build their houses, barn, bake house, dock, tabernacle, and tent-house school. They owned all things in common. Smoking, alcohol, and dancing were prohibited. The members lived in their own homes but ate communally. All their social life revolved around the church. Some of the members worked at jobs outside the community. Others cut wood and took it to the mill on Blakely Island to earn a living.

In 1916 rumors began to circulate within the community regarding Gourley's misappropriation of funds. A general meeting forced his ouster, and an elder, Abba Green, took his place as leader of the community. Gourley soon afterward moved to Georgia and was later killed in a train wreck. The commune lasted a few years longer and then disbanded. It is said that a bootlegger then took over their vacant buildings until the property was divided and sold. A book with a section that focuses on the Lopez Island Community is LeWarne's *Utopias on Puget Sound, 1885–1915.*

Lord's Farm (1889–1902), at what is now Woodcliff Lake, New Jersey, was formed by Paul Blaudin Mnason, whose original name was Mason T. Huntsman. The fifteen members held all goods in common and practiced celibacy, nonre-

sistance, and vegetarianism. They owned 18 acres of land, donated by one member, and leased an additional 150 acres from the father of two members named Blaudina and Titus. Among the other members were Gary Storms and his sister, Chauncy Roe, and a man who came from England named Billy Wilson. It is estimated that 3,000 persons visited the Lord's Farm before it closed.

Neighbors, however, resented the presence of Mnason and his followers. A locally-recruited mob once grabbed him, cut his hair, and pulled out his whiskers. Later he was arrested for Sabbath-breaking and blasphemy, as well as for conspiracy to defraud, kidnapping, rape, and running a disorderly house. None of these charges held up in court except that of blasphemy, and Mnason was fined for "allowing himself to be adored as a Son of God." Still later, all the members of this commune were arrested by the man who leased the land to them, on a charge that the community was conspiring to defraud him of his land. After six months in jail the entire group was released and the charges were dropped. A book with a section that focuses on the Lord's Farm is Hinds' *American Communities.*

Los Angeles Fellowship Farm (1912–1926), northeast of Puente, California, was a cooperative farming community established by the Rev. George Littlefield, who had earlier established **Fellowship Farm** in Massachusetts and **Fruit Crest** in Missouri, and Los Angeles dentist Kate E. Buck. They purchased 75 acres of land and soon had 12 families there. The membership eventually grew to as many as 60 persons, including an advocate of nudism who acted as the colony's first secretary, and a religious fanatic who spent his weekends preaching on the streets of Los

Angeles. By 1926 the community had lost its cooperative nature and most of its members. The land was then taken over by the Maple Water Company. A book with a section that focuses on the Los Angeles Fellowship Farm is Hine's *California's Utopian Communities.*

Lost Colony of Cropperville *see* **Cropperville**

Lystra (1899–1902), located in Virginia, was a religious commune of 25 members, who may have been related in some way to the community of **Friedheim**. Nothing about Lystra or the religious outlook of its members has been preserved.

Macedonia Cooperative (1937–1957), near Clarksville, Georgia, was a farming commune established on 1,000 acres of timberland at the foot of the Blue Ridge Mountains by Columbia University education professor Morris Mitchell. He hoped to demonstrate that such a project could avoid the mistakes reportedly being made by the government-sponsored cooperative farms of Roosevelt's New Deal.

During World War II, however, this commune became a pacifist center, and most of the members then were conscientious objectors. They had a sawmill, cooperative store, dairy, apiary, and woodworking shop where they made children's blocks for sale. They also had ten houses serviced by electricity and heated by woodstoves, and a nursery school. At its height there were 27 members.

The commune experienced great resentment from neighbors who opposed their pacifist position. They were accused of being members of the Communist Party, "nigger lovers," atheists, and "free lovers." They were able to overcome some of this resentment, however, when in November 1947 they held a timber stand demonstration and barbecue for the people of the county. State and federal forestry men gave support to this event.

The Macedonia Cooperative Community never prospered, and in September 1957 the members decided to sell the property, and move to the **New Meadow Run** commune at Farmington, Pennsylvania. Eight of them set up a different pacifist commune at **Canterbury**, New Hampshire. Books with sections that focus on the Macedonia Cooperative Community are Infield's *Cooperative Communities at Work* and *Utopia and Experiment.*

McKean County Association (1842–1844), 12 miles southwest of Smethport, Pennsylvania, and near present-day Marvindale, was a colony of German immigrants led by the Rev. George Ginal, a Universalist minister. The approximately 550 participants were all members of the Society of Industry, a cooperative organization of which Ginal was the agent. The society was founded, according to Ginal, on "the principle of community of property, money and furniture accepted, and is sustained by the cooperation of its members; and equal distribution of profits being made half-yearly."

The commune set up two branches, Teutonia and Ginalsburg, on their 37,000 acres of undeveloped land. Among the buildings they erected were a store, steam sawmill, tannery, pottery, two schoolhouses, and between 70 and 80 log cabins and frame homes, none of which are still standing. It is not clear as to why this commune came to an end within two years. Books with sections that focus on the McKean County Association are Mulkream and Pugh's *A*

Traveler's Guide to Historic Western Pennsylvania and Noyes' *History of American Socialisms.*

Magnolia (1896), at Shepherd, Texas, was a land-development cooperative that was also known as the East Texas Cooperative Association. It encompassed 479 acres of land and had perhaps 25 members. It failed, according to an item in the *Coming Nation*, because the membership fee of $300 was too low.

Mahanaim (1745–1750), in Pulaski County, Virginia probably near the present town of New River, was set up by the three Eckerlin brothers — Samuel, Gabriel, and Israel — after they were expelled from **Ephrata**. Because of its location, this commune was also sometimes called New River. One other former member from the Ephrata Seventh-day Baptist commune joined them, as did for a short time Alexander Mack, the aging German pastor who organized the first congregation of the Church of the Brethren in 1708. Eventually, by recruiting other German settlers in the area, Mahanaim grew to about ten members. They constructed a crude dwelling, adopted a lifestyle much like that at Ephrata, and survived for about five years. But fears of an impending Indian attack and a successful attempt at reconciliation with the head of Ephrata eventually led the group to give up this communal experiment and return to the parent body.

Manahar Cooperative Fellowship *see* **Bhoodan Center**

Manchester Union *see* **Ontario Union**

Manlius Perfectionists (1849–1855), at Manlius, New York, was a commune of perhaps ten members who followed the teachings of John Humphrey Noyes (see **Putney Corporation**). They were closely related to the **Oneida** Perfectionist community and it is believed that the members moved there when this community closed.

Marlboro Association (1841–1845), at Oakland, some 40 miles northeast of Cincinnati, Ohio, was formed by 24 persons opposed to the use of money and favoring common ownership of property. They were led by Dr. Abraham Brooke and his brother, Edward Brooke, who each owned farms that they contributed to this experiment. One of these contained a large orchard. The members later connected the two farms originally owned by the Brookes by purchasing another that lay between them.

The Brooke brothers were active in the anti-slavery movement and had helped many slaves escape to Canada by way of the underground railway before they organized this commune. Another prominent member was Joseph Lukens, who had also been active in the anti-slavery movement and who died before the Marlboro Association experiment ended. His sister-in-law was married to Edward Brooke.

Dr. Abraham Brooke left the commune in 1843 to form another community, **Dr. Abraham Brooke's Experiment**, at a nearby location. He later said he disliked the Marlboro Association because its members did not "practice communism with enough thoroughness." Books with sections that focus on the Marlboro Association are Bestor's *American Phalanxes, the Fourierist Phase of Socialism in the United States* and Perrin's *History of Stark County.*

Martha's Vineyard Cooperative (1900), on Martha's Vineyard Island, off Cape

Cod, Massachusetts, was a cooperative farm of about five members that was established for a short time by the Brotherhood of the New Age (*see* **Southern Co-operative Association**).

Martindale (1959–present), near Martindale, Montana, is a Hutterite Brüderhof (see **Bon Homme**) that had 93 members in 1964 and was then led by John Wipf.

Maryfarm (1935–1946), also known as Our Lady Star of the Sea Farm, was the first of several communal farms established by the Catholic Worker movement. It was initially located on an acre-size lot next to what is now Wolf Pond Park on Staten Island, New York, but it was moved in April 1936 to a location three miles from Easton, Pennsylvania.

The Catholic Worker movement itself grew out of a joint undertaking by Peter Maurin, a French émigré who had come to the United States with doctrines of radical Catholicism and anarchism, and Dorothy Day, who had been a journalist for newspapers published by the Industrial Workers of the World, Socialists, and Communists before her conversion to Catholicism. Maurin and Day established a newspaper, *The Catholic Worker*, which went on sale in 1933 for one penny a copy. The newspaper in its early years reached a top circulation of 150,000. But its popularity dropped drastically during the war because of the movement's pacifist position. The paper is still sold for just one penny.

Maurin, as a result of experiences in Europe, had come to the conclusion that there was a need for a nonviolent revolutionary movement grounded in the prayer life of the church, the labor movement, agriculture, and the arts — a movement aimed at establishing a just social order. Both he and Dorothy Day believed that a society in tune with the teachings of Jesus and the Roman Catholic Church would have no place for exploitation of one human by another, or for war, or for racial and religious discrimination.

The two of them set up Houses of Hospitality in New York, Chicago, Minneapolis, and many other cities as aid stations for the sick, the homeless, and the jobless. They established farming communes in the country to experiment in the new lifestyle. These Catholic Worker farms usually were started where land was donated to the movement. They were not only operated according to communal principles but served as rehabilitation centers for those who needed rest from the taxing work at the Houses of Hospitality in the city.

The communal farms were usually directly related to one or another of the Houses of Hospitality, and they often provided some of the food for the soup kitchens run by these city establishments. In the summer they became centers for conferences of the Catholic Worker movement.

None of the farms lasted for any great length of time, but when one of these communes was abandoned another would shortly thereafter be organized to take its place. There are still several of these Catholic Worker farm communes operating in states such as New York, Massachusetts, and California. (None of the current ones are listed here because they were established after 1963.)

The Catholic Worker movement has become widely known for its pacifism. The members urged neutrality during the Spanish Civil War, when the hierarchy of the Catholic Church was giving support to Franco and the Fascists, while Socialists and Communists throughout the world were supporting the Spanish Loyalists. The movement opposed World War II, nuclear weapons, and the Vietnam War. As Dorothy Day once said, "Love is indeed a harsh and dreadful thing to ask of us, but it is the only answer."

Maryfarm, according to Dorothy Day, was initiated to bring about a "new society in which it will be easier for men to be good." The New York property contained a house with eight bedrooms. From its wide porch the members could overlook Raritan Bay. Day said that the participants, numbering about 15 at any one time, spent as much time in heated discussions as they did in gardening.

When the commune was moved to Pennsylvania, the location contained 28 acres and had two level fields — though most of the land was hilly — and it included an eight-acre section of woodland. It also had a house with three bedrooms, a barn, and a carriage shed. They purchased the land with funds donated primarily by a Southern school teacher, who gave the money on the condition that the members provide her with a summer home on the farm. The land, however, had no water supply. They had to use storage cisterns to catch rainwater from the roofs. There were a few peach trees, some apple and cherry trees, some raspberry bushes, and a half acre of asparagus. Friends donated money for a cow, as well as furniture and other needs. The members planted corn and built a number of other houses.

Throughout most of the year the farm was filled with groups of visiting students and children from the slums of New York City. Dorothy Day lived there when she was not traveling or engaged in work at one of the Houses of Hospitality, as did Peter Maurin. The commune closed in a dispute over ownership of the land. Books with sections that focus on Maryfarm are three by Day: *House of Hospitality*, *The Long Loneliness*, and *Loaves and Fishes*.

Maryfarm (1945–1947), at Newburgh, New York, was a Catholic Worker farm (see **Maryfarm** on Staten Island) with a large house and about 15 members. Both Peter Maurin, a founder of the Catholic Worker movement, and poet Maxwell Bodenheim were participants there for a short time.

Maxwell (1900–present), about five miles northeast of Scotland, South Dakota, is a Hutterite Brüderhof (see **Bon Homme**) that moved to Manitoba, Canada, in 1919 because of the hostility they were facing in the United States during World War I. They returned to their South Dakota lands in 1947. They had 68 members in 1964 and were led by Joseph Hofer.

May Valley Cooperative Community (1956–1977), at Renton, Washington, was a cooperative housing community organized by followers of Ralph Borsodi (see **Bayard Lane Homestead Community**) and members of the Seattle Co-op Housing Association. It had about 30 resident members and many nonresident shareowners. Its leader was John Affolter.

In 1977 the membership decided to end the cooperative nature of May Valley and become instead a homeowners' association. However, part of the membership under Affolter's leadership decided to continue their cooperative lifestyle in a commune they call Teramanto (Loving Earth in Esperanto). This occupies some of the land formerly held by the May Valley Cooperative Community.

Melbourne Village (1947–1969), at Melbourne, Florida, was a homestead community established by followers of Ralph Borsodi and his Green Revolution Movement (see **Bayard Lane Homestead Community**). Its membership grew to about 700 before it ceased to operate as a homesteading community. Borsodi himself moved there from New York to set up a school advocating his principles. He called it Melbourne University. Several persons who had worked with him at the Dayton Homesteads in Dayton, Ohio, also settled at Melbourne Village. These included Mrs. George H. Wood, Miss Margaret Hutchinson, and Mrs. Elizabeth Nutting.

Memnonia Institute (1856), at Yellow Springs, Ohio, was a 20-member cooperative community devoted to vegetarianism and water cure practices. It was established by Mary Gove Nichols (1810–1884) and her husband, Thomas Low Nichols (1815–1901), publishers of *Nichols' Monthly*, a magazine devoted to vegetarianism and water cure practices. They chose this site because the Yellow Springs Water Cure establishment was available for lease, and they selected the name "Memnonia" because this was the name of the Egyptian God of Waters.

Mrs. Nichols was not only an author, reformer, and water cure physician, but she was well-known for her support of mesmerism, spiritualism, temperance, and dress reform. She was also a friend of author Edgar Allan Poe. Her husband, also a published author, was a hydrotherapist and pioneer dietician. They had both previously been members of the Fourierist **North American Phalanx** and anarchist **Modern Times** communes.

The members of Memnonia, besides availing themselves of the water cure treatment, made elaborate plans to establish "a harmonious society throughout all the earth." Educator Horace Mann and others on the faculty of Antioch College in Yellow Springs were openly hostile to this commune, and it failed within the year.

Nichols and his wife then joined the Catholic Church and spent several years lecturing to students at Catholic institutions throughout the Mississippi Valley. Then, just before the start of the Civil War, they moved to England and became well-known in British spiritualist and vegetarian circles. Mr. Nichols founded the London magazine *Herald of Health* and edited it until 1886. Both of them wrote separate autobiographies. Books with sections that focus on the Memnonia Institute are Adams and Hutter's *The Mad Forties* and Fogarty's *All Things New*.

Memphis Colony *see* **South Western Colony**

Metropolitan Institute of Texas *see* **Burning Bush**

Miami (1948–present), near Pendroy, Montana, is a Hutterite Brüderhof (see **Bon Homme**) that was led by Issak Wurtz and had 80 members in 1964.

Michigan St. Benedict's Farm (1938–1953), at South Lyon, Michigan, was a Catholic Worker communal farm (see **Maryfarm** on Staten Island) established on land donated by the father of a Detroit priest. The ten members raised produce on their 100 acres for the movement's St. Francis House of Hospitality in Detroit. They called the large building on their property Marybrook, and they used this not only as living quarters but as a retreat house for college students.

Middlesex Community (1882), in Middlesex County, Virginia, was a Jewish agricultural commune (see **Sicily Island**) of about 30 people. The exact location is now unknown. This commune should not be confused with another Jewish agricultural settlement that was started one year later in the same county, **Water View**.

Milford (1910–1918), along the James River in Beadle County, South Dakota, was a 100-member Hutterite Brüderhof (see **Bone Homme**). This commune moved to Alberta, Canada, in 1918 because of hostility directed at them during World War I. They still exist there.

Miller Ranch (1949–present), near Choteau, Montana, is a Hutterite Brüderhof (see **Bon Homme**). It had 98 members in 1964 and David Hofer was their leader.

Millerdale Colony see **Hand County Brüderhof**

Millfort (1948–present), near Augusta, Montana, is a Hutterite Brüderhof (see **Bon Homme**) that had 97 members in 1964 and was led by Joseph Kleinsasser.

Milltown Brüderhof see **Tripp**

Mixville Association (1843–1844), at the village of Mixville, New York, now known as Wiscoy, was a Fourierist community (see **Social Reform Unity**) said to have numbered 78 members. Although it is not known what goods they produced, they likely made use of the steep drop of some of the waterfalls on Wiscoy Creek to power their workshops.

Modern Times (1851–1860), on 700-800 acres of land at the site of the present town of Brentwood, Long Island, New York, was the third and last anarchist commune established by Josiah Warren (see **Equity**). According to a newspaper report published in April 1853, the community had 70 members at that time. By the end of that year this number had grown to at least 100. The same newspaper item said that a single lot in the community costs only $1.50 to $2 while elsewhere the cost for the same type of property would be $50 to $500.

Most of the houses at Modern Times were constructed of sun-burnt bricks manufactured from lime and gravel by a process Warren had invented some years earlier. Such structures could be built at a very low cost. As he had done at his Equity Store in Cincinnati, Warren based all the work at the commune on each individual's labor time, and no one was permitted to make any kind of profit. Members were paid in labor certificates instead of money. They took pride in the fact that the community had no other rules or formal leadership.

Modern Times was described by an English visitor, A.C. Cuddon, as having "broad avenues, tree-lined streets, and pretty cottages, surrounded by strawberry beds and well-tilled gardens." There were manufacturing enterprises of various kinds, and the members did some farming. There was also a primary school for the small children.

Stephen Pearl Andrews, a well-known sociologist and inventor of an international language (Alwato), was a prominent member. Another was Dr. Thomas Low Nichols, who preached a system of free love and advocated "water cure" methods to heal all ills. After leaving Modern Times, Nichols and his wife set up a health commune in Ohio called the **Memnoia Institute**. Still another member, Henry Edgar, was a leading Comtian Positivist, and, after the demise of Modern Times, tried to set up a Positivist community on the site, but without success. Theron C. Leland, formerly a member of the Board of Directors of the **Sodus Bay Phalanx** and a resident in the **Ontario Union** commune, also joined Modern Times after the Fourierist movement collapsed.

Much opposition to the community came from outsiders because of its supposedly dangerous doctrines of food and sex. Apparently some of the members experimented with strange diets of nuts, fruits, and beans, and other members practiced polygamy. Andrews himself spoke out against the institution of marriage as a social evil, and spoke of the crimes committed in its name, such as prostitution. Eventually the controversy over these ideas reached the pages of the *New York Tribune*, with Andrews defending Warren's views on anarchy and publisher Horace Greeley and author Henry James attacking them.

The 1857 depression undermined the community's manufacturing enterprises, and the Modern Times commune closed in 1860. Books with sections that focus on Modern Times are Bailie's *Josiah Warren* and Calverton's *Where Angels Dared to Tread*.

Modjeska's Farm (1876–1877), at Anaheim, California, was a commune of ten intellectual radicals from Poland who wished to create a second Brook Farm. The participants, bitter over Russian domination of their homeland, emigrated from Kracòw, Poland. They had developed the plans and constitution for the community at the Polish home of Count Charles Bozenta Chalapowski and his actress wife, Helena Modjeska (1840–1909), after whom they named the project.

The members included the Count and his wife; their son, Rudolphe Modjeska; Henryk Sienkiewicz, later to write the best-selling novel *Quo Vadis*; Paprocki, a painter; Julian Sypniewski, his wife, and two children; and Anusia, a 16-year-old girl hired to care for the children. They sent Sienkiewicz and Sypniewski ahead to locate the land for their experiment. The rest followed in July 1876.

Anaheim was chosen for the site because many of the residents there spoke German, a language the Poles could more readily use than English. They lived in a frame house of two bedrooms, a dining room, and a parlor. By the second day in the fields, every member had sore arms and lame backs. Sypniewski was the only one among them with any knowledge of farming, and his experience was with the fundamentally different climate and soil in Poland. A visitor to the farm some weeks after the group was settled reported that he found the members practicing a Wagner opera while one of their mules and a cow were dying from improper food.

After six months, the members of Modjeska's Farm found they had spent $15,000 with no returns. At this point, in the spring of 1877, they sold the property. Most of them were homesick and returned to Poland. Madame Modjeska, however, stayed in the United States and perfected her English. She went back on the stage and experienced many later triumphs with actors Edwin Booth and Otis Skinner. A book with a section that focuses on Modjeska's Farm is Hine's *California's Utopian Communities*.

Mohegan Colony (1923–1969), at Mohegan Lake near Peekskill, New York, was an anarchist community set up by Harry Kelley, who had been one of the founders of the **Ferrer Colony**. He left Ferrer because of a dispute over the leadership there. At its height, the Mohegan Colony had about 300 members. They established a progressive school in 1928, organized much like the Ferrer Modern School. It was closed by 1950.

Life at Mohegan became rich and diverse during the 1930s and 1940s because of the many artists and writers who settled there. There were regular performances of plays, dance recitals and concerts, as well as lectures and poetry readings. Folk singers Pete Seeger and Joan Baez, actor Boris Karloff, and poet Edgar Lee Masters all performed there. Author Richard Wright penned his classic novel, *Native Son*, while living in the colony, and composer Harold Rome wrote several pieces of music there. Writer Mike Gold also stayed there while recuperating from an illness.

In 1966 a nursery school was set up in the partially-abandoned school building. Then, about 1969, with the membership and interest in the communal lifestyle declining rapidly, Mohegan was turned into a homesteaders' association, and it has continued to operate as such ever since. Jacques Rudome was the last commune leader.

In 1995 the membership of the homesteaders' association voted to form a park district in order to spread the cost of maintaining the property among all property owners. Today, old-timers believe the Mohegan Colony is just like any other Westchester County community — a middle-class neighborhood where few residents are aware of the area's anarchist and communal past.

Montecello Colony (1898), at Montecello, Florida, was a cooperative colony that was started in February and failed by September because of "poor land," according to an article in an issue of the *Coming Nation* that was published in 1898. There were perhaps ten members.

Montrose (1950–1967), first at Montrose, Colorado, and then at Palisades, Colorado, was a cooperative community that once had about 35 members. One of these was Griscom Morgan, now the leader of the **Vale** commune in Ohio.

Morehouse Union (1843–1844), located at what is now the village of Piseco, New York, was a Fourierist community (see **Social Reform Unity**) of about 50 members. Their land came from one member, Andrew K. Morehouse, who owned vast acreages in several counties of the state. He offered this mostly woodland property for the commune on condition that the members clear it of trees within a three-year period.

Mr. Morehouse and a relative named Brown were the officers of the commune. Morehouse furnished all the necessities and Brown kept the accounts. The other members, who spent the winter clearing the land and planting rye and potatoes, mostly suffered starvation conditions. By March 1844, most of them had departed in the realization that, according to one member, "the whole would soon fall into the hands of Mr. Morehouse."

Morristown (1874–1876), in Washington County, Utah, was a United Order Mormon commune for two years that was based on the model at **St. George**. It had about 50 members.

Moses Montefiore Colony (1884–1885), in Pratt County, Kansas, was a Jewish agricultural community (see **Sicily**

Island) of about 50 members. They disbanded because these urbanites from Eastern Europe had great difficulties in trying to farm.

Mount Airy (1925–1931), at Croton-on-Hudson, New York, was an anarchist community formed by 35 members from the **Mohegan Colony**. They were led by Harry Kelley, who had earlier participated in setting up both the **Ferrer Colony** and the Mohegan Colony.

Mt. Carmel (1874), Utah, was for a short time a Mormon United Order settlement patterned after the one at **St. George**. It had about 200 members, but they disbanded in a quarrel with 150 of them moving to **Orderville**, where they helped to form that commune.

Mount Lebanon (1787–1947), in Columbia County, New York, about two miles from the town of New Lebanon, was a Shaker community established by Joseph Meacham, a leader of the **Watervliet** Shaker commune. This was the most prosperous of all the Shaker communities, and it was the second Shaker commune to be "gathered." The members owned 3,000 acres of land, much of it on a hillside. At one point Mount Lebanon had as many as 600 members.

In time, Mount Lebanon became the central ministry or directing body for all the Shaker communes, and as such sent three members west to take the Shaker message into Ohio, Indiana, and Kentucky. Most of the early Shaker industries, particularly those of woodworking, were developed at Mount Lebanon. This commune was justifiably famous for its wooden chairs and oval boxes, but the members also manufactured baskets, brooms, floor mops, wire and horsehair sieves, mats, fans, dusters, and medicinal herbs and extracts. They grew sweet corn, garden seeds, and sheep for market.

In 1839 this community had 125 buildings including a new church, school house, infirmary, several barns, tannery, brick shop and kiln, machine shop, sawmill, gristmill, laundry, dairy, blacksmith shop, fulling mill, hatter's shop, three-story woodshed, and many dwellings. The community was noted for its system of wooden aqueducts that carried water to all the kitchens.

Mount Lebanon was the home of Elder Frederick Evans (1808–1893), one of the best known leaders of the Shaker movement. The son of a middle-class English family, he came to the United States in 1820, began a search for the ideal community, and finally joined the Shakers in 1830. He had earlier been associated with the Owenite **Kendal** community. He had also worked with his brother, George Henry Evans, in the printing of *The Workingman's Advocate, The Daily Sentinel, The Bible of Reason,* and *Young America*, all publications that advocated such ideas as freedom of public lands, equal rights for women, the abolition of slavery and wage slavery, and non-imprisonment for debts. Before he joined the Shakers, Evans had been a materialist and free-thinker, and throughout his life he was interested in arbitration, sanitation, dietary reform, and scientific agriculture. He continued to advocate many reforms after he joined the Shakers, calling in newspaper articles and giving speeches in favor of public education for all up to the age of 21, opposition to war, and tolerance for the Mormons. In the field of government he wanted to apply Shaker principles to state legislatures by limiting state senates to women and state houses to men, both bodies to be made up of celibates. He corresponded with Henry George on the single tax issue and with the Russian author Tolstoy on cooperation and nonresistance.

Another prominent member of Mount Lebanon was Daniel Fraser, the son of a Scottish silk weaver. Before Fraser came to the United States in 1834, he worked in Great Britain with Michael Thomas Sadler, a member of Parliament, for the advocacy of child labor laws. His purpose in emigrating was to found a worker's community, but the Mount Lebanon society turned out to be what he was seeking. He wrote articles on many subjects, including the universal ownership of land and equal justice for all men and women, as well as on hygiene and dietetics. For many years Fraser carried on an extensive correspondence about political economy with British writer John Ruskin.

Mount Lebanon was visited by many dignitaries and written about by the noted authors Charles Dickens; Don Lorenzo de Zavala, a Mexican; and Dr. Don Ramon de la Sagra, a Spaniard.

When Mount Lebanon dissolved in 1947, the remaining members moved to the **Hancock** Shaker settlement in Massachusetts. Their property now belongs to the Darrow School, and the Shaker meeting house is that school's library. Books with sections that focus on Mount Lebanon are Andrews' *The People Called Shakers* and Melcher's *The Shaker Adventure*.

Mountain Cove (1851–1860), north of Fayetteville, West Virginia, was a spiritualist commune organized by James D. Scott and Ira S. Hitchcock. The idea for such a community originated out of table rappings at a spiritualist meeting in Auburn, New York.

Mountain Cove had over 100 members who gathered to await the second coming of Christ, which was predicted to take place at this location. The com-mune disbanded when the hopes of the members were not fulfilled. The best known participant was Thomas Lake Harris, a spiritualist preacher and poet who later organized the **Brotherhood of New Life** and **Fountain Grove** spiritualist communes. Books with sections that focus particularly on Mountain Cove are Hine's *California's Utopian Communities* and Noyes' *History of American Socialisms*.

Mutual Aid Cooperative Association (1883–1890), near Glenallen, Missouri, was a communal settlement of 25 members established by Alcander Longley (see **Fourier Phalanx**). Almost nothing is known about this experiment except that all the property of the members was held in common, in accord with Longley's Christian communist principles, and that it probably closed because of a lack of capital.

Mutual Home Association (1896–1909), bordering the waterfront of Puget Sound, 13 miles west of Tacoma, Washington, was a cooperative colony established by advocates of socialism who followed the teachings of Edward Bellamy (see **Ruskin Commonwealth**). The founding members were Oliver A. Verity, George H. Allen, and Frank Odell, all of whom had been members of the earlier **Glennis Cooperative Industrial Company**.

By 1905 there were 120 persons in the Mutual Home Association, and they owned more than 200 acres of land and 68 homes. Members joined by paying into the common treasury an amount equal to the price of the land they planned to farm. Each person was permitted to start any industry they wished, the land being the only thing they held in common. An elected board of trustees conducted affairs for the community. Eventually the commune had two blacksmith shops, a carpenter shop, several other businesses, and a weekly newspaper called *Discontent: Mother of Progress.*

Elbert Hubbard, essayist, lecturer, and founder of the **Roycrofters** Community, visited and gave a lecture there. Other visitors included many radicals, such as Bill Haywood of the Industrial Workers of the World (IWW), and Communist Party leaders William Z. Foster and Elizabeth Gurley Flynn. In time the commune became a center for anarchists. Emma Goldman, the great anarchist leader and orator, gave lectures there, and one of the members, James Edward Morton, Jr., widely promoted the anarchist cause. Portraits of revolutionary heros — Karl Marx, Ferdinand Lassalle, Peter Kropotkin, and Michael Bakunin — hung on the school room walls.

In 1901, three members were arrested — on the basis of the notorious Comstock Act that was often used during that period to suppress radical and unpopular views — for mailing obscene literature. They were quickly acquitted, but shortly thereafter two women members were indicted on the same charge because of their books and articles relating to sex and the emancipation of women. One of them was convicted and fined $100. Also the federal authorities often delayed and interfered with the commune's mailing of their *Discontent* newspaper.

By 1908 the Mutual Home Association was beginning to decline as a commune. An amendment to their articles of incorporation, adopted in 1909, allowed for the sale of property to individual owners. This depleted the holdings of the association and ended its promise of available land for incoming members. However the area remained a center where anarchists and other radicals could live in relatively isolated comfort until long after World War II. Books with sections that focus on the Mutual Home Association are Hinds' *American Communities* and LeWarne's *Utopias on Puget Sound, 1885–1915.*

Mutual Land Emigration and Cooperative Colonization Company (1869–1874), in Nehama County, Kansas, was organized in London, England, by James Redford and James Murray. They recruited about 50 families (perhaps 150 people) to join the cooperative farming venture, which was located on 740 acres. When the cooperative nature of the experiment ended for reasons unknown, many of the participants remained in the area as individual farmers.

Nantmel (1747–1752), in Chester County, Pennsylvania, was a Seventh-day Baptist commune established near the present-day village of Knauertown. It was organized by Israel Seymour, a sailor and a pirate captain before his religious conversion. He joined the Seventh-day Baptist community at **Ephrata** and later the **Broad River** Seventh-day Baptist commune, but he stayed at neither of them for very long, finding life there too strict. Seymour next went to Chester County as an evangelist for the Seventh-day Baptist movement and, with the help of some Brothers from Ephrata, erected a community house for the new commune. It was modeled on the plan at Ephrata, with both sexes, though separated, being housed in the same building. Nantmel had about ten members.

Although Seymour agreed to follow the celibacy rule of Ephrata at Nantmel, he was never really happy with it. He fell in love with Johanna Henrich

Hagemann, a young woman who had been sent from Ephrata to perfect her English under Seymour's tutelage. The resulting marriage, an unhappy one, broke up the Nantmel settlement.

Seymour afterward reportedly engaged in a series of frauds that resulted in the death of his father-in-law, the abandonment of his wife, and his own flight to South Carolina, where he enlisted in the army to fight the Indians. During one engagement, his horse was shot out from under him and he had to be rescued by fellow soldiers. This close escape so affected Seymour that he vowed to mend his ways.

He retired from the army and soon began plans to establish another Seventh-day Baptist commune without the authorization of the leadership at Ephrata.

Narcoosee (1894–1898), on East Tohopekaliga Lake, 21 miles south of Orlando, Florida, was a seven-member Shaker colony organized by Benjamin Gates of the **Mount Lebanon** Shaker commune, after that commune purchased 7,000 acres of land at this location for a new settlement. The members had 900 head of cattle, fruit trees, rice fields, grape vines, and even a windmill with a 5,000-gallon water tank for irrigation purposes. But they gave up this unprofitable venture in 1898, and a small tourist camp now occupies the site.

Nashoba (1825–1828), established on 2,000 acres of land bordering the Wolf River in Tennessee, about 14 miles west of Memphis, was founded by British author and advocate of women's equality, Frances Wright (1795–1852), as a means of freeing slaves. It was her plan to purchase 50 to 100 slaves, educate them, and free them after a period of work in the communal atmosphere.

The example, she argued, "would eventually lead to the ending of slavery, this country's greatest social evil."

She communicated her plans to the former presidents Thomas Jefferson, James Madison, and James Monroe, as well as to Chief Justice John Marshall, and to future president Andrew Jackson. Both Jefferson and Madison approved, but with caution. Jackson suggested that she purchase some of the newly acquired Indian Territory land in Tennessee, formerly owned by the Chickasaw Indians, which she did. The name that she chose, Nashoba, was the name the Indians had for the area.

Wright also published a pamphlet describing her plans that cited the Moravian, Shaker, and Rappite communes as examples of the success of communitarianism. However, she was the most enthusiastic about Robert Owen's **New Harmony** commune, visiting there many times to lecture and get support from its members for her project. She patterned Nashoba as closely as she could after New Harmony, and she traveled to Europe in 1827 with Robert Dale Owen to raise money for her project.

Nashoba was open not only to freed slaves but to "good men of all countries" who could come there to live, teach, and manage the affairs of the commune. The settlement got underway with the purchase and gift of 12 slaves. Wright and her sister, George Flower and his family, and James Richardson moved there as well. At one point there were about 40 persons living at Nashoba, including 30 partially freed slaves. There were a number of visitors who came to see how the project was progressing. One of these was British author Frances Trollope, who wrote about Nashoba in her book *Domestic Manners of the Americans*.

Trollope found the project disappointing, and her stay there was brief.

Unfortunately while Wright was in Europe raising funds, she left Nashoba in the hands of one of the white members, James Richardson, an unfortunate choice. He preached equality of sex relations between the slave women and the white men of the community, and the reports of this caused a great scandal among outside supporters of the project. At the same time the hope that the slaves would follow their patron's example of hard work and self-education was proving a failure. Having just been freed from the overseer's whip, and unable to appreciate Wright's idealism, they took advantage of their situation by loafing and indulging themselves.

There were other difficulties as well, hinted at by this report that appeared in the *Nashoba Gazette*, the commune's newspaper. "If there be introduced into such a society thoughts of evil and unkindness, feelings of intolerance and words of dissension, it can not prosper. That which produces in the world only commonplace jealousies and everyday squabbles, is sufficient to destroy a community."

In December 1827, Wright turned over the estate to a board of trustees that included her sister Camilla Wright; James Richardson and George Flower of Nashoba; General Lafayette, who was a close friend of hers; Robert Owen, his son Robert Dale Owen and William Maclure of New Harmony; Richardson Whitby, who had been educated in a Shaker commune and then lived at both New Harmony and Nashoba; and Cadwallader Colden and Robert Jenkins, both of whom had taken a great interest in the commune.

But by February 1, 1828, Frances Wright and Robert Dale Owen realized that the plan was failing, so they decided to abandon it. Nashoba was closed that year. Wright then moved to New Harmony to help Owen edit the *New Harmony Gazette* until 1830. As a final act on behalf of the black residents of Nashoba, she sailed with them to Haiti in January 1830, where their emancipation was completed. On her return to the United States, Wright went on a series of nationwide lecture tours. She defended equal rights for women, attacked religion and the influence of churches in politics, and attacked the existing system of education based on authority. She further discussed birth control, more equal property distribution, and the need for workers to organize politically. In 1831 she married William Phiquepal D'Arusmout, a coworker of hers when she was living at New Harmony. The marriage ended in divorce. But to the end of her life she argued for the gradual emancipation of slaves through education. Books with sections that focus on Nashoba are Bestor's *Backwoods Utopias: The Sectarian and Owenite Phases of Communitarian Socialism in America, 1663–1828* and Madison's *Critics and Crusaders*.

Nauvoo (1839–1846), at Nauvoo, Illinois, was the largest of the Mormon United Order settlements (see **Kirtland**). Before the first Mormons moved to this location, it was a place of only six or seven dwellings called Commerce. But with their arrival, the city grew at an amazing speed. They named it "Nauvoo" because the word means "beautiful place" in Hebrew. Within five years it had become the largest city in Illinois, greatly surpassing Chicago in size. In 1841 the population was over 3,000, and in 1842 it increased to about 10,000. By October 1845 it was reported that Nau-

Stone carving retrieved from the Mormon Temple ruins at Nauvoo after the building was destroyed by an arsonist (photo by author).

voo had a population of 20,000 and between 7,000 and 8,000 houses. With such a large population, it was virtually impossible to maintain the communal nature of the United Order system. The church leadership began to encourage a system of tithing wherever the United Order broke down. However the United Order remained the ideal for which Mormons were expected to strive throughout their sojourn at Nauvoo.

The residents dug drainage ditches to overcome the problem of low and swampy land infested by malaria mosquitoes. This drainage left the area with fertile river bottom land for farming. A hill site was designated for a temple, and the business district was plotted.

Joseph Smith, Jr., the founder of the Mormon religion, was fortunate in securing a liberal charter from the state of Illinois that permitted the Nauvoo leaders to levy and disburse taxes, set up their own courts, and maintain an independent militia. A charter was also granted to their university, the first municipal university in the United States. Its president was a graduate of Trinity College, Dublin, and the courses taught included mathematics, languages, ancient and modern literature, church history, and other subjects.

One million dollars was raised for the construction of the temple, an elaborate building that combined Venetian, Egyptian, Grecian, and Byzantine architecture. It was built of gray limestone and its baptismal fount was supported by 12 carved oxen. The city newspaper, *Times and Seasons*, unfortunately says little about the economy of Nauvoo. Its pages are mostly filled with religious and political matters. However, there were at least a few mills, a wagon shop, two quarries, and a match and powder factory. The main economic base was farming.

The more successful this city and the Mormons became, the more hostile grew their neighbors. But the militia of Nauvoo held would-be attackers at bay. Smith, desiring a political climate more favorable to the community, announced his own candidacy for president of the United States. Sidney Rigdon ran as the vice-presidential candidate. Smith reasoned that, because the Mormons represented such a large voting block in the state, they might gain enough votes to force enactment of the legislation they were promoting. Among other things, Smith advocated that the U.S. government should purchase all slaves and grant them immediate emancipation.

On election day in 1844, the Mormons were met at polling places by mobs intent on preventing them from voting. Shortly afterward Smith himself was arrested with his brother Hyrum on trumped-up charges of rioting and treason. Both were subsequently killed on June 7, 1844, by an angry mob that stormed the Carthage, Illinois, jail in which they were being held.

The state legislature then moved to repeal the charter they had given Nauvoo, and orders were issued directing the Mormons to leave Illinois. Most of the residents left Nauvoo early in 1846 and headed west under the leadership of Brigham Young. He was then president of the Council of Twelve, the ruling body of the church. These Mormons eventually settled in Utah.

But not all the Mormons at Nauvoo accepted Young's leadership. The members of Smith's own family refused to go with him and remained in Nauvoo. Rigdon led a faction of his supporters away from Nauvoo to settle in Pittsburgh, Pennsylvania. Lyman Wight led his group from Nauvoo to Texas, where they established **Zodiac**. James Strang took followers to Wisconsin and set up the **Voree** commune. Charles B. Thompson went to Iowa and started **Preparation**. Alpheus Cutler, Austin Cowles, James Emmet, and Gladden Bishop, all leading members of the church, also led different groups to other places. Cowles, Emmet, and Bishop did not start new communes, but the followers of Cutler did at Cliterall, Minnesota, where they are known as the **Cutlerite Mormons**.

Much of the property at Nauvoo was damaged or destroyed after the Mormons left, even though a small band of Mormons and "Jack Mormons" (gentile friends) fought gallantly against the large force of anti–Mormons in defense of the city. The great temple, which was nearly completed, was burned to the ground. A group of French socialists in 1849 leased the land from the few remaining Mormons to set up a different kind of commune there, **Icarian Nauvoo**.

Today much of the swampy land that the Nauvoo residents drained for their farms is completely covered by water stored above the Keokuk Dam. Dozens of historically interesting Mormon buildings that have since been restored and can be visited include the Joseph Smith homestead and the old Mansion House, or hotel, that stands nearby. Visitors can also see the graves of Joseph, Emma, and Hyrum Smith near the homestead. Books with sections that focus on Nauvoo are Davis' *The Story of the Church* and Flanders' *Nauvoo: Kingdom on the Mississippi*.

Nazareth (1743–1844), at Nazareth, Pennsylvania, was a Moravian General Economy community whose first members came from **Savannah**, the earliest of the American Moravian communes, after Savannah disbanded. The members purchased 5,000 acres of land for their community from George Whitfield, a man later to become a leader among the American Methodists. The site was 12 miles north of **Bethlehem**, another Moravian commune. They built homes, a church, and divided the community into four villages: Nazareth, Gnadenthal, Christiansbrunn, and Friedensthal. A noted school for boys was started at Nazareth in 1743.

As at Bethlehem, the Nazareth members gave up their General Economy system in 1762, turning instead to the Herrnhut system of management used at the Moravian communities in Europe. And before the Herrnhut system was disbanded in 1844, the population of Nazareth grew to about 800 members. The town of Nazareth was incorporated in 1856.

One large building, Whitfield House, or Ephrata as it was called by the Moravians, was completed in 1755. It can still be seen, as can the Gray House, a log cabin built in 1740. This is the oldest remaining Moravian building in Pennsylvania.

Nazareth House (1941), at Ramsey, Illinois, was a Catholic Worker farm (see **Maryfarm** on Staten Island) that probably had about ten members. It was in operation for only a few months.

Nehalem Valley Cooperative Colony (1886–1892), at Mist, Oregon, was organized on December 5, 1886, as the Columbia Cooperative Colony. The 50 members, all lumberjacks, held their property collectively. They paid a membership fee of $500 to join, which could be paid in either cash or goods. The men worked together eight hours each day in the lumbering trade, and their aim was to provide "houses and employment for members," with "justice for all." The community is said to have failed because of "surrounding opposition and lack of funds."

Neudorf *see* **Tripp**

Nevada Colony (1916–1918), at Fallon, Nevada, was a community of 150 socialists established by C.V. Eggleston (1855–?), a former treasurer for the **Llano del Rio** commune in California. The members lived in adobe houses, engaged in farming, and published *The Nevada Colonist*. Their 1,600 acres were good for farming and well-irrigated by the waters of the Lahonton Dam. But preparations for the settlement were inadequate. The members had been promised schools and industries at the time they joined, and none of these were provided.

Many complaints about Eggleston's leadership resulted in his expulsion. R.E. Bray (1862–?) then assumed the leadership, but apparently he was no better as an organizer. The colony finally closed, most of the members having already left to join in the efforts of World War I or for the purpose of metal prospecting in the Nevada and Arizona desert. The colony was greatly in debt when it closed. There are no remnants. A book with a section that focuses on the Nevada Colony is Wooster's *Communities of the Past and Present*.

New Elm Springs (1900–1918), on the James River about eight miles from Dimock, South Dakota, was a Hutterite Brüderhof (see **Bon Homme**) of about 100 members. They moved to Alberta, Canada, in 1918, and still maintain the commune there today. Their land in South Dakota was occupied in 1936 by Hutterites from Canada who thus formed a second **New Elm Springs** Brüderhof.

New Elm Springs (1936–present), on the border of Hutchinson and Hanson counties, South Dakota, is a Hutterite Brüderhof (see **Bon Homme**) formed by Hutterites from Canada. In 1964 they had 125 members and were led by Sam Wollman.

New England Committee for Nonviolent Action Farm (1962–1972), just west of Voluntown, Connecticut, was a pacifist community started by Robert and Marjorie Swann as a training school for nonviolent action. This commune was also called the Polaris Action Farm because of the leadership that the members gave to the campaign to stop the launching of Polaris nuclear submarines.

The members occupied a 200-year-old farmhouse, raised their own food on the farm, and occasionally worked for local farmers. They numbered about ten, although there were usually many students and visitors living for short periods of time at the commune as well.

Most of the energies and time of the members were directed to peace actions (walks, pickets, and civil disobedience demonstrations) throughout the eastern United States, and most of them spent time in jail because of their protests against the military machine. Several times hostile war-supporting neighbors entered the community to attack them and throw rocks through the windows of their house, and in 1966 antagonists burned down their barn. The members published a monthly, *Direct Action*, said to have had over 2,000 subscribers. An article with information that focuses on the New England Committee for Nonviolent Action Farm can be found in the *New York Times*, November 29, 1965, "Even Pacifism Requires Training: A Nonviolent Group Learning Art of Self Defense."

New Gloucester *see* **Sabbathday Lake Village**

New Harmony (1825–1828), in Indiana, where the present town of New Harmony is located, was the first and largest of several communes established by the followers of Robert Owen. The land was formerly the site of Rapp's **Harmony** community in that state. Owen purchased the 30,000 acres with his own money, $150,000.

Communitarian-evangelist Robert Owen (1771–1858) was born at Newton, Wales. He left school at age 9 to work as a cotton spinner. By 1799 he had become part owner and head of the New Lanark cotton mills in Scotland. There he organized a model community in which, instead of employing children in the mills, he built schools for them. He kept the mills in good repair and tried to take care of his laborer's needs. Owen's basic tenet was "circumstances form character." He wrote extensively on the subject of proper social conditions and tried to get the British government interested in building "villages of cooperation." He believed these villages should be partly agricultural and partly industrial. In time he decided to establish one himself in the United States and thus show that the scheme was practical.

Even before Owen's autumn 1824 arrival in the United States, small but active societies had sprung up in various cities to promote his plans for setting up communal villages. The New York Society for Promoting Communities planned to set up one around 1820 in Virginia. Another was planned for

New Harmony Dormitory Number Two, built by the Rappites in 1822, was used as a school by the Owenites (New Harmony State Historic Site).

Kentucky in 1822, and one for somewhere in the West in 1823. Edward P. Page petitioned Congress to grant land in Florida for such a settlement, also in 1823. And in that year a group in Philadelphia projected a community in which members of the Philadelphia Academy of Sciences showed great interest. None of these plans came to fruition, although some of the Philadelphia scientists joined New Harmony after it was established.

Owen traveled widely in 1825, announcing to vast audiences that he had "come to this country to introduce an entire new system of society; to change it from an ignorant, selfish system to an enlightened social system which shall gradually unite all interests into one, and remove all causes for contest between individuals." Humankind, he argued, is but a creature of the environment. Change the environment and within a short time people will change.

Owen's message stirred the enthusiasm of the nation as few speakers have

before or since. President John Quincy Adams, for example, made a special trip to the old Hall of Representatives in the Capitol to hear Owen give a three-hour lecture. It was only the fourth day of Adams' presidency. That very afternoon Congress had battled over the most controversial of his nominations to the Cabinet, that of Henry Clay to be secretary of state. Few men would have been willing to sit through a three-hour speech on anything by anyone after such a day. Yet here was the president listening in rapt attention to Owen's lecture advocating a system of voluntary communism. And with President Adams in the audience was his predecessor, James Monroe, together with some of the justices of the Supreme Court and many members of Congress.

The same was true in other lecture halls. City fathers and social leaders everywhere turned out to hear Owen speak about establishing "villages of cooperation" across the land. The fact that Owen was a rich, self-made industrialist gave him credentials that people in this new and rapidly-industrializing nation could well appreciate.

Within a matter of months Owen had established his New Harmony commune in Indiana, and because it was located on the land formerly occupied and developed by the members of Rapp's commune, it included a regularly laid out village with streets running at right angles to one another. There was a public square surrounded by large brick buildings that the Rappites had formerly used for a church, a school, and other community purposes. Owen's followers had little difficulty in turning these structures into housing, workshops, and assembly halls. However there was widespread criticism when the Owenites turned the large, brick Rappite church to secular uses. The press failed to note that a second church at New Harmony was made available by the members to any preacher who wished to use it.

By the summer of 1825, 800 colonists had gathered at New Harmony, most of them coming from the small but active societies that had formed across the country to promote Owen's plans. Owen himself did not move there, but he put one of his sons, William, in charge of preparing for its occupants. The father continued to lecture throughout the country about the advantages of cooperation. The number of members increased to 900 by October. Among these were some prominent intellectuals, including the noted geologists William Maclure and Gerald Troost, zoologist Thomas Say, botanist Charles Alexander Le Sueur, and the well-known educators Joseph Neef and Madame Fretegeot.

Other prominent members included Thomas Pears, a Pittsburgh capitalist; William Pelham, a newspaperman and former Ohio postmaster; Josiah

Warren, an anarchist who later established **Equity** and two other anarchist communes; and Frances Wright, the British author and advocate of women's equality who founded the **Nashoba** commune.

All able-bodied persons were expected to work under the guidance of a committee appointed by Owen, and all received "labor credits" for their work, which they could exchange for food and other goods at the New Harmony public store.

Life in the community, at least for the first few months, was varied, enlightened, and rather carefree. A weekly dance was held on Tuesday nights. Concerts were on Thursday and Friday. Wednesday was the evening for public discussion, and there were frequent lectures on a variety of subjects such as religion, economics, and science. Parades and drills, meetings of the Female Social Society and the Philanthropic Lodge of Masons filled the week with social activities.

The approximately 200 children were regarded as belonging to the community and lived together away from their parents. The educational plan for them, which was somewhat based on principles developed by the Swiss educator Johann Pestallozzi, was to train them for the first five years in the efficient use of their bodies through physical exercise. For the next five years the children were to learn by observation and to be given some practical work experience. Then they were to be taught definite occupations, philosophy and scientific knowledge. Finally, they were to receive technical training.

Because of the success of this educational program, the New Harmony commune is now considered to be the birthplace for several common U.S. institutions. Among these are the first kindergarten, the first infant school, the first trade school, and the first free library.

Although the educational program was good, the level of production at New Harmony was not. According to the otherwise rather positive report that appeared in the October 1825 issue of the *New Harmony Gazette*, the commune had only 137 skilled craftsmen out of a population of about 900, including 17 boot and shoe makers, 8 hat manufacturers, a butcher, a baker, a brewer, a tailor, a blacksmith, and some carpenters and bricklayers. The community also lacked agriculturists, for the list included only 36 farmers and field laborers, and 2 gardeners. The author of the *Gazette* article continued, "With the machinery now on hand, our operations in the wool business should turn out one hundred and sixty pounds of yarn per day, but the want of spinners reduces the business much below that amount. The fulling and dressing departments have, at present, neither regular superintendents or workmen; consequently they are not prosecuted with effect. The cotton-spinning establishment is equal to producing between three and four hundred pounds of yarn per week, and is under very good direction; but skillful and steady hands are much wanting, which time will furnish from our present population. The dyehouse is a spacious brick building, furnished with copper vessels capable of containing between 1,500 and 2,000 gallons; and will probably compare in convenience with any other in the United States. At present, this valuable establishment is doing nothing, for want of a skillful person to undertake the direction of it."

Reports of the residents show that what was lacking was not primarily "skillful persons" but persons who wished to work at all. The community was apparently filled with people who wanted to be supported by Owen's generosity without having to do much to deserve it. There was constant bickering among the members and arguments over authority and commune assignments. And, according to one visitor, throughout the two and a half years that Owen's New Harmony existed the members "continued strangers to each other in spite of all their meetings, their balls, their frequent occasions of congregating in the hall, and all their pretense of cooperation."

One particularly destructive member, Paul Brown, kept insisting that Owen turn over all his holdings at New Harmony and all he owned elsewhere to the entire membership. Brown also argued against the keeping of account books as unbecoming to a communal society.

By January 1826 Owen, somewhat in despair, ended his direct leadership of New Harmony and replaced this with a Community Equality, which provided for lawmaking to be in the hands of an assembly of all male residents. About March, there was a split that resulted in the formation of two new communities, each taking possession of different parts of the commune land while the original commune retained the rest. One of these was formed by about 70 English farmers who had come as a group to participate in the experiment and had soon become disgusted with the way farming was carried on at New Harmony. They called their establishment Febia-Paveli after a translation of the area's latitude and longitude into letters of the alphabet. The other was named Macluria in honor of William Maclure, a geologist. It had about 150 members, most of whom were the families of backwoodsmen, according to a visitor.

Still another breakoff group, intended to be composed of the most intellectual members, was planned but never successfully established. It included Maclure, Robert L. Jennings, a former Universalist minister, and two of Owen's sons, William and Robert Dale. This group wanted to take over the main part of New Harmony and exclude all the "summer soldiers and sunshine patriots" who crowded the settlement. The elder Robert Owen, however, recognized the danger in this approach and squelched the plan before his sons and the others could implement it.

Owen in May then reorganized New Harmony into four occupational divisions and introduced paper money for trade. In September he reorganized it again, this time as a "trust" under the dictates of three managers. In January 1827, Owen tried still once more to reorganize the community but failed. By April he was selling the property to individuals, and he himself departed for England in June. The last remnants of the New Harmony commune died early in 1828.

Despite the rapid dissolution of New Harmony, much can be said for Owen's theories and teachings in other areas of social progress. He exerted a particularly powerful influence on the English labor movement, and the famous Rochdale consumer cooperative, started by British weavers in 1844, was among the products of his thought. In *Socialism, Utopian and Scientific*, the Marxist Friedrich Engels stated that almost every progressive activity in England during the 19th century bore the mark of Owen's work.

The town of New Harmony, after the dissolution of the commune, became a center for scientists and engineers, many of whom were originally attracted there by hopes for the experiment. The Minerva Club, the first organized women's society in the United States, was started at New Harmony, as was the Workingmen's Institute that set up libraries and workers clubs throughout Indiana and Illinois. The Thespian Society, a drama club established by former New Harmony commune members who continued to live in the area, lasted for 50 years. Furthermore, the presence at New Harmony of Maclure's large collection of geological works was probably responsible for the town being the headquarters for the U.S. Geological Survey from 1839 to 1856.

Owen's son, Robert Dale Owen, stayed in Indiana after his father returned to England and later won a seat in the Indiana state legislature where he tried to improve the legal standing of women. He was largely responsible for the improved state divorce laws and for the state's providing free tax-supported schools. He was elected to the U.S. Congress in 1843, where he was an advocate of birth control, universal education, and the abolition of slavery. He introduced the bill into Congress that helped establish the Smithsonian Institution, and he served as minister to Naples from 1855 to 1858.

A visit to New Harmony today can be quite rewarding. Among the Rappite buildings that can be seen are a two-story community house, some factory buildings, and some smaller homes. Homes that were built by Owen's followers are also still standing, including Robert Dale Owen's house and a house that had been used by Rapp and then added to by geologist William Maclure. Books with sections that focus on New Harmony are Bestor's *Backwoods Utopias: The Sectarian and Owenite Phases of Communitarian Socialism in America, 1663–1828*, Harvey's *Robert Owen,*

Social Idealist, and Noyes' *History of American Socialisms*.

New Harmony (1874–1877), Utah, a town named after the famous commune established by Robert Owen, was for three years a Mormon United Order settlement patterned after the one established at **St. George**. It had about 75 members.

New Helvetia (1844–1846), by the Osage River, about five miles from Westphalia, Missouri, was a 43-member Swiss commune founded by utopian novelist and labor leader Andreas Dietsch (1807–1845). He was a self-educated brush maker from Alsace who had moved to Switzerland and written a book projecting a utopian society, *Das tausent jährige Reich* (The Millennium).

The book's hero, a traveling journeyman, comes upon a utopian colony where everyone is cheerful and busy, though there is no compulsion to work. The novel's colony is the result of the generosity of a benevolent nobleman who has turned over his castle and land to the communalists. The hero plans to remain in the place and marry one of the young women when the novel ends with the author's wife poking him in the ribs to wake him up. At the heart of Dietsch's suggestions, in both his later pamphlets on political matters and in this novel, was the hope for the patronage of some rich benefactor in order to set his utopian scheme in motion. No such benefactor appeared, however, though his book had enough appeal to attract a large number of followers.

In 1843 Dietsch decided to start his utopian colony in Missouri, which he had read would be a good area for colonization. He reached St. Louis on August 31, 1844, with 42 of his followers, 18 of them children. They included two tailors, two cabinet makers, a brick maker, a mechanic, three blacksmiths, a furrier, and a bookbinder. Dietsch, with a committee of eight, went to Westphalia, then a town of log cabins, and contracted for 363 acres of land on which to start the commune.

One of Dietsch's friends who he was planning to take with him to the United States was William Weitling (see **Communia**). But Weitling was jailed for blasphemy in Zurich just before Dietsch departed. Weitling later did come to the country and he participated in the leadership of **Communia**, but this was after Dietsch had died.

Life at New Helvetia was not what Dietsch's followers had expected. They disliked the weather since they were not used to the rapid changes in the Midwestern climate, and they had trouble procuring sufficient food for the entire colony. Disease was also a problem. They built one large log house, which was so inadequate that some of the members had to live with farm families in nearby Westphalia. Also there was much dissension and there were charges that the management was mishandling funds. The commune was finally disbanded after Dietsch died. Some of the members then moved to Communia.

The records of Osage County show that Rosetta Dietsch, one of his daughters, sold the tract of land in 1859. It is today owned by William Vogel. In 1947, a search of the land revealed a number of troughs to indicate a burial place near what was once the New Helvetia house and garden. Also found was a rusty pair of broken scissors. A book with a section that focuses on New Helvetia is Wittke's *We Who Built America: The Saga of the Immigrant*.

New House of Israel (1895–1920), between the towns of Livingston and

Leggett in Polk County, Texas, was established by a sect from Canada known as the Flying Roll, or the Israelites. They were a vegetarian group that followed the Mosaic law. The male members wore long hair and beards. They built a church on their 144-acre tract of land, which they named the New House of Israel. The land had been donated to them by a family that they converted in the area. Eventually this commune grew in size to 75 families, perhaps 250 people. When their "high priest" died, no one took his place and the families began to move away. By the middle 1920s, the commune had become a ghost town.

New Icaria (1878–1898), at Corning, Iowa, was a 39-member community of Cabet's followers (see **Icaria** in Texas) formed after the breakup of Corning's **Icaria**. It was composed of the older, more staid members of that community. The rest formed **Jeune Icarie**.

New Jerusalem (1788–1844), on the west bank of the Seneca Lake between the present towns of Dundee to the south and Dresden to the north, was established in August 1788 by the followers of Jemima Wilkinson (1752–1819). It had 260 members by 1790.

Wilkinson was a farmer's daughter whose interest in religion was aroused when she heard a sermon by George Whitfield, the noted Methodist evangelist. Several years later, during a severe illness, she went into a prolonged trance and claimed she had died and was now inhabited by the "Spirit of Life" come from God "to warn a lost and guilty, gossiping, dying world to flee from the wrath to come." In 1776 she took the name "Public Universal Friend" and began to hold open air meetings. This was during the post–

Revolutionary War period in the United States, a time when there was wide interest in prophetic messages about how God was acting as the punisher of corrupt religion and politics. Wilkinson's pleasant countenance and magnetic personality attracted many.

The "Friend" was soon leading processions on horseback through Rhode Island and Connecticut, establishing churches at New Milford, Connecticut, and East Greenwich and South Kingston, Rhode Island. Among her supporters were R.I. William Potter, a former state treasurer of Rhode Island; James Parker, a prominent judge in that state; and Stephen Hopkins, the governor of Connecticut.

But there was much opposition to her preaching from people who charged she was breaking up families by her call to celibacy. She went to Philadelphia in 1783 where she was at first well received by the local Quakers who liked the fact that she opposed slavery and conducted worship in much the way they did. She preached to large audiences in that city, but again faced hostility. Stones were thrown at her when she tried to speak at Worcester, about 25 miles from Philadelphia. However at Worcester she did convert, among others, David Wagener and members of his family. He later became a leading member of the New Jerusalem commune.

The "Friend" returned to New England in 1787 with plans to establish the New Jerusalem settlement. She delegated three followers — Richard Smith, Thomas Hathaway, and Abraham Dayton — to find the right location, and by August 1788, 25 persons, among whom were Judge Parker and his family, moved onto the Seneca Lake location. But the "Friend" was not among them, as she had nearly drowned crossing a river on horseback and was recovering

Jemima Wilkinson's home, now a private residence, stands on a hill a distance away from her New Jerusalem commune (photo by author).

from the illness that followed. She did not join the commune until two years later, although she was kept well informed about its progress by Sarah Richards, one of the members who visited the "Friend" regularly to report on activities there.

The early settlers suffered from lack of food and the hardness of the winter, but they were able to trade with the surrounding Indians for some of their necessities. They planted about 12 acres and made an application to Governor George Clinton for a grant of more land. Eventually they were able to acquire a total of 14,040 acres, which they held in common. The land was surveyed into lots and divided among them, some members getting more and some less, according to their ability. Their primary crop was wheat. They erected a grist mill, saw mill, log meeting house, and fine home for Wilkinson, the "Public Universal Friend."

The members were industrious, held worship services much like Quaker meetings, and expressed their opposition to slavery, insisting that slaveholders set their subjects free. At least one escaped slave, Cloe Towerhill, was a member of this commune. The "Public Universal Friend" also had the respect of the Indians in the area, who called her "great woman preacher." Some historians give her credit for helping to pacify the Indians of western New York state, an unsettled region prior to her arrival.

In time, however, dissension arose over the allotment of the plots of land. Judge Parker and William Potter broke with the "Friend," engaging her in a legal battle that was poorly settled and resulted in the jailing of one member, George Sisson, for the debts. Another suit over the land was instituted at a later date by Enoch Malin and his wife, Eliza Richards, daughter of Sarah Richards. The two had eloped to be secretly married. The case was not settled until long after the death of the "Friend," though to the advantage of the commune.

Troubles within the colony

became so severe that it was decided to send Abraham Dayton to Canada to find new land to which they might all move. Dayton, a former Quaker, convinced the governor of Canada to grant his request for land, but the governor then rescinded the agreement when he discovered that these communalists were not "true Quakers." He gave the land only to Dayton and his family. At this point Dayton decided to abandon New Jerusalem and move to Canada.

Another problem that beset the community was the gradual withdrawal of the "Friend" from the rest of the members. She developed a habit of demanding gifts from her followers, saying, "The Friend hath need of these things." Then, after a new house was completed for her about 20 miles from the center of the settlement, she moved there and became somewhat of a recluse, seldom participating in the life of the community. This house is still standing is is designated by a historical marker. Following the death of the "Friend," this house became a shrine for her followers. It is now a private residence and stands four miles north of the present town of Branchport.

In her final years, the "Friend" suffered from dropsy and lost her early beauty, even to the point of becoming disfigured. Lucy Brown, Rachel Malin, and Margaret Malin were the attendants in her last hours of illness. She died on July 1, 1819, and was buried on a hillside near her house.

The community continued until 1844 under the leadership of Rachel and Margaret Malin. After Margaret Malin died, leadership passed to James Brown, Jr., who accepted a division of the estate and dissolution of the commune. In these latter years there was much dissension among the members. This apparently was caused by three late-comers to the community — Michael H. Barton, who arrived in 1830, George Clark, and Osa Hymes. Barton left the community in anger, later going to Ohio to campaign for the election of President Harrison. The early death of the president eclipsed his hopes for a political appointment.

Rachel Malin died in 1848 and the remainder of the estate was conveyed to her relatives. The "Friend's" mansion went to the wife of George Clark. It was later purchased as a home for disabled soldiers, and then it went into private hands. A book with a section that focuses on New Jerusalem is Cleveland's *History and Directory of Yates County*.

New Meadow Run (1957–present), at Farmington, Pennsylvania, also called the Farmington Brüderhof or the Oak Lake Community, is a commune established by members of the Society of Brothers (see **Woodcrest**). They own a former luxury hotel and are led by Eberhard Arnold, Jr., the son of the founder of the Society of Brothers in Germany. There are about 200 members. When the **Macedonia Cooperative** commune closed in 1957, its remaining members joined New Meadow Run.

New Mexico Molokan Colony (1924), near Raton, New Mexico, was a Molokan farming commune (see **Freedom Colony**) of perhaps 30 members. There was another Molokan commune, the **Raton Molokan Colony**, nearby, and the members undoubtedly kept in close touch with one another.

New Norway *see* **Oleana**

New Odessa (1882–1888), near Glendale, Oregon, was a Jewish agricultural commune (see **Sicily Island**) that was set up by Jewish university students and idealistic communists from Southwestern Russia. They went under the name "Sons of the Free," and they originally gathered together in a cooperative housing arrangement on Pell Street in New York City, which they called Am Olam. There they became acquainted with William Frey (Vladimir Konstantinovich Geins) who, though not Jewish, had communal experience in running the **Progressive Community** of Cedar Vale, Kansas. They asked Frey to help them establish their New Odessa commune.

With his help, they located 750 acres of land in Douglas County, Oregon, and the 25 youth, some of whom had gained experience working for private farmers near Hartford, Connecticut, moved to Oregon to start their commune. At first they tried to grow oats, wheat, barley, and potatoes, but only about one-fourth of their land was cultivatable. Then they cut trees to market for railroad ties as well as firewood. This did not bring in much income. However they were able to construct a large building to live in, and their membership grew to 40 by 1884. Frey left the commune that year, returning to New York City to run a cooperative laundry for a short time before moving to England.

In 1887, a fire wrecked the New Odessa community building and destroyed their library. The whole operation was abandoned in 1888. Throughout the history of this commune there were constant battles and arguments among the members over ideological issues such as what constitutes Jewish identity and how much freedom must exist for a community to be truly socialist, as well as debates over Frey's leadership and the rigid structures he insisted on instituting. A book with a section on New Odessa is the *Jewish Encyclopedia* article "Agricultural Colonies in the United States," by Reizenstein.

New Philadelphia (1832–1871) was formed by 250 departing members from Rapp's **Harmony** community in Pennsylvania. They were led by Count de Leon (Bernhard Müller—1787–1834), who had caused much dissension within Rapp's commune when he tried to take over the leadership. The Count was particularly opposed to Rapp's insistence on celibacy among the members. When the majority in the Rappite commune elected to keep Rapp as their leader, the Count and his supporters were given $5,000 on the condition that they leave and relinquish any further claims on the Rappites.

The New Philadelphia group settled first at Phillipsburg (now Monaca), Pennsylvania, some ten miles away and across the river from Rapp's commune. They purchased 800 acres there and survived for more than a year. But the Count was a poor manager and by September 1833, being in economic straits, they found it necessary to voyage down the Ohio and Mississippi rivers and settle at Grand Encore on the Red River in Natchitoches Parish, Louisiana. Then, following the death of the Count (some say from cholera), they moved to a place they called Germantown, eight miles north of Minden, in Webster Parish, Louisiana. The commune broke up peacefully after the Civil War. Some cabins, reputedly theirs, still stand at Germantown.

One of the Count's followers was Jacob Zundel, who had been with Rapp from the beginning until the schism took place. He then worked with Count de Leon until the Count died. Zundel next joined the Mormons at **Nauvoo** and began writing to his former colleagues in Rapp's colony, urging them to also join the Mormons. Zundel even tried to arrange several conferences that never took place between the Mormons and the Rappites. It is said that some of the other followers of Count de Leon joined the **Bethel** commune after New Philadelphia was disbanded. Books with sections that focus on New Philadelphia are Bestor's *Backwoods Utopias: The Sectarian and Owenite Phases of Communitarian Socialism in America*, and Nordhoff's *The Communistic Societies of the United States*.

New River *see* **Mahanaim**

New Rockport (1948–present), near Choteau, Montana, is a Hutterite Brüderhof (see **Bon Homme**), It was led by Peter Hofer in 1964 and had 131 members.

New Ulm (1855–1858), at New Ulm, Minnesota, was a cooperative community established by the Turnerbund of North America, a German socialist organization. They purchased the property for this commune from a German land society that had named the place after the town of Ulm in Württemburg, Germany. It included 23 log houses scattered over a three-mile area. The community leader was William Pfaender, and the membership grew from 23 to 600 before the commune closed. Most of them were Germans from Cincinnati, Ohio. They established a cooperative sawmill, engaged in farming, and, for about a year, had a communal store. After the sawmill burned to the ground, they decided to disband the commune. Many members continued to live in the area, and some were killed there during the Sioux uprising of 1862. A book with a section that focuses on New Ulm is Wittke's *We Who Built America: The Saga of the Immigrant*.

Newark Ashram (1941–1945), in Newark, New Jersey, was a community of pacifists who supported themselves by working in the Newark area. They were located at 37 Wright Street. There were perhaps ten members, and they were led by Robin Rae. Dave Dellinger, the founder of the **St. Francis Acres** anarchist commune, was briefly a member of the Newark Ashram.

Newark Perfectionists (1849–1855), at Newark, New Jersey, was a commune of about ten members. They followed the teachings of John Humphrey Noyes, who had set up both the **Putney Corporation** and **Oneida** communes. When the Newark Perfectionists disbanded, all the members moved to Oneida.

Newborns (1725–1727), also known as the Baumanites, formed a commune at Germantown, now part of Philadelphia, in 1725. There were possibly as many as 25 members and they were led by Matthias Bauman. He had been a poor, uneducated day-laborer in Germany when he fell ill in 1701. After he recovered from his delirium, Bauman claimed he had gone to heaven and returned with the power of prophecy. He began to preach about his new powers, but had little success in Germany. So he emigrated to America in 1719 and began to conduct revival meetings at Oley and surrounding towns in Pennsylvania. It is said that he made "many converts." Part of his success came from the fact that he taught that all followers would be free of sin and could never sin again. He told them to dispense with the Bible, sacraments, prayer, worship, and marriage. One of those he tried to convert, without success, was Joseph Conrad

Beissel, the leader of the **Ephrata** commune. Bauman's teachings led to a great deal of conflict between his followers and members of other German sects in the area. Perhaps the Baumanites decided to form the commune in order to mutually protect themselves from their opponents. Bauman died in 1727, and the leadership of the commune was then taken by two members named Kuhlwein and Jotter (first names unknown). Within a short time the commune disbanded. Many of the participants are said to have later joined the **Emmaus** Moravian community. A book with a section that focuses on the Newborns is Sachse's *The German Sectarians of Pennsylvania, 1708–1800: A Critical and Legendary History of the Ephrata Cloister and the Dunkers.*

Newllano (1917–1938), a few miles south of Leesville, Louisiana, was established by socialist Job Harriman of the **Llano del Rio** commune on 20,000 acres of land that he purchased, which included an abandoned lumber town. By January 1918 there were 300 members living there in 100 abandoned lumber shacks, some larger homes, and an 18-room hotel. There was also a store, warehouses, and a small school. The members tried to farm, but drought ruined their first crop. They also sold cord wood that they processed at a lumber mill that came with the land.

Difficulties in the early years and later conflicts between the participants caused the size of the membership to fluctuate greatly. Harriman was away much of the time, beset by legal problems surrounding the dissolution of his California commune. The leadership of Newllano thus rested in the hands of journalist Ernest Wooster, osteopath Robert K. Williams, and dancing instructor George T. Pickett, all of whom had been members of the earlier Llano del Rio experiment. Pickett was the better organizer and eventually became the primary director. He had a great deal of enthusiasm and optimism, and once ran for U.S. Congress from Louisiana on a platform designed by the Townshend old-age pension plan movement.

Pickett established new industries, including a brick kiln, dairy, and printing press, and he started a rice farm and a citrus grove. He also encouraged two leading socialist journalists, Kate Richards and Frank O'Hare, to move their highly-successful *American Vanguard* (formerly *American Rip Saw*) newspaper to Newllano in 1923. William E. Zeuch came that same year and made an agreement with the members of Newllano to establish a college on 40 acres of their land. Zeuch turned this into another commune that he called *Commonwealth College.* Other prominent members included Theodore Cuno, an affluent socialist publisher from Germany who had participated in deliberations of the First International and had briefly worked with Karl Marx and Friedrich Engels; Septer Baldwin, the manager of Pickett's rice farm; Ole Synoground, a construction engineer; Carl Henry "Dad" Gleeser, the editor of the Newllano paper, the *Colonist*; Ed Merrill, artist and former IWW leader; Mack and John Rust, inventors of the Rust cotton picker; and Harry Weatherwax, a former Communist Party organizer who took a dim view of this commune but stayed because he liked its social life.

Dancing, picnics, concerts, silent movies, forums, May Day parades, and sports activities were a regular part of life at Newllano. They had a park, play areas, and a swimming pool. Their library contained 7,000 books. The standard of living, though certainly quite low, was higher than that generally found elsewhere in the rural South during the 1920s. Every home had electricity, most had running water, and all families received daily deliveries of ice.

Pickett was an advocate of industrial schools. He established one called the Kid Kolony at Newllano. He also set up a highly publicized kindergarten and a day nursery. And, for a time, residents could take college-level courses at the adjacent Commonwealth College commune. After Commonwealth College moved to Arkansas, Lowell H. Coats, a former college president from Idaho, set up a junior college at the commune, a school that lasted for about a year. The struggle over Pickett's leadership, along with fires that destroyed some of the commune buildings and an ever recurring need for financial assistance, created many problems. Pickett tried unsuccessfully to get financial support from the federal government; he even tried to get the commune established as a site for one of the Farm Security Administration cooperative farms, but to no avail. Open revolt against Pickett's leadership broke out on May Day 1935, and a new group of directors took over. From then until 1936, when the courts appointed a receiver, the colony was divided into warring factions that at least once fired shots at each other. Before the dispute ended, many from both sides had been arrested.

The colony continued to operate until 1938 under directors appointed by the receiver. The property was then liquidated. Until sometime after World War II, the *Llano Colonist*, a mimeographed news sheet, was circulated among former members. It contained reminiscences of the old colony. Pickett himself stayed at his home in the town that still bears the name Newllano

until he died in 1962. The main buildings of the commune are still standing, although they are now privately owned. Books with sections that focus on Newllano are Conkin's *Two Paths to Utopia: The Hutterites and the Llano Colony* and Koch's *Educational Commune: The Story of Commonwealth College*.

Niksur Cooperative Association (1897–1900), at Lawrence, now Wahkon, in Mille Lacs County, Minnesota, was a communal settlement of about 50 members, some of whom were also members of the early American labor union known as the Knights of Labor. The members had 500 acres of land. They manufactured wooden ware, advocated practical socialism, and published *The Niksur Magazine*. Charles D. Raymer, a Minneapolis bookseller, was the commune's president. Nelson L. Nash was the vice-president, and Ernest B. Mayo was the secretary-treasurer. Another active member was Peter McGaughey of the Knights of Labor. This commune was also sometimes called the Pioneer Association.

Nineveh *see* **Bethel**

Nojoshing Community (1849–1898), in Milwaukee, Wisconsin, was established as a farming commune by two Franciscan priests from Bavaria—Father Anthony Keppler and Father Matthias Steiger. Their aim was to give lay Catholics the opportunity and right to live in a structured and corporate environment, such as exists in the Franciscan monasteries.

The commune had 167 members, both men and women, and it was named after the Indian designation for the area (meaning tongue of land running into Lake Michigan). The two priests died of cholera in 1851, but the community continued for more than 45 years thereafter. The members lived in one large brick building that stood near the present site of the St. Francis Seminary in Milwaukee. A book with a section that focuses on Nojoshing is Hinds' *American Communities*.

Norfolk Brüderhof *see* Evergreen Community

North American Phalanx (1843–1856) was located at a place still called Phalanx, which is about five miles southwest of Red Bank, New Jersey, and two miles from Vanderburg. This was the most successful of all the Fourierist experiments set up after the first one, **Social Reform Unity**. It had 112 members, many of whom came from Albany, New York, and New York City. They began community life in September 1843, on 637 acres of land.

There were two farmhouses on the property when the first families arrived to take possession of it. Such housing was obviously inadequate, and so they began immediately to build their phalanx house which, when completed, was 40 by 80 feet in size and two stories high. They also built shops and mills, planted crops, and engaged in brick making and raising cows. The produce they harvested (corn, potatoes, and tomatoes) was considered among the best raised in the area.

Much of the stock in this commune was owned by nonresidents, one of them newspaper publisher Horace Greeley. Thus, questions about policy for the community were often decided in meetings by stockholders who did not live at the North American Phalanx and so were among those least involved. The residents who were most active in the leadership were Charles Sears, John Gray, John S. Bucklin, Leeman Stockwell, George B. Arnold, and Alcander Longley. Longley later became a member of the **Clermont Phalanx**, was the leader of the **Fourier Phalanx**, and set up five short-lived, non–Fourierist communes of his own in various parts of Missouri.

Two types of conflict developed there, one over whether there should be more authoritarian leadership or more democracy and the other over religion. The religious issue finally led to the withdrawal of a group of members in 1853, after ten years of relatively successful phalanx life. They were led by Marcus Spring, who insisted that the community should sustain a preacher to cultivate the moral and religious aspects of the phalanx. Spring's group departed to establish still another Fourierist commune, the **Raritan Bay Union** in New Jersey.

A fire destroyed two of the North American Phalanx mills and the business office on September 10, 1854, resulting in a loss of about $10,000 in assets. The members asked their non-resident stock holders to provide funds for the rebuilding of the mills, but instead these men pulled out of the enterprise altogether. The resident members then tried to rebuild the structures themselves, but were forced by lack of financing to disband early in 1856. All that remains today of the original North American Phalanx buildings is an old hotel, still partially in use.

North Bloomfield Association *see* **Bloomfield Union Association**

North Union (1822–1889), at Shaker Heights, now a suburb of Cleveland, Ohio, was a Shaker commune (see **Watervliet**) established on land provided by Ralph Russell. The first presiding elder of this community was

Ashbel Kitchell. The next was Matthew Houston, followed by David Spinning, and then Samuel Russell. At its high point, North Union had as many as 300 members, divided into three "families."

David Baird, one of the most prolific of all Shaker inventors, lived here. He invented a revolving harrow, an automatic spring, and one type of Babbitt metal. This was also the home of James S. Prescott, an early advocate of eugenics and a relative of the historian William Prescott. When George Ingels of this community was drafted into the army in 1862, Shakers Benjamin Gates and Frederick Evans of Watervliet went to Washington to petition President Lincoln to exempt Shakers from serving in the war.

The members had a four-story sandstone gristmill (built in 1843), saw mill, horse barn, cow barn, grain barn, tannery, office building, and a number of residences. They manufactured brooms, stocking yarn, lumber, and wooden ware, and they sold milk and vegetables to people in nearby Cleveland. What were later known as the Shaker Lakes were developed by members of North Union from small swampy pools on Doan Brook, which ran through their property.

When this commune dissolved on October 24, 1889, they sold their property to a real estate company. None of the buildings still stand. The remaining 17 members moved to the **Union Village** and Watervliet Shaker communes.

Northampton Association of Education and Industry (1842–1846), at a place now within the city of Northampton, Massachusetts, was a commune in which the members prided themselves in having no religious creed or forms of worship. For this reason outsiders often called them "Nothingarians."

The commune was founded by ten people, including David Mack, Samuel L. Hill, George W. Benson, and William Adam. They purchased 500 acres of land for about $31,000 in an area known as Broughton's Meadows (now Florence), about two and a half miles from the business center of Northampton. It included a silk factory, six homes, and a saw mill. In time the commune membership grew to 130, and many more homes were built.

People applying to join the Northampton Association were not asked about their religious and moral beliefs, but only if they could be useful to the association. Every member's labor was considered of equal value, and so they were paid for it in equal amounts. According to Benson, there was always plenty of food, and no one suffered for the necessities and comforts of life. "All were satisfied with simplicity, both in diet and dress." Despite their rejection of religious values, they constantly argued, according to Benson, about matters of religion and worship. However they were united in opposition to slavery. David Riggles, a black reformer who had befriended Frederick Douglas after the latter's escape from slavery, was a member, and Douglas visited Riggles there at least once. Sojourner Truth, the first black woman orator to speak against slavery, was also a member for a brief period of time.

In 1843, the Northampton Association members organized a boarding school that was designed to unite study with labor. William Adam was the first director of this school. He was succeeded by David Mack. Pupils were recruited from various places, including Europe.

The members of the commune met for discussion sessions once a week, and there were often bitter conflicts over the management of the enterprises. The commune was dissolved by mutual consent on November 1, 1846. A book with a section that focuses on the Northampton Association is Noyes' *History of American Socialisms*.

Oak Lake Community *see* **New Meadow Run**

Oberlin Colony (1833–1846), at what is now the town of Oberlin, Ohio, was a Protestant commune of about 50 members who pooled their resources and put all their surplus into the costs of "spreading the Gospel." They named the settlement after the German theologian and evangelist Johann Friedrich Oberlin, and they agreed to maintain "as perfect a community of interest as though we held a community property." Their leader was John Shipherd. One member who joined the commune in 1837, Dr. Isaac Jennings, looked on private property as the chief source of all evil and unsuccessfully advocated a complete communism of goods for the membership.

The Oberlin Colony took a strong stand against slavery and provided one of the rest stops on the underground railway that helped slaves to escape to Canada. The members furthermore had great interest in Christian education. They helped to found a college in the hopes of improving learning among the surrounding farm communities where most people were relatively parochial and showed little interest in further education. They named their school after the commune. Oberlin College, which from the beginning was a co-educational institution, was the first school in the United States to award degrees to women.

When the town of Oberlin was incorporated in 1846, the members of the commune abandoned their cooperative system. An article with a section that focuses on the Oberlin Colony is McKinley's "A Guide to the Communistic Communities of Ohio" in the January 1937 issue of the *Ohio State Archaeological and Historical Quarterly*.

Ohio Phalanx (1843–1845), sometimes referred to as the Western Fourier Association, was located at what is now Bellaire, Ohio. The membership, which reached 100, was drawn from Fourierist groups in Pittsburgh, Pennsylvania, and Canton, Ohio (see **Social Reform Unity**). They had 2000 acres of land that lay along the western bank of the Ohio River. There were already two frame houses and ten log cabins on the property when they purchased it, and much of the land was under cultivation.

The organizer of this commune was Elijah P. Grant (1808–1874), and some of its leading members were H.H. VanAmringe and James D. Thornburg. VanAmringe joined the **Trumbull Phalanx** after the Ohio Phalanx closed. Its property was sold at public auction on September 17, 1845.

Oleana (1852–1857), also called New Norway, was founded on Little Kettle Creek in Potter County, Pennsylvania. It was established by the famous Norwegian violinist Olaus Borneman Bull (1810–1880), and had 800 Norwegian immigrant members.

"Ole" Bull's purpose in establishing this settlement, which encompassed 11,144 acres of land, was to "found a New Norway, consecrated to liberty, baptized with independence, and protected by the Union's mighty flag." He planned four villages: Oleana (now a town), New Norway, New Bergen (now called Carter Camp), and Walhalla. In time, 300 houses and a hotel were built to accommodate the members.

They farmed cooperatively. Former secretary of state and presidential candidate Henry Clay gave the colonists blooded horses and other friends gave them farming equipment and cows. Bull, in order to establish an industry for the commune, agreed to build 2,000 cannons for the U.S. government and leased a deserted foundry for this purpose.

When Bull went on a concert tour in 1853, he contracted yellow fever in Panama, where his violin was also stolen. To add to Bull's problems, he returned to Oleana to find he did not have a clear title to the land. He tried to repurchase it from the rightful owner, but his savings were now rapidly dwindling. The community disbanded in 1857. The foundation to Bull's uncompleted home can still be seen in nearby Ole Bull State Park. A book with a section that focuses on Oleana is Mulkearn and Pugh's *A Traveler's Guide to Historic Western Pennsylvania*.

Oneida (1848–1881), the commune that gave its name to the present town in New York, was a Perfectionist community organized by John Humphrey Noyes, after the forced closing of his **Putney Corporation** in Vermont. When the first members came to the new site, they had 40 acres with an unpainted frame house, an abandoned Indian hut, and an old Indian saw mill. At that time they were so poor that they had to sleep on the floor of the frame house. They existed on a diet of bread, milk, potatoes, and beans, with milk gravy substituting for butter.

They depended on agriculture and horticulture for their income. Some of the members also engaged in logging, milling, and clearing swamps. In time they set up a blacksmith shop and began making animal traps, the design for which was based on a patent by Samuel Newhouse, one of the members of this commune.

By 1878 their number had grown to 268, and applications for membership poured in at all times though only a few applicants were accepted. They had increased their land holdings to 654 acres, and they had constructed two large brick buildings, a number of houses, and a school that were all heated by steam. One of the brick buildings was four stories high. Their trap trade had become quite lucrative and they were canning fruit for sale, as well as selling the rustic furniture they made. They owned a large stable of horses, sold milk from their cows, manufactured silk, and raised farm crops in abundance. They even owned a sloop that sailed the Hudson River. The community library contained between 5,000 and 6,000 volumes. They also had a photographic studio, a fine arts center, and a print shop where they produced a newspaper and many other publications.

The production of fine Oneida silverware, for which they became particularly well known, was an industry that was started at the **Wallingford** Perfectionist commune before moving to Oneida. They were so successful economically, in fact, that to operate all their industries they had to hire as many as 200 outside laborers, as well as a number of fruit pickers.

Here, as at all the other Perfectionist communes, the members held mutual criticism sessions and practiced "complex marriage," a system that apparently worked well at Oneida. Those selected to bear children saw themselves as being "living sacrifices to God and true communism." The children were reared in a community nursery and their parents neither had special rights to them nor seemed to show any special interest in them. They were the community's children. In later years, after the dissolution of Oneida as a commune, these same children became the efficient and resourceful managers of the highly successful, well-managed businesses of the Oneida industrial complex.

In principle the members of Oneida took no action without general agreement of all the members. Whenever there was strong objection to a plan, they put off its implementation until there could be further discussion so as to reach an agreement. The work of the members was done, whenever possible, by the "bee" system, with one member of the group reading a novel or play aloud to accompany all others at work on a single project.

The demise of the commune came about due to strong opposition from outsiders who were horrified by its practice of complex marriage. In 1879, Noyes decided to abandon this aspect of the community's life and persuade the others of the wisdom of this deci-sion. The members then married among themselves. Noyes also decided that it would be best if he departed from the community as outside opposition might abate once he was no longer there. He emigrated to Canada, where for a year's time he directed the community life from a distance. In 1881 the members decided to change the nature of the community from that of a commune to a joint-stock company.

Noyes died in 1886 at Niagara Falls. The joint-stock company is still in existence, and their buildings, many of which were the factories and homes of the original commune, are still in use. The Mansion, built in 1860 as a large community center, is now used as a resident hotel. Books with sections that focus on Oneida are Hinds' *American Communities*, Nordhoff's *The Communistic Societies of the United States*, and Noyes' *History of American Socialisms*.

One-Mention Community (1843–1844), in Monroe County, Pennsylvania, was a commune of about 40 persons who

Main building of the Oneida commune as it looked in 1875 (drawing by Lois Will).

purchased 800 acres of land unseen for their settlement. Although they were followers of Robert Owen (see **New Harmony**), they belonged to an urban movement that went by the name of the One-Mention Society, and they called themselves "One-Mentionists." The name for their organization was derived from Biblical scripture, probably from the phrase Paul used in the New Testament to "Be of one mind." The movement had branches in Newark, New York, Brooklyn, Philadelphia, and some other cities. The One-Mentionists combined a Protestant outlook with Owen's dream of creating villages of cooperation.

The leaders of this commune were Dr. Humbert, Mr. Horner, Mr. Scott, and Mr. Hudson. When they arrived at the site, they found that the land was poor and rocky. There was one log cabin and a few animals, but they had to provide all the farm implements, some machinery, and more stock. After many months of hard labor they had only cleared about 40 acres. Visitors from the city branches of the society did not give very enthusiastic reports about the project, and a special committee assigned by the organization to look into the matter painted a quite negative picture of the One-Mention Community.

There were disagreements among the members and Mr. Hudson decided to leave this project and establish another at **Goose Pond**, Pennsylvania, where the land was more developed. The whole project was abandoned in 1844.

Ontario Union (1844–1845), also called the Manchester Union, was a Fourierist commune (see **Social Reform Unity**) that occupied 284 acres of land, five miles north of Canadaigua in Ontario County, New York (on the boundary between Hopewell and Manchester townships). The 150 members had a saw mill, flour and grist mill, and a spoke factory. Theron C. Leland was a member and director there after the **Sodus Bay Phalanx** closed. It is not known why the Ontario Union failed after 14 months of relatively successful commune life.

Ora Labora Community (1862–1868), in Huron County, Michigan, between Caseville and Bay Port, was a commune of about 30 German Methodists under the leadership of Emil Baur. The members came from Ohio and Pennsylvania, and they built ten homes. But during the Civil War, a number of members left to join the Union Army, and the commune was never afterward able to accumulate enough capital to sustain itself.

Order of St. Michael (1954–1972) was an Episcopalian commune established at Gary, Indiana, and named for the Archangel Michael. The five members were totally committed to the renewal of the church, shared all their worldly goods, and took a nonviolent and pacifist position in regard to war and social conflict. They worked at jobs outside the commune in order to finance the experiment. The leader was Jim Driver.

The members moved their commune in 1960 to a 120-acre farm near Crown Point, Indiana. The membership then grew to more than 20 before their land was taken away from them by the construction company from which the land was rented.

Order of Theocracy (1910–1931), at Fort Myers, Florida, was established by followers of Cyrus Teed from **Estero**, after Teed died. The leader was Annie G. Ordway, who had been Teed's closest assistant, and the approximately ten members advocated Teed's teachings regarding "cellular cosmogony" and the idea that the surface of the earth is concave rather than convex. They lived together communally in a single residence.

Orderville (1874–1885), Utah, was a commune formed while Brigham Young traveled throughout Utah from one Mormon community to another, attempting to revive the Joseph Smith's United Order (see **St. George**). It was established mainly by people from the disbanded commune at Mt. Carmel, Utah, who believed that the settlement there was not communal enough. They pooled their wealth, established a system of common labor, and made all decisions by common consent. The membership grew to over 700 and lasted some years longer than any of the St. George–type United Order communes.

The property of the Orderville members included several hundred acres of land, houses, agricultural machinery, sawmills, cattle and horses, hogs, sheep, and chickens. They built a store room, shoe shop, bakery, blacksmith shop, carpenter shop, coopers shop, tannery, woolen factory, barns, schoolhouse, and even a telegraph office during this communal period.

Members were not given wages or wage credits for their work, but they were allowed to take what they needed from a common storehouse. They met every morning and evening for worship, ate at a common table, and carried on the activities of the settlement under the supervision of a board of directors. They adopted a wage and price system in 1883 in order to increase incentive, but this brought dissension among them and finally the abandonment of the United Order system. A major factor in

this demise was a boom in mining in southern Utah following the panic of 1873. Thus neighbors outside of the commune who were employed by the mines began to do so much better financially than those within that the church authorities advised them to drop the communal aspects of Orderville. Today the town is a farming and grazing community of about 400 persons.

Our Lady of the Wayside (1941–1952), at Avon, Ohio, was a Catholic Worker farm (see **Maryfarm** on Staten Island) led by Bill Gauchet and his wife. It had about 15 members.

Our Lady Star of the Sea Farm *see* **Maryfarm**

Painted Woods (1882–1887), near Bismark, North Dakota, was a Jewish agricultural commune (see **Sicily Island**). Although it started with only 20 families, it grew to 54 families within a year's time — 213 people. They farmed 160 acres of land, but their crops were several times destroyed by prairie fires and drought. This finally forced them to disband. Most of the members then moved to other parts of the state.

Palestine (1891–1900), four miles from Bad Axe, Michigan, was a Jewish agricultural settlement (see **Sicily Island**) established by about 45 people from Russia, many of whom had previously been peddlers. They paid $12 an acre for the property. Their land was wild, but good, and they erected a few log houses and bought some horses and cows. They received support from the Beth-El Hebrew Relief Society of Detroit and the Baron de Hirsch Fund, but they soon ran into difficulties because they lacked sufficient funds to hold them through the initial unproductive years of farming. By April 1900, only eight families remained on the property; by the end of the year all were gone.

Panaca (1874–1875), Nevada, was a **St. George**–type of United Order Mormon commune established at the urging of Erastus Snow, Miles Andrus, and Angus Cannon. It had about 150 members.

Paragonah (1874–1877), Utah, was a Mormon United Order commune for several years. Its economy was based on the **St. George** plan. There were about 150 members.

Paris (1874–1876), near Kanab, Utah, was a Mormon United Order commune based on the model adopted at the **St. George** commune. There were about 30 members who were organized by John R. Young.

Parishfield (1948–1967), first at Brighton and then Detroit, Michigan, was a Protestant community established as an educational center for lay churchmen. It had perhaps 25 members who were committed to the belief that communal life constitutes the center for any church renewal.

The members became deeply involved in Detroit's Industrial Mission project after 1956, and began to exemplify a style of direct action and presence in the urban community that somewhat resembled the worker-priest movement in France. They eventually disbanded the commune because they felt that the church as a whole had become isolated from the human struggle and that they themselves had lost their leverage on it. An article with information that focuses on Parishfield is Winter's "The Parishfield Community," *The Christian Century*, June 14, 1967.

Peace Union Settlement (1843–1844), also known as Friedens-Verein, was in Limestone township, Warren County, Pennsylvania. It had about 30 German immigrant members and was led by Andreas Bernardus Smolnikar (b. 1795), a former Benedictine monk and professor of Biblical studies at a university in Austria. He had been a member of the Fourierist commune **Social Reform Unity** before he established this one, and he had published five volumes propounding his views that were printed in Philadelphia.

The members of the Peace Union Settlement owned 10,000 acres of fertile but wild land. However, their experiment lasted no more than a year because Smolnikar was such a poor manager.

By 1845 Smolnikar was wandering about the country claiming to be the "Ambassador Extraordinary of Christ and Apostle of Peace." He believed that Jesus had appointed him to bring peace to all nations. He even announced that this appointment happened at exactly 5 P.M. on January 5, 1837. Smolnikar also claimed to have established two other "Peace Union" communities, but this is doubtful since no substantiating record can be found for either of them. A book with a section that focuses on the Peace Union Settlement is Calverton's *Where Angels Dared to Tread*.

Pearl Creek (1949–present), in Beadle County, South Dakota, is a Hutterite Brüderhof (see **Bon Homme**) established by a river of that name. In 1964 it had 186 members and the leader was Michael Waldner.

Penn-Craft Community (1937–1962), near Uniontown, Pennsylvania, was started by the American Friends Service Committee as an experimental community for the rehabilitation of unemployed coal miners. They had a knitting factory, cooperative store, and other cooperative enterprises. Although the 250 members voted on all community decisions, managers were appointed from the outside by the Friends Service Committee.

At first the cooperative nature of this community was quite attractive to the membership, but with each passing year this aspect seemed less important to them. One problem was that the land allotted to each family was too small for full-scale farming and too large for part-time farming. Penn-Craft still exists as a housing community, but not as a commune. Its cooperative enterprises were disbanded in 1962, and the former cooperative store is now privately owned. A book with a section that focuses on the Penn-Craft Community is Infield's *Utopia and Experiment*.

Peoria Street Fellowship *see* **Church of Hope**

Peter Maurin Farm (1950–1962), on Staten Island, New York, was a Catholic Worker farm (see **Maryfarm** on Staten Island) named after the founder of the Catholic Worker movement. It had about 15 members. They had 22 acres of land, containing a brown-shingled farmhouse, and they raised asparagus and tomatoes for their House of Hospitality in New York City. They also had a bakery that could produce 100 loaves of bread at a time. For the first ten years Beth Rogers was the director, and then Jean Walsh, a nurse, took her place. Other members included Hans Tunnesen, A Norwegian seaman who built a chapel for the farm; Joe Cotter, an electrician; Agnes Sidney; Dick Barber, and Joe Roche. They frequently faced harassment by county building inspectors and other officials.

Philadelphia Industrial Association (1845–1847) was a Fourierist commune (see **Social Reform Unity**) that was established on the farm of William McCartney. This was on the west side of the St. Joseph River, in German Township, about two and a half miles from South Bend, Indiana. It had 70 resident members as well as 30 nonresident members. McCartney was the president and William C. Talcott was treasurer. When the commune disbanded, Talcott said that the failure was due to McCartney holding back his best land and only providing a tract of broken, marshy soil near the river. McCartney fared well, according to Talcott, because when he took back the land after the commune broke up, it was all cleared and improved.

Pigeon River (1846), just north of the mouth of the Pigeon River in Sheboygan County, Wisconsin, was a commune formed by about ten Fourierists (see **Social Reform Unity**) who had worked with a group at Sheboygan Falls, Wisconsin, in planning the **Spring Farm Association** commune. The members of Pigeon River, however, disagreed with the others over where their commune should be established. Both experiments were started in the same year and in the same county, but this one lasted just a few months. The names of only two members of the Pigeon River commune are known: Newton Goodell of Sheboygan Falls and William Seaman, who had previously been a member of the **Wisconsin Phalanx**.

Pilgrims (1817–1825) were a gypsy-like communal group that came to the United States in 1817 from Ascot Corner, Canada, and settled for a time at South Woodstock, Vermont. Their leader was Isaac Bullard, a man who had devoted himself to Christ after recovering from a long illness. Their membership increased from eight to forty during the stay in Vermont. Among those who joined this commune were Joseph Ball, a minister; Peter Ball, the owner of a farm where the commune members lived in 1817; and a man named Cummings, who acted as the chief speaker for the group even though he took his instructions from Bullard.

Bullard was an absolute dictator. The property of the group was held in common but distributed only according to Bullard's wishes. He even married and unmarried members at his personal whim, and rewarded or punished them. He ordered his followers to discard all things of civilization, and the members then clothed themselves in bear skins and leather girdles, let their beards grow (Bullard's was red), never combed their hair, and imposed rigid fasts on themselves. Finding no scriptural command to wash, they decided that filth must be a virtue and never bathed. They carried this to such an extreme that they sometimes even rolled in the dust until it covered their bodies.

The group left South Woodstock in the fall of 1817 and traveled by foot westward, stopping at Bennington, Vermont; Troy, New York (where they stayed briefly with the Shakers at **Watervliet**); Sussex, New Jersey; Cincinnati, Ohio; and eventually settling on Pilgrim Island, 30 miles below New Madrid, Missouri. At one point their membership grew to 300. But dissensions began to plague them in Missouri and many members left the group, including the families of Peter and Joseph Ball. Also some riverboat men joined the commune temporarily to rob them of all their money. By 1820 a visitor reported that there were only six people left in the commune, and Bullard was too ill to talk to anyone. Books with sections that focus on the Pilgrims are Flint's *Recollections of the Last Ten Years in the Valley of the Mississippi* and Ludlum's *Social Ferment in Vermont, 1791–1850.*

Pine Valley (1874–1875), about 20 miles north of St. George, Utah, was a Mormon commune patterned after the **St. George** United Order model. It was organized by Erastus Snow, Miles Andrus, and Angus Cannon, and had about 100 members.

Pinto (1874–1875), south of Newcastle in Washington County, Utah, was a 50-member Mormon United Order community of the type established first at **St. George**. The organizers here, as at **Pine Valley**, were Erastus Snow, Miles Andrus, and Angus Cannon.

Pioneer Association *see* **Niksur Cooperative Association**

Pisgah Grande (1914–1920), east of Santa Susana, California, and along the Los Angeles–Ventura county line, was established in 1914 by "Father" Finis E. Yoakum as a Pentecostal religious commune. Yoakum was previously head of a gospel mission to the destitute in Los Angeles. He purchased the 3,200-acre cattle ranch, located in an isolated spot and fed by bountiful springs, and there gathered 75 followers. They planted gardens, drank goat's milk, and feasted on honey. They also erected a two-story headquarters and individual dwellings, as well as a communal dining hall, post office, and school building. They had a watchtower in which they kept a flame constantly burning.

Yoakum died in August 1920. His two sons and James Cheek, who acted as manager for the colony, tried to keep things going. But the project failed after the county health officer condemned its unsanitary facilities and a Los Angeles County grand jury began an investigation of its communal practices.

Most of the crumbling buildings are still standing, including the headquarters, post office, and prayer tower high on a hill. The site can be reached by a private extension of the Las Llajas Canyon Road. A book with a section that focuses on Pisgah Grande is Hine's *California's Utopian Communities*.

Plainview (1959–present), north of Ipswich, South Dakota, is a Hutterite Brüderhof (see **Bon Homme**) that had 97 members in 1964 and was then led by Joseph Wipf.

Platte Brüderhof *see* **Charles Mix Brüderhof**

Plattsburg Community (1878–1879), at Plattsburg, Missouri, was a religious commune of 12 persons, most of whom were members of the same family. Little else is known about this community, except that William Frey of the **Investigating Community** offered them his commune's land after it closed. The Plattsburg members responded that they did not want to move.

Pleasant Hill (1806–1910), in Mercer County, Kentucky, about seven miles east of Harrodsburg and fifteen north of Danville, was a Shaker community of about 500 members organized into eight "families." The commune was established when Elisha Thomas gave his 140-acre farm to the Shakers. Eventually their property covered 4,200 acres.

The first leaders of this community were John Meacham, son of Joseph Meacham of the **Watervliet** Shaker commune in New York, and Lucy Smith.

Micajah Burnett, a civil engineer and architect, designed their buildings of fine Georgian architecture. One of these was an office building that had a widely admired spiral staircase.

John Dunlavy, another member, wrote comprehensive essays on Shaker theology. He most clearly summed up the Shaker stance for religious communism in his work *The Manifesto*, written in 1818. For him sharing property with others was the only way to show equality and universal love. He pointed out that faith in the brotherhood of man was meaningless without concrete actions in this direction.

The members of Pleasant Hill owned a saw and grist mill, a woolen mill, a cooper's shop, a cobbler's shop, a carding and fulling mill, a linseed-oil mill, a paper mill, and a tanyard. They raised fine stock, were successful in agriculture, preserved fruits and pickles for sale, made brooms, packaged garden seeds, cloth and straw hats. They set up the first water system in Kentucky by opening a spring at the foot of a hill and using wooden force pumps, driven by horses, to pump water to the various houses of the commune. They also designed a four-wheel dump cart that they manufactured and sold extensively.

During the Civil War armies of both the North and South foraged off the community, taking away many of their horses and wagons. Because the Shaker stance against slavery was well-known, the Confederate soldiers were particularly hostile to the members of this community. However the Southern general John Morgan, who had been born near the settlement, protected them against his own troops.

Dr. W.F. Pennybaker was the leading trustee of Pleasant Hill at the time of this commune's dissolution. He gave the deed for the land to George Bohon of Harrodsburg to be held in trust, the condition being that the 12 remaining residents be cared for as long as they lived. Bohon was also to use some of the property for the Pennybaker Home for Girls. In 1925 the last member of Pleasant Hill, Sister Mary Settles, died at the age of 87.

About 20 stone buildings remain, the first built in 1809. One of these buildings, the former guest house, has been turned into a Shaker museum. The area is now called Shakertown and is a popular tourist site.

Point Hope (1854–1861), at Berlin Heights, Ohio, was formed initially by Francis Barry and a few others as a commune called Davis House. In 1860, Barry and 19 other free thinkers, including some from the anarchist **Modern Times** commune in New York, moved from this house onto some nearby farming property that they owned collectively. At this point they adopted the name Point Hope. They grew fruit successfully and tried to promote their ideas in the surrounding villages. One member, James Arrington Clay, had been jailed in Gardiner, Maine, for his theology of nonresistance and free love. Clay had published two periodicals there and a book on his prison experiences.

After the first few months of communal life, the members of Point Hope changed their name to the Industrial Fraternity. They closed the experiment the following year for unknown reasons.

Point Loma (1897–1942) near San Diego, California, was a Theosophist commu-

nity established by Katherine Tingley (1847–1929), the leader of one of the factions of this movement of psychical thought and Eastern mysticism. Its teachings were first brought to the United States in 1875 by Madame Elena Petrovna Blavatsky (1831–1891), who was also instrumental in spreading Theosophy throughout the world. This system of philosophic and religious thought is based on claims of a mystic insight into the nature of God and the laws of the universe. To a theosophist, the truest knowledge comes not through reason or the senses, but through direct communion of the soul with divine reality.

Tingley was also a noted proponent of slum relief projects, crusades for education of children around the world, and campaigns for world peace and the abolition of capital punishment. At Point Loma she aimed to achieve a nucleus of universal brotherhood without distinctions of race, creed, caste, sex, or color. She also hoped to promote the study of Eastern religious literature and to investigate the psychical powers latent in humankind.

Built on 330 acres of land, Point Loma had three large buildings, groups of smaller bungalows and tents for living quarters, a Greek theater, gardens, orchards, and a forest of Eucalyptus trees that were planted by the members. There were more than 500 participants in this commune by 1910, most of them well-educated middle class and upper middle class individuals. These included sporting goods manufacturer Albert G. Spaulding, Pittsburgh promoter and fruit grower William Chase Temple, former president of the American Screw Company Clark Thurston, and Georgia manufacturer W. Ross White.

The members received no wages for their work, only food and clothing.

The Greek Theater was regularly used by the residents of Point Loma for lavish productions (drawings by Lois Will).

The men wore uniforms and the women wore simple, if not identical, garments. They ate in two communal dining halls. All children were cared for in a communal nursery or in special bungalows and were permitted to visit with their parents only on Sundays.

Theosophists from all over the world sent children to be educated at the Point Loma school, which Tingley called Raja Yoga after the Sanskrit term meaning "kingly union." The number of students averaged 300, and there were 65 teachers. Among other studies, the children were given good grounding in instrumental and vocal music. The community had a noted orchestra which conductor Walter Damrosch praised when he gave a guest performance there. They also had a theater production company that regularly performed plays by Shakespeare.

When Tingley died on July 11, 1929, leadership passed to Gottfried de Purucker, a scholar in Sanskrit literature. But the costs of running Point Loma far exceeded its income, most from donations, and the community declined. In 1940, in order to satisfy creditors, they sold all their land except that which immediately surrounded the central buildings. Then in 1942, the U.S. government purchased the rest of the land and buildings for wartime housing, and the community closed. The remaining members moved to a secluded spot at Covina, California, but were unable to maintain community life there.

Few of the buildings of Point Loma remain today. The temple was destroyed by fire many years ago. The others are now part of Point Loma College, owned by the Church of the Nazarene. The

Greek Theater is still intact and open to visitors. It has a plaque reading "First Greek Theater in America. Built A.D. 1901 by the Universal Brotherhood and Theosophical Society under the leadership of Katherine Tingley. The Society occupied these premises from 1897 to 1942." A book with a section that focuses on Point Loma is Hine's *California's Utopian Communities.*

Polaris Action Farm *see* **New England Committee for Nonviolent Action Farm**

Port Richmond Phalanx *see* **Social Reform Unity**

Powelton Neighbors (1947–1970), in Philadelphia, Pennsylvania, was an interracial cooperative housing community established by the American Friends Service Committee. Their stated purpose was to erect housing that might stop further deterioriation of a neighborhood near the University of Pennsylvania. The approximately 50 members sponsored a nursery school, social action committee, art class, babysitting cooperative, and recreational activities such as folk dancing. They won two awards for outstanding progress in urban renewal. The cooperative aspects of the community diminished, however, as the members got better jobs outside the community and thus became more affluent.

Prairie Home Colony (1868–1888), at what is now Silkville, Kansas, was a Fourierist community (see **Social Reform Unity**) that was also called the Kansas Cooperative Farm and Silkville. It was established by French aristocrat Ernest Valeton de Boissière (1810–1894), who had worked closely with novelist Victor Hugo and had allied himself with the radical wing of the Republican Party in France. After Napoleon took power and began to deal harshly with such radicals, he had to flee to the United States.

Ernest de Boissière first settled in New Orleans and contributed $10,000 to construct a Methodist Episcopal school for orphaned black children. This gesture caused a great deal of resentment in Southern aristocratic circles, where there was much opposition to the education of children of former slaves. It was, therefore, made clear to de Boissière that he was no longer welcome in the South.

He then moved to Kansas in 1868 and purchased 3,156 acres about 20 miles south of Ottawa for the purpose of establishing a Fourierist phalanx. His plan was for the members to raise cows and grow grapes and mulberry trees so that they could produce wine, silk, and cheese. Charles Sears, a former leader of the **North American Phalanx**, and Albert Brisbane, the foremost American proponent of Fourierism, helped de Boissière find the right land and set up the commune.

While the number of residents varied from year to year, it is probable that there were never more than 50 at any one time. The land included a large peach orchard, 400 apple trees and a number of other kinds of fruit trees. The members planted about 1,200 grape vines and 70 acres of mulberry trees. In time, they were producing 224 yards of silk ribbon each day. They later set up their cheese factory that had a capacity of producing 1,200 pounds of cheese per day.

Although the silk received favorable comments at the Philadelphia Exposition in 1876, the community did not particularly prosper. In 1884 de Boissière returned to his estates in France.

View of the Prairie Home Colony as it appeared in 1877 (drawing by Lois Will).

Within four years the rest of the members abandoned the commune, and in 1892 de Boissière gave the white limestone buildings to the Odd Fellows for an orphanage, now known as the De-Boissière Odd Fellows Orphans' Home and Industrial School Association of Kansas. These buildings are still being used for this purpose. Books with sections that focus on the Prairie Home Colony are Hinds' *American Communities* and Nordhoff's *The Communistic Societies of the United States*.

Prairie Home Community (1844), near West Liberty, Ohio, was organized by John O. Wattles, Valentine Nicholson, and others who had become interested in such a project after attending a convention of socialists in New York City. There were about 130 members, most of whom were Hicksite Quaker farm families, and they had 500 acres of land. Half this land was hilly and well-timbered and the rest was good farmland.

The commune had a large two-story frame house, a log cabin, a flour mill, and an old saw mill. The members practiced vegetarianism and from time to time assisted runaway slaves. Their one principle of organization was the golden rule. "Do unto others as ye would have others do unto you." There was apparently little direction of work within the commune, and it was expected that the members would volunteer to do jobs whenever the need arose. Orson S. Murray, editor of a paper devoted to communalism called the *Regenerator*, was a member here for a brief period. When he tried to bring his printing equipment to the Prairie Home Community, the boat that was transporting it was wrecked on Lake Erie and the equipment lost. He later organized his own Ohio commune, **Fruit Hills**. Other prominent members included an Englishman named John Wood and a Dr. Hard.

The commune also owned a small farm nine miles north called Highland Home. It included a farm house in which 12 members lived. Both Prairie Home and its satellite farm closed before the end of the year, probably because of the lack of organizational structure. A number of members moved to other communes, and Wattles went on to join the Fourierist **Clermont Phalanx** and then to set up two communes of his own, **The Brotherhood** and the **Grand Prairie Harmonial Association**. A book with a section that focuses on the Prairie Home Community is Noyes' *History of American Socialisms*.

Preparation (1853–1858), in Preparation Canyon State Park, Monona County, Iowa, was a Mormon commune established by Charles B. Thompson. He was born into a Quaker family, became a Methodist as a young man, and then joined the Mormons at **Kirtland**. In 1848, while promoting the Mormon cause in St. Louis, Missouri, he had a revelation in which an angel appointed him to be the "Chief Teacher and Interpreter of the Book of Mormon." In time he gathered 500 followers to set up a United Order community on the 160 acres of land in Iowa. There he published a newspaper, *The Preparation News*, and set up a post office with himself as postmaster. But his dictatorial methods led to a revolt in the community and he was expelled from it in October 1858. The matter was taken to court, and the land was then divided among the members. Thereafter the commune ceased to exist. A book with a section that focuses on Preparation is Allen's *Northwestern Iowa: Its History and Traditions — 1804–1926*.

Price City (1875–1882), at what is now Price, Utah, was a communal settlement of Mormons that followed the **Orderville** United Order model. There may have been as many as 200 members. This commune was dissolved following the passage of the Edmunds antipolygamy law by Congress, which forced many of the Mormon leaders into hiding.

Progressive Community (1871–1878), at Cedar Vale, Kansas, was a communal settlement of about ten members, including a Russian sculptor, Russian astronomer, American clergyman who had embraced spiritualism, and American health-food doctor. Their stated purpose was "to achieve both communism and individual freedom, or to lead persons of all kinds of opinions to labor together for their common welfare. If there was to be any law, it should be only for the regulation of industry or hours of work."

The commune was organized by Stephen Briggs and William Frey (Vladimir Konstantinovich Geins, 1839–1888). The latter came from Odessa, Russia, and had possibly been a member of the radical Land and Liberty Party that worked to overthrow the czar. He came to the United States in 1868, with the intention of joining the **Oneida** commune, but instead he and his family joined the **Reunion Community**, just at the time that commune was beginning to disband.

Other members included Avrahm Yarmolinsky and a family named Right. They had 320 acres of land, some stock, and a number of fruit trees. At Frey's insistence, they practiced "mutual criticism," as used at Oneida. However, disagreements among the members over questions of religion and socialism led to the splitting of this commune in July 1875, and Frey's formation of a different one nearby called the **Investigating Community**. Frey was particularly disgusted with the fact that the Progressive Community had been taken over by a group of spiritualists and health-food faddists. Books with sections that focus on the Progressive Community are Fogarty's *All Things New* and Nordhoff's *The Communistic Societies of the United States*.

Providence Cooperative Farm (1939–1952), near Cruger, Mississippi, was an interracial project started by Sherwood Eddy with the aim of alleviating some of the poverty suffered by sharecroppers in Mississippi. It was designed to operate much like the **Delta Cooperative Farm** that Eddy had established earlier in the same state, and some of the 25 members came from there.

This commune encompassed 2,888 acres of land purchased with donations from supporters in Northern states. Eddy appointed A.E. Cox as the overall director of the commune, although the various managers of specific projects were elected by the membership at regular meetings. Of greatest importance to the commune and to the surrounding community that it serviced as well was the medical clinic, which was operated by Dr. David R. Minter.

As at the Delta Cooperative Farm, the members of this commune were under frequent verbal attacks from the surrounding community because of the member's insistence on racial inclusiveness. And there were some incidents of open hostility toward them. When the experiment closed in 1942, due to the departure of many of the members and most of the trained leadership because of the availability of high-paying jobs during World War II, the land was divided into individual plots and allocated to the remaining members. Dr. Minter continued his clinic there for a long time after this commune closed, treating thousands of tenant farmer patients. A book with a section that focuses on the Providence Cooperative Farm is Eddy's *Eighty Adventurous Years.*

Puget Sound Cooperative Colony (1887–1892) was a land-development cooperative located at Port Angeles, Washington. It was organized by George Venable Smith (1843–1919), a lawyer in Seattle, and he promoted the plan through a newspaper called *The Model Commonwealth.* He also held a convention in Seattle for would-be members. The delegates who aimed to provide "houses and employment for members" with "justice for all" adopted a constitution for the project on May 4, 1887. They also elected 11 trustees to oversee the property.

Smith had secured a large tract of wooded land that was incorporated with a capital stock of $100,000. Members purchased lots on the property for $20 to $200, depending on the size and location. Smith went on a tour through a number of states to advertise the commune, and one of his stops was the **Union Colony** in Colorado from which a few members came.

By late summer in 1887 the commune's saw mill had turned out about 250,000 feet of lumber. There was also a brick kiln, blacksmiths and wagonmakers shops, stables, a butcher shop, and a greenhouse to provide vegetables for the 239 members. Most of them engaged in fishing for a living. They lived in tents until they were able to build some homes and a large building where they cooked and ate together called the "East End Hotel."

Because they were unable to raise sufficient funds to build a railroad on the site, they constructed a steamship to transport the wood, fish, and other marketable products they produced. They called this ship the *Angeles.* Wages were paid on a sliding scale based on the cost of good purchased outside the community. The members never did complete their plans for streets, regular houses, and several hotels.

Shortly after they began community life, dissension broke out among the members over the elected leadership. In

February 1988, Smith and others were deposed and a new board was elected. It was headed by Fred R. Thompson and Thomas Malony.

The commune closed because of lawsuits brought against the directors by dissatisfied shareholders and creditors. Today a large pulp-paper mill occupies the site. A book with a section that focuses on the Puget Sound Cooperative Colony is LeWarne's *Utopias on the Puget Sound, 1885–1915*.

Putney Corporation (1843–1847), at Putney, Vermont, was the first Perfectionist community organized by John Humphrey Noyes (1811–1886). The 40 members, who called themselves "Bible Communists," believed that perfection in life is possible through communion with God, and that people must share all personal possessions and live as one family. They established a system of mutual criticism in which each member was evaluated by the other members in the hope of achieving personal improvement. They also practiced a system of complex marriage in which each commune member had the possibility of sexual access to every other member, with his or her consent and under the general supervision of community leaders.

Noyes had been called by some as "the greatest of the Vermont prophets." He was the son of a congressman and a first cousin to President Rutherford B. Hayes. He entered Dartmouth College at the age of 15, preparing himself for a legal profession, but after he was converted by the noted evangelist Charles Finney, Noyes decided instead to become a preacher. Though he rapidly earned his preacher's license, he lost it just as quickly because he insisted on upholding the doctrine of Perfectionism: that is, the belief that conversion offers complete release from sin. He also upheld another doctrine that was considered heresy by orthodox theologians: the belief that the Second Coming of Christ had occurred within a single generation of Christ's first appearance in Palestine, and thus the basis had already been laid for the establishment of Christ's kingdom.

For several years Noyes met and worked with groups of Perfectionists in New York and Massachusetts, and he tried to interest leading reformers of the day in this theological stance. Then he returned to his home in Putney and urged other believers in Perfectionism to join him there.

The members included Noyes and his wife, his brother George, the families of John Skinner and John Miller, as well as others whose names are no longer known. They lived in a number of Putney houses and worked on the surrounding farms and at various trades within the town. They considered any kind of work dignified, and the women members had equal rights with men. Children were raised by the community as a whole. They were treated permissively, being allowed to sleep each morning until they awoke, and they were given ample time for play and a loving, noncoercive environment in which to develop.

The system of "complex marriage" integral to all the Perfectionist communes was not quite the system of "free love" that some have described it, since while any couple could join together freely, sexual relations were permissible only if both parties were willing and children were conceived only after agreement by the rest of the community. The limiting of births under such a system, Noyes argued, could be achieved through a male's control of his climax.

Perhaps the most important feature of the Putney Corporation was Noyes' system of mutual criticism. The effect of these mutual criticism sessions seems to have been somewhat similar to group psychotherapy, permitting the expression of grievances before they became explosive. The whole community selected the "standing committee of criticism," and changed it from time to time so that all members might give as well as receive such criticism. In the words of Noyes, "Mutual criticism subordinates the I-spirit to the We-spirit."

The community in Putney was closed in 1847 after Noyes was arrested on a charge of adultery. He gave bond for his appearance at trial and then fled quickly to Oneida, New York, where a number of his supporters gathered in another communal experiment that was started in 1848 (see **Oneida**).

The village of Putney never seemed to recover from the shock of Noyes' arrest and the fact that they had harbored such a community. There are still houses in the village that were used by the Perfectionists, but the present-day residents do not welcome inquiries about them and none are designated by markers. Books with sections that focus on the Putney Corporation are Calverton's *Where Angels Dared to Tread*, Holloway's *Heavens on Earth*, Nordhoff's *The Communistic Societies of the United States*, and Noyes' *History of American Socialisms*.

Putney Perfectionists (1849–1851), at Putney, Vermont, was a commune of perhaps five followers of John Humphrey Noyes, who lived as a community in the same town where he had established his original Perfectionist **Putney Corporation**. Since hostility against Noyes and the Perfectionists in this town was overwhelming, the members of this commune must have maintained strict secrecy of their lifestyle. It is believed they moved to **Oneida** when the commune disbanded.

Rankin Colony (1878–1879), at Muscoda, Wisconsin, was a Christian commune founded by J.S. Rankin that was "on good land, in a desirable location and ready to welcome Christian people who would join in cooperative labor." Rankin was the editor of the *Free Flag* newspaper in Muscoda. There were perhaps ten members.

Raritan Bay Union (1853–1855), at Englewood, now part of Perth Amboy, New Jersey, was a Fourierist phalanx (see **Social Reform Unity**) founded by about 30 members who left the **North American Phalanx** over a religious conflict. These members disagreed with the others because they believed that the commune should hire a religious leader to strengthen the moral and religious aspects of the phalanx.

The Raritan Bay Union derived its name from its location at the mouth of the Raritan River overlooking Raritan Bay. The leader was Marcus Spring (1810–1874), formerly a commission merchant in New York City. Other prominent members included Mrs. Tyndale from Philadelphia, Clement O. Read, George S. Arnold, Joseph L. Pennock, and Theodore and Angelina Grimke Weld. The latter was one of the two Grimke sisters, well-known for their pioneering work in the women's rights movement and their active opposition to slavery. Here, as at the North American Phalanx, religion became a major issue of contention. When the members finally decided to abandon the project, the property reverted to Spring, who then continued to live there.

Rational Brethren of Oxford *see* **Coal Creek**

One of the houses used by the members of Reba Place (photo by Norman Stockwell).

Raton Molokan Colony (1924), near Raton, New Mexico, was a Molokan farming commune (see **Freedom Colony**) closely allied to the **New Mexico Molokan Colony**. It had about 30 members.

Reba Place (1957–present), in Evanston, Illinois, is a community started by three Mennonites and named after the street on which their property is located. The three leaders had been students together at Goshen College, a Mennonite institution in Indiana. They chose Evanston for their experiment because at the time there were a number of Mennonite conscientious objectors working out their alternative service at Evanston General Hospital. They thought this group of young men might provide an initial base for their membership.

Although they did not eventually attract any of the conscientious objectors to join their community, they did succeed in attracting others and by 1973 the community had expanded from a single apartment into nine separate houses with a membership of 180 persons. The members work at various jobs in Evanston and Chicago. A number of them are hospital workers. They pool their earnings and use them for the community as a whole.

One of the three founders, Virgil Vogt, has said that one of the reasons for establishing this commune was that "We believe that if the Church is to reflect the Mennonite tradition, it must be reorganized into communal Christian communities." The Reba Place founders also attempted to reverse the rather conservative rural outlook of most American Mennonite congregations by insisting that Christianity is an urban movement, therefore the Church should focus its work in urban centers.

The membership is no longer strictly Mennonite, but is now nondenominational and interracial in character. All the members, however, are pacifists and regularly take part in civil rights, peace, and political struggles within the Chicago-Evanston urban area as a whole. A book with a section that focuses on Reba Place is Roberts' *The New Communes: Coming Together in America*.

Red Banks (1807–1810) at what is now Henderson, Kentucky, was a small Shaker settlement (see **Watervliet**) of probably fewer than 25 members. It grew out of the recruiting trip that Issacher Bates, Richard McNemar, and Matthew Houston took to the Midwest on behalf of the **Mount Lebanon** Shaker community. In 1810, the entire commune closed and joined with two other Shaker communities, **Straight Creek** and **Eagle Creek**, to form the **West Union** Shaker commune in Indiana.

Reformed Methodist Farm (1814–1816), located on the state line between Bennington, Vermont, and Hoosick, New York, was a communal establishment formed by 12 persons who seceded from the Methodist Episcopal Church in the towns of Whitingham and Readsborough, Vermont, on January 16, 1814. Their land covered several hundred acres, and among the members were Elijah Bailey, James Bailey, Ezra Amadon, Ebeneezer Davis, William Lake, and Caleb Whiting.

They were mechanics, farmers, and local preachers opposed to the ruling authority of bishops within the Methodist Episcopal Church. They felt that such a form of church government was basically undemocratic, and they advocated a system in which each congregation could set its own rules. They also opposed slavery and believed that disease could be healed by prayer alone.

Although the members of this commune were forced to give up their experiment after two years because of lack of funds to pay for the land and "as the cold season was coming on," they did eventually establish the Reformed Methodist Church that over the years grew to about 3,000 members in the United States and Canada. This denomination is today rapidly declining in membership. A book with a section that focuses on the Reformed Methodist Farm is Clark's *The Small Sects in America*.

Relief (1881), at an unknown place called Principia that was probably in Bolinger County, Missouri, was a communal settlement of perhaps ten members, organized by Alcander Longley (see **Fourier Phalanx**). He was an advocate of Christian communism who had belonged to several other communes and organized six of his own. The experiment did not last a full year, and is thought to have failed because of lack of capital.

Réunion (1855–1875) was a Fourierist community founded by Victor Considérant (1808–1893) on the south bank of the Trinity River, three miles west of Dallas, Texas. Considérant had been a close associate of Fourier's in France and he was the first person to try to apply Fourier's theories (see **Social Reform Unity**) by organizing some phalanx-type communes in France. He had also helped Fourier to establish the monthly magazine *Le Phalanstère*. After Fourier's death in 1837, Considérant became the accepted head of the Fourierist movement in France. He established a library in Paris that was devoted to Fourier's work, began a daily newspaper, and set up Fourierist societies wherever he could.

Following the Revolution of 1848, Considérant was elected to the Constitutional Assembly in Paris where he introduced legislation in support of the right of women to vote. It failed to pass. In 1849 he was accused of treason for his role in an armed demonstration against Napoleon's Roman Expedition. Considérant fled to Belgium and then to the United States, where he purchased 61,500 acres for the Réunion project. It was promoted in Europe through the Societé de Colonisation Européa—Américaine au Texas. The main part of this land was near Dallas, but some of it was also near Houston, and the rest was in Uvalde County, Texas.

On June 16, 1855, the first group of immigrants planning to join the Réunion commune arrived at the property. They came from France, Belgium, and Switzerland. Their ship landed at Houston and they traveled by oxcart from there to Dallas. Only two of them were farmers; the rest were artisans and some highly educated professionals, including scientists, authors, musicians, artists, and naturalists. In time the membership of Réunion rose to about 500. For two years they suffered successive droughts, a grasshopper infestation, and hostility from the Know-Nothing Party in the Texas legislature.

Considérant abandoned the project in 1858 because it was failing to fulfill his Fourierist dreams. With his wife and mother-in-law, Mme. Clarice Vigorureaux (a gifted writer), he moved to San Antonio. He later became an American citizen, but in 1869 he returned to Paris where he died in obscurity.

Many of the other members tried to continue the Réunion project before the community sold its assets and disbanded in 1875. Some of the descendants of the Réunion commune became famous in the history of Dallas and the state of Texas. Today the crumbling foundations of a single house that was built in 1859 for the widow of one of the commune members, Alphonse Delord, as well as some graves of members in the old Fishtrap Cemetery are all that remain of this commune. A book with a section that focuses on Réunion is Bestor's *American Phalanxes, the Fourierist Phase of Socialism in the United States.*

Reunion Community (1868–1870) was a settlement of 27 members located at Reunion, near Oronogo, in Jasper County, Missouri. It was established by Alcander Longley (see **Fourier Phalanx**), who lived in two Fourierist communes, established another, and then set up five Christian communist communes, this being the first of the latter. This commune was also called the True Family.

As in all of Longley's experiments, the property was held in common by the membership. It is probably that this commune collapsed because of too little capital. A book with a section that focuses on Longley's Reunion Community is Bliss's *The Encyclopedia of Social Reform.*

Richards Colony (1906–1918), in Sanborn County, South Dakota, was a Hutterite Brüderhof (see **Bon Homme**) that had about 100 members. They moved to Alberta, Canada, in 1918, where they still exist.

Rimrock (1963–present), near Sunburst, Montana, is a Hutterite Brüderhof (see **Bon Homme**). It had 82 members in 1964 and was led by Peter Hofer.

Rising Star Community (1853–1857), at Stelvideo in Darke County, Ohio, a few miles north of Greenville, was a cooperative settlement of 13 persons led by John S. Patterson. They owned 400 acres of land, a two-story frame house, and a large saw mill that was run by steam. The members claimed to be liberal in all things, and there was no effort to achieve unity in religion, politics, diet, or other social practices. However, the dress reform movement of Amelia Bloomer was so popular here that neighbors began to call the community "Bloomertown." In 1856 the members began to publish a periodical called the *Social Revolutionist*. It is not known why this commune disbanded, but when it did, Patterson moved the periodical to the **Berlin Community** at Berlin Heights, Ohio.

Riverside (1949–present), near Huron, South Dakota, is a Hutterite Brüderhof (see **Bon Homme**) that had 101 members in 1964 and was led by John Waldner.

Robin Hill (1927), at Media, Pennsylvania, was established as a single-tax community (see **Fairhope**) of about ten members. Galen Wood was the president and Isaac Dornblum the vice-president. The members were never able to secure a necessary loan from the banks for any improvements on their leased land and so they soon gave up the project. A book with a section that focuses on Robin Hill is Huntington's *Enclaves of Economic Rent for 1931.*

Rockport (1890–1934), in Hutchinson County, South Dakota, was a Hutterite Brüderhof (see **Bon Homme**) that was settled about six miles north of the **Elm Spring** commune. The approximately 100 members moved to Canada where

the colony is still maintained. A different Brüderhof, also called Rockport, now occupies the land.

Rockport (1934–present), in Hutchinson County, South Dakota, is a Hutterite Brüderhof established by members of the **Bon Homme** Hutterite commune on the vacant lands of the former **Rockport** Brüderhof that had moved to Canada. In 1964 there were 140 members, and this commune was led by Daniel Wipf.

Rockport in Montana (1948–present), near Pendroy, Montana, is a Hutterite Brüderhof (see **Bon Homme**) with 78 members in 1964. It was led then by John Kleinsasser.

Rockville (1874–1875), Utah, was a **St. George**–type of Mormon United Order commune for nearly a year. There were about 100 members, most of them fruit farmers.

Rosedale (1901–present), near Alexandria, South Dakota, is a Hutterite Brüderhof (see **Bon Homme**) founded by members of the **Tripp** Brüderhof. They moved to Manitoba, Canada, in 1918, but returned to South Dakota in 1945. In 1964 there were 147 members and their minister was Joseph Waldner.

Rosenhayn (1882–1889), near Deerfield, New Jersey, was a Jewish agricultural settlement (see **Sicily Island**) that had 250 members at its high point before it ceased to be cooperative. The community was sponsored by the Hebrew Immigrant Aid Society, and was one of the few Jewish settlements in New Jersey that was organized as a cooperative, although there were many such Jewish communes in other states. The members built a clothing factory and farmed. The settlement continued after 1889, but by then the members had discarded its cooperative nature.

Roycrofters (1896–1915), at East Aurora, Erie County, New York, was established by lecturer, publisher, and essayist Elbert Hubbard (1856–1915). At first this was just a publishing venture in imitation of the Kelmscott Press, set up in England by socialist artist and writer William Morris. However Hubbard soon saw that he could attract laborers and assistants to join him in this project if he designed his company as a commune.

In 1896 he placed an advertisement in his magazine *Philistine* that read: "all good Philistines ... welcome to seats at the table and a place to sleep — of course without charge. All men and women, however, who remain over one night are expected to work for the public good at least two hours a day. There is type setting, proof reading, copying and addressing wrappers to do, besides ... cooking, washing, and then there is a good big wood pile." Many people came to Roycrofters to stay for a period of time. At one point there may have been as many as 500 persons living and working there on the farm, in the Roycrofters bank, printing plant, book bindery, furniture shop, and blacksmith shop. Some of them lived in a building that was called the Roycroft Phalanxtry.

All the company profits, including fees that came from Hubbard's lectures, went, according to Hubbard, "into the common fund of the Roycrofters — the benefit is for all." A big income producer was Hubbard's well-known essay "Message to Garcia" (1899), an account of a U.S. Army officer's daring search through the Cuban jungle for the Cuban rebel Garcia. The officer carried word of American support for the rebel. The essay was reprinted again and again due to popular demand.

The members of Roycrofters ate at a common table, held meetings, educational studies, and sports events together, and they used a common library that Hubbard established. When Hubbard visited and gave a lecture at the **Mutual Home Association** in Washington, one of the families there departed and moved to Roycrofters.

Hubbard died in the sinking of the *Lusitania*, and this effectively ended the commune, although the Roycroft publishing enterprise continued for some years afterward as a purely commercial enterprise. A book with a section that focuses on the Roycrofters is Champney's *Love and Glory: The Story of Elbert Hubbard*.

Runnymede (1916), near Palo Alto, California, was a commune of about 100 Little Landers (see **San Ysidro Little Landers**). They had strict physical and financial requirements for membership.

Ruskin Commonwealth (1894–1901), founded by Julius A. Wayland (1854–1912), was located first at Tennessee City, Tennessee, (at what is now Ruskin, Tennessee) and finally at what is now Ruskin, Georgia. Wayland was an advocate of the socialist ideas of Edward Bellamy (1850–1898), who in 1888 published the best-selling utopian novel, *Looking Backward*. The book was an immediate success, selling almost one million copies by the early 1890s. It became, according to one historian, "one of the most influential books ever published in this country and on a par with *Uncle Tom's Cabin*."

Looking Backward described a system of reform that was at once appealing and seemingly practicable. Almost at once the book became a focal point for Nationalist clubs that sprang up everywhere with the sole aim of advocating a new socialist order. The first of these was formed in Boston, and within two years there were more than 150 such clubs throughout the country. The members published periodicals, conducted forums, and participated in political campaigns. They called themselves Nationalists because their aim "was to nationalize the functions of production and distribution," to bring "the entire system of the country under the same popular government which now extends to a few comparatively trifling functions called political."

Under capitalism, Bellamy argued, a man is driven by dire need. Yet fear, the lash of want, is "on the whole the weakest as well as certainly the cruelest of incentives." Nationalism, he claimed — giving each person an equal share of the total income and rewarding special effort with prized degrees of rank and prestige — is certain to develop a healthy and desirable kind of incentive to keep the economy on an even keel.

Bellamy himself never participated in the Ruskin Commonwealth or any of the other communes that were established by advocates of his ideas, nor did he join the Nationalist movement, but he did help to build many National Clubs that advocated experiments and thrusts toward socialism.

Wayland also espoused the ideas of English artist, poet, and socialist William Morris (1834–1896), who also wrote a utopian novel, *News from Nowhere*, that described a socialist society quite different from that of Bellamy's. Wayland apparently was never aware that Morris wrote his book as an antidote to the rather mechanical society depicted in *Looking Backward*.

Despite his affection for the ideas of Bellamy and Morris, Wayland decided to name his commune after another English socialist, John Ruskin (1819–1900), a man who did not write any utopian novels but who was perhaps the most influential writer on art and social issues of his time. Ruskin believed that education, morality, and healthy social conditions were needed to produce good art and good citizens.

Wayland was a native of Indiana. He made a modest fortune in job printing and also real estate at Pueblo, Colorado. However in 1893 he decided to sell his printing business and return to Indiana to promote his ideas about socialism. He established a weekly newspaper, *The Coming Nation*, that fostered the ideas of Bellamy and other socialists. His paper was a product of the moralistic, prohibitionist, Bible Belt Midwest, as he was. Its pages were filled with rambling anecdotes and epigrams, and it was highly popular. Within six months there was a paid-up subscription list of 14,000, and Wayland was selling an additional 3,000 copies through street sales. By July 1894, there were 60,000 subscribers.

When Wayland established the Ruskin Commonwealth commune, he decided that anyone contributing $100 to the project or anyone securing 200 subscribers to his paper could become a charter member. He moved his printing plant to Tennessee City, where he had purchased 1,000 acres of land for the colony. But the land was poor and the combination of socialists and anarchists attracted to the experiment led to violent disagreements. Also the colonists were unprepared for the cold winter that year in Tennessee, and so there was much sickness.

By January 1895 there were so many complaints against Wayland's leadership that he sold the paper to the members and withdrew from the commune, giving them full title to the land. Wayland later went on to edit and publish the equally popular socialist paper *Appeal to Reason.*

J.H. Dodson took Wayland's place as president. Dodson moved the commune to Cave Mills (now Ruskin), not far away and within the same county, where the land was better and they could obtain two fine farms, a large flour mill, a store, and a post office. They also had a good stream of water there and two large caves that provided an attraction for visitors.

The internal conflicts did not abate, however, and in 1899 a majority of the members decided to move the commune to Duke, Georgia. The town is now called Ruskin. There they joined a group of 35 people who had only recently oranized themselves as the **American Settlers Co-operative Association.** These people already had nearly 800 acres of land with more than 50 houses, so it seemed almost perfect to merge the two groups. This brought the membership up to 284, perhaps the highest number to ever belong to the Ruskin Commonwealth at one time. There were doctors, lawyers, mechanics, teachers, and businessmen, though most of the members had farming backgrounds. But again, the communalists found that the land was poor and disagreements over the management soon broke out.

They did engage in woodworking, broom manufacturing, leatherworking, making shingles, marketing of cereal coffee, general farming, and, of course, publishing *The Coming Nation.* At various times this commune also tried to run a bakery, laundry, grist mill, blacksmith shop, photographic shop, chewing-gum factory, and a saw mill. They built a general store, an executive office, a hotel, a post office, and a railroad station. They also established a school, a women's club, a theater group, a brass band, a lyceum, and a library of over 1,500 volumes. Each member worked a nine-hour day, and each family lived in their own home. But, by the end of 1901, so many members had departed that the commune could not continue. Some joined other communal experiments — **Cooperative Industrial College, Fairhope,** and **Kinder Lou.** Today there is nothing left to mark the Ruskin Commonwealth's existence but the town name. A book with sections that focus on the Ruskin Commonwealth is Hinds' *American Communities.*

Rys (1897–1900), at Vontay near Dabneys, Virginia, was a communal settlement of perhaps 40 Bohemian immigrants. The members paid an initiation fee of $50 and agreed to add a sum to this amount each week after they joined the commune. They purchased an old plantation and lived according to a pattern in which everyone shared alike in the products raised. They disbanded because of dissension, and most of the participants then moved to Baltimore and New York City. Books with sections that focus on Rys are Cápek's *The Cechs (Bohemians) in America* and Miller's *Some Tennessee Utopias.*

Sabbathday Lake Village (1794–present), at Sabbathday Lake, south of Poland, Maine, is a Shaker commune (see **Watervliet**) that was also once known as New Gloucester. The community is located on the side of a hill that slopes down to Sabbathday Lake. At one time the land holdings of this Shaker commune totaled 2,000 acres. The members constructed a saw mill, grist mill, machine shop, several large

Shops and stable on the Sabbathday Lake Shaker Community (courtesy of United Society of Shakers).

barns, a central brick dormitory with a chapel in one wing, and a number of small workshops. They marketed garden seeds, brooms, dry measures, wire sieves, spinning wheels, and oak staves for molasses hogsheads. They also sold pickles and herbs.

Hewitt Chandler invented a mowing machine there that they profitably manufactured. He also invented a way of bending the oak staves without setting them up in casks, a method that greatly simplified the manufacturing of these items. In 1823 Sabbathday Lake Village had 150 members divided into three "families," and in 1995 there were still eight aging members, all women. The Shakers have for many years refused to accept any new recruits.

Sage Creek (1961–present), near Chester, Montana, is a Hutterite Brüderhof (see **Bon Homme**) that had 106 members in 1964 and was led by Paul Wipf.

St. Benedict's Farm (1938–1960), at Upton, Massachusetts, was a Catholic Worker farm (see **Maryfarm** on Staten Island) that was established on 100 acres of land that contained a farmhouse, an old schoolhouse that they converted into a residence, and a barn. Five months after the commune was established, a hurricane leveled their barn.

In 1952, there were 31 members living here. One of the leaders at that time was Carl Paulson, a man who spent the war years in a conscientious objectors camp. He later became a manufacturer of stained glass objects and was able to employ several of the members to work with him in this trade. Other members included John Magee, the former head of the Catholic Worker House of Hospitality in Boston; Ade Bethune, an artist for *The Catholic Worker* newspaper; Bill Sheehan, who was the cook for the commune; and Dave Wilson, the commune carpenter.

St. Francis Acres (1947–1973), at Glen Gardner, New Jersey, was an anarchist community established by Dave Dellinger, one of the leaders of the peace movement in the 1960s. It was named after St. Francis of Assisi, who they quoted as saying, "But my lord Bishop, if we held any property, armed force would become necessary for protection. For property gives rise to lawsuits and to wars which in various ways destroy all love of God and of fellowmen. Our brotherhood, therefore, will not hold any property." The community had a printing press and began the magazine *Liberation*, which after Dellinger left the community was moved to New York City. They also printed many other publications, although their press was damaged by vandals in 1964. There were about 15 members.

St. Francis Farm (1941–1945), at Shrewsbury, Vermont, was a Catholic Worker farm (see **Maryfarm** on Staten Island) that had about 15 members.

St. George (1874–1878), a town in Utah, became for a period of four years, a 300-member Mormon commune, closely patterned after the original **Kirtland** United Order. The commune was started after Brigham Young visited this village, which was then in particular need of economic revivalism. He decided to reinstitute the United Order system that had been abandoned by the Mormons for almost 30 years after they arrived in Utah.

With revivalistic fervor Young convinced the residents of St. George that the United Order was the only way for Mormons to live. The town's economy soon revitalized. Small, inefficiently worked fields were combined to improve their yields. Every able man was put to work and was paid in labor credits.

Money was taken out of circulation. Household necessities were supplied as families needed them, and at the end of the year the books were balanced. The success of St. George's United Order led Young and other leaders of the church to go about organizing the system throughout the Utah communities.

Students of Mormon history now distinguish four distinct types of United Orders growing out of this movement, two of which fit into the category of communes: the St. George–type, of which there were at least 25 examples, and a type used at **Orderville**, of which there were eight. A book with a section that focuses on St. George is Allen's *The Second United Order Among the Mormons*.

St. Isadore's Farm (1946–1947), near Aitken, Minnesota, was a Catholic Worker farm (see **Maryfarm** on Staten Island) named for the patron saint of farmers. It had 15 members and was established by Larry Heaney and Martin Paul, who later also set up **Holy Family Farm** in Missouri. Other members included Al Reser and his wife, who had edited the *Chicago Catholic Worker* newspaper, and Don Humphrey from Milwaukee, Wisconsin. Together they built a few cabins and started farming. But the struggle for survival in this remote area was too much for them and the commune lasted for just more than one year. One of their children died there of a rare pancreatic disorder, and one of the members was drafted into the army, which was quite demoralizing to the pacifist membership.

St. Louis-Western Colony (1871), at Evans, Colorado, was a cooperative community modeled after the **Union Colony** at Greeley. The approximately 100 members were organized by the

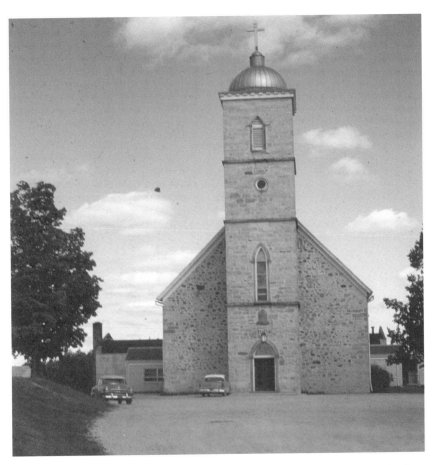

Church built by members of St. Nazianz as it stands today (photo by author).

Rev. A.C. Todd of Oakdale, Illinois, who set up the recruitment headquarters in St. Louis, Missouri. The community collapsed because of bad management. A book with a section that focuses on the St. Louis-Western Colony is Willard's *The Union Colony of Greeley, Colorado, 1869–1871*.

St. Nazianz (1854–1896), in Manitowoc County, Wisconsin, was a Catholic commune named after a Greek saint. The location has since become a village by that name. The communal settle-ment was founded by Ambrose Oschswald (1801–1873), a German Catholic priest who had published in 1848 *Mystischen Schriften*, a work that predicted that the New Jerusalem would arrive before 1900. For this he was condemned by the archbishop of Baden and relieved of his parish. However his followers established the St. Nazianz Association and 113 of them traveled with him from Freiburg, Germany to the United States to begin this commune as an example of commitment in the midst of a corrupt world.

The land they occupied extended seven miles from east to west and three miles from north to south. They erected log houses for the unmarried brothers and sisters, who were encouraged to remain celibate. Married members lived in a nearby village but obtained all their supplies and work assignments from St. Nazianz. Eventually the commune grew to 450 members. They farmed, operated a dairy, and produced straw and knit goods.

After the death of Oschswald, it was decided that no more married couples could join the commune and that the property should be controlled by a joint stock company composed of former members. Then, in 1874, no more single members were permitted to join. When the remaining ones had all died, the property was taken over by the Catholic Society of Our Divine Savior, which still makes use of the original buildings. The church, constructed by this commune in the 1860s, is also still in use. Books with sections that focus on St. Nazianz are Fogarty's *All Things New* and Quaife's *Wisconsin, Its History and Its People.*

St. Theresa's Village (1938–1940) was a Catholic cooperative experiment aimed at helping starving families not being reached by the various relief programs of Roosevelt's New Deal. It began on a 160-acre tract of land near Bolling, about ten miles from Greenville, Alabama. The land contained some crude houses. After two years, the commune was moved to another location near Greenville, a site bordering Highway 31. The experiment was initiated by Father Arthur W. Terminiello, a traveling priest of the Catholic Central Missions of Alabama and rural life director for his diocese, and it had the support of Bishop Toolen of Alabama.

Seven sharecropper families — six white and one black — joined the experiment. Each family was allowed two acres for their own use. The rest of the land was farmed cooperatively. Each family was also permitted their own chickens. Other livestock, including a few pigs, some mules, cows, steers, and one bull, were cooperatively owned. Father Terminiello, who lived at the commune and commuted to work in Greenville, appointed 18-year-old Dan Shaw as manager. The commune closed because of financial difficulties. An article with information that focuses on St. Theresa's Village is Sylvester's "Dynamite in Alabama," *Commonweal*, September 30, 1938

Salem-on-Erie *see* **Brotherhood of the New Life**

Saline Valley Farms (1932–1953), five miles from Saline, Michigan, was a cooperative farming community started in 1932. It had about 60 members and was organized by Harold Studley Gray. They owned 590 acres that included an orchard, filling station, greenhouse, woodworking shop, cooperative store, cannery, and 16 homes. The community closed in 1953, eclipsed, according to Gray, by the affluence of the post–World War II economy. A book with a section that focuses on the Saline Valley Farms is Infield's *Cooperative Communities at Work.*

San Fernando Farm (1945–1956), at Sylmar, now a suburb of Los Angeles County, California, was a pacifist commune organized in 1945 by four Quakers who were conscientious objectors during World War II and had been interned in Civilian Public Service Camps because of their refusal to participate in the war effort. The commune was located at what is now 13890 Sayre Street in this

Los Angeles suburb. The 20 members did part-time farming and worked at various trades in Los Angeles. They pooled their income and made decisions by unanimous consent. They also built their own homes and avoided going into debt, even for building materials. The community finally closed in 1956 because the city of Los Angeles began to encroach on their property.

San Fernando Little Landers (1916), in the San Fernando Valley of California, was a community of approximately 100 Little Landers (see **San Ysidro Little Landers**).

San Ysidro Little Landers (1909–1916), in Tiajuana Valley, 14 miles south of San Diego and 2 miles from the Mexican border, was a commune organized by William Ellsworth Smythe (1861–1922). He believed that anyone could support themselves and their family on a single acre of land, as long as the land was well-irrigated. Smythe had gone to California from New England. He lectured and wrote extensively on the land problem and in time gathered a large following.

Those who advocated his acre-plan were called Little Landers because they believed in purchasing large lots cooperatively, irrigating the land, and then subdividing it into small plots, or "little lands." In their communes, they authorized the leadership to market all food raised on these acre plots so that there was no intermediary to sap away profits.

The members of San Ysidro had 550 acres of land altogether in an area that has since become part of the city of San Diego. About a dozen families joined Smythe there the first year, but by 1913 the colony had 116 families, or about 300 people. A flood in January 1915 hit the colony so hard that the

members had to apply for relief. By the end of the next year the last colonist had departed.

The Little Landers movement declined as the members of the communes found their holdings too small to be economically sound. In February 1919 Smythe finally gave up plans for establishing further colonies and began to promote the reclamation of land for private farms to be sold to returning World War I servicemen, under the auspices of the national Forward the Land League. Books with sections that focus on the San Ysidro Little Landers are Conkin's *Tomorrow a New World* and Hine's *California's Utopian Communities*.

Santa Rosa Altruria (1895–1896), within the city of Santa Rosa, California, was a Christian Socialist commune founded by former members of **Altruria**. There may have been as many as ten members, and the project only lasted about eight months.

Savannah (1735–1740), on the edge of the town of Savannah, Georgia, was the first of ten Moravian communal settlements in America. It was established under a program called the General Economy, in which all land and property was held in common. In comparison to the other Moravian communes in the United States founded between 1740 and 1853, this one was a failure. Its structure was not well-developed and it lasted for only five years.

The Moravian Church had established other such communes in Europe before they began their American experiments. The church itself was formed in Bohemia after the death of the religious reformer and martyr John Huss (1369–1415). Basing themselves on his teachings, the members stressed the sole authority of the Bible; simplicity in worship; receiving the Lord's Supper in faith without authoritative human explanation; and disciplined Christian living. At first they called themselves the *Unitas Fratrum* (Unity of Brethren), but later were named Moravians. The church had gained a large following in Bohemia and Moravia by the time of the Thirty Years War (1618–1648). But then persecution and exile nearly destroyed the movement.

Many of the members had to flee from Moravia to Saxony because of their beliefs. There they settled on the lands of Count Nicholas von Zinzendorf (1700–1760), one of their converts. They built a communal town on his property that they called Herrnhut, and they chose Zinzendorf as one of their leaders. Within five years Herrnhut had achieved a population of more than 500. In time they also founded other such towns at other locations in Europe. They did not practice as strict a communal system at Herrnhut as they were to do later under the General Economy at Savannah, but within the Herrnhut system no one was allowed to own any property except a member of the church. The church controlled all spiritual and industrial pursuits.

In 1733 Zinzendorf decided to establish a mission in the American colonies. He had earlier visited this country briefly in an attempt to make contacts with and unite some of the German sectarians who had migrated to Pennsylvania. He sent nine members, under the leadership of Augustus Gottlieb Spangenberg (1704–1792), to Georgia to start their Savannah commune.

More members came in 1736 with Bishop David Nitschmann, who ordained one of them, Anton Seifert, as the first pastor for the Savannah commune. Eventually there was a total of 47 members at Savannah. This was the place where John Wesley, the founder of Methodism, first met Spangenberg and other Moravians who helped to influence his radical departure from the general practices of the Church of England.

Before the Moravians left Europe for America, they had acquired two grants of land, each 500 acres, on the Ogeechee River west of Savannah. But they never occupied this land, remaining instead at their settlement in Savannah.

As in the Moravian Herrnhuts of Europe, the Savannah communalists divided their membership into "choirs" according to age, sex, and station in life. At the head of each choir was an elder or deaconess. This organizational division is still maintained today within the Moravian Church, although the communal aspects of their life have long since been abandoned. The choir system proved to be a fine educational device. Teachers accommodated their subject matter and methods to the age and sex of the group at hand. Children, even of preschool age, were taken care of in this church-school system. At the age of 18 months they were placed in nurseries and from there into the various stages of the choir structure. Educational historians today give Zinzendorf, the one who designed this choir system, credit for being about 200 years ahead of his time in developing this kind of age-differentiated education. The Savannah Moravians also established a school for the Indians at Irene, a few miles north of this town.

When Spain threatened an invasion of Georgia in the late 1730s, the non–Moravian residents in the town of Savannah organized a defense militia. The Moravians, however, refused to participate because this would violate their article of faith against bearing arms.

Hostility quickly developed against these pacifists, and some threats were made on their lives. Thus, after a communal vote, the Moravians decided to leave Savannah and found a new settlement to the north. Some members left for Pennsylvania as early as 1737, but others remained to pay off their Trustees of Georgia for the Ogeechee land. By the middle of 1740 every member had departed for the north, leaving no traces of the Savannah settlement. Some of the departing members set up **Emmaus** and others started **Nazareth**, both in Pennsylvania. A book with a section that focuses on Savannah is Sessler's *Communal Pietism Among Early American Moravians.*

Savoy (1817–1825), at Savoy, Massachusetts, in the Berkshire Mountains about 18 miles east of the New York state line, was an 80-member Shaker settlement abandoned because of severe drought. The members then moved to the **Watervliet** and **Mount Lebanon** Shaker communes.

Schneeberg *see* **Snow Hill**

Scipio (1874–1877), Utah, was a Mormon United Order community based on the **St. George** model until shortly after the death of Brigham Young, the Mormon leader, in Salt Lake City. It had about 230 members.

Shalam (1884–1901), also called the Children's Land, was founded by spiritualist J.B. Newbrough (1828–1891) near Dona Ana, New Mexico. He was a dentist by profession and is credited with the invention of the rubber dental plate. He also was a member of Spear's **Harmonia** commune for two years. While in a trance-like state, Newbrough composed a new Bible that he called

"Oahspee." It was in the pages of this work that he recorded the command to create a spiritualist community.

Newbrough and his followers, known as Faithists, planned the community as a training center for 3,000 orphans who would be raised as vegetarians, communalists, spiritualists, and opponents of city life. A.M. Howland, a rich convert, provided most of the money for the purchase of 1,000 acres of land. Many Faithists gathered there, but the settlement never grew to more than 150 participants, most of them adults and just a few orphans. They lived in shacks and tents while constructing their three buildings: Fraturnum, a 20-room mansion of Spanish design; Temple of Tae, a circular one-story church; and Studio, a windowless retreat for Dr. Newbrough's periods of contemplation. Some years after he died, the community closed, primarily because of lack of interest in continuing the project. The Faithist cult still exists, but it has few adherents. A book with a section that focuses on Shalam is Hinds' *American Communities.*

Shalom (1837–1842), at Wawarsing, in Ulster County, New York, was the first of a number of Jewish cooperative farming communities that were established in the United States. The name "Shalom" means peace in Hebrew. It was hoped that by setting up such an all–Jewish community, the members could escape from the discrimination they faced in America and that their families had experienced for centuries in Europe. This commune was different from most of the other Jewish agricultural communities in that its population was composed of Jews from Central and Western Europe rather than poor immigrants from Eastern Europe, and it was the only such commune established before the extensive Russo-Jewish immigration of 1881–1882. An earlier proposal to set up a Jewish agricultural commune on Grand Island in the Niagara River never materialized.

The initial membership of Shalom was 13 families from New York City, possibly some of Portuguese origin since they later collected funds for a Portuguese synagogue in that city. Led by Moses Cohen they settled on 500 acres of land on a barren plateau in the Shawangunk Mountains. Contracts for erecting houses, a store, two factories, a synagogue, an art gallery, and a museum were given to a builder in the area. The members farmed but could not make this pay. They also made fur caps and quill pens in their factories, and they repaired secondhand clothing that was shipped to them from New York City.

Replacements came as some of the original members moved away, but there were probably never more than about 35 members of Shalom at any one time. The commune finally closed because their farming and manufacturing did not produce enough income to sustain the community. A book with a section that focuses on Shalom is Carmer's *The Hudson*.

Shenandoah (1753–1764), on the north fork of the Shenandoah River, near the present town of Strasburg, Virginia, was a Seventh-day Baptist community plagued by Indian attacks. It was founded by Heinrich Sangmeister and Anton Höllenthal, who had departed from **Ephrata** shortly after the Eckerlin brothers were expelled from there. Altogether there were 26 members, one of whom was Samuel Eckerlin. He came there after the destruction of his **Cheat River** commune in West Virginia.

The members of Shenandoah purchased 365 acres of land. They erected cabins and a community house, designing their community on the model used at Ephrata. At first they made their living by teaching school and binding books, but later they established a pottery industry.

The Indian troubles that plagued them came to a head in July 1764, when it seemed a major Indian war was at hand. Some of the members quickly moved to Germantown and others joined Ephrata. When the troubles were over, a few of the members returned to the Shenandoah property as permanent settlers, but no attempt was made to revive the community.

Shiloh (1895–1948), on a pine-covered hill overlooking the Adroscoggin River, not far from Freeport, Maine, was established in 1895 by The Kingdom, Incorporated, a sect also known as The Holy Ghost and Us Society. This sect was led by fundamentalist Baptist preacher Frank Weston Sandford (1862–1948), who told his followers that in a vision he had been instructed to build the commune for them. He displayed a shovel, wheelbarrow, and copper penny he had found on the road. "A great temple," he said, "will grow from this small beginning."

The community in time contained several buildings with about 500 rooms, including dormitories, an infirmary, a playhouse for children, and other types of communal halls. The main building was topped by a tower five stories high called the Eye of the Needle. This was used as a place of constant prayer. The members opposed smoking, drinking, cosmetics, jewelry, and even haircuts. They ate but two meals a day and practiced occasional fasting. There were 600 members in 1911, including a Japanese lady, an African prince, and a wealthy Texan.

The once elegant buildings of Shiloh are now worn by weather and time (drawing by Lois Will).

That year Sandford announced the end of the world was at hand and the whole commune gave itself to a life of prayer. But when the "day of doom" failed to materialize, he produced another revelation calling for a worldwide mission of conversion. He purchased a 150-ton sailing vessel, the *Coronet*, and set off from Portland with a crew of 45 commune members. The trip ended in disaster. Eight of the crew died of scurvy, and Sandford was shortly thereafter arrested and convicted of manslaughter. He was sentenced to the federal penitentiary at Atlanta, where he served seven years.

After Sandford's return to the community, the members became quite secretive about their activities. There was a shooting at Shiloh in 1946 when a mentally unbalanced veteran of World War II tried to enter the establishment.

The veteran and a Shiloh guard were killed in the exchange of fire, and the police investigation revealed that Sandford, long thought dead, was still alive at age 83. He died two years later. His son Frank now runs the sect, though its headquarters have been moved to Dublin, New Hampshire.

Since Sandford's death, the Shiloh members have given up their communal lifestyle. Recently a large, well-carpeted room in the main building at Shiloh was opened to the public for regularly scheduled worship services. A book with a section that focuses on Shiloh is Rich's *State O'Maine*.

Shirley (1793–1908), about two miles from Shirley, Massachusetts, and about 40 miles north of Boston, was a Shaker community (see **Watervliet**) that had extensive apple orchards and was noted for the brooms, cider, and applesauce that the members sold. The property they owned covered 2,000 acres, and in 1823 there were 150 members divided into three "families."

This commune was started after four prosperous farmers in the area — Elijah and Ivory Wilds, John Warren, and Nathan Willard — were converted to Shakerism. They all had been members of the Congregational Church in Shirley, and their attempt to get the other members of that church to embrace the Shaker movement led to a schism within the church. Willard gave the initial land for the Shirley commune.

The Shaker community had an infirmary, house for the aged, school, laundry, cotton factory, and various barns and dwellings. When the commune closed, the remaining members moved to the **Hancock** and **Harvard** Shaker communes. The Shirley property was then sold to the state for an industrial school for boys. The meeting house at Shirley was transported in 1961 to the site of Alcott's **Fruitlands**. It is now part of the Shaker museum there.

Shunesburg (1874–1876), near Rockville, Utah, was a Mormon settlement of about 50 members organized into a commune on the **St. George** United Order plan.

Sicily Island (1881–1882), in Catahoula Parish, Louisiana, was the first of a number of Jewish agricultural communes, most of which were established in the late 1800s. All of them were aided by the concerted efforts of European and American settlement organizations, such as the Alliance Israélite Universelle (headquartered in Paris), the Hebrew Immigrant Aid Society (headquartered in New York City), the Baron de Hirsch Fund, the Montifiore Agricultural Aid Society, and the Jewish Agricultural and Colonial Association. The communes were promoted among immigrants from Eastern Europe as structures through which the age-old problems of anti–Semitism might be overcome and in which Jews might once again, after centuries of urban living, become agriculturists and owners of the land.

Not all the settlements so promoted were communes. Several, particularly those of southern New Jersey and Texas, were only individualistic farming communities. But it made little difference to the immigrants what kind of lifestyle and economic system were advocated. They were happy to have any place to settle and to begin life anew.

The residents of most of these communities had to constantly ask for more funds from the sponsoring organizations in order to continue. Having been peddlers and small shopkeepers in Europe, living a precarious hand-to-mouth existence, they were ill-prepared for farming and they did not usually recognize the long-term planning and patience necessary for engaging in farm life.

But the few somewhat successful Jewish agricultural communes proved that Jews could indeed be good farmers and gave symbolic hope to those in Europe and elsewhere who wanted to establish a Jewish homeland in Israel. When some of the pioneer Zionist agricultural settlements were started in Israel, the members recalled the experience of the American agriculturists, as did the members of the short-lived Biro-Bidjan agricultural settlement for Jews in Soviet Russia.

At Sicily Island most of the 125 members were teachers, students, artists, merchants, craftsmen, and peddlers.

They all came from Russia — 35 families from Kiev and 25 from Elizabethgrad. They were organized in Russia and led by Herman Rosenthal (1843–1917), who later also helped set up the Jewish agricultural commune called **Crémieux** and subsequently became head of the Slavonic Department of the New York Public Library.

They lived in three old plantation homes left over from pre–Civil War times, until they were able to secure lumber from New Orleans. The New Orleans committee of the Alliance Israélite Universelle also provided horses, farm implements, poultry, and other farming needs. The members planted corn, cotton, and vegetables on their 5,000 acres of land, and they built fences. But the Mississippi River floods of 1882 swept everything away and the group had to abandon their project. Some of the participants then moved to Texas, others to Kansas and Missouri. A few families followed Rosenthal to Crémieux, and some joined the **Arkansas** Jewish commune. Books with sections that focus on Sicily Island are Fogarty's *All Things New*, Postel and Koppman's *A Jewish Tourist Guide to the United States*, and the *Jewish Encyclopedia* article "Agricultural Colonies in the United States" by Reizenstein.

Silkville *see* **Prairie Home Colony**

Skaneateles (1843–1846), two miles north of Skaneateles, New York, was a commune organized by abolitionist John Anderson Collins (1810–1879). It was based on the denunciation of individual property ownership, negation of all force in settling problems, easy divorce, universal education, and vegetarianism. There were 150 members and they owned 350 acres of land, purchased by Collins and three other members of this commune.

Collins had previously been the general agent for the Massachusetts Anti-Slavery Society, but then he became convinced that the abolition of slavery was just part of the great social reformation needed — a "reformation that would free all humankind." He had traveled abroad to raise money for the antislavery cause and was editor of an antislavery periodical, the *Monthly Garland*, from 1840 to 1841. In 1843 he conducted a series of antislavery meetings that ended with his call for the establishment of separate communities "that would indeed be free of the evils of society."

All religious doctrines were denied at the Skaneateles commune, and the members published a magazine, *The Communitist*, through which they attacked the teachings of the Fourierist communal movement. *The New York Weekly Tribune*, which supported Fourierism, called the Skaneateles commune "crude and inefficient."

The members at Skaneateles worked well together at first, but then a small faction led by Q.A. Johnson began to mobilize against the leadership of Collins. They caused much dissension and by the summer of 1845 most of the members had left. The commune was closed in May 1846, and three months later Collins publicly renounced "the principles we entertained, both in relation to government and society, as false in theory and pernicious in their practical tendencies." Thereafter he gave up all schemes for social improvement and moved to California to mine the sands of the Klamath River for gold, a project that also ended in failure. A book with a section that focuses on Skaneateles is Noyes' *History of American Socialisms*.

Skyview Acres (1949–present), at Pomona, New York, is a homestead community established by followers of Ralph Borsodi (see **Bayard Lane Homestead Community**). In 1954 the community had 156 acres of land and 221 members. Most, though not all, of the adult members are professional workers. Community decisions are made at community-wide meetings in which each family is allowed one vote. One of their leaders was Jim Best.

Snowhill (1788–1894), in Franklin County, Pennsylvania, three miles north of Waynesboro, was a 30-member Seventh-day Baptist community established under the leadership of Peter Lehman (1757–1823). At first it went by the name of Schneeberg after the Schneeberger family that provided the land. Life at Snowhill was much like that at **Ephrata**, although the buildings were more modern. Stone houses were built here in 1793, 1835, 1838, and 1843. The community house was erected in 1814.

As Ephrata declined in membership, many of its activities were shifted to Snowhill. After Lehman died in 1823, he was succeeded by Andreas Fahnestock, with Andreas Schneeberger and Abraham Ely as assistant deacons.

Social Freedom (1874–1880), in Chesterfield County, Virginia, was an anarchist farming community of 15 members. They owned 333 acres of land on which they raised medicinal herbs. They also sold lumber, ground grain for other farmers, and did coopering. They lived in one building, had no constitution, and were governed by "free criticism." A book with a section that focuses on Social Freedom is Nordhoff's *The Communistic Societies of the United States*.

Social Reform Unity (1842–1843), located at Goose Pond, Pennsylvania,

was the first of 31 Fourierist communes established in the United States. The site was at the foot of the Pocono Mountains, about 18 miles north of Stroudsburg. There were about 20 members, most of them mechanics, from Brooklyn, New York.

The Fourierist movement was promoted in the United States by Albert Brisbane (1809–1890), a man now almost forgotten, but one who stood foremost among the social planners of the 1840s. He was the older brother of famous journalist Arthur Brisbane. As a young man, Albert Brisbane went to Europe to study under the most eminent philosophers of the day, including Hegel in Berlin. He toyed with the ideas of Saint Simon and met Karl Marx, but he eventually became convinced that Charles Fourier (1772–1837), in Paris, had devised the ideal state for society. Brisbane even compared Fourier's accomplishments to those of Columbus, Copernicus, and Newton. Over a period of two years, he took daily lessons with Fourier and grasped his system so thoroughly that Brisbane became an excellent interpreter of Fourierist thought.

The essential kernel of this was that human nature, though basically good, is corrupted by commerce, and that harmonious association will release humankind from this corruption. The system of association, which Fourier developed in every detail, was intended to make manual labor dignified and attractive, abolish inequality and poverty, and achieve the highest scientific development and general human perfection. "The error of Reformers," Fourier wrote in 1829, "is to condemn this or that abuse of society, whereas they should condemn the whole system of Society itself, which is a circle of abuses and defects throughout."

After much study, Fourier had concluded that there were a total of 12 human passions or instincts. "Happiness," he wrote, "consists in the continued satisfaction of the twelve passions harmoniously developed." He hoped to achieve this satisfaction by the proper and voluntary division of labor in a social structure he called a phalanx (his name for a commune). In practice, Fourier's plan was extremely mechanical, requiring a specific number of people to do a specific series of tasks in an area of certain size. Fourier divided the work of each phalanx into necessary labor, useful labor, and pleasing labor, with the highest wages being paid for necessary labor and the lowest for pleasing labor. By allowing each member to choose the nature of their work and to change the particular occupation every hour or so, Fourier hoped to eliminate any distasteful elements such as compulsion and monotony. Each phalanx was to be designed around a large central building called the Phalanxtry, and the finances were to be arranged on a joint-stock basis with members either purchasing or earning shares and receiving dividends according to their investments.

After Brisbane returned to the United States in 1834, he organized Fourierist study groups in New York City and Philadelphia and wrote a book about Fourier's proposals, *The Social Destiny of Man*. To fit conditions there he modified Fourier's estimate of the number of persons needed to establish an ideal phalanx from more than 1,600 persons to only 400, provided they had sufficient capital, and he made a few other adjustments to Fourier's grand plan.

One of Brisbane's first converts was newspaper publisher Horace Greeley. For two months they co-published a weekly called *Future* that was devoted to the ideas of Fourier, and after Greeley founded *The Tribune* he continued to support Brisbane's ideas by giving him a daily column in the paper. Other intellectual leaders that Brisbane converted included William Henry Channing, Charles A. Dana, Parke Godwin, and George Ripley, the head of the transcendentalist **Brook Farm** experiment. Ripley was so convinced that Fourierism was the future that he changed the rather relaxed atmosphere at the Brook Farm commune into the rigid restraints of a Fourierist phalanx, and renamed the experiment the Brook Farm Phalanx. The members also changed the name of their magazine from the *Harbinger* to the *Phalanx*.

But none of the 31 phalanxes established in the United States actually met Brisbane's specifications for the adequate number of people and capital, and so he himself did not give any of them his support. Late in 1843, he returned to Paris to make a study of Fourier's unpublished writings. He devoted the rest of his life to travel and invention.

This first Fourierist commune, Social Reform Unity, owned 2,000 acres of land but had no members with any experience in farming. After ten months of effort they were only able to clear an acre and a half of the land. They also had a small house with about four rooms and a saw mill, as well as some pigs, poultry and oxen, all of which were on the property when the members arrived. Their leaders were C.H. Little and a Mr. Mackenzie.

After a little less than a year, the members voted to disband, even though Article 62 of their constitution specifically stated: "The question or subject of the dissolution of this Unity shall never be entertained, admitted or discussed in any of the meetings of the same." The property was later occupied by the Owenite **Goose Pond** commune. Books with sections that focus on Social Reform Unity are Bestor's *American Phalanxes, the Fourierist Phase of Socialism in the United States* and Noyes' *History of American Socialisms.*

Societas Fraternia (1879), near Anaheim, California, was a diet-reform commune established by a Dr. Schlesinger. The members said they were seeking to return to the kind of community in which the early Christians lived, as described in Acts, and they believed that the total reform of food intake was the first step to such a community. They lived in circular rooms because they believed this aided in the movement of air.

In May 1879, Dr. Schlesinger was taken to court by some hostile citizens of Anaheim who charged that a newborn baby in the community was slowly starving to death on a diet of scraped apple, rice, and barley water. This court action led to the demise of the commune. It is not known how many members were living there at the time, but probably no more than five. A book with a section that focuses on the Societas Fraternia is Hine's *California's Utopian Communities.*

Sodus Bay Phalanx (1844–1847), also called the Sodus Phalanx, was a Fourierist settlement (see **Social Reform Unity**) located on land formerly owned by the **Groveland** Shakers at Sodus Point, New York. In all, the members of this commune had 1,400 acres of land, 300 of which had been cleared before they occupied the property.

The Shakers left a "manor house," a barn, and a gristmill, all of which are still standing. The phalanx members built other barns, a sawmill, a tannery, and a brick kiln. They planted barley, corn, beans, hay, oats, peas, potatoes, parsnips, and fruit trees. Also they kept cows, sheep, and hogs. They made some of their other income at carpentry, masonry, blacksmithing, shoemaking, tailoring, and the production of charcoal.

At its height the Sodus Bay Phalanx had about 300 members, including ministers, teachers, doctors, and representatives of several other trades and professions. One of these members, Benjamin Fish, was the owner of a store and flour mill in Rochester, New York, 35 miles west of Sodus Point. He was one of that city's wealthiest citizens. Unlike other rich Fourierists, Fish was quite willing to take on the hardships of community life and was one of the first to move to the Sodus location. When the phalanx was in the organizing stages he acted as its president, although Roswell G. Murray replaced him in that office before the actual occupation of the land. Fish was then given the job of provisioning the community. He remained faithful to the commune to the end, even after most of the other members had departed.

John S. Gildersleeve was the largest stockholder in this enterprise, having been given his stock in return for farmland that he added to the Shaker tract. Another large stockholder was John Smith. Alonzo M. Watson, who joined Sodus Bay some time after it was established, came from the defunct **Jefferson County Industrial Association**, the Fourierst commune he had organized and of which he had been president. Shortly after his arrival at Sodus Bay, he was elected its president also.

Another important member of the board of directors, although he was not a resident member, was Theron C. Leland, who was in charge of the Rochester office of the American Industrial Union, the short-lived federation of Fourierist communities in the New York area. Leland later became a director and resident member of the Fourierist **Ontario Union**, and when the U.S. Fourierist movement collapsed, he migrated toward the anarchist thinking of Josiah Warren, eventually joining Warren's **Modern Times** commune. When the weekly *American Socialist* was started in 1876, Leland became a frequent correspondent, writing articles in support of Warren's ideas.

Religious controversy and typhoid fever contributed to the collapse of the Sodus Bay Phalanx. The conservatives in the religious conflict focussed their charge on two members, Lorenzo Mabbett and Asa Anthony, who they said were at fault for working to bring in the hay on the Sabbath. Both men were subsequently exonerated because the action prevented weather damage to the hay, but this was after a bitter fight that split the board of directors into two warring factions. To their credit, both Mabbett and Anthony were among the members who remained with the phalanx long after most others had departed. As to the typhoid fever, at one point 49 of the members were on the sick list at the same time.

Even though some of the buildings are still standing, they cannot be visited as they are now privately owned under the name "Alasa Farms."

Sonyea *see* **Groveland**

South Union (1807–1922), 16 miles southwest of Bowling Green, Kentucky, and near the present town of South Union, was a Shaker community (see **Watervliet**) that once had 400 members, organized into four "families."

They owned 6,000 acres of land, part of which is now one of the outstanding stock farms in Kentucky.

The initial land for this commune was given by Jesse McComb, a landowner in the area who gave all he owned to "the one true faith." Benjamin Youngs was the head of South Union at the beginning. He was succeeded by Elder Harvey Eads and then Elder John Rankin. Eads was a particularly accomplished leader, for he was a tailor, shoemaker, seedsman, wool carder, teamster, tin and sheet-iron worker, painter, hatter, printer, writer, and even a dentist. He had been placed among the Shakers shortly after his birth, and spent all 84 years of his life among the Shaker communes of Kentucky.

Because slaveowners who joined the commune were required to free their slaves, the membership eventually included 40 ex-slaves who had also made the decision to join South Union. Under Eads' leadership, the commune adopted a policy of hiring slaves from the surrounding owners and paying the slaves wages so that they might purchase their own freedom. John Finch, an English economist who wrote about his visit to the United States, said of Kentucky in 1844 that "the Shakers in their midst, all free, wealthy and happy, are an everlasting reproach upon their accursed slavery system."

South Union was famous for its fine stock — cattle, hogs, sheep, and chickens — its orchards, corn, wheat, rye, oats, and silk worms. From the silk produced here, the members made kerchiefs that were worn in all the Shaker communities. The members also made palm leaf bonnets, brooms, packaged garden seeds, and canned preserves. They had a grist mill, a tannery, a tailor shop, a shoemaker's shop, a carpenter's shop, a blacksmith shop, a meeting house erected in 1810, and many other buildings. Because there was a sulfur spring nearby, they even erected a hotel and store for visitors who came to the community to improve their health.

During the Civil War, South Union lost buildings, stock, and other properties (valued at over $100,000) as marauding troops occupied their land. The commune members fed at least 50,000 meals to hungry soldiers of both the Northern and Southern armies, and after the war they adopted 20 orphans from Tennessee.

When South Union closed in 1922, the estate was sold at auction. Seven of the ten remaining members moved to the **Mount Lebanon** Shaker commune. The other three accepted $10,000 each as their share of the property and remained in Kentucky. Two of the three became man and wife.

South Western Colony (1871), on the South Platte River about 25 miles east of Evans, Colorado, was a cooperative community initiated by D.S. Green of Denver. It had about 75 members and was also known as the Tennessee or Memphis Colony because many members came from Memphis. They named the town they started to build Green City, but the community collapsed before the year's end because of bad management. A book with a section that focuses on the South Western Colony is Willard's *The Union Colony of Greeley, Colorado, 1869–1871.*

Southern Co-operative Association (1900–1904), at Apalachicola, Florida, was a Swedenborgian commune established by the Rev. Harry C. Vrooman, who secured 1,700 acres of land on Apalachicola Bay for the project. It was one of the projects of an organization called the Brotherhood of the New Age, which later changed its name to the National Production Company and eventually merged with the Cooperative Association of America. They had one other cooperative community in Massachusetts, the **Martha's Vineyard Cooperative**.

Some of the 17 members of the Southern Co-operative Association had previously belonged to the **Christian Commonwealth** in Georgia. They lived here by farming and fishing for which they had three sailboats and two seine boats. Each member invested $100 when they joined the commune. They lived separately in five houses but ate together in a central dining hall. The experiment came to an end when Vrooman departed and moved to Indianapolis, Indiana.

Spink County Colony (1905–present), on the James River about ten miles south of Frankfort, South Dakota, is a Hutterite Brüderhof (see **Bon Homme**) that moved to Alberta, Canada, in 1918, but returned to their South Dakota lands in 1942. John Wipf was their minister in 1964 and there were then 76 members.

Spirit Fruit Society (1899–1908), first at Lisbon, Ohio, and then at Ingleside, Illinois, was a spiritualist community organized by Jacob Beilhart (1867–1908). he was an ex–Seventh-day Adventist minister who held that every person is but a "part, or cell, of the Universal Body." He further proclaimed that if people allowed, the Universal Life would flow into them and eliminate self and all its desires.

Beilhart purchased a small, five-acre farm at Lisbon and there began publication of his spiritualist newspaper, *Spirit Fruit*. Some of his followers soon joined him on the farm. They held all things in common and claimed a worldwide following of over one million people — a great exaggeration as the commune itself probably never had more than 30 members. In 1906 they moved to the Ingleside location, near Fox Lake, Illinois, and built a 35-room house there on the 90 acres that they purchased. It was a cement structure with steam heating. They also rented some farming land to grow crops. In time, these communalists came under newspaper attack as an alleged free-love group and they decided to disband. Books with sections that focus on the Spirit Fruit Society are Fogarty's *All Things New* and Hinds' *American Communities*.

Spring Creek (1945–present), near Lewiston, Montana, is a Hutterite Brüderhof (see **Bon Homme**) that was led by Paul Walter in 1964 and had 51 members.

Spring Farm Association (1846–1848), in Sheboygan County, Wisconsin, about 20 miles from Lake Michigan, was a Fourierist commune (see **Social Reform Unity**). It was organized by a group at Sheboygan Falls, Wisconsin, and had perhaps 25 members, among whom were farmers, carpenters, joiners, and blacksmiths. The leaders were Dr. P. Cody of Ohio and E.C. Trowbridge. They had 30 acres of land that they cultivated until the commune disbanded for some unknown reason. Some of those with whom they had made plans for this commune disagreed as to its location and broke off from the rest to establish, in the same year and same county, the **Pigeon River** Fourierist commune.

Spring Lake *see* **Colony of Equality**

Spring Valley Brüderhof (1963–present), near Wessington Springs, South Dakota, is a Hutterite commune (see **Bon Homme**) that had 73 members in 1964 and was led by John Wurtz.

Springdale (1875–1882), about three miles northwest of Rockville, Utah, and near the entrance to Zion National Park, was a Mormon United Order communal settlement founded on the plan in use at **Orderville**. It had about 100 members and lasted until the U.S. government passed the Edmunds antipoligamy act of 1882, which forced some of the Mormon leaders to go into hiding.

Springdale (1959–present), near White Sulphur Springs, Montana, is a Hutterite Brüderhof (see **Bon Homme**). It had 97 members in 1964 and their leader was Peter Wipf.

Springfield Industrial Works *see* **Union Manufacturing Company**

Straight Creek (1808–1810), at what is now Georgetown in Guernsey County, Ohio, was a Shaker commune (see **Watervliet**) of probably about 25 members. In 1810 they joined with the members at **Red Banks** and at **Eagle Creek** to form the **West Union** Shaker commune.

Straight Edge Community (1899–1907), at 240 Sixth Avenue in New York City, was a cooperative community organized by Willard F. Copeland, the son of a Methodist minister. He hoped through the work of this commune to apply "the Golden Rule to business and social relations." The 18 members started various industries to give jobs to unemployed workers. These included printing, sign making, and bread baking. They also ran a work-play school for children, teaching them regular school subjects and practical crafts such as box making, cooking, washing, ironing, house building, sewing, paper folding, and gardening.

They used a time-card system to calculate work done in their industries, and regularly shifted assignments so that everyone was given a chance to do the most desirable work. After 1900 they purchased a farm on Staten Island that they named "The Land of the Living." Here they planned to raise food for a cooperative kitchen in the city. But this did not succeed and so they sold the farm and bought four acres on the western slope of the Palisades at Alpine, New Jersey, to be used as a summer camp for the children of the workers. They named the camp "La Hacienda." The members occasionally published *The Straight Edge* to explain their work and tell about the activities of the commune. After the commune closed, the industries the members had started were continued until 1918. A book with a section that focuses on the Straight Edge Community is Hinds' *American Communities*.

Sunrise Cooperative Farm (1933–1936), 18 miles south of Saginaw, Michigan, was a Jewish community established by Eli Greenblatt and Joseph Cohen, who had been one of the leaders of the **Ferrer Colony**. Cohen was an anarchist, as were many of the members of this commune. There were also socialists, however, who were members of the Arbeiter Ring of the Jewish National Workers Alliance. They allowed no professed Communists to join because, Cohen argued, the Communists' main activity "consisted in disrupting labor organizations."

The members paid $500 to join ($600 for a couple and $150 for each child) and were expected to bring clothing and furniture with them. Most of the members had been workers in the needle trades, and only a few had farming experience. There were also painters, carpenters, butchers, a baker, a shoemaker, three graduate teachers, a chemist, and a civil engineer, totaling 312 members.

The property included 500 acres of timberland, 5,000 acres of pasture, and 3,500 acres of tillable land. It also included 80 buildings, a gas station, blacksmith shop, school, post office, children's center, central kitchen, carpenter's shop, dining hall, and bakery. An elected executive committee administered the affairs of the colony, though this was fully controlled by Cohen. The crops and livestock they raised in 1935 won 15 ribbons at the county fair, and the members published a newspaper, the *Sunrise News*, in both English and Yiddish. When conflicts began to beset the membership, an opposing faction published an opposition paper in Yiddish only.

The experiment was relatively successful financially, although the income was never sufficient to cover all the expenses. During its second year, the colonists applied for and received a $12,500 loan from the U.S. government's Farm Credit Administration. They later applied for other funds from federal and state agencies. Internal dissension, however, was apparently the main factor in causing the colony to close. After this happened, the land was then appropriated by the government and used for the Sunrise Valley Farms of the Federal Resettlement Association. Books with sections that focus on the Sunrise Cooperative Farm are Fogarty's *American Utopianism* and Infield's *Cooperative Communities at Work*.

Sunrise Cooperative Farms (1930–

1935), at what is now Roosevelt, New Jersey, was a Jewish cooperative farm (see **Sicily Island**) of about 300 members. It was organized by Benjamin Brown, an immigrant from the Ukraine and an active promoter of Jewish cooperatives. He had earlier been a member of the **Clarion Colony**. When this commune closed, the land was sold to the government's Division of Subsistence Homesteads for the Jersey Homesteads project, which Brown was named to head. A book with a section that focuses on the Sunrise Cooperative Farms is Conkin's *Tomorrow a New World*.

Sunset (1876–1882), between Halbrook and Joseph City, Arizona, on the bend of the Little Colorado River, was a Mormon United Order commune of about 100 members. It was designed after the plan in use at **Orderville**. All traces of this commune and town are now gone.

Swanendael (1663–1664), near Lewes, Delaware, was the first communal experiment in America. The members were all Mennonites from Holland and they were led by Pieter Cornelisz Plockhoy of Zeirik Zee. Their hope was to recreate the kind of cooperative lifestyle that existed among the earliest Christians, a society of love and holding all things in common as described in the Book of Acts. According to Acts, the first Christians sold all their possessions and distributed their wealth among all who had need. "The whole group of believers was united, heart and soul; no one claimed for his own use anything that he had, as everything they owned was held in common.... None of their members was ever in want, as all those who owned land or houses would sell them, and bring the money from them to present it to the apostles; it was then distributed to any members who might be in need" (Acts 5:32–35).

Their leader, Plockhoy, is still spoken of in Mennonite circles as "the father of modern socialism," though he is virtually ignored in most history books on the development of social theory. Although he grew up in Holland, he lived in England during the revolutionary times of Oliver Cromwell (1642–1659), with whom he was acquainted, and he worked closely with many of the political reformers of that period, including Samuel Hartlib and the Levelers, Giles Culvert and William Walwyn. It is also said that Plockhoy was a friend of the poet John Milton.

In 1659 Plockhoy published several works in London, the best known of which is titled: *A Way Propounded to Make the Poor in These and Other Nations Happy, by Bringing Together a Fit, Suitable and Well Qualified People Unto One Household-Government, or Little-Common-Wealth.* In these works he expounded the values of cooperation and called for the establishment of cooperative settlements. His teachings actually led to the start of such cooperative communities in London, Southampton, and Ireland. But the overthrow of Cromwell and the restoration of the Stuarts to the throne in 1660 put a stop to all such experiments.

Plockhoy was forced to flee from England. By 1661 he was back in Holland, now negotiating with the Amsterdam authorities for the right to set up an experimental community in the New World. This, like the ones in England, would "aim to perfect the equality of all classes — economic, social, and political."

The negotiations were completed in 1663, and in July of that year "41 souls" led by Plockhoy sailed from Holland for their new home in Delaware.

The scant record of their community shows that they shared all things in common, refused to keep slaves, practiced religious toleration for all but Catholics and "stiff-necked Quakers," and had the first free school in the New World.

The Swanendael commune might have lasted for many years had it not been for the fierce economic rivalry that existed between the English and Dutch colonists of the New World. The region that the Dutch claimed as New Netherland in the 1600s included parts of what are now Connecticut, Delaware, New Jersey, and New York. The English also had settlements in those areas as well as in Maryland, Massachusetts, New Hampshire, North Carolina, Rhode Island, Pennsylvania, and Virginia. The rivalry between the two nations became so intense that in 1664 the English sent a fleet of warships to capture all of New Netherland for the Duke of York. The Dutch were quickly defeated and Governor Peter Stuyvesant was forced to surrender to the English. What was left of New Netherland became the English colony of New York.

When the English arrived in Delaware to wipe out all the Dutch settlements, they seemed to take particular delight in leveling Swanendael. The English commander, Sir Robert Carr, likely viewed such an egalitarian society as a threat to his own social position because he singled it out for savagery not accorded the other Dutch settlements. He later wrote boastfully, "I destroyed the Quaking colony of Plockhoy to a naile." Those members of Swanendael who were not killed were likely sold as slaves to work in various English settlements that were then being established in the New World. There were no more attempts to establish a Mennonite commune in the United States until nearly 300 years later (see **Reba Place Fellowship**).

Plockhoy and his wife may have been away from the Swanendael commune at the time of the English attack because he was luckily able to escape the fate of the other members, and he remained in hiding in the Delaware area for the next 30 years, apparently living among some of the Dutch families that continued to farm there under the governing of the English. In 1694, now old and blind, Plockhoy wandered into the village of Germantown, Pennsylvania, with his wife leading him. There he found a home among fellow Mennonites, and lived on their charity for the few remaining years of his life. An article with a section that particularly focuses on Swanendael is Harder's "Plockhoy, Pieter Cornelisz," in *The Mennonite Encyclopedia: A Comprehensive Reference Work on the Anabaptist-Mennonite Movement.*

Sylvania Phalanx (1843–1844), at what is now Greeley, Pennsylvania, was founded by Fourierists (see **Social Reform Unity**) from New York City. Newspaper publisher Horace Greeley (1811–1872) was the largest stockholder in this commune, and he took over much of the land when it disbanded. This undoubtedly accounts for the name of the town that now stands at the location of the Sylvania Phalanx.

Altogether the 150 members owned 2,394 acres of which about 100 acres had been cleared before they began commune life. They purchased the saw-and-grist mill that was already on the land, put up some temporary buildings, and constructed their phalanxtry or central structure. Among the industries they started was a shoemaking business. They also farmed.

Greeley acted as treasurer for the

phalanx, Thomas W. Whitley was president, J.D. Pierson its vice-president, and J.T.S. Smith, its secretary. At one point Greeley, who always championed women's rights, declared that he thought women should rule the community.

A frost in July 1884 destroyed all their crops and left many of the members destitute. They therefore decided to dissolve the project on August 10, 1844. By 1866 no remains of this experiment could be found.

Synanon Foundation (1958–1980) commune in Santa Monica, California, was a highly structured, strongly conformist drug therapy establishment. It was set up in a three-story brick building by reformed alcoholic and former statistician Charles Dederich. The commune was later moved to beach-front property in that city.

Dederich firmly believed that all addicts could learn how to live without the use of drugs through rugged encounter sessions in which they acted out their inner hostilities. Learning the truth about themselves apparently helped them stay off drugs or alcohol. His rehabilitation program proved highly successful and members joined the commune in great numbers, many of them nonaddicts attracted by Synanon's lifestyle.

By 1972 there were 1,800 members. Related communes were established after 1963 elsewhere in California, in San Francisco and in Tulare and Marin counties.

Financially, Synanon literally went from begging dry bread and wilted vegetables in its early days to founding its own successful businesses. One woman reportedly donated $1,000,000 to the commune. In addition, a series of changes occurred within the commune itself. It became less of a drug treatment center and more of a religious cult, with its members giving up cigarettes and the female members shaving their heads. There were also reports of widespread divorces and "changing partners" within the community, as well as child abuse.

In 1978, two of the members were arrested for placing a diamondback rattlesnake in the mailbox of a Los Angeles attorney who had just won a judgment against Synanon on behalf of a married couple who said the wife was kidnapped and abused by members of the commune.

As more public agencies — including one county grand jury, the state department of health, and the attorney general's office — began to step up reviews of Synanon's operations, Dederich himself became openly hostile to those outside the commune. At a press conference in 1977, after he learned the health department was instituting a probe of the movement, Dederich exploded: "If they want to come on our property, we will surround each one of them with ten guys twice their size within one foot of them and say, 'All right, inspect, punk.'" He resigned as director and board chairman of Synanon in 1978. Also that year the commune reportedly bought $63,000 worth of weapons and ammunition for its own protection.

With a series of legal actions pending against the commune on the part of private complainants and public authorities, Synanon lost its members as rapidly as it had earlier gained them. In July 1980, Dederich and the two members who mailed the rattlesnake pleaded no contest to the charge of conspiracy to commit murder, and Dederich was then sentenced to five years probation on agreement that he would sever all connections with the Synanon organization. The commune closed shortly thereafter. A book with a section that focuses on the Synanon Foundation is Mitchell's *The Light on Synanon*.

Tahanto (1909–1940), across a small lake from Ayer, Massachusetts, was a single-tax community (see **Fairhope**) established on land that Boston paper manufacturer Fiske Warren bought from the **Harvard** Shaker community. The members maintained apple orchards, sold lumber, and made wooden boxes. Although Warren did not live in this community, the approximately 20 members closed Tahanto shortly after his death. A book with a section that focuses on Tahanto is Huntington's *Enclaves of Single Tax or Economic Rent*.

Tanguy Homesteads (1945–1973), at Glen Mills, Pennsylvania, was a housing community organized by Robert Wilson and other students at Pendle Hill College. Most of the members were Quakers and pacifists. Rochdale cooperative principles prevailed, and business meetings were held according to the model of a Quaker meeting. There were 110 members in 1959.

Temple Home (1905–1913), at Oceano, California, was a cooperative colony formed by a group of 50 Theosophists from **Point Loma** who had disagreed with most of the members there on particular aspects of Theosophist philosophy. They were led by Dr. William H. Dower and Mrs. Francia A. LaDue, who purchased about 100 acres of fertile land and built a sanitorium as the focus for their community. Later they changed the name to Halcyon. Their stated purpose was to set up a colony "wherein all the land will be owned all of the time by all of the people; where all the means of production and distribution, tools, ma-

chinery, and natural resources, will be owned by the people — the community — and where Capital and Labor may meet on equal terms with no special privileges to either."

Participants received living expenses, half an acre of land on which to grow vegetables, and $10 a month. Unlike the colony at Point Loma, children lived with their parents and attended public school in the nearby town of Arroyo Grande. The commune's monthly magazine, the *Temple Artisan*, was published to promote Theosophist principles. The group ceased to live as a cooperative colony in 1913, although they have continued as an independent Theosophical society at this location.

The old Victorian mansion in which the sanitorium was located stands at Highway 1 and 25th Street at the east end of Oceano. It is now headquarters for the Halcyon Theosophist's trailer camp. Also, six or seven community buildings still stand, and there is a graveyard where Dower, LaDue, and some other members of the commune are buried. A book with a section that focuses on Temple Home is Hine's *California's Utopian Communities*.

Tennessee Colony *see* **South Western Colony**

Teutonia Society of United Germans (1827–1831), Columbiana County, Ohio, was a commune founded by language teacher Peter Kaufman, who had lived for one year at Rapp's **Harmony** commune. The commune had perhaps ten members and it is unknown why it closed, but it has been suggested that the members just became bored with community life and moved away.

Thompson (1831), at Thompson, Ohio, was a Mormon United Order community composed of 60 members of the church who came to Ohio from Colesville, New York, with the church's founder, Joseph Smith, Jr. The village of Thompson is only about 20 miles from **Kirtland**, where the first Mormon commune was established and where Smith himself settled, so there was a close relationship between the two communes. Shortly after the Mormon settlement of **Zion** in Missouri was started, the members of Thompson closed their community and decided to move there.

Thompson Colony (1880), near Salina, Kansas, was named after Elizabeth Rowell Thompson, a philanthropist who gave support to a number of cooperative projects, including this one. The members worked the fields in common and held their farm tools in common, but maintained separate homes and gardens. They were expected to repay their benefactor in annual installments, and then, when repayment was completed they had the option of continuing the commune or giving up this cooperative lifestyle and returning to an individualistic one. Although it is not known how many members there were, the original plan was for the commune to have about 25 families, a number thought to be the ideal for such a project. Perhaps there were 30 members in all. The commune collapsed because the drought of 1880 destroyed their crops. A book with a section that focuses on the Thompson Colony is Fogarty's *All Things New*.

Tolstoy Farm (1963–present), about five miles from Davenport, Washington, is an anarchist community that is still active. It was established in 1963 by Huw and Sylvia Williams. Anyone who wishes to may join this community, and no one can be forced to leave. In 1969, they had 40 members, 180 acres of land, 13 homes, and an experimental schoolhouse for children.

At Tolstoy, every member is allowed to decide for themselves how much they wish to participate in the communal life. As a result there has been much disagreement over who will do the work. The long-range building and farming jobs (which have greatest importance and are somewhat creative) are the ones always completed by eager volunteers, but the clean-up and woodcutting chores are never done happily; only constant reminders and much guilt resolves the problem attached to these tasks. One enthusiast says that the supper meal, followed by games, folk music, and story reading, is the highlight of each day at the Tolstoy Farm. A book with a section that focuses on Tolstoy Farm is Fairfield's *Communes U.S.A.: A Personal Tour*.

Toquerville (1874–1875), Utah, was a **St. George**–type Mormon United Order commune for one year. It had about 75 members.

Touro (1883), in Comanche County, Kansas, was an agricultural commune (see **Sicily Island**) of Russian Jews, numbering about 30. They maintained their language and customs throughout the short life of the settlement.

Trabuco College (1942–1947), in the hills behind Laguna Beach, some 50 miles southeast of Los Angeles, California, was a pacifist meditation center and commune created by English writer Henry Fitzgerald Heard (1890–1971), known to his readers as Gerald Heard. He was the author of several prize-winning mysteries and essays in the field of popular science. He moved to southern California in 1938 and came under the influence of the Vedanta Center in Hollywood, as did the two other British writers, Aldous Huxley and Christopher Isherwood, both friends of Heard's. This contact with the Vedanta group intensified Heard's desire to create a community that would train persons in a new form of spirituality, one that might counteract fascism and war.

After he selected the site, Heard began to construct a Mediterranean brick building to house the commune members. It was designed for about 30 people, though there were never more than 12 members there, most of them women. The construction was supervised by Felix Greene, later known for his political radicalism and support of China's new Communist government. Huxley assisted Heard in writing the prospectus for Trabuco College, though he never joined the commune.

Heard also erected a round, windowless building that was always kept dark inside, a structure where members spent three hour-long periods of meditation each day. None of the buildings had heat or electricity and the meals the members ate were sparse and mostly vegetarian in nature. The members were also expected to lead a celibate life. When Heard eventually closed the community, he donated the buildings to the Vedanta Society.

Trapelo (1927–1940), at Weston, Massachusetts, was a single-tax enclave (see **Fairhope**) of 98 acres and about 30 members. They maintained a boarding school for more than 100 boys and girls, called the Cambridge School, that prepared youth for college entrance.

John R.P. French was the headmaster, and there were 17 teachers. The enclave also managed the Trapelo Golf Club. However, interest in maintaining the community declined over the years and so it closed. A book with a section that focuses on Trapelo is Huntington's *Enclaves of Economic Rent for 1931.*

Tripp (1878–1922), located on the James River near Milltown, South Dakota, was a Hutterite Brüderhof formed by members from **Bon Homme**. It was also often called Neudorf. When the **Harmony** Rappites in Pennsylvania offered land at Tidioute, Pennsylvania, to the Hutterites, the colony moved there, but they did not prosper in Pennsylvania and returned to their South Dakota home within two years, now calling themselves the Milltown Brüderhof. There were about 100 members and they eventually all moved to Manitoba, Canada, where the colony still exists today.

True Church of Philadelphia or Brotherly Love *see* **Irenia**

True Family *see* **Reunion Community**

Trumbull Phalanx (1844–1848), on Eagle Creek about eight miles west of Warren, Ohio, was a Fourierist community (see **Social Reform Unity**) organized by Nathan C. Meeker, an editor on Horace Greeley's *New York Tribune*. It had 200 members who together purchased 1,500 acres of land from Mr. Rood and Eli Barnum, a relative of the circus entrepreneur P.T. Barnum.

On the property was a grist mill, a vegetable-oil pressing mill, a two-story brick house, and a large barn. The members added several other houses, a tannery, a wagon shop, a flaxseed mill, a shoe shop, a blacksmith shop, a wooden-bowl factory, granaries, two saw mills, a school, and a community building. They planted wheat, oats, corn, potatoes, turnips, buckwheat, broom corn, peach trees, and garden

Children of the Hutterite community (photo by Burton Buller).

vegetables. They also raised cows, horses, and oxen. E.H. VanAmringe moved here from the **Ohio Phalanx** to become one of the Trumbull Phalanx leaders.

The dissolution of the phalanx was announced on December 3, 1847, but on May 27, 1848, a reorganization of the commune was announced. Nothing more was heard of it after July 15, 1848, so it can be assumed that it closed shortly thereafter. Apparently the problem that led to the Trumbull Phalanx's closure was that much of the land was swampy and therefore disease spread with relative ease throughout the commune. One of the granaries, painted red, is now used as a cheese factory. One of their mills is also still standing.

Tschetter (1896–1918), on the James River in Hutchison County, South Dakota, was a Hutterite Brüderhof (see **Bon Homme**) named for a leading member, Lorenz Tschetter. The approx-

imately 100 members moved their community to Alberta, Canada, where they are still in existence. In 1941 the South Dakota land was occupied by a division of the Barrackman Brüderhof in Canada, which then changed its name to the **Tschetter Colony**.

Tschetter Colony (1941–present) is a Hutterite Brüderhof (see **Bon Homme**) in Hutchinson County, South Dakota, that was formed by a division of the Barrackman Hutterite colony in Manitoba, Canada. It is located on the land of the earlier Tschetter Colony, which moved to Canada in 1918. In 1964 they had 104 members, and their leader was David Dekker.

Tuolume Cooperative Farms (1946–1959), on the north side of the Tuolume River, southwest of Modesto, California, was a pacifist community established in 1946 by several families who wanted to separate themselves from the ever-increasing militarism of American society. They owned 155 acres of land, four houses, barns, and some storage sheds. They raised cows, goats, corn, walnuts, and pomegranates. The 17 members lived separately as families and took funds from the communal treasury according to their needs. They had a business meeting every month and rotated work selections on a weekly basis. They sold the farm when they dispersed.

Turner Brüderhof (1957–present), near Turner, Montana, is a Hutterite commune (see **Bon Homme**) that had 75 members in 1964 and was led by John Hofer.

Turtle Creek *see* **Union Village**

Tusculum (1849–1851), near what is now Boerne, Texas, was a commune established by six German students, five of whom had previously lived at the **Bettina** commune. They selected the name "Tusculum" after the home of Roman orator Cicero.

The members were Christian Flatch, Wilhelm Friedrich, Leopold Schultz, Adam Vogt, Philip Zoeller, and Fritz Kramer. When they abandoned this project for reasons unknown, they sold the land to a neighboring farmer for about one-fourth of the price they paid for it. All six students were later among the founders of the town of Boerne. A book with a section that focuses on Tusculum is Biesele's *The History of the German Settlements in Texas, 1831–1861.*

Tyringham (1792–1875), on the side of Mount Horeb, one mile from the town of Tyringham, Massachusetts, was a Shaker settlement (see **Watervliet**) that was originally called Fernside because

their land was built on the fernside of a valley.

The buildings in this commune were constructed on such a steep slope that there were two stories on the upper side and four on the lower. Their barn was large enough to hold 40 yoke of oxen. At one point Tyringham had 100 members.

After the commune closed, the property was sold and became a resort called the Tyringham Forest Association. The land has since passed into private hands.

Ucopia (1950–1973), first at Wildomar and then San Marcos, California, was established by Walter Milsap and others loyal to the socialist ideals of the **Llano del Rio** community. It had perhaps ten members. The name is an abbreviation of United Cooperative Industries, the overall title they gave to a series of enterprises they managed on a cooperative basis.

Ukiah Brotherhood (1912–1918), near the Russian River, 15 miles north of Ukiah, California, was a Molokan farming commune (see **Freedom Colony**) of about 50 members. The participants came from San Francisco and each family had their own small house on the 500 acres of land. After this commune closed, the members all moved back to San Francisco.

Union (1804–1810), at Clark's Crossing, about two miles north of Potsdam, New York, was a cooperative venture of ten families (about 35 people) led by a Vermont shoemaker named William Bullard.

The members owned 2,427 acres of land that they purchased by pooling their resources. They kept an accurate accounting of all the labor and materials that each member provided, and apportioned the proceeds according to work done. During the first few years the commune prospered, but in time arguments over the distribution of profits arose. Some said that they should not be based on the pro rata cooperative system but should be divided equally. These disagreements increased over time and finally led to the dissolution of the commune. The land was then divided equally among the members. Some of their buildings were reportedly still standing in 1934. A book with a section that focuses on Union is Hough's *A History of St. Lawrence and Franklin Counties, New York.*

Union Association *see* **Bloomfield Union Association**

Union Colony (1869–1871), at Greeley, Colorado, was a cooperative venture originated by Nathaniel C. Meeker (1817–1897), the agricultural editor of Horace Greeley's *New York Weekly Tribune,* and promoted with great enthusiasm by the publisher. Neither of these men actually participated in the community, but the members eventually named their town Greeley in honor of Horace Greeley.

All participants were required to be of good moral character and advocates of temperance. They paid a membership fee of $155, which entitled them to a parcel of farming land that they had to improve within a year's time in order to gain title.

Transportation from New York, Boston, Buffalo, Cleveland, and Chicago was arranged for the colonists at a reduced rate. Altogether they had 11,900 acres. When they arrived, they lived in tents until the town was surveyed, streets laid out, and trees planted. By May 1870 there were 40 wooden houses,

a schoolhouse, a town hall, bridges over the Poudre River, and irrigation canals. They fenced in the farm lands by 1871.

There was some confusion at the beginning, particularly over the lack of housing, and some members left in disgust. But before the community dropped its cooperative features at the end of 1871, the experiment had grown to about 700 members before it disbanded. A book with a section that focuses on the Union Colony is Willard's *The Union Colony of Greeley, Colorado, 1869–1871.*

Union Grove (1856–1858), somewhere in Meeker County, Minnesota, was set up by about 30 members who came from the **Hopedale** community in Massachusetts. They purchased 800 acres of land for their communal experiment and erected 13 crude dwellings. But they were forced to disband because of Indian troubles and lack of capital. Hoped-for funds to keep the community solvent were expected from the people at Hopedale but they never came.

Union Home (1844–1846), at Huntsville, Indiana, was a community of about 25 persons organized by abolitionist Hiram Mendenhall from nearby Unionsport. Because their purpose — that of opposing slavery — was not popular in the days before the Civil War, little is now known of their activities. However, there are indications that they raised money to help in the antislavery struggle and perhaps even aided escaped slaves in their flight to Canada. (Many slaves fled from Tennessee up through Kentucky, Indiana, and Michigan to Canada.) The members lost a great deal of money trying to keep this project going, and when they dissolved it there was financial loss to all, especially to

Mendenhall, who bore the largest expense of this experiment. A book with a section that focuses on Union Home is Tucker's *History of Randolph County, Indiana*.

Union Manufacturing Company (1878), at Springfield, Vermont, was a cooperative enterprise of about 40 members who lived together in a single building. Their leader was J.A.H. Ellis. The commune was first called Springfield Industrial Works.

Union Mills Company (1892–1896), of Nehalem in Tillamook County, Oregon, was a commune of perhaps 20 lumbermen who held all property in common and worked an eight-hour day. They distributed their earnings equally, regardless of the type of work done. Members joined the community by purchasing stock at $100 a share. The failure of this commune has been attributed to the depressed market conditions of the time.

Union Village (1806–1912), in Warren County, Ohio, four miles from Lebanon, was the first of a series of Shaker settlements (see **Watervliet**) established outside of the New England states. It was first called Turtle Creek, but the name was later changed to Union Village. The commune was established on 4,500 acres of fertile Miami River bottom land, and there were as many as 600 members at one point. However, mob violence was a recurring problem there.

This community was formed as a result of the western trip of John Meacham, Benjamin Youngs, and Issacher Bates, who were sent out from the **Mount Lebanon** Shaker settlement on a recruiting mission. Their first convert in Ohio was Malcom Worley, a landowner who donated some of the land

for Union Village. Soon afterward the three Shaker leaders converted Richard McNemar (1770–1839), a preacher who had at that time the largest Presbyterian church in southern Ohio. McNemar and his family, along with most of the members of his congregation, joined the Shakers to form the initial membership of Union Village. In time McNemar became one of the ablest leaders for the Shaker movement in the Midwest. A skilled preacher and writer, he also had knowledge of the weaving, bookbinding, chairmaking, and printing trades.

David Darrow was named as the first elder at Union Village. He came from the Mount Lebanon Shaker commune, as did his three assistants — Solomon King, Ruth Farrington, and Hortense Goodrich. After Darrow died, Eldress Freegift Wells took his place. Wells was particularly jealous of McNemar and brought a medium to the commune to impute him. Though McNemar was later vindicated, the incident broke his spirit.

Union Village was a stock raising center for the Shakers, who bred Durham cattle there for export to Europe. The members also developed the breed of hogs known as Poland-China, and they raised fine sheep, garden seeds, and corn. They manufactured bricks, steel, pipes, leather, hollow ware, woolen yarn, brooms, medicinal herbs and extracts, syrup or sarsaparilla, and palm-leaf bonnets. They owned a grist mill, two sawmills, a tailor shop, a shoemaking shop, a blacksmith shop, and a wagonmaking shop. Their meeting house was constructed in 1809.

Mob violence was a recurring problem for this commune. It was agitated in part by an anti–Shaker newspaper called the *Western Star*, published in Lebanon. On August 27, 1810, a group of 500 armed men with at least 1,000 followers, and led by an ex–Shaker, came to the settlement intent on tarring and feathering McNemar and sending the rest of the members "back to New York." The Shakers invited the leaders into their community to inspect it, and soon the group dispersed. But violence occurred again in 1813, 1817, 1819, and 1824.

When the commune finally closed, the remaining members went to four Shaker communes — **South Union, Canterbury**, Watervliet, and Mount Lebanon. Some of their land and 26 of their buildings became part of the Lebanon State Prison Farm. The rest of their land was purchased by Otterbein College.

United Christians (1836–1837), at what is now Berea, Ohio, was a commune of about 60 Methodists who held their property in common and transacted business through a board of 12 Apostles. They were gathered together by the Rev. Henry O. Sheldon and James Gilruth. The members farmed and actively participated in the antislavery movement.

They had purchased over 1,000 acres of land for the experiment. On that property, they built some houses and purchased others, bought and repaired a sawmill and gristmill, and planted crops. The members had regular Sunday services — the first conducted in that area — and Sheldon built the Methodist Church that is still standing there. But dissension soon developed over the leadership of the apostles and the community disbanded in 1837.

Sheldon and Gilruth, who both remained in the area after the commune closed, disagreed on what to name the village that was then beginning to form there. Sheldon wanted to call it Berea; Gilruth wanted it named Tabor. A toss of a coin decided the matter in favor of Sheldon, who also became its first postmaster. The two men, however, cooperated in establishing the Berea Lyceum, which was a high school, and local residents for a time called their village Lyceum.

When the Methodists were looking for a place to found Baldwin-Wallace College, they discovered a ready environment there among the former members of the commune. A book with a section that focuses on the United Christians is Coats' *A History of Cuyahoga County and the City of Cleveland*.

Use *see* **Brotherhood of the New Life**

Utah Molokan Colony (1917) was a Molokan farming community (see **Freedom Colony**) that may have had 30 members. The Utah Historical Society once requested permission to erect a marker at the grave site of one of the members, but her son refused permission and so the location of this commune has since been forgotten.

Utilitarian Association of United Interests (1845–1848), near Mukwonago, Wisconsin, was an Owenite (see **New Harmony**) community that was established by 16 mechanics and their families from London (about 40 persons). It is thought that they may have come to the United States to participate in the Owenite **Colony of Equality** that was located 13 miles away in the same county, but decided to set up their own commune instead. They purchased a 200 acre farm near Mukwonago. However, after three years of struggle to make the project successful, they were finally "starved out"; most of the members then moved to Milwaukee.

Utopia (1847–1850), on the banks of the Ohio River in Clermont County, Ohio, about 35 miles from Cincinnati, was an anarchist colony of about 15 people established by Josiah Warren (see **Equity**). Today the place still bears the name "Utopia." The land had been abandoned by a Fourierist commune known as the **Clermont Phalanx,** and some of the members at Equity were former members of that phalanx who had not yet left the project. Together they had only 10 dollars with which to start the new commune.

Warren and his group in time built several houses, two brick stores, and a steam saw and grist mill. The commune closed in 1850 because of Warren's departure. Some of the members then moved to Minnesota, where land at that time was relatively cheap.

Vale (1950–present), near Antioch College at Yellow Springs, Ohio, is a nonsectarian cooperative community led by Griscom Morgan, son of Arthur E. Morgan, former president of Antioch College and founder of the **Celo Community** in North Carolina. The approximately 20 members maintained a school for the first three grades and kindergarten until 1985. They also rent apartments to students at Antioch College and work at various jobs in Yellow Springs to provide income for the community. Some of their funds are allocated to peace, civil rights, and other political causes. The commune occupies about 40 acres. A book with a section that focuses on Vale is Roberts' *The New Communes: Coming Together in America.*

Valley Forge (1826) also known as the Friendly Association for Mutual Interests, was established on George Washington's campsite at Valley Forge, Penn-

sylvania, by 15 Owenites. They patterned their community after Owen's commune called **New Harmony.** The members came from Philadelphia, Pennsylvania, and Wilmington, Delaware, and there is fragmentary evidence that those from Philadelphia were Quakers. They developed a constitution that was dated January 19, 1826.

Shortly after they settled on the property, however, bitter religious attacks were directed against them in the local press. The charge was that they were atheists and destroyers of the church. By September the members had dispersed. Some of them reportedly joined the Shaker **Watervliet** commune.

Van Eden Farms (1939–1949), near Burgaw, North Carolina, was a cooperative agricultural settlement started in the fall of 1939 for refugees from German fascism, both Jews and non–Jews. The project was planned by Dr. Alvin Johnson and financed by the Refugee Economic Corporation. It had 23 members, none of whom had previously been farmers. The project closed in 1949, most of the members having already left to obtain jobs in city factories.

Van Houton Fields (1940–1970), at West Nyack, Rockland County, New York, was a community organized by followers of Ralph Borsodi and his Green Revolution Movement (see **Bayard Lane Homestead Community**). It had about 75 members, who had a cooperative buying system and a cooperative wage system for home building.

Virgin City (1874–1877), Utah, was a **St. George**–type Mormon United Order commune for several years. It had about

The Voree printing plant on Beaver Island now serves as a museum (photo by Tammy McDonough).

75 members. The system was dropped there after Brigham Young, who had visited Virgin City to initiate the plan, died.

Voree (1844–1856), started at a place about two miles west of Burlington, Wisconsin, and then moved to Beaver Island in the northern part of Lake Michigan, was a Mormon commune. It was organized by James Jesse Strang, who departed from **Nauvoo** with several hundred followers after the murder of Joseph Smith, Jr., the founder of the Mormon religion.

Strang (1813–1856) was a former schoolteacher, lawyer, and small town newspaper editor in Burlington, Wisconsin. He visited Nauvoo in 1844 and there embraced Mormonism. On the day Smith was killed, just five months after Strang had become a Mormon, he claimed he had been ordained by angels to assume the leadership of the church. He exhibited a letter, which he said was written by Smith, instructing him to

found a Wisconsin branch of the church. Most of the Mormon leadership repudiated him, but one who did support Strang was Joseph Smith's brother, William.

By 1847 Strang had produced a large number of revelations; had, like Joseph Smith, found sacred tablets that he translated; and had given out many creedal pronouncements, including one that gave instructions for ordering of his commune and others that provided for the construction of a temple and a home for himself.

He moved the settlement to Beaver Island in 1847, and by 1849 his followers had erected the city of St. James on that island. Strang was crowned king there in 1850. The membership of Voree reached a high of 2,500 at this time. In 1852 and 1854 Strang was elected to the Michigan state legislature.

Although he initially opposed polygamy, practiced by some of the Mormons who had gone to Utah, he now had a revelation that allowed the practice among his members and he himself took three more wives. Eventually Strang's commandments and dictatorial methods caused dissension among his followers. He was killed in 1856 by mob action organized by an ex-member, Dr. Hezekiah McCulloch, who had previously been Strang's trusted advisor.

The members now scattered, many of them forced to do so by people from the mainland who invaded Beaver Island and pushed them into boats that took them away. The Strangite branch of Mormonism still exists, although it has a very small membership and no communal base. The only remnants of the Voree community are a harbor light on the island, said to have been erected by the Mormons, and a building (built in 1850) that was used as the printing shop for the community. A book with a sec-

tion that focuses on Voree is Mathison's *Faiths, Cults and Sects in America.*

Wachovia (1753–1856), which covered 98,985 acres in present-day Forsyth County, North Carolina, including the area now occupied by the city of Winston-Salem, was a Moravian community that operated under a system called the General Economy (see **Bethlehem**). The Moravians purchased the land from Lord Granville, speaker in the English House of Commons, and the title was held by David Nitschmann and Nathaniel Seidel.

The Moravians particularly liked the area because it contained several Indian tribes whom they hoped to convert. These tribes were the Creek, Catawaba, Cherokee, and Chickasaw.

The 12 initial settlers took over an abandoned hunter's cabin and began to

The Lick-Boner House of the Moravian community at Salem as it appears today (courtesy of Old Salem).

build houses, a church, barns, and some workshops. By 1800 the population of Wachovia had reached 1,147, and the members were living in seven towns, all of which were operated under the single church leadership. These were Bethabara (Old Town), started in 1753; Bethania (New Town), started in 1759; Salem, started in 1766; and Winston, Friedberg, Friedland, and Hope, all started in 1849.

Salem had at least 30 dwelling houses, a congregation house, a single brethren's house, a community store, a tavern, waterworks, and a fire department. Water was supplied to every house in Salem by an elaborate system of conduits that carried the liquid a mile and a half. When President George Washington visited in 1791, he was "especially pleased with the waterworks." (Winston and Salem were not united into one city until 1913, long after the communal life of this settlement ended.)

During the American Revolution, British captives were kept at Wachovia, and colonial ammunition was stored in Salem. A hospital there provided care for the wounded. When the English General Cornwallis passed in pursuit of General Greene, the British troops destroyed much of the property in Bethabara and Salem.

As at the Moravian community of Bethlehem, the General Economy system at Wachovia was dropped in 1849 and replaced by the somewhat less communal Herrnhut system used in the European Moravian communities. Within seven years all forms of communalism at Wachovia had been discarded. Today one can visit the restored Moravian village of Salem within the city of Winston-Salem. Books with sections that focus on Wachovia are Fries' *The Road to Salem* and Sessler's *Communal Pietism Among Early American Moravians.*

Wallingford (1851–1881), at Wallingford, Connecticut, was a Perfectionist community of 38 members who practiced the teachings of John Humphrey Noyes (see **Putney Corporation**). They erected a community mansion as well as a number of smaller buildings, engaged in farming, the making of match boxes, silk manufacturing, and printing. Charles Cragin developed a process of silver plating there that eventually led to the manufacturing of the well-known Oneida brand of silverware. This is still produced at **Oneida,** where the production company was moved shortly after Cragin perfected it. The members of Wallingford closed their commune after they decided to change their economic system into that of a joint stock company.

Warm Springs Colony (1871), on the French Broad River in Madison County, North Carolina, was organized at a meeting of the Cooper Institute in New York City. The exact location is unknown, but it may have been near what is now the town of Hot Springs. Each member paid $100 for a share in the community, and a mortgage was taken on 1,500 acres of land that included a hotel and mineral springs. Some of the members constructed a dam on the river to provide a good supply of water; a store was opened, and a few homes were built. However, most of the 50 members preferred to live in the hotel. One of these was Eugene L. Fischer, who had originally intended to join **Icarian Nauvoo.** When Warm Springs closed he migrated to the **German Socialist Colony.**

Warren Range (1913–1920), probably south of Red Lodge, Montana, was a

Hutterite Brüderhof (see **Bon Homme**) of about 100 members. They moved to Alberta, Canada, in 1920, where they presumably still exist.

Washington (1874–1875), Utah, was a 250 member Mormon commune patterned after the **St. George** United Order system for a brief period of time.

Washington Colony (1881–1884), at the town of Whatcom, Washington, now part of the city of Bellingham, was a cooperative land venture composed of about 75 people from Kansas who wanted to move west. Members paid $100 a share for stock in the company. They built homes, a saw mill, and a wharf. But disputes over titles to the land disrupted the community and when the land reverted to a creditor as a result of a lawsuit, the Washington Colony closed. A book with a section that focuses on the Washington Colony is LeWarne's *Utopias on Puget Sound, 1885–1915*.

Washington Community (1833), near Washington D.C., was a Jewish agricultural commune (see **Sicily Island**) of about 45 members. It is unknown why this community closed after only a few months of existence.

Water View (1883–1886), on the Rappahannock River in Middlesex County, Virginia, was a Jewish agricultural commune (see **Sicily Island**) of about 20 members. They engaged in farming under the leadership of Joseph Friedenwald of Baltimore. This commune should not be confused with the earlier Jewish agricultural settlement called **Middlesex**, which was in the same county.

Watervliet (1776–1938), seven miles northwest of Albany, New York, once known as Niskayuna, was the first of 28 Shaker communes established in the United States. It was "gathered" and led by Mother Ann Lee (1736–1784), the person who brought the Shaker movement to the United States. At its height it had 350 members.

Officially known as the United Society of Believers in Christ's Second Appearing, the Shakers were founded in England as an offshoot of the Quakers and as a result of the spiritual impetus of the French Camisards. They were called Shakers because, during religious meetings, their intense emotions caused them to quiver and shake.

Ann Lee (or Lees), was the daughter of a blacksmith in Manchester, England. She could neither read nor write when she joined the society in 1758, then under the leadership of Jane and James Wardley. She had worked in a cotton factory, as a cook, and as a cutter of hatter's fur. She married a blacksmith by the name of Abraham Staderin (or Standley) and had four children, all of whom died in infancy. Her enthusiasm for Shakerism led her to roam the streets every day preaching a "war on lust." This eventually led to her persecution and imprisonment in 1770 for "profanation of the Sabbath." But during her stay in prison she had a revelation of "the mystery of iniquity, or the root and foundation of human depravity." She became convinced that Christ's second coming had already occurred within herself, as it could in anyone after confession of their sins. Mother Ann also became sure that sexual intercourse and lusts of the flesh were at the root of most human evils.

In 1774 she brought the movement and nine of its disciples (including her husband, brother, and a niece) to New

York. One of her followers, John Hocknell, purchased the tract of swampy and wooded land that was to form the location for this commune at Niskayuna up the Hudson River. Seven of the followers moved there to build some cabins and start clearing the land, but Mother Ann and her husband remained in New York City eking out a living — she by taking in washing and he as a blacksmith. Her husband soon renounced Shakerism and deserted her for another woman. Mother Ann then joined the others at Niskayuna to start the communal experiment. Hocknell went back to England and returned with his own family and another family named Partington, increasing the membership of the commune to about 15.

For three and a half years the community existed in relative isolation. The members erected a few buildings and held religious meetings. But in time the group became known to the surrounding farmers and villagers because they constantly preached against war and would not bear arms or take an oath. They were accused of pro–British sympathies, and in 1780 Mother Ann, as well as five others, was arrested and held on charges of high treason. These Shakers were released several months later.

In 1781 Mother Ann began to tour the New England states holding meetings in many places and organizing small groups of "believers." Again she suffered many incidents of persecution because of her preaching, once even being stoned by an angry crowd. She returned to Watervliet in 1783 completely worn out, and died there in 1784.

The leadership of Watervliet then passed to Elder James Whitaker (1751–1787), who was one of the nine who had originally come with Mother Ann from England. He was a weaver by trade and a gifted public speaker. He had been arrested with Mother Ann, had accompanied her on the tour of the New England states, and had been badly beaten by mobs at that time. After Father James died in 1787, he was succeeded by Father Joseph Meacham (1741–1796), a former Baptist preacher. Meacham was one of Mother Ann's first American converts. He picked Lucy Wright (1760–1821), another early American convert, to assist him in leading "the female line" of the commune. When Meacham died in 1796, Lucy Wright assumed the entire administration of the enterprise.

To this day Shakers consider Mother Ann somewhat of a deity. While holding many beliefs of orthodox Christianity, they reject the Virgin birth and the resurrection of the body, adhere to a system of seven heavens and seven hells, and preach a hierarchy of Holy Spirits and angels. The members also believe that God includes both male and female, and that just as the eternal Christ in Jesus is male so the eternal Christ in Ann Lee is female. These two, then, consisted the father and mother of all the children of God.

In the late 1850s, the Shaker movement reached its peak membership. At that time there were about 6,000 persons in all the Shaker communes. Today there is still one of these Shaker communes in existence, **Sabbathday Lake Village** in Maine.

From the outset, the Shakers were pacifists and opponents of slavery. But the two most prominent features of Shakerism were their practice of holding goods in common and their insistence on celibacy. In the communes there was no private ownership of any kind. Separate doorways and stairways, separate residence floors, separate tables for eating, and even separate pews for worship kept men and women apart while they lived under the same roofs. It was considered "contrary to order" for a man and a woman to touch or even to be alone together.

The members carefully followed the precepts of their founder, Mother Ann, who said they should earnestly do their work as though they had 1,000 years to live and at the same time as though they were going to die tomorrow. The result was craftsmanship reminiscent of the best medieval artisans, yet as technically advanced as any other products of the day. Into the back and legs of every chair they made, the Shaker craftsperson seemingly put their whole life purpose. Every basket of fruit that they shipped to the market was carefully inspected to make sure that the apples in the middle and bottom layers were as fresh and ripe as those on top.

The Shaker movement attracted some outstanding humanitarian leaders. One of these was Frederick Evans, who joined the Shakers in 1830 after a distinguished career as publisher of labor, antislavery, and women's rights periodicals. As a Shaker, he continued to call for such reforms and for free public education for everyone up to 21 years of age, opposition to war, and opposition to imprisonment for debts. He met with President Abraham Lincoln and Secretary of War Stanton, along with another Shaker leader, Benjamin Gates, to request the exemption of Shakers from participating in the Civil War, a petition that Lincoln granted.

Another Shaker with strong humanitarian interests was Daniel Fraser, son of a Scottish silk weaver, who, before he came to the United States and joined the Shakers in 1834, had helped to lead the movement for the enactment of child labor laws in the United States. Fraser, as a Shaker, wrote extensively in support of universal ownership of land, equal justice for all, hygiene, and dietetics. Both Evans and Fraser in time became prominent leaders of Shaker communes.

The Shakers are well known for the exceptionally fine and functional furniture they made. Less familiar are the many inventions that poured from their settlements. The flat broom, now used in almost every household, was invented by a Shaker brother in 1798. They made the first one-horse buggies, the first screw propeller, the first circular harrow, the first threshing machine, the first pea sheller, the first apple corer, the first clothespin, the first cut nails. They also invented metal pen points and a static electricity generator for shock therapy, in this case to cure rheumatism and not psychiatric disorders. Furthermore, they were the first producers of commercial seed, and they developed herbal medicines that sold widely throughout nineteenth century America. This, of course, is only a partial list of their inventions.

Their inventiveness was not just in practical matters, but extended to the arts as well, particularly to music. Here they drew from the themes of American revival hymns and spirituals, to which they added a simplified alphabetical notation system of their own (designed so that anyone might be able to sing), and wove the inspired product into the ritual of dance. Their close-order "marching" type of dance expressed unity and discipline for the Shakers, and the closeness but physical separation of the men and women represented the commune's celibacy in the face of temptation. Their songs were expressive of their understanding and determination to be perfect in the sight of God.

The Shaker movement had a marked influence on American letters. Three novels by William Dean Howells were based on Shaker material: *The Undiscovered Country, A Parting and a Meeting*, and *The Day of Their Wedding*. Hawthorne's *Shaker Bridal* and *The Canterbury Pilgrims* were also about them, as were novels by Catherine Sedgewick and Kate Douglas Wiggins. One of the characters in Melville's *Moby Dick* came from this "crazy society of Neskyeuna Shakers," and Artimas Ward found them an apt subject for humor.

The commune at Watervliet was divided into four separate "families." They increased the land they owned to 4,500 acres, and on this land grew fruit and vegetables which they marketed in tin cans. They also raised sheep and cattle. Their Watervliet library had 400 volumes, mostly religious works but some of popular science.

The noted garden-seed business conducted at a number of the Shaker communes began in 1790 when Elder Joseph Turner first offered seeds for sale. Ebeneezer Allen, another Watervliet member, invented a "printing box" for hand printing the seed bags, and by 1811 they were raising $300 worth of seeds each year, a great deal of money at that time. Trustees David Osborn and Morrel Baker contributed much to the improvement of the seed stock through the careful selection of parent plants. The Shaker broom-making industry also first started here in 1798, and one of the members invented the needle with an eye in the middle for sewing these brooms. This tool was later adapted by Elias Howe in his invention of the first practical sewing machine.

When the community closed in 1938, the three remaining members — all women — moved to the **Mount**

Lebanon Shaker settlement in New York. The red-brick buildings of the Watervliet commune are still standing and are now used for a county home for the poor and infirm. The graveyard where Mother Ann and others are buried is also there. Books with sections that focus on Watervliet and the Shaker movement are Andrews' *The People Called Shakers* and Melcher's *The Shaker Adventure*.

Watervliet in Ohio (1806–1910), six miles south of Dayton, was a Shaker settlement (see **Watervliet**) first known as Beaver Creek and then as Beulah. It was a publishing center for the Shaker society in the Midwest, and at one point this commune had as many as 100 members.

John Patterson, the first settler in the Beaver Creek area, was one of the first members of this commune. He, John Huston, and John and William Stewart gave the initial land for the settlement after they were converted to Shakerism. Eventually the commune encompassed a total of 1,300 acres.

Richard McNemar, one of the leading Shakers of **Union Village**, came there to establish and supervise the printing plant. In 1833 they published a collection of hymns, most of which were probably written by McNemar. The members also made wooden ware, woolens, wagons, brooms, and ironware for sale. Their log meeting house was constructed in 1810, grist mill in 1812, tannery in 1813, and cooper's shop in 1814. They also had, besides their printing plant, a saw mill and a woolen mill. When this commune was disbanded, the few remaining members moved to Union Village.

Wayne Produce Association (1921–1965), at McKinnon, Georgia, was a cooperative community of 75 coal and iron miners, woodsmen, and industrial workers of Finnish nationality. One of the leaders was Isaac Ahlborg. They occupied 3,000 acres of land. Some of the members earlier had been associated with the Industrial Workers of the World, the Communist Party, or the Workers Party.

The commune had a dairy, store, blacksmith shop, sawmill, lodging house, cottages, Finnish bath (which outsiders enjoyed using as much as did members), and one of the best vegetable and corn gardens in the county. They also raised cows, chickens, and pigs. Every other Saturday night, visitors were invited to a dance. When the community disbanded, the land was sold to the Brunswick Pulp and Paper Company. There were only a few remaining members at the time. A book with a section that focuses on the Wayne Produce Association is Wooster's *Communities of the Past and Present.*

West Union (1810–1827), located on a 2,000-acre tract of land about ten miles north of Vincennes, Indiana, near the town of Busseron, was a Shaker community (see **Watervliet**) organized by Issacher Bates. The place at that time was called Busro Creek and is now known as Shaker Prairie.

The membership of three other Shaker communes—**Red Banks, Straight Creek,** and **Eagle Creek**—was consolidated to form this one. Eventually the membership at West Union grew to 300, organized into three "families." Archibald Meacham, son of Joseph Meacham of Watervliet, was the spiritual leader for this group.

Although they had been promised freedom of worship and protection by Indiana Governor William Henry Harrison, the commune members faced trouble from the beginning. There were occasional attacks on the settlement by Indians as well as by bands of marauding soldiers during the War of 1812. The commune also suffered from floods, fire, hostile neighbors, and malaria.

The members raised stock and took produce for sale on flatboats down the Mississippi to New Orleans. They had a grist mill, saw mill, and distillery. In 1820 they built a three-story 25-room community house that had 60 windows, 21 fireplaces, and two kitchens.

After they decided to close this commune, the remaining members moved to either the **Union Village** or the Watervliet Shaker settlements. All of the land was sold by 1837, and the last house constructed was torn down by 1882.

Western Fourier Association *see* **Ohio Phalanx.**

Western New York Industrial Association *see* **Social Reform Unity.**

White Oak Shakers (1898), at White Oak, Georgia, on the Atlantic Coast and about 20 miles north of the Florida State line was a short-lived Shaker community (see **Watervliet**) of about ten members. Little is known about them or why this commune lasted for such a short time.

Whitewater (1824–1907) was a Shaker commune in Hamilton County, Ohio, about 15 miles west of Cincinnati. It was organized by Miriam Agnew, her husband Joseph, and his brother Brant. At one time this community had 150 members organized into three "families." They owned 1,500 acres of land.

The members erected a brick meeting house in 1827. They packaged garden seeds and made brooms for sale, raised stock, and did general farming. They were particularly adept at bookbinding, and so taught this art to other Shaker communities. However, the commune was unable to produce enough income to support the members and they had to be subsidized by other Shaker communities. So Whitewater was ordered dissolved by the center of the Shaker ministry at **Mount Lebanon.**

Willard Cooperative Colony (1895–1896) was organized at Harriman, Tennessee, although the 50-member group established their commune on 1,000 acres of land in Cherokee County, North Carolina. They named it for the temperance movement leader Frances Willard.

Besides promoting the causes of temperance and cooperation, the members favored bringing all Protestant churches together into one united denomination. They were, however, never able to complete the $21,000 payment for the land and so they had to disband. Among the members was the Rev. Ralph Albertson, who persuaded many of the members to join him when he later established the **Christian Commonwealth** commune in Georgia.

Wilson Range (1963–present), near Stanford, Montana, is a Hutterite Brüderhof (see **Bon Homme**) with 75 members in 1964 and Elias Walter as their leader.

Wisconsin Phalanx (1844–1850), at what is now Ripon, Wisconsin, was one of the most successful of the many Fourierist communes (see **Social Reform Unity**). It was organized by people in Southport (now Kenosha), Wisconsin, and eventually had 180 resident members. They purchased 1,793 acres of land on which they raised 10,000 bushels of wheat in one season, as well as corn, potatoes, buckwheat, peas, beans, and garden vegetables of all types. They also had cattle, horses, sheep, and chickens.

The members built two long houses, or phalanxtrys. One of these is still in use today as a low-income apartment house. They also erected a saw mill, grist mill, stone schoolhouse, wash house, hen house, blacksmith shop, and a communal kitchen. A question that divided the membership from time to time was whether to build separate residences for all the families or to construct a bigger and better phalanxtry for all to live in, as dictated by Fourierist principles. The phalanxtry concept won out each time a vote was taken, but only by a small majority. On the question of meals, however, the member families were permitted to choose for themselves whether to eat boarding house–style or in their own apartments.

Warren B. Chase (1813–1891), a local preacher in the Methodist Episcopal Church and a man who later became a leader in the spiritualist movement and ran for public office on the radical Free-Soiler ticket, was the chairman of the phalanx. Benjamin Wright was its president and Stephen Bates its secretary. Other prominent members included L.M. Parsons, who replaced Wright as president in 1845, and Michael Frank, chairman of the committee that drafted the commune's constitution. Publisher Christopher Latham Sholes, the inventor of the first typewriter, was a proponent of the Wisconsin Phalanx and printed a great deal about it in his newspaper, the *Southport Telegraph* (now the *Kenosha Telegraph*).

During the life of this phalanx, the members organized themselves and their neighbors into a town under the guidance of the Wisconsin state legisla-

Phalanx building of the Wisconsin Phalanx is used for low-income housing today (photo by author).

ture. It was incorporated as the town of Ceresco in honor of Ceres, the Roman goddess of agriculture. Only later did the citizens change the name to Ripon. Three members of the phalanx were elected to the state senate, and one was a candidate for governor. Some of the members also attended both state constitutional conventions. Today the town of Ripon claims one other distinction — being the birthplace of the Republican Party.

The Wisconsin Phalanx came to an end on January 29, 1850, when the members voted to dissolve the commune and put their land up for public sale. Many of the members continued to live in the area after the experiment ended.

Wolf Creek (1875–1930), in the valley of the James River near Freeman, South Dakota, was a Hutterite Brüderhof established by the first division of **Bon Homme**. The commune was led by Darius Walter, and it had about 100 members before they moved to Alberta, Canada, in 1930, because of harassment in the United States. Their land was later reclaimed by the **Beadle County Colony** of Hutterites.

Wolf Creek (1960–present), near Harlem, Montana, is a Hutterite Brüderhof (see **Bon Homme**). They had 55 members in 1964. The leader at that time was Joseph Hofer.

Women of the Wilderness (1694–1720), established on a ridge overlooking Wissahickon Creek, now part of Fairmont Park in Philadelphia, Pennsylvania, was a German pietist commune led by Johann Kelpius. The members, all men, never numbered more than 40. They devoted themselves to meditation, wrote music, studied astrology, and waited the end of the world. The name chosen for this commune comes from the Bible where, in the book of Revelations, it says women emerged from the wilderness to deliver the true church. It was a rather strange name for them to choose since they never permitted any women members.

Their leader, Kelpius (1673–1708), was born in Transylvania and was a man of great learning. He earned a doctorate from Helmstadt University in Germany, could read five languages, wrote and scored music, and possessed a wide reputation as a sage and a saint. In Germany, he worked closely with Johann Jacob Zimmerman, a theologian, mathematician, and astronomer who had determined, by exact mathematical calculations of the Biblical text, that the Millennium would come in the year 1694. It was Zimmerman's plan to take a company of 40 men from Germany to the forests of the New World where they could await this great event. After Zimmerman died unexpectedly before he and his followers could leave for the New World, Kelpius assumed leadership. The group, then numbering somewhat less than 40, sailed for America early in 1694.

They arrived at Bohemia Landing, Maryland, on June 22, and then proceeded to Germantown, Pennsylvania, where Kelpius immediately began to search for a site for their settlement. "Hermit Lane" and "Hermit Creek" in Fairmont Park today designate the general location of this commune.

The members built a log house, 40 feet square, and called it a Tabernacle. Therein they conducted religious and musical services. They held all possessions in common and believed that celibacy was necessary to achieve perfection. Much of their time was devoted to prayer and meditation. They also cultivated medicinal plants and gave religious instruction to the German settlers and Indians in the area. The commune members had a number of telescopes and other astronomical instruments with which they pursued studies in astrology.

When 1694 passed, the members concluded that the reason they were denied the privilege of witnessing this great Millennium must be because they still had less than 40 commune participants. So Daniel Falckner, the business manager for the group, went back to Germany to find more recruits to bring their number up to the mystic 40. While there, Falckner wrote a book about Pennsylvania that was widely circulated by groups promoting emigration to the New World. Falckner returned to Pennsylvania in 1700 with his brother, Justus, and others. But Justus Falckner only stayed at the commune for a few months because he found that he could not totally share the beliefs of the members. He later became a prominent Lutheran minister in America. Daniel Falckner, in his final years, also served as a Lutheran minister.

Music was particularly important to the commune members. They had an orchestra of sorts, printed the first volume of music to appear in America — a book of original hymns with musical scores by Kelpius — and gave the first known musical recital in Pennsylvania at the ordination of Justus Falckner in 1703. The instruments used for this recital were a viol, oboe, trumpet, and kettledrum.

One of the more prominent members of the commune was Heinrich Bernhard Köster (1662–1749), a man with a reputation for scholarship that almost equaled that of Kelpius. Köster disagreed with Kelpius on some fundamental issues that are now forgotten and departed from the commune in 1696 to establish his own settlement (see **Irenia**). In 1697 he wrote the first

Latin work to be composed in America, a highly mystical dissertation. No printer could be found to handle such a complex text and so it awaited publication until Köster returned to Germany in 1699.

After Kelpius died, Johann Gottfried Seelig took over as the commune leader. The job later passed to Conrad Matthai. But by 1720 the settlement was no more, although some of the former members continued to live as hermits in the woods around Wissahickon Creek.

When John Greenleaf Whittier wrote his poem *Pennsylvania Pilgrim*, he commemorated Kelpius in the following lines:

Deep in the woods, where the small river slid
Snake-like in shade, the Helmstadt mystic hid
Weird as a wizard, over arts forbid.

A book with a section that focuses on the Women of the Wilderness is Calverton's *Where Angels Dared to Tread.*

Women's Commonwealth (1874–1906), at Belton, Texas, until 1898, and then at Washington, D.C., was organized by Mrs. Martha (White) McWhirter (1829–1904). She was the mother of 12 and a devoted member of the Methodist Church. She had a conversion experience that convinced her to start a religious revival among her acquaintances. The result was the formation of this commune in which almost all the members were women, though there were four men at one point. The members preached celibacy and were eccentric in both religion and dress.

At the beginning the Women's Commonwealth members were persecuted by their neighbors, who derisively called them the "sanctified band." The rented homes they lived in were stoned on occasion, and some members were cruelly beaten. One was abducted and confined to a mental institution by her husband after she joined the group. To earn a living, they took in washing, wove carpets, and did nursing. By 1880 they had become accepted by the townsfolk and were running a boarding house, which became known as "the best hotel in Belton." They also ran two small hotels in Waco, Texas, for a few years, and McWhirter became the only female member of the Board of Trade there.

Their membership reached more than 50 before they left Belton for Washington. It is said that when they announced they were leaving, the entire town begged them to stay. The old McWhirter house in Belton is still standing. A bullet hole in the door remains as a visible reminder of the harassment this community experienced in its earliest days.

McWhirter moved the commune to Washington in the hope that the members might improve themselves and have some influence on the workings of Congress. They set up their commune in the Mount Pleasant area of Washington, at 1437 Kenneshaw Avenue, and they were incorporated in that city on October 30, 1902. Shortly after their arrival, they purchased a 119-acre farm in Montgomery County, Maryland. Two years later, McWhirter died at the age of 77. The leadership then passed to Fannie Haltzclaw. However, the commune closed soon afterward, the membership having dropped to 18. Some of the last members continued to live at their Maryland farm until the 1930s, but not as a commune. Books with sections that focus on the Women's Commonwealth are Fogarty's *All Things New* and Wooster's *Communities of the Past and Present.*

Sunday morning meeting at Woodcrest or wedding of one of the Woodcrest Members (photo by Heinrich Barth).

Woodcrest (1954–present), near Rifton, New York, is a Society of Brothers commune, modeled after the Hutterite Brüderhofs but without any direct relationship to them. The members are followers of Eberhard Arnold, a German theologian who once was the secretary of the German Christian Student Union. He was an advocate of Christian socialism and proclaimed that the economic injustice of the world has to be overcome through love.

As early as 1920, Arnold gathered several families together for an experiment in Christian communal living. This community thrived in rural Germany for more than ten years. But with the advent of Hitler's fascism and draft for the army, the members were forced to flee from Germany to England and then to Paraguay. Some of them came to the United States and joined the **Forest River** Hutterite Brüderhof, with disastrous results to that commune. Oth-

ers came and set up Woodcrest. By 1956 Woodcrest had grown to 167 members. They now also have two other communities in the United States — one at Norfolk, Connecticut (the **Deerspring Community**), and the other at Farmington, Pennsylvania (**New Meadow Run**), as well as one in England. At Woodcrest the members raise garden crops on their 110 acres and manufacture toys and play equipment that they sell by mail order throughout the United States. They have a school for children up to the eighth grade (older children go to the public school) and a publishing house. They also support a ministry to prisoners at the nearby maximum security prison in Green Haven, New York. The members of this community are quite open to welcoming visitors. Books with sections that focus on Woodcrest are Conkin's *Two Paths to Utopia: The Hutterites and the Llano Colony* and Zablocki's *The Joyful Community*.

Woodruff (1877–1882), Arizona, was a Mormon United Order commune that followed the model first enacted at **Orderville**. It had about 150 members.

Yellow Springs (1825–1826), at Yellow Springs, Ohio, was an Owenite community of 200 people, the first such formed after the establishment of **New Harmony**. It grew out of a series of meetings held in Cincinnati, Ohio, in November and December 1824, at which Robert Owen was the guest speaker. The nucleus of the membership came from the congregation of the New Jerusalem Swedenborgian Church in Cincinnati. With their minister, Daniel Roe, they decided to purchase 720 acres for the experiment.

The members included teachers, mechanics, merchants, farmers, laborers, and a number of professional men. They lived at Yellow Springs in a common house and divided their labor equally. Each family had a private room, but they ate together in a communal dining hall. They set up a school to "teach all things useful, except religion," and members were encouraged to give lectures on any subject of their choice. The Sabbath was put aside as a day of rest and recreation, when members could engage in walks, rides, games such as ten pins, and public lectures. Dancing was promoted as a most valuable means of physical and social culture.

Dissension over distribution of earnings brought the experiment to a close at the end of 1826. As a newspaper account put it, "Mechanics, whose single day's labor brought two dollars into the common stock, insisted that they should, in justice, work only half as long as the agriculturist, whose work brought but one." Robert Owen himself went to Yellow Springs in January 1826,

to look into the problem, as did geologist and New Harmony member William Maclure. Maclure later said that there was only one Yellow Spring member he could fully trust — a man named Caleb Lowns.

By the time the experiment ended, only half the purchase price had been paid for the land, and so it was deeded back to the original owners. The site is now occupied by Antioch College.

York Society of Integral Cooperators (1882–1883), in Taney County, Missouri, was a commune established by Henry E. Sharpe of the Knights of Labor, one of the most important early labor unions in the United States. Sharpe was head of the Cooperative Colony Aid Association and one of five members of a special Cooperative Board that was an organ of the Knights of Labor. The prospectus for this commune stated "that if a sufficient number of people, of sufficient variety of skill, go apart to a sufficiently friendly locality, with sufficient funds for operations, they can from their own hands, by their own industry, obtain and fashion all those things according to their own ideas of equity."

The commune had 50 members and 1,000 acres of land. They also organized a Knights of Labor unit within the community. Sharpe lectured widely on the values of cooperation and eventually was named chairman of the Cooperative Board. He also set up a Cooperative Aid Association to assist the York Society of Integral Cooperators. The secretary of the Kansas branch of this Aid Association was E.E. Barnum, circus promoter P.T. Barnum's nephew. But other members of the Knights of Labor disliked Sharpe's high-handed methods and charged him with "kidnapping." Even though an inquiry found the evidence against Sharpe was insufficient, he was suspended from the Cooperative Board and later expelled from the Knights of Labor. This brought an end to his commune. Sharpe, in 1889, joined a communal experiment in Brazil. A book with a section that focuses on the York Society of Integral Cooperators is Fogarty's *All Things New*.

Yuba City Molokan Colony (1917), near Yuba City, California, was a Molokan farming commune (see **Freedom Colony**) of approximately 30 members.

Zion (1831–1833), at a place now within the city limits of Kansas City, Missouri, was a Mormon United Order commune established by Oliver Cowdery and Parley Pratt, who had come to the state from **Kirtland** in Ohio as part of an effort to spread the Mormon gospel among the Indians. Cowdery and Pratt purchased 40 acres of land for their settlement and gave it the name Zion to designate it as the promised land of the Mormons.

Although they never had much contact with any Indians in the area, Cowdery and Pratt did convert many of the white settlers and by 1832 the population of Zion reached more than 1,200 people, or about one-third of the total population of Jackson County at that time.

They laid a cornerstone for their temple and built many houses on the property. But mob violence directed against the Mormons forced them to abandon the experiment. They were attacked because of religious prejudice and resentment against their promotion of the idea that the Indians were entitled to inhabit and inherit the promised land. The primary reason for hostility against the Mormons in Missouri, however, came from the fact that this was a border state at a time when there was growing national concern over the question of slavery. The Mormons, as nonslaveholders, were regarded as possible, if not actual, abolitionists. Nearly 300 of their homes were burned by one anti–Mormon mob. The members of Zion had to flee to Clay County, Missouri, where they lived noncommunally for a time, and then part of the group went to Caldwell County, to a place they named **Far West**. The rest went to Daviess County, where Lyman Wight had already started another Mormon community, **Adam-ondi-Ahman.**

Zion (1861–1862), three miles northwest of South Webber, Utah, was a Mormon community (see **Kirtland**) established by Joseph Morris, an Englishman who claimed to be the "Seventh Angel" foretold by Daniel in the Bible. It numbered about 500 members and was destroyed by a military posse from Salt Lake City, sent to arrest the now-excommunicated Morris. He died in the ensuing three-day battle along with five other members. The followers who survived the onslaught broke into dissenting groups and scattered into other states. Some now compose a small Mormon sect known as the Morrisites. A book with a section that focuses on Zion is O'Dea's *The Mormons.*

Zion City (1901–1939), at Zion, Illinois, 42 miles north of Chicago, was founded by Australian fundamentalist and divine healer John Alexander Dowie (1847–1907), who established the Christian Catholic Church. Dowie had come to the United States in 1888. He lived first on the West Coast and then moved to the Chicago area to conduct missions of divine healing. His evangelistic methods were so effective they were later copied by evangelist Billy Sunday. Part of Dowie's power rested in his impressive appearance. He had an enormous brow, large eyes, and an extensive beard.

Dowie combined his revival meetings and mass healing sessions with verbal attacks on medical doctors and traditional church leaders. The Chicago clergymen and physicians were so offended that, in 1895, they united to bring more than 100 charges against him in the courts of law. But Dowie successfully defended himself against all of these charges.

He decided to set up Zion City as a place where his followers (then claimed to number more than 50,000) could gather to pursue their faith without pressures from the outside world. At that point he was calling himself "Elijah the Restorer," or, as he also sometimes put it, "Elijah the Third," John the Baptist being "Elijah the Second." Within a few years, 5,000 of his followers had joined him in Zion City.

The members constructed a temple, schools, a college, a bank, a hotel, a publishing house, and many industries, including a noted lace factory. The extensive publications that were printed on the Zion City press were put out in a half a dozen languages for worldwide distribution. Dowie forbade smoking; the eating of pork, clams, and oysters; and the use of playing cards. He permitted no theaters, dance halls, drug stores, physicians' offices, or secret lodges, and whistles blew at regular times of the day for public prayers. No trains were permitted to stop at the Zion City railroad station on Sundays because this was the holy day.

Though the community as a whole owned all the industries, Dowie controlled the decision-making process, and his dictatorial leadership upset many of the members, particularly after

he entered politics with the founding of a short-lived Theocratic Party at Zion City. Dowie established this party to "reform American politics."

In 1903 he led a mission to London that failed, and in 1904 he led a mission to New York City, taking 3,000 of his followers with him on this crusade. He erected a baptismal font in Madison Square Garden and conducted a campaign filled with circus-like antics. The mission cost $300,000 and produced negligible results. Dowie then headed for Mexico in 1905, in the hope of better success there. While in Mexico, he suffered a stroke. At this point a storm of criticism erupted over his leadership of Zion.

The members deposed Dowie in 1906 because of his financial mismanagement. Zion City was then badly in debt. Wilbur Glenn Voliva (1870–1942), a man who had been Dowie's most trusted friend and the person to whom Dowie had given his power of attorney when he was away from the commune on evangelistic tours, now took over the leadership. Although Dowie was able to secure a court order that required the commune members to provide him with lifetime support, he died a bitter man.

Voliva proved to be a much better administrator that Dowie, and he was able to overcome the community's financial problems and pay off all its debts. But he is best known for his belief that the world is flat rather than round. He based this on a literal interpretation of the Bible. He further held that Hades is beneath the Earth, that the stars are as small as they appear, that the moon is self luminous, and that the sun is but a few feet in diameter. He regarded all astronomers as "poor, ignorant, conceited fools."

Besides promoting his flat earth

beliefs, Voliva predicted that the world would end in 1923, then in 1927, then in 1930, and then in 1935. He also concluded that a fire that destroyed the Zion City Temple in 1937 was the work of the devil, and he predicted that he himself would live to the age of 120 on a special diet of buttermilk and nuts. Voliva died, however, at the age of 72. By then he had lost his control as overseer of the Christian Catholic Church, and the titles to the Zion City real estate were then transferred to individual ownership in 1939. This ended what remained of any communal life at Zion City.

Today the Christian Catholic Church still functions at Zion in a newly-built temple, although some of its theological teachings have been liberalized. Zion Home, a block-long frame building erected by the commune in 1904, was recently torn down, though its dome is preserved on the corner of the property where it once stood. Shiloh House, built as a residence for Dowie, is open for tours in the summer. Books with sections that focus on Zion City are Braden's *Those Who Believe: A Study of Modern American Cults and Minority Religious Movements,* Calverton's *Where Angels Dared to Tread,* and Gardner's *Fads and Fallacies in the Name of Science.*

Zion Hill (1830–1835), near Ossining, New York, was a commune established by Robert Matthews, a farmer and a carpenter who was so caught up in the religious revival movement of 1816 that he became an active advocate of temperance and vegetarianism. By 1830 he was wandering the streets of Albany prophesying that the city would soon be destroyed. He began to call himself Matthias and asserted he was a Jew, although he had previously been a member of the Presbyterian church. He further said that the only true Christians were those who were unshaven.

Soon Matthews had gathered a few followers (perhaps ten), including a wealthy merchant named Benjamin Folger and noted suffragette and anti-slavery orator Sojourner Truth, into the communal settlement near Ossining. He wore gorgeous robes and some of his followers were said to think of him as both the Messiah and God. However, the commune soon evolved into a free love community with spiritual marriages taking place under the direction of Matthews. He was arrested in 1835 on a charge of having murdered his chief disciple, Elijah Pierson. Sojourner Truth testified on his behalf at the trial and later entered a slander suit against his detractors. Matthews was acquitted on the murder charge but then imprisoned on an assault charge brought against him by his married daughter. His imprisonment effectively brought an end to the commune. A book with a section that focuses on Zion Hill is Stone's *Matthias and His Impostures.*

Zions Order of the Sons of Levi (1960–present), ten miles southwest of Mansfield, Missouri, is a religious and pacifist community that sees its mission as one of service to neighbors. The members hold all property in common, wear diamond-shaped pendants as symbols of their community, and the men wear beards. The approximately 95 members were led by Marl V. Kilgore until he died in 1989. Now they are led by his eldest son, Nathan. For a time they published a newsletter called *Moon Reports on Sunny Things with Little Twinkling Stars.* Visitors are welcomed to "come in peace, stay in peace, and live in peace."

Baümler's house at Zoar as it looked in 1875 (drawing by Lois Will).

Zoar (1819–1898) was named after the scriptural reference to the place where Lot went after fleeing from Sodom and Gomorra. Founded by a group of German pietists under the leadership of Joseph Bimeler, it was located where the town of Zoar, Ohio, now stands. In 1832 the membership numbered nearly 500.

Joseph Michael Baümler (Bimeler is the Americanized spelling) was born in 1778, probably at Wüttemburg, Germany. A weaver by trade, he had joined a persecuted sect of pietists and became their leader about ten years prior to their departure for the United States. The group landed at Philadelphia on August 14, 1817, and were cared for by Quakers for a short time. Through the assistance of these Quakers, Bimeler was able to purchase 5,600 acres of land in Tuscarawas County, Ohio, and the group then moved there to establish their settlement.

Bimeler was known to his follow-ers as a saint. It is probable that his physical appearance, as well as his tremendous drive and intelligence, contributed to this reverence. He was anything but handsome because he had one large protruding eye, and he walked with a limp.

At first Bimeler had no intention of his followers pooling all their goods and living by a communal style of life, but he soon discovered that they must do so if they were to be able to pay for the land. "In heaven there is only communism," one of the members told visitor William Alfred Hinds in the 1870s, "and why should it not be our aim to prepare ourselves in this world for the society we are sure to enter there?" At the same time as they pooled all their goods, the members opted for celibacy until the land was fully paid for. Marriage was reintroduced sometime between 1828 and 1830, and Bimeler himself then took a wife.

Members were either first-class (on a probationary basis until they signed the Covenant), or second-class (accorded full voting privileges and allowed to hold a leadership office). The first-class members could withdraw at any time and take out any money they had deposited into the common fund. The Covenant that the second-class members signed, however, was an agreement to surrender all property rights. Elections were held by ballot once a year, women voting as well as men. The officers were three trustees, a standing committee of five, a cashier, and an agent to relate to the outside world. The trustees directed the activities of the society and the standing committee mediated any disagreements between the members and the trustees.

A court suit was once brought against Zoar by some disgruntled former members, but the U.S. Supreme Court held for Zoar. In its decision, the justices said that the Bimeler administration was "not only not fraudulent but above reproach," and further he was "a man of great energy and high capacity for business."

Children of this commune were separated from their parents at age 3 and boarded in large houses, one for boys and one for girls. They attended school both summer and winter until age 15. In other houses several families lived together, though they managed their own affairs and cooked their own meals. Many of the commune enterprises did exceptionally well, including a brewery, flour mill, saw mill, linen mill, tannery, and dye house. They raised wheat, corn, oats, sheep, and cows.

Bimeler died on August 27, 1853, long before the commune formally closed, but his authority remained in the community, where members con-sidered all his writings as sacred and continued to look to them for daily guidance. Jacob Sylvan and Christian Weebel followed him as spiritual leaders and trustees, and then Jacob Ackerman was elected as head.

By 1874 the members of Zoar owned 7,200 acres of land, reputed to be worth more than $1,000,000. One project, an ironworks, failed, but it was kept going for some time even though it was a drain on their economy because the communalists did not want the outsiders employed there to lose their jobs.

The communal form of life was abandoned in 1898 as a result of agitation for individual rights coming primarily from a descendant of Bimeler and printed in a paper that he published for the society.

Today Bimeler's home is a museum called the King's Palace Memorial Museum. It is owned by the Ohio Archaeological and Historical Society. Also to be seen at Zoar is a two and a half acre garden that the members of the commune designed from a description of New Jerusalem in the biblical Book of Revelations. Books with sections that focus on Zoar are Hinds' *American Communities* and Nordhoff's *The Communistic Societies of the United States.*

Zodiac (1847–1853), first on the Perdernales River about four miles southwest of Fredericksburg, Texas, and then near Longhorn State Park, five or six miles south of Burnet, Texas, was a Mormon communal settlement established by Lyman Wight, one of the original members of **Kirtland.** Wight had earlier set up a Mormon commune in Missouri that was called **Adam-ondi-Ahman** and he was later one of the leaders at **Nauvoo** in Illinois.

When Brigham Young took most of the Mormons on their journey from

Nauvoo to Utah, Wight rejected Young's leadership and led followers to Fredericksburg, partly because he was convinced that the promised land lay in Texas. The 150 members of Zodiac built a grist mill at their site, with millstones that they obtained from France. They used this to grind grain not only for themselves but for many of the surrounding non–Mormon farmers. Most of the members of Zodiac came from farms in the Midwest, and they did so well at agriculture that they were asked to teach their methods to many German immigrants who had moved into the area. Wight himself was elected to be a chief justice in Fredericksburg.

Relations between the Mormons of Zodiac and the surrounding non–Mormons were relatively peaceful except when politics intervened. This was because the members of Zodiac opposed the system used for elections in the area. It was local practice to hold the polls open for a week so that any voter wishing to change a vote during that time could replace their ballot with another. The Mormons argued that this was quite undemocratic.

A flood in 1850 destroyed the Zodiac mill and took a number of lives as well as most of the commune crops. The members therefore decided in 1851 to move to the new location near Burnet. That property had a lake and waterfall so that they could rebuild their mill, as well as construct log dwellings and a schoolhouse. They brought the grinding stones for the mill from their first location, after they found them buried under four feet of mud left by the flood. Non–Mormon farmers brought their grain from great distances to the Zodiac mill to be ground. In 1853 Wight believed he had a call from heaven to move on and so he sold his rights to the place. Zodiac was disbanded after that, although the mill was still in use until 1881. Wight died in 1858 while traveling near San Antonio. He was taken to Fredericksburg for burial and his grave today is tended by a delegation from the Mormon church in Utah. All that remains at Zodiac's second location are the traces of the mill race and a small cemetery marking the site. A book with a section that focuses on Zodiac is Davis' *The Story of the Church.*

Appendix 1: Communes by Year of Formation

1663–1664	Swanendael
1684–1727	Bohemia Manor
1694–1720	Women of the Wilderness
1696–1699	Irenia
1725–1727	Newborns
1732–1934	Ephrata
1735–1740	Savannah
1740–1835	Emmaus
1741–1844	Bethlehem
1743–1844	Nazareth
1745–1750	Mahanaim
1747–1752	Nantmel
1751–1758	Cheat River
1752–1760	Bermudian
1753–1764	Shenandoah
1753–1856	Wachovia
1754–1844	Lititz
1756–1783	Broad River
1769–1781	Harvard New Lighters
1774–1808	Hope
1776–1938	Watervliet
1787–1947	Mount Lebanon
1788–1894	Snowhill
1788–1844	New Jerusalem
1790–1960	Hancock
1790–1917	Enfield
1792–1992	Caterbury
1792–1875	Tyringham
1793–1932	Alfred
1793–1923	Enfield-2
1793–1918	Harvard
1793–1908	Shirley
1794–present	Sabbathday Lake
1797–1798	Dorrilites
1804–1810	Union
1804–1903	Harmony
1806–1912	Union Village
1806–1910	Watervliet-2
1806–1910	Pleasant Hill
1807–1922	South Union
1807–1810	Red Banks
1808–1819	Gorham
1808–1810	Straight Creek
1808–1810	Eagle Creek
1810–1827	West Union
1814–1816	Reformed Methodist Farm
1817–1825	Savoy
1817–1820	Pilgrims
1819–1898	Zoar
1822–1889	North Union

1822–1825	Darby Plaines
1824–1907	Whitwater
1825–1828	New Harmony
1825–1826	Yellow Springs
1825–1828	Nashoba
1825–1832	Coal Creek
1825–1826	Goshen Community
1826–1827	Blue Spring
1826–1826	Valley Forge
1826–1827	Forrestville
1826–1826	Franklin
1826–1829	Kendal
1826–1895	Groveland
1827–1827	Jeffersonville
1827–1831	Teutonia Society of Germans
1830–1832	Equity
1830–1838	Kirtland
1830–1835	Zion Hill
1831–1831	Thompson
1831–1833	Zion
1832–1871	New Philadelphia
1833–1846	Oberlin Colony
1833–1835	First Com. Of Man's Free Brotherhood
1836–1837	United Christians
1837–1839	Far West
1837–1842	Shalom
1838–1846	Adam–ondi–Ahman
1839–1846	Nauvoo
1841–1847	Brook Farm
1841–1845	Marlboro Association
1842–1868	Hopedale
1842–1846	Northampton Association
1842–1844	McKean County Association
1842–1843	Social Reform Unity
1843–1932	Amana
1843–1845	Fruitlands
1843–1845	Clarkson Association
1843–1844	Congregation of Saints
1843–1844	Lamoille Agricultural Association
1843–1844	Jefferson County Association
1843–1844	Mixville Association
1843–1844	Sylvania Phalanx
1843–1844	Morehouse Union
1843–1845	Brook's Experiment
1843–1846	Skaneateles
1843–1844	Peace Union
1843–1856	North American Phalanx
1843–1846	LaGrange Phalanx
1843–1845	Ohio Phalanx
1843–1847	Putney Corporation
1843–1846	Colony of Equality
1843–1844	One-Mention Community
1843–1850	Gorstville
1844–1844	Goose Pond
1844–1844	Prairie Home
1844–1847	Bloomfield Association
1844–1844	Leraysville Phalanx
1844–1848	Alphadelphia Phalanx
1844–1847	Sodus Bay Phalanx
1844–1845	Iowa Pioneer Phalanx
1844–1845	Ontario Union
1844–1846	Clermont Phalanx
1844–1848	Trumbull Phalanx
1844–1850	Wisconsin Phalanx
1844–1881	Bethel
1844–1846	New Helvetia
1844–1846	Union Home
1844–1856	Voree
1845–1847	Philadelphia Industrial Association
1845–1845	Columbian Phalanx
1845–1845	Canton Phalanx
1845–1846	Integral Phalanx
1845–1848	Fruit Hills
1845–1846	Grand Prairie Community
1845–1846	Kristeen Community
1845–1848	Utilitarian Assn. of United Interests
1846–1848	Spring Farm Association
1846–1846	Pigeon River
1846–1862	Bishop Hill
1846–1860	Jackson Family
1847–1848	Bettina
1847–1847	The Brotherhood
1847–1850	Utopia
1847–1853	Zodiac
1847–1856	Communia
1848–1881	Oneida

1848–1848	Icaria
1849–1851	Tusculum
1849–1898	Nojoshing Community
1849–1860	Icarian Nauvoo
1849–1855	Brooklyn Perfectionists
1849–1855	Newark Perfectionists
1849–1855	Cambridge Perfectionists
1849–1855	Manlius Perfectionists
1849–1851	Putney Perfectionists
1850–1853	Ephriam
1850–1850	Forty-Eighters Colony
1851–1852	Hopewell
1851–1853	Jasper Colony
1851–1881	Wallingford
1851–1860	Modern Times
1851–1860	Mountain Cove
1852–1863	Harmonia
1852–1857	Oleana
1853–1855	Raritan Bay Union
1853–1858	Preparation
1853–1853	Grand Prairie Harmonial Association
1853–1857	Rising Star Community
1853–1864	Ephriam
1854–1896	St. Nazianz
1855–1875	Reunion
1855–1881	Aurora
1855–1858	New Ulm
1856–1856	Memnoia Institute
1856–1858	Union Grove
1857–1879	Germania Company
1857–1860	Anaheim
1858–1864	Cheltenham
1858–1858	Fourier Phalanx
1860–1878	Icaria
1860–1861	Harmonial Vegetarian Society
1860–1860	Point Hope
1861–1881	Brotherhood of the New Life
1861–1862	Zion
1861–1897	Adonai Shomo
1862–1864	Celesta
1862–1868	Ora Labra
1865–1866	Berlin Community
1867–1881	Kingdom of Heaven
1868–1888	Prairie Home Colony

1868–1870	Reunion Community
1869–1871	German Colonization Company
1869–1874	Mutual Land Emigration Colony
1869–1871	Union Colony
1871–1877	Progressive Community
1871–1871	South Western Colony
1871–1871	St. Louis-Western Colony
1871–1873	Chicago-Colorado Colony
1871–1871	Warm Springs Colony
1872–1877	Friendship Community
1873–1877	Bennett Co-operative Colony
1873–1878	German Socialist Colony
1874–1880	Social Freedom
1874–1878	St. George
1874–1875	Washington
1874–1875	Rockville
1874–1877	Virgin City
1874–1875	Toquerville
1874–1877	Kanab
1874–1877	Johnson
1874–1876	Paris
1874–1875	Pine Valley
1874–1875	Pinto
1874–1876	Morristown
1874–1876	Shunesburg
1874–1874	Mt. Carmel
1874–1877	Leeds
1874–1877	Harrisburgh
1874–1877	Glendale
1874–1875	Panaca
1874–1877	Hebron
1874–1877	Bellview
1874–1877	Kanara
1874–1877	Kanosh
1874–1877	New Harmony
1874–1877	Holden
1874–1877	Scipio
1874–1877	Paragonah
1874–1880	Glenwood
1874–present	Bon Homme
1874–1885	Orderville
1874–1875	Dawn Valcour

1874–1906	Women's Commonwealth
1875–1930	Wolf Creek
1875–1882	Springdale
1875–1882	Kingston
1875–1882	Price City
1875–1882	Bunkerville
1875–1892	Fountain Grove
1875–1875	Investigating Community
1875–1877	Cedar Vale Benevolent Society
1876–1877	Modjeska's Farm
1876–1882	Allen's Camp
1876–1882	Sunset
1877–1918	Elm Spring
1877–1880	Home
1877–1882	Woodruff
1877–1880	Esperanza
1877–1878	Kane County Community
1877–1877	Hayes Socialists
1878–1922	Tripp
1878–1898	New Icaria
1878–1886	Jeune Icarie
1878–1878	Union Manufacturing Company
1878–1878	Ancora Community
1878–1878	Plattsburgh Community
1878–1879	Rankin Colony
1879–1879	Societas Fraternia
1880–1882	Koresh Community
1880–1880	Thompson Colony
1881–1886	Idaria Speranza
1881–1884	Joyful
1881–1882	Sicily Island
1881–1881	Relief
1882–1887	Painted Woods
1882–1888	Beersheba
1882–1882	Carp Lake
1882–1882	Middlesex Community
1882–1885	Cotopaxi
1882–1885	Cremieux
1882–1888	New Odessa
1882–1889	Rosenhayn
1882–1883	York Society of Integral Cooperation
1882–1885	Bethlehem-Yehuda
1883–1886	Water View

1883–1883	Arkansas Community
1883–1883	Washington Community
1883–1883	Hebron
1883–1883	Touro
1883–1883	Leeser
1883–1890	Mutual Aid Cooperative Association
1884–1901	Shalam
1884–1885	Moses Montefiore Colony
1885–1888	Lasker
1885–1903	Koreshan
1885–1892	Kaweah Co-op Commonwealth
1886–1918	Jamesville
1886–1886	Gilead
1886–1892	Nehalem Valley
1887–1892	Puget Sound Cooperative Community
1887–1887	Calavaros County Community
1889–1902	Lord's Farm
1890–1934	Rockport
1890–1891	Koreshan Unity
1891–1900	Palestine
1892–1896	Union Mills Company
1892–1901	Chesterfield
1893–1898	Winters Island
1893–1896	Hiawatha Village Association
1894–1965	Estero
1894–1896	Glennis Cooperative Industrial Co.
1894–1895	Altruist Community
1894–1898	Narcoosee
1894–1901	Colorado Cooperative Company
1894–1896	Altruria
1894–1901	Ruskin Commonwealth
1894–1896	Kinder Lou
1894–present	Fairhope
1894–1898	Grander Age Colony
1895–1896	Willard Cooperative Colony
1895–1948	Shiloh
1895–1896	Cloverdale Altruria
1895–1896	Santa Rosa Altruria

1895–1920	New House of Israel
1896–1918	Tschetter
1896–1909	Mutual Home Association
1896–1901	Home Employment Company
1896–1900	Christian Commonwealth
1896–1897	Liberty Cooperative Association
1896–1897	Christian Commonwealth
1896–1896	Magnolia
1896–1915	Roycrofters
1897–1905	Freedom Colony
1897–1942	Point Loma
1897–1907	Equality Colony
1897–1900	Rys
1897–1900	Niksur Cooperative Association
1898–1898	White Oak Shakers
1898–1912	Cooperative Brotherhood
1898–1899	American Settlers Co-op Association
1898–1898	Montecello Colony
1899–1907	Straight Edge Community
1899–1902	Cooperative Industrial College
1899–1902	Commonwealth of Israel
1899–1900	Friedheim
1899–1902	Lystra
1899–1904	Christian Social Association
1899–1908	Spirit Fruit Society
1900–1904	Southern Co-operative Association
1900–1906	Freeland Association
1900–present	Maxwell
1900–present	Arden
1900–1900	Martha's Vineyard Cooperative
1900–1918	New Elm Springs
1901–1907	Altruist Community
1901–1939	Zion City
1901–present	Rosedale
1903–present	House of David

1905–present	Spink County Colony
1905–1913	Temple Home
1905–1936	Beadle County Colony
1906–1916	Askov
1906–present	Horon Colony
1906–1918	Richards Colony
1906–1907	Helicon Home
1907–1918	Buffalo Colony
1907–1908	Fellowship Farm
1909–1916	San Ysidro Little Landers
1909–present	Free Acres
1909–1940	Tahanto
1910–1918	Milford
1910–1915	Clarion
1910–1931	Order of Theocracy
1911–1940	Halidon
1911–1920	Lopez Island Community
1911–1912	Fruit Crest
1912–present	Lewiston Colony
1912–1940	Fellowship Farm Cooperative
1912–1926	Los Angeles Fellowship Farm
1912–1912	Freedom Colony
1912–1918	Ukiah Brotherhood
1913–1920	Warren Range
1913–1970	Cutlerite Mormons
1913–1916	Bohemian Cooperative
1913–present	Gould Farm
1913–1919	Burning Bush
1914–1920	Pisgah Grande
1914–1918	Llano del Rio
1914–1918	Army of Industry
1915–1963	Divine's Peace Mission
1915–1950	Ferrer Colony
1916–1916	Runnymede
1916–1916	San Fernando Little Landers
1916–1916	Cupertino
1916–1916	Hayward Heath
1916–1918	Nevada Colony
1916–1920	Glendale Molokan Colony
1917–1917	Yuba City Molokan Colony
1917–1917	Utah Molokan Colony
1917–1957	Bellville

1917–1938	Newllano
1918–1954	Holy City
1921–1965	Wayne Produce Association
1923–1963	Heaven City
1923–1940	Commonwealth College
1923–1969	Mohegan
1923–1969	Chatham
1923–1924	Harmonia
1923–present	Ananda Ashram
1924–1924	New Mexico Molokan Colony
1924–1924	Raton Molokan Colony
1925–1925	Belle Terre
1925–1931	Mount Airy
1925–1925	Ink
1927–1927	Robin Hill
1927–1940	Gilpin's Point
1927–1940	Trapelo
1929–1932	Atherton Stewardship Community
1929–present	Cohasset Ashram
1930–present	Israelite City of David
1930–1935	Sunrise Cooperative Farms
1931–1933	Christian Commonwealth Colony
1932–1953	Saline Valley Farms
1932–1961	Highlander Folk School
1933–1934	Cooperative Subsistence Colony
1933–1936	Sunrise Cooperative Farm
1934–present	Rockport
1935–1946	Maryfarm
1936–1942	Delta Cooperative Farm
1936–present	New Elm Springs
1937–1957	Macedonia Cooperative
1937–1962	Penn-Craft
1937–1964	Bayard Lane Homestead
1937–present	Celo Community
1938–1940	St. Theresa's Village
1938–1953	St. Benedict's Farm-1
1938–1960	St. Benedict's Farm-2
1939–1952	Providence Cooperative Farm
1939–1942	Van Eden Farms
1939–1942	Cropperville
1940–1945	Fellowship Farm
1940–1970	Van Houton Fields
1940–present	Bryn Gweld
1941–present	Tschetter Colony
1941–1946	Bass Lake Farm
1941–1945	Newark Ashram
1941–1952	Our Lady of the Wayside
1941–1941	Nazareth House
1941–1945	Christ the Worker Farm
1941–1945	St. Francis Farm
1941–1941	Alcuin Community
1942–1968	Eskdale
1942–present	Koinonia
1942–1947	Trobuco College
1943–1943	Cape May
1943–1943	Aptos
1944–1946	Colchester
1944–present	Huron
1945–1973	Tanguy
1945–present	Ayers
1945–present	Spring Creek
1945–1947	Maryfarm
1945–1956	San Fernando Farm
1945–present	Kirkridge
1945–present	Bethany
1946–1959	Tuolumne
1946–1947	St. Isador's Farm
1947–present	Birch Creek
1947–present	Deerfield
1947–1973	St. Francis Acres
1947–1969	Melbourne Village
1947–1970	Powelton Neighbors
1947–1953	Holy Family Farm
1948–present	Graceville
1948–present	Millfort
1948–present	New Rockport
1948–present	Miami
1948–present	Rockport
1948–1967	Parishfield
1949–present	Hand County
1949–present	Charles Mix
1949–present	Glendale
1949–present	Riverside
1949–present	Pearl Creek
1949–present	Miller Ranch
1949–1957	Fountain of the World

1949–present	Skyview Acres		1957–1957	Canterbury
1950–present	Blumengard		1958–present	Evergreen Community
1950–1962	Peter Maurin Farm		1958–present	Big Stone
1950–present	Forest River		1958–1980	Synanon
1950–present	Vale		1959–present	Martindale
1950–1973	Ucopia		1959–present	Plainview
1950–1967	Montrose		1959–present	Springdale
1951–present	Glacier		1959–1964	Amity
1951–present	Hillside		1960–1972	Bhoodan Center
1951–present	Koinonia Foundation		1960–present	Espanola
1952–1961	Christian Faith and Life Community		1960–present	Wolf Creek
			1960–present	Zions Order of the Sons of Levi
1953–1954	Hickory Hill			
1953–1960	Brotherhood Community		1960–1963	Baring Street Fellowship
1954–present	Woodcrest		1961–present	Hillside
1954–1972	Order of St. Michael		1961–present	Sage Creek
1954–1956	Kingwood		1962–1981	Ecumenical Institute
1955–present	Clark		1962–1972	Nonviolent Action Farm
1955–present	Camphill		1962–1963	Brown House
1956–1977	May Valley		1963–present	Clover Leaf
1956–1967	Fountain of the World		1963–present	Spring Valley
1956–1956	Falsington		1963–present	Duncan Ranch
1956–present	Turner		1963–present	Rimrock
1956–present	Reba Place		1963–present	Hilldale
1957–1965	Church of Hope		1963–present	Wilson Range
1957–present	New Meadow Run		1963–present	Tolstoy Farm

Appendix 2: Government Projects

The government's New Deal cooperative farms and communities resembled the nongovernmental communal colonies in many ways. This was partly because the U.S. Farm Security Administration made careful studies of the Shaker communes, Amana , and other successful communitarian projects in planning these New Deal ones.

Milburn L. Wilson of the U.S. Department of the Interior was the first administrator of these projects. He announced, on October 14, 1933, that his Division of Subsistence Homesteads would concentrate on three types: (1) communities of part-time farmers near industrial employment; (2) all rural colonies; and (3) a few experimental villages with new industries. He said that either a local corporation or a federal corporation would construct the communities, but they would only be placed where there was strong local backing and frequently only with the cooperation of the state colleges of agriculture. The plan was to eventually allow the participants, over a 30-year time period, to purchase their own homes at low rates of interest. Various arrangements for this were worked out by the several government agencies involved. But by the time Congress ordered the program dissolved, only a few of the homes had been purchased by the members of the cooperative communities.

For the most part, the farms were economic failures. Few of them ever showed a profit, a fact that the opposition endlessly restated. In the U.S. Congress and elsewhere across the nation, controversy raged over the economic policies and ideological commitment of those administering the program. The owners of cotton plantations, large orchards, and truck farms were the strongest opponents of these government experiments. They recognized them as a threat to the continuation of a system of cheap migrant and sharecropper labor.

Yet the program and cooperative industries initiated and maintained by the federal grants went a long way toward bettering the life situation of share-croppers and migrant workers. And, though every manner of abuse was heaped on the New Deal administration for coddling drifters and wasting the taxpayers' money, this program will undoubtedly go down in history as one of the great experiments in social engineering conducted during the New Deal years. (For more information, see Conkin's *Tomorrow a New World*.)

Below is a list of the 145 New Deal projects:

Name	Dates	Location	Members
Arthurdale	1933–1948	Reedsville, West Virginia	450
Dayton Homesteads	1933–1937	Dayton, Ohio	100
Cumberland Homesteads	1933–1942	Cressville, Tennessee	750
Panderlea Homesteads	1933–1944	Wallace, North Carolina	550
Piedmont Homesteads	1934–1941	Jasper County, Georgia	150
Tygart Valley Homesteads	1934–1944	Dailey, West Virginia	300
Westmorland Homesteads	1934–1945	Greenburg, Pennsylvania	750
Richton Homesteads	1934–1941	Richton, Mississippi	75
Shenandoah Homesteads	1934–1941	Shenandoah Mountains, Virginia	475
Jersey Homesteads	1934–1940	Highstown, New Jersey	600
Granger Homesteads	1934–1942	Granger, Iowa	252
Mantuska Valley	1935–1941	Palmer, Alaska	1,024
Red House	1935–1942	Eleanor, West Virginia	450
Woodlake	1935–1942	Wood County, Texas	300
Austin Homesteads	1935–1942	Austin, Minnesota	150
Bankhead Farms	1935–1937	Jasper, Alabama	300
Bauxart Gardens	1935–1937	Beaumont, Texas	150
Decatur Homesteads	1935–1937	Decatur, Indiana	150
El Monte Homesteads	1935–1937	El Monte, California	300
Hattiesburg Homesteads	1935–1944	Hattiesburg, Mississippi	75
Houston Gardens	1935–1937	Houston, Texas	300
McComb Homesteads	1935–1942	McComb, Mississippi	60
Magnolia Homesteads	1935–1944	Meridian, Mississippi	75
San Fernando Homesteads	1935–1937	Roseda, California	125
Tupelo Homesteads	1935–1937	Tupelo, Mississippi	75
Wichita Gardens	1935–1937	Wichita Falls, Texas	175
Dalworthington Gardens	1935–1937	Arlington, Texas	250
Longview Homesteads	1935–1936	Longview, Washington	175
Palmerdale Homesteads	1935–1942	Birmingham, Alabama	300
Phoenix Homesteads	1935–1937	Phoenix, Arizona	75
Three Rivers Gardens	1935–1944	Three Rivers, Texas	150
Cahaba	1935–1942	Trussville, Alabama	850
Cherry Lake Farms	1935–1942	Madison, Florida	500
Duluth Homesteads	1935–1942	Duluth, Minnesota	250
Pine Mountain Valley	1935–1940	Harris County, Georgia	600
Albert Lea Homesteads	1935–1941	Albert Lea, Minnesota	40

Name	Dates	Location	Members
Ashwood Plantation	1935–1942	Lee County, South Carolina	475
Bosque Farms	1935–1942	Jarles, New Mexico	900
Chicot Farms	1935–1942	Chicot County, Arkansas	250
Fairbury Farmsteads	1935–1941	Jefferson County, Nebraska	30
Grand Island Farmsteads	1935–1941	Hall County, Nebraska	30
Irwinville	1935–1941	Irwinville, Georgia	300
Kearney Homesteads	1935–1941	Buffalo County, Nebraska	30
Ropesville Farms	1935–1941	Hockley County, Texas	250
St. Francis River Farms	1935–1942	Forrest City, Arkansas	250
Skyline Farms	1935–1941	Jackson County, Arkansas	500
South Sioux City Farms	1935–1941	Dakota County, Nebraska	75
Wichita Valley Farms	1935–1941	Wichita County, Texas	300
Wolf Creek	1935–1941	Grady County, Georgia	75
Dyess Colony	1936–1942	Wilson, Arkansas	1,500
Aberdeen Gardens	1936–1942	Newport News, Virginia	400
Greenwood Homesteads	1936–1942	Birmingham, Alabama	250
Lake County Homesteads	1936–1942	Chicago, Illinois	150
Mount Olive Homesteads	1936–1942	Birmingham, Alabama	250
Biscoe Farms	1936–1941	Prairie County, Arkansas	250
Christian-Trigg Farms	1936–1941	Hopkinsville, Kentucky	300
Clover Bend Farms	1936–1941	Lawrence County, Alabama	300
Dasha Farms	1936–1941	Desha County, Arkansas	250
Drummond Project	1936–1941	Bayfield, Wisconsin	100
Escambia Farms	1936–1941	Okaloosa County, Florida	250
Gee's Bend Farms	1936–1941	Wilcox County, Alabama	300
Hinds Farms	1936–1941	Hinds County, Mississippi	250
Ironwood Homesteads	1936–1942	Ironwood, Michigan	400
Kinsey Flats	1936–1941	Custer County, Maryland	250
La Forge Farms	1936–1941	Sikeston, Missouri	300
Lonoke Farms	1936–1940	Lonoke, Arkansas	150
Lucedale Farms	1936–1941	George County, Mississippi	300
McLennan Farms	1936–1941	McLennan County, Texas	60
Mounds Farms	1936–1941	Madison Parish, Louisiana	450
Orangeburg Farms	1936–1941	Orangeburg, South Carolina	250
Plum Bayou	1936–1941	Jefferson County, Arkansas	600
Prairie Farms	1936–1941	Macon County, Arkansas	100
Sabine Farms	1936–1941	Harrison County, Texas	250
Saginaw Valley Farms	1936–1941	Saginaw, Michigan	100
Sublimity Farms	1936–1941	London, Kentucky	200
Sam Houston Farms	1936–1941	Harris County, Texas	250
Tiverton Farms	1936–1941	Sumter County, Texas	80
Townes Farms	1936–1941	Crittenden County, Arkansas	100
Transylvania Farms	1936–1941	Transylvania, Louisiana	450
Trumann Farms	1936–1942	Poinsette County, Arkansas	150
Loup City Farmsteads	1937–1942	Loup City, Nebraska	30

Name	Dates	Location	Members
Scottsbluff Farmsteads	1937–1942	Scotts Bluff County, Nebraska	75
Burlington Project	1937–1942	Burlington, North Dakota	100
Falls City Farmsteads	1937–1942	Falls City, Nebraska	30
Lakeview Farms	1937–1941	Helena, Arkansas	400
Sioux Falls Farms	1937–1942	Sioux Falls, South Dakota	45
Greenbelt	1937–1952	Berwyn Heights, Maryland	3,000
Roanoke Farms	1938–1942	Halifax, North Carolina	600
Deshee Farm	1938–1944	Vincennes, Indiana	100
Mineral King Farms	1938–1942	Visalia, California	10
Lake Dick Farm	1938–1942	Altheimer, Arkansas	300
Osage Farms	1938–1942	Pettis County, Missouri	100
Arizona Part-Time Farms	1938–1942	Chandler, Arizona	300
Casa Grande Valley Farms	1938–1943	Florence, Arizona	150
Greenhills	1938–1949	Cincinnati, Ohio	2,000
Thornton Farms	1938–1942	Thornton, California	5
Greendale	1938–1951	Milwaukee, Wisconsin	1,900
Flint River Farms	1938–1942	Montezuma, Georgia	400
Scuppernog Farms	1938–1942	Cresswell, North Carolina	350
Pembroke Farms	1938–1942	Pembroke, North Carolina	200
Two Rivers Farmsteads	1938–1942	Waterloo, Nebraska	150
Terribonne Association	1939–1942	Terrebone Parish, Louisiana	250
Misco Homestead Assn.	1939–1942	Wilson, Arkansas	143
Grenada Homestead Corp.	1939–1942	Grenada, Mississippi	17
Bolivar Homestead Corp.	1939–1942	Cleveland, Mississippi	68
Drew Homestead Corp.	1939–1942	Indeanola, Mississippi	19
Natchitoches Farmstead Assn.	1939–1942	Powhaton, Louisiana	46
Peach Orchard Bluff Homestead Assn.	1939–1942	Augusta, Arkansas	45
Woodruff Homestead Assn.	1939–1942	Augusta, Arkansas	9
Ashley Homestead Assn.	1939–1942	Hamburg, Arkansas	55
Poinsett Homestead Assn.	1939–1942	Marked Tree, Arkansas	80
Talla Bena Farmstead Assn.	1939–1942	Tallulah, Louisiana	72
Moro Homestead Assn.	1939–1942	Marianna, Arkansas	27
Torras Farmstead Assn.	1939–1942	New Roads, Louisiana	56
Minorca Farmstead Assn.	1939–1942	Ferriday, Louisiana	16
Pulaski Homestead Assn.	1939–1941	Little Rock, Arkansas	36
Bayou Bourbeaux Farmstead Assn.	1940–1942	Clarence, Louisiana	27
Portage Farms	1940–1942	Caruthersville, Missouri	66
Twist Leasing Cooperative Assn.	1940–1942	Twist, Arkansas	270
Clarksdale Homestead Assn.	1940–1942	Turrel, Arkansas	121

Name	Dates	Location	Members
Jefferson Cooperative Leasing Assn.	1940–1942	Pine Bluff, Arkansas	53
Tallahatchie Cooperative Assn.	1940–1941	Swann Lake, Mississippi	70
East Carroll Parish Farmstead Assn.	1940–1942	Lake Providence, Louisiana	7
Independence Farms	1940–1942	Kennett, Missouri	34
Calahoula Farmstead Assn.	1940–1942	Jonesville, Louisiana	33
Lomaland Farmstead Assn.	1940–1942	St. Joseph, Louisiana	13
Mileston Farms	1940–1942	Mileston, Mississippi	300
Tensus Farmstead Assn.	1940–1942	St. Joseph, Louisiana	29
Blairstown Farmstead Assn.	1940–1942	Clinton, Louisiana	38
Autauga Cooperative Leasing Assn.	1940–1942	Prattsville, Alabama	40
Coy Cooperative Leasing Assn.	1940–1942	Camden, Alabama	22
Meadville Homestead Corp.	1940–1942	Meadville, Mississippi	12
Pontotoc Cooperative Leasing Assn.	1941–1942	Pontotoc, Mississippi	26
Lincoln Cooperative Leasing Assn.	1941–1942	Simsboro, Louisiana	115
Arkansas River Cooperative Assn.	1941–1942	Little Rock, Arkansas	22
Reulah Cooperative Leasing Assn.	1941–1942	St. Francisville, Louisiana	35
Spivey Cooperative Leasing Assn.	1941–1942	Hamburg, Arkansas	22
Sumter Cooperative Leasing Assn.	1941–1942	Sumter, South Carolina	18
Little River Cooperative Leasing Assn.	1941–1942	Ashdown, Arkansas	30
Black Belt Cooperative Leasing Assn.	1941–1942	Greensboro, Alabama	73
Macon Lake Cooperative Leasing Assn.	1941–1942	Lake Village, Arkansas	45
Glades Farm	1941–1942	Jefferson County, Florida	150
Rio Farms	1941–1945	Edcouch, Texas	20
Grassland Farms	1942–1942	Harpersville, Alabama	40
Allandale	1942–1943	Richland County, South Carolina	300

Bibliography

Adams, Frank, "Highlander Folk School: Getting Information, Going Back and Teaching It," *Harvard Educational Review,* November 1972.

_____, *Unearthing Seeds of Fire: The Idea of Highlander.* J. F. Blair, Winston-Salem, NC, 1975.

Adams, Grace, and Edward Hutter, *The Mad Forties.* Harper and Brothers, New York, 1942.

Albertson, Ralph, "A Survey of Mutualistic Communities in America," *Iowa Journal of History and Politics,* October, 1936.

Allen, Arthur Francis, *Northwestern Iowa: Its History and Traditions — 1804–1926.* Chicago, 1927.

Allen, E.J., *The Second United Order Among the Mormons.* New York, 1936.

Alyea, Paul E., and Blanche Alyea, *Fairhope 1894–1954.* University, Ala., 1956.

American Guide Series, compiled and written by the Federal Writer's Project and the Writers' Program, 1936–1943, 153 vols. The first edition of many of these state, waterway, and area guides contain good general information about early communes in the specified area.

Anderson, Nels, *Desert Saints: The Mormon Frontier in Utah.* University of Chicago Press, Chicago, 1942.

Andrews, Edward D., *The People Called Shakers,* Dover Publications, New York, 1963.

Armytage, W.H.G., *Heavens Below: Utopian Experiments in England, 1560–1960.* Routledge and K. Paul London, 1961.

Arndt, Karl J.R., *George Rapp's Harmony Society, 1785–1847.* Farleigh Dickenson University, Rutherford, N.J., 1972.

Arnold, Emmy, *Torches Together: The Beginning and Early Years of the Brüderhof Communities.* Plough Publishing House, Rifton, N.Y., 1964.

Arrington, L.J., *Great Basin Kingdom: An Economic History of the Latter Day Saints, 1830–1960.* University of Utah Press, Salt Lake City, Utah, 1993.

Bailie, William, *Josiah Warren.* Arno Press, New York, 1972.

Ballou, Adin, *History of the Hopedale Community.* Thompson & Hill, Lowell, Mass., 1897.

Banfield, Edward C., *Government Project.* Free Press, Glencoe, Ill., 1951.

Bates, E.S., *American Faith: Its Religious, Political and Economic Foundations.* W. W. Norton & Company, New York, 1940.

Battle, J.H., *Counties of Warren, Benton, Jasper, and Newton, Indiana.* F. A. Battey, Chicago, 1883.

Beam, Maurice, *Cults in America.* Macfadden-Bartell Corp., New York, 1964.

Bellamy, Edward, *Looking Backward.* Belknap Press of Harvard University, Cambridge, Mass., 1967.

Berneri, Marie Louise, *Journey Through Utopia.* Freedom Press, London, 1950.

Bestor, A.E., *American Phalanxes, the Fourierist Phase of Socialism in the United States.* Doctoral thesis, Yale University, 1938.

_____, *Backwood's Utopias: The Sectarian and Owenite Phases of Communitarian Socialism in America, 1663–1828.* University of Pennsylvania, Philadelphia, 1950.

Bethany Fellowship School Catalog, Minneapolis, 1962.

Biessele, Rudolph L., *The History of the German Settlements in Texas, 1831–1861.* Von Boeckmann-Jones, Austin, Tex., 1930.

Bishop, Claire H., *All Things Common.* Harper, New York, 1952.

Blair, Don, *The New Harmony Story.* New Harmony Publications Committee, New Harmony, Ind., 1959.

Bliss, William Dwight Porter, ed., *The Encyclopedia of Social Reform.* Greenwood Press, Westport, Ct., 1970.

Boaz, Ruth, "My Thirty Years with Father Divine," *Ebony,* May 1965.

Bole, J.A., *The Harmony Society: A Chapter in German American Culture History.* American Germanica Press, Philadelphia, 1904.

Borsodi, Ralph, *Education and Living.* Suffern, N.Y., 1948.

Braden, Charles Samuel, *Those Who Believe: A Study of Modern American Cults and Minority Religious Movements.* New York, 1953.

Bridges, Leonard Hal, *American Mysticism.* Harper & Row, New York, 1970.

Broome, Isaac, *Last Days of the Ruskin Co-Operative Association.* C. H. Kerr & Company, Chicago, 1902.

Brown, Ralph H., *Historical Geography of the United States.* Harcourt Brace College Publishers, New York, 1948.

Buber, Martin, *Paths in Utopia.* Beacon Press, Boston, 1985.

Buchen, Gustave William, *Historic Sheboygan County.* Sheboygan, Wisc., 1944.

Burton, Katherine, *Paradise Planters: The Story of Brook Farm.* Longmans, Green, London, 1939.

Bushee, F.A., "Communistic Societies in the United States," *Political Science Quarterly,* December 1905.

Calverton, V.F., *Where Angels Dared to Tread.* Books for Libraries Press, Freeport, N.Y., 1969.

Capek, Thomas, *The Cechs (Bohemians) in America.* Arno Press, New York, 1969.

Carmer, Carl, *Dark Trees in the Wind.* W. Sloane Associates, New York, 1949.

_____, *The Hudson,* Grosset & Dunlap, New York. 1968.

_____, *Listen for a Lonesome Drum.* Syracuse University Press, Syracuse, N.Y., 1995.

Carpenter, Garrett R., "Silkville: A Kansas Attempt in the History of Fourierist Utopias, 1869–1892," *The Emporia State Research Studies.* Emporia, Kan., December, 1954.

Case, John and Rosemary C.R. Taylor, *Co-ops, Communes and Collectives.* Pantheon Books, New York, 1979.

Champney, Freeman, *Art & Glory: The Story of Elbert Hubbard,* Crown Publishers, New York, 1968.

Clark, E.T., *The Small Sects in America.* Cokesbury Press, Nashville, Tenn., 1937.

Clark, Henry, ed., *Manpower for Mission.* Chicago, 1967.

Cleland, Robert Glass, *From Wilderness to Empire: A History of California.* Knopf, New York, 1962.

Cleveland, Stafford C., *History and Directory of Yates County.* W. E. Morrison, Ovid, N.Y., 1976.

Coats, William R., *A History of Cuyahoga County and the City of Cleveland.* The American Historical Society, Chicago, 1924.

Codman, J.T., *Brook Farm: Historic and Personal Memoirs.* Arena Publishing Company, Boston, 1894.

"Commune Directory," *Alternatives Newsmagazine,* Alternatives Foundations, San Francisco, 1971.

Conkin, Paul K., *Tomorrow a New World.* Da Capo Press, New York, 1976.

_____. *Two Paths to Utopia: The Hutterites and the Llano Colony,* Greenwood Press, Westport, Ct., 1983.

Coulter, E. Merton, *Georgia, A Short History.* University of North Carolina Press, Chapel Hill, N.C., 1960.

Curtis, Edith Roelker, *A Season in Utopia: The Story of Brook Farm.* Russel & Russel, Camden, N.J., 1961.

Cross, Ira B., *A History of the Labor Movement in California.* University of California Press, Berkeley, CA, 1935.

Cross, W.R., *The Burned-Over District: The Social and Intellectual History of Enthusiastic Religion in Western New York, 1800–1850.* Octabon Books, New York, 1981.

Cryer, Newman, "Chicago's Ecumenical Institute: Laboratory for Tomorrow's Church," *Together,* March 1966.

Davidson, Gabriel, "Agricultural Colonies in the United States," *The Universal Jewish Encyclopedia,* Issac Landman, ed., 10 vols. New York, 1939.

_____. *Our Jewish Farmers and the Story of the Jewish Agricultural Society,* L. B. Fischer, New York, 1943.

Davis, I.S., *The Story of the Church.* R.L.D.S. Press, Independence, Mo., 1964.

Day, Dorothy, *House of Hospitality.* London, 1939.

_____. *Loaves and Fishes.* Harper & Row, New York, 1963.

_____. *The Long Loneliness.* Harper, New York, 1959.

Deem, David Bruce, "Cropperville," *History of Butler County, Missouri,* Butler County Historical Society, no date.

Deets, L.E., *The Hutterites: A Study in Social Cohesion.* Porcupine Press, Philadelphia, 1975.

Desroches, Henri, *The American Shakers,* University of Massachusetts Press, Amherst, Ma., 1971.

Dickens, Charles, *American Notes and Pictures from Italy.* Oxford University Press, New York, 1957.

Dobbs, C.R., *Freedom's Will: The Society of the Separatists of Zoar.* New York, 1947.

Dombrowski, James, *The Early Days of Christian Socialism in America,* Octagon Books, New York, 1936.

Doty, William J., ed., *The Historic Annals of Southwestern New York.* Lewis Historical Publishing Company, Inc., New York, 1940.

Douglas, D.W., and Grace Lumpkin, "Communistic Settlements," *Encyclopedia of the Social Sciences,* Edwin R.A. Seligman, ed. New York, 1931.

Douglas, Margaret Stoneman, *The Everglades: River of Grass.* Pineapple Press, Sarasota, Fl., 1988.

Duino, Russell, "Utopian Theme with Variations: John Murray Spear and His Kiantone Domain," *Pennsylvania History,* April 1962.

Dunn, Ethel, *American Molokans and Canadian Dukhobors: Economic Position and Ethnic Identity.* Paper presented at the 1973 International Congress of Anthropological and Ethnological Sciences, held in Chicago.

Duss, J.S., *The Harmonists, a Personal History.* Harmonia Associates, Ambridge, Pa., 1970.

Easum, Chester V., *The Americanization of Carl Schurz.* The University of Chicago Press, Chicago, 1929.

Eaton, Joseph W., and Saul M. Katz, *Research Guide on Cooperative Group Farming.* H. W. Wilson Company, New York, 1942.

_____, and Weil, Robert J., "The Mental Health of the Hutterites," *Scientific American,* December 1953.

Eddy, George Sherwood, *Eighty Adventurous Years.* Harper, New York, 1955.

Edmonds, Walter D., *The First Hundred Years (1848–1948), Oneida Community.* Oneida, N.Y., 1948.

Egbert, Donald E., and Stow Parsons, eds., *Socialism in American Life.* Princeton University Press, Princeton, 1952.

Elkins, Harvey, *Fifteen Years in the Senior Order of Shakers.* Dartmouth Press, Hanover, N.H., 1853.

"Established Communities U.S.A.," *A Way Out,* publication of the School of Living, January 1964.

Evans, J.H., *Joseph Smith, An American Prophet.* Deseret Book Co., Salt Lake City, Ut., 1989.

Fairfield, Richard, *Communes U.S.A.: A Personal Tour.* Penguin Books, Baltimore, 1972.

Fetsinger, Leon, Henry W. Riecken, and Stanley Schachter, *When Prophecy Fails.* University of Minnesota Press, Minneapolis, 1956.

Feuer, Lewis S., "The Influence of American Communist Colonies on Engels and Marx," *The Western Political Quarterly,* September, 1966.

Fitzgerald, George R., *Communes: Their Goals, Hopes, Problems.* Paulist Press, New York, 1971.

Flanders, Robert B., *Nauvoo: Kingdom on the Mississippi.* University of Illinois Press, Urbana, Ill., 1965.

Flint, Timothy, *Recollections of the Last Ten Years in the Valley of the Mississippi.* De Capo Press, Carbondale, Ill., 1968.

Fogarty, Robert S., *All Things New.* University of Chicago Press, Chicago, 1990.

_____, *Dictionary of American Communal and Utopian History.* Greenwood Press, Westport, Ct., 1980.

_____. *American Utopianism*. F. E. Peacock, Itasca, Ill., 1972.

Ford, Edsel, "The Harmonial Vegetarian Society," *Arkansas Democrat*, February 5, 1961.

Fox, Wendall P., "The Kendal Community," *Ohio Archaeological and Historical Society Quarterly*, January 1911.

Fries, Adelaide L., *The Road to Salem*. John F. Blair, Winston-Salem, N.C., 1993.

Gaddis, Merrill Elmer, *Christian Perfectionism in America*. Doctoral thesis, University of Chicago, 1929.

Gardner, Martin, *Fads and Fallacies in the Name of Science*. Dover Publications, New York, 1957.

Gaskins, J.W., "Arden: A Modern As You Like It," *Independent*, August 10, 1911.

Geddes, J.A., *The United Order Among the Mormons (Missouri Phase)*. AMS Press, New York, 1975.

Gerrin, Florence, "Arden — A Social Experiment," *American City*, July 1916.

Gide, Charles, *Communist and Co-Operative Colonies*. Crowell, New York, 1931.

Ginger, Ray, *The Bending Cross: A Biography of Eugene Victor Debs*. Russel & Russel, Camden, N.J., 1969.

Goldberg, Robert Alan. *Back to the Soil: The Jewish Farmers of Clarion, Utah, and Their World*. University of Utah Press, Salt Lake City, 1949.

Gollin, Gillian L., *Moravians in Two Worlds: A Study of Changing Communities*. Columbia University Press, New York, 1967.

Grant, H. Roger, "Utopias that Failed: The Ante-Bellum Years," *Western Illinois Regional Studies*, Vol. 2, No. 1, Spring 1979.

Greenwalt, Emmett A., *The Point Loma Community in California, 1897–1942: A Theosophical Experiment*. AMS Press, New York, 1979.

Harder, Leland, "Plockhoy, Pietr Cornelisz," *The Mennonite Encyclopedia: A Comprehensive Reference Work on the Anabaptist-Mennonite Movement*, 4 vols., (IV, pg. 195). Hillsboro, Kan., 1959.

Harrison, F.C., *Quest for the New Moral World: Robert Owen and the Owenites in Britain and America*. Routledge and K. Paul, New York, 1969.

Harvey, Rowland Hill, *Robert Owen, Social Idealist*. University of California Press, Berkeley, Calif., 1949.

Hawthorne, Nathaniel, *The Blithedale Romance*. Norton, New York, 1978.

Hayden, Dolores, *Seven American Utopias: The Architecture of Communitarian Socialism*, MIT Press, Cambridge, MA, 1976.

Hedgepath, William, and Denis Stock, *The Alternative: Communal Life in New America*. Macmillan, New York, 1971.

Hendricks, R.J., *Bethel and Aurora: An Experiment in Communism as Practical Christianity, with Some Account of Past and Present Ventures in Collective Living*. Press of the Pioneers, New York, 1933.

Hennacy, Ammon, *The Book of Ammon*. Hennacy Press, Phoenix, 1970.

Hertzler, J.O., *The History of Utopian Thought*. Cooper Square Publishers, New York, 1965.

Hillquit, Morris, *History of Socialism in the United States*. Dover Publications, New York, 1971.

Hinds, W.A., *American Communities*. Corinth Books, New York, 1961 (reprint of 1878 edition). Also 3rd edition, C. H. Kerr Co., Chicago, 1908.

Hine, Robert V., *California's Utopian Communities.* Yale University Press, New Haven, Conn., 1953.

History of Clayton County, Iowa. Inter-state Publishing Company, Chicago, 1882.

History of Laclede, Camden, Dallas, Webster, Wright, Texas, Pulaski, Phelps and Dent Counties, Missouri, Southern Historical Press, Greenville, S.C., 1974.

History of Waukesha County, Wisconsin, Waukesha County Museum and Waukesha County Historical Society, Waukesha, Wisc., 1989.

Holand, Hjalmar R., *Old Peninsula Days: Tales and Sketches of the Door County Peninsula.* Wm. Caxton, Sister Bay, Wisc., 1990.

Holloway, Mark, *Heavens on Earth.* Dover Publications, New York, 1951.

Hoover, Mildred Brooke, Hero Eugene Rensch, and Ethel Grace Rensch, *Historic Spots in California.* Stanford University Press, Stanford, Calif., 1966.

Hostetler, John A., "Aspects of Personality in a Communal Society," *Socialization and Communication in Primary Groups,* Thomas R. Williams, ed. The Hague, Netherlands, 1975.

_____, *Hutterite Society.* Johns Hopkins University, Baltimore, 1974.

Hough, Franklin B., *A History of St. Lawrence and Franklin Counties, New York.* Regional Publishing Company, Baltimore, 1970.

Houriet, Robert, *Getting Back Together.* Coward, McCann & Geoghegan, New York, 1971.

Howard, Timothy Edward, *A History of St. Joseph County, Indiana.* The Lewis Publishing Company, Chicago, 1907.

Hudson, David, *History of Jemima Wilkinson.* AMS Press, New York, 1972.

Huntington, Charles White, *Enclaves of Economic Rent for 1931.* F. Warren, Harvard, Mass., 1931.

_____, *Enclaves of Single Tax or Economic Rent.* F. Warren, Harvard, Mass., 1921.

_____, "Children of the Hutterites," *Natural History,* February 1981.

Infield, Henrik. *Cooperative Communities at Work.* Dryden Press, New York, 1945.

_____, ed., *Cooperative Communities at Work.* Dryden Press, New York, 1950.

_____, *Utopia and Experiment.* Kennikat Press, Port Washington, N.Y., 1971.

The Intentional Communities, 1959 Yearbook of the Fellowship of Intentional Communities. Yellow Springs, Ohio, August 1, 1960.

Itemized Observer, Nov. 16, 1933, article on Oregon Subsistence Colony. Dallas, Oregon.

James, B.B., *The Labadist Colony in Maryland.* AMS Press, New York, 1973.

James, Eleanor, "The Sanctificationists of Belton," *The American West,* Summer 1965.

Jerome, Judson, *Families of Eden: Communes and the New Anarchism.* Seabury Press, New York, 1974.

Johnson, C., *Robert Owen in the United States.* Humanities Press, New York, 1970.

Jones, W. Paul, "Communes and Christian Intentional Community," *The Christian Century,* Jan. 17, 1973.

Journal of Jasper Danckaerts, 1679–80, Bartlett B. James and J. Franklin Jameson. HarperCollins, New York, 1969.

Kagen, Paul, *New World Utopias: A Photographic History of the Search for Community.* Penguin Books, New York, 1975.

Kanter, Rosebeth Moss, *Commitment and Community: Communes and Utopia in Sociological Perspective.* Harvard University Press, Harvard, Mass., 1972.

Kaplan, Bert, and Thomas Plaut, *Personality in a Communal Society.* University Press of Kansas, Lawrence, Kans., 1956.

Katz, Elia, *Armed Love.* Rinehart and Winston, New York, 1971.

Kegel, Charles H., "Ruskin's St. George in America," *American Quarterly,* Winter 1957.

Kent, Alexander, "Cooperative Communities in the United States," U.S. Department of Labor *Bulletin,* VI, July, 1901.

Keyes, Elisha W., *History of Dane County.* Madison, Wis., 1906.

Knoedler, C.F., *The Harmony Society.* Vantage Press, New York, 1954.

Koch, Raymond and Charlotte, *Educational Commune: The Story of Commonwealth College.* Schocken Books, New York, 1972.

Lane, Margaret, *Frances Wright and the Great Experiment.* Rowman and Littlefield, Totowa, N.J., 1972.

LeWarne, Charles Pierce, *Utopias on Puget Sound, 1885–1915,* University of Washington Press, Seattle, Wash. 1975.

Lockwood, G.B., *The New Harmony Movement.* D. Appleton and Company, New York, 1905.

Longley, Alcander, *Communism: The Right Way and the Best Way for All to Live.* The Altruist Community, St. Louis, 1880.

Ludlum, David M., *Social Ferment in Vermont, 1791–1850.* Columbia University Press, New York, 1939.

McBee, A.E., *From Utopia to Florence: The Story of a Transcendentalist Community in Northampton, Mass., 1830–1852.* Porcupine Press, Philadelphia, 1975.

McKinley, K.W., "A Guide to the Communistic Communities of Ohio," *Ohio State Archaeological and Historical Quarterly,* January 1937.

MacLean, J.P., *Bibliography of Shaker Literature.* B. Franklin, New York, 1971.

Madison, C.A., *Critics and Crusaders,* Henry Holt and Company, New York, 1971.

Mannheim, Karl, *Ideology and Utopia: An Introduction to the Sociology of Knowledge.* Harcourt, Brace and Co., New York, 1936.

Manuel, Frank E., and Fritzie P., *Utopias: An Anthology of Ideal Societies.* Free Press, New York, 1971.

Martin, J.H., *Historical Sketch of Bethlehem in Pennsylvania.* AMS Press, New York, 1971.

Martineau, Harriet, *Society in America.* Anchor Books, Garden City, N.Y., 1962.

Mathison, R.R., *Faiths, Cults and Sects in America.* Bobbs-Merrill, Indianapolis, 1960.

Maximillian, Prince of Wied, "Travels in the Interior of North America, 1832–1834," *Early Western Travels,* R.C. Thwaites, ed., A. H. Clark Company, Cleveland, 1906.

Melcher, M.F., *The Shaker Adventure.* Shaker Museum Foundation, Inc., Albany, N.Y., 1986.

Melish, John, *Travels Through the United States of America.* Johnson Reprint Corporation, New York, 1970.

Mikkelsen, M.Z., *The Bishop Hill Colony: A Religious Communistic Settlement in Henry County, Illinois.* John Hopkins Press, Baltimore, 1892.

Miller, Ernest I., *Some Tennessee Utopias.* Master's thesis, University of Tennessee, August 1941.

Miller, William D., *A Harsh and Dreadful Love: Dorothy Day and the Catholic Worker Movement.* Liveright, New York, 1972.

Miller, Timothy. *American Communes: A Bibliography.* Garland Pub., New York, 1990.

Mitchell, Dave, *The Light on Synanon.* Seaview Books, New York, 1980.

Moore, R. Laurence, *European Socialists and the American Promised Land.* Oxford University Press, New York, 1970.

Morgan, Arthur E., *Nowhere Is Somewhere: How History Makes Utopias and How Utopias Make History.* Greenwood Publishing Group, Westport, Ct., 1976.

Morse, Flo, *Yankee Communes: Another American Way.* Harcourt Brace Jovanovich, New York, 1971.

Mulkearn, Lois, and Edwin V. Pugh, *A Traveler's Guide to Historic Western Pennsylvania.* University of Pittsburgh Press, Pittsburgh, 1954.

Mumford, Lewis, *The Story of Utopias.* Boni and Liveright, New York, 1922.

Muncy, Raymond Lee, *Sex and Marriage in Utopian Communities: Nineteenth-Century America.* Indiana University Press, Bloomington, Ind., 1973.

Murray, John J., *The Heritage of the Middle West.* Oklahoma University Press, Norman, Okla., 1958.

New York Times, "Even Pacifism Requires Training: A Nonviolent Group Learning Art of Self Defense," November 29, 1965.

Nordhoff, Charles, *The Communistic Societies of the United States.* Hillary House Publishers, New York, 1961 (reprint of 1875 edition).

Noyes, George W., ed., *John Humphrey Noyes: The Putney Community.* Oneida, N.Y., 1931.

Noyes, John Humphrey, *History of American Socialisms.* Dover Publications, New York, 1966.

Noyes, Pierrepont, *My Father's House: An Oneida Boyhood.* P. Smith, Gloucester, Mass., 1966.

Nuttall, Thomas, "Journal of Travels into Arkansas Territory During the Year 1819," *Early Western Travels,* R.G. Thwaites, ed. A. H. Clark Company, Cleveland, 1905.

O'Brien, Harriet E., *Lost Utopias.* Brookline, Mass., 1947.

O'Dea, Thomas F., *The Mormons.* University of Chicago Press, Chicago, 1957.

One Hundred Years in Pine County, Pine County, Minn., Historical Society Publication, 1949.

Oreate, Jean, "You Can Help Bend History," *Chicago, The Quarterly Magazine of Mid-America,* Autumn 1966 (on the Ecumentical Institute).

Palmer, Elice Mary, *The Cutlerite Settlement of Clitherall, Minnesota.* Master's thesis, North Dakota State University, 1963.

Parker, Robert A., *A Yankee Saint: John Humphrey Noyes and the Oneida Community.* Archon Books, Hamden, Ct., 1973.

Pease, William H. and Jane H., *Black Utopia.* State Historical Society of Wisconsin, Madison, Wis., 1963.

Perkins, A.J.G., and Theresa Wolfson, *Frances Wright: Free Enquirer.* Porcupine Press, Philadelphia, 1972.

Perrin, William Henry, *History of Stark County.* Baskin and Battey, Chicago, 1881.

Peters, Victor, *All Things in Common: The Hutteran Way of Life.* University of Minnesota Press, Minneapolis, 1965.

Piehl, Mel, *Breaking Bread: The Catholic Worker and the Origin of Catholic Radicalism in America.* Temple University Press, Philadelphia, 1982.

Postal, Bernard, and Lionel Koppman, *A Jewish Tourist's Guide to the United States,* Jewish Publication Society of America, Philadelphia, 1954.

Quaife, Milo M., *Wisconsin, Its History and Its People,* Chicago, no date.

_____, *The Kingdom of Saint James.* Yale University Press, New Haven, Conn., 1930.

_____, *Lake Michigan.* Ameron, New York, 1949.

Randall, E.O., *History of the Zoar Society.* AMS Press, New York, 1971.

Ransom, Harley, *Pioneer Recollections.* Historical Pub. Co., Vinton, Iowa, 1941.

Regenerator, issues of April 14, 1845; August 4, 1845; August 18, 1845; September 7, 1846. Warren County, Ohio.

Reizenstein, Milton, "Agricultural Colonies (United States)," *Jewish Encyclopedia,* Isadore Singer, ed., Vol. I. New York, 1901.

Rerick, J.C., *Counties of LaGrange and Noble, Indiana.* F. A. Battey & Co., Chicago, 1882.

Rich, Louise Dickinson, *State O'Maine.* Harper & Row, New York, 1964.

Richter, Peyton E., *Utopias: Social Ideals and Communal Experiments.* Holbrook Press, Boston, 1971.

Riley, Marvin P., *The Hutterite Brethren.* State University, Brookings, South Dakota, 1965.

Roberts, Ron E., *The New Communes: Coming Together in America.* Prentice-Hall, Englewood Cliffs, N.J., 1971.

Robertson, Constance Noyes, *Oneida Community: The Breakup, 1876–1881.* Syracuse University Press, Syracuse, N.Y., 1972.

Rose, Stephen C., "The Ecumenical Institute: Ode to a Dying Church," *Christianity and Crisis,* November 11, 1968.

Ross, Marie, *Child of Icaria.* Hyperion Press, Westport, Ct., 1976.

Rosskam, Edwin, *Roosevelt, New Jersey.* Grossman, New York, 1972.

Rupp, I.D., *An Original History of the Religious Denominations at Present Existing in the United States.* AMS Press, New York, 1975.

Sanborn, F.B., *Bronson Alcott at Alcott House, England, and Fruitlands, New England (1842–1844).* Folcroft Library Editions, Folcroft, Pa., 1974.

Sachse, J.F., *The German Pietists of Provincial Pennsylvania, 1694–1708.* AMS Press, New York, 1970.

_____, *The German Sectarians of Pennsylvania, 1708–1800: A Critical and Legendary History of the Ephrata Cloister and the Dunkers.* AMS Press, New York, 1971.

Savacool, Harry M., "Kirkridge," *Church Management,* December 1949.

Schneider, Herbert W., and Grace Lawton, *A Prophet and a Pilgrim.* Columbia University Press, New York, 1942.

Schroeder, Theodore, "Anarchism and the Lord's Farm," *The Open Court,* October 1919.

Schulz-Behrend, George, "Andreas Dietsch and Helvetia, Missouri." *Swiss Record* (Yearbook of the Swiss-American Historical Society), March 1950.

Sears, Clara Endicott, *Bronson Alcott's Fruitlands,* Porcupine Press, Philadelphia, 1975.

Sessler, J.J., *Communal Pietism Among Early American Moravians.* AMS Press, New York, 1971.

Shambaugh, B.M.H., "Amana Society," *Encyclopedia of Religion and Ethics,* James Hastings, ed. New York, 1951.

_____, *Amana That Was and Amana That Is.* B. Blom, Iowa City, Iowa, 1932.

Shaw, Albert, *Icaria: A Chapter in the History of Communism.* AMS Press, New York, 1973.

Sheehan, Arthur, *Peter Maurin, Gay Believer.* Hanover House, Garden City, New York, 1959.

Sheffeld, C.A., ed., *History of Florence, Massachusetts: Including a Complete Account of the Northampton Association of Education and Industry.* Florence, Mass., 1885.

Shepard, O., *Peddlar's Progress: The Life of Bronson Alcott.* Telegraph Books, 1986.

Shepperson, Wilbur, *Retreat to Nevada: A Socialist Colony of World War I,* University of Nevada Press, Reno, NV, 1966.

Simons, Richard, "A Utopian Failure," *Indiana History Bulletin,* February 1941.

Sinclair, Upton, *The Autobiography of Upton Sinclair.* Harcourt, Brace & World, New York, 1962.

Skinner, C.M., *American Communes: Practical Socialism in the United States.* Brooklyn Daily Eagle, Brooklyn, N.Y., 1901.

Smith, Charles Henry, *The Story of the Mennonites.* Faith and Life Press, Newton, Kans., 1957.

Smyrl, Edwin, "The Burning Bush," *Southwestern Historical Quarterly 3,* 1947.

The Social Revolutionist, Darke County, Ohio, January 1856.

Stegner, Wallace, *Mormon Country.* Duell, Sloan & Pierce, New York, 1942.

Stokes, K.D., "The Land of Shalam," *New Mexico Historical Review,* January and April 1958.

Stone, William L., *Matthias and His Impostures,* Harper & Brothers, New York, 1835.

Story of the Atherton Adventure, paper written by members of the Reorganized Church of Latter Day Saints. Independence, Mo., no date.

Swainson, W.P., *Thomas Lake Harris and His Occult Teaching.* W. Rider & Son, Ltd., London, 1922.

Swank, George, *Painter Kranz.* Garland Press, Galva, Il., 1978.

Swift, Lindsay, *Brook Farm, Its Members, Scholars and Visitors.* Corinth Books, New York, 1961.

Sylvester, Harry, "Dynamite in Alabama," *Commonweal,* September 30, 1938.

Taylor, B.B., "Communistic Societies of America," *Encyclopedia of Religion and Ethics,* James Hastings, ed. New York, 1951.

Teselle, Sallie, *The Family, Communes and Utopian Societies.* Harper & Row, New York, 1972.

Thompson, Zadock, *History of Vermont,* Vol. II. Published by author, Burlington, Vt., 1853.

Thrupp, Sylvia L., *Millennial Dreams in Action: Comparative Studies in Society and History.* Schocken Books, New York, 1970.

Todd, Ian, and Michael Wheeler, *Utopia.* Harmony Books, New York, 1978.

Tucker, E., *History of Randolph County, Indiana.* Whipporwill Publications, Evansville, Ind., 1975.

Tyler, Alice Felt, *Freedom's Ferment.* University of Minnesota Press, Minneapolis, 1944.

_____, "William Pfander and the Founding of New Ulm," *Minnesota History,* Vol. 30, 1949.

Ulrick, Polly, "Start Small Conquer the World," *Chicago,* August, 1976 (on the Ecumenical Institute).

Veysey, Laurence, *The Communal Experience: Anarchist and Mystical Counter-Culture in America.* Harper & Row, New York, 1973.

Waterman, William Randall, *Frances Wright.* AMS Press, New York, 1967.

Wayland, Julius A., *Leaves of Life.* Hyperon Press, Westport, Ct., 1975.

Webber, Everett, *Escape to Utopia: The Communal Movement in America.* Hastings House Publishers, New York, 1959.

Whitworth, John McKelvie, *God's Blueprints.* Routledge and K. Paul, London, 1975.

Willard, James Field, *The Union Colony of Greeley, Colorado, 1869–1871.* Boulder, Colo., 1918.

Williams, E.M., "The Monastic Orders of Provincial Ephrata," *Lancaster County Pennsylvania, A History,* H.M.J. Klein and E.M. Williams, eds. Lewis Historical Publishing Company, New York, 1924.

Williams, Julia Elizabeth, *An Analytical Tabulation of the North American Utopian Communities by Type, Longevity and Location.* Master's thesis, University of Iowa, 1939.

Wilson, William E., *The Angel and the Serpent: The Story of New Harmony.* Indiana University Press, Bloomington, Ind., 1964.

Winter, Gibson, "The Parishfield Community," *The Christian Century,* June 14, 1967.

Wisbey, Herbert, *Pioneer Prophetess,* Cornell University Press, Ithica, NY, 1964 (about Jemima Wilkenson).

Wittke, Carl, *We Who Built America: The Saga of the Immigrant.* Press of Case Western Reserve University, Cleveland, 1967.

Woods, John, "Two Years' Residence in the Settlement on the English Prairie in Illinois Country," *Early Western Travels,* R.C. Thwaites, ed. A. H. Clark Company, Cleveland, 1904.

Wooster, E.S., *Communities of the Past and Present.* AMS Press, New York, 1974.

Young, Marguerite, *Angel in the Forest; a Fairy Tale of Two Utopias.* Dalkey Archive Press, Normal, Il., 1994.

Young, Sid, *The Crisis in Llano Colony 1935–36.* Published by author, Los Angeles, 1936.

Zablocki, Benjamin, *The Joyful Community.* Penguin Books, Baltimore, 1971.

Zornow, William, *Kansas, the Jayhawk State,* University of Oklahoma Press, Norman, Okla., 1959.

Index

The New Oxford Book
of English Verse

The New
Oxford Book
of English Verse

1250–1950

CHOSEN AND EDITED BY

Helen Gardner

1972
Oxford University Press
New York and Oxford

© OXFORD UNIVERSITY PRESS 1972
Library of Congress Catalogue Card Number
Printed in the United States of America

PREFACE

The Oxford Book of English Verse, 1250–1900, chosen and edited by Arthur Quiller-Couch, appeared in 1900. It rapidly established itself as the classic anthology of English poetry, running through twenty-one impressions in the next forty years and selling nearly half a million copies. The judgement of readers confirmed, to quote the editor's preface, that he had so managed his task 'as to serve those who already love poetry and to implant that love in some young minds not yet initiated'. In 1939 Sir Arthur revised his anthology, 'having come to regret some inclusions and omissions of indolence', and extended it by nearly a hundred pages to bring it down to 1918. The revision hardly affected the first three-quarters of the original book where only some forty items were omitted and some forty added. It was after Keats, in the section that had always given least satisfaction, that Sir Arthur made most changes, dropping some seventy poems, and adding roughly the equivalent number, before extending into the first twenty years of this century. The revision did not change the nature of the anthology. It remained what it had originally been, an anthology of lyrical verse, inspired by the most famous of Victorian anthologies, Palgrave's *Golden Treasury*.

The present edition is not a revision of Q's revision but a new anthology. Like my predecessor, I have tried 'to range over the whole field of English verse' and 'to choose the best'. But any anthology that thus aims at being classic will reflect not only the personal taste of the anthologist but also the critical consensus of the age in which it is compiled. Q was of his age in holding that to choose the best meant to choose numbers 'either lyrical or epigrammatic'. This involved the virtual exclusion of Pope, the representation of poets such as Dryden, Byron, Tennyson, and Browning solely by their lyrics, and the neglect of the tradition of satiric, political, epistolary, and didactic verse in English. Since 1900 the concept of the 'best' has widened beyond the lyrical, and the reputations of poets and of individual poems have changed. Nobody today would give twenty pages to Herrick while giving only seven to Donne and five to Herbert; and it seems safe to say that nobody today would not include such famous poems as 'Ulysses', 'My Last Duchess', and 'Dover Beach' as being finely characteristic of their authors' best work.

In making this new anthology I have in many ways followed my predecessor's example. Although I have widened the range of poetry he drew upon, I have followed him in excluding dramatic verse. Here context is all-important. I have also followed him in giving full representation to major poets, and have treated Hopkins, Hardy, Yeats, and Eliot, the four greatest poets of the last hundred years, as he treated Keats and Shelley. I have also not attempted to avoid the familiar, believing with him that 'the best is the best, though a hundred judges have declared it so'. I have also agreed with him in modernizing the spelling throughout (even, as far as is possible, in the medieval poems), with the exception that I have not tampered with the spelling of poems in Scots, and have left Spenser's archaic spelling as an integral part of his deliberate attempt to 'affect the ancients'. I have also, like him, resisted the temptation to gloss, except for the occasional glossing of an obsolete word; and have kept the pages free of references, hiding them away in notes at the back of the volume. On the other hand, I have not followed him in including American poets. Since I have both enlarged the range of verse he drew upon and extended my terminal date to include a particularly rich period of English verse, I reluctantly decided that I must confine myself to poets writing in these islands. It seemed impossible to do justice to American poetry without seriously restricting the selection from English. I have made one exception, and included a handful of poems by Ezra Pound, since, though he kept American nationality, he was at the centre of the modern movement in England. I hesitated whether in a book of English Verse, poems in the Scottish dialect should be included. But I decided that the Scots would be less offended at their inclusion under this title than at the omission of the Border Ballads and Burns, which are part of the cultural heritage of England as well as of Scotland.

The present volume attempts to represent the range of English nondramatic poetry from 1250 to 1950. It includes no poet who had not established himself by 1950, although I have not felt it necessary to confine myself with absolute strictness to poems published before that date. The end of the Second World War is a genuine terminus, the impetus of the so-called modern movement having spent itself, and the last hundred pages of Q's anthology are a warning of the danger—and the unfairness—of attempting to select from poets in mid-passage. Unlike Q I have excerpted from long poems, supplying titles for the extracts. Those curious for the source of such excerpts will find references in the notes at the close. Q regarded himself as an anthologist, or 'gatherer of flowers', and did not scruple to omit verses, or to lift a couple or so of verses from a poem, give them a title, and print them as a complete poem without signalization. Such a practice runs contrary to modern feeling. Considerations of space make some shortenings inevitable; but it can be assumed that all the items here, which are not patently extracts, or noted as such in the Notes and References, are complete poems, unless an omission is signalized by dots, or, if the omission is substantial, by an asterisk. In the latter case, the extent of the omission is indicated in a note.

The poets are arranged chronologically by date of birth, with a few exceptions. For example, I have played a little with the dates at the close of the sixteenth century to place those, like Sidney or Marlowe, who died before 1600 and are strictly Elizabethans, before poets like Greville and Ralegh who survived into the Jacobean period, and I have placed Traherne before Dryden, since he died before Dryden's major works were written. I have followed Q in grouping together poems from the Song Books, though I place them at the end and not at the beginning of the Elizabethan period; and in collecting the Ballads and placing them before the Restoration poets. On the whole, and as far as it can be ascertained, the poems of individual poets are printed in order of composition, or in order of publication.

No anthologist can hope to win approval for all his inclusions and exclusions; but I hope that some who regret the absence of old favourites will discover new loves, and be stimulated to explore further some poets with whom they are not familiar. Q's bias was towards the lyrical and the poem of personal joys and sorrows. This anthology balances against poems of the private life poems that deal with public events, and historic occasions, or express convictions, religious, moral, or political. Together with what may be felt to be a too generous proportion of satire, I have also included familiar verse, and that distinctive English achievement, light verse. As well as attempting to represent the range of English poetry, I have tried to represent a poet's own range, and wherever I could have included poems of tribute to other poets. I can only hope that readers will find half the pleasure that I have found in reading and re-reading for this anthology, in the richest and most continuously lively poetic tradition in the world.

Since I was first invited to revise the Oxford Book, over ten years ago I have had cause to be grateful to many people for suggestions and discussions. My greatest debt is to the late Mr. John Hayward for many delightful hours discussing his own anthology, the *Penguin Book of English Verse*, and his *Oxford Book of Nineteenth-Century English Verse*. Among colleagues I must particularly thank Mr. John Buxton, Miss Katherine Duncan-Jones, and Professor Norman Davis, who encouraged and assisted me in modernizing medieval texts. By great good fortune, just as I was settling down to make final choices, Mrs. Bridget Bertram offered me her services as research assistant. As well as giving invaluable assistance in checking texts, tracing sources, and preparing copy for the press, she brought critical judgement and taste to our discussions of the contents. Finally I have to thank Mrs. M. A. Gordon, who, by relieving me of all domestic cares, made possible the completion of my task far sooner than without her I could have accomplished it.

HELEN GARDNER

Oxford University
1972

ACKNOWLEDGEMENTS

The editor gratefully acknowledges permission to reproduce copyright poems in this book.

W. H. Auden: 'O Where are you going', Copyright 1934 and renewed 1962 by W. H. Auden; 'As I walked out one evening', 'Lullaby', 'Musée des Beaux Arts', 'In Memory of W. B. Yeats', Copyright 1940 and renewed 1968 by W. H. Auden; 'The Shield of Achilles', copyright 1952 by W. H. Auden. All from *Collected Shorter Poems 1927–1957*. Reprinted by permission of Faber & Faber Ltd., and Random House, Inc.

Hilaire Belloc: 'Matilda' and 'The Statesman' from *Cautionary Verses*. Published 1941 by Alfred A. Knopf, Inc. Reprinted by permission of Gerald Duckworth & Co. Ltd. and Alfred A. Knopf, Inc.; 'On a General Election' from *Sonnets and Verse* (Gerald Duckworth & Co. Ltd.). Reprinted by permission of A. D. Peters and Company.

John Betjeman: 'Death of King George V', 'Parliament Hill Fields', and 'The Cottage Hospital'. Reprinted by permission of John Murray (Publishers) Ltd. and Houghton Mifflin Company.

Laurence Binyon: 'For the Fallen' from *Collected Poems* and 'The Burning of the Leaves' (section i) from *The Burning of the Leaves*. Reprinted by permission of Mrs. Nicolete Gray and The Society of Authors on behalf of the Laurence Binyon Estate.

Edmund Blunden: from *Collected Poems*, 1972. Reprinted by permission of Gerald Duckworth & Co. Ltd.

Robert Bridges: from *The Poetical Works of Robert Bridges*. Reprinted by permission of The Clarendon Press, Oxford.

G. K. Chesterton: from *The Collected Poems of G. K. Chesterton*. Reprinted by permission of A. P. Watt & Son on behalf of Miss D. E. Collins and Methuen & Co. Ltd.

W. H. Davies: from *Collected Poems*. Copyright 1963 by Jonathan Cape Ltd. Reprinted by permission of Jonathan Cape Ltd. on behalf of Mrs. H. M. Davies and Wesleyan University Press, publishers.

Cecil Day-Lewis: from *Collected Poems 1954*. Copyright 1954 by C. Day-Lewis. Reprinted by permission of Jonathan Cape Ltd., The Hogarth Press and Harold Matson Company, Inc.

Keith Douglas: from *Collected Poems*. Reprinted by permission of Faber & Faber Ltd. and Chilmark Press.

T. S. Eliot: from *Collected Poems 1909–1962*. Copyright 1936, by Harcourt Brace Jovanovich, Inc.; copyright © 1943, 1963, 1964 by T. S. Eliot.

ACKNOWLEDGEMENTS

Reprinted by permission of Faber & Faber Ltd. and Harcourt Brace Jovanovich, Inc.

William Empson: from *Collected Poems*. Copyright © 1949 by William Empson. Reprinted by permission of Chatto and Windus Ltd. and Harcourt Brace Jovanovich, Inc.

Roy Fuller: 'Translation' from *Collected Poems*. Reprinted by permission of André Deutsch Ltd. 'The Statue' from *Collected Poems*. Reprinted by permission of André Deutsch Ltd. and Curtis Brown Ltd.

Robert Graves: from *Collected Poems 1965*. Reprinted by permission of A. P. Watt and Son on behalf of Mr. Robert Graves.

Thomas Hardy: from *Collected Poems*. Copyright © 1925 by The Macmillan Company. Reprinted by permission of the Trustees of the Hardy Estate, The Macmillan Company of Canada Ltd., and Macmillan London and Basingstoke.

Ralph Hodgson: 'The Bells of Heaven' and 'The Hammers' from *Collected Poems*. Reprinted by permission of Mrs. Hodgson, St. Martin's Press, Inc., The Macmillan Company of Canada Ltd., and Macmillan London and Basingstoke.

A. E. Housman: from *The Collected Poems*. Copyright 1922 by Holt, Rinehart & Winston, Inc., Copyright 1936, 1950 by Barclays Bank Ltd. Copyright © 1964 by Robert E. Symons; 'On Wenlock Edge', 'On the Idle Hill of Summer', and 'Into My Heart an Air that Kills' from 'A Shropshire Lad'—Authorized Edition—from *Collected Poems*. Copyright 1939, 1940, © 1959 by Holt Rinehart and Winston Inc. Copyright © 1967, 1968 by Robert E. Symons. Reprinted by permission of The Society of Authors as the literary representative of the Estate of A. E. Housman, and Jonathan Cape Ltd. as publishers, and Holt, Rinehart & Winston, Inc.

James Joyce: from *Chamber Music* and in the U.S. from *Collected Poems*. Copyright © 1918 by B. W. Huebsch, renewed 1946 by Nora Joyce. Reprinted by permission of The Society of Authors as the literary representative of the Estate of James Joyce, Jonathan Cape Ltd. on behalf of the Executors of the Joyce Estate, and The Viking Press Inc.

Rudyard Kipling: 'Mandalay' from *Barrack Room Ballads*; 'Danny Deever' from *Departmental Ditties*; 'Cities and Thrones and Powers' from *Puck of Pook's Hill*; 'The Way Through the Woods' from *Rewards and Fairies*; 'Recessional' from *The Five Nations*. Reprinted by permission of A. P. Watt & Son on behalf of Mrs. George Bambridge and Macmillan & Co. Ltd. All the above poems are also reprinted by permission of Doubleday and Company, Inc. from their *Rudyard Kipling's Definitive Edition*.

D. H. Lawrence: 'Piano' (Copyright © 1920 by B. W. Huebsch, Inc., copyright renewed 1948 by Frieda Lawrence); 'Snake' (Copyright © 1923, © renewed 1951 by Frieda Lawrence); 'Bavarian Gentians' (Copyright 1933 by Frieda Lawrence); 'Giorno dei Morti' from *The Complete Poems*

ACKNOWLEDGEMENTS

(William Heinemann Ltd.) edited by Vivian de Sola Pinto and Warren Roberts. Reprinted by permission of Laurence Pollinger Ltd. on behalf of the Estate of the Late Mrs. Frieda Lawrence, and The Viking Press, Inc. of New York.

Alun Lewis: from *Raider's Dawn*. Reprinted by permission of George Allen & Unwin Ltd.

Louis MacNeice: from *The Collected Poems* edited by E. R. Dodds. Copyright © The Estate of Louis MacNeice 1966. Reprinted by permission of Faber & Faber Ltd. and Oxford University Press, Inc.

John Masefield: 'Cargoes' (Copyright 1912 by The Macmillan Company, renewed 1940 by John Masefield) and 'Up on the Downs' (Copyright 1917 by John Masefield, renewed 1945 by John Masefield) from *Poems*. Reprinted by permission of The Society of Authors as the literary representative of the Estate of John Masefield, and The Macmillan Company of New York.

Alice Meynell: 'Renouncement', and 'Christ in the Universe', Reprinted by permission of Miss Sylvia Mulvey on behalf of the Literary Executors of Alice Meynell.

Edwin Muir: From *Collected Poems 1921–1958*. Copyright © 1960 by Willa Muir. Reprinted by permission of Faber & Faber Ltd. and Oxford University Press, Inc.

Wilfred Owen: from *Collected Poems*. Copyright Chatto & Windus Ltd. 1944, © 1963. Reprinted by permission of Chatto & Windus Ltd. on behalf of the Executors of the Estate of Harold Owen, and New Directions Publishing Corp., New York.

Oxford Book of Ballads, edited by James Kinsley. Reprinted by permission of the editor and The Clarendon Press, Oxford.

Ezra Pound: 'The River-Merchant's Wife: A Letter', 'Hugh Selwyn Mauberly III, IV, V' from *Collected Shorter Poems* (and from *Personae* in the U.S.) and 'Canto LXXXI' from *The Cantos of Ezra Pound*. *Personae* Copyright © 1926 by Ezra Pound. *The Cantos* Copyright © 1948 by Ezra Pound. Reprinted by permission of Faber & Faber Ltd. and New Directions Publishing Corporation.

Kathleen Raine: from *The Collected Poems*. Copyright © 1956 by Kathleen Raine, Hamish Hamilton, London. Reprinted by permission of the publishers.

Henry Reed: from *A Map of Verona*. Reprinted by permission of Jonathan Cape Ltd.

Anne Ridler: from *A Matter of Life and Death*. © by Anne Ridler, 1952. Reprinted by permission of Faber & Faber Ltd. and The Macmillan Company of New York.

Isaac Rosenberg: 'August 1914' and 'Break of Day in the Trenches' from

ACKNOWLEDGEMENTS

xii

The New Oxford Book
of English Verse

ANONYMOUS

1

Cuckoo Song

SUMMER is y-comen in,
　　Loudè sing, cuckoo!
Groweth seed and bloweth meed
And spring'th the woodè now—
　　　Sing cuckoo!

Ewè bleateth after lamb,
　　Low'th after calfè cow;
Bullock starteth, buckè farteth.
　　Merry sing, cuckoo!

　　Cuckoo, Cuckoo!
Well sing'st thou, cuckoo:
　　Ne swike thou never now!

Sing cuckoo, now! Sing, cuckoo!
Sing cuckoo! Sing, cuckoo, now!

2

In Praise of Mary

OF one that is so fair and bright,
　　Velut maris stella,
Brighter than the dayès light,
　　Parens et puella,
I cry to thee; thou see to me!
Lady, pray thy son for me,
　　Tam pia,
That I motè come to thee
　　Maria.

Lady, flower of allè thing,
　　Rosa sine spina,
Thou borè Jesu, heavenès king
　　Gratia divina.

swike] cease

2 see to me] look on me

1

ANONYMOUS

Of allė thou bear'st the prize,
Lady, queen of Paradise
Electa.
Maidė mildė mother is
Effecta.

Of carė conseil thou art best
Felix fecundata,
Of allė weary thou art rest,
Mater honorata.
Beseech him with mildė mood
That for us allė shed his blood
In cruce,
That we moten come to him
In luce.

All this worėld were forlore
Eva peccatrice,
Till our Loverd was y-bore
De te genetrice.
With '*Ave*' it went away
Thuster night, and com'th the day
Salutis.
The wellė springeth out of thee
Virtutis.

Well he wot he is thy son
Ventre quem portąsti;
He will not wernė thee thy boon,
Parvum quem lactasti.
So hendė and so good he is,
He haveth brought us to bliss
Superni,
That hath y-dit the foulė pit
Inferni.

Of carė . . . best] In distress you are the best counsellor
Thuster] dark   wernė] deny   hendė] gracious
                       y-dit] shut

2

3

The Irish Dancer

I AM of Ireland
And of the holy land
    Of Ireland.
Good sir, pray I thee,
Of sainté charity
Come and dance with me
    In Ireland.

4

The Maid of the Moor

MAIDEN in the moor lay,
    In the moor lay,
Seven nighté full,
Seven nighté full,
Maiden in the moor lay,
    In the moor lay
Seven nighté full and a day.

Well was heré meat;
    What was heré meat?
The primérole and the—
The primérole and the—
Well was heré meat;
    What was heré meat?
The primérole and the violet.

Well was heré dring;
    What was heré dring?
The coldé water of the—
The coldé water of the—
Well was heré dring;
    What was heré dring?
The coldé water of the wellé-spring.

Well was heré bower
    What was heré bower?
The redé rose and the—
The redé rose and the—
Well was heré bower;
    What was heré bower?
The redé rose and the lily-flower.

5 *The Virgin's Song*

JESU, sweetè sonè dear,
On poorful bed liest thou here,
 And that me grieveth sore;
For thy cradle is as a bere,
Ox and assè be thy fere:
 Weep I may therefóre.

Jesu, sweetè, be not wroth,
Though I n'avè clout ne cloth
 Thee on for to fold,
Thee on to foldè ne to wrap,
For I n'avè clout ne lap;
 But lay thou thy feet to my pap
 And wite thee from the cold.

WILLIAM LANGLAND

?1330–?1400

6 *Et Incarnatus Est*

LOVE is the plant of peace and most precious of virtues;
For heaven hold it ne might, so heavy it seemed,
Till it had on earth yoten himself.
Was never leaf upon linden lighter thereafter,
As when it had of the fold flesh and blood taken;
Then was it portative and piercing as the point of a needle.
May no armour it let, neither high walls.
For-thy is love leader of our Lord's folk of heaven.

bere] byre	fere] companions	Thee . . . fold] to fold thee in
	lap] fold	wite] keep
6 yoten] poured out	fold] earth	portative] light to carry
	let] hinder	

4

GEOFFREY CHAUCER

?1343–1400

7

The Complaint of Troilus

'O PALACE, whilom crown of houses all,
Enlumìnèd with sun of allè bliss!
O ring, fro which the ruby is outfall,
O cause of woe, that cause hast been of liss!
Yet since I may no bet, fain would I kiss
Thy coldè doorès, durst I for this rout;
And farewell shrine, of which the saint is out! . . .'

From thennèsforth he rideth up and down,
And everything come him to rémembránce,
As he rode forby places of the town
In which he whilom had all his pleasánce.
'Lo, yonder saw I last my lady dance;
And in that temple, with her eyen clear,
Me caughtè first my rightè lady dear.

'And yonder have I heard full lustily
My dearè heartè laugh; and yonder play
Saw I her onès eek full blissfully.
And yonder onès to me gan she say,
"Now goodè sweetè, love me well, I pray;"
And yond so goodly gan she me behold,
That to the death mine heart is to her hold.

'And at that corner, in the yonder house
Heard I my allerliefest lady dear
So womanly, with voice melodious,
Singen so well, so goodly, and so clear,
That in my soulè yet me think'th I hear
The blissful sound; and in that yonder place
My lady first me took unto her grace.

*

liss] joy   onès] once   allerliefest] most beloved

5

'O star, of which I lost have all the light,
With hearté sore well ought I to bewail,
That ever dark in torment, night by night,
Toward my death with wind in steer I sail:
For which the tenthé night, if that I fail
The guiding of thy beamés bright an hour,
My ship and me Charybdis will devour.'

*

'Was there none other brooch you listé let
To fiefé with your newé love,' quod he,
'But thilké brooch that I, with tearés wet,
You gave, as for a rémembránce of me?
None other cause, alas, ne haddé ye
But for despite, and eek for that ye meant
All utterly to shewen your entent.

'Through which I see that clean out of your mind
Ye have me cast; and I ne can nor may,
For all this world, within my hearté find
To unloven you a quarter of a day!
In cursèd time I born was, wellaway,
That you, that do me all this woe endure,
Yet love I best of any creatúre!'

8   *Love Unfeigned*

O YOUNGÉ freshé folkés, he or she,
In which that love upgroweth with your age,
Repaireth home from worldly vanity,
And of your heart upcasteth the viságe
To thilké God that after his imáge
You made, and thinketh all n'is but a fair
This world, and passeth soon as flowers fair.

And loveth him, the which that right for love
Upon a cross, our soulés for to buy,
First starf, and rose, and sit in heaven above;
For he n'ill falsen no wight, dare I say,
That will his heart all wholly on him lay.
And since he best to love is, and most meek,
What needeth feignèd lovés for to seek?

To fiefé . . . love] to endow your new love with   8   starf] died

6

9 *Balade*

HIDE, Absalom, thy giltè tresses clear;
Esther, lay thou thy meekness all a-down;
Hide, Jonathan, all thy friendly mannér;
Penelope and Marcia Catóun
Make of your wifehood no comparisón;
Hide ye your beauties, Isolde and Elaine:
My lady com'th, that all this may distain.

Thy fairè body let it not appear,
Lavine; and thou, Lucrece of Romè town,
And Polixene, that boughten love so dear,
And Cleopatre, with all thy passión,
Hide ye your truth of love and your renown;
And thou, Thisbe, that hast for love such pain:
My lady com'th, that all this may distain.

Hero, Dido, Laodámia, all y-fere,
And Phyllis, hanging for thy Demophon,
And Cánacé, espièd by thy chere,
Hypsípylé, betraysèd with Jasón,
Make of your truthè neither boast ne soun;
Nor Hypermestre or Ariadne, ye twain:
My lady com'th, that all this may distain.

10 *Madam Eglantine*

THERE was also a nun, a Prioress,
That of her smiling was full simple and coy;
Her greatest oath was but by Saint Loy;
And she was clepèd Madam Eglantine.
Full well she sang the servicè divine,
Entunèd in her nose full seemély,
And French she spake full fair and fetisly,
After the school of Stratford-attè-Bow,
For French of Paris was to her unknow.

distain] outshine   espièd by thy chere] found out by thy looks

10 coy] demure   fetisly] elegantly

At meaté well y-taught was she withal;
She let no morsel from her lippés fall,
Ne wet her fingers in her saucé deep;
Well could she carry a morsel and well keep
That no droppé ne fell upon her breast.
In courtesy was set full much her lest.
Her over-lippé wipèd she so clean
That in her cup there was no farthing seen
Of greasé, when she drunken had her draught.
Full seemély after her meat she raught.
And sikerly she was of great desport,
And full pleasánt, and amiable of port,
And peynèd her to counterfeité cheer
Of court, and been estately of mannér
And to ben holden digne of reverence.
But, for to speaken of her consciénce,
She was so charitable and so pitóus
She wouldé weep, if that she saw a mouse
Caught in a trap, if it were dead or bled.
Of smallé houndés had she that she fed
With roasted flesh, or milk and wastel-bread.
But sore wept she if one of them were dead,
Or if men smote it with a yardé smart;
And all was consciénce and tender heart.
Full seemély her wimple pinchèd was;
Her nosé tretys, her eyen grey as glass,
Her mouth full small, and thereto soft and red;
But sikerly she had a fair forehéad;
It was almost a spanné broad, I trow;
For, hardily, she was not undergrow.
Full fetis was her cloak, as I was ware.
Of small corál about her arm she bore
A pair of beadés, gauded all with green,
And thereon hung a brooch of gold full sheen,
On which there was first writ a crownèd 'A',
And after *Amor vincit omnia.*

deep] deeply   keep] take care   lest] mind
peynèd her . . .] took pains to imitate the manners of the court
digne] worthy   wastel-bread] fine white bread   yardé] stick
smart] sharply   pinchèd] pleated   tretys] shapely
A pair . . . green] a rosary with larger beads of green

ANONYMOUS

11 *Quia Amore Langueo*

IN the vale of restless mind
I sought in mountain and in mead,
Trusting a true love for to find.
Upon an hill then took I heed;
A voice I heard—and near I yede—
In great dolóur complaining tho:
'See, dear soul, my sidès bleed,
Quia amore langueo.

Upon this mount I found a tree;
Under this tree a man sitting;
From head to foot wounded was he,
His hartè-blood I saw bleeding;
A seemly man to be a king
A gracious face to look unto.
I asked him how he had paining.
He said: '*Quia amore langueo.*

'I am true love that false was never:
My sister, man's soul, I lovèd her thus;
Because I would on no wise dissever,
I left my kingdom glorious;
I purveyed her a place full precious;
She flit; I followed; I loved her so
That I suffered these painès piteous,
Quia amore langueo.

'My fair love and my spousè bright,
I saved her fro beating and she hath me bet;
I clothed her in grace and heavenly light,
This bloody surcote she hath on me set.
For longing love I will not let;
Sweetè strokès be these, lo!
I have lovèd her ever as I het,
Quia amore langueo.

near I yede] I went nearer   tho] then
Quia amore langueo] I am sick with love (Canticles 2:5)   het] promised

'I crowned her with bliss, and she me with thorn;
I led her to chamber, and she me to die;
I brought her to worship, and she me to scorn;
I did her reverence, and she me villainy.
To love that loveth is no maistrý;
  Her hate made never my love her foe;
Ask then no mo questions why,
  Quia amore langueo.

'Look unto mine handès, man!
These gloves were given me when I her sought;
They be not white, but red and wan,
  Embroidered with blood, my spouse them bought;
They will not off, I leave them nought,
  I woo her with them wherever she go;
These hands full friendly for her fought,
  Quia amore langueo.

'Marvel not, man, though I sit still;
  My love hath shod me wonder strait;
She buckled my feet, as was her will,
  With sharpè nails—well thou mayst wait!
In my love was never deceit,
  For all my members I have opened her to;
My body I made her heartès bait,
  Quia amore langueo.

'In my side I have made her nest;
  Look in me how wide a wound is here!
This is her chamber, here shall she rest,
  That she and I may sleep in fere.
Here may she wash, if any filth were,
  Here is succour for all her woe;
Come if she will, she shall have cheer,
  Quia amore langueo.

To love . . . maistrý] To love one that loves is no hard task
wan] discoloured   wonder strait] wonderfully tight
          wait] see   in fere] together

'I will abide till she be ready,
I will her sue if she say nay;
If she be reckėless, I will be ready,
If she be dangerous, I will her pray.
If she do weep, then bid I nay;
    Mine arms be spread to clip her me to;
Cry onės: I come. Now, soul, assay!
    Quia amore langueo.

'I sit on an hill for to see far,
I look to the vale; my spouse I see:
Now runs she awayward, now comes she nearer,
Yet fro mine eye-sight she may not be.
Some wait their prey to make her flee;
    I run tofore to chastise her foe.
Recover, my soul, again to me,
    Quia amore langueo.

'My sweetė spouse, will we go play?
Apples be ripe in my gardéne
I shall clothe thee,in new array,
    Thy meat shall be milk, honey, and wine.
Now, dear soul, let us go dine,
    Thy sustenance is in my scrippė, lo!
Tarry not now, fair spousė mine,
    Quia amore langueo.

'If thou be foul, I shall make thee clean;
If thou be sick, I shall thee heal,
If thou ought mourn, I shall bemene.
    Spouse, why wilt thou nought with me deal?
Thou foundest never love so leal;
    What wilt thou, soul, that I shall do?
I may of unkindness thee appeal,
    Quia amore langueo.

dangerous] haughty   bid I nay] I shall beg her not to
wait] lie in wait for   Recover] return   bemene] condole
                thee appeal] accuse thee

ANONYMOUS

'What shall I do now with my spouse?
Abide I will her gentleness.
Would she look onès out of her house
Of fleshly affections and uncleanness,
Her bed is made, her bolster is bliss,
Her chamber is chosen, such are no mo.
Look out at the windows of kindness,
Quia amore langueo.

'Long and love thou never so high,
Yet is my love more than thine may be;
Thou gladdest, thou weepest, I sit thee by;
Yet might thou, spouse, look onès at me!
Spouse, should I always feedè thee
With childès meat? Nay, love, not so!
I prove thy love with adversity,
Quia amore langueo.

'My spouse is in chamber, hold your peace;
Make no noise, but let her sleep.
My babe shall suffer no disease,
I may not hear my dear child weep;
For with my pap I shall her keep.
No wonder though I tend her to:
This hole in my side had never been so deep,
But *quia amore langueo.*

'Wax not weary, mine own dear wife:
What meed is aye to live in comfórt?
For in tribulation I run more rife
Oftentimes than in disport;
In wealth, in woe, ever I support,
Then, dear soul, go never me fro!
Thy meed is markèd, when thou art mort,
Quia amore langueo.

prove] test   run more rife] run to help more quickly
markèd] assigned   mort] dead

12

12
I Sing of a Maiden

I SING of a maiden
That is makéless:
King of all kingés
To her son she ches.

He came all so stillé
There his mother was
As dew in Aprílle
That falleth on the grass.

He came all so stillé
To his mother's bower
As dew in Aprílle
That falleth on the flower.

He came all so stillé
There his mother lay
As dew in Aprílle
That falleth on the spray.

Mother and maiden
Was never none but she;
Well may such a lady
Goddés mother be.

13
Adam lay y-bounden

ADAM lay y-bounden
Bounden in a bond;
Four thousand winter
Thought he not too long;
And all was for an apple
An apple that he took,
As clerkés finden written
In theiré book.

makéless] matchless, without a mate   ches] chose
      all so stillé] as silently

13   clerkés] learned men

Ne had the apple taken been,
The apple taken been,
Ne haddè never our Lady
A been heaven's queen.
Blessed be the time
That apple taken was!
Therefore we may singen
'*Deo Gratias!*'

14

I Have a Gentle Cock

I HAVE a gentle cock
Croweth me day;
He doth me risen early
My matins for to say.

I have a gentle cock
Comen he is of great;
His comb is of red corál
His tail is of jet.

I have a gentle cock
Comen he is of kind;
His comb is of red corál
His tail is of inde.

His leggès been of azure
So gentle and so small;
His spurrès are of silver white
Into the wortèwale.

His eyen are of crystal
Locken all in amber;
And every night he percheth him
In my lady's chamber.

14 doth] makes   of great] of great family   of kind] of noble stock
        inde] indigo   wortèwale] root   Locken] set

15

Jankin

'KYRIĔ', so 'Kyriĕ',
  Jankin singeth merry,
With '*eléison*'.

As I went on Yulĕ day
  In our procession,
Knew I jolly Jankin
  By his merry tone—
  Kyrie eléison.

Jankin began the office
  On the Yulĕ day,
And yet me think'th it does me good
  So merry gan he say
  '*Kyrie eléison*'

Jankin read the pistle
  Full fair and full well,
And yet me think'th it does me good,
  As ever have I sel.
  Kyrie eléison.

Jankin at the *Sanctus*
  Crack'th a merry note,
And yet me think'th it does me good—
  I payĕd for his coat.
  Kyrie eléison.

Jankin cracketh notĕs
  An hundred on a knot
And yet he hack'th them smaller
  Than wortĕs to the pot.
  Kyrie eléison.

As . . . sel] as I hope always to be happy
Crack'th . . . note] divides the note into short ones

Jankin at the *Agnus*
Beareth the pax-bread;
He twinkèlèd but said nought,
And on my foot he tread.
Kyrie eléison.

Benedicamus Domino,
Christ from shame me shield!
Deo gratias thereto—
Alas I go with child!
Kyrie eléison.

CHARLES OF ORLEANS
?1394–1465

16   *A Lover's Confession*

MY ghostly father, I me confess,
First to God and then to you,
That at a window—wot ye how?
I stole a kiss of great sweetness,
Which done was out avisedness;
But it is done, not undone, now.
My ghostly father, I me confess,
First to God and then to you.
But I restore it shall doubtless
Again, if so be that I mow;
And that to God I make avow,
And else I ask forgivèness.
My ghostly father, I me confess,
First to God and then to you,
That at a window—wot ye how?
I stole a kiss of great sweetness.

16   out avisedness] without thought

ANONYMOUS

17   *Corpus Christi Carol*

Lully, lullay, lully, lullay,
The falcon hath borne my make away.

He bore him up, he bore him down;
He bore him into an orchard brown.

In that orchard there was an hall,
That was hanged with purple and pall.

And in that hall there was a bed;
It was hanged with gold so red.

And in that bed there lieth a knight,
His woundès bleeding day and night.

By that bed's side there kneeleth a may,
And she weepeth both night and day.

And by that bed's side there standeth a stone,
Corpus Christi written thereon.

18   *The Jolly Shepherd*

CAN I not sing but 'hoy'
When the jolly shepherd made so much joy?

The shepherd upon a hill he sat;
He had on him his tabard and his hat,
His tar-box, his pipe and his flagát;
His name was called Jolly, Jolly Wat,
    For he was a good herdsboy.
      With hoy!
    For in his pipe he made so much joy.

make] mate   *may*] maid
   18 *flagát*] flask

The shepherd upon a hill was laid;
His dog to his girdle was taid.
He had not slept but a little braid
But *'Gloria in excelsis'* was to him said.
  With hoy!
 For in his pipe he made so much joy.

The shepherd on a hill he stood;
Round about him his sheep they yood;
He put his hand under his hood;
He saw a star as red as blood.
  With hoy!
 For in his pipe he made so much joy.

'Now farewell Mall, and also Will;
For my love go ye all still
Until I come again you till;
And evermore, Will, ring well thy bell.'
  With hoy!
 For in his pipe he made so much joy.

'Now must I go there Christ was born;
Farewell, I come again to-morn.
Dog, keep well my sheep fro the corn,
And warn well Warrock when I blow my horn.'
  With hoy!
 For in his pipe he made so much joy.

The shepherd said anon-right:
'I will go see yon ferly sight,
Whereas the angel singeth on height,
And the star that shineth so bright.'
  With hoy!
 For in his pipe he made so much joy.

When Wat to Bethlehem come was
He sweat: he had gone faster than a pace.
He found Jesu in a simple place
Between an ox and an ass.
  With hoy!
 For in his pipe he made so much joy.

braid] moment   yood] went

'Jesu, I offer to thee here my pipe,
My skirt, my tar-box, and my scrip;
Home to my fellows now will I skip,
And also look unto my sheep.'
    With hoy!
  For in his pipe he made so much joy.

'Now farewell, mine own herdsman Wat.'
'Yea, for God, Lady, even so I hat.
Lull well Jesu in thy lap,
And farewell, Joseph, with thy round cap.'
    With hoy!
  For in his pipe he made so much joy.

'Now may I well both hop and sing
For I have been at Christès bearing.
Home to my fellows now will I fling.
Christ of heaven to his bliss us bring!'
    With hoy!
  For in his pipe he made so much joy.

19   *The Bridal Morn*

THE maidens came
    When I was in my mother's bower;
I had all that I would.
    The bailey beareth the bell away;
    The lily, the rose, the rose I lay.
The silver is white, red is the gold;
  The robes they lay in fold.
    The bailey beareth the bell away;
    The lily, the rose, the rose I lay.
And through the glass window shines the sun.
How should I love, and I so young?
    The bailey beareth the bell away;
    The lily, the rose, the rose I lay.

WILLIAM CORNISH

d. 1524

20

The Knight and the Lady

THE knight knocked at the castle gate;
The lady marvelled who was thereat.

To call the porter he would not blin;
The lady said he should not come in.

The portress was a lady bright;
Strangèness that lady hight.

She askèd him what was his name;
He said, 'Desire, your man, Madame.'

She said, 'Desire, what do ye here?'
He said, 'Madame, as your prisoner.'

He was counselled to brief a bill,
And show my lady his own will.

'Kindness', said she, 'would it bear,'
'And Pity', said she, 'would be there.'

Thus how they did we cannot say;
We left them there and went our way.

ANONYMOUS

21

Western Wind

WESTERN wind, when will thou blow,
The small rain down can rain?
Christ, if my love were in my arms
And I in my bed again!

20 blin] cease   brief a bill] draw up a petition

WILLIAM DUNBAR

?1460–1520

22

Timor Mortis Conturbat Me

I THAT in heill wes and gladnes
Am trublit now with gret seiknes
And feblit with infirmite:
Timor mortis conturbat me.

Our plesance here is all vane glory,
This fals warld is bot transitory,
The flesche is brukle, the Fend is sle:
Timor mortis conturbat me.

The stait of man dois change and vary,
Now sound, now seik, now blith, now sary,
Now dansand mery, now like to dee:
Timor mortis conturbat me.

No stait in erd heir standis sickir;
As with the wynd wavis the wickir
Wavis this warldis vanite:
Timor mortis conturbat me.

On to the ded gois all estatis,
Princis, prelotis, and potestatis,
Baith riche and pur of all degre:
Timor mortis conturbat me.

He takis the knychtis in to feild,
Anarmit under helme and scheild;
Victour he is at all mellie:
Timor mortis conturbat me.

Timor mortis conturbat me] The fear of Death troubles me (Office of the Dead)
brukle] feeble   sle] cunning   sickir] sure   wickir] willow

That strang unmercifull tyrand
Takis, on the moderis breist sowkand,
The bab full of benignite:
Timor mortis conturbat me.

He takis the campion in the stour,
The capitane closit in the tour,
The lady in bour full of bewte:
Timor mortis conturbat me.

He sparis no lord for his piscence,
Na clerk for his intelligence,
His awfull strak may no man fle:
Timor mortis conturbat me. . . .

I se that makaris amang the laif
Playis heir ther pageant, syne gois to graif;
Sparit is nocht ther faculte:
Timor mortis conturbat me.

He hes done petuously devour
The noble Chaucer of makaris flour,
The Monk of Bury, and Gower, all thre:
Timor mortis conturbat me.

*

Sen he hes all my brether tane
He will nocht lat me lif alane;
On forse I man his nyxt prey be:
Timor mortis conturbat me.

Sen for the deid remeid is none
Best is that we for deid dispone
Eftir our deid that live may we:
Timor mortis conturbat me.

campion] champion   piscence] puissance   stour] fight
     makaris] poets   the laif] the rest

23 *The Lord is Risen*

DONE is a battell on the dragon blak,
Our campioun Chryst confountet hes his force;
The yettis of hell ar brokin with a crak,
The signe triumphall rasit is of the croce,
The divillis trymmillis with hiddous voce,
The saulis ar borrowit and to the blis can go,
Chryst with his blud our ransonis dois indoce:
Surrexit dominus de sepulchro.

Dungin is the deidly dragon Lucifer,
The crewall serpent with the mortall stang,
The auld kene tegir with his teith on char
Quhilk in a wait hes lyne for us so lang,
Thinking to grip us in his clowis strang:
The mercifull lord wald nocht that it wer so,
He maid him for to felye of that fang:
Surrexit dominus de sepulchro.

He for our saik that sufferit to be slane
And lyk a lamb in sacrifice wes dicht,
Is lyk a lyone rissin up agane,
And as a gyane raxit him on hicht:
Sprungin is Aurora radius and bricht,
On loft is gone the glorius Appollo,
The blisfull day depairtit fro the nycht:
Surrexit dominus de sepulchro.

The grit victour agane is rissin on hicht
That for our querrell to the deth wes woundit;
The sone that wox all paill now schynis bricht,
And, dirknes clerit, our fayth is now refoundit:
The knell of mercy fra the hevin is soundit,
The Cristin ar deliverit of thair wo,
The Jowis and thair errour ar confoundit:
Surrexit dominus de sepulchro.

yettis] gates   borrowit] ransomed   indoce] endorse
Dungin] struck down   on char] ajar, open
to felye of that fang] fail of his booty   dicht] made ready
raxit him] raised himself up

The fo is chasit, the battell is done ceis,
The presone brokin, the jevellouris fleit and flemit,
The weir is gon, confermit is the peis,
The fetteris lowsit and the dungeoun temit,
The ransoun maid, the presoneris redemit,
The feild is win, ourcummin is the fo,
Dispulit of the tresur that he yemit:
Surrexit dominus de sepulchro.

JOHN SKELTON

?1460–1529

24   *Philip Sparrow*

PLA ce bo!
Who is there, who?
Di le xi!
Dame Margery,
Fa, re, my, my.
Wherefore and why, why?
For the soul of Philip Sparrow
That was late slain at Carrow,
Among the Nunnés Black.
For that sweet soulés sake,
And for all sparrows' souls,
Set in our bead-rolls,
Pater noster qui,
With an *Ave Mari,*
And with the corner of a Creed,
The more shall be your meed.

When I remember again
How my Philip was slain,
Never half the pain
Was between you twain,
Pyramus and Thisbe,
As then befell to me.

24 jevellouris . . .] gaolers terrified and put to flight
     temit] emptied   yemit] kept

24

I wept and I wailed,
The tearès down hailed,
But nothing it availed
To call Philip again
Whom Gib, our cat, hath slain.

Gib, I say, our cat,
Worried her on that
Which I lovèd best.
It cannot be exprest
My sorrowful heaviness,
But all without redress!
For within that stound,
Half slumbering, in a sound
I fell down to the ground.

Unneth I cast mine eyes
Toward the cloudy skies.
But when I did behold
My sparrow dead and cold,
No creature but that would
Have ruèd upon me,
To behold and see
What heaviness did me pang:
Wherewith my hands I wrang,
That my sinews cracked,
As though I had been racked,
So pained and so strained
That no life wellnigh remained.

I sighed and I sobbed,
For that I was robbed
Of my sparrow's life.
O maiden, widow, and wife,
Of what estate ye be,
Of high or low degree,
Great sorrow then ye might see,
And learn to weep at me!
Such pains did me fret
That mine heart did beat,

stound] moment   sound] swoon   Unneth] hardly

My visage pale and dead,
Wan, and blue as lead:
The pangs of hateful death
Wellnigh had stopped my breath.

*

Like Andromach, Hector's wife,
Was weary of her life,
When she had lost her joy,
Noble Hector of Troy;
In like manner alsó
Increaseth my deadly woe,
For my sparrow is go.

It was so pretty a fool,
It would sit on a stool,
And learned after my school
For to keep his cut,
With 'Philip, keep your cut!'

It had a velvet cap,
And would sit upon my lap
And seek after small worms,
And sometime white bread-crumbs;
And many times and oft
Between my breastès soft
It would lie and rest;
It was proper and prest.

Sometime he would gasp
When he saw a wasp;
A fly or a gnat,
He would fly at that;
And prettily he would pant
When he saw an ant.
Lord, how he would pry
After the butterfly!
Lord, how he would hop
After the gressop!

go] gone   keep his cut] behave himself   prest] alert
                   gressop] grasshopper

And when I said, 'Phip, Phip!'
Then he would leap and skip,
And take me by the lip.
Alas, it will me slo
That Philip is gone me fro!

Si in i qui ta tes
Alas, I was evil at ease!
De pro fun dis cla ma vi,
When I saw my sparrow die!

*

The Requiem Mass

Lauda, anima mea, Dominum!
To weep with me look that ye come
All manner of birdės in your kind;
See none be left behind
To mourning look that ye fall
With dolorous songs funeral,
Some to sing, and some to say,
Some to weep, and some to pray,
Every bird in his lay.
The goldfinch, the wagtail;
The jangling jay to rail,
The fleckèd pie to chatter
Of this dolorous matter;
And robin redbreast,
He shall be the priest
The requiem mass to sing,
Softly warbeling,
With help of the red-sparrow,
And the chattering swallow,
This hearse for to hallow;
The lark with his long toe;
The spink, and the martinet alsó;
The shoveller with his broad beak;
The dotterel, that foolish peke,
And also the mad coot,
With a bald face to toot;

slo] slay   red-sparrow] sedge-warbler
  spink] chaffinch   shoveller] spoonbill

27

JOHN SKELTON

The fieldfare and the snite;
The crow and the kite;
The raven, called Rolfè,
His plain-song to sol-fa;
The partridge, the quail;
The plover with us to wail;
The woodhack, that singeth 'chur'
Hoarsely, as he had the mur;
The lusty chanting nightingale;
The popinjay to tell her tale,
That toteth oft in a glass,
Shall read the Gospel at mass;
The mavis with her whistle
Shall read there the Pistle.
But with a large and a long
To keep just plain-song,
Our chanters shall be the cuckoo,
The culver, the stockdowe,
With 'peewit' the lapwing,
The Versicles shall sing.

The bittern with his bumpè,
The crane with his trumpè,
The swan of Maeander,
The goose and the gander,
The duck and the drake,
Shall watch at this wake;
The peacock so proud,
Because his voice is loud,
And hath a glorious tail,
He shall sing the Grail;
The owl, that is so foul,
Must help us to howl;
The heron so gaunt,
And the cormorant,
With the pheasant,
And the gaggling gant,
And the churlish chough;
The knot and the ruff;

snite] snipe   woodhack] woodpecker   mur] catarrh
popinjay] parrot   toteth] peeps   Grail] Gradual

28

The barnacle, the buzzard,
With the wild mallard;
The divendop to sleep;
The water-hen to weep;
The puffin and the teal
Money they shall deal
To poorè folk at large,
That shall be their charge;
The seamew and the titmouse;
The woodcock with the longè nose;
The throstle with her warbling;
The starling with her brabling;
The rook, with the osprey
That putteth fishes to a fray;
And the dainty curlew,
With the turtle most true.

At this *Placebo*
We may not well forgo
The countering of the coe;
The stork alsó,
That maketh his nest
In chimneys to rest;
Within those walls
No broken galls
May there abide
Of cuckoldry side,
Or else philosophy
Maketh a great lie.

The ostrich, that will eat
An horseshoe so great,
In the stead of meat,
Such fervent heat
His stomach doth fret;
He cannot well fly,
Nor sing tunably,
Yet at a brayd
He hath well assayed
To sol-fa above E-la.
Fa, lorell, *fa, fa!*

countering] improvising   coe] jackdaw   at a brayd] at a push

Ne quando
Male cantando,
The best that we can,
To make him our bell-man,
And let him ring the bells.
He can do nothing else.

Chanticleer, our cock,
Must tell what is of the clock
By the astrology
That he hath naturally
Conceivèd and caught,
And was never taught
By Albumazer
The astronomer,
Nor by Ptolomy
Prince of astronomy,
Nor yet by Haly;
And yet he croweth daily
And nightly the tides
That no man abides,
With Partlot his hen,
Whom now and then
He plucketh by the head
When he doth her tread.

The bird of Araby,
That potentially
May never die,
And yet there is none
But one alone;
A phoenix it is
This hearse that must bless
With aromatic gums
That cost great sums,
The way of thurification
To make a fumigation,
Sweet of reflare,
And redolent of air,
This corse for to cense
With great reverence,

reflare] perfume

As Patriarch or Pope
In a black cope.
While he censeth the hearse,
He shall sing the verse,
Liber a me,
In *de, la, sol, re,*
Softly B molle
For my sparrow's soul.
Pliny sheweth all
In his *Story Natural*
What he doth find
Of this phoenix kind;
Of whose incineration
There riseth a new creation
Of the same fashion
Without alteration,
Saving that old age
Is turned into corage
Of fresh youth again;
This matter true and plain,
Plain matter indeed,
Who so list to read.

But for the eagle doth fly
Highest in the sky,
He shall be the sub-dean,
The choir to demean,
As provost principal,
To teach them their Ordinal;
Also the noble falcon,
With the ger-falcon,
The tarsel gentil,
They shall mourn soft and still
In their amice of gray;
The saker with them shall say
Dirige for Philip's soul;
The goshawk shall have a roll
The choristers to control;
The lanners and the merlins
Shall stand in their mourning-gowns;

demean] conduct   saker] hawk   lanners] falcons

The hobby and the musket
The censers and the cross shall fet;
The kestrel in all this wark
Shall be holy-water clerk.

And now the dark cloudy night
Chaseth away Phoebus bright,
Taking his course toward the west,
God send my sparrow's soul good rest!
Requiem aeternam dona eis, Domine! . . .

from A Garland of Laurel

(i)

25   *To Mistress Margery Wentworth*

WITH marjoram gentle,
    The flower of goodlihead,
Embroiderèd the mantle
    Is of your maidenhead.
Plainly, I cannot glose;
    Ye be, as I devine,
The pretty primrose,
    The goodly columbine.
With marjoram gentle,
    The flower of goodlihead,
Embroiderèd the mantle
    Is of your maidenhead.
Benign, courteous, and meek,
    With wordès well devised;
In you, who list to seek,
    Be virtues well comprised.
With marjoram gentle,
    The flower of goodlihead,
Embroiderèd the mantle
    Is of your maidenhead.

hobby] small falcon   musket] sparrow-hawk

25   glose] flatter

(ii)

26   *To Mistress Isabel Pennell*

BY Saint Mary, my lady,
Your mammy and your daddy
Brought forth a goodly baby!

My maiden Isabel,
Reflaring rosabel.
The fragrant camomel;
  The ruddy rosary,
The sovereign rosemary,
The pretty strawberry;
  The columbine, the nept,
The jelofer well set,
The proper violet:
  Ennewèd your colour
Is like the daisy flower
After the April shower;
  Star of the morrow gray,
The blossom on the spray,
The freshest flower of May;
  Maidenly demure,
Of womanhood the lure;
Wherefore, I make you sure,
  It were an heavenly health,
It were an endless wealth,
A life for God himself,
  To hear this nightingale
Among the birdès small
Warbling in the vale,
    'Dug, dug,
    Jug, jug,
      Good year and good luck!'
      With 'Chuck, chuck, chuck, chuck!'

Reflaring rosabel] redolent rosebud		rosary] rose-bush
nept] mint	jelofer] gillyflower	Ennewèd] freshened

33

(iii)

27

To Mistress Margaret Hussey

MERRY Margaret,
   As midsummer flower,
Gentle as falcon
Or hawk of the tower:
With solace and gladness,
Much mirth and no madness,
All good and no badness;
   So joyously,
   So maidenly,
   So womanly
   Her demeaning
   In everything,
   Far, far passing
   That I can indite,
   Or suffice to write
Of Merry Margaret
   As midsummer flower,
Gentle as falcon
Or hawk of the tower.
   As patient and as still
And as full of good will
As fair Isaphill,
Coriander,
Sweet pomander,
Good Cassander,
Steadfast of thought,
Well made, well wrought,
Far may be sought
Ere that ye can find
So courteous, so kind,
As Merry Margaret,
   This midsummer flower,
Gentle as falcon
Or hawk of the tower.

Isaphill] Hypsipyle   Cassander] Cassandra

SIR THOMAS WYATT

c. 1503–1542

28 *Remembrance*

THEY flee from me, that sometime did me seek
With naked foot, stalking in my chamber.
I have seen them gentle, tame, and meek,
   That now are wild, and do not remember
   That sometime they put themselves in danger
      To take bread at my hand; and now they range
      Busily seeking with a continual change.

Thanked be fortune it hath been otherwise
   Twenty times better; but once, in special,
In thin array, after a pleasant guise,
   When her loose gown from her shoulders did fall,
   And she me caught in her arms long and small,
      Therewith all sweetly did me kiss
      And softly said, 'Dear heart, how like you this?'

It was no dream; I lay broad waking:
   But all is turned, thorough my gentleness,
Into a strange fashion of forsaking;
   And I have leave to go of her goodness,
   And she also to use newfangleness.
      But since that I so kindly am served,
      I would fain know what she hath deserved.

29 *To His Lute*

MY lute, awake! perform the last
Labour that thou and I shall waste,
   And end that I have now begun;
For when this song is sung and past,
   My lute, be still, for I have done.

As to be heard where ear is none,
As lead to grave in marble stone,
　My song may pierce her heart as soon.
Should we then sigh, or sing, or moan?
　No, no, my lute, for I have done.

The rocks do not so cruelly
Repulse the waves continually,
　As she my suit and affection;
So that I am past remedy,
　Whereby my lute and I have done.

Proud of the spoil that thou hast got
Of simple hearts thorough love's shot,
　By whom, unkind, thou hast them won,
Think not he hath his bow forgot,
　Although my lute and I have done.

Vengeance shall fall on thy disdain,
That mak'st but game on earnest pain;
　Think not alone under the sun
Unquit to cause thy lovers plain,
　Although my lute and I have done.

Perchance thee lie withered and old,
The winter nights that are so cold,
　Plaining in vain unto the moon;
Thy wishes then dare not be told.
　Care then who list, for I have done.

And then may chance thee to repent
The time that thou hast lost and spent
　To cause thy lovers sigh and swoon;
Then shalt thou know beauty but lent,
　And wish and want as I have done.

Now cease, my lute! this is the last
Labour that thou and I shall waste,
　And ended is that we begun;
Now is this song both sung and past.
　My lute, be still, for I have done.

30   *An Appeal*

AND wilt thou leave me thus?
    Say nay, say nay, for shame!
    To save thee from the blame
    Of all my grief and grame.
And wilt thou leave me thus?
    Say nay! say nay!

And wilt thou leave me thus,
    That hath loved thee so long
    In wealth and woe among?
    And is thy heart so strong
As for to leave me thus?
    Say nay! say nay!

And wilt thou leave me thus,
    That hath given thee my heart,
    Never for to depart
    Neither for pain nor smart;
And wilt thou leave me thus?
    Say nay! say nay!

And wilt thou leave me thus,
    And have no more pity
    Of him that loveth thee?
    Hélas! thy cruelty!
And wilt thou leave me thus?
    Say nay! say nay!

31   *Steadfastness*

FORGET not yet the tried intent
Of such a truth as I have meant;
My great travail so gladly spent
            Forget not yet!

        30 grame] vexation

37

Forget not yet when first began
The weary life ye know, since whan
The suit, the service, none tell can;
 Forget not yet!

Forget not yet the great assays,
The cruel wrong, the scornful ways,
The painful patience in denays,
 Forget not yet!

Forget not yet, forget not this,
How long ago hath been, and is,
The mind that never meant amiss
 Forget not yet!

Forget not then thine own approved,
The which so long hath thee so loved,
Whose steadfast faith yet never moved;
 Forget not this!

32   *Farewell*

 WHAT should I say,
  Since faith is dead,
 And truth away
  From you is fled?
 Should I be led
  With doubleness?
  Nay, nay, mistress!

 I promised you,
  And you promised me,
 To be as true,
  As I would be.
 But since I see
  Your double heart,
  Farewell my part!

      31   denays] denials

Though for to take
It is not my mind,
But to forsake
One so unkind,
And as I find
So will I trust,
Farewell, unjust!

Can ye say nay,
But that you said
That I alway
Should be obeyed?
And thus betrayed,
Or that I wist,
Farewell, unkissed!

33   *In Eternum*

In eternum I was once determed
For to have loved and my mind affirmed,
That with my heart it should be confirmed
        In eternum.

Forthwith I found the thing that I might like,
And sought with love to warm her heart alike,
For, as methought, I should not see the like
        In eternum.

To trace this dance I put myself in press;
Vain hope did lead and bade I should not cease
To serve, to suffer, and still to hold my peace
        In eternum.

With this first rule I furthered me apace,
That, as methought, my troth had taken place
With full assurance to stand in her grace
        In eternum.

It was not long ere I by proof had found
That feeble building is on feeble ground;
For in her heart this word did never sound,
        In eternum.

In eternum then from my heart I kest
That I had first determined for the best;
Now in the place another thought doth rest,
    In eternum.

HENRY HOWARD, EARL OF SURREY

?1517–1547

34   *In Windsor Castle*

So cruel prison how could betide, alas,
As proud Windsor, where I in lust and joy
With a king's son my childish years did pass
In greater feast than Priam's sons of Troy?
Where each sweet place returns a taste full sour;
The large green courts where we were wont to hove
With eyes cast up unto the maidens' tower,
And easy sighs, such as folk draw in love;
The stately sales, the ladies bright of hue,
The dances short, long tales of great delight,
With words and looks that tigers could but rue,
Where each of us did plead the other's right;
The palm-play where, despoilèd for the game,
With dazèd eyes oft we by gleams of love
Have missed the ball and got sight of our dame,
To bait her eyes, which kept the leads above;
The gravelled ground, with sleeves tied on the helm,
On foaming horse, with swords and friendly hearts,
With cheer, as though the one should overwhelm,
Where we have fought and chasèd oft with darts;
With silver drops the meads yet spread for ruth,
In active games of nimbleness and strength,
Where we did strain, trailèd by swarms of youth,
Our tender limbs that yet shot up in length;
The secret groves which oft we made resound
Of pleasant plaint and of our ladies' praise,
Recording soft what grace each one had found,
What hope of speed, what dread of long delays;

34   sales] chambers

The wild forest, the clothèd holts with green,
With reins avaled, and swift ybreathèd horse,
With cry of hounds and merry blasts between,
Where we did chase the fearful hart a force;
The void walls eke that harboured us each night,
Wherewith, alas! revive within my breast
The sweet accord, such sleeps as yet delight,
The pleasant dreams, the quiet bed of rest,
The secret thoughts imparted with such trust,
The wanton talk, the divers change of play,
The friendship sworn, each promise kept so just,
Wherewith we passed the winter nights away.
And with this thought the blood forsakes my face,
The tears berain my cheeks of deadly hue,
The which as soon as sobbing sighs, alas!
Upsuppèd have, thus I my plaint renew:
'O place of bliss, renewer of my woes,
Give me account where is my noble fere,
Whom in thy walls thou didst each night enclose,
To other lief, but unto me most dear.'
Echo, alas! that doth my sorrow rue,
Returns thereto a hollow sound of plaint.
Thus I alone, where all my freedom grew,
In prison pine with bondage and restraint;
And with remembrance of the greater grief
To banish the less, I find my chief relief.

35   *Spring*

THE sootè season, that bud and bloom forth brings,
    With green hath clad the hill and eke the vale.
The nightingale with feathers new she sings;
    The turtle to her make hath told her tale.
Summer is come, for every spray now springs.
    The hart hath hung his old head on the pale;
The buck in brake his winter coat he flings;
    The fishes float with new repairèd scale;

avaled] slackened   fere] companion   lief] beloved
        35   make] mate

41

The adder all her slough away she slings;
  The swift swallow pursueth the flies small;
The busy bee her honey now she mings;
  Winter is worn that was the flowers' bale.
And thus I see among these pleasant things
Each care decays; and yet my sorrow springs.

36   *Consolation*

  WHEN raging love with extreme pain
    Most cruelly distrains my heart,
  When that my tears, as floods of rain,
    Bear witness of my woeful smart;
      When sighs have wasted so my breath
      That I lie at the point of death,

  I call to mind the navy great
    That the Greeks brought to Troyė town,
  And how the boistous winds did beat
    Their ships, and rent their sails adown;
      Till Agamemnon's daughter's blood
      Appeased the gods that them withstood.

  And how that in those ten years' war
    Full many a bloody deed was done,
  And many a lord that came full far
    There caught his bane, alas! too soon;
      And many a good knight overrun,
      Before the Greeks had Helen won.

  Then think I thus: sith such repair,
    So long time war of valiant men,
  Was all to win a lady fair,
    Shall I not learn to suffer then,
      And think my life well spent to be,
      Serving a worthier wight than she?

35 mings] remembers

Therefore I never will repent,
But pains contented still endure;
For like as when, rough winter spent,
The pleasant spring straight draweth in ure,
So, after raging storms of care,
Joyful at length may be my fare.

37   *The Seafarer*

O HAPPY dames, that may embrace
The fruit of your delight,
Help to bewail the woeful case
And eke the heavy plight
Of me, that wonted to rejoice
The fortune of my pleasant choice;
Good ladies, help to fill my mourning voice.

In ship, freight with rememberance
Of thoughts and pleasures past,
He sails that hath in governance
My life while it will last;
With scalding sighs, for lack of gale,
Furthering his hope, that is his sail,
Toward me, the sweet port of his avail.

Alas! how oft in dreams I see
Those eyes that were my food;
Which sometime so delighted me,
That yet they do me good;
Wherewith I wake with his return,
Whose absent flame did make me burn:
But when I find the lack, Lord, how I mourn!

When other lovers in arms across
Rejoice their chief delight,
Drownèd in tears, to mourn my loss
I stand the bitter night
In my window, where I may see
Before the winds how the clouds flee.
Lo! what a mariner love hath made me!

37   avail] disembarking

And in green waves when the salt flood
   Doth rise by rage of wind,
A thousand fancies in that mood
   Assail my restless mind.
Alas! now drencheth my sweet foe,
That with the spoil of my heart did go,
And left me; but, alas! why did he so?

And when the seas wax calm again
   To chase fro me annoy,
My doubtful hope doth cause me plain;
   So dread cuts off my joy.
Thus is my wealth mingled with woe,
And of each thought a doubt doth grow;
'Now he comes! Will he come? Alas, no, no!'

38   *The Happy Life*

MARTIAL, the things for to attain
The happy life be these, I find:
The riches left, not got with pain;
The fruitful ground, the quiet mind;
The equal friend; no grudge nor strife;
No charge of rule nor governance;
Without disease the healthful life;
The household of continuance;
The mean diet, no delicate fare;
Wisdom joined with simplicity;
The night dischargèd of all care
Where wine may bear no sovereignty;
The chaste wife wise, without debate;
Such sleeps as may beguile the night;
Contented with thine own estate;
Neither wish death, nor fear his might.

ROBERT WEVER

c. 1550

39 *In Youth is Pleasure*

IN a herber green, asleep where I lay,
The birds sang sweet in the mids of the day;
I dreamèd fast of mirth and play.
In youth is pleasure, in youth is pleasure.

Methought I walked still to and fro,
And from her company could not go;
But when I waked it was not so.
In youth is pleasure, in youth is pleasure.

Therefore my heart is surely pight
Of her alone to have a sight,
Which is my joy and heart's delight.
In youth is pleasure, in youth is pleasure.

THOMAS SACKVILLE, EARL OF DORSET

1536–1608

40 *The Shield of War*

LASTLY, stood War, in glittering arms yclad,
With visage grim, stern looks, and blackly hued;
In his right hand a naked sword he had,
That to the hilts was all with blood imbrued;
And in his left, that kings and kingdoms rued,
Famine and fire he held, and therewithal
He razèd towns and threw down towers and all.

39   herber] arbour   pight] fixed

45

Cities he sacked and realms, that whilom flowered
In honour, glory, and rule above the best,
He overwhelmed and all their fame devoured,
Consumed, destroyed, wasted, and never ceased,
Till he their wealth, their name, and all oppressed;
His face forhewed with wounds, and by his side
There hung his targe, with gashes deep and wide.

In midst of which, depainted there, we found
Deadly Debate, all full of snaky hair,
That with a bloody fillet was ybound,
Out-breathing nought but discord everywhere.
And round about were portrayed, here and there,
The hugy hosts, Darius and his power,
His kings, princes, his peers, and all his flower:

Whom great Macedo vanquished there in fight
With deep slaughter, despoiling all his pride,
Pierced through his realms and daunted all his might.
Duke Hannibal beheld I there beside,
In Canna's field victor how he did ride,
And woeful Romans that in vain withstood,
And consul Paulus covered all in blood.

Yet saw I more: the fight at Thrasimene,
And Trebery field, and eke when Hannibal
And worthy Scipio last in arms were seen
Before Carthago gate, to try for all
The world's empire, to whom it should befall;
There saw I Pompey and Caesar clad in arms,
Their hosts allied and all their civil harms:

With conquerors' hands, forbathed in their own blood,
And Caesar weeping over Pompey's head.
Yet saw I Sulla and Marius where they stood,
Their great cruelty and the deep bloodshed
Of friends; Cyrus I saw and his host dead,
And how the queen with great despite hath flung
His head in blood of them she overcome.

Xerxes, the Persian king, yet saw I there
  With his huge host that drank the rivers dry,
Dismounted hills, and made the vales uprear,
  His host and all yet saw I plain, perdy!
  Thebes I saw, all razed how it did lie
    In heaps of stones, and Tyrus put to spoil,
    With walls and towers flat evened with the soil.

But Troy, alas! methought, above them all,
  It made mine eyes in very tears consume,
When I beheld the woeful weird befall,
  That by the wrathful will of gods was come;
  And Jove's unmovèd sentence and foredoom
    On Priam king and on his town so bent,
    I could not lin, but I must there lament.

And that the more, sith destiny was so stern
  As, force perforce, there might no force avail,
But she must fall, and by her fall we learn
  That cities, towers, wealth, world, and all shall quail.
  No manhood, might, nor nothing mought prevail;
    All were there prest full many a prince and peer,
    And many a knight that sold his death full dear:

Not worthy Hector, worthiest of them all,
  Her hope, her joy; his force is now for nought.
O Troy, Troy, Troy, there is no boot but bale;
  The hugy horse within thy walls is brought;
  Thy turrets fall, thy knights, that whilom fought
    In arms amid the field, are slain in bed,
    Thy gods defiled and all thy honour dead.

The flames upspring and cruelly they creep
  From wall to roof till all to cinders waste;
Some fire the houses where the wretches sleep;
  Some rush in here, some run in there as fast;
  In every where or sword or fire they taste;
    The walls are torn, the towers whirled to the ground;
    There is no mischief but may there be found.

lin] cease   prest] ready

47

Cassandra yet there saw I how they haled
From Pallas' house, with spercled tress undone,
Her wrists fast bound, and with Greeks' rout empaled;
And Priam eke, in vain how did he run
To arms, whom Pyrrhus with despite hath done
To cruel death, and bathed him in the baign
Of his son's blood, before the altar slain.

But how can I describe the doleful sight
That in the shield so livelike fair did shine?
Sith in this world I think was never wight
Could have set forth the half, not half so fine.
I can no more but tell how there is seen
Fair Ilium fall in burning red gledes down,
And from the soil great Troy, Neptunus' town.

GEORGE GASCOIGNE

1542–1577

41   *A Farewell*

'AND if I did, what then?
    Are you aggrieved therefore?
The sea hath fish for every man,
    And what would you have more?'

Thus did my mistress once
    Amaze my mind with doubt;
And popped a question for the nonce,
    To beat my brains about.

Whereto I thus replied:
    'Each fisherman can wish,
That all the seas at every tide
    Were his alone to fish.

---

40 spercled] flowing   baign] bath   gledes] embers

'And so did I, in vain,
  But since it may not be,
Let such fish there as find the gain,
  And leave the loss for me.

'And with such luck and loss
  I will content myself,
Till tides of turning time may toss
  Such fishers on the shelf.

'And when they stick on sands,
  That every man may see,
Then will I laugh and clap my hands,
  As they do now at me.'

SIR EDWARD DYER

1543-1607

42   *My Mind to Me a Kingdom Is*

MY mind to me a kingdom is
  Such perfect joy therein I find,
That it excels all other bliss
That world affords or grows by kind.
    Though much I want which most would have,
    Yet still my mind forbids to crave.

No princely pomp, no wealthy store,
No force to win the victory,
No wily wit to salve a sore,
No shape to feed a loving eye;
    To none of these I yield as thrall,
    For why? my mind doth serve for all.

I see how plenty suffers oft,
And hasty climbers soon do fall;
I see that those which are aloft
Mishap doth threaten most of all;
    They get with toil, they keep with fear;
    Such cares my mind could never bear.

Content I live, this is my stay,
I seek no more than may suffice,
I press to bear no haughty sway;
Look, what I lack my mind supplies.
   Lo, thus I triumph like a king,
   Content with that my mind doth bring.

Some have too much, yet still do crave,
I little have, and seek no more:
They are but poor, though much they have,
And I am rich with little store:
   They poor, I rich; they beg, I give;
   They lack, I leave; they pine, I live.

I laugh not at another's loss,
I grudge not at another's gain;
No worldly waves my mind can toss,
My state at one doth still remain.
   I fear no foe, I fawn no friend;
   I loathe not life, nor dread no end.

Some weigh their pleasure by their lust,
Their wisdom by their rage of will;
Their treasure is their only trust,
A cloaked craft their store of skill:
   But all the pleasure that I find
   Is to maintain a quiet mind.

My wealth is health and perfect ease,
My conscience clear my chief defence;
I neither seek by bribes to please,
Nor by desert to breed offence.
   Thus do I live, thus will I die;
   Would all did so, as well as I.

43   *A Silent Love*

THE lowest trees have tops, the ant her gall,
The fly her spleen, the little spark his heat;
The slender hairs cast shadows, though but small,
And bees have stings, although they be not great;
   Seas have their source, and so have shallow springs;
   And love is love, in beggars and in kings.

Where waters smoothest run, there deepest are the fords,
The dial stirs, yet none perceives it move;
The firmest faith is found in fewest words,
The turtles do not sing, and yet they love;
    True hearts have ears and eyes, no tongues to speak;
    They hear and see, and sigh, and then they break.

SIR PHILIP SIDNEY

1554–1586

44   *Ye goat-herd Gods that love the
grassy mountains*

Strephon. Ye goat-herd Gods that love the grassy mountains,
    Ye Nymphs which haunt the springs in pleasant valleys,
    Ye Satyrs joyed with free and quiet forests,
    Vouchsafe your silent ears to plaining music,
    Which to my woes gives still an early morning,
    And draws the dolour on till weary evening.

Klaius. O Mercury, foregoer to the evening,
    O heavenly huntress of the savage mountains,
    O lovely star, entitled of the morning,
    While that my voice doth fill these woeful valleys,
    Vouchsafe your silent ears to plaining music,
    Which oft hath Echo tired in secret forests.

Strephon. I that was once free burgess of the forests,
    Where shade from sun and sport I sought in evening,
    I that was once esteemed for pleasant music,
    Am banished now among the monstrous mountains
    Of huge despair, and foul affliction's valleys,
    Am grown a shriek-owl to myself each morning.

Klaius. I that was once delighted every morning,
    Hunting the wild inhabiters of forests,
    I that was once the music of these valleys,
    So darkened am, that all my day is evening,
    Heart-broken so, that molehills seem high mountains,
    And fill the vales with cries instead of music.

Strephon. Long since, alas, my deadly swannish music
    Hath made itself a crier of the morning,
    And hath with wailing strength climbed highest mountains;
    Long since my thoughts more desert be than forests;
    Long since I see my joys come to their evening,
    And state thrown down to over-trodden valleys.

Klaius. Long since the happy dwellers of these valleys
    Have prayed me leave my strange exclaiming music,
    Which troubles their day's work and joys of evening;
    Long since I hate the night, more hate the morning;
    Long since my thoughts chase me like beasts in forests,
    And make me wish myself laid under mountains.

Strephon. Meseems I see the high and stately mountains
    Transform themselves to low dejected valleys;
    Meseems I hear in these ill-changed forests
    The nightingales do learn of owls their music;
    Meseems I feel the comfort of the morning
    Turned to the mortal serene of an evening.

Klaius. Meseems I see a filthy cloudy evening
    As soon as sun begins to climb the mountains;
    Meseems I feel a noisome scent, the morning
    When I do smell the flowers of these valleys;
    Meseems I hear, when I do hear sweet music,
    The dreadful cries of murdered men in forests.

Strephon. I wish to fire the trees of all these forests;
    I give the sun a last farewell each evening;
    I curse the fiddling finders out of music;
    With envy I do hate the lofty mountains,
    And with despite despise the humble valleys;
    I do detest night, evening, day, and morning.

Klaius. Curse to myself my prayer is, the morning;
    My fire is more, than can be made with forests;
    My state more base, than are the basest valleys;
    I wish no evenings more to see, each evening;
    Shamèd I hate myself in sight of mountains,
    And stop mine ears, lest I grow mad with music.

Strephon. For she, whose parts maintained a perfect music,
  Whose beauties shined more than the blushing morning,
  Who much did pass in state the stately mountains,
  In straightness passed the cedars of the forests,
  Hath cast me, wretch, into eternal evening,
  By taking her two suns from these dark valleys.

Klaius. For she, with whom compared, the Alps are valleys,
  She, whose least word brings from the spheres their music,
  At whose approach the sun rose in the evening,
  Who, where she went, bore in her forehead morning,
  Is gone, is gone from these our spoilèd forests,
  Turning to deserts our best pastured mountains.

Strephon. These mountains witness shall, so shall these valleys,
Klaius. These forests eke, made wretched by our music,
  Our morning hymn this is, and song at evening.

45   *The Bargain*

    MY true love hath my heart, and I have his,
      By just exchange, one for the other given.
    I hold his dear, and mine he cannot miss,
      There never was a better bargain driven.
    His heart in me keeps me and him in one,
      My heart in him his thoughts and senses guides;
    He loves my heart, for once it was his own,
      I cherish his, because in me it bides.
    His heart his wound receivèd from my sight,
      My heart was wounded with his wounded heart;
    For as from me on him his hurt did light,
      So still methought in me his hurt did smart.
        Both equal hurt, in this change sought our bliss:
        My true love hath my heart and I have his.

46 *Philomela*

THE Nightingale, as soon as April bringeth
Unto her rested sense a perfect waking,
While late-bare Earth, proud of new clothing, springeth,
Sings out her woes, a thorn her song-book making;
And mournfully bewailing,
Her throat in tunes expresseth
What grief her breast oppresseth,
For Tereus' force on her chaste will prevailing.

O Philomela fair, O take some gladness
That here is juster cause of plaintful sadness!
Thine earth now springs, mine fadeth;
Thy thorn without, my thorn my heart invadeth.

Alas! she hath no other cause of anguish
But Tereus' love, on her by strong hand wroken;
Wherein she suffering, all her spirits languish,
Full womanlike complains her will was broken.
But I, who, daily craving,
Cannot have to content me,
Have more cause to lament me,
Since wanting is more woe than too much having.

O Philomela fair, O take some gladness
That here is juster cause of plaintful sadness!
Thine earth now springs, mine fadeth;
Thy thorn without, my thorn my heart invadeth.

47 *Sleep, baby mine, Desire*

SLEEP, baby mine, Desire, nurse Beauty singeth,
Thy cries, O baby, set mine head on aching;
The babe cries, 'Way, thy love doth keep me waking'.

Lully, lully, my babe, hope cradle bringeth
Unto my children always good rest taking;
The babe cries, 'Way, thy love doth keep me waking'.

Since, baby mine, from me thy watching springeth,
Sleep then a little, pap content is making;
The babe cries, 'Nay, for that abide I waking'.

48   *A Farewell*

OFT have I mused, but now at length I find,
    Why those that die, men say they do depart.
'Depart!'—a word so gentle, to my mind,
    Weakly did seem to paint death's ugly dart.
But now the stars, with their strange course, do bind
    Me one to leave, with whom I leave my heart;
I hear a cry of spirits faint and blind,
    That, parting thus, my chiefest part I part.
Part of my life, the lothèd part to me,
    Lives to impart my weary clay some breath;
But that good part, wherein all comforts be,
    Now dead, doth show departure is a death—
      Yea, worse than death; death parts both woe and joy.
      From joy I part, still living in annoy.

49   *To Sleep*

COME, Sleep, O Sleep, the certain knot of peace,
    The baiting-place of wit, the balm of woe,
The poor man's wealth, the prisoner's release,
    The indifferent judge between the high and low;
With shield of proof shield me from out the press
    Of those fierce darts Despair at me doth throw:
O make in me those civil wars to cease;
    I will good tribute pay, if thou do so.
Take thou of me smooth pillows, sweetest bed,
    A chamber deaf to noise and blind to light,
A rosy garland and a weary head;
    And if these things, as being thine by right,
      Move not thy heavy grace, thou shalt in me,
      Livelier than elsewhere, Stella's image see.

50 *To the Sad Moon*

WITH how sad steps, O Moon, thou climb'st the skies!
  How silently, and with how wan a face!
  What! may it be that even in heavenly place
That busy archer his sharp arrows tries?
Sure, if that long-with-love-acquainted eyes
  Can judge of love, thou feel'st a lover's case:
  I read it in thy looks; thy languished grace
To me, that feel the like, thy state descries.
Then, even of fellowship, O Moon, tell me,
  Is constant love deemed there but want of wit?
Are beauties there as proud as here they be?
  Do they above love to be loved, and yet
    Those lovers scorn whom that love doth possess?
    Do they call 'virtue' there—ungratefulness?

51 *Voices at the Window*

'WHO is it that this dark night
    Underneath my window plaineth?'
It is one who from thy sight
    Being, ah! exiled, disdaineth
Every other vulgar light.

'Why, alas! and are you he?
    Be not yet those fancies changèd?'
Dear, when you find change in me,
    Though from me you be estrangèd,
Let my change to ruin be.

'Well, in absence this will die;
    Leave to see and leave to wonder.'
Absence sure will help, if I
    Can learn how myself to sunder
From what in my heart doth lie.

'But time will these thoughts remove;
  Time doth work what no man knoweth.'
Time doth as the subject prove;
  With time still the affection groweth
In the faithful turtle dove.

'What if you new beauties see,
  Will not they stir new affection?'
I will think they pictures be,
  Image-like, of saint's perfection,
Poorly counterfeiting thee.

'But your reason's purest light
  Bids you leave such minds to nourish.'
Dear, do reason no such spite;
  Never doth thy beauty flourish
More than in my reason's sight.

'But the wrongs love bears will make
  Love at length leave undertaking.'
No, the more fools it do shake,
  In a ground of so firm making
Deeper still they drive the stake.

'Peace, I think that some give ear;
  Come no more lest I get anger.'
Bliss, I will my bliss forbear,
  Fearing, sweet, you to endanger;
But my soul shall harbour there.

'Well, begone, begone, I say,
  Lest that Argus' eyes perceive you.'
Oh, unjustest Fortune's sway,
  Which can make me thus to leave you,
And from louts to run away.

52 *Desire*

THOU blind man's mark, thou fool's self-chosen snare,
 Fond fancy's scum, and dregs of scattered thought,
Band of all evils, cradle of causeless care,
 Thou web of will, whose end is never wrought;
 Desire, desire! I have too dearly bought,
With price of mangled mind, thy worthless ware;
 Too long, too long, asleep thou hast me brought,
Who should my mind to higher things prepare.
 But yet in vain thou hast my ruin sought,
In vain thou mad'st me to vain things aspire,
In vain thou kindlest all thy smoky fire;
 For virtue hath this better lesson taught,
Within myself to seek my only hire,
Desiring nought but how to kill desire.

53 *Splendidis Longum Valedico Nugis*

LEAVE me, O Love, which reachest but to dust,
 And thou, my mind, aspire to higher things!
Grow rich in that which never taketh rust:
 Whatever fades, but fading pleasure brings.
Draw in thy beams, and humble all thy might
 To that sweet yoke where lasting freedoms be;
Which breaks the clouds and opens forth the light
 That doth both shine and give us sight to see.
O take fast hold! let that light be thy guide
 In this small course which birth draws out to death,
And think how evil becometh him to slide
 Who seeketh Heaven, and comes of heavenly breath.
 Then farewell, world! thy uttermost I see:
 Eternal Love, maintain thy life in me!

CHIDIOCK TICHBORNE

d. 1586

54 *Elegy*

MY prime of youth is but a frost of cares,
  My feast of joy is but a dish of pain,
My crop of corn is but a field of tares,
  And all my good is but vain hope of gain;
    The day is past, and yet I saw no sun,
    And now I live, and now my life is done.

My tale was heard and yet it was not told,
  My fruit is fallen and yet my leaves are green,
My youth is spent and yet I am not old,
  I saw the world and yet I was not seen;
    My thread is cut and yet it is not spun,
    And now I live, and now my life is done.

I sought my death and found it in my womb,
  I looked for life and saw it was a shade,
I trod the earth and knew it was my tomb,
  And now I die, and now I was but made;
    My glass is full, and now my glass is run,
    And now I live, and now my life is done.

EDMUND SPENSER

?1552–1599

55 *The Lay to Eliza*

YE dayntye Nymphs, that in this blessed Brooke
    Doe bathe your brest,
Forsake your watry bowres, and hether looke,
    At my request:
And eke you Virgins, that on Parnasse dwell,
Whence floweth Helicon the learned well,
    Helpe me to blaze
    Her worthy praise,
Which in her sexe doth all excell.

Of fayre Elisa be your silver song,
    That blessed wight:
The flowre of Virgins, may shee florish long,
    In princely plight.
For shee is Syrinx daughter without spotte,
Which Pan the shepheards God of her begot:
    So sprong her grace
    Of heavenly race,
No mortall blemishe may her blotte.

See, where she sits upon the grassie greene,
    (O seemely sight)
Yclad in Scarlot like a mayden Queene,
    And Ermines white.
Upon her head a Cremosin coronet,
With Damaske roses and Daffadillies set:
    Bayleaves betweene,
    And Primroses greene
Embellish the sweete Violet.

Tell me, have ye seene her angelick face,
    Like Phoebe fayre?
Her heavenly haveour, her princely grace
    Can you well compare?
The Redde rose medled with the White yfere,
In either cheeke depeincten lively chere.
    Her modest eye,
    Her Majestie,
Where have you seene the like, but there?

I sawe Phoebus thrust out his golden hedde,
    Upon her to gaze:
But when he sawe, how broade her beames did spredde,
    It did him amaze.
He blusht to see another Sunne belowe,
Ne durst againe his fyrye face out showe:
    Let him, if he dare,
    His brightnesse compare
With hers, to have the overthrowe.

medled] mingled   yfere] together

Shewe thy selfe, Cynthia, with thy silver rayes,
    And be not abasht:
When shee the beames of her beauty displayes,
    O how art thou dasht?
But I will not match her with Latonaes seede,
Such follie great sorow to Niobe did breede.
    Now she is a stone,
    And makes dayly mone,
Warning all other to take heede.

Pan may be proud, that ever he begot
    Such a Bellibone,
And Syrinx rejoyse, that ever was her lot
    To bear such an one.
Soone as my younglings cryen for the dam,
To her will I offer a milkwhite Lamb:
    Shee is my goddesse plaine,
    And I her shepherds swayne,
Albee forswonck and forswatt I am.

I see Calliope speede her to the place,
    Where my Goddesse shines:
And after her the other Muses trace,
    With their Violines.
Bene they not Bay braunches, which they doe beare,
All for Elisa in her hand to weare?
    So sweetely they play,
    And sing all the way,
That it a heaven is to heare.

Lo how finely the graces can it foote
    To the Instrument:
They dauncen deffly, and singen soote,
    In their meriment.
Wants not a fourth grace, to make the daunce even?
Let that rowme to my Lady be yeven:
    She shalbe a grace,
    To fyll the fourth place,
And reigne with the rest in heaven.

Bellibone] goodly one   forswonck and forswatt] tired and sweaty

And whither rennes this bevie of Ladies bright,
      Raunged in a rowe?
They bene all Ladyes of the lake behight,
      That unto her goe.
Chloris, that is the chiefest Nymph of al,
Of Olive braunches beares a Coronall:
      Olives bene for peace,
      When wars doe surcease:
Such for a Princesse bene principall.

Ye shepheards daughters, that dwell on the greene,
      Hye you there apace:
Let none come there, but that Virgins bene,
      To adorne her grace.
And when you come, whereas shee is in place,
See, that your rudenesse doe not you disgrace:
      Binde your fillets faste,
      And gird in your waste,
For more finesse, with a tawdrie lace.

Bring hether the Pincke and purple Cullambine,
      With Gelliflowres:
Bring Coronations, and Sops in wine,
      Worne of Paramoures.
Strowe me the ground with Daffadowndillies,
And Cowslips, and Kingcups, and loved Lillies:
      The pretie Pawnce,
      And the Chevisaunce,
Shall match with the fayre flowre Delice.

Now ryse up, Elisa, decked as thou art,
      In royall aray:
And now ye daintie Damsells may depart
      Echeone her way,
I feare, I have troubled your troupes to longe:
Let dame Elisa thanke you for her song.
      And if you come hether,
      When Damsines I gether,
I will part them all you among.

Sops in wine] pinks   Pawnce] pansy   Chevisaunce] ?

56 *Easter*

MOST glorious Lord of lyfe, that on this day,
   Didst make thy triumph over death and sin:
And having harrowd hell, didst bring away
   Captivity thence captive us to win:
This joyous day, deare Lord, with joy begin,
And grant that we, for whom thou diddest dye,
   Being with thy deare blood clene washt from sin,
May live for ever in felicity.
And that thy love we weighing worthily,
   May likewise love thee for the same againe:
And for thy sake that all lyke deare didst buy,
   With love may one another entertayne.
   So let us love, deare love, lyke as we ought,
   Love is the lesson which the Lord us taught.

57 *Epithalamion*

YE learned sisters which have oftentimes
Beene to me ayding, others to adorne:
Whom ye thought worthy of your gracefull rymes,
That even the greatest did not greatly scorne
To heare theyr names sung in your simple layes,
But joyed in theyr prayse.
And when ye list your owne mishaps to mourne,
Which death, or love, or fortunes wreck did rayse,
Your string could soone to sadder tenor turne,
And teach the woods and waters to lament
Your dolefull dreriment.
Now lay those sorrowfull complaints aside,
And having all your heads with girland crownd,
Helpe me mine owne loves prayses to resound,
Ne let the same of any be envide
So Orpheus did for his owne bride,
So I unto my selfe alone will sing,
The woods shall to me answer and my Eccho ring.

Early before the worlds light giving lampe,
His golden beame upon the hils doth spred,
Having disperst the nights unchearefull dampe,
Doe ye awake, and with fresh lusty hed,
Go to the bowre of my beloved love,
My truest turtle dove,
Bid her awake; for Hymen is awake,
And long since ready forth his maske to move,
With his bright Tead that flames with many a flake,
And many a bachelor to waite on him,
In theyr fresh garments trim.
Bid her awake therefore and soone her dight,
For lo the wished day is come at last,
That shall for al the paynes and sorrowes past,
Pay to her usury of long delight:
And whylest she doth her dight,
Doe ye to her of joy and solace sing,
That all the woods may answer and your eccho ring.

Bring with you all the Nymphes that you can heare
Both of the rivers and the forrests greene:
And of the sea that neighbours to her neare,
Al with gay girlands goodly wel beseene.
And let them also with them bring in hand,
Another gay girland
For my fayre love of lillyes and.of roses,
Bound truelove wize with a blew silke riband.
And let them make great store of bridale poses,
And let them eeke bring store of other flowers
To deck the bridale bowers.
And let the ground whereas her foot shall tread,
For feare the stones her tender foot should wrong
Be strewed with fragrant flowers all along,
And diapred lyke the discolored mead.
Which done, doe at her chamber dore awayt,
For she will waken strayt,
The whiles doe ye this song unto her sing,
The woods shall to you answer and your Eccho ring.

Tead] torch

Ye Nymphes of Mulla which with carefull heed,
The silver scaly trouts doe tend full well,
And greedy pikes which use therein to feed,
(Those trouts and pikes all others doo excell)
And ye likewise which keepe the rushy lake,
Where none doo fishes take,
Bynd up the locks the which hang scatterd light,
And in his waters which your mirror make,
Behold your faces as the christall bright,
That when you come whereas my love doth lie,
No blemish she may spie.
And eke ye lightfoot mayds which keepe the deere,
That on the hoary mountayne use to towre,
And the wylde wolves which seeke them to devoure,
With your steele darts doo chace from comming neer
Be also present heere,
To helpe to decke her and to help to sing,
That all the woods may answer and your eccho ring.

Wake now, my love, awake; for it is time.
The Rosy Morne long since left Tithones bed,
All ready to her silver coche to clyme,
And Phoebus gins to shew his glorious hed.
Hark how the cheerefull birds do chaunt theyr laies
And carroll of loves praise.
The merry Larke hir mattins sings aloft,
The thrush replyes, the Mavis descant playes,
The Ouzell shrills, the Ruddock warbles soft,
So goodly all agree with sweet consent,
To this dayes merriment.
Ah my deere love, why doe ye sleepe thus long,
When meeter were that ye should now awake,
T'awayt the comming of your joyous make,
And hearken to the birds lovelearned song,
The deawy leaves among.
For they of joy and pleasance to you sing,
That all the woods them answer and theyr eccho ring.

My love is now awake out of her dreame,
And her fayre eyes, like stars that dimmed were
With darksome cloud, now shew theyr goodly beams
More bright then Hesperus his head doth rere.
Come now, ye damzels, daughters of delight,
Helpe quickly her to dight,
But first come, ye fayre houres which were begot
In Joves sweet paradice, of Day and Night,
Which doe the seasons of the yeare allot,
And al that ever in this world is fayre
Doe make and still repayre.
And ye three handmayds of the Cyprian Queene,
The which doe still adorne her beauties pride,
Helpe to addorne my beautifullest bride:
And as ye her array, still throw betweene
Some graces to be seene,
And as ye use to Venus, to her sing,
The whiles the woods shal answer and your eccho ring.

Now is my love all ready forth to come;
Let all the virgins therefore well awayt,
And ye fresh boyes that tend upon her groome
Prepare your selves; for he is comming strayt.
Set all your things in seemely good aray
Fit for so joyfull day,
The joyfulst day that ever sunne did see.
Faire Sun, shew forth thy favourable ray,
And let thy lifull heat not fervent be
For feare of burning her sunshyny face,
Her beauty to disgrace.
O fayrest Phoebus, father of the Muse,
If ever I did honour thee aright,
Or sing the thing, that mote thy mind delight,
Doe not thy servants simple boone refuse,
But let this day, let this one day, be myne,
Let all the rest be thine.
Then I thy soverayne prayses loud wil sing,
That all the woods shal answer and theyr eccho ring.

Harke how the Minstrels gin to shrill aloud
Their merry Musick that resounds from far,
The pipe, the tabor, and the trembling Croud,
That well agree withouten breach or jar.
But most of all the Damzels doe delite,
When they their tymbrels smyte,
And thereunto doe daunce and carrol sweet,
That all the sences they doe ravish quite,
The whyles the boyes run up and downe the street,
Crying aloud with strong confused noyce,
As if it were one voyce.
Hymen, io, Hymen, Hymen, they do shout,
That even to the heavens theyr shouting shrill
Doth reach, and all the firmament doth fill,
To which the people standing all about,
As in approvance doe thereto applaud
And loud advance her laud,
And evermore they Hymen, Hymen sing,
That al the woods them answer and theyr eccho ring.

Loe where she comes along with portly pace
Lyke Phoebe from her chamber of the East,
Arysing forth to run her mighty race,
Clad all in white, that seemes a virgin best.
So well it her beseemes that ye would weene
Some angell she had beene.
Her long loose yellow locks lyke golden wyre,
Sprinckled with perle, and perling flowres a tweene,
Doe lyke a golden mantle her attyre,
And being crowned with a girland greene,
Seeme lyke some mayden Queene.
Her modest eyes abashed to behold
So many gazers, as on her do stare,
Upon the lowly ground affixed are.
Ne dare lift up her countenance too bold,
But blush to heare her prayses sung so loud,
So farre from being proud.
Nathlesse doe ye still loud her prayses sing.
That all the woods may answer and your eccho ring.

Croud] fiddle

67

Tell me, ye merchants daughters, did ye see
So fayre a creature in your towne before,
So sweet, so lovely, and so mild as she,
Adornd with beautyes grace and vertues store,
Her goodly eyes lyke Saphyres shining bright,
Her forehead yvory white,
Her cheekes lyke apples which the sun hath rudded,
Her lips lyke cherryes charming men to byte,
Her brest like to a bowle of creame uncrudded,
Her paps lyke lyllies budded,
Her snowie necke lyke to a marble towre,
And all her body like a pallace fayre,
Ascending uppe with many a stately stayre,
To honors seat and chastities sweet bowre.
Why stand ye still, ye virgins, in amaze,
Upon her so to gaze,
Whiles ye forget your former lay to sing,
To which the woods did answer and your eccho ring.

But if ye saw that which no eyes can see,
The inward beauty of her lively spright,
Garnisht with heavenly guifts of high degree,
Much more then would ye wonder at that sight,
And stand astonisht lyke to those which red
Medusaes mazeful hed.
There dwels sweet love and constant chastity,
Unspotted fayth and comely womanhood,
Regard of honour and mild modesty,
There vertue raynes as Queene in royal throne,
And giveth lawes alone.
The which the base affections doe obay,
And yeeld theyr services unto her will,
Ne thought of thing uncomely ever may
Thereto approch to tempt her mind to ill.
Had ye once seene these her celestial threasures,
And unrevealed pleasures,
Then would ye wonder and her prayses sing,
That al the woods should answer and your echo ring.

mazeful] amazing

Open the temple gates unto my love,
Open them wide that she may enter in,
And all the postes adorne as doth behove,
And all the pillours deck with girlands trim,
For to recyve this Saynt with honour dew,
That commeth in to you.
With trembling steps and humble reverence,
She commeth in, before th'almighties vew,
Of her, ye virgins, learne obedience,
When so ye come into those holy places,
To humble your proud faces:
Bring her up to th'high altar, that she may
The sacred ceremonies there partake,
The which do endlesse matrimony make,
And let the roring Organs loudly play
The praises of the Lord in lively notes,
The whiles with hollow throates
The Choristers the joyous Antheme sing,
That al the woods may answere and their eccho ring.

Behold whiles she before the altar stands
Hearing the holy priest that to her speakes
And blesseth her with his two happy hands,
How the red roses flush up in her cheekes,
And the pure snow with goodly vermill stayne,
Like crimsin dyde in grayne,
That even th'Angels which continually
About the sacred Altare doe remaine,
Forget their service and about her fly,
Ofte peeping in her face that seemes more fayre,
The more they on it stare.
But her sad eyes still fastened on the ground,
Are governed with goodly modesty,
That suffers not one looke to glaunce awry,
Which may let in a little thought unsownd.
Why blush ye, love, to give to me your hand,
The pledge of all our band?
Sing ye, sweet Angels, Alleluya sing,
That all the woods may answere and your eccho ring.

Now al is done; bring home the bride againe,
Bring home the triumph of our victory,
Bring home with you the glory of her gaine,
With joyance bring her and with jollity.
Never had man more joyfull day then this,
Whom heaven would heape with blis.
Make feast therefore now all this live long day,
This day for ever to me holy is,
Poure out the wine without restraint or stay,
Poure not by cups, but by the belly full,
Poure out to all that wull,
And sprinkle all the postes and wals with wine,
That they may sweat, and drunken be withall.
Crowne ye God Bacchus with a coronall,
And Hymen also crowne with wreathes of vine,
And let the Graces daunce unto the rest;
For they can doo it best:
The whiles the maydens doe theyr carroll sing,
To which the woods shal answer and theyr eccho ring.

Ring ye the bels, ye yong men of the towne,
And leave your wonted labors for this day:
This day is holy; doe ye write it downe,
That ye for ever it remember may.
This day the sunne is in his chiefest hight,
With Barnaby the bright,
From whence declining daily by degrees,
He somewhat loseth of his heat and light,
When once the Crab behind his back he sees.
But for this time it ill ordained was,
To chose the longest day in all the yeare,
And shortest night, when longest fitter weare:
Yet never day so long, but late would passe.
Ring ye the bels, to make it weare away,
And bonefiers make all day,
And daunce about them, and about them sing,
That all the woods may answer, and your eccho ring.

Ah when will this long weary day have end,
And lende me leave to come unto my love?
How slowly do the houres theyr numbers spend!
How slowly does sad Time his feathers move!
Hast thee, O fayrest Planet, to thy home
Within the Westerne fome:
Thy tyred steedes long since have need of rest.
Long though it be, at last I see it gloome,
And the bright evening star with golden creast
Appeare out of the East.
Fayre childe of beauty, glorious lampe of love,
That all the host of heaven in rankes doost lead,
And guydest lovers through the nightes dread,
How chearefully thou lookest from above,
And seemst to laugh atweene thy twinkling light
As joying in the sight
Of these glad many which for joy doe sing,
That all the woods them answer and their echo ring.

Now ceasse, ye damsels, your delights forepast;
Enough is it, that all the day was youres:
Now day is doen, and night is nighing fast:
Now bring the Bryde into the brydall boures.
Now night is come, now soone her disaray,
And in her bed her lay;
Lay her in lillies and in violets,
And silken courteins over her display,
And odourd sheetes, and Arras coverlets.
Behold how goodly my faire love does ly
In proud humility;
Like unto Maia, when as Jove her tooke,
In Tempe, lying on the flowry gras,
Twixt sleepe and wake, after she weary was,
With bathing in the Acidalian brooke.
Now it is night, ye damsels may be gon,
And leave my love alone,
And leave likewise your former lay to sing:
The woods no more shal answere, nor your echo ring.

Now welcome night, thou night so long expected,
That long daies labour doest at last defray,
And all my cares, which cruell love collected,
Hast sumd in one, and cancelled for aye:
Spread thy broad wing over my love and me,
That no man may us see,
And in thy sable mantle us enwrap,
From feare of perrill and foule horror free.
Let no false treason seeke us to entrap,
Nor any dread disquiet once annoy
The safety of our joy:
But let the night be calme and quietsome,
Without tempestuous storms or sad afray:
Lyke as when Jove with fayre Alcmena lay,
When he begot the great Tirynthian groome:
Or lyke as when he with thy selfe did lie,
And begot Majesty.
And let the mayds and yongmen cease to sing:
Ne let the woods them answer, nor theyr eccho ring.

Let no lamenting cryes, nor dolefull teares,
Be heard all night within nor yet without:
Ne let false whispers, breeding hidden feares,
Breake gentle sleepe with misconceived dout.
Let no deluding dreames, nor dreadful sights
Make sudden sad affrights;
Ne let housefyres, nor lightnings helpelesse harmes,
Ne let the Pouke, nor other evill sprights,
Ne let mischivous witches with theyr charmes,
Ne let hob Goblins, names whose sence we see not,
Fray us with things that be not.
Let not the shriech Oule, nor the Storke be heard,
Nor the night Raven that still deadly yels,
Nor damned ghosts cald up with mighty spels,
Nor griesly vultures make us once affeard,
Ne let th'unpleasant Quyre of Frogs still croking
Make us to wish theyr choking.
Let none of these theyr drery accents sing;
Ne let the woods them answer, nor theyr eccho ring.

But let stil Silence trew night watches keepe,
That sacred peace may in assurance rayne,
And tymely sleep, when it is tyme to sleepe,
May poure his limbs forth on your pleasant playne,
The whiles an hundred little winged loves,
Like divers fethered doves,
Shall fly and flutter round about your bed,
And in the secret darke, that none reproves,
Their prety stealthes shal worke, and snares shal spread
To filch away sweet snatches of delight,
Conceald through covert night.
Ye sonnes of Venus, play your sports at will,
For greedy pleasure, carelesse of your toyes,
Thinks more upon her paradise of joyes,
Then what ye do, albe it good or ill.
All night therefore attend your merry play,
For it will soone be day:
Now none doth hinder you, that say or sing,
Ne will the woods now answer, nor your Eccho ring.

Who is the same, which at my window peepes?
Or whose is that faire face, that shines so bright,
Is it not Cinthia, she that never sleepes,
But walkes about high heaven al the night?
O fayrest goddesse, do thou not envy
My love with me to spy:
For thou likewise didst love, though now unthought,
And for a fleece of woll, which privily
The Latmian shephard once unto thee brought,
His pleasures with thee wrought.
Therefore to us be favorable now;
And sith of wemens labours thou hast charge,
And generation goodly dost enlarge,
Encline thy will t'effect our wishfull vow,
And the chast wombe informe with timely seed,
That may our comfort breed:
Till which we cease our hopefull hap to sing,
Ne let the woods us answere, nor our Eccho ring.

And thou, great Juno, which with awful might
The lawes of wedlock still dost patronize,
And the religion of the faith first plight
With sacred rites hast taught to solemnize:
And eeke for comfort often called art
Of women in their smart,
Eternally bind thou this lovely band,
And all thy blessings unto us impart.
And thou, glad Genius, in whose gentle hand
The bridale bowre and geniall bed remaine,
Without blemish or staine,
And the sweet pleasures of theyr loves delight
With secret ayde doest succour and supply,
Till they bring forth the fruitfull progeny,
Send us the timely fruit of this same night.
And thou, fayre Hebe, and thou, Hymen free,
Grant that it may so be.
Til which we cease your further prayse to sing,
Ne any woods shal answer, nor your Eccho ring.

And ye high heavens, the temple of the gods,
In which a thousand torches flaming bright
Doe burne, that to us wretched earthly clods
In dreadful darknesse lend desired light;
And all ye powers which in the same remayne,
More then we men can fayne,
Poure out your blessing on us plentiously
And happy influence upon us raine,
That we may raise a large posterity,
Which from the earth, which they may long possesse,
With lasting happinesse,
Up to your haughty pallaces may mount,
And for the guerdon of theyr glorious merit
May heavenly tabernacles there inherit,
Of blessed Saints for to increase the count.
So let us rest, sweet love, in hope of this,
And cease till then our tymely joyes to sing,
The woods no more us answer, nor our eccho ring.

Song, made in lieu of many ornaments,
With which my love should duly have bene dect,
Which cutting off through hasty accidents,
Ye would not stay your dew time to expect,
But promist both to recompens,
Be unto her a goodly ornament,
And for short time an endlesse moniment.

from The Faerie Queene

(i)

The Cave of Despair

58

ERE long they come, where that same wicked wight
  His dwelling has, low in an hollow cave,
Farre underneath a craggie clift ypight,
  Darke, dolefull, drearie, like a greedie grave,
  That still for carrion carcases doth crave:
On top whereof aye dwelt the ghastly Owle,
  Shrieking his balefull note, which ever drave
Farre from that haunt all other chearefull fowle;
And all about it wandring ghostes did waile and howle.

And all about old stockes and stubs of trees,
  Whereon nor fruit, nor leafe was ever seene,
Did hang upon the ragged rocky knees;
  On which had many wretches hanged beene,
  Whose carcases were scattered on the greene,
And throwne about the cliffs. Arrived there,
  That bare-head knight for dread and dolefull teene,
Would faine have fled, ne durst approchen neare,
But th'other forst him stay, and comforted in feare.

That darkesome cave they enter, where they find
  That cursed man, low sitting on the ground,
Musing full sadly in his sullein mind;
  His griesie lockes, long growen, and unbound,
  Disordred hong about his shoulders round,
And hid his face; through which his hollow eyne
  Lookt deadly dull, and stared as astound;
His raw-bone cheekes through penurie and pine
Were shronke into his jawes, as he did never dine.

His garment nought but many ragged clouts,
  With thornes together pind and patched was,
The which his naked sides he wrapt abouts;
  And him beside there lay upon the gras
  A drearie corse, whose life away did pas,
All wallowd in his owne yet luke-warme blood,
  That from his wound yet welled fresh, alas;
In which a rustie knife fast fixed stood,
And made an open passage for the gushing flood.

Which piteous spectacle, approving trew
  The wofull tale that Trevisan had told,
When as the gentle Redcrosse knight did vew,
  With firie zeale he burnt in courage bold,
  Him to avenge, before his bloud were cold,
And to the villein said, 'Thou damned wight,
  The author of this fact we here behold,
What justice can but judge against thee right,
With thine owne bloud to price his bloud, here shed in sight?'

'What franticke fit' (quoth he) 'hath thus distraught
  Thee, foolish man, so rash a doome to give?
What justice ever other judgement taught
  But he should die who merites not to live?
  None else to death this man despayring drive
But his owne guiltie mind deserving death.
  Is then unjust to each his due to give?
Or let him die that loatheth living breath?
Or let him die at ease that liveth here uneath?

'Who travels by the wearie wandring way
  To come unto his wished home in haste,
And meetes a flood, that doth his passage stay,
  Is not great grace to helpe him over past,
  Or free his feet, that in the myre sticke fast?
Most envious man, that grieves at neighbours good,
  And fond, that joyest in the woe thou hast,
Why wilt not let him passe, that long hath stood
Upon the banke, yet wilt thy selfe not passe the flood?

'He there does now enjoy eternall rest
 And happie ease, which thou doest want and crave,
And further from it daily wanderest:
 What if some litle paine the passage have,
 That makes fraile flesh to feare the bitter wave?
Is not short paine well borne, that brings long ease,
 And layes the soule to sleepe in quiet grave?
Sleepe after toyle, port after stormie seas,
Ease after warre, death after life does greatly please.'

The knight much wondred at his suddeine wit,
 And said, 'The terme of life is limited,
Ne may a man prolong, nor shorten it;
 The souldier may not move from watchfull sted,
 Nor leave his stand, untill his Captaine bed.'
'Who life did limit by almightie doome,'
 (Quoth he) 'knowes best the termes established;
And he that points the Centonell his roome
Doth license him depart at sound of morning droome.

'Is not his deed, what ever thing is donne,
 In heaven and earth? did not he all create
To die againe? all ends that was begonne.
 Their times in his eternall booke of fate
 Are written sure, and have their certaine date.
Who then can strive with strong necessitie,
 That holds the world in his still chaunging state,
Or shunne the death ordaynd by destinie?
When houre of death is come, let none aske whence, nor why.

'The lenger life, I wote the greater sin,
 The greater sin, the greater punishment:
All those great battels, which thou boasts to win,
 Through strife and bloud-shed and avengement,
 Now praysd, hereafter deare thou shalt repent:
For life must life, and bloud must bloud repay.
 Is not enough thy evill life forespent?
For he that once hath missed the right way,
The further he doth goe, the further he doth stray.

'Then do no further goe, no further stray,
But here lie downe, and to thy rest betake,
Th'ill to prevent, that life ensewen may.
For what hath life, that may it loved make,
And gives not rather cause it to forsake?
Feare, sicknesse, age, losse, labour, sorrow, strife,
Paine, hunger, cold, that makes the hart to quake;
And ever fickle fortune rageth rife,
All which, and thousands mo do make a loathsome life.'

(ii)

59　　　　*The Bower of Bliss*

EFTSOONES they heard a most melodious sound,
Of all that mote delight a daintie eare,
Such as attonce might not on living ground,
Save in this Paradise, be heard elswhere:
Right hard it was, for wight which did it heare,
To read what manner musicke that mote bee:
For all that pleasing is to living eare,
Was there consorted in one harmonee,
Birdes, voyces, instruments, windes, waters, all agree.

The joyous birdes shrouded in chearefull shade,
Their notes unto the voyce attempred sweet;
Th'Angelicall soft trembling voyces made
To th'instruments divine respondence meet:
The silver sounding instruments did meet
With the base murmure of the waters fall:
The waters fall with difference discreet,
Now soft, now loud, unto the wind did call:
The gentle warbling wind low answered to all.

There, whence that Musick seemed heard to bee,
Was the faire Witch her selfe now solacing,
With a new Lover, whom through sorceree
And witchcraft she from farre did thither bring:
There she had him now layd a slombering,
In secret shade, after long wanton joyes:
Whilst round about them pleasauntly did sing
Many faire Ladies, and lascivious boyes,
That ever mixt their song with light licentious toyes.

And all that while, right over him she hong,
　With her false eyes fast fixed in his sight,
As seeking medicine, whence she was stong,
　Or greedily depasturing delight:
And oft inclining downe with kisses light,
For feare of waking him, his lips bedewd,
　And through his humid eyes did sucke his spright,
Quite molten into lust and pleasure lewd;
Wherewith she sighed soft, as if his case she rewd.

The whiles some one did chaunt this lovely lay;
　'Ah see, who so faire thing doest faine to see,
In springing flowre the image of thy day;
　Ah see the Virgin Rose, how sweetly shee
　Doth first peepe forth with bashfull modestee,
That fairer seemes, the lesse ye see her may;
　Lo, see soone after, how more bold and free
Her bared bosome she doth broad display;
Loe, see soone after, how she fades, and falles away.

'So passeth, in the passing of a day,
　Of mortall life the leafe, the bud, the flowre,
Ne more doth flourish after first decay,
　That earst was sought to decke both bed and bowre,
　Of many a Ladie, and many a Paramowre:
Gather therefore the Rose, whilest yet is prime,
　For soone comes age, that will her pride deflowre:
Gather the Rose of love, whilest yet is time,
Whilest loving thou mayst loved be with equall crime.'

(iii)

60　*The Garden of Adonis*

IN that same Gardin all the goodly flowres,
　Wherewith dame Nature doth her beautifie,
And decks the girlonds of her paramoures,
　Are fetcht: there is the first seminarie
　Of all things that are borne to live and die,
According to their kindes. Long worke it were,
　Here to account the endlesse progenie
Of all the weedes that bud and blossome there;
But so much as doth need, must needs be counted here.

It sited was in fruitfull soyle of old,
   And girt in with two walles on either side;
The one of yron, the other of bright gold,
    That none might thorough breake, nor overstride:
   And double gates it had, which opened wide,
By which both in and out men moten pas;
   Th'one faire and fresh, the other old and dride:
Old Genius the porter of them was,
Old Genius, the which a double nature has.

He letteth in, he letteth out to wend,
   All that to come into the world desire;
A thousand thousand naked babes attend
    About him day and night, which doe require,
    That he with fleshly weedes would them attire:
Such as him list, such as eternall fate
   Ordained hath, he clothes with sinfull mire,
And sendeth forth to live in mortall state,
Till they againe returne backe by the hinder gate.

After that they againe returned beene,
   They in that Gardin planted be againe;
And grow afresh, as they had never seene
    Fleshly corruption, nor mortall paine.
    Some thousand yeares so doen they there remaine;
And then of him are clad with other hew,
   Or sent into the chaungefull world againe,
Till thither they returne, where first they grew:
So like a wheele around they runne from old to new.

Ne needs there Gardiner to set, or sow,
   To plant or prune: for of their owne accord
All things, as they created were, doe grow,
    And yet remember well the mightie word,
    Which first was spoken by th'Almightie lord,
That bad them to increase and multiply:
   Ne doe they need with water of the ford,
Or of the clouds to moysten their roots dry;
For in themselves eternall moisture they imply.

Infinite shapes of creatures there are bred,
　　And uncouth formes, which none yet ever knew,
And every sort is in a sundry bed
　　Set by it selfe, and ranckt in comely rew:
　　Some fit for reasonable soules t'indew,
Some made for beasts, some made for birds to weare,
　　And all the fruitfull spawne of fishes hew
In endlesse rancks along enraunged were,
That seem'd the Ocean could not containe them there.

Daily they grow, and daily forth are sent
　　Into the world, it to replenish more;
Yet is the stocke not lessened, nor spent,
　　But still remaines in everlasting store,
　　As it at first created was of yore.
For in the wide wombe of the world there lyes,
　　In hatefull darkenesse and in deepe horrore,
An huge eternall Chaos, which supplyes
The substances of natures fruitfull progenyes.

All things from thence doe their first being fetch,
　　And borrow matter, whereof they are made,
Which when as forme and feature it does ketch,
　　Becomes a bodie, and doth then invade
　　The state of life, out of the griesly shade.
That substance is eterne, and bideth so,
　　Ne when the life decayes, and forme does fade,
Doth it consume, and into nothing go,
But chaunged is, and often altred to and fro.

The substance is not chaunged, nor altered,
　　But th'only forme and outward fashion;
For every substance is conditioned
　　To change her hew, and sundry formes to don,
　　Meet for her temper and complexion:
For formes are variable and decay,
　　By course of kind, and by occasion;
And that faire flowre of beautie fades away,
As doth the lilly fresh before the sunny ray.

Great enimy to it, and to all the rest,
    That in the Gardin of Adonis springs,
Is wicked Time, who with his scyth addrest,
    Does mow the flowring herbes and goodly things,
    And all their glory to the ground downe flings,
Where they doe wither, and are fowly mard:
    He flyes about, and with his flaggy wings
Beates downe both leaves and buds without regard,
Ne ever pittie may relent his malice hard.

Yet pittie often did the gods relent,
    To see so faire things mard, and spoyled quight:
And their great mother Venus did lament
    The losse of her deare brood, her deare delight:
    Her hart was pierst with pittie at the sight,
When walking through the Gardin, them she spyde,
    Yet no'te she find redresse for such despight.
For all that lives, is subject to that law:
All things decay in time, and to their end do draw.

But were it not, that Time their troubler is,
    All that in this delightfull Gardin growes,
Should happie be, and have immortall blis,
    For here all plentie, and all pleasure flowes
    And sweet love gentle fits emongst them throwes,
Without fell rancor, or fond gealosie;
    Franckly each paramour his leman knowes,
Each bird his mate, ne any does envie
Their goodly meriment, and gay felicitie.

There is continuall spring, and harvest there
    Continuall, both meeting at one time:
For both the boughes doe laughing blossomes beare,
    And with fresh colours decke the wanton Prime,
    And eke attonce the heavy trees they clime,
Which seeme to labour under their fruits lode:
    The whiles the joyous birdes make their pastime
Emongst the shadie leaves, their sweet abode,
And their true loves without suspition tell abrode.

no'te] could not

(iv)

61   *The Masque of Cupid*

THE first was Fancy, like a lovely boy,
  Of rare aspect, and beautie without peare;
Matchable either to that ympe of Troy,
  Whom Jove did love, and chose his cup to beare,
  Or that same daintie lad, which was so deare,
To great Alcides, that when as he dyde,
  He wailed womanlike with many a teare,
And every wood, and every valley wyde
He fild with Hylas name; the Nymphes eke Hylas cryde.

His garment neither was of silke nor say,
  But painted plumes, in goodly order dight,
Like as the sunburnt Indians do aray
  Their tawney bodies, in their proudest plight:
  As those same plumes, so seemd he vaine and light,
That by his gate might easily appeare;
  For still he far'd as dauncing in delight,
And in his hand a windy fan did beare,
That in the idle aire he mov'd still here and there.

And him beside marcht amorous Desyre,
  Who seemd of riper yeares, then th'other Swaine,
Yet was that other swayne this elders syre, ,
  And gave him being, commune to them twaine:
  His garment was disguised very vaine,
And his embrodered Bonet sat awry;
  Twixt both his hands few sparkes he close did straine,
Which still he blew, and kindled busily,
That soone they life conceiv'd, and forth in flames did fly.

Next after him went Doubt, who was yclad
  In a discolour'd cote, of straunge disguyse,
That at his backe a brode Capuccio had,
  And sleeves dependant Albanese-wyse:

Capuccio] hood

He lookt askew with his mistrustfull eyes,
And nicely trode, as thornes lay in his way,
  Or that the flore to shrinke he did avyse,
And on a broken reed he still did stay
His feeble steps, which shrunke, when hard theron he lay.

With him went Daunger, cloth'd in ragged weed,
  Made of Beares skin, that him more dreadfull made,
Yet his owne face was dreadfull, ne did need
  Straunge horrour, to deforme his griesly shade;
  A net in th'one hand, and a rustie blade
In th'other was, this Mischiefe, that Mishap;
  With th'one his foes he threatned to invade,
With th'other he his friends ment to enwrap:
For whom he could not kill, he practizd to entrap.

Next him was Feare, all arm'd from top to toe,
  Yet thought himselfe not safe enough thereby,
But feard each shadow moving to and fro,
  And his owne armes when glittering he did spy,
  Or clashing heard, he fast away did fly,
As ashes pale of hew, and wingyheeld;
  And evermore on daunger fixt his eye,
Gainst whom he alwaies bent a brasen shield,
Which his right hand unarmed fearefully did wield.

With him went Hope in rancke, a handsome Mayd,
  Of chearefull looke and lovely to behold;
In silken samite she was light arayd,
  And her faire lockes were woven up in gold;
  She alway smyld, and in her hand did hold
An holy water Sprinckle, dipt in deowe,
  With which she sprinckled favours manifold,
On whom she list, and did great liking sheowe,
Great liking unto many, but true love to feowe.

And after them Dissemblance, and Suspect
  Marcht in one rancke, yet an unequall paire:
For she was gentle, and of milde aspect,
  Courteous to all, and seeming debonaire,

Goodly adorned, and exceeding faire:
Yet was that all but painted, and purloynd,
 And her bright browes were deckt with borrowed haire:
Her deedes were forged, and her words false coynd,
And alwaies in her hand two clewes of silke she twynd.

But he was foule, ill favoured, and grim,
 Under his eyebrowes looking still askaunce;
And ever as Dissemblance laught on him,
 He lowrd on her with daungerous eyeglaunce;
 Shewing his nature in his countenance;
His rolling eyes did never rest in place,
 But walkt each where, for feare of hid mischaunce,
Holding a lattice still before his face,
Through which he still did peepe, as forward he did pace.

Next him went Griefe, and Fury matcht yfere;
 Griefe all in sable sorrowfully clad,
Downe hanging his dull head with heavy chere,
 Yet inly being more, then seeming sad:
 A paire of Pincers in his hand he had,
With which he pinched people to the hart,
 That from thenceforth a wretched life they lad,
In wilfull languor and consuming smart,
Dying each day with inward wounds of dolours dart.

But Fury was full ill appareiled
 In rags, that naked nigh she did appeare,
With ghastly lookes and dreadfull drerihed;
 For from her backe her garments she did teare,
 And from her head oft rent her snarled heare:
In her right hand a firebrand she did tosse
 About her head, still roming here and there;
As a dismayed Deare in chace embost,
Forgetfull of his safety, hath his right way lost.

After them went Displeasure and Pleasance,
 He looking lompish and full sullein sad,
And hanging downe his heavy countenance;
 She chearefull fresh and full of joyance glad,

clewes] skeins   snarled] tangled   embost] hard-pressed

As if no sorrow she ne felt ne drad;
That evill matched paire they seemd to bee
    An angry Waspe th'one in a viall had
Th'other in hers an hony-lady Bee;
Thus marched these sixe couples forth in faire degree.

(v)

62   *The Hill of the Graces*

UNTO this place when as the Elfin Knight
    Approcht, him seemed that the merry sound
Of a shrill pipe he playing heard on hight,
    And many feete fast thumping th'hollow ground,
    That through the woods their Eccho did rebound.
He nigher drew, to weete what mote it be;
    There he a troupe of Ladies dauncing found
Full merrily, and making gladfull glee,
And in the midst a Shepheard piping he did see.

He durst not enter into th'open greene,
    For dread of them unwares to be descryde,
For breaking of their daunce, if he were seene;
    But in the covert of the wood did byde,
    Beholding all, yet of them unespyde.
There he did see, that pleased much his sight,
    That even he him selfe his eyes envyde,
An hundred naked maidens lilly white,
All raunged in a ring, and dauncing in delight.

All they without were raunged in a ring,
    And daunced round; but in the midst of them
Three other Ladies did both daunce and sing,
    The whilest the rest them round about did hemme,
    And like a girlond did in compasse stemme:
And in the middest of those same three, was placed
    Another Damzell, as a precious gemme,
Amidst a ring most richly well enchaced,
That with her goodly presence all the rest much graced.

62 stemme] surround

86

Looke how the Crowne, which Ariadne wore
  Upon her yvory forehead that same day,
That Theseus her unto his bridale bore,
  When the bold Centaures made that bloudy fray,
  With the fierce Lapithes, which did them dismay;
Being now placed in the firmament,
  Through the bright heaven doth her beams display,
And is unto the starres an ornament,
Which round about her move in order excellent.

Such was the beauty of this goodly band,
  Whose sundry parts were here too long to tell:
But she that in the midst of them did stand,
  Seem'd all the rest in beauty to excell,
  Crownd with a rosie girlond, that right well
Did her beseeme. And ever, as the crew
  About her daunst, sweet flowres, that far did smell,
And fragrant odours they uppon her threw;
But most of all, those three did her with gifts endew.

Those were the Graces, daughters of delight,
  Handmaides of Venus, which are wont to haunt
Uppon this hill, and daunce there day and night:
  Those three to men all gifts of grace do graunt,
  And all, that Venus in her selfe doth vaunt,
Is borrowed of them. But that faire one,
  That in the midst was placed paravaunt,
Was she to whom that shepheard pypt alone,
That made him pipe so merrily, as never none.

She was to weete that jolly Shepheards lasse,
  Which piped there unto that merry rout,
That jolly shepheard, which there piped, was
  Poore Colin Clout (who knowes not Colin Clout?)
  He pypt apace, whilest they him daunst about.
Pype, jolly shepheard, pype thou now apace
  Unto thy love, that made thee low to lout:
Thy love is present there with thee in place,
Thy love is there advaunst to be another Grace.

(vi)

63   *Nature's Reply to Mutability*

So having ended, silence long ensewed,
    Ne Nature to or fro spake for a space,
But with firme eyes affixt, the ground still viewed.
    Meane while, all creatures, looking in her face,
    Expecting th'end of this so doubtfull case,
Did hang in long suspence what would ensew,
    To whether side should fall the soveraigne place:
At length, she looking up with chearefull view,
The silence brake, and gave her doome in speeches few.

'I well consider all that ye have sayd,
    And find that all things stedfastnes doe hate
And changed be: yet being rightly wayd
    They are not changed from their first estate;
    But by their change their being doe dilate:
And turning to themselves at length againe,
    Doe worke their owne perfection so by fate:
Then over them Change doth not rule and raigne:
But they raigne over change, and doe their states maintaine.

'Cease therefore, daughter, further to aspire,
    And thee content thus to be rul'd by me:
For thy decay thou seekst by thy desire;
    But time shall come that all shall changed bee,
    And from thenceforth, none no more change shall see.'
So was the Titaness put downe and whist,
    And Jove confirm'd in his imperiall see.
Then was that whole assembly quite dismist,
And Nature's selfe did vanish, whither no man wist.

*

When I bethinke me on that speech whyleare,
    Of Mutability, and well it way:
Me seemes, that though she all unworthy were
    Of the Heav'ns Rule; yet very sooth to say,
    In all things else she beares the greatest sway.
Which makes me loath this state of life so tickle,
    And love of things so vaine to cast away;
Whose flowring pride, so fading and so fickle,
Short Time shall soon cut down with his consuming sickle.

Then gin I thinke on that which Nature sayd,
  Of that same time when no more Change shall be,
But stedfast rest of all things firmely stayd
  Upon the pillours of Eternity,
  That is contrayr to Mutabilitie:
For, all that moveth, doth in Change delight:
  But thence-forth all shall rest eternally
With Him that is the God of Sabbaoth hight:
O that great Sabbaoth God, graunt me that Sabaoths sight.

ANTHONY MUNDAY

1553–1633

64   *Beauty Bathing*

BEAUTY sat bathing by a spring
  Where fairest shades did hide her;
The winds blew calm, the birds did sing,
  The cool streams ran beside her.
My wanton thoughts enticed mine eye
  To see what was forbidden:
But better memory said, fie!
  So vain desire was chidden.
    Hey nonny, nonny, etc.

Into a slumber then I fell,
  When fond imagination
Seemed to see, but could not tell
  Her feature or her fashion.
But even as babes in dreams do smile,
  And sometime fall a-weeping,
So I awaked, as wise this while,
  As when I fell a-sleeping.
    Hey nonny, nonny, etc.

JOHN LYLY
?1554–1606

65   *A Serving-Men's Song*

Granichus. O! for a bowl of fat Canary,
        Rich Palermo, sparkling Sherry,
        Some nectar else, from Juno's dairy;
        O! these draughts would make us merry.

Psyllus. O! for a wench (I deal in faces,
        And in other daintier things);
        Tickled am I with her embraces,
        Fine dancing in such fairy rings.

Manes. O! for a plump fat leg of mutton,
        Veal, lamb, capon, pig, and coney;
        None is happy but a glutton,
        None an ass but who wants money.

Chorus. Wines (indeed) and girls are good,
        But brave victuals feast the blood;
        For wenches, wine, and lusty cheer,
        Jove would leap down to surfeit here.

66   *Cards and Kisses*

CUPID and my Campaspe played
At cards for kisses, Cupid paid;
He stakes his quiver, bow, and arrows,
His mother's doves, and team of sparrows;
Loses them too; then, down he throws
The coral of his lip, the rose
Growing on's cheek (but none knows how);
With these, the crystal of his brow,
And then the dimple of his chin:
All these did my Campaspe win.
At last, he set her both his eyes;
She won, and Cupid blind did rise.
    O Love! has she done this to thee?
    What shall (alas!) become of me?

67   *Welcome to Spring*

WHAT bird so sings, yet so does wail?
O! 'tis the ravished nightingale.
Jug, Jug, Jug, Jug, Tereu, she cries,
And still her woes at midnight rise.
Brave prick song! who is 't now we hear?
None but the lark so shrill and clear;
How at heaven's gates she claps her wings,
The morn not waking till she sings.
Hark, hark, with what a pretty throat
Poor Robin Redbreast tunes his note;
Hark how the jolly cuckoos sing
Cuckoo, to welcome in the spring,
Cuckoo, to welcome in the spring.

NICHOLAS BRETON
?1545–1626

68   *The Ploughman's Song*

IN the merry month of May,
In a morn by break of day,
Forth I walked by the wood side,
Whereas May was in his pride.
There I spied all alone
Phyllida and Corydon.
Much ado there was, God wot,
He would love and she would not.
She said, never man was true;
He said, none was false to you.
He said, he had loved her long;
She said, love should have no wrong.
Corydon would kiss her then;
She said, maids must kiss no men,
Till they did for good and all.
Then she made the shepherd call
All the heavens to witness truth,
Never loved a truer youth.

Thus with many a pretty oath,
Yea and nay, and faith and troth,
Such as silly shepherds use,
When they will not love abuse,
Love, which had been long deluded,
Was with kisses sweet concluded:
And Phyllida with garlands gay
Was made the Lady of the May.

69 *A Cradle Song*

COME, little babe, come, silly soul,
Thy father's shame, thy mother's grief,
Born as I doubt to all our dole,
And to thyself unhappy chief:
　　Sing lullaby and lap it warm,
　　Poor soul that thinks no creature harm.

Thou little think'st and less dost know
The cause of this thy mother's moan;
Thou want'st the wit to wail her woe,
And I myself am all alone;
　　Why dost thou weep? why dost thou wail,
　　And knowest not yet what thou dost ail?

Come, little wretch! Ah, silly heart!
Mine only joy, what can I more?
If there be any wrong thy smart,
That may the destinies implore,
　　'Twas I, I say, against my will:
　　I wail the time, but be thou still.

And dost thou smile? O! thy sweet face!
Would God himself he might thee see!
No doubt thou wouldst soon purchase grace,
I know right well, for thee and me:
　　But come to mother, babe, and play,
　　For father false is fled away.

Sweet boy, if it by fortune chance
Thy father home again to send,
If death do strike me with his lance,
Yet mayst thou me to him commend;
    If any ask thy mother's name,
    Tell how by love she purchased blame.

Then will his gentle heart soon yield;
I know him of a noble mind;
Although a lion in the field,
A lamb in town thou shalt him find:
    Ask blessing, babe, be not afraid!
    His sugared words hath me betrayed.

Then mayst thou joy and be right glad,
Although in woe I seem to moan;
Thy father is no rascal lad,
A noble youth of blood and bone;
    His glancing looks, if he once smile,
    Right honest women may beguile.

Come, little boy, and rock asleep!
Sing lullaby, and be thou still!
I, that can do nought else but weep,
Will sit by thee and wail my fill:
    God bless my babe, and lullaby,
    From this thy father's quality.

70   *Wooing in a Dream*

    SHALL we go dance the hay, the hay?
    Never pipe could ever play
    Better shepherd's roundelay.

    Shall we go sing the song, the song?
    Never Love did ever wrong.
    Fair maids, hold hands all along.

    Shall we go learn to woo, to woo?
    Never thought came ever to,
    Better deed could better do.

Shall we go learn to kiss, to kiss?
Never heart could ever miss
Comfort, where true meaning is.

Thus at base they run, they run,
When the sport was scarce begun.
But I waked, and all was done.

THOMAS LODGE

?1558–1625

71   *Rosalind's Madrigal*

LOVE in my bosom like a bee
        Doth suck his sweet;
Now with his wings he plays with me,
        Now with his feet.
Within mine eyes he makes his nest,
His bed amidst my tender breast;
My kisses are his daily feast,
And yet he robs me of my rest.
        Ah, wanton, will ye?

And if I sleep, then percheth he
        With pretty flight,
And makes his pillow of my knee
        The livelong night.
Strike I my lute, he tunes the string;
He music plays if so I sing;
He lends me every lovely thing;
Yet cruel he my heart doth sting.
        Whist, wanton, still ye!

Else I with roses every day
        Will whip you hence,
And bind you, when you long to play,
        For your offence.

I'll shut mine eyes to keep you in,
I'll make you fast it for your sin,
I'll count your power not worth a pin.
Alas! what hereby shall I win
   If he gainsay me?

What if I beat the wanton boy
   With many a rod?
He will repay me with annoy,
   Because a god.
Then sit thou safely on my knee,
And let thy bower my bosom be;
Lurk in mine eyes, I like of thee.
O Cupid, so thou pity me,
   Spare not, but play thee!

GEORGE PEELE

?1558–1596

72   *Oenone and Paris*

Oenone.   Fair and fair, and twice so fair,
        As fair as any may be;
        The fairest shepherd on our green,
        A Love for any lady.
Paris.   Fair and fair, and twice so fair,
        As fair as any may be;
        Thy Love is fair for thee alone,
        And for no other lady.
Oenone.   My Love is fair, my Love is gay,
        As fresh as bin the flowers in May;
        And of my Love my roundelay,
        My merry, merry, merry, roundelay,
        Concludes with Cupid's curse:
        They that do change old love for new,
        Pray gods they change for worse.
Together. They that do change old love for new,
        Pray gods they change for worse.

95

Oenone. Fair and fair, and twice so fair,
    As fair as any may be;
    The fairest shepherd on our green,
    A Love for any lady.
Paris. Fair and fair, and twice so fair,
    As fair as any may be;
    Thy Love is fair for thee alone,
    And for no other lady.
Oenone. My Love can pipe, my Love can sing,
    My Love can many a pretty thing,
    And of his lovely praises ring
    My merry, merry, merry roundelays.
    Amen to Cupid's curse:
    They that do change old love for new,
    Pray gods they change for worse.
Together. They that do change old love for new,
    Pray gods they change for worse.

73   *What Thing is Love?*

WHAT thing is love? for sure love is a thing.
It is a prick, it is a sting,
It is a pretty, pretty thing;
It is a fire, it is a coal,
Whose flame creeps in at every hole;
And as my wit doth best devise,
Love's dwelling is in ladies' eyes,
From whence do glance love's piercing darts,
That make such holes into our hearts;
And all the world herein accord,
Love is a great and mighty lord;
And when he list to mount so high,
With Venus he in heaven doth lie,
And evermore hath been a god,
Since Mars and she played even and odd.

74   *Farewell to Arms*
       To Queen Elizabeth

HIS golden locks time hath to silver turned;
    O time too swift, O swiftness never ceasing!
His youth 'gainst time and age hath ever spurned,
    But spurned in vain; youth waneth by increasing:
Beauty, strength, youth, are flowers but fading seen;
Duty, faith, love, are roots, and ever green.

His helmet now shall make a hive for bees;
    And, lovers' sonnets turned to holy psalms,
A man-at-arms must now serve on his knees,
    And feed on prayers, which are age's alms:
But though from court to cottage he depart,
His saint is sure of his unspotted heart.

And when he saddest sits in homely cell,
    He'll teach his swains this carol for a song:
'Blest be the hearts that wish my sovereign well,
    Curst be the souls that think her any wrong.'
Goddess, allow this aged man his right,
To be your beadsman now, that was your knight.

75   *Bethsabe's Song*

HOT sun, cool fire, tempered with sweet air,
Black shade, fair nurse, shadow my white hair:
Shine, sun; burn, fire; breathe, air, and ease me;
Black shade, fair nurse, shroud me and please me:
Shadow, my sweet nurse, keep me from burning,
Make not my glad cause cause of mourning.
        Let not my beauty's fire
        Inflame unstaid desire,
        Nor pierce any bright eye
        That wandereth lightly.

76   *A Summer Song*

> WHEN as the rye reach to the chin,
> And chopcherry, chopcherry ripe within,
> Strawberries swimming in the cream,
> And school-boys playing in the stream;
>   Then O, then O, then O my true love said,
>   Till that time come again,
>   She could not live a maid.

77   *The Voice from the Well*

> FAIR maiden, white and red,
> Comb me smooth, and stroke my head;
> And thou shalt have some cockle bread.
> Gently dip, but not too deep,
> For fear thou make the golden beard to weep.
> Fair maid, white and red,
> Comb me smooth, and stroke my head;
> And every hair a sheave shall be,
> And every sheave a golden tree.

ROBERT GREENE

1558–1592

78   *Sephestia's Lullaby*

> WEEP not, my wanton, smile upon my knee;
> When thou art old there's grief enough for thee.
>   Mother's wag, pretty boy,
>   Father's sorrow, father's joy.
>   When thy father first did see
>   Such a boy by him and me,
>   He was glad, I was woe:
>   Fortune changed made him so,
>   When he left his pretty boy,
>   Last his sorrow, first his joy.

Weep not, my wanton, smile upon my knee;
When thou art old there's grief enough for thee.
    Streaming tears that never stint,
    Like pearl drops from a flint,
    Fell by course from his eyes,
    That one another's place supplies:
    Thus he grieved in every part,
    Tears of blood fell from his heart,
    When he left his pretty boy,
    Father's sorrow, father's joy.

Weep not, my wanton, smile upon my knee;
When thou art old there's grief enough for thee.
    The wanton smiled, father wept;
    Mother cried, baby lept;
    More he crowed, more we cried;
    Nature could not sorrow hide.
    He must go, he must kiss
    Child and mother, baby bliss;
    For he left his pretty boy,
    Father's sorrow, father's joy.

Weep not, my wanton, smile upon my knee;
When thou art old there's grief enough for thee.

79 *Samela*

LIKE to Diana in her summer weed,
Girt with a crimson robe of brightest dye,
        Goes fair Samela.
Whiter than be the flocks that straggling feed,
When washed by Arethusa's fount they lie,
        Is fair Samela.
As fair Aurora in her morning gray,
Decked with the ruddy glister of her love,
        Is fair Samela.
Like lovely Thetis on a calmèd day,
When as her brightness Neptune's fancy move,
        Shines fair Samela.

Her tresses gold, her eyes like glassy streams,
Her teeth are pearl, the breasts are ivory
   Of fair Samela.
Her cheeks like rose and lily yield forth gleams,
Her brows bright arches framed of ebony:
   Thus fair Samela.
Passeth fair Venus in her bravest hue,
And Juno in the show of majesty,
   For she's Samela.
Pallas in wit, all three, if you will view,
For beauty, wit, and matchless dignity,
   Yield to Samela.

ROBERT SOUTHWELL

1561–1595

80   *The Burning Babe*

As I in hoary winter's night stood shivering in the snow,
Surprised I was with sudden heat which made my heart to glow;
And lifting up a fearful eye to view what fire was near,
A pretty Babe all burning bright did in the air appear;
Who, scorchèd with excessive heat, such floods of tears did shed,
As though his floods should quench his flames which with his tears
 were fed.
'Alas!' quoth he, 'but newly born in fiery heats I fry,
Yet none approach to warm their hearts or feel my fire but I.
My faultless breast the furnace is, the fuel wounding thorns;
Love is the fire, and sighs the smoke, the ashes shame and scorns;
The fuel justice layeth on, and mercy blows the coals;
The metal in this furnace wrought are men's defilèd souls:
For which, as now on fire I am to work them to their good,
So will I melt into a bath to wash them in my blood.'
With this he vanished out of sight and swiftly shrunk away,
And straight I callèd unto mind that it was Christmas day.

81   *New Prince, New Pomp*

BEHOLD, a silly tender Babe
    In freezing winter night
In homely manger trembling lies,
    Alas, a piteous sight!

The inns are full; no man will yield
    This little pilgrim bed,
But forced he is with silly beasts
    In crib to shroud his head.

Despise him not for lying there,
    First, what he is inquire;
An orient pearl is often found
    In depth of dirty mire.

Weigh not his crib, his wooden dish,
    Nor beasts that by him feed;
Weigh not his Mother's poor attire,
    Nor Joseph's simple weed.

This stable is a Prince's court,
    This crib his chair of state;
The beasts are parcel of his pomp,
    The wooden dish his plate.

The persons in that poor attire
    His royal liveries wear;
The Prince himself is come from heaven;
    This pomp is prizèd there.

With joy approach, O Christian wight,
    Do homage to thy King;
And highly praise his humble pomp,
    Which he from heaven doth bring.

82   *New Heaven, New War*

COME to your heaven, you heavenly choirs!
Earth hath the heaven of your desires;
Remove your dwelling to your God,
A stall is now his best abode;
Sith men their homage do deny,
Come, angels, all their fault supply.

His chilling cold doth heat require,
Come, seraphins, in lieu of fire;
This little ark no cover hath,
Let cherubs' wings his body swathe;
Come, Raphael, this Babe must eat,
Provide our little Toby meat.

Let Gabriel be now his groom,
That first took up his earthly room;
Let Michael stand in his defence,
Whom love hath linked to feeble sense;
Let graces rock when he doth cry,
And angels sing his lullaby.

The same you saw in heavenly seat,
Is he that now sucks Mary's teat;
Agnize your King a mortal wight,
His borrowed weed lets not your sight;
Come, kiss the manger where he lies,
That is your bliss above the skies.

This little Babe, so few days old,
Is come to rifle Satan's fold;
All hell doth at his presence quake,
Though he himself for cold do shake;
For in this weak unarmèd wise
The gates of hell he will surprise.

With tears he fights and wins the field,
His naked breast stands for a shield;
His battering shot are babish cries,
His arrows looks of weeping eyes,
His martial ensigns cold and need,
And feeble flesh his warrior's steed.

His camp is pitchèd in a stall,
His bulwark but a broken wall;
The crib his trench, hay-stalks his stakes,
Of shepherds he his muster makes;
And thus, as sure his foe to wound,
The angels' trumps alarum sound.

My soul, with Christ join thou in fight;
Stick to the tents that he hath pight;
Within his crib is surest ward,
This little Babe will be thy guard;
If thou wilt foil thy foes with joy,
Then flit not from this heavenly boy.

? ROBERT SOUTHWELL

83   *Upon the Image of Death*

BEFORE my face the picture hangs,
    That daily should put me in mind
Of those cold qualms and bitter pangs,
    That shortly I am like to find:
        But yet, alas, full little I
        Do think hereon that I must die.

I often look upon a face
    Most ugly, grisly, bare, and thin;
I often view the hollow place,
    Where eyes and nose' had sometimes been;
        I see the bones across that lie,
        Yet little think that I must die.

I read the label underneath,
    That telleth me whereto I must;
I see the sentence eke that saith
    'Remember, man, that thou art dust!'
        But yet, alas, but seldom I
        Do think indeed that I must die.

82 pight] pitched

Continually at my bed's head
  A hearse doth hang, which doth me tell,
That I ere morning may be dead,
    Though now I feel myself full well:
      But yet, alas, for all this, I
      Have little mind that I must die.

The gown which I do use to wear,
  The knife wherewith I cut my meat,
And eke that old and ancient chair
  Which is my only usual seat;
    All these do tell me I must die,
    And yet my life amend not I.

My ancestors are turned to clay,
  And many of my mates are gone;
My youngers daily drop away,
  And can I think to 'scape alone?
    No, no, I know that I must die,
    And yet my life amend not I.

Not Solomon, for all his wit,
  Nor Samson, though he were so strong,
No king nor person ever yet
  Could 'scape, but death laid him along:
    Wherefore I know that I must die,
    And yet my life amend not I.

Though all the East did quake to hear
  Of Alexander's dreadful name,
And all the West did likewise fear
  To hear of Julius Caesar's fame,
    Yet both by death in dust now lie.
    Who then can 'scape, but he must die?

If none can 'scape death's dreadful dart,
  If rich and poor his beck obey,
If strong, if wise, if all do smart,
  Then I to 'scape shall have no way.
    Oh! grant me grace, O God, that I
    My life may mend, sith I must die.

THOMAS NASHE
1567–1601

84 *Spring*

SPRING, the sweet spring, is the year's pleasant king;
Then blooms each thing, then maids dance in a ring,
Cold doth not sting, the pretty birds do sing:
Cuckoo, jug-jug, pu-we, to-witta-woo!

The palm and may make country houses gay,
Lambs frisk and play, the shepherds pipe all day,
And we hear aye birds tune this merry lay:
Cuckoo, jug-jug, pu-we, to-witta-woo!

The fields breathe sweet, the daisies kiss our feet,
Young lovers meet, old wives a-sunning sit;
In every street these tunes our ears do greet:
Cuckoo, jug-jug, pu-we, to-witta-woo!
Spring, the sweet spring!

85 *In Time of Pestilence*

ADIEU, farewell earth's bliss,
This world uncertain is;
Fond are life's lustful joys,
Death proves them all but toys,
None from his darts can fly.
I am sick, I must die.
Lord, have mercy on us!

Rich men, trust not in wealth,
Gold cannot buy you health;
Physic himself must fade,
All things to end are made.
The plague full swift goes by.
I am sick, I must die.
Lord, have mercy on us!

THOMAS NASHE

Beauty is but a flower
Which wrinkles will devour;
Brightness falls from the air,
Queens have died young and fair,
Dust hath closed Helen's eye.
I am sick, I must die.
       Lord, have mercy on us!

Strength stoops unto the grave,
Worms feed on Hector brave,
Swords may not fight with fate,
Earth still holds ope her gate.
Come! come! the bells do cry.
I am sick, I must die.
       Lord, have mercy on us!

Wit with his wantonness
Tasteth death's bitterness;
Hell's executioner
Hath no ears for to hear
What vain art can reply.
I am sick, I must die.
       Lord, have mercy on us!

Haste, therefore, each degree,
To welcome destiny.
Heaven is our heritage,
Earth but a player's stage;
Mount we unto the sky.
I am sick, I must die.
       Lord, have mercy on us!

CHRISTOPHER MARLOWE
1564-1593

from Hero and Leander

(i)

86   *Love at First Sight*

ON this feast day, oh, cursèd day and hour!
Went Hero thorough Sestos, from her tower
To Venus' temple, where unhappily,
As after chanced, they did each other spy.
So fair a church as this had Venus none;
The walls were of discoloured jasper stone,
Wherein was Proteus carvèd, and o'erhead
A lively vine of green sea-agate spread,
Where by one hand light-headed Bacchus hung,
And with the other wine from grapes out-wrung.
Of crystal shining fair the pavement was;
The town of Sestos called it Venus' glass.
There might you see the gods in sundry shapes,
Committing heady riots, incest, rapes:
For know that underneath this radiant floor
Was Danae's statue in a brazen tower;
Jove slyly stealing from his sister's bed
To dally with Idalian Ganymede,
And for his love Europa bellowing loud,
And tumbling with the rainbow in a cloud;
Blood-quaffing Mars heaving the iron net
Which limping Vulcan and his Cyclops set;
Love kindling fire to burn such towns as Troy;
Silvanus weeping for the lovely boy
That now is turned into a cypress tree,
Under whose shade the wood-gods love to be.
And in the midst a silver altar stood;
There Hero sacrificing turtles' blood,
Vailed to the ground, veiling her eyelids close,
And modestly they opened as she rose:

vailed] sank

Thence flew love's arrow with the golden head,
And thus Leander was enamourèd.
Stone-still he stood, and evermore he gazed,
Till with the fire that from his countenance blazed
Relenting Hero's gentle heart was strook;
Such force and virtue hath an amorous look.

It lies not in our power to love or hate,
For will in us is over-ruled by fate.
When two are stripped, long ere the course begin,
We wish that one should lose, the other win;
And one especially do we affect
Of two gold ingots, like in each respect.
The reason no man knows; let it suffice,
What we behold is censured by our eyes.
Where both deliberate, the love is slight;
Who ever loved, that loved not at first sight?

(ii)

87   *Amorous Neptune*

WITH that he stripped him to the ivory skin,
And crying, 'Love, I come', leaped lively in.
Whereat the sapphire-visaged god grew proud,
And made his capering Triton sound aloud,
Imagining that Ganymede, displeased,
Had left the heavens; therefore on him he seized.
Leander strived; the waves about him wound,
And pulled him to the bottom, where the ground
Was strewed with pearl, and in low coral groves
Sweet singing mermaids sported with their loves
On heaps of heavy gold, and took great pleasure
To spurn in careless sort the shipwreck treasure:
For here the stately azure palace stood,
Where kingly Neptune and his train abode.
The lusty god embraced him, called him love,
And swore he never should return to Jove.
But when he knew it was not Ganymede,
For under water he was almost dead,
He heaved him up, and looking on his face,
Beat down the bold waves with his triple mace,

Which mounted up, intending to have kissed him,
And fell in drops like tears, because they missed him.
Leander, being up, began to swim,
And looking back, saw Neptune follow him;
Whereat aghast, the poor soul 'gan to cry:
'O! let me visit Hero ere I die!'
The god put Helle's bracelet on his arm,
And swore the sea should never do him harm.
He clapped his plump cheeks, with his tresses played,
And smiling wantonly, his love bewrayed.
He watched his arms, and as they opened wide,
At every stroke betwixt them would he slide,
And steal a kiss, and then run out and dance,
And as he turned, cast many a lustful glance,
And threw him gaudy toys to please his eye,
And dive into the water, and there pry
Upon his breast, his thighs, and every limb,
And up again, and close beside him swim,
And talk of love. Leander made reply:
'You are deceived, I am no woman, I.'
Thereat smiled Neptune, and then told a tale,
How that a shepherd, sitting in a vale,
Played with a boy so lovely fair and kind,
As for his love both earth and heaven pined;
That of the cooling river durst not drink
Lest water-nymphs should pull him from the brink;
And when he sported in the fragrant lawns,
Goat-footed satyrs and up-staring fauns
Would steal him thence. Ere half this tale was done,
'Ay me!' Leander cried, 'the enamoured sun,
That now should shine on Thetis' glassy bower,
Descends upon my radiant Hero's tower.
O! that these tardy arms of mine were wings!'
And as he spake, upon the waves he springs.

88   *The Passionate Shepherd to His Love*

COME live with me and be my love,
And we will all the pleasures prove,
That hills and valleys, dales and fields,
And all the craggy mountains yields.

There we will sit upon the rocks,
And see the shepherds feed their flocks,
By shallow rivers to whose falls
Melodious birds sing madrigals.

And I will make thee beds of roses
With a thousand fragrant posies,
A cap of flowers, and a kirtle
Embroidered all with leaves of myrtle;

A gown made of the finest wool
Which from our pretty lambs we pull;
Fair linèd slippers for the cold,
With buckles of the purest gold;

A belt of straw and ivy buds,
With coral clasps and amber studs:
And if these pleasures may thee move,
Come live with me and be my love.

The shepherds' swains shall dance and sing
For thy delight each May morning:
If these delights thy mind may move,
Then live with me and be my love.

SIR WALTER RALEGH

?1552-1618

89   *The Nymph's Reply to the Shepherd*

If all the world and love were young,
And truth in every shepherd's tongue,
These pretty pleasures might me move
To live with thee and be thy love.

Time drives the flocks from field to fold,
When rivers rage and rocks grow cold,
And Philomel becometh dumb;
The rest complains of cares to come.

The flowers do fade, and wanton fields
To wayward winter reckoning yields;
A honey tongue, a heart of gall,
Is fancy's spring, but sorrow's fall.

Thy gowns, thy shoes, thy beds of roses,
Thy cap, thy kirtle, and thy posies
Soon break, soon wither, soon forgotten,
In folly ripe, in reason rotten.

Thy belt of straw and ivy buds,
Thy coral clasps and amber studs,
All these in me no means can move
To come to thee and be thy love.

But could youth last and love still breed,
Had joys no date nor age no need,
Then these delights my mind might move
To live with thee and be thy love.

90   *Walsingham*

'As you came from the holy land
     Of Walsingham,
Met you not with my true love
     By the way as you came?'

'How shall I know your true love,
     That have met many one
As I went to the holy land,
     That have come, that have gone?'

'She is neither white nor brown,
     But as the heavens fair,
There is none hath a form so divine
     In the earth or the air.'

'Such an one did I meet, good Sir,
     Such an angelic face,
Who like a queen, like a nymph did appear
     By her gait, by her grace.'

'She hath left me here all alone,
    All alone as unknown,
Who sometimes did me lead with herself,
    And me loved as her own.'

'What's the cause that she leaves you alone
    And a new way doth take,
Who loved you once as her own
    And her joy did you make?'

'I have loved her all my youth,
    But now old as you see,
Love likes not the falling fruit
    From the withered tree.

'Know that Love is a careless child,
    And forgets promise past;
He is blind, he is deaf when he list
    And in faith never fast.

'His desire is a dureless content
    And a trustless joy;
He is won with a world of despair
    And is lost with a toy.

'Of womenkind such indeed is the love
    Or the word love abused,
Under which many childish desires
    And conceits are excused.

'But true Love is a durable fire
    In the mind ever burning;
Never sick, never old, never dead,
    From itself never turning.'

91   *The Passionate Man's Pilgrimage*
        Supposed to be written by One at the Point of Death

GIVE me my scallop-shell of quiet,
My staff of faith to walk upon,
My scrip of joy, immortal diet,
My bottle of salvation,
My gown of glory, hope's true gage,
And thus I'll take my pilgrimage.

Blood must be my body's balmer,
No other balm will there be given,
Whilst my soul like a white palmer
Travels to the land of heaven,
Over the silver mountains,
Where spring the nectar fountains;
And there I'll kiss
The bowl of bliss,
And drink my eternal fill
On every milken hill.
My soul will be a-dry before,
But after it will ne'er thirst more.

And by the happy blissful way
More peaceful pilgrims I shall see,
That have shook off their gowns of clay
And go apparelled fresh like me.
I'll bring them first
To slake their thirst,
And then to taste those nectar suckets,
At the clear wells
Where sweetness dwells,
Drawn up by saints in crystal buckets.

And when our bottles and all we
Are filled with immortality,
Then the holy paths we'll travel,
Strewed with rubies thick as gravel,
Ceilings of diamonds, sapphire floors,
High walls of coral and pearl bowers.

From thence to heaven's bribeless hall
Where no corrupted voices brawl,
No conscience molten into gold,
Nor forged accusers bought and sold,
No cause deferred, nor vain-spent journey,
For there Christ is the King's Attorney,
Who pleads for all without degrees,
And he hath angels, but no fees.

When the grand twelve million jury
Of our sins with sinful fury
'Gainst our souls black verdicts give,
Christ pleads his death, and then we live.
Be thou my speaker, taintless pleader,
Unblotted lawyer, true proceeder;
Thou movest salvation even for alms,
Not with a bribed lawyer's palms.

And this is my eternal plea
To him that made heaven, earth and sea:
Seeing my flesh must die so soon,
And want a head to dine next noon,
Just at the stroke when my veins start and spread,
Set on my soul an everlasting head.
Then am I ready, like a palmer fit,
To tread those blest paths which before I writ.

92   *The Lie*

Go, soul, the body's guest,
　Upon a thankless arrant;
Fear not to touch the best;
　The truth shall be thy warrant.
　Go, since I needs must die,
　And give the world the lie.

92   arrant] errand

Say to the court, it glows
  And shines like rotten wood;
Say to the church, it shows
  What's good, and doth no good:
    If church and court reply,
    Then give them both the lie.

Tell potentates, they live
  Acting by others' action,
Not loved unless they give,
  Not strong but by affection:
    If potentates reply,
    Give potentates the lie.

Tell men of high condition
  That manage the estate,
Their purpose is ambition,
  Their practice only hate:
    And if they once reply,
    Then give them all the lie.

Tell them that brave it most,
  They beg for more by spending,
Who, in their greatest cost,
  Seek nothing but commending:
    And if they make reply,
    Then give them all the lie.

Tell zeal it wants devotion;
  Tell love it is but lust;
Tell time it metes but motion;
  Tell flesh it is but dust:
    And wish them not reply,
    For thou must give the lie.

Tell age it daily wasteth;
  Tell honour how it alters;
Tell beauty how she blasteth;
  Tell favour how it falters:
    And as they shall reply,
    Give every one the lie.

Tell wit how much it wrangles
  In tickle points of niceness;
Tell wisdom she entangles
  Herself in over-wiseness:
    And when they do reply,
    Straight give them both the lie.

Tell physic of her boldness;
  Tell skill it is prevention;
Tell charity of coldness;
  Tell law it is contention:
    And as they do reply,
    So give them still the lie.

Tell fortune of her blindness;
  Tell nature of decay;
Tell friendship of unkindness;
  Tell justice of delay:
    And if they will reply,
    Then give them all the lie.

Tell arts they have no soundness,
  But vary by esteeming;
Tell schools they want profoundness,
  And stand too much on seeming:
    If arts and schools reply,
    Give arts and schools the lie.

Tell faith it's fled the city;
  Tell how the country erreth;
Tell, manhood shakes off pity;
  Tell, virtue least preferreth:
    And if they do reply,
    Spare not to give the lie.

So when thou hast, as I
  Commanded thee, done blabbing,
Although to give the lie
  Deserves no less than stabbing,
    Stab at thee he that will,
    No stab thy soul can kill.

93 *All the World's a Stage*

WHAT is our life? A play of passion,
Our mirth the music of division.
Our mother's wombs the tiring-houses be,
Where we are dressed for this short comedy.
Heaven the judicious sharp spectator is,
That sits and marks still who doth act amiss.
Our graves that hide us from the searching sun
Are like drawn curtains when the play is done.
Thus march we, playing, to our latest rest.
Only we die in earnest, that 's no jest.

94 ❧ *Epitaph*

EVEN such is Time, which takes in trust
Our youth, our joys, and all we have,
And pays us but with age and dust;
Who in the dark and silent grave,
When we have wandered all our ways,
Shuts up the story of our days:
And from which earth, and grave, and dust,
The Lord shall raise me up, I trust.

FULKE GREVILLE, LORD BROOKE
1554–1628

95 *Myra*

I, WITH whose colours Myra dressed her head,
I, that ware posies of her own hand-making,
I, that mine own name in the chimneys read
By Myra finely wrought ere I was waking;
Must I look on, in hope time coming may
With change bring back my turn again to play?

I, that on Sunday at the church-stile found
A garland sweet, with true-love knots in flowers,
Which I to wear about mine arm was bound,
    That each of us might know that all was ours;
        Must I now lead an idle life in wishes,
        And follow Cupid for his loaves and fishes?

I, that did wear the ring 'her mother left,
    I, for whose love she gloried to be blamed,
I, with whose eyes her eyes committed theft,
    I, who did make her blush when I was named;
        Must I lose ring, flowers, blush, theft, and go naked,
        Watching with sighs, till dead love be awakèd?

I, that, when drowsy Argus fell asleep,
    Like jealousy o'erwatchèd with desire,
Was ever warnèd modesty to keep,
    While her breath, speaking, kindled Nature's fire;
        Must I look on a-cold, while others warm them?
        Do Vulcan's brothers in such fine nets arm them?

Was it for this that I might Myra see
    Washing the water, with her beauties, white?
Yet would she never write her love to me.
    Thinks wit of change, while thoughts are in delight?
        Mad girls must safely love, as they may leave;
        No man can print a kiss; lines may deceive.

96   *Chorus Sacerdotum*

OH wearisome condition of Humanity!
Born under one law, to another bound:
Vainly begot, and yet forbidden vanity;
Created sick, commanded to be sound:
What meaneth Nature by these diverse laws?
Passion and Reason self-division cause:
Is it the mark or majesty of Power
To make offences that it may forgive?
Nature herself doth her own self deflower,
To hate those errors she herself doth give.

For how should man think that he may not do,
If Nature did not fail, and punish too?
Tyrant to others, to herself unjust,
Only commands things difficult and hard,
Forbids us all things which it knows is lust,
Makes easy pains, impossible reward.
If Nature did not take delight in blood,
She would have made more easy ways to good.
We that are bound by vows and by promotion,
With pomp of holy sacrifice and rites,
To teach belief in good and still devotion,
To preach of Heaven's wonders and delights:
Yet when each of us in his own heart looks,
He finds the God there, far unlike his books.

GEORGE CHAPMAN

1559–1634

Bridal Song

97

O! COME, soft rest of cares, come Night,
  Come, naked Virtue's only tire,
The reapèd harvest of the light,
  Bound up in sheaves of sacred fire.
      Love calls to war;
        Sighs his alarms,
      Lips his swords are
        The field his arms.

Come, Night, and lay thy velvet hand
  On glorious Day's outfacing face;
And all thy crownèd flames command,
  For torches to our nuptial grace.
      Love calls to war;
        Sighs his alarms,
      Lips his swords are
        The field his arms.

MARK ALEXANDER BOYD

1563–1601

98   *Sonnet*

FRA bank to bank, fra wod to wod, I rin
   Ourhailit with my feble fantasie,
Like til a leif that fallis from a tree
   Or til a reid ourblawin with the wind.
Twa gods guides me: the ane of them is blind,
   Yea, and a bairn brocht up in vanitie;
The nixt a wyf ingenrit of the sea,
And lichter nor a dauphin with hir fin.
   Unhappie is the man for evirmair
   That teils the sand and sawis in the air;
But twyse unhappier is he, I lairn,
   That feidis in his hairt a mad desyre,
   And follows on a woman throw the fyre,
Led by a blind and teichit by a bairn.

SAMUEL DANIEL

1562–1619

Sonnets to Delia

99   (i)

FAIR is my Love, and cruel as she's fair
   Her brow shades frowns, although her eyes are sunny;
Her smiles are lightning, though her pride despair;
   And her disdains are gall, her favours honey.
A modest maid, decked with a blush of honour,
   Whose feet do tread green paths of youth and love,
The wonder of all eyes that look upon her,
   Sacred on earth, designed a saint above!

98   teils] tills

Chastity and Beauty, which were deadly foes,
    Live reconcilèd friends within her brow;
And had she Pity to conjoin with those,
    Then who had heard the plaints I utter now?
      For had she not been fair, and thus unkind,
      My Muse had slept, and none had known my mind.

100   (ii)

WHEN men shall find thy flower, thy glory, pass,
    And thou with careful brow sitting alone
Receivèd hast this message from thy glass,
    That tells thee truth and says that all is gone,
Fresh shalt thou see in me the wounds thou madest,
    Though spent thy flame, in me the heat remaining;
I that have loved thee thus before thou fadest,
    My faith shall wax, when thou art in thy waning.
The world shall find this miracle in me,
    That fire can burn when all the matter's spent;
Then what my faith hath been thyself shalt see,
    And that thou wast unkind thou mayst repent.
      Thou mayst repent that thou hast scorned my tears,
      When winter snows upon thy sable hairs.

101   (iii)

BEAUTY, sweet Love, is like the morning dew,
    Whose short refresh upon the tender green
Cheers for a time, but till the sun doth shew,
    And straight 'tis gone as it had never been.
Soon doth it fade that makes the fairest flourish
    Short is the glory of the blushing rose,
The hue which thou so carefully dost nourish,
    Yet which at length thou must be forced to lose.
When thou, surcharged with burden of thy years,
    Shalt bend thy wrinkles homeward to the earth,
And that in beauty's lease expired appears
    The date of age, the calends of our death—
      But ah! no more; this must not be foretold,
      For women grieve to think they must be old.

102   (iv)

CARE-CHARMER Sleep, son of the sable Night,
  Brother to Death, in silent darkness born,
Relieve my languish, and restore the light,
  With dark forgetting of my cares return.
And let the day be time enough to mourn
  The shipwreck of my ill-adventured youth;
Let waking eyes suffice to wail their scorn,
  Without the torment of the night's untruth.
Cease, dreams, the images of day-desires,
  To model forth the passions of the morrow;
Never let rising sun approve you liars,
  To add more grief to aggravate my sorrow.
    Still let me sleep, embracing clouds in vain;
    And never wake to feel the day's disdain.

103   (v)

LET others sing of knights and paladins
  In agèd accents and untimely words;
Paint shadows in imaginary lines,
  Which well the reach of their high wits records:
But I must sing of thee, and those fair eyes
  Authentic shall my verse in time to come;
When yet the unborn shall say, 'Lo where she lies,
  Whose beauty made him speak that else was dumb.'
These are the arks, the trophies I erect,
  That fortify thy name against old age;
And these thy sacred virtues must protect
  Against the dark, and Time's consuming rage.
    Though the error of my youth in them appear,
    Suffice they shew I lived and loved thee dear.

104   *Heavenly Eloquence*

POWER above powers, O heavenly Eloquence,
  That with the strong rein of commanding words
Dost manage, guide, and master the eminence
  Of men's affections, more than all their swords,
Shall we not offer to thy excellence
  The richest treasure that our wit affords?

Thou that canst do much more with one poor pen,
    Than all the powers of princes can effect;
And draw, divert, dispose and fashion men,
    Better than force or rigour can direct!
Should we this ornament of glory then,
    As the unmaterial fruits of shades, neglect?

Or should we careless come behind the rest
    In power of words, that go before in worth;
When as our accent's equal to the best,
    Is able greater wonders to bring forth?
When all that ever hotter spirits expressed
    Comes bettered by the patience of the north.

And who, in time, knows whither we may vent
    The treasure of our tongue, to what strange shores
This gain of our best glory shall be sent,
    To enrich unknowing nations with our stores?
What worlds in the yet unformèd Occident
    May come refined with the accents that are ours?

Or who can tell for what great work in hand
    The greatness of our style is now ordained?
What powers it shall bring in, what spirits command?
    What thoughts let out, what humours keep restrained?
What mischief it may powerfully withstand;
    And what fair ends may thereby be attained?

And as for Poesy, mother of this force,
    That breeds, brings forth, and nourishes this might,
Teaching it in a loose, yet measured course,
    With comely motions how to go upright;
And fostering it with bountiful discourse,
    Adorns it thus in fashions of delight:

What should I say? since it is well approved
    The speech of Heaven, with whom they have commerce,
That only seem out of themselves removed,
    And do with more than human skills converse:
Those numbers, wherewith Heaven and Earth are moved,
    Show weakness speaks in prose, but power in verse.

105   *Ulysses and the Siren*

Siren. Come, worthy Greek! Ulysses, come;
    Possess these shores with me!
The winds and seas are troublesome
    And here we may be free.
Here may we sit and view their toil
    That travail in the deep,
And joy the day in mirth the while
    And spend the night in sleep.

Ulysses. Fair nymph, if fame or honour were
    To be attained with ease,
Then would I come and rest me there,
    And leave such toils as these.
But here it dwells, and here must I
    With danger seek it forth:
To spend the time luxuriously
    Becomes not men of worth.

Siren. Ulysses, O! be not deceived
    With that unreal name;
This honour is a thing conceived
    And rests on others' fame;
Begotten only to molest
    Our peace, and to beguile
The best thing of our life, our rest,
    And give us up to toil.

Ulysses. Delicious nymph, suppose there were
    Nor honour nor report,
Yet manliness would scorn to wear
    The time in idle sport;
For toil doth give a better touch
    To make us feel our joy,
And ease finds tediousness as much
    As labour yields annoy.

Siren. Then pleasure likewise seems the shore,
      Whereto tends all your toil,
   Which you forgo to make it more,
      And perish oft the while.
   Who may disport them diversely
      Find never tedious day,
   And ease may have variety,
      As well as action may.

Ulysses. But natures of the noblest frame
      These toils and dangers please;
   And they take comfort in the same
      As much as you in ease;
   And with the thought of actions past
      Are recreated still;
   When pleasure leaves a touch at last,
      To shew that it was ill.

Siren. That doth opinion only cause,
      That's out of custom bred,
   Which makes us many other laws,
      Than ever nature did.
   No widows wail for our delights,
      Our sports are without blood;
   The world we see by warlike wights
      Receives more hurt than good.

Ulysses. But yet the state of things require
      These motions of unrest;
   And these great spirits of high desire
      Seem born to turn them best;
   To purge the mischiefs that increase
      And all good order mar,
   For oft we see a wicked peace
      To be well changed for war.

Siren. Well, well, Ulysses, then I see
      I shall not have thee here;
   And therefore I will come to thee
      And take my fortunes there.
   I must be won that cannot win,
      Yet lost were I not won,
   For beauty hath created been
      T'undo, or be undone.

106 *Shadows*

ARE they shadows that we see?
  And can shadows pleasure give?
Pleasures only shadows be,
    Cast by bodies we conceive,
      And are made the things we deem
      In those figures which they seem.

But these pleasures vanish fast,
  Which by shadows are expressed;
Pleasures are not, if they last;
    In their passing is their best.
      Glory is most bright and gay
      In a flash and so away.

Feed apace, then, greedy eyes
  On the wonder you behold;
Take it sudden as it flies,
    Though you take it not to hold.
      When your eyes have done their part,
      Thought must length it in the heart.

107 *Love is a Sickness*

LOVE is a sickness full of woes,
  All remedies refusing;
A plant that with most cutting grows,
  Most barren with best using.
      Why so?
More we enjoy it, more it dies;
If not enjoyed, it sighing cries,
      Hey ho.
Love is a torment of the mind,
  A tempest everlasting;
And Jove hath made it of a kind,
  Not well, nor full nor fasting.
      Why so?
More we enjoy it, more it dies;
If not enjoyed, it sighing cries,
      Hey ho.

MICHAEL DRAYTON
1563–1631

Sonnets to Idea

108

(i)

AN evil spirit, your beauty, haunts me still,
 Wherewith, alas! I have been long possessed,
Which ceaseth not to tempt me to each ill,
 Nor gives me once but one poor minute's rest;
In me it speaks, whether I sleep or wake,
 And when by means to drive it out I try,
With greater torments then it me doth take,
 And tortures me in most extremity;
Before my face it lays down my despairs,
 And hastes me on unto a sudden death,
Now tempting me to drown myself in tears,
 And then in sighing to give up my breath.
  Thus am I still provoked to every evil
  By this good wicked spirit, sweet angel devil.

109

(ii)

DEAR, why should you command me to my rest,
 When now the night doth summon all to sleep?
Methinks this time becometh lovers best;
 Night was ordained together friends to keep.
How happy are all other living things,
 Which though the day disjoin by several flight,
The quiet evening yet together brings,
 And each returns unto his love at night.
O thou that art so courteous else to all,
 Why shouldst thou, Night, abuse me only thus,
That every creature to his kind dost call,
 And yet 'tis thou dost only sever us?
  Well could I wish it would be ever day,
  If, when night comes, you bid me go away.

110

(iii)

CALLING to mind since first my love begun,
  The uncertain times oft varying in their course,
How things still unexpectedly have run,
  As't please the Fates, by their resistless force,
Lastly, mine eyes amazedly have seen
  Essex great fall, Tyrone his peace to gain,
The quiet end of that long-living Queen,
  This King's fair entrance, and our peace with Spain,
We and the Dutch at length ourselves to sever.
  Thus the world doth, and evermore shall reel,
Yet to my Goddess am I constant ever,
  Howe'er blind Fortune turn her giddy wheel.
    Though heaven and earth prove both to me untrue,
    Yet am I still inviolate to you.

111

(iv)

SINCE there 's no help, come let us kiss and part.
  Nay, I have done; you get no more of me,
And I am glad, yea, glad with all my heart,
  That thus so cleanly I myself can free;
Shake hands for ever, cancel all our vows,
  And when we meet at any time again,
Be it not seen in either of our brows
  That we one jot of former love retain.
Now at the last gasp of Love's latest breath,
  When, his pulse failing, Passion speechless lies,
When Faith is kneeling by his bed of death,
  And Innocence is closing up his eyes,
    Now if thou wouldst, when all have given him over,
    From death to life thou mightst him yet recover.

To the Virginian Voyage

YOU brave heroic minds
  Worthy your country's name,
    That honour still pursue;
    Go and subdue!
Whilst loitering hinds
  Lurk here at home with shame.

Britons, you stay too long:
  Quickly aboard bestow you,
    And with a merry gale
    Swell your stretched sail
With vows as strong
  As the winds that blow you.

Your course securely steer,
  West and by south forth keep
    Rocks, lee-shores, nor shoals
    When Eolus scowls
You need not fear;
  So absolute the deep.

And cheerfully at sea
  Success you still entice
    To get the pearl and gold,
    And ours to hold
VIRGINIA,
  Earth's only paradise.

Where nature hath in store
  Fowl, venison, and fish,
    And the fruitfullest soil
    Without your toil
Three harvests more,
  All greater than your wish.

And the ambitious vine
  Crowns with his purple mass
    The cedar reaching high
    To kiss the sky,
The cypress, pine,
  And useful sassafras.

To whom the Golden Age
  Still nature's laws doth give,
    No other cares attend,
    But them to defend
From winter's rage,
  That long there doth not live.

When as the luscious smell
  Of that delicious land
    Above the seas that flows
    The clear wind throws,
Your hearts to swell
  Approaching the dear strand;

In kenning of the shore
  (Thanks to God first given)
    O you the happiest men,
    Be frolic then!
Let cannons roar,
  Frighting the wide heaven.

And in regions far,
  Such heroes bring ye forth
    As those from whom we came;
    And plant our name
Under that star
  Not known unto our North.

And as there plenty grows
  Of laurel everywhere—
    Apollo's sacred tree—
    You it may see
A poet's brows
  To crown, that may sing there.

Thy *Voyages* attend,
  Industrious Hakluyt,
    Whose reading shall inflame
    Men to seek fame,
And much commend
  To after times thy wit.

113   *First Steps up Parnassus*

My dearly lovèd friend, how oft have we
In winter evenings (meaning to be free)
To some well-chosen place used to retire,
And there with moderate meat, and wine, and fire,
Have passed the hours contentedly with chat;
Now talked of this, and then discoursed of that,
Spoke our own verses 'twixt ourselves, if not
Other men's lines which we by chance had got,
Or some stage pieces famous long before,
Of which your happy memory had store;
And I remember you much pleasèd were
Of those who livèd long ago to hear,
As well as of those of these latter times
Who have enriched our language with their rhymes,
And in succession, how still up they grew,
Which is the subject that I now pursue.
For from my cradle you must know that I
Was still inclined to noble Poesie,
And when that once *Pueriles* I had read,
And newly had my *Cato* construèd,
In my small self I greatly marvelled then,
Amongst all other, what strange kind of men
These poets were; and, pleasèd with the name,
To my mild tutor merrily I came
(For I was then a proper goodly page,
Much like a pigmy, scarce ten years of age),
Clasping my slender arms about his thigh,
'O my dear master, cannot you' (quoth I)
'Make me a poet? Do it, if you can,
And you shall see I'll quickly be a man.'
Who me thus answered smiling, 'Boy,' (quoth he)
'If you'll not play the wag, but I may see
You ply your learning, I will shortly read
Some poets to you.' Phoebus be my speed!
To't hard went I, when shortly he began,
And first read to me honest Mantuan,
Then Virgil's *Eglogues*; being entered thus,
Methought I straight had mounted Pegasus,
And in his full career could make him stop,
And bound upon Parnassus' bi-cleft top.

114 *Verses Made the Night before he Died*

So well I love thee as without thee I
Love nothing; if I might choose, I'd rather die
Than be one day debarred thy company.

Since beasts and plants do grow and live and move,
Beasts are those men that such a life approve:
He only lives that deadly is in love.

The corn, that in the ground is sown, first dies,
And of one seed do many ears arise;
Love, this world's corn, by dying multiplies.

The seeds of love first by thy eyes were thrown
Into a ground untilled, a heart unknown
To bear such fruit, till by thy hands 'twas sown.

Look as your looking-glass by chance may fall,
Divide, and break in many pieces small,
And yet shows forth the selfsame face in all,

Proportions, features, graces, just the same,
And in the smallest piece as well the name
Of fairest one deserves as in the richest frame;

So all my thoughts are pieces but of you,
Which put together makes a glass so true
As I therein no other's face but yours can view.

WILLIAM SHAKESPEARE
1564–1616

115   *Courser and Jennet*

But, lo! from forth a copse that neighbours by,
A breeding jennet, lusty, young, and proud,
Adonis' trampling courser doth espy,
    And forth she rushes, snorts and neighs aloud:
        The strong-necked steed, being tied unto a tree,
        Breaketh his rein, and to her straight goes he.

Imperiously he leaps, he neighs, he bounds,
And now his woven girths he breaks asunder;
The bearing earth with his hard hoof he wounds,
    Whose hollow womb resounds like heaven's thunder;
        The iron bit he crusheth 'tween his teeth,
        Controlling what he was controllèd with.

His ears up-pricked, his braided hanging mane,
    Upon his compassed crest now stand on end;
His nostrils drink the air, and forth again,
    As from a furnace, vapours doth he send:
        His eye, which scornfully glisters like fire,
        Shows his hot courage and his high desire.

Sometime he trots, as if he told the steps,
    With gentle majesty and modest pride;
Anon he rears upright, curvets and leaps,
    As who should say, 'Lo! thus my strength is tried;
        And this I do to captivate the eye
        Of the fair breeder that is standing by.'

What recketh he his rider's angry stir,
    His flattering 'Holla', or his 'Stand, I say'?
What cares he now for curb or pricking spur,
    For rich caparisons or trappings gay?
        He sees his love, and nothing else he sees,
        For nothing else with his proud sight agrees.

jennet] Spanish mare

133

Look, when a painter would surpass the life,
  In limning out a well-proportioned steed,
His art with nature's workmanship at strife,
  As if the dead the living should exceed;
    So did this horse excel a common one,
    In shape, in courage, colour, pace and bone.

Round-hoofed, short-jointed, fetlocks shag and long,
  Broad breast, full eye, small head, and nostril wide,
High crest, short ears, straight legs and passing strong,
  Thin mane, thick tail, broad buttock, tender hide:
    Look, what a horse should have he did not lack,
    Save a proud rider on so proud a back.

Sometime he scuds far off, and there he stares;
  Anon he starts at stirring of a feather;
To bid the wind a base he now prepares,
  And whether he run or fly they know not whether;
    For through his mane and tail the high wind sings,
    Fanning the hairs, who wave like feathered wings.

He looks upon his love, and neighs unto her;
  She answers him as if she knew his mind;
Being proud, as females are, to see him woo her,
  She puts on outward strangeness, seems unkind,
    Spurns at his love and scorns the heat he feels,
    Beating his kind embracements with her heels.

Then, like a melancholy malcontent,
  He vails his tail that, like a falling plume,
Cool shadow to his melting buttock lent:
  He stamps, and bites the poor flies in his fume.
    His love, perceiving how he was enraged,
    Grew kinder, and his fury was assuaged.

His testy master goeth about to take him;
  When lo! the unbacked breeder, full of fear,
Jealous of catching, swiftly doth forsake him,
  With her the horse, and left Adonis there.
    As they were mad, unto the wood they hie them,
    Out-stripping crows that strive to over-fly them.

116   *An Outcry upon Opportunity*

'O OPPORTUNITY! thy guilt is great,
    'Tis thou that execut'st the traitor's treason;
Thou set'st the wolf where he the lamb may get;
    Whoever plots the sin, thou point'st the season;
    'Tis thou that spurn'st at right, at law, at reason;
        And in thy shady cell, where none may spy him,
        Sits Sin to seize the souls that wander by him.

'Thou mak'st the vestal violate her oath;
    Thou blow'st the fire when temperance is thawed;
Thou smother'st honesty, thou murder'st troth;
    Thou foul abettor! thou notorious bawd!
    Thou plantest scandal and displacest laud:
        Thou ravisher, thou traitor, thou false thief,
        Thy honey turns to gall, thy joy to grief!

'Thy secret pleasure turns to open shame,
    Thy private feasting to a public fast,
Thy smoothing titles to a ragged name,
    Thy sugared tongue to bitter wormwood taste:
    Thy violent vanities can never last.
        How comes it, then, vile Opportunity,
        Being so bad, such numbers seek for thee?

'When wilt thou be the humble suppliant's friend,
    And bring him where his suit may be obtained?
When wilt thou sort an hour great strifes to end?
    Or free that soul which wretchedness hath chained?
    Give physic to the sick, ease to the pained?
        The poor, lame, blind, halt, creep, cry out for thee;
        But they ne'er meet with Opportunity.

'The patient dies while the physician sleeps;
    The orphan pines while the oppressor feeds;
Justice is feasting while the widow weeps;
    Advice is sporting while infection breeds:
    Thou grant'st no time for charitable deeds:
        Wrath, envy, treason, rape, and murder's rages,
        Thy heinous hours wait on them as their pages.

                    sort] choose

Spring and Winter

(i)

WHEN daisies pied and violets blue
  And lady-smocks all silver-white
And cuckoo-buds of yellow hue
  Do paint the meadows with delight,
The cuckoo then, on every tree,
Mocks married men; for thus sings he,
    Cuckoo!
Cuckoo, cuckoo! O, word of fear,
Unpleasing to a married ear!

When shepherds pipe on oaten straws,
  And merry larks are ploughmen's clocks,
When turtles tread, and rooks, and daws,
  And maidens bleach their summer smocks,
The cuckoo then, on every tree,
Mocks married men; for thus sings he,
    Cuckoo!
Cuckoo, cuckoo! O, word of fear,
Unpleasing to a married ear!

(ii)

WHEN icicles hang by the wall,
  And Dick the shepherd blows his nail,
And Tom bears logs into the hall,
  And milk comes frozen home in pail;
When blood is nipped, and ways be foul,
Then nightly sings the staring owl.
Tu-whit, to-who! a merry note,
While greasy Joan doth keel the pot.

When all aloud the wind doth blow,
  And coughing drowns the parson's saw,
And birds sit brooding in the snow,
  And Marian's nose looks red and raw,

118   keel] cool

When roasted crabs hiss in the bowl,
Then nightly sings the staring owl,
Tu-whit, tu-who! a merry note,
While greasy Joan doth keel the pot.

Fairy Songs

(i)

119

OVER hill, over dale,
  Thorough bush, thorough brier,
Over park, over pale,
  Thorough flood, thorough fire,
I do wander everywhere,
Swifter than the moonë's sphere;
And I serve the fairy queen,
To dew her orbs upon the green:
The cowslips tall her pensioners be;
In their gold coats spots you see;
Those be rubies, fairy favours,
In those freckles live their savours:
I must go seek some dew-drops here,
And hang a pearl in every cowslip's ear.

120

(ii)

YOU spotted snakes with double tongue,
  Thorny hedgehogs, be not seen;
Newts and blind-worms, do no wrong;
  Come not near our fairy queen.

  Philomel, with melody,
    Sing in our sweet lullaby;
Lulla, lulla, lullaby; lulla, lulla, lullaby!
    Never harm,
    Nor spell nor charm,
  Come our lovely lady nigh.
  So, good night, with lullaby.

Weaving spiders, come not here;
Hence, you long-legged spinners, hence!
Beetles black, approach not near;
Worm nor snail, do no offence.

Philomel, with melody,
Sing in our sweet lullaby;
Lulla, lulla, lullaby; lulla, lulla, lullaby!
Never harm,
Nor spell nor charm,
Come our lovely lady nigh.
So, good night, with lullaby.

Songs sung in Arden

121   (i)

BLOW, blow, thou winter wind,
Thou art not so unkind
As man's ingratitude;
Thy tooth is not so keen,
Because thou art not seen,
Although thy breath be rude.
Heigh-ho! sing, heigh-ho! unto the green holly:
Most friendship is feigning, most loving mere folly.
Then heigh-ho! the holly!
This life is most jolly.

Freeze, freeze, thou bitter sky,
That dost not bite so nigh
As benefits forgot:
Though thou the waters warp,
Thy sting is not so sharp
As friend remembered not.
Heigh-ho! sing, heigh-ho! unto the green holly:
Most friendship is feigning, most loving mere folly.
Then heigh-ho! the holly!
This life is most jolly.

122   (ii)

IT was a lover and his lass,
    With a hey, and a ho, and a hey nonino,
That o'er the green corn-field did pass,
    In spring time, the only pretty ring time,
When birds do sing, hey ding a ding, ding;
Sweet lovers love the spring.

Between the acres of the rye,
    With a hey, and a ho, and a hey nonino,
Those pretty country folks would lie,
    In spring time, the only pretty ring time,
When birds do sing, hey ding a ding, ding;
Sweet lovers love the spring.

This carol they began that hour,
    With a hey, and a ho, and a hey nonino,
How that a life was but a flower
    In spring time, the only pretty ring time,
When birds do sing, hey ding a ding, ding;
Sweet lovers love the spring.

And therefore take the present time,
    With a hey, and a ho, and a hey nonino;
For love is crowned with the prime
    In spring time, the only pretty ring time,
When birds do sing, hey ding a ding, ding;
Sweet lovers love the spring.

Feste's Songs

123   (i)

O MISTRESS mine, where are you roaming?
O! stay and hear; your true love's coming,
    That can sing both high and low.
Trip no further, pretty sweeting;
Journeys end in lovers meeting,
    Every wise man's son doth know.

What is love? 'Tis not hereafter;
Present mirth hath present laughter;
   What's to come is still unsure.
In delay there lies no plenty;
Then come kiss me, sweet and twenty;
   Youth's a stuff will not endure.

124   (ii)

COME away, come away, death,
   And in sad cypress let me be laid.
Fly away, fly away, breath;
   I am slain by a fair cruel maid.
My shroud of white, stuck all with yew,
     O! prepare it.
My part of death, no one so true
     Did share it.

Not a flower, not a flower sweet,
   On my black coffin let there be strown;
Not a friend, not a friend greet
   My poor corpse, where my bones shall be thrown.
A thousand thousand sighs to save,
     Lay me, O! where
Sad true lover never find my grave,
     To weep there.

125   (iii)

WHEN that I was and a little tiny boy,
   With hey, ho, the wind and the rain;
A foolish thing was but a toy,
   For the rain it raineth every day.

But when I came to man's estate,
   With hey, ho, the wind and the rain;
'Gainst knaves and thieves men shut their gate,
   For the rain it raineth every day.

But when I came, alas! to wive,
  With hey, ho, the wind and the rain;
By swaggering could I never thrive,
  For the rain it raineth every day.

But when I came unto my beds,
  With hey, ho, the wind and the rain;
With toss-pots still had drunken heads,
  For the rain it raineth every day.

A great while ago the world begun,
  With hey, ho, the wind and the rain;
But that's all one, our play is done,
  And we'll strive to please you every day.

126   *At the Moated Grange*

TAKE, O! take those lips away,
  That so sweetly were forsworn,
And those eyes, the break of day,
  Lights that do mislead the morn;
But my kisses bring again,
      Bring again,
Seals of love, but sealed in vain,
      Sealed in vain.

127   *Dirge for Fidele*

FEAR no more the heat o' the sun,
  Nor the furious winter's rages;
Thou thy worldly task hast done,
  Home art gone, and ta'en thy wages.
Golden lads and girls all must,
As chimney-sweepers, come to dust.

Fear no more the frown o' the great,
  Thou art past the tyrant's stroke;
Care no more to clothe and eat,
  To thee the reed is as the oak.
The sceptre, learning, physic, must
All follow this, and come to dust.

Fear no more the lightning-flash,
   Nor the all-dreaded thunder-stone;
Fear not slander, censure rash;
   Thou hast finished joy and moan.
All lovers young, all lovers must
Consign to thee, and come to dust.

No exorciser harm thee!
Nor no witchcraft charm thee!
Ghost unlaid forbear thee!
Nothing ill come near thee!
Quiet consummation have,
And renownèd be thy grave!

128   *Autolycus Sings*

WHEN daffodils begin to peer,
   With heigh! the doxy, over the dale,
Why, then comes in the sweet o' the year;
   For the red blood reigns in the winter's pale.

The white sheet bleaching on the hedge,
   With heigh! the sweet birds, O, how they sing!
Doth set my pugging tooth on edge,
   For a quart of ale is a dish for a king.

The lark, that tirra-lirra chants,
   With heigh! with heigh! the thrush and the jay,
Are summer songs for me and my aunts,
   While we lie tumbling in the hay.

Ariel's Songs

129   (i)

COME unto these yellow sands,
   And then take hands:
Curtsied when you have, and kissed
   The wild waves whist,
Foot it featly here and there;
And, sweet sprites, the burden bear.

Hark, hark!
　Bow, wow
The watch-dogs bark,
　Bow, wow,
Hark, hark! I hear
The strain of strutting Chanticleer
Cry, Cock-a-diddle-dow.

130　　　　　　　(ii)

FULL fathom five thy father lies;
　Of his bones are coral made;
Those are pearls that were his eyes:
　Nothing of him that doth fade,
But doth suffer a sea-change
Into something rich and strange:
Sea nymphs hourly ring his knell.
　　　　　　Ding-dong!
　Hark! now I hear them,
　　　　　Ding-dong, bell!

131　　　　　　　(iii)

WHERE the bee sucks, there suck I,
In a cowslip's bell I lie,
There I couch when owls do cry,
On the bat's back I do fly
After summer merrily.
　Merrily, merrily, shall I live now
　Under the blossom that hangs on the bough.

132　　　　　*Sweet Music's Power*

ORPHEUS with his lute made trees
And the mountain tops that freeze
　Bow themselves when he did sing:
To his music plants and flowers
Ever sprung; as sun and showers
　There had made a lasting spring.

Every thing that heard him play,
Even the billows of the sea,
  Hung their heads and then lay by.
In sweet music is such art,
  Killing care and grief of heart
  Fall asleep, or, hearing, die.

133   *A Bridal Song*

ROSES, their sharp spines being gone,
Not royal in their smells alone,
  But in their hue;
Maiden pinks, of odour faint,
Daisies smell-less, yet most quaint,
  And sweet thyme true;

Primrose, firstborn child of Ver,
Merry springtime's harbinger,
  With her bells dim;
Oxlips in their cradles growing,
Marigolds on death-beds blowing,
  Larks'-heels trim:

All dear Nature's children sweet
Lie 'fore bride and bridegroom's feet,
  Blessing their sense.
Not an angel of the air,
Bird melodious or bird fair,
  Be absent hence.

The crow, the slanderous cuckoo, nor
The boding raven, nor chough hoar,
  Nor chattering pie,
May on our bride-house perch or sing,
Or with them any discord bring,
  But from it fly.

Sonnets

134

(i)

SHALL I compare thee to a summer's day?
  Thou art more lovely and more temperate:
Rough winds do shake the darling buds of May,
  And summer's lease hath all too short a date:
Sometime too hot the eye of heaven shines,
  And often is his gold complexion dimmed;
And every fair from fair sometime declines,
  By chance, or nature's changing course untrimmed;
But thy eternal summer shall not fade,
  Nor lose possession of that fair thou owest,
Nor shall death brag thou wanderest in his shade,
  When in eternal lines to time thou growest;
    So long as men can breathe, or eyes can see,
    So long lives this, and this gives life to thee.

135

(ii)

WHEN in disgrace with fortune and men's eyes
  I all alone beweep my outcast state,
And trouble deaf heaven with my bootless cries,
  And look upon myself, and curse my fate,
Wishing me like to one more rich in hope,
  Featured like him, like him with friends possessed,
Desiring this man's art, and that man's scope,
  With what I most enjoy contented least;
Yet in these thoughts myself almost despising,
  Haply I think on thee, and then my state,
Like to the lark at break of day arising
  From sullen earth, sings hymns at heaven's gate;
    For thy sweet love remembered such wealth brings
    That then I scorn to change my state with kings.

136   (iii)

W HEN to the sessions of sweet silent thought
 I summon up remembrance of things past,
I sigh the lack of many a thing I sought,
 And with old woes new wail my dear time's waste:
Then can I drown an eye, unused to flow,
 For precious friends hid in death's dateless night,
And weep afresh love's long since cancelled woe,
 And moan the expense of many a vanished sight:
Then can I grieve at grievances foregone,
 And heavily from woe to woe tell o'er
The sad account of fore-bemoanèd moan,
 Which I new pay as if not paid before.
  But if the while I think on thee, dear friend,
  All losses are restored and sorrows end.

137   (iv)

T HY bosom is endearèd with all hearts,
 Which I by lacking have supposed dead;
And there reigns love, and all love's loving parts,
 And all those friends which I thought buried.
How many a holy and obsequious tear
 Hath dear religious love stolen from mine eye,
As interest of the dead, which now appear
 But things removed that hidden in thee lie!
Thou art the grave where buried love doth live,
 Hung with the trophies of my lovers gone,
Who all their parts of me to thee did give,
 That due of many now is thine alone.
  Their images I loved I view in thee,
  And thou, all they, hast all the all of me.

138   (v)

Not marble, nor the gilded monuments
    Of princes, shall outlive this powerful rhyme;
But you shall shine more bright in these contents
    Than unswept stone, besmeared with sluttish time.
When wasteful war shall statues overturn,
    And broils root out the work of masonry,
Nor Mars his sword nor war's quick fire shall burn
    The living record of your memory.
'Gainst death and all oblivious enmity
    Shall you pace forth; your praise shall still find room
Even in the eyes of all posterity
    That wear this world out to the ending doom.
        So, till the judgement that yourself arise,
        You live in this, and dwell in lovers' eyes.

139   (vi)

Like as the waves make towards the pebbled shore,
    So do our minutes hasten to their end;
Each changing place with that which goes before,
    In sequent toil all forwards do contend.
Nativity, once in the main of light,
    Crawls to maturity, wherewith being crowned,
Crooked eclipses 'gainst his glory fight,
    And Time that gave doth now his gift confound.
Time doth transfix the flourish set on youth
    And delves the parallels in beauty's brow,
Feeds on the rarities of nature's truth,
    And nothing stands but for his scythe to mow.
        And yet to times in hope my verse shall stand,
        Praising thy worth, despite his cruel hand.

140

(vii)

WHEN I have seen by Time's fell hand defaced
  The rich proud cost of outworn buried age;
When sometime lofty towers I see down razed,
  And brass eternal slave to mortal rage;
When I have seen the hungry ocean gain
  Advantage on the kingdom of the shore,
And the firm soil win of the watery main,
  Increasing store with loss, and loss with store;
When I have seen such interchange of state,
  Or state itself confounded to decay,
Ruin hath taught me thus to ruminate,
  That Time will come and take my Love away.
    This thought is as a death, which cannot choose
    But weep to have that which it fears to lose.

141

(viii)

SINCE brass, nor stone, nor earth, nor boundless sea,
  But sad mortality o'ersways their power,
How with this rage shall beauty hold a plea,
  Whose action is no stronger than a flower?
O, how shall summer's honey breath hold out
  Against the wrackful siege of battering days,
When rocks impregnable are not so stout,
  Nor gates of steel so strong, but Time decays?
O fearful meditation! Where, alack,
  Shall Time's best jewel from Time's chest lie hid?
Or what strong hand can hold his swift foot back?
  Or who his spoil of beauty can forbid?
    O, none, unless this miracle have might,
    That in black ink my love may still shine bright.

142   (ix)

TIRED with all these, for restful death I cry;
    As to behold desert a beggar born,
And needy nothing trimmed in jollity,
    And purest faith unhappily forsworn,
And gilded honour shamefully misplaced,
    And maiden virtue rudely strumpeted,
And right perfection wrongfully disgraced,
    And strength by limping sway disabled,
And art made tongue-tied by authority,
    And folly, doctor-like, controlling skill,
And simple truth miscalled simplicity,
    And captive good attending captain ill.
        Tired with all these, from these would I be gone,
        Save that, to die, I leave my Love alone.

143   (x)

THAT time of year thou mayst in me behold
    When yellow leaves, or none, or few, do hang
Upon those boughs which shake against the cold,
    Bare ruined choirs, where late the sweet birds sang.
In me thou seest the twilight of such day
    As after sunset fadeth in the west;
Which by and by black night doth take away,
    Death's second self, that seals up all in rest.
In me thou seest the glowing of such fire,
    That on the ashes of his youth doth lie,
As the death-bed whereon it must expire,
    Consumed with that which it was nourished by.
        This thou perceiv'st, which makes thy love more strong,
        To love that well which thou must leave ere long.

144 (xi)

FAREWELL! thou art too dear for my possessing,
    And like enough thou know'st thy estimate:
The charter of thy worth gives thee releasing;
    My bonds in thee are all determinate.
For how do I hold thee but by thy granting?
    And for that riches where is my deserving?
The cause of this fair gift in me is wanting,
    And so my patent back again is swerving.
Thyself thou gav'st, thy own worth then not knowing,
    Or me, to whom thou gav'st it, else mistaking;
So thy great gift, upon misprision growing,
    Comes home again, on better judgement making.
      Thus have I had thee, as a dream doth flatter,
      In sleep a king, but, waking, no such matter.

145 (xii)

THEN hate me when thou wilt; if ever, now;
    Now, while the world is bent my deeds to cross,
Join with the spite of fortune, make me bow,
    And do not drop in for an after-loss:
Ah! do not, when my heart hath 'scaped this sorrow,
    Come in the rearward of a conquered woe;
Give not a windy night a rainy morrow,
    To linger out a purposed overthrow.
If thou wilt leave me, do not leave me last,
    When other petty griefs have done their spite,
But in the onset come; so shall I taste
    At first the very worst of fortune's might.
      And other strains of woe, which now seem woe,
      Compared with loss of thee will not seem so.

146   (xiii)

THEY that have power to hurt and will do none,
    That do not do the thing they most do show,
Who, moving others, are themselves as stone,
    Unmovèd, cold, and to temptation slow—
They rightly do inherit heaven's graces,
    And husband nature's riches from expense;
They are the Lords and owners of their faces,
    Others, but stewards of their excellence.
The summer's flower is to the summer sweet,
    Though to itself it only live and die;
But if that flower with base infection meet,
    The basest weed outbraves his dignity:
       For sweetest things turn sourest by their deeds;
       Lilies that fester smell far worse than weeds.

147   (xiv)

How like a winter hath my absence been
    From thee, the pleasure of the fleeting year!
What freezings have I felt, what dark days seen!
    What old December's bareness everywhere!
And yet this time removed was summer's time,
    The teeming autumn, big with rich increase,
Bearing the wanton burden of the prime,
    Like widowed wombs after their lords' decease:
Yet this abundant issue seemed to me
    But hope of orphans and unfathered fruit;
For summer and his pleasures wait on thee,
    And, thou away, the very birds are mute.
       Or, if they sing, 'tis with so dull a cheer,
       That leaves look pale, dreading the winter's near.

148   (xv)

FROM you have I been absent in the spring,
 When proud pied April, dressed in all his trim,
Hath put a spirit of youth in every thing,
 That heavy Saturn laughed and leaped with him.
Yet nor the lays of birds, nor the sweet smell
 Of different flowers in odour and in hue,
Could make me any summer's story tell,
 Or from their proud lap pluck them where they grew:
Nor did I wonder at the lily's white,
 Nor praise the deep vermilion in the rose;
They were but sweet, but figures of delight,
 Drawn after you, you pattern of all those.
  Yet seemed it winter still, and, you away,
  As with your shadow I with these did play.

149   (xvi)

WHEN in the chronicle of wasted time
 I see descriptions of the fairest wights,
And beauty making beautiful old rhyme,
 In praise of ladies dead and lovely knights,
Then, in the blazon of sweet beauty's best,
 Of hand, of foot, of lip, of eye, of brow,
I see their antique pen would have expressed
 Even such a beauty as you master now.
So all their praises are but prophecies
 Of this our time, all you prefiguring;
And, for they looked but with divining eyes,
 They had not skill enough your worth to sing:
  For we, which now behold these present days,
  Have eyes to wonder, but lack tongues to praise.

150   (xvii)

O! NEVER say that I was false of heart,
  Though absence seemed my flame to qualify.
As easy might I from myself depart
  As from my soul, which in thy breast doth lie:
That is my home of love; if I have ranged,
  Like him that travels, I return again,
Just to the time, not with the time exchanged,
  So that myself bring water for my stain.
Never believe, though in my nature reigned
  All frailties that besiege all kinds of blood,
That it could so preposterously be stained,
  To leave for nothing all thy sum of good;
    For nothing this wide universe I call,
    Save thou, my rose; in it thou art my all.

151   (xviii)

LET me not to the marriage of true minds
  Admit impediments. Love is not love
Which alters when it alteration finds,
  Or bends with the remover to remove.
O, no! it is an ever-fixèd mark,
  That looks on tempests and is never shaken;
It is the star to every wandering bark,
  Whose worth's unknown, although his height be taken.
Love's not Time's fool, though rosy lips and cheeks
  Within his bending sickle's compass come;
Love alters not with his brief hours and weeks,
  But bears it out even to the edge of doom.
    If this be error, and upon me proved,
    I never writ, nor no man ever loved.

152 (xix)

THE expense of spirit in a waste of shame
 Is lust in action; and till action, lust
Is perjured, murderous, bloody, full of blame,
 Savage, extreme, rude, cruel, not to trust;
Enjoyed, no sooner but despised straight;
 Past reason hunted; and no sooner had,
Past reason hated, as a swallowed bait,
 On purpose laid to make the taker mad:
Mad in pursuit, and in possession so;
 Had, having, and in quest to have, extreme;
A bliss in proof, and proved, a very woe;
 Before, a joy proposed; behind, a dream.
  All this the world well knows; yet none knows well
  To shun the heaven that leads men to this hell.

153 (xx)

POOR soul, the centre of my sinful earth,
 My sinful earth these rebel powers array,
Why dost thou pine within and suffer dearth,
 Painting thy outward walls so costly gay?
Why so large cost, having so short a lease,
 Dost thou upon thy fading mansion spend?
Shall worms, inheritors of this excess,
 Eat up thy charge? Is this thy body's end?
Then, soul, live thou upon thy servant's loss,
 And let that pine to aggravate thy store;
Buy terms divine in selling hours of dross;
 Within be fed, without be rich no more:
  So shalt thou feed on Death, that feeds on men,
  And Death once dead, there's no more dying then.

154   *The Phoenix and the Turtle*

LET the bird of loudest lay,
  On the sole Arabian tree,
  Herald sad and trumpet be,
To whose sound chaste wings obey.

But thou shrieking harbinger,
  Foul precurrer of the fiend,
  Augur of the fever's end,
To this troop come thou not near.

From this session interdict
  Every fowl of tyrant wing,
  Save the eagle, feathered king;
Keep the obsequy so strict.

Let the priest in surplice white
  That defunctive music can,
  Be the death-divining swan,
Lest the requiem lack his right.

And thou treble-dated crow,
  That thy sable gender mak'st
  With the breath thou giv'st and tak'st,
'Mongst our mourners shalt thou go.

Here the anthem doth commence:
  Love and constancy is dead;
  Phoenix and the turtle fled
In a mutual flame from hence.

So they loved, as love in twain
  Had the essence but in one;
  Two distincts, division none;
Number there in love was slain.

Hearts remote, yet not asunder;
  Distance, and no space was seen
  'Twixt the turtle and his queen;
But in them it were a wonder.

can] knows

So between them love did shine,
  That the turtle saw his right
  Flaming in the phoenix' sight;
Either was the other's mine.

Property was thus appalled,
  That the self was not the same;
  Single nature's double name
Neither two nor one was called.

Reason, in itself confounded,
  Saw division grow together,
  To themselves yet either neither,
Simple were so well compounded:

That it cried, 'How true a twain
  Seemeth this concordant one!
  Love hath reason, reason none,
If what parts can so remain.'

Whereupon it made this threne
  To the phoenix and the dove,
  Co-supremes and stars of love,
As chorus to their tragic scene.

THRENOS

Beauty, truth, and rarity,
Grace in all simplicity,
Here enclosed in cinders lie.

Death is now the phoenix' nest;
And the turtle's loyal breast
To eternity doth rest,

Leaving no posterity:
'Twas not their infirmity,
It was married chastity.

Truth may seem, but cannot be;
Beauty brag, but 'tis not she;
Truth and beauty buried be.

Property] individuality   threne] lament

To this urn let those repair
That are either true or fair;
For these dead birds sigh a prayer.

THOMAS CAMPION
1567–1620

155   *Integer Vitae*

THE man of life upright,
  Whose guiltless heart is free
From all dishonest deeds
  Or thought of vanity:

The man whose silent days
  In harmless joys are spent,
Whom hopes cannot delude,
  Nor sorrow discontent:

That man needs neither towers
  Nor armour for defence,
Nor secret vaults to fly
  From thunder's violence.

He only can behold
  With unaffrighted eyes
The horrors of the deep
  And terrors of the skies.

Thus scorning all the cares
  That fate or fortune brings,
He makes the heaven his book,
  His wisdom heavenly things,

Good thoughts his only friends,
  His wealth a well-spent age,
The earth his sober inn
  And quiet pilgrimage.

156 *Among the Shades*

WHEN thou must home to shades of underground,
    And there arrived, a new admirèd guest,
The beauteous spirits do engirt thee round,
    White Iope, blithe Helen and the rest,
To hear the stories of thy finished love
From that smooth tongue, whose music hell can move:

Then wilt thou speak of banqueting delights,
    Of masks and revels which sweet youth did make,
Of tourneys and great challenges of knights,
    And all these triumphs for thy beauty's sake.
When thou hast told these honours done to thee,
Then tell, O! tell, how thou didst murder me.

157 *Devotion*

FOLLOW your saint, follow with accents sweet;
Haste you, sad notes, fall at her flying feet.
There, wrapped in cloud of sorrow, pity move,
And tell the ravisher of my soul I perish for her love.
    But if she scorns my never-ceasing pain,
Then burst with sighing in her sight, and ne'er return again.

All that I sung still to her praise did tend.
Still she was first, still she my songs did end.
Yet she my love and music both doth fly,
The music that her echo is, and beauty's sympathy.
    Then let my notes pursue her scornful flight;
It shall suffice that they were breathed, and died for her delight.

158 *Follow thy Fair Sun*

FOLLOW thy fair sun, unhappy shadow.
    Though thou be black as night,
    And she made all of light,
Yet follow thy fair sun, unhappy shadow.

Follow her whose light thy light depriveth.
   Though here thou liv'st disgraced,
   And she in heaven is placed,
Yet follow her whose light the world reviveth.

Follow those pure beams whose beauty burneth,
   That so have scorchèd thee,
   As thou still black must be,
Till her kind beams thy black to brightness turneth.

Follow her, while yet her glory shineth.
   There comes a luckless night,
   That will dim all her light;
And this the black unhappy shade divineth.

Follow still, since so thy fates ordainèd.
   The sun must have his shade,
   Till both at once do fade,
The sun still proved, the shadow still disdainèd.

159   *Laura*

    ROSE-CHEEKED Laura, come;
  Sing thou smoothly with thy beauty's
  Silent music, either other
     Sweetly gracing.

    Lovely forms do flow
  From concent divinely framèd;
  Heaven is music, and thy beauty's
     Birth is heavenly.

    These dull notes we sing
  Discords need for helps to grace them;
  Only beauty purely loving
     Knows no discord;

    But still moves delight,
  Like clear springs renewed by flowing,
  Ever perfect, ever in them-
     selves eternal.

160   *In Praise of Neptune*

OF Neptune's empire let us sing,
At whose command the waves obey,
To whom the rivers tribute pay,
   Down the high mountains sliding;
To whom the scaly nation yields
Homage for the crystal fields
         Wherein they dwell;
And every sea-god pays a gem,
Yearly out of his watery cell,
To deck great Neptune's diadem.

The Tritons dancing in a ring,
Before his palace gates, do make
The water with their echoes quake,
   Like the great thunder sounding:
The sea-nymphs chant their accents shrill;
   And the Sirens, taught to kill
         With their sweet voice,
Make every echoing rock reply,
Unto their gentle murmuring noise,
The praise of Neptune's empery.

161   *Winter Nights*

NOW winter nights enlarge
   The number of their hours,
And clouds their storms discharge
   Upon the airy towers.
Let now the chimneys blaze,
   And cups o'erflow with wine;
Let well-tuned words amaze
   With harmony divine.
Now yellow waxen lights
   Shall wait on honey Love,
While youthful revels, masks, and courtly sights
   Sleep's leaden spells remove.

This time doth well dispense
  With lovers' long discourse.
Much speech hath some defence
  Though beauty no remorse.
All do not all things well:
  Some measures comely tread,
Some knotted riddles tell,
  Some poems smoothly read.
The Summer hath his joys,
  And Winter his delights.
Though Love and all his pleasures are but toys,
  They shorten tedious nights.

162　　　　　　　　　*A Lover's Plea*

SHALL I come, sweet Love, to thee,
  When the evening beams are set?
Shall I not excluded be?
  Will you find no feignèd let?
Let me not, for pity, more
Tell the long hours at your door.

Who can tell what thief or foe
  In the covert of the night
For his prey will work my woe,
  Or through wicked foul despite?
So may I die unredressed,
Ere my long love be possessed.

But to let such dangers pass,
  Which a lover's thoughts disdain,
'Tis enough in such a place
  To attend love's joys in vain.
Do not mock me in thy bed,
While these cold nights freeze me dead.

163   *Love-Charms*

THRICE toss these oaken ashes in the air;
Thrice sit thou mute in this enchanted chair;
Then thrice three times tie up this true love's knot,
And murmur soft: 'She will, or she will not.'

Go burn these poisonous weeds in yon blue fire,
These screech-owl's feathers and this prickling briar,
This cypress gathered at a dead man's grave,
That all thy fears and cares an end may have.

Then come, you fairies, dance with me a round;
Melt her hard heart with your melodious sound.
In vain are all the charms I can devise;
She hath an art to break them with her eyes.

164   *Cherry-Ripe*

THERE is a garden in her face,
   Where roses and white lilies grow;
A heavenly paradise is that place,
   Wherein all pleasant fruits do flow.
There cherries grow which none may buy,
Till 'Cherry-ripe' themselves do cry.

Those cherries fairly do enclose
   Of orient pearl a double row,
Which when her lovely laughter shows,
   They look like rosebuds filled with snow.
Yet them nor peer nor prince can buy,
Till 'Cherry-ripe' themselves do cry.

Her eyes like angels watch them still;
   Her brows like bended bows do stand,
Threatening with piercing frowns to kill
   All that attempt with eye or hand
Those sacred cherries to come nigh,
Till 'Cherry-ripe' themselves do cry.

165   *O Come Quickly!*

NEVER weather-beaten sail more willing bent to shore,
   Never tired pilgrim's limbs affected slumber more,
Than my weary spright now longs to fly out of my troubled breast.
   O! come quickly, sweetest Lord, and take my soul to rest.

Ever blooming are the joys of Heaven's high Paradise.
   Cold age deafs not there our ears, nor vapour dims our eyes;
Glory there the sun outshines, whose beams the blessed only see.
   O! come quickly, glorious Lord, and raise my spright to thee.

ANONYMOUS

166   *Hierusalem, my Happy Home*

HIERUSALEM, my happy home,
   When shall I come to thee?
When shall my sorrows have an end
   Thy joys when shall I see?

O happy harbour of the saints,
   O sweet and pleasant soil
In thee no sorrow may be found
   No grief, no care, no toil. . . .

No dampish mist is seen in thee,
   Nor cold nor darksome night;
There every soul shines as the sun,
   There God himself gives light.

There lust and lucre cannot dwell,
   There envy bears no sway;
There is no hunger, heat nor cold,
   But pleasure every way.

Hierusalem, Hierusalem,
   God grant I once may see
Thy endless joys, and of the same
   Partaker aye to be.

Thy walls are made of precious stones,
  Thy bulwarks diamonds square;
Thy gates are of right orient pearl,
  Exceeding rich and rare.

Thy turrets and thy pinnacles
  With carbuncles do shine;
Thy very streets are paved with gold,
  Surpassing clear and fine.

Thy houses are of ivory,
  Thy windows crystal clear,
Thy tiles are made of beaten gold,
  O God, that I were there.

Within thy gates nothing doth come
  That is not passing clean;
No spider's web, no dirt, no dust,
  No filth may there be seen.

Ah, my sweet home, Hierusalem,
  Would God I were in thee!
Would God my woes were at an end,
  Thy joys that I might see! . . .

Thy gardens and thy gallant walks
  Continually are green;
There grows such sweet and pleasant flowers
  As nowhere else are seen . . .

Quite through the streets with silver sound
  The flood of life doth flow;
Upon whose banks on every side
  The wood of life doth grow.

There trees for evermore bear fruit
  And evermore do spring;
There evermore the angels sit
  And evermore do sing.

There David stands with harp in hand
    As master of the Quire;
Ten thousand times that man were blest
    That might this music hear.

Our Lady sings *Magnificat*
    With tune surpassing sweet;
And all the virgins bear their parts
    Sitting about her feet.

Te Deum doth Saint Ambrose sing,
    Saint Austin doth the like;
Old Simeon and Zachary
    Have not their songs to seek.

There Magdalen hath left her moan
    And cheerfully doth sing,
With blessed saints whose harmony
    In every street doth ring.

Hierusalem, my happy home,
    Would God I were in thee!
Would God my woes were at an end,
    Thy joys that I might see!

from Song-Books

(i)

167   *The Herdmen*

WHAT pleasure have great princes,
    More dainty to their choice,
Than herdmen wild, who careless
    In quiet life rejoice,
And Fortune's fate not fearing
Sing sweet in summer morning?

Their dealings plain and rightful
    Are void of all deceit;
They never know how spiteful
    It is to kneel and wait
On favourite presumptuous,
Whose pride is vain and sumptuous.

All day their flocks each tendeth;
　At night they take their rest,
More quiet than who sendeth
　His ship into the East,
Where gold and pearl are plenty,
But getting very dainty.

For lawyers and their pleading
　They esteem it not a straw;
They think that honest meaning
　Is of itself a law;
Where conscience judgeth plainly,
They spend no money vainly.

O happy who thus liveth,
　Not caring much for gold,
With clothing which sufficeth
　To keep him from the cold.
Though poor and plain his diet,
Yet merry it is and quiet.

(ii)

168　　　　　　　*Philon the Shepherd*

WHILE that the sun with his beams hot
　Scorchèd the fruits in vale and mountain,
Philon the shepherd, late forgot,
　Sitting besides a crystal fountain
In shadow of a green oak tree,
Upon his pipe this song played he:
　'Adieu love, adieu love, untrue love!
　Your mind is light, soon lost for new love.

'So long as I was in your sight,
　I was as your heart, your soul, your treasure;
And evermore you sobbed, you sighed,
　Burning in flames beyond all measure.
Three days endured your love to me,
And it was lost in other three.
　Adieu love, adieu love, untrue love!
　Your mind is light, soon lost for new love.

'Another shepherd you did see,
  To whom your heart was soon enchainèd;
Full soon your love was lept from me;
  Full soon my place he had obtainèd.
Soon came a third your love to win,
And we were out, and he was in.
    Adieu love, adieu love, untrue love!
    Your mind is light, soon lost for new love.

'Sure you have made me passing glad,
  That you your mind so soon removèd,
Before that I the leisure had,
  To choose you for my best belovèd;
For all my love was past and done,
Two days before it was begun.
    Adieu love, adieu love, untrue love!
    Your mind is light, soon lost for new love.'

(iii)

169   *A Pedlar*

FINE knacks for ladies, cheap, choice, brave and new!
  Good pennyworths! but money cannot move.
I keep a fair but for the Fair to view;
  A beggar may be liberal of love.
Though all my wares be trash, the heart is true.

Great gifts are guiles and look for gifts again;
  My trifles come as treasures from my mind.
It is a precious jewel to be plain;
  Sometimes in shell the orient'st pearls we find.
Of others take a sheaf, of me a grain.

Within this pack pins, points, laces, and gloves,
  And divers toys fitting a country fair,
But in my heart, where duty serves and loves,
  Turtles and twins, court's brood, a heavenly pair.
Happy the heart that thinks of no removes!

(iv)

170 *Tears*

WEEP you no more, sad fountains;
  What need you flow so fast?
Look how the snowy mountains
  Heaven's sun doth gently waste.
    But my sun's heavenly eyes
      View not your weeping,
      That now lies sleeping
    Softly, now softly lies
      Sleeping.

Sleep is a reconciling,
  A rest that peace begets.
Doth not the sun rise smiling
  When fair at even he sets?
    Rest you then, rest, sad eyes,
      Melt not in weeping,
      While she lies sleeping
    Softly, now softly lies
      Sleeping.

(v)

171 *My Lady's Tears*

I SAW my lady weep,
  And Sorrow proud to be advancèd so
In those fair eyes where all perfections keep.
  Her face was full of woe;
But such a woe, believe me, as wins more hearts,
Than Mirth can do with her enticing parts.

  Sorrow was there made fair,
  And Passion wise, tears a delightful thing;
Silence beyond all speech a wisdom rare.
  She made her sighs to sing,
And all things with so sweet a sadness move,
As made my heart at once both grieve and love.

O fairer than aught else
The world can show, leave off in time to grieve.
Enough, enough your joyful looks excels;
    Tears kills the heart, believe.
  O! strive not to be excellent in woe,
Which only breeds your beauty's overthrow.

(vi)

Sister, Awake!

172

SISTER, awake! close not your eyes!
    The day her light discloses,
And the bright morning doth arise
    Out of her bed of roses.

See the clear sun, the world's bright eye,
    In at our window peeping:
Lo, how he blusheth to espy
    Us idle wenches sleeping!

Therefore awake! make haste, I say,
    And let us, without staying,
All in our gowns of green so gay
    Into the Park a-maying!

(vii)

No Other Choice

173

FAIN would I change that note
To which fond Love hath charmed me
Long, long to sing by rote,
Fancying that that harmed me:
Yet when this thought doth come,
'Love is the perfect sum
    Of all delight,'
I have no other choice
Either for pen or voice
    To sing or write.

O Love! they wrong thee much
That say thy sweet is bitter,
When thy rich fruit is such
As nothing can be sweeter.
Fair house of joy and bliss,
Where truest pleasure is,
    I do adore thee:
I know thee what thou art,
I serve thee with my heart,
    And fall before thee.

(viii)

174

Passing By

THERE is a Lady sweet and kind,
Was never face so pleased my mind;
I did but see her passing by,
And yet I love her till I die.

Her gesture, motion, and her smiles,
Her wit, her voice my heart beguiles,
Beguiles my heart, I know not why,
And yet I love her till I die.

Cupid is wingèd and doth range,
Her country so my love doth change:
But change she earth, or change she sky,
Yet will I love her till I die.

(ix)

175

The Awakening

ON a time the amorous Silvy
Said to her shepherd, 'Sweet, how do ye?
Kiss me this once and then God be wi' ye,
    My sweetest dear!
Kiss me this once and then God be wi' ye.
For now the morning draweth near.'

With that, her fairest bosom showing,
Opening her lips, rich perfumes blowing,
She said, 'Now kiss me and be going,
      My sweetest dear!
Kiss me this once and then be going,
For now the morning draweth near.'

With that the shepherd waked from sleeping,
And spying where the day was peeping,
He said, 'Now take my soul in keeping,
      My sweetest dear!
Kiss me and take my soul in keeping,
Since I must go, now day is near.'

(x)

176   *A Madrigal*

MY Love in her attire doth show her wit,
   It doth so well become her:
For every season she hath dressings fit,
   For winter, spring, and summer.
No beauty she doth miss,
   When all her robes are on:
But Beauty's self she is,
   When all her robes are gone.

177   *Aubade*

STAY, O sweet, and do not rise!
   The light that shines comes from thine eyes;
The day breaks not: it is my heart,
   Because that you and I must part.
      Stay! or else my joys will die
      And perish in their infancy.

HENRY CHETTLE

c. 1560–*c.* 1607

178   *Diaphenia*

DIAPHENIA, like the daffodowndilly,
    White as the sun, fair as the lily,
Heigh ho, how I do love thee!
    I do love thee as my lambs
    Are beloved of their dams;
How blest were I if thou wouldst prove me!

Diaphenia, like the spreading roses,
    That in thy sweets all sweets encloses,
Fair sweet, how I do love thee!
    I do love thee as each flower
    Loves the sun's life-giving power,
For, dead, thy breath to life might move me.

Diaphenia, like to all things blessèd,
    When all thy praises are expressèd,
Dear joy, how I do love thee!
    As the birds do love the spring,
    Or the bees their careful king:
Then in requite, sweet virgin, love me!

SIR HENRY WOTTON

1568–1639

179   *Elizabeth of Bohemia*

YOU meaner beauties of the night,
    That poorly satisfy our eyes
More by your number than your light,
    You common people of the skies;
    What are you when the moon shall rise?

You curious chanters of the wood,
　That warble forth Dame Nature's lays,
Thinking your passions understood
　　By your weak accents; what's your praise
　　When Philomel her voice shall raise?

You violets that first appear,
　By your pure purple mantles known
Like the proud virgins of the year,
　　As if the spring were all your own;
　　What are you when the rose is blown?

So, when my mistress shall be seen
　In form and beauty of her mind,
By virtue first, then choice, a Queen,
　　Tell me, if she were not designed
　　The eclipse and glory of her kind.

180　*Upon the Sudden Restraint of the Earl of Somerset,
then falling from favour, 1615.*

DAZZLED thus with height of place,
Whilst our hopes our wits beguile,
No man marks the narrow space
'Twixt a prison and a smile.

Then, since Fortune's favours fade,
You that in her arms do sleep,
Learn to swim, and not to wade,
For the hearts of Kings are deep.

But, if Greatness be so blind
As to trust in towers of air,
Let it be with Goodness lined,
That at least the fall be fair.

Then, though darkened, you shall say,
When friends fail, and Princes frown,
Virtue is the roughest way,
But proves at night a bed of down.

181 *The Character of a Happy Life*

HOW happy is he born and taught
That serveth not another's will;
Whose armour is his honest thought,
And simple truth his utmost skill!

Whose passions not his masters are;
Whose soul is still prepared for death,
Untied unto the world by care
Of public fame or private breath;

Who envies none that chance doth raise,
Nor vice; who never understood
How deepest wounds are given by praise;
Nor rules of state, but rules of good;

Who hath his life from rumours freed;
Whose conscience is his strong retreat;
Whose state can neither flatterers feed,
Nor ruin make oppressors great;

Who God doth late and early pray
More of His grace than gifts to lend;
And entertains the harmless day
With a religious book or friend;

—This man is freed from servile bands
Of hope to rise or fear to fall:
Lord of himself, though not of lands,
And having nothing, yet hath all.

SIR JOHN DAVIES

1569–1626

182   *The Praise of Dancing*

'DANCING, bright lady, then began to be,
  When the first seeds whereof the world did spring,
The fire, air, earth, and water, did agree
  By Love's persuasion, nature's mighty king,
  To leave their first discorded combating,
    And in a dance such measure to observe,
    As all the world their motion should preserve.

'Since when they still are carried in a round,
  And changing come one in another's place;
Yet do they neither mingle nor confound,
  But every one doth keep the bounded space
  Wherein the dance doth bid it turn or trace.
    This wondrous miracle did Love devise,
    For dancing is love's proper exercise.

'Like this he framed the gods' eternal bower,
  And of a shapeless and confusèd mass,
By his through-piercing and digesting power,
  The turning vault of heaven formèd was,
  Whose starry wheels he hath so made to pass,
    As that their movings do a music frame,
    And they themselves still dance unto the same.

*

'For that brave sun, the father of the day,
  Doth love this earth, the mother of the night;
And, like a reveller in rich array,
  Doth dance his galliard in his leman's sight,
  Both back and forth and sideways passing light.
    His gallant grace doth so the gods amaze,
    That all stand still and at his beauty gaze.

'But see the earth when she approacheth near,
　　How she for joy doth spring and sweetly smile;
But see again her sad and heavy cheer,
　　When changing places he retires a while;
　　But those black clouds he shortly will exile,
　　　　And make them all before his presence fly,
　　　　As mists consumed before his cheerful eye.

'Who doth not see the measure of the moon?
　　Which thirteen times she danceth every year,
And ends her pavan thirteen times as soon
　　As doth her brother, of whose golden hair
　　She borroweth part, and proudly doth it wear.
　　　　Then doth she coyly turn her face aside,
　　　　That half her cheek is scarce sometimes descried.

'Next her, the pure, subtle, and cleansing fire
　　Is swiftly carried in a circle even,
Though Vulcan be pronounced by many a liar
　　The only halting god that dwells in heaven;
　　But that foul name may be more fitly given
　　　　To your false fire, that far from heaven is fall,
　　　　And doth consume, waste, spoil, disorder all.

'And now behold your tender nurse, the air,
　　And common neighbour that aye runs around;
How many pictures and impressions fair
　　Within her empty regions are there found,
　　Which to your senses dancing do propound?
　　　　For what are breath, speech, echoes, music, winds,
　　　　But dancings of the air, in sundry kinds?

'For, when you breathe, the air in order moves,
　　Now in, now out, in time and measure true,
And when you speak, so well she dancing loves,
　　That doubling oft and oft redoubling new
　　With thousand forms she doth herself endue;
　　　　For all the words that from your lips repair
　　　　Are nought but tricks and turnings of the air.

'Hence is her prattling daughter, Echo, born,
　That dances to all voices she can hear.
There is no sound so harsh that she doth scorn,
　Nor any time wherein she will forbear
　　The airy pavement with her feet to wear;
　　　And yet her hearing sense is nothing quick,
　　　For after time she endeth every trick.

'And thou, sweet music, dancing's only life,
　The ear's sole happiness, the air's best speech,
Lodestone of fellowship, charming rod of strife,
　The soft mind's paradise, the sick mind's leech,
　　With thine own tongue thou trees and stones canst teach,
　　　That when the air doth dance her finest measure,
　　　Then art thou born, the gods' and men's sweet pleasure.

'Lastly, where keep the winds their revelry,
　Their violent turnings and wild whirling hays,
But in the air's tralucent gallery?
　Where she herself is turned a hundred ways,
　While with those maskers wantonly she plays.
　　　Yet in this misrule they such rule embrace
　　　As two, at once, encumber not the place.

'If then fire, air, wandering and fixed lights,
　In every province of the imperial sky,
Yield perfect forms of dancing to your sights,
　In vain I teach the ear that which the eye,
　With certain view, already doth descry;
　　　But for your eyes perceive not all they see,
　　　In this I will your senses' master be.

'For lo! the sea that fleets about the land,
　And like a girdle clips her solid waist,
Music and measure both doth understand;
　For his great crystal eye is always cast
　Up to the moon, and on her fixèd fast;
　　　And as she danceth in her pallid sphere,
　　　So danceth he about the centre here.

　　　hays] country dances

177

'Sometimes his proud green waves in order set,
   One after other, flow unto the shore;
Which when they have with many kisses wet,
   They ebb away in order, as before;
     And to make known his courtly love the more,
      He oft doth lay aside his three-forked mace,
      And with his arms the timorous earth embrace.

'Only the earth doth stand forever still:
   Her rocks remove not, nor her mountains meet,
Although some wits enriched with learning's skill
   Say heaven stands firm and that the earth doth fleet,
   And swiftly turneth underneath their feet;
     Yet, though the earth is ever steadfast seen,
     On her broad breast hath dancing ever been.

'For those blue veins that through her body spread,
   Those sapphire streams which from great hills do spring,
The earth's great dugs, for every wight is fed
   With sweet fresh moisture from them issuing,
   Observe a dance in their wild wandering;
     And still their dance begets a murmur sweet,
     And still the murmur with the dance doth meet.'

183   *Affliction*

If aught can teach us aught, Affliction's looks,
   Making us look into ourselves so near,
Teach us to know ourselves beyond all books,
   Or all the learned schools that ever were.

This mistress lately plucked me by the ear,
   And many a golden lesson hath me taught;
Hath made my senses quick, and reason clear,
   Reformed my will, and rectified my thought.

So do the winds and thunders cleanse the air;
   So working seas settle and purge the wine;
So lopped and prunèd trees do flourish fair;
   So doth the fire the drossy gold refine.

Neither Minerva nor the learned Muse,
    Nor rules of art, nor precepts of the wise,
Could in my brain those beams of skill infuse,
    As but the glance of this dame's angry eyes.

She within lists my ranging mind hath brought,
    That now beyond myself I list not go;
Myself am centre of my circling thought,
    Only myself I study, learn, and know.

I know my body's of so frail a kind
    As force without, fevers within, can kill;
I know the heavenly nature of my mind,
    But 'tis corrupted both in wit and will;

I know my soul hath power to know all things,
    Yet is she blind and ignorant in all;
I know I am one of nature's little kings,
    Yet to the least and vilest things am thrall.

I know my life's a pain and but a span,
    I know my sense is mocked with everything;
And to conclude, I know myself a man,
    Which is a proud, and yet a wretched thing.

184   *The Soul and the Body*

BUT how shall we this union well express?
    Nought ties the soul; her subtlety is such,
She moves the body, which she doth possess,
    Yet no part toucheth, but by virtue's touch.

Then dwells she not therein as in a tent;
    Nor as a pilot in his ship doth sit;
Nor as the spider in his web is pent;
    Nor as the wax retains the print in it;

Nor as a vessel water doth contain;
    Nor as one liquor in another shed;
Nor as the heat doth in the fire remain;
    Nor as a voice throughout the air is spread.

But as the fair and cheerful morning light
  Doth here and there her silver beams impart,
And in an instant doth herself unite
  To the transparent air, in all and part;

Still resting whole, when blows the air divide,
  Abiding pure, when the air is most corrupted,
Throughout the air her beams dispersing wide,
  And when the air is tossed, not interrupted:

So doth the piercing soul the body fill,
  Being all in all, and all in part diffused,
Indivisible, incorruptible still,
  Not forced, encountered, troubled or confused.

And as the sun above the light doth bring,
  Though we behold it in the air below,
So from the eternal Light the soul doth spring,
  Though in the body she her powers do show.

JOHN DONNE

1572–1631

185   *Seek True Religion!*

                    THOUGH Truth and Falsehood be
Near twins, yet Truth a little elder is.
Be busy to seek her; believe me this:
He's not of none, nor worst, that seeks the best.
To adore, or scorn an image, or protest,
May all be bad. Doubt wisely; in strange way
To stand inquiring right is not to stray;
To sleep or run wrong is. On a huge hill,
Craggèd and steep, Truth stands, and he that will
Reach her, about must and about must go,
And what the hill's suddenness resists, win so.
Yet strive so, that before age, death's twilight,
Thy soul rest, for none can work in that night.

To will implies delay; therefore now do.
Hard deeds the body's pains; hard knowledge too,
The mind's endeavours reach; and mysteries
Are like the sun, dazzling, yet plain to all eyes.
Keep the truth which thou hast found; men do not stand
In so ill case here that God hath with his hand
Signed kings blank charters to kill whom they hate,
Nor are they vicars, but hangmen to Fate.
Fool and wretch, wilt thou let thy soul be tied
To man's laws, by which she shall not be tried
At the last day? Will it then boot thee
To say a Philip or a Gregory,
A Harry, or a Martin taught thee this?
Is not this excuse for mere contraries
Equally strong? Cannot both sides say so?
That thou mayst rightly obey Power, her bounds know;
Those passed, her nature and name's changed; to be
Then humble to her is idolatry.
As streams are Power is; those blest flowers that dwell
At the rough stream's calm head thrive and prove well,
But having left their roots and themselves given
To the stream's tyrannous rage, alas, are driven
Through mills and rocks and woods, and at last, almost
Consumed in going, in the sea are lost.
So perish souls which more choose men's unjust
Power from God claimed than God himself to trust.

186   *To His Mistress Desiring to Travel with*
        Him as His Page

BY our first strange and fatal interview,
By all desires which thereof did ensue,
By our long starving hopes, by that remorse
Which my words' masculine persuasive force
Begot in thee, and by the memory
Of hurts which spies and rivals threatened me,
I calmly beg; but by thy parents' wrath,
By all pains which want and divorcement hath,

185   mere] absolute

181

I conjure thee; and all those oaths which I
And thou have sworn, to seal joint constancy,
Here I unswear, and overswear them thus:
Thou shalt not love by means so dangerous.
Temper, O fair Love, love's impetuous rage,
Be my true mistress still, not my feigned page.
I'll go, and, by thy kind leave, leave behind
Thee, only worthy to nurse in my mind
Thirst to come back; O, if thou die before,
From other lands my soul towards thee shall soar.
Thy else almighty beauty cannot move
Rage from the seas, nor thy love teach them love,
Nor tame wild Boreas' harshness: thou hast read
How roughly he in pieces shiverèd
Fair Orithea, whom he swore he loved.
Fall ill or good, 'tis madness to have proved
Dangers unurged; feed on this flattery,
That absent lovers one in the other be.
Dissemble nothing, not a boy, nor change
Thy body's habit, nor mind's; be not strange
To thyself only; all will spy in thy face
A blushing womanly discovering grace.
Richly clothed apes are called apes, and as soon
Eclipsed as bright, we call the moon the moon.
Men of France, changeable chameleons,
Spittles of diseases, shops of fashions,
Love's fuellers, and the rightest company
Of players, which upon the world's stage be,
Will quickly know thee, and know thee; and alas,
The indifferent Italian, as we pass
His warm land, well content to think thee page,
Will haunt thee, with such lust and hideous rage
As Lot's fair guests were vexed: but none of these,
Nor spongy hydroptic Dutch, shall thee displease,
If thou stay here. O stay here; for, for thee
England is only a worthy gallery,
To walk in expectation, till from thence
Our great King call thee into his presence.
When I am gone, dream me some happiness;
Nor let thy looks our long-hid love confess;
Nor praise, nor dispraise me, bless, nor curse
Openly love's force; nor in bed fright thy nurse

With midnight's startings, crying out, 'O, O,
Nurse, O, my love is slain; I saw him go
O'er the white Alps, alone; I saw him, I,
Assailed, fight, taken, stabbed, bleed, fall, and die.'
Augur me better chance, except dread Jove
Think it enough for me to have had thy love.

187   *A Storm at Sea*

BUT when I waked, I saw that I saw not;
I, and the sun, which should teach me, had forgot
East, west, day, night; and I could but say,
If the world had lasted, now it had been day.
Thousands our noises were, yet we 'mongst all
Could none by his right name, but thunder, call:
Lightning was all our light, and it rained more
Than if the sun had drunk the sea before.
Some coffined in their cabins lie, equally
Grieved that they are not dead, and yet must die;
And as sin-burdened souls from graves will creep
At the last day, some forth their cabins peep,
And tremblingly ask, 'What news?' and do hear so,
Like jealous husbands, what they would not know.
Some, sitting on the hatches, would seem there
With hideous gazing to fear away fear.
There note they the ship's sicknesses, the mast
Shaked with this ague, and the hold and waist
With a salt dropsy clogged, and all our tacklings
Snapping, like too-high-stretchèd treble strings.
And from our tattered sails rags drop down so,
As from one hanged in chains a year ago.
Even our ordnance, placed for our defence,
Strive to break loose, and 'scape away from thence.
Pumping hath tired our men, and what's the gain?
Seas into seas thrown, we suck in again;
Hearing hath deafed our sailors, and if they
Knew how to hear, there's none knows what to say.
Compared to these storms, death is but a qualm,
Hell somewhat lightsome, and the Bermuda calm.
Darkness, light's elder brother, his birth-right
Claims o'er this world, and to heaven hath chased light.

All things are one, and that one none can be,
Since all forms uniform deformity
Doth cover; so that we, except God say
Another *Fiat*, shall have no more day.
So violent, yet long, these furies be,
That though thine absence starve me, I wish not thee.

188   *Song*

Go and catch a falling star,
    Get with child a mandrake root,
Tell me where all past years are,
    Or who cleft the Devil's foot;
Teach me to hear mermaids singing,
Or to keep off envy's stinging,
                And find
                What wind
Serves to advance an honest mind.

If thou beest born to strange sights,
    Things invisible to see,
Ride ten thousand days and nights
    Till Age snow white hairs on thee;
Thou, when thou return'st, wilt tell me
All strange wonders that befell thee,
                And swear
                No where
Lives a woman true and fair.

If thou find'st one, let me know;
    Such a pilgrimage were sweet.
Yet do not; I would not go,
    Though at next door we might meet.
Though she were true when you met her,
And last till you write your letter,
                Yet she
                Will be
False, ere I come, to two or three.

189   *The Apparition*

WHEN by thy scorn, O murderess, I am dead,
And that thou think'st thee free
From all solicitation from me,
Then shall my ghost come to thy bed,
And thee, fained vestal, in worse arms shall see·
Then thy sick taper will begin to wink,
And he, whose thou art then, being tired before,
Will, if thou stir, or pinch to wake him, think
    Thou call'st for more,
And in false sleep will from thee shrink,
And then, poor aspen wretch, neglected thou
Bathed in a cold quicksilver sweat wilt lie
    A verier ghost than I;
What I will say, I will not tell thee now,
Lest that preserve thee; and since my love is spent,
I had rather thou shouldst painfully repent,
Than by my threatenings rest still innocent.

190   *Song*

SWEETEST love, I do not go
    For weariness of thee,
Nor in hope the world can show
    A fitter love for me;
        But since that I
Must die at last, 'tis best
To use myself in jest
    Thus by fained deaths to die.

Yesternight the sun went hence,
    And yet is here today,
He hath no desire nor sense,
    Nor half so short a way:
        Then fear not me,
But believe that I shall make
Speedier journeys, since I take
    More wings and spurs than he.

O how feeble is man's power,
　That if good fortune fall,
Cannot add another hour,
　Nor a lost hour recall!
　　But come bad chance,
And we join to it our strength,
And we teach it art and length,
　Itself o'er us to advance.

When thou sigh'st, thou sigh'st not wind,
　But sigh'st my soul away,
When thou weep'st, unkindly kind,
　My life's blood doth decay.
　　It cannot be
That thou lov'st me, as thou sayst,
If in thine my life thou waste,
　Thou art the best of me.

Let not thy divining heart
　Forethink me any ill,
Destiny may take thy part,
　And may thy fears fulfil.
　　But think that we
Are but turned aside to sleep;
They who one another keep
　Alive, ne'er parted be.

191　　　　　　*The Undertaking*

I HAVE done one braver thing
　Than all the Worthies did,
Yet a braver thence doth spring,
　Which is, to keep that hid.

It were but madness now to impart
　The skill of specular stone.
When he which can have learned the art
　To cut it can find none.

So, if I now should utter this,
　Others (because no more
Such stuff to work upon, there is)
　Would love but as before.

But he who loveliness within
  Hath found, all outward loathes;
For he who colour loves, and skin,
  Loves but their oldest clothes.

If, as I have, you also do
  Virtue attired in woman see,
And dare love that, and say so too,
  And forget the He and She;

And if this love, though placèd so,
  From profane men you hide,
Which will no faith on this bestow,
  Or, if they do, deride:

Then you have done a braver thing
  Than all the Worthies did,
And a braver thence will spring,
  Which is, to keep that hid.

192 *A Valediction: forbidding Mourning*

As virtuous men pass mildly away,
  And whisper to their souls to go,
Whilst some of their sad friends do say
  'The breath goes now,' and some say, 'No':

So let us melt, and make no noise,
  No tear-floods, nor sigh-tempests move,
'Twere profanation of our joys
  To tell the laity our love.

Moving of the earth brings harms and fears,
  Men reckon what it did and meant;
But trepidation of the spheres,
  Though greater far, is innocent.

Dull sublunary lovers' love
  (Whose soul is sense) cannot admit
Absence, because it doth remove
  Those things which elemented it.

But we by a love so much refined
   That ourselves know not what it is,
Inter-assurèd of the mind,
   Care less eyes, lips and hands to miss.

Our two souls therefore, which are one,
   Though I must go, endure not yet
A breach, but an expansion
   Like gold to airy thinness beat.

If they be two, they are two so
   As stiff twin compasses are two;
Thy soul, the fixed foot, makes no show
   To move, but doth, if the other do.

And though it in the centre sit,
   Yet when the other far doth roam,
It leans, and hearkens after it,
   And grows erect, as it comes home.

Such wilt thou be to me, who must
   Like the other foot, obliquely run;
Thy firmness makes my circle just,
   And makes me end where I begun.

193   *The Ecstasy*

WHERE, like a pillow on a bed,
   A pregnant bank swelled up, to rest
The violet's reclining head,
   Sat we two, one another's best.

Our hands were firmly cemented
   With a fast balm, which thence did spring;
Our eye-beams twisted, and did thread
   Our eyes upon one double string;

So to entergraft our hands, as yet
   Was all our means to make us one,
And pictures on our eyes to get
   Was all our propagation.

As 'twixt two equal armies Fate
   Suspends uncertain victory,
Our souls (which to advance their state
   Were gone out) hung 'twixt her and me.

And whilst our souls negotiate there,
   We like sepulchral statues lay;
All day the same our postures were,
   And we said nothing all the day.

If any, so by love refined
   That he soul's language understood,
And by good love were grown all mind,
   Within convenient distance stood,

He (though he knew not which soul spake,
   Because both meant, both spake the same)
Might thence a new concoction take,
   And part far purer than he came.

This ecstasy doth unperplex
   (We said) and tell us what we love,
We see by this, it was not sex,
   We see, we saw not what did move:

But as all several souls contain
   Mixture of things, they know not what,
Love these mixed souls doth mix again,
   And makes both one, each this and that.

A single violet transplant,
   The strength, the colour, and the size,
(All which before was poor and scant)
   Redoubles still, and multiplies.

When love with one another so
   Interinanimates two souls,
That abler soul, which thence doth flow,
   Defects of loneliness controls.

We then, who are this new soul, know
  Of what we are composed, and made,
For the atomies of which we grow
  Are souls, whom no change can invade.

But, O alas! so long, so far
  Our bodies why do we forbear?
They are ours, though they are not we; we are
  The intelligences, they the sphere.

We owe them thanks, because they thus
  Did us, to us, at first convey,
Yielded their forces, sense, to us,
  Nor are dross to us, but allay.

On man heaven's influence works not so,
  But that it first imprints the air;
So soul into the soul may flow,
  Though it to body first repair.

As our blood labours to beget
  Spirits, as like souls as it can;
Because such fingers need to knit
  That subtle knot, which makes us man;

So must pure lovers' souls descend
  To affections, and to faculties,
Which sense may reach and apprehend,
  Else a great Prince in prison lies.

To our bodies turn we then, that so
  Weak men on love revealed may look;
Love's mysteries in souls do grow,
  But yet the body is his book.

And if some lover, such as we,
  Have heard this dialogue of one,
Let him still mark us, he shall see
  Small change, when we're to bodies gone.

194   *The Sun Rising*

Busy old fool, unruly Sun,
        Why dost thou thus,
Through windows and through curtains call on us?
Must to thy motions lovers' seasons run?
        Saucy pedantic wretch, go chide
        Late school-boys, and sour 'prentices,
    Go tell court-huntsmen that the King will ride,
    Call country ants to harvest offices;
Love, all alike, no season knows, nor clime,
Nor hours, days, months, which are the rags of time.

    Thy beams, so reverend and strong
        Why shouldst thou think?
I could eclipse and cloud them with a wink,
But that I would not lose her sight so long:
        If her eyes have not blinded thine,
        Look, and tomorrow late tell me,
    Whether both the Indias of spice and mine
    Be where thou left'st them, or lie here with me.
Ask for those kings whom thou saw'st yesterday,
And thou shalt hear, 'All here in one bed lay.'

    She's all States, and all Princes I;
        Nothing else is.
Princes do but play us; compared to this,
All honour's mimic; all wealth alchemy.
        Thou, Sun, art half as happy as we,
        In that the world's contracted thus;
    Thine age asks ease, and since thy duties be
    To warm the world, that's done in warming us.
Shine here to us, and thou art everywhere;
This bed thy centre is, these walls thy sphere.

195   *The Anniversary*

ALL Kings, and all their favourites,
  All glory of honours, beauties, wits,
The sun itself, which makes times, as they pass,
Is elder by a year now than it was
When thou and I first one another saw:
All other things to their destruction draw,
    Only our love hath no decay;
This no tomorrow hath, nor yesterday,
Running it never runs from us away,
But truly keeps his first, last, everlasting day.

  Two graves must hide thine and my corse;
    If one might, death were no divorce.
Alas, as well as other Princes, we
(Who Prince enough in one another be)
Must leave at last in death these eyes and ears,
Oft fed with true oaths, and with sweet salt tears;
    But souls where nothing dwells but love
(All other thoughts being inmates) then shall prove
This, or a love increasèd there above,
When bodies to their graves, souls from their graves remove.

  And then we shall be throughly blest;
    But we no more than all the rest.
Here upon earth we're Kings, and none but we
Can be such Kings, nor of such subjects be;
Who is so safe as we? where none can do
Treason to us, except one of us two.
    True and false fears let us refrain,
Let us love nobly, and live, and add again
Years and years unto years, till we attain
To write threescore: this is the second of our reign.

196 *The Canonization*

For God's sake hold your tongue, and let me love,
　　Or chide my palsy, or my gout,
My five gray hairs, or ruined fortune flout;
With wealth your state, your mind with arts improve;
　　Take you a course, get you a place,
　　Observe his Honour, or his Grace,
And the King's real, or his stamped face
　　Contemplate; what you will, approve,
　　　　So you will let me love.

Alas, alas, who's injured by my love?
　　What merchant's ships have my sighs drowned?
Who says my tears have overflowed his ground?
When did my colds a forward spring remove?
　　When did the heats which my veins fill
　　Add one man to the plaguy Bill?
Soldiers find wars, and lawyers find out still
　　Litigious men, which quarrels move,
　　　　Though she and I do love.

Call us what you will, we're made such by love;
　　Call her one, me another fly,
We're tapers too, and at our own cost die,
And we in us find the Eagle and the Dove;
　　The Phoenix riddle hath more wit
　　By us; we two, being one, are it,
So, to one neutral thing both sexes fit.
　　We die and rise the same, and prove
　　　　Mysterious by this love.

We can die by it, if not live by love,
　　And if unfit for tombs or hearse
Our legend be, it will be fit for verse;
And if no piece of chronicle we prove,
　　We'll build in sonnets pretty rooms;
　　As well a well-wrought urn becomes
The greatest ashes, as half-acre tombs;
　　And by these hymns all shall approve
　　　　Us canonized for love;

And thus invoke us: 'You, whom reverend Love
   Made one another's hermitage;
You, to whom love was peace, that now is rage;
Who did the whole world's soul extract, and drove
    Into the glasses of your eyes,
    So made such mirrors, and such spies,
That they did all to you epitomize,
     Countries, towns, courts: beg from above
     A pattern of your love!'

197   *A Nocturnal upon St Lucy's Day,*
           being the shortest day

'Tis the year's midnight, and it is the day's,
Lucy's, who scarce seven hours herself unmasks;
   The sun is spent, and now his flasks
   Send forth light squibs, no constant rays;
    The world's whole sap is sunk;
The general balm the hydroptic earth hath drunk,
Whither, as to the bed's-feet, life is shrunk,
Dead and interred; yet all these seem to laugh,
Compared with me, who am their epitaph.

Study me then, you who shall lovers be
At the next world, that is, at the next spring:
   For I am every dead thing,
   In whom love wrought new alchemy.
    For his art did express
A quintessence even from nothingness,
From dull privations, and lean emptiness:
He ruined me, and I am re-begot
Of absence, darkness, death: things which are not.

All others, from all things, draw all that's good,
Life, soul, form, spirit, whence they being have;
   I, by Love's limbeck, am the grave
   Of all, that's nothing. Oft a flood
    Have we two wept, and so
Drowned the whole world, us two; oft did we grow
To be two Chaoses, when we did show
Care to ought else; and often absences
Withdrew our souls, and made us carcasses.

     197 limbeck] alchemical still

But I am by her death (which word wrongs her)
Of the first nothing the elixir grown;
   Were I a man, that I were one,
   I needs must know; I should prefer,
     If I were any beast,
Some ends, some means; yea plants, yea stones detest
And love; all, all some properties invest;
If I an ordinary nothing were,
As shadow, a light, and body must be here.

But I am None; nor will my sun renew.
You lovers, for whose sake the lesser sun
   At this time to the Goat is run
   To fetch new lust, and give it you,
     Enjoy your summer all;
Since she enjoys her long night's festival,
Let me prepare towards her, and let me call
This hour her vigil, and her eve, since this
Both the year's and the day's deep midnight is.

198   *The Relic*

      WHEN my grave is broke up again
      Some second guest to entertain,
     (For graves have learned that woman-head
     To be to more than one a bed)
        And he that digs it, spies
A bracelet of bright hair about the bone,
      Will he not let us alone,
And think that there a loving couple lies
Who thought that this device might be some way
To make their souls, at the last busy day,
Meet at this grave, and make a little stay?

       If this fall in a time, or land,
       Where mis-devotion doth command,
        Then he that digs us up will bring
        Us to the Bishop and the King,

197   elixir] essence   to the Goat] to the zodiacal sign of Capricorn

To make us relics; then
Thou shalt be a Mary Magdalen, and I
    A something else thereby;
All women shall adore us, and some men;
And since at such times miracles are sought,
I would that age were by this paper taught
What miracles we harmless lovers wrought.

First, we loved well and faithfully,
   Yet knew not what we loved, nor why;
Difference of sex no more we knew
   Than our guardian angels do;
    Coming and going we
Perchance might kiss, but not between those meals;
    Our hands ne'er touched the seals,
Which nature, injured by late law, sets free:
These miracles we did; but now alas,
All measure, and all language, I should pass,
Should I tell what a miracle she was.

Holy Sonnets

199   (i)

THOU hast made me, and shall thy work decay?
  Repair me now, for now mine end doth haste;
  I run to death, and death meets me as fast,
And all my pleasures are like yesterday.
I dare not move my dim eyes any way;
  Despair behind, and death before doth cast
  Such terror, and my feebled flesh doth waste
By sin in it, which it towards hell doth weigh.
Only thou art above, and when towards thee
  By thy leave I can look, I rise again;
But our old subtle foe so tempteth me
  That not one hour I can myself sustain.
    Thy grace may wing me to prevent his art,
    And thou like adamant draw mine iron heart.

200

(ii)

AT the round earth's imagined corners blow
　　Your trumpets, angels, and arise, arise
　　From death, you numberless infinities
Of souls, and to your scattered bodies go:
All whom the flood did, and fire shall o'erthrow,
　　All whom war, dearth, age, agues, tyrannies,
　　Despair, law, chance hath slain, and you whose eyes
Shall behold God, and never taste death's woe.
But let them sleep, Lord, and me mourn a space,
　　For if above all these my sins abound,
'Tis late to ask abundance of thy grace
　　When we are there. Here on this lowly ground
　　　Teach me how to repent: for that's as good
　　　As if thou hadst sealed my pardon with thy blood.

201

(iii)

DEATH, be not proud, though some have callèd thee
　　Mighty and dreadful, for thou art not so;
　　For those whom thou think'st thou dost overthrow
Die not, poor Death, nor yet canst thou kill me.
From rest and sleep, which but thy pictures be,
　　Much pleasure—then, from thee much more must flow;
　　And soonest our best men with thee do go,
Rest of their bones and soul's delivery.
Thou'rt slave to fate, chance, kings and desperate men,
　　And dost with poison, war, and sickness dwell;
　　And poppy or charms can make us sleep as well,
And better than thy stroke. Why swell'st thou then?
　　　One short sleep past, we wake eternally,
　　　And death shall be no more. Death, thou shalt die.

202   (iv)

BATTER my heart, three-personed God, for you
   As yet but knock, breathe, shine, and seek to mend;
   That I may rise and stand, o'erthrow me and bend
Your force to break, blow, burn, and make me new.
I, like an usurped town to another due,
   Labour to admit you, but O, to no end.
   Reason, your viceroy in me, me should defend,
But is captived and proves weak or untrue.
Yet dearly I love you and would be loved fain,
   But am betrothed unto your enemy.
Divorce me, untie, or break that knot again,
   Take me to you, imprison me, for I,
     Except you enthrall me, never shall be free,
     Nor ever chaste except you ravish me.

203   *A Hymn*

WILT thou forgive that sin where I begun,
   Which is my sin, though it were done before?
Wilt thou forgive those sins through which I run,
   And do them still, though still I do deplore?
     When thou hast done, thou hast not done,
      For I have more.

Wilt thou forgive that sin by which I won
   Others to sin? and made my sin their door?
Wilt thou forgive that sin which I did shun
   A year or two, but wallowed in a score?
     When thou hast done, thou hast not done,
      For I have more.

I have a sin of fear, that when I have spun
   My last thread, I shall perish on the shore;
Swear by thyself, that at my death thy Sun
   Shall shine as it shines now, and heretofore;
     And, having done that, thou hast done,
      I have no more.

BEN JONSON
?1573-1637

204 *Hymn to Diana*

QUEEN and huntress, chaste and fair,
  Now the sun is laid to sleep,
Seated in thy silver chair,
  State in wonted manner keep:
    Hesperus entreats thy light,
    Goddess excellently bright.

Earth, let not thy envious shade
  Dare itself to interpose;
Cynthia's shining orb was made
  Heaven to clear when day did close:
    Bless us then with wishèd sight,
    Goddess excellently bright.

Lay thy bow of pearl apart,
  And thy crystal-shining quiver;
Give unto the flying hart
  Space to breathe, how short soever:
    Thou that mak'st a day of night—
    Goddess excellently bright.

205 *Simplex Munditiis*

STILL to be neat, still to be drest,
As you were going to a feast;
Still to be powdered, still perfumed,
Lady, it is to be presumed,
Though art's hid causes are not found,
All is not sweet, all is not sound.

Give me a look, give me a face
That makes simplicity a grace;
Robes loosely flowing, hair as free:
Such sweet neglect more taketh me
Than all the adulteries of art;
They strike mine eyes, but not my heart.

199

206   *To Celia*

DRINK to me only with thine eyes,
    And I will pledge with mine;
Or leave a kiss but in the cup
    And I'll not look for wine.
The thirst that from the soul doth rise
    Doth ask a drink divine;
But might I of Jove's nectar sup,
    I would not change for thine.

I sent thee late a rosy wreath,
    Not so much honouring thee
As giving it a hope that there
    It could not withered be;
But thou thereon didst only breathe,
    And sent'st it back to me;
Since when it grows, and smells, I swear,
    Not of itself but thee!

207   *The Shadow*

FOLLOW a shadow, it still flies you;
    Seem to fly it, it will pursue:
So court a mistress, she denies you;
    Let her alone, she will court you.
        Say, are not women truly, then,
        Styled but the shadows of us men?

At morn and even, shades are longest;
    At noon they are or short or none:
So men at weakest, they are strongest,
    But grant us perfect, they're not known.
        Say, are not women truly, then,
        Styled but the shadows of us men?

Epitaphs

(i)

208

On my First Daughter

HERE lies to each her parents' ruth
Mary, the daughter of their youth:
Yet, all Heaven's gifts being Heaven's due,
It makes the father less to rue.
At six months' end she parted hence
With safety of her innocence;
Whose soul Heaven's Queen (whose name she bears)
In comfort of her mother's tears,
Hath placed amongst her virgin-train;
Where, while that severed doth remain,
This grave partakes the fleshly birth,
Which cover lightly, gentle earth.

(ii)

209

On my Son

Farewell, thou child of my right hand, and joy;
   My sin was too much hope of thee, loved boy.
Seven years thou wert lent to me, and I thee pay,
   Exacted by thy fate, on the just day.
O, could I lose all father now! For why
   Will man lament the state he should envy?
To have so soon 'scaped world's and flesh's rage,
   And, if no other misery, yet age?
Rest in soft peace, and, asked, say here doth lie
   Ben Jonson, his best piece of poetry.
For whose sake, henceforth, all his vows be such
   As what he loves may never like too much.

(iii)

210

On Solomon Pavy
A child of Queen Elizabeth's Chapel

WEEP with me, all you that read
    This little story;
And know, for whom a tear you shed
    Death's self is sorry.
'Twas a child that so did thrive
    In grace and feature,
As Heaven and Nature seemed to strive
    Which owned the creature.
Years he numbered scarce thirteen
    When Fates turned cruel,
Yet three filled Zodiacs had he been
    The Stage's jewel;
And did act (what now we moan)
    Old men so duly,
As sooth the Parcae thought him one,
    He played so truly.
So, by error, to his fate
    They all consented;
But, viewing him since, alas, too late!
    They have repented;
And have sought, to give new birth,
    In baths to steep him;
But, being so much too good for earth,
    Heaven vows to keep him.

211

Inviting a Friend to Supper

TONIGHT, grave Sir, both my poor house and I
    Do equally desire your company:
Not that we think us worthy such a guest,
    But that your worth will dignify our feast
With those that come; whose grace may make that seem
    Something, which else could hope for no esteem.

It is the fair acceptance, Sir, creates
    The entertainment perfect: not the cates.
Yet shall you have, to rectify your palate,
    An olive, capers, or some better salad,
Ushering the mutton; with a short-legged hen,
    If we can get her, full of eggs, and then
Lemons, and wine for sauce; to these a cony
    Is not to be despaired of for our money;
And though fowl now be scarce, yet there are clerks,
    The sky not falling, think we may have larks.
I'll tell you of more, and lie, so you will come:
    Of partridge, pheasant, wood-cock, of which some
May yet be there; and godwit, if we can;
    Knot, rail and ruff too. How so ere, my man
Shall read a piece of Virgil, Tacitus,
    Livy, or of some better book to us,
Of which we'll speak our minds, amidst our meat;
    And I'll profess no verses to repeat:
To this, if ought appear which I not know of,
    That will the pastry, not my paper show of.
Digestive cheese and fruit there sure will be;
    But that which most doth take my Muse and me
Is a pure cup of rich Canary wine,
    Which is the Mermaid's now, but shall be mine;
Of which had Horace or Anacreon tasted,
    Their lives, as do their lines, till now had lasted.
Tobacco, nectar, or the Thespian spring
    Are all but Luther's beer, to this I sing.
Of this we will sup free, but moderately,
    And we will have no Pooly or Parrot by;
Nor shall our cups make any guilty men,
    But at our parting we will be as when
We innocently met. No simple word
    That shall be uttered at our mirthful board
Shall make us sad next morning, or affright
    The liberty that we'll enjoy tonight.

Pooly or Parrot] two well-known informers

212 *The Witches' Charm*

THE owl is abroad, the bat, and the toad,
  And so is the cat-a-mountain;
The ant and the mole sit both in a hole,
  And frog peeps out o'the fountain;
The dogs they do bay, and the timbrels play,
  The spindle is now a-turning;
The moon it is red, and the stars are fled,
  But all the sky is a-burning:
The ditch is made, and our nails the spade,
With pictures full, of wax and of wool;
Their livers I stick with needles quick:
There lacks but the blood to make up the flood.

213 *The Return of Astraea*

LOOK, look! rejoice and wonder!
  That you offending mortals are
  (For all your crimes) so much the care
Of him that bears the thunder!

Jove can endure no longer
  Your great ones should your less invade,
  Or that your weak, though bad, be made
A prey unto the stronger.

And therefore means to settle
  Astraea in her seat again;
  And let down in his golden chain
The age of better metal.

Which deed he doth the rather
  That even envy may behold
  Time not enjoyed his head of gold
Alone beneath his father.

But that his care conserveth,
  As time, so all time's honours too;
  Regarding still what heaven should do,
And not what earth deserveth.

214   *The Triumph of Charis*

SEE the Chariot at hand here of Love,
  Wherein my Lady rideth!
Each that draws is a swan or a dove,
  And well the car Love guideth.
As she goes, all hearts do duty
          Unto her beauty;
And enamoured do wish, so they might
          But enjoy such a sight,
That they still were to run by her side,
Thorough swords, thorough seas, whither she would ride.

Do but look on her eyes, they do light
  All that Love's world compriseth!
Do but look on her hair, it is bright
  As Love's star when it riseth!
Do but mark, her forehead's smoother
          Than words that soothe her;
And from her arched brows such a grace
          Sheds itself through the face,
As alone there triumphs to the life
All the gain, all the good, of the elements' strife.

Have you seen but a bright lily grow
  Before rude hands have touched it?
Have you marked but the fall of the snow
  Before the soil hath smutched it?
Have you felt the wool of the beaver,
          Or swan's down ever?
Or have smelt of the bud of the brier,
          Or the nard in the fire?
Or have tasted the bag of the bee?
O so white, O so soft, O so sweet is she!

215   *Ode to Himself*

WHERE dost thou careless lie,
    Buried in ease and sloth?
Knowledge that sleeps doth die;
And this security,
    It is the common moth,
That eats on wits, and arts, and oft destroys them both.

Are all the Aonian springs
    Dried up? lies Thespia waste?
Doth Clarius' harp want strings,
That not a nymph now sings?
    Or droop they as disgraced,
To see their seats and bowers by chattering pies defaced?

If hence thy silence be,
    As 'tis too just a cause,
Let this thought quicken thee:
Minds that are great and free
    Should not on fortune pause,
'Tis crown enough to virtue still, her own applause.

What though the greedy fry
    Be taken with false baits
Of worded balladry
And think it poesy?
    They die with their conceits,
And only piteous scorn upon their folly waits.

Then take in hand thy lyre,
    Strike in thy proper strain;
With Japhet's line, aspire
Sol's chariot for new fire,
    To give the world again:
Who aided him will thee, the issue of Jove's brain.

And since our dainty age
    Cannot endure reproof,
Make not thyself a page
To that strumpet the Stage,
    But sing high and aloof,
Safe from the wolf's black jaw, and the dull ass's hoof.

216 *The Dream*

OR scorn or pity on me take,
I must the true relation make,
  I am undone tonight;
 Love, in a subtle dream disguised,
 Hath both my heart and me surprised,
Whom never yet he durst attempt awake;
Nor will he tell me for whose sake
  He did me the delight,
    Or spite,
 But leaves me to enquire
 In all my wild desire,
  Of sleep again, who was his aid;
  And sleep so guilty and afraid
As since he dares not come within my sight.

217 *To the Immortal Memory and Friendship of that*
   Noble Pair, Sir Lucius Cary and
     Sir Henry Morison.

I. i

BRAVE infant of Saguntum, clear
Thy coming forth in that great year,
When the prodigious Hannibal did crown
His rage with razing your immortal town.
Thou, looking then about,
E'er thou wert half got out,
Wise child, didst hastily return
And mad'st thy mother's womb thine urn.
How summed a circle didst thou leave mankind
Of deepest lore, could we the centre find!

I. ii

Did wiser Nature draw thee back
From out the horror of that sack?
Where shame, faith, honour, and regard of right
Lay trampled on; the deeds of death and night

Urged, hurried forth, and hurled
Upon the affrighted world;
Sword, fire, and famine, with fell fury met,
And all on utmost ruin set;
As, could they but life's miseries foresee,
No doubt all infants would return like thee.

I. iii

For what is life, if measured by the space,
Not by the act?
Or maskèd man, if valued by his face,
Above his fact?
Here's one out-lived his peers,
And told forth fourscore years;
He vexèd time, and busied the whole State,
Troubled both foes and friends;
But ever to no ends:
What did this stirrer but die late?
How well at twenty had he fallen or stood!
For three of his fourscore he did no good.

II. i

He entered well, by virtuous parts,
Got up and thrived with honest arts:
He purchased friends and fame and honours then,
And had his noble name advanced with men;
But, weary of that flight,
He stooped in all men's sight
To sordid flatteries, acts of strife,
And sunk in that dead sea of life
So deep as he did then death's waters sup;
But that the cork of Title buoyed him up.

II. ii

Alas, but Morison fell young:
He never fell, thou fall'st, my tongue.
He stood, a soldier to the last right end,
A perfect patriot, and a noble friend,
But most, a virtuous son.
All offices were done

By him, so ample, full, and round,
In weight, in measure, number, sound,
As, though his age imperfect might appear,
His life was of humanity the sphere.

II. iii

Go now, and tell out days summed up with fears,
And make them years;
Produce thy mass of miseries on the stage,
To swell thine age;
Repeat of things a throng,
To shew thou hast been long,
Not lived; for life doth her great actions spell
By what was done and wrought
In season, and so brought
To light: her measures are—how well
Each syllable answered, and was formed, how fair:
These make the lines of life, and that's her air.

III. i

It is not growing like a tree
In bulk, doth make man better be;
Or standing long an oak, three hundred year,
To fall a log at last, dry, bald, and sere:
A lily of a day
Is fairer far in May,
Although it fall and die that night,
It was the plant and flower of light.
In small proportions we just beauty see,
And in short measures life may perfect be.

III. ii

Call, noble Lucius, then for wine,
And let thy looks with gladness shine:
Accept this garland, plant it on thy head,
And think, nay, know, thy Morison's not dead.
He leaped the present age,
Possessed with holy rage,
To see that bright eternal Day,
Of which we priests and poets say
Such truths as we expect for happy men,
And there he lives with memory; and Ben

III. iii

Jonson, who sung this of him e'er he went
Himself to rest,
Or taste a part of that full joy he meant
To have expressed,
In this bright Asterism:
Where it were friendship's schism
(Were not his Lucius long with us to tarry)
To separate these twi-
Lights, the Dioscuri,
And keep the one half from his Harry.
But fate doth so alternate the design,
Whilst that in heaven, this light on earth must shine.

IV. i

And shine as you exalted are!
Two names of friendship, but one star:
Of hearts the union: and those not by chance
Made, or indentured, or leased out to advance
The profits for a time.
No pleasures vain did chime,
Of rhymes, or riots, at your feasts,
Orgies of drink or feigned protests;
But simple love of greatness and of good,
That knits brave minds and manners more than blood.

IV. ii

This made you first to know the Why
You liked, then after, to apply
That liking; and approach so one the t'other,
Till either grew a portion of the other:
Each stylèd by his end
The copy of his friend.
You lived to be the great surnames
And titles by which all made claims
Unto the Virtue—nothing perfect done
But as a Cary or a Morison.

IV. iii

And such a force the fair example had,
As they that saw
The good, and durst not practise it, were glad
That such a law
Was left yet to mankind;
Where they might read, and find
Friendship in deed was written, not in words:
And with the heart, not pen,
Of two so early men,
Whose lines her rolls were, and records;
Who, e'er the first down bloomèd on the chin,
Had sowed these fruits and got the harvest in.

218   *Death and Love*

Though I am young, and cannot tell
    Either what Death or Love is well,
Yet I have heard they both bear darts,
    And both do aim at human hearts;
And then again I have been told
    Love wounds with heat, as Death with cold;
So that I fear they do but bring
    Extremes to touch, and mean one thing.

As in a ruin, we it call
    One thing to be blown up or fall;
Or to our end like way may have,
    By a flash of lightning or a wave:
So Love's inflamèd shaft or brand
    May kill as soon as Death's cold hand;
Except Love's fires the virtue have
    To fright the frost out of the grave.

219   *To the Memory of my Beloved*
Mr. William Shakespeare

I, THEREFORE, will begin. Soul of the Age!
   The applause, delight, the wonder of our Stage!
My Shakespeare, rise; I will not lodge thee by
   Chaucer, or Spenser, or bid Beaumont lie
A little further, to make thee a room:
   Thou art a monument, without a tomb,
And art alive still, while thy book doth live,
   And we have wits to read and praise to give.
That I not mix thee so, my brain excuses;
   I mean with great, but disproportioned Muses:
For, if I thought my judgement were of years,
   I should commit thee surely with thy peers,
And tell how far thou didst our Lyly out-shine,
   Or sporting Kyd, or Marlowe's mighty line.
And though thou hadst small Latin and less Greek,
   From thence to honour thee, I would not seek
For names; but call forth thundering Æschylus,
   Euripides, and Sophocles to us,
Paccuvius, Accius, him of Cordova dead,
   To life again, to hear thy buskin tread,
And shake a stage; or, when thy socks were on,
   Leave thee alone, for the comparison
Of all that insolent Greece or haughty Rome
   Sent forth, or since did from their ashes come.
Triumph, my Britain, thou hast one to show
   To whom all scenes of Europe homage owe.
He was not of an age but for all time!
   And all the Muses still were in their prime
When, like Apollo, he came forth to warm
   Our ears, or, like a Mercury, to charm!
Nature herself was proud of his designs,
   And joyed to wear the dressing of his lines!
Which were so richly spun and woven so fit
   As, since, she will vouchsafe no other wit.
The merry Greek, tart Aristophanes,
   Neat Terence, witty Plautus, now not please,

But antiquated and deserted lie
  As they were not of Nature's family.
Yet must I not give Nature all: thy Art,
  My gentle Shakespeare, must enjoy a part.
For though the poet's matter Nature be,
  His Art doth give the fashion. And that he
Who casts to write a living line must sweat,
  (Such as thine are) and strike the second heat
Upon the Muses' anvil: turn the same
  (And himself with it) that he thinks to frame;
Or for the laurel he may gain a scorn,
  For a good poet's made as well as born.
And such wert thou. . . .

RICHARD BARNFIELD

1574–1627

220   *Philomel*

As it fell upon a day
In the merry month of May,
Sitting in a pleasant shade
Which a grove of myrtles made,
Beasts did leap and birds did sing,
Trees did grow and plants did spring;
Every thing did banish moan
Save the nightingale alone.
She, poor bird, as all forlorn,
Leaned her breast up-till a thorn,
And there sung the dolefullest ditty,
That to hear it was great pity.
Fie, fie, fie, now would she cry,
Teru, teru, by and by,
That to hear her so complain
Scarce I could from tears refrain;
For her griefs so lively shown
Made me think upon mine own.
Ah! thought I, thou mourn'st in vain,
None takes pity on thy pain;

Senseless trees, they cannot hear thee,
Ruthless beasts, they will not cheer thee;
King Pandion, he is dead,
All thy friends are lapped in lead;
All thy fellow birds do sing
Careless of thy sorrowing. . . .

JOHN FLETCHER
1579–1625

221 *Hymn to Pan*

SING his praises that doth keep
   Our flocks from harm,
Pan, the father of our sheep;
   And arm in arm
Tread we softly in a round,
Whilst the hollow neighbouring ground
Fills the music with her sound.

Pan, O great god Pan, to thee
   Thus do we sing!
Thou that keep'st us chaste and free
   As the young spring:
Ever be thy honour spoke
From that place the morn is broke
To that place day doth unyoke!

222 *Aspatia's Song*

LAY a garland on my hearse of the dismal yew;
Maidens, willow branches bear; say I died true:
My love was false, but I was firm from my hour of birth;
Upon my buried body lay lightly, gentle earth.

223 *Away, Delights*

AWAY, delights! go seek some other dwelling,
    For I must die.
Farewell, false love! thy tongue is ever telling
    Lie after lie.
For ever let me rest now from thy smarts;
    Alas, for pity go
    And fire their hearts
That have been hard to thee! Mine was not so.

Never again deluding love shall know me,
    For I will die;
And all those griefs that think to overgrow me
    Shall be as I:
For ever will I sleep, while poor maids cry—
    'Alas, for pity stay,
    And let us die
With thee! Men cannot mock us in the clay.'

224 *Love's Emblems*

NOW the lusty spring is seen;
    Golden yellow, gaudy blue,
    Daintily invite the view:
Everywhere on every green
Roses blushing as they blow
    And enticing men to pull,
Lilies whiter than the snow,
    Woodbines of sweet honey full:
        All love's emblems, and all cry,
        'Ladies, if not plucked, we die.'

Yet the lusty spring hath stayed;
    Blushing red and purest white
    Daintily to love invite
Every woman, every maid:

Cherries kissing as they grow,
  And inviting men to taste,
Apples even ripe below,
  Winding gently to the waist:
    All love's emblems, and all cry,
    'Ladies, if not plucked, we die.'

225   *Hear, Ye Ladies*

  HEAR, ye ladies that despise
    What the mighty Love has done;
  Fear examples and be wise:
    Fair Callisto was a nun;
  Leda, sailing on the stream
    To deceive the hopes of man,
  Love accounting but a dream,
    Doted on a silver swan;
      Danaë, in a brazen tower,
      Where no love was, loved a shower.

  Hear, ye ladies that are coy,
    What the mighty Love can do;
  Fear the fierceness of the boy:
    The chaste Moon he makes to woo;
  Vesta, kindling holy fires,
    Circled round about with spies,
  Never dreaming loose desires,
    Doting at the altar dies;
      Ilion, in a short hour, higher
      He can build, and once more fire.

JOHN WEBSTER
?1580–?1625

226 *A Dirge*

CALL for the robin-redbreast and the wren,
Since o'er shady groves they hover,
And with leaves and flowers do cover
The friendless bodies of unburied men.
Call unto his funeral dole
The ant, the field-mouse, and the mole,
To rear him hillocks that shall keep him warm,
And (when gay tombs are robbed) sustain no harm;
But keep the wolf far thence, that's foe to men,
For with his nails he'll dig them up again.

227 *The Shrouding of the Duchess of Malfi*

HARK! now everything is still,
The screech-owl and the whistler shrill,
Call upon our dame aloud,
And bid her quickly don her shroud!
Much you had of land and rent;
Your length in clay's now competent:
A long war disturbed your mind;
Here your perfect peace is signed.
Of what is't fools make such vain keeping?
Sin their conception, their birth weeping,
Their life a general mist of error,
Their death a hideous storm of terror.
Strew your hair with powders sweet,
Don clean linen, bathe your feet,
And—the foul fiend more to check—
A crucifix let bless your neck:
'Tis now full tide 'tween night and day;
End your groan and come away.

228 *Vanitas Vanitatum*

ALL the flowers of the spring
Meet to perfume our burying;
These have but their growing prime,
And man does flourish but his time:
Survey our progress from our birth—
We are set, we grow, we turn to earth.
Courts adieu, and all delights,
All bewitching appetites!
Sweetest breath and clearest eye
Like perfumes go out and die;
And consequently this is done
As shadows wait upon the sun.
Vain the ambition of kings
Who seek by trophies and dead things
To leave a living name behind,
And weave but nets to catch the wind.

RICHARD CORBET

1582-1635

229 *The Fairies' Farewell*

FAREWELL, rewards and Fairies,
  Good housewives now may say,
For now foul sluts in dairies
  Do fare as well as they;
And though they sweep their hearths no less
  Than maids were wont to do,
Yet who of late for cleanliness
  Finds sixpence in her shoe?

Lament, lament, old Abbies,
  The fairies' lost command;
They did but change priests' babies,
  But some have changed your land;

And all your children sprung from thence
   Are now grown Puritans,
Who live as changelings ever since
   For love of your domains.

At morning and at evening both
   You merry were and glad,
So little care of sleep or sloth
   These pretty ladies had.
When Tom came home from labour,
   Or Ciss to milking rose,
Then merrily, merrily went their tabor,
   And nimbly went their toes.

Witness those rings and roundelays
   Of theirs, which yet remain,
Were footed in Queen Mary's days
   On many a grassy plain;
But since of late Elizabeth,
   And later James, came in
They never danced on any heath
   As when the time hath been.

By which we note the Fairies
   Were of the old profession;
Their songs were Ave Marys,
   Their dances were procession.
But now, alas, they all are dead,
   Or gone beyond the seas,
Or farther for Religion fled,
   Or else they take their ease.

A tell-tale in their company
   They never could endure,
And whoso kept not secretly
   Their mirth, was punished sure.
It was a just and Christian deed
   To pinch such black and blue:
O, how the Common wealth doth need
   Such Justices as you.

Now they have left our quarters
    A Register they have
Who looketh to their Charters,
    A man both wise and grave;
An hundred of their merry pranks
    By one that I could name
Are kept in store, con twenty thanks
    To William for the same.

I marvel who his cloak would turn
    When Puck had led him round,
Or where those walking fires would burn,
    Where Cureton would be found;
How Broker would appear to be
    For whom this Age doth mourn;
But that their spirits live in thee,
    In thee, old William Chourne.

To William Chourne of Staffordshire
    Give laud and praises due,
Who every meal can mend your cheer
    With tales both old and true.
To William all give audience,
    And pray ye for his noddle,
For all the Fairies' evidence
    Were lost if that were addle.

PHINEAS FLETCHER

1582–1650

230   *'Drop, Drop, Slow Tears'*

DROP, drop, slow tears
    and bathe those beauteous feet,
Which brought from heaven
    the news and Prince of peace:
Cease not, wet eyes,
    his mercies to entreat;
To cry for vengeance
    sin doth never cease:

In your deep floods
   drown all my faults and fears;
Nor let his eye
   see sin, but through my tears.

LORD HERBERT OF CHERBURY
1583–1648

231   *Elegy over a Tomb*

MUST I then see, alas! eternal night
   Sitting upon those fairest eyes,
And closing all those beams, which once did rise
   So radiant and bright,
That light and heat in them to us did prove
   Knowledge and Love?

Oh, if you did delight no more to stay
   Upon this low and earthly stage,
But rather chose an endless heritage,
   Tell us at least, we pray,
Where all the beauties that those ashes owed
   Are now bestowed?

Doth the sun now his light with yours renew?
   Have waves the curling of your hair?
Did you restore unto the sky and air
   The red, and white, and blue?
Have you vouchsafed to flowers since your death
   That sweetest breath?

Had not Heaven's lights else in their houses slept,
   Or to some private life retired?
Must not the sky and air have else conspired?
   And in their regions wept?
Must not each flower else the earth could breed
   Have been a weed?

But thus enriched may we not yield some cause
  Why they themselves lament no more?
That must have changed the course they held before,
    And broke their proper laws,
Had not your beauties given this second birth
    To Heaven and Earth?

Tell us—for oracles must still ascend,
  For those that crave them at your tomb—
Tell us, where are those beauties now become,
    And what they now intend:
Tell us, alas, that cannot tell our grief,
    Or hope relief.

232   *To his Watch*
           When he could not sleep

Uncessant minutes, whilst you move you tell
  The time that tells our life, which though it run
  Never so fast or far, your new begun
Short steps shall overtake; for though life well

May 'scape his own account, it shall not yours;
  You are Death's auditors, that both divide
And sum what ere that life inspired endures
  Past a beginning, and through you we bide

THE DOOM of Fate, whose unrecalled decree
  You date, bring, execute; making what's new,
  Ill and good, old, for as we die in you,
You die in Time, Time in Eternity.

233   *Ode on a Question Moved:*
 Whether Love Should Continue Forever

Having interred her Infant-birth,
  The watery ground that late did mourn
  Was strewed with flowers for the return
Of the wished Bridegroom of the earth.

The well accorded birds did sing
   Their hymns unto the pleasant time,
   And in a sweet consorted chime
Did welcome in the cheerful Spring.

To which soft whistles of the wind,
   And warbling murmurs of a brook,
   And varied notes of leaves that shook,
An harmony of parts did bind.

While doubling joy unto each other,
   All in so rare consent was shown,
   No happiness that came alone,
Nor pleasure that was not another.

When with a love none can express,
   That mutually happy pair,
   Melander and Celinda fair,
The season with their loves did bless.

Walking thus towards a pleasant grove,
   Which did, it seemed, in new delight
   The pleasures of the time unite
To give a triumph to their love,

They stayed at last, and on the grass
   Reposèd so, as o'er his breast
   She bowed her gracious head to rest,
Such a weight as no burden was.

While over either's compassed waist
   Their folded arms were so composed
   As if in straightest bonds enclosed
They suffered for joys they did taste.

Long their fixed eyes to Heaven bent
   Unchangèd, they did never move,
   As if so great and pure a love
No glass but it could represent.

When with a sweet, though troubled, look
   She first brake silence, saying, 'Dear friend,
   O that our love might take no end,
Or never had beginning took!

'I speak not this with a false heart,'
  (Wherewith his hand she gently strained)
  'Or that would change a love maintained
With so much faith on either part.

'Nay, I protest, though Death with his
  Worst counsel should divide us here,
  His terrors could not make me fear
To come where your loved presence is.

'Only if love's fire with the breath
  Of life be kindled, I doubt
  With our last air 'twill be breathed out,
And quenchèd with the cold of death.

'That if affection be a line,
  Which is closed up in our last hour;
  O how 'twould grieve me, any power
Could force so dear a love as mine!'

She scarce had done when his shut eyes
  An inward joy did represent,
  To hear Celinda thus intent
To a love he so much did prize.

Then with a look, it seemed, denied
  All earthly power but hers, yet so
  As if to her breath he did owe
This borrowed life, he thus replied:

'O you, wherein they say souls rest
  Till they descend, pure heavenly fires,
  Shall lustful and corrupt desires
With your immortal seed be blest?

'And shall our love, so far beyond
  That low and dying appetite,
  And which so chaste desires unite,
Not hold in an eternal bond?

'Is it because we should decline,
  And wholly from our thoughts exclude,
  Objects that may the sense delude,
And study only the Divine?

'No, sure; for if none can ascend
　　Even to the visible degree
　　Of things created, how should we
The invisible comprehend?

'Or rather since that Power expressed
　　His greatness in his works alone,
　　Being here best in his creatures known,
Why is he not loved in them best?

'But is't not true, which you pretend,
　　That since our love and knowledge here
　　Only as parts of life appear,
So they with it should take their end?

'O no, Beloved, I am most sure,
　　Those virtuous habits we acquire,
　　As being with the soul entire,
Must with it evermore endure.

'For if where sins and vice reside
　　We find so foul a guilt remain,
　　As never dying in his stain,
Still punished in the soul doth bide;

'Much more that true and real joy,
　　Which in a virtuous love is found,
　　Must be more solid in its ground
Than Fate or Death can e'er destroy.

'Else should our souls in vain elect,
　　And vainer yet were Heaven's laws,
　　When to an everlasting Cause
They gave a perishing Effect.

'Nor here on earth then, nor above,
　　Our good affection can impair;
　　For where God doth admit the fair,
Think you that he excludeth Love?

'These eyes again then, eyes shall see,
  And hands again these hands enfold,
  And all chaste pleasures can be told
Shall with us everlasting be.

'For if no use of sense remain
  When bodies once this life forsake,
  Or they could no delight partake,
Why should they ever rise again?

'And if every imperfect mind
  Make love the end of knowledge here,
  How perfect will our love be, where
All imperfection is refined?

'Let then no doubt, Celinda, touch,
  Much less your fairest mind invade;
  Were not our souls immortal made,
Our equal loves can make them such.

'So when one wing can make no way,
  Two joinèd can themselves dilate,
  So can two persons propagate,
When singly either would decay.

'So when from hence we shall be gone
  And be no more, nor you, nor I,
  As one another's mystery,
Each shall be both, yet both but one.'

This said, in her up-lifted face,
  Her eyes, which did that beauty crown,
  Were like two stars, that having fallen down
Look up again to find their place:

While such a moveless silent peace
  Did seize on their becalmèd sense,
  One would have thought some Influence
Their ravished spirits did possess.

SIR JOHN BEAUMONT
1583–1627

234   *Of My Dear Son, Gervase Beaumont*

CAN I, who have for others oft compiled
The songs of Death, forget my sweetest child,
Which, like a flower crushed, with a blast is dead,
And ere full time hangs down his smiling head,
Expecting with clear hope to live anew
Among the angels, fed with heavenly dew?
We have this sign of joy, that many days,
While on the earth his struggling spirit stays,
The name of Jesus in his mouth contains
His only food, his sleep, his ease from pains.
O may that sound be rooted in my mind,
Of which in him such strong effect I find.
Dear Lord, receive my son, whose winning love
To me was like a friendship, far above
The course of nature or his tender age,
Whose looks could all my bitter griefs assuage;
Let his pure soul ordained seven years to be
In that frail body, which was part of me,
Remain my pledge in Heaven, as sent to show
How to this port at every step I go.

AURELIAN TOWNSHEND
?1583–?1651

235   *A Dialogue betwixt Time and a Pilgrim*

Pilgrim. Agèd man, that mows these fields.
Time.   Pilgrim, speak; what is thy will?
Pilgrim. Whose soil is this, that such sweet pasture yields?
        Or who art thou, whose foot stands never still?
        Or where am I? *Time.* In love.
Pilgrim. His Lordship lies above.

Time. Yes, and below, and round about
  Wherein all sorts of flowers are growing
  Which, as the early Spring puts out,
   Time falls as fast a-mowing.
Pilgrim. If thou art Time, these flowers have lives,
   And then I fear
  Under some lily she I love
   May now be growing there.
Time. And in some thistle or some spire of grass
  My scythe thy stalk before hers come may pass.
Pilgrim. Wilt thou provide it may? *Time.* No.
Pilgrim. Allege the cause.
Time. Because Time cannot alter but obey Fate's laws.
Chorus. Then happy those whom Fate, that is the stronger,
  Together twists their threads, and yet draws hers the longer.

?FRANCIS BEAUMONT

?1584–1616

236 *On the Tombs in Westminster Abbey*

MORTALITY, behold, and fear,
What a change of flesh is here!
Think how many royal bones
Sleep within this heap of stones,
Hence removed from beds of ease,
Dainty fare, and what might please,
Fretted roofs, and costly shows,
To a roof that flats the nose:
Which proclaims all flesh is grass;
How the world's fair glories pass;
That there is no trust in health,
In youth, in age, in greatness, wealth;
For if such could have reprieved
Those had been immortal lived.
Know from this the world's a snare,
How that greatness is but care,
How all pleasures are but pain,
And how short they do remain:

For here they lie had realms and lands,
That now want strength to stir their hands;
Where from their pulpits sealed with dust
They preach: 'In greatness is no trust'.
Here's an acre sown indeed
With the richest royalest seed,
That the earth did e'er suck in
Since the first man died for sin.
Here the bones of birth have cried,
'Though Gods they were, as men they died'.
Here are sands (ignoble things)
Dropped from the ruined sides of kings;
With whom the poor man's earth being shown
The difference is not easily known.
Here's a world of pomp and state,
Forgotten, dead, disconsolate;
Think, then, this scythe that mows down kings
Exempts no meaner mortal things.
Then bid the wanton lady tread
Amid these mazes of the dead;
And these truly understood
More shall cool and quench the blood
Than her many sports aday,
And her nightly wanton play.
Bid her paint till day of doom,
To this favour she must come.
Bid the merchant gather wealth,
The usurer exact by stealth,
The proud man beat it from his thought,
Yet to this shape all must be brought.

WILLIAM DRUMMOND OF HAWTHORNDEN
1585–1649

237 *Madrigal*

LIKE the Idalian queen,
Her hair about her eyne,
With neck and breast's ripe apples to be seen,
At first glance of the morn
In Cyprus' gardens gathering those fair flowers
Which of her blood were born,
I saw, but fainting saw, my paramours.
The Graces naked danced about the place,
The winds and trees amazed
With silence on her gazed,
The flowers did smile, like those upon her face;
And as their aspen stalks those fingers band,
That she might read my case,
A hyacinth I wished me in her hand.

238 *Inexorable*

MY thoughts hold mortal strife;
I do detest my life,
And with lamenting cries,
Peace to my soul to bring,
Oft call that prince which here doth monarchise:
—But he, grim-grinning King,
Who caitiffs scorns, and doth the blest surprise,
Late having decked with beauty's rose his tomb,
Disdains to crop a weed, and will not come.

239   *The World a Hunt*

THE World a-hunting is:
The prey poor Man, the Nimrod fierce is Death;
His speedy greyhounds are
Lust, Sickness, Envy, Care,
Strife that ne'er falls amiss,
With all those ills which haunt us while we breathe.
Now if by chance we fly
Of these the eager chase,
Old Age with stealing pace
Casts up his nets, and there we panting die.

240   *Saint John Baptist*

THE last and greatest Herald of Heaven's King,
    Girt with rough skins, hies to the deserts wild,
Among that savage brood the woods forth bring,
    Which he than man more harmless found and mild.
His food was locusts, and what young doth spring
    With honey that from virgin hives distilled;
Parched body, hollow eyes, some uncouth thing
    Made him appear, long since from earth exiled.
There burst he forth: 'All ye, whose hopes rely
    On God, with me amidst these deserts mourn;
    Repent, repent, and from old errors turn!'
Who listened to his voice, obeyed his cry?
        Only the echoes, which he made relent,
        Rung from their marble caves 'Repent! Repent!'

GILES FLETCHER
?1588–1623

241   *The Celestial City*

IN midst of this City celestial
Where the eternal Temple should have rose,
Lightened the Idea Beatifical:
End and beginning of each thing that grows,
Whose self no end, nor yet beginning knows,
   That hath no eyes to see, nor ears to hear,
   Yet sees and hears, and is all eye, all ear,
That nowhere is contained, and yet is everywhere.

Changer of all things, yet immutable,
Before, and after all, the first, and last,
That moving all, is yet immoveable,
Great without quantity, in whose forecast,
Things past are present, things to come are past,
   Swift without motion, to whose open eye
   The hearts of wicked men unbreasted lie,
At once absent and present to them, far and nigh.

It is no flaming lustre made of light,
No sweet consent or well-timed harmony,
Ambrosia for to feast the appetite,
Or flowery odour mixed with spicery,
No soft embrace or pleasure bodily;
   And yet it is a kind of inward feast,
   A harmony that sounds within the breast,
An odour, light, embrace, in which the soul doth rest,

A heavenly feast no hunger can consume,
A light unseen, yet shines in every place,
A sound no time can steal, a sweet perfume
No winds can scatter, an entire embrace
That no satiety can e'er unlace.
   Ingraced into so high a favour there,
   The saints with their beau-peers whole worlds outwear,
And things unseen do see, and things unheard do hear.

JOHN FORD

?1586–1639

242 *Love's Martyrs*

OH no more, no more! too late
  Sighs are spent; the burning tapers
Of a life as chaste as Fate,
  Pure as are unwritten papers,
  Are burnt out; no heat, no light
  Now remains; 'tis ever night.
Love is dead; let lovers' eyes,
  Locked in endless dreams,
  The extremes of all extremes,
Ope no more, for now Love dies.
  Now Love dies, implying
Love's Martyrs must be ever, ever dying.

SIR FRANCIS KYNASTON

1587–1642

243 *To Cynthia: On Concealment of her Beauty*

DO not conceal thy radiant eyes,
The star-light of serenest skies,
Lest wanting of their heavenly light,
They turn to Chaos' endless night.

Do not conceal those tresses fair,
The silken snares of thy curled hair,
Lest finding neither gold, nor ore,
The curious silk-worm work no more.

Do not conceal those breasts of thine,
More snow white than the Apennine,
Lest if there be like cold or frost,
The lily be forever lost.

Do not conceal that fragrant scent,
Thy breath, which to all flowers hath lent
Perfumes, lest it being suppressed,
No spices grow in all the East.

Do not conceal thy heavenly voice,
Which makes the hearts of Gods rejoice,
Lest Music hearing no such thing,
The nightingale forget to sing.

Do not conceal, nor yet eclipse
Thy pearly teeth with coral lips,
Lest that the seas cease to bring forth
Gems, which from thee have all their worth.

Do not conceal no beauty, grace,
That's either in thy mind or face,
Lest virtue overcome by vice
Make men believe no Paradise.

GEORGE WITHER

1588–1667

244 *I Loved a Lass*

I LOVED a lass, a fair one,
  As fair as e'er was seen;
She was indeed a'rare one,
  Another Sheba queen.
But, fool as then I was,
  I thought she loved me too,
But now, alas, she's left me,
  Falero, lero, loo.

Her hair like gold did glister,
  Each eye was like a star;
She did surpass her sister,
  Which passed all others far.
She would me 'honey' call,
  She'd, O! she'd kiss me too;
But now, alas, she's left me,
  Falero, lero, loo.

In summer time to Medley
  My love and I would go;
The boatmen there stood ready,
  My love and I to row.
For cream there would we call,
  For cakes, and for prunes too;
But now, alas, she's left me,
  Falero, lero, loo.

Many a merry meeting
  My love and I have had;
She was my only sweeting,
  She made my heart full glad,
The tears stood in her eyes,
  Like to the morning dew;
But now, alas, she's left me,
  Falero, lero, loo.

And as abroad we walkèd,
  As lovers' fashion is,
Oft as we sweetly talkèd
  The sun should steal a kiss,
The wind upon her lips
  Likewise most sweetly blew;
But now, alas, she's left me,
  Falero, lero, loo.

Her cheeks were like the cherry,
  Her skin as white as snow;
When she was blithe and merry,
  She angel-like did show.
Her waist exceeding small,
  The fives did fit her shoe;
But now, alas, she's left me,
  Falero, lero, loo.

In summer time or winter
  She had her heart's desire;
I still did scorn to stint her
  From sugar, sack, or fire;
The world went round about,
  No cares we ever knew;
But now, alas, she's left me,
  Falero, lero, loo.

As we walked home together
   At midnight through the town,
To keep away the weather
   O'er her I'd cast my gown.
No cold my love should feel,
   Whate'er the heavens could do;
But now, alas, she's left me,
   Falero, lero, loo.

Like doves we would be billing,
   And clip and kiss so fast,
Yet she would be unwilling
   That I should kiss the last;
They're Judas' kisses now,
   Since that they proved untrue.
For now, alas, she's left me,
   Falero, lero, loo.

To maidens' vows and swearing
   Henceforth no credit give,
You may give them the hearing
   But never them believe.
They are as false as fair,
   Unconstant, frail, untrue;
For mine, alas, has left me,
   Falero, lero, loo.

'Twas I that paid for all things,
   'Twas others drank the wine,
I cannot now recall things,
   Live, but a fool to pine.
'Twas I that beat the bush,
   The bird to others flew,
For she, alas, hath left me,
   Falero, lero, loo.

If ever that Dame Nature,
   For this false lover's sake,
Another pleasing creature
   Like unto her would make,
Let her remember this,
   To make the other true,
For this, alas, hath left me,
   Falero, lero, loo.

No riches now can raise me,
 No want make me despair,
No misery amaze me,
 Nor yet for want I care;
I have lost a world itself,
 My earthly heaven, adieu,
Since she, alas, hath left me,
 Falero, lero, loo.

245   *A Lover's Resolution*

SHALL I, wasting in despair,
Die because a woman's fair?
Or make pale my cheeks with care
'Cause another's rosy are?
Be she fairer than the day,
Or the flowery meads in May,
 If she be not so to me,
 What care I how fair she be?

Should my heart be grieved or pined
'Cause I see a woman kind?
Or a well disposèd nature
Joinèd with a lovely feature?
Be she meeker, kinder, than
Turtle-dove or pelican,
 If she be not so to me,
 What care I how kind she be?

Shall a woman's virtues move
Me to perish for her love?
Or her well-deserving known
Make me quite forget mine own?
Be she with that goodness blest
Which may gain her name of Best,
 If she be not such to me,
 What care I how good she be?

'Cause her fortune seems too high,
Shall I play the fool and die?
Those that bear a noble mind,
Where they want of riches find,

Think what with them they would do
That without them dare to woo.
    And unless that mind I see,
    What care I though great she be?

Great, or good, or kind, or fair,
I will ne'er the more despair;
If she love me, this believe,
I will die ere she shall grieve.
If she slight me when I woo,
I can scorn and let her go.
    For if she be not for me,
    What care I for whom she be?

WILLIAM BROWNE OF TAVISTOCK

1591–1643

246   *The Sirens' Song*

STEER, hither steer your wingèd pines,
    All beaten mariners!
Here lie Love's undiscovered mines,
    A prey to passengers;
Perfumes far sweeter than the best
Which make the Phoenix' urn and nest.
    Fear not your ships,
Nor any to oppose you save our lips;
    But come on shore,
Where no joy dies till Love hath gotten more.

For swelling waves our panting breasts,
    Where never storms arise,
Exchange, and be awhile our guests:
    For stars gaze on our eyes.
The compass Love shall hourly sing,
And as he goes about the ring,
    We will not miss
To tell each point he nameth with a kiss.
    Then come on shore,
Where no joy dies till Love hath gotten more.

Epitaphs

(i)

247
In Obitum *M.S. x° Maij, 1614*

MAY! Be thou never graced with birds that sing,
       Nor Flora's pride!
In thee all flowers and roses spring,
       Mine only died.

(ii)

248 *Epitaph on the Countess Dowager of Pembroke*

UNDERNEATH this sable hearse
Lies the subject of all verse;
Sidney's sister, Pembroke's mother:
Death, ere thou hast slain another
Fair and learned and good as she,
Time shall throw a dart at thee.

ROBERT HERRICK

1591–1674

249 *When He would Have his Verses Read*

IN sober mornings do not thou rehearse
The holy incantation of a verse;
But when that men have both well drunk and fed,
Let my enchantments then be sung or read.
When laurel spurts i'the fire, and when the hearth
Smiles to itself and gilds the roof with mirth;
When up the Thyrse is raised, and when the sound
Of sacred Orgies flies around, around,
When the rose reigns, and locks with ointments shine,
Let rigid Cato read these lines of mine.

250 *Upon Julia's Voice*

So smooth, so sweet, so silvery, is thy voice
As, could they hear, the damned would make no noise,
But listen to thee (walking in thy chamber)
Melting melodious words to lutes of amber.

251 *Delight in Disorder*

A SWEET disorder in the dress
Kindles in clothes a wantonness:
A lawn about the shoulders thrown
Into a fine distraction:
An erring lace, which here and there
Enthrals the crimson stomacher:
A cuff neglectful, and thereby
Ribbands to flow confusedly:
A winning wave, deserving note,
In the tempestuous petticoat:
A careless shoe-string, in whose tie
I see a wild civility:
Do more bewitch me than when art
Is too precise in every part.

252 *To Dianeme*

SWEET, be not proud of those two eyes
Which starlike sparkle in their skies;
Nor be you proud that you can see
All hearts your captives, yours yet free;
Be you not proud of that rich hair
Which wantons with the love-sick air;
Whenas that ruby which you wear,
Sunk from the tip of your soft ear,
Will last to be a precious stone
When all your world of beauty's gone.

253 *Corinna's Going a-Maying*

GET up, get up for shame! the blooming morn
Upon her wings presents the god unshorn.
  See how Aurora throws her fair
  Fresh-quilted colours through the air:
    Get up, sweet slug-a-bed, and see
    The dew-bespangling herb and tree.
Each flower has wept, and bowed toward the east,
Above an hour since; yet you not drest,
  Nay! not so much as out of bed?
  When all the birds have matins said,
    And sung their thankful hymns; 'tis sin,
    Nay, profanation to keep in,
Whenas a thousand virgins on this day
Spring sooner than the lark to fetch in May.

Rise and put on your foliage, and be seen
To come forth, like the spring-time, fresh and green,
  And sweet as Flora. Take no care
  For jewels for your gown or hair:
    Fear not; the leaves will strew
    Gems in abundance upon you:
Besides, the childhood of the day has kept,
Against you come, some orient pearls unwept.
  Come, and receive them while the light
  Hangs on the dew-locks of the night:
    And Titan on the eastern hill
    Retires himself, or else stands still
Till you come forth. Wash, dress, be brief in praying:
Few beads are best when once we go a-Maying.

Come, my Corinna, come; and coming, mark
How each field turns a street, each street a park
  Made green and trimmed with trees: see how
  Devotion gives each house a bough
    Or branch; each porch, each door, ere this,
    An ark, a tabernacle is,
Made up of white-thorn neatly interwove,
As if here were those cooler shades of love.

Can such delights be in the street
And open fields, and we not see't?
Come, we'll abroad: and let's obey
The proclamation made for May,
And sin no more, as we have done, by staying;
But, my Corinna, come, let's go a-Maying.

There's not a budding boy or girl this day
But is got up and gone to bring in May.
    A deal of youth ere this is come
    Back, and with white-thorn laden home.
    Some have dispatched their cakes and cream,
    Before that we have left to dream:
And some have wept and wooed, and plighted troth,
And chose their priest, ere we can cast off sloth:
    Many a green-gown has been given;
    Many a kiss, both odd and even;
    Many a glance too has been sent
    From out the eye, love's firmament:
Many a jest told of the keys betraying
This night, and locks picked: yet we're not a-Maying!

Come, let us go, while we are in our prime,
And take the harmless folly of the time!
    We shall grow old apace, and die
    Before we know our liberty.
    Our life is short, and our days run
    As fast away as does the sun.
And as a vapour or a drop of rain,
Once lost, can ne'er be found again:
    So when or you or I are made
    A fable, song, or fleeting shade,
    All love, all liking, all delight
    Lies drowned with us in endless night.
Then, while time serves, and we are but decaying,
Come, my Corinna, come, let's go a-Maying.

254   *To the Virgins, to Make Much of Time*

GATHER ye rosebuds while ye may,
  Old Time is still a-flying:
And this same flower that smiles to-day
  To-morrow will be dying.

The glorious lamp of heaven, the sun,
  The higher he's a-getting,
The sooner will his race be run,
  And nearer he's to setting.

That age is best which is the first,
  When youth and blood are warmer;
But being spent, the worse, and worst
  Times still succeed the former.

Then be not coy, but use your time,
  And while ye may, go marry:
For having lost but once your prime,
  You may for ever tarry.

255   *A Meditation for His Mistress*

You are a tulip seen today,
But, dearest, of so short a stay
That where you grew scarce man can say.

You are a lovely July-flower,
Yet one rude wind or ruffling shower
Will force you hence, and in an hour.

You are a sparkling rose i'th'bud,
Yet lost ere that chaste flesh and blood
Can shew where you or grew or stood.

You are a full-spread fair-set vine,
And can with tendrils love entwine,
Yet dried ere you distill your wine.

You are like balm enclosèd well
In amber, or some crystal shell,
Yet lost ere you transfuse your smell.

You are a dainty violet,
Yet withered ere you can be set
Within the virgins' coronet.

You are the queen all flowers among,
But die you must, fair maid, ere long,
As he, the maker of this song.

256 *To Anthea, Who May Command Him Anything*

BID me to live, and I will live
    Thy Protestant to be;
Or bid me love, and I will give
    A loving heart to thee.

A heart as soft, a heart as kind,
    A heart as sound and free
As in the whole world thou canst find,
    That heart I'll give to thee.

Bid that heart stay, and it will stay
    To honour thy decree:
Or bid it languish quite away,
    And 't shall do so for thee.

Bid me to weep, and I will weep
    While I have eyes to see:
And, having none, yet I will keep
    A heart to weep for thee.

Bid me despair, and I'll despair
    Under that cypress-tree:
Or bid me die, and I will dare
    E'en death to die for thee.

Thou art my life, my love, my heart,
    The very eyes of me:
And hast command of every part
    To live and die for thee.

257 *To Meadows*

Ye have been fresh and green,
   Ye have been filled with flowers,
And ye the walks have been
   Where maids have spent their hours.

You have beheld how they
   With wicker arks did come
To kiss and bear away
   The richer cowslips home.

You've heard them sweetly sing,
   And seen them in a round:
Each virgin like a spring,
   With honeysuckles crowned.

But now we see none here
   Whose silvery feet did tread
And with dishevelled hair
   Adorned this smoother mead.

Like unthrifts, having spent
   Your stock and needy grown,
You're left here to lament
   Your poor estates, alone.

258 *To Daffodils*

Fair daffodils, we weep to see
   You haste away so soon;
As yet the early-rising sun
   Has not attained his noon.
      Stay, stay
     Until the hasting day
      Has run
     But to the evensong;
And, having prayed together, we
   Will go with you along.

We have short time to stay as you,
   We have as short a spring;
As quick a growth to meet decay,
   As you, or anything.
      We die
     As your hours do, and dry
      Away
     Like to the summer's rain;
Or as the pearls of morning's dew,
   Ne'er to be found again.

259   *To the Most Fair and Lovely Mistress*
          Anne Soame, now Lady Abdie

So smell those odours that do rise
From out the wealthy spiceries;
So smells the flower of blooming clove,
Or roses smothered in the stove;
So smells the air of spicèd wine,
Or essences of jessamine;
So smells the breath about the hives,
When well the work of honey thrives,
And all the busy factors come
Laden with wax and honey home;
So smell those neat and woven bowers,
All over-arched with orange flowers,
And almond blossoms, that do mix
To make rich these aromatics;
So smell those bracelets and those bands
Of amber chafed between the hands,
When thus enkindled they transpire
A noble perfume from the fire.
The wine of cherries, and to these,
The cooling breath of raspberries,
The smell of morning's milk and cream,
Butter of cowslips mixed with them,
Of roasted warden or baked pear,
These are not to be reckoned here;
Whenas the meanest part of her
Smells like the maiden-pomander.
Thus sweet she smells, or what can be
More liked by her, or loved by me.

260 *Upon Julia's Clothes*

WHENAS in silks my Julia goes,
Then, then, methinks, how sweetly flows
That liquefaction of her clothes!

Next, when I cast mine eyes and see
That brave vibration each way free,
—O how that glittering taketh me!

261 *Comfort to a Youth that had Lost his Love*

WHAT needs complaints,
When she a place
Has with the race
   Of saints?

In endless mirth
She thinks not on
What's said or done
   In Earth.

She sees no tears,
Or any tone
Of thy deep groan
   She hears:

Nor does she mind
Or think on't now
That ever thou
   Wast kind;

But changed above,
She likes not there,
As she did here,
   Thy love.

Forbear therefore,
And lull asleep
Thy woes, and weep
   No more.

HENRY KING

1592–1669

Exequy upon His Wife

ACCEPT, thou shrine of my dead saint,
Instead of dirges this complaint;
And for sweet flowers to crown thy hearse,
Receive a strew of weeping verse
From thy grieved friend, whom thou mightst see
Quite melted into tears for thee.
  Dear loss! since thy untimely fate
My task hath been to meditate
On thee, on thee! Thou art the book,
The library, whereon I look
Though almost blind. For thee, loved clay,
I languish out, not live, the day,
Using no other exercise
But what I practise with mine eyes.
By which wet glasses I find out
How lazily time creeps about
To one that mourns. This, only this,
My exercise and business is:
So I compute the weary hours
With sighs dissolvèd into showers.
  Nor wonder if my time go thus
Backward and most preposterous:
Thou hast benighted me. Thy set
This eve of blackness did beget,
Who wast my day (though overcast
Before thou hadst thy noon-tide past)
And I remember must in tears
Thou scarce hadst seen so many years
As day tells hours. By thy clear sun
My love and fortune first did run;
But thou wilt never more appear
Folded within my hemisphere,
Since both thy light and motion,
Like a fled star, is fallen and gone,
And 'twixt me and my soul's dear wish
The earth now interposèd is,

Which such a strange eclipse doth make
As ne'er was read in almanac.
   I could allow thee for a time
To darken me and my sad clime;
Were it a month, a year, or ten,
I would thy exile live till then;
And all that space my mirth adjourn,
So thou wouldst promise to return
And, putting off thy ashy shroud,
At length disperse this sorrow's cloud.
   But woe is me! the longest date
Too narrow is to calculate
These empty hopes. Never shall I
Be so much blest as to descry
A glimpse of thee, till that day come
Which shall the earth to cinders doom,
And a fierce fever must calcine
The body of this world, like thine,
My little world! That fit of fire
Once off, our bodies shall aspire
To our souls' bliss: then we shall rise,
And view ourselves with clearer eyes
In that calm region where no night
Can hide us from each other's sight.
   Meantime thou hast her, Earth: much good
May my harm do thee. Since it stood
With Heaven's will I might not call
Her longer mine, I give thee all
My short-lived right and interest
In her, whom living I loved best:
With a most free and bounteous grief,
I give thee what I could not keep.
Be kind to her, and prithee look
Thou write into thy Doomsday book
Each parcel of this rarity,
Which in thy casket shrined doth lie.
See that thou make thy reckoning straight,
And yield her back again by weight;
For thou must audit on thy trust
Each grain and atom of this dust,
As thou wilt answer him that lent,
Not gave thee, my dear monument.

So close the ground, and 'bout her shade
Black curtains draw: my bride is laid.
    Sleep on, my Love, in thy cold bed
Never to be disquieted.
My last good night! Thou wilt not wake
Till I thy fate shall overtake:
Till age, or grief, or sickness must
Marry my body to that dust
It so much loves; and fill the room
My heart keeps empty in thy tomb.
Stay for me there: I will not fail
To meet thee in that hollow vale.
And think not much of my delay;
I am already on the way,
And follow thee with all the speed
Desire can make, or sorrows breed.
Each minute is a short degree
And every hour a step towards thee.
At night when I betake to rest,
Next morn I rise nearer my west
Of life, almost by eight hours sail
Than when sleep breathed his drowsy gale.
    Thus from the sun my bottom steers,
And my day's compass downward bears.
Nor labour I to stem the tide
Through which to thee I swiftly glide.
    'Tis true, with shame and grief I yield;
Thou, like the van, first took'st the field
And gotten hast the victory
In thus adventuring to die
Before me, whose more years might crave
A just precedence in the grave.
But hark! my pulse, like a soft drum,
Beats my approach, tells thee I come;
And slow howe'er my marches be
I shall at last sit down by thee.
    The thought of this bids me go on
And wait my dissolution
With hope and comfort. Dear, (forgive
The crime) I am content to live
Divided, with but half a heart,
Till we shall meet and never part.

263 *Sic Vita*

LIKE to the falling of a star,
Or as the flights of eagles are,
Or like the fresh spring's gaudy hue,
Or silver drops of morning dew,
Or like a wind that chafes the flood,
Or bubbles which on water stood:
Even such is man, whose borrowed light
Is straight called in, and paid to night.

The wind blows out, the bubble dies;
The spring entombed in autumn lies;
The dew dries up, the star is shot;
The flight is past: and man forgot.

FRANCIS QUARLES

1592–1644

264 *My Beloved is Mine and I am His*

EVEN like two little bank-dividing brooks,
    That wash the pebbles with their wanton streams,
And having ranged and searched a thousand nooks,
    Meet both at length in silver-breasted Thames
        Where in a greater current they conjoin:
So I my Best-Beloved's am, so he is mine.

Even so we met; and after long pursuit
    Even so we joined; we both became entire;
No need for either to renew a suit,
    For I was flax and he was flames of fire:
        Our firm united souls did more than twine,
So I my Best-Beloved's am, so he is mine.

If all those glittering monarchs that command
  The servile quarters of this earthly ball
Should tender in exchange their shares of land,
    I would not change my fortunes for them all:
      Their wealth is but a counter to my coin;
The world's but theirs, but my Beloved's mine.

Nay, more: if the fair Thespian ladies all
  Should heap together their diviner treasure,
That treasure should be deemed a price too small
    To buy a minute's lease of half my pleasure.
      'Tis not the sacred wealth of all the Nine
Can buy my heart from him, or his from being mine.

Nor time, nor place, nor chance, nor death can bow
  My least desires unto the least remove;
He's firmly mine by oath, I his by vow;
    He's mine by faith, and I am his by love;
      He's mine by water, I am his by wine;
Thus I my Best-Beloved's am, thus he is mine.

He is my altar, I his holy place;
  I am his guest, and he my living food;
I'm his by penitence, he mine by grace;
    I'm his by purchase, he is mine by blood;
      He's my supporting elm, and I his vine:
Thus I my Best-Beloved's am, thus he is mine.

He gives me wealth, I give him all my vows;
  I give him songs, he gives me length of days;
With wreaths of grace he crowns my conquering brows;
    And I his temples with a crown of praise,
      Which he accepts as an everlasting sign,
That I my Best-Beloved's am; that he is mine.

265   *Epigram*

    MY soul, sit thou a patient looker-on;
    Judge not the play before the play is done:
    Her plot has many changes; every day
    Speaks a new scene; the last act crowns the play.

GEORGE HERBERT
1593–1633

266 *Redemption*

HAVING been tenant long to a rich Lord,
  Not thriving, I resolvèd to be bold,
And make a suit unto him, to afford
  A new small-rented lease, and cancel the old.
In heaven at his manor I him sought:
  They told me there that he was lately gone
About some land, which he had dearly bought
  Long since on earth, to take possession.
I straight returned, and knowing his great birth,
  Sought him accordingly in great resorts:
  In cities, theatres, gardens, parks, and courts.
At length I heard a ragged noise and mirth
    Of thieves and murderers: there I him espied,
    Who straight, *Your suit is granted*, said, and died.

267 *Bitter-Sweet*

AH my dear angry Lord,
Since thou dost love, yet strike;
Cast down, yet help afford;
Sure I will do the like.

I will complain, yet praise;
I will bewail, approve;
And all my sour-sweet days
I will lament, and love.

268 *Affliction*

WHEN first thou didst entice to thee my heart
        I thought the service brave:
So many joys I writ down for my part,
        Besides what I might have
Out of my stock of natural delights,
Augmented with thy gracious benefits.

I lookèd on thy furniture so fine,
    And made it fine to me:
Thy glorious household-stuff did me entwine
    And 'tice me unto thee.
Such stars I counted mine: both heaven and earth
Paid me my wages in a world of mirth.

What pleasures could I want, whose King I served
    Where joys my fellows were?
Thus argued into hopes, my thoughts reserved
    No place for grief or fear.
Therefore my sudden soul caught at the place,
And made her youth and fierceness seek thy face.

At first thou gav'st me milk and sweetnesses;
    I had my wish and way:
My days were strewed with flowers and happiness;
    There was no month but May.
But with my years sorrow did twist and grow,
And made a party unawares for woe.

My flesh began unto my soul in pain,
    'Sicknesses cleave my bones;
Consuming agues dwell in every vein,
    And tune my breath to groans.'
Sorrow was all my soul; I scarce believed,
Till grief did tell me roundly, that I lived.

When I got health, thou took'st away my life,
    And more; for my friends die:
My mirth and edge was lost; a blunted knife
    Was of more use than I.
Thus thin and lean, without a fence or friend,
I was blown through with every storm and wind.

Whereas my birth and spirit rather took
    The way that takes the town;
Thou didst betray me to a lingering book,
    And wrap me in a gown.
I was entangled in a world of strife,
Before I had the power to change my life.

Yet, for I threatened oft the siege to raise,
           Not simpering all mine age,
Thou often didst with academic praise
           Melt and dissolve my rage.
I took thy sweetened pill, till I came where
I could not go away, nor persevere.

Yet lest perchance I should too happy be
           In my unhappiness,
Turning my purge to food, thou throwest me
           Into more sicknesses.
Thus doth thy power cross-bias me, not making
Thine own gift good, yet me from my ways taking.

Now I am here, what thou wilt do with me
           None of my books will show:
I read, and sigh, and wish I were a tree;
           For sure then I should grow
To fruit or shade: at least some bird would trust
Her household to me, and I should be just.

Yet, though thou troublest me, I must be meek;
           In weakness must be stout.
Well, I will change the service, and go seek
           Some other master out.
Ah, my dear God! though I am clean forgot,
Let me not love thee, if I love thee not.

269 *Prayer*

PRAYER, the Church's banquet, Angels' age,
  God's breath in man returning to his birth,
The soul in paraphrase, heart in pilgrimage,
  The Christian plummet, sounding heaven and earth;
Engine against the Almighty, sinner's tower,
  Reversèd thunder, Christ-side-piercing spear,
The six-days' world transposing in an hour,
  A kind of tune, which all things hear and fear;

Softness, and peace, and joy, and love, and bliss,
    Exalted manna, gladness of the best,
    Heaven in ordinary, man well drest,
The milky way, the bird of Paradise,
      Church-bells beyond the stars heard, the soul's blood,
    The land of spices; something understood.

270   *Denial*

      WHEN my devotions could not pierce
           Thy silent ears;
Then was my heart broken, as was my verse;
        My breast was full of fears
           And disorder.

      My bent thoughts, like a brittle bow,
           Did fly asunder:
Each took his way: some would to pleasure go,
        Some to the wars and thunder
           Of alarms.

      As good go anywhere, they say,
           As to benumb
Both knees and heart, in crying night and day,
        Come, come, my God, O come,
           But no hearing.

      O that thou shouldst give dust a tongue
           To cry to thee,
And then not hear it crying! all day long
        My heart was in my knee,
           But no hearing.

      Therefore my soul lay out of sight,
           Untuned, unstrung;
My feeble spirit, unable to look right,
        Like a nipped blossom, hung
           Discontented.

      O cheer and tune my heartless breast,
           Defer no time;
That so thy favours granting my request,
        They and my mind may chime,
           And mend my rhyme.

271 *Virtue*

SWEET day, so cool, so calm, so bright,
The bridal of the earth and sky:
The dew shall weep thy fall tonight,
        For thou must die.

Sweet rose, whose hue angry and brave
Bids the rash gazer wipe his eye:
Thy root is ever in its grave,
        And thou must die.

Sweet spring, full of sweet days and roses,
A box where sweets compacted lie:
My music shows ye have your closes,
        And all must die.

Only a sweet and virtuous soul,
Like seasoned timber never gives;
But though the whole world turn to coal,
        Then chiefly lives.

272 *The Collar*

I STRUCK the board, and cried, 'No more!
        I will abroad.
What? shall I ever sigh and pine?
My lines and life are free; free as the road,
  Loose as the wind, as large as store.
      Shall I be still in suit?
Have I no harvest but a thorn
To let me blood, and not restore
What I have lost with cordial fruit?
           Sure there was wine
Before my sighs did dry it: there was corn
    Before my tears did drown it.
  Is the year only lost to me?
    Have I no bays to crown it?

No flowers, no garlands gay? all blasted?
                All wasted?
Not so, my heart: but there is fruit,
             And thou hast hands.
Recover all thy sigh-blown age
On double pleasures: leave thy cold dispute
Of what is fit, and not. Forsake thy cage,
             Thy rope of sands,
Which petty thoughts have made, and made to thee
  Good cable, to enforce and draw,
             And be thy law,
  While thou didst wink and wouldst not see.
             Away; take heed:
             I will abroad.
Call in thy death's head there: tie up thy fears.
             He that forbears
    To suit and serve his need,
             Deserves his load.'
But as I raved and grew more fierce and wild
             At every word,
  Methoughts I heard one calling, 'Child!'
    And I replied, 'My Lord'.

273   *The Pulley*

    WHEN God at first made man,
Having a glass of blessings standing by,
'Let us', said he, 'pour on him all we can:
Let the world's riches, which dispersèd lie,
          Contract into a span.'

    So strength first made a way;
Then beauty flowed, then wisdom, honour, pleasure;
When almost all was out, God made a stay,
Perceiving that, alone of all his treasure,
          Rest in the bottom lay.

    'For if I should', said he,
'Bestow this jewel also on my creature,
He would adore my gifts instead of me,
And rest in Nature, not the God of Nature:
          So both should losers be.

'Yet let him keep the rest,
But keep them with repining restlessness;
Let him be rich and weary, that at least,
If goodness lead him not, yet weariness
                         May toss him to my breast.'

274   *The Flower*

How fresh, O Lord, how sweet and clean
Are thy returns! even as the flowers in spring,
      To which, besides their own demean,
The late-past frosts tributes of pleasure bring,
                  Grief melts away
                  Like snow in May,
As if there were no such cold thing.

Who would have thought my shrivelled heart
Could have recovered greenness? It was gone
      Quite underground; as flowers depart
To see their mother-root, when they have blown;
                  Where they together
                  All the hard weather,
Dead to the world, keep house unknown.

These are thy wonders, Lord of power,
Killing and quickening, bringing down to hell
      And up to heaven in an hour;
Making a chiming of a passing-bell.
                  We say amiss,
                  This or that is.
Thy word is all, if we could spell.

O that I once past changing were,
Fast in thy Paradise, where no flower can wither!
      Many a spring I shoot up fair,
Offering at heaven, growing and groaning thither:
                  Nor doth my flower
                  Want a spring shower,
My sins and I joining together.

But while I grow in a straight line,
Still upwards bent, as if heaven were mine own,
    Thy anger comes and I decline:
What frost to that? what pole is not the zone,
                Where all things burn,
                When thou dost turn,
    And the least frown of thine is shown?

    And now in age I bud again,
After so many deaths I live and write;
    I once more smell the dew and rain,
And relish versing: O my only light,
                It cannot be
                That I am he
    On whom thy tempests fell all night.

    These are thy wonders, Lord of love,
To make us see we are but flowers that glide;
    Which when we once can find and prove,
Thou hast a garden for us, where to bide.
                Who would be more,
                Swelling through store,
    Forfeit their Paradise by their pride.

275   *Easter*

    I GOT me flowers to straw thy way,
        I got me boughs off many a tree;
    But thou wast up by break of day,
        And brought'st thy sweets along with thee.

    The sun arising in the East,
        Though he give light, and the East perfume;
    If they should offer to contest
        With thy arising they presume.

    Can there be any day but this,
        Though many suns to shine endeavour?
    We count three hundred, but we miss:
        There is but one, and that one ever.

276   *Discipline*

THROW away thy rod,
Throw away thy wrath:
            O my God,
Take the gentle path.

For my heart's desire
Unto thine is bent:
            I aspire
To a full consent.

Not a word or look
I affect to own,
            But by book,
And thy book alone.

Though I fail, I weep;
Though I halt in pace,
            Yet I creep
To the throne of grace.

Then let wrath remove;
Love will do the deed;
            For with love
Stony hearts will bleed.

Love is swift of foot,
Love's a man of war,
            And can shoot,
And can hit from far.

Who can 'scape his bow?
That which wrought on thee,
            Brought thee low,
Needs must work on me.

Throw away thy rod:
Though man frailties hath,
            Thou art God:
Throw away thy wrath.

277 *Love*

LOVE bade me welcome; yet my soul drew back,
        Guilty of dust and sin.
But quick-eyed Love, observing me grow slack
        From my first entrance in,
Drew nearer to me, sweetly questioning,
        If I lacked anything.

'A guest', I answered, 'worthy to be here.'
        Love said, 'You shall be he.'
'I, the unkind, ungrateful? Ah, my dear,
        I cannot look on thee.'
Love took my hand, and smiling did reply,
        'Who made the eyes but I?'

'Truth, Lord, but I have marred them; let my shame
        Go where it doth deserve.'
'And know you not', says Love, 'who bore the blame?'
        'My dear, then I will serve.'
'You must sit down', says Love, 'and taste my meat.'
        So I did sit and eat.

ANONYMOUS

278 *Preparations*

YET if His Majesty, our sovereign lord,
Should of his own accord
Friendly himself invite,
And say 'I'll be your guest to-morrow night,'
How should we stir ourselves, call and command
All hands to work! 'Let no man idle stand!
'Set me fine Spanish tables in the hall;
See they be fitted all;
Let there be room to eat
And order taken that there want no meat.
See every sconce and candlestick made bright,
That without tapers they may give a light.

'Look to the presence: are the carpets spread,
The dazie o'er the head,
The cushions in the chairs,
And all the candles lighted on the stairs?
Perfume the chambers, and in any case
Let each man give attendance in his place!'
Thus, if the king were coming, would we do;
And 'twere good reason too;
For 'tis a duteous thing
To show all honour to an earthly king,
And after all our travail and our cost,
So he be pleased, to think no labour lost.
But at the coming of the King of Heaven
All 's set at six and seven;
We wallow in our sin,
Christ cannot find a chamber in the inn.
We entertain him always like a stranger,
And, as at first, still lodge him in the manger.

THOMAS CAREW

?1595–1640

279   *On the Death of Donne*

THE Muses' garden, with pedantic weeds
O'erspread, was purged by thee; the lazy seeds
Of servile imitation thrown away;
And fresh invention planted. Thou didst pay
The debts of our penurious bankrupt age,
Licentious thefts, that make poetic rage
A mimic fury, when our souls must be
Possessed, or with Anacreon's ecstasy,
Or Pindar's, not their own; the subtle cheat
Of sly exchanges, and the juggling feat
Of two-edged words, or whatsoever wrong
By ours was done the Greek or Latin tongue,
Thou hast redeemed, and opened us a mine
Of rich and pregnant fancy, drawn a line
Of masculine expression, which, had good
Old Orpheus seen, or all the ancient brood

Our superstitious fools admire and hold
Their lead more precious than thy burnished gold,
Thou hadst been their Exchequer, and no more
They each in other's dust had raked for ore.
Thou shalt yield no precedence but of time,
And the blind fate of language, whose tuned chime
More charms the outward sense. Yet thou mayst claim
From so great disadvantage greater fame;
Since to the awe of thy imperious wit
Our stubborn language bends, made only fit
With her tough thick-ribbed hoops to gird about
Thy giant fancy, which had proved too stout
For their soft melting phrases. As in time
They had the start, so did they cull the prime
Buds of invention many a hundred year,
And left the rifled fields, besides the fear
To touch their harvest; yet from those bare lands
Of what is purely thine, thy only hands
(And that thy smallest work) have gleanèd more
Than all those times and tongues could reap before.
  But thou art gone, and thy strict laws will be
Too hard for libertines in Poetry.
They will repeal the goodly exiled train
Of gods and goddesses, which in thy just reign
Were banished nobler poems; now, with these,
The silenced tales of the *Metamorphoses*
Shall stuff their lines, and swell the windy page,
Till Verse, refined by thee, in this last age
Turn ballad rhyme, or those old idols be
Adored again with new apostasy.

280   *Song*

    ASK me no more where Jove bestows,
    When June is past, the fading rose;
    For in your beauty's orient deep
    These flowers, as in their causes, sleep.

    Ask me no more whither doth stray
    The golden atoms of the day;
    For in pure love heaven did prepare
    Those powders to enrich your hair.

Ask me no more whither doth haste
The nightingale when May is past;
For in your sweet dividing throat
She winters and keeps warm her note.

Ask me no more where those stars light
That downwards fall in dead of night;
For in your eyes they sit, and there
Fixed become as in their sphere.

Ask me no more if east or west
The Phoenix builds her spicy nest;
For unto you at last she flies,
And in your fragrant bosom dies.

281   *Persuasions to Enjoy*

IF the quick spirits in your eye
Now languish and anon must die;
If every sweet and every grace
Must fly from that forsaken face;
    Then, Celia, let us reap our joys
    Ere Time such goodly fruit destroys.

Or if that golden fleece must grow
For ever free from agèd snow;
If those bright suns must know no shade,
Nor your fresh beauties ever fade;
    Then, fear not, Celia, to bestow
    What, still being gathered, still must grow.

Thus either Time his sickle brings
In vain, or else in vain his wings.

282   *To My Inconstant Mistress*

WHEN thou, poor Excommunicate
  From all the joys of love, shalt see
The full reward and glorious fate
  Which my strong faith shall purchase me,
  Then curse thine own inconstancy!

A fairer hand than thine shall cure
  That heart which thy false oaths did wound;
And to my soul a soul more pure
  Than thine shall by Love's hand be bound,
  And both with equal glory crowned.

Then shalt thou weep, entreat, complain
  To Love, as I did once to thee;
When all thy tears shall be as vain
  As mine were then: for thou shalt be
  Damned for thy false apostasy.

283   *On the Lady Mary Villiers*

THE Lady Mary Villiers lies
Under this stone; with weeping eyes
The parents that first gave her birth,
And their sad friends, laid her in earth.
If any of them, Reader, were
Known unto thee, shed a tear;
Or if thyself possess a gem
As dear to thee, as this to them,
Though a stranger to this place,
Bewail in theirs thine own hard case:
  For thou perhaps at thy return
  Mayst find thy Darling in an urn.

JAMES SHIRLEY

1596–1666

284   *Piping Peace*

YOU virgins that did late despair
  To keep your wealth from cruel men,
Tie up in silk your careless hair:
  Soft peace is come again.

Now lovers' eyes may gently shoot
   A flame that will not kill;
The drum was angry, but the lute
   Shall whisper what you will.

Sing Io, Io! for his sake
   That hath restored your drooping heads;
With choice of sweetest flowers make
   A garden where he treads;

Whilst we whole groves of laurel bring,
   A petty triumph to his brow,
Who is the Master of our spring
   And all the bloom we owe.

285   *Death the Leveller*

THE glories of our blood and state
   Are shadows, not substantial things;
There is no armour against Fate;
   Death lays his icy hand on kings:
        Sceptre and Crown
        Must tumble down,
And in the dust be equal made
With the poor crooked scythe and spade.

Some men with swords may reap the field,
   And plant fresh laurels where they kill:
But their strong nerves at last must yield;
   They tame but one another still:
        Early or late
        They stoop to fate,
And must give up their murmuring breath
When they, pale captives, creep to death.

The garlands wither on your brow;
   Then boast no more your mighty deeds!
Upon Death's purple altar now
   See where the victor-victim bleeds.
        Your heads must come
        To the cold tomb:
Only the actions of the just
Smell sweet and blossom in their dust.

WILLIAM STRODE
1602–1645

286   *Chloris in the Snow*

I SAW fair Chloris walk alone,
When feathered rain came softly down,
As Jove descending from his Tower
To court her in a silver shower:
The wanton snow flew to her breast,
Like pretty birds into their nest,
But, overcome with whiteness there,
For grief it thawed into a tear:
    Thence falling on her garments' hem,
    To deck her, froze into a gem.

WILLIAM HABINGTON
1605–1654

287   *Nox nocti indicat Scientiam*

WHEN I survey the bright
    Celestial sphere;
So rich with jewels hung that Night
    Doth like an Ethiop bride appear:

My soul her wings doth spread
    And heavenward flies,
The Almighty's mysteries to read
    In the large volumes of the skies.

For the bright firmament
    Shoots forth no flame
So silent, but is eloquent
    In speaking the Creator's name.

No unregarded star
        Contracts its light
Into so small a character,
  Removed far from our human sight;

But if we steadfast look
        We shall discern
In it, as in some holy book,
  How man may heavenly knowledge learn.

It tells the Conqueror
        That far-stretched power,
Which his proud dangers traffic for,
  Is but the triumph of an hour;

That from the farthest North,
        Some nation may,
Yet undiscovered, issue forth,
  And o'er his new-got conquest sway;

Some nation yet shut in
        With hills of ice
May be let out to scourge his sin,
  Till they shall equal him in vice.

And then they likewise shall
        Their ruin have;
For as yourselves your Empires fall,
  And every Kingdom hath a grave.

Thus those celestial fires,
        Though seeming mute,
The fallacy of our desires
  And all the pride of life confute:—

For they have watched since first
        The world had birth:
And found sin in itself accurst,
  And nothing permanent on Earth.

288 *Pretty Sport*

FINE young folly, though you were
That fair beauty I did swear,
Yet you ne'er could reach my heart.
For we courtiers learn at school
Only with your sex to fool:
Y'are not worth the serious part.

When I sigh and kiss your hand,
Cross my arms and wondering stand,
Holding parley with your eye,
Then dilate on my desires;
Swear the sun ne'er shot such fires:
All is but a handsome lie.

When I eye your curl or lace,
Gentle soul, you think your face
Straight some murder doth commit,
And your virtue doth begin
To grow scrupulous of my sin,
When I talk to show my wit.

Therefore, Madam, wear no cloud
Nor to check my love grow proud,
For in sooth I much do doubt,
'Tis the powder in your hair,
Not your breath, perfumes the air,
And your clothes that set you out.

Yet though truth has this confessed
And I vow I love in jest,
When I next begin to court,
And protest an amorous flame,
You'll swear I in earnest am.
Bedlam! this is pretty sport.

THOMAS RANDOLPH
1605–1635

289 *An Ode to Master Anthony Stafford*
   to Hasten Him into the Country

COME, spur away,
I have no patience for a longer stay,
 But must go down,
And leave the chargeable noise of this great town:
 I will the country see,
 Where old simplicity,
  Though hid in gray,
  Doth look more gay
Than foppery in plush and scarlet clad.
 Farewell, you city wits, that are
  Almost at civil war—
'Tis time that I grow wise, when all the world grows mad.

  More of my days
I will not spend to gain an idiot's praise;
 Or to make sport
For some slight Puisne of the Inns of Court.
 Then, worthy Stafford, say,
 How shall we spend the day?
  With what delights
  Shorten the nights?
When from this tumult we are got secure,
 Where mirth with all her freedom goes,
  Yet shall no finger lose;
Where every word is thought, and every thought is pure?

  There from the tree
We'll cherries pluck, and pick the strawberry;
 And every day
Go see the wholesome country girls make hay,
 Whose brown hath lovelier grace
 Than any painted face
  That I do know
  Hyde Park can show:

Where I had rather gain a kiss than meet
  (Though some of them in greater state
    Might court my love with plate)
The beauties of the Cheap, and wives of Lombard Street.

    But think upon
Some other pleasures: these to me are none.
    Why do I prate
Of women, that are things against my fate!
    I never mean to wed
    That torture t o my bed:
     My Muse is she
     My love shall be.
Let clowns get wealth and heirs: when I am gone
  And the great bugbear, grisly Death,
    Shall take this idle breath,
If I a poem leave, that poem is my son.

    Of this no more!
We'll rather taste the bright Pomona's store.
    No fruit shall 'scape
Our palates, from the damson to the grape.
    Then, full, we'll seek a shade,
    And hear what music's made;
     How Philomel
     Her tale doth tell,
And how the other birds do fill the quire;
  The thrush and blackbird lend their throats,
    Warbling melodious notes;
We will all sports enjoy which others but desire.

    Ours is the sky,
Where, at what fowl we please, our hawk shall fly:
    Nor will we spare
To hunt the crafty fox or timorous hare;
    But let our hounds run loose
    In any ground they'll choose;
     The buck shall fall,
     The stag, and all.
Our pleasures must from their own warrants be,
  For to my Muse, if not to me,
    I'm sure all game is free:
Heaven, earth, are all but parts of her great royalty.

And when we mean
To taste of Bacchus' blessings now and then,
And drink by stealth
A cup or two to noble Barkley's health,
I'll take my pipe and try
The Phrygian melody;
Which he that hears,
Lets through his ears
A madness to distemper all the brain:
Then I another pipe will take
And Doric music make,
To civilize with graver notes our wits again.

290   *Upon his Picture*

WHEN age hath made me what I am not now;
And every wrinkle tells me where the plough
Of time hath furrowed; when an ice shall flow
Through every vein, and all my head wear snow;
When death displays his coldness in my cheek
And I myself in my own picture seek,
Not finding what I am, but what I was,
In doubt which to believe, this or my glass;
Yet though I alter, this remains the same
As it was drawn, retains the primitive frame
And first complexion; here will still be seen
Blood on the cheek, and down upon the chin.
Here the smooth brow will stay, the lively eye,
The ruddy lip, and hair of youthful dye.
Behold what frailty we in man may see
Whose shadow is less given to change than he.

SIR WILLIAM DAVENANT
1606-1668

291 *Aubade*

THE lark now leaves his watery nest,
 And climbing shakes his dewy wings.
He takes this window for the East,
 And to implore your light he sings—
Awake, awake! the morn will never rise
Till she can dress her beauty at your eyes.

The merchant bows unto the seaman's star,
 The ploughman from the sun his season takes;
But still the lover wonders what they are
 Who look for day before his mistress wakes.
Awake, awake! break through your veils of lawn!
Then draw your curtains, and begin the dawn!

292 *Endimion Porter and Olivia*

Olivia.   Before we shall again behold
 In his diurnal race the world's great eye,
  We may as silent be and cold
 As are the shades where buried lovers lie.

Endimion.   Olivia, 'tis no fault of love
 To lose ourselves in death, but O, I fear
  When life and knowledge is above
 Restored to us, I shall not know thee there.

Olivia.   Call it not Heaven, my love, where we
 Ourselves shall see, and yet each other miss:
  So much of Heaven I find in thee
 As, thou unknown, all else privation is.

Endimion.   Why should we doubt, before we go
 To find the knowledge which shall ever last,
  That we may there each other know?
 Can future knowledge quite destroy the past?

Olivia. When at the bowers in the Elysian shade
    I first arrive, I shall examine where
     They dwell who love the highest virtue made;
    For I am sure to find Endimion there.

Endimion. From this vexed world when we shall both retire,
    Where all are lovers, and where all rejoice,
     I need not seek thee in the Heavenly quire;
    For I shall know Olivia by her voice.

293   *The Philosopher and the Lover*
      to a Mistress Dying

 Lover.   Your beauty, ripe and calm and fresh
      As eastern summers are,
     Must now, forsaking time and flesh,
      Add light to some small star.

Philosopher. Whilst she yet lives, were stars decayed,
      Their light by hers relief might find;
     But Death will lead her to a shade
      Where Love is cold and Beauty blind.

 Lover.   Lovers, whose priests all poets are,
      Think every mistress, when she dies,
     Is changed at least into a star:
      And who dares doubt the poets wise?

Philosopher. But ask not bodies doomed to die
      To what abode they go;
     Since Knowledge is but Sorrow's spy,
      It is not safe to know.

294   *The Soldier Going to the Field*

     PRESERVE thy sighs, unthrifty girl,
      To purify the air;
     Thy tears to thread instead of pearl
      On bracelets of thy hair.

The trumpet makes the echo hoarse
  And wakes the louder drum;
Expense of grief gains no remorse
  When sorrow should be dumb.

For I must go where lazy Peace
  Will hide her drowsy head,
And, for the sport of Kings, increase
  The number of the dead.

But first I'll chide thy cruel theft:
  Can I in war delight,
Who being of my heart bereft
  Can have no heart to fight?

Thou know'st the sacred Laws of old
  Ordained a thief should pay,
To quit him of his theft, sevenfold
  What he had stolen away.

Thy payment shall but double be;
  O then with speed resign
My own seduced heart to me,
  Accompanied with thine.

EDMUND WALLER

1606–1687

295   *Go, Lovely Rose*

Go, lovely Rose—
Tell her that wastes her time and me,
  That now she knows,
When I resemble her to thee,
How sweet and fair she seems to be.

Tell her that's young,
And shuns to have her graces spied,
  That hadst thou sprung
In deserts where no men abide,
Thou must have uncommended died.

Small is the worth
Of beauty from the light retired:
    Bid her come forth,
Suffer herself to be desired,
And not blush so to be admired.

    Then die—that she
The common fate of all things rare
    May read in thee;
How small a part of time they share
That are so wondrous sweet and fair!

296   *Old Age*

THE seas are quiet when the winds give o'er;
So calm are we when passions are no more.
For then we know how vain it was to boast
Of fleeting things, so certain to be lost.
Clouds of affection from our younger eyes
Conceal that emptiness which age descries.

The soul's dark cottage, battered and decayed,
Lets in new light through chinks that Time has made:
Stronger by weakness, wiser men become
As they draw near to their eternal home.
Leaving the old, both worlds at once they view
That stand upon the threshold of the new.

SIR RICHARD FANSHAWE

1608–1666

297   *Ode on His Majesty's Proclamation,*
Commanding the Gentry to Reside on their Estates:
                1630

NOW war is all the world about,
And everywhere Erynnis reigns,
Or else, the torch so late put out,
            The stench remains.

Holland for many years hath been
Of Christian tragedies the stage,
Yet seldom hath she played a scene
      Of bloodier rage.

And France that was not long composed,
With civil drums again resounds,
And ere the old are fully closed
      Receives new wounds.

The great Gustavus in the west
Plucks the Imperial Eagle's wing,
Than whom the earth did ne'er invest
      A fiercer king;

Revenging lost Bohemia,
And the proud wrongs which Tilly did,
And tempereth the German clay
      With Spanish blood.

What should I tell of Polish bands,
And the bloods boiling in the North?
'Gainst whom the furied Russians
      Their troops bring forth:

Both confident. This in his purse,
And needy valour set on work;
He in his axe, which oft did worse
      The invading Turk.

Who now sustains a Persian storm:
There hell, that made it, suffers schism:
This war, forsooth, was to reform
      Mahometism.

Only the island which we sow,
(A world without the world) so far
From present wounds, it cannot show
      An ancient scar.

SIR RICHARD FANSHAWE

White Peace, the beautifullest of things
Seems here her everlasting rest
To fix, and spreads her downy wings
          Over the nest.

As when great Jove, usurping reign,
From the plagued world did her exile,
And tied her with a golden chain
          To one blest isle;

Which in a sea of plenty swam,
And turtles sang on every bough;
A safe retreat to all that came,
          As ours is now.

Yet we, as if some foe were here,
Leave the despisèd fields to clowns,
And come to save ourselves as 'twere
          In wallèd towns.

Hither we bring wives, babes, rich clothes
And gems; till now my Sovereign
The growing evil doth oppose:
          Counting in vain

His care preserves us from annoy
Of enemies his realms to invade,
Unless he force us to enjoy
          The peace he made.

To roll themselves in envied leisure
He therefore sends the landed heirs,
Whilst he proclaims not his own pleasure
          So much as theirs.

The sap and blood of the land, which fled
Into the root, and choked the heart,
Are bid their quickening power to spread
          Through every part.

SIR RICHARD FANSHAWE

O, 'twas an act not for my Muse
To celebrate, nor the dull Age
Until the country air infuse
          A purer rage!

And if the fields as thankful prove
For benefits received, as seed,
They will, to quite so great a love,
          A Virgil breed.

A Tityrus, that shall not cease
The Augustus of our world to praise
In equal verse, author of peace
          And halcyon days.

Nor let the gentry grudge to go
Into those places whence they grew,
But think them blest they may do so.
          Who would pursue

The smoky glory of the town,
That may go till his native earth,
And by the shining fire sit down
          Of his own hearth,

Free from the griping scrivener's bands,
And the more biting mercer's books;
Free from the bait of oilèd hands
          And painted looks?

The country too, even chops for rain:
You that exhale it by your power
Let the fat drops fall down again
          In a full shower.

And you bright beauties of the time,
That waste yourselves here in a blaze,
Fix to your orb and proper clime
          Your wandering rays.

Let no dark corner of the land
Be unembellished with one gem,
And those which here too thick do stand
          Sprinkle on them.

Believe me, ladies, you will find
In that sweet life more solid joys,
More true contentment to the mind
        Than all town toys.

Nor Cupid there less blood doth spill,
But heads his shafts with chaster love,
Not feathered with a sparrow's quill,
        But of a dove.

There shall you hear the nightingale,
The harmless siren of the wood,
How prettily she tells a tale
        Of rape and blood.

The lyric lark, with all beside
Of nature's feathered quire, and all
The commonwealth of flowers in its pride
        Behold you shall.

The lily, queen, the royal rose,
The gillyflower, prince of the blood,
The courtier tulip, gay in clothes,
        The regal bud,

The violet, purple senator,
How they do mock the pomp of state,
And all that at the surly door
        Of great ones wait.

Plant trees you may, and see them shoot
Up with your children, to be served
To your clean boards, and the fairest fruit
        To be preserved.

And learn to use their several gums;
'Tis innocence in the sweet blood
Of cherry, apricots and plums
        To be imbrued.

JOHN MILTON
1608–1674

298   *Hymn on the Morning of Christ's Nativity,*
Composed 1629

IT was the winter wild,
While the Heaven-born Child
    All meanly wrapped in the rude manger lies;
Nature in awe to him
Had doffed her gaudy trim,
    With her great Master so to sympathize;
It was no season then for her
To wanton with the sun, her lusty paramour.

Only with speeches fair
She woos the gentle air
    To hide her guilty front with innocent snow,
And on her naked shame,
Pollute with sinful blame,
    The saintly veil of maiden white to throw,
Confounded that her Maker's eyes
Should look so near upon her foul deformities.

But he her fears to cease
Sent down the meek-eyed Peace;
    She, crowned with olive green, came softly sliding
Down through the turning sphere,
His ready harbinger,
    With turtle wing the amorous clouds dividing,
And waving wide her myrtle wand,
She strikes a universal peace through sea and land.

No war or battle's sound
Was heard the world around:
    The idle spear and shield were high up-hung;
The hookèd chariot stood
Unstained with hostile blood;
    The trumpet spake not to the armèd throng,
And kings sat still with awful eye,
As if they surely knew their sovran Lord was by.

But peaceful was the night
Wherein the Prince of Light
   His reign of peace upon the earth began:
The winds with wonder whist
Smoothly the waters kissed,
   Whispering new joys to the mild ocean,
Who now hath quite forgot to rave,
While birds of calm sit brooding on the charmèd wave.

The stars with deep amaze
Stand fixed in steadfast gaze,
   Bending one way their precious influence,
And will not take their flight,
For all the morning light,
   Or Lucifer that often warned them thence;
But in their glimmering orbs did glow,
Until their Lord himself bespake, and bid them go.

And though the shady gloom
Had given day her room,
   The sun himself withheld his wonted speed,
And hid his head for shame,
As his inferior flame
   The new-enlightened world no more should need;
He saw a greater Sun appear
Than his bright throne or burning axle-tree could bear.

The shepherds on the lawn,
Or ere the point of dawn,
   Sat simply chatting in a rustic row;
Full little thought they than
That the mighty Pan
   Was kindly come to live with them below;
Perhaps their loves or else their sheep,
Was all that did their silly thoughts so busy keep.

When such music sweet
Their hearts and ears did greet,
   As never was by mortal finger strook,
Divinely warbled voice
Answering the stringèd noise
   As all their souls in blissful rapture took:
The air such pleasure loth to lose,
With thousand echoes still prolongs each heavenly close.

Nature that heard such sound
Beneath the hollow round
   Of Cynthia's seat, the airy region thrilling,
Now was almost won
To think her part was done,
   And that her reign had here its last fulfilling;
She knew such harmony alone
Could hold all heaven and earth in happier union.

At last surrounds their sight
A globe of circular light,
   That with long beams the shame-faced Night arrayed,
The helmèd Cherubim
And sworded Seraphim
   Are seen in glittering ranks with wings displayed,
Harping in loud and solemn quire,
With unexpressive notes to Heaven's new-born heir.

Such music (as 'tis said)
Before was never made,
   But when of old the sons of morning sung,
While the Creator great
His constellations set,
   And the well-balanced world on hinges hung,
And cast the dark foundations deep,
And bid the weltering waves their oozy channel keep.

Ring out, ye crystal spheres,
Once bless our human ears
   (If ye have power to touch our senses so),
And let your silver chime
Move in melodious time,
   And let the bass of heaven's deep organ blow;
And with your ninefold harmony
Make up full consort to the angelic symphony.

For if such holy song
Enwrap our fancy long,
   Time will run back and fetch the age of gold,
And speckled Vanity
Will sicken soon, and die,
   And leprous Sin will melt from earthly mould,
And hell itself will pass away
And leave her dolorous mansions to the peering day.

Yea, Truth and Justice then
Will down return to men,
    Orbed in a rainbow; and, like glories wearing,
Mercy will sit between,
Throned in celestial sheen,
    With radiant feet the tissued clouds down-steering,
And heaven, as at some festival,
Will open wide the gates of her high palace hall.

But wisest Fate says no,
This must not yet be so;
    The Babe lies yet in smiling infancy,
That on the bitter cross
Must redeem our loss,
    So both himself and us to glorify;
Yet first, to those ychained in sleep,
The wakeful trump of doom must thunder through the deep.

With such a horrid clang
As on Mount Sinai rang,
    While the red fire and smouldering clouds out-brake:
The aged Earth, aghast
With terror of that blast,
    Shall from the surface to the centre shake,
When at the world's last session
The dreadful Judge in middle air shall spread his throne.

And then at last our bliss
Full and perfect is,
    But now begins; for from this happy day
The old Dragon underground,
In straiter limits bound,
    Not half so far casts his usurpèd sway,
And, wroth to see his kingdom fail,
Swinges the scaly horror of his folded tail.

The oracles are dumb,
No voice or hideous hum
    Runs through the archèd roof in words deceiving.
Apollo from his shrine
Can no more divine,
    With hollow shriek the steep of Delphos leaving.
No nightly trance or breathèd spell
Inspires the pale-eyed priest from the prophetic cell.

The lonely mountains o'er,
And the resounding shore,
  A voice of weeping heard, and loud lament,
From haunted spring and dale,
Edged with poplar pale,
  The parting Genius is with sighing sent;
With flower-inwoven tresses torn
The nymphs in twilight shade of tangled thickets mourn.

In consecrated earth,
And on the holy hearth,
  The Lars and Lemures moan with midnight plaint;
In urns and altars round,
A drear and dying sound
  Affrights the flamens at their service quaint;
And the chill marble seems to sweat,
While each peculiar power forgoes his wonted seat.

Peor and Baälim
Forsake their temples dim,
  With that twice-battered god of Palestine;
And moonèd Ashtaroth,
Heaven's queen and mother both,
  Now sits not girt with tapers' holy shine;
The Libyc Hammon shrinks his horn,
In vain the Tyrian maids their wounded Thammuz mourn.

And sullen Moloch fled,
Hath left in shadows dread
  His burning idol all of blackest hue;
In vain with cymbals' ring
They call the grisly king,
  In dismal dance about the furnace blue;
The brutish gods of Nile as fast,
Isis and Orus, and the dog Anubis haste.

Nor is Osiris seen
In Memphian grove or green,
  Trampling the unshowered grass with lowings loud;
Nor can he be at rest
Within his sacred chest,
  Nought but profoundest hell can be his shroud,
In vain with timbreled anthems dark
The sable-stolèd sorcerers bear his worshipped ark.

He feels from Judah's land
The dreaded Infant's hand,
   The rays of Bethlehem blind his dusky eyn;
Nor all the gods beside,
Longer dare abide,
   Not Typhon huge ending in snaky twine:
Our Babe, to show his Godhead true,
Can in his swaddling bands control the damnèd crew.

So when the sun in bed,
Curtained with cloudy red,
   Pillows his chin upon an orient wave,
The flocking shadows pale
Troop to the infernal jail,
   Each fettered ghost slips to his several grave,
And the yellow-skirted fays
Fly after the night-steeds, leaving their moon-loved maze.

But see, the Virgin blest
Hath laid her Babe to rest:
   Time is our tedious song should here have ending;
Heaven's youngest teemèd star,
Hath fixed her polished car,
   Her sleeping Lord with handmaid lamp attending;
And all about the courtly stable,
Bright-harnessed angels sit in order serviceable.

299   *At a Solemn Music*

BLEST pair of Sirens, pledges of heaven's joy,
Sphere-born harmonious sisters, Voice and Verse,
Wed your divine sounds, and mixed power employ
Dead things with inbreathed sense able to pierce,
And to our high-raised phantasy present
That undisturbèd song of pure concent,
Ay sung before the sapphire-coloured throne
To him that sits thereon,
With saintly shout and solemn jubilee,
Where the bright Seraphim in burning row
Their loud uplifted angel-trumpets blow,
And the Cherubic host in thousand quires
Touch their immortal harps of golden wires,

With those just spirits that wear victorious palms,
Hymns devout and holy psalms
Singing everlastingly;
That we on earth with undiscording voice
May rightly answer that melodious noise:
As once we did, till disproportioned sin
Jarred against Nature's chime, and with harsh din
Broke the fair music that all creatures made
To their great Lord, whose love their motion swayed
In perfect diapason, whilst they stood
In first obedience and their state of good.
O may we soon again renew that song,
And keep in tune with heaven, till God ere long
To his celestial consort us unite,
To live with him, and sing in endless morn of light.

from Comus

(i)

300   *Comus speaks*

THE star that bids the shepherd fold
Now the top of heaven doth hold,
And the gilded car of day
His glowing axle doth allay
In the steep Atlantic stream;
And the slope sun his upward beam
Shoots against the dusky pole,
Pacing toward the other goal
Of his chamber in the east.
Meanwhile welcome joy and feast,
Midnight shout and revelry,
Tipsy dance and jollity.
Braid your locks with rosy twine,
Dropping odours, dropping wine.
Rigour now is gone to bed;
And Advice with scrupulous head,
Strict Age, and sour Severity,
With their grave saws, in slumber lie.
We that are of purer fire,
Imitate the starry quire,
Who in their nightly watchful spheres,
Lead in swift round the months and years.

The sounds and seas with all their finny drove
Now to the moon in wavering morris move
And on the tawny sands and shelves
Trip the pert fairies and the dapper elves;
By dimpled brook and fountain-brim,
The wood-nymphs, decked with daisies trim,
Their merry wakes and pastimes keep:
What hath night to do with sleep?
Night hath better sweets to prove,
Venus now wakes, and wakens Love. . . .
Come, knit hands, and beat the ground,
In a light fantastic round.

(ii)

301

The Lady Sings

SWEET Echo, sweetest nymph, that liv'st unseen
      Within thy airy shell
  By slow Meander's margent green,
And in the violet-embroidered vale
    Where the lovelorn nightingale
Nightly to thee her sad song mourneth well:
Canst thou not tell me of a gentle pair
    That likest thy Narcissus are?
       O if thou have
    Hid them in some flowery cave,
      Tell me but where,
  Sweet queen of parley, daughter of the sphere;
  So mayst thou be translated to the skies,
And give resounding grace to all heaven's harmonies.

(iii)

302

Sabrina

The Spirit. Sabrina fair,
      Listen where thou art sitting
    Under the glassy, cool, translucent wave,
      In twisted braids of lilies knitting
    The loose train of thy amber-dropping hair;
      Listen for dear honour's sake,
      Goddess of the silver lake,
      Listen and save.

Listen and appear to us
In name of great Oceanus,
By the earth-shaking Neptune's mace,
And Tethys' grave majestic pace,
By hoary Nereus' wrinkled look,
And the Carpathian wizard's hook,
By scaly Triton's winding shell,
And old soothsaying Glaucus' spell,
By Leucothea's lovely hands,
And her son that rules the strands,
By Thetis' tinsel-slippered feet,
And the songs of Sirens sweet,
By dead Parthenope's dear tomb,
And fair Ligea's golden comb,
Wherewith she sits on diamond rocks
Sleeking her soft alluring locks;
By all the nymphs that nightly dance
Upon thy streams with wily glance,
Rise, rise, and heave thy rosy head
From thy coral-paven bed,
And bridle in thy headlong wave,
Till thou our summons answered have.
                              Listen and save!

Sabrina.   By the rushy-fringèd bank,
Where grows the willow and the osier dank,
      My sliding chariot stays,
Thick set with agate, and the azurn sheen
      Of turkis blue, and emerald green,
            That in the channel strays.
      Whilst from off the waters fleet
      Thus I set my printless feet
      O'er the cowslip's velvet head,
            That bends not as I tread.
      Gentle swain, at thy request
            I am here!

(iv)

303

The Spirit Epiloguizes

To the ocean now I fly,
And those happy climes that lie
Where day never shuts his eye,
Up in the broad fields of the sky.
There I suck the liquid air,
All amidst the gardens fair
Of Hesperus, and his daughters three
That sing about the golden tree.
Along the crispèd shades and bowers
Revels the spruce and jocund Spring;
The Graces and the rosy-bosomed Hours
Thither all their bounties bring,
That there eternal summer dwells;
And west winds with musky wing
About the cedarn alleys fling
Nard and cassia's balmy smells.
Iris there with humid bow
Waters the odorous banks that blow
Flowers of more mingled hue
Than her purfled scarf can shew,
And drenches with Elysian dew
(List, mortals, if your ears be true)
Beds of hyacinth and roses,
Where young Adonis oft reposes,
Waxing well of his deep wound,
In slumber soft, and on the ground
Sadly sits the Assyrian queen.
But far above in spangled sheen
Celestial Cupid, her famed son, advanced,
Holds his dear Psyche, sweet entranced
After her wandering labours long,
Till free consent the gods among
Make her his eternal bride,
And from her fair unspotted side
Two blissful twins are to be born,
Youth and Joy; so Jove hath sworn.

But now my task is smoothly done,
I can fly, or I can run
Quickly to the green earth's end,
Where the bowed welkin slow doth bend,
And from thence can soar as soon
To the corners of the moon.
　　Mortals, that would follow me,
Love Virtue, she alone is free;
She can teach ye how to climb
Higher than the sphery chime;
Or, if Virtue feeble were,
Heaven itself would stoop to her.

304　　　　　　　　　*Lycidas*

*Monody on the Death of a Friend drowned in his
passage from Chester on the Irish Seas, 1637*

YET once more, O ye laurels, and once more,
Ye myrtles brown, with ivy never sere,
I come to pluck your berries harsh and crude,
And with forced fingers rude
Shatter your leaves before the mellowing year.
Bitter constraint, and sad occasion dear,
Compels me to disturb your season due;
For Lycidas is dead, dead ere his prime,
Young Lycidas, and hath not left his peer.
Who would not sing for Lycidas? He knew
Himself to sing, and build the lofty rhyme.
He must not float upon his watery bier
Unwept, and welter to the parching wind,
Without the meed of some melodious tear.
　　Begin then, Sisters of the sacred well
That from beneath the seat of Jove doth spring,
Begin, and somewhat loudly sweep the string.
Hence with denial vain and coy excuse;
So may some gentle Muse
With lucky words favour my destined urn,
And as he passes turn,
And bid fair peace be to my sable shroud.
For we were nursed upon the self-same hill
Fed the same flock, by fountain, shade, and rill.

Together both, ere the high lawns appeared
Under the opening eyelids of the morn,
We drove afield, and both together heard
What time the grey-fly winds her sultry horn,
Battening our flocks with the fresh dews of night,
Oft till the star that rose, at evening, bright
Toward heaven's descent had sloped his westering wheel.
Meanwhile the rural ditties were not mute,
Tempered to the oaten flute;
Rough Satyrs danced, and Fauns with cloven heel
From the glad sound would not be absent long,
And old Damoetas loved to hear our song.

But O the heavy change, now thou art gone,
Now thou art gone, and never must return!
Thee, Shepherd, thee the woods and desert caves,
With wild thyme and the gadding vine o'ergrown,
And all their echoes mourn.
The willows and the hazel copses green,
Shall now no more be seen,
Fanning their joyous leaves to thy soft lays.
As killing as the canker to the rose,
Or taint-worm to the weanling herds that graze,
Or frost to flowers, that their gay wardrobe wear,
When first the white-thorn blows;
Such, Lycidas, thy loss to shepherd's ear.

Where were ye, Nymphs, when the remorseless deep
Closed o'er the head of your loved Lycidas?
For neither were ye playing on the steep,
Where your old bards, the famous Druids, lie,
Nor on the shaggy top of Mona high,
Nor yet where Deva spreads her wizard stream.
Ay me, I fondly dream,
Had ye been there!—for what could that have done?
What could the Muse herself that Orpheus bore,
The Muse herself, for her enchanting son
Whom universal nature did lament,
When by the rout that made the hideous roar
His gory visage down the stream was sent,
Down the swift Hebrus to the Lesbian shore?

Alas! what boots it with uncessant care
To tend the homely slighted shepherd's trade,
And strictly meditate the thankless Muse?

Were it not better done, as others use,
To sport with Amaryllis in the shade,
Or with the tangles of Neaera's hair?
Fame is the spur that the clear spirit doth raise
(That last infirmity of noble mind)
To scorn delights, and live laborious days;
But the fair guerdon when we hope to find,
And think to burst out into sudden blaze,
Comes the blind Fury with the abhorrèd shears,
And slits the thin-spun life. 'But not the praise,'
Phoebus replied, and touched my trembling ears:
'Fame is no plant that grows on mortal soil,
Nor in the glistering foil
Set off to the world, nor in broad rumour lies,
But lives and spreads aloft by those pure eyes
And perfect witness of all-judging Jove;
As he pronounces lastly on each deed,
Of so much fame in heaven expect thy meed.'

O fountain Arethuse, and thou honoured flood,
Smooth-sliding Mincius, crowned with vocal reeds,
That strain I heard was of a higher mood.
But now my oat proceeds,
And listens to the herald of the sea,
That came in Neptune's plea.
He asked the waves, and asked the felon winds,
What hard mishap hath doomed this gentle swain?
And questioned every gust of rugged wings
That blows from off each beakèd promontory;
They knew not of his story,
And sage Hippotades their answer brings,
That not a blast was from his dungeon strayed;
The air was calm, and on the level brine
Sleek Panope with all her sisters played.
It was that fatal and perfidious bark,
Built in the eclipse, and rigged with curses dark,
That sunk so low that sacred head of thine.

Next Camus, reverend sire, went footing slow,
His mantle hairy, and his bonnet sedge,
Inwrought with figures dim, and on the edge
Like to that sanguine flower inscribed with woe.
'Ah, who hath reft,' quoth he, 'my dearest pledge?'

Last came, and last did go,
The Pilot of the Galilean lake;
Two massy keys he bore of metals twain
(The golden opes, the iron shuts amain).
He shook his mitred locks, and stern bespake:
'How well could I have spared for thee, young swain,
Enow of such as for their bellies' sake
Creep and intrude and climb into the fold!
Of other care they little reckoning make
Than how to scramble at the shearers' feast,
And shove away the worthy bidden guest.
Blind mouths! that scarce themselves know how to hold
A sheep-hook, or have learned aught else the least
That to the faithful herdman's art belongs!
What recks it them? What need they? They are sped;
And when they list, their lean and flashy songs
Grate on their scrannel pipes of wretched straw;
The hungry sheep look up, and are not fed,
But swoln with wind, and the rank mist they draw,
Rot inwardly, and foul contagion spread;
Besides what the grim wolf with privy paw
Daily devours apace, and nothing said;
But that two-handed engine at the door
Stands ready to smite once, and smite no more.'
   Return, Alphéus, the dread voice is past
That shrunk thy streams; return, Sicilian Muse,
And call the vales, and bid them hither cast
Their bells and flowerets of a thousand hues.
Ye valleys low, where the mild whispers use
Of shades and wanton winds and gushing brooks,
On whose fresh lap the swart star sparely looks,
Throw hither all your quaint enamelled eyes,
That on the green turf suck the honied showers,
And purple all the ground with vernal flowers.
Bring the rathe primrose that forsaken dies,
The tufted crow-toe, and pale jessamine,
The white pink, and the pansy freaked with jet,
The glowing violet,
The musk rose, and the well-attired woodbine,
With cowslips wan that hang the pensive head,
And every flower that sad embroidery wears.
Bid amaranthus all his beauty shed,
And daffadillies fill their cups with tears,

To strew the laureate hearse where Lycid lies.
For so to interpose a little ease,
Let our frail thoughts dally with false surmise;
Ay me! whilst thee the shores and sounding seas
Wash far away, where'er thy bones are hurled,
Whether beyond the stormy Hebrides,
Where thou perhaps under the whelming tide
Visit'st the bottom of the monstrous world;
Or whether thou, to our moist vows denied,
Sleep'st by the fable of Bellerus old,
Where the great Vision of the guarded mount
Looks toward Namancos, and Bayona's hold.
Look homeward, Angel, now, and melt with ruth:
And, O ye dolphins, waft the hapless youth.
　　Weep no more, woeful shepherds, weep no more,
For Lycidas, your sorrow, is not dead,
Sunk though he be beneath the watery floor;
So sinks the day-star in the ocean bed,
And yet anon repairs his drooping head,
And tricks his beams, and with new-spangled ore
Flames in the forehead of the morning sky:
So Lycidas sunk low, but mounted high,
Through the dear might of him that walked the waves,
Where, other groves and other streams along,
With nectar pure his oozy locks he laves,
And hears the unexpressive nuptial song,
In the blest kingdoms meek of joy and love.
There entertain him all the saints above,
In solemn troops and sweet societies,
That sing, and singing in their glory move,
And wipe the tears for ever from his eyes.
Now, Lycidas, the shepherds weep no more;
Henceforth thou art the Genius of the shore,
In thy large recompense, and shalt be good
To all that wander in that perilous flood.
　　Thus sang the uncouth swain to the oaks and rills,
While the still morn went out with sandals grey;
He touched the tender stops of various quills,
With eager thought warbling his Doric lay.
And now the sun had stretched out all the hills,
And now was dropped into the western bay;
At last he rose, and twitched his mantle blue:
Tomorrow to fresh woods, and pastures new.

305   *On His Blindness*

WHEN I consider how my light is spent,
　　Ere half my days, in this dark world and wide,
　　And that one talent which is death to hide
　　Lodged with me useless, though my soul more bent
To serve therewith my Maker, and present
　　My true account, lest he returning chide,
　　'Doth God exact day-labour, light denied?'
　　I fondly ask. But Patience, to prevent
That murmur, soon replies: 'God doth not need
　　Either man's work or his own gifts; who best
　　Bear his mild yoke, they serve him best. His state
Is kingly: thousands at his bidding speed,
　　And post o'er land and ocean without rest;
　　They also serve who only stand and wait.'

306   *On the Late Massacre in Piedmont*

AVENGE, O Lord, thy slaughtered saints, whose bones
　　Lie scattered on the Alpine mountains cold,
　　Even them who kept thy truth so pure of old
　　When all our fathers worshipped stocks and stones,
Forget not; in thy book record their groans
　　Who were thy sheep, and in their ancient fold
　　Slain by the bloody Piedmontese that rolled
　　Mother with infant down the rocks. Their moans
The vales redoubled to the hills, and they
　　To heaven. Their martyred blood and ashes sow
　　O'er all the Italian fields, where still doth sway
The triple tyrant, that from these may grow
　　A hundredfold, who, having learnt thy way,
　　Early may fly the Babylonian woe.

307 *On His Dead Wife*

METHOUGHT I saw my late espousèd saint
  Brought to me like Alcestis from the grave,
  Whom Jove's great son to her glad husband gave,
  Rescued from death by force, though pale and faint.
Mine, as whom washed from spot of childbed taint
  Purification in the old Law did save,
  And such as yet once more I trust to have
  Full sight of her in heaven without restraint,
Came vested all in white, pure as her mind.
  Her face was veiled, yet to my fancied sight
  Love, sweetness, goodness, in her person shined
So clear as in no face with more delight.
  But O as to embrace me she inclined,
  I waked, she fled, and day brought back my night.

from Paradise Lost

(i)

308 *Immortal Hate*

THERE the companions of his fall, o'erwhelmed
With floods and whirlwinds of tempestuous fire,
He soon discerns, and weltering by his side
One next himself in power, and next in crime,
Long after known in Palestine, and named
Beelzebub. To whom the Arch-Enemy,
And thence in heaven called Satan, with bold words
Breaking the horrid silence thus began:
  'If thou beest he—but O how fallen! how changed
From him, who in the happy realms of light,
Clothed with transcendent brightness didst outshine
Myriads though bright—if he whom mutual league,
United thoughts and counsels, equal hope
And hazard in the glorious enterprise,
Joined with me once, now misery hath joined
In equal ruin: into what pit thou seest
From what highth fallen, so much the stronger proved
He with his thunder, and till then who knew
The force of those dire arms? Yet not for those,

Nor what the potent Victor in his rage
Can else inflict, do I repent or change,
Though changed in outward lustre, that fixed mind
And high disdain, from sense of injured merit,
That with the mightiest raised me to contend
And to the fierce contention brought along
Innumerable force of Spirits armed
That durst dislike his reign, and me preferring,
His utmost power with adverse power opposed
In dubious battle on the plains of heaven,
And shook his throne. What though the field be lost?
All is not lost; the unconquerable will,
And study of revenge, immortal hate,
And courage never to submit or yield:
And what is else not to be overcome?
That glory never shall his wrath or might
Extort from me. To bow and sue for grace
With suppliant knee, and deify his power
Who from the terror of this arm so late
Doubted his empire, that were low indeed,
That were an ignominy and shame beneath
This downfall; since by fate the strength of gods
And this empyreal substance cannot fail,
Since through experience of this great event,
In arms not worse, in foresight much advanced,
We may with more successful hope resolve
To wage by force or guile eternal war
Irreconcilable to our grand Foe,
Who now triumphs, and in the excess of joy
Sole reigning holds the tyranny of heaven.'

(ii)

309 *Holy Light*

HAIL, holy Light, offspring of Heaven first-born,
Or of the Eternal coeternal beam
May I express thee unblamed? since God is light,
And never but in unapproachèd light
Dwelt from eternity, dwelt then in thee,
Bright effluence of bright essence increate.
Or hear'st thou rather pure ethereal stream,
Whose fountain who shall tell? Before the sun,

Before the heavens thou wert, and at the voice
Of God, as with a mantle didst invest
The rising world of waters dark and deep,
Won from the void and formless infinite.
Thee I revisit now with bolder wing,
Escaped the Stygian pool, though long detained
In that obscure sojourn, while in my flight
Through utter and through middle darkness borne
With other notes than to the Orphean lyre
I sung of Chaos and eternal Night,
Taught by the Heavenly Muse to venture down
The dark descent, and up to reascend,
Though hard and rare. Thee I revisit safe,
And feel thy sovran vital lamp; but thou
Revisit'st not these eyes, that roll in vain
To find thy piercing ray, and find no dawn;
So thick a drop serene hath quenched their orbs,
Or dim suffusion veiled. Yet not the more
Cease I to wander where the Muses haunt
Clear spring, or shady grove, or sunny hill,
Smit with the love of sacred song; but chief
Thee, Sion, and the flowery brooks beneath
That wash thy hallowed feet, and warbling flow,
Nightly I visit; nor sometimes forget
Those other two equalled with me in fate,
So were I equalled with them in renown,
Blind Thamyris and blind Maeonides,
And Tiresias and Phineus prophets old:
Then feed on thoughts that voluntary move
Harmonious numbers, as the wakeful bird
Sings darkling, and in shadiest covert hid
Tunes her nocturnal note. Thus with the year
Seasons return; but not to me returns
Day, or the sweet approach of even or morn,
Or sight of vernal bloom, or summer's rose,
Or flocks, or herds, or human face divine;
But cloud instead, and ever-during dark
Surrounds me, from the cheerful ways of men
Cut off, and for the book of knowledge fair
Presented with a universal blank
Of Nature's works to me expunged and rased,
And wisdom at one entrance quite shut out.
So much the rather thou, celestial Light,

Shine inward, and the mind through all her powers
Irradiate, there plant eyes, all mist from thence
Purge and disperse, that I may see and tell
Of things invisible to mortal sight.

(iii)

Evening in Paradise

310

NOW came still evening on, and twilight grey
Had in her sober livery all things clad;
Silence accompanied, for beast and bird,
They to their grassy couch, these to their nests
Were slunk, all but the wakeful nightingale;
She all night long her amorous descant sung;
Silence was pleased. Now glowed the firmament
With living sapphires; Hesperus that led
The starry host, rode brightest, till the moon
Rising in clouded majesty, at length
Apparent queen unveiled her peerless light,
And o'er the dark her silver mantle threw;
   When Adam thus to Eve: 'Fair consort, the hour
Of night, and all things now retired to rest,
Mind us of like repose; since God hath set
Labour and rest, as day and night to men
Successive, and the timely dew of sleep
Now falling with soft slumbrous weight inclines
Our eyelids; other creatures all day long
Rove idle, unemployed, and less need rest;
Man hath his daily work of body or mind
Appointed, which declares his dignity,
And the regard of Heaven on all his ways;
While other animals unactive range,
And of their doings God takes no account.
Tomorrow ere fresh morning streak the east
With first approach of light, we must be risen,
And at our pleasant labour, to reform
Yon flowery arbours, yonder alleys green,
Our walks at noon, with branches overgrown,
That mock our scant manuring and require
More hands than ours to lop their wanton growth.
Those blossoms also, and those dropping gums,
That lie bestrewn unsightly and unsmooth,

Ask riddance, if we mean to tread with ease;
Meanwhile, as nature wills, night bids us rest.'
    To whom thus Eve with perfect beauty adorned:
'My author and disposer, what thou bid'st
Unargued I obey; so God ordains.
God is thy law, thou mine; to know no more
Is woman's happiest knowledge, and her praise.
With thee conversing, I forget all time,
All seasons, and their change, all please alike.
Sweet is the breath of morn, her rising sweet,
With charm of earliest birds; pleasant the sun,
When first on this delightful land he spreads
His orient beams, on herb, tree, fruit, and flower,
Glistering with dew; fragrant the fertile earth
After soft showers; and sweet the coming on
Of grateful evening mild, then silent night
With this her solemn bird, and this fair moon
And these the gems of heaven, her starry train:
But neither breath of morn, when she ascends
With charm of earliest birds, nor rising sun
On this delightful land, nor herb, fruit, flower,
Glistering with dew, nor fragrance after showers,
Nor grateful evening mild, nor silent night
With this her solemn bird, nor walk by moon
Or glittering starlight, without thee is sweet.

(iv)

311   *The Banishment*

    So spake our mother Eve, and Adam heard
Well pleased, but answered not; for now too nigh
The Archangel stood, and from the other hill
To their fixed station, all in bright array
The Cherubim descended; on the ground
Gliding metéorous, as evening mist
Risen from a river o'er the marish glides,
And gathers ground fast at the labourer's heel
Homeward returning. High in front advanced,
The brandished sword of God before them blazed
Fierce as a comet; which with torrid heat,
And vapour as the Libyan air adust,

Began to parch that temperate clime; whereat
In either hand the hastening Angel caught
Our lingering parents, and to the eastern gate
Led them direct, and down the cliff as fast
To the subjected plain; then disappeared.
They, looking back, all the eastern side beheld
Of Paradise, so late their happy seat,
Waved over by that flaming brand, the gate
With dreadful faces thronged and fiery arms.
Some natural tears they dropped, but wiped them soon;
The world was all before them, where to choose
Their place of rest, and Providence their guide:
They hand in hand, with wandering steps and slow,
Through Eden took their solitary way.

from Samson Agonistes

312

(i)

O HOW comely it is and how reviving
To the spirits of just men long oppressed,
When God into the hands of their deliverer
Puts invincible might
To quell the mighty of the earth, the oppressor,
The brute and boisterous force of violent men,
Hardy and industrious to support
Tyrannic power, but raging to pursue
The righteous and all such as honour truth!
He all their ammunition
And feats of war defeats
With plain heroic magnitude of mind
And celestial vigour armed;
Their armouries and magazines contemns,
Renders them useless, while
With winged expedition
Swift as the lightning glance he executes
His errand on the wicked, who surprised,
Lose their defence, distracted and amazed.
  But patience is more oft the exercise
Of saints, the trial of their fortitude,
Making them each his own deliverer,

And victor over all
That tyranny or fortune can inflict;
Either of these is in thy lot,
Samson, with might endued
Above the sons of men; but sight bereaved
May chance to number thee with those
Whom patience finally must crown.

313   (ii)

ALL is best, though we oft doubt,
What the unsearchable dispose
Of Highest Wisdom brings about,
And ever best found in the close.
Oft he seems to hide his face,
But unexpectedly returns
And to his faithful champion hath in place
Bore witness gloriously; whence Gaza mourns,
And all that band them to resist
His uncontrollable intent:
His servants he, with new acquist
Of true experience from this great event,
With peace and consolation hath dismissed,
And calm of mind, all passion spent.

SIR JOHN SUCKLING

1609–1642

314   *A Doubt of Martyrdom*

O FOR some honest lover's ghost,
    Some kind unbodied post
    Sent from the shades below!
    I strangely long to know
Whether the nobler chaplets wear
Those that their mistress' scorn did bear
    Or those that were used kindly.

For whatsoe'er they tell us here
    To make those sufferings dear,
     'Twill there, I fear, be found
    That to the being crowned
To have loved alone will not suffice,
Unless we also have been wise
    And have our loves enjoyed.

What posture can we think him in
    That, here unloved, again
     Departs, and's thither gone
    Where each sits by his own?
Or how can that Elysium be
Where I my mistress still must see
    Circled in other's arms?

For there the judges all are just,
    And Sophonisba must
     Be his whom she held dear,
    Not his who loved her here.
The sweet Philoclea, since she died,
Lies by her Pirocles his side,
    Not by Amphialus.

Some bays, perchance, or myrtle bough
    For difference crowns the brow
     Of those kind souls that were
    The noble martyrs here:
And if that be the only odds
(As who can tell?), ye kinder gods,
    Give me the woman here!

315   *The Constant Lover*

    OUT upon it, I have loved
      Three whole days together!
    And am like to love three more,
      If it hold fair weather.

    Time shall moult away his wings
      Ere he shall discover
    In the whole wide world again
      Such a constant lover.

But a pox upon't, no praise
    There is due at all to me:
Love with me had made no stay,
    Had it any been but she.

Had it any been but she,
    And that very very face,
There had been at least ere this
    A dozen dozen in her place.

316   *Why so Pale and Wan*

WHY so pale and wan, fond lover?
        Prithee, why so pale?
Will, when looking well can't move her,
        Looking ill prevail?
        Prithee, why so pale?

Why so dull and mute, young sinner?
        Prithee, why so mute?
Will, when speaking well can't win her,
        Saying nothing do 't?
        Prithee, why so mute?

Quit, quit for shame! This will not move;
        This cannot take her.
If of herself she will not love,
        Nothing can make her:
        The devil take her!

SIDNEY GODOLPHIN

1610–1643

317   *Wise Men and Shepherds*

LORD, when the wise men came from far,
Led to thy cradle by a star,
Then did the shepherds too rejoice,
Instructed by thy angel's voice.
Blest were the wise men in their skill,
And shepherds in their harmless will.

Wise men, in tracing Nature's laws,
Ascend unto the highest cause;
Shepherds with humble fearfulness
Walk safely, though their light be less.
Though wise men better know the way,
It seems no honest heart can stray.

There is no merit in the wise
But love, the shepherds' sacrifice.
Wise men, all ways of knowledge passed,
To the shepherds' wonder come at last.
To know can only wonder breed,
And not to know is wonder's seed.

A wise man at the altar bows,
And offers up his studied vows,
And is received. May not the tears,
Which spring too from a shepherd's fears,
And sighs upon his frailty spent,
Though not distinct, be eloquent?

'Tis true, the object sanctifies
All passions which within us rise,
But since no creature comprehends
The cause of causes, end of ends,
He who himself vouchsafes to know
Best pleases his creator so.

When then our sorrows we apply
To our own wants and poverty,
When we look up in all distress,
And our own misery confess,
Sending both thanks and prayers above,
Then, though we do not know, we love.

JAMES GRAHAM, MARQUIS OF MONTROSE
1612–1650

318   *I'll Never Love Thee More*

MY dear and only love, I pray
   That little world of thee
Be governed by no other sway
   Than purest monarchy;
For if confusion have a part
   (Which virtuous souls abhor),
And hold a synod in thine heart,
   I'll never love thee more.

Like Alexander I will reign,
   And I will reign alone;
My thoughts did evermore disdain
   A rival on my throne.
He either fears his fate too much,
   Or his deserts are small,
That dares not put it to the touch,
   To gain or lose it all.

And in the empire of thine heart,
   Where I should solely be,
If others do pretend a part
   Or dare to vie with me,
Or if Committees thou erect,
   And go on such a score,
I'll laugh and sing at thy neglect,
   And never love thee more.

But if thou wilt prove faithful then,
   And constant of thy word,
I'll make thee glorious by my pen
   And famous by my sword;
I'll serve thee in such noble ways
   Was never heard before;
I'll crown and deck thee all with bays,
   And love thee more and more.

319   *Epitaph on Charles I*

GREAT, good and just, could I but rate
My grief to thy too rigid fate!
I'd weep the world in such a strain
As it would once deluge again:
But since thy loud-tongued blood demands supplies
More from Briareus' hands than Argus' eyes,
I'll tune thy elegies to trumpet sounds,
And write thy epitaph in blood and wounds.

THOMAS JORDAN
?1612–1685

320   *The Epicure*
Sung by one in the Habit of a Town Gallant

LET us drink and be merry, dance, joke, and rejoice,
With Claret and Sherry, Theorbo and Voice;
The changeable world to our joy is unjust,
All treasure uncertain, then down with your dust.
   In frolic dispose your pounds, shillings and pence,
   For we shall be nothing a hundred years hence.

We'll kiss and be free with Nan, Betty, and Philly,
Have oysters and lobsters, and maids by the belly;
Fish-dinners will make a lass spring like a flea,
Dame Venus (Love's goddess) was born of the sea.
   With her and with Bacchus we'll tickle the sense,
   For we shall be past it a hundred years hence.

Your most beautiful bit that hath all eyes upon her,
That her honesty sells for a hogo of honour;
Whose lightness and brightness doth shine in such splendour
That none but the stars are thought fit to attend her,
   Though now she be pleasant and sweet to the sense,
   Will be damnably mouldy a hundred years hence.

320 hogo] taint, or flavour

Then why should we turmoil in cares and in fears,
Turn all our tranquillity to sighs and to tears?
Let's eat, drink and play till the worms do corrupt us,
'Tis certain that *post mortem nulla Voluptas.*
　　Let's deal with our damsels, that we may from thence
　　Have broods to succeed us a hundred years hence. . . .

RICHARD CRASHAW

?1612–1649

321　　　　　　　　*On Hope*
By Way of Question and Answer Between
Abraham Cowley and Richard Crashaw

Cowley.　　*Hope, whose weak being ruined is*
　　Alike if it succeed and if it miss;
　　Whom ill and good doth equally confound,
　　And both the horns of Fate's dilemma wound;
　　　　Vain shadow! that doth vanish quite
　　　　Both at full noon and perfect night.
　　　　The Fates have not a possibility
　　　　　　Of blessing thee.
　　If things then from their ends we happy call,
　　'Tis Hope is the most hopeless thing of all.

Crashaw.　　Dear Hope! Earth's dowry and Heaven's debt,
　　The entity of things that are not yet.
　　Subtlest but surest being! thou by whom
　　Our nothing hath a definition.
　　　　Fair cloud of fire, both shade and light,
　　　　Our life in death, our day in night.
　　　　Fates cannot find out a capacity
　　　　　　Of hurting thee;
　　From thee their thin dilemma with blunt horn
　　Shrinks, like the sick moon at the wholesome morn.

320　*post mortem* . . .] there is no pleasure after death

RICHARD CRASHAW

Cowley.   *Hope, thou bold taster of delight,*
Who, instead of doing so, devour'st it quite;
Thou bring'st us an estate, yet leav'st us poor,
By clogging it with legacies before.
    The joys which we entire should wed
    Come deflowered virgins to our bed.
    Good fortunes without gain imported be,
       So mighty custom's paid to thee.
For joy, like wine, kept close doth better taste:
If it take air before, its spirits waste.

Crashaw.   Thou art Love's legacy under lock
Of Faith, the steward of our growing stock.
Our crown-lands lie above, yet each meal brings
A seemly portion for the sons of kings.
    Nor will the virgin joys we wed
    Come less unbroken to our bed
    Because that from the bridal cheek of bliss
       Thou thus steal'st down a distant kiss:
Hope's chaste kiss wrongs no more joy's maidenhead,
Than spousal rites prejudge the marriage-bed.

    Fair Hope! our earlier Heaven! by thee
Young Time is taster to Eternity.
The generous wine with age grows strong, not sour,
Nor need we kill thy fruit to smell thy flower.
Thy golden head never hangs down
    Till in the lap of Love's full noon
    It falls and dies: Oh no, it melts away
       As doth the dawn into the day,
As lumps of sugar lose themselves, and twine
Their subtle essence with the soul of wine.

Cowley.   *Hope, Fortune's cheating lottery,*
Where for one prize an hundred blanks there be;
Fond archer Hope, who tak'st thine aim so far
That still or short or wide thine arrows are.
    Thine empty cloud the eye itself deceives
    With shapes that our own fancy gives:
    A cloud which gilt and painted now appears
       But must drop presently in tears.
When thy false beams o'er Reason's light prevail,
By ignes fatui, *not North stars, we sail.*

Crashaw. Fortune, alas, above the world's law wars;
    Hope kicks the curled heads of conspiring stars.
    Her keel cuts not the waves, where our winds stir,
    And Fate's whole lottery is one blank to her.
     Her shafts and she fly far above,
     And forage in the fields of light and love.
     Sweet Hope! kind cheat! fair fallacy! by thee
      We are not where or what we be,
    But what and where we would be: thus art thou
    Our absent presence, and our future now.

Cowley. *Brother of Fear! more gaily clad,*
    The merrier fool of the two, yet quite as mad.
    Sire of Repentance! child of fond Desire,
    That blows the chymic's and the lover's fire,
     Still leading them insensibly on
     With the strange witchcraft of Anon.
     By thee the one doth changing Nature through
     Her endless labyrinths pursue,
    And the other chases woman, while she goes
    More ways and turns than hunted Nature knows.

Crashaw. Faith's sister! nurse of fair Desire!
    Fear's antidote! a wise and well-stayed fire,
    Tempered 'twixt cold despair and torrid joy,
    Queen Regent in young Love's minority.
     Though the vexed chymic vainly chases
     His fugitive gold through all her faces,
     And loves more fierce, more fruitless fires assay
      One face more fugitive than all they,
    True Hope's a glorious huntress, and her chase
    The God of Nature in the field of Grace.

322   *The Shepherds' Hymn*

Tityrus. Gloomy night embraced the place
     Where the noble Infant lay.
    The Babe looked up and showed his face;
     In spite of darkness, it was day.
    It was thy day, Sweet, and did rise
    Not from the East, but from thine eyes.

Thyrsis. Winter chid aloud, and sent
  The angry North to wage his wars;
 The North forgot his fierce intent
  And left perfumes instead of scars.
 By those sweet eyes' persuasive powers,
 Where he meant frost, he scattered flowers.

Both. We saw thee in thy balmy nest,
  Bright dawn of our eternal day!
 We saw thine eyes break from their East
  And chase the trembling shades away.
 We saw thee, and we blessed the sight;
 We saw thee by thine own sweet light.

Tityrus. Poor world, said I, what wilt thou do
  To entertain this starry stranger?
 Is this the best thou canst bestow,
  A cold, and not too cleanly manger?
 Contend, ye powers of heaven and earth,
 To fit a bed for this huge birth.

Thyrsis. Proud world, said I, cease your contest,
  And let the mighty Babe alone,
 The phoenix builds the phoenix' nest,
  Love's architecture is his own.
 The Babe whose birth embraves this morn
 Made his own bed ere he was born.

Tityrus. I saw the curled drops, soft and slow,
  Come hovering o'er the place's head,
 Offering their whitest sheets of snow,
  To furnish the fair infant's bed.
 Forbear, said I, be not too bold;
 Your fleece is white, but 'tis too cold.

Thyrsis. I saw the obsequious Seraphins
  Their rosy fleece of fire bestow,
 For well they now can spare their wings,
  Since Heaven itself lies here below.
 Well done, said I, but are you sure
 Your down, so warm, will pass for pure?

Tityrus.   No, no, your King's not yet to seek
        Where to repose his royal head;
See, see, how soon his new-bloomed cheek
        'Twixt mother's breasts is gone to bed!
Sweet choice, said we; no way but so,
Not to lie cold, yet sleep in snow.

Both.   We saw thee in thy balmy nest,
        Bright dawn of our eternal day!
We saw thine eyes break from their East
        And chase the trembling shades away.
We saw thee and we blessed the sight;
We saw thee by thine own sweet light.

Full Chorus. Welcome, all wonders in one sight!
        Eternity shut in a span,
Summer in winter, day in night,
        Heaven in earth and God in Man;
Great little one! whose all embracing birth
Lifts earth to heaven, stoops heaven to earth.

Welcome! though not to gold nor silk,
        To more than Caesar's birthright is:
Two sister-seas of virgin-milk,
        With many a rarely-tempered kiss
That breathes at once both Maid and Mother,
Warms in the one, cools in the other.

She sings thy tears asleep, and dips
        Her kisses in thy weeping eye,
She spreads the red leaves of thy lips
        That in their buds yet blushing lie,
She 'gainst those mother-diamonds tries
The points of her young eagle's eyes.

Welcome! though not to those gay flies
        Gilded in the beams of earthly kings,
Slippery souls in smiling eyes,
        But to poor shepherds, home-spun things,
Whose wealth's their flock, whose wit to be
Well read in their simplicity.

Yet when young April's husband showers
   Shall bless the fruitful Maia's bed,
We'll bring the first-born of her flowers
   To kiss thy feet and crown thy head.
To thee, dread Lamb! whose love must keep
The shepherds more than they their sheep.

To thee, meek Majesty, soft King
   Of simple graces and sweet loves,
Each of us his lamb will bring
   Each his pair of silver doves;
Till burnt at last in fire of thy fair eyes,
Our selves become our own best sacrifice.

323   *A Hymn to the Name and Honour of*
the Admirable Saint Teresa

Love, thou art absolute, sole Lord
Of life and death. To prove the word,
We'll now appeal to none of all
Those thy old soldiers, great and tall,
Ripe men of martyrdom, that could reach down
With strong arms their triumphant crown:
Such as could with lusty breath
Speak loud into the face of death
Their great Lord's glorious name; to none
Of those whose spacious bosoms spread a throne
For Love at large to fill. Spare blood and sweat,
And see him take a private seat,
Making his mansion in the mild
And milky soul of a soft child.
Scarce hath she learnt to lisp the name
Of martyr, yet she thinks it shame
Life should so long play with that breath
Which spent can buy so brave a death.
She never undertook to know
What death with love should have to do;
Nor hath she e'er yet understood
Why to show love, she should shed blood.
Yet though she cannot tell you why,
She can love, and she can die.

Scarce hath she blood enough to make
A guilty sword blush for her sake;
Yet hath she a heart dare hope to prove
How much less strong is death than love. . . .

Since 'tis not to be had at home,
She'll travel for a martyrdom.
No home for hers confesses she,
But where she may a martyr be.
She'll to the Moors and trade with them
For this unvalued Diadem;
She'll offer them her dearest breath,
With Christ's name in't, in change for death.
She'll bargain with them, and will give
Them God, and teach them how to live
In him; or, if they this deny,
For him she'll teach them how to die.
So shall she leave amongst them sown
Her Lord's blood, or at least her own.
Farewell then, all the world, adieu!
Teresa is no more for you.
Farewell all pleasures, sports, and joys,
Never till now esteemèd toys!
Farewell whatever dear may be,
Mother's arms or father's knee!
Farewell house, and farewell home!
She's for the Moors and martyrdom.

Sweet not so fast! Lo, thy fair Spouse,
Whom thou seek'st with so swift vows,
Calls thee back, and bids thee come
To embrace a milder martyrdom. . . .

O how oft shalt thou complain
Of a sweet and subtle pain!
Of intolerable joys!
Of a death, in which who dies
Loves his death, and dies again,
And would forever so be slain;
And lives and dies, and knows not why
To live, but that he thus may never leave to die!
How kindly will thy gentle heart
Kiss the sweetly-killing dart,

And close in his embraces keep
Those delicious wounds that weep
Balsam to heal themselves with! Thus,
When these thy deaths so numerous
Shall all at last die into one,
And melt thy soul's sweet mansion;
Like a soft lump of incense, hasted
By too hot a fire, and wasted
Into perfuming clouds, so fast
Shalt thou exhale to heaven at last,
In a resolving sigh, and then,
O what? Ask not the tongues of men.

    Angels cannot tell. Suffice
Thyself shall feel thine own full joys,
And hold them fast forever. There,
So soon as thou shalt first appear,
The Moon of maiden stars, thy white
Mistress, attended by such bright
Souls as thy shining self, shall come,
And in her first ranks make thee room;
Where 'mongst her snowy family
Immortal welcomes wait for thee.
O what delight, when revealed Life shall stand
And teach thy lips heaven with his hand,
On which thou now mayst to thy wishes
Heap up thy consecrated kisses!
What joys shall seize thy soul, when she
Bending her blessed eyes on thee,
Those second smiles of heaven, shall dart
Her mild rays through thy melting heart!
Angels, thy old friends, there shall greet thee,
Glad at their own home now to meet thee.
All thy good works which went before,
And waited for thee at the door,
Shall own thee there, and all in one
Weave a constellation
Of crowns with which the King, thy Spouse,
Shall build up thy triumphant brows.

All thy old woes shall now smile on thee,
And thy pains sit bright upon thee;
All thy sorrows here shall shine,
And thy sufferings be divine.
Tears shall take comfort, and turn gems,
And wrongs repent to diadems.
Even thy deaths shall live, and new
Dress the soul that erst they slew.
Thy wounds shall blush to such bright scars
As keep account of the Lamb's wars.
Those rare works where thou shalt leave writ
Love's noble history, with wit
Taught thee by none but him, while here
They feed our souls, shall clothe thine there.
Each heavenly word, by whose hid flame
Our hard hearts shall strike fire, the same
Shall flourish on thy brows, and be
Both fire to us, and flame to thee;
Whose light shall live bright in thy face
By glory, in our hearts by grace.
Thou shalt look round about, and see
Thousands of crowned souls throng to be
Themselves thy crown; sons of thy vows,
The virgin-births, with which thy sovereign Spouse
Made fruitful thy fair soul. Go now,
And with them all about thee bow
To him. 'Put on', he'll say, 'put on,
My rosy Love, that thy rich zone,
Sparkling with the sacred flames
Of thousand souls, whose happy names
Heaven keeps upon thy score: thy bright
Life brought them first to kiss the light
That kindled them to stars; and so
Thou with the Lamb, thy Lord, shalt go;
And whereso'er he sets his white
Steps, walk with him those ways of light,
Which who in death would live to see
Must learn in life to die like thee.'

324

The Flaming Heart
Upon the Book and Picture of
the Seraphical Saint Teresa

O THOU undaunted daughter of desires!
By all thy dower of lights and fires;
By all the eagle in thee, all the dove;
By all thy lives and deaths of love;
By thy large draughts of intellectual day,
And by thy thirsts of love more large than they;
By all thy brim-filled bowls of fierce desire,
By thy last morning's draught of liquid fire;
By the full kingdom of that final kiss
That seized thy parting soul, and sealed thee His,
By all the Heavens thou hast in Him
(Fair sister of the seraphim!);
By all of Him we have in thee;
Leave nothing of myself in me.
Let me so read thy life, that I
Unto all life of mine may die!

325

An Epitaph upon Husband and Wife
Who died and were buried together

To these whom death again did wed
This grave's the second marriage-bed.
For though the hand of Fate could force
'Twixt soul and body a divorce,
It could not sever man and wife,
Because they both lived but one life.
Peace, good reader, do not weep;
Peace, the lovers are asleep.
They, sweet turtles, folded lie
In the last knot that love could tie.
Let them sleep, let them sleep on,
Till this stormy night be gone,
And the eternal morrow dawn;
Then the curtains will be drawn,
And they wake into a light
Whose day shall never die in night.

SAMUEL BUTLER

1613–1680

from Hudibras

(i)

326   *Presbyterian Knight*

WHEN civil fury first grew high,
And men fell out they knew not why;
When hard words, jealousies and fears
Set folks together by the ears,
And made them fight like mad or drunk
For Dame Religion as for punk,
Whose honesty they all durst swear for,
Though not a man of them knew wherefore;
When Gospel-trumpeter, surrounded
With long-eared rout, to battle sounded,
And pulpit, drum ecclesiastic,
Was beat with fist instead of a stick:
Then did Sir Knight abandon dwelling
And out he rode a Colonelling.

*

For his Religion it was fit
To match his learning and his wit:
'Twas Presbyterian true blue,
For he was of that stubborn crew
Of errant Saints, whom all men grant
To be the true Church Militant:
Such as do build their Faith upon
The holy Text of pike and gun;
Decide all controversies by
Infallible artillery;
And prove their Doctrine orthodox
By Apostolic blows and knocks;
Call fire and sword and desolation
A godly-thorough-Reformation,
Which always must be carried on
And still be doing, never done,

As if Religion were intended
For nothing else but to be mended.
A sect whose chief devotion lies
In odd perverse antipathies,
In falling out with that or this,
And finding somewhat still amiss;
More peevish, cross and splenetick
Than dog distract or monkey sick;
That with more care keep holy-day
The wrong, than others the right way;
Compound for sins they are inclined to,
By damning those they have no mind to;
Still so perverse and opposite
As if they worshipped God for spite.
The selfsame thing they will abhor
One way, and long another for.
Free-will they one way disavow,
Another, nothing else allow.
All piety consists therein
In them, in other men all sin.
Rather than fail they will defy
That which they love most tenderly,
Quarrel with minced pies, and disparage
Their best and dearest friend, plum-porridge;
Fat pig and goose itself oppose,
And blaspheme custard through the nose.
The Apostles of this fierce Religion,
Like Mahomet's, were ass and widgeon,
To whom our Knight by fast instinct
Of wit and temper was so linked
As if hypocrisy and nonsense
Had got the advowson of his conscience.

(ii)

327 *Independent Squire*

A SQUIRE he had whose name was Ralph,
That in the adventure went his half.
(Though writers, for more stately tone,
Do call him Ralpho: 'tis all one:
And when we can with metre safe,
We'll call him so, if not plain Raph.)

*

His knowledge was not far behind
The Knight's, but of another kind,
And he another way came by it:
Some call it gifts, and some New Light;
A liberal art, that costs no pains
Of study, industry or brains.
His wits were sent him for a token,
But in the carriage cracked and broken.
Like commendation ninepence, crooked
With to and from my love, it looked.
He ne'er considered it, as loath
To look a gift-horse in the mouth,
And very wisely would lay forth
No more upon it than 'twas worth.
But as he got it freely, so
He spent it frank and freely too.
For Saints themselves will sometimes be
Of gifts that cost them nothing, free.
By means of this, with *hem* and *cough*,
Prolongers to enlightened snuff,
He could deep mysteries unriddle
As easily as thread a needle;
For as of vagabonds we say
That they are ne'er beside their way,
Whate'er men speak by this New Light,
Still they are sure to be i'th' right.
'Tis a dark-lantern of the Spirit,
Which none see by but those that bear it:
A Light that falls down from on high
For spiritual trades to cozen by;
An *Ignis Fatuus* that bewitches,
And leads men into pools and ditches,
To make them dip themselves, and sound
For Christendom in dirty pond;
To dive like wildfowl for Salvation,
And fish to catch Regeneration.
This Light inspires, and plays upon
The nose of Saint like bagpipe-drone,
And speaks through hollow empty soul,
As through a trunk or whispering hole,
Such language as no mortal ear
But spiritual eavesdroppers can hear.

So Phoebus or some friendly Muse
Into small poets song infuse,
Which they at secondhand rehearse
Through reed or bagpipe, verse for verse.

JOHN CLEVELAND

1613–1658

328   *Epitaph on the Earl of Strafford*

HERE lies wise and valiant dust,
Huddled up 'twixt fit and just,
Strafford, who was hurried hence
'Twixt treason and convenience.
He spent his time here in a mist,
A Papist, yet a Calvinist;
His Prince's nearest joy and grief,
He had, yet wanted, all relief;
The prop and ruin of the State,
The peoples' violent love and hate;
One in extremes loved and abhorred.
Riddles lie here, or in a word,
Here lies blood, and let it lie
Speechless still, and never cry.

ABRAHAM COWLEY

1618–1667

329   *The Wish*

WELL then! I now do plainly see
This busy world and I shall ne'er agree.
The very honey of all earthly joy
Does of all meats the soonest cloy;
    And they, methinks, deserve my pity
Who for it can endure the stings,
The crowd, and buzz, and murmurings,
    Of this great hive, the city.

Ah, yet, ere I descend to the grave,
May I a small house and large garden have;
And a few friends, and many books, both true,
Both wise, and both delightful too!
    And since love ne'er will from me flee,
A mistress moderately fair,
And good as guardian angels are,
    Only beloved and loving me.

O fountains! when in you shall I
Myself eased of unpeaceful thoughts espy?
O fields! O woods! when, when shall I be made
The happy tenant of your shade?
    Here's the spring-head of Pleasure's flood:
Here's wealthy Nature's treasury,
Where all the riches lie that she
    Has coined and stamped for good.

Pride and ambition here
Only in far-fetched metaphors appear;
Here nought but winds can hurtful murmurs scatter,
And nought but Echo flatter.
    The gods, when they descended, hither
From heaven did always choose their way:
And therefore we may boldly say
    That 'tis the way too thither.

How happy here should I
And one dear She live, and embracing die!
She who is all the world, and can exclude,
In deserts, solitude.
    I should have then this only fear:
Lest men, when they my pleasures see,
Should hither throng to live like me,
    And so make a city here.

330   *Drinking*

THE thirsty earth soaks up the rain,
And drinks and gapes for drink again;
The plants suck in the earth, and are
With constant drinking fresh and fair;
The sea itself (which one would think
Should have but little need of drink)
Drinks ten thousand rivers up,
So filled that they o'erflow the cup.
The busy Sun (and one would guess
By 's drunken fiery face no less)
Drinks up the sea, and when he's done,
The Moon and Stars drink up the Sun:
They drink and dance by their own light,
They drink and revel all the night:
Nothing in Nature's sober found,
But an eternal health goes round.
Fill up the bowl, then, fill it high,
Fill all the glasses there—for why
Should every creature drink but I?
Why, man of morals, tell me why?

331   *On the Death of Mr. William Harvey*

IT was a dismal and a fearful night,
Scarce could the morn drive on the unwilling light,
When Sleep, Death's image, left my troubled breast
        By something liker Death possest.
My eyes with tears did uncommanded flow,
        And on my soul hung the dull weight
        Of some intolerable fate.
What bell was that? Ah me! too much I know.

My sweet companion, and my gentle peer,
Why hast thou left me thus unkindly here,
Thy end forever, and my life to moan?
        O thou hast left me all alone!
Thy soul and body, when death's agony
        Besieged around thy noble heart,
        Did not with more reluctance part
Than I, my dearest Friend, do part from thee.

My dearest Friend, would I had died for thee!
Life and this world henceforth will tedious be.
Nor shall I know hereafter what to do
    If once my griefs prove tedious too.
Silent and sad I walk about all day,
      As sullen ghosts stalk speechless by
      Where their hid treasures lie;
Alas, my treasure's gone, why do I stay?

He was my friend, the truest friend on earth;
A strong and mighty influence joined our birth.
Nor did we envy the most sounding name
    By Friendship given of old to Fame.
None but his brethren he, and sisters, knew
      Whom the kind youth preferred to me;
      And even in that we did agree,
For much above myself I loved them too.

Say, for you saw us, ye immortal lights,
How oft unwearied have we spent the nights,
Till the Ledaean stars, so famed for love,
    Wondered at us from above?
We spent them not in toys, in lusts, or wine,
      But search of deep Philosophy,
      Wit, Eloquence, and Poetry,
Arts which I loved, for they, my Friend, were thine.

Ye fields of Cambridge, our dear Cambridge, say,
Have ye not seen us walking every day?
Was there a tree about which did not know
    The love betwixt us two?
Henceforth, ye gentle trees, forever fade;
      Or your sad branches thicker join
      And into darksome shades combine,
Dark as the grave wherein my friend is laid. . . .

RICHARD LOVELACE
1618–1657

332   *To Lucasta, Going to the Wars*

TELL me not, sweet, I am unkind,
    That from the nunnery
Of thy chaste breast and quiet mind
    To war and arms I fly.

True, a new mistress now I chase,
    The first foe in the field;
And with a stronger faith embrace
    A sword, a horse, a shield.

Yet this inconstancy is such
    As you too shall adore;
I could not love thee, dear, so much,
    Loved I not honour more.

333   *The Grasshopper:*
To My Noble Friend, Mr. Charles Cotton

O THOU that swing'st upon the waving hair
    Of some well-fillèd oaten-beard,
Drunk every night with a delicious tear
    Dropped thee from heaven, where now thou art reared.

The joys of earth and air are thine entire,
    That with thy feet and wings dost hop and fly;
And when thy poppy works thou dost retire
    To thy carved acorn-bed to lie.

Up with the day, the sun thou welcom'st then,
    Sport'st in the gilt-plaits of his beams,
And all these merry days mak'st merry men,
    Thyself, and melancholy streams.

But ah, the sickle! golden ears are cropped;
    Ceres and Bacchus bid good-night;
Sharp frosty fingers all your flowers have topped
    And what scythes spared, winds shave off quite.

Poor verdant fool! and now green ice! thy joys,
 Large and as lasting as thy perch of grass,
Bid us lay in 'gainst winter rain, and poise
 Their floods with an o'er flowing glass.

Thou best of men and friends! we will create
 A genuine summer in each other's breast;
And spite of this cold time and frozen fate
 Thaw us a warm seat to our rest.

Our sacred hearths shall burn eternally
 As vestal flames; the north-wind, he
Shall strike his frost-stretched wings, dissolve and fly
 This Etna in epitome.

Dropping December shall come weeping in,
 Bewail the usurping of his reign;
But when in showers of old Greek we begin
 Shall cry he hath his crown again!

Night as clear Hesper shall our tapers whip
 From the light casements where we play,
And the dark hag from her black mantle strip,
 And stick there everlasting day.

Thus richer than untempted kings are we,
 That asking nothing, nothing need:
Though Lord of all what seas embrace, yet he
 That wants himself is poor indeed.

334   *To Althea, from Prison*

When Love with unconfinèd wings
 Hovers within my gates;
And my divine Althea brings
 To whisper at the grates;
When I lie tangled in her hair,
 And fettered to her eye;
The Gods that wanton in the air
 Know no such liberty.

When flowing cups run swiftly round
  With no allaying Thames,
Our careless heads with roses bound
  Our hearts with loyal flames;
When thirsty grief in wine we steep,
  When healths and draughts go free,
Fishes that tipple in the deep
  Know no such liberty.

When, like committed linnets, I
  With shriller throat shall sing
The sweetness, mercy, majesty,
  And glories of my King;
When I shall voice aloud how good
  He is, how great should be,
Enlargèd winds that curl the flood
  Know no such liberty.

Stone walls do not a prison make,
  Nor iron bars a cage;
Minds innocent and quiet take
  That for an hermitage;
If I have freedom in my love,
  And in my soul am free;
Angels alone that soar above
  Enjoy such liberty.

ANDREW MARVELL

1621–1678

335
An Horation Ode
upon Cromwell's Return from Ireland,
1650

THE forward youth that would appear
Must now forsake his Muses dear,
  Nor in the shadows sing
  His numbers languishing.

'Tis time to leave the books in dust,
And oil the unusèd armour's rust,
    Removing from the wall
    The corslet of the hall.

So restless Cromwell could not cease
In the inglorious arts of peace,
    But through adventurous war
    Urgèd his active star:

And like the three-forked lightning, first
Breaking the clouds where it was nurst,
    Did thorough his own side
    His fiery way divide:

For 'tis all one to courage high,
The emulous, or enemy;
    And with such, to enclose
    Is more than to oppose.

Then burning through the air he went
And palaces and temples rent;
    And Caesar's head at last
    Did through his laurels blast.

'Tis madness to resist or blame
The force of angry Heaven's flame;
    And if we would speak true,
    Much to the man is due,

Who, from his private gardens, where
He lived reservèd and austere
    (As if his highest plot
    To plant the bergamot),

Could by industrious valour climb
To ruin the great work of time,
    And cast the Kingdom old
    Into another mould.

Though Justice against Fate complain,
And plead the ancient rights in vain—
    But those do hold or break
    As men are strong or weak—

ANDREW MARVELL

Nature, that hateth emptiness,
Allows of penetration less,
    And therefore must make room
    Where greater spirits come.

What field of all the civil wars
Where his were not the deepest scars?
    And Hampton shows what part
    He had of wiser art;

Where, twining subtle fears with hope,
He wove a net of such a scope
    That Charles himself might chase
    To Car'sbrook's narrow case;

That thence the Royal Actor borne
The tragic scaffold might adorn:
    While round the armèd bands
    Did clap their bloody hands.

He nothing common did or mean
Upon that memorable scene,
    But with his keener eye
    The axe's edge did try;

Nor called the Gods, with vulgar spite,
To vindicate his helpless right;
    But bowed his comely head
    Down, as upon a bed.

This was that memorable hour
Which first assured the forcèd power:
    So when they did design
    The Capitol's first line,

A bleeding head, where they begun,
Did fright the architects to run;
    And yet in that the State
    Foresaw its happy fate!

And now the Irish are ashamed
To see themselves in one year tamed:
    So much one man can do
    That does both act and know.

331

They can affirm his praises best,
And have, though overcome, confest
    How good he is, how just
    And fit for highest trust;

Nor yet grown stiffer with command,
But still in the Republic's hand—
    How fit he is to sway
    That can so well obey!

He to the Commons' feet presents
A Kingdom for his first year's rents,
    And, what he may, forbears
    His fame, to make it theirs:

And has his sword and spoils ungirt
To lay them at the public's skirt.
    So when the falcon high
    Falls heavy from the sky,

She, having killed, no more does search
But on the next green bough to perch,
    Where, when he first does lure,
    The falconer has her sure.

What may not then our Isle presume
While victory his crest does plume?
    What may not others fear,
    If thus he crown each year?

As Caesar he, ere long, to Gaul,
To Italy an Hannibal,
    And to all States not free
    Shall climacteric be.

The Pict no shelter now shall find
Within his particoloured mind,
    But from this valour sad
    Shrink underneath the plaid,

Happy, if in the tufted brake
The English hunter him mistake,
    Nor lay his hounds in near
    The Caledonian deer.

But thou, the War's and Fortune's son,
March indefatigably on;
    And for the last effect,
    Still keep thy sword erect:

Besides the force it has to fright
The spirits of the shady night,
    The same arts that did gain
    A power, must it maintain.

336   *The Definition of Love*

MY Love is of a birth as rare
As 'tis for object strange and high:
It was begotten by Despair
Upon Impossibility.

Magnanimous Despair alone
Could show me so divine a thing,
Where feeble Hope could ne'er have flown
But vainly flapped its tinsel wing.

And yet I quickly might arrive
Where my extended soul is fixt,
But Fate does iron wedges drive,
And always crowds itself betwixt.

For Fate with jealous eye does see
Two perfect Loves; nor lets them close:
Their union would her ruin be,
And her tyrannic power depose.

And therefore her decrees of steel
Us as the distant Poles have placed,
(Though Love's whole World on us doth wheel)
Not by themselves to be embraced.

Unless the giddy Heaven fall,
And Earth some new convulsion tear;
And, us to join, the World should all
Be cramped into a planisphere.

As lines so Loves oblique may well
Themselves in every angle greet:
But ours so truly parallel,
Though infinite, can never meet.

Therefore the Love which us doth bind
But Fate so enviously debars,
Is the conjunction of the Mind,
And opposition of the Stars.

337   *To His Coy Mistress*

HAD we but world enough, and time,
This coyness, Lady, were no crime.
We would sit down and think which way
To walk and pass our long love's day.
Thou by the Indian Ganges' side
Shouldst rubies find: I by the tide
Of Humber would complain. I would
Love you ten years before the Flood,
And you should, if you please, refuse
Till the conversion of the Jews.
My vegetable love should grow
Vaster than empires, and more slow;
An hundred years should go to praise
Thine eyes and on thy forehead gaze;
Two hundred to adore each breast;
But thirty thousand to the rest;
An age at least to every part,
And the last age should show your heart;
For, Lady, you deserve this state,
Nor would I love at lower rate.
    But at my back I always hear
Time's wingèd chariot hurrying near;
And yonder all before us lie
Deserts of vast eternity.
Thy beauty shall no more be found,
Nor, in thy marble vault, shall sound
My echoing song: then worms shall try
That long preserved virginity,
And your quaint honour turn to dust,
And into ashes all my lust:

The grave's a fine and private place,
But none, I think, do there embrace.
  Now therefore, while the youthful hue
Sits on thy skin like morning dew,
And while thy willing soul transpires
At every pore with instant fires,
Now let us sport us while we may,
And now, like amorous birds of prey,
Rather at once our time devour
Than languish in his slow-chapt power.
Let us roll all our strength and all
Our sweetness up into one ball,
And tear our pleasures with rough strife
Thorough the iron gates of life:
Thus, though we cannot make our sun
Stand still, yet we will make him run.

338   *The Garden*

HOW vainly men themselves amaze
To win the palm, the oak, or bays,
And their uncessant labours see
Crowned from some single herb or tree,
Whose short and narrow-vergèd shade
Does prudently their toils upbraid;
While all flowers and all trees do close
To weave the garlands of repose!

Fair Quiet, have I found thee here,
And Innocence, thy sister dear?
Mistaken long, I sought you then
In busy companies of men:
Your sacred plants, if here below,
Only among the plants will grow:
Society is all but rude
To this delicious solitude.

No white nor red was ever seen
So amorous as this lovely green.
Fond lovers, cruel as their flame,
Cut in these trees their mistress' name:

Little, alas! they know or heed
How far these beauties hers exceed!
Fair trees! wheresoe'er your barks I wound,
No name shall but your own be found.

When we have run our passions' heat,
Love hither makes his best retreat:
The gods, that mortal beauty chase,
Still in a tree did end their race;
Apollo hunted Daphne so,
Only that she might laurel grow;
And Pan did after Syrinx speed
Not as a nymph, but for a reed.

What wondrous life is this I lead!
Ripe apples drop about my head;
The luscious clusters of the vine
Upon my mouth do crush their wine;
The nectarine and curious peach
Into my hands themselves do reach;
Stumbling on melons, as I pass,
Ensnared with flowers, I fall on grass.

Meanwhile the mind from pleasure less
Withdraws into its happiness;
The mind, that Ocean where each kind
Does straight its own resemblance find;
Yet it creates, transcending these,
Far other worlds, and other seas;
Annihilating all that's made
To a green thought in a green shade.

Here at the fountain's sliding foot,
Or at some fruit-tree's mossy root,
Casting the body's vest aside,
My soul into the boughs does glide;
There, like a bird, it sits and sings,
Then whets and combs its silver wings,
And, till prepared for longer flight,
Waves in its plumes the various light.

Such was that happy Garden-state
While man there walked without a mate:
After a place so pure and sweet,
What other help could yet be meet!
But 'twas beyond a mortal's share
To wander solitary there:
Two paradises 'twere in one,
To live in Paradise alone.

How well the skilful gardener drew
Of flowers and herbs this dial new!
Where, from above, the milder sun
Does through a fragrant zodiac run:
And, as it works, the industrious bee
Computes its time as well as we.
How could such sweet and wholesome hours
Be reckoned, but with herbs and flowers.

339   *Bermudas*

WHERE the remote Bermudas ride
In the ocean's bosom unespied,
From a small boat, that rowed along,
The listening winds received this song.
   'What should we do but sing his praise
That led us through the watery maze,
Unto an isle so long unknown,
And yet far kinder than our own?
Where he the huge sea-monsters wracks,
That lift the deep upon their backs.
He lands us on a grassy stage,
Safe from the storms' and prelates' rage.
He gave us this eternal spring,
Which here enamels everything;
And sends the fowls to us in care,
On daily visits through the air.
He hangs in shades the orange bright,
Like golden lamps in a green night,
And does in the pomegranates close
Jewels more rich than Ormus shows.
He makes the figs our mouths to meet,
And throws the melons at our feet;

But apples plants of such a price
No tree could ever bear them twice.
With cedars, chosen by his hand,
From Lebanon, he stores the land;
And makes the hollow seas that roar
Proclaim the ambergris on shore.
He cast (of which we rather boast)
The Gospel's pearl upon our coast,
And in these rocks for us did frame
A temple, where to sound his Name.
Oh let our voice his praise exalt,
Till it arrive at heaven's vault,
Which thence, perhaps, rebounding may
Echo beyond the Mexique Bay.'
    Thus sung they, in the English boat,
An holy and a cheerful note,
And all the way, to guide their chime,
With falling oars they kept the time.

340   *The Fair Singer*

To make a final conquest of all me,
Love did compose so sweet an enemy,
In whom both beauties to my death agree,
Joining themselves in fatal harmony;
That while she with her eyes my heart does bind,
She with her voice might captivate my mind.

I could have fled from one but singly fair:
My disentangled soul itself might save,
Breaking the curlèd trammels of her hair.
But how should I avoid to be her slave,
Whose subtle art invisibly can wreath
My fetters of the very air I breath?

It had been easy fighting in some plain,
Where victory might hang in equal choice;
But all resistance against her is vain,
Who has the advantage both of eyes and voice;
And all my forces needs must be undone,
She having gainèd both the wind and sun.

341   *The Picture of Little T.C. in*
a Prospect of Flowers

SEE with what simplicity
This nymph begins her golden days!
In the green grass she loves to lie,
And there with her fair aspect tames
The wilder flowers, and gives them names;
But only with the roses plays,
           And them does tell
What colour best becomes them, and what smell.

Who can foretell for what high cause
This darling of the gods was born?
Yet this is she whose chaster laws
The wanton Love shall one day fear,
And, under her command severe,
See his bow broke and ensigns torn.
           Happy who can
Appease this virtuous enemy of man!

O then let me in time compound
And parley with those conquering eyes,
Ere they have tried their force to wound;
Ere with their glancing wheels they drive
In triumph over hearts that strive,
And them that yield but more despise:
           Let me be laid,
Where I may see thy glories from some shade.

Meantime, whilst every verdant thing
Itself does at thy beauty charm,
Reform the errors of the Spring;
Make that the tulips may have share
Of sweetness, seeing they are fair,
And roses of their thorns disarm;
           But most procure
That violets may a longer age endure.

But O, young beauty of the woods,
Whom Nature courts with fruits and flowers,
Gather the flowers, but spare the buds;
Lest Flora, angry at thy crime
To kill her infants in their prime,
Do quickly make the example yours;
And ere we see,
Nip in the blossom all our hopes and thee.

342 *The Mower to the Glow-worms*

YE living lamps, by whose dear light
The nightingale does sit so late
And studying all the summer night,
Her matchless songs does meditate;

Ye country comets, that portend
No war, nor prince's funeral,
Shining unto no higher end
Than to presage the grasses' fall;

Ye glow-worms, whose officious flame
To wandering mowers shows the way,
That in the night have lost their aim,
And after foolish fires do stray;

Your courteous lights in vain you waste,
Since Juliana here is come,
For she my mind hath so displaced
That I shall never find my home.

343 *The Garden of Appleton House,*
Laid out by Lord Fairfax in Figure of a Fort

WHEN in the east the morning ray
Hangs out the colours of the day,
The bee through these known alleys hums
Beating the dian with its drums.
Then flowers their drowsy eyelids raise,
Their silken ensigns each displays,
And dries its pan yet dank with dew,
And fills its flask with odours new.

These, as their Governor goes by,
In fragrant volleys they let fly;
And to salute their Governess
Again as great a charge they press:
None for the Virgin Nymph, for she
Seems with the flowers a flower to be.
And think so still! though not compare
With breath so sweet, or cheek so fair.

Well shot, ye firemen! Oh how sweet
And round your equal fires do meet,
Whose shrill report no ear can tell,
But echoes to the eye and smell.
See how the flowers, as at parade,
Under their colours stand displayed:
Each regiment in order grows,
That of the tulip, pink and rose.

But when the vigilant patrol
Of stars walks round about the Pole,
Their leaves, that to the stalks are curled,
Seem to their staves the ensigns furled.
Then in some flower's beloved hut
Each bee as sentinel is shut;
And sleeps so too: but, if once stirred,
She runs you through, or asks the Word.

O thou, that dear and happy isle,
The Garden of the World erewhile,
Thou Paradise of four seas,
Which Heaven planted us to please,
But, to exclude the World, did guard
With watery, if not flaming, sword:
What luckless apple did we taste
To make us mortal, and thee waste?

Unhappy! shall we never more
That sweet militia restore,
When gardens only had their towers,
And all the garrisons were flowers,
When roses only arms might bear,
And men did rosy garlands wear?
Tulips, in several colours barred,
Were then the Switzers of our guard.

The gardener had the soldier's place,
And his more gentle forts did trace.
The nursery of all things green
Was then the only magazine.
The winter quarters were the stoves,
Where he the tender plants removes.
But war all this doth overgrow:
We ordnance plant and powder sow.

HENRY VAUGHAN

1621–1695

344 *The Retreat*

HAPPY those early days, when I
Shined in my angel-infancy!
Before I understood this place
Appointed for my second race,
Or taught my soul to fancy aught
But a white celestial thought;
When yet I had not walked above
A mile or two from my first love,
And looking back, at that short space,
Could see a glimpse of his bright face;
When on some gilded cloud, or flower,
My gazing soul would dwell an hour,
And in those weaker glories spy
Some shadows of eternity;
Before I taught my tongue to wound
My conscience with a sinful sound,
Or had the black art to dispense
A several sin to every sense,
But felt through all this fleshly dress
Bright shoots of everlastingness.

O how I long to travel back,
And tread again that ancient track!
That I might once more reach that plain
Where first I left my glorious train;

From whence the enlightened spirit sees
That shady City of Palm-trees.
But ah! my soul with too much stay
Is drunk, and staggers in the way.
Some men a forward motion love,
But I by backward steps would move,
And when this dust falls to the urn
In that state I came, return.

345   *Peace*

My soul, there is a country
    Far beyond the stars,
Where stands a wingèd sentry
    All skilful in the wars:
There above noise and danger
    Sweet Peace sits crowned with smiles,
And One born in a manger
    Commands the beauteous files.
He is thy gracious friend
    And—O my soul, awake!—
Did in pure love descend
    To die here for thy sake.
If thou canst get but thither,
    There grows the flower of Peace,
The Rose that cannot wither,
    Thy fortress, and thy ease.
Leave then thy foolish ranges
    For none can thee secure,
But one who never changes,
    Thy God, thy life, thy cure.

346

They are all gone into the world of light!
    And I alone sit lingering here;
Their very memory is fair and bright,
    And my sad thoughts doth clear.

It glows and glitters in my cloudy breast
   Like stars upon some gloomy grove,
Or those faint beams in which this hill is dressed,
   After the sun's remove.

I see them walking in an air of glory,
   Whose light doth trample on my days:
My days, which are at best but dull and hoary,
   Mere glimmering and decays.

O holy Hope! and high Humility,
   High as the heavens above!
These are your walks, and you have showed them me,
   To kindle my cold love.

Dear beauteous Death! the jewel of the Just,
   Shining nowhere but in the dark;
What mysteries do lie beyond thy dust,
   Could man outlook that mark!

He that hath found some fledged bird's nest may know,
   At first sight, if the bird be flown;
But what fair well or grove he sings in now,
   That is to him unknown.

And yet, as angels in some brighter dreams
   Call to the soul, when man doth sleep;
So some strange thoughts transcend our wonted themes,
   And into glory peep.

If a star were confined into a tomb,
   Her captive flames must needs burn there;
But when the hand that locked her up gives room,
   She'll shine through all the sphere.

O Father of eternal life, and all
   Created glories under thee!
Resume thy spirit from this world of thrall
   Into true liberty.

Either disperse these mists, which blot and fill
   My perspective still as they pass,
Or else remove me hence unto that hill,
   Where I shall need no glass.

347 *The World*

I SAW Eternity the other night
Like a great Ring of pure and endless light,
    All calm as it was bright;
And round beneath it, Time, in hours, days, years,
    Driven by the spheres,
Like a vast shadow moved, in which the world
    And all her train were hurled.
The doting Lover in his quaintest strain
    Did there complain;
Near him, his lute, his fancy, and his flights,
    Wit's sour delights;
With gloves and knots, the silly snares of pleasure;
    Yet his dear treasure
All scattered lay, while he his eyes did pour
    Upon a flower.

The darksome Statesman hung with weights and woe,
Like a thick midnight fog, moved there so slow
    He did nor stay nor go;
Condemning thoughts, like sad eclipses, scowl
    Upon his soul,
And clouds of crying witnesses without
    Pursued him with one shout.
Yet digged the mole, and, lest his ways be found,
    Worked under ground,
Where he did clutch his prey; but One did see
    That policy.
Churches and altars fed him, perjuries
    Were gnats and flies;
It rained about him blood and tears, but he
    Drank them as free.

The fearful Miser on a heap of rust
Sat pining all his life there, did scarce trust
    His own hands with the dust;
Yet would not place one piece above, but lives
    In fear of thieves.
Thousands there were as frantic as himself,
    And hugged each one his pelf.

The downright Epicure placed heaven in sense
    And scorned pretence;
While others, slipped into a wide excess,
    Said little less;
The weaker sort, slight, trivial wares enslave,
    Who think them brave;
And poor despisèd Truth sat counting by
    Their victory.

Yet some, who all this while did weep and sing,
And sing and weep, soared up into the Ring;
    But most would use no wing.
'O fools', said I, 'thus to prefer dark night
    Before true light,
To live in grots, and caves, and hate the day
    Because it shows the way,
The way which from this dead and dark abode
    Leads up to God,
A way where you might tread the sun, and be
    More bright than he.'
But as I did their madness so discuss,
    One whispered thus,
This Ring the Bridegroom did for none provide
    But for his Bride.

348   *Man*

WEIGHING the steadfastness and state
Of some mean things which here below reside,
Where birds like watchful clocks the noiseless date
    And intercourse of times divide,
Where bees at night get home and hive, and flowers
    Early, as well as late,
Rise with the sun, and set in the same bowers;

I would (said I) my God would give
The staidness of these things to man! for these
To his divine appointments ever cleave,
    And no new business breaks their peace;
The birds nor sow, nor reap, yet sup and dine,
    The flowers without clothes live,
Yet Solomon was never dressed so fine.

Man hath still either toys, or care,
He hath no root, nor to one place is tied,
But ever restless and irregular
    About this earth doth run and ride,
He knows he hath a home, but scarce knows where,
        He says it is so far
That he hath quite forgot how to go there.

    He knocks at all doors, strays and roams,
Nay, hath not so much wit as some stones have,
Which in the darkest nights point to their homes
    By some hid sense their Maker gave;
Man is the shuttle, to whose winding quest
        And passage through these looms
God ordered motion, but ordained no rest.

349
           The Night

    THROUGH that pure Virgin-shrine,
That sacred veil drawn o'er thy glorious noon
That men might look and live as glow-worms shine,
    And face the moon,
  Wise Nicodemus saw such light
  As made him know his God by night.

    Most blest believer he!
Who in that land of darkness and blind eyes
Thy long-expected healing wings could see,
    When thou didst rise,
  And what can never more be done
  Did at midnight speak with the Sun!

    O who will tell me where
He found thee at that dead and silent hour!
What hallowed solitary ground did bear
    So rare a flower,
  Within whose sacred leaves did lie
  The fullness of the Deity.

No mercy-seat of gold,
No dead and dusty cherub, nor carved stone,
But his own living works did my Lord hold
  And lodge alone;
 Where trees and herbs did watch and peep
 And wonder, while the Jews did sleep.

  Dear night! this world's defeat;
The stop to busy fools; care's check and curb;
The day of spirits; my soul's calm retreat
  Which none disturb!
 Christ's progress, and his prayer time;
 The hours to which high Heaven doth chime.

  God's silent searching flight:
When my Lord's head is filled with dew, and all
His locks are wet with the clear drops of night;
  His still soft call;
 His knocking time; the soul's dumb watch,
 When spirits their fair kindred catch.

  Were all my loud, evil days
Calm and unhaunted as is thy dark tent,
Whose peace but by some angel's wing or voice
  Is seldom rent,
 Then I in Heaven all the long year
 Would keep and never wander here.

  But living where the sun
Doth all things wake, and where all mix and tire
Themselves and others, I consent and run
  To every mire,
 And by this world's ill-guiding light,
 Err more than I can do by night.

  There is in God, some say,
A deep, but dazzling darkness, as men here
Say it is late and dusky, because they
  See not all clear.
 O for that night! where I in him
 Might live invisible and dim.

350

The Waterfall

WITH what deep murmurs through time's silent stealth
Doth thy transparent, cool, and watery wealth
       Here flowing fall,
       And chide and call,
As if his liquid loose retinue stayed
Lingering, and were of this steep place afraid,
       The common pass
       Where, clear as glass,
       All must descend
       Not to an end;
But quickened by this deep and rocky grave,
Rise to a longer course more bright and brave.

      Dear stream! dear bank, where often I
      Have sat, and pleased my pensive eye,
      Why, since each drop of thy quick store
      Runs thither, whence it flowed before,
      Should poor souls fear a shade or night,
      Who came, sure, from a sea of light?
      Or since those drops are all sent back
      So sure to thee, that none doth lack,
      Why should frail flesh doubt any more
      That what God takes, he'll not restore?
      O useful Element and clear!
      My sacred wash and cleanser here,
      My first consigner unto those
      Fountains of life, where the Lamb goes,
      What sublime truths, and wholesome themes
      Lodge in thy mystical, deep streams!
      Such as dull man can never find,
      Unless that Spirit lead his mind,
      Which first upon thy face did move,
      And hatched all with his quickening love.
      As this loud brook's incessant fall
      In streaming rings restagnates all,
      Which reach by course the bank, and then
      Are no more seen, just so pass men.
      O my invisible estate,
      My glorious liberty, still late!
      Thou art the channel my soul seeks,
      Not this with cataracts and creeks.

351 *Quickness*

FALSE life! a foil and no more, when
                Wilt thou be gone?
Thou foul deception of all men
That would not have the true come on.

Thou art a moon-like toil; a blind
                Self-posing state;
A dark contest of waves and wind;
A mere tempestuous debate.

Life is a fixed, discerning light,
                A knowing joy;
No chance, or fit; but ever bright,
And calm and full, yet doth not cloy.

'Tis such a blissful thing, that still
                Doth vivify,
And shine and smile, and hath the skill
To please without Eternity.

Thou art a toilsome mole, or less,
                A moving mist;
But life is what none can express,
A quickness which my God hath kissed.

THOMAS STANLEY

1625–1678

352 *The Magnet*

ASK the Empress of the night
   How the hand which guides her sphere,
Constant in unconstant light,
   Taught the waves her yoke to bear,
And did thus by loving force
Curb or tame the rude sea's course.

Ask the female palm how she
  First did woo her husband's love;
And the magnet, ask how he
  Doth the obsequious iron move;
Waters, plants and stones know this,
That they love, not what love is.

Be not then less kind than these,
  Or from love exempt alone;
Let us twine like amorous trees,
  And like rivers melt in one;
Or if thou more cruel prove
Learn of steel and stones to love.

JOHN BUNYAN

1628–1688

353   *The Shepherd Boy Sings in*
the Valley of Humiliation

HE that is down needs fear no fall,
  He that is low, no pride;
He that is humble ever shall
  Have God to be his guide.

I am content with what I have,
  Little be it or much:
And, Lord, contentment still I crave,
  Because Thou savest such.

Fullness to such a burden is
  That go on pilgrimage:
Here little, and hereafter bliss,
  Is best from age to age.

THOMAS TRAHERNE
1638–1674

354   *News*

NEWS from a foreign country came
As if my treasure and my wealth lay there;
So much it did my heart inflame,
'Twas wont to call my Soul into mine ear;
Which thither went to meet
The approaching sweet,
And on the threshold stood
To entertain the unknown Good.
It hovered there
As if 'twould leave mine ear,
And was so eager to embrace
The joyful tidings as they came,
'Twould almost leave its dwelling-place
To entertain the same.

As if the tidings were the things,
My very joys themselves, my foreign treasure—
Or else did bear them on their wings—
With so much joy they came, with so much pleasure.
My Soul stood at the gate
To recreate
Itself with bliss, and to
Be pleased with speed. A fuller view
It fain would take,
Yet journeys back would make
Unto my heart; as if 'twould fain
Go out to meet, yet stay within
To fit a place to entertain
And bring the tidings in.

What sacred instinct did inspire
My soul in childhood with a hope so strong?
What secret force moved my desire
To expect my joys beyond the seas, so young?
Felicity I knew
Was out of view,

And being here alone,
I saw that happiness was gone
    From me! For this
    I thirsted absent bliss,
And thought that sure beyond the seas,
    Or else in something near at hand—
I knew not yet—since naught did please
    I knew—my Bliss did stand.

But little did the infant dream
That all the treasures of the world were by:
    And that himself was so the cream
And crown of all which round about did lie.
        Yet thus it was: the Gem,
           The Diadem,
    The ring enclosing all
That stood upon this earthy ball,
        The Heavenly eye,
    Much wider than the sky,
Wherein they all included were,
  The glorious Soul, that was the King
Made to possess them, did appear
    A small and little thing!

ANONYMOUS

Ballads and Songs

355   *Thomas the Rhymer*

TRUE Thomas lay on Huntlie bank,
    A ferlie he spied wi' his e'e;
And there he saw a ladye bright
    Come riding down by the Eildon Tree.

Her shirt was o' the grass-green silk,
    Her mantle o' the velvet fine;
At ilka tett of her horse's mane
    Hung fifty siller bells and nine.

355   ferlie] marvel   ilka tett] each tuft

True Thomas, he pulled aff his cap
  And louted low down to his knee:
'All hail, thou mighty Queen of Heaven!
  For thy peer on earth I never did see.'

'O no, O no, Thomas,' she said,
  'That name does not belang to me;
I am but the Queen of fair Elfland
  That am hither come to visit thee.

'Harp and carp, Thomas,' she said,
  'Harp and carp along wi' me,
And if ye dare to kiss my lips,
  Sure of your bodie I will be.'

'Betide me weal, betide me woe,
  That weird shall never daunton me.'
Syne he has kissed her rosy lips
  All underneath the Eildon Tree.

'Now ye maun go wi' me,' she said,
  'True Thomas, ye maun go wi' me;
And ye maun serve me seven years
  Through weal or woe, as may chance to be.'

She mounted on her milk-white steed,
  She's ta'en True Thomas up behind;
And aye whene'er her bridle rung
  The steed flew swifter than the wind.

O they rade on, and farther on—
  The steed gaed swifter than the wind—
Until they reached a desart wide
  And living land was left behind.

'Light down, light down now, True Thomas,
  And lean your head upon my knee;
Abide and rest a little space
  And I will shew you ferlies three.

carp] sing

354

'O see ye not yon narrow road
　So thick beset with thorns and briers?
That is the path of righteousness,
　Though after it but few enquires.

'And see ye not that braid, braid road
　That lies across that lily leven?
That is the path of wickedness,
　Though some call it the road to heaven.

'And see not ye that bonny road
　That winds about the fernie brae?
That is the road to fair Elfland,
　Where thou and I this night maun gae.

'But, Thomas, ye maun hold your tongue
　Whatever ye may hear or see,
For if you speak word in Elflyn land
　Ye'll ne'er get back to your ain countrie.'

O they rade on, and farther on,
　And they waded through rivers aboon the knee,
And they saw neither sun nor moon
　But they heard the roaring of the sea.

It was mirk, mirk night and there was nae stern light
　And they waded through red blude to the knee;
For a' the blude that's shed on earth
　Rins through the springs o' that countrie.

Syne they came on to a garden green
　And she pu'd an apple frae a tree:
'Take this for thy wages, True Thomas,
　It will give thee the tongue that can never lie.'

'My tongue is mine ain,' True Thomas said,
　'A gudely gift ye wad gie to me;
I neither dought to buy nor sell
　At fair or tryst where I may be;

lily leven] lovely lea　　　stern] star　　　dought] dare　　　tryst] market

355

'I dought neither speak to prince or peer
    Nor ask of grace from fair ladye.'
'Now hold thy peace,' the lady said,
    For as I say, so must it be.'

He has gotten a coat of the even cloth
    And a pair of shoes of velvet green;
And till seven years were gane and past
    True Thomas on earth was never seen.

356   *Tam Lin*

O I FORBID you, maidens a'
    That wear gowd on your hair,
To come, or gae by Carterhaugh,
    For young Tom-lin is there.

There's nane that gaes by Carterhaugh
    But they leave him a wad;
Either their rings, or green mantles,
    Or else their maidenhead.

Janet has kilted her green kirtle,
    A little aboon her knee;
And she has broded her yellow hair
    A little aboon her bree;
And she's awa to Carterhaugh
    As fast as she can hie.

When she cam to Carterhaugh
    Tom-lin was at the well,
And there she fand his steed standing
    But away was himsel.

She had na pu'd a double rose,
    A rose but only tway,
Till up then started young Tom-lin,
    Says, 'Lady, thou's pu' nae mae.

356   wad] forfeit   at the well] under enchantment

'Why pu's thou the rose, Janet,
  And why breaks thou the wand?
Or why comes thou to Carterhaugh
  Withoutten my command?'

'Carterhaugh it is my ain,
  My daddie gave it me;
I'll come and gang by Carterhaugh
  And ask nae leave at thee.'

Janet has kilted her green kirtle
  A little aboon her knee,
And she has snooded her yellow hair
  A little aboon her bree,
And she is to her father's ha,
  As fast as she can hie.

Four and twenty ladies fair
  Were playing at the ba',
And out then cam the fair Janet,
  Ance the flower amang them a'.

Four and twenty ladies fair
  Were playing at the chess,
And out then cam the fair Janet,
  As green as onie glass.

Out then spak an auld grey knight,
  Lay o'er the castle-wa',
And says, 'Alas, fair Janet, for thee,
  But we'll be blamed a'.'

'Haud your tongue, ye auld-faced knight,
  Some ill death may ye die,
Father my bairn on whom I will,
  I'll father nane on thee.'

Out then spak her father dear,
  And he spak meek and mild,
'And ever alas, sweet Janet,' he says,
  'I think thou gaes wi' child.'

'If that I gae wi' child, father,
    Mysel maun bear the blame;
There's ne'er a laird about your ha',
    Shall get the bairn's name.

'If my Love were an earthly knight,
    As he's an elfin grey;
I wad na gie my ain true-love
    For nae lord that ye hae.

'The steed that my true-love rides on,
    Is lighter than the wind;
Wi' siller he is shod before,
    Wi' burning gowd behind.'

Janet has kilted her green kirtle
    A little aboon her knee;
And she has snooded her yellow hair
    A little aboon her bree;
And she's awa to Carterhaugh
    As fast as she can hie.

When she cam to Carterhaugh,
    Tom-lin was at the well;
And there she fand his steed standing,
    But away was himsel.

She had na pu'd a double rose,
    A rose but only tway,
Till up then started young Tom-lin,
    Says, 'Lady, thou pu's nae mae.

'Why pu's thou the rose, Janet,
    Amang the groves sae green,
And a' to kill the bonie babe
    That we gat us between.'

'O tell me, tell me, Tom-lin', she says,
    'For's sake that died on tree,
If e'er ye was in holy chapel,
    Or Christendom did see.'

'Roxbrugh he was my grandfather,
   Took me with him to bide,
And ance it fell upon a day
   That wae did me betide.

'Ance it fell upon a day,
   A cauld day and a snell,
When we were frae the hunting come
   That frae my horse I fell.

'The queen o' Fairies she caught me,
   In yon green hill to dwell,
And pleasant is the fairy-land;
   But, an eerie tale to tell!

'Ay at the end of seven years
   We pay a tiend to hell;
I am sae fair and fu' o' flesh
   I'm feared it be mysel.

'But the night is Halloween, lady,
   The morn is Hallowday;
Then win me, win me, an ye will,
   For weel I wat ye may.

'Just at the mirk and midnight hour
   The fairy folk will ride;
And they that wad their truelove win,
   At Milescross they maun bide.'

'But how shall I thee ken, Tom-lin,
   O how my true-love know,
Amang sae mony unco knights
   The like I never saw.'

'O first let pass the black, lady,
   And syne let pass the brown;
But quickly run to the milk-white steed,
   Pu ye his rider down;

snell] bitter   tiend] tithe

'For I'll ride on the milk-white steed,
　And ay nearest the town;
Because I was an earthly knight
　They gie me that renown.

'My right hand will be gloved, lady,
　My left hand will be bare;
Cockt up shall my bonnet be,
　And kaimed down shall my hair;
And thae's the tokens I gie thee,
　Nae doubt I will be there.

'They'll turn me in your arms, lady,
　Into an ask and adder,
But hald me fast and fear me not,
　I am your bairn's father.

'They'll turn me to a bear sae grim,
　And then a lion bold;
But hold me fast and fear me not,
　As ye shall love your child.

'Again they'll turn me in your arms
　To a red het gaud of airn;
But hold me fast and fear me not,
　I'll do to you nae harm.

'And last they'll turn me, in your arms,
　Into the burning lead;
Then throw me into well-water,
　O throw me in wi' speed!

'And then I'll be your ain true-love,
　I'll turn a naked knight:
Then cover me wi' your green mantle,
　And cover me out o'sight.'

Gloomy, gloomy was the night,
　And eerie was the way,
As fair Jenny in her green mantle
　To Milescross she did gae.

ask] eft, lizard　　　　het gaud of airn] hot iron bar

About the middle o' the night
 She heard the bridles ring;
This lady was as glad at that
 As any earthly thing.

First she let the black pass by,
 And syne she let the brown;
But quickly she ran to the milk-white steed
 And pu'd the rider down.

Sae weel she minded what he did say
 And young Tom-lin did win;
Syne covered him wi' her green mantle
 As blythe's a bird in spring.

Out then spak the queen o' Fairies,
 Out of a bush o' broom;
'Them that has gotten young Tom-lin,
 Has gotten a stately groom.'

Out then spak the queen o' Fairies,
 And an angry queen was she;
'Shame betide her ill-fared face,
 And an ill death may she die,
For she's ta'en awa the boniest knight
 In a' my companie.

'But had I kenned, Tom-lin,' she says,
 'What now this night I see,
I wad hae ta'en out thy twa grey e'en,
 And put in twa een o' tree.'

357   *Sir Patrick Spence*

THE king sits in Dumferling toune,
 Drinking the blude-reid wine:
'O whar will I get a guid sailor,
 To sail this schip of mine?'

tree] wood

Up and spak an eldern knicht,
　　Sat at the king's richt kne:
'Sir Patrick Spence is the best sailor,
　　That sails upon the se.'

The king has written a braid letter,
　　And signed it wi' his hand;
And sent it to Sir Patrick Spence,
　　Was walking on the sand.

The first line that Sir Patrick red,
　　A loud lauch lauched he:
The next line that Sir Patrick red,
　　The teir blinded his e'e.

'O wha is this has don this deid,
　　This ill deid don to me;
To send me out this time o' the yeir,
　　To sail upon the se?

'Mak haste, mak haste, my mirry men all,
　　Our guid schip sails the morne.'
'O say na sae, my master deir,
　　For I feir a deadlie storme.

'Late, late yestreen I saw the new moone
　　Wi' the auld moone in hir arme;
And I feir, I feir, my deir master,
　　That we will com to harme.'

O our Scots nobles wer richt laith
　　To weet their cork-heiled schoone;
Bot lang owre a' the play wer played,
　　Thair hats they swam aboone.

O lang, lang may thair ladies sit
　　Wi' thair fans into their hand,
Or eir they se Sir Patrick Spence
　　Cum sailing to the land.

O lang, lang may the ladies stand
　　Wi' thair gold kems in their hair,
Waiting for thair ain deir lords,
　　For they'll se thame na mair.

Haf owre, haf owre to Aberdour,
  It's fiftie fadom deip:
And thair lies guid Sir Patrick Spence,
  Wi' the Scots lords at his feit.

358   *Edward, Edward*

'WHY dois your brand sae drop wi' bluid,
    Edward, Edward?
Why dois your brand sae drop wi' bluid?
    And why sae sad gang yee, O?'
'O, I hae killed my hauke sae guid,
    Mither, mither:
O, I hae killed my hauke sae guid:
    And I had nae mair bot hee, O.'

'Your haukis bluid was nevir sae reid,
    Edward, Edward.
Your haukis bluid was nevir sae reid,
    My deir son I tell thee, O.'
'O, I hae killed my reid-roan steid,
    Mither, mither:
O, I hae killed my reid-roan steid,
    That erst was sae fair and free, O.'

'Your steid was auld, and ye hae gat mair,
    Edward, Edward:
Your steid was auld, and ye hae gat mair,
    Sum other dule ye drie, O.'
'O, I hae killed my fadir deir,
    Mither, mither,
O, I hae killed my fadir deir,
    Alas! and wae is me, O!'

'And whatten penance wul ye drie for that,
    Edward, Edward?
And whatten penance will ye drie for that?
    My deir son, now tell me, O.'
'Ile set my feit in yonder boat,
    Mither, mither:
Ile set my feit in yonder boat,
    And Ile fare ovir the sea, O.'

  358   dule ye drie] grief you are suffering

'And what wul ye doe wi' your towirs and your ha',
    Edward, Edward?
And what wul ye doe wi' your towirs and your ha',
    That were sae fair to see, O?'
'Ile let them stand til they doun fa',
    Mither, mither:
Ile let them stand til they doun fa',
    For here nevir mair maun I bee, O.'

'And what wul ye leive to your bairns and your wife,
    Edward, Edward?
And what wul ye leive to your bairns and your wife,
    Whan ye gang ovir the sea, O?'
'The warldis room, let thame beg throw life,
    Mither, mither:
The warldis room, let thame beg throw life,
    For thame nevir mair wul I see, O.'

'And what wul ye leive to your ain mither deir,
    Edward, Edward?
And what wul ye leive to your ain mither deir?
    My deir son, now tell me, O.'
'The curse of hell frae me sall ye beir,
    Mither, mither:
The curse of hell frae me sall ye beir,
    Sic counseils ye gave to me, O.'

359   *Mary Hamilton*

O MARY HAMILTON to the kirk is gane
    Wi' ribbons in her hair;
An' the king thocht mair o' Marie
    Then onie that were there.

Mary Hamilton's to the preaching gane
    Wi' ribbons on her breast;
An' the king thocht mair o' Marie
    Than he thocht o' the priest.

Syne word is through the palace gane,
    I heard it tauld yestreen,
The king loes Mary Hamilton
    Mair than he loes his queen.

A sad tale through the town is gaen,
  A sad tale on the morrow:
Oh Mary Hamilton has born a babe
  And slain it in her sorrow.

And down then cam the auld queen,
  Goud tassels tied her hair:
'What did ye wi' the wee wee bairn
  That I heard greet sae sair?'

'There ne'er was a bairn into my room,
  An' as little designs to be;
'T was but a stitch o' my sair side
  Cam owre my fair bodie.'

'Rise up now, Marie,' quo' the queen,
  'Rise up, an' come wi' me,
For we maun ride to Holyrood
  A gay wedding to see.'

The queen was drest in scarlet fine,
  Her maidens all in green;
An' every town that they cam through
  Took Marie for the queen.

But little wist Marie Hamilton
  As she rode oure the lea
That she was gaun to Edinbro' town
  Her doom to hear and dree.

When she cam to the Netherbow Port
  She laughed loud laughters three;
But when she reached the gallows-tree
  The tears blinded her e'e.

'Yestreen the queen had four Maries,
  The nicht she'll hae but three;
There's Marie Seaton, an' Marie Beaton,
  An' Marie Carmichael, an' me.

dree] suffer

'Oh aften have I dressed my queen
  An' put gowd in her hair;
The gallows-tree is my reward
  An' shame maun be my share.

'Oh aften hae I dressed my queen
  An' saft, saft made her bed;
An' now I've got for my reward
  The gallows-tree to tread.

'There's a health to all gallant sailors
  That sail upon the sea:
Oh never let on to my father and mither
  The death that I maun dee.

'An' I charge ye, all ye mariners,
  When ye sail owre the main,
Let neither my father nor mither know
  But that I'm comin hame.

'Oh little did my mither ken,
  That day she cradled me,
What lands I was to tread in
  Or what death I should dee.'

360   *The Wife of Usher's Well*

THERE lived a wife at Usher's Well
  And a wealthy wife was she;
She had three stout and stalwart sons
  And sent them o'er the sea.

They hadna been a week from her,
  A week but barely ane,
Whan word came to the carline wife
  That her three sons were gane.

They hadna been a week from her,
  A week but barely three,
Whan word came to the carline wife
  That her sons she'd never see.

360 carline] old

366

'I wish the wind may never cease,
   Nor fishes in the flood,
Till my three sons come hame to me
   In earthly flesh and blood.'

It fell about the Martinmas
   Whan nights are lang and mirk,
The carline wife's three sons came hame
   And their hats were o' the birk.

It neither grew in syke nor ditch
   Nor yet in ony sheugh,
But at the gates o' Paradise
   That birk grew fair eneugh.

'Blow up the fire, my maidens,
   Bring water from the well;
For a' my house shall feast this night
   Since my three sons are well.'

And she has made to them a bed,
   She's made it large and wide,
And she's ta'en her mantle her about,
   Sat down at the bed-side.

Up then crew the red, red cock
   And up and crew the gray;
The eldest to the youngest said,
   ' 'Tis time we were away.'

The cock he hadna crawed but once
   And clapped his wings at a'
Whan the youngest to the eldest said,
   'Brother, we must awa.

'The cock doth craw, the day doth daw,
   The channerin' worm doth chide;
Gin we be mist out o' our place
   A sair pain we maun bide.

---

birk] birch   syke] small stream
sheugh] trench   channerin'] fretting

'Fare ye weel, my mother dear;
    Fareweel to barn and byre;
And fare ye weel, the bonny lass
    That kindles my mother's fire.'

361   *A Lyke-Wake Dirge*

THIS ae nighte, this ae nighte,
    —*Every nighte and alle,*
Fire and fleet and candle-lighte,
    And Christe receive thy saule.

When thou from hence away art past,
    —*Every nighte and alle,*
To Whinny-muir thou com'st at last;
    And Christe receive thy saule.

If ever thou gavest hosen and shoon,
    —*Every nighte and alle,*
Sit thee down and put them on;
    And Christe receive thy saule.

If hosen and shoon thou ne'er gav'st nane
    —*Every nighte and alle,*
The whinnes sall prick thee to the bare bane;
    And Christe receive thy saule.

From Whinny-muir when thou mayst pass,
    —*Every nighte and alle,*
To Brig o' Dread thou com'st at last;
    And Christe receive thy saule.

From Brig o' Dread when thou mayst pass,
    —*Every nighte and alle,*
To Purgatory fire thou com'st at last;
    And Christe receive thy saule.

If ever thou gavest meat or drink,
    —*Every nighte and alle,*
The fire sall never make thee shrink;
    And Christe receive thy saule.

If meat or drink thou ne'er gav'st nane,
  —*Every nighte and alle,*
The fire will burn thee to the bare bane;
  And Christe receive thy saule.

This ae nighte, this ae nighte,
  —*Every nighte and alle,*
Fire and fleet and candle-lighte,
  And Christe receive thy saule.

362   *Loving Mad Tom*

FROM the hag and hungry goblin
That into rags would rend ye
All the spirits that stand by the naked man
In the Book of Moons defend ye!
That of your five sound senses
You never be forsaken
Nor wander from yourselves with Tom
Abroad to beg your bacon.

        While I do sing 'Any food, any feeding,
        Feeding, drink, or clothing'
        Come dame or maid, be not afraid,
        Poor Tom will injure nothing.

O thirty bare years have I
Twice twenty been enragèd,
And of forty been three times fifteen
In durance soundly cagèd
On the lordly lofts of Bedlam,
With stubble soft and dainty,
Brave bracelets strong, sweet whip's ding dong,
With wholesome hunger plenty.

        And now I sing etc.

With a thought I took for Maudlin
And a cruise of cockle pottage
With a thing thus tall, sky bless you all,
I befell into this dotage.

I slept not since the Conquest,
Till then I never waked,
Till the roguish boy of love where I lay
Me found and stripped me naked.

And now I sing etc.

When I short have shorn my sour face
And swigged my horny barrel
In an oaken inn I pound my skin
As a suit of gilt apparel.
The moon's my constant Mistress
And the lonely owl my marrow,
The flaming drake and the nightcrow make
Me music to my sorrow.

And now I sing etc.

The palsy plagues my pulses
When I prig their pigs or pullen,
Your culvers take, or matchless make
Your chanticleer, or sullen;
When I want provant, with Humphrey
I sup; and when benighted
I repose in Paul's with waking souls,
Yet never am affrighted.

But I do sing etc.

I know more than Apollo,
For oft when he lies sleeping
I see the stars at bloody wars
In the wounded welkin weeping;
The moon embrace her shepherd
And the queen of Love her warrior,
While the first doth horn the star of morn
And the next the heavenly Farrier.

While I do sing etc.

provant] provisions   Humphrey . . . Paul's] Persons loitering in
St Paul's were said to be 'dining with Duke Humphrey', i.e. going supperless

370

The Gipsy snap and Pedro
Are none of Tom's comrades.
The punk I scorn and the cutpurse sworn
And the roaring boys' bravado.
The meek, the white, the gentle,
Me handle, touch, and spare not,
But those that cross Tom Rynosseros
Do what the panther dare not.

    Although I sing etc.

With an host of furious fancies,
Whereof I am commander,
With a burning spear, and a horse of air,
To the wilderness I wander.
By a knight of ghosts and shadows
I summoned am to tourney,
Ten leagues beyond the wide world's end.
Me thinks it is no journey.

    Yet will I sing etc.

JOHN DRYDEN

1631–1700

363   *London After the Great Fire, 1666*

METHINKS already from this chymic flame
I see a city of more precious mould,
Rich as the town which gives the Indies name,
With silver paved and all divine with gold.

Already, labouring with a mighty fate,
She shakes the rubbish from her mounting brow,
And seems to have renewed her charter's date,
Which Heaven will to the death of time allow.

More great than human now and more August,
New deified she from her fires does rise:
Her widening streets on new foundations trust,
And, opening, into larger parts she flies.

Before, she like some shepherdess did show
Who sat to bathe her by a river's side,
Not answering to her fame, but rude and low,
Nor taught the beauteous arts of modern pride.

Now like a maiden queen she will behold
From her high turrets hourly suitors come;
The East with incense and the West with gold
Will stand like suppliants to receive her doom.

The silver Thames, her own domestic flood,
Shall bear her vessels like a sweeping train,
And often wind, as of his mistress proud,
With longing eyes to meet her face again.

The wealthy Tagus and the wealthier Rhine
The glory of their towns no more shall boast,
And Seine, that would with Belgian rivers join,
Shall find her lustre stained and traffic lost.

The venturous merchant who designed more far
And touches on our hospitable shore,
Charmed with the splendour of this northern star,
Shall here unlade him and depart no more.

364   *The Crown Prince of Dullness*

ALL human things are subject to decay,
And, when Fate summons, monarchs must obey:
This Flecknoe found, who, like Augustus, young
Was called to empire, and had governed long:
In prose and verse was owned without dispute,
Through all the realms of Nonsense, absolute.
This aged Prince now flourishing in peace,
And blest with issue of a large increase,
Worn out with business, did at length debate
To settle the succession of the State:
And pondering which of all his sons was fit
To reign, and wage immortal war with Wit,
Cried, ' 'Tis resolved; for Nature pleads that he
Should only rule who most resembles me:

Shadwell alone my perfect image bears,
Mature in dullness from his tender years.
Shadwell alone, of all my sons, is he
Who stands confirmed in full stupidity.
The rest to some faint meaning make pretence,
But Shadwell never deviates into sense.
Some beams of Wit on other souls may fall,
Strike through, and make a lucid interval;
But Shadwell's genuine night admits no ray,
His rising fogs prevail upon the day:
Besides, his goodly fabric fills the eye,
And seems designed for thoughtless majesty:
Thoughtless as monarch oaks, that shade the plain,
And, spread in solemn state, supinely reign.'

from Absalom and Achitophel

(i)

365   *Achitophel: the Earl of Shaftesbury*

So several factions from this first ferment
Work up to foam, and threat the government.
Some by their friends, more by themselves thought wise,
Opposed the power to which they could not rise.
Some had in courts been great and, thrown from thence,
Like fiends were hardened in impenitence.
Some by their Monarch's fatal mercy grown
From pardoned rebels kinsmen to the throne
Were raised in power and public office high:
Strong bands, if bands ungrateful men could tie.
  Of these the false Achitophel was first,
A name to all succeeding ages curst:
For close designs and crooked counsels fit,
Sagacious, bold, and turbulent of wit,
Restless, unfixed in principles and place,
In power unpleased, impatient of disgrace;
A fiery soul, which, working out its way,
Fretted the pigmy body to decay
And o'er-informed the tenement of clay.
A daring pilot in extremity,
Pleased with the danger, when the waves went high,

He sought the storms; but, for a calm unfit,
Would steer too nigh the sands to boast his wit.
Great wits are sure to madness near allied
And thin partitions do their bounds divide;
Else, why should he, with wealth and honour blest,
Refuse his age the needful hours of rest?
Punish a body which he could not please,
Bankrupt of life, yet prodigal of ease?
And all to leave what with his toil he won
To that unfeathered two-legged thing, a son,
Got, while his soul did huddled notions try,
And born a shapeless lump, like anarchy.
In friendship false, implacable in hate,
Resolved to ruin or to rule the state;
To compass this the triple bond he broke,
The pillars of the public safety shook,
And fitted Israel for a foreign yoke;
Then, seized with fear, yet still affecting fame,
Usurped a patriot's all-atoning name.
So easy still it proves in factious times
With public zeal to cancel private crimes.
How safe is treason and how sacred ill,
Where none can sin against the people's will,
Where crowds can wink and no offence be known,
Since in another's guilt they find their own!
 Yet fame deserved no enemy can grudge;
The statesman we abhor, but praise the judge.
In Israel's courts ne'er sat an Abbethdin
With more discerning eyes or hands more clean,
Unbribed, unsought, the wretched to redress,
Swift of despatch and easy of access.
Oh! had he been content to serve the crown
With virtues only proper to the gown,
Or had the rankness of the soil been freed
From cockle that oppressed the noble seed,
David for him his tuneful harp had strung
And Heaven had wanted one immortal song.
But wild Ambition loves to slide, not stand,
And Fortune's ice prefers to Virtue's land.

(ii)

366   *Zimri: the Duke of Buckingham*

A NUMEROUS host of dreaming Saints succeed,
Of the true old enthusiastic breed:
'Gainst form and order they their power employ,
Nothing to build and all things to destroy.
But far more numerous was the herd of such
Who think too little and who talk too much. . . .
Such were the tools; but a whole Hydra more
Remains of sprouting heads too long to score.
    Some of their chiefs were Princes of the land;
In the first rank of these did Zimri stand,
A man so various that he seemed to be
Not one, but all mankind's epitome:
Stiff in opinions, always in the wrong,
Was everything by starts and nothing long;
But, in the course of one revolving moon,
Was chemist, fiddler, statesman, and buffoon;
Then all for women, painting, rhyming, drinking,
Besides ten thousand freaks that died in thinking.
Blest madman, who could every hour employ
With something new to wish or to enjoy!
Railing and praising were his usual themes,
And both, to show his judgement, in extremes:
So over-violent or over-civil
That every man with him was God or Devil.
In squandering wealth was his peculiar art;
Nothing went unrewarded but desert.
Beggared by fools, whom still he found too late,
He had his jest, and they had his estate.
He laughed himself from Court; then sought relief
By forming parties, but could ne'er be chief:
For, spite of him, the weight of business fell
On Absalom and wise Achitophel;
Thus wicked but in will, of means bereft,
He left not faction, but of that was left.

367   *Vox Populi*

HE preaches to the crowd that power is lent,
But not conveyed, to kingly government;
That claims successive bear no binding force;
That Coronation Oaths are things of course;
Maintains the multitude can never err,
And sets the people in the papal chair.
The reason's obvious: interest never lies;
The most have still their interest in their eyes;
The power is always theirs, and power is ever wise.
Almighty Crowd, thou shortenest all dispute;
Power is thy essence, Wit thy attribute!
Nor faith nor reason make thee at a stay,
Thou leap'st o'er all eternal truths, in thy Pindaric way!
Athens, no doubt, did righteously decide,
When Phocion and when Socrates were tried:
As righteously they did those dooms repent;
Still they were wise, whatever way they went.
Crowds err not, though to both extremes they run;
To kill the Father, and, recall the Son.
Some think the fools were most as times went then,
But now the world's o'er-stocked with prudent men.
The common cry is even religion's test;
The Turk's is, at Constantinople, best;
Idols in India, Popery at Rome;
And our own worship only true at home.
And true but for the time; 'tis hard to know
How long we please it shall continue so.
This side today, and that tomorrow burns;
So all are God-a'mighties in their turns.
A tempting doctrine, plausible and new;
What fools our fathers were, if this be true!

368 *To the Memory of Mr. Oldham*

FAREWELL, too little and too lately known,
Whom I began to think and call my own;
For sure our souls were near allied, and thine
Cast in the same poetic mould with mine.
One common note on either lyre did strike,
And knaves and fools we both abhorred alike:
To the same goal did both our studies drive,
The last set out the soonest did arrive.
Thus Nisus fell upon the slippery place,
While his young friend performed and won the race.
O early ripe! to thy abundant store
What could advancing age have added more?
It might (what Nature never gives the young)
Have taught the numbers of thy native tongue.
But Satire needs not those, and Wit will shine
Through the harsh cadence of a rugged line.
A noble error, and but seldom made,
When poets are by too much force betrayed.
Thy generous fruits, though gathered ere their prime
Still showed a quickness; and maturing time
But mellows what we write to the dull sweets of Rhyme.
Once more, hail and farewell; farewell, thou young,
But ah too short, Marcellus of our tongue;
Thy brows with ivy, and with laurels bound;
But Fate and gloomy Night encompass thee around.

369 *Confessio Fidei*

WHAT weight of ancient witness can prevail,
If private reason hold the public scale?
But, gracious God, how well dost thou provide
For erring judgements an unerring guide!
Thy throne is darkness in the abyss of light,
A blaze of glory that forbids the sight.
O teach me to believe thee thus concealed,
And search no farther than thyself revealed;
But her alone for my director take,
Whom thou hast promised never to forsake!

My thoughtless youth was winged with vain desires;
My manhood, long misled by wandering fires,
Followed false lights; and when their glimpse was gone
My pride struck out new sparkles of her own.
Such was I, such by nature still I am;
Be thine the glory and be mine the shame!
Good life be now my task; my doubts are done;
What more could fright my faith than Three in One?
Can I believe eternal God could lie
Disguised in mortal mould and infancy,
That the great Maker of the world could die?
And, after that, trust my imperfect sense
Which calls in question his omnipotence?
Can I my reason to my faith compel,
And shall my sight and touch and taste rebel?
Superior faculties are set aside;
Shall their subservient organs be my guide?
Then let the moon usurp the rule of day,
And winking tapers show the sun his way;
For what my senses can themselves perceive
I need no revelation to believe.

370   *Farewell, Ungrateful Traitor*

FAREWELL, ungrateful traitor,
Farewell, my perjured swain,
Let never injured creature
Believe a man again.
The pleasure of possessing
Surpasses all expressing,
But 'tis too short a blessing,
And love too long a pain.

'Tis easy to deceive us
In pity of your pain,
But when we love you leave us
To rail at you in vain.
Before we have descried it
There is no bliss beside it,
But she that once has tried it
Will never love again.

378

The passion you pretended
Was only to obtain,
But when the charm is ended
The charmer you disdain.
Your love by ours we measure
Till we have lost our treasure,
But dying is a pleasure,
When living is a pain.

371   *Alexander's Feast: or The Power of Music.*
          An Ode in Honour of St. Cecilia's Day,
                    1967

I

'TWAS at the royal feast, for Persia won
          By Philip's warlike son:
       Aloft in awful state
       The god-like hero sate
          On his imperial throne:
       His valiant peers were placed around;
Their brows with roses and with myrtles bound.
          (So should desert in arms be crowned:)
The lovely Thaïs by his side,
Sat like a blooming Eastern bride
In flower of youth and beauty's pride.
          Happy, happy, happy pair!
          None but the Brave
          None but the Brave
          None but the Brave deserves the Fair.

CHORUS

Happy, happy, happy pair!
None but the Brave
None but the Brave
None but the Brave deserves the Fair.

II

Timotheus placed on high
          Amid the tuneful choir,
          With flying fingers touched the lyre:
The trembling notes ascend the sky,
                    And heavenly joys inspire.

379

The song began from Jove;
Who left his blissful seats above,
(Such is the power of mighty Love.)
A dragon's fiery form belied the god:
Sublime on radiant spires he rode,
  When he to fair Olympia pressed,
   And while he sought her snowy breast:
Then, round her slender waist he curled,
And stamped an image of himself, a sovereign of the world.
The listening crowd admire the lofty sound,
'A present Deity,' they shout around:
'A present Deity,' the vaulted roofs rebound.
   With ravished ears
   The Monarch hears,
   Assumes the god,
   Affects to nod,
  And seems to shake the spheres.

CHORUS

With ravished ears
The Monarch hears,
Assumes the god,
Affects to nod,
And seems to shake the spheres.

III

The praise of Bacchus then the sweet musician sung,
  Of Bacchus ever fair and ever young;
   The jolly god in triumph comes;
   Sound the trumpets, beat the drums:
    Flushed with a purple grace
    He shows his honest face;
Now give the hautboys breath: he comes, he comes!
 'Bacchus, ever fair and young,
  Drinking joys did first ordain;
 Bacchus' blessings are a treasure;
 Drinking is the soldier's pleasure;
   Rich the treasure,
   Sweet the pleasure;
  Sweet is pleasure after pain.'

CHORUS

Bacchus' blessings are a treasure;
Drinking is the soldier's pleasure;
  Rich the treasure,
  Sweet the pleasure;
Sweet is pleasure after pain.

IV

Soothed with the sound the King grew vain,
  Fought all his battles o'er again;
And thrice he routed all his foes, and thrice he slew the slain.
    The master saw the madness rise,
    His glowing cheeks, his ardent eyes;
    And while he heaven and earth defied,
    Changed his hand, and checked his pride.
      He chose a mournful Muse
      Soft pity to infuse:
    He sung Darius great and good,
      By too severe a fate,
    Fallen, fallen, fallen, fallen,
      Fallen from his high estate
          And weltering in his blood;
    Deserted at his utmost need
    By those his former bounty fed;
    On the bare earth exposed he lies,
    With not a friend to close his eyes.

With downcast looks the joyless victor sate,
  Revolving in his altered soul
    The various turns of chance below;
  And, now and then, a sigh he stole,
  And tears began to flow.

CHORUS

Revolving in his altered soul
  The various turns of chance below;
And, now and then, a sigh he stole,
  And tears began to flow.

381

V

The mighty master smiled to see
That love was in the next degree:
'Twas but a kindred sound to move,
For pity melts the mind to love.
    Softly sweet, in Lydian measures
    Soon he soothed his soul to pleasures.
    'War', he sung, 'is toil and trouble;
    Honour but an empty bubble.
      Never ending, still beginning,
    Fighting still, and still destroying;
      If the world be worth thy winning,
    Think, O think it worth enjoying.
      Lovely Thaïs sits beside thee,
      Take the good the Gods provide thee.'

The many rend the skies with loud applause;
So Love was crowned, but Music won the cause.
    The Prince, unable to conceal his pain,
      Gazed on the Fair
      Who caused his care,
    And sighed and looked, sighed and looked,
    Sighed and looked, and sighed again:
At length, with love and wine at once oppressed,
The vanquished victor sunk upon her breast.

CHORUS

The Prince, unable to conceal his pain,
    Gazed on the Fair
    Who caused his care,
    And sighed and looked, sighed and looked,
    Sighed and looked, and sighed again:
At length, with love and wine at once oppressed,
The vanquished victor sunk upon her breast.

VI

Now strike the golden lyre again,
A louder yet, and yet a louder strain.
Break his bands of sleep asunder,
And rouse him, like a rattling peal of thunder.

Hark, hark, the horrid sound
      Has raised up his head,
      As awaked from the dead,
   And amazed he stares around.
'Revenge, revenge!' Timotheus cries,
      'See the Furies arise!
   See the snakes that they rear,
   How they hiss in their hair,
   And the sparkles that flash from their eyes!
      Behold a ghastly band,
      Each a torch in his hand!
Those are Grecian ghosts that in battle were slain,
                     And unburied remain
                     Inglorious on the plain.
         Give the vengeance due
         To the valiant crew.
Behold how they toss their torches on high,
      How they point to the Persian abodes,
And glittering temples of their hostile gods!'
The Princes applaud with a furious joy,
And the King seized a flambeau, with zeal to destroy;
         Thaïs led the way
         To light him to his prey,
And, like another Helen, fired another Troy.

CHORUS

And the King seized a flambeau, with zeal to destroy;
         Thaïs led the way
         To light him to his prey,
And, like another Helen, fired another Troy.

VII

      Thus, long ago,
Ere heaving bellows learned to blow,
      While organs yet were mute;
Timotheus, to his breathing flute
      And sounding lyre,
Could swell the soul to rage, or kindle soft desire.
      At last divine Cecilia came,
      Inventress of the vocal frame;

The sweet Enthusiast, from her sacred store,
      Enlarged the former narrow bounds,
      And added length to solemn sounds,
With Nature's mother wit, and arts unknown before.
      Let old Timotheus yield the prize,
          Or both divide the crown;
          He raised a mortal to the skies,
          She drew an angel down.

GRAND CHORUS

At last divine Cecilia came,
      Inventress of the vocal frame;
The sweet Enthusiast, from her sacred store,
      Enlarged the former narrow bounds,
      And added length to solemn sounds,
With Nature's mother wit, and arts unknown before.
      Let old Timotheus yield the prize,
          Or both divide the crown;
          He raised a mortal to the skies,
          She drew an angel down.

372   *Songs from* The Secular Masque

Diana. With horns and with hounds I waken the day,
      And hie to my woodland walks away;
      I tuck up my robe, and am buskined soon,
      And tie to my forehead a waxing moon.
      I course the fleet stag, unkennel the fox,
      And chase the wild goats o'er summits of rocks;
      With shouting and hooting we pierce through the sky,
      And Echo turns hunter and doubles the cry.

Chorus. *Then our age was in its prime,*
          Free from rage, and free from crime,
          A very merry, dancing, drinking,
          Laughing, quaffing, and unthinking time.

Mars.   Inspire the vocal brass, inspire;
       The world is past its infant age:
          Arms and honour,
          Arms and honour,
       Set the martial mind on fire,
       And kindle manly rage.
       Mars has looked the sky to red;
       And Peace, the lazy good, is fled.
       Plenty, Peace, and Pleasure fly;
          The sprightly green
       In woodland walks no more is seen;
       The sprightly green has drunk the Tyrian dye.

Momus. Thy sword within the scabbard keep,
         And let mankind agree;
       Better the world were fast asleep.
         Than kept awake by thee.
       The fools are only thinner,
         With all our cost and care;
       But neither side a winner,
         For things are as they were.

Venus. Calms appear when storms are past,
       Love will have his hour at last:
       Nature is my kindly care;
       Mars destroys, and I repair;
       Take me, take me, while you may;
       Venus comes not every day.

Chorus. *All, all of a piece throughout:*
       Thy chase had a beast in view;
       Thy wars brought nothing about;
       Thy lovers were all untrue.
       'Tis well an old age is out,
       And time to begin a new.

CHARLES SACKVILLE,
EARL OF DORSET
1638–1706

373   *Song*

Written at Sea in the First Dutch War (1665),
the night before an Engagement

To all you ladies now at land
   We men at sea indite;
But first would have you understand
   How hard it is to write:
The Muses now, and Neptune too,
We must implore to write to you—
      With a fa, la, la, la, la.

For though the Muses should prove kind,
   And fill our empty brain,
Yet if rough Neptune rouse the wind
   To wave the azure main,
Our paper, pen, and ink, and we,
Roll up and down our ships at sea—
      With a fa, la, la, la, la.

Then if we write not by each post,
   Think not we are unkind;
Nor yet conclude our ships are lost
   By Dutchmen or by wind:
Our tears we'll send a speedier way,
The tide shall bring them twice a day—
      With a fa, la, la, la, la.

The King with wonder and surprise
   Will swear the seas grow bold,
Because the tides will higher rise
   Than e'er they did of old:
But let him know it is our tears
Bring floods of grief to Whitehall stairs—
      With a fa, la, la, la, la.

Should foggy Opdam chance to know
  Our sad and dismal story,
The Dutch would scorn so weak a foe,
  And quit their fort at Goree:
For what resistance can they find
From men who've left their hearts behind?—
    With a fa, la, la, la, la.

Let wind and weather do its worst,
  Be you to us but kind;
Let Dutchmen vapour, Spaniards curse,
  No sorrow we shall find:
'Tis then no matter how things go,
Or who's our friend, or who's our foe—
    With a fa, la, la, la, la.

To pass our tedious hours away
  We throw a merry main,
Or else at serious ombre play;
  But why should we in vain
Each other's ruin thus pursue?
We were undone when we left you—
    With a fa, la, la, la, la.

But now our fears tempestuous grow
  And cast our hopes away;
Whilst you, regardless of our woe,
  Sit careless at a play:
Perhaps permit some happier man
To kiss your hand, or flirt your fan—
    With a fa, la, la, la, la.

When any mournful tune you hear,
  That dies in every note
As if it sighed with each man's care
  For being so remote,
Think then how often love we've made
To you, when all those tunes were played—
    With a fa, la, la, la, la.

In justice you cannot refuse
  To think of our distress,
When we for hopes of honour lose
  Our certain happiness:
All those designs are but to prove
Ourselves more worthy of your love—
    With a fa, la, la, la, la.

And now we've told you all our loves,
  And likewise all our fears,
In hopes this declaration moves
  Some pity for our tears:
Let's hear of no inconstancy—
We have too much of that at sea—
    With a fa, la, la, la, la.

SIR CHARLES SEDLEY

1639–1701

374   *To Celia*

NOT, Celia, that I juster am
  Or better than the rest!
For I would change each hour, like them,
  Were not my heart at rest.

But I am tied to very thee
  By every thought I have;
Thy face I only care to see,
  Thy heart I only crave.

All that in woman is adored
  In thy dear self I find—
For the whole sex can but afford
  The handsome and the kind.

Why then should I seek further store,
  And still make love anew?
When change itself can give no more,
  'Tis easy to be true!

375 *Song*

LOVE still has something of the sea,
   From whence his mother rose;
No time his slaves from Doubt can free,
   Nor give their thoughts repose:

They are becalmed in clearest days,
   And in rough weather tost;
They wither under cold delays,
   Or are in tempests lost.

One while they seem to touch the port,
   Then straight into the main,
Some angry wind in cruel sport
   The vessel drives again.

At first Disdain and Pride they fear,
   Which if they chance to 'scape,
Rivals and Falsehood soon appear
   In a more dreadful shape.

By such degrees to Joy they come,
   And are so long withstood,
So slowly they receive the sum,
   It hardly does them good.

'Tis cruel to prolong a pain,
   And to defer a joy,
Believe me, gentle Celemene,
   Offends the wingèd Boy.

An hundred thousand oaths your fears
   Perhaps would not remove;
And if I gazed a thousand years
   I could no deeper love.

376 *Phyllis Knotting*

HEARS not my Phyllis how the birds
　　Their feathered mates salute?
They tell their passion in their words;
　　Must I alone be mute?
Phyllis, *without frown or smile,*
Sat and knotted all the while.

The God of Love in thy bright eyes
　　Does like a tyrant reign;
But in thy heart a child he lies,
　　Without his dart or flame.
Phyllis, *without frown or smile,*
Sat and knotted all the while.

So many months in silence past,
　　And yet in raging love,
Might well deserve one word at last
　　My passion should approve.
Phyllis, *without frown or smile,*
Sat and knotted all the while.

Must then your faithful swain expire,
　　And not one look obtain,
Which he, to sooth his fond desire,
　　Might pleasingly explain?
Phyllis, *without frown or smile,*
Sat and knotted all the while.

APHRA BEHN

1640–1689

377 *Song*

LOVE in fantastic triumph sate
　　Whilst bleeding hearts around him flowed,
For whom fresh pains he did create
　　And strange tyrannic power he showed:

From thy bright eyes he took his fires,
    Which round about in sport he hurled;
But 'twas from mine he took desires
    Enough to undo the amorous world.

From me he took his sighs and tears,
    From thee his pride and cruelty;
From me his languishments and fears,
    And every killing dart from thee.
Thus thou and I the god have armed
    And set him up a deity;
But my poor heart alone is harmed,
    Whilst thine the victor is, and free!

JOHN WILMOT, EARL OF ROCHESTER

1647–1680

378   *The Mistress*

An age in her embraces passed
    Would seem a winter's day,
Where life and light with envious haste
    Are torn and snatched away.

But oh, how slowly minutes roll
    When absent from her eyes,
That feed my love, which is my soul:
    It languishes and dies.

For then no more a soul, but shade,
    It mournfully does move
And haunts my breast, by absence made
    The living tomb of love.

You wiser men, despise me not
    Whose lovesick fancy raves
On shades of souls, and heaven knows what:
    Short ages live in graves.

Whene'er those wounding eyes, so full
  Of sweetness, you did see,
Had you not been profoundly dull,
  You had gone mad like me.

Nor censure us, you who perceive
  My best beloved and me
Sigh and lament, complain and grieve:
  You think we disagree.

Alas! 'tis sacred jealousy,
  Love raised to an extreme:
The only proof 'twixt her and me
  We love, and do not dream.

Fantastic fancies fondly move
  And in frail joys believe,
Taking false pleasure for true love;
  But pain can ne'er deceive.

Kind jealous doubts, tormenting fears,
  And anxious cares, when past,
Prove our hearts' treasure fixed and dear,
  And make us blest at last.

379   *Return*

ABSENT from thee, I languish still;
  Then ask me not, when I return?
The straying fool 'twill plainly kill
  To wish all day, all night to mourn.

Dear! from thine arms then let me fly,
  That my fantastic mind may prove
The torments it deserves to try
  That tears my fixed heart from my love.

When, wearied with a world of woe,
  To thy safe bosom I retire
Where love and peace and truth does flow,
  May I contented there expire,

Lest, once more wandering from that heaven,
   I fall on some base heart unblest,
Faithless to thee, false, unforgiven,
   And lose my everlasting rest.

380   *Love and Life*

ALL my past life is mine no more;
   The flying hours are gone,
Like transitory dreams given o'er
Whose images are kept in store
   By memory alone.

Whatever is to come is not:
   How can it then be mine?
The present moment's all my lot,
And that, as fast as it is got,
   Phyllis, is wholly thine.

Then talk not of inconstancy,
   False hearts, and broken vows;
If I, by miracle, can be
This livelong minute true to thee,
   'Tis all that heaven allows.

381   *Homo Sapiens*

WERE I (who to my cost already am
One of those strange, prodigious creatures, man)
A spirit free to choose, for my own share,
What case of flesh and blood I pleased to wear,
I'd be a dog, a monkey, or a bear,
Or anything but that vain animal
Who is so proud of being rational.
   The senses are too gross, and he'll contrive
A sixth, to contradict the other five,
And before certain instinct, will prefer
Reason, which fifty times for one does err;
Reason, an *ignis fatuus* in the mind,
Which, leaving light of nature, sense, behind,

Pathless and dangerous wandering ways it takes
Through error's fenny bogs and thorny brakes;
Whilst the misguided follower climbs with pain
Mountains of whimseys, heaped in his own brain;
Stumbling from thought to thought, falls headlong down
Into doubt's boundless sea, where, like to drown,
Books bear him up awhile, and make him try
To swim with bladders of philosophy;
In hopes still to o'ertake the escaping light,
The vapour dances in his dazzling sight
Till, spent, it leaves him to eternal night.
Then old age and experience, hand in hand,
Lead him to death, and make him understand,
After a search so painful and so long,
That all his life he has been in the wrong.
Huddled in dirt the reasoning engine lies,
Who was so proud, so witty, and so wise.

MATTHEW PRIOR

1664–1721

382   *To a Child of Quality*
Five Years Old, 1704. The Author then Forty

LORDS, knights, and squires, the numerous band
   That wear the fair Miss Mary's fetters,
Were summoned by her high command
   To show their passion by their letters.

My pen amongst the rest I took,
   Lest those bright eyes, that cannot read,
Should dart their kindling fires, and look
   The power they have to be obeyed.

Nor quality, nor reputation,
   Forbid me yet my flame to tell;
Dear Five-years-old befriends my passion,
   And I may write till she can spell.

For, while she makes her silkworms beds
   With all the tender things I swear;
Whilst all the house my passion reads,
   In papers round her baby's hair;

She may receive and own my flame,
   For, though the strictest prudes should know it,
She'll pass for a most virtuous dame,
   And I for an unhappy poet.

Then too, alas! when she shall tear
   The lines some younger rival sends,
She'll give me leave to write, I fear,
   And we shall still continue friends.

For, as our different ages move,
   'Tis so ordained (would Fate but mend it!)
That I shall be past making love
   When she begins to comprehend it.

383
A Letter
To Lady Margaret Cavendish Holles-Harley,
when a Child

MY noble, lovely, little Peggy,
Let this my First Epistle beg ye,
At dawn of morn, and close of even,
To lift your heart and hands to Heaven.
In double beauty say your prayer:
Our Father first, then *Notre Père.*
And, dearest child, along the day,
In every thing you do and say,
Obey and please my lord and lady,
So God shall love and angels aid ye.

If to these precepts you attend,
No second letter need I send,
And so I rest your constant friend.

384   *Jinny the Just*

RELEASED from the noise of the butcher and baker
Who, my old friends be thanked, did seldom forsake her,
And from the soft duns of my landlord the Quaker,

From chiding the footmen and watching the lasses,
From Nell that burned milk too, and Tom that brake glasses
(Sad mischiefs through which a good housekeeper passes!)

From some real care but more fancied vexation,
From a life parti-coloured half reason half passion,
Here lies after all the best wench in the nation.

From the Rhine to the Po, from the Thames to the Rhone,
Joanna or Janneton, Jinny or Joan,
'Twas all one to her by what name she was known.

For the idiom of words very little she heeded,
Provided the matter she drove at succeeded,
She took and gave languages just as she needed.

So for kitchen and market, for bargain and sale,
She paid English or Dutch or French down on the nail,
But in telling a story she sometimes did fail;

Then begging excuse as she happened to stammer,
With respect to her betters but none to her grammar,
Her blush helped her out and her jargon became her.

Her habit and mien she endeavoured to frame
To the different *gout* of the place where she came,
Her outside still changed, but her inside the same:

At the Hague in her slippers and hair as the mode is,
At Paris all falbalowed fine as a goddess,
And at censuring London in smock sleeves and bodice.

She ordered affairs that few people could tell
In what part about her that mixture did dwell
Of Frau, or Mistress, or Mademoiselle.

For her surname and race let the heralds e'en answer;
Her own proper worth was enough to advance her,
And he who liked her little valued her grandsire.

But from what house soever her lineage may come
I wish my own Jinny but out of her tomb,
Though all her relations were there in her room.

Of such terrible beauty she never could boast
As with absolute sway o'er all hearts rules the roast
When J—— bawls out to the chair for a toast;

But of good household features her person was made,
Nor by faction cried up, nor of censure afraid,
And her beauty was rather for use than parade.

Her blood so well mixed and flesh so well pasted
That, though her youth faded, her comeliness lasted;
The blue was worn off but the plum was well tasted.

Less smooth than her skin, and less white than her breast,
Was this polished stone beneath which she lies pressed:
Stop, reader, and sigh while thou think'st on the rest.

With a just trim of virtue her soul was endued,
Not affectedly pious nor secretly lewd
She cut even between the coquette and the prude;

And her will with her duty so equally stood
That, seldom opposed, she was commonly good,
And did pretty well, doing just what she would.

Declining all power she found means to persuade,
Was then most regarded when most she obeyed,
The mistress in truth when she seemed but the maid.

Such care of her own proper actions she took
That on'other folks lives she had no time to look,
So censure and praise were struck out of her book.

Her thought still confined to its own little sphere,
She minded not who did excel or did err
But just as the matter related to her.

Then too when her private tribunal was reared
Her mercy so mixed with her judgement appeared
That her foes were condemned and her friends always cleared.

Her religion so well with her learning did suit
That in practice sincere and in controverse mute,
She showed she knew better to live than dispute.

Some parts of the Bible by heart she recited,
And much in historical chapters delighted,
But in points about faith she was something short-sighted;

So notions and modes she referred to the schools,
And in matters of conscience adhered to two rules:
To advise with no bigots and jest with no fools.

And scrupling but little, enough she believed,
By charity ample small sins she retrieved,
And when she had new clothes she always received.

Thus still whilst her morning unseen fled away,
In ordering the linen and making the tea,
That she scarce could have time for the psalms of the day;

And while after dinner the night came so soon
That half she proposed very seldom was done;
With twenty God bless me's, how this day is gone!

While she read and accounted and paid and abated,
Ate and drank, played and worked, laughed and cried, loved
    and hated,
As answered the end of her being created:

In the midst of her age came a cruel disease,
Which neither her broths nor receipts could appease;
So down dropped her clay, may her soul be at peace.

Retire from this sepulchre all the profane,
Ye that love for debauch, or that marry for gain;
Retire lest ye trouble the Manes of J——.

But thou that know'st love above interest or lust,
Strew the myrtle and rose on this once beloved dust,
And shed one pious tear upon Jinny the Just.

Tread soft on her grave, and do right to her honour,
Let neither rude hand nor ill tongue light upon her,
Do all the small favours that now can be done her.

And when what thou liked shall return to her clay,
For so I'm persuaded she must do one day,
Whatever fantastic J—— Asgill may say,

When as I have done now, thou shalt set up a stone
For something however distinguished or known,
May some pious friend the misfortune bemoan,
And make thy concern by reflection his own.

385   *Written in the Beginning of*
         Mezeray's History of France

WHATE'ER thy countrymen have done
By law and wit, by sword and gun,
   In thee is faithfully recited:
And all the living world, that view
Thy work, give thee the praises due,
   At once instructed and delighted.

Yet for the fame of all these deeds
What beggar in the Invalides,
   With lameness broke, with blindness smitten,
Wished ever decently to die,
To have been either Mezeray
   Or any monarch he has written?

It strange, dear Author, yet it true is,
That down from Pharamond to Louis
   All covet life, yet call it pain;
All feel the ill, yet shun the cure:
Can sense this paradox endure?
   Resolve me, Cambray or Fontaine.

The man in graver Tragic known,
Though his best part long since was done,
   Still on the stage desires to tarry;
And he who played the Harlequin
After the jest still loads the scene,
   Unwilling to retire, though weary.

386 *Answer to Chloe Jealous*

DEAR Chloe, how blubbered is that pretty face!
Thy cheek all on fire, and thy hair all uncurled.
Prithee, quit this caprice; and (as old Falstaff says)
Let us e'en talk a little like folks of this world.

How canst thou presume thou hast leave to destroy
The beauties which Venus but lent to thy keeping?
Those looks were designed to inspire love and joy:
More ordinary eyes may serve people for weeping.

To be vexed at a trifle or two that I writ
Your judgement at once and my passion you wrong:
You take that for fact which will scarce be found wit:
'Od's life! must one swear to the truth of a song?

What I speak, my fair Chloe, and what I write, shows
The difference there is betwixt Nature and Art:
I court others in verse, but I love thee in prose;
And they have my whimsies, but thou hast my heart.

The God of us verse-men, you know, child, the sun
How after his journeys he sets up his rest:
If at morning o'er Earth 'tis his fancy to run,
At night he reclines on his Thetis's breast.

So when I am wearied with wandering all day,
To thee, my delight, in the evening I come;
No matter what beauties I saw in my way,
They were but my visits, but thou art my home.

Then finish, dear Chloe, this pastoral war,
And let us like Horace and Lydia agree:
For thou art a girl as much brighter than her
As he was a poet sublimer than me.

WILLIAM CONGREVE

1670–1729

387 *Pious Selinda*

PIOUS Selinda goes to prayers,
　If I but ask the favour;
And yet the tender fool's in tears,
　When she believes I'll leave her.

Would I were free from this restraint,
　Or else had hopes to win her;
Would she would make of me a saint,
　Or I of her a sinner.

388 *False though she be*

FALSE though she be to me and love,
　I'll ne'er pursue revenge;
For still the charmer I approve
　Though I deplore her change.

In hours of bliss we oft have met:
　They could not always last;
And though the present I regret,
　I'm grateful for the past.

JONATHAN SWIFT

1667–1745

389 *A Description of the Morning*

NOW hardly here and there a hackney-coach
Appearing, showed the ruddy morn's approach.
Now Betty from her master's bed had flown,
And softly stole to discompose her own.
The slipshod 'prentice from his master's door
Had pared the dirt and sprinkled round the floor.

Now Moll had whirled her mop with dexterous airs,
Prepared to scrub the entry and the stairs.
The youth with broomy stumps began to trace
The kennel-edge, where wheels had worn the place.
The small-coal-man was heard with cadence deep,
'Till drowned in shriller notes of chimney-sweep.
Duns at his Lordship's gate began to meet,
And brickdust Moll had screamed through half a street.
The turnkey now his flock returning sees,
Duly let out a-nights to steal for fees.
The watchful bailiffs take their silent stands,
And schoolboys lag, with satchels in their hands.

390   *Verses on the Death of Doctor Swift*

THE time is not remote when I
Must by the course of nature die:
When I foresee my special friends
Will try to find their private ends:
Though it is hardly understood
Which way my death can do them good;
Yet, thus methinks I hear 'em speak:
'See how the Dean begins to break,
Poor gentleman, he droops apace,
You plainly find it in his face;
That old vertigo in his head
Will never leave him till he's dead:
Besides, his memory decays,
He recollects not what he says,
He cannot call his friends to mind,
Forgets the place where last he dined,
Plies you with stories o'er and o'er—
He told them fifty times before.
How does he fancy we can sit
To hear his out-of-fashioned wit?
But he takes up with younger folks,
Who for his wine will bear his jokes,
Faith, he must make his stories shorter,
Or change his comrades once a quarter;
In half the time he talks them round,
There must another set be found.

For poetry, he's past his prime,
He takes an hour to find a rhyme;
His fire is out, his wit decayed,
His fancy sunk, his muse a jade.
I'd have him throw away his pen,
But there's no talking to some men.'

And then their tenderness appears,
By adding largely to my years:
'He's older than he would be reckoned,
And well remembers Charles the Second.'

'He hardly drinks a pint of wine,
And that, I doubt, is no good sign.
His stomach too begins to fail:
Last year we thought him strong and hale,
But now he's quite another thing;
I wish he may hold out till spring.'

Then hug themselves, and reason thus;
'It is not yet so bad with us.'

*

Suppose me dead; and then suppose
A club assembled at the Rose,
Where from discourse of this and that
I grow the subject of their chat;
And, while they toss my name about,
With favour some, and some without,
One quite indifferent in the cause
My character impartial draws:

'The Dean, if we believe report,
Was never ill-received at Court;
As for his works in verse and prose,
I own myself no judge of those;
Nor can I tell what critics thought 'em,
But this I know, all people bought 'em;
As with a moral view designed
To cure the vices of mankind;
His vein, ironically grave,
Exposed the fool, and lashed the knave;
To steal a hint was never known,
But what he writ was all his own.

He never thought an honour done him
Because a Duke was proud to own him;
Would rather slip aside, and choose
To talk with wits in dirty shoes;
Despised the fools with Stars and Garters,
So often seen caressing Chartres;
He never courted men in station
Nor persons had in admiration;
Of no man's greatness was afraid,
Because he sought for no man's aid.
Though trusted long in great affairs
He gave himself no haughty airs;
Without regarding private ends
Spent all his credit for his friends;
And only chose the wise and good,
No flatterers, no allies in blood;
But succoured virtue in distress,
And seldom failed of good success,
As numbers in their hearts must own,
Who, but for him, had been unknown.

With Princes kept a due decorum,
But never stood in awe before 'em;
And to her Majesty, God bless her,
Would speak as free as to her dresser;
She thought it his peculiar whim,
Nor took it ill as come from him.
He followed David's lesson just,
"In Princes never put thy trust."
And would you make him truly sour,
Provoke him with "a slave in power";
The Irish senate, if you named,
With what impatience he declaimed!
Fair LIBERTY was all his cry;
For her he stood prepared to die;
For her he boldly stood alone;
For her he oft exposed his own.
Two kingdoms, just as faction led,
Had set a price upon his head,
But not a traitor could be found
To sell him for six hundred pound.

Had he but spared his tongue and pen
He might have rose like other men;
But power was never in his thought,
And wealth he valued not a groat;
Ingratitude he often found,
And pitied those who meant the wound;
But kept the tenor of his mind
To merit well of human kind;
Nor made a sacrifice of those
Who still were true, to please his foes.
He laboured many a fruitless hour
To reconcile his friends in power;
Saw mischief by a faction brewing,
While they pursued each other's ruin.
But, finding vain was all his care,
He left the Court in mere despair.'

*

'Perhaps I may allow, the Dean
Had too much satire in his vein,
And seemed determined not to starve it
Because no age could more deserve it.
Yet malice never was his aim:
He lashed the vice, but spared the name.
No individual could resent
Where thousands equally were meant.
His satire points at no defect
But what all mortals may correct;
For he abhorred that senseless tribe,
Who call it humour when they jibe;
He spared a hump or crooked nose
Whose owners set not up for beaux.
True genuine dullness moved his pity,
Unless it offered to be witty.
Those who their ignorance confessed
He ne'er offended with a jest,
But laughed to hear an idiot quote
A verse from Horace, learned by rote.

He knew an hundred pleasant stories,
With all the turns of Whigs and Tories:
Was cheerful to his dying day,
And friends would let him have his way.

405

He gave the little wealth he had
To build a house for fools and mad:
And shewed by one satiric touch
No nation wanted it so much;
That kingdom he hath left his debtor,
I wish it soon may have a better.'

391   *The Day of Judgement*

WITH a whirl of thought oppressed
I sink from reverie to rest.
An horrid vision seized my head,
I saw the graves give up their dead.
Jove, armed with terrors, burst the skies,
And thunder roars, and lightning flies!
Amazed, confused, its fate unknown,
The world stands trembling at his throne.
While each pale sinner hangs his head,
Jove, nodding, shook the Heavens, and said,
'Offending race of human kind,
By nature, reason, learning, blind;
You who through frailty stepped aside,
And you who never fell—through pride;
You who in different sects have shammed,
And come to see each other damned;
(So some folks told you, but they knew
No more of Jove's designs than you):
The world's mad business now is o'er,
And I resent these pranks no more.
I to such blockheads set my wit!
I damn such fools!—Go, go, you're bit.'

ISAAC WATTS

1674–1748

392   *The Day of Judgement*

WHEN the fierce North-wind with his airy forces
Rears up the Baltic to a foaming fury;
And the red lightning with a storm of hail comes
                 Rushing amain down;

How the poor sailors stand amazed and tremble,
While the hoarse thunder, like a bloody trumpet,
Roars a loud onset to the gaping waters,
                 Quick to devour them.

Such shall the noise be, and the wild disorder
(If things eternal may be like these earthly),
Such the dire terror when the great Archangel
                 Shakes the creation;

Tears the strong pillars of the vault of Heaven,
Breaks up old marble, the repose of princes;
See the graves open, and the bones arising,
                 Flames all around them.

Hark, the shrill outcries of the guilty wretches!
Lively bright horror and amazing anguish
Stare through their eyelids, while the living worm lies
                 Gnawing within them.

Thoughts, like old vultures, prey upon their heart-strings,
And the smart twinges, when their eye beholds the
Lofty Judge frowning, and a flood of vengeance
                 Rolling afore him.

Hopeless immortals! how they scream and shiver,
While devils push them to the pit wide-yawning,
Hideous and gloomy, to receive them headlong
                 Down to the centre!

Stop here, my fancy: (all away, ye horrid
Doleful ideas!) come, arise to Jesus,
How he sits God-like! and the saints around him
                 Throned, yet adoring!

O may I sit there when he comes triumphant,
Dooming the nations! then ascend to glory,
While our Hosannas all along the passage
                Shout the Redeemer!

393   *Sweet Muse, Descend*

SWEET Muse, descend and bless the shade,
    And bless the evening grove;
Business, and noise, and day are fled,
    And every care but love.

But hence, ye wanton young and fair,
    Mine is a purer flame;
No Phyllis shall infect the air,
    With her unhallowed name.

Jesus has all my powers possessed,
    My hopes, my fears, my joys:
He, the dear Sovereign of my breast,
    Shall still command my voice.

Some of the fairest choirs above
    Shall flock around my song,
With joy to hear the name they love
    Sound from a mortal tongue.

His charms shall make my numbers flow,
    And hold the falling floods,
While silence sits on every bough,
    And bends the listening woods.

I'll carve our passion on the bark,
    And every wounded tree
Shall drop and bear some mystic mark
    That Jesus died for me.

The swains shall wonder when they read,
    Inscribed on all the grove,
That Heaven itself came down, and bled
    To win a mortal's love.

JOHN GAY

1685–1732

394   *Over the Hills and Far Away*

Macheath. Were I laid on Greenland's coast,
           And in my arms embraced my lass,
           Warm amidst eternal frost,
           Too soon the half-year's night would pass.
Polly.   Were I sold on Indian soil,
           Soon as the burning day was closed,
           I could mock the sultry toil
           When on my charmer's breast reposed.
Macheath. And I would love you all the day,
Polly.   Every night would kiss and play,
Macheath. If with me you'd fondly stray
Polly.   Over the hills and far away.

395   *Youth and Love*

YOUTH's the season made for joys,
      Love is then our duty,
She alone who that employs,
      Well deserves her beauty.
        Let's be gay,
        While we may,
Beauty's a flower despised in decay.
Chorus. Youth's the season, etc.

Let us drink and sport today,
      Ours is not to-morrow.
Love with Youth flies swift away,
      Age is nought but sorrow.
        Dance and sing,
        Time's on the wing.
Life never knows the return of spring.
Chorus. Let us drink, etc.

396 *Song*

O RUDDIER than the cherry,
O sweeter than the berry,
O Nymph more bright
Than moonshine night,
Like kidlings blithe and merry.
Ripe as the melting cluster,
No lily has such lustre,
Yet hard to tame,
As raging flame,
And fierce as storms that bluster.

ALEXANDER POPE

1688–1744

397 *Sylvan Delights*

SEE what delights in sylvan scenes appear!
Descending Gods have found Elysium here.
In woods bright Venus with Adonis strayed,
And chaste Diana haunts the forest-shade.
Come, lovely nymph, and bless the silent hours,
When swains from shearing seek their nightly bowers;
When weary reapers quit the sultry field,
And crowned with corn, their thanks to Ceres yield,
This harmless grove no lurking viper hides,
But in my breast the serpent Love abides.
Here bees from blossoms sip the rosy dew,
But your Alexis knows no sweets but you.
Oh deign to visit our forsaken seats,
The mossy fountains, and the green retreats!
Where'er you walk, cool gales shall fan the glade,
Trees, where you sit, shall crowd into a shade:
Where'er you tread, the blushing flowers shall rise,
And all things flourish where you turn your eyes.

398   *A Little Learning*

A LITTLE learning is a dangerous thing;
Drink deep, or taste not the Pierian spring:
There shallow draughts intoxicate the brain,
And drinking largely sobers us again.
Fired at first sight with what the Muse imparts,
In fearless youth we tempt the heights of Arts;
While from the bounded level of our mind
Short views we take, nor see the lengths behind,
But, more advanced, behold with strange surprise
New distant scenes of endless science rise!
So pleased at first the towering Alps we try,
Mount o'er the vales, and seem to tread the sky;
The eternal snows appear already past,
And the first clouds and mountains seem the last:
But those attained, we tremble to survey
The growing labours of the lengthened way;
The increasing prospect tires our wandering eyes,
Hills peep o'er hills, and Alps on Alps arise!

from The Rape of the Lock

(i)

399   *The Toilet*

AND now, unveiled, the Toilet stands displayed,
Each silver vase in mystic order laid.
First, robed in white, the Nymph intent adores,
With head uncovered, the Cosmetic powers.
A heavenly Image in the glass appears,
To that she bends, to that her eyes she rears;
The inferior Priestess, at her altar's side,
Trembling, begins the sacred rites of Pride.
Unnumbered treasures ope at once, and here
The various offerings of the world appear;
From each she nicely culls with curious toil,
And decks the Goddess with the glittering spoil.
This casket India's glowing gems unlocks,
And all Arabia breathes from yonder box.

The tortoise here and elephant unite,
Transformed to combs, the speckled and the white.
Here files of pins extend their shining rows,
Puffs, powders, patches, Bibles, billet-doux.
Now awful Beauty puts on all its arms;
The fair each moment rises in her charms,
Repairs her smiles, awakens every grace,
And calls forth all the wonders of her face;
Sees by degrees a purer blush arise,
And keener lightnings quicken in her eyes.
The busy sylphs surround their darling care,
These set the head, and those divide the hair,
Some fold the sleeve, whilst others plait the gown;
And Betty's praised for labours not her own.

(ii)

400   *The Voyage on the Thames*

NOT with more glories, in the ethereal plain,
The Sun first rises o'er the purpled main,
Than, issuing forth, the rival of his beams
Launched on the bosom of the silver Thames.
Fair nymphs and well-dressed youths around her shone,
But every eye was fixed on her alone.
On her white breast a sparkling cross she wore,
Which Jews might kiss, and Infidels adore.
Her lively looks a sprightly mind disclose,
Quick as her eyes, and as unfixed as those:
Favours to none, to all she smiles extends;
Oft she rejects, but never once offends.
Bright as the sun, her eyes the gazers strike,
And, like the sun, they shine on all alike,
Yet graceful ease, and sweetness void of pride,
Might hide her faults, if Belles had faults to hide:
If to her share some female errors fall,
Look on her face, and you'll forget 'em all.

*

But now secure the painted vessel glides,
The sun-beams trembling on the floating tides;
While melting music steals upon the sky,
And softened sounds along the waters die;

Smooth flow the waves, the Zephyrs gently play,
Belinda smiled, and all the world was gay.
All but the Sylph,—with careful thoughts oppressed,
The impending woe sat heavy on his breast.
He summons straight his denizens of air;
The lucid squadrons round the sails repair:
Soft o'er the shrouds aerial whispers breathe,
That seemed but Zephyrs to the train beneath.
Some to the sun their insect-wings unfold,
Waft on the breeze, or sink in clouds of gold;
Transparent forms, too fine for mortal sight,
Their fluid bodies half dissolved in light.
Loose to the wind their airy garments flew,
Thin glittering textures of the filmy dew,
Dipped in the richest tincture of the skies,
Where light disports in ever-mingling dyes,
While every beam new transient colours flings,
Colours that change whene'er they wave their wings.

401

An Epistle
To Miss Blount, On her Leaving the Town
after the Coronation

As some fond virgin, whom her mother's care
Drags from the town to wholesome country air,
Just when she learns to roll a melting eye,
And hear a spark, yet think no danger nigh;
From the dear man unwilling she must sever,
Yet takes one kiss before she parts forever:
Thus from the world fair Zephalinda flew,
Saw others happy, and with sighs withdrew;
Not that their pleasures caused her discontent,
She sighed not that *They* stayed, but that *She* went.
She went, to plain-work, and to purling brooks,
Old-fashioned halls, dull aunts, and croaking rooks:
She went from opera, park, assembly, play,
To morning-walks, and prayers three hours a day,
To part her time 'twixt reading and Bohea,
To muse, and spill her solitary tea,
Or o'er cold coffee trifle with the spoon;
Count the slow clock, and dine exact at noon,

Divert her eyes with pictures in the fire,
Hum half a tune, tell stories to the squire;
Up to her godly garret after seven,
There starve and pray, for that's the way to heaven.
    Some Squire, perhaps, you take delight to rack;
Whose game is Whisk, whose treat a toast in sack;
Who visits with a gun, presents you birds,
Then gives a smacking buss, and cries, 'No words!'
Or with his hound comes hallowing from the stable,
Makes love with nods, and knees beneath a table;
Whose laughs are hearty, though his jests are coarse,
And loves you best of all things—but his horse.
    In some fair evening, on your elbow laid,
You dream of triumphs in the rural shade;
In pensive thought recall the fancied scene,
See Coronations rise on every green;
Before you pass the imaginary sights
Of Lords, and Earls, and Dukes, and gartered Knights,
While the spread fan o'ershades your closing eyes;
Then give one flirt, and all the vision flies.
Thus vanish sceptres, coronets, and balls,
And leave you in lone woods, or empty walls!
    So when your slave, at some dear idle time,
(Not plagued with head-aches, or the want of rhyme)
Stands in the streets, abstracted from the crew,
And while he seems to study, thinks of you;
Just when his fancy points your sprightly eyes,
Or sees the blush of Parthenissa rise,
Gay pats my shoulder, and you vanish quite,
Streets, chairs, and coxcombs rush upon my sight;
Vexed to be still in town, I knit my brow,
Look sour, and hum a tune, as you may now.

402   *Elegy to the Memory of an Unfortunate Lady*

    WHAT beckoning ghost, along the moonlight shade
Invites my step, and points to yonder glade?
'Tis she!—But why that bleeding bosom gored,
Why dimly gleams the visionary sword?
Oh, ever beauteous, ever friendly! tell,
Is it, in Heaven, a crime to love too well?

To bear too tender, or too firm a heart,
To act a Lover's or a Roman's part?
Is there no bright reversion in the sky
For those who greatly think, or bravely die?

Why bade ye else, ye Powers, her soul aspire
Above the vulgar flight of low desire?
Ambition first sprung from your blest abodes,
The glorious fault of angels and of gods;
Thence to their images on earth it flows,
And in the breasts of kings and heroes glows.
Most souls, 'tis true, but peep out once an age,
Dull sullen prisoners in the body's cage:
Dim lights of life, that burn a length of years
Useless, unseen, as lamps in sepulchres;
Like Eastern kings a lazy state they keep,
And close confined in their own palace sleep.

From these perhaps (ere Nature bade her die)
Fate snatched her early to the pitying sky.
As into air the purer spirits flow,
And separate from their kindred dregs below;
So flew the soul to its congenial place,
Nor left one virtue to redeem her race.

But thou, false guardian of a charge too good,
Thou, mean deserter of thy brother's blood!
See on these ruby lips the trembling breath,
These cheeks, now fading at the blast of death;
Cold is that breast which warmed the world before,
And those love-darting eyes must roll no more.
Thus, if eternal justice rules the ball,
Thus shall your wives, and thus your children fall:
On all the line a sudden vengeance waits,
And frequent hearses shall besiege your gates.
These passengers shall stand, and pointing say
(While the long funerals blacken all the way)
'Lo! these were they, whose souls the Furies steeled
And cursed with hearts unknowing how to yield.'
Thus unlamented pass the proud away,
The gaze of fools, and pageant of a day!
So perish all whose breast ne'er learned to glow
For others' good, or melt at others' woe.

What can atone (Oh ever-injured shade!)
Thy fate unpitied, and thy rites unpaid?

No friend's complaint, no kind domestic tear
Pleased thy pale ghost, or graced thy mournful bier.
By foreign hands thy dying eyes were closed,
By foreign hands thy decent limbs composed,
By foreign hands thy humble grave adorned,
By strangers honoured, and by strangers mourned!
What though no friends in sable weeds appear,
Grieve for an hour, perhaps, then mourn a year,
And bear about the mockery of woe
To midnight dances, and the public show?
What though no weeping Loves thy ashes grace,
Nor polished marble emulate thy face?
What though no sacred earth allow thee room,
Nor hallowed dirge be muttered o'er thy tomb?
Yet shall thy grave with rising flowers be dressed,
And the green turf lie lightly on thy breast:
There shall the morn her earliest tears bestow,
There the first roses of the year shall blow;
While angels with their silver wings o'ershade
The ground, now sacred by thy relics made.
    So peaceful rests, without a stone, a name,
What once had beauty, titles, wealth, and fame.
How loved, how honoured once, avails thee not,
To whom related, or by whom begot;
A heap of dust alone remains of thee:
'Tis all thou art, and all the proud shall be!
    Poets themselves must fall, like those they sung;
Deaf the praised ear, and mute the tuneful tongue.
Even he, whose soul now melts in mournful lays,
Shall shortly want the generous tear he pays;
Then from his closing eyes thy form shall part,
And the last pang shall tear thee from his heart;
Life's idle business at one gasp be o'er,
The Muse forgot, and thou beloved no more!

403   *On a Certain Lady at Court*

I KNOW the thing that's most uncommon;
    (Envy, be silent, and attend!)
I know a reasonable woman,
    Handsome and witty, yet a friend.

Not warped by passion, awed by rumour,
    Not grave through pride, or gay through folly,
An equal mixture of good humour,
    And sensible soft melancholy.

'Has she no faults then' (Envy says) 'Sir?'
    Yes, she has one, I must aver;
When all the world conspires to praise her,
    The woman's deaf, and does not hear.

404   *Know Thyself*

KNOW then thyself, presume not God to scan;
The proper study of mankind is Man.
Placed on this isthmus of a middle state,
A being darkly wise and rudely great:
With too much knowledge for the Sceptic side,
With too much weakness for the Stoic's pride,
He hangs between; in doubt to act or rest,
In doubt to deem himself a God or Beast,
In doubt his mind or body to prefer;
Born but to die, and reasoning but to err;
Alike in ignorance, his reason such
Whether he thinks too little or too much:
Chaos of thought and passion, all confused;
Still by himself abused, or disabused;
Created half to rise and half to fall;
Great lord of all things, yet a prey to all;
Sole judge of truth, in endless error hurled:
The glory, jest, and riddle of the world!

405   *The Duke of Buckingham*

IN the worst inn's worst room, with mat half-hung,
The floors of plaster, and the walls of dung,
On once a flock-bed, but repaired with straw,
With tape-tied curtains, never meant to draw,
The George and Garter dangling from that bed
Where tawdry yellow strove with dirty red,
Great Villiers lies—alas, how changed from him,
That life of pleasure, and that soul of whim!

Gallant and gay, in Cliveden's proud alcove,
The bower of wanton Shrewsbury and love;
Or just as gay, at Council, in a ring
Of mimicked statesmen, and their merry King.
No Wit to flatter, left of all his store!
No fool to laugh at, which he valued more.
There, victor of his health, of fortune, friends,
And fame, this lord of useless thousands ends.

Characters

(i)

406   *Atticus*

PEACE to all such! But were there one whose fires
True Genius kindles, and fair Fame inspires;
Blest with each talent and each art to please,
And born to write, converse, and live with ease;
Should such a man, too fond to rule alone,
Bear, like the Turk, no brother near the throne,
View him with scornful, yet with jealous eyes,
And hate for arts that caused himself to rise;
Damn with faint praise, assent with civil leer,
And without sneering, teach the rest to sneer;
Willing to wound, and yet afraid to strike,
Just hint a fault, and hesitate dislike;
Alike reserved to blame, or to commend,
A timorous foe, and a suspicious friend;
Dreading even fools, by flatterers besieged,
And so obliging, that he ne'er obliged;
Like Cato give his little Senate laws,
And sit attentive to his own applause;
While Wits and Templars every sentence raise,
And wonder with a foolish face of praise—
Who but must laugh, if such a man there be?
Who would not weep, if Atticus were he!

(ii)

407

Sporus

LET Sporus tremble—'What? That thing of silk,
Sporus, that mere white curd of ass's milk?
Satire or sense, alas, can Sporus feel,
Who breaks a butterfly upon a wheel?'
   Yet let me flap this bug with gilded wings,
This painted child of dirt, that stinks and stings;
Whose buzz the witty and the fair annoys,
Yet wit ne'er tastes, and beauty ne'er enjoys:
So well-bred spaniels civilly delight
In mumbling of the game they dare not bite.
Eternal smiles his emptiness betray,
As shallow streams run dimpling all the way.
Whether in florid impotence he speaks,
And, as the prompter breathes, the puppet squeaks;
Or at the ear of Eve, familiar Toad,
Half-froth, half-venom, spits himself abroad,
In puns, or politics, or tales, or lies,
Or spite, or smut, or rhymes, or blasphemies.
His wit all see-saw, between that and this,
Now high, now low, now Master up, now Miss,
And he himself one vile antithesis.
Amphibious thing! that acting either part,
The trifling head, or the corrupted heart,
Fop at the toilet, flatterer at the board,
Now trips a lady, and now struts a lord.
Eve's tempter thus the rabbins have exprest,
A cherub's face, a reptile all the rest;
Beauty that shocks you, parts that none will trust,
Wit that can creep, and pride that licks the dust.

(iii)

408

Chloe

'YET Chloe sure was formed without a spot'—
Nature in her then erred not, but forgot.
'With every pleasing, every prudent part,
Say, what can Chloe want?'—She wants a heart.

She speaks, behaves, and acts just as she ought;
But never, never, reached one generous thought.
Virtue she finds too painful an endeavour,
Content to dwell in decencies forever.
So very reasonable, so unmoved,
As never yet to love, or to be loved.
She, while her lover pants upon her breast,
Can mark the figures on an Indian chest;
And when she sees her friend in deep despair,
Observes how much a chintz exceeds mohair.
Forbid it Heaven, a favour or a debt
She e'er should cancel—but she may forget.
Safe is your secret still in Chloe's ear;
But none of Chloe's shall you ever hear.
Of all her Dears she never slandered one,
But cares not if a thousand are undone.
Would Chloe know if you're alive or dead?
She bids her footman put it in her head.
Chloe is prudent—would you too be wise?
Then never break your heart when Chloe dies.

409   *Apologia pro Vita Sua*

NOT Fortune's worshipper, nor Fashion's fool,
Not Lucre's madman, nor Ambition's tool,
Not proud, nor servile: be one poet's praise
That, if he pleased, he pleased by manly ways:
That flattery, even to kings, he held a shame,
And thought a lie in verse or prose the same:
That not in Fancy's maze he wandered long,
But stooped to Truth, and moralised his song:
That not for Fame, but Virtue's better end,
He stood the furious foe, the timid friend,
The damning critic, half-approving wit,
The coxcomb hit, or fearing to be hit;
Laughed at the loss of friends he never had,
The dull, the proud, the wicked, and the mad;
The distant threats of vengeance on his head,
The blow unfelt, the tear he never shed,
The tale revived, the lie so oft o'erthrown,
The imputed trash, and dullness not his own,

The morals blackened when the writings 'scape,
The libelled person, and the pictured shape;
Abuse, on all he loved, or loved him, spread,
A friend in exile, or a father dead;
The whisper, that to greatness still too near,
Perhaps yet vibrates on his Sovereign's ear—
Welcome, for thee, fair Virtue, all the past:
For thee, fair Virtue, welcome even the last!

410 *The Triumph of Vice*

VIRTUE may choose the high or low degree,
'Tis just alike to Virtue, and to me;
Dwell in a monk, or light upon a king,
She's still the same, beloved, contented thing.
Vice is undone, if she forgets her birth,
And stoops from Angels to the dregs of Earth:
But 'tis the fall degrades her to a whore;
Let Greatness own her, and she's mean no more:
Her birth, her beauty, crowds and courts confess,
Chaste matrons praise her, and grave bishops bless;
In golden chains the willing world she draws,
And hers the Gospel is, and hers the Laws,
Mounts the tribunal, lifts her scarlet head,
And sees pale Virtue carted in her stead.
Lo! at the wheels of her triumphal car,
Old England's Genius, rough with many a scar,
Dragged in the dust! His arms hang idly round,
His flag inverted trails along the ground!
Our youth, all liveried o'er with foreign gold,
Before her dance: behind her crawl the old!
See thronging millions to the pagod run,
And offer country, parent, wife, or son!
Hear her black trumpet through the land proclaim,
That 'NOT TO BE CORRUPTED IS THE SHAME'.
In soldier, churchman, patriot, man in power,
'Tis avarice all, ambition is no more!
See, all our nobles begging to be slaves!
See, all our fools aspiring to be knaves!
The wit of cheats, the courage of a whore,
Are what ten thousand envy and adore:

All, all look up, with reverential awe,
At crimes that 'scape, or triumph o'er the Law:
While truth, worth, wisdom, daily they decry—
'Nothing is sacred now but villainy.'
   Yet may this verse (if such a verse remain)
Show there was one who held it in disdain.

411   *The Power of Ridicule*

Ask you what provocation I have had?
The strong antipathy of Good to Bad.
When Truth or Virtue an affront endures,
The affront is mine, my friend, and should be yours.
Mine, as a foe professed to false pretence,
Who think a coxcomb's honour like his sense;
Mine, as a friend to every worthy mind;
And mine as man, who feel for all mankind.
   F. You're strangely proud.
                    P. So proud, I am no slave:
So impudent, I own myself no knave:
So odd, my country's ruin makes me grave.
Yes, I am proud; I must be proud to see
Men not afraid of God, afraid of me:
Safe from the Bar, the Pulpit, and the Throne,
Yet touched and shamed by Ridicule alone.
   O sacred weapon! left for Truth's defence,
Sole dread of Folly, Vice, and Insolence!
To all but Heaven-directed hands denied,
The Muse may give thee, but the God must guide;
Reverent I touch thee! but with honest zeal;
To rouse the watchmen of the public weal,
To Virtue's work provoke the tardy Hall,
And goad the Prelate slumbering in his stall.
Ye tinsel Insects! whom a Court maintains,
That counts your beauties only by your stains,
Spin all your cobwebs o'er the eye of day!
The Muse's wing shall brush you all away:
All his Grace preaches, all his Lordship sings,
All that makes Saints of Queens, and Gods of Kings,
All, all but Truth, drops dead-born from the press,
Like the last Gazette, or the last Address.

412   *The Triumph of Dullness*

IN vain, in vain,—the all-composing hour
Resistless falls: the Muse obeys the Power.
She comes! She comes! The sable throne behold
Of Night primaeval, and of Chaos old!
Before her, Fancy's gilded clouds decay,
And all its varying rainbows die away.
Wit shoots in vain its momentary fires,
The meteor drops, and in a flash expires.
As one by one, at dread Medea's strain,
The sickening stars fade off the ethereal plain;
As Argus' eyes by Hermes' wand opprest,
Closed one by one to everlasting rest;
Thus at her felt approach, and secret might,
Art after Art goes out, and all is Night.
See skulking Truth to her old cavern fled,
Mountains of Casuistry heaped o'er her head!
Philosophy, that leaned on Heaven before,
Shrinks to her second cause, and is no more.
Physic of Metaphysic begs defence,
And Metaphysic calls for aid on Sense!
See Mystery to Mathematics fly!
In vain! they gaze, turn giddy, rave and die.
Religion blushing veils her sacred fires,
And unawares Morality expires.
Nor public flame, nor private, dares to shine;
Nor human spark is left, nor glimpse divine!
Lo! thy dread Empire, Chaos, is restored;
Light dies before thy uncreating word:
Thy hand, great Anarch, lets the curtain fall;
And Universal Darkness buries All.

HENRY CAREY

d. 1743

413   *Sally in our Alley*

OF all the girls that are so smart
  There's none like pretty Sally;
She is the darling of my heart,
  And she lives in our alley.
There is no lady in the land
  Is half so sweet as Sally;
She is the darling of my heart,
  And she lives in our alley.

Her father he makes cabbage-nets,
  And through the streets does cry 'em;
Her mother she sells laces long
  To such as please to buy 'em:
But sure such folks could ne'er beget
  So sweet a girl as Sally!
She is the darling of my heart,
  And she lives in our alley.

When she is by, I leave my work,
  I love her so sincerely;
My master comes like any Turk,
  And bangs me most severely:
But let him bang his bellyful,
  I'll bear it all for Sally;
She is the darling of my heart,
  And she lives in our alley.

Of all the days that's in the week
  I dearly love but one day—
And that's the day that comes betwixt
  A Saturday and Monday;
For then I'm drest all in my best
  To walk abroad with Sally;
She is the darling of my heart,
  And she lives in our alley.

My master carries me to church,
  And often am I blamed
Because I leave him in the lurch
  As soon as text is named;
I leave the church in sermon-time
  And slink away to Sally;
She is the darling of my heart,
  And she lives in our alley.

When Christmas comes about again,
  O, then I shall have money;
I'll hoard it up, and box and all
  I'll give it to my honey:
And would it were ten thousand pounds,
  I'd give it all to Sally,
She is the darling of my heart,
  And she lives in our alley.

My master and the neighbours all,
  Make game of me and Sally,
And, but for her, I'd better be
  A slave and row a galley;
But when my seven long years are out,
  O, then I'll marry Sally;
O, then we'll wed, and then we'll bed—
  But not in our alley!

ANONYMOUS

414   *The Vicar of Bray*

In good King Charles's golden days,
  When loyalty no harm meant;
A furious High-Church man I was,
  And so I gained preferment.
Unto my flock I daily preached,
  'Kings are by God appointed,
And damned are those who dare resist,
  Or touch the Lord's Anointed.'

And this is Law, I will maintain
　　Unto my dying day, Sir,
That whatsoever King shall reign,
　　I will be Vicar of Bray, Sir!

When royal James possessed the Crown,
　　And Popery grew in fashion,
The Penal Law I hooted down,
　　And read the Declaration:
The Church of Rome I found would fit
　　Full well my constitution,
And I had been a Jesuit
　　But for the Revolution.
　　　　And this is Law, etc.

When William our Deliverer came
　　To heal the Nation's grievance,
I turned the cat in pan again,
　　And swore to him allegiance:
Old principles I did revoke,
　　Set Conscience at a distance,
Passive Obedience is a joke,
　　A jest is Non-Resistance.
　　　　And this is Law, etc.

When glorious Anne became our Queen,
　　The Church of England's glory,
Another face of things was seen,
　　And I became a Tory:
Occasional Conformists base
　　I damned, and Moderation,
And thought the Church in danger was
　　From such prevarication.
　　　　And this is Law, etc.

When George in pudding time came o'er,
　　And moderate men looked big, Sir,
My principles I changed once more,
　　And so became a Whig, Sir:
And thus preferment I procured
　　From our Faith's Great Defender,
And almost every day abjured
　　The Pope and the Pretender.
　　　　And this is Law, etc.

426

The illustrious House of Hanover,
  And Protestant Succession,
To these I lustily will swear,
  Whilst they can keep possession:
For in my Faith and Loyalty
  I never once will falter,
But George my lawful King shall be,
  Except the times should alter.
    And this is Law, etc.

JOHN BYROM

1692–1763

415   *My Spirit Longeth for Thee*

MY spirit longeth for thee
  Within my troubled breast,
Although I be unworthy
  Of so divine a guest.

Of so divine a guest
  Unworthy though I be,
Yet has my heart no rest
  Unless it come from thee.

Unless it come from thee,
  In vain I look around;
In all that I can see,
  No rest is to be found.

No rest is to be found
  But in thy blessed Love;
O! let my wish be crowned,
  And send it from above!

JAMES THOMSON
1700–1748

416 *A Winter Night*

WITH the fierce rage of winter deep suffused,
An icy gale, oft shifting, o'er the pool
Breathes a blue film, and in its mid-career
Arrests the bickering stream. The loosened ice,
Let down the flood, and half dissolved by day,
Rustles no more; but to the sedgy bank
Fast grows, or gathers round the pointed stone,
A crystal pavement, by the breath of Heaven
Cemented firm; till, seized from shore to shore,
The whole imprisoned river growls below.
Loud rings the frozen earth, and hard reflects
A double noise; while at his evening watch
The village dog deters the nightly thief;
The heifer lows; the distant water-fall
Swells in the breeze; and, with the hasty tread
Of traveller, the hollow-sounding plain
Shakes from afar. The full ethereal round,
Infinite worlds disclosing to the view,
Shines out intensely keen; and, all one cope
Of starry glitter, glows from Pole to Pole.
From Pole to Pole the rigid influence falls
Through the still night, incessant, heavy, strong,
And seizes Nature fast. It freezes on;
Till morn, late-rising o'er the drooping world,
Lifts her pale eye unjoyous.

417 *Spring Flowers*

ALONG the blushing borders bright with dew,
And in yon mingled wilderness of flowers,
Fair-handed Spring unbosoms every grace:
Throws out the snow-drop and the crocus first;
The daisy, primrose, violet darkly blue,

And polyanthus of unnumbered dyes;
The yellow wall-flower, stained with iron brown,
And lavish stock that scents the garden round:
From the soft wing of vernal breezes shed,
Anemonies; auriculas, enriched
With shining meal o'er all their velvet leaves;
And full ranunculas, of glowing red.
Then comes the tulip-race, where Beauty plays
Her idle freaks: from family diffused
To family, as flies the father-dust,
The varied colours run; and while they break
On the charmed eye, the exulting florist marks,
With secret pride, the wonders of his hand.
No gradual bloom is wanting; from the bud,
First-born of Spring, to Summer's musky tribes:
Nor hyacinths, deep-purpled; nor jonquils,
Of potent fragrance; nor narcissus fair,
As o'er the fabled fountain hanging still;
Nor broad carnations, nor gay-spotted pinks;
Nor, showered from every bush, the damask-rose:
Infinite numbers, delicacies, smells,
With hues on hues expression cannot paint,
The breath of Nature, and her endless bloom.

418   *The Autumnal Moon*

THE western sun withdraws the shortened day,
And humid evening, gliding o'er the sky
In her chill progress, to the ground condensed
The vapours throws. Where creeping waters ooze,
Where marshes stagnate, and where rivers wind,
Cluster the rolling fogs, and swim along
The dusky-mantled lawn. Meanwhile the moon
Full-orbed, and breaking through the scattered clouds,
Shews her broad visage in the crimsoned east.
Turned to the sun direct, her spotted disc,
(Where mountains rise, umbrageous dales descend,
And oceans roll, as optic tube descries)
A smaller earth, gives all its blaze again,
Void of its flame, and sheds a softer day.
Now through the passing cloud she seems to stoop,

Now up the pure cerulean rides sublime.
Wide the pale deluge floats, and streaming mild
O'er the skied mountain to the shadowy vale,
While rocks and floods reflect the quivering gleam,
The whole air whitens with a boundless tide
Of silver radiance, trembling round the world.

CHARLES WESLEY

1707–1788

419   *Wrestling Jacob*

COME, O thou Traveller unknown,
   Whom still I hold, but cannot see,
My company before is gone,
   And I am left alone with thee,
With thee all night I mean to stay,
And wrestle till the break of day.

I need not tell thee who I am,
   My misery, or sin declare,
Thyself hast called me by my name,
   Look on thy hands, and read it there,
But who, I ask thee, who art thou?
Tell me thy name, and tell me now.

In vain thou strugglest to get free,
   I never will unloose my hold:
Art thou the Man that died for me?
   The secret of thy love unfold.
Wrestling I will not let thee go,
Till I thy name, thy nature know.

Wilt thou not yet to me reveal
   Thy new, unutterable name?
Tell me, I still beseech thee, tell;
   To know it now resolved I am.
Wrestling I will not let thee go,
Till I thy name, thy nature know.

'Tis all in vain to hold thy tongue,
   Or touch the hollow of my thigh:
Though every sinew be unstrung,
   Out of my arms thou shalt not fly.
Wrestling I will not let thee go,
Till I thy name, thy nature know.

What though my shrinking flesh complain,
   And murmur to contend so long,
I rise superior to my pain,
   When I am weak then I am strong,
And when my all of strength shall fail,
I shall with the God-Man prevail.

My strength is gone, my nature dies,
   I sink beneath thy weighty hand,
Faint to revive, and fall to rise;
   I fall, and yet by faith I stand,
I stand, and will not let thee go,
Till I thy name, thy nature know.

Yield to me now—for I am weak;
   But confident in self-despair:
Speak to my heart, in blessings speak,
   Be conquered by my instant prayer,
Speak, or thou never hence shalt move,
And tell me, if thy name is Love.

'Tis Love, 'tis Love! Thou died'st for me,
   I hear thy whisper in my heart.
The morning breaks, the shadows flee:
   Pure Universal Love thou art;
To me, to all, thy bowels move,
Thy nature and thy name is Love.

My prayer hath power with God; the Grace
   Unspeakable I now receive,
Through Faith I see thee face to face,
   I see thee face to face, and live:
In vain I have not wept, and strove,
Thy nature and thy name is Love.

I know thee, Saviour, who thou art,
   Jesus, the feeble sinner's friend;
Nor wilt thou with the night depart,
   But stay, and love me to the end;
Thy mercies never shall remove,
Thy nature and thy name is Love.

The Sun of Righteousness on me
   Hath rose with healing in his wings,
Withered my nature's strength; from thee
   My soul its life and succour brings,
My help is all laid up above;
Thy nature and thy name is Love.

Contented now upon my thigh
   I halt, till life's short journey end;
All helplessness, all weakness I,
   On thee alone for strength depend,
Nor have I power, from thee, to move;
Thy nature and thy name is Love.

Lame as I am, I take the prey,
   Hell, earth, and sin with ease o'ercome;
I leap for joy, pursue my way,
   And as a bounding hart fly home,
Through all eternity to prove
Thy nature and thy name is Love.

SAMUEL JOHNSON

1709–1784

420   *The Scholar's Life*

WHEN first the college rolls receive his name,
The young enthusiast quits his ease for fame;
Through all his veins the fever of renown
Burns from the strong contagion of the gown;
O'er Bodley's dome his future labours spread,
And Bacon's mansion trembles o'er his head.

Are these thy views? Proceed, illustrious youth,
And Virtue guard thee to the throne of Truth!
Yet should thy soul indulge the generous heat,
Till captive Science yields her last retreat;
Should Reason guide thee with her brightest ray,
And pour on misty Doubt resistless day;
Should no false Kindness lure to loose delight,
Nor Praise relax, nor Difficulty fright;
Should tempting Novelty thy cell refrain,
And Sloth effuse her opiate fumes in vain;
Should Beauty blunt on fops her fatal dart,
Nor claim the triumph of a lettered heart;
Should no Disease thy torpid veins invade,
Nor Melancholy's phantoms haunt thy shade;
Yet hope not life from grief or danger free,
Nor think the doom of man reversed for thee:
Deign on the passing world to turn thine eyes,
And pause awhile from letters, to be wise;
There mark what ills the scholar's life assail,
Toil, envy, want, the patron, and the jail.
See nations slowly wise, and meanly just,
To buried merit raise the tardy bust.
If dreams yet flatter, once again attend,
Hear Lydiat's life, and Galileo's end.

421   *Charles XII of Sweden*

On what foundation stands the warrior's pride,
How just his hopes let Swedish Charles decide;
A frame of adamant, a soul of fire,
No dangers fright him, and no labours tire;
O'er love, o'er fear, extends his wide domain,
Unconquered lord of pleasure and of pain;
No joys to him pacific sceptres yield,
War sounds the trump, he rushes to the field;
Behold surrounding kings their power combine,
And one capitulate, and one resign;
Peace courts his hand, but spreads her charms in vain;
'Think nothing gained,' he cries, 'till nought remain,
On Moscow's walls till Gothic standards fly,
And all be mine beneath the polar sky.'

The march begins in military state,
And nations on his eye suspended wait;
Stern Famine guards the solitary coast,
And Winter barricades the realms of Frost;
He comes, not want and cold his course delay;—
Hide, blushing Glory, hide Pultowa's day:
The vanquished hero leaves his broken bands,
And shows his miseries in distant lands;
Condemned a needy supplicant to wait,
While ladies interpose, and slaves debate.
But did not Chance at length her error mend?
Did no subverted empire mark his end?
Did rival monarchs give the fatal wound?
Or hostile millions press him to the ground?
His fall was destined to a barren strand,
A petty fortress, and a dubious hand;
He left the name, at which the world grew pale,
To point a moral, or adorn a tale.

422   *The Power of Prayer*

WHERE then shall Hope and Fear their objects find?
Must dull Suspence corrupt the stagnant mind?
Must helpless man, in ignorance sedate,
Roll darkling down the torrent of his fate?
Must no dislike alarm, no wishes rise,
No cries attempt the mercies of the skies?
Enquirer, cease, petitions yet remain,
Which heaven may hear, nor deem religion vain.
Still raise for good the supplicating voice,
But leave to heaven the measure and the choice,
Safe in his power, whose eyes discern afar
The secret ambush of a specious prayer.
Implore his aid, in his decisions rest,
Secure whate'er he gives, he gives the best.
Yet when the sense of sacred presence fires,
And strong devotion to the skies aspires,
Pour forth thy fervours for a healthful mind,
Obedient passions, and a will resigned;
For love, which scarce collective man can fill;
For patience, sovereign o'er transmuted ill;

For faith, that panting for a happier seat,
Counts death kind Nature's signal of retreat:
These goods for man the laws of heaven ordain,
These goods he grants, who grants the power to gain;
With these celestial wisdom calms the mind,
And makes the happiness she does not find.

423   *A Short Song of Congratulation*

LONG-EXPECTED one-and-twenty,
Lingering year at last is flown:
Pomp and pleasure, pride and plenty,
Great Sir John, are all your own.

Loosened from the minor's tether,
Free to mortgage or to sell,
Wild as wind, and light as feather,
Bid the slaves of thrift farewell.

Call the Betties, Kates, and Jennies,
Every name that laughs at care;
Lavish of your grandsire's guineas,
Show the spirit of an heir.

All that prey on vice and folly
Joy to see their quarry fly;
Here the gamester light and jolly,
There the lender grave and sly.

Wealth, Sir John, was made to wander,
Let it wander as it will;
See the jockey, see the pander,
Bid them come and take their fill.

When the bonny blade carouses,
Pockets full, and spirits high,
What are acres? What are houses?
Only dirt, or wet or dry.

If the guardian or the mother
Tell the woes of wilful waste,
Scorn their counsel, scorn their pother:
You can hang or drown at last!

424　　　　*On the Death of Mr. Robert Levet*
　　　　　　　A Practiser in Physic

CONDEMNED to Hope's delusive mine,
　　As on we toil from day to day,
By sudden blasts or slow decline
　　Our social comforts drop away.

Well tried through many a varying year,
　　See Levet to the grave descend;
Officious, innocent, sincere,
　　Of every friendless name the friend.

Yet still he fills affection's eye,
　　Obscurely wise and coarsely kind;
Nor, lettered Arrogance, deny
　　Thy praise to merit unrefined.

When fainting nature called for aid,
　　And hovering death prepared the blow,
His vigorous remedy displayed
　　The power of art without the show.

In Misery's darkest cavern known,
　　His useful care was ever nigh,
Where hopeless Anguish poured his groan,
　　And lonely Want retired to die.

No summons mocked by chill delay,
　　No petty gain disdained by pride;
The modest wants of every day
　　The toil of every day supplied.

His virtues walked their narrow round,
　　Nor made a pause, nor left a void;
And sure the Eternal Master found
　　The single talent well employed.

The busy day, the peaceful night,
　　Unfelt, uncounted, glided by;
His frame was firm—his powers were bright,
　　Though now his eightieth year was nigh.

Then with no fiery throbbing pain,
  No cold gradations of decay,
Death broke at once the vital chain,
  And freed his soul the nearest way.

WILLIAM SHENSTONE

1714–1763

425   *Written at an Inn at Henley*

To thee, fair freedom! I retire
  From flattery, cards, and dice, and din:
Nor art thou found in mansions higher
  Than the low cot, or humble inn.

'Tis here with boundless power I reign;
  And every health which I begin
Converts dull port to bright champagne,
  Such freedom crowns it, at an inn.

I fly from pomp, I fly from plate!
  I fly from falsehood's specious grin!
Freedom I love, and form I hate,
  And choose my lodgings at an inn.

Here, waiter! take my sordid ore,
  Which lackeys else might hope to win;
It buys what courts have not in store,
  It buys me freedom, at an inn.

And now once more I shape my way
  Through rain or shine, through thick or thin,
Secure to meet, at close of day,
  With kind reception, at an inn.

Whoe'er has travelled life's dull round,
  Where'er his stages may have been,
May sigh to think he still has found
  The warmest welcome at an inn.

THOMAS GRAY
1716–1771

426   *Ode on a Distant Prospect of Eton College*

YE distant spires, ye antique towers,
That crown the watery glade,
Where grateful Science still adores
Her Henry's holy shade;
And ye that from the stately brow
Of Windsor's heights the expanse below
Of grove, of lawn, of mead survey,
Whose turf, whose shade, whose flowers among
Wanders the hoary Thames along
His silver-winding way.

Ah, happy hills, ah, pleasing shade,
Ah, fields beloved in vain,
Where once my careless childhood strayed,
A stranger yet to pain!
I feel the gales, that from ye blow,
A momentary bliss bestow,
As waving fresh their gladsome wing,
My weary soul they seem to soothe,
And, redolent of joy and youth,
To breathe a second spring.

Say, Father Thames, for thou hast seen
Full many a sprightly race
Disporting on thy margent green
The paths of pleasure trace,
Who foremost now delight to cleave
With pliant arm thy glassy wave?
The captive linnet which enthrall?
What idle progeny succeed
To chase the rolling circle's speed,
Or urge the flying ball?

While some on earnest business bent
Their murmuring labours ply
'Gainst graver hours, that bring constraint
To sweeten liberty:
Some bold adventurers disdain
The limits of their little reign,
And unknown regions dare descry:
Still as they run they look behind,
They hear a voice in every wind,
And snatch a fearful joy.

Gay hope is theirs by fancy fed,
Less pleasing when possessed;
The tear forgot as soon as shed,
The sunshine of the breast:
Theirs buxom health of rosy hue,
Wild wit, invention ever-new,
And lively cheer of vigour born;
The thoughtless day, the easy night,
The spirits pure, the slumbers light,
That fly the approach of morn.

Alas, regardless of their doom,
The little victims play!
No sense have they of ills to come,
Nor care beyond today:
Yet see how all around 'em wait
The ministers of human fate,
And black Misfortune's baleful train!
Ah, show them where in ambush stand
To seize their prey the murtherous band!
Ah, tell them, they are men!

These shall the fury Passions tear,
The vultures of the mind,
Disdainful Anger, pallid Fear,
And Shame that skulks behind;
Or pining Love shall waste their youth,
Or Jealousy with rankling tooth,
That inly gnaws the secret heart,
And Envy wan, and faded Care,
Grim-visaged comfortless Despair,
And Sorrow's piercing dart.

439

Ambition this shall tempt to rise,
Then whirl the wretch from high,
To bitter Scorn a sacrifice,
And grinning Infamy.
The stings of Falsehood those shall try,
And hard Unkindness' altered eye,
That mocks the tear it forced to flow;
And keen Remorse with blood defiled,
And moody Madness laughing wild
Amid severest woe.

Lo, in the vale of years beneath
A grisly troop are seen,
The painful family of Death,
More hideous than their Queen:
This racks the joints, this fires the veins,
That every labouring sinew strains,
Those in the deeper vitals rage:
Lo, Poverty, to fill the band,
That numbs the soul with icy hand,
And slow-consuming Age.

To each his sufferings: all are men,
Condemned alike to groan;
The tender for another's pain,
The unfeeling for his own.
Yet ah! why should they know their fate?
Since sorrow never comes too late,
And happiness too swiftly flies.
Thought would destroy their paradise.
No more; where ignorance is bliss,
'Tis folly to be wise.

427   *On the Death of Richard West*

IN vain to me the smiling mornings shine,
    And reddening Phoebus lifts his golden fire:
The birds in vain their amorous descant join,
    Or cheerful fields resume their green attire:

These ears, alas! for other notes repine,
    A different object do these eyes require.
My lonely anguish melts no heart but mine;
    And in my breast the imperfect joys expire.
Yet morning smiles the busy race to cheer,
    And new-born pleasure brings to happier men;
The fields to all their wonted tribute bear;
    To warm their little loves the birds complain.
I fruitless mourn to him that cannot hear,
    And weep the more because I weep in vain.

428   *Ode on the Death of a Favourite Cat*
           Drowned in a Tub of Gold Fishes

'TWAS on a lofty vase's side,
Where China's gayest art had dyed
    The azure flowers, that blow;
Demurest of the tabby kind,
The pensive Selima reclined,
    Gazed on the lake below.

Her conscious tail her joy declared;
The fair round face, the snowy beard,
    The velvet of her paws,
Her coat that with the tortoise vies,
Her ears of jet and emerald eyes,
    She saw; and purred applause.

Still had she gazed; but 'midst the tide
Two angel forms were seen to glide,
    The Genii of the stream:
Their scaly armour's Tyrian hue
Through richest purple to the view
    Betrayed a golden gleam.

The hapless nymph with wonder saw:
A whisker first and then a claw,
    With many an ardent wish,
She stretched in vain to reach the prize.
What female heart can gold despise?
    What cat's averse to fish?

Presumptuous maid! with looks intent
Again she stretched, again she bent,
    Nor knew the gulf between.
(Malignant Fate sat by and smiled)
The slippery verge her feet beguiled,
    She tumbled headlong in.

Eight times emerging from the flood
She mewed to every watery god,
    Some speedy aid to send.
No dolphin came, no Nereid stirred:
Nor cruel Tom nor Susan heard.
    A favourite has no friend!

From hence, ye beauties, undeceived,
Know, one false step is ne'er retrieved,
    And be with caution bold.
Not all that tempts your wandering eyes
And heedless hearts is lawful prize;
    Nor all that glisters gold.

429

Elegy
Written in a Country Churchyard

THE curfew tolls the knell of parting day,
The lowing herd wind slowly o'er the lea,
The ploughman homeward plods his weary way,
And leaves the world to darkness and to me.

Now fades the glimmering landscape on the sight,
And all the air a solemn stillness holds,
Save where the beetle wheels his droning flight,
And drowsy tinklings lull the distant folds;

Save that from yonder ivy-mantled tower
The moping owl does to the moon complain
Of such as, wandering near her secret bower,
Molest her ancient solitary reign.

Beneath those rugged elms, that yew-tree's shade,
Where heaves the turf in many a mouldering heap,
Each in his narrow cell for ever laid,
The rude forefathers of the hamlet sleep.

The breezy call of incense-breathing morn,
The swallow twittering from the straw-built shed,
The cock's shrill clarion or the echoing horn,
No more shall rouse them from their lowly bed.

For them no more the blazing hearth shall burn,
Or busy housewife ply her evening care:
No children run to lisp their sire's return,
Or climb his knees the envied kiss to share.

Oft did the harvest to their sickle yield,
Their furrow oft the stubborn glebe has broke;
How jocund did they drive their team afield!
How bowed the woods beneath their sturdy stroke!

Let not Ambition mock their useful toil,
Their homely joys and destiny obscure;
Nor Grandeur hear, with a disdainful smile,
The short and simple annals of the poor.

The boast of heraldry, the pomp of power,
And all that beauty, all that wealth e'er gave,
Awaits alike the inevitable hour.
The paths of glory lead but to the grave.

Nor you, ye Proud, impute to these the fault,
If Memory o'er their tomb no trophies raise,
Where through the long-drawn aisle and fretted vault
The pealing anthem swells the note of praise.

Can storied urn or animated bust
Back to its mansion call the fleeting breath?
Can Honour's voice provoke the silent dust,
Or Flattery soothe the dull cold ear of Death?

Perhaps in this neglected spot is laid
Some heart once pregnant with celestial fire;
Hands that the rod of empire might have swayed,
Or waked to ecstasy the living lyre.

But Knowledge to their eyes her ample page
Rich with the spoils of time did ne'er unroll;
Chill Penury repressed their noble rage,
And froze the genial current of the soul.

Full many a gem of purest ray serene
The dark unfathomed caves of ocean bear:
Full many a flower is born to blush unseen,
And waste its sweetness on the desert air.

Some village-Hampden that with dauntless breast
The little tyrant of his fields withstood;
Some mute inglorious Milton here may rest,
Some Cromwell guiltless of his country's blood.

The applause of listening senates to command,
The threats of pain and ruin to despise,
To scatter plenty o'er a smiling land,
And read their history in a nation's eyes,

Their lot forbade: nor circumscribed alone
Their growing virtues, but their crimes confined;
Forbade to wade through slaughter to a throne,
And shut the gates of mercy on mankind,

The struggling pangs of conscious truth to hide,
To quench the blushes of ingenuous shame,
Or heap the shrine of Luxury and Pride
With incense kindled at the Muse's flame.

Far from the madding crowd's ignoble strife
Their sober wishes never learned to stray;
Along the cool sequestered vale of life
They kept the noiseless tenor of their way.

Yet even these bones from insult to protect
Some frail memorial still erected nigh,
With uncouth rhymes and shapeless sculpture decked,
Implores the passing tribute of a sigh.

Their name, their years, spelt by the unlettered muse,
The place of fame and elegy supply:
And many a holy text around she strews,
That teach the rustic moralist to die.

For who to dumb Forgetfulness a prey,
This pleasing anxious being e'er resigned,
Left the warm precincts of the cheerful day,
Nor cast one longing lingering look behind?

On some fond breast the parting soul relies,
Some pious drops the closing eye requires;
Even from the tomb the voice of Nature cries,
Even in our ashes live their wonted fires.

For thee who, mindful of the unhonoured dead,
Dost in these lines their artless tale relate;
If chance, by lonely Contemplation led,
Some kindred spirit shall inquire thy fate,

Haply some hoary-headed swain may say,
'Oft have we seen him at the peep of dawn
Brushing with hasty steps the dews away
To meet the sun upon the upland lawn.

'There at the foot of yonder nodding beech
That wreathes its old fantastic roots so high,
His listless length at noontide would he stretch,
And pore upon the brook that babbles by.

'Hard by yon wood, now smiling as in scorn,
Muttering his wayward fancies he would rove,
Now drooping, woeful wan, like one forlorn,
Or crazed with care, or crossed in hopeless love.

'One morn I missed him on the customed hill,
Along the heath and near his favourite tree;
Another came; nor yet beside the rill,
Nor up the lawn, nor at the wood was he;

'The next with dirges due in sad array
Slow through the church-way path we saw him borne.
Approach and read (for thou canst read) the lay,
Graved on the stone beneath yon aged thorn.'

The Epitaph

Here rests his head upon the lap of earth
A youth to Fortune and to Fame unknown.
Fair Science frowned not on his humble birth,
And Melancholy marked him for her own.

Large was his bounty and his soul sincere,
Heaven did a recompense as largely send:
He gave to Misery all he had, a tear,
He gained from Heaven ('twas all he wished) a friend.

No farther seek his merits to disclose,
Or draw his frailties from their dread abode,
(There they alike in trembling hope repose)
The bosom of his Father and his God.

430 *The Bard*

I. 1

'RUIN seize thee, ruthless king!
Confusion on thy banners wait,
Though fanned by Conquest's crimson wing
They mock the air with idle state.
Helm nor hauberk's twisted mail,
Nor even thy virtues, tyrant, shall avail
To save thy secret soul from nightly fears,
From Cambria's curse, from Cambria's tears!'
Such were the sounds, that o'er the crested pride
Of the first Edward scattered wild dismay,
As down the steep of Snowdon's shaggy side
He wound with toilsome march his long array.
Stout Gloucester stood aghast in speechless trance:
'To arms!' cried Mortimer, and couched his quivering lance.

I. 2

On a rock, whose haughty brow
Frowns o'er old Conway's foaming flood,
Robed in the sable garb of woe,
With haggard eyes the Poet stood;
(Loose his beard and hoary hair
Streamed, like a meteor, to the troubled air)
And, with a master's hand and prophet's fire,
Struck the deep sorrows of his lyre.
'Hark, how each giant-oak and desert cave
Sighs to the torrent's awful voice beneath!
O'er thee, oh King! their hundred arms they wave
Revenge on thee in hoarser murmurs breathe;
Vocal no more, since Cambria's fatal day,
To high-born Hoel's harp or soft Llewellyn's lay.

I. 3

'Cold is Cadwallo's tongue,
That hushed the stormy main:
Brave Urien sleeps upon his craggy bed:
Mountains, ye mourn in vain
Modred, whose magic song
Made huge Plinlimmon bow his cloud-topped head.
On dreary Arvon's shore they lie,
Smeared with gore and ghastly pale:
Far, far aloof the affrighted ravens sail;
The famished eagle screams and passes by.
Dear lost companions of my tuneful art,
Dear as the light that visits these sad eyes,
Dear as the ruddy drops that warm my heart,
Ye died amidst your dying country's cries—
No more I weep. They do not sleep.
On yonder cliffs, a grisly band,
I see them sit, they linger yet,
Avengers of their native land;
With me in dreadful harmony they join,
And weave with bloody hands the tissue of thy line.

II. 1

' "Weave the warp and weave the woof,
The winding-sheet of Edward's race.
Give ample room and verge enough
The characters of hell to trace.
Mark the year and mark the night,
When Severn shall re-echo with affright
The shrieks of death, through Berkeley's roofs that ring,
Shrieks of an agonizing King!
She-wolf of France, with unrelenting fangs,
That tear'st the bowels of thy mangled mate,
From thee be born who o'er thy country hangs
The scourge of Heaven. What terrors round him wait!
Amazement in his van, with Flight combined,
And Sorrow's faded form, and Solitude behind.

II. 2

' "Mighty Victor, mighty Lord,
Low on his funeral couch he lies!
No pitying heart, no eye, afford
A tear to grace his obsequies.
Is the sable warrior fled?
Thy son is gone. He rests among the dead.
The swarm that in thy noon-tide beam were born?
Gone to salute the rising morn.
Fair laughs the morn and soft the zephyr blows,
While proudly riding o'er the azure realm
In gallant trim the gilded vessel goes;
Youth on the prow and Pleasure at the helm;
Regardless of the sweeping whirlwind's sway,
That, hushed in grim repose, expects his evening-prey.

II. 3

' "Fill high the sparkling bowl,
The rich repast prepare,
Reft of a crown, he yet may share the feast:
Close by the regal chair
Fell Thirst and Famine scowl
A baleful smile upon their baffled guest.
Heard ye the din of battle bray,
Lance to lance and horse to horse?
Long years of havoc urge their destined course,
And through the kindred squadrons mow their way.
Ye Towers of Julius, London's lasting shame,
With many a foul and midnight murther fed,
Revere his consort's faith, his father's fame,
And spare the meek usurper's holy head.
Above, below, the rose of snow,
Twined with her blushing foe, we spread:
The bristled Boar in infant-gore
Wallows beneath the thorny shade.
Now, brothers, bending o'er the accursed loom,
Stamp we our vengeance deep and ratify his doom.

III. 1

' "Edward, lo! to sudden fate
(Weave we the woof. The thread is spun.)
Half of thy heart we consecrate.
(The web is wove. The work is done.)"
Stay, oh stay! nor thus forlorn
Leave me unblessed, unpitied, here to mourn:
In yon bright track, that fires the western skies,
They melt, they vanish from my eyes.
But oh! what solemn scenes on Snowdon's height
Descending slow their glittering skirts unroll?
Visions of glory, spare my aching sight,
Ye unborn ages, crowd not on my soul!
No more our long-lost Arthur we bewail.
All-hail, ye genuine kings, Britannia's issue, hail!

III. 2

'Girt with many a baron bold
Sublime their starry fronts they rear;
And gorgeous dames, and statesmen old
In bearded majesty, appear.
In the midst a form divine!
Her eye proclaims her of the Briton-line;
Her lion-port, her awe-commanding face,
Attempered sweet to virgin-grace.
What strings symphonious tremble in the air,
What strains of vocal transport round her play!
Hear from the grave, great Taliessin, hear;
They breathe a soul to animate thy clay.
Bright Rapture calls and, soaring as she sings,
Waves in the eye of heaven her many-coloured wings.

III. 3

'The verse adorn again
Fierce war and faithful love,
And truth severe, by fairy fiction dressed.
In buskined measures move
Pale Grief and pleasing Pain,
With Horror, tyrant of the throbbing breast.

A voice as of the cherub-choir
Gales from blooming Eden bear;
And distant warblings lessen on my ear,
That lost in long futurity expire.
Fond impious man, think'st thou yon sanguine cloud,
Raised by thy breath, has quenched the orb of day?
Tomorrow he repairs the golden flood,
And warms the nations with redoubled ray.
Enough for me: with joy I see
The different doom our fates assign.
Be thine despair and sceptred care;
To triumph, and to die, are mine.'
He spoke, and headlong from the mountain's height
Deep in the roaring tide he plunged to endless night.

WILLIAM COLLINS

1721–1759

431   *Ode to Simplicity*

O THOU by Nature taught
To breathe her genuine thought,
In numbers warmly pure and sweetly strong:
 Who first on mountains wild
 In Fancy, loveliest child,
Thy babe or Pleasure's, nursed the powers of song!

Thou, who with hermit heart
Disdain'st the wealth of art,
And gauds and pageant weeds and trailing pall:
 But com'st a decent maid
 In Attic robe arrayed,
O chaste unboastful nymph, to thee I call!

By all the honeyed store
On Hybla's thymy shore,
By all her blooms and mingled murmurs dear;
 By her, whose love-lorn woe
 In evening musings slow
Soothed sweetly sad Electra's poet's ear:

By old Cephisus deep,
   Who spread his wavy sweep
In warbled wanderings round thy green retreat,
   On whose enamelled side
   When holy Freedom died
No equal haunt allured thy future feet.

   O sister meek of Truth,
   To my admiring youth
Thy sober aid and native charms infuse!
   The flowers that sweetest breathe,
   Though Beauty culled the wreath,
Still ask thy hand to range their ordered hues.

   While Rome could none esteem
   But Virtue's patriot theme,
You loved her hills and led her laureate band:
   But stayed to sing alone
   To one distinguished throne,
And turned thy face, and fled her altered land.

   No more, in hall or bower,
   The passions own thy power,
Love, only Love, her forceless numbers mean:
   For thou hast left her shrine,
   Nor olive more nor vine
Shall gain thy feet to bless the servile scene.

   Though taste, though genius bless
   To some divine excess,
Faints the cold work till thou inspire the whole;
   What each, what all supply
   May court, may charm our eye,
Thou, only thou canst raise the meeting soul!

   Of these let others ask
   To aid some mighty task:
I only seek to find thy temperate vale,
   Where oft my reed might sound
   To maids and shepherds round,
And all thy sons, O Nature, learn my tale.

432   *How Sleep the Brave*

HOW sleep the brave, who sink to rest
By all their country's wishes blest!
When Spring, with dewy fingers cold,
Returns to deck their hallowed mould,
She there shall dress a sweeter sod
Than Fancy's feet have ever trod.

By fairy hands their knell is rung,
By forms unseen their dirge is sung;
There Honour comes, a pilgrim grey,
To bless the turf that wraps their clay,
And Freedom shall awhile repair
To dwell a weeping hermit there!

433   *Ode to Evening*

IF aught of oaten stop or pastoral song
May hope, chaste Eve, to soothe thy modest ear,
      Like thy own solemn springs,
      Thy springs and dying gales,
O nymph reserved, while now the bright-haired sun
Sits in yon western tent, whose cloudy skirts,
      With brede ethereal wove,
      O'erhang his wavy bed;
Now air is hushed, save where the weak-eyed bat
With short shrill shriek flits by on leathern wing,
      Or where the beetle winds
      His small but sullen horn,
As oft he rises midst the twilight path,
Against the pilgrim borne in heedless hum:
      Now teach me, maid composed,
      To breathe some softened strain,
Whose numbers stealing through thy darkening vale
May not unseemly with its stillness suit;
      As musing slow, I hail
      Thy genial loved return!

For when thy folding star arising shows
His paly circlet, at his warning lamp
    The fragrant Hours, and elves
    Who slept in flowers the day,
And many a nymph who wreathes her brows with sedge,
And sheds the freshening dew, and, lovelier still,
    The Pensive Pleasures sweet,
    Prepare thy shadowy car.
Then lead, calm votaress, where some sheety lake
Cheers the lone heath, or some time-hallowed pile,
    Or upland fallows grey,
    Reflect its last cool gleam.
But when chill blustering winds or driving rain
Forbid my willing feet, be mine the hut
    That from the mountain's side
    Views wilds and swelling floods,
And hamlets brown, and dim-discovered spires,
And hears their simple bell, and marks o'er all
    Thy dewy fingers draw
    The gradual dusky veil.
While Spring shall pour his showers, as oft he wont,
And bathe thy breathing tresses, meekest Eve!
    While Summer loves to sport
    Beneath thy lingering light;
While sallow Autumn fills thy lap with leaves,
Or Winter, yelling through the troublous air,
    Affrights thy shrinking train,
    And rudely rends thy robes;
So long, sure-found beneath the sylvan shed,
Shall Fancy, Friendship, Science, rose-lipped Health,
    Thy gentlest influence own,
    And hymn thy favourite name!

434   *Dirge in Cymbeline*

    To fair Fidele's grassy tomb
      Soft maids and village hinds shall bring
    Each opening sweet of earliest bloom,
      And rifle all the breathing spring.

No wailing ghost shall dare appear
    To vex with shrieks this quiet grove;
But shepherd lads assemble here,
    And melting virgins own their love.

No withered witch shall here be seen,
    No goblins lead their nightly crew;
The female fays shall haunt the green,
    And dress thy grave with pearly dew!

The red-breast oft at evening hours
    Shall kindly lend his little aid:
With hoary moss and gathered flowers,
    To deck the ground where thou art laid.

When howling winds and beating rain
    In tempests shake the sylvan cell,
Or midst the chase on every plain,
    The tender thought on thee shall dwell.

Each lonely scene shall thee restore,
    For thee the tear be duly shed:
Beloved, till life could charm no more,
    And mourned, till Pity's self be dead.

435   *The Stormy Hebrides*

UNBOUNDED is thy range; with varied style
    Thy Muse may, like those feathery tribes which spring
    From their rude rocks, extend her skirting wing
Round the moist marge of each cold Hebrid isle,
To that hoar pile which still its ruin shows:
    In whose small vaults a pigmy-folk is found,
Whose bones the delver with his spade upthrows,
    And culls them, wondering, from the hallowed ground!
Or thither, where beneath the showery west
    The mighty kings of three fair realms are laid;
Once foes, perhaps, together now they rest.
    No slaves revere them and no wars invade:

Yet frequent now, at midnight's solemn hour,
　The rifted mounds their yawning cells unfold,
And forth the monarchs stalk with sovereign power
　In pageant robes, and wreathed with sheeny gold,
And on their twilight tombs aerial council hold.

But O, o'er all, forget not Kilda's race,
　On whose bleak rocks, which brave the wasting tides,
　Fair Nature's daughter, Virtue, yet abides!
Go, just as they, their blameless manners trace!
Then to my ear transmit some gentle song
　Of those whose lives are yet sincere and plain,
Their bounded walks the ragged cliffs along,
　And all their prospect but the wintry main.
With sparing temperance, at the needful time,
　They drain the sainted spring or, hunger-pressed,
Along the Atlantic rock undreading climb,
　And of its eggs despoil the solan's nest.
Thus blest in primal innocence they live,
　Sufficed and happy with that frugal fare
Which tasteful toil and hourly danger give.
　Hard is their shallow soil, and bare;
Nor ever vernal bee was heard to murmur there!

CHRISTOPHER SMART

1722–1771

436　　　　*A Song to David*

O THOU, that sitst upon a throne,
With harp of high majestic tone,
　To praise the King of kings;
And voice of heaven-ascending swell,
Which, while its deeper notes excel,
　Clear, as a clarion, rings:

To bless each valley, grove and coast,
And charm the cherubs to the post
　Of gratitude in throngs;
To keep the days on Zion's mount,
And send the year to his account,
　With dances and with songs:

O Servant of God's holiest charge,
The minister of praise at large,
  Which thou mayst now receive;
From thy blest mansion hail and hear,
From topmost eminence appear
  To this the wreath I weave.

*

O DAVID, highest in the list
Of worthies, on God's ways insist,
  The genuine word repeat:
Vain are the documents of men,
And vain the flourish of the pen
  That keeps the fool's conceit.

PRAISE above all—for praise prevails;
Heap up the measure, load the scales,
  And good to goodness add:
The generous soul her Saviour aids,
But peevish obloquy degrades;
  The Lord is great and glad.

For ADORATION all the ranks
Of angels yield eternal thanks,
  And DAVID in the midst;
With God's good poor, which, last and least
In man's esteem, thou to thy feast,
  O blessed bride-groom, bidst.

For ADORATION seasons change,
And order, truth, and beauty range,
  Adjust, attract, and fill:
The grass the polyanthus cheques;
And polished porphyry reflects,
  By the descending rill.

Rich almonds colour to the prime
For ADORATION; tendrils climb,
  And fruit-trees pledge their gems;
And Ivis with her gorgeous vest
Builds for her eggs her cunning nest,
  And bell-flowers bow their stems.

Ivis] humming bird

With vinous syrup cedars spout;
From rocks pure honey gushing out,
   For ADORATION springs:
All scenes of painting crowd the map
Of nature; to the mermaid's pap
    The scalèd infant clings.

The spotted ounce and playsome cubs
Run rustling 'mongst the flowering shrubs,
   And lizards feed the moss;
For ADORATION beasts embark,
While waves upholding halcyon's ark
    No longer roar and toss.

While Israel sits beneath his fig,
With coral root and amber sprig
   The weaned adventurer sports;
Where to the palm the jasmin cleaves,
For ADORATION 'mongst the leaves
    The gale his peace reports.

Increasing days their reign exalt,
Nor in the pink and mottled vault
   The opposing spirits tilt;
And, by the coasting reader spied,
The silverlings and crusions glide
    For ADORATION gilt.

For ADORATION ripening canes
And cocoa's purest milk detains
   The western pilgrim's staff;
Where rain in clasping boughs inclosed,
And vines with oranges disposed,
    Embower the social laugh.

Now labour his reward receives,
For ADORATION counts his sheaves
   To peace, her bounteous prince;
The nectarine his strong tint imbibes,
And apples of ten thousand tribes,
    And quick peculiar quince.

The wealthy crops of whitening rice,
'Mongst thyine woods and groves of spice,
   For ADORATION grow;
And, marshalled in the fencèd land,
The peaches and pomegranates stand,
   Where wild carnations blow.

The laurels with the winter strive;
The crocus burnishes alive
   Upon the snow-clad earth;
For ADORATION myrtles stay
To keep the garden from dismay,
   And bless the sight from dearth.

The pheasant shows his pompous neck;
And ermine, jealous of a speck,
   With fear eludes offence:
The sable, with his glossy pride,
For ADORATION is descried,
   Where frosts the wave condense.

The cheerful holly, pensive yew,
And holy thorn, their trim renew;
   The squirrel hoards his nuts:
All creatures batten o'er their stores,
And careful nature all her doors
   For ADORATION shuts.

For ADORATION, DAVID's psalms
Lift up the heart to deeds of alms;
   And he, who kneels and chants,
Prevails his passions to control,
Finds meat and medicine to the soul,
   Which for translation pants.

For ADORATION, beyond match,
The scholar bullfinch aims to catch
   The soft flute's ivory touch;
And, careless on the hazel spray,
The daring redbreast keeps at bay
   The damsel's greedy clutch.

For ADORATION, in the skies,
The Lord's philosopher espies
   The Dog, the Ram, and Rose;
The planets ring, Orion's sword;
Nor is his greatness less adored
   In the vile worm that glows.

For ADORATION on the strings
The western breezes work their wings,
   The captive ear to sooth.—
Hark! 'tis a voice—how still, and small—
That makes the cataracts to fall,
   Or bids the sea be smooth.

For ADORATION, incense comes
From bezoar, and Arabian gums;
   And on the civet's fur.
But as for prayer, or ere it faints,
Far better is the breath of saints
   Than galbanum and myrrh.

For ADORATION from the down,
Of damsons to the anana's crown,
   God sends to tempt the taste;
And while the luscious zest invites,
The sense, that in the scene delights,
   Commands desire be chaste.

For ADORATION, all the paths
Of grace are open, all the baths
   Of purity refresh;
And all the rays of glory beam
To deck the man of God's esteem,
   Who triumphs o'er the flesh.

For ADORATION, in the dome
Of Christ the sparrows find an home;
   And on his olives perch:
The swallow also dwells with thee,
O man of God's humility,
   Within his Saviour's CHURCH.

strings] strings of the Æolian harp   anana] pineapple

Sweet is the dew that falls betimes,
And drops upon the leafy limes;
　　Sweet Hermon's fragrant air:
Sweet is the lily's silver bell,
And sweet the wakeful tapers smell
　　That watch for early prayer.

Sweet the young nurse with love intense,
Which smiles o'er sleeping innocence;
　　Sweet when the lost arrive:
Sweet the musician's ardour beats,
While his vague mind's in quest of sweets
　　The choicest flowers to hive.

Sweeter in all the strains of love,
The language of thy turtle dove,
　　Paired to thy swelling chord;
Sweeter with every grace endued,
The glory of thy gratitude,
　　Respired unto the Lord.

Strong is the horse upon his speed;
Strong in pursuit the rapid glede,
　　Which makes at once his game:
Strong the tall ostrich on the ground;
Strong through the turbulent profound
　　Shoots xiphias to his aim.

Strong is the lion—like a coal
His eye-ball—like a bastion's mole
　　His chest against the foes:
Strong, the gier-eagle on his sail,
Strong against tide, the enormous whale
　　Emerges as he goes.

But stronger still, in earth and air,
And in the sea, the man of prayer;
　　And far beneath the tide;
And in the seat to faith assigned,
Where ask is have, where seek is find,
　　Where knock is open wide.

xiphias] the sword-fish

Beauteous the fleet before the gale;
Beauteous the multitudes in mail,
    Ranked arms and crested heads:
Beauteous the garden's umbrage mild,
Walk, water, meditated wild,
    And all the bloomy beds.

Beauteous the moon full on the lawn;
And beauteous, when the veil's withdrawn,
    The virgin to her spouse:
Beauteous the temple decked and filled,
When to the heaven of heavens they build
    Their heart-directed vows.

Beauteous, yea beauteous more than these,
The shepherd king upon his knees,
    For his momentous trust;
With wish of infinite conceit,
For man, beast, mute, the small and great,
    And prostrate dust to dust.

Precious the bounteous widow's mite;
And precious, for extreme delight,
    The largess from the churl:
Precious the ruby's blushing blaze,
And alba's blest imperial rays,
    And pure cerulean pearl.

Precious the penitential tear;
And precious is the sigh sincere,
    Acceptable to God:
And precious are the winning flowers,
In gladsome Israel's feast of bowers,
    Bound on the hallowed sod.

More precious that diviner part
Of David, even the Lord's own heart,
    Great, beautiful, and new:
In all things where it was intent,
In all extremes, in each event,
    Proof—answering true to true.

Glorious the sun in mid career;
Glorious the assembled fires appear;
   Glorious the comet's train:
Glorious the trumpet and alarm;
Glorious the almighty stretched-out arm;
   Glorious the enraptured main:

Glorious the northern lights astream;
Glorious the song, when God's the theme
   Glorious the thunder's roar:
Glorious hosanna from the den;
Glorious the catholic amen;
   Glorious the martyr's gore:

Glorious—more glorious is the crown
Of him that brought salvation down
   By meekness, called thy Son;
Thou that stupendous truth believed,
And now the matchless deed's achieved,
   DETERMINED, DARED, and DONE.

437   *The Nativity of Our Lord and Saviour*

WHERE is this stupendous stranger?
   Swains of Solyma advise,
Lead me to my Master's manger,
   Shew me where my Saviour lies.

O most Mighty! O most Holy!
   Far beyond the seraph's thought,
Art thou then so mean and lowly,
   As unheeded prophets taught?

O the magnitude of meekness!
   Worth from worth immortal sprung;
O the strength of infant weakness,
   If eternal is so young!

If so young and thus eternal,
   Michael tune the shepherd's reed,
Where the scenes are ever vernal.
   And the loves be love indeed!

See the God blasphemed and doubted
    In the schools of Greece and Rome,
See the powers of darkness routed,
    Taken at their utmost gloom.

Nature's decorations glisten
    Far above their usual trim;
Birds on box and laurels listen,
    As so near the cherubs hymn.

Boreas now no longer winters
    On the desolated coast;
Oaks no more are riven in splinters
    By the whirlwind and his host.

Spinks and ouzels sing sublimely
    'We too have a Saviour born';
Whiter blossoms burst untimely
    On the blest Mosaic thorn.

God all-bounteous,,all creative,
    Whom no ills from good dissuade,
Is incarnate and a native
    Of the very world he made.

OLIVER GOLDSMITH

1730–1774

438   *Song*

WHEN lovely woman stoops to folly,
    And finds too late that men betray,
What charm can sooth her melancholy,
    What art can wash her guilt away?

The only art her guilt to cover,
    To hide her shame from every eye,
To give repentance to her lover,
    And wring his bosom—is to die.

439 *Sweet Auburn*

SWEET Auburn, loveliest village of the plain,
Where health and plenty cheered the labouring swain,
Where smiling spring its earliest visit paid,
And parting summer's lingering blooms delayed,
Dear lovely bowers of innocence and ease,
Seats of my youth, when every sport could please,
How often have I loitered o'er thy green,
Where humble happiness endeared each scene!
How often have I paused on every charm,
The sheltered cot, the cultivated farm,
The never failing brook, the busy mill,
The decent church that topped the neighbouring hill,
The hawthorn bush, with seats beneath the shade,
For talking age, and whispering lovers made!
How often have I blest the coming day,
When toil remitting lent its turn to play,
And all the village train from labour free
Led up their sports beneath the spreading tree,
While many a pastime circled in the shade,
The young contending as the old surveyed;
And many a gambol frolicked o'er the ground,
And slights of art and feats of strength went round;
And still as each repeated pleasure tired,
Succeeding sports the mirthful band inspired;
The dancing pair that simply sought renown
By holding out to tire each other down;
The swain mistrustless of his smutted face,
While secret laughter tittered round the place;
The bashful virgin's side-long looks of love,
The matron's glance that would those looks reprove!
These were thy charms, sweet village; sports like these,
With sweet succession taught even toil to please;
These round thy bowers their cheerful influence shed
These were thy charms—but all these charms are fled.
    Sweet smiling village, loveliest of the lawn,
Thy sports are fled, and all thy charms withdrawn;
Amidst thy bowers the tyrant's hand is seen
And desolation saddens all thy green:
One only master grasps the whole domain,
And half a tillage stints thy smiling plain;

No more thy glassy brook reflects the day,
But choked with sedges, works its weedy way;
Along thy glades, a solitary guest,
The hollow sounding bittern guards its nest;
Amidst thy desert walks the lapwing flies,
And tires their echoes with unvaried cries.
Sunk are thy bowers, in shapeless ruin all,
And the long grass o'ertops the mouldering wall;
And trembling, shrinking from the spoiler's hand,
Far, far away thy children leave the land.
   Ill fares the land, to hastening ills a prey,
Where wealth accumulates, and men decay:
Princes and lords may flourish, or may fade;
A breath can make them, as a breath has made;
But a bold peasantry, their country's pride,
When once destroyed, can never be supplied.

THOMAS OSBERT MORDAUNT

1730–1809

440   *Sound, Sound the Clarion*

SOUND, sound the clarion, fill the fife!
   Throughout the sensual world proclaim,
One crowded hour of glorious life
   Is worth an age without a name.

JOHN SCOTT OF AMWELL

1730–1783

441   *The Drum*

I HATE that drum's discordant sound,
Parading round, and round, and round:
To thoughtless youth it pleasure yields,
And lures from cities and from fields,
To sell their liberty for charms
Of tawdry lace, and glittering arms;
And when Ambition's voice commands,
To march, and fight, and fall, in foreign lands.

I hate that drum's discordant sound,
Parading round, and round, and round:
To me it talks of ravaged plains,
And burning towns, and ruined swains,
And mangled limbs, and dying groans,
And widows' tears, and orphans' moans;
And all that Misery's hand bestows.
To fill the catalogue of human woes.

WILLIAM COWPER

1731–1800

442   *Light Shining out of Darkness*

GOD moves in a mysterious way,
  His wonders to perform;
He plants his footsteps in the sea,
  And rides upon the storm.

Deep in unfathomable mines
  Of never failing skill
He treasures up his bright designs,
  And works his sovereign will.

Ye fearful saints, fresh courage take,
  The clouds ye so much dread
Are big with mercy, and shall break
  In blessings on your head.

Judge not the Lord by feeble sense,
  But trust him for his grace;
Behind a frowning providence,
  He hides a smiling face.

His purposes will ripen fast,
  Unfolding every hour;
The bud may have a bitter taste,
  But sweet will be the flower.

Blind unbelief is sure to err,
  And scan his work in vain;
God is his own interpreter,
  And he will make it plain.

443   *The Shrubbery*
      Written in a Time of Affliction

OH, happy shades—to me unblest,
  Friendly to peace, but not to me,
How ill the scene that offers rest,
  And heart that cannot rest, agree!

This glassy stream, that spreading pine,
  Those alders quivering to the breeze,
Might sooth a soul less hurt than mine,
  And please, if any thing could please.

But fixed unalterable care
  Foregoes not what she feels within,
Shows the same sadness everywhere,
  And slights the season and the scene.

For all that pleased in wood or lawn,
  While peace possessed these silent bowers,
Her animating smile withdrawn,
  Has lost its beauties and its powers.

The saint or moralist should tread
  This moss-grown alley, musing, slow;
They seek, like me, the secret shade,
  But not, like me, to nourish woe.

Me fruitful scenes and prospects waste
  Alike admonish not to roam;
These tell me of enjoyments past,
  And those of sorrows yet to come.

444   *On the Loss of the Royal George*

1782

TOLL for the brave—
The brave! that are no more:
  All sunk beneath the wave,
Fast by their native shore.
  Eight hundred of the brave,
Whose courage well was tried,
  Had made the vessel heel
And laid her on her side;
  A land-breeze shook the shrouds,
And she was overset;
  Down went the Royal George,
With all her crew complete.

  Toll for the brave—
Brave Kempenfelt is gone,
  His last sea-fight is fought,
His work of glory done.
  It was not in the battle,
No tempest gave the shock,
  She sprang no fatal leak,
She ran upon no rock;
  His sword was in the sheath,
His fingers held the pen,
  When Kempenfelt went down
With twice four hundred men.

  Weigh the vessel up,
Once dreaded by our foes,
  And mingle with your cup
The tears that England owes;
  Her timbers yet are sound,
And she may float again,
  Full charged with England's thunder,
And plough the distant main;
  But Kempenfelt is gone,
His victories are o'er;
  And he and his eight hundred
Must plough the wave no more.

445   *The Poplar-Field*

THE poplars are felled, farewell to the shade
And the whispering sound of the cool colonnade,
The winds play no longer, and sing in the leaves,
Nor Ouse on his bosom their image receives.

Twelve years have elapsed since I last took a view
Of my favourite field and the bank where they grew,
And now in the grass behold they are laid,
And the tree is my seat that once lent me a shade.

The blackbird has fled to another retreat
Where the hazels afford him a screen from the heat,
And the scene where his melody charmed me before,
Resounds with his sweet-flowing ditty no more.

My fugitive years are all hasting away,
And I must ere long lie as lowly as they,
With a turf on my breast, and a stone at my head,
Ere another such grove shall arise in its stead.

'Tis a sight to engage me, if any thing can,
To muse on the perishing pleasures of man;
Though his life be a dream, his enjoyments, I see,
Have a being less durable even than he.

446   *The Castaway*

OBSCUREST night involved the sky,
    The Atlantic billows roared,
When such a destined wretch as I,
    Washed headlong from on board,
Of friends, of hope, of all bereft,
His floating home for ever left.

No braver chief could Albion boast
    Than he with whom he went,
Nor ever ship left Albion's coast,
    With warmer wishes sent.
He loved them both, but both in vain,
Nor him beheld, nor her again.

Not long beneath the whelming brine,
   Expert to swim, he lay;
Nor soon he felt his strength decline,
   Or courage die away;
But waged with death a lasting strife,
Supported by despair of life.

He shouted: nor his friends had failed
   To check the vessel's course,
But so the furious blast prevailed,
   That, pitiless perforce,
They left their outcast mate behind,
And scudded still before the wind.

Some succour yet they could afford;
   And, such as storms allow,
The cask, the coop, the floated cord,
   Delayed not to bestow.
But he (they knew) nor ship, nor shore,
Whate'er they gave, should visit more.

Nor, cruel as it seemed, could he
   Their haste himself condemn,
Aware that flight, in such a sea,
   Alone could rescue them;
Yet bitter felt it still to die
Deserted, and his friends so nigh.

He long survives, who lives an hour
   In ocean, self-upheld;
And so long he, with unspent power,
   His destiny repelled;
And ever, as the minutes flew,
Entreated help, or cried—Adieu!

At length, his transient respite past,
   His comrades, who before
Had heard his voice in every blast,
   Could catch the sound no more.
For then, by toil subdued, he drank
The stifling wave, and then he sank.

No poet wept him: but the page
   Of narrative sincere,
That tells his name, his worth, his age,
   Is wet with Anson's tear.
And tears by bards or heroes shed
Alike immortalize the dead.

I therefore purpose not, or dream,
   Descanting on his fate,
To give the melancholy theme
   A more enduring date:
But misery still delights to trace
Its semblance in another's case.

No voice divine the storm allayed,
   No light propitious shone;
When, snatched from all effectual aid,
   We perished, each alone:
But I beneath a rougher sea,
And whelmed in deeper gulfs than he.

THOMAS CHATTERTON

1752–1770

447　　　*Song from Ælla*

O! SYNGE untoe mie roundelaie,
O! droppe the brynie teare wythe mee,
Daunce ne moe atte hallie daie,
Lycke a reynynge ryver bee;
     Mie love ys dedde,
     Gon to hys death-bedde,
     Al under the wyllowe tree.

Blacke hys cryne as the wyntere nyghte,
Whyte hys rode as the sommer snowe,
Rodde hys face as the mornynge lyghte,
Cale he lyes ynne the grave belowe;
     Mie love ys dedde,
     Gon to hys deathe-bedde,
     Al under the wyllowe tree.

447　cryne] hair　　　rode] complexion　　　Cale] cold

471

Swote hys tyngue as the throstles note,
Quycke ynn daunce as thoughte canne bee,
Defte hys taboure, codgelle stote,
O! hee lyes bie the wyllowe tree;
  Mie love ys dedde,
   Gonne to hys deathe-bedde,
   Alle underre the wyllowe tree.

Harke! the ravenne flappes hys wynge,
In the briered delle belowe;
Harke! the dethe-owle loude dothe synge,
To the nyghte-mares as heie goe;
  Mie love ys dedde,
   Gonne to hys deathe-bedde,
   Al under the wyllowe tree.

See! the whyte moone sheenes onne hie;
Whyterre ys mie true loves shroude;
Whyterre yanne the mornynge skie,
Whyterre yanne the evenynge cloude;
  Mie love ys dedde,
   Gon to hys deathe-bedde,
   Al under the wyllowe tree.

Heere, uponne mie true loves grave,
Schalle the baren fleurs be layde,
Nee one hallie Seyncte to save
Al the celness of a mayde.
  Mie love ys dedde,
   Gonne to hys death-bedde,
   Alle under the wyllowe tree.

Wythe mie hondes I'lle dente the brieres
Rounde his hallie corse to gre,
Ouphante fairie, lyghte youre fyres,
Heere mie boddie stylle schalle bee.
  Mie love ys dedde,
   Gon to hys death-bedde,
   Al under the wyllowe tree.

heie] they   celness] coldness   Ouphante] Elfin

Comme, wythe acorne-coppe & thorne,
Drayne mie hartys blodde awaie;
Lyfe and all yttes goode I scorne,
Daunce bie nete, or feaste by daie.
   Mie love ys dedde,
   Gon to hys death-bedde,
   Al under the wyllowe tree.

Waterre wytches, crownede wythe reytes,
Bere mee to yer leathalle tyde.
I die; I comme; mie true love waytes.
Thos the damselle spake, and dyed.

GEORGE CRABBE

1754–1832

448   *Rural Life*

  I GRANT indeed that fields and flocks have charms
For him that grazes or for him that farms;
But when amid such pleasing scenes I trace
The poor laborious natives of the place,
And see the mid-day sun, with fervid ray,
On their bare heads and dewy temples play;
While some, with feebler heads and fainter hearts,
Deplore their fortune, yet sustain their parts:
Then shall I dare these real ills to hide
In tinsel trappings of poetic pride?
  No; cast by Fortune on a frowning coast,
Which neither groves nor happy valleys boast;
Where other cares than those the Muse relates,
And other shepherds dwell with other mates;
By such examples taught, I paint the Cot,
As Truth will paint it, and as Bards will not:
Nor you, ye poor, of lettered scorn complain,
To you the smoothest song is smooth in vain;
O'ercome by labour, and bowed down by time,
Feel you the barren flattery of a rhyme?
Can poets soothe you, when you pine for bread,
By winding myrtles round your ruined shed?

Can their light tales your weighty griefs o'erpower,
Or glad with airy mirth the toilsome hour?
   Lo! where the heath, with withering brake grown o'er,
Lends the light turf that warms the neighbouring poor;
From thence a length of burning sand appears,
Where the thin harvest waves its withered ears;
Rank weeds, that every art and care defy,
Reign o'er the land, and rob the blighted rye:
There thistles stretch their prickly arms afar,
And to the ragged infant threaten war;
There poppies nodding, mock the hope of toil;
There the blue bugloss paints the sterile soil;
Hardy and high, above the slender sheaf,
The slimy mallow waves her silky leaf;
O'er the young shoot the charlock throws a shade,
And clasping tares cling round the sickly blade;
With mingled tints the rocky coasts abound,
And a sad splendour vainly shines around.

   So looks the nymph whom wretched arts adorn,
Betrayed by man, then left for man to scorn;
Whose cheek in vain assumes the mimic rose,
While her sad eyes the troubled breast disclose;
Whose outward splendour is but folly's dress,
Exposing most, when most it gilds distress.

449 *The Lady of the Manor*

   NEXT died the Lady who yon Hall possessed;
And here they brought her noble bones to rest.
In Town she dwelt;—forsaken stood the Hall:
Worms ate the floors, the tapestry fled the wall:
No fire the kitchen's cheerless grate displayed;
No cheerful light the long-closed sash conveyed;
The crawling worm, that turns a summer-fly,
Here spun his shroud and laid him up to die
The winter-death:—upon the bed of state,
The bat shrill-shrieking wooed his flickering mate;
To empty rooms the curious came no more,
From empty cellars turned the angry poor,
And surly beggars cursed the ever-bolted door.
To one small room the steward found his way,
Where tenants followed to complain and pay;

Yet no complaint before the Lady came,
The feeling servant spared the feeble dame;
Who saw her farms with his observing eyes,
And answered all requests with his replies:—
She came not down, her falling groves to view;
Why should she know, what one so faithful knew?
Why come, from many clamorous tongues to hear,
What one so just might whisper in her ear?
Her oaks or acres, why with care explore;
Why learn the wants, the sufferings of the poor;
When one so knowing all their worth could trace,
And one so piteous governed in her place?

    Lo! now, what dismal sons of Darkness come,
To bear this daughter of Indulgence home;
Tragedians all, and well arranged in black!
Who nature, feeling, force, expression lack;
Who cause no tear, but gloomily pass by,
And shake their sables in the wearied eye,
That turns disgusted from the pompous scene,
Proud without grandeur, with profusion, mean!
The tear for kindness past affection owes;
For worth deceased the sigh from reason flows;
E'en well-feigned passion for our sorrows call,
And real tears for mimic miseries fall:
But this poor farce has neither truth nor art,
To please the fancy or to touch the heart;
Unlike the darkness of the sky, that pours
On the dry ground its fertilizing showers;
Unlike to that which strikes the soul with dread,
When thunders roar and forky fires are shed;
Dark but not awful, dismal but yet mean,
With anxious bustle moves the cumbrous scene;
Presents no objects tender or profound,
But spreads its cold unmeaning gloom around.

    When woes are feigned, how ill such forms appear;
And oh! how needless, when the woe's sincere.

    Slow to the vault they come, with heavy tread,
Bending beneath the Lady and her lead;
A case of elm surrounds that ponderous chest,
Close on that case the crimson velvet's pressed;
Ungenerous this, that to the worm denies,
With niggard caution, his appointed prize;

For now, ere yet he works his tedious way,
Through cloth and wood and metal to his prey,
That prey dissolving shall a mass remain,
That fancy loathes and worms themselves disdain.
　　　But see! the master-mourner makes his way,
To end his office for the coffined clay;
Pleased that our rustic men and maids behold
His plate like silver, and his studs like gold,
As they approach to spell the age, the name,
And all the titles of the illustrious dame.—
This as (my duty done) some scholar read,
A village-father looked disdain and said:
'Away, my friends! why take such pains to know
What some brave marble soon in church shall show?
Where not alone her gracious name shall stand,
But how she lived—the blessing of the land;
How much we all deplored the noble dead,
What groans we uttered and what tears we shed;
Tears, true as those, which in the sleepy eyes
Of weeping cherubs on the stone shall rise;
Tears, true as those, which, ere she found her grave,
The noble Lady to our sorrows gave.'

450　　　　　　*Peter Grimes; the Outcast*

THUS by himself compelled to live each day,
To wait for certain hours the tide's delay;
At the same times the same dull views to see,
The bounding marsh-bank and the blighted tree;
The water only, when the tides were high,
When low, the mud half-covered and half-dry;
The sun-burnt tar that blisters on the planks,
And bank-side stakes in their uneven ranks;
Heaps of entangled weeds that slowly float,
As the tide rolls by the impeded boat.
　　When tides were neap, and, in the sultry day,
Through the tall bounding mud-banks made their way,
Which on each side rose swelling, and below
The dark warm flood ran silently and slow;
There anchoring, Peter chose from man to hide,
There hang his head, and view the lazy tide
In its hot slimy channel slowly glide;

Where the small eels that left the deeper way
For the warm shore, within the shallows play;
Where gaping mussels, left upon the mud,
Slope their slow passage to the fallen flood;—
Here dull and hopeless he'd lie down and trace
How sidelong crabs had scrawled their crooked race;
Or sadly listen to the tuneless cry
Of fishing gull or clanging golden-eye;
What time the sea-birds to the marsh would come,
And the loud bittern, from the bull-rush home,
Gave from the salt-ditch side the bellowing boom:
He nursed the feelings these dull scenes produce,
And loved to stop beside the opening sluice;
Where the small stream, confined in narrow bound,
Ran with a dull, unvaried, saddening sound;
Where all, presented to the eye or ear,
Oppressed the soul with misery, grief, and fear.

451 *Frenzy*

THEN was I cast from out my state;
   Two fiends of darkness led my way;
They waked me early, watched me late,
   My dread by night, my plague by day!
Oh! I was made their sport, their play,
   Through many a stormy troubled year;
And how they used their passive prey
   Is sad to tell:—but you shall hear.

*

Those fiends upon a shaking fen
   Fixed me, in dark tempestuous night;
There never trod the foot of men,
   There flocked the fowl in wintry flight;
There danced the moor's deceitful light
   Above the pool where sedges grow;
And when the morning-sun shone bright,
   It shone upon a field of snow.

They hung me on a bough so small,
　The rook could build her nest no higher;
They fixed me on the trembling ball
That crowns the steeple's quivering spire;
They set me where the seas retire,
　But drown with their returning tide;
And made me flee the mountain's fire,
　When rolling from its burning side.

I've hung upon the ridgy steep
　Of cliffs, and held the rambling brier;
I've plunged below the billowy deep,
　Where air was sent me to respire;
I've been where hungry wolves retire;
　And (to complete my woes) I've ran
Where Bedlam's crazy crew conspire
　Against the life of reasoning man.

I've furled in storms the flapping sail,
　By hanging from the topmast-head;
I've served the vilest slaves in jail,
　And picked the dunghill's spoil for bread;
I've made the badger's hole my bed,
　I've wandered with a gipsy crew;
I've dreaded all the guilty dread,
　And done what they would fear to do.

On sand, where ebbs and flows the flood,
　Midway they placed and bade me die;
Propped on my staff, I stoutly stood
　When the swift waves came rolling by;
And high they rose, and still more high,
　Till my lips drank the bitter brine;
I sobbed convulsed, then cast mine eye,
　And saw the tide's re-flowing sign.

And then, my dreams were such as nought
　Could yield but my unhappy case;
I've been of thousand devils caught,
　And thrust into that horrid place,
Where reign dismay, despair, disgrace;
　Furies with iron fangs were there,
To torture that accursed race,
　Doomed to dismay, disgrace, despair.

452   *His Late Wife's Wedding-Ring*

THE ring so worn, as you behold,
So thin, so pale, is yet of gold:
The passion such it was to prove;
Worn with life's cares, love yet was love.

WILLIAM BLAKE

1757–1827

453   *To the Muses*

WHETHER on Ida's shady brow,
   Or in the chambers of the East,
The chambers of the sun, that now
   From ancient melody have ceased;

Whether in Heaven ye wander fair,
   Or the green corners of the earth,
Or the blue regions of the air,
   Where the melodious winds have birth;

Whether on crystal rocks ye rove,
   Beneath the bosom of the sea
Wandering in many a coral grove,
   Fair Nine, forsaking Poetry!

How have you left the ancient love
   That bards of old enjoyed in you!
The languid strings do scarcely move!
   The sound is forced, the notes are few!

454   *The Prince of Love*

HOW sweet I roamed from field to field,
   And tasted all the summer's pride,
'Till I the prince of love beheld,
   Who in the sunny beams did glide!

He showed me lilies for my hair,
   And blushing roses for my brow;
He led me through his gardens fair,
   Where all his golden pleasures grow.

With sweet May dews my wings were wet,
   And Phoebus fired my vocal rage;
He caught me in his silken net,
   And shut me in his golden cage.

He loves to sit and hear me sing,
   Then, laughing, sports and plays with me;
Then stretches out my golden wing,
   And mocks my loss of liberty.

455   *Piping Down the Valleys Wild*

PIPING down the valleys wild,
Piping songs of pleasant glee,
On a cloud I saw a child,
And he laughing said to me:

'Pipe a song about a Lamb!'
So I piped with merry cheer.
'Piper, pipe that song again.'
So I piped: he wept to hear.

'Drop thy pipe, thy happy pipe,
Sing thy songs of happy cheer.'
So I sung the same again,
While he wept with joy to hear.

'Piper, sit thee down and write
In a book, that all may read.'
So he vanished from my sight,
And I plucked a hollow reed,

And I made a rural pen,
And I stained the water clear,
And I wrote my happy songs
Every child may joy to hear.

456 *The Divine Image*

To Mercy, Pity, Peace, and Love
All pray in their distress;
And to these virtues of delight
Return their thankfulness.

For Mercy, Pity, Peace, and Love
Is God, our father dear,
And Mercy, Pity, Peace, and Love,
Is Man, his child and care.

For Mercy has a human heart,
Pity a human face,
And Love, the human form divine,
And Peace, the human dress.

Then every man, of every clime,
That prays in his distress,
Prays to the human form divine,
Love, Mercy, Pity', Peace.

And all must love the human form,
In heathen, turk, or jew;
Where Mercy, Love, and Pity dwell
There God is dwelling too.

457 *Holy Thursday*

'TWAS on a Holy Thursday, their innocent faces clean,
The children walking two and two, in red and blue and green,
Grey-headed beadles walked before, with wands as white as snow,
Till into the high dome of Paul's they like Thames' waters flow.

O what a multitude they seemed, these flowers of London town!
Seated in companies they sit, with radiance all their own.
The hum of multitudes was there, but multitudes of lambs,
Thousands of little boys and girls raising their innocent hands.

Now like a mighty wind they raise to Heaven the voice of song,
Or like harmonious thunderings the seats of Heaven among.
Beneath them sit the aged men, wise guardians of the poor;
Then cherish pity, lest you drive an angel from your door.

458   *Hear the Voice of the Bard*

HEAR the voice of the Bard!
Who present, past, and future sees;
Whose ears have heard
The Holy Word
That walked among the ancient trees,

Calling the lapsèd soul,
And weeping in the evening dew;
That might control
The starry pole,
And fallen, fallen light renew!

'O Earth, O Earth, return!
Arise from out the dewy grass;
Night is worn,
And the morn
Rises from the slumberous mass.

Turn away no more;
Why wilt thou turn away?
The starry floor,
The watery shore,
Is given thee till the break of day.'

459   *The Clod and the Pebble*

'LOVE seeketh not itself to please,
Nor for itself hath any care,
But for another gives its ease,
And builds a Heaven in Hell's despair.'

So sung a little Clod of Clay
Trodden with the cattle's feet,
But a Pebble of the brook
Warbled out these metres meet:

'Love seeketh only self to please,
To bind another to its delight,
Joys in another's loss of ease,
And builds a Hell in Heaven's despite.'

460

The Sick Rose

O ROSE, thou art sick!
The invisible worm
That flies in the night,
In the howling storm.

Has found out thy bed
Of crimson joy,
And his dark secret love
Does thy life destroy.

461

The Tiger

TIGER! Tiger! burning bright
In the forests of the night,
What immortal hand or eye
Could frame thy fearful symmetry?

In what distant deeps or skies
Burned the fire of thine eyes?
On what wings dare he aspire?
What the hand dare seize the fire?

And what shoulder, and what art,
Could twist the sinews of thy heart?
And when thy heart began to beat,
What dread hand? And what dread feet?

What the hammer? What the chain?
In what furnace was thy brain?
What the anvil? What dread grasp
Dare its deadly terrors clasp?

When the stars threw down their spears,
And watered heaven with their tears,
Did he smile his work to see?
Did he who made the Lamb make thee?

Tiger! Tiger! burning bright
In the forests of the night,
What immortal hand or eye
Dare frame thy fearful symmetry?

462 *London*

I WANDER through each chartered street,
Near where the chartered Thames does flow,
And mark in every face I meet
Marks of weakness, marks of woe.

In every cry of every man,
In every infant's cry of fear,
In every voice, in every ban,
The mind-forged manacles I hear.

How the chimney-sweeper's cry
Every blackening church appalls;
And the hapless soldier's sigh
Runs in blood down palace walls.

But most through midnight streets I hear
How the youthful harlot's curse
Blasts the newborn infant's tear,
And blights with plagues the marriage hearse.

463 *To Tirzah*

WHATE'ER is born of Mortal Birth
Must be consumed with the Earth,
To rise from Generation free:
Then what have I to do with thee?

The Sexes sprung from Shame and Pride,
Blowed in the morn; in evening died;
But Mercy changed Death into Sleep;
The Sexes rose to work and weep.

Thou, Mother of my Mortal Part,
With cruelty didst mould my heart,
And with false self-deceiving tears
Didst bind my Nostrils, Eyes, and Ears;

Didst close my tongue in senseless clay,
And me to Mortal Life betray:
The Death of Jesus set me free:
Then what have I to do with thee?

464 *The Secrets of the Earth*

THE eternal gates' terrific porter lifted the northern bar:
Thel entered in and saw the secrets of the land unknown.
She saw the couches of the dead, and where the fibrous roots
Of every heart on earth infixes deep its restless twists:
A land of sorrows and of tears where never smile was seen.

She wandered in the land of clouds through valleys dark, listening
Dolours and lamentations; waiting oft beside a dewy grave
She stood in silence, listening to the voices of the ground,
Till to her own grave plot she came, and there she sat down,
And heard this voice of sorrow breathed from the hollow pit.

'Why cannot the Ear be closed to its own destruction?
Or the glistening Eye to the poison of a smile?
Why are Eyelids stored with arrows ready drawn,
Where a thousand fighting men in ambush lie?
Or an Eye of gifts and graces showering fruits and coined gold?
Why a Tongue impressed with honey from every wind?
Why an Ear, a whirlpool fierce to draw creations in?
Why a Nostril wide inhaling terror, trembling, and affright?
Why a tender curb upon the youthful burning boy?
Why a little curtain of flesh on the bed of our desire?'

465 *Never Seek to Tell thy Love*

NEVER seek to tell thy love
Love that never told can be;
For the gentle wind does move
Silently, invisibly.

I told my love, I told my love,
I told her all my heart,
Trembling, cold, in ghastly fears—
Ah, she doth depart.

Soon as she was gone from me
A traveller came by
Silently, invisibly—
O, was no deny.

466   *Eternity*

> HE who bends to himself a joy
> Does the wingèd life destroy;
> But he who kisses the joy as it flies
> Lives in eternity's sunrise.

467   *Jerusalem*

> AND did those feet in ancient time
> Walk upon England's mountains green?
> And was the holy Lamb of God
> On England's pleasant pastures seen?
>
> And did the Countenance Divine
> Shine forth upon our clouded hills?
> And was Jerusalem builded here
> Among these dark Satanic Mills?
>
> Bring me my Bow of burning gold!
> Bring me my Arrows of desire!
> Bring me my Spear! O clouds, unfold!
> Bring me my Chariot of fire!
>
> I will not cease from Mental Fight,
> Nor shall my Sword sleep in my hand,
> Till we have built Jerusalem
> In England's green and pleasant land.

468   *The Vision of Beulah*

> THOU hearest the nightingale begin the Song of Spring.
> The lark sitting upon his earthy bed, just as the morn
> Appears, listens silent; then springing from the waving cornfield, loud
> He leads the Choir of Day: trill, trill, trill, trill,
> Mounting upon the wings of light into the great expanse,
> Re-echoing against the lovely blue and shining heavenly shell,
> His little throat labours with inspiration; every feather
> On throat and breast and wings vibrates with the effluence Divine.

All Nature listens silent to him, and the awful Sun
Stands still upon the mountain looking on this little bird
With eyes of soft humility and wonder, love and awe.
Then loud from their green covert all the birds begin their song:
The thrust, the linnet and the goldfinch, robin and the wren,
Awake the Sun from his sweet reverie upon the mountain.
The nightingale again assays his song, and through the day
And through the night warbles luxuriant, every bird of song
Attending his loud harmony with admiration and love.

Thou perceivest the flowers put forth their precious odours,
And none can tell how from so small a centre comes such sweets,
Forgetting that within that centre Eternity expands
Its ever-during doors that Og and Anak fiercely guard.
First, e'er the morning breaks, joy opens in the flowery bosoms,
Joy even to tears, which the Sun rising dries; first the wild thyme
And meadow-sweet, downy and soft, waving among the reeds,
Light springing on the air, lead the sweet dance: they wake
The honeysuckle sleeping on the oak; the flaunting beauty
Revels along upon the wind; the white-thorn, lovely may,
Opens her many lovely eyes listening; the rose still sleeps,
None dare to wake her; soon she bursts her crimson-curtained bed
And comes forth in the majesty of beauty; every flower,
The pink, the jessamine, the wall-flower, the carnation,
The jonquil, the mild lily, opes her heavens; every tree
And flower and herb soon fill the air with an innumerable dance,
Yet all in order sweet and lovely. Men are sick with love.

ROBERT BURNS

1759–1796

469   *Address to the Unco Guid*

O YE wha are sae guid yoursel,
    Sae pious and sae holy,
Ye've nought to do but mark and tell
    Your neebour's fauts and folly!
Whase life is like a weel-gaun mill,
    Supplied wi' store o' water,
The heapet happer's ebbing still,
    And still the clap plays clatter.

Hear me, ye venerable Core,
    As counsel for poor mortals,
That frequent pass douce Wisdom's door
    For glaikit Folly's portals;
I, for their thoughtless, careless sakes,
    Would here propone defences,
Their donsie tricks, their black mistakes,
    Their failings and mischances.

Ye see your state wi' theirs compared,
    And shudder at the niffer;
But cast a moment's fair regard
    What maks the mighty differ?
Discount what scant occasion gave,
    That purity ye pride in,
And (what's aft mair than a' the lave)
    Your better art o' hiding.

Think, when your castigated pulse
    Gies now and then a wallop,
What ragings must his veins convulse,
    That still eternal gallop:
Wi' wind and tide fair i' your tail,
    Right on ye scud your sea-way;
But in the teeth o' baith to sail,
    It maks an unco leeway.

See Social-life and Glee sit down,
    All joyous and unthinking,
Till, quite transmugrified, they're grown
    Debauchery and Drinking:
O would they stay to calculate
    The eternal consequences;
Or your more dreaded hell to state,
    Damnation of expenses!

Ye high, exalted, virtuous Dames,
    Tied up in godly laces,
Before ye gie poor Frailty names,
    Suppose a change o' cases;

douce] sober   glaikit] giddy   donsie] unlucky
                    niffer] exchange

A dear-loved lad, convenience snug,
 A treacherous inclination—
But, let me whisper i' your lug,
 Ye're aiblins nae temptation.

Then gently scan your brother Man,
 Still gentler sister Woman;
Though they may gang a kennin wrang,
 To step aside is human:
One point must still be greatly dark,
 The moving *Why* they do it:
And just as lamely can ye mark,
 How far perhaps they rue it.

Who made the heart, 'tis *He* alone
 Decidedly can try us,
He knows each chord, its various tone,
 Each spring, its various bias:
Then at the balance let's be mute,
 We never can adjust it;
What's *done* we partly may compute,
 But know not what's resisted.

470 *Auld Lang Syne*

SHOULD auld acquaintance be forgot,
 And never brought to min'?
Should auld acquaintance be forgot,
 And auld lang syne?

  For auld lang syne, my dear,
   For auld lang syne,
  We'll tak a cup o' kindness yet,
   For auld lang syne.

We twa hae run about the braes,
 And pu'd the gowans fine;
But we've wandered mony a weary foot
 Sin' auld lang syne.

aiblins] perhaps a kennin] a little
470 gowans] daisies

We twa hae paidled i' the burn,
   From morning sun till dine;
But seas between us braid hae roared
   Sin' auld lang syne.

And there's a hand, my trusty fiere,
   And gie's a hand o' thine:
And we'll tak a right guid-willie waught,
   For auld lang syne.

And surely ye'll be your pint-stowp,
   And surely I'll be mine;
And we'll tak a cup o' kindness yet
   For auld lang syne.

471   *John Anderson, my Jo*

JOHN ANDERSON my jo, John,
   When we were first acquent,
Your locks were like the raven,
   Your bonnie brow was brent;
But now your brow is beld, John,
   Your locks are like the snow;
But blessings on your frosty pow,
   John Anderson, my jo.

John Anderson my jo, John,
   We clamb the hill thegither;
And mony a canty day, John,
   We've had wi' ane anither:
Now we maun totter down, John,
   And hand in hand we'll go,
And sleep thegither at the foot,
   John Anderson, my jo.

472   *The Silver Tassie*

Go fetch to me a pint o' wine,
   An' fill it in a silver tassie;
That I may drink, before I go,
   A service to my bonnie lassie.

That boat rocks at the pier o' Leith,
   Fu' loud the wind blaws frae the ferry,
The ship rides by the Berwick-law,
   And I maun leave my bonnie Mary.

The trumpets sound, the banners fly,
   The glittering spears are rankèd ready;
The shouts o' war are heard afar,
   The battle closes thick and bloody;
But it's no the roar o' sea or shore
   Wad mak me langer wish to tarry;
Nor shout o' war that's heard afar,
   It's leaving thee, my bonnie Mary.

473   *The Banks o' Doon*

Ye banks and braes o' bonnie Doon,
   How can ye bloom sae fresh and fair?
How can ye chant, ye little birds,
   And I sae weary fu' o' care?
Thou'lt break my heart, thou warbling bird,
   That wantons thro' the flowering thorn:
Thou minds me o' departed joys,
   Departed never to return.

Aft hae I roved by bonnie Doon,
   To see the rose and woodbine twine;
And ilka bird sang o' its love,
   And fondly sae did I o' mine.
Wi' lightsome heart I pu'd a rose,
   Fu' sweet upon its thorny tree;
And my fause lover stole my rose,
   But ah! he left the thorn wi' me.

474   *A Red, Red Rose*

My love is like a red, red rose
   That's newly sprung in June:
My love is like the melody
   That's sweetly played in tune.

As fair art thou, my bonnie lass,
  So deep in love am I:
And I will love thee still, my dear,
  Till a' the seas gang dry.

Till a' the seas gang dry, my dear,
  And the rocks melt wi' the sun:
And I will love thee still, my dear,
  While the sands o' life shall run.

And fare thee weel, my only love,
  And fare thee weel a while!
And I will come again, my love,
  Thou' it were ten thousand mile.

475   *Bonnie Lesley*

O SAW ye bonnie Lesley
  As she gaed o'er the Border?
She's gane, like Alexander,
  To spread her conquests farther.

To see her is to love her,
  And love but her for ever;
For Nature made her what she is,
  And never made anither!

Thou art a queen, fair Lesley,
  Thy subjects we, before thee:
Thou art divine, fair Lesley,
  The hearts o' men adore thee.

The Deil he could na skaith thee,
  Or aught that wad belang thee;
He'd look into thy bonnie face,
  And say, 'I canna wrang thee.'

The Powers aboon will tent thee;
  Misfortune sha'na steer thee;
Thou'rt like themsel' sae lovely,
  That ill they'll ne'er let near thee.

475 tent] take care of   steer] molest

Return again, fair Lesley,
　　Return to Caledonie!
That we may brag we hae a lass
　　There's nane again sae bonnie.

476　　*Robert Bruce's March to Bannockburn*

SCOTS, wha hae wi' Wallace bled,
Scots, wham Bruce has aften led,
Welcome to your gory bed,
　　Or to victory!

Now's the day, and now's the hour;
See the front o' battle lour,
See approach proud Edward's power—
　　Chains and slavery!

Wha will be a traitor knave?
Wha can fill a coward's grave?
Wha sae base as be a slave?—
　　Let him turn, and flee!

Wha for Scotland's King and Law
Freedom's sword will strongly draw,
Freeman stand or freeman fa',
　　Let him follow me!

By Oppression's woes and pains,
By your sons in servile chains,
We will drain our dearest veins,
　　But they shall be free!

Lay the proud usurpers low!
Tyrants fall in every foe!
Liberty's in every blow!
　　Let us do, or die!

477   *O wert Thou in the Cauld Blast*

O WERT thou in the cauld blast,
   On yonder lea, on yonder lea,
My plaidie to the angry airt,
   I'd shelter thee, I'd shelter thee.
Or did misfortune's bitter storms
   Around thee blaw, around thee blaw,
Thy bield should be my bosom,
   To share it a', to share it a'.

Or were I in the wildest waste,
   Sae black and bare, sae black and bare,
The desert were a Paradise,
   If thou wert there, if thou wert there.
Or were I monarch o' the globe,
   Wi' thee to reign, wi' thee to reign,
The brightest jewel in my crown
   Wad be my queen, wad be my queen.

SAMUEL ROGERS

1763–1855

478   *A Wish*

MINE be a cot beside the hill;
   A bee-hive's hum shall soothe my ear;
A willowy brook, that turns a mill,
   With many a fall shall linger near.

The swallow oft beneath my thatch
   Shall twitter from her clay-built nest;
Oft shall the pilgrim lift the latch
   And share my meal, a welcome guest.

Around my ivied porch shall spring
   Each fragrant flower that drinks the dew;
And Lucy at her wheel shall sing
   In russet gown and apron blue.

477   bield] shelter

The village church among the trees,
    Where first our marriage vows were given,
With merry peals shall swell the breeze
    And point with taper spire to Heaven.

WILLIAM WORDSWORTH

1770–1850

Lucy

479

(i)

STRANGE fits of passion have I known:
    And I will dare to tell,
But in the Lover's ear alone,
    What once to me befell.

When she I loved looked every day
    Fresh as a rose in June,
I to her cottage bent my way,
    Beneath an evening-moon.

Upon the moon I fixed my eye,
    All over the wide lea;
With quickening pace my horse drew nigh
    Those paths so dear to me.

And now we reached the orchard-plot;
    And, as we climbed the hill,
The sinking moon to Lucy's cot
    Came near, and nearer still.

In one of those sweet dreams I slept,
    Kind Nature's gentlest boon!
And all the while my eyes I kept
    On the descending moon.

My horse moved on; hoof after hoof
    He raised, and never stopped:
When down behind the cottage roof,
    At once, the bright moon dropped.

What fond and wayward thoughts will slide
Into a Lover's head!
'O mercy!' to myself I cried,
'If Lucy should be dead!'

480   (ii)

SHE dwelt among the untrodden ways
  Beside the springs of Dove,
A Maid whom there were none to praise
  And very few to love:

A violet by a mossy stone
  Half hidden from the eye!
Fair as a star, when only one
  Is shining in the sky.

She lived unknown, and few could know
  When Lucy ceased to be;
But she is in her grave, and oh,
  The difference to me!

481   (iii)

I TRAVELLED among unknown men,
  In lands beyond the sea;
Nor, England! did I know till then
  What love I bore to thee.

'Tis past, that melancholy dream!
  Nor will I quit thy shore
A second time; for still I seem
  To love thee more and more.

Among thy mountains did I feel
  The joy of my desire;
And she I cherished turned her wheel
  Beside an English fire.

Thy mornings showed, thy nights concealed,
  The bowers where Lucy played;
And thine too is the last green field
  That Lucy's eyes surveyed.

482   **(iv)**

THREE years she grew in sun and shower;
Then Nature said, 'A lovelier flower
  On earth was never sown;
This child I to myself will take;
She shall be mine, and I will make
  A lady of my own.

'Myself will to my darling be
Both law and impulse: and with me
  The girl, in rock and plain,
In earth and heaven, in glade and bower,
Shall feel an overseeing power
  To kindle or restrain.

'She shall be sportive as the fawn
That wild with glee across the lawn
  Or up the mountain springs;
And hers shall be the breathing balm,
And hers the silence and the calm
  Of mute insensate things.

'The floating clouds their state shall lend
To her; for her the willow bend;
  Nor shall she fail to see
Even in the motions of the storm
Grace that shall mould the maiden's form
  By silent sympathy.

'The stars of midnight shall be dear
To her; and she shall lean her ear
  In many a secret place
Where rivulets dance their wayward round,
And beauty born of murmuring sound
  Shall pass into her face.

'And vital feelings of delight
Shall rear her form to stately height,
    Her virgin bosom swell;
Such thoughts to Lucy I will give
While she and I together live
    Here in this happy dell.'

Thus Nature spake—The work was done—
How soon my Lucy's race was run!
    She died, and left to me
This heath, this calm and quiet scene;
The memory of what has been,
    And never more will be.

483   (v)

A SLUMBER did my spirit seal;
    I had no human fears:
She seemed a thing that could not feel
    The touch of earthly years.

No motion has she now, no force;
    She neither hears nor sees;
Rolled round in earth's diurnal course,
    With rocks, and stones, and trees.

484   *Resolution and Independence*

THERE was a roaring in the wind all night;
The rain came heavily and fell in floods;
But now the sun is rising calm and bright;
The birds are singing in the distant woods;
Over his own sweet voice the stock-dove broods;
The jay makes answer as the magpie chatters;
And all the air is filled with pleasant noise of waters.

All things that love the sun are out of doors;
The sky rejoices in the morning's birth;
The grass is bright with rain-drops;—on the moors
The hare is running races in her mirth;
And with her feet she from the plashy earth
Raises a mist; that, glittering in the sun,
Runs with her all the way, wherever she doth run.

I was a Traveller then upon the moor;
I saw the hare that raced about with joy;
I heard the woods and distant waters roar;
Or heard them not, as happy as a boy:
The pleasant season did my heart employ:
My old remembrances went from me wholly;
And all the ways of men, so vain and melancholy.

But, as it sometimes chanceth, from the might
Of joy in minds that can no further go,
As high as we have mounted in delight
In our dejection do we sink as low;
To me that morning did it happen so;
And fears and fancies thick upon me came;
Dim sadness—and blind thoughts, I knew not, nor could name.

I heard the sky-lark warbling in the sky;
And I bethought me of the playful hare:
Even such a happy Child of earth am I;
Even as these blissful creatures do I fare;
Far from the world I walk, and from all care;
But there may come another day to me—
Solitude, pain of heart, distress, and poverty.

My whole life I have lived in pleasant thought,
As if life's business were a summer mood;
As if all needful things would come unsought
To genial faith, still rich in genial good;
But how can he expect that others should
Build for him, sow for him, and at his call
Love him, who for himself will take no heed at all?

I thought of Chatterton, the marvellous Boy,
The sleepless Soul that perished in his pride;
Of Him who walked in glory and in joy
Following his plough, along the mountain-side:
By our own spirits are we deified:
We Poets in our youth begin in gladness;
But thereof come in the end despondency and madness.

Now, whether it were by peculiar grace,
A leading from above, a something given,
Yet it befell that, in this lonely place,
When I with these untoward thoughts had striven,
Beside a pool bare to the eye of heaven
I saw a Man before me unawares:
The oldest man he seemed that ever wore grey hairs.

As a huge stone is sometimes seen to lie
Couched on the bald top of an eminence;
Wonder to all who do the same espy,
By what means it could thither come, and whence;
So that it seems a thing endued with sense:
Like a sea-beast crawled forth, that on a shelf
Of rock or sand reposeth, there to sun itself;

Such seemed this Man, not all alive nor dead,
Nor all asleep—in his extreme old age:
His body was bent double, feet and head
Coming together in life's pilgrimage;
As if some dire constraint of pain, or rage
Of sickness felt by him in times long past,
A more than human weight upon his frame had cast.

Himself he propped, limbs, body, and pale face,
Upon a long grey staff of shaven wood:
And, still as I drew near with gentle pace,
Upon the margin of that moorish flood
Motionless as a cloud the old Man stood,
That heareth not the loud winds when they call;
And moveth all together, if it move at all.

At length, himself unsettling, he the pond
Stirred with his staff, and fixedly did look
Upon the muddy water, which he conned,
As if he had been reading in a book:
And now a stranger's privilege I took;
And, drawing to his side, to him did say,
'This morning gives us promise of a glorious day'.

A gentle answer did the old Man make,
In courteous speech which forth he slowly drew:
And him with further words I thus bespake,
'What occupation do you there pursue?
This is a lonesome place for one like you.'
Ere he replied, a flash of mild surprise
Broke from the sable orbs of his yet-vivid eyes.

His words came feebly, from a feeble chest,
But each in solemn order followed each,
With something of a lofty utterance drest—
Choice word and measured phrase, above the reach
Of ordinary men; a stately speech;
Such as grave Livers do in Scotland use,
Religious men, who give to God and man their dues.

He told, that to these waters he had come
To gather leeches, being old and poor:
Employment hazardous and wearisome!
And he had many hardships to endure:
From pond to pond he roamed, from moor to moor;
Housing, with God's good help, by choice or chance;
And in this way he gained an honest maintenance.

The old Man still stood talking by my side;
But now his voice to me was like a stream
Scarce heard; nor word from word could I divide;
And the whole body of the Man did seem
Like one whom I had met with in a dream;
Or like a man from some far region sent,
To give me human strength, by apt admonishment.

My former thoughts returned: the fear that kills;
And hope that is unwilling to be fed;
Cold, pain, and labour, and all fleshly ills;
And mighty Poets in their misery dead.
—Perplexed, and longing to be comforted,
My question eagerly did I renew,
'How is it that you live, and what is it you do?'

He with a smile did then his words repeat;
And said that, gathering leeches, far and wide
He travelled; stirring thus about his feet
The waters of the pools where they abide.
'Once I could meet with them on every side;
But they have dwindled long by slow decay;
Yet still I persevere, and find them where I may.'

While he was talking thus, the lonely place,
The old Man's shape, and speech—all troubled me:
In my mind's eye I seemed to see him pace
About the weary moors continually,
Wandering about alone and silently.
While I these thoughts within myself pursued,
He, having made a pause, the same discourse renewed.

And soon with this he other matter blended,
Cheerfully uttered, with demeanour kind,
But stately in the main; and when he ended,
I could have laughed myself to scorn to find
In that decrepit Man so firm a mind.
'God,' said I, 'be my help and stay secure;
I'll think of the Leech-gatherer on the lonely moor!'

485   *My heart leaps up*

MY heart leaps up when I behold
    A rainbow in the sky:
So was it when my life began;
So is it now I am a man;
So be it when I shall grow old,
    Or let me die!
The Child is father of the Man;
And I could wish my days to be
Bound each to each by natural piety.

486   *Upon Westminster Bridge*
         Sept. 3, 1802

EARTH has not anything to show more fair:
    Dull would he be of soul who could pass by
    A sight so touching in its majesty:
This City now doth, like a garment, wear
The beauty of the morning; silent, bare,
    Ships, towers, domes, theatres, and temples lie
    Open unto the fields, and to the sky;
All bright and glittering in the smokeless air.
Never did sun more beautifully steep
    In his first splendour, valley, rock, or hill;
Ne'er saw I, never felt, a calm so deep!
    The river glideth at his own sweet will:
Dear God! the very houses seem asleep;
    And all that mighty heart is lying still!

487   *On the Extinction of the Venetian Republic,*
         1802

ONCE did She hold the gorgeous East in fee;
    And was the safeguard of the West: the worth
    Of Venice did not fall below her birth,
Venice, the eldest Child of Liberty.
She was a maiden City, bright and free;
    No guile seduced, no force could violate;
    And, when she took unto herself a Mate,
She must espouse the everlasting Sea.
And what if she had seen those glories fade,
    Those titles vanish, and that strength decay;
Yet shall some tribute of regret be paid
    When her long life hath reached its final day:
Men are we, and must grieve when even the Shade
    Of that which once was great, is passed away.

488 *To Toussaint L'Ouverture*
Leader of the African Slaves of San Domingo,
Imprisoned by Napoleon

TOUSSAINT, the most unhappy man of men!
   Whether the whistling rustic tend his plough
   Within thy hearing, or thy head be now
Pillowed in some deep dungeon's earless den;—
O miserable Chieftain! where and when
   Wilt thou find patience! Yet die not; do thou
   Wear rather in thy bonds a cheerful brow:
Though fallen thyself, never to rise again,
Live, and take comfort. Thou hast left behind
   Powers that will work for thee; air, earth, and skies;
There's not a breathing of the common wind
   That will forget thee; thou hast great allies;
   Thy friends are exultations, agonies,
And love, and man's unconquerable mind.

489

IT is not to be thought of that the Flood
   Of British freedom, which, to the open sea
   Of the world's praise, from dark antiquity
Hath flowed, 'with pomp of waters, unwithstood',—
Roused though it be full often to a mood
   Which spurns the check of salutary bands,—
   That this most famous Stream in bogs and sands
Should perish; and to evil and to good
Be lost for ever. In our halls is hung
   Armoury of the invincible Knights of old:
We must be free or die, who speak the tongue
   That Shakespeare spake; the faith and morals hold
Which Milton held.—In every thing we are sprung
   Of Earth's first blood, have titles manifold.

490   *The Solitary Reaper*

BEHOLD her, single in the field,
  Yon solitary Highland Lass!
Reaping and singing by herself;
  Stop here, or gently pass!
Alone she cuts and binds the grain,
And sings a melancholy strain;
O listen! for the vale profound
Is overflowing with the sound.

No nightingale did ever chaunt
  More welcome notes to weary bands
Of travellers in some shady haunt,
  Among Arabian sands:
A voice so thrilling ne'er was heard
In spring-time from the cuckoo-bird,
Breaking the silence of the seas
Among the farthest Hebrides.

Will no one tell me what she sings?—
  Perhaps the plaintive numbers flow
For old, unhappy, far-off things,
  And battles long ago:
Or is it some more humble lay,
Familiar matter of to-day?
Some natural sorrow, loss, or pain,
That has been, and may be again?

Whate'er the theme, the maiden sang
  As if her song could have no ending;
I saw her singing at her work,
  And o'er the sickle bending;—
I listened, motionless and still;
And, as I mounted up the hill,
The music in my heart I bore,
Long after it was heard no more.

491 *Daffodils*

I WANDERED lonely as a cloud
   That floats on high o'er vales and hills,
When all at once I saw a crowd,
   A host, of golden daffodils;
Beside the lake, beneath the trees,
Fluttering and dancing in the breeze.

Continuous as the stars that shine
   And twinkle on the Milky Way,
They stretched in never-ending line
   Along the margin of a bay:
Ten thousand saw I at a glance,
Tossing their heads in sprightly dance.

The waves beside them danced, but they
   Out-did the sparkling waves in glee:
A poet could not but be gay,
   In such a jocund company:
I gazed—and gazed—but little thought
What wealth the show to me had brought:

For oft, when on my couch I lie
   In vacant or in pensive mood,
They flash upon that inward eye
   Which is the bliss of solitude;
And then my heart with pleasure fills,
And dances with the daffodils.

492 *A Complaint*

THERE is a change—and I am poor;
Your love hath been, nor long ago,
A fountain at my fond heart's door,
Whose only business was to flow;
And flow it did; not taking heed
Of its own bounty, or my need.

What happy moments did I count!
Blest was I then all bliss above!
Now, for that consecrated fount
Of murmuring, sparkling, living love,
What have I? shall I dare to tell?
A comfortless and hidden well.

A well of love—it may be deep—
I trust it is,—and never dry:
What matter? if the waters sleep
In silence and obscurity.
—Such change, and at the very door
Of my fond heart, hath made me poor.

493   *Personal Talk*

I AM not one who much or oft delight
    To season my fireside with personal talk,—
    Of friends, who live within an easy walk,
Or neighbours, daily, weekly, in my sight:
And, for my chance-acquaintance, ladies bright,
    Sons, mothers, maidens withering on the stalk,
    These all wear out of me, like forms, with chalk
Painted on rich men's floors, for one feast-night.
Better than such discourse doth silence long,
    Long, barren silence, square with my desire;
To sit without emotion, hope, or aim,
    In the loved presence of my cottage-fire,
And listen to the flapping of the flame,
Or kettle whispering its faint undersong.

494

THE world is too much with us; late and soon,
    Getting and spending, we lay waste our powers:
    Little we see in Nature that is ours;
We have given our hearts away, a sordid boon!
This sea that bares her bosom to the moon;
    The winds that will be howling at all hours,
    And are up-gathered now like sleeping flowers;
For this, for everything, we are out of tune;

It moves us not.—Great God! I'd rather be
    A Pagan suckled in a creed outworn;
So might I, standing on this pleasant lea,
    Have glimpses that would make me less forlorn;
Have sight of Proteus rising from the sea;
    Or hear old Triton blow his wreathèd horn.

495   *Ode*
*Intimations of Immortality from Recollections
of Early Childhood*

THERE was a time when meadow, grove, and stream,
    The earth, and every common sight,
        To me did seem
    Apparelled in celestial light,
The glory and the freshness of a dream.
It is not now as it hath been of yore;—
        Turn wheresoe'er I may,
        By night or day,
The things which I have seen I now can see no more.

        The rainbow comes and goes,
        And lovely is the rose;
        The moon doth with delight
Look round her when the heavens are bare;
        Waters on a starry night
        Are beautiful and fair;
    The sunshine is a glorious birth;
    But yet I know, where'er I go,
That there hath passed away a glory from the earth.

Now, while the birds thus sing a joyous song,
    And while the young lambs bound
        As to the tabor's sound,
To me alone there came a thought of grief:
A timely utterance gave that thought relief,
        And I again am strong:
The cataracts blow their trumpets from the steep;
No more shall grief of mine the season wrong;
I hear the echoes through the mountains throng,
The winds come to me from the fields of sleep,

And all the earth is gay;
    Land and sea
Give themselves up to jollity,
    And with the heart of May
Doth every beast keep holiday;—
      Thou Child of Joy,
Shout round me, let me hear thy shouts, thou happy
Shepherd-boy!

Ye blessed creatures, I have heard the call
    Ye to each other make; I see
The heavens laugh with you in your jubilee;
    My heart is at your festival,
    My head hath its coronal,
The fullness of your bliss, I feel—I feel it all.
      O evil day! if I were sullen
      While Earth herself is adorning,
        This sweet May-morning,
      And the children are culling
        On every side,
    In a thousand valleys far and wide,
    Fresh flowers; while the sun shines warm,
And the babe leaps up on his mother's arm:—
    I hear, I hear, with joy I hear!
    —But there's a tree, of many, one,
A single field which I have looked upon,
Both of them speak of something that is gone:
      The pansy at my feet
      Doth the same tale repeat:
Whither is fled the visionary gleam?
Where is it now, the glory and the dream?

Our birth is but a sleep and a forgetting:
The Soul that rises with us, our life's Star,
      Hath had elsewhere its setting,
      And cometh from afar:
    Not in entire forgetfulness,
    And not in utter nakedness,
But trailing clouds of glory do we come
      From God, who is our home:
Heaven lies about us in our infancy!

Shades of the prison-house begin to close
  Upon the growing Boy,
But he beholds the light, and whence it flows,
  He sees it in his joy;
The Youth, who daily farther from the east
  Must travel, still is Nature's priest,
   And by the vision splendid
   Is on his way attended;
At length the Man perceives it die away,
And fade into the light of common day.

Earth fills her lap with pleasures of her own;
  Yearnings she hath in her own natural kind;
And, even with something of a mother's mind,
   And no unworthy aim,
  The homely nurse doth all she can
To make her foster-child, her inmate Man,
  Forget the glories he hath known,
And that imperial palace whence he came.

Behold the Child among his new-born blisses,
A six years' darling of a pigmy size!
See, where 'mid work of his own hand he lies,
Fretted by sallies of his mother's kisses,
With light upon him from his father's eyes!
See, at his feet, some little plan or chart,
Some fragment from his dream of human life,
Shaped by himself with newly-learnèd art;
  A wedding or a festival,
  A mourning or a funeral;
   And this hath now his heart,
  And unto this he frames his song:
   Then will he fit his tongue
To dialogues of business, love, or strife;
   But it will not be long
   Ere this be thrown aside,
   And with new joy and pride
The little actor cons another part;
Filling from time to time his 'humorous stage'
With all the Persons, down to palsied Age,
That Life brings with her in her equipage;
   As if his whole vocation
   Were endless imitation.

Thou, whose exterior semblance doth belie
      Thy soul's immensity;
Thou best philosopher, who yet dost keep
Thy heritage, thou eye among the blind,
That, deaf and silent, read'st the eternal deep,
Haunted for ever by the eternal mind,—
      Mighty prophet! Seer blest!
      On whom those truths do rest,
Which we are toiling all our lives to find,
In darkness lost, the darkness of the grave;
Thou, over whom thy Immortality
Broods like the Day, a master o'er a slave,
A presence which is not to be put by;
Thou little Child, yet glorious in the might
Of heaven-born freedom on thy being's height,
Why with such earnest pains dost thou provoke
The years to bring the inevitable yoke,
Thus blindly with thy blessedness at strife?
Full soon thy soul shall have her earthly freight,
And custom lie upon thee with a weight,
Heavy as frost, and deep almost as life!

      O joy! that in our embers
      Is something that doth live,
      That nature yet remembers
      What was so fugitive!
The thought of our past years in me doth breed
Perpetual benediction: not indeed
For that which is most worthy to be blest—
Delight and liberty, the simple creed
Of childhood, whether busy or at rest,
With new-fledged hope still fluttering in his breast:—
      Not for these I raise
      The song of thanks and praise;
    But for those obstinate questionings
    Of sense and outward things,
    Fallings from us, vanishings;
    Blank misgivings of a Creature
Moving about in worlds not realized,
High instincts before which our mortal Nature
Did tremble like a guilty thing surprised:
      But for those first affections,
      Those shadowy recollections,

Which, be they what they may,
Are yet the fountain-light of all our day,
Are yet a master-light of all our seeing;
Uphold us, cherish, and have power to make
Our noisy years seem moments in the being
Of the eternal Silence: truths that wake,
  To perish never:
Which neither listlessness, nor mad endeavour,
  Nor Man nor Boy,
Nor all that is at enmity with joy,
Can utterly abolish or destroy!
  Hence in a season of calm weather
    Though inland far we be,
Our souls have sight of that immortal sea
    Which brought us hither,
  Can in a moment travel thither,
And see the children sport upon the shore,
And hear the mighty waters rolling evermore.

Then sing, ye birds, sing, sing a joyous song!
    And let the young lambs bound
    As to the tabor's sound!
We in thought will join your throng,
    Ye that pipe and ye that play,
    Ye that through your hearts to-day
    Feel the gladness of the May!
What though the radiance which was once so bright
Be now for ever taken from my sight,
    Though nothing can bring back the hour
Of splendour in the grass, of glory in the flower;
    We will grieve not, rather find
    Strength in what remains behind;
    In the primal sympathy
    Which having been must ever be;
    In the soothing thoughts that spring
    Out of human suffering;
    In the faith that looks through death,
In years that bring the philosophic mind.

And O ye Fountains, Meadows, Hills, and Groves,
Forbode not any severing of our loves!
Yet in my heart of hearts I feel your might;
I only have relinquished one delight
To live beneath your more habitual sway.
I love the brooks which down their channels fret,
Even more than when I tripped lightly as they;
The innocent brightness of a new-born Day
          Is lovely yet;
The clouds that gather round the setting sun
Do take a sober colouring from an eye
That hath kept watch o'er man's mortality;
Another race hath been, and other palms are won.
Thanks to the human heart by which we live,
Thanks to its tenderness, its joys, and fears,
To me the meanest flower that blows can give
Thoughts that do often lie too deep for tears.

from The Prelude

Childhood and School-Time

496
(i)

FAIR seed-time had my soul, and I grew up
Fostered alike by beauty and by fear;
Much favoured in my birthplace, and no less
In that beloved Vale to which, ere long,
I was transplanted. Well I call to mind
('Twas at an early age, ere I had seen
Nine summers) when upon the mountain slope
The frost and breath of frosty wind had snapped
The last autumnal crocus, 'twas my joy
To wander half the night among the cliffs
And the smooth hollows, where the woodcocks ran
Along the open turf. In thought and wish
That time, my shoulder all with springes hung,
I was a fell destroyer. On the heights
Scudding away from snare to snare, I plied
My anxious visitation, hurrying on,
Still hurrying, hurrying onward; moon and stars
Were shining o'er my head; I was alone,

And seemed to be a trouble to the peace
That was among them. Sometimes it befell
In these night-wanderings, that a strong desire
O'erpowered my better reason, and the bird
Which was the captive of another's toils
Became my prey; and, when the deed was done
I heard among the solitary hills
Low breathings coming after me, and sounds
Of indistinguishable motion, steps
Almost as silent as the turf they trod.
Nor less in springtime when on southern banks
The shining sun had from his knot of leaves
Decoyed the primrose flower, and when the vales
And woods were warm, was I a plunderer then
In the high places, on the lonesome peaks
Where'er, among the mountains and the winds,
The mother-bird had built her lodge. Though mean
My object, and inglorious, yet the end
Was not ignoble. Oh! when I have hung
Above the raven's nest, by knots of grass
And half-inch fissures in the slippery rock
But ill sustained, and almost, as it seemed,
Suspended by the blast which blew amain,
Shouldering the naked crag; Oh! at that time,
While on the perilous ridge I hung alone,
With what strange utterance did the loud dry wind
Blow through my ears! the sky seemed not a sky
Of earth, and with what motion moved the clouds!

497   (ii)

WISDOM and Spirit of the universe!
Thou Soul that art the Eternity of Thought!
That giv'st to forms and images a breath
And everlasting motion! not in vain,
By day or star-light thus from my first dawn
Of childhood didst thou intertwine for me
The passions that build up our human soul,
Not with the mean and vulgar works of man,
But with high objects, with enduring things,

With life and nature, purifying thus
The elements of feeling and of thought,
And sanctifying, by such discipline,
Both pain and fear, until we recognize
A grandeur in the beatings of the heart.

   Nor was this fellowship vouchsafed to me
With stinted kindness. In November days,
When vapours, rolling down the valleys, made
A lonely scene more lonesome; among woods
At noon, and 'mid the calm of summer nights,
When, by the margin of the trembling lake,
Beneath the gloomy hills I homeward went
In solitude, such intercourse was mine;
'Twas mine among the fields both day and night,
And by the waters all the summer long.

   And in the frosty season, when the sun
Was set, and visible for many a mile
The cottage windows through the twilight blazed,
I heeded not the summons:—happy time
It was, indeed, for all of us; to me
It was a time of rapture: clear and loud
The village clock tolled six; I wheeled about,
Proud and exulting, like an untired horse,
That cares not for his home.—All shod with steel,
We hissed along the polished ice, in games
Confederate, imitative of the chase
And woodland pleasures, the resounding horn,
The pack loud bellowing, and the hunted hare.
So through the darkness and the cold we flew,
And not a voice was idle; with the din,
Meanwhile, the precipices rang aloud,
The leafless trees, and every icy crag
Tinkled like iron, while the distant hills
Into the tumult sent an alien sound
Of melancholy, not unnoticed, while the stars,
Eastward, were sparkling clear, and in the west
The orange sky of evening died away.

Not seldom from the uproar I retired
Into a silent bay, or sportively
Glanced sideway, leaving the tumultuous throng,
To cut across the image of a star
That gleamed upon the ice: and oftentimes
When we had given our bodies to the wind,
And all the shadowy banks, on either side,
Came sweeping through the darkness, spinning still
The rapid line of motion; then at once
Have I, reclining back upon my heels,
Stopped short, yet still the solitary cliffs
Wheeled by me, even as if the earth had rolled
With visible motion her diurnal round;
Behind me did they stretch in solemn train
Feebler and feebler, and I stood and watched
Till all was tranquil as a dreamless sleep.

498

SURPRISED by joy—impatient as the wind
I turned to share the transport—Oh! with whom
But thee, deep buried in the silent tomb,
That spot which no vicissitude can find?
Love, faithful love, recalled thee to my mind—
But how could I forget thee? Through what power,
Even for the least division of an hour,
Have I been so beguiled as to be blind
To my most grievous loss!—That thought's return
Was the worst pang that sorrow ever bore,
Save one, one only, when I stood forlorn,
Knowing my heart's best treasure was no more;
That neither present time, nor years unborn
Could to my sight that heavenly face restore.

499 *Valediction to the River Duddon*

I THOUGHT of Thee, my partner and my guide,
 As being past away.—Vain sympathies!
 For, backward, Duddon! as I cast my eyes,
I see what was, and is, and will abide;
Still glides the Stream, and shall for ever glide;
 The Form remains, the Function never dies;
 While we, the brave, the mighty, and the wise,
We Men, who in our morn of youth defied
The elements, must vanish;—be it so!
 Enough, if something from our hands have power
 To live, and act, and serve the future hour;
And if, as toward the silent tomb we go,
 Through love, through hope, and faith's transcendent
  dower,
We feel that we are greater than we know.

500 *Mutability*

FROM low to high doth dissolution climb,
 And sink from high to low, along a scale
 Of awful notes, whose concord shall not fail;
A musical but melancholy chime,
Which they can hear who meddle not with crime,
 Nor avarice, nor over-anxious care.
 Truth fails not; but her outward forms that bear
The longest date do melt like frosty rime,
That in the morning whitened hill and plain
And is no more; drop like the tower sublime
 Of yesterday, which royally did wear
His crown of weeds, but could not even sustain
 Some casual shout that broke the silent air,
Or the unimaginable touch of Time.

501 *Extempore Effusion upon the Death of James Hogg*

WHEN first, descending from the moorlands,
I saw the stream of Yarrow glide
Along a bare and open valley,
The Ettrick Shepherd was my guide.

When last along its banks I wandered,
Through groves that had begun to shed
Their golden leaves upon the pathways,
My steps the Border-minstrel led.

The mighty Minstrel breathes no longer,
'Mid mouldering ruins low he lies;
And death upon the braes of Yarrow,
Has closed the Shepherd-poet's eyes:

Nor has the rolling year twice measured,
From sign to sign, its steadfast course,
Since every mortal power of Coleridge
Was frozen at its marvellous source;

The rapt One, of the godlike forehead,
The heaven-eyed creature sleeps in earth:
And Lamb, the frolic and the gentle,
Has vanished from his lonely hearth.

Like clouds that rake the mountain-summits,
Or waves that own no curbing hand,
How fast has brother followed brother,
From sunshine to the sunless land!

Yet I, whose lids from infant slumber
Were earlier raised, remain to hear
A timid voice, that asks in whispers,
'Who next will drop and disappear?'

Our haughty life is crowned with darkness,
Like London with its own black wreath,
On which with thee, O Crabbe! forth-looking,
I gazed from Hampstead's breezy heath.

As if but yesterday departed,
Thou too art gone before; but why,
O'er ripe fruit, seasonably gathered,
Should frail survivors heave a sigh?

Mourn rather for that holy spirit,
Sweet as the spring, as ocean deep;
For her who, ere her summer faded,
Has sunk into a breathless sleep.

No more of old romantic sorrows,
For slaughtered youth or love-lorn maid!
With sharper grief is Yarrow smitten,
And Ettrick mourns with her their poet dead.

SIR WALTER SCOTT

1771–1832

502   *Patriotism*

BREATHES there the man, with soul so dead,
Who never to himself hath said,
    This is my own, my native land!
Whose heart hath ne'er within him burned,
As home his footsteps he hath turned,
    From wandering on a foreign strand!
If such there breathe, go, mark him well;
For him no Minstrel raptures swell;
High though his titles, proud his name,
Boundless his wealth as wish can claim;
Despite those titles, power, and pelf,
The wretch, concentred all in self,
Living, shall forfeit fair renown,
And, doubly dying, shall go down
To the vile dust, from whence he sprung,
Unwept, unhonoured, and unsung.

O Caledonia! stern and wild,
Meet nurse for a poetic child!
Land of brown heath and shaggy wood,
Land of the mountain and the flood,
Land of my sires! what mortal hand
Can e'er untie the filial band,
That knits me to thy rugged strand!
Still as I view each well-known scene,
Think what is now, and what hath been,

Seems as, to me, of all bereft,
Sole friends thy woods and streams were left;
And thus I love them better still,
Even in extremity of ill.
By Yarrow's stream still let me stray,
Though none should guide my feeble way;
Still feel the breeze down Ettrick break,
Although it chill my withered cheek;
Still lay my head by Teviot Stone,
Though there, forgotten and alone,
The Bard may draw his parting groan.

503   *Lochinvar*

O, YOUNG Lochinvar is come out of the west,
Through all the wide Border his steed was the best;
And save his good broadsword he weapons had none,
He rode all unarmed, and he rode all alone.
So faithful in love, and so dauntless in war,
There never was knight like the young Lochinvar.

He stayed not for brake, and he stopped not for stone,
He swam the Eske river where ford there was none;
But ere he alighted at Netherby gate,
The bride had consented, the gallant came late:
For a laggard in love, and a dastard in war,
Was to wed the fair Ellen of brave Lochinvar.

So boldly he entered the Netherby Hall,
Among bride's-men, and kinsmen, and brothers, and all:
Then spoke the bride's father, his hand on his sword,
(For the poor craven bridegroom said never a word)
'O come ye in peace here, or come ye in war,
Or to dance at our bridal, young Lord Lochinvar?'

'I long wooed your daughter, my suit you denied;—
Love swells like the Solway, but ebbs like its tide—
And now am I come, with this lost love of mine,
To lead but one measure, drink one cup of wine.
There are maidens in Scotland more lovely by far,
That would gladly be bride to the young Lochinvar.'

The bride kissed the goblet: the knight took it up,
He quaffed off the wine, and he threw down the cup.
She looked down to blush, and she looked up to sigh,
With a smile on her lips, and a tear in her eye.
He took her soft hand, ere her mother could bar,—
'Now tread we a measure!' said the young Lochinvar.

So stately his form and so lovely her face,
That never a hall such a galliard did grace;
While her mother did fret, and her father did fume,
And the bridegroom stood dangling his bonnet and plume;
And the bride-maidens whispered, "'Twere better by far,
To have matched our fair cousin with young Lochinvar.'

One touch to her hand, and one word in her ear,
When they reached the hall-door, and the charger stood near;
So light to the croup the fair lady he swung,
So light to the saddle before her he sprung!
'She is won! we are gone, over bank, bush, and scaur;
They'll have fleet steeds that follow,' quoth young Lochinvar.

There was mounting 'mong Graemes of the Netherby clan;
Forsters, Fenwicks, and Musgraves, they rode and they ran:
There was racing and chasing on Cannobie Lee,
But the lost bride of Netherby ne'er did they see.
So daring in love, and so dauntless in war,
Have ye e'er heard of gallant like young Lochinvar?

504 *Soldier, Rest!*

SOLDIER, rest! thy warfare o'er,
  Sleep the sleep that knows not breaking;
Dream of battled fields no more,
  Days of danger, nights of waking.
In our isle's enchanted hall,
  Hands unseen thy couch are strewing,
Fairy strains of music fall,
  Every sense in slumber dewing.
Soldier, rest! thy warfare o'er,
Dream of fighting fields no more:
Sleep the sleep that knows not breaking,
Morn of toil, nor night of waking.

No rude sound shall reach thine ear,
  Armour's clang, or war-steed champing,
Trump nor pibroch summon here
  Mustering clan, or squadron tramping.
Yet the lark's shrill fife may come
  At the day-break from the fallow,
And the bittern sound his drum,
  Booming from the sedgy shallow.
Ruder sounds shall none be near,
Guards nor warders challenge here,
Here's no war-steed's neigh and champing,
Shouting clans, or squadrons stamping.

Huntsman, rest! thy chase is done;
  While our slumbrous spells assail ye,
Dream not, with the rising sun,
  Bugles here shall sound reveille.
Sleep! the deer is in his den;
  Sleep! thy hounds are by thee lying;
Sleep! nor dream in yonder glen,
  How thy gallant steed lay dying.
Huntsman, rest! thy chase is done,
Think not of the rising sun,
For at dawning to assail ye,
Here no bugles sound reveille.

505   *The Rover's Farewell*

A WEARY lot is thine, fair maid,
  A weary lot is thine!
To pull the thorn thy brow to braid,
  And press the rue for wine.
A lightsome eye, a soldier's mien,
  A feather of the blue,
A doublet of the Lincoln green—
  No more of me you knew,
          My Love!
No more of me you knew.

'This morn is merry June, I trow,
　　The rose is budding fain;
But she shall bloom in winter snow
　　Ere we two meet again.'
—He turned his charger as he spake
　　Upon the river shore,
He gave his bridle-reins a shake,
　　Said 'Adieu for evermore,
　　　　My Love!
And adieu for evermore.'

506　　　　　*Madge Wildfire's Song*

PROUD Maisie is in the wood,
　　Walking so early;
Sweet Robin sits on the bush,
　　Singing so rarely.

'Tell me, thou bonny bird,
　　When shall I marry me?'
—'When six braw gentlemen
　　Kirkward shall carry ye.'

'Who makes the bridal bed,
　　Birdie, say truly?'
—'The grey-headed sexton
　　That delves the grave duly.

'The glow-worm o'er grave and stone
　　Shall light thee steady;
The owl from the steeple sing
　　Welcome, proud lady!'

507　　　　　*Lucy Ashton's Song*

LOOK not thou on beauty's charming;
Sit thou still when kings are arming;
Taste not when the wine-cup glistens;
Speak not when the people listens;
Stop thine ear against the singer;
From the red gold keep thy finger;
Vacant heart and hand and eye,
Easy live and quiet die.

SAMUEL TAYLOR COLERIDGE
1772–1834

508   *Frost at Midnight*

THE Frost performs its secret ministry,
Unhelped by any wind. The owlet's cry
Came loud—and hark, again! loud as before.
The inmates of my cottage, all at rest,
Have left me to that solitude, which suits
Abstruser musings: save that at my side
My cradled infant slumbers peacefully.
'Tis calm indeed! so calm, that it disturbs
And vexes meditation with its strange
And extreme silentness. Sea, hill, and wood,
This populous village! Sea, and hill, and wood,
With all the numberless goings-on of life,
Inaudible as dreams! the thin blue flame
Lies on my low-burnt fire, and quivers not;
Only that film, which fluttered on the grate,
Still flutters there, the sole unquiet thing.
Methinks, its motion in this hush of nature
Gives it dim sympathies with me who live,
Making it a companionable form,
Whose puny flaps and freaks the idling Spirit
By its own moods interprets, everywhere
Echo or mirror seeking of itself,
And makes a toy of Thought.

                       But O! how oft,
How oft, at school, with most believing mind,
Presageful, have I gazed upon the bars,
To watch that fluttering *stranger*! and as oft
With unclosed lids, already had I dreamt
Of my sweet birth-place, and the old church-tower,
Whose bells, the poor man's only music, rang
From morn to evening, all the hot Fair-day,
So sweetly, that they stirred and haunted me
With a wild pleasure, falling on mine ear
Most like articulate sounds of things to come!
So gazed I, till the soothing things I dreamt,
Lulled me to sleep, and sleep prolonged my dreams!

And so I brooded all the following morn,
Awed by the stern preceptor's face, mine eye
Fixed with mock study on my swimming book:
Save if the door half opened, and I snatched
A hasty glance, and still my heart leaped up,
For still I hoped to see the *stranger's* face,
Townsman, or aunt, or sister more beloved,
My play-mate when we both were clothed alike!

    Dear Babe, that sleepest cradled by my side,
Whose gentle breathings, heard in this deep calm,
Fill up the interspersèd vacancies
And momentary pauses of the thought!
My babe so beautiful! it thrills my heart
With tender gladness, thus to look at thee,
And think that thou shalt learn far other lore,
And in far other scenes! For I was reared
In the great city, pent 'mid cloisters dim,
And saw nought lovely but the sky and stars.
But *thou*, my babe! shalt wander like a breeze
By lakes and sandy shores, beneath the crags
Of ancient mountain, and beneath the clouds,
Which image in their bulk both lakes and shores
And mountain crags: so shalt thou see and hear
The lovely shapes and sounds intelligible
Of that eternal language, which thy God
Utters, who from eternity doth teach
Himself in all, and all things in himself.
Great universal Teacher! he shall mould
Thy spirit, and by giving make it ask.

    Therefore all seasons shall be sweet to thee,
Whether the summer clothe the general earth
With greenness, or the redbreast sit and sing
Betwixt the tufts of snow on the bare branch
Of mossy apple-tree, while the nigh thatch
Smokes in the sun-thaw; whether the eave-drops fall
Heard only in the trances of the blast,
Or if the secret ministry of frost
Shall hang them up in silent icicles,
Quietly shining to the quiet Moon.

509 *The Rime of the Ancient Mariner*

PART I

An ancient Mariner meeteth three Gallants bidden to a wedding-feast, and detaineth one.

IT is an ancient Mariner
And he stoppeth one of three.
'By thy long grey beard and glittering eye,
Now wherefore stopp'st thou me?

The Bridegroom's doors are opened wide,
And I am next of kin;
The guests are met, the feast is set:
Mayst hear the merry din.'

He holds him with his skinny hand,
'There was a ship,' quoth he.
'Hold off! unhand me, grey-beard loon!'
Eftsoons his hand dropt he.

The Wedding-Guest is spellbound by the eye of the old seafaring man, and constrained to hear his tale.

He holds him with his glittering eye—
The Wedding-Guest stood still,
And listens like a three years' child:
The Mariner hath his will.

The Wedding-Guest sat on a stone:
He cannot choose but hear;
And thus spake on that ancient man,
The bright-eyed Mariner.

'The ship was cheered, the harbour cleared,
Merrily did we drop
Below the kirk, below the hill,
Below the lighthouse top.

The Mariner tells how the ship sailed southward with a good wind and fair weather, till it reached the Line.

The Sun came up upon the left,
Out of the sea came he!
And he shone bright, and on the right
Went down into the sea.

Higher and higher every day,
Till over the mast at noon—'
The Wedding-Guest here beat his breast,
For he heard the loud bassoon.

SAMUEL TAYLOR COLERIDGE

The Wedding-
Guest heareth the
bridal music; but
the Mariner con-
tinueth his tale.

The bride hath paced into the hall,
Red as a rose is she;
Nodding their heads before her goes
The merry minstrelsy.

The Wedding-Guest he beat his breast,
Yet he cannot choose but hear;
And thus spake on that ancient man,
The bright-eyed Mariner.

The ship driven by a
storm toward the
South Pole.

'And now the STORM-BLAST came, and he
Was tyrannous and strong:
He struck with his o'ertaking wings,
And chased us south along.

With sloping masts and dipping prow,
As who pursued with yell and blow
Still treads the shadow of his foe,
And forward bends his head,
The ship drove fast, loud roared the blast,
And southward aye we fled.

And now there came both mist and snow,
And it grew wondrous cold:
And ice, mast-high, came floating by,
As green as emerald.

The land of ice, and
of fearful sounds,
where no living
thing was to be seen.

And through the drifts the snowy clifts
Did send a dismal sheen:
Nor shapes of men nor beasts we ken—
The ice was all between.

The ice was here, the ice was there,
The ice was all around:
It cracked and growled, and roared and howled,
Like noises in a swound!

Till a great sea-bird,
called the Albatross,
came through the
snow-fog, and was
received with great
joy and hospitality.

At length did cross an Albatross,
Thorough the fog it came;
As if it had been a Christian soul,
We hailed it in God's name.

It ate the food it ne'er had eat,
And round and round it flew.
The ice did split with a thunder-fit;
The helmsman steered us through!

And lo! the
Albatross proveth a
bird of good omen,
and followeth the
ship as it returned
northward through
fog and floating ice.

And a good south wind sprung up behind;
The Albatross did follow,
And every day, for food or play,
Came to the mariners' hollo!

In mist or cloud, on mast or shroud,
It perched for vespers nine;
Whiles all the night, through fog-smoke white,
Glimmered the white Moon-shine.'

The ancient Mariner
inhospitably killeth
the pious bird of
good omen.

'God save thee, ancient Mariner!
From the fiends, that plague thee thus!—
Why look'st thou so?'—'With my cross-bow
I shot the ALBATROSS.'

PART II

'The Sun now rose upon the right:
Out of the sea came he,
Still hid in mist, and on the left
Went down into the sea.

And the good south wind still blew behind,
But no sweet bird did follow,
Nor any day for food or play
Came to the mariners' hollo!

His shipmates cry
out against the
ancient Mariner, for
killing the bird of
good luck.

And I had done a hellish thing,
And it would work 'em woe:
For all averred, I had killed the bird
That made the breeze to blow.
Ah wretch! said they, the bird to slay,
That made the breeze to blow!

<table>
<tr><td>

But when the fog
cleared off, they
justify the same, and
thus make them-
selves accomplices in
the crime.

</td><td>

Nor dim nor red, like God's own head,
The glorious Sun uprist:
Then all averred, I had killed the bird
That brought the fog and mist.
'Twas right, said they, such birds to slay,
That bring the fog and mist.

</td></tr>
</table>

The fair breeze
continues; the ship
enters the Pacific
Ocean, and sails
northward, even till
it reaches the Line.

The fair breeze blew, the white foam flew,
The furrow followed free;
We were the first that ever burst
Into that silent sea.

Down dropt the breeze, the sails dropt down,
'Twas sad as sad could be;
And we did speak only to break
The silence of the sea!

The ship hath been
suddenly becalmed.

All in a hot and copper sky,
The bloody Sun, at noon,
Right up above the mast did stand,
No bigger than the Moon.

Day after day, day after day,
We stuck, nor breath nor motion;
As idle as a painted ship
Upon a painted ocean.

And the Albatross
begins to be
avenged.

Water, water, every where,
And all the boards did shrink;
Water, water, every where,
Nor any drop to drink.

The very deep did rot: O Christ!
That ever this should be!
Yea, slimy things did crawl with legs
Upon the slimy sea.

About, about, in reel and rout
The death-fires danced at night;
The water, like a witch's oils,
Burnt green, and blue and white.

A Spirit had
followed them; one
of the invisible in-
habitants of this
planet, neither
departed souls nor
angels; concerning whom the learned Jew Josephus, and the Platonic Constanti-
nopolitan, Michael Psellus, may be consulted. They are very numerous, and there
is no climate or element without one or more.

And some in dreams assurèd were
Of the Spirit that plagued us so;
Nine fathom deep he had followed us
From the land of mist and snow.

And every tongue, through utter drought,
Was withered at the root;
We could not speak, no more than if
We had been choked with soot.

The shipmates, in
their sore distress,
would fain throw
the whole guilt on
the ancient Mariner:
in sign whereof they
hang the dead sea-
bird round his neck.

Ah! well a-day! What evil looks
Had I from old and young!
Instead of the cross, the Albatross
About my neck was hung.'

Part III

'There passed a weary time. Each throat
Was parched, and glazed each eye.
A weary time! a weary time!
How glazed each weary eye,

The ancient Mariner
beholdeth a sign in
the element afar off.

When looking westward, I beheld
A something in the sky.

At first it seemed a little speck,
And then it seemed a mist;
It moved and moved, and took at last
A certain shape, I wist.

A speck, a mist, a shape, I wist!
And still it neared and neared:
As if it dodged a water-sprite,
It plunged and tacked and veered.

At its nearer
approach, it seemeth
him to be a ship;
and at a dear ran-
som he freeth his
speech from the
bonds of thirst.

With throats unslaked, with black lips baked,
We could nor laugh nor wail;
Through utter drought all dumb we stood!
I bit my arm, I sucked the blood,
And cried, A sail! a sail!

With throats unslaked, with black lips baked,
Agape they heard me call:

A flash of joy;

Gramercy! they for joy did grin,
And all at once their breath drew in,
As they were drinking all.

And horror follows.
For can it be a ship
that comes onward
without wind or
tide?

See! see! (I cried) she tacks no more!
Hither to work us weal;
Without a breeze, without a tide,
She steadies with upright keel!

The western wave was all a-flame.
The day was well nigh done!
Almost upon the western wave
Rested the broad bright Sun;
When that strange shape drove suddenly
Betwixt us and the Sun.

It seemeth him but
the skeleton of a
ship.

And straight the Sun was flecked with bars,
(Heaven's Mother send us grace!)
As if through a dungeon-grate he peered
With broad and burning face.

And its ribs are seen
as bars on the face
of the setting Sun.
The Spectre-
Woman and her
Death-mate, and no
other on board the
skeleton ship.

Alas! (thought I, and my heart beat loud)
How fast she nears and nears!
Are those *her* sails that glance in the Sun,
Like restless gossameres?

Are those *her* ribs through which the Sun
Did peer, as through a grate?
And is that Woman all her crew?
Is that a DEATH? and are there two?
Is DEATH that woman's mate?

Like vessel, like
crew! Death and
Life-in-Death have
diced for the ship's
crew, and she (the
latter) winneth the
ancient Mariner.

Her lips were red, *her* looks were free,
Her locks were yellow as gold:
Her skin was as white as leprosy,
The Night-mare LIFE-IN-DEATH was she,
Who thicks man's blood with cold.

The naked hulk alongside came,
And the twain were casting dice;
"The game is done! I've won! I've won!"
Quoth she, and whistles thrice.

No twilight within the courts of the Sun.

The Sun's rim dips; the stars rush out:
At one stride comes the dark;
With far-heard whisper, o'er the sea,
Off shot the spectre-bark.

At the rising of the Moon,

We listened and looked sideways up!
Fear at my heart, as at a cup,
My life-blood seemed to sip!
The stars were dim, and thick the night,
The steersman's face by his lamp gleamed white;
From the sails the dew did drip—
Till clomb above the eastern bar
The hornèd Moon, with one bright star
Within the nether tip.

One after another,

One after one, by the star-dogged Moon,
Too quick for groan or sigh,
Each turned his face with a ghastly pang,
And cursed me with his eye.

His shipmates drop down dead.

Four times fifty living men,
(And I heard nor sigh nor groan)
With heavy thump, a lifeless lump,
They dropped down one by one.

But Life-in-Death begins her work on the ancient Mariner.

The souls did from their bodies fly,—
They fled to bliss or woe!
And every soul, it passed me by,
Like the whizz of my cross-bow!'

PART IV

The Wedding-Guest feareth that a Spirit is talking to him;

'I fear thee, ancient Mariner!
I fear thy skinny hand!
And thou art long, and lank, and brown,
As is the ribbed sea-sand.

I fear thee and thy glittering eye,
And thy skinny hand, so brown.'—
'Fear not, fear not, thou Wedding-Guest!
This body dropt not down.

But the ancient
Mariner assureth
him of his bodily
life, and proceedeth
to relate his horrible
penance.

Alone, alone, all, all alone,
Alone on a wide wide sea!
And never a saint took pity on
My soul in agony.

He despiseth the
creatures of the
calm,

The many men, so beautiful!
And they all dead did lie:
And a thousand thousand slimy things
Lived on; and so did I.

And envieth that
they should live,
and so many lie
dead.

I looked upon the rotting sea,
And drew my eyes away;
I looked upon the rotting deck,
And there the dead men lay.

I looked to heaven, and tried to pray;
But or ever a prayer had gusht,
A wicked whisper came, and made
My heart as dry as dust.

I closed my lids, and kept them close,
And the balls like pulses beat;
For the sky and the sea, and the sea and the sky
Lay like a load on my weary eye,
And the dead were at my feet.

But the curse liveth
for him in the eye of
the dead men.

The cold sweat melted from their limbs,
Nor rot nor reek did they:
The look with which they looked on me
Had never passed away.

An orphan's curse would drag to hell
A spirit from on high;
But oh! more horrible than that
Is the curse in a dead man's eye!
Seven days, seven nights, I saw that curse,
And yet I could not die.

In his loneliness and fixedness he yearneth towards the journeying Moon, and the stars that still sojourn, yet still move onward; and every-where the blue sky belongs to them, and is their appoint-ed rest, and their native country and their own natural homes, which they enter unannounced, as lords that are certainly expected and yet there is a silent joy at their arrival.

The moving Moon went up the sky,
And no where did abide:
Softly she was going up,
And a star or two beside—

Her beams bemocked the sultry main,
Like April hoar-frost spread;
But where the ship's huge shadow lay,
The charmèd water burnt alway
A still and awful red.

By the light of the Moon he beholdeth God's creatures of the great calm.

Beyond the shadow of the ship,
I watched the water-snakes:
They moved in tracks of shining white,
And when they reared, the elfish light
Fell off in hoary flakes.

Within the shadow of the ship
I watched their rich attire:
Blue, glossy green, and velvet black,
They coiled and swam; and every track
Was a flash of golden fire.

Their beauty and their happiness.

O happy living things! no tongue
Their beauty might declare:
A spring of love gushed from my heart,

He blesseth them in his heart.

And I blessed them unaware:
Sure my kind Saint took pity on me,
And I blessed them unaware.

The spell begins to break.

The self-same moment I could pray;
And from my neck so free
The Albatross fell off, and sank
Like lead into the sea.'

PART V

'Oh sleep! it is a gentle thing,
Beloved from pole to pole!
To Mary Queen the praise be given!
She sent the gentle sleep from Heaven,
That slid into my soul.

534

By grace of the holy
Mother, the ancient
Mariner is refreshed
with rain.

The silly buckets on the deck,
That had so long remained,
I dreamt that they were filled with dew;
And when I awoke, it rained.

My lips were wet, my throat was cold,
My garments all were dank;
Sure I had drunken in my dreams,
And still my body drank.

I moved, and could not feel my limbs:
I was so light—almost
I thought that I had died in sleep,
And was a blessed ghost.

He heareth sounds
and seeth strange
sights and
commotions in the
sky and the element.

And soon I heard a roaring wind:
It did not come anear;
But with its sound it shook the sails,
That were so thin and sere.

The upper air burst into life!
And a hundred fire-flags sheen,
To and fro they were hurried about!
And to and fro, and in and out,
The wan stars danced between.

And the coming wind did roar more loud,
And the sails did sigh like sedge;
And the rain poured down from one black cloud;
The Moon was at its edge.

The thick black cloud was cleft, and still
The Moon was at its side:
Like waters shot from some high crag,
The lightning fell with never a jag,
A river steep and wide.

The bodies of the
ship's crew are
inspired and the ship
moves on;

The loud wind never reached the ship,
Yet now the ship moved on!
Beneath the lightning and the Moon
The dead men gave a groan.

535

They groaned, they stirred, they all uprose,
Nor spake, nor moved their eyes;
It had been strange, even in a dream,
To have seen those dead men rise.

The helmsman steered, the ship moved on;
Yet never a breeze up-blew;
The mariners all 'gan work the ropes,
Where they were wont to do;
They raised their limbs like lifeless tools—
We were a ghastly crew.

The body of my brother's son
Stood by me, knee to knee:
The body and I pulled at one rope,
But he said nought to me.'

'I fear thee, ancient Mariner!'
'Be calm, thou Wedding-Guest!
'Twas not those souls that fled in pain,
Which to their corses came again,
But a troop of spirits blest:

But not by the souls
of the men, nor by
daemons of earth or
middle air, but by a
blessed troop of
angelic spirits, sent
down by the invoca-
tion of the guardian
saint.

For when it dawned—they dropped their arms,
And clustered round the mast;
Sweet sounds rose slowly through their mouths,
And from their bodies passed.

Around, around, flew each sweet sound,
Then darted to the Sun;
Slowly the sounds came back again,
Now mixed, now one by one.

Sometimes a-dropping from the sky
I heard the sky-lark sing;
Sometimes all little birds that are,
How they seemed to fill the sea and air
With their sweet jargoning!

And now 'twas like all instruments,
Now like a lonely flute;
And now it is an angel's song,
That makes the heavens be mute.

It ceased; yet still the sails made on
A pleasant noise till noon,
A noise like of a hidden brook
In the leafy month of June,
That to the sleeping woods all night
Singeth a quiet tune.

Till noon we quietly sailed on,
Yet never a breeze did breathe:
Slowly and smoothly went the ship,
Moved onward from beneath.

The lonesome Spirit from the South Pole carries on the ship as far as the Line, in obedience to the angelic troop, but still requireth vengeance.

Under the keel nine fathom deep,
From the land of mist and snow,
The spirit slid: and it was he
That made the ship to go.
The sails at noon left off their tune,
And the ship stood still also.

The Sun, right up above the mast,
Had fixed her to the ocean:
But in a minute she 'gan stir,
With a short uneasy motion—
Backwards and forwards half her length
With a short uneasy motion.

Then like a pawing horse let go,
She made a sudden bound:
It flung the blood into my head,
And I fell down in a swound.

The Polar Spirit's fellow-daemons, the invisible inhabitants of the element, take part in his wrong; and two of them relate, one to the other, that penance long and heavy for the ancient Mariner hath been accorded to the Polar Spirit, who returneth southward.

How long in that same fit I lay,
I have not to declare;
But ere my living life returned,
I heard and in my soul discerned
Two voices in the air.

"Is it he?" quoth one, "Is this the man?
By him who died on cross,
With his cruel bow he laid full low
The harmless Albatross.

The spirit who bideth by himself
In the land of mist and snow,
He loved the bird that loved the man
Who shot him with his bow."

The other was a softer voice,
As soft as honey-dew:
Quoth he, "The man hath penance done,
And penance more will do.'"

PART VI

FIRST VOICE

' "But tell me, tell me! speak again,
Thy soft response renewing—
What makes that ship drive on so fast?
What is the ocean doing?"

SECOND VOICE

"Still as a slave before his lord,
The ocean hath no blast;
His great bright eye most silently
Up to the Moon is cast—

If he may know which way to go;
For she guides him smooth or grim.
See, brother, see! how graciously
She looketh down on him."

FIRST VOICE

The Mariner hath been cast into a trance; for the angelic power causeth the vessel to drive northward faster than human life could endure.

"But why drives on that ship so fast,
Without or wave or wind?"

SECOND VOICE

"The air is cut away before,
And closes from behind.

Fly, brother, fly! more high, more high!
Or we shall be belated:
For slow and slow that ship will go,
When the Mariner's trance is abated."

The supernatural motion is retarded; the Mariner awakes, and his penance begins anew.

I woke, and we were sailing on
As in a gentle weather:
'Twas night, calm night, the moon was high;
The dead men stood together.

All stood together on the deck,
For a charnel-dungeon fitter:
All fixed on me their stony eyes,
That in the Moon did glitter.

The pang, the curse, with which they died,
Had never passed away:
I could not draw my eyes from theirs,
Nor turn them up to pray.

The curse is finally expiated.

And now this spell was snapt: once more
I viewed the ocean green,
And looked far forth, yet little saw
Of what had else been seen—

Like one, that on a lonesome road
Doth walk in fear and dread,
And having once turned round walks on,
And turns no more his head;
Because he knows, a frightful fiend
Doth close behind him tread.

But soon there breathed a wind on me,
Nor sound nor motion made:
Its path was not upon the sea,
In ripple or in shade.

It raised my hair, it fanned my cheek
Like a meadow-gale of spring—
It mingled strangely with my fears,
Yet it felt like a welcoming.

Swiftly, swiftly flew the ship,
Yet she sailed softly too:
Sweetly, sweetly blew the breeze—
On me alone it blew.

And the ancient
Mariner beholdeth
his native country.

Oh! dream of joy! is this indeed
The light-house top I see?
Is this the hill? is this the kirk?
Is this mine own countree?

We drifted o'er the harbour-bar,
And I with sobs did pray—
O let me be awake, my God!
Or let me sleep alway.

The harbour-bay was clear as glass,
So smoothly it was strewn!
And on the bay the moonlight lay,
And the shadow of the Moon.

The rock shone bright, the kirk no less,
That stands above the rock:
The moonlight steeped in silentness
The steady weathercock.

And the bay was white with silent light,
Till rising from the same,

The angelic spirits
leave the dead
bodies,

Full many shapes, that shadows were,
In crimson colours came.

And appear in their
own forms of light.

A little distance from the prow
Those crimson shadows were:
I turned my eyes upon the deck—
Oh, Christ! what saw I there!

Each corse lay flat, lifeless and flat,
And, by the holy rood!
A man all light, a seraph-man,
On every corse there stood.

This seraph-band, each waved his hand:
It was a heavenly sight!
They stood as signals to the land,
Each one a lovely light;

This seraph-band, each waved his hand,
No voice did they impart—
No voice; but oh! the silence sank
Like music on my heart.

But soon I heard the dash of oars,
I heard the Pilot's cheer;
My head was turned perforce away
And I saw a boat appear.

The Pilot and the Pilot's boy,
I heard them coming fast:
Dear Lord in Heaven! it was a joy
The dead men could not blast.

I saw a third—I heard his voice:
It is the Hermit good!
He singeth loud his godly hymns
That he makes in the wood.
He'll shrieve my soul, he'll wash away
The Albatross's blood.'

PART VII

The Hermit of the
Wood,

'This Hermit good lives in that wood
Which slopes down to the sea.
How loudly his sweet voice he rears!
He loves to talk with marineres
That come from a far countree.

He kneels at morn, and noon, and eve—
He hath a cushion plump:
It is the moss that wholly hides
The rotted old oak-stump.

The skiff-boat neared: I heard them talk,
"Why, this is strange, I trow!
Where are those lights so many and fair,
That signal made but now?"

Approacheth the
ship with wonder.

"Strange, by my faith!" the Hermit said—
"And they answered not our cheer!
The planks looked warped! and see those sails
How thin they are and sere!
I never saw aught like to them,
Unless perchance it were

Brown skeletons of leaves that lag
My forest-brook along;
When the ivy-tod is heavy with snow,
And the owlet whoops to the wolf below,
That eats the she-wolf's young."

"Dear Lord! it hath a fiendish look—
(The Pilot made reply)
I am a-feared"—"Push on, push on!"
Said the Hermit cheerily.

The boat came closer to the ship,
But I nor spake nor stirred;
The boat came close beneath the ship,
And straight a sound was heard.

The ship suddenly sinketh.

Under the water it rumbled on,
Still louder and more dread:
It reached the ship, it split the bay;
The ship went down like lead.

The ancient Mariner is saved in the Pilot's boat.

Stunned by that loud and dreadful sound,
Which sky and ocean smote,
Like one that hath been seven days drowned
My body lay afloat;
But swift as dreams, myself I found
Within the Pilot's boat.

Upon the whirl, where sank the ship,
The boat spun round and round;
And all was still, save that the hill
Was telling of the sound.

I moved my lips—the Pilot shrieked
And fell down in a fit;
The holy Hermit raised his eyes,
And prayed where he did sit.

I took the oars: the Pilot's boy,
Who now doth crazy go
Laughed loud and long, and all the while
His eyes went to and fro.
"Ha! Ha!" quoth he, "full plain I see,
The Devil knows how to row."

And now, all in my own countree,
I stood on the firm land!
The Hermit stepped forth from the boat,
And scarcely he could stand.

"O shrieve me, shrieve me, holy man!"
The Hermit crossed his brow.
"Say quick," quoth he, "I bid thee say—
What manner of man art thou?"

Forthwith this frame of mine was wrenched
With a woful agony,
Which forced me to begin my tale;
And then it left me free.

Since then, at an uncertain hour,
That agony returns:
And till my ghastly tale is told,
This heart within me burns.

I pass, like night, from land to land;
I have strange power of speech;
That moment that his face I see,
I know the man that must hear me:
To him my tale I teach.

What loud uproar bursts from that door!
The wedding-guests are there:
But in the garden-bower the bride
And bride-maids singing are:
And hark the little vesper bell,
Which biddeth me to prayer!

O Wedding-Guest! this soul hath been
Alone on a wide wide sea:
So lonely 'twas, that God himself
Scarce seemèd there to be.

O sweeter than the marriage-feast,
'Tis sweeter far to me,
To walk together to the kirk
With a goodly company!—

To walk together to the kirk
And all together pray,
While each to his great Father bends,
Old men, and babes, and loving friends
And youths and maidens gay!

And to teach, by his own example, love and reverence to all things that God made and loveth.

Farewell, farewell! but this I tell
To thee, thou Wedding-Guest!
He prayeth well, who loveth well
Both man and bird and beast.

He prayeth best, who loveth best
All things both great and small;
For the dear God who loveth us,
He made and loveth all.'

The Mariner, whose eye is bright,
Whose beard with age is hoar,
Is gone: and now the Wedding-Guest
Turned from the bridegroom's door.

He went like one that hath been stunned,
And is of sense forlorn:
A sadder and a wiser man,
He rose the morrow morn.

510   *Kubla Khan*

In Xanadu did Kubla Khan
   A stately pleasure-dome decree:
Where Alph, the sacred river, ran
Through caverns measureless to man
   Down to a sunless sea.
So twice five miles of fertile ground
   With walls and towers were girdled round:
And there were gardens bright with sinuous rills
Where blossomed many an incense-bearing tree;
And here were forests ancient as the hills,
Enfolding sunny spots of greenery.

But O, that deep romantic chasm which slanted
Down the green hill athwart a cedarn cover!
A savage place! as holy and enchanted
As e'er beneath a waning moon was haunted
By woman wailing for her demon-lover!
And from this chasm, with ceaseless turmoil seething,
As if this earth in fast thick pants were breathing,
A mighty fountain momently was forced;
Amid whose swift half-intermitted burst
Huge fragments vaulted like rebounding hail,
Or chaffy grain beneath the thresher's flail:
And 'mid these dancing rocks at once and ever
It flung up momently the sacred river.
Five miles meandering with a mazy motion
Through wood and dale the sacred river ran,
Then reached the caverns measureless to man,
And sank in tumult to a lifeless ocean:
And 'mid this tumult Kubla heard from far
Ancestral voices prophesying war!

    The shadow of the dome of pleasure
      Floated midway on the waves;
    Where was heard the mingled measure
      From the fountain and the caves.
It was a miracle of rare device,
A sunny pleasure-dome with caves of ice!

    A damsel with a dulcimer
      In a vision once I saw:
    It was an Abyssinian maid,
      And on her dulcimer she played,
    Singing of Mount Abora.
    Could I revive within me,
      Her symphony and song,
To such a deep delight 'twould win me,
That with music loud and long,
I would build that dome in air,
That sunny dome! those caves of ice!
And all who heard should see them there,
And all should cry, Beware! Beware!
His flashing eyes, his floating hair!

Weave a circle round him thrice,
  And close your eyes with holy dread,
  For he on honey-dew hath fed,
And drunk the milk of Paradise.

511   *Dejection: an Ode*

    Late, late yestreen I saw the new Moon,
    With the old Moon in her arms;
    And I fear, I fear, my Master dear!
    We shall have a deadly storm.
             Ballad of Sir Patrick Spence

WELL! If the Bard was weather-wise, who made
  The grand old ballad of Sir Patrick Spence,
  This night, so tranquil now, will not go hence
Unroused by winds, that ply a busier trade
Than those which mould yon cloud in lazy flakes,
Or the dull sobbing draft, that moans and rakes
Upon the strings of this Æolian lute,
    Which better far were mute.
  For lo! the New-moon winter-bright!
  And overspread with phantom light,
  (With swimming phantom light o'erspread
  But rimmed and circled by a silver thread)
I see the old Moon in her lap, foretelling
  The coming-on of rain and squally blast.
And oh! that even now the gust were swelling,
  And the slant night-shower driving loud and fast!
Those sounds which oft have raised me, whilst they awed,
    And sent my soul abroad,
Might now perhaps their wonted impulse give,
Might startle this dull pain, and make it move and live!

A grief without a pang, void, dark, and drear,
  A stifled, drowsy, unimpassioned grief,
  Which finds no natural outlet, no relief,
    In word, or sigh, or tear—
O Lady! in this wan and heartless mood,
To other thoughts by yonder throstle wooed,

All this long eve, so balmy and serene,
Have I been gazing on the western sky,
   And its peculiar tint of yellow green:
And still I gaze—and with how blank an eye!
And those thin clouds above, in flakes and bars,
That give away their motion to the stars;
Those stars, that glide behind them or between,
Now sparkling, now bedimmed, but always seen:
Yon crescent Moon, as fixed as if it grew
In its own cloudless, starless lake of blue;
I see them all so excellently fair,
I see, not feel, how beautiful they are!

     My genial spirits fail;
     And what can these avail
To lift the smothering weight from off my breast?
     It were a vain endeavour,
     Though I should gaze for ever
On that green light that lingers in the west:
I may not hope from outward forms to win
The passion and the life, whose fountains are within.

O Lady! we receive but what we give,
And in our life alone does Nature live:
Ours is her wedding garment, ours her shroud!
   And would we aught behold, of higher worth,
Than that inanimate cold world allowed
To the poor loveless ever-anxious crowd,
   Ah! from the soul itself must issue forth
A light, a glory, a fair luminous cloud
     Enveloping the Earth—
And from the soul itself must there be sent
   A sweet and potent voice, of its own birth,
Of all sweet sounds the life and element!

O pure of heart! thou need'st not ask of me
What this strong music in the soul may be!
What, and wherein it doth exist,
This light, this glory, this fair luminous mist,
This beautiful and beauty-making power.
   Joy, virtuous Lady! Joy that ne'er was given,
Save to the pure, and in their purest hour,
Life, and Life's effluence, cloud at once and shower,

Joy, Lady! is the spirit and the power,
Which wedding Nature to us gives in dower
  A new Earth and new Heaven,
Undreamt of by the sensual and the proud—
Joy is the sweet voice, Joy the luminous cloud—
    We in ourselves rejoice!
And thence flows all that charms or ear or sight,
  All melodies the echoes of that voice,
All colours a suffusion from that light.

There was a time when, though my path was rough,
  This joy within me dallied with distress,
And all misfortunes were but as the stuff
  Whence Fancy made me dreams of happiness:
For hope grew round me, like the twining vine,
And fruits, and foliage, not my own, seemed mine.
But now afflictions bow me down to earth:
Nor care I that they rob me of my mirth;
    But oh! each visitation
Suspends what nature gave me at my birth,
  My shaping spirit of Imagination.
For not to think of what I needs must feel,
  But to be still and patient, all I can;
And haply by abstruse research to steal
  From my own nature all the natural man—
  This was my sole resource, my only plan:
Till that which suits a part infects the whole,
And now is almost grown the habit of my soul.

Hence, viper thoughts, that coil around my mind,
    Reality's dark dream!
I turn from you, and listen to the wind,
  Which long has raved unnoticed. What a scream
Of agony by torture lengthened out
That lute sent forth! Thou Wind, that rav'st without,
  Bare crag, or mountain-tairn, or blasted tree,
Or pine-grove whither woodman never clomb,
Or lonely house, long held the witches' home,
  Methinks were fitter instruments for thee,
Mad Lutanist! who in this month of showers,
Of dark-brown gardens, and of peeping flowers,

Mak'st Devils' yule, with worse than wintry song,
The blossoms, buds, and timorous leaves among.
   Thou Actor, perfect in all tragic sounds!
Thou mighty Poet, e'en to frenzy bold!
     What tell'st thou now about?
    'Tis of the rushing of an host in rout,
  With groans, of trampled men, with smarting wounds—
At once they groan with pain, and shudder with the cold!
But hush! there is a pause of deepest silence!
   And all that noise, as of a rushing crowd,
With groans, and tremulous shudderings—all is over—
It tells another tale, with sounds less deep and loud!
     A tale of less affright,
     And tempered with delight,
As Otway's self had framed the tender lay,—
      'Tis of a little child
      Upon a lonesome wild,
Not far from home, but she hath lost her way:
And now moans low in bitter grief and fear,
And now screams loud, and hopes to make her mother hear.

'Tis midnight, but small thoughts have I of sleep:
Full seldom may my friend such vigils keep!
Visit her, gentle Sleep! with wings of healing,
  And may this storm be but a mountain-birth,
May all the stars hang bright above her dwelling,
  Silent as though they watched the sleeping Earth!
     With light heart may she rise,
     Gay fancy, cheerful eyes,
  Joy lift her spirit, joy attune her voice;
To her may all things live, from pole to pole,
Their life the eddying of her living soul!
   O simple spirit, guided from above,
Dear Lady! friend devoutest of my choice,
Thus may'st thou ever, evermore rejoice.

512   *Time Real and Imaginary: an Allegory*

    ON the wide level of a mountain's head
    (I knew not where, but 'twas some faery place),
    Their pinions, ostrich-like, for sails outspread,
    Two lovely children run an endless race,

A sister and a brother!
This far outstripped the other;
Yet ever runs she with reverted face,
And looks and listens for the boy behind:
For he, alas! is blind!
O'er rough and smooth with even step he passed,
And knows not whether he be first or last.

513   *Work without Hope*

ALL Nature seems at work. Slugs leave their lair—
The bees are stirring—birds are on the wing—
And Winter, slumbering in the open air,
Wears on his smiling face a dream of Spring!
And I, the while, the sole unbusy thing,
Nor honey make, nor pair, nor build, nor sing.

Yet well I ken the banks where amaranths blow,
Have traced the fount whence streams of nectar flow.
Bloom, O ye amaranths! bloom for whom ye may,
For me ye bloom not! Glide, rich streams, away!
With lips unbrightened, wreathless brow, I stroll:
And would you learn the spells that drowse my soul?
Work without Hope draws nectar in a sieve,
And Hope without an object cannot live.

WALTER SAVAGE LANDOR
1775–1864

514   *Corinna, to Tanagra, from Athens*

TANAGRA! think not I forget
    Thy beautifully storeyed streets;
Be sure my memory bathes yet
    In clear Thermodon, and yet greets
The blythe and liberal shepherd-boy
Whose sunny bosom swells with joy
When we accept his matted rushes
Upheaved with sylvan fruit; away he bounds, and blushes.

I promise to bring back with me
   What thou with transport wilt receive,
The only proper gift for thee,
   Of which no mortal shall bereave
In later times thy mouldering walls,
Until the last old turret falls;
   A crown, a crown from Athens won,
A crown no God can wear, beside Latona's son.

There may be cities who refuse
   To their own child the honours due,
And look ungently on the Muse;
   But ever shall those cities rue
The dry, unyielding, niggard breast,
Offering no nourishment, no rest,
   To that young head which soon shall rise
Disdainfully, in might and glory, to the skies.

Sweetly where caverned Dirce flows
   Do white-armed maidens chaunt my lay,
Flapping the while with laurel-rose
   The honey-gathering tribes away;
And sweetly, sweetly Attick tongues
Lisp your Corinna's early songs;
   To her with feet more graceful come
The verses that have dwelt in kindred breasts at home.

O let thy children lean aslant
   Against the tender mother's knee,
And gaze into her face, and want
   To know what magic there can be
In words that urge some eyes to dance,
While others as in holy trance
   Look up to heaven: be such my praise!
Why linger? I must haste, or lose the Delphic bays.

515

MOTHER, I cannot mind my wheel;
   My fingers ache, my lips are dry:
O, if you felt the pain I feel!
   But O, who ever felt as I?

No longer could I doubt him true—
    All other men may use deceit;
He always said my eyes were blue,
    And often swore my lips were sweet.

To Ianthe

516

(i)

PAST ruined Ilion Helen lives,
    Alcestis rises from the shades;
Verse calls them forth; 'tis verse that gives
    Immortal youth to mortal maids.

Soon shall Oblivion's deepening veil
    Hide all the peopled hills you see,
The gay, the proud, while lovers hail
    These many summers you and me.

517

(ii)

FROM you, Ianthe, little troubles pass
    Like little ripples down a sunny river;
Your pleasures spring like daisies in the grass,
    Cut down, and up again as blithe as ever.

518   *Dirce*

STAND close around, ye Stygian set,
    With Dirce in one boat conveyed!
Or Charon, seeing, may forget
    That he is old and she a shade.

519   *Rose Aylmer*

AH, what avails the sceptred race!
   Ah, what the form divine!
What every virtue, every grace!
   Rose Aylmer, all were thine.

Rose Aylmer, whom these wakeful eyes
   May weep, but never see,
A night of memories and sighs
   I consecrate to thee.

520   *Ternissa*

TERNISSA! you are fled!
   I say not to the dead,
But to the happy ones who rest below:
   For, surely, surely, where
   Your voice and graces are,
Nothing of death can any feel or know.
   Girls who delight to dwell
   Where grows most asphodel,
Gather to their calm breasts each word you speak:
   The mild Persephone
   Places you on her knee,
And your cool palm smoothes down stern Plato's cheek.

521

I STROVE with none, for none was worth my strife.
Nature I loved and, next to Nature, Art:
I warmed both hands before the fire of life;
It sinks, and I am ready to depart.

522

DEATH stands above me, whispering low
   I know not what into my ear:
Of his strange language all I know
   Is, there is not a word of fear.

CHARLES LAMB
1775-1834

523 *The Old Familiar Faces*

I HAVE had playmates, I have had companions,
In my days of childhood, in my joyful school-days,
All, all are gone, the old familiar faces.

I have been laughing, I have been carousing,
Drinking late, sitting late, with my bosom cronies,
All, all are gone, the old familiar faces.

I loved a love once, fairest among women:
Closed are her doors on me, I must not see her—
All, all are gone, the old familiar faces.

I have a friend, a kinder friend has no man;
Like an ingrate, I left my friend abruptly;
Left him, to muse on the old familiar faces.

Ghost-like I paced round the haunts of my childhood,
Earth seemed a desert I was bound to traverse,
Seeking to find the old familiar faces.

Friend of my bosom, thou more than a brother,
Why wert not thou born in my father's dwelling?
So might we talk of the old familiar faces—

How some they have died, and some they have left me,
And some are taken from me; all are departed;
All, all are gone, the old familiar faces.

THOMAS CAMPBELL
1777–1844

524   *Ye Mariners of England*

YE Mariners of England
  That guard our native seas!
Whose flag has braved a thousand years
  The battle and the breeze!
Your glorious standard launch again
  To match another foe;
And sweep through the deep,
  While the stormy winds do blow!
While the battle rages loud and long
  And the stormy winds do blow.

The spirits of your fathers
  Shall start from every wave—
For the deck it was their field of fame,
  And Ocean was their grave:
Where Blake and mighty Nelson fell
  Your manly hearts shall glow,
As ye sweep through the deep,
  While the stormy winds do blow!
While the battle rages loud and long
  And the stormy winds do blow.

Britannia needs no bulwarks,
  No towers along the steep;
Her march is o'er the mountain-waves,
  Her home is on the deep.
With thunders from her native oak
  She quells the floods below,
As they roar on the shore,
  When the stormy winds do blow!
When the battle rages loud and long,
  And the stormy winds do blow.

The meteor flag of England
  Shall yet terrific burn;
Till danger's troubled night depart
  And the star of peace return.

555

Then, then, ye ocean-warriors!
  Our song and feast shall flow
To the fame of your name,
    When the storm has ceased to blow!
When the fiery fight is heard no more,
    And the storm has ceased to blow.

525   *Hohenlinden*

ON Linden, when the sun was low,
All bloodless lay the untrodden snow,
And dark as winter was the flow
  Of Iser, rolling rapidly.

But Linden saw another sight,
When the drum beat, at dead of night,
Commanding fires of death to light
  The darkness of her scenery.

By torch and trumpet fast arrayed,
Each horseman drew his battle blade,
And furious every charger neighed
  To join the dreadful revelry.

Then shook the hills, with thunder riven;
Then rushed the steed, to battle driven;
And, louder than the bolts of heaven,
  Far flashed the red artillery.

But redder yet that light shall glow,
On Linden's hills of stainèd snow;
And bloodier yet, the torrent flow
  Of Iser, rolling rapidly.

'Tis morn; but scarce yon level sun
Can pierce the war-clouds, rolling dun,
Where furious Frank, and fiery Hun,
  Shout in their sulphurous canopy.

The combat deepens. On, ye brave,
Who rush to glory, or the grave!
Wave, Munich, all thy banners wave,
  And charge with all thy chivalry!

Few, few shall part, where many meet!
The snow shall be their winding sheet,
And every turf, beneath their feet,
    Shall be a soldier's sepulchre.

THOMAS MOORE

1779–1852

526   *The Light of Other Days*

OFT, in the stilly night,
    Ere slumber's chain has bound me,
Fond Memory brings the light
    Of other days around me:
    The smiles, the tears
    Of boyhood's years,
    The words of love then spoken;
        The eyes that shone,
        Now dimmed and gone,
    The cheerful hearts now broken!
Thus, in the stilly night,
    Ere slumber's chain has bound me,
Sad Memory brings the light
    Of other days around me.

When I remember all
    The friends, so linked together,
I've seen around me fall
    Like leaves in wintry weather,
        I feel like one
        Who treads alone
    Some banquet-hall deserted,
        Whose lights are fled,
        Whose garlands dead,
    And all but he departed!
Thus, in the stilly night,
    Ere slumber's chain has bound me.
Sad Memory brings the light
    Of other days around me.

527   *At the Mid Hour of Night*

AT the mid hour of night, when stars are weeping, I fly
To the lone vale we loved, when life shone warm in thine eye;
    And I think that, if spirits can steal from the regions of air
    To revisit past scenes of delight, thou wilt come to me there,
And tell me our love is remembered even in the sky.

Then I sing the wild song it once was such rapture to hear,
When our voices commingling breathed like one on the ear;
    And as Echo far off through the vale my sad orison rolls,
    I think, O my love! 'tis thy voice from the Kingdom of Souls
Faintly answering still the notes that once were so dear.

JAMES LEIGH HUNT
1784–1859

528   *The Nile*

IT flows through old hushed Egypt and its sands,
    Like some grave mighty thought threading a dream,
    And times and things, as in that vision, seem
Keeping along it their eternal stands,—
Caves, pillars, pyramids, the shepherd bands
    That roamed through the young world, the glory extreme
    Of high Sesostris, and that southern beam,
The laughing queen that caught the world's great hands.
Then comes a mightier silence, stern and strong,
As of a world left empty of its throng,
    And the void weighs on us; and then we wake,
And hear the fruitful stream lapsing along
    Twixt villages, and think how we shall take
    Our own calm journey on for human sake.

529   *Abou Ben Adhem*

ABOU BEN ADHEM (may his tribe increase!)
Awoke one night from a deep dream of peace,
And saw, within the moonlight in his room,
Making it rich, and like a lily in bloom,
An angel writing in a book of gold:—
Exceeding peace had made Ben Adhem bold,
And to the presence in the room he said,
    'What writest thou?'—The vision raised its head,
And with a look made of all sweet accord,
Answered, 'The names of those who love the Lord.'
'And is mine one?' said Abou. 'Nay, not so,'
Replied the angel. Abou spoke more low,
But cheerly still; and said, 'I pray thee, then,
Write me as one that loves his fellow men.'
    The angel wrote, and vanished. The next night
It came again with a great wakening light,
And showed the names whom love of God had blest,
And lo! Ben Adhem's name led all the rest.

530   *Jenny Kissed Me*

JENNY kissed me when we met,
    Jumping from the chair she sat in;
Time, you thief, who love to get
    Sweets into your list, put that in!
Say I'm weary, say I'm sad,
    Say that health and wealth have missed me,
Say I'm growing old, but add,
    Jenny kissed me.

THOMAS LOVE PEACOCK
1785–1866

531   *The War Song of Dinas Vawr*

THE mountain sheep are sweeter,
But the valley sheep are fatter;
We therefore deemed it meeter
To carry off the latter.
We made an expedition;
We met a host, and quelled it;
We forced a strong position,
And killed the men who held it.

On Dyfed's richest valley,
Where herds of kine were brousing,
We made a mighty sally,
To furnish our carousing.
Fierce warriors rushed to meet us;
We met them, and o'erthrew them:
They struggled hard to beat us;
But we conquered them, and slew them.

As we drove our prize at leisure,
The king marched forth to catch us:
His rage surpassed all measure,
But his people could not match us.
He fled to his hall-pillars;
And, ere our force we led off,
Some sacked his house and cellars,
While others cut his head off.

We there, in strife bewildering,
Spilt blood enough to swim in:
We orphaned many children,
And widowed many women.
The eagles and the ravens
We glutted with our foemen;
The heroes and the cravens,
The spearmen and the bowmen.

We brought away from battle,
And much their land bemoaned them,
Two thousand head of cattle,
And the head of him who owned them:
Ednyfed, king of Dyfed,
His head was borne before us;
His wine and beasts supplied our feasts,
And his overthrow, our chorus.

532 *Newark Abbey*

August, 1842, with a reminiscence of August, 1807

I GAZE where August's sunbeam falls
Along these gray and lonely walls,
Till in its light absorbed appears
The lapse of five-and thirty years.
  If change there be, I trace it not
In all this consecrated spot:
No new imprint of Ruin's march
On roofless wall and frameless arch:
The woods, the hills, the fields, the stream,
Are basking in the selfsame beam:
The fall, that turns the unseen mill,
As then it murmured, murmurs still.
It seems as if in one were cast
The present and the imaged past;
Spanning, as with a bridge sublime,
That fearful lapse of human time;
That gulf, unfathomably spread
Between the living and the dead.
  For all too well my spirit feels
The only change this scene reveals.
The sunbeams play, the breezes stir,
Unseen, unfelt, unheard by her,
Who, on that long-past August day,
Beheld with me these ruins gray.
  Whatever span the fates allow,
Ere I shall be as she is now,
Still, in my bosom's inmost cell,
Shall that deep-treasured memory dwell;
That, more than language can express,
Pure miracle of loveliness,

Whose voice so sweet, whose eyes so bright,
Were my soul's music, and its light,
In those blest days when life was new,
And hope was false, but love was true.

533   *Rich and Poor*

THE poor man's sins are glaring;
In the face of ghostly warning
        He is caught in the fact
        Of an overt act—
Buying greens on Sunday morning.

The rich man's sins are hidden
In the pomp of wealth and station;
        And escape the sight
        Of the children of light,
Who are wise in their generation.

The rich man has a kitchen,
And cooks to dress his dinner;
        The poor who would roast
        To the baker's must post,
And thus becomes a sinner.

The rich man has a cellar,
And a ready butler by him;
        The poor must steer
        For his pint of beer
Where the saint can't choose but spy him.

The rich man's painted windows
Hide the concerts of the quality;
        The poor can but share
        A cracked fiddle in the air,
Which offends all sound morality.

The rich man is invisible
In the crowd of his gay society;
        But the poor man's delight
        Is a sore in the sight,
And a stench in the nose of piety.

The rich man has a carriage
Where no rude eye can flout him;
    The poor man's bane
    Is a third class train,
With the day-light all about him.

The rich man goes out yachting,
Where sanctity can't pursue him;
    The poor goes afloat
    In a fourpenny boat,
Where the bishop groans to view him.

GEORGE GORDON NOEL, LORD BYRON

1788–1824

534

SHE walks in beauty, like the night
    Of cloudless climes and starry skies;
And all that's best of dark and bright
    Meet in her aspect and her eyes:
Thus mellowed to that tender light
    Which heaven to gaudy day denies.

One shade the more, one ray the less,
    Had half impaired the nameless grace
Which waves in every raven tress,
    Or softly lightens o'er her face;
Where thoughts serenely sweet express
    How pure, how dear their dwelling-place.

And on that cheek, and o'er that brow,
    So soft, so calm, yet eloquent,
The smiles that win, the tints that glow,
    But tell of days in goodness spent,
A mind at peace with all below,
    A heart whose love is innocent.

535

WHEN we two parted
    In silence and tears,
Half broken-hearted
    To sever for years,
Pale grew thy cheek and cold,
    Colder thy kiss;
Truly that hour foretold
    Sorrow to this.

The dew of the morning
    Sunk chill on my brow—
It felt like the warning
    Of what I feel now.
Thy vows are all broken,
    And light is thy fame;
I hear thy name spoken,
    And share in its shame.

They name thee before me,
    A knell to mine ear;
A shudder comes o'er me—
    Why wert thou so dear?
They know not I knew thee,
    Who knew thee too well:—
Long, long shall I rue thee,
    Too deeply to tell.

In secret we met—
    In silence I grieve,
That thy heart could forget,
    Thy spirit deceive.
If I should meet thee
    After long years,
How should I greet thee?
    With silence and tears.

536 *The Eve of Waterloo*

THERE was a sound of revelry by night,
  And Belgium's Capital had gathered then
  Her Beauty and her Chivalry, and bright
  The lamps shone o'er fair women and brave men;
  A thousand hearts beat happily; and when
  Music arose with its voluptuous swell,
  Soft eyes looked love to eyes which spake again,
  And all went merry as a marriage bell;
But hush! hark! a deep sound strikes like a rising knell!

Did ye not hear it?—No; 'twas but the wind,
  Or the car rattling o'er the stony street;
  On with the dance! let joy be unconfined;
  No sleep till morn, when Youth and Pleasure meet
  To chase the glowing Hours with flying feet—
  But hark!—that heavy sound breaks in once more,
  As if the clouds its echo would repeat;
  And nearer, clearer, deadlier than before!
Arm! Arm! it is—it is—the cannon's opening roar!

Within a windowed niche of that high hall
  Sate Brunswick's fated chieftain; he did hear
  That sound the first amidst the festival,
  And caught its tone with Death's prophetic ear;
  And when they smiled because he deemed it near,
  His heart more truly knew that peal too well
  Which stretched his father on a bloody bier,
  And roused the vengeance blood alone could quell;
He rushed into the field, and, foremost fighting, fell.

Ah! then and there was hurrying to and fro,
  And gathering tears, and tremblings of distress,
  And cheeks all pale, which but an hour ago
  Blushed at the praise of their own loveliness;
  And there were sudden partings, such as press
  The life from out young hearts, and choking sighs
  Which ne'er might be repeated; who could guess
  If ever more should meet those mutual eyes,
Since upon night so sweet such awful morn could rise!

And there was mounting in hot haste: the steed,
  The mustering squadron, and the clattering car,
  Went pouring forward with impetuous speed,
  And swiftly forming in the ranks of war;
  And the deep thunder peal on peal afar;
  And near, the beat of the alarming drum
  Roused up the soldier ere the morning star;
  While thronged the citizens with terror dumb,
Or whispering, with white lips—'The foe! They come!
    they come!'

And wild and high the 'Cameron's Gathering' rose!
  The war-note of Lochiel, which Albyn's hills
  Have heard, and heard, too, have her Saxon foes:—
  How in the noon of night that pibroch thrills,
  Savage and shrill! But with the breath which fills
  Their mountain-pipe, so fill the mountaineers
  With the fierce native daring which instils
  The stirring memory of a thousand years,
And Evan's, Donald's fame rings in each clansman's ears!

And Ardennes waves above them her green leaves,
  Dewy with nature's tear-drops, as they pass,
  Grieving, if aught inanimate e'er grieves,
  Over the unreturning brave,—alas!
  Ere evening to be trodden like the grass
  Which now beneath them, but above shall grow
  In its next verdure, when this fiery mass
  Of living valour, rolling on the foe
And burning with high hope, shall moulder cold and low.

Last noon beheld them full of lusty life,
  Last eve in Beauty's circle proudly gay,
  The midnight brought the signal-sound of strife,
  The morn the marshalling in arms,—the day
  Battle's magnificently-stern array!
  The thunder-clouds close o'er it, which when rent
  The earth is covered thick with other clay
  Which her own clay shall cover, heaped and pent,
Rider and horse,—friend, foe,—in one red burial blent!

537   *The Dying Gladiator*

I SEE before me the Gladiator lie:
   He leans upon his hand—his manly brow
   Consents to death, but conquers agony,
   And his drooped head sinks gradually low—
   And through his side the last drops, ebbing slow
   From the red gash, fall heavy, one by one,
   Like the first of a thunder-shower; and now
   The arena swims around him—he is gone,
Ere ceased the inhuman shout which hailed the wretch
     who won.

He heard it, but he heeded not—his eyes
   Were with his heart and that was far away;
   He recked not of the life he lost nor prize,
   But where his rude hut by the Danube lay,
   There were his young barbarians all at play,
   There was their Dacian mother—he, their sire,
   Butchered to make a Roman holiday—
   All this rushed with his blood—Shall he expire
And unavenged?—Arise! ye Goths, and glut your ire!

538   *from* The Prisoner of Chillon

A KIND of change came in my fate,
My keepers grew compassionate;
I know not what had made them so,
They were inured to sights of woe,
But so it was:—my broken chain
With links unfastened did remain,
And it was liberty to stride,
Along my cell from side to side,
And up and down, and then athwart,
And tread it over every part;
And round the pillars one by one,
Returning where my walk begun,
Avoiding only, as I trod,
My brothers' graves without a sod;

For if I thought with heedless tread
My step profaned their lowly bed,
My breath came gaspingly and thick,
And my crushed heart felt blind and sick.

I made a footing in the wall,
  It was not therefrom to escape,
For I had buried one and all,
  Who loved me in a human shape;
And the whole earth would henceforth be
A wider prison unto me:
No child, no sire, no kin had I,
No partner in my misery;
I thought of this, and I was glad,
For thought of them had made me mad;
But I was curious to ascend
To my barred windows, and to bend
Once more, upon the mountains high,
The quiet of a loving eye.

I saw them, and they were the same,
They were not changed like me in frame;
I saw their thousand years of snow
On high—their wide long lake below,
And the blue Rhone in fullest flow;
I heard the torrents leap and gush
O'er channelled rock and broken bush;
I saw the white-walled distant town,
And whiter sails go skimming down;
And then there was a little isle,
Which in my very face did smile,
  The only one in view;
A small green isle, it seemed no more,
Scarce broader than my dungeon floor,
But in it there were three tall trees,
And o'er it blew the mountain breeze,
And by it there were waters flowing,
And on it there were young flowers growing,
  Of gentle breath and hue.
The fish swam by the castle wall,
And they seemed joyous each and all;
The eagle rode the rising blast,
Methought he never flew so fast

As then to me he seemed to fly;
And then new tears came in my eye,
And I felt troubled—and would fain
I had not left my recent chain;
And when I did descend again,
The darkness of my dim abode
Fell on me as a heavy load;
It was as is a new-dug grave,
Closing o'er one we sought to save,—
And yet my glance, too much opprest,
Had almost need of such a rest.

It might be months, or years, or days,
   I kept no count, I took no note,
I had no hope my eyes to raise,
   And clear them of their dreary mote;
At last men came to set me free;
   I asked not why, and recked not where;
It was at length the same to me,
Fettered or fetterless to be
   I learned to love despair.
And thus when they appeared at last,
And all my bonds aside were cast,
These heavy walls to me had grown
A hermitage—and all my own!
And half I felt as they were come
To tear me from a second home:
With spiders I had friendship made,
And watched them in their sullen trade,
Had seen the mice by moonlight play,
And why should I feel less than they?
We were all inmates of one place,
And I, the monarch of each race,
Had power to kill—yet, strange to tell!
In quiet we had learned to dwell;
My very chains and I grew friends,
So much a long communion tends
To make us what we are:—even I
Regained my freedom with a sigh.

539 *Prometheus*

TITAN! to whose immortal eyes
 The sufferings of mortality,
  Seen in their sad reality,
Were not as things that gods despise;
What was thy pity's recompense?
A silent suffering, and intense;
The rock, the vulture, and the chain,
All that the proud can feel of pain,
The agony they do not show,
The suffocating sense of woe,
 Which speaks but in its loneliness,
And then is jealous lest the sky
Should have a listener, nor will sigh
 Until its voice is echoless.

Titan! to thee the strife was given
 Between the suffering and the will,
  Which torture where they cannot kill;
And the inexorable Heaven,
And the deaf tyranny of Fate,
The ruling principle of Hate,
Which for its pleasure doth create
The things it may annihilate,
Refused thee even the boon to die:
The wretched gift Eternity
Was thine—and thou hast borne it well.
All that the Thunderer wrung from thee
Was but the menace which flung back
On him the torments of thy rack;
The fate thou didst so well foresee,
But would not to appease him tell;
And in thy Silence was his Sentence,
And in his Soul a vain repentance,
And evil dread so ill dissembled,
That in his hand the lightnings trembled.

Thy Godlike crime was to be kind,
 To render with thy precepts less
  The sum of human wretchedness,
And strengthen Man with his own mind;

But baffled as thou wert from high,
Still in thy patient energy,
In the endurance, and repulse
    Of thine impenetrable Spirit,
Which Earth and Heaven could not convulse,
    A mighty lesson we inherit:
Thou art a symbol and a sign
    To Mortals of their fate and force;
Like thee, Man is in part divine,
    A troubled stream from a pure source;
And Man in portions can foresee
His own funereal destiny;
His wretchedness, and his resistance,
And his sad unallied existence:
To which his Spirit may oppose
Itself—an equal to all woes,
    And a firm will, and a deep sense,
Which even in torture can descry
    Its own concentered recompense,
Triumphant where it dares defy,
And making Death a Victory.

540   *Italy versus England*

WITH all its sinful doings, I must say,
    That Italy's a pleasant place to me,
Who love to see the sun shine every day,
    And vines (not nailed to walls) from tree to tree
Festooned, much like the back scene of a play,
    Or melodrame, which people flock to see,
When the first act is ended by a dance
In vineyards copied from the South of France.

I like on autumn evenings to ride out,
    Without being forced to bid my groom be sure
My cloak is round his middle strapped about,
    Because the skies are not the most secure;
I know too that, if stopped upon my route,
    Where the green alleys windingly allure,
Reeling with grapes red wagons choke the way.—
In England 'twould be dung, dust, or a dray.

I also like to dine on becaficas,
   To see the sun set, sure he'll rise to-morrow,
Not through a misty morning twinkling weak as
   A drunken man's dead eye in maudlin sorrow,
But with all Heaven to himself; the day will break as
   Beauteous as cloudless, nor be forced to borrow
That sort of farthing candlelight which glimmers
Where reeking London's smoky cauldron simmers.

I love the language, that soft bastard Latin,
   Which melts like kisses from a female mouth,
And sounds as if it should be writ on satin,
   With syllables which breathe of the sweet South,
And gentle liquids gliding all so pat in,
   That not a single accent seems uncouth,
Like our harsh northern whistling, grunting guttural,
Which we're obliged to hiss, and spit, and sputter all.

I like the women too (forgive my folly!),
   From the rich peasant cheek of ruddy bronze,
And large black eyes that flash on you a volley
   Of rays that say a thousand things at once,
To the high Dama's brow, more melancholy,
   But clear, and with a wild and liquid glance,
Heart on her lips, and soul within her eyes,
Soft as her clime, and sunny as her skies.

Eve of the land which still is Paradise!
   Italian Beauty! didst thou not inspire
Raphael, who died in thy embrace, and vies
   With all we know of Heaven, or can desire,
In what he hath bequeathed us?—in what guise,
   Though flashing from the fervour of the lyre,
Would *words* describe thy past and present glow,
While yet Canova can create below?

'England! with all thy faults I love thee still',
   I said at Calais, and have not forgot it;
I like to speak and lucubrate my fill;
   I like the government (but that is not it);
I like the freedom of the press and quill;
   I like the Habeas Corpus (when we've got it);
I like a Parliamentary debate,
Particularly when 'tis not too late;

I like the taxes, when they're not too many;
   I like a seacoal fire, when not too dear;
I like a beef-steak, too, as well as any;
   Have no objection to a pot of beer;
I like the weather,—when it is not rainy,
   That is, I like two months of every year.
And so God save the Regent, Church, and King!
Which means that I like all and every thing.

Our standing army, and disbanded seamen,
   Poor's rate, Reform, my own, the nation's debt,
Our little riots just to show we're free men,
   Our trifling bankruptcies in the Gazette,
Our cloudy climate, and our chilly women,
   All these I can forgive, and those forget,
And greatly venerate our recent glories,
And wish they were not owing to the Tories.

541   *So, we'll go no more a-roving*

So, we'll go no more a-roving
   So late into the night,
Though the heart be still as loving,
   And the moon be still as bright.

For the sword outwears its sheath,
   And the soul wears out the breast,
And the heart must pause to breathe,
   And love itself have rest.

Though the night was made for loving,
   And the day returns too soon,
Yet we'll go no more a-roving
   By the light of the moon.

542 *Growing Old*

BUT now at thirty years my hair is grey—
    (I wonder what it will be like at forty?
I thought of a peruke the other day—)
    My heart is not much greener; and, in short, I
Have squandered my whole summer while 'twas May,
    And feel no more the spirit to retort; I
Have spent my life, both interest and principal,
And deem not, what I deemed, my soul invincible.

No more—no more—Oh! never more on me
    The freshness of the heart can fall like dew,
Which out of all the lovely things we see
    Extracts emotions beautiful and new;
Hived in our bosoms like the bag o' the bee.
    Think'st thou the honey with those objects grew?
Alas! 'twas not in them, but in thy power
To double even the sweetness of a flower.

No more—no more—Oh! never more, my heart,
    Canst thou be my sole world, my universe!
Once all in all, but now a thing apart,
    Thou canst not be my blessing or my curse:
The illusion's gone for ever, and thou art
    Insensible, I trust, but none the worse,
And in thy stead I've got a deal of judgement,
Though Heaven knows how it ever found a lodgement.

My days of love are over; me no more
    The charms of maid, wife, and still less of widow,
Can make the fool of which they made before,—
    In short, I must not lead the life I did do;
The credulous hope of mutual minds is o'er,
    The copious use of claret is forbid too,
So for a good old-gentlemanly vice,
I think I must take up with avarice.

Ambition was my idol, which was broken
    Before the shrines of Sorrow, and of Pleasure;
And the two last have left me many a token
    O'er which reflection may be made at leisure:

Now, like Friar Bacon's Brazen Head, I've spoken,
　'Time is, Time was, Time's past': a chymic treasure
Is glittering Youth, which I have spent betimes—
My heart in passion, and my head on rhymes.

What is the end of Fame? 'tis but to fill
　A certain portion of uncertain paper:
Some liken it to climbing up a hill,
　Whose summit, like all hills, is lost in vapour;
For this men write, speak, preach, and heroes kill,
　And bards burn what they call their 'midnight taper',
To have, when the original is dust,
A name, a wretched picture and worse bust.

What are the hopes of man? Old Egypt's King
　Cheops erected the first Pyramid
And largest, thinking it was just the thing
　To keep his memory whole, and mummy hid;
But somebody or other rummaging,
　Burglariously broke his coffin's lid:
Let not a monument give you or me hopes,
Since not a pinch of dust remains of Cheops.

But I, being fond of true philosophy,
　Say very often to myself, 'Alas!
All things that have been born were born to die,
　And flesh (which Death mows down to hay) is grass;
You've passed your youth not so unpleasantly,
　And if you had it o'er again—'twould pass—
So thank your stars that matters are no worse,
And read your Bible, sir, and mind your purse.'

543　　　　　*The Isles of Greece*

THE isles of Greece! the isles of Greece
　Where burning Sappho loved and sung,
Where grew the arts of war and peace,
　Where Delos rose, and Phœbus sprung!
Eternal summer gilds them yet,
But all, except their sun, is set.

The Scian and the Teian muse,
  The hero's harp, the lover's lute,
Have found the fame your shores refuse:
  Their place of birth alone is mute
To sounds which echo further west
Than your sires' 'Islands of the Blest.'

The mountains look on Marathon—
  And Marathon looks on the sea;
And musing there an hour alone,
  I dreamed that Greece might still be free;
For standing on the Persians' grave,
I could not deem myself a slave.

A king sate on the rocky brow
  Which looks o'er sea-born Salamis;
And ships, by thousands, lay below,
  And men in nations;—all were his!
He counted them at break of day—
And when the sun set, where were they?

And where are they? and where art thou,
  My country? On thy voiceless shore
The heroic lay is tuneless now—
  The heroic bosom beats no more!
And must thy lyre, so long divine,
Degenerate into hands like mine?

'Tis something in the dearth of fame,
  Though linked among a fettered race,
To feel at least a patriot's shame,
  Even as I sing, suffuse my face;
For what is left the poet here?
For Greeks a blush—for Greece a tear.

Must *we* but weep o'er days more blest?
  Must *we* but blush?—Our fathers bled.
Earth! render back from out thy breast
  A remnant of our Spartan dead!
Of the three hundred grant but three,
To make a new Thermopylæ!

What, silent still? and silent all?
   Ah! no;—the voices of the dead
Sound like a distant torrent's fall,
   And answer, 'Let one living head,
But one, arise,—we come, we come!'
'Tis but the living who are dumb.

In vain—in vain: strike other chords;
   Fill high the cup with Samian wine!
Leave battles to the Turkish hordes,
   And shed the blood of Scio's vine!
Hark! rising to the ignoble call—
How answers each bold Bacchanal!

You have the Pyrrhic dance as yet;
   Where is the Pyrrhic phalanx gone?
Of two such lessons, why forget
   The nobler and the manlier one?
You have the letters Cadmus gave—
Think ye he meant them for a slave?

Fill high the bowl with Samian wine!
   We will not think of themes like these!
It made Anacreon's song divine:
   He served—but served Polycrates—
A tyrant; but our masters then
Were still, at least, our countrymen.

The tyrant of the Chersonese
   Was freedom's best and bravest friend;
That tyrant was Miltiades!
   O that the present hour would lend
Another despot of the kind!
Such chains as his were sure to bind.

Fill high the bowl with Samian wine!
   On Suli's rock, and Parga's shore,
Exists the remnant of a line
   Such as the Doric mothers bore;
And there, perhaps, some seed is sown,
The Heracleidan blood might own.

Trust not for freedom to the Franks—
 They have a king who buys and sells;
In native swords and native ranks
 The only hope of courage dwells:
But Turkish force and Latin fraud
Would break your shield, however broad.

Fill high the bowl with Samian wine!
 Our virgins dance beneath the shade—
I see their glorious black eyes shine;
 But gazing on each glowing maid,
My own the burning tear-drop laves,
To think such breasts must suckle slaves.

Place me on Sunium's marbled steep,
 Where nothing, save the waves and I,
May hear our mutual murmurs sweep;
 There, swan-like, let me sing and die:
A land of slaves shall ne'er be mine—
Dash down yon cup of Samian wine!

544   *Love and Death:*
       Last Lines

I WATCHED thee when the foe was at our side,
 Ready to strike at him—or thee and me,
Were safety hopeless—rather than divide
 Aught with one loved save love and liberty.

I watched thee on the breakers, when the rock
 Received our prow and all was storm and fear,
And bade thee cling to me through every shock;
 This arm would be thy bark, or breast thy bier.

I watched thee when the fever glazed thine eyes,
 Yielding my couch and stretched me on the ground,
When overworn with watching, ne'er to rise
 From thence if thou an early grave hadst found.

The earthquake came, and rocked the quivering wall,
 And men and nature reeled as if with wine.
Whom did I seek around the tottering hall?
 For thee. Whose safety first provide for? Thine.

And when convulsive throes denied my breath
  The faintest utterance to my fading thought,
To thee—to thee—e'en in the gasp of death
  My spirit turned, oh! oftener than it ought.

Thus much and more; and yet thou lov'st me not,
  And never wilt! Love dwells not in our will.
Nor can I blame thee, though it be my lot
  To strongly, wrongly, vainly love thee still.

CHARLES WOLFE

1791–1823

545   *The Burial of Sir John Moore
after Corunna*

NOT a drum was heard, not a funeral note,
  As his corse to the rampart we hurried;
Not a soldier discharged his farewell shot
  O'er the grave where our hero we buried.

We buried him darkly at dead of night,
  The sods with our bayonets turning,
By the struggling moonbeam's misty light
  And the lanthorn dimly burning.

No useless coffin enclosed his breast,
  Not in sheet or in shroud we wound him;
But he lay like a warrior taking his rest
  With his martial cloak around him.

Few and short were the prayers we said,
  And we spoke not a word of sorrow;
But we steadfastly gazed on the face that was dead,
  And we bitterly thought of the morrow.

We thought, as we hollowed his narrow bed
  And smoothed down his lonely pillow,
That the foe and the stranger would tread o'er his head,
  And we far away on the billow!

Lightly they'll talk of the spirit that's gone,
  And o'er his cold ashes upbraid him—
But little he'll reck, if they let him sleep on
  In the grave where a Briton has laid him.

But half of our heavy task was done
  When the clock struck the hour for retiring;
And we heard the distant and random gun
  That the foe was sullenly firing.

Slowly and sadly we laid him down,
  From the field of his fame fresh and gory;
We carved not a line, and we raised not a stone,
  But we left him alone with his glory.

PERCY BYSSHE SHELLEY

1792–1822

546   *Ozymandias*

I MET a traveller from an antique land
Who said: Two vast and trunkless legs of stone
Stand in the desert . . . Near them, on the sand,
Half sunk, a shattered visage lies, whose frown,
And wrinkled lip, and sneer of cold command,
Tell that its sculptor well those passions read
Which yet survive, stamped on these lifeless things,
The hand that mocked them, and the heart that fed:
And on the pedestal these words appear:
'My name is Ozymandias, king of kings:
Look on my works, ye Mighty, and despair!'
Nothing beside remains. Round the decay
Of that colossal wreck, boundless and bare
The lone and level sands stretch far away.

547 *England in 1819*

AN old, mad, blind, despised, and dying king,—
Princes, the dregs of their dull race, who flow
Through public scorn,—mud from a muddy spring,—
Rulers who neither see, nor feel, nor know,
But leech-like to their fainting country cling,
Till they drop, blind in blood, without a blow,—
A people starved and stabbed in the untilled field,—
An army, which liberticide and prey
Makes as a two-edged sword to all who wield,—
Golden and sanguine laws which tempt and slay;
Religion Christless, Godless—a book sealed;
A Senate,—Time's worst statute unrepealed,—
Are graves, from which a glorious Phantom may
Burst, to illumine our tempestuous day.

548 *from* Prometheus Unbound

A Voice in the Air sings

LIFE of Life! thy lips enkindle
    With their love the breath between them;
And thy smiles before they dwindle
    Make the cold air fire; then screen them
In those looks, where whoso gazes
Faints, entangled in their mazes.

Child of Light! thy limbs are burning
    Through the vest which seems to hide them;
As the radiant lines of morning
    Through the clouds ere they divide them;
And this atmosphere divinest
Shrouds thee wheresoe'er thou shinest.

Fair are others; none beholds thee,
    But thy voice sounds low and tender
Like the fairest, for it folds thee
    From the sight, that liquid splendour,
And all feel, yet see thee never,
As I feel now, lost for ever!

Lamp of Earth! where'er thou movest
   Its dim shapes are clad with brightness,
And the souls of whom thou lovest
   Walk upon the winds with lightness,
Till they fail, as I am failing,
Dizzy, lost, yet unbewailing!

Asia Replies

My soul is an enchanted boat,
   Which, like a sleeping swan, doth float
Upon the silver waves of thy sweet singing;
   And thine doth like an angel sit
   Beside the helm conducting it,
Whilst all the winds with melody are ringing.
   It seems to float ever, for ever,
   Upon that many-winding river,
   Between mountains, woods, abysses,
   A paradise of wildernesses!
Till, like one in slumber bound,
Borne to the ocean, I float down, around,
Into a sea profound, of ever-spreading sound:

   Meanwhile thy spirit lifts its pinions
   In music's most serene dominions;
Catching the winds that fan that happy heaven.
   And we sail on, away, afar,
   Without a course, without a star,
But, by the instinct of sweet music driven;
   Till through Elysian garden islets
   By thee, most beautiful of pilots,
   Where never mortal pinnace glided,
   The boat of my desire is guided:
Realms where the air we breathe is love,
Which in the winds and on the waves doth move,
Harmonizing this earth with what we feel above.

   We have passed Age's icy caves,
   And Manhood's dark and tossing waves,
And Youth's smooth ocean, smiling to betray:
   Beyond the glassy gulfs we flee
   Of shadow-peopled Infancy,
Through Death and Birth, to a diviner day;

A paradise of vaulted bowers,
Lit by downward-gazing flowers,
And watery paths that wind between
Wildernesses calm and green,
Peopled by shapes too bright to see,
And rest, having beheld; somewhat like thee;
Which walk upon the sea, and chant melodiously!

549   *Ode to the West Wind*

I

O WILD West Wind, thou breath of Autumn's being,
   Thou from whose unseen presence the leaves dead
Are driven like ghosts from an enchanter fleeing,

   Yellow, and black, and pale, and hectic red,
Pestilence-stricken multitudes! O thou
   Who chariotest to their dark wintry bed

The wingèd seeds, where they lie cold and low,
   Each like a corpse within its grave, until
Thine azure sister of the Spring shall blow

   Her clarion o'er the dreaming earth, and fill
(Driving sweet buds like flocks to feed in air)
   With living hues and odours plain and hill;

Wild Spirit, which art moving everywhere;
Destroyer and preserver; hear, O hear!

II

Thou on whose stream, 'mid the steep sky's commotion,
   Loose clouds like earth's decaying leaves are shed,
Shook from the tangled boughs of heaven and ocean,

   Angels of rain and lightning! there are spread
On the blue surface of thine airy surge,
   Like the bright hair uplifted from the head

Of some fierce Maenad, even from the dim verge
   Of the horizon to the zenith's height,
The locks of the approaching storm. Thou dirge

Of the dying year, to which this closing night
Will be the dome of a vast sepulchre,
  Vaulted with all thy congregated might

Of vapours, from whose solid atmosphere
Black rain, and fire, and hail will burst: O hear!

III

Thou who didst waken from his summer dreams
  The blue Mediterranean, where he lay,
Lulled by the coil of his crystalline streams,

  Beside a pumice isle in Baiae's bay,
And saw in sleep old palaces and towers
  Quivering within the wave's intenser day,

All overgrown with azure moss, and flowers
  So sweet, the sense faints picturing them! Thou
For whose path the Atlantic's level powers

  Cleave themselves into chasms, while far below
The sea-blooms and the oozy woods which wear
  The sapless foliage of the ocean, know

Thy voice, and suddenly grow gray with fear,
And tremble and despoil themselves: O hear!

IV

If I were a dead leaf thou mightest bear;
  If I were a swift cloud to fly with thee;
A wave to pant beneath thy power, and share

  The impulse of thy strength, only less free
Than thou, O uncontrollable! if even
  I were as in my boyhood, and could be

The comrade of thy wanderings over heaven,
  As then, when to outstrip thy skiey speed
Scarce seemed a vision—I would ne'er have striven

  As thus with thee in prayer in my sore need.
O! lift me as a wave, a leaf, a cloud!
  I fall upon the thorns of life! I bleed!

A heavy weight of hours has chained and bowed
One too like thee—tameless, and swift, and proud.

V

Make me thy lyre, even as the forest is:
   What if my leaves are falling like its own?
The tumult of thy mighty harmonies

   Will take from both a deep autumnal tone,
Sweet though in sadness. Be thou, Spirit fierce,
   My spirit! Be thou me, impetuous one!

Drive my dead thoughts over the universe,
   Like withered leaves, to quicken a new birth;
And, by the incantation of this verse,

   Scatter, as from an unextinguished hearth
Ashes and sparks, my words among mankind!
   Be through my lips to unawakened earth

The trumpet of a prophecy! O Wind,
If Winter comes, can Spring be far behind?

550   *Ode to a Skylark*

HAIL to thee, blithe spirit!
   Bird thou never wert—
That from heaven or near it
   Pourest thy full heart
In profuse strains of unpremeditated art.

Higher still and higher
   From the earth thou springest,
Like a cloud of fire;
   The blue deep thou wingest,
And singing still dost soar, and soaring ever singest.

In the golden lightning
   Of the sunken sun,
O'er which clouds are brightening,
   Thou dost float and run,
Like an unbodied joy whose race is just begun.

The pale purple even
  Melts around thy flight;
Like a star of heaven,
  In the broad daylight
Thou art unseen, but yet I hear thy shrill delight—

Keen as are the arrows
  Of that silver sphere
Whose intense lamp narrows
  In the white dawn clear,
Until we hardly see, we feel that it is there.

All the earth and air
  With thy voice is loud,
As, when night is bare,
  From one lonely cloud
The moon rains out her beams, and heaven is overflowed.

What thou art we know not;
  What is most like thee?
From rainbow clouds there flow not
  Drops so bright to see,
As from thy presence showers a rain of melody:—

Like a poet hidden
  In the light of thought,
Singing hymns unbidden,
  Till the world is wrought
To sympathy with hopes and fears it heeded not:

Like a high-born maiden
  In a palace tower,
Soothing her love-laden
  Soul in secret hour
With music sweet as love, which overflows her bower:

Like a glow-worm golden
  In a dell of dew,
Scattering unbeholden
  Its aërial hue
Among the flowers and grass which screen it from the view:

Like a rose embowered
　　In its own green leaves,
By warm winds deflowered,
　　Till the scent it gives
Makes faint with too much sweet these heavy-winged thieves:

Sound of vernal showers
　　On the twinkling grass,
Rain-awakened flowers—
　　All that ever was
Joyous and clear and fresh—thy music doth surpass.

Teach us, sprite or bird,
　　What sweet thoughts are thine:
I have never heard
　　Praise of love or wine
That panted forth a flood of rapture so divine.

Chorus hymeneal,
　　Or triumphal chant,
Matched with thine would be all
　　But an empty vaunt—
A thing wherein we feel there is some hidden want.

What objects are the fountains
　　Of thy happy strain?
What fields, or waves, or mountains?
　　What shapes of sky or plain?
What love of thine own kind? what ignorance of pain?

With thy clear keen joyance
　　Languor cannot be:
Shadow of annoyance
　　Never came near thee:
Thou lovest, but ne'er knew love's sad satiety.

Waking or asleep,
　　Thou of death must deem
Things more true and deep
　　Than we mortals dream,
Or how could thy notes flow in such a crystal stream?

We look before and after,
    And pine for what is not:
Our sincerest laughter
    With some pain is fraught;
Our sweetest songs are those that tell of saddest thought.

Yet, if we could scorn
    Hate and pride and fear,
If we were things born
    Not to shed a tear,
I know not how thy joy we ever should come near.

Better than all measures
    Of delightful sound,
Better than all treasures
    That in books are found,
Thy skill to poet were, thou scorner of the ground!

Teach me half the gladness
    That thy brain must know;
Such harmonious madness
    From my lips would flow,
The world should listen then, as I am listening now.

551   *To Maria Gisborne in England, from Italy*

YOU are not here! the quaint witch Memory sees,
In vacant chairs, your absent images,
And points where once you sat, and now should be
But are not.—I demand if ever we
Shall meet as then we met;—and she replies,
Veiling in awe her second-sighted eyes;
'I know the past alone—but summon home
My sister Hope,—she speaks of all to come.'
But I, an old diviner, who knew well
Every false verse of that sweet oracle,
Turned to the sad enchantress once again,
And sought a respite from my gentle pain,
In citing every passage o'er and o'er
Of our communion—how on the sea-shore
We watched the ocean and the sky together,
Under the roof of blue Italian weather;

How I ran home through last year's thunder-storm,
And felt the transverse lightning linger warm
Upon my cheek—and how we often made
Feasts for each other, where good will outweighed
The frugal luxury of our country cheer,
As well it might, were it less firm and clear
Than ours must ever be;—and how we spun
A shroud of talk to hide us from the sun
Of this familiar life, which seems to be
But is not:—or is but quaint mockery
Of all we would believe, and sadly blame
The jarring and inexplicable frame
Of this wrong world:—and then anatomize
The purposes and thoughts of men whose eyes
Were closed in distant years;—or widely guess
The issue of the earth's great business,
When we shall be as we no longer are—
Like babbling gossips safe, who hear the war
Of winds, and sigh, but tremble not;—or how
You listened to some interrupted flow
Of visionary rhyme,—in joy and pain
Struck from the inmost fountains of my brain,
With little skill perhaps;—or how we sought
Those deepest wells of passion or of thought
Wrought by wise poets in the waste of years,
Staining their sacred waters with our tears;
Quenching a thirst ever to be renewed! . . .
                        You are now
In London, that great sea, whose ebb and flow
At once is deaf and loud, and on the shore
Vomits its wrecks, and still howls on for more.
Yet in its depth what treasures! You will see
That which was Godwin,—greater none than he
Though fallen—and fallen on evil times—to stand
Among the spirits of our age and land,
Before the dread tribunal of *to come*
The foremost,—while Rebuke cowers pale and dumb.
You will see Coleridge—he who sits obscure
In the exceeding lustre and the pure
Intense irradiation of a mind,
Which, with its own internal lightning blind,
Flags wearily through darkness and despair—
A cloud-encircled meteor of the air,

A hooded eagle among blinking owls.—
You will see Hunt—one of those happy souls
Which are the salt of the earth, and without whom
This world would smell like what it is—a tomb;
Who is, what others seem; his room no doubt
Is still adorned with many a cast from Shout,
With graceful flowers tastefully placed about;
And coronals of bay from ribbons hung,
And brighter wreaths in neat disorder flung;
The gifts of the most learned among some dozens
Of female friends, sisters-in-law, and cousins.
And there is he with his eternal puns,
Which beat the dullest brain for smiles, like duns
Thundering for money at a poet's door;
Alas! it is no use to say, 'I'm poor!'
Or oft in graver mood, when he will look
Things wiser than were ever read in book,
Except in Shakespeare's wisest tenderness.—
You will see Hogg,—and I cannot express
His virtues,—though I know that they are great,
Because he locks, then barricades the gate
Within which they inhabit;—of his wit
And wisdom, you'll cry out when you are bit.
He is a pearl within an oyster shell,
One of the richest of the deep;—and there
Is English Peacock, with his mountain Fair,
Turned into a Flamingo;—that shy bird
That gleams i' the Indian air—have you not heard
When a man marries, dies, or turns Hindoo,
His best friends hear no more of him?—but you
Will see him, and will like him too, I hope,
With the milk-white Snowdonian Antelope
Matched with this cameleopard—his fine wit
Makes such a wound, the knife is lost in it;
A strain too learned for a shallow age,
Too wise for selfish bigots; let his page,
Which charms the chosen spirits of the time,
Fold itself up for the serener clime
Of years to come, and find its recompense
In that just expectation.—Wit and sense,
Virtue and human knowledge; all that might
Make this dull world a business of delight,

Are all combined in Horace Smith.—And these,
With some exceptions, which I need not tease
Your patience by descanting on,—are all
You and I know in London.
                                    I recall
My thoughts, and bid you look upon the night.
As water does a sponge, so the moonlight
Fills the void, hollow, universal air—
What see you?—unpavilioned Heaven is fair,
Whether the moon, into her chamber gone,
Leaves midnight to the golden stars, or wan
Climbs with diminished beams the azure steep;
Or whether clouds sail o'er the inverse deep,
Piloted by the many-wandering blast,
And the rare stars rush through them dim and fast:—
All this is beautiful in every land.—
But what see you beside?—a shabby stand
Of Hackney coaches—a brick house or wall
Fencing some lonely court, white with the scrawl
Of our unhappy politics;—or worse—
A wretched woman reeling by, whose curse
Mixed with the watchman's, partner of her trade,
You must accept in place of serenade—
Or yellow-haired Pollonia murmuring
To Henry, some unutterable thing.
I see a chaos of green leaves and fruit
Built round dark caverns, even to the root
Of the living stems that feed them—in whose bowers
There sleep in their dark dew the folded flowers;
Beyond, the surface of the unsickled corn
Trembles not in the slumbering air, and borne
In circles quaint, and ever-changing dance,
Like wingèd stars the fire-flies flash and glance,
Pale in the open moonshine, but each one
Under the dark trees seems a little sun,
A meteor tamed; a fixed star gone astray
From the silver regions of the milky way;—
Afar the Contadino's song is heard,
Rude, but made sweet by distance—and a bird
Which cannot be the Nightingale, and yet
I know none else that sings so sweet as it
At this late hour;—and then all is still—
Now—Italy or London, which you will!

552 *Mourn not for Adonais*

PEACE, peace! he is not dead, he doth not sleep—
He hath awakened from the dream of life—
'Tis we, who lost in stormy visions, keep
With phantoms an unprofitable strife,
And in mad trance, strike with our spirit's knife
Invulnerable nothings.—*We* decay
Like corpses in a charnel; fear and grief
Convulse us and consume us day by day,
And cold hopes swarm like worms within our living clay.

He has outsoared the shadow of our night;
Envy and calumny and hate and pain,
And that unrest which men miscall delight,
Can touch him not and torture not again;
From the contagion of the world's slow stain
He is secure, and now can never mourn
A heart grown cold, a head grown gray in vain;
Nor, when the spirit's self has ceased to burn,
With sparkless ashes load an unlamented urn.

He lives, he wakes—'tis Death is dead, not he;
Mourn not for Adonais.—Thou young Dawn,
Turn all thy dew to splendour, for from thee
The spirit thou lamentest is not gone;
Ye caverns and ye forests, cease to moan!
Cease, ye faint flowers and fountains, and thou Air,
Which like a mourning veil thy scarf hadst thrown
O'er the abandoned Earth, now leave it bare
Even to the joyous stars which smile on its despair!

He is made one with Nature: there is heard
His voice in all her music, from the moan
Of thunder, to the song of night's sweet bird;
He is a presence to be felt and known
In darkness and in light, from herb and stone,
Spreading itself where'er that Power may move
Which has withdrawn his being to its own;
Which wields the world with never-wearied love,
Sustains it from beneath, and kindles it above.

He is a portion of the loveliness
Which once he made more lovely: he doth bear
His part, while the one Spirit's plastic stress
Sweeps through the dull dense world, compelling there,
All new successions to the forms they wear;
Torturing the unwilling dross that checks its flight
To its own likeness, as each mass may bear;
And bursting in its beauty and its might
From trees and beasts and men into the Heaven's light.

The splendours of the firmament of time
May be eclipsed, but are extinguished not;
Like stars to their appointed height they climb,
And death is a low mist which cannot blot
The brightness it may veil. When lofty thought
Lifts a young heart above its mortal lair,
And love and life contend in it, for what
Shall be its earthly doom, the dead live there
And move like winds of light on dark and stormy air.

*

The One remains, the many change and pass;
Heaven's light forever shines, Earth's shadows fly;
Life, like a dome of many-coloured glass,
Stains the white radiance of Eternity,
Until Death tramples it to fragments.—Die,
If thou wouldst be with that which thou dost seek!
Follow where all is fled!—Rome's azure sky,
Flowers, ruins, statues, music, words, are weak
The glory they transfuse with fitting truth to speak.

Why linger, why turn back, why shrink, my Heart?
Thy hopes are gone before: from all things here
They have departed; thou shouldst now depart!
A light is passed from the revolving year,
And man, and woman; and what still is dear
Attracts to crush, repels to make thee wither.
The soft sky smiles,—the low wind whispers near:
'Tis Adonais calls! oh, hasten thither,
No more let Life divide what Death can join together.

That Light whose smile kindles the Universe,
That Beauty in which all things work and move,
That Benediction which the eclipsing Curse
Of birth can quench not, that sustaining Love
Which through the web of being blindly wove
By man and beast and earth and air and sea,
Burns bright or dim, as each are mirrors of
The fire for which all thirst; now beams on me,
Consuming the last clouds of cold mortality.

The breath whose might I have invoked in song
Descends on me; my spirit's bark is driven,
Far from the shore, far from the trembling throng
Whose sails were never to the tempest given;
The massy earth and spherèd skies are riven!
I am borne darkly, fearfully, afar;
Whilst, burning through the inmost veil of Heaven,
The soul of Adonais, like a star,
Beacons from the abode where the Eternal are.

553   *Hellas*

THE world's great age begins anew,
    The golden years return,
The earth doth like a snake renew
    Her winter weeds outworn:
Heaven smiles, and faiths and empires gleam
Like wrecks of a dissolving dream.

A brighter Hellas rears its mountains
    From waves serener far;
A new Peneus rolls his fountains
    Against the morning star;
Where fairer Tempes bloom, there sleep
Young Cyclads on a sunnier deep.

A loftier Argo cleaves the main,
    Fraught with a later prize;
Another Orpheus sings again,
    And loves, and weeps, and dies;
A new Ulysses leaves once more
Calypso for his native shore.

O write no more the tale of Troy,
  If earth Death's scroll must be—
Nor mix with Laian rage the joy
  Which dawns upon the free,
Although a subtler Sphinx renew
Riddles of death Thebes never knew.

Another Athens shall arise,
  And to remoter time
Bequeath, like sunset to the skies,
  The splendour of its prime;
And leave, if naught so bright may live,
All earth can take or Heaven can give.

Saturn and Love their long repose
  Shall burst, more bright and good
Than all who fell, than One who rose,
  Than many unsubdued:
Not gold, not blood, their altar dowers,
But votive tears and symbol flowers.

O cease! must hate and death return?
  Cease! must men kill and die?
Cease! drain not to its dregs the urn
  Of bitter prophecy!
The world is weary of the past—
O might it die or rest at last!

554   *To ....*

ONE word is too often profaned
  For me to profane it;
One feeling too falsely disdained
  For thee to disdain it;
One hope is too like despair
  For prudence to smother;
And pity from thee more dear
  Than that from another.

I can give not what men call love:
    But wilt thou accept not
The worship the heart lifts above
    And the heavens reject not,
The desire of the moth for the star,
    Of the night for the morrow,
The devotion to something afar
    From the sphere of our sorrow?

555

MUSIC, when soft voices die,
Vibrates in the memory;
Odours, when sweet violets sicken,
Live within the sense they quicken.

Rose leaves, when the rose is dead,
Are heaped for the beloved's bed;
And so thy thoughts, when thou art gone,
Love itself shall slumber on.

556
Song

A WIDOW bird sate mourning for her love
    Upon a wintry bough;
The frozen wind crept on above,
    The freezing stream below.

There was no leaf upon the forest bare,
    No flower upon the ground,
And little motion in the air
    Except the mill-wheel's sound.

557
A Lament

O WORLD! O life! O time!
On whose last steps I climb,
    Trembling at that where I had stood before;
When will return the glory of your prime?
      No more—Oh, never more!

Out of the day and night
A joy has taken flight;
　Fresh spring, and summer, and winter hoar,
Move my faint heart with grief, but with delight
　　No more—Oh, never more!

558　　　　　　　　*A Dirge*

ROUGH wind, that moanest loud
　Grief too sad for song;
Wild wind, when sullen cloud
　Knells all the night long;
Sad storm, whose tears are vain,
Bare woods, whose branches strain,
Deep caves and dreary main,—
　Wail, for the world's wrong!

JOHN CLARE

1793–1864

559　　　　　　　　*February*

THE snow has left the cottage top;
　The thatch moss grows in brighter green;
And eaves in quick succession drop,
　Where grinning icicles have been,
Pit-patting with a pleasant noise
　In tubs set by the cottage-door;
While ducks and geese, with happy joys,
　Plunge in the yard-pond brimming o'er.

The sun peeps through the window-pane;
　Which children mark with laughing eye,
And in the wet street steal again
　To tell each other spring is nigh:
Then, as young hope the past recalls,
　In playing groups they often draw,
To build beside the sunny walls
　Their spring-time huts of sticks or straw.

And oft in pleasure's dreams they hie
  Round homesteads by the village side,
Scratching the hedgerow mosses by,
  Where painted pooty shells abide,
Mistaking oft the ivy spray
  For leaves that come with budding spring,
And wondering, in their search for play,
  Why birds delay to build and sing.

The milkmaid singing leaves her bed,
  As glad as happy thoughts can be,
While magpies chatter o'er her head
  As jocund in the change as she:
Her cows around the closes stray,
  Nor lingering wait the foddering-boy,
Tossing the molehills in their play,
  And staring round with frolic joy.

The shepherd now is often seen
  Near warm banks o'er his hook to bend,
Or o'er a gate or stile to lean,
  Chattering to a passing friend:
Ploughmen go whistling to their toils,
  And yoke again the rested plough;
And, mingling o'er the mellow soils,
  Boys shout, and whips are noising now.

The barking dogs, by lane and wood,
  Drive sheep afield from foddering ground;
And Echo, in her summer mood,
  Briskly mocks the cheering sound.
The flocks, as from a prison broke,
  Shake their wet fleeces in the sun,
While, following fast, a misty smoke
  Reeks from the moist grass as they run.

No more behind his master's heels
  The dog creeps on his winter-pace;
But cocks his tail, and o'er the fields
  Runs many a wild and random chase,
Following, in spite of chiding calls,
  The startled cat with harmless glee,
Scaring her up the weed-green walls,
  Or mossy mottled apple-tree.

As crows from morning perches fly,
  He barks and follows them in vain;
E'en larks will catch his nimble eye,
  And off he starts and barks again,
With breathless haste and blinded guess,
  Oft following where the hare hath gone,
Forgetting, in his joy's excess,
  His frolic puppy-days are done.

The hedgehog, from his hollow root,
  Sees the wood-moss clear of snow,
And hunts the hedge for fallen fruit—
  Crab, hip, and winter-bitten sloe;
But often checked by sudden fears,
  As shepherd-dog his haunt espies,
He rolls up in a ball of spears,
  And all his barking rage defies.

The gladdened swine bolt from the sty,
  And round the yard in freedom run,
Or stretching in their slumbers lie
  Beside the cottage in the sun.
The young horse whinnies to his mate,
  And, sickening from the thresher's door,
Rubs at the straw-yard's banded gate,
  Longing for freedom on the moor.

The small birds think their wants are o'er,
  To see the snow-hills fret again,
And, from the barn's chaff-littered door,
  Betake them to the greening plain.
The woodman's robin startles coy,
  Nor longer to his elbow comes,
To peck, with hunger's eager joy,
  'Mong mossy stulps the littered crumbs.

'Neath hedge and walls that screen the wind,
  The gnats for play will flock together;
And e'en poor flies some hope will find
  To venture in the mocking weather;
From out their hiding-holes again,
  With feeble pace, they often creep
Along the sun-warmed window-pane,
  Like dreaming things that walk in sleep.

The mavis thrush with wild delight,
  Upon the orchard's dripping tree,
Mutters, to see the day so bright,
  Fragments of young Hope's poesy:
And oft Dame stops her buzzing wheel
  To hear the robin's note once more,
Who tootles while he pecks his meal
  From sweetbrier hips beside the door.

The sunbeams on the hedges lie,
  The south wind murmurs summer-soft;
The maids hang out white clothes to dry
  Around the elder-skirted croft:
A calm of pleasure listens round,
  And almost whispers winter by;
While Fancy dreams of summer's sound,
  And quiet rapture fills the eye.

Thus Nature of the spring will dream
  While south winds thaw; but soon again
Frost breathes upon the stiffening stream,
  And numbs it into ice: the plain
Soon wears its mourning garb of white;
  And icicles, that fret at noon,
Will eke their icy tails at night
  Beneath the chilly stars and moon.

Nature soon sickens of her joys,
  And all is sad and dumb again.
Save merry shouts of sliding boys
  About the frozen furrowed plain.
The foddering-boy forgets his song,
  And silent goes with folded arms;
And croodling shepherds bend along,
  Crouching to the whizzing storms.

560 *I am*

I AM: yet what I am none cares or knows,
　My friends forsake me like a memory lost;
I am the self-consumer of my woes,
　They rise and vanish in oblivious host,
Like shades in love and death's oblivion lost;
And yet I am, and live with shadows tost

Into the nothingness of scorn and noise,
　Into the living sea of waking dreams,
Where there is neither sense of life nor joys,
　But the vast shipwreck of my life's esteems;
And e'en the dearest—that I loved the best—
Are strange—nay, rather stranger than the rest.

I long for scenes where man has never trod,
　A place where woman never smiled or wept;
There to abide with my Creator, God,
　And sleep as I in childhood sweetly slept:
Untroubling and untroubled where I lie,
The grass below—above the vaulted sky.

561

　　LOVE lives beyond
The tomb, the earth, which fades like dew!
　　I love the fond,
The faithful, and the true.

　　Love lives in sleep,
The happiness of healthy dreams:
　　Eve's dews may weep,
But love delightful seems.

　　'Tis seen in flowers,
And in the morning's pearly dew;
　　In earth's green hours,
And in the heaven's eternal blue.

　　'Tis heard in spring
When light and sunbeams, warm and kind,
　　On angel's wing
Bring love and music to the mind.

And where is voice,
So young, so beautiful, and sweet
As nature's choice,
Where spring and lovers meet?

Love lives beyond
The tomb, the earth, the flowers, and dew.
I love the fond,
The faithful, young, and true.

JOHN KEATS

1795–1821

562   *On First Looking into Chapman's Homer*

MUCH have I travelled in the realms of gold,
  And many goodly states and kingdoms seen;
  Round many western islands have I been
Which bards in fealty to Apollo hold.
Oft of one wide expanse had I been told
  That deep-browed Homer ruled as his demesne:
  Yet did I never breathe its pure serene
Till I heard Chapman speak out loud and bold:
Then felt I like some watcher of the skies
  When a new planet swims into his ken;
Or like stout Cortez, when with eagle eyes
  He stared at the Pacific—and all his men
Looked at each other with a wild surmise—
  Silent, upon a peak in Darien.

563   *The Song of the Indian Maid*

BENEATH my palm-trees, by the river side,
I sat a-weeping: in the whole world wide
There was no one to ask me why I wept,—
    And so I kept
Brimming the water-lily cups with tears
    Cold as my fears.

Beneath my palm-trees, by the river side,
I sat a-weeping: what enamoured bride,
Cheated by shadowy wooer from the clouds,
   But hides and shrouds
Beneath dark palm-trees by a river side?

And as I sat, over the light blue hills
There came a noise of revellers: the rills
Into the wide stream came of purple hue—
   'Twas Bacchus and his crew!
The earnest trumpet spake, and silver thrills
From kissing cymbals made a merry din—
   'Twas Bacchus and his kin!
Like to a moving vintage down they came,
Crowned with green leaves, and faces all on flame;
All madly dancing through the pleasant valley,
   To scare thee, Melancholy!
O then, O then, thou wast a simple name!
And I forgot thee, as the berried holly
By shepherds is forgotten, when in June
Tall chestnuts keep away the sun and moon:—
   I rushed into the folly!

Within his car, aloft, young Bacchus stood,
Trifling his ivy-dart, in dancing mood,
   With sidelong laughing;
And little rills of crimson wine imbrued
His plump white arms and shoulders, enough white
   For Venus' pearly bite;
And near him rode Silenus on his ass,
Pelted with flowers as he on did pass
   Tipsily quaffing.

'Whence came ye, merry Damsels! whence came ye,
So many, and so many, and such glee?
Why have ye left your bowers desolate,
   Your lutes, and gentler fate?'—
'We follow Bacchus! Bacchus on the wing,
   A-conquering!
Bacchus, young Bacchus! good or ill betide,
We dance before him thorough kingdoms wide:—
Come hither, lady fair, and joinèd be
   To our wild minstrelsy!'

'Whence came ye, jolly Satyrs! whence came ye,
So many, and so many, and such glee?
Why have ye left your forest haunts, why left
   Your nuts in oak-tree cleft?'—
'For wine, for wine we left our kernel tree;
For wine we left our heath, and yellow brooms,
   And cold mushrooms;
For wine we follow Bacchus through the earth;
Great god of breathless cups and chirping mirth!
Come hither, lady fair, and joinèd be
   To our mad minstrelsy!'

Over wide streams and mountains great we went,
And, save when Bacchus kept his ivy tent,
Onward the tiger and the leopard pants,
   With Asian elephants:
Onward these myriads—with song and dance,
With zebras striped, and sleek Arabians' prance,
Web-footed alligators, crocodiles,
Bearing upon their scaly backs, in files,
Plump infant laughers mimicking the coil
Of seamen, and stout galley-rowers' toil:
With toying oars and silken sails they glide,
   Nor care for wind and tide.

Mounted on panthers' furs and lions' manes,
From rear to van they scour about the plains;
A three days' journey in a moment done;
And always, at the rising of the sun,
About the wilds they hunt with spear and horn.
   On spleenful unicorn.

I saw Osirian Egypt kneel adown
   Before the vine-wreath crown!
I saw parched Abyssinia rouse and sing
   To the silver cymbals' ring!
I saw the whelming vintage hotly pierce
   Old Tartary the fierce!
The kings of Ind their jewel-sceptres vail,
And from their treasures scatter pearlèd hail;
Great Brahma from his mystic heaven groans,
   And all his priesthood moans,
Before young Bacchus' eye-wink turning pale.

Into these regions came I, following him,
Sick-hearted, weary—so I took a whim
To stray away into these forests drear,
    Alone, without a peer:
And I have told thee all thou mayest hear.

564   *Ode to a Nightingale*

MY heart aches, and a drowsy numbness pains
  My sense, as though of hemlock I had drunk,
Or emptied some dull opiate to the drains
  One minute past, and Lethe-wards had sunk:
'Tis not through envy of thy happy lot,
  But being too happy in thy happiness,
    That thou, light-wingèd Dryad of the trees,
      In some melodious plot
Of beechen green, and shadows numberless,
  Singest of summer in full-throated ease.

O for a draught of vintage! that hath been
  Cooled a long age in the deep-delvèd earth,
Tasting of Flora and the country-green,
  Dance, and Provençal song, and sunburnt mirth!
O for a beaker full of the warm South!
  Full of the true, the blushful Hippocrene,
    With beaded bubbles winking at the brim,
      And purple-stainèd mouth;
That I might drink, and leave the world unseen,
  And with thee fade away into the forest dim:

Fade far away, dissolve, and quite forget
  What thou among the leaves hast never known,
The weariness, the fever, and the fret
  Here, where men sit and hear each other groan;
Where palsy shakes a few, sad, last grey hairs,
  Where youth grows pale, and spectre-thin, and dies;
    Where but to think is to be full of sorrow
      And leaden-eyed despairs;
Where Beauty cannot keep her lustrous eyes,
  Or new Love pine at them beyond to-morrow.

Away! away! for I will fly to thee,
  Not charioted by Bacchus and his pards,
But on the viewless wings of Poesy,
  Though the dull brain perplexes and retards:
Already with thee! tender is the night,
    And haply the Queen-Moon is on her throne,
      Clustered around by all her starry Fays;
          But here there is no light,
    Save what from heaven is with the breezes blown
      Through verdurous glooms and winding mossy ways.

I cannot see what flowers are at my feet,
  Nor what soft incense hangs upon the boughs,
But, in embalmèd darkness, guess each sweet
  Wherewith the seasonable month endows
The grass, the thicket, and the fruit-tree wild;
    White hawthorn, and the pastoral eglantine;
      Fast fading violets covered up in leaves;
          And mid-May's eldest child,
    The coming musk-rose, full of dewy wine,
      The murmurous haunt of flies on summer eves.

Darkling I listen; and for many a time
  I have been half in love with easeful Death,
Called him soft names in many a musèd rhyme,
  To take into the air my quiet breath;
Now more than ever seems it rich to die,
    To cease upon the midnight with no pain,
      While thou art pouring forth thy soul abroad
          In such an ecstasy!
    Still wouldst thou sing, and I have ears in vain—
      To thy high requiem become a sod.

Thou wast not born for death, immortal Bird!
  No hungry generations tread thee down;
The voice I hear this passing night was heard
  In ancient days by emperor and clown:
Perhaps the self-same song that found a path
    Through the sad heart of Ruth, when, sick for home,
      She stood in tears amid the alien corn;
          The same that oft times hath
    Charmed magic casements, opening on the foam
      Of perilous seas, in faery lands forlorn.

Forlorn! the very word is like a bell
  To toll me back from thee to my sole self!
Adieu! the fancy cannot cheat so well
  As she is famed to do, deceiving elf.
Adieu! adieu! thy plaintive anthem fades
    Past the near meadows, over the still stream,
      Up the hill-side; and now 'tis buried deep
        In the next valley-glades:
  Was it a vision, or a waking dream?
  Fled is that music:—do I wake or sleep?

565   *Ode on a Grecian Urn*

THOU still unravished bride of quietness,
  Thou foster-child of Silence and slow Time,
Sylvan historian, who canst thus express
  A flowery tale more sweetly than our rhyme:
What leaf-fringed legend haunts about thy shape
  Of deities or mortals, or of both,
    In Tempe or the dales of Arcady?
  What men or gods are these? What maidens loth?
What mad pursuit? What struggle to escape?
    What pipes and timbrels? What wild ecstasy?

Heard melodies are sweet, but those unheard
  Are sweeter; therefore, ye soft pipes, play on;
Not to the sensual ear, but, more endeared,
  Pipe to the spirit ditties of no tone:
Fair youth, beneath the trees, thou canst not leave
  Thy song, nor ever can those trees be bare;
    Bold Lover, never, never canst thou kiss,
Though winning near the goal—yet, do not grieve;
    She cannot fade, though thou hast not thy bliss,
  For ever wilt thou love, and she be fair!

Ah, happy, happy boughs! that cannot shed
  Your leaves, nor ever bid the Spring adieu;
And, happy melodist, unwearièd,
  For ever piping songs for ever new;

More happy love! more happy, happy love!
 For ever warm and still to be enjoyed,
  For ever panting and for ever young;
All breathing human passion far above,
 That leaves a heart high-sorrowful and cloyed,
  A burning forehead, and a parching tongue.

Who are these coming to the sacrifice?
 To what green altar, O mysterious priest,
Lead'st thou that heifer lowing at the skies,
 And all her silken flanks with garlands drest?
What little town by river or sea-shore,
 Or mountain-built with peaceful citadel,
  Is emptied of this folk, this pious morn?
And, little town, thy streets for evermore
 Will silent be; and not a soul, to tell
  Why thou art desolate, can e'er return.

O Attic shape! fair attitude! with brede
 Of marble men and maidens overwrought,
With forest branches and the trodden weed;
 Thou, silent form! dost tease us out of thought
As doth eternity. Cold Pastoral!
 When old age shall this generation waste,
  Thou shalt remain, in midst of other woe
Than ours, a friend to man, to whom thou sayst,
 'Beauty is truth, truth beauty,—that is all
  Ye know on earth, and all ye need to know.'

566   *Ode to Psyche*

O GODDESS! hear these tuneless numbers, wrung
 By sweet enforcement and remembrance dear,
And pardon that thy secrets should be sung
 Even into thine own soft-conchèd ear:
Surely I dreamed today, or did I see
 The wingèd Psyche with awakened eyes?
I wandered in a forest thoughtlessly,
 And, on the sudden, fainting with surprise,

Saw two fair creatures, couchèd side by side
  In deepest grass, beneath the whispering roof
  Of leaves and trembled blossoms, where there ran
      A brooklet, scarce espied:
'Mid hushed, cool-rooted flowers fragrant-eyed,
  Blue, silver-white, and budded Tyrian.
They lay calm-breathing on the bedded grass;
  Their arms embracèd, and their pinions too;
  Their lips touched not, but had not bade adieu,
As if disjoinèd by soft-handed slumber,
And ready still past kisses to outnumber
  At tender eye-dawn of aurorean love:
      The wingèd boy I knew
  But who wast thou, O happy, happy dove?
      His Psyche true!

O latest-born and loveliest vision far
  Of all Olympus' faded hierarchy!
Fairer than Phoebe's sapphire-regioned star,
  Or Vesper, amorous glow-worm of the sky;
Fairer than these, though temple thou hast none,
      Nor altar heaped with flowers;
Nor Virgin choir to make delicious moan
      Upon the midnight hours;
No voice, no lute, no pipe, no incense sweet
  From chain-swung censer teeming;
No shrine, no grove, no oracle, no heat
  Of pale-mouthed prophet dreaming.

O brightest! though too late for antique vows,
  Too, too late for the fond believing lyre,
When holy were the haunted forest boughs,
  Holy the air, the water, and the fire;
Yet even in these days so far retired
  From happy pieties, thy lucent fans,
  Fluttering among the faint Olympians,
I see, and sing, by my own eyes inspired.
So let me be thy choir, and make a moan
      Upon the midnight hours;
Thy voice, thy lute, thy pipe, thy incense sweet
  From swingèd censer teeming:
Thy shrine, thy grove, thy oracle, thy heat
  Of pale-mouthed prophet dreaming.

Yes, I will be thy priest, and build a fane
    In some untrodden region of my mind,
Where branchèd thoughts, new grown with pleasant pain,
    Instead of pines shall murmur in the wind:
Far, far around shall those dark-clustered trees
    Fledge the wild-ridgèd mountains steep by steep;
And there by zephyrs, streams, and birds, and bees,
    The moss-lain Dryads shall be lulled to sleep;
And in the midst of this wide quietness
A rosy sanctuary will I dress
With the wreathed trellis of a working brain,
    With buds, and bells, and stars without a name,
With all the gardener Fancy e'er could feign,
    Who, breeding flowers, will never breed the same;
And there shall be for thee all soft delight
        That shadowy thought can win,
A bright torch, and a casement ope at night,
        To let the warm Love in!

567   *Ode on Melancholy*

No, no! go not to Lethe, neither twist
    Wolf's-bane, tight-rooted, for its poisonous wine;
Nor suffer thy pale forehead to be kist
    By nightshade, ruby grape of Proserpine;
Make not your rosary of yew-berries,
    Nor let the beetle, nor the death-moth be
        Your mournful Psyche, nor the downy owl
A partner in your sorrow's mysteries;
    For shade to shade will come too drowsily,
        And drown the wakeful anguish of the soul.

But when the melancholy fit shall fall
    Sudden from heaven like a weeping cloud,
That fosters the droop-headed flowers all,
    And hides the green hill in an April shroud;
Then glut thy sorrow on a morning rose,
    Or on the rainbow of the salt sand-wave,
        Or on the wealth of globèd peonies;
Or if thy mistress some rich anger shows,
    Emprison her soft hand, and let her rave,
        And feed deep, deep upon her peerless eyes.

She dwells with Beauty—Beauty that must die;
    And Joy, whose hand is ever at his lips
Bidding adieu; and aching Pleasure nigh,
    Turning to poison while the bee-mouth sips:
Ay, in the very temple of Delight
    Veiled Melancholy has her sovran shrine,
        Though seen of none save him whose strenuous tongue
Can burst Joy's grape against his palate fine;
    His soul shall taste the sadness of her might,
        And be among her cloudy trophies hung.

568   *To Autumn*

SEASON of mists and mellow fruitfulness!
    Close bosom-friend of the maturing sun;
Conspiring with him how to load and bless
    With fruit the vines that round the thatch-eaves run;
To bend with apples the mossed cottage-trees,
    And fill all fruit with ripeness to the core;
        To swell the gourd, and plump the hazel shells
With a sweet kernel; to set budding more,
    And still more, later flowers for the bees,
    Until they think warm days will never cease,
        For Summer has o'erbrimmed their clammy cells.

Who hath not seen thee oft amid thy store?
    Sometimes whoever seeks abroad may find
Thee sitting careless on a granary floor,
    Thy hair soft-lifted by the winnowing wind,
Or on a half-reaped furrow sound asleep,
    Drowsed with the fume of poppies, while thy hook
        Spares the next swath and all its twinèd flowers;
And sometimes like a gleaner thou dost keep
    Steady thy laden head across a brook;
    Or by a cider-press, with patient look,
        Thou watchest the last oozings hours by hours.

Where are the songs of Spring? Ay, where are they?
    Think not of them, thou hast thy music too,—
While barred clouds bloom the soft-dying day,
    And touch the stubble-plains with rosy hue;

Then in a wailful choir the small gnats mourn
  Among the river sallows, borne aloft
    Or sinking as the light wind lives or dies;
And full-grown lambs loud bleat from hilly bourn;
  Hedge-crickets sing; and now with treble soft
  The redbreast whistles from a garden-croft;
    And gathering swallows twitter in the skies.

569   *Stanzas*

        IN a drear-nighted December,
          Too happy, happy tree,
        Thy branches ne'er remember
          Their green felicity:
        The north cannot undo them,
        With a sleety whistle through them;
        Nor frozen thawings glue them
          From budding at the prime.

        In a drear-nighted December,
          Too happy, happy brook,
        Thy bubblings ne'er remember
          Apollo's summer look;
        But with a sweet forgetting,
        They stay their crystal fretting,
        Never, never petting
          About the frozen time.

        Ah! would 'twere so with many
          A gentle girl and boy!
        But were there ever any
          Writhed not at passèd joy?
        To know the change and feel it,
        When there is none to heal it,
        Nor numbèd sense to steel it,
          Was never said in rhyme.

570   *La Belle Dame Sans Merci*

'O WHAT can ail thee, knight-at-arms,
    Alone and palely loitering?
The sedge has withered from the lake,
    And no birds sing.

'O what can ail thee, knight-at-arms,
    So haggard and so woe-begone?
The squirrel's granary is full,
    And the harvest's done.

'I see a lily on thy brow
    With anguish moist and fever dew;
And on thy cheek a fading rose
    Fast withereth too.'

'I met a lady in the meads,
    Full beautiful—a faery's child,
Her hair was long, her foot was light,
    And her eyes were wild.

'I made a garland for her head,
    And bracelets too, and fragrant zone;
She looked at me as she did love,
    And made sweet moan.

'I set her on my pacing steed
    And nothing else saw all day long,
For sideways would she lean, and sing
    A faery's song.

'She found me roots of relish sweet,
    And honey wild and manna dew,
And sure in language strange she said,
    "I love thee true!"

'She took me to her elfin grot,
    And there she wept and sighed full sore;
And there I shut her wild, wild eyes
    With kisses four.

'And there she lullèd me asleep,
  And there I dreamed—Ah! woe betide!
The latest dream I ever dreamed
  On the cold hill's side.

'I saw pale kings and princes too,
  Pale warriors, death-pale were they all;
Who cried—"La belle Dame sans Merci
  Hath thee in thrall!"

'I saw their starved lips in the gloam
  With horrid warning gapèd wide,
And I awoke and found me here
  On the cold hill's side.

'And this is why I sojourn here
  Alone and palely loitering,
Though the sedge is withered from the lake,
  And no birds sing.'

571   *Last Sonnet*

BRIGHT star, would I were steadfast as thou art—
  Not in lone splendour hung aloft the night,
And watching, with eternal lids apart,
  Like Nature's patient sleepless Eremite,
The moving waters at their priest-like task
  Of pure ablution round earth's human shores,
Or gazing on the new soft-fallen mask
  Of snow upon the mountains and the moors—
No—yet still steadfast, still unchangeable,
  Pillowed upon my fair love's ripening breast,
To feel for ever its soft fall and swell,
  Awake for ever in a sweet unrest,
    Still, still to hear her tender-taken breath,
    And so live ever—or else swoon to death.

572 *To Fanny Brawne*

THIS living hand, now warm and capable
Of earnest grasping, would, if it were cold
And in the icy silence of the tomb,
So haunt thy days and chill thy dreaming nights
That thou wouldst wish thine own heart dry of blood
So in my veins red life might stream again,
And thou be conscience-calmed—see here it is—
I hold it towards you.

GEORGE DARLEY

1795–1846

573

WHEREFORE, unlaurelled Boy,
    Whom the contemptuous Muse will not inspire,
With a sad kind of joy,
    Still sing'st thou to thy solitary lyre?

The melancholy winds
    Pour through unnumbered reeds their idle woes:
And every Naiad finds
    A stream to weep her sorrow as it flows.

Her sighs unto the air
    The wood-maid's native oak doth broadly tell:
And Echo's fond despair
    Intelligible rocks re-syllable.

Wherefore then should not I,
    Albeit no haughty Muse my breast inspire,
Fated of grief to die,
    Impart it to a solitary lyre?

574 *Serenade of a Loyal Martyr*

SWEET in her green cell the Flower of Beauty slumbers,
  Lulled by the faint breezes sighing through her hair;
Sleeps she, and hears not the melancholy numbers
  Breathed to my sad lute amid the lonely air?

Down from the high cliffs the rivulet is teeming
  To wind round the willow banks that lure him from above:
O that in tears from my rocky prison streaming,
  I too could glide to the bower of my love!

Ah! where the woodbines with sleepy arms have wound her
  Opes she her eyelids at the dream of my lay,
Listening like the dove, while the fountains echo round her,
  To her lost mate's call in the forests far away?

Come then, my Bird!—for the peace thou ever bearest,
  Still heaven's messenger of comfort to me,
Come!—this fond bosom, my faithfullest! my fairest!
  Bleeds with its death-wound, but deeper yet for thee.

from Nepenthe

575 *The Phoenix*

O BLEST unfabled Incense Tree,
That burns in glorious Araby,
With red scent chalicing the air,
Till earth-life grow Elysian there!

Half buried to her flaming breast
In this bright tree, she makes her nest,
Hundred-sunned Phoenix! when she must
Crumble at length to hoary dust!

Her gorgeous death-bed! her rich pyre
Burnt up with aromatic fire!
Her urn, sight high from spoiler men!
Her birth-place when self-born again!

The mountainless green wilds among,
Here ends she her unechoing song!
With amber tears and odorous sighs
Mourned by the desert where she dies!

Laid like the young fawn mossily
In sun-green vales of Araby,
I woke, hard by the Phoenix tree
That with shadeless boughs flamed over me,
And upward called by a dumb cry
With moonbroad orbs of wonder, I
Beheld the immortal Bird on high
Glassing the great sun in her eye.
Steadfast she gazed upon his fire,
Still her destroyer and her sire!
As if to his her soul of flame
Had flown already, whence it came;
Like those that sit and glare so still,
Intense with their death struggle, till
We touch, and curdle at their chill!—
But breathing yet while she doth burn
    The deathless Daughter of the sun!
Slowly to crimson embers turn
    The beauties of the brightsome one.
O'er the broad nest her silver wings
Shook down their wasteful glitterings;
Her brinded neck high-arched in air
Like a small rainbow faded there;
But brighter glowed her plumy crown
Mouldering to golden ashes down;
With fume of sweet woods, to the skies,
Pure as a Saint's adoring sighs,
Warm as a prayer in Paradise,
Her life-breath rose in sacrifice!
The while with shrill triumphant tone
Sounding aloud, aloft, alone,
Ceaseless her joyful deathwail she
Sang to departing Araby!
    Deep melancholy wonder drew
Tears from my heartspring at that view.
Like cresset shedding its last flare
Upon some wistful mariner,

The Bird, fast blending with the sky,
Turned on me her dead-gazing eye
Once—and as surge to shallow spray
Sank down to vapoury dust away!

O, fast her amber blood doth flow
 From the heart-wounded Incense Tree,
Fast as earth's deep-embosomed woe
 In silent rivulets to the sea!

Beauty may weep her fair first-born,
 Perchance in as resplendent tears,
Such golden dewdrops bow the corn
 When the stern sickleman appears.

But oh! such perfume to a bower
 Never allured sweet-seeking bee,
As to sip fast that nectarous shower
 A thirstier minstrel drew in me!

576   *Hundred-Gated Thebes*

HUNDRED-GATED City! thou
With gryphoned arch and avenue
For denizen giants, serve they now
But to let one poor mortal through?
Wide those streaming gates of war
Ran once with many a conqueror,
Horseman and chariot, to the sound
Of the dry serpent blazoning round
Theban Sesostris' dreaded name.
Where is now the loud acclaim?
Where the trample and the roll,
Shaking staid Earth like a mole?
Sunk to a rush's sigh!—Farewell,
Thou bleached wilderness o'erblown
By treeless winds, unscythable
Sandbanks, with peeping rocks bestrown,
That for thy barrenness seem'st to be
The bed of some retreated sea!
City of Apis, shrine and throne,

Fare thee well! dispeopled sheer
Of thy mighty millions, here
Giant thing inhabits none,
But vast Desolation!

THOMAS HOOD
1799-1845

577   *I Remember, I Remember*

I REMEMBER, I remember,
The house where I was born,
The little window where the sun
Came peeping in at morn;
He never came a wink too soon,
Nor brought too long a day,
But now, I often wish the night
Had borne my breath away!

I remember, I remember,
The roses, red and white,
The violets, and the lily-cups,
Those flowers made of light!
The lilacs where the robin built,
And where my brother set
The laburnum on his birthday,—
The tree is living yet!

I remember, I remember,
Where I was used to swing,
And thought the air must rush as fresh
To swallows on the wing;
My spirit flew in feathers then,
That is so heavy now,
And summer pools could hardly cool
The fever on my brow!

I remember, I remember,
The fir trees dark and high;
I used to think their slender tops
Were close against the sky:
It was a childish ignorance,
But now 'tis little joy
To know I'm farther off from heaven
Than when I was a boy.

578   *Silence*

THERE is a silence where hath been no sound,
   There is a silence where no sound may be,
   In the cold grave—under the deep, deep sea,
Or in wide desert where no life is found,
Which hath been mute, and still must sleep profound;
   No voice is hushed—no life treads silently,
   But clouds and cloudy shadows wander free,
That never spoke, over the idle ground:
But in green ruins, in the desolate walls,
   Of antique palaces, where Man hath been,
Though the dun fox, or wild hyena, calls,
   And owls, that flit continually between,
Shriek to the echo, and the low winds moan,
There the true Silence is, self-conscious and alone.

579   *Ruth*

SHE stood breast high amid the corn,
Clasped by the golden light of morn,
Like the sweetheart of the sun,
Who many a glowing kiss had won.

On her cheek an autumn flush,
Deeply ripened;—such a blush
In the midst of brown was born,
Like red poppies grown with corn.

Round her eyes her tresses fell,
Which were blackest none could tell,
But long lashes veiled a light,
That had else been all too bright.

And her hat, with shady brim,
Made her tressy forehead dim;—
Thus she stood amid the stooks,
Praising God with sweetest looks:—

Sure, I said, heaven did not mean,
Where I reap thou shouldst but glean,
Lay thy sheaf adown and come,
Share my harvest and my home.

580   *The Death-Bed*

WE watched her breathing through the night,
Her breathing soft and low,
As in her breast the wave of life
Kept heaving to and fro!

So silently we seemed to speak—
So slowly moved about!
As we had lent her half our powers
To eke her living out!

Our very hopes belied our fears
Our fears our hopes belied—
We thought her dying when she slept,
And sleeping when she died!

For when the morn came dim and sad—
And chill with early showers,
Her quiet eyelids closed—she had
Another morn than ours!

THOMAS BABINGTON MACAULAY, LORD MACAULAY

1800–1859

581 *A Jacobite's Epitaph*

To my true king I offered free from stain
Courage and faith; vain faith, and courage vain.
For him I threw lands, honours, wealth, away,
And one dear hope, that was more prized than they.
For him I languished in a foreign clime,
Gray-haired with sorrow in my manhood's prime;
Heard on Lavernia Scargill's whispering trees,
And pined by Arno for my lovelier Tees;
Beheld each night my home in fevered sleep,
Each morning started from the dream to weep;
Till God, who saw me tried too sorely, gave
The resting-place I asked, an early grave.
O thou, whom chance leads to this nameless stone,
From that proud country which was once mine own,
By those white cliffs I never more must see,
By that dear language which I spake like thee,
Forget all feuds, and shed one English tear
O'er English dust. A broken heart lies here.

WILLIAM BARNES

1801–1886

582 *A Winter Night*

It was a chilly winter's night;
 And frost was glittering on the ground,
And evening stars were twinkling bright;
 And from the gloomy plain around
  Came no sound,
But where, within the wood-girt tower,
The churchbell slowly struck the hour;

As if that all of human birth
  Had risen to the final day,
And soaring from the worn-out earth
  Were called in hurry and dismay,
      Far away;
And I alone of all mankind
Were left in loneliness behind.

583   *The Mother's Dream*

I'D a dream to-night
As I fell asleep,
Oh! the touching sight
Makes me still to weep:
Of my little lad,
Gone to leave me sad,
Aye, the child I had,
But was not to keep.

As in heaven high,
I my child did seek,
There, in train, came by
Children fair and meek,
Each in lily white,
With a lamp alight;
Each was clear to sight,
But they did not speak.

Then, a little sad,
Came my child in turn,
But the lamp he had,
Oh! it did not burn;
He, to clear my doubt,
Said, half turned about,
'Your tears put it out;
Mother, never mourn.'

584 *The Storm-Wind*

WHEN the swift-rolling brook, swollen deep,
  Rushes on by the alders, full speed,
And the wild-blowing winds lowly sweep
  O'er the quivering leaf and the weed,
And the willow tree writhes in each limb
Over sedge-beds that reel by the brim—

The man that is staggering by
  Holds his hat to his head by the brim;
And the girl as her hair-locks outfly,
  Puts a foot out, to keep herself trim,
And the quivering wavelings o'erspread
The small pool where the bird dips his head.

But out at my house, in the lee
  Of the nook, where the winds die away,
The light swimming airs, round the tree
  And the low-swinging ivy stem, play
So soft that a mother that's nigh
Her still cradle, may hear her babe sigh.

585 *Musings*

BEFORE the falling summer sun
  The boughs are shining all as gold,
And down below them waters run,
  As there in former years they rolled;
The poolside wall is glowing hot,
  The pool is in a dazzling glare,
And makes it seem as, ah! 'tis not,
  A summer when my life was fair.

The evening, gliding slowly by,
  Seems one of those that long have fled;
The night comes on to star the sky
  As then it darkened round my head.
A girl is standing by yon door,
  As one in happy times was there,
And this day seems, but is no more,
  A day when all my life was fair.

We hear from yonder feast the hum
   Of voices, as in summers past;
And hear the beatings of the drum
   Again come throbbing on the blast.
There neighs a horse in yonder plot,
   As once there neighed our petted mare,
And summer seems, but ah! is not
   The summer when our life was fair.

WINTHROP MACKWORTH PRAED
1802–1839

586   *Good-Night to the Season*

GOOD-NIGHT to the Season! 'tis over!
   Gay dwellings no longer are gay;
The courtier, the gambler, the lover,
   Are scattered like swallows away:
There's nobody left to invite one,
   Except my good uncle and spouse;
My mistress is bathing at Brighton,
   My patron is sailing at Cowes:
For want of a better employment,
   Till Ponto and Don can get out,
I'll cultivate rural enjoyment,
   And angle immensely for trout.

Good-night to the Season!—the lobbies,
   Their changes, and rumours of change,
Which startled the rustic Sir Bobbies,
   And made all the Bishops look strange:
The breaches, and battles, and blunders,
   Performed by the Commons and Peers;
The Marquis's eloquent thunders,
   The Baronet's eloquent ears:
Denouncings of Papists and treasons,
   Of foreign dominion and oats;
Misrepresentations of reasons,
   And misunderstandings of notes.

Good-night to the Season!—the buildings
   Enough to make Inigo sick;
The paintings, and plasterings, and gildings
   Of stucco, and marble, and brick;
The orders deliciously blended,
   From love of effect, into one;
The club-houses only intended,
   The palaces only begun;
The hell where the fiend, in his glory,
   Sits staring at putty and stones,
And scrambles from story to story,
   To rattle at midnight his bones.

Good-night to the Season! the dances,
   The fillings of hot little rooms,
The glancings of rapturous glances,
   The fancyings of fancy costumes;
The pleasures which Fashion makes duties,
   The praisings of fiddles and flutes,
The luxury of looking at beauties,
   The tedium of talking to mutes;
The female diplomatists, planners
   Of matches for Laura and Jane,
The ice of her Ladyship's manners,
   The ice of his Lordship's champagne.

Good-night to the Season! the rages
   Led off by the chiefs of the throng,
The Lady Matilda's new pages,
   The Lady Eliza's new song;
Miss Fennel's macaw, which at Boodle's
   Is held to have something to say;
Mrs. Splenetic's musical poodles,
   Which bark 'Batti Batti' all day;
The pony Sir Araby sported,
   As hot and as black as a coal,
And the Lion his mother imported,
   In bearskins and grease, from the Pole.

Good-night to the Season! the Toso,
   So very majestic and tall;
Miss Ayton, whose singing was so-so,
   And Pasta, divinest of all;

The labour in vain of the Ballet,
  So sadly deficient in stars;
The foreigners thronging the Alley,
  Exhaling the breath of cigars;
The 'loge' where some heiress, how killing,
  Environed with Exquisites sits,
The lovely one out of her drilling,
  The silly ones out of their wits.

Good-night to the Season! the splendour
  That beamed in the Spanish Bazaar;
Where I purchased—my heart was so tender—
  A card-case,—a pasteboard guitar,—
A bottle of perfume,—a girdle,—
  A lithographed Riego full-grown,
Whom Bigotry drew on a hurdle
  That artists might draw him on stone,—
A small panorama of Seville,—
  A trap for demolishing flies,—
A caricature of the Devil,—
  And a look from Miss Sheridan's eyes.

Good-night to the Season! the flowers
  Of the grand horticultural fête,
When boudoirs were quitted for bowers,
  And the fashion was not to be late;
When all who had money and leisure
  Grew rural o'er ices and wines,
All pleasantly toiling for pleasure,
  All hungrily pining for pines,
And making of beautiful speeches,
  And marring of beautiful shows,
And feeding on delicate peaches,
  And treading on delicate toes.

Good-night to the Season! another
  Will come with its trifles and toys,
And hurry away like its brother,
  In sunshine, and odour, and noise.
Will it come with a rose or a briar?
  Will it come with a blessing or curse?
Will its bonnets be lower or higher?
  Will its morals be better or worse?

Will it find me grown thinner or fatter,
Or fonder of wrong or of right,
Or married,—or buried?—no matter,
Good-night to the Season, Good-night!

THOMAS LOVELL BEDDOES
1803–1849

587
Song from the Waters

THE swallow leaves her nest,
The soul my weary breast;
But therefore let the rain
On my grave
Fall pure; for why complain?
Since both will come again
O'er the wave.

The wind dead leaves and snow
Doth hurry to and fro;
And, once, a day shall break
O'er the wave,
When a storm of ghosts shall shake
The dead, until they wake
In the grave.

588
Wolfram's Dirge

IF thou wilt ease thine heart
Of love and all its smart,
Then sleep, dear, sleep;
And not a sorrow
Hang any tear on your eyelashes;
Lie still and deep,
Sad soul, until the sea-wave washes
The rim o' th' sun to-morrow,
In eastern sky.

But wilt thou cure thy heart
Of love and all its smart,
   Then die, dear, die;
'Tis deeper, sweeter,
  Than on a rose bank to lie dreaming
    With folded eye;
  And then alone, amid the beaming
Of love's stars, thou'lt meet her
    In eastern sky.

589   *Sybylla's Dirge*

WE do lie beneath the grass
  In the moonlight, in the shade
Of the yew-tree. They that pass
  Hear us not. We are afraid
    They would envy our delight,
    In our graves by glow-worm night.
Come follow us, and smile as we;
  We sail to the rock in the ancient waves,
Where the snow falls by thousands into the sea,
  And the drowned and the shipwrecked have
      happy graves.

590   *Dream-Pedlary*

IF there were dreams to sell,
  What would you buy?
Some cost a passing bell;
  Some a light sigh,
That shakes from Life's fresh crown
Only a roseleaf down.
If there were dreams to sell,
Merry and sad to tell,
And the crier rung the bell,
  What would you buy?

A cottage lone and still,
  With bowers nigh,
Shadowy, my woes to still,
  Until I die.
Such pearl from Life's fresh crown
Fain would I shake me down.
Were dreams to have at will,
This would best heal my ill,
  This would I buy.

But there were dreams to sell,
  Ill didst thou buy;
Life is a dream, they tell,
  Waking, to die.
Dreaming a dream to prize,
Is wishing ghosts to rise;
  And, if I had the spell
  To call the buried, well,
    Which one would I?

If there are ghosts to raise,
  What shall I call,
Out of hell's murky haze,
  Heaven's blue hall?
Raise my loved long-lost boy
To lead me to his joy.
  There are no ghosts to raise;
  Out of death lead no ways;
    Vain is the call.

Know'st thou not ghosts to sue?
  No love thou hast.
Else lie, as I will do,
  And breathe thy last.
So out of Life's fresh crown
Fall like a rose-leaf down.
  Thus are the ghosts to woo;
  Thus are all dreams made true,
    Ever to last!

ELIZABETH BARRETT BROWNING
1806–1861

Sonnets from the Portuguese

591   (i)

I THOUGHT once how Theocritus had sung
  Of the sweet years, the dear and wished-for years,
  Who each one in a gracious hand appears
To bear a gift for mortals, old or young:
And, as I mused it in his antique tongue,
  I saw, in gradual vision through my tears,
  The sweet, sad years, the melancholy years,
Those of my own life, who by turns had flung
A shadow across me. Straightway I was 'ware,
  So weeping, how a mystic Shape did move
Behind me, and drew me backward by the hair;
  And a voice said in mastery, while I strove,—
'Guess now who holds thee?'—'Death,' I said. But, there,
  The silver answer rang,—'Not Death, but Love.'

592   (ii)

IF thou must love me, let it be for naught
  Except for love's sake only. Do not say,
  'I love her for her smile—her look—her way
Of speaking gently,—for a trick of thought
That falls in well with mine, and certes brought
  A sense of pleasant ease on such a day'—
  For these things in themselves, Beloved, may
Be changed, or change for thee—and love, so wrought,
May be unwrought so. Neither love me for
  Thine own dear pity's wiping my cheeks dry:
A creature might forget to weep, who bore
  Thy comfort long, and lose thy love thereby!
But love me for love's sake, that evermore
  Thou mayst love on, through love's eternity.

593   (iii)

WHEN our two souls stand up erect and strong,
   Face to face, silent, drawing nigh and nigher,
   Until the lengthening wings break into fire
At either curvèd point,—what bitter wrong
Can the earth do to us, that we should not long
   Be here contented? Think! In mounting higher,
   The angels would press on us, and aspire
To drop some golden orb of perfect song
Into our deep, dear silence. Let us stay
   Rather on earth, Beloved—where the unfit
Contrarious moods of men recoil away
   And isolate pure spirits, and permit
A place to stand and love in for a day,
   With darkness and the death-hour rounding it.

EDWARD FITZGERALD

1809–1883

594   *from* The Rubaiyat of Omar Khayyam

A BOOK of Verses underneath the Bough,
A Jug of Wine, a Loaf of Bread—and Thou
   Beside me singing in the Wilderness—
O, Wilderness were Paradise enow!

Some for the Glories of This World; and some
Sigh for the Prophet's Paradise to come;
   Ah, take the Cash, and let the Credit go,
Nor heed the rumble of a distant Drum!

Look to the blowing Rose about us—'Lo,
Laughing,' she says, 'into the world I blow.
   At once the silken tassel of my Purse
Tear, and its Treasure on the Garden throw.'

And those who husbanded the Golden grain
And those who flung it to the winds like Rain,
   Alike to no such aureate Earth are turned
As, buried once, Men want dug up again.

The Worldly Hope men set their Hearts upon
Turns Ashes—or it prospers; and anon,
    Like Snow upon the Desert's dusty Face,
Lighting a little hour or two—is gone.

Think, in this battered Caravanserai
Whose Portals are alternate Night and Day,
    How Sultan after Sultan with his Pomp
Abode his destined Hour, and went his way.

They say the Lion and the Lizard keep
The Courts where Jamshyd gloried and drank deep:
    And Bahram, that great Hunter—the wild Ass
Stamps o'er his Head, but cannot break his Sleep.

I sometimes think that never blows so red
The Rose as where some buried Caesar bled;
    That every Hyacinth the Garden wears
Dropt in her Lap from some once lovely Head.

And this reviving Herb whose tender Green
Fledges the River-Lip on which we lean—
    Ah, lean upon it lightly! for who knows
From what once lovely Lip it springs unseen!

Ah, my Beloved, fill the Cup that clears
To-DAY of past Regrets and future Fears:
    To-morrow!—Why, To-morrow I may be
Myself with Yesterday's Seven thousand Years.

For some we loved, the loveliest and the best
That from his Vintage rolling Time hath prest,
    Have drunk their Cup a Round or two before,
And one by one crept silently to rest.

And we, that now make merry in the Room
They left, and Summer dresses in new bloom,
    Ourselves must we beneath the Couch of Earth
Descend—ourselves to make a Couch—for whom?

Ah, make the most of what we yet may spend,
Before we too into the Dust descend;
    Dust into Dust, and under Dust to lie,
Sans Wine, sans Song, sans Singer, and—sans End!

ALFRED, LORD TENNYSON
1809–1892

595   *Mariana*

WITH blackest moss the flower-pots
   Were thickly crusted, one and all:
The rusted nails fell from the knots
   That held the pear to the gable-wall.
The broken sheds looked sad and strange:
   Unlifted was the clinking latch;
   Weeded and worn the ancient thatch
Upon the lonely moated grange.
     She only said, 'My life is dreary,
       He cometh not,' she said;
     She said, 'I am aweary, aweary,
       I would that I were dead!'

Her tears fell with the dews at even;
   Her tears fell ere the dews were dried;
She could not look on the sweet heaven,
   Either at morn or eventide.
After the flitting of the bats,
   When thickest dark did trance the sky,
   She drew her casement-curtain by,
And glanced athwart the glooming flats.
     She only said, 'The night is dreary,
       He cometh not,' she said;
     She said, 'I am aweary, aweary,
       I would that I were dead!'

Upon the middle of the night,
   Waking she heard the night-fowl crow:
The cock sung out an hour ere light:
   From the dark fen the oxen's low
Came to her: without hope of change,
   In sleep she seemed to walk forlorn,
   Till cold winds woke the gray-eyed morn
About the lonely moated grange.

She only said, 'The day is dreary,
    He cometh not,' she said;
She said, 'I am aweary, aweary,
    I would that I were dead!'

About a stone-cast from the wall
    A sluice with blackened waters slept,
And o'er it many, round and small,
    The clustered marish-mosses crept.
Hard by a poplar shook alway,
    All silver-green with gnarlèd bark:
For leagues no other tree did mark
The level waste, the rounding gray.
        She only said, 'My life is dreary,
            He cometh not,' she said;
        She said, 'I am aweary, aweary,
            I would that I were dead!'

And ever when the moon was low,
    And the shrill winds were up and away,
In the white curtain, to and fro,
    She saw the gusty shadow sway.
But when the moon was very low,
    And wild winds bound within their cell,
The shadow of the poplar fell
Upon her bed, across her brow.
        She only said, 'The night is dreary,
            He cometh not,' she said;
        She said, 'I am aweary, aweary,
            I would that I were dead!'

All day within the dreamy house,
    The doors upon their hinges creaked;
The blue fly sung in the pane; the mouse
    Behind the mouldering wainscot shrieked,
Or from the crevice peered about.
    Old faces glimmered through the doors,
    Old footsteps trod the upper floors,
Old voices called her from without.
        She only said, 'My life is dreary,
            He cometh not,' she said;
        She said, 'I am aweary, aweary,
            I would that I were dead!'

The sparrow's chirrup on the roof,
  The slow clock ticking, and the sound
Which to the wooing wind aloof
  The poplar made, did all confound
Her sense; but most she loathed the hour
  When the thick-moted sunbeam lay
  Athwart the chambers, and the day
Was sloping toward his western bower.
    Then, said she, 'I am very dreary,
      He will not come,' she said;
    She wept, 'I am aweary, aweary,
      Oh God, that I were dead!'

596   *The Lady of Shalott*

PART I

On either side the river lie
Long fields of barley and of rye,
That clothe the wold and meet the sky;
And through the field the road runs by
    To many-towered Camelot;
And up and down the people go,
Gazing where the lilies blow
Round an island there below,
    The island of Shalott.

Willows whiten, aspens quiver,
Little breezes dusk and shiver
Through the wave that runs for ever
By the island in the river
    Flowing down to Camelot.
Four gray walls, and four gray towers,
Overlook a space of flowers,
And the silent isle imbowers
    The Lady of Shalott.

By the margin, willow-veiled,
Slide the heavy barges trailed
By slow horses; and unhailed
The shallop flitteth silken-sailed
    Skimming down to Camelot:
But who hath seen her wave her hand?
Or at the casement seen her stand?
Or is she known in all the land,
    The Lady of Shalott?

Only reapers, reaping early
In among the bearded barley,
Hear a song that echoes cheerly
From the river winding clearly,
    Down to towered Camelot:
And by the moon the reaper weary,
Piling sheaves in uplands airy,
Listening, whispers ' 'Tis the fairy
    Lady of Shalott.'

PART II

There she weaves by night and day
A magic web with colours gay.
She has heard a whisper say,
A curse is on her if she stay
    To look down to Camelot.
She knows not what the curse may be,
And so she weaveth steadily,
And little other care hath she,
    The Lady of Shalott.

And moving through a mirror clear
That hangs before her all the year,
Shadows of the world appear.
There she sees the highway near
    Winding down to Camelot:
There the river eddy whirls,
And there the surly village-churls,
And the red cloaks of market girls,
    Pass onward from Shalott.

Sometimes a troop of damsels glad,
An abbot on an ambling pad,
Sometimes a curly shepherd-lad,
Or long-haired page in crimson clad,
    Goes by to towered Camelot;
And sometimes through the mirror blue
The knights come riding two and two:
She hath no loyal knight and true,
    The Lady of Shalott.

But in her web she still delights
To weave the mirror's magic sights,
For often through the silent nights
A funeral, with plumes and lights
    And music, went to Camelot:
Or when the moon was overhead,
Came two young lovers lately wed;
'I am half sick of shadows,' said
    The Lady of Shalott.

PART III

A bow-shot from her bower-eaves,
He rode between the barley-sheaves,
The sun came dazzling through the leaves,
And flamed upon the brazen greaves
    Of bold Sir Lancelot.
A red-cross knight for ever kneeled
To a lady in his shield,
That sparkled on the yellow field,
    Beside remote Shalott.

The gemmy bridle glittered free,
Like to some branch of stars we see
Hung in the golden Galaxy.
The bridle bells rang merrily
    As he rode down to Camelot:
And from his blazoned baldric slung
A mighty silver bugle hung,
And as he rode his armour rung,
    Beside remote Shalott.

All in the blue unclouded weather
Thick-jewelled shone the saddle-leather,
The helmet and the helmet-feather
Burned like one burning flame together,
    As he rode down to Camelot.
As often through the purple night,
Below the starry clusters bright,
Some bearded meteor, trailing light,
    Moves over still Shalott.

His broad clear brow in sunlight glowed;
On burnished hooves his war-horse trode;
From underneath his helmet flowed
His coal-black curls as on he rode,
    As he rode down to Camelot.
From the bank and from the river
He flashed into the crystal mirror,
'Tirra lirra,' by the river
    Sang Sir Lancelot.

She left the web, she left the loom,
She made three paces through the room,
She saw the water-lily bloom,
She saw the helmet and the plume,
    She looked down to Camelot.
Out flew the web and floated wide;
The mirror cracked from side to side;
'The curse is come upon me,' cried
    The Lady of Shalott.

PART IV

In the stormy east-wind straining,
The pale yellow woods were waning,
The broad stream in his banks complaining,
Heavily the low sky raining
    Over towered Camelot;
Down she came and found a boat
Beneath a willow left afloat,
And round about the prow she wrote
    The Lady of Shalott.

And down the river's dim expanse
Like some bold seër in a trance,
Seeing all his own mischance—
With a glassy countenance
  Did she look to Camelot.
And at the closing of the day
She loosed the chain, and down she lay;
The broad stream bore her far away,
  The Lady of Shalott.

Lying, robed in snowy white
That loosely flew to left and right—
The leaves upon her falling light—
Through the noises of the night
  She floated down to Camelot:
And as the boat-head wound along
The willowy hills and fields among,
They heard her singing her last song,
  The Lady of Shalott.

Heard a carol, mournful, holy,
Chanted loudly, chanted slowly,
Till her blood was frozen slowly,
And her eyes were darkened wholly,
  Turned to towered Camelot.
For ere she reached upon the tide
The first house by the water-side,
Singing in her song she died,
  The Lady of Shalott.

Under tower and balcony,
By garden-wall and gallery,
A gleaming shape she floated by,
Dead-pale between the houses high,
  Silent into Camelot.
Out upon the wharfs they came,
Knight and burgher, lord and dame,
And round the prow they read her name,
  The Lady of Shalott.

Who is this? and what is here?
And in the lighted palace near
Died the sound of royal cheer;
And they crossed themselves for fear,

All the knights at Camelot:
But Lancelot mused a little space;
He said, 'She has a lovely face;
God in his mercy lend her grace,
    The Lady of Shalott.'

597   *Song of the Lotos-Eaters*

THERE is sweet music here that softer falls
Than petals from blown roses on the grass,
Or night-dews on still waters between walls
Of shadowy granite, in a gleaming pass;
Music that gentlier on the spirit lies,
Than tired eyelids upon tired eyes;
Music that brings sweet sleep down from the blissful skies.
Here are cool mosses deep,
And through the moss the ivies creep,
And in the stream the long-leaved flowers weep,
And from the craggy ledge the poppy hangs in sleep.

Why are we weighed upon with heaviness,
And utterly consumed with sharp distress,
While all things else have rest from weariness?
All things have rest: why should we toil alone,
We only toil, who are the first of things,
And make perpetual moan,
Still from one sorrow to another thrown:
Nor ever fold our wings,
And cease from wanderings,
Nor steep our brows in slumber's holy balm;
Nor harken what the inner spirit sings,
'There is no joy but calm!'
Why should we only toil, the roof and crown of things?

Lo! in the middle of the wood,
The folded leaf is wooed from out the bud
With winds upon the branch, and there
Grows green and broad, and takes no care,
Sun-steeped at noon, and in the moon
Nightly dew-fed; and turning yellow
Falls, and floats adown the air.

Lo! sweetened with the summer light,
The full-juiced apple, waxing over-mellow,
Drops in a silent autumn night.
All its allotted length of days,
The flower ripens in its place,
Ripens and fades, and falls, and hath no toil,
Fast-rooted in the fruitful soil.

Hateful is the dark-blue sky,
Vaulted o'er the dark-blue sea.
Death is the end of life; ah, why
Should life all labour be?
Let us alone. Time driveth onward fast,
And in a little while our lips are dumb.
Let us alone. What is it that will last?
All things are taken from us, and become
Portions and parcels of the dreadful Past.
Let us alone. What pleasure can we have
To war with evil? Is there any peace
In ever climbing up the climbing wave?
All things have rest, and ripen toward the grave
In silence; ripen, fall and cease:
Give us long rest or death, dark death, or dreamful ease.

How sweet it were, hearing the downward stream,
With half-shut eyes ever to seem
Falling asleep in a half-dream!
To dream and dream, like yonder amber light,
Which will not leave the myrrh-bush on the height;
To hear each other's whispered speech;
Eating the Lotos day by day,
To watch the crisping ripples on the beach,
And tender curving lines of creamy spray;
To lend our hearts and spirits wholly
To the influence of mild-minded melancholy;
To muse and brood and live again in memory,
With those old faces of our infancy
Heaped over with a mound of grass,
Two handfuls of white dust, shut in an urn of brass!

Dear is the memory of our wedded lives,
And dear the last embraces of our wives
And their warm tears: but all hath suffered change:
For surely now our household hearths are cold:
Our sons inherit us: our looks are strange:
And we should come like ghosts to trouble joy.
Or else the island princes over-bold
Have eat our substance, and the minstrel sings
Before them of the ten years' war in Troy,
And our great deeds, as half-forgotten things.
Is there confusion in the little isle?
Let what is broken so remain.
The Gods are hard to reconcile:
'Tis hard to settle order once again.
There *is* confusion worse than death,
Trouble on trouble, pain on pain,
Long labour unto agèd breath,
Sore task to hearts worn out by many wars
And eyes grown dim with gazing on the pilot-stars.

But, propt on beds of amaranth and moly,
How sweet (while warm airs lull us, blowing lowly)
With half-dropt eyelid still,
Beneath a heaven dark and holy,
To watch the long bright river drawing slowly
His waters from the purple hill—
To hear the dewy echoes calling
From cave to cave through the thick-twinèd vine—
To watch the emerald-coloured water falling
Through many a woven acanthus-wreath divine!
Only to hear and see the far-off sparkling brine,
Only to hear were sweet, stretched out beneath the pine.

The Lotos blooms below the barren peak:
The Lotos blows by every winding creek:
All day the wind breathes low with mellower tone:
Through every hollow cave and alley lone
Round and round the spicy downs the yellow Lotos-dust is blown.
We have had enough of action, and of motion we,
Rolled to starboard, rolled to larboard, when the surge was
    seething free,
Where the wallowing monster spouted his foam-fountains in the
    sea.

Let us swear an oath, and keep it with an equal mind,
In the hollow Lotos-land to live and lie reclined
On the hills like Gods together, careless of mankind.
For they lie beside their nectar, and the bolts are hurled
Far below them in the valleys, and the clouds are lightly curled
Round their golden houses, girdled with the gleaming world:
Where they smile in secret, looking over wasted lands,
Blight and famine, plague and earthquake, roaring deeps and fiery
    sands,
Clanging fights, and flaming towns, and sinking ships, and praying
    hands.
But they smile, they find a music centred in a doleful song
Steaming up, a lamentation and an ancient tale of wrong,
Like a tale of little meaning though the words are strong;
Chanted from an ill-used race of men that cleave the soil,
Sow the seed, and reap the harvest with enduring toil,
Storing yearly little dues of wheat, and wine and oil;
Till they perish and they suffer—some, 'tis whispered—down in
    hell
Suffer endless anguish, others in Elysian valleys dwell,
Resting weary limbs at last on beds of asphodel.
Surely, surely, slumber is more sweet than toil, the shore
Than labour in the deep mid-ocean, wind and wave and oar;
Oh rest ye, brother mariners, we will not wander more.

598   *Ulysses*

IT little profits that an idle king,
By this still hearth, among these barren crags,
Matched with an agèd wife, I mete and dole
Unequal laws unto a savage race,
That hoard, and sleep, and feed, and know not me.

I cannot rest from travel: I will drink
Life to the lees: all times I have enjoyed
Greatly, have suffered greatly, both with those
That loved me, and alone; on shore, and when
Through scudding drifts the rainy Hyades
Vext the dim sea: I am become a name;
For always roaming with a hungry heart
Much have I seen and known; cities of men

And manners, climates, councils, governments,
Myself not least, but honoured of them all;
And drunk delight of battle with my peers,
Far on the ringing plains of windy Troy.

   I am a part of all that I have met;
Yet all experience is an arch wherethrough
Gleams that untravelled world, whose margin fades
For ever and for ever when I move.
How dull it is to pause, to make an end,
To rust unburnished, not to shine in use!
As though to breathe were life. Life piled on life
Were all too little, and of one to me
Little remains: but every hour is saved
From that eternal silence, something more,
A bringer of new things; and vile it were
For some three suns to store and hoard myself,
And this gray spirit yearning in desire
To follow knowledge like a sinking star,
Beyond the utmost bound of human thought.

   This is my son, mine own Telemachus,
To whom I leave the sceptre and the isle—
Well-loved of me, discerning to fulfil
This labour, by slow prudence to make mild
A rugged people, and through soft degrees
Subdue them to the useful and the good.
Most blameless is he, centred in the sphere
Of common duties, decent not to fail
In offices of tenderness, and pay
Meet adoration to my household gods,
When I am gone. He works his work, I mine.

   There lies the port; the vessel puffs her sail:
There gloom the dark broad seas. My mariners,
Souls that have toiled, and wrought, and thought with me—
That ever with a frolic welcome took
The thunder and the sunshine, and opposed
Free hearts, free foreheads—you and I are old;
Old age hath yet his honour and his toil;
Death closes all: but something ere the end,
Some work of noble note, may yet be done,
Not unbecoming men that strove with Gods.

The lights begin to twinkle from the rocks:
The long day wanes: the slow moon climbs: the deep
Moans round with many voices. Come, my friends,
'Tis not too late to seek a newer world.
Push off, and sitting well in order smite
The sounding furrows; for my purpose holds
To sail beyond the sunset, and the baths
Of all the western stars, until I die.
It may be that the gulfs will wash us down:
It may be we shall touch the Happy Isles,
And see the great Achilles, whom we knew.
Though much is taken, much abides; and though
We are not now that strength which in old days
Moved earth and heaven; that which we are, we are;
One equal temper of heroic hearts,
Made weak by time and fate, but strong in will
To strive, to seek, to find, and not to yield.

599

O THAT 'twere possible,
  After long grief and pain,
To find the arms of my true-love
  Round me once again! . . .

A shadow flits before me—
  Not thou, but like to thee.
Ah God! that it were possible
  For one short hour to·see
The souls we loved, that they might tell us
  What and where they be. . . .

600

BREAK, break, break,
  On thy cold gray stones, O Sea!
And I would that my tongue could utter
  The thoughts that arise in me.

O well for the fisherman's boy,
  That he shouts with his sister at play!
O well for the sailor lad,
  That he sings in his boat on the bay!

And the stately ships go on
  To their haven under the hill;
But O for the touch of a vanished hand,
  And the sound of a voice that is still!

Break, break, break,
  At the foot of thy crags, O Sea!
But the tender grace of a day that is dead
  Will never come back to me.

601   *Tears, Idle Tears*

TEARS, idle tears, I know not what they mean,
Tears from the depth of some divine despair
Rise in the heart, and gather to the eyes,
In looking on the happy Autumn-fields,
And thinking of the days that are no more.

Fresh as the first beam glittering on a sail,
That brings our friends up from the underworld,
Sad as the last which reddens over one
That sinks with all we love below the verge;
So sad, so fresh, the days that are no more.

Ah, sad and strange as in dark summer dawns
The earliest pipe of half-awakened birds
To dying ears, when unto dying eyes
The casement slowly grows a glimmering square;
So sad, so strange, the days that are no more.

Dear as remembered kisses after death,
And sweet as those by hopeless fancy feigned
On lips that are for others; deep as love,
Deep as first love, and wild with all regret;
O Death in Life, the days that are no more.

602 *Now Sleeps the Crimson Petal*

NOW sleeps the crimson petal, now the white;
Nor waves the cypress in the palace walk;
Nor winks the gold fin in the porphyry font:
The fire-fly wakens: waken thou with me.

Now droops the milkwhite peacock like a ghost,
And like a ghost she glimmers on to me.

Now lies the Earth all Danaë to the stars,
And all thy heart lies open unto me.

Now slides the silent meteor on, and leaves
A shining furrow, as thy thoughts in me.

Now folds the lily all her sweetness up,
And slips into the bosom of the lake:
So fold thyself, my dearest, thou, and slip
Into my bosom and be lost in me.

603 *Blow, Bugle, Blow*

THE splendour falls on castle walls
    And snowy summits old in story:
The long light shakes across the lakes,
    And the wild cataract leaps in glory.
Blow, bugle, blow, set the wild echoes flying,
Blow, bugle; answer, echoes, dying, dying, dying.

O hark, O hear! how thin and clear,
    And thinner, clearer, farther going!
O sweet and far from cliff and scar
    The horns of Elfland faintly blowing!
Blow, let us hear the purple glens replying:
Blow, bugle; answer, echoes, dying, dying, dying.

O love, they die in yon rich sky,
    They faint on hill or field or river:
Our echoes roll from soul to soul,
    And grow for ever and for ever.
Blow, bugle, blow, set the wild echoes flying,
And answer, echoes, answer, dying, dying, dying.

from In Memoriam

604

(i)

OLD Yew, which graspest at the stones
　　That name the under-lying dead,
　　Thy fibres net the dreamless head,
Thy roots are wrapt about the bones.

The seasons bring the flower again,
　　And bring the firstling to the flock;
　　And in the dusk of thee, the clock
Beats out the little lives of men.

O not for thee the glow, the bloom,
　　Who changest not in any gale,
　　Nor branding summer suns avail
To touch thy thousand years of gloom:

And gazing on thee, sullen tree,
　　Sick for thy stubborn hardihood,
　　I seem to fail from out my blood
And grow incorporate into thee.

605

(ii)

Dark house, by which once more I stand
　　Here in the long unlovely street,
　　Doors, where my heart was used to beat
So quickly, waiting for a hand,

A hand that can be clasped no more—
　　Behold me, for I cannot sleep,
　　And like a guilty thing I creep
At earliest morning to the door.

He is not here; but far away
　　The noise of life begins again,
　　And ghastly through the drizzling rain
On the bald street breaks the blank day.

606   (iii)

CALM is the morn without a sound,
    Calm as to suit a calmer grief,
    And only through the faded leaf
The chestnut pattering to the ground:

Calm and deep peace on this high wold,
    And on these dews that drench the furze,
    And all the silvery gossamers
That twinkle into green and gold:

Calm and still light on yon great plain
    That sweeps with all its autumn bowers,
    And crowded farms and lessening towers,
To mingle with the bounding main:

Calm and deep peace in this wide air,
    These leaves that redden to the fall;
    And in my heart, if calm at all,
If any calm, a calm despair:

Calm on the seas, and silver sleep,
    And waves that sway themselves in rest,
    And dead calm in that noble breast
Which heaves but with the heaving deep.

607   (iv)

TONIGHT the winds begin to rise
    And roar from yonder dropping day:
    The last red leaf is whirled away,
The rooks are blown about the skies;

The forest cracked, the waters curled,
    The cattle huddled on the lea;
    And wildly dashed on tower and tree
The sunbeam strikes along the world:

And but for fancies, which aver
   That all thy motions gently pass
   Athwart a plane of molten glass,
I scarce could brook the strain and stir

That makes the barren branches loud;
   And but for fear it is not so,
   The wild unrest that lives in woe
Would dote and pore on yonder cloud

That rises upward always higher,
   And onward drags a labouring breast,
   And topples round the dreary west,
A looming bastion fringed with fire.

608   (v)

I DREAMED there would be Spring no more,
   That Nature's ancient power was lost:
   The streets were black with smoke and frost,
They chattered trifles at the door:

I wandered from the noisy town,
   I found a wood with thorny boughs:
   I took the thorns to bind my brows,
I wore them like a civic crown:

I met with scoffs, I met with scorns
   From youth and babe and hoary hairs:
   They called me in the public squares
The fool that wears a crown of thorns:

They called me fool, they called me child:
   I found an angel of the night;
   The voice was low, the look was bright;
He looked upon my crown and smiled:

He reached the glory of a hand,
   That seemed to touch it into leaf:
   The voice was not the voice of grief,
The words were hard to understand.

609 (vi)

Now fades the last long streak of snow,
  Now burgeons every maze of quick
  About the flowering squares, and thick
By ashen roots the violets blow.

Now rings the woodland loud and long,
  The distance takes a lovelier hue,
  And drowned in yonder living blue
The lark becomes a sightless song.

Now dance the lights on lawn and lea,
  The flocks are whiter down the vale,
  And milkier every milky sail
On winding stream or distant sea;

Where now the seamew pipes, or dives
  In yonder greening gleam, and fly
  The happy birds, that change their sky
To build and brood; that live their lives

From land to land; and in my breast
  Spring wakens too; and my regret
  Becomes an April violet,
And buds and blossoms like the rest.

610 (vii)

THERE rolls the deep where grew the tree.
  O earth, what changes hast thou seen!
  There where the long street roars, hath been
The stillness of the central sea.

The hills are shadows, and they flow
  From form to form, and nothing stands;
  They melt like mist, the solid lands,
Like clouds they shape themselves and go.

But in my spirit will I dwell,
  And dream my dream, and hold it true;
  For though my lips may breathe adieu,
I cannot think the thing farewell.

611   (viii)

LOVE is and was my Lord and King,
    And in his presence I attend
    To hear the tidings of my friend,
Which every hour his couriers bring.

Love is and was my King and Lord,
    And will be, though as yet I keep
    Within his court on earth, and sleep
Encompassed by his faithful guard,

And hear at times a sentinel
    Who moves about from place to place,
    And whispers to the worlds of space,
In the deep night, that all is well.

612

COME into the garden, Maud,
    For the black bat, night, has flown,
Come into the garden, Maud,
    I am here at the gate alone;
And the woodbine spices are wafted abroad,
    And the musk of the rose is blown.

For a breeze of morning moves,
    And the planet of Love is on high,
Beginning to faint in the light that she loves
    On a bed of daffodil sky,
To faint in the light of the sun she loves,
    To faint in his light, and to die.

All night have the roses heard
    The flute, violin, bassoon;
All night has the casement jessamine stirred
    To the dancers dancing in tune;
Till a silence fell with the waking bird,
    And a hush with the setting moon.

I said to the lily, 'There is but one
  With whom she has heart to be gay.
When will the dancers leave her alone?
  She is weary of dance and play.'
Now half to the setting moon are gone,
  And half to the rising day;
Low on the sand and loud on the stone
  The last wheel echoes away.

I said to the rose, 'The brief night goes
  In babble and revel and wine.
O young lord-lover, what sighs are those,
  For one that will never be thine?
But mine, but mine,' so I sware to the rose,
  'For ever and ever, mine.'

And the soul of the rose went into my blood,
  As the music clashed in the hall;
And long by the garden lake I stood,
  For I heard your rivulet fall
From the lake to the meadow and on to the wood,
  Our wood, that is dearer than all;

From the meadow your walks have left so sweet
  That whenever a March-wind sighs
He sets the jewel-print of your feet
  In violets blue as your eyes,
To the woody hollows in which we meet
  And the valleys of Paradise.

The slender acacia would not shake
  One long milk-bloom on the tree;
The white lake-blossom fell into the lake
  As the pimpernel dozed on the lea;
But the rose was awake all night for your sake,
  Knowing your promise to me;
The lilies and roses were all awake,
  They sighed for the dawn and thee.

Queen rose of the rosebud garden of girls,
   Come hither, the dances are done,
In gloss of satin and glimmer of pearls,
   Queen lily and rose in one;
Shine out, little head, sunning over with curls,
   To the flowers, and be their sun.

There has fallen a splendid tear
   From the passion-flower at the gate.
She is coming, my dove, my dear;
   She is coming, my life, my fate;
The red rose cries, 'She is near, she is near;'
   And the white rose weeps, 'She is late;'
The larkspur listens, 'I hear, I hear;'
   And the lily whispers, 'I wait.'

She is coming, my own, my sweet,
   Were it ever so airy a tread,
My heart would hear her and beat,
   Were it earth in an earthy bed;
My dust would hear her and beat,
   Had I lain for a century dead;
Would start and tremble under her feet,
   And blossom in purple and red.

613   *Tithonus*

THE woods decay, the woods decay and fall,
The vapours weep their burthen to the ground,
Man comes and tills the field and lies beneath,
And after many a summer dies the swan.
Me only cruel immortality
Consumes: I wither slowly in thine arms,
Here at the quiet limit of the world,
A white-haired shadow roaming like a dream
The ever-silent spaces of the East,
Far-folded mists, and gleaming halls of morn.

Alas! for this gray shadow, once a man—
So glorious in his beauty and thy choice,
Who madest him thy chosen, that he seemed
To his great heart none other than a God!

I asked thee, 'Give me immortality.'
Then didst thou grant mine asking with a smile,
Like wealthy men who care not how they give.
But thy strong Hours indignant worked their wills,
And beat me down and marred and wasted me,
And though they could not end me, left me maimed
To dwell in presence of immortal youth,
Immortal age beside immortal youth,
And all I was, in ashes. Can thy love,
Thy beauty, make amends, though even now,
Close over us, the silver star, thy guide,
Shines in those tremulous eyes that fill with tears
To hear me? Let me go: take back thy gift:
Why should a man desire in any way
To vary from the kindly race of men,
Or pass beyond the goal of ordinance
Where all should pause, as is most meet for all?

A soft air fans the cloud apart; there comes
A glimpse of that dark world where I was born.
Once more the old mysterious glimmer steals
From thy pure brows, and from thy shoulders pure,
And bosom beating with a heart renewed.
Thy cheek begins to redden through the gloom,
Thy sweet eyes brighten slowly close to mine,
Ere yet they blind the stars, and the wild team
Which love thee, yearning for thy yoke, arise,
And shake the darkness from their loosened manes,
And beat the twilight into flakes of fire.

Lo! ever thus thou growest beautiful
In silence, then before thine answer given
Departest, and thy tears are on my cheek.

Why wilt thou ever scare me with thy tears,
And make me tremble lest a saying learnt,
In days far-off, on that dark earth, be true?
'The Gods themselves cannot recall their gifts.'

Ay me! ay me! with what another heart
In days far-off, and with what other eyes
I used to watch—if I be he that watched—
The lucid outline forming round thee; saw
The dim curls kindle into sunny rings;
Changed with thy mystic change, and felt my blood
Glow with the glow that slowly crimsoned all
Thy presence and thy portals, while I lay,
Mouth, forehead, eyelids, growing dewy-warm
With kisses balmier than half-opening buds
Of April, and could hear the lips that kissed
Whispering I knew not what of wild and sweet,
Like that strange song I heard Apollo sing,
While Ilion like a mist rose into towers.

Yet hold me not for ever in thine East:
How can my nature longer mix with thine?
Coldly thy rosy shadows bathe me, cold
Are all thy lights, and cold my wrinkled feet
Upon thy glimmering thresholds, when the steam
Floats up from those dim fields about the homes
Of happy men that have the power to die,
And grassy barrows of the happier dead.
Release me, and restore me to the ground;
Thou seëst all things, thou wilt see my grave:
Thou wilt renew thy beauty morn by morn;
I earth in earth forget these empty courts,
And thee returning on thy silver wheels.

614   *In the Valley of Cauteretz*

ALL along the valley, stream that flashest white,
Deepening thy voice with the deepening of the night,
All along the valley, where thy waters flow,
I walked with one I loved two and thirty years ago.
All along the valley, while I walked today,
The two and thirty years were a mist that rolls away;
For all along the valley, down thy rocky bed,
Thy living voice to me was as the voice of the dead,
And all along the valley, by rock and cave and tree,
The voice of the dead was a living voice to me.

615   *Crossing the Bar*

SUNSET and evening star,
  And one clear call for me!
And may there be no moaning of the bar,
  When I put out to sea,

But such a tide as moving seems asleep,
  Too full for sound and foam,
When that which drew from out the boundless deep
  Turns again home.

Twilight and evening bell,
  And after that the dark!
And may there be no sadness of farewell,
  When I embark;

For though from out our bourne of Time and Place
  The flood may bear me far,
I hope to see my Pilot face to face
  When I have crost the bar.

ROBERT BROWNING

1812–1889

616   *My Last Duchess*

THAT's my last Duchess painted on the wall,
Looking as if she were alive. I call
That piece a wonder, now: Frà Pandolf's hands
Worked busily a day, and there she stands.
Will 't please you sit and look at her? I said
'Frà Pandolf' by design, for never read
Strangers like you that pictured countenance,
The depth and passion of its earnest glance,
But to myself they turned (since none puts by
The curtain I have drawn for you, but I)
And seemed as they would ask me, if they durst,
How such a glance came there; so, not the first
Are you to turn and ask thus. Sir, 't was not
Her husband's presence only, called that spot

Of joy into the Duchess' cheek: perhaps
Frà Pandolf chanced to say 'Her mantle laps
Over my lady's wrist too much,' or 'Paint
Must never hope to reproduce the faint
Half-flush that dies along her throat:' such stuff
Was courtesy, she thought, and cause enough
For calling up that spot of joy. She had
A heart—how shall I say?—too soon made glad,
Too easily impressed; she liked whate'er
She looked on, and her looks went everywhere.
Sir, 't was all one! My favour at her breast,
The dropping of the daylight in the West,
The bough of cherries some officious fool
Broke in the orchard for her, the white mule
She rode with round the terrace—all and each
Would draw from her alike the approving speech,
Or blush, at least. She thanked men,—good! but thanked
Somehow—I know not how—as if she ranked
My gift of a nine-hundred-years-old name
With anybody's gift. Who'd stoop to blame
This sort of trifling? Even had you skill
In speech—(which I have not)—to make your will
Quite clear to such an one, and say, 'Just this
Or that in you disgusts me; here you miss,
Or there exceed the mark'—and if she let
Herself be lessoned so, nor plainly set
Her wits to yours, forsooth, and made excuse,
—E'en then would be some stooping; and I choose
Never to stoop. Oh sir, she smiled, no doubt,
Whene'er I passed her; but who passed without
Much the same smile? This grew; I gave commands;
Then all smiles stopped together. There she stands
As if alive. Will 't please you rise? We'll meet
The company below, then. I repeat,
The Count your master's known munificence
Is ample warrant that no just pretence
Of mine for dowry will be disallowed;
Though his fair daughter's self, as I avowed
At starting, is my object. Nay, we'll go
Together down, sir. Notice Neptune, though,
Taming a sea-horse, thought a rarity,
Which Claus of Innsbruck cast in bronze for me!

617 *The Lost Mistress*

ALL's over, then: does truth sound bitter
　　As one at first believes?
Hark, 'tis the sparrows' good-night twitter
　　About your cottage eaves!

And the leaf-buds on the vine are woolly,
　　I noticed that, to-day;
One day more bursts them open fully
　　—You know the red turns gray.

To-morrow we meet the same then, dearest?
　　May I take your hand in mine?
Mere friends are we,—well, friends the merest
　　Keep much that I resign:

For each glance of the eye so bright and black,
　　Though I keep with heart's endeavour,—
Your voice, when you wish the snowdrops back,
　　Though it stay in my soul for ever!—

Yet I will but say what mere friends say,
　　Or only a thought stronger;
I will hold your hand but as long as all may,
　　Or so very little longer!

618 *Home Thoughts from Abroad*

OH, to be in England
Now that April's there,
And whoever wakes in England
Sees, some morning, unaware,
That the lowest boughs and the brushwood sheaf
Round the elm-tree bole are in tiny leaf,
While the chaffinch sings on the orchard bough
In England—now!

And after April, when May follows,
And the whitethroat builds, and all the swallows!
Hark, where my blossomed pear-tree in the hedge
Leans to the field and scatters on the clover
Blossoms and dewdrops—at the bent spray's edge—
That's the wise thrush; he sings each song twice over,
Lest you should think he never could recapture
The first fine careless rapture!
And though the fields look rough with hoary dew
All will be gay when noontide wakes anew
The buttercups, the little children's dower
—Far brighter than this gaudy melon-flower!

619   *Home Thoughts from the Sea*

NOBLY, nobly Cape Saint Vincent to the North-west died away;
Sunset ran, one glorious blood-red, reeking into Cadiz Bay;
Bluish 'mid the burning water, full in face Trafalgar lay;
In the dimmest North-east distance dawned Gibraltar grand and
    gray;
'Here and here did England help me: how can I help England?'—
    say,
Whoso turns as I, this evening, turn to God to praise and pray,
While Jove's planet rises yonder, silent over Africa.

620   *Meeting at Night*

THE gray sea and the long black land;
And the yellow half-moon large and low;
And the startled little waves that leap
In fiery ringlets from their sleep,
As I gain the cove with pushing prow,
And quench its speed i' the slushy sand.

Then a mile of warm sea-scented beach;
Three fields to cross till a farm appears;
A tap at the pane, the quick sharp scratch
And blue spurt of a lighted match,
And a voice less loud, through its joys and fears,
Than the two hearts beating each to each!

621 *Parting at Morning*

ROUND the cape of a sudden came the sea,
And the sun looked over the mountain's rim:
And straight was a path of gold for him,
And the need of a world of men for me.

622 *Love among the Ruins*

WHERE the quiet-coloured end of evening smiles,
    Miles and miles
On the solitary pastures where our sheep
    Half-asleep
Tinkle homeward through the twilight, stray or stop
    As they crop—
Was the site once of a city great and gay,
    (So they say)
Of our country's very capital, its prince
    Ages since
Held his court in, gathered councils, wielding far
    Peace or war.

Now,—the country does not even boast a tree,
    As you see,
To distinguish slopes of verdure, certain rills
    From the hills
Intersect and give a name to, (else they run
    Into one)
Where the domed and daring palace shot its spires
    Up like fires
O'er the hundred-gated circuit of a wall
    Bounding all,
Made of marble, men might march on nor be pressed,
    Twelve abreast.

And such plenty and perfection, see, of grass
    Never was!
Such a carpet as, this summer time, o'erspreads
    And embeds
Every vestige of the city, guessed alone,
    Stock or stone—

Where a multitude of men breathed joy and woe
      Long ago;
Lust of glory pricked their hearts up, dread of shame
      Struck them tame;
And that glory and that shame alike, the gold
      Bought and sold.

Now,—the single little turret that remains
      On the plains,
By the caper overrooted, by the gourd
      Overscored,
While the patching houseleek's head of blossom winks
      Through the chinks—
Marks the basement whence a tower in ancient time
      Sprang sublime,
And a burning ring, all round, the chariots traced
      As they raced,
And the monarch and his minions and his dames
      Viewed the games.

And I know, while thus the quiet-coloured eve
      Smiles to leave
To their folding, all our many-tinkling fleece
      In such peace,
And the slopes and rills in undistinguished grey
      Melt away—
That a girl with eager eyes and yellow hair
      Waits me there
In the turret whence the charioteers caught soul
      For the goal,
When the king looked, where she looks now, breathless, dumb
      Till I come.

But he looked upon the city, every side,
      Far and wide,
All the mountains topped with temples, all the glades'
      Colonnades,
All the causeys, bridges, aqueducts,—and then,
      All the men!
When I do come, she will speak not, she will stand,
      Either hand

On my shoulder, give her eyes the first embrace
    Of my face,
Ere we rush, ere we extinguish sight and speech
    Each on each.

In one year they sent a million fighters forth
    South and North,
And they built their gods a brazen pillar high
    As the sky,
Yet reserved a thousand chariots in full force—
    Gold, of course.
Oh heart! oh blood that freezes, blood that burns!
    Earth's returns
For whole centuries of folly, noise and sin!
    Shut them in,
With their triumphs and their glories and the rest!
    Love is best!

623   *Up at a Villa—Down in the City*
As distinguished by an Italian person of Quality

HAD I but plenty of money, money enough and to spare,
The house for me, no doubt, were a house in the city-square;
Ah, such a life, such a life, as one leads at the window there!

Something to see, by Bacchus, something to hear, at least!
There, the whole day long, one's life is a perfect feast;
While up at a villa one lives, I maintain it, no more than a beast.

Well now, look at our villa! stuck like the horn of a bull
Just on a mountain-edge as bare as the creature's skull,
Save a mere shag of a bush with hardly a leaf to pull!
—I scratch my own, sometimes, to see if the hair's turned wool.

But the city, oh the city—the square with the houses! Why?
They are stone-faced, white as a curd, there's something to take the
    eye!
Houses in four straight lines, not a single front awry;
You watch who crosses and gossips, who saunters, who hurries by;
Green blinds, as a matter of course, to draw when the sun gets high;
And the shops with fanciful signs which are painted properly.

What of a villa? Though winter be over in March by rights,
'Tis May perhaps ere the snow shall have withered well off the
    heights:
You've the brown ploughed land before, where the oxen steam and
    wheeze,
And the hills over-smoked behind by the faint grey olive-trees.

Is it better in May, I ask you? You've summer all at once;
In a day he leaps complete with a few strong April suns.
'Mid the sharp short emerald wheat, scarce risen three fingers well,
The wild tulip, at end of its tube, blows out its great red bell
Like a thin clear bubble of blood, for the children to pick and sell.

Is it ever hot in the square? There's a fountain to spout and splash!
In the shade it sings and springs; in the shine such foam-bows flash
On the horses with curling fish-tails, that prance and paddle and pash
Round the lady atop in her conch—fifty gazers do not abash,
Though all that she wears is some weeds round her waist in a sort of
    sash.

All the year long at the villa, nothing to see though you linger,
Except yon cypress that points like death's lean lifted forefinger.
Some think fireflies pretty, when they mix i' the corn and mingle,
Or thrid the stinking hemp till the stalks of it seem a-tingle.
Late August or early September, the stunning cicala is shrill,
And the bees keep their tiresome whine round the resinous firs on the
    hill.
Enough of the seasons,—I spare you the months of the fever and chill.

Ere you open your eyes in the city, the blessed church-bells begin:
No sooner the bells leave off than the diligence rattles in:
You get the pick of the news, and it costs you never a pin.
By-and-by there's the travelling doctor gives pills, lets blood, draws
    teeth;
Or the Pulcinello-trumpet breaks up the market beneath.
At the post-office such a scene-picture—the new play, piping hot!
And a notice how, only this morning, three liberal thieves were shot.
Above it, behold the Archbishop's most fatherly of rebukes,
And beneath, with his crown and his lion, some little new law of the
    Duke's!
Or a sonnet with flowery marge, to the Reverend Don So-and-so
Who is Dante, Boccaccio, Petrarca, Saint Jerome and Cicero,

'And moreover,' (the sonnet goes rhyming,) 'the skirts of Saint Paul
    has reached,
'Having preached us those six Lent-lectures more unctuous than ever
    he preached.'
Noon strikes,—here sweeps the procession! our Lady borne smiling
    and smart
With a pink gauze gown all spangles, and seven swords stuck in her
    heart!
Bang-whang-whang goes the drum, *tootle-te-tootle* the fife;
No keeping one's haunches still: it's the greatest pleasure in life.

But bless you, it's dear—it's dear! fowls, wine, at double the rate.
They have clapped a new tax upon salt, and what oil pays passing the
    gate
It's a horror to think of. And so, the villa for me, not the city!
Beggars can scarcely be choosers: but still—ah, the pity, the pity!
Look, two and two go the priests, then the monks with cowls and
    sandals,
And the penitents dressed in white shirts, a-holding the yellow candles;
One, he carries a flag up straight, and another a cross with handles,
And the Duke's guard brings up the rear, for the better prevention of
    scandals:
Bang-whang-whang goes the drum, *tootle-te-tootle* the fife.
Oh, a day in the city-square, there is no such pleasure in life!

624   *A Toccata of Galuppi's*

Oh Galuppi, Baldassaro, this is very sad to find!
I can hardly misconceive you; it would prove me deaf and blind;
But although I take your meaning, 'tis with such a heavy mind!

Here you come with your old music, and here's all the good it brings.
What, they lived once thus at Venice where the merchants were the
    kings,
Where Saint Mark's is, where the Doges used to wed the sea with
    rings?

Ay, because the sea's the street there; and 'tis arched by . . . what
    you call
. . . Shylock's bridge with houses on it, where they kept the carnival:
I was never out of England—it's as if I saw it all.

Did young people take their pleasure when the sea was warm in May?
Balls and masks begun at midnight, burning ever to mid-day,
When they made up fresh adventures for the morrow, do you say?

Was a lady such a lady, cheeks so round and lips so red,—
On her neck the small face buoyant, like a bell-flower on its bed,
O'er the breast's superb abundance where a man might base his head?

Well, and it was graceful of them—they'd break talk off and afford
—She, to bite her mask's black velvet—he, to finger on his sword,
While you sat and played Toccatas, stately at the clavichord?

What? Those lesser thirds so plaintive, sixths diminished, sigh on
    sigh,
Told them something? Those suspensions, those solutions—'Must we
    die?'
Those commiserating sevenths—'Life might last! we can but try!'

'Were you happy?'—'Yes.'—'And are you still as happy?'—'Yes.
    And you?'
—'Then, more kisses!'—'Did I stop them, when a million seemed
    so few?'
Hark, the dominant's persistence till it must be answered to!

So, an octave struck the answer. Oh, they praised you, I dare say!
'Brave Galuppi! that was music! good alike at grave and gay!
'I can always leave off talking when I hear a master play!'

Then they left you for their pleasure: till in due time, one by one,
Some with lives that came to nothing, some with deeds as well undone,
Death stepped tacitly and took them where they never see the sun.

But when I sit down to reason, think to take my stand nor swerve,
While I triumph o'er a secret wrung from nature's close reserve,
In you come with your cold music till I creep thro' every nerve.

Yes, you, like a ghostly cricket, creaking where a house was burned:
'Dust and ashes, dead and done with, Venice spent what Venice earned.
'The soul, doubtless, is immortal—where a soul can be discerned.

'Yours for instance: you know physics, something of geology,
'Mathematics are your pastime; souls shall rise in their degree;
'Butterflies may dread extinction,—you'll not die, it cannot be!

667

'As for Venice and her people, merely born to bloom and drop,
'Here on earth they bore their fruitage, mirth and folly were the crop:
'What of soul was left, I wonder, when the kissing had to stop?

'Dust and ashes!' So you creak it, and I want the heart to scold.
Dear dead women, with such hair, too—what's become of all the gold
Used to hang and brush their bosoms? I feel chilly and grown old.

625   *Love in a Life*

> ROOM after room,
> I hunt the house through
> We inhabit together.
> Heart, fear nothing, for, heart, thou shalt find her—
> Next time, herself!—not the trouble behind her
> Left in the curtain, the couch's perfume!
> As she brushed it, the cornice-wreath blossomed anew:
> Yon looking-glass gleamed at the wave of her feather.
>
> Yet the day wears,
> And door succeeds door;
> I try the fresh fortune—
> Range the wide house from the wing to the centre.
> Still the same chance! she goes out as I enter.
> Spend my whole day in the quest,—who cares?
> But 'tis twilight, you see,—with such suites to explore,
> Such closets to search, such alcoves to importune!

626   *Two in the Campagna*

> I WONDER do you feel to-day
>   As I have felt since, hand in hand,
> We sat down on the grass, to stray
>   In spirit better through the land,
> This morn of Rome and May?
>
> For me, I touched a thought, I know,
>   Has tantalized me many times,
> (Like turns of thread the spiders throw
>   Mocking across our path) for rhymes
> To catch at and let go.

Help me to hold it! First it left
  The yellowing fennel, run to seed
There, branching from the brickwork's cleft,
  Some old tomb's ruin: yonder weed
Took up the floating weft,

Where one small orange cup amassed
  Five beetles,—blind and green they grope
Among the honey-meal: and last,
  Everywhere on the grassy slope
I traced it. Hold it fast!

The champaign with its endless fleece
  Of feathery grasses everywhere!
Silence and passion, joy and peace,
  An everlasting wash of air—
Rome's ghost since her decease.

Such life here, through such lengths of hours,
  Such miracles performed in play,
Such primal naked forms of flowers,
  Such letting nature have her way
While heaven looks from its towers!

How say you? Let us, O my dove,
  Let us be unashamed of soul,
As earth lies bare to heaven above!
  How is it under our control
To love or not to love?

I would that you were all to me,
  You that are just so much, no more.
Nor yours nor mine, nor slave nor free!
  Where does the fault lie? What the core
O' the wound, since wound must be?

I would I could adopt your will,
  See with your eyes, and set my heart
Beating by yours, and drink my fill
  At your soul's springs,—your part my part
In life, for good and ill.

No. I yearn upward, touch you close,
  Then stand away. I kiss your cheek,
Catch your soul's warmth,—I pluck the rose
  And love it more than tongue can speak—
Then the good minute goes.

Already how am I so far
  Out of that minute? Must I go
Still like the thistle-ball, no bar,
  Onward, whenever light winds blow,
Fixed by no friendly star?

Just when I seemed about to learn!
  Where is the thread now? Off again!
The old trick! Only I discern—
  Infinite passion, and the pain
Of finite hearts that yearn.

627   *Confessions*

WHAT is he buzzing in my ears?
  'Now that I come to die,
Do I view the world as a vale of tears?'
  Ah, reverend sir, not I!

What I viewed there once, what I view again
  Where the physic bottles stand
On the table's edge,—is a suburb lane,
  With a wall to my bedside hand.

That land sloped, much as the bottles do,
  From a house you could descry
O'er the garden-wall: is the curtain blue
  Or green to a healthy eye?

To mine, it serves for the old June weather
  Blue above lane and wall;
And that farthest bottle labelled 'Ether'
  Is the house o'ertopping all.

At a terrace, somewhere near the stopper,
  There watched for me, one June,
A girl: I know, sir, it's improper,
  My poor mind's out of tune.

Only, there was a way . . . you crept
    Close by the side, to dodge
Eyes in the house, two eyes except:
    They styled their house 'The Lodge.'

What right had a lounger up their lane?
    But, by creeping very close,
With the good wall's help,—their eyes might strain
    And stretch themselves to Oes,

Yet never catch her and me together,
    As she left the attic, there,
By the rim of the bottle labelled 'Ether',
    And stole from stair to stair,

And stood by the rose-wreathed gate. Alas,
    We loved, sir—used to meet:
How sad and bad and mad it was—
    But then, how it was sweet!

628   *May and Death*

I WISH that when you died last May,
    Charles, there had died along with you
Three parts of spring's delightful things;
    Ay, and, for me, the fourth part too.

A foolish thought, and worse, perhaps!
    There must be many a pair of friends
Who, arm in arm, deserve the warm
    Moon-births and the long evening-ends.

So, for their sake, be May still May!
    Let their new time, as mine of old,
Do all it did for me: I bid
    Sweet sights and sounds throng manifold.

Only, one little sight, one plant,
    Woods have in May, that starts up green
Save a sole streak which, so to speak,
    Is spring's blood, spilt its leaves between,—

That, they might spare; a certain wood
  Might miss the plant; their loss were small:
But I,—whene'er the leaf grows there,
  Its drop comes from my heart, that's all.

629   *Apparent Failure*

      'We shall soon lose a celebrated building.'
                          Paris Newspaper

No, for I'll save it! Seven years since,
  I passed through Paris, stopped a day
To see the baptism of your Prince;
  Saw, made my bow, and went my way:
Walking the heat and headache off,
  I took the Seine-side, you surmise,
Thought of the Congress, Gortschakoff,
  Cavour's appeal and Buol's replies,
So sauntered till—what met my eyes?

Only the Doric little Morgue!
  The dead-house where you show your drowned:
Petrarch's Vaucluse makes proud the Sorgue,
  Your Morgue has made the Seine renowned.
One pays one's debt in such a case;
  I plucked up heart and entered,—stalked,
Keeping a tolerable face
  Compared with some whose cheeks were chalked:
Let them! No Briton's to be baulked!

First came the silent gazers; next,
  A screen of glass, we're thankful for;
Last, the sight's self, the sermon's text,
  The three men who did most abhor
Their life in Paris yesterday,
  So killed themselves: and now, enthroned
Each on his copper couch, they lay
  Fronting me, waiting to be owned.
I thought, and think, their sin's atoned.

Poor men, God made, and all for that!
    The reverence struck me; o'er each head
Religiously was hung its hat,
    Each coat dripped by the owner's bed,
Sacred from touch: each had his berth,
    His bounds, his proper place of rest,
Who last night tenanted on earth
    Some arch, where twelve such slept abreast,—
Unless the plain asphalte seemed best.

How did it happen, my poor boy?
    You wanted to be Buonaparte
And have the Tuileries for toy,
    And could not, so it broke your heart?
You, old one by his side, I judge,
    Were, red as blood, a socialist,
A leveller! Does the Empire grudge
    You've gained what no Republic missed?
Be quiet, and unclench your fist!

And this—why, he was red in vain,
    Or black,—poor fellow that is blue!
What fancy was it turned your brain?
    Oh, women were the prize for you!
Money gets women, cards and dice
    Get money, and ill-luck gets just
The copper couch and one clear nice
    Cool squirt of water o'er your bust,
The right thing to extinguish lust!

It's wiser being good than bad;
    It's safer being meek than fierce:
It's fitter being sane than mad.
    My own hope is, a sun will pierce
The thickest cloud earth ever stretched;
    That, after Last, returns the First,
Though a wide compass round be fetched;
    That what began best, can't end worst,
Nor what God blessed once, prove accurst.

630 *Epilogue to Asolando*

AT the midnight in the silence of the sleep-time,
    When you set your fancies free,
Will they pass to where—by death, fools think, imprisoned—
Low he lies who once so loved you, whom you loved so,
    —Pity me?

Oh to love so, be so loved, yet so mistaken!
    What had I on earth to do
With the slothful, with the mawkish, the unmanly?
Like the aimless, helpless, hopeless, did I drivel!
    —Being—who?

One who never turned his back but marched breast forward,
    Never doubted clouds would break,
Never dreamed, though right were worsted, wrong would triumph,
Held we fall to rise, are baffled to fight better,
    Sleep to wake.

No, at noonday in the bustle of man's work-time
    Greet the unseen with a cheer!
Bid him forward, breast and back as either should be,
'Strive and thrive!' cry, 'Speed,—fight on, fare ever
    There as here!'

EDWARD LEAR

1812–1888

631 *How pleasant to know Mr. Lear*

'HOW pleasant to know Mr. Lear!'
    Who has written such volumes of stuff!
Some think him ill-tempered and queer,
    But a few think him pleasant enough.

His mind is concrete and fastidious,
    His nose is remarkably big;
His visage is more or less hideous,
    His beard it resembles a wig.

He has ears, and two eyes, and ten fingers,
　　Leastways if you reckon two thumbs;
Long ago he was one of the singers,
　　But now he is one of the dumbs.

He sits in a beautiful parlour,
　　With hundreds of books on the wall
He drinks a great deal of Marsala,
　　But never gets tipsy at all.

He has many friends, laymen and clerical,
　　Old Foss is the name of his cat:
His body is perfectly spherical,
　　He weareth a runcible hat.

When he walks in a waterproof white,
　　The children run after him so!
Calling out, 'He's come out in his night-
　　gown, that crazy old Englishman, oh!'

He weeps by the side of the ocean,
　　He weeps on the top of the hill;
He purchases pancakes and lotion,
　　And chocolate shrimps from the mill.

He reads but he cannot speak Spanish,
　　He cannot abide ginger-beer:
Ere the days of his pilgrimage vanish,
　　How pleasant to know Mr. Lear!

632　　　　　*The Owl and the Pussy-Cat*

THE Owl and the Pussy-Cat went to sea
　　In a beautiful pea-green boat,
They took some honey, and plenty of money,
　　Wrapped up in a five-pound note.
The Owl looked up to the stars above,
　　And sang to a small guitar,
'O lovely Pussy! O Pussy, my love,
　　What a beautiful Pussy you are,
　　　　　You are,
　　　　　You are!
　　What a beautiful Pussy you are!'

Pussy said to the Owl, 'You elegant fowl!
  How charmingly sweet you sing!
O let us be married! too long we have tarried:
  But what shall we do for a ring?'
They sailed away for a year and a day,
  To the land where the Bong-tree grows,
And there in a wood a Piggy-wig stood,
  With a ring at the end of his nose,
      His nose,
      His nose,
  With a ring at the end of his nose.

'Dear Pig, are you willing to sell for one shilling
  Your ring?' Said the Piggy, 'I will.'
So they took it away, and were married next day
  By the Turkey who lives on the hill.
They dined on mince, and slices of quince,
  Which they ate with a runcible spoon;
And hand in hand, on the edge of the sand,
  They danced by the light of the moon,
      The moon,
      The moon,
  They danced by the light of the moon.

EMILY BRONTË

1818–1848

633   *Spellbound*

THE night is darkening round me,
The wild winds coldly blow;
But a tyrant spell has bound me
And I cannot, cannot go.

The giant trees are bending
Their bare boughs weighed with snow.
And the storm is fast descending,
And yet I cannot go.

Clouds beyond clouds above me,
Wastes beyond wastes below;
But nothing drear can move me;
I will not, cannot go.

634   *The Old Stoic*

RICHES I hold in light esteem,
And Love I laugh to scorn;
And lust of Fame was but a dream
That vanished with the morn—

And if I pray, the only prayer
That moves my lips for me
Is—'Leave the heart that now I bear,
And give me liberty.'

Yes, as my swift days near their goal,
'Tis all that I implore—
Through life and death, a chainless soul,
With courage to endure!

635   *Remembrance*

COLD in the earth—and the deep snow piled above thee,
Far, far removed, cold in the dreary grave!
Have I forgot, my only Love, to love thee,
Severed at last by Time's all-severing wave?

Now, when alone, do my thoughts no longer hover
Over the mountains, on that northern shore,
Resting their wings where heath and fern-leaves cover
Thy noble heart for ever, ever more?

Cold in the earth—and fifteen wild Decembers
From those brown hills have melted into spring—
Faithful indeed is the spirit that remembers
After such years of change and suffering!

Sweet Love of youth, forgive if I forget thee
While the world's tide is bearing me along:
Other desires and other hopes beset me,
Hopes which obscure, but cannot do thee wrong!

No later light has lightened up my heaven;
No second morn has ever shone for me:
All my life's bliss from thy dear life was given—
All my life's bliss is in the grave with thee.

But, when the days of golden dreams had perished,
And even Despair was powerless to destroy,
Then did I learn how existence could be cherished,
Strengthened, and fed without the aid of joy;

Then did I check the tears of useless passion,
Weaned my young soul from yearning after thine;
Sternly denied its burning wish to hasten
Down to that tomb already more than mine!

And, even yet, I dare not let it languish,
Dare not indulge in Memory's rapturous pain;
Once drinking deep of that divinest anguish,
How could I seek the empty world again?

636   *The Visionary*

SILENT is the house: all are laid asleep:
One alone looks out o'er the snow-wreaths deep,
Watching every cloud, dreading every breeze
That whirls the wildering drift, and bends the groaning trees.

Cheerful is the hearth, soft the matted floor;
Not one shivering gust creeps through pane or door;
The little lamp burns straight, its rays shoot strong and far:
I trim it well, to be the wanderer's guiding-star.

Frown, my haughty sire! chide, my angry dame;
Set your slaves to spy; threaten me with shame:
But neither sire nor dame, nor prying serf shall know,
What angel nightly tracks that waste of frozen snow.

What I love shall come like visitant of air,
Safe in secret power from lurking human snare;
Who loves me, no word of mine shall e'er betray,
Though for faith unstained my life must forfeit pay.

Burn, then, little lamp; glimmer straight and clear—
Hush! a rustling wing stirs, methinks, the air:
He for whom I wait, thus ever comes to me;
Strange Power! I trust thy might; trust thou my constancy.

637   *The Prisoner*

'STILL let my tyrants know, I am not doomed to wear
Year after year in gloom, and desolate despair;
A messenger of Hope comes every night to me,
And offers for short life, eternal liberty.

'He comes with western winds, with evening's wandering airs,
With that clear dusk of heaven that brings the thickest stars,
Winds take a pensive tone, and stars a tender fire,
And visions rise, and change, that kill me with desire.

'Desire for nothing known in my maturer years,
When Joy grew mad with awe, at counting future tears.
When, if my spirit's sky was full of flashes warm,
I knew not whence they came, from sun or thunder-storm.

'But, first, a hush of peace—a soundless calm descends;
The struggle of distress, and fierce impatience ends;
Mute music soothes my breast—unuttered harmony,
That I could never dream, till Earth was lost to me.

'Then dawns the Invisible; the Unseen its truth reveals;
My outward sense is gone, my inward essence feels:
Its wings are almost free—its home, its harbour found,
Measuring the gulf, it stoops and dares the final bound.

'O! dreadful is the check—intense the agony—
When the ear begins to hear, and the eye begins to see;
When the pulse begins to throb, the brain to think again;
The soul to feel the flesh, and the flesh to feel the chain.

'Yet I would lose no sting, would wish no torture less;
The more that anguish racks, the earlier it will bless;
And robed in fires of hell, or bright with heavenly shine,
If it but herald death, the vision is divine!'

638 *Last Lines*

'The following are the last lines my sister Emily ever wrote.'
(Charlotte Brontë)

No coward soul is mine,
No trembler in the world's storm-troubled sphere:
I see Heaven's glories shine,
And faith shines equal, arming me from fear.

O God within my breast,
Almighty, ever-present Deity!
Life—that in me has rest,
As I—undying Life—have power in thee!

Vain are the thousand creeds
That move men's hearts: unutterably vain;
Worthless as withered weeds,
Or idlest froth amid the boundless main,

To waken doubt in one
Holding so fast by thine infinity;
So surely anchored on
The steadfast rock of immortality.

With wide-embracing love
Thy spirit animates eternal years,
Pervades and broods above,
Changes, sustains, dissolves, creates, and rears.

Though earth and man were gone,
And suns and universes ceased to be,
And thou were left alone,
Every existence would exist in thee.

There is not room for Death,
Nor atom that his might could render void:
Thou—thou art Being and Breath,
And what thou art may never be destroyed.

ARTHUR HUGH CLOUGH

1819–1861

639   *Say Not the Struggle Nought Availeth*

SAY not the struggle nought availeth,
   The labour and the wounds are vain,
The enemy faints not, nor faileth,
   And as things have been, things remain.

If hopes were dupes, fears may be liars;
   It may be, in yon smoke concealed,
Your comrades chase e'en now the fliers,
   And, but for you, possess the field.

For while the tired waves, vainly breaking,
   Seem here no painful inch to gain,
Far back through creeks and inlets making
   Came, silent, flooding in, the main,

And not by eastern windows only,
   When daylight comes, comes in the light,
In front the sun climbs slow, how slowly,
   But westward, look, the land is bright.

640   *Where Lies the Land?*

WHERE lies the land to which the ship would go?
Far, far ahead, is all her seamen know.
And where the land she travels from? Away,
Far, far behind, is all that they can say.

On sunny noons upon the deck's smooth face,
Linked arm in arm, how pleasant here to pace;
Or, o'er the stern reclining, watch below
The foaming wake far widening as we go.

On stormy nights when wild north-westers rave,
How proud a thing to fight with wind and wave!
The dripping sailor on the reeling mast
Exults to bear, and scorns to wish it past.

Where lies the land to which the ship would go?
Far, far ahead, is all her seamen know.
And where the land she travels from? Away,
Far, far behind, is all that they can say.

641 *The Latest Decalogue*

THOU shalt have one God only; who
Would be at the expense of two?
No graven images may be
Worshipped, except the currency:
Swear not at all; for, for thy curse
Thine enemy is none the worse:
At church on Sunday to attend
Will serve to keep the world thy friend:
Honour thy parents; that is, all
From whom advancement may befall:
Thou shalt not kill; but need'st not strive
Officiously to keep alive:
Do not adultery commit;
Advantage rarely comes of it:
Thou shalt not steal; an empty feat,
When it's so lucrative to cheat:
Bear not false witness; let the lie
Have time on its own wings to fly:
Thou shalt not covet; but tradition
Approves all forms of competition.

The sum of all is, thou shalt love,
If anybody, God above:
At any rate shall never labour
More than thyself to love thy neighbour.

642 *How Pleasant it is to have Money*

As I sat at the café, I said to myself,
They may talk as they please about what they call pelf,
They may sneer as they like about eating and drinking,
But help it I cannot, I cannot help thinking,
  How pleasant it is to have money, heigh ho!
  How pleasant it is to have money.

I sit at my table *en grand seigneur*,
And when I have done, throw a crust to the poor;
Not only the pleasure, one's self, of good living,
But also the pleasure of now and then giving.
  So pleasant it is to have money, heigh ho!
  So pleasant it is to have money.

It was but last winter I came up to Town,
But already I'm getting a little renown;
I make new acquaintance where'er I appear;
I am not too shy, and have nothing to fear.
  So pleasant it is to have money, heigh ho!
  So pleasant it is to have money.

I drive through the streets, and I care not a damn;
The people they stare, and they ask who I am;
And if I should chance to run over a cad,
I can pay for the damage if ever so bad.
  So pleasant it is to have money, heigh ho!
  So pleasant it is to have money.

We stroll to our box and look down on the pit,
And if it weren't low should be tempted to spit;
We loll and we talk until people look up,
And when it's half over we go out and sup.
  So pleasant it is to have money, heigh ho!
  So pleasant it is to have money.

The best of the tables and best of the fare—
And as for the others, the devil may care;
It isn't our fault if they dare not afford
To sup like a prince and be drunk as a lord.
  So pleasant it is to have money, heigh ho!
  So pleasant it is to have money.

We sit at our tables and tipple champagne;
Ere one bottle goes, comes another again;
The waiters they skip and they scuttle about,
And the landlord attends us so civilly out.
  So pleasant it is to have money, heigh ho!
  So pleasant it is to have money.

It was but last winter I came up to town,
But already I'm getting a little renown;
I get to good houses without much ado,
Am beginning to see the nobility too.
   So pleasant it is to have money, heigh ho!
   So pleasant it is to have money.

O dear! what a pity they ever should lose it!
For they are the gentry that know how to use it;
So grand and so graceful, such manners, such dinners,
But yet, after all, it is we are the winners.
   So pleasant it is to have money, heigh ho!
   So pleasant it is to have money.

Thus I sat at my table *en grand seigneur*,
And when I had done threw a crust to the poor;
Not only the pleasure, one's self, of good eating,
But also the pleasure of now and then treating.
   So pleasant it is to have money, heigh ho!
   So pleasant it is to have money.

They may talk as they please about what they call pelf,
And how one ought never to think of one's self,
And how pleasures of thought surpass eating and drinking—
My pleasure of thought is the pleasure of thinking
   How pleasant it is to have money, heigh ho!
   How pleasant it is to have money.

A gondola here, and a gondola there,
'Tis the pleasantest fashion of taking the air.
To right and to left; stop, turn, and go yonder,
And let us repeat, o'er the tide as we wander,
   How pleasant it is to have money, heigh ho!
   How pleasant it is to have money.

643   *There is No God*

'THERE is no God,' the wicked saith,
  'And truly it's a blessing,
For what he might have done with us
  It's better only guessing.'

'There is no God,' a youngster thinks,
  'Or really, if there may be,
He surely didn't mean a man
  Always to be a baby.'

'There is no God, or if there is,'
  The tradesman thinks, ' 'twere funny
If he should take it ill in me
  To make a little money.'

'Whether there be,' the rich man says,
  'It matters very little,
For I and mine, thank somebody,
  Are not in want of victual.'

Some others, also, to themselves
  Who scarce so much as doubt it,
Think there is none, when they are well,
  And do not think about it.

But country folks who live beneath
  The shadow of the steeple;
The parson and the parson's wife,
  And mostly married people;

Youths green and happy in first love,
  So thankful for illusion;
And men caught out in what the world
  Calls guilt, in first confusion;

And almost everyone when age,
  Disease, or sorrows strike him,
Inclines to think there is a God,
  Or something very like him.

MATTHEW ARNOLD
1822–1888

644   *The Song of Callicles*

THROUGH the black, rushing smoke-bursts,
Thick breaks the red flame;
All Etna heaves fiercely
Her forest-clothed frame.

Not here, O Apollo!
Are haunts meet for thee.
But, where Helicon breaks down
In cliff to the sea,

Where the moon-silvered inlets
Send far their light voice
Up the still vale of Thisbe,
O speed, and rejoice!

On the sward at the cliff-top
Lie strewn the white flocks,
On the cliff-side the pigeons
Roost deep in the rocks.

In the moonlight the shepherds,
Soft lulled by the rills,
Lie wrapt in their blankets
Asleep on the hills.

—What forms are these coming
So white through the gloom?
What garments out-glistening
The gold-flowered broom?

What sweet-breathing presence
Out-perfumes the thyme?
What voices enrapture
The night's balmy prime?—

'Tis Apollo comes leading
His choir, the Nine.
—The leader is fairest,
But all are divine.

They are lost in the hollows!
They stream up again!
What seeks on this mountain
The glorified train?—

They bathe on this mountain,
In the spring by their road;
Then on to Olympus,
Their endless abode.

—Whose praise do they mention?
Of what is it told?—
What will be for ever;
What was from of old.

First hymn they the Father
Of all things; and then,
The rest of immortals,
The action of men.

The day in his hotness,
The strife with the palm;
The night in her silence,
The stars in their calm.

645   *To Marguerite*

YES! in the sea of life enisled,
With echoing straits between us thrown,
Dotting the shoreless watery wild,
We mortal millions live *alone*.
The islands feel the enclasping flow,
And then their endless bounds they know.

But when the moon their hollows lights,
And they are swept by balms of spring,
And in their glens, on starry nights,
The nightingales divinely sing;
And lovely notes, from shore to shore,
Across the sounds and channels pour—

Oh! then a longing like despair
Is to their farthest caverns sent;
For surely once, they feel, we were
Parts of a single continent!
Now round us spreads the watery plain—
Oh might our marges meet again!

Who ordered, that their longing's fire
Should be, as soon as kindled, cooled?
Who renders vain their deep desire?—
A God, a God their severance ruled!
And bade betwixt their shores to be
The unplumbed, salt, estranging sea.

646   *Sohrab Dead*

So, on the bloody sand, Sohrab lay dead;
And the great Rustum drew his horseman's cloak
Down o'er his face, and sate by his dead son.
As those black granite pillars, once high-reared
By Jemshid in Persepolis, to bear
His house, now 'mid their broken flights of steps
Lie prone, enormous, down the mountain side—
So in the sand lay Rustum by his son.
    And night came down over the solemn waste,
And the two gazing hosts, and that sole pair,
And darkened all; and a cold fog, with night,
Crept from the Oxus. Soon a hum arose,
As of a great assembly loosed, and fires
Began to twinkle through the fog; for now
Both armies moved to camp, and took their meal;
The Persians took it on the open sands
Southward, the Tartars by the river marge;
And Rustum and his son were left alone.
    But the majestic river floated on,

Out of the mist and hum of that low land,
Into the frosty starlight, and there moved,
Rejoicing, through the hushed Chorasmian waste,
Under the solitary moon; he flowed
Right for the polar star, past Orgunjè,
Brimming, and bright, and large; then sands begin
To hem his watery march, and dam his streams,
And split his currents; that for many a league
The shorn and parcelled Oxus strains along
Through beds of sand and matted rushy isles—
Oxus, forgetting the bright speed he had
In his high mountain-cradle in Pamere,
A foiled circuitous wanderer—till at last
The longed-for dash of waves is heard, and wide
His luminous home of waters opens, bright
And tranquil, from whose floor the new-bathed stars
Emerge, and shine upon the Aral Sea.

647 *Requiescat*

STREW on her roses, roses,
   And never a spray of yew!
In quiet she reposes;
   Ah, would that I did too!

Her mirth the world required;
   She bathed it in smiles of glee.
But her heart was tired, tired,
   And now they let her be.

Her life was turning, turning,
   In mazes of heat and sound.
But for peace her soul was yearning,
   And now peace laps her round.

Her cabined, ample spirit,
   It fluttered and failed for breath.
To-night it doth inherit
   The vasty hall of death.

648   *The Scholar Gipsy*

Go, for they call you, shepherd, from the hill;
    Go, shepherd, and untie the wattled cotes!
        No longer leave thy wistful flock unfed,
    Nor let thy bawling fellows rack their throats,
        Nor the cropped herbage shoot another head.
            But when the fields are still,
    And the tired men and dogs all gone to rest,
        And only the white sheep are sometimes seen
        Cross and recross the strips of moon-blanched green,
    Come, shepherd, and again begin the quest!

Here, where the reaper was at work of late—
    In this high field's dark corner, where he leaves
        His coat, his basket, and his earthen cruse,
    And in the sun all morning binds the sheaves,
        Then here, at noon, comes back his stores to use—
            Here will I sit and wait,
    While to my ear from uplands far away
        The bleating of the folded flocks is borne,
        With distant cries of reapers in the corn—
    All the live murmur of a summer's day.

Screened is this nook o'er the high, half-reaped field,
    And here till sun-down, shepherd! will I be.
        Through the thick corn the scarlet poppies peep,
    And round green roots and yellowing stalks I see
        Pale pink convolvulus in tendrils creep;
            And air-swept lindens yield
    Their scent, and rustle down their perfumed showers
        Of bloom on the bent grass where I am laid,
        And bower me from the August sun with shade;
    And the eye travels down to Oxford's towers.

And near me on the grass lies Glanvil's book—
   Come, let me read the oft-read tale again!
     The story of the Oxford scholar poor,
   Of pregnant parts and quick inventive brain,
      Who, tired of knocking at preferment's door,
        One summer-morn forsook
   His friends, and went to learn the gipsy-lore,
     And roamed the world with that wild brotherhood,
     And came, as most men deemed, to little good,
   But came to Oxford and his friends no more.

But once, years after, in the country-lanes,
   Two scholars, whom at college erst he knew,
     Met him, and of his way of life enquired;
   Whereat he answered; that the gipsy-crew,
      His mates, had arts to rule as they desired
        The workings of men's brains,
   And they can bind them to what thoughts they will.
     'And I,' he said, 'the secret of their art,
     When fully learned, will to the world impart;
   But it needs heaven-sent moments for this skill.'

This said, he left them, and returned no more.—
   But rumours hung about the country-side,
     That the lost Scholar long was seen to stray,
   Seen by rare glimpses, pensive and tongue-tied,
      In hat of antique shape, and cloak of grey,
        The same the gipsies wore.
   Shepherds had met him on the Hurst in spring;
     At some lone alehouse in the Berkshire moors,
     On the warm ingle-bench, the smock-frocked boors
   Had found him seated at their entering,

But, 'mid their drink and clatter, he would fly.
   And I myself seem half to know thy looks,
     And put the shepherds, wanderer! on thy trace;
   And boys who in lone wheatfields scare the rooks
      I ask if thou hast passed their quiet place;
        Or in my boat I lie
   Moored to the cool bank in the summer-heats,
     'Mid wide grass meadows which the sunshine fills,
     And watch the warm, green-muffled Cumner hills,
   And wonder if thou haunt'st their shy retreats.

For most, I know, thou lov'st retired ground!
  Thee at the ferry Oxford riders blithe,
    Returning home on summer-nights, have met
  Crossing the stripling Thames at Bab-lock-hithe,
    Trailing in the cool stream thy fingers wet,
      As the punt's rope chops round;
  And leaning backward in a pensive dream,
    And fostering in thy lap a heap of flowers
    Plucked in shy fields and distant Wychwood bowers,
  And thine eyes resting on the moonlit stream.

And then they land, and thou art seen no more!—
  Maidens, who from the distant hamlets come
    To dance around the Fyfield elm in May,
  Oft through the darkening fields have seen thee roam,
    Or cross a stile into the public way.
      Oft thou hast given them store
  Of flowers—the frail-leafed, white anemony,
    Dark bluebells drenched with dews of summer eves,
    And purple orchises with spotted leaves—
  But none hath words she can report of thee.

And, above Godstow Bridge, when hay-time's here
  In June, and many a scythe in sunshine flames,
    Men who through those wide fields of breezy grass
  Where black-winged swallows haunt the glittering Thames,
    To bathe in the abandoned lasher pass,
      Have often passed thee near
  Sitting upon the river bank o'ergrown;
    Marked thine outlandish garb, thy figure spare,
    Thy dark vague eyes, and soft abstracted air—
  But, when they came from bathing, thou wast gone!

At some lone homestead in the Cumner hills,
  Where at her open door the housewife darns,
    Thou hast been seen, or hanging on a gate
  To watch the threshers in the mossy barns.
    Children, who early range these slopes and late
      For cresses from the rills,
  Have known thee eying, all an April-day,
    The springing pastures and the feeding kine;
    And marked thee, when the stars come out and shine,
  Through the long dewy grass move slow away.

In autumn, on the skirts of Bagley Wood—
   Where most the gipsies by the turf-edged way
     Pitch their smoked tents, and every bush you see
   With scarlet patches tagged and shreds of grey,
     Above the forest-ground called Thessaly—
       The blackbird, picking food,
   Sees thee, nor stops his meal, nor fears at all;
     So often has he known thee past him stray,
     Rapt, twirling in thy hand a withered spray,
And waiting for the spark from heaven to fall.

And once, in winter, on the causeway chill
   Where home through flooded fields foot-travellers go,
     Have I not passed thee on the wooden bridge,
   Wrapt in thy cloak and battling with the snow,
     Thy face toward Hinksey and its wintry ridge?
       And thou hast climbed the hill,
   And gained the white brow of the Cumner range;
     Turned once to watch, while thick the snowflakes fall,
     The line of festal light in Christ-Church hall—
Then sought thy straw in some sequestered grange.

But what—I dream! Two hundred years are flown
   Since first thy story ran through Oxford halls,
     And the grave Glanvil did the tale inscribe
   That thou wert wandered from the studious walls
     To learn strange arts, and join a gipsy-tribe;
       And thou from earth art gone
   Long since, and in some quiet churchyard laid—
     Some country-nook, where o'er thy unknown grave
     Tall grasses and white flowering nettles wave,
Under a dark, red-fruited yew-tree's shade.

—No, no, thou hast not felt the lapse of hours!
   For what wears out the life of mortal men?
     'Tis that from change to change their being rolls;
   'Tis that repeated shocks, again, again,
     Exhaust the energy of strongest souls
       And numb the elastic powers.
Till having used our nerves with bliss and teen,
   And tired upon a thousand schemes our wit,
     To the just-pausing Genius we remit
Our worn-out life, and are—what we have been.

Thou hast not lived, why shouldst thou perish, so?
  Thou hadst *one* aim, *one* business, *one* desire;
    Else wert thou long since numbered with the dead!
  Else hadst thou spent, like other men, thy fire!
    The generations of thy peers are fled,
      And we ourselves shall go;
  But thou possessest an immortal lot,
    And we imagine thee exempt from age
    And living as thou liv'st on Glanvil's page,
  Because thou hadst—what we, alas! have not.

For early didst thou leave the world, with powers
  Fresh, undiverted to the world without,
    Firm to their mark, not spent on other things;
  Free from the sick fatigue, the languid doubt,
    Which much to have tried, in much been baffled, brings.
      O life unlike to ours!
  Who fluctuate idly without term or scope,
    Of whom each strives, nor knows for what he strives,
    And each half lives a hundred different lives;
  Who wait like thee, but not, like thee, in hope.

Thou waitest for the spark from heaven! and we,
  Light half-believers of our casual creeds,
    Who never deeply felt, nor clearly willed,
  Whose insight never has borne fruit in deeds,
    Whose vague resolves never have been fulfilled;
      For whom each year we see
  Breeds new beginnings, disappointments new;
    Who hesitate and falter life away,
    And lose to-morrow the ground won to-day—
  Ah! do not we, wanderer, await it too?

Yes, we await it!—but it still delays,
  And then we suffer! and amongst us one,
    Who most has suffered, takes dejectedly
  His seat upon the intellectual throne;
    And all his store of sad experience he
      Lays bare of wretched days;
  Tells us his misery's birth and growth and signs,
    And how the dying spark of hope was fed,
    And how the breast was soothed, and how the head,
  And all his hourly varied anodynes.

This for our wisest! and we others pine,
 And wish the long unhappy dream would end,
  And waive all claim to bliss, and try to bear;
 With close-lipped patience for our only friend,
  Sad patience, too near neighbour to despair—
   But none has hope like thine!
 Thou through the fields and through the woods dost stray,
  Roaming the country-side, a truant boy,
  Nursing thy project in unclouded joy,
 And every doubt long blown by time away.

O born in days when wits were fresh and clear,
 And life ran gaily as the sparkling Thames;
  Before this strange disease of modern life,
 With its sick hurry, its divided aims,
  Its heads o'ertaxed, its palsied hearts, was rife—
   Fly hence, our contact fear!
 Still fly, plunge deeper in the bowering wood!
  Averse, as Dido did with gesture stern
  From her false friend's approach in Hades turn,
 Wave us away, and keep thy solitude!

Still nursing the unconquerable hope,
 Still clutching the inviolable shade,
  With a free, onward impulse brushing through,
 By night, the silvered branches of the glade—
  Far on the forest-skirts, where none pursue.
   On some mild pastoral slope
 Emerge, and resting on the moonlit pales
  Freshen thy flowers as in former years
  With dew, or listen with enchanted ears,
 From the dark dingles, to the nightingales!

But fly our paths, our feverish contact fly!
 For strong the infection of our mental strife,
  Which though it gives no bliss, yet spoils for rest;
 And we should win thee from thy own fair life,
  Like us distracted, and like us unblest.
   Soon, soon thy cheer would die,
 Thy hopes grow timorous, and unfixed thy powers,
  And thy clear aims be cross and shifting made;
  And then thy glad perennial youth would fade,
 Fade, and grow old at last, and die like ours.

Then fly our greetings, fly our speech and smiles!
  —As some grave Tyrian trader, from the sea,
    Descried at sunrise an emerging prow
  Lifting the cool-haired creepers stealthily,
    The fringes of a southward-facing brow
      Among the Ægæan isles;
  And saw the merry Grecian coaster come,
    Freighted with amber grapes, and Chian wine,
    Green, bursting figs, and tunnies steeped in brine—
  And knew the intruders on his ancient home,

The young light-hearted masters of the waves—
  And snatched his rudder, and shook out more sail;
    And day and night held on indignantly
  O'er the blue Midland waters with the gale,
    Betwixt the Syrtes and soft Sicily,
      To where the Atlantic raves
  Outside the western straits; and unbent sails
    There, where down cloudy cliffs, through sheets of foam,
    Shy traffickers, the dark Iberians come;
  And on the beach undid his corded bales.

649   *Thyrsis*

A Monody, to commemorate the author's friend,
Arthur Hugh Clough, who died at Florence, 1861

How changed is here each spot man makes or fills!
  In the two Hinkseys nothing keeps the same;
    The village street its haunted mansion lacks,
  And from the sign is gone Sibylla's name,
    And from the roofs the twisted chimney-stacks—
      Are ye too changed, ye hills?
  See, 'tis no foot of unfamiliar men
    To-night from Oxford up your pathway strays!
    Here came I often, often, in old days—
  Thyrsis and I; we still had Thyrsis then.

Runs it not here, the track by Childsworth Farm,
　　Past the high wood, to where the elm-tree crowns
　　　The hill behind whose ridge the sunset flames?
　The signal-elm, that looks on Ilsley Downs,
　　　The Vale, the three lone weirs, the youthful Thames?—
　　　　This winter-eve is warm,
　　Humid the air! leafless, yet soft as spring,
　　　The tender purple spray on copse and briers!
　　And that sweet city with her dreaming spires,
　She needs not June for beauty's heightening,

Lovely all times she lies, lovely to-night!—
　　Only, methinks, some loss of habit's power
　　　Befalls me wandering through this upland dim.
　Once passed I blindfold here, at any hour;
　　　Now seldom come I, since I came with him.
　　　　That single elm-tree bright
　　Against the west—I miss it! is it gone?
　　　We prized it dearly; while it stood, we said,
　　　Our friend, the Gipsy-Scholar, was not dead;
　While the tree lived, he in these fields lived on.

Too rare, too rare, grow now my visits here,
　　But once I knew each field, each flower, each stick;
　　　And with the country-folk acquaintance made
　By barn in threshing-time, by new-built rick.
　　　Here, too, our shepherd-pipes we first assayed.
　　　　Ah me! this many a year
　　My pipe is lost, my shepherd's holiday!
　　　Needs must I lose them, needs with heavy heart
　　　Into the world and wave of men depart;
　But Thyrsis of his own will went away.

It irked him to be here, he could not rest.
　　He loved each simple joy the country yields,
　　　He loved his mates; but yet he could not keep,
　For that a shadow loured on the fields,
　　　Here with the shepherds and the silly sheep.
　　　　Some life of men unblest
　　He knew, which made him droop, and filled his head.
　　　He went; his piping took a troubled sound
　　　Of storms that rage outside our happy ground;
　He could not wait their passing, he is dead.

So, some tempestuous morn in early June,
  When the year's primal burst of bloom is o'er,
    Before the roses and the longest day—
  When garden-walks and all the grassy floor
    With blossoms red and white of fallen May
      And chestnut-flowers are strewn—
So have I heard the cuckoo's parting cry,
  From the wet field, through the vext garden-trees,
  Come with the volleying rain and tossing breeze:
The bloom is gone, and with the bloom go I!

Too quick despairer, wherefore wilt thou go?
  Soon will the high Midsummer pomps come on,
    Soon will the musk carnations break and swell,
  Soon shall we have gold-dusted snapdragon,
    Sweet-William with his homely cottage-smell,
      And stocks in fragrant blow;
Roses that down the alleys shine afar,
  And open, jasmine-muffled lattices,
  And groups under the dreaming garden-trees,
And the full moon, and the white evening-star.

He hearkens not! light comer, he is flown!
  What matters it? next year he will return,
    And we shall have him in the sweet spring-days,
  With whitening hedges, and uncrumpling fern,
    And blue-bells trembling by the forest-ways,
      And scent of hay new-mown.
But Thyrsis never more we swains shall see;
  See him come back, and cut a smoother reed,
  And blow a strain the world at last shall heed—
For Time, not Corydon, hath conquered thee!

Alack, for Corydon no rival now!—
  But when Sicilian shepherds lost a mate,
    Some good survivor with his flute would go,
  Piping a ditty sad for Bion's fate;
    And cross the unpermitted ferry's flow,
      And relax Pluto's brow,
And make leap up with joy the beauteous head
  Of Proserpine, among whose crowned hair
  Are flowers first opened on Sicilian air,
And flute his friend, like Orpheus, from the dead.

O easy access to the hearer's grace
  When Dorian shepherds sang to Proserpine!
    For she herself had trod Sicilian fields,
  She knew the Dorian water's gush divine,
    She knew each lily white which Enna yields,
      Each rose with blushing face;
  She loved the Dorian pipe, the Dorian strain.
    But ah, of our poor Thames she never heard!
    Her foot the Cumner cowslips never stirred;
  And we should tease her with our plaint in vain!

Well! wind-dispersed and vain the words will be,
  Yet, Thyrsis, let me give my grief its hour
    In the old haunt, and find our tree-topped hill!
  Who, if not I, for questing here hath power?
    I know the wood which hides the daffodil,
      I know the Fyfield tree,
  I know what white, what purple fritillaries
    The grassy harvest of the river-fields,
    Above by Ensham, down by Sandford, yields,
  And what sedged brooks are Thames's tributaries;

I know these slopes; who knows them if not I?—
  But many a dingle on the loved hill-side,
    With thorns once studded, old, white-blossomed trees,
  Where thick the cowslips grew, and far descried
    High towered the spikes of purple orchises,
      Hath since our day put by
  The coronals of that forgotten time;
    Down each green bank hath gone the ploughboy's team,
    And only in the hidden brookside gleam
  Primroses, orphans of the flowery prime.

Where is the girl, who by the boatman's door,
  Above the locks, above the boating throng,
    Unmoored our skiff when through the Wytham flats,
  Red loosestrife and blond meadow-sweet among
    And darting swallows and light water-gnats,
      We tracked the shy Thames shore?
  Where are the mowers, who, as the tiny swell
    Of our boat passing heaved the river-grass,
    Stood with suspended scythe to see us pass?—
  They all are gone, and thou art gone as well!

Yes, thou art gone! and round me too the night
  In ever-nearing circle weaves her shade.
    I see her veil draw soft across the day,
  I feel her slowly chilling breath invade
    The cheek grown thin, the brown hair sprent with grey;
      I feel her finger light
  Laid pausefully upon life's headlong train;—
    The foot less prompt to meet the morning dew,
    The heart less bounding at emotion new,
  And hope, once crushed, less quick to spring again.

And long the way appears, which seemed so short
  To the less practised eye of sanguine youth;
    And high the mountain-tops, in cloudy air,
  The mountain-tops where is the throne of Truth,
    Tops in life's morning-sun so bright and bare!
      Unbreachable the fort
  Of the long-battered world uplifts its wall;
    And strange and vain the earthly turmoil grows,
    And near and real the charm of thy repose,
  And night as welcome as a friend would fall.

But hush! the upland hath a sudden loss
  Of quiet!—look, adown the dusk hill-side,
    A troop of Oxford hunters going home,
  As in old days, jovial and talking, ride!
    From hunting with the Berkshire hounds they come.
      Quick! let me fly, and cross
  Into yon farther field!—'Tis done; and see,
    Backed by the sunset, which doth glorify
    The orange and pale violet evening-sky,
  Bare on its lonely ridge, the Tree! the Tree!

I take the omen! Eve lets down her veil,
  The white fog creeps from bush to bush about,
    The west unflushes, the high stars grow bright,
  And in the scattered farms the lights come out.
    I cannot reach the signal-tree to-night,
      Yet, happy omen, hail!
  Hear it from thy broad lucent Arno-vale,
    (For there thine earth-forgetting eyelids keep
    The morningless and unawakening sleep
  Under the flowery oleanders pale),

Hear it, O Thyrsis, still our tree is there!—
   Ah, vain! These English fields, this upland dim,
     These brambles pale with mist engarlanded,
  That lone, sky-pointing tree, are not for him;
     To a boon southern country he is fled,
       And now in happier air,
  Wandering with the great Mother's train divine
     (And purer or more subtle soul than thee,
     I trow, the mighty Mother doth not see)
  Within a folding of the Apennine,

Thou hearest the immortal chants of old!—
   Putting his sickle to the perilous grain
     In the hot cornfield of the Phrygian king,
  For thee the Lityerses-song again
     Young Daphnis with his silver voice doth sing;
       Sings his Sicilian fold,
  His sheep, his hapless love, his blinded eyes—
     And how a call celestial round him rang,
     And heavenward from the fountain-brink he sprang,
  And all the marvel of the golden skies.

There thou art gone, and me thou leavest here
   Sole in these fields! yet will I not despair.
     Despair I will not, while I yet descry
  'Neath the mild canopy of English air
     That lonely tree against the western sky.
       Still, still these slopes, 'tis clear,
  Our Gipsy-Scholar haunts, outliving thee!
     Fields where soft sheep from cages pull the hay,
     Woods with anemonies in flower till May,
  Know him a wanderer still; then why not me?

A fugitive and gracious light he seeks,
   Shy to illumine; and I seek it too.
     This does not come with houses or with gold,
  With place, with honour, and a flattering crew;
     'Tis not in the world's market bought and sold—
       But the smooth-slipping weeks
  Drop by, and leave its seeker still untired;
     Out of the heed of mortals he is gone,
     He wends unfollowed, he must house alone;
  Yet on he fares, by his own heart inspired.

Thou too, O Thyrsis, on like quest wast bound;
  Thou wanderedst with me for a little hour!
    Men gave thee nothing; but this happy quest,
If men esteemed thee feeble, gave thee power,
    If men procured thee trouble, gave thee rest.
      And this rude Cumner ground,
  Its fir-topped Hurst, its farms, its quiet fields,
    Here cam'st thou in thy jocund youthful time,
    Here was thine height of strength, thy golden prime!
And still the haunt beloved a virtue yields.

What though the music of thy rustic flute
  Kept not for long its happy, country tone;
    Lost it too soon, and learnt a stormy note
Of men contention-tost, of men who groan,
    Which tasked thy pipe too sore, and tired thy throat—
      It failed, and thou wast mute!
  Yet hadst thou alway visions of our light,
    And long with men of care thou couldst not stay,
    And soon thy foot resumed its wandering way,
Left human haunt, and on alone till night.

Too rare, too rare, grow now my visits here!
  'Mid city-noise, not, as with thee of yore,
    Thyrsis! in reach of sheep-bells is my home.
  —Then through the great town's harsh, heart-wearying roar,
    Let in thy voice a whisper often come,
      To chase fatigue and fear:
Why faintest thou? I wandered till I died.
  Roam on! The light we sought is shining still.
  Dost thou ask proof? Our tree yet crowns the hill,
Our Scholar travels yet the loved hill-side.

650 *Dover Beach*

THE sea is calm to-night.
The tide is full, the moon lies fair
Upon the straits;—on the French coast the light
Gleams and is gone; the cliffs of England stand,
Glimmering and vast, out in the tranquil bay.
Come to the window, sweet is the night-air!
Only, from the long line of spray
Where the sea meets the moon-blanched land,
Listen! you hear the grating roar
Of pebbles which the waves draw back, and fling,
At their return, up the high strand,
Begin, and cease, and then again begin,
With tremulous cadence slow, and bring
The eternal note of sadness in.

Sophocles long ago
Heard it on the Ægæan, and it brought
Into his mind the turbid ebb and flow
Of human misery; we
Find also in the sound a thought,
Hearing it by this distant northern sea.

The Sea of Faith
Was once, too, at the full, and round earth's shore
Lay like the folds of a bright girdle furled.
But now I only hear
Its melancholy, long, withdrawing roar,
Retreating, to the breath
Of the night-wind, down the vast edges drear
And naked shingles of the world.

Ah, love, let us be true
To one another! for the world, which seems
To lie before us like a land of dreams,
So various, so beautiful, so new,
Hath really neither joy, nor love, nor light,
Nor certitude, nor peace, nor help for pain;
And we are here as on a darkling plain
Swept with confused alarms of struggle and flight,
Where ignorant armies clash by night.

651 *The Last Word*

CREEP into thy narrow bed,
Creep, and let no more be said!
Vain thy onset! all stands fast.
Thou thyself must break at last.

Let the long contention cease!
Geese are swans, and swans are geese.
Let them have it how they will!
Thou art tired; best be still.

They out-talked thee, hissed thee, tore thee?
Better men fared thus before thee;
Fired their ringing shot and passed,
Hotly charged—and sank at last.

Charge once more, then, and be dumb!
Let the victors, when they come,
When the forts of folly fall,
Find thy body by the wall!

WILLIAM CORY

1823–1892

652 *Mimnermus in Church*

YOU promise heavens free from strife,
    Pure truth, and perfect change of will;
But sweet, sweet is this human life,
    So sweet, I fain would breathe it still;
Your chilly stars I can forgo,
This warm kind world is all I know.

You say there is no substance here,
    One great reality above:
Back from that void I shrink in fear,
    And child-like hide myself in love:
Show me what angels feel. Till then
I cling, a mere weak man, to men.

You bid me lift my mean desires
 From faltering lips and fitful veins
To sexless souls, ideal quires,
 Unwearied voices, wordless strains:
My mind with fonder welcome owns
One dear dead friend's remembered tones.

Forsooth the present we must give
 To that which cannot pass away;
All beauteous things for which we live
 By laws of time and space decay.
But Oh, the very reason why
I clasp them, is because they die.

653   *Heraclitus*

THEY told me, Heraclitus, they told me you were dead,
They brought me bitter news to hear and bitter tears to shed.
I wept as I remembered how often you and I
Had tired the sun with talking and sent him down the sky.

And now that thou art lying, my dear old Carian guest,
A handful of grey ashes, long, long ago at rest,
Still are thy pleasant voices, thy nightingales, awake;
For Death, he taketh all away, but them he cannot take.

COVENTRY PATMORE

1823–1896

654   *Departure*

IT was not like your great and gracious ways!
Do you, that have nought other to lament,
Never, my Love, repent
Of how, that July afternoon,
You went,
With sudden, unintelligible phrase,
And frightened eye,
Upon your journey of so many days,
Without a single kiss, or a good-bye?

I knew, indeed, that you were parting soon;
And so we sáte, within the low sun's rays,
You whispering to me, for your voice was weak,
Your harrowing praise.
Well, it was well,
To hear you such things speak,
And I could tell
What made your eyes a growing gloom of love,
As a warm South-wind sombres a March grove.
And it was like your great and gracious ways
To turn your talk on daily things, my Dear,
Lifting the luminous, pathetic lash
To let the laughter flash,
Whilst I drew near,
Because you spoke so low that I could scarcely hear.
But all at once to leave me at the last,
More at the wonder than the loss aghast,
With huddled, unintelligible phrase,
And frightened eye,
And go your journey of all days
With not one kiss, or a good-bye,
And the only loveless look the look with which you passed:
'Twas all unlike your great and gracious ways.

655   *A Farewell*

WITH all my will, but much against my heart,
We two now part.
My Very Dear,
Our solace is, the sad road lies so clear.
It needs no art,
With faint, averted feet
And many a tear,
In our opposèd paths to persevere.
Go thou to East, I West.
We will not say
There's any hope, it is so far away.
But, O, my Best,
When the one darling of our widowhead,
The nursling, Grief,
Is dead,

And no dews blur our eyes
To see the peach-bloom come in evening skies,
Perchance we may,
Where now this night is day,
And even through faith of still averted feet,
Making full circle of our banishment,
Amazèd meet;
The bitter journey to the bourne so sweet
Seasoning the termless feast of our content
With tears of recognition never dry.

656   *Winter*

I, SINGULARLY moved
To love the lovely that are not beloved,
Of all the Seasons, most
Love Winter, and to trace
The sense of the Trophonian pallor on her face.
It is not death, but plenitude of peace;
And the dim cloud that does the world enfold
Hath less the characters of dark and cold
Than warmth and light asleep,
And correspondent breathing seems to keep
With the infant harvest, breathing soft below
Its eider coverlet of snow.
Nor is in field or garden anything
But, duly looked into, contains serene
The substance of things hoped for, in the Spring,
And evidence of Summer not yet seen.
On every chance-mild day
That visits the moist shaw,
The honeysuckle, 'sdaining to be crost
In urgence of sweet life by sleet or frost,
'Voids the time's law
With still increase
Of leaflet new, and little, wandering spray;
Often, in sheltering brakes,
As one from rest disturbed in the first hour,
Primrose or violet bewildered wakes,
And deems 'tis time to flower;

Though not a whisper of her voice he hear,
The buried bulb does know
The signals of the year,
And hails far Summer with his lifted spear.
The gorse-field dark, by sudden, gold caprice,
Turns, here and there, into a Jason's fleece;
Lilies, that soon in Autumn slipped their gowns of green,
And vanished into earth,
And came again, ere Autumn died, to birth,
Stand full-arrayed, amidst the wavering shower,
And perfect for the Summer, less the flower;
In nook of pale or crevice of crude bark,
Thou canst not miss,
If close thou spy, to mark
The ghostly chrysalis,
That, if thou touch it, stirs in its dream dark;
And the flushed Robin, in the evenings hoar,
Does of Love's Day, as if he saw it, sing;
But sweeter yet than dream or song of Summer or Spring
Are Winter's sometime smiles, that seem to well
From infancy ineffable;
Her wandering, languorous gaze,
So unfamiliar, so without amaze,
On the elemental, chill adversity,
The uncomprehended rudeness; and her sigh
And solemn, gathering tear,
And look of exile from some great repose, the sphere
Of ether, moved by ether only, or
By something still more tranquil.

657   *Magna est Veritas*

HERE, in this little Bay,
Full of tumultuous life and great repose,
Where, twice a day,
The purposeless, glad ocean comes and goes,
Under high cliffs, and far from the huge town,
I sit me down.
For want of me the world's course will not fail;
When all its work is done, the lie shall rot;
The truth is great, and shall prevail,
When none cares whether it prevail or not.

WILLIAM ALLINGHAM

1824–1889

658 *The Fairies*

Up the airy mountain,
  Down the rushy glen,
We daren't go a-hunting
  For fear of little men;
Wee folk, good folk,
  Trooping all together;
Green jacket, red cap,
  And white owl's feather!

Down along the rocky shore
  Some make their home,
They live on crispy pancakes
  Of yellow tide-foam;
Some in the reeds
  Of the black mountain lake,
With frogs for their watch-dogs,
  All night awake.

High on the hill-top
  The old King sits;
He is now so old and gray
  He's nigh lost his wits.
With a bridge of white mist
  Columbkill he crosses,
On his stately journeys
  From Slieveleague to Rosses;
Or going up with music
  On cold starry nights
To sup with the Queen
  Of the gay Northern Lights.

They stole little Bridget
  For seven years long;
When she came down again
  Her friends were all gone.

They took her lightly back,
  Between the night and morrow,
They thought that she was fast asleep,
  But she was dead with sorrow.
They have kept her ever since
  Deep within the lake,
On a bed of flag-leaves,
  Watching till she wake.

By the craggy hill-side,
  Through the mosses bare,
They have planted thorn-trees
  For pleasure here and there.
Is any man so daring
  As dig them up in spite,
He shall find their sharpest thorns
  In his bed at night.

Up the airy mountain,
  Down the rushy glen,
We daren't go a-hunting
  For fear of little men;
Wee folk, good folk,
  Trooping all together;
Green jacket, red cap,
  And white owl's feather!

DANTE GABRIEL ROSSETTI

1828–1882

659   *The Blessed Damozel*

THE blessed damozel leaned out
  From the gold bar of Heaven;
Her eyes were deeper than the depth
  Of waters stilled at even;
She had three lilies in her hand,
  And the stars in her hair were seven.

Her robe, ungirt from clasp to hem,
  No wrought flowers did adorn,
But a white rose of Mary's gift,
  For service meetly worn;
Her hair that lay along her back
  Was yellow like ripe corn.

Herseemed she scarce had been a day
  One of God's choristers;
The wonder was not yet quite gone
  From that still look of hers;
Albeit, to them she left, her day
  Had counted as ten years.

(To one, it is ten years of years.
  . . . Yet now, and in this place,
Surely she leaned o'er me—her hair
  Fell all about my face. . .
Nothing: the autumn fall of leaves.
  The whole year sets apace.)

It was the rampart of God's house
  That she was standing on;
By God built over the sheer depth
  The which is Space begun;
So high, that looking downward thence
  She scarce could see the sun.

It lies in Heaven, across the flood
  Of ether, as a bridge.
Beneath, the tides of day and night
  With flame and darkness ridge
The void, as low as where this earth
  Spins like a fretful midge.

Around her, lovers, newly met
  'Mid deathless love's acclaims,
Spoke evermore among themselves
  Their heart remembered names;
And the souls mounting up to God
  Went by her like thin flames.

And still she bowed herself and stooped
  Out of the circling charm;
Until her bosom must have made
  The bar she leaned on warm,
And the lilies lay as if asleep
  Along her bended arm.

From the fixed place of Heaven she saw
  Time like a pulse shake fierce
Through all the worlds. Her gaze still strove
  Within the gulf to pierce
Its path; and now she spoke as when
  The stars sang in their spheres.

The sun was gone now; the curled moon
  Was like a little feather
Fluttering far down the gulf; and now
  She spoke through the still weather.
Her voice was like the voice the stars
  Had when they sang together.

(Ah sweet! Even now, in that bird's song,
  Strove not her accents there,
Fain to be hearkened? When those bells
  Possessed the mid-day air,
Strove not her steps to reach my side
  Down all the echoing stair?)

'I wish that he were come to me,
  For he will come,' she said.
'Have I not prayed in Heaven?—on earth,
  Lord, Lord, has he not prayed?
Are not two prayers a perfect strength?
  And shall I feel afraid?

'When round his head the aureole clings,
  And he is clothed in white,
I'll take his hand and go with him
  To the deep wells of light;
We will step down as to a stream,
  And bathe there in God's sight.

'We two will stand beside that shrine,
    Occult, withheld, untrod,
Whose lamps are stirred continually
    With prayer sent up to God;
And see our old prayers, granted, melt
    Each like a little cloud.

'We two will lie i' the shadow of
    That living mystic tree
Within whose secret growth the Dove
    Is sometimes felt to be,
While every leaf that His plumes touch
    Saith His Name audibly.

'And I myself will teach to him,
    I myself, lying so,
The songs I sing here; which his voice
    Shall pause in, hushed and slow,
And find some knowledge at each pause,
    Of some new thing to know.'

(Alas! We two, we two, thou sayst!
    Yea, one wast thou with me
That once of old. But shall God lift
    To endless unity
The soul whose likeness with thy soul
    Was but its love for thee?)

'We two,' she said, 'will seek the groves
    Where the lady Mary is,
With her five handmaidens, whose names
    Are five sweet symphonies,
Cecily, Gertrude, Magdalen,
    Margaret and Rosalys.

'Circlewise sit they, with bound locks
    And foreheads garlanded;
Into the fine cloth white like flame
    Weaving the golden thread,
To fashion the birth-robes for them
    Who are just born, being dead.

'He shall fear, haply, and be dumb:
   Then will I lay my cheek
To his, and tell about our love,
   Not once abashed or weak:
And the dear Mother will approve
   My pride, and let me speak.

'Herself shall bring us, hand in hand,
   To Him round whom all souls
Kneel, the clear-ranged unnumbered heads
   Bowed with their aureoles:
And angels meeting us shall sing
   To their citherns and citoles.

'There will I ask of Christ the Lord
   Thus much for him and me:—
Only to live as once on earth
   With Love,—only to be,
As then awhile, for ever now
   Together, I and he.'

She gazed and listened and then said,
   Less sad of speech than mild,—
'All this is when he comes.' She ceased.
   The light thrilled towards her, filled
With angels in strong level flight.
   Her eyes prayed, and she smiled.

(I saw her smile.) But soon their path
   Was vague in distant spheres:
And then she cast her arms along
   The golden barriers,
And laid her face between her hands,
   And wept. (I heard her tears.)

660   *The Woodspurge*

THE wind flapped loose, the wind was still,
Shaken out dead from tree and hill:
I had walked on at the wind's will,—
I sat now, for the wind was still.

Between my knees my forehead was,—
My lips, drawn in, said not Alas!
My hair was over in the grass,
My naked ears heard the day pass.

My eyes, wide open, had the run
Of some ten weeds to fix upon;
Among those few, out of the sun,
The woodspurge flowered, three cups in one.

From perfect grief there need not be
Wisdom or even memory:
One thing then learnt remains to me,—
The woodspurge has a cup of three.

661   *Even So*

So it is, my dear.
All such things touch secret strings
For heavy hearts to hear.
So it is, my dear.

Very like indeed:
Sea and sky, afar, on high,
Sand and strewn seaweed,—
Very like indeed.

But the sea stands spread
As one wall with the flat skies,
Where the lean black craft like flies
Seem well-nigh stagnated,
Soon to drop off dead.

Seemed it so to us
When I was thine and thou wast mine,
And all these things were thus,
But all our world in us?

Could we be so now?
Not if all beneath heaven's pall
Lay dead but I and thou,
Could we be so now!

715

662   *Sudden Light*

I HAVE been here before,
    But when or how I cannot tell:
I know the grass beyond the door,
    The sweet keen smell,
The sighing sound, the lights around the shore.

You have been mine before,—
    How long ago I may not know:
But just when at that swallow's soar
    Your neck turned so,
Some veil did fall,—I knew it all of yore.

Has this been thus before?
    And shall not thus time's eddying flight
Still with our lives our love restore
    In death's despite,
And day and night yield one delight once more?

663   *A Superscription*

LOOK in my face; my name is Might-have-been;
    I am also called No-more, Too-late, Farewell;
    Unto thine ear I hold the dead-sea shell
Cast up thy Life's foam-fretted feet between;
Unto thine eyes the glass where that is seen
    Which had Life's form and Love's, but by my spell
    Is now a shaken shadow intolerable,
Of ultimate things unuttered the frail screen.
Mark me, how still I am! But should there dart
    One moment through thy soul the soft surprise
    Of that winged Peace which lulls the breath of sighs,—
Then shalt thou see me smile, and turn apart
Thy visage to mine ambush at thy heart
    Sleepless with cold commemorative eyes.

GEORGE MEREDITH
1828–1909

664   *Love in the Valley*

UNDER yonder beech-tree single on the green-sward,
  Couchèd with her arms behind her golden head,
Knees and tresses folded to slip and ripple idly,
  Lies my young love sleeping in the shade.
Had I the heart to slide an arm beneath her,
  Press her parting lips as her waist I gather slow,
Waking in amazement she could not but embrace me:
  Then would she hold me and never let me go?

Shy as the squirrel and wayward as the swallow,
  Swift as the swallow along the river's light
Circleting the surface to meet his mirrored winglets,
  Fleeter she seems in her stay than in her flight.
Shy as the squirrel that leaps among the pine-tops,
  Wayward as the swallow overhead at set of sun,
She whom I love is hard to catch and conquer,
  Hard, but O the glory of the winning were she won!

When her mother tends her before the laughing mirror,
  Tying up her laces, looping up her hair,
Often she thinks, were this wild thing wedded,
  More love should I have, and much less care.
When her mother tends her before the lighted mirror,
  Loosening her laces, combing down her curls,
Often she thinks, were this wild thing wedded,
  I should miss but one for many boys and girls.

Heartless she is as the shadow in the meadows
  Flying to the hills on a blue and breezy noon.
No, she is athirst and drinking up her wonder:
  Earth to her is young as the slip of the new moon.
Deals she an unkindness, 'tis but her rapid measure,
  Even as in a dance; and her smile can heal no less:
Like the swinging May-cloud that pelts the flowers with hailstones
  Off a sunny border, she was made to bruise and bless.

Lovely are the curves of the white owl sweeping
   Wavy in the dusk lit by one large star.
Lone on the fir-branch, his rattle-note unvaried,
   Brooding o'er the gloom, spins the brown eve-jar.
Darker grows the valley, more and more forgetting:
   So were it with me, if forgetting could be willed.
Tell the grassy hollow that holds the bubbling well-spring,
   Tell it to forget the source that keeps it filled.

Stepping down the hill with her fair companions,
   Arm in arm, all against the raying West,
Boldly she sings, to the merry tune she marches,
   Brave in her shape, and sweeter unpossessed.
Sweeter, for she is what my heart first awaking
   Whispered the world was; morning light is she.
Love that so desires would fain keep her changeless;
   Fain would fling the net, and fain have her free.

Happy happy time, when the white star hovers
   Low over dim fields fresh with bloomy dew,
Near the face of dawn, that draws athwart the darkness,
   Threading it with colour, like yewberries the yew.
Thicker crowd the shades as the grave East deepens
   Glowing, and with crimson a long cloud swells.
Maiden still the morn is; and strange she is, and secret;
   Strange her eyes; her cheeks are cold as cold sea-shells.

*

Mother of the dews, dark eye-lashed twilight,
   Low-lidded twilight, o'er the valley's brim,
Rounding on thy breast sings the dew-delighted skylark,
   Clear as though the dewdrops had their voice in him.
Hidden where the rose-flush drinks the rayless planet,
   Fountain-full he pours the spraying fountain-showers.
Let me hear her laughter, I would have her ever
   Cool as dew in twilight, the lark above the flowers.

All the girls are out with their baskets for the primrose;
   Up lanes, woods through, they troop in joyful bands.
My sweet leads: she knows not why, but now she loiters,
   Eyes the bent anemones, and hangs her hands.

Such a look will tell that the violets are peeping,
    Coming the rose: and unaware a cry
Springs in her bosom for odours and for colour,
    Covert and the nightingale; she knows not why.

*

Hither she comes; she comes to me; she lingers,
    Deepens her brown eyebrows, while in new surprise
High rise the lashes in wonder of a stranger;
    Yet am I the light and living of her eyes.
Something friends have told her fills her heart to brimming,
    Nets her in her blushes, and wounds her, and tames.—
Sure of her haven, O like a dove alighting,
    Arms up, she dropped: our souls were in our names.

*

Could I find a place to be alone with heaven,
    I would speak my heart out: heaven is my need.
Every woodland tree is flushing like the dogwood,
    Flashing like the whitebeam, swaying like the reed.
Flushing like the dogwood crimson in October;
    Streaming like the flag-reed South-West blown;
Flashing as in gusts the sudden-lighted whitebeam:
    All seem to know what is for heaven alone.

665   *Phoebus with Admetus*

WHEN by Zeus relenting the mandate was revoked,
    Sentencing to exile the bright Sun-God,
Mindful were the ploughmen of who the steer had yoked,
    Who: and what a track showed the upturned sod!
Mindful were the shepherds as now the noon severe
    Bent a burning eyebrow to brown evetide,
How the rustic flute drew the silver to the sphere,
    Sister of his own, till her rays fell wide.
                God! of whom music
                And song and blood are pure,
                The day is never darkened
                That had thee here obscure.

Chirping none, the scarlet cicalas crouched in ranks:
    Slack the thistle-head piled its down-silk grey:
Scarce the stony lizard sucked hollows in his flanks:
    Thick on spots of umbrage our drowsed flocks lay.
Sudden bowed the chestnuts beneath a wind unheard,
    Lengthened ran the grasses, the sky grew slate:
Then amid a swift flight of winged seed white as curd,
    Clear of limb a Youth smote the master's gate.
              God! of whom music
              And song and blood are pure,
              The day is never darkened
              That had thee here obscure.

Water, first of singers, o'er rocky mount and mead,
    First of earthly singers, the sun-loved rill,
Sang of him, and flooded the ripples on the reed,
    Seeking whom to waken and what ear fill.
Water, sweetest soother to kiss a wound and cool,
    Sweetest and divinest, the sky-born brook,
Chuckled, with a whimper, and made a mirror-pool
    Round the guest we welcomed, the strange hand shook.
              God! of whom music
              And song and blood are pure,
              The day is never darkened
              That had thee here obscure.

Many swarms of wild bees descended on our fields:
    Stately stood the wheatstalk with head bent high:
Big of heart we laboured at storing mighty yields,
    Wool and corn, and clusters to make men cry!
Hand-like rushed the vintage; we strung the bellied skins
    Plump, and at the sealing the Youth's voice rose:
Maidens clung in circle, on little fists their chins;
    Gentle beasties through pushed a cold long nose.
              God! of whom music
              And song and blood are pure,
              The day is never darkened
              That had thee here obscure.

Foot to fire in snowtime we trimmed the slender shaft:
    Often down the pit spied the lean wolf's teeth
Grin against his will, trapped by masterstrokes of craft;
    Helpless in his froth-wrath as green logs seethe!

Safe the tender lambs tugged the teats, and winter sped
  Whirled before the crocus, the year's new gold.
Hung the hooky beak up aloft the arrowhead
  Reddened through his feathers for our dear fold.
        God! of whom music
        And song and blood are pure,
        The day is never darkened
        That had thee here obscure.

Tales we drank of giants at war with Gods above:
  Rocks were they to look on, and earth climbed air!
Tales of search for simples, and those who sought of love
  Ease because the creature was all too fair.
Pleasant ran our thinking that while our work was good,
  Sure as fruits for sweat would the praise come fast.
He that wrestled stoutest and tamed the billow-brood
  Danced in rings with girls, like a sail-flapped mast.
        God! of whom music
        And song and blood are pure,
        The day is never darkened
        That had thee here obscure.

Lo, the herb of healing, when once the herb is known,
  Shines in shady woods bright as new-sprung flame.
Ere the string was tightened we heard the mellow tone,
  After he had taught how the sweet sounds came.
Stretched about his feet, labour done, 'twas as you see
  Red pomegranates tumble and burst hard rind.
So began contention to give delight and be
  Excellent in things aimed to make life kind.
        God! of whom music
        And song and blood are pure,
        The day is never darkened
        That had thee here obscure.

You with shelly horns, rams! and promontory goats,
  You whose browsing beards dip in coldest dew!
Bulls, that walk the pastures in kingly-flashing coats!
  Laurel, ivy, vine, wreathed for feasts not few!
You that build the shade-roof, and you that court the rays,
  You that leap besprinkling the rock stream-rent:
He has been our fellow, the morning of our days;
  Us he chose for housemates, and this way went.

God! of whom music
And song and blood are pure,
The day is never darkened
That had thee here obscure.

666 *Lucifer in Starlight*

ON a starred night Prince Lucifer uprose.
Tired of his dark dominion swung the fiend
Above the rolling ball in cloud part screened,
Where sinners hugged their spectre of repose.
Poor prey to his hot fit of pride were those.
And now upon his western wing he leaned,
Now his huge bulk o'er Afric's sands careened,
Now the black planet shadowed Arctic snows.
Soaring through wider zones that pricked his scars
With memory of the old revolt from Awe,
He reached a middle height, and at the stars,
Which are the brain of heaven, he looked, and sank.
Around the ancient track marched, rank on rank,
The army of unalterable law.

from Modern Love

667 (i)

MARK where the pressing wind shoots javelin-like
Its skeleton shadow on the broad-backed wave!
Here is a fitting spot to dig Love's grave;
Here where the ponderous breakers plunge and strike,
And dart their hissing tongues high up the sand:
In hearing of the ocean, and in sight
Of those ribbed wind-streaks running into white.
If I the death of Love had deeply planned,
I never could have made it half so sure,
As by the unblest kisses which upbraid
The full-waked sense; or failing that, degrade!
'Tis morning: but no morning can restore
What we have forfeited. I see no sin:
The wrong is mixed. In tragic life, God wot,
No villain need be! Passions spin the plot:
We are betrayed by what is false within.

668   (ii)

WE saw the swallows gathering in the sky,
And in the osier-isle we heard them noise.
We had not to look back on summer joys,
Or forward to a summer of bright dye:
But in the largeness of the evening earth
Our spirits grew as we went side by side.
The hour became her husband and my bride.
Love, that had robbed us so, thus blessed our dearth!
The pilgrims of the year waxed very loud
In multitudinous chatterings, as the flood
Full brown came from the West, and like pale blood
Expanded to the upper crimson cloud.
Love, that had robbed us of immortal things,
This little moment mercifully gave,
Where I have seen across the twilight wave
The swan sail with her young beneath her wings.

669   (iii)

THUS piteously Love closed what he begat:
The union of this ever-diverse pair!
These two were rapid falcons in a snare,
Condemned to do the flitting of the bat.
Lovers beneath the singing sky of May,
They wandered once; clear as the dew on flowers:
But they fed not on the advancing hours:
Their hearts held cravings for the buried day.
Then each applied to each that fatal knife,
Deep questioning, which probes to endless dole.
Ah, what a dusty answer gets the soul
When hot for certainties in this our life!—
In tragic hints here see what evermore
Moves dark as yonder midnight ocean's force,
Thundering like ramping hosts of warrior horse,
To throw that faint thin line upon the shore!

CHRISTINA GEORGINA ROSSETTI
1830–1894

670   *A Birthday*

MY heart is like a singing bird
  Whose nest is in a watered shoot;
My heart is like an apple-tree
  Whose boughs are bent with thickset fruit;
My heart is like a rainbow shell
  That paddles in a halcyon sea;
My heart is gladder than all these
  Because my love is come to me.

Raise me a dais of silk and down;
  Hang it with vair and purple dyes;
Carve it in doves and pomegranates,
  And peacocks with a hundred eyes;
Work it in gold and silver grapes,
  In leaves and silver fleurs-de-lys;
Because the birthday of my life
  Is come, my love is come to me.

671   *Song*

WHEN I am dead, my dearest,
  Sing no sad songs for me;
Plant thou no roses at my head,
  Nor shady cypress tree:
Be the green grass above me
  With showers and dewdrops wet;
And if thou wilt, remember,
  And if thou wilt, forget.

I shall not see the shadows,
  I shall not feel the rain;
I shall not hear the nightingale
  Sing on, as if in pain;
And dreaming through the twilight
  That doth not rise nor set,
Haply I may remember,
  And haply may forget.

672   *Uphill*

DOES the road wind uphill all the way?
  Yes, to the very end.
Will the day's journey take the whole long day?
  From morn to night, my friend.

But is there for the night a resting-place?
  A roof for when the slow, dark hours begin.
May not the darkness hide it from my face?
  You cannot miss that inn.

Shall I meet other wayfarers at night?
  Those who have gone before.
Then must I knock, or call when just in sight?
  They will not keep you standing at that door.

Shall I find comfort, travel-sore and weak?
  Of labour you shall find the sum.
Will there be beds for me and all who seek?
  Yea, beds for all who come.

673   *Remember*

REMEMBER me when I am gone away,
  Gone far away into the silent land;
  When you can no more hold me by the hand,
Nor I half turn to go yet turning stay.
Remember me when no more day by day
  You tell me of our future that you planned:
  Only remember me; you understand
It will be late to counsel then or pray.
Yet if you should forget me for a while
  And afterwards remember, do not grieve:
  For if the darkness and corruption leave
  A vestige of the thoughts that once I had,
Better by far you should forget and smile
  Than that you should remember and be sad.

674

THE irresponsive silence of the land,
The irresponsive sounding of the sea,
  Speak both one message of one sense to me:—
'Aloof, aloof, we stand aloof, so stand
Thou too aloof, bound with the flawless band
  Of inner solitude; we bind not thee;
  But who from thy self-chain shall set thee free?
What heart shall touch thy heart? What hand thy hand?'—
And I am sometimes proud and sometimes meek,
  And sometimes I remember days of old
When fellowship seemed not so far to seek ,
  And all the world and I seemed much less cold,
  And at the rainbow's foot lay surely gold,
And hope felt strong, and life itself not weak.

675   *Rest*

O EARTH, lie heavily upon her eyes;
Seal her sweet eyes weary of watching, Earth;
  Lie close around her; leave no room for mirth
With its harsh laughter, nor for sound of sighs.
She hath no questions, she hath no replies,
  Hushed in and curtained with a blessed dearth
  Of all that irked her from the hour of birth;
With stillness that is almost Paradise.
Darkness more clear than noonday holdeth her,
  Silence more musical than any song;
Even her very heart has ceased to stir:
Until the morning of Eternity
Her rest shall not begin nor end, but be;
  And when she wakes she will not think it long.

676   *Echo*

COME to me in the silence of the night;
    Come in the speaking silence of a dream;
Come with soft rounded cheeks and eyes as bright
        As sunlight on a stream;
            Come back in tears,
O memory, hope, love of finished years.

O dream how sweet, too sweet, too bitter sweet,
    Whose wakening should have been in Paradise,
Where souls brimfull of love abide and meet;
        Where thirsting longing eyes
            Watch the slow door
That opening, letting in, lets out no more.

Yet come to me in dreams that I may live
    My very life again though cold in death:
Come back to me in dreams, that I may give
        Pulse for pulse, breath for breath:
            Speak low, lean low,
As long ago, my love, how long ago.

677   *A Pause of Thought*

I LOOKED for that which is not, nor can be,
    And hope deferred made my heart sick in truth:
    But years must pass before a hope of youth
        Is resigned utterly.

I watched and waited with a steadfast will:
    And though the object seemed to flee away
    That I so longed for, ever day by day
        I watched and waited still.

Sometimes I said: 'This thing shall be no more;
    My expectation wearies and shall cease;
    I will resign it now and be at peace':
        Yet never gave it o'er.

Sometimes I said: 'It is an empty name
  I long for; to a name why should I give
  The peace of all the days I have to live?'—
    Yet gave it all the same.

Alas, thou foolish one! alike unfit
  For healthy joy and salutary pain:
  Thou knowest the chase useless, and again
    Turnest to follow it.

678   *Twice*

        I TOOK my heart in my hand
          (O my love, O my love),
        I said: Let me fall or stand,
          Let me live or die,
        But this once hear me speak—
          (O my love, O my love)—
        Yet a woman's words are weak;
          You should speak, not I.

        You took my heart in your hand
          With a friendly smile,
        With a critical eye you scanned,
          Then set it down,
        And said: It is still unripe,
          Better wait awhile;
        Wait while the skylarks pipe,
          Till the corn grows brown.

        As you set it down it broke—
          Broke, but I did not wince;
        I smiled at the speech you spoke,
          At your judgement that I heard:
        But I have not often smiled
          Since then, nor questioned since,
        Nor cared for corn-flowers wild,
          Nor sung with the singing bird.

I take my heart in my hand,
   O my God, O my God,
My broken heart in my hand,
   Thou hast seen, judge thou.
My hope was written on sand,
   O my God, O my God:
Now let thy judgement stand—
   Yea, judge me now.

This contemned of a man,
   This marred one heedless day,
This heart take thou to scan
   Both within and without:
Refine with fire its gold,
   Purge thou its dross away—
Yea, hold it in thy hold,
   Whence none can pluck it out.

I take my heart in my hand—
   I shall not die, but live—
Before thy face I stand;
   I, for thou callest such:
All that I have I bring,
   All that I am I give,
Smile thou and I shall sing,
   But shall not question much.

679   *Somewhere or Other*

SOMEWHERE or other there must surely be
   The face not seen, the voice not heard,
The heart that not yet—never yet—ah me!
   Made answer to my word.

Somewhere or other, may be near or far;
   Past land and sea, clean out of sight;
Beyond the wandering moon, beyond the star
   That tracks her night by night.

Somewhere or other, may be far or near;
   With just a wall, a hedge, between;
With just the last leaves of the dying year
   Fallen on a turf grown green.

680   *Marvel of Marvels*

MARVEL of marvels, if I myself shall behold
With mine own eyes my King in his city of gold;
Where the least of lambs is spotless white in the fold,
Where the least and last of saints in spotless white is stoled,
Where the dimmest head beyond a moon is aureoled.
O saints, my beloved, now mouldering to mould in the mould,
Shall I see you lift your heads, see your cerements unrolled,
See with these very eyes? who now in darkness and cold
Tremble for the midnight cry, the rapture, the tale untold,
'The Bridegroom cometh, cometh, his Bride to enfold.'

Cold it is, my beloved since your funeral bell was tolled:
Cold it is, O my King, how cold alone on the wold.

CHARLES LUTWIDGE DODGSON (LEWIS CARROLL)
1832–1898

681   *Jabberwocky*

'TWAS brillig, and the slithy toves
    Did gyre and gimble in the wabe:
All mimsy were the borogoves,
      And the mome raths outgrabe.

'Beware the Jabberwock, my son!
    The jaws that bite, the claws that catch!
Beware the Jubjub bird, and shun
      The frumious Bandersnatch!'

He took his vorpal sword in hand:
    Long time the manxome foe he sought—
So rested he by the Tumtum tree,
      And stood awhile in thought.

And, as in uffish thought he stood,
    The Jabberwock, with eyes of flame,
Came whiffling through the tulgey wood,
      And burbled as it came!

One, two! One, two! And through and through
    The vorpal blade went snicker-snack!
He left it dead, and with its head
    He went galumphing back.

'And hast thou slain the Jabberwock?
    Come to my arms, my beamish boy!
O frabjous day! Callooh! Callay!'
    He chortled in his joy.

'Twas brillig, and the slithy toves
    Did gyre and gimble in the wabe:
All mimsy were the borogoves,
    And the mome raths outgrabe.

682   *The White Knight's Song*

I'LL tell thee everything I can:
    There's little to relate,
I saw an aged aged man,
    A-sitting on a gate.
'Who are you, aged man?' I said.
    'And how is it you live?'
And his answer trickled through my head,
    Like water through a sieve.

He said 'I look for butterflies
    That sleep among the wheat:
I make them into mutton-pies,
    And sell them in the street.
I sell them unto men', he said,
    'Who sail on stormy seas;
And that's the way I get my bread—
    A trifle, if you please.'

But I was thinking of a plan
    To dye one's whiskers green,
And always use so large a fan
    That they could not be seen.
So, having no reply to give
    To what the old man said,
I cried 'Come, tell me how you live!'
    And thumped him on the head.

His accents mild took up the tale:
   He said 'I go my ways,
And when I find a mountain-rill,
   I set it in a blaze;
And thence they make a stuff they call
   Rowland's Macassar-Oil—
Yet two-pence-halfpenny is all
   They give me for my toil.'

But I was thinking of a way
   To feed oneself on batter
And so go on from day to day
   Getting a little fatter.
I shook him well from side to side,
   Until his face was blue:
'Come, tell me how you live,' I cried,
   'And what it is you do!'

He said 'I hunt for haddocks' eyes
   Among the heather bright,
And work them into waistcoat-buttons
   In the silent night.
And these I do not sell for gold
   Or coin of silvery shine,
But for a copper halfpenny,
   And that will purchase nine.

I sometimes dig for buttered rolls,
   Or set limed twigs for crabs:
I sometimes search the grassy knolls
   For wheels of Hansom-cabs.
And that's the way' (he gave a wink)
   'By which I get my wealth—
And very gladly will I drink
   Your Honour's noble health.'

I heard him then, for I had just
   Completed my design
To keep the Menai bridge from rust
   By boiling it in wine.
I thanked him much for telling me
   The way he got his wealth,
But chiefly for his wish that he
   Might drink my noble health.

And now, if e'er by chance I put
  My fingers into glue,
Or madly squeeze a right-hand foot
  Into a left-hand shoe,
Or if I drop upon my toe
  A very heavy weight,
I weep, for it reminds me so
Of that old man I used to know—
Whose look was mild, whose speech was slow
Whose hair was whiter than the snow,
Whose face was very like a crow,
With eyes, like cinders, all aglow,
Who seemed distracted with his woe,
Who rocked his body to and fro,
And muttered mumblingly and low,
As if his mouth were full of dough,
Who snorted like a buffalo—
That summer evening long ago,
  A-sitting on a gate.

RICHARD WATSON DIXON

1833–1900

683   *Song*

THE feathers of the willow
Are half of them grown yellow
  Above the swelling stream;
And ragged are the bushes,
And rusty now the rushes,
  And wild the clouded gleam.

The thistle now is older,
His stalk begins to moulder,
  His head is white as snow;
The branches all are barer,
The linnet's song is rarer,
  The robin pipeth now.

WILLIAM MORRIS
1834–1896

684 *Summer Dawn*

PRAY but one prayer for me 'twixt thy closed lips;
　Think but one thought of me up in the stars.
The summer night waneth, the morning light slips,
　Faint and grey 'twixt the leaves of the aspen,
　　betwixt the cloud-bars,
That are patiently waiting there for the dawn:
　Patient and colourless, though Heaven's gold
Waits to float through them along with the sun.
Far out in the meadows, above the young corn,
　The heavy elms wait, and restless and cold
The uneasy wind rises; the roses are dun;
Through the long twilight they pray for the dawn,
Round the lone house in the midst of the corn.
　Speak but one word to me over the corn,
　Over the tender, bowed locks of the corn.

685 *Riding Together*

FOR many, many days together
　The wind blew steady from the East;
For many days hot grew the weather,
　About the time of our Lady's Feast.

For many days we rode together,
　Yet met we neither friend nor foe;
Hotter and clearer grew the weather,
　Steadily did the East wind blow.

We saw the trees in the hot, bright weather,
　Clear-cut, with shadows very black,
As freely we rode on together
　With helms unlaced and bridles slack.

And often as we rode together,
　We, looking down the green-banked stream,
Say flowers in the sunny weather,
　And saw the bubble-making bream.

And in the night lay down together,
  And hung above our heads the rood,
Or watched night-long in the dewy weather,
  The while the moon did watch the wood.

Our spears stood bright and thick together,
  Straight out the banners streamed behind,
As we galloped on in the sunny weather,
  With faces turned towards the wind.

Down sank our threescore spears together,
  As thick we saw the pagans ride;
His eager face in the clear fresh weather,
  Shone out that last time by my side.

Up the sweep of the bridge we dashed together,
  It rocked to the crash of the meeting spears,
Down rained the buds of the dear spring weather,
  The elm-tree flowers fell like tears.

There as we rolled and writhed together,
  I threw my arms above my head,
For close by my side, in the lovely weather,
  I saw him reel and fall back dead,

I and the slayer met together,
  He waited the death-stroke there in his place,
With thoughts of death, in the lovely weather,
  Gapingly mazed at my maddened face.

Madly I fought as we fought together;
  In vain: the little Christian band
The pagans drowned, as in stormy weather,
  The river drowns low-lying land.

They bound my blood-stained hands together,
  They bound his corpse to nod by my side:
Then on we rode, in the bright March weather,
  With clash of cymbals did we ride.

We ride no more, no more together;
  My prison-bars are thick and strong,
I take no heed of any weather,
  The sweet Saints grant I live not long.

686   *A Garden by the Sea*

I KNOW a little garden-close,
Set thick with lily and red rose,
Where I would wander if I might
From dewy morn to dewy night,
And have one with me wandering.

And though within it no birds sing,
And though no pillared house is there,
And though the apple-boughs are bare
Of fruit and blossom, would to God
Her feet upon the green grass trod,
And I beheld them as before.

There comes a murmur from the shore,
And in the close two fair streams are,
Drawn from the purple hills afar,
Drawn down unto the restless sea:
Dark hills whose heath-bloom feeds no bee,
Dark shore no ship has ever seen,
Tormented by the billows green
Whose murmur comes unceasingly
Unto the place for which I cry.
For which I cry both day and night,
For which I let slip all delight,
Whereby I grow both deaf and blind,
Careless to win, unskilled to find,
And quick to lose what all men seek.

Yet tottering as I am and weak,
Still have I left a little breath
To seek within the jaws of death
An entrance to that happy place,
To seek the unforgotten face,
Once seen, once kissed, once reft from me
Anigh the murmuring of the sea.

JAMES THOMSON ('B.V.')

1834–1882

from The City of Dreadful Night

(i)

687 *The City*

Lo, thus, as prostrate, 'In the dust I write
  My heart's deep languor and my soul's sad tears.'
Yet why evoke the spectres of black night
  To blot the sunshine of exultant years?
Why disinter dead faith from mouldering hidden?
Why break the seals of mute despair unbidden,
  And wail life's discords into careless ears?

Because a cold rage seizes one at whiles
  To show the bitter old and wrinkled truth
Stripped naked of all vesture that beguiles,
  False dreams, false hopes, false masks and modes of youth;
Because it gives some sense of power and passion
In helpless impotence to try to fashion
  Our woe in living words howe'er uncouth.

Surely I write not for the hopeful young,
  Or those who deem their happiness of worth,
Or such as pasture and grow fat among
  The shows of life and feel nor doubt nor dearth,
Or pious spirits with a God above them
To sanctify and glorify and love them,
  Or sages who foresee a heaven on earth.

For none of these I write, and none of these
  Could read the writing if they deigned to try:
So may they flourish, in their due degrees,
  On our sweet earth and in their unplaced sky.
If any cares for the weak words here written,
It must be some one desolate, Fate-smitten,
  Whose faith and hope are dead, and who would die.

Yes, here and there some weary wanderer
   In that same city of tremendous night,
Will understand the speech, and feel a stir
   Of fellowship in all-disastrous fight;
'I suffer mute and lonely, yet another
Uplifts his voice to let me know a brother
   Travels the same wild paths though out of sight.'

O sad Fraternity, do I unfold
   Your dolorous mysteries shrouded from of yore?
Nay, be assured; no secret can be told
   To any who divined it not before:
None uninitiate by many a presage
Will comprehend the language of the message,
   Although proclaimed aloud for evermore.

*

The street-lamps burn amidst the baleful glooms,
   Amidst the soundless solitudes immense
Of rangèd mansions dark and still as tombs.
   The silence which benumbs or strains the sense
Fulfils with awe the soul's despair unweeping:
Myriads of habitants are ever sleeping,
   Or dead, or fled from nameless pestilence!

Yet as in some necropolis you find
   Perchance one mourner to a thousand dead,
So there; worn faces that look deaf and blind
   Like tragic masks of stone. With weary tread,
Each wrapt in his own doom, they wander, wander,
Or sit foredone and desolately ponder
   Through sleepless hours with heavy drooping head.

Mature men chiefly, few in age or youth,
   A woman rarely, now and then a child:
A child! If here the heart turns sick with ruth
   To see a little one from birth defiled,
Or lame or blind, as preordained to languish
Through youthless life, think how it bleeds with anguish
   To meet one erring in that homeless wild.

They often murmur to themselves, they speak
  To one another seldom, for their woe
Broods maddening inwardly and scorns to wreak
  Itself abroad; and if at whiles it grow
To frenzy which must rave, none heeds the clamour,
Unless there waits some victim of like glamour,
  To rave in turn, who lends attentive show.

The City is of Night, but not of Sleep;
  There sweet sleep is not for the weary brain;
The pitiless hours like years and ages creep,
  A night seems termless hell. This dreadful strain
Of thought and consciousness which never ceases,
Or which some moments' stupor but increases,
  This, worse than woe, makes wretches there insane.

They leave all hope behind who enter there:
  One certitude while sane they cannot leave,
One anodyne for torture and despair;
  The certitude of Death, which no reprieve
Can put off long; and which, divinely tender,
But waits the outstretched hand to promptly render
  That draught whose slumber nothing can bereave.

(ii)

688   *The City's Queen*

ANEAR the centre of that northern crest
  Stands out a level upland bleak and bare,
From which the city east and south and west
  Sinks gently in long waves; and thronèd there
An Image sits, stupendous, superhuman,
The bronze colossus of a wingèd Woman,
  Upon a graded granite base foursquare.

Low-seated she leans forward massively,
  With cheek on clenched left hand, the forearm's might
Erect, its elbow on her rounded knee;
  Across a clasped book in her lap the right
Upholds a pair of compasses; she gazes
With full set eyes, but wandering in thick mazes
  Of sombre thought beholds no outward sight.

Words cannot picture her; but all men know
　　That solemn sketch the pure sad artist wrought
Three centuries and threescore years ago,
　　With phantasies of his peculiar thought:
The instruments of carpentry and science
Scattered about her feet, in strange alliance
　　With the keen wolf-hound sleeping undistraught;

Scales, hour-glass, bell, and magic-square above;
　　The grave and solid infant perched beside,
With open winglets that might bear a dove,
　　Intent upon its tablets, heavy-eyed;
Her folded wings as of a mighty eagle,
But all too impotent to lift the regal
　　Robustness of her earth-born strength and pride;

And with those wings, and that light wreath which seems
　　To mock her grand head and the knotted frown
Of forehead charged with baleful thoughts and dreams,
　　The household bunch of keys, the housewife's gown
Voluminous, indented, and yet rigid
As if a shell of burnished metal frigid,
　　The feet thick-shod to tread all weakness down;

The comet hanging o'er the waste dark seas,
　　The massy rainbow curved in front of it
Beyond the village with the masts and trees;
　　The snaky imp, dog-headed, from the Pit,
Bearing upon its batlike leathern pinions
Her name unfolded in the sun's dominions,
　　The 'MELENCOLIA' that transcends all wit.

Thus has the artist copied her, and thus
　　Surrounded to expound her form sublime,
Her fate heroic and calamitous;
　　Fronting the dreadful mysteries of Time,
Unvanquished in defeat and desolation,
Undaunted in the hopeless conflagration
　　Of the day setting on her baffled prime.

the pure sad artist] Albrecht Dürer

Baffled and beaten back she works on still,
  Weary and sick of soul she works the more,
Sustained by her indomitable will:
  The hands shall fashion and the brain shall pore,
And all her sorrow shall be turned to labour,
Till Death the friend-foe piercing with his sabre
  That mighty heart of hearts ends bitter war.

But as if blacker night could dawn on night,
  With tenfold gloom on moonless night unstarred,
A sense more tragic than defeat and blight,
  More desperate than strife with hope debarred,
More fatal than the adamantine Never
Encompassing her passionate endeavour,
  Dawns glooming in her tenebrous regard:

The sense that every struggle brings defeat
  Because Fate holds no prize to crown success;
That all the oracles are dumb or cheat
  Because they have no secret to express;
That none can pierce the vast black veil uncertain
Because there is no light beyond the curtain;
  That all is vanity and nothingness.

Titanic from her high throne in the north,
  That City's sombre Patroness and Queen,
In bronze sublimity she gazes forth
  Over her Capital of teen and threne,
Over the river with its isles and bridges,
The marsh and moorland, to the stern rock-ridges,
  Confronting them with a coëval mien.

The moving moon and stars from east to west
  Circle before her in the sea of air;
Shadows and gleams glide round her solemn rest.
  Her subjects often gaze up to her there:
The strong to drink new strength of iron endurance,
The weak new terrors; all, renewed assurance
  And confirmation of the old despair.

ALGERNON CHARLES SWINBURNE
1837–1909

689   Chorus from *Atalanta in Calydon*

WHEN the hounds of spring are on winter's traces,
    The mother of months in meadow or plain
Fills the shadows and windy places
    With lisp of leaves and ripple of rain;
And the brown bright nightingale amorous
Is half assuaged for Itylus,
For the Thracian ships and the foreign faces,
    The tongueless vigil, and all the pain.

Come with bows bent and with emptying of quivers,
    Maiden most perfect, lady of light,
With a noise of winds and many rivers,
    With a clamour of waters, and with might;
Bind on thy sandals, O thou most fleet,
Over the splendour and speed of thy feet;
For the faint east quickens, the wan west shivers,
    Round the feet of the day and the feet of the night.

Where shall we find her, how shall we sing to her,
    Fold our hands round her knees, and cling?
O that man's heart were as fire and could spring to her,
    Fire, or the strength of the streams that spring!
For the stars and the winds are unto her
As raiment, as songs of the harp-player;
For the risen stars and the fallen cling to her,
    And the southwest-wind and the west-wind sing.

For winter's rains and ruins are over,
    And all the season of snows and sins;
The days dividing lover and lover,
    The light that loses, the night that wins;
And time remembered is grief forgotten,
And frosts are slain and flowers begotten,
And in green underwood and cover
    Blossom by blossom the spring begins.

The full streams feed on flower of rushes,
    Ripe grasses trammel a travelling foot,
The faint fresh flame of the young year flushes
    From leaf to flower and flower to fruit;
And fruit and leaf are as gold and fire,
And the oat is heard above the lyre,
And the hoofèd heel of a satyr crushes
    The chestnut-husk at the chestnut-root.

And Pan by noon and Bacchus by night,
    Fleeter of foot than the fleet-foot kid,
Follows with dancing and fills with delight
    The Mænad and the Bassarid;
And soft as lips that laugh and hide
The laughing leaves of the trees divide,
And screen from seeing and leave in sight
    The god pursuing, the maiden hid.

The ivy falls with the Bacchanal's hair
    Over her eyebrows hiding her eyes;
The wild vine slipping down leaves bare
    Her bright breast shortening into sighs;
The wild vine slips with the weight of its leaves,
But the berried ivy catches and cleaves
To the limbs that glitter, the feet that scare
    The wolf that follows, the fawn that flies.

690   *A Leave-Taking*

LET us go hence, my songs; she will not hear.
Let us go hence together without fear;
Keep silence now, for singing-time is over,
And over all old things and all things dear.
She loves not you nor me as we all love her.
Yea, though we sang as angels in her ear,
        She would not hear.

743

Let us rise up and part; she will not know.
Let us go seaward as the great winds go,
Full of blown sand and foam; what help is here?
There is no help, for all these things are so,
And all the world is bitter as a tear.
And how these things are, though ye strove to show,
     She would not know.

Let us go home and hence; she will not weep.
We gave love many dreams and days to keep,
Flowers without scent, and fruits that would not grow,
Saying, 'If thou wilt, thrust in thy sickle and reap.'
All is reaped now; no grass is left to mow;
And we that sowed, though all we fell on sleep,
     She would not weep.

Let us go hence and rest; she will not love.
She shall not hear us if we sing hereof,
Nor see love's ways, how sore they are and steep.
Come hence, let be, lie still; it is enough.
Love is a barren sea, bitter and deep;
And though she saw all heaven in flower above,
     She would not love.

Let us give up, go down; she will not care.
Though all the stars made gold of all the air,
And the sea moving saw before it move
One moon-flower making all the foam-flowers fair;
Though all those waves went over us, and drove
Deep down the stifling lips and drowning hair,
     She would not care.

Let us go hence, go hence; she will not see.
Sing all once more together; surely she,
She too, remembering days and words that were,
Will turn a little toward us, sighing; but we,
We are hence, we are gone, as though we had not been there.
Nay, and though all men seeing had pity on me,
     She would not see.

691   *The Garden of Proserpine*

HERE, where the world is quiet;
    Here, where all trouble seems
Dead winds' and spent waves' riot
    In doubtful dreams of dreams;
I watch the green field growing
For reaping folk and sowing,
For harvest-time and mowing,
    A sleepy world of streams.

I am tired of tears and laughter,
    And men that laugh and weep;
Of what may come hereafter
    For men that sow to reap:
I am weary of days and hours,
Blown buds of barren flowers,
Desires and dreams and powers
    And everything but sleep.

Here life has death for neighbour,
    And far from eye or ear
Wan waves and wet winds labour,
    Weak ships and spirits steer;
They drive adrift, and whither
They wot not who make thither;
But no such winds blow hither,
    And no such things grow here.

No growth of moor or coppice,
    No heather-flower or vine,
But bloomless buds of poppies,
    Green grapes of Proserpine,
Pale beds of blowing rushes
Where no leaf blooms or blushes
Save this whereout she crushes
    For dead men deadly wine.

Pale, without name or number,
  In fruitless fields of corn,
They bow themselves and slumber
  All night till light is born;
And like a soul belated,
In hell and heaven unmated,
By cloud and mist abated
  Comes out of darkness morn.

Though one were strong as seven,
  He too with death shall dwell,
Nor wake with wings in heaven,
  Nor weep for pains in hell;
Though one were fair as roses,
His beauty clouds and closes;
And well though love reposes,
  In the end it is not well.

Pale, beyond porch and portal,
  Crowned with calm leaves, she stands
Who gathers all things mortal
  With cold immortal hands;
Her languid lips are sweeter
Than love's who fears to greet her
To men that mix and meet her
  From many times and lands.

She waits for each and other,
  She waits for all men born;
Forgets the earth her mother,
  The life of fruits and corn;
And spring and seed and swallow
Take wing for her and follow
Where summer song rings hollow
  And flowers are put to scorn.

There go the loves that wither,
  The old loves with wearier wings;
And all dead years draw thither,
  And all disastrous things;
Dead dreams of days forsaken,
Blind buds that snows have shaken,
Wild leaves that winds have taken,
  Red strays of ruined springs.

We are not sure of sorrow,
   And joy was never sure;
To-day will die to-morrow;
   Time stoops to no man's lure;
And love, grown faint and fretful,
With lips but half regretful
Sighs, and with eyes forgetful
   Weeps that no loves endure.

From too much love of living,
   From hope and fear set free,
We thank with brief thanksgiving
   Whatever gods may be
That no life lives for ever;
That dead men rise up never;
That even the weariest river
   Winds somewhere safe to sea.

Then star nor sun shall waken,
   Nor any change of light:
Nor sound of waters shaken,
   Nor any sound or sight:
Nor wintry leaves nor vernal,
Nor days nor things diurnal;
Only the sleep eternal
   In an eternal night.

692   *Ave atque Vale*

IN MEMORY OF CHARLES BAUDELAIRE

Nous devrions pourtant lui porter quelques fleurs;
Les morts, les pauvres morts, ont de grandes douleurs,
Et quand Octobre souffle, émondeur des vieux arbres,
Son vent mélancolique à l'entour de leurs marbres,
Certe, ils doivent trouver les vivants bien ingrats.
           —'Les Fleurs du Mal.'

SHALL I strew on thee rose or rue or laurel,
   Brother, on this that was the veil of thee?
   Or quiet sea-flower moulded by the sea,
Or simplest growth of meadow-sweet or sorrel,
   Such as the summer-sleepy Dryads weave,
   Waked up by snow-soft sudden rains at eve?

747

Or wilt thou rather, as on earth before,
  Half-faded fiery blossoms, pale with heat
  And full of bitter summer, but more sweet
To thee than gleanings of a northern shore
  Trod by no tropic feet?

For always thee the fervid languid glories
  Allured of heavier suns in mightier skies;
  Thine ears knew all the wandering watery sighs
Where the sea sobs round Lesbian promontories,
  The barren kiss of piteous wave to wave
  That knows not where is that Leucadian grave
Which hides too deep the supreme head of song.
  Ah, salt and sterile as her kisses were,
  The wild sea winds her and the green gulfs bear
Hither and thither, and vex and work her wrong,
  Blind gods that cannot spare.

Thou sawest, in thine old singing season, brother,
  Secrets and sorrows unbeheld of us:
  Fierce loves, and lovely leaf-buds poisonous,
Bare to thy subtler eye, but for none other
  Blowing by night in some unbreathed-in clime;
  The hidden harvest of luxurious time,
Sin without shape, and pleasure without speech;
  And where strange dreams in a tumultuous sleep
  Make the shut eyes of stricken spirits weep;
And with each face thou saw'st the shadow on each,
  Seeing as men sow men reap.

O sleepless heart and sombre soul unsleeping,
  That were athirst for sleep and no more life
  And no more love, for peace and no more strife!
Now the dim gods of death have in their keeping
  Spirit and body and all the springs of song,
  Is it well now where love can do no wrong,
Where stingless pleasure has no foam or fang
  Behind the unopening closure of her lips?
  Is it not well where soul from body slips
And flesh from bone divides without a pang
  As dew from flower-bell drips?

It is enough; the end and the beginning
   Are one thing to thee, who art past the end.
   O hand unclasped of unbeholden friend,
For thee no fruits to pluck, no palms for winning,
   No triumph and no labour and no lust,
   Only dead yew-leaves and a little dust.
O quiet eyes wherein the light saith nought,
   Whereto the day is dumb, nor any night
   With obscure finger silences your sight,
Nor in your speech the sudden soul speaks thought,
   Sleep, and have sleep for light.

Now all strange hours and all strange loves are over,
   Dreams and desires and sombre songs and sweet,
   Hast thou found place at the great knees and feet
Of some pale Titan-woman like a lover,
   Such as thy vision here solicited,
   Under the shadow of her fair vast head,
The deep division of prodigious breasts,
   The solemn slope of mighty limbs asleep,
   The weight of awful tresses that still keep
The savour and shade of old-world pine-forests
   Where the wet hill-winds weep?

Hast thou found any likeness for thy vision?
   O gardener of strange flowers, what bud, what bloom,
   Hast thou found sown, what gathered in the gloom?
What of despair, of rapture, of derision,
   What of life is there, what of ill or good?
   Are the fruits grey like dust or bright like blood?
Does the dim ground grow any seed of ours,
   The faint fields quicken any terrene root,
   In low lands where the sun and moon are mute
And all the stars keep silence? Are there flowers
   At all, or any fruit?

Alas, but though my flying song flies after,
   O sweet strange elder singer, thy more fleet
   Singing, and footprints of thy fleeter feet,
Some dim derision of mysterious laughter
   From the blind tongueless warders of the dead,
   Some gainless glimpse of Proserpine's veiled head,

Some little sound of unregarded tears
  Wept by effaced unprofitable eyes,
  And from pale mouths some cadence of dead sighs—
These only, these the hearkening spirit hears,
  Sees only such things rise.

Thou art far too far for wings of words to follow,
  Far too far off for thought or any prayer.
  What ails us with thee, who art wind and air?
What ails us gazing where all seen is hollow?
  Yet with some fancy, yet with some desire,
  Dreams pursue death as winds a flying fire,
Our dreams pursue our dead and do not find.
  Still, and more swift than they, the thin flame flies,
  The low light fails us in elusive skies,
Still the foiled earnest ear is deaf, and blind
  Are still the eluded eyes.

Not thee, O never thee, in all time's changes,
  Not thee, but this the sound of thy sad soul,
  The shadow of thy swift spirit, this shut scroll
I lay my hand on, and not death estranges
  My spirit from communion of thy song—
  These memories and these melodies that throng
Veiled porches of a Muse funereal—
  These I salute, these touch, these clasp and fold
  As though a hand were in my hand to hold,
Or through mine ears a mourning musical
  Of many mourners rolled.

I among these, I also, in such station
  As when the pyre was charred, and piled the sods,
  And offering to the dead made, and their gods,
The old mourners had, standing to make libation,
  I stand, and to the gods and to the dead
  Do reverence without prayer or praise, and shed
Offering to these unknown, the gods of gloom,
  And what of honey and spice my seedlands bear,
  And what I may of fruits in this chilled air,
And lay, Orestes-like, across the tomb
  A curl of severed hair.

But by no hand nor any treason stricken,
  Not like the low-lying head of Him, the King,
  The flame that made of Troy a ruinous thing,
Thou liest, and on this dust no tears could quicken
  There fall no tears like theirs that all men hear
  Fall tear by sweet imperishable tear
Down the opening leaves of holy poets' pages.
  Thee not Orestes, not Electra mourns;
  But bending us-ward with memorial urns
The most high Muses that fulfil all ages
  Weep, and our God's heart yearns.

For, sparing of his sacred strength, not often
  Among us darkling here the lord of light
  Makes manifest his music and his might
In hearts that open and in lips that soften
  With the soft flame and heat of songs that shine.
  Thy lips indeed he touched with bitter wine,
And nourished them indeed with bitter bread;
  Yet surely from his hand thy soul's food came,
  The fire that scarred thy spirit at his flame
Was lighted, and thine hungering heart he fed
  Who feeds our hearts with fame.

Therefore he too now at thy soul's sunsetting,
  God of all suns and songs, he too bends down
  To mix his laurel with thy cypress crown,
And save thy dust from blame and from forgetting.
  Therefore he too, seeing all thou wert and art,
  Compassionate, with sad and sacred heart,
Mourns thee of many his children the last dead,
  And hallows with strange tears and alien sighs
  Thine unmelodious mouth and sunless eyes,
And over thine irrevocable head
  Sheds light from the under skies.

And one weeps with him in the ways Lethean,
  And stains with tears her changing bosom chill:
  That obscure Venus of the hollow hill,
That thing transformed which was the Cytherean,
  With lips that lost their Grecian laugh divine
  Long since, and face no more called Erycine;

751

A ghost, a bitter and luxurious god.
   Thee also with fair flesh and singing spell
   Did she, a sad and second prey, compel
Into the footless places once more trod,
   And shadows hot from hell.

And now no sacred staff shall break in blossom,
   No choral salutation lure to light
   A spirit sick with perfume and sweet night
And love's tired eyes and hands and barren bosom.
   There is no help for these things; none to mend
   And none to mar; not all our songs, O friend,
Will make death clear or make life durable.
   Howbeit with rose and ivy and wild vine
   And with wild notes about this dust of thine
At least I fill the place where white dreams dwell
   And wreathe an unseen shrine.

Sleep; and if life was bitter to thee, pardon,
   If sweet, give thanks; thou hast no more to live;
   And to give thanks is good, and to forgive.
Out of the mystic and the mournful garden
   Where all day through thine hands in barren braid
   Wove the sick flowers of secrecy and shade,
Green buds of sorrow and sin, and remnants grey,
   Sweet-smelling, pale with poison, sanguine-hearted,
   Passions that sprang from sleep and thoughts that started,
Shall death not bring us all as thee one day
   Among the days departed?

For thee, O now a silent soul, my brother,
   Take at my hands this garland, and farewell.
   Thin is the leaf, and chill the wintry smell,
And chill the solemn earth, a fatal mother,
   With sadder than the Niobean womb,
   And in the hollow of her breasts a tomb.
Content thee, howsoe'er, whose days are done;
   There lies not any troublous thing before,
   Nor sight nor sound to war against thee more,
For whom all winds are quiet as the sun,
   All waters as the shore.

A Forsaken Garden

IN a coign of the cliff between lowland and highland,
    At the sea-down's edge between windward and lee,
Walled round with rocks as an inland island,
    The ghost of a garden fronts the sea.
A girdle of brushwood and thorn encloses
    The steep square slope of the blossomless bed
Where the weeds that grew green from the graves of its roses
            Now lie dead.

The fields fall southward, abrupt and broken,
    To the low last edge of the long lone land.
If a step should sound or a word be spoken,
    Would a ghost not rise at the strange guest's hand?
So long have the grey bare walks lain guestless,
    Through branches and briars if a man make way,
He shall find no life but the sea-wind's, restless
            Night and day.

The dense hard passage is blind and stifled
    That crawls by a track none turn to climb
To the strait waste place that the years have rifled
    Of all but the thorns that are touched not of time.
The thorns he spares when the rose is taken;
    The rocks are left when he wastes the plain.
The wind that wanders, the weeds wind-shaken,
            These remain.

Not a flower to be pressed of the foot that falls not;
    As the heart of a dead man the seed-plots are dry;
From the thicket of thorns whence the nightingale calls not,
    Could she call, there were never a rose to reply.
Over the meadows that blossom and wither
    Rings but the note of a sea-bird's song;
Only the sun and the rain come hither
            All year long.

The sun burns sere and the rain dishevels
    One gaunt bleak blossom of scentless breath.
Only the wind here hovers and revels
    In a round where life seems barren as death.

Here there was laughing of old, there was weeping,
    Haply, of lovers none ever will know,
Whose eyes went seaward a hundred sleeping
        Years ago.

Heart handfast in heart as they stood, 'Look thither,'
    Did he whisper? 'look forth from the flowers to the sea;
For the foam-flowers endure when the rose-blossoms wither,
    And men that love lightly may die—but we?'
And the same wind sang and the same waves whitened,
    And or ever the garden's last petals were shed,
In the lips that had whispered, the eyes that had lightened,
        Love was dead.

Or they loved their life through, and then went whither?
    And were one to the end—but what end who knows?
Love deep as the sea as a rose must wither,
    As the rose-red seaweed that mocks the rose.
Shall the dead take thought for the dead to love them?
    What love was ever as deep as a grave?
They are loveless now as the grass above them
        Or the wave.

All are at one now, roses and lovers,
    Not known of the cliffs and the fields and the sea.
Not a breath of the time that has been hovers
    In the air now soft with a summer to be.
Not a breath shall there sweeten the seasons hereafter
    Of the flowers or the lovers that laugh now or weep,
When as they that are free now of weeping and laughter
        We shall sleep.

Here death may deal not again for ever;
    Here change may come not till all change end.
From the graves they have made they shall rise up never,
    Who have left nought living to ravage and rend.
Earth, stones, and thorns of the wild ground growing,
    While the sun and the rain live, these shall be;
Till a last wind's breath upon all these blowing
        Roll the sea.

Till the slow sea rise and the sheer cliff crumble,
  Till terrace and meadow the deep gulfs drink,
Till the strength of the waves of the high tides humble
  The fields that lessen, the rocks that shrink,
Here now in his triumph where all things falter,
  Stretched out on the spoils that his own hand spread,
As a god self-slain on his own strange altar,
       Death lies dead.

THOMAS HARDY

1840–1928

694

I LOOK into my glass,
And view my wasting skin,
And say, 'Would God it came to pass
My heart had shrunk as thin!'

For then, I, undistrest
By hearts grown cold to me,
Could lonely wait my endless rest
With equanimity.

But Time, to make me grieve,
Part steals, lets part abide;
And shakes this fragile frame at eve
With throbbings of noontide.

695

I NEED not go
Through sleet and snow
To where I know
She waits for me;
She will tarry me there
Till I find it fair,
And have time to spare
From company.

When I've overgot
The world somewhat,
When things cost not
Such stress and strain,
Is soon enough
By cypress sough
To tell my Love
I am come again.

And if some day,
When none cries nay,
I still delay
To seek her side,
(Though ample measure
Of fitting leisure
Await my pleasure)
She will not chide.

What—not upbraid me
That I delayed me,
Nor ask what stayed me
So long? Ah, no!—
New cares may claim me,
New loves inflame me,
She will not blame me,
But suffer it so.

696   *Wives in the Sere*

NEVER a careworn wife but shows,
        If a joy suffuse her,
Something beautiful to those
        Patient to peruse her,
Some one charm the world unknows
        Precious to a muser,
Haply what, ere years were foes,
        Moved her mate to choose her.

But, be it a hint of rose
    That an instant hues her,
Or some early light or pose
    Wherewith thought renews her—
Seen by him at full, ere woes
    Practised to abuse her—
Sparely comes it, swiftly goes,
    Time again subdues her.

The Darkling Thrush

I LEANT upon a coppice gate
    When Frost was spectre-gray,
And Winter's dregs made desolate
    The weakening eye of day.
The tangled bine-stems scored the sky
    Like strings of broken lyres,
And all mankind that haunted nigh
    Had sought their household fires.

The land's sharp features seemed to be
    The Century's corpse outleant,
His crypt the cloudy canopy,
    The wind his death-lament.
The ancient pulse of germ and birth
    Was shrunken hard and dry,
And every spirit upon earth
    Seemed fervourless as I.

At once a voice arose among
    The bleak twigs overhead
In a full-hearted evensong
    Of joy illimited;
An agèd thrush, frail, gaunt, and small,
    In blast-beruffled plume,
Had chosen thus to fling his soul
    Upon the growing gloom.

So little cause for carolings
    Of such ecstatic sound
Was written on terrestrial things
    Afar or nigh around,

That I could think there trembled through
  His happy good-night air
Some blessed Hope, whereof he knew
  And I was unaware.

698   *The Self-Unseeing*

HERE is the ancient floor,
Footworn and hollowed and thin,
Here was the former door
Where the dead feet walked in.

She sat here in her chair,
Smiling into the fire;
He who played stood there,
Bowing it higher and higher.

Childlike, I danced in a dream;
Blessings emblazoned that day;
Everything glowed with a gleam;
Yet we were looking away!

699   *In Tenebris*

WINTERTIME nighs;
But my bereavement-pain
It cannot bring again:
  Twice no one dies.

Flower-petals flee;
But, since it once hath been,
No more that severing scene
  Can harrow me.

Birds faint in dread:
I shall not lose old strength
In the lone frost's black length:
  Strength long since fled!

Leaves freeze to dun;
But friends can not turn cold
This season as of old
    For him with none.

Tempests may scath;
But love can not make smart
Again this year his heart
    Who no heart hath.

Black is night's cope;
But death will not appal
One who, past doubtings all,
    Waits in unhope.

700 *Shut Out that Moon*

CLOSE up the casement, draw the blind,
    Shut out that stealing moon,
She wears too much the guise she wore
    Before our lutes were strewn
With years-deep dust, and names we read
    On a white stone were hewn.

Step not forth on the dew-dashed lawn
    To view the Lady's Chair,
Immense Orion's glittering form,
    The Less and Greater Bear:
Stay in; to such sights we were drawn
    When faded ones were fair.

Brush not the bough for midnight scents
    That come forth lingeringly,
And wake the same sweet sentiments
    They breathed to you and me
When living seemed a laugh, and love
    All it was said to be.

Within the common lamp-lit room
    Prison my eyes and thought;
Let dingy details crudely loom,
    Mechanic speech be wrought:
Too fragrant was Life's early bloom,
    Too tart the fruit it brought!

759

701 *On the Departure Platform*

WE kissed at the barrier; and passing through
She left me, and moment by moment got
Smaller and smaller, until to my view
      She was but a spot;

A wee white spot of muslin fluff
That down the diminishing platform bore
Through hustling crowds of gentle and rough
      To the carriage door.

Under the lamplight's fitful glowers,
Behind dark groups from far and near,
Whose interests were apart from ours,
      She would disappear,

Then show again, till I ceased to see
That flexible form, that nebulous white;
And she who was more than my life to me
      Had vanished quite.

We have penned new plans since that fair fond day,
And in season she will appear again—
Perhaps in the same soft white array—
      But never as then!

—'And why, young man, must eternally fly
A joy you'll repeat, if you love her well?'
—O friend, nought happens twice thus; why,
      I cannot tell!

702 *A Church Romance*

(*Mellstock: circa 1835*)

SHE turned in the high pew, until her sight
Swept the west gallery, and caught its row
Of music-men with viol, book, and bow
Against the sinking sad tower-window light.

She turned again; and in her pride's despite
One strenuous viol's inspirer seemed to throw
A message from his string to her below,
Which said: 'I claim thee as my own forthright!'

Thus their hearts' bond began, in due time signed.
And long years thence, when Age had scared Romance,
At some old attitude of his or glance
That gallery-scene would break upon her mind,
With him as minstrel, ardent, young, and trim,
Bowing 'New Sabbath' or 'Mount Ephraim'.

703   *The Roman Road*

THE Roman Road runs straight and bare
As the pale parting-line in hair
Across the heath. And thoughtful men
Contrast its days of Now and Then,
And delve, and measure, and compare;

Visioning on the vacant air
Helmed legionaries, who proudly rear
The Eagle, as they pace again
     The Roman Road.

But no tall brass-helmed legionnaire
Haunts it for me. Uprises there
A mother's form upon my ken,
Guiding my infant steps, as when
We walked that ancient thoroughfare,
     The Roman Road.

704   *After the Visit*

COME again to the place
Where your presence was as a leaf that skims
Down a drouthy way whose ascent bedims
  The bloom on the farer's face.

  Come again, with the feet
That were light on the green as a thistledown ball,
And those mute ministrations to one and to all
  Beyond a man's saying sweet.

Until then the faint scent
Of the bordering flowers swam unheeded away,
And I marked not the charm in the changes of day
    As the cloud-colours came and went.

Through the dark corridors
Your walk was so soundless I did not know
Your form from a phantom's of long ago
    Said to pass on the ancient floors,

Till you drew from the shade,
And I saw the large luminous living eyes
Regard me in fixed inquiring-wise
    As those of a soul that weighed,

Scarce consciously,
The eternal question of what Life was,
And why we were there, and by whose strange laws
    That which mattered most could not be.

705   *Beyond the Last Lamp*
              (*Near Tooting Common*)

WHILE rain, with eve in partnership,
Descended darkly, drip, drip, drip,
Beyond the last lone lamp I passed
    Walking slowly, whispering sadly,
     Two linked loiterers, wan, downcast;
Some heavy thought constrained each face,
And blinded them to time and place.

The pair seemed lovers, yet absorbed
In mental scenes no longer orbed
By love's young rays. Each countenance
    As it slowly, as it sadly
     Caught the lamplight's yellow glance,
Held in suspense a misery
At things which had been or might be.

When I retrod that watery way
Some hours beyond the droop of day,
Still I found pacing there the twain
    Just as slowly, just as sadly,
      Heedless of the night and rain.
One could but wonder who they were
And what wild woe detained them there.

Though thirty years of blur and blot
Have slid since I beheld that spot,
And saw in curious converse there
    Moving slowly, moving sadly
      That mysterious tragic pair,
Its olden look may linger on—
All but the couple; they have gone.

Whither? Who knows, indeed. . . . And yet
To me, when nights are weird and wet,
Without those comrades there at tryst
    Creeping slowly, creeping sadly,
      That lone lane does not exist.
There they seem brooding on their pain,
And will, while such a lane remain.

706 *The Going*

WHY did you give no hint that night
That quickly after the morrow's dawn,
And calmly, as if indifferent quite,
You would close your term here, up and be gone
    Where I could not follow
    With wing of swallow
To gain one glimpse of you ever anon!

    Never to bid good-bye,
    Or lip me the softest call,
Or utter a wish for a word, while I
Saw morning harden upon the wall,
    Unmoved, unknowing
    That your great going
Had place that moment, and altered all.

Why do you make me leave the house
And think for a breath it is you I see
At the end of the alley of bending boughs
Where so often at dusk you used to be;
      Till in darkening dankness
      The yawning blankness
Of the perspective sickens me!

      You were she who abode
      By those red-veined rocks far West,
You were the swan-necked one who rode
Along the beetling Beeny Crest,
      And, reining nigh me,
      Would muse and eye me,
While Life unrolled us its very best.

Why, then, latterly did we not speak,
Did we not think of those days long dead,
And ere your vanishing strive to seek
That time's renewal? We might have said,
      'In this bright spring weather
      We'll visit together
Those places that once we visited.'

      Well, well! All's past amend,
      Unchangeable. It must go.
I seem but a dead man held on end
To sink down soon. . . . O you could not know
      That such swift fleeing
      No soul foreseeing—
Not even I—would undo me so!

707

      I FOUND her out there
      On a slope few see,
      That falls westwardly
      To the salt-edged air,
      Where the ocean breaks
      On the purple strand,
      And the hurricane shakes
      The solid land.

I brought her here,
And have laid her to rest
In a noiseless nest
No sea beats near.
She will never be stirred
In her loamy cell
By the waves long heard
And loved so well.

So she does not sleep
By those haunted heights
The Atlantic smites
And the blind gales sweep,
Whence she often would gaze
At Dundagel's famed head,
While the dipping blaze
Dyed her face fire-red;

And would sigh at the tale
Of sunk Lyonnesse,
As a wind-tugged tress
Flapped her cheek like a flail;
Or listen at whiles
With a thought-bound brow
To the murmuring miles
She is far from now.

Yet her shade, maybe,
Will creep underground
Till it catch the sound
Of that western sea
As it swells and sobs
Where she once domiciled,
And joy in its throbs
With the heart of a child.

708   *The Haunter*

HE does not think that I haunt here nightly:
    How shall I let him know
That whither his fancy sets him wandering
    I, too, alertly go?—

Hover and hover a few feet from him
    Just as I used to do,
But cannot answer the words he lifts me—
    Only listen thereto!

When I could answer he did not say them:
    When I could let him know
How I would like to join in his journeys
    Seldom he wished to go.
Now that he goes and wants me with him
    More than he used to do,
Never he sees my faithful phantom
    Though he speaks thereto.

Yes, I companion him to places
    Only dreamers know,
Where the shy hares print long paces,
    Where the night rooks go;
Into old aisles where the past is all to him,
    Close as his shade can do,
Always lacking the power to call to him,
    Near as I reach thereto!

What a good haunter I am, O tell him!
    Quickly make him know
If he but sigh since my loss befell him
    Straight to his side I go.
Tell him a faithful one is doing
    All that love can do
Still that his path may be worth pursuing,
    And to bring peace thereto.

709   *At Castle Boterel*

As I drive to the junction of lane and highway,
    And the drizzle bedrenches the waggonette,
I look behind at the fading byway,
    And see on its slope, now glistening wet,
        Distinctly yet

Myself and a girlish form benighted
 In dry March weather. We climb the road
Beside a chaise. We had just alighted
 To ease the sturdy pony's load
  When he sighed and slowed.

What we did as we climbed, and what we talked of
 Matters not much, nor to what it led,—
Something that life will not be balked of
 Without rude reason till hope is dead,
  And feeling fled.

It filled but a minute. But was there ever
 A time of such quality, since or before,
In that hill's story? To one mind never,
 Though it has been climbed, foot-swift, foot-sore,
  By thousands more.

Primaeval rocks form the road's steep border,
 And much have they faced there, first and last,
Of the transitory in Earth's long order;
 But what they record in colour and cast
  Is—that we two passed.

And to me, though Time's unflinching rigour,
 In mindless rote, has ruled from sight
The substance now, one phantom figure
 Remains on the slope, as when that night
  Saw us alight.

I look and see it there, shrinking, shrinking,
 I look back at it amid the rain
For the very last time; for my sand is sinking,
 And I shall traverse old love's domain
  Never again.

710 *The Phantom Horsewoman*

QUEER are the ways of a man I know:
    He comes and stands
    In a careworn craze,
    And looks at the sands
    And the seaward haze
    With moveless hands
    And face and gaze,
    Then turns to go . . .
And what does he see when he gazes so?

They say he sees as an instant thing
    More clear than to-day,
    A sweet soft scene
    That was once in play
    By that briny green;
    Yes, notes alway
    Warm, real, and keen,
    What his back years bring—
A phantom of his own figuring.

Of this vision of his they might say more:
    Not only there
    Does he see this sight,
    But everywhere
    In his brain—day, night,
    As if on the air
    It were drawn rose-bright—
    Yea, far from that shore
Does he carry this vision of heretofore:

A ghost-girl-rider. And though, toil-tried
    He withers daily,
    Time touches her not,
    But she still rides gaily
    In his rapt thought
    On that shagged and shaly
    Atlantic spot,
    And as when first eyed
Draws rein and sings to the swing of the tide.

711   *The Oxen*

CHRISTMAS EVE, and twelve of the clock.
    'Now they are all on their knees,'
An elder said as we sat in a flock
    By the embers in hearthside ease.

We pictured the meek mild creatures where
    They dwelt in their strawy pen,
Nor did it occur to one of us there
    To doubt they were kneeling then.

So fair a fancy few would weave
    In these years! Yet, I feel,
If someone said on Christmas Eve,
    'Come; see the oxen kneel,

'In the lonely barton by yonder coomb
    Our childhood used to know,'
I should go with him in the gloom,
    Hoping it might be so.

712   *Great Things*

SWEET cyder is a great thing,
    A great thing to me,
Spinning down to Weymouth town
    By Ridgway thirstily,
And maid and mistress summoning
    Who tend the hostelry:
O cyder is a great thing,
    A great thing to me!

The dance it is a great thing,
    A great thing to me,
With candles lit and partners fit
    For night-long revelry;
And going home when day-dawning
    Peeps pale upon the lea:
O dancing is a great thing,
    A great thing to me!

Love is, yea, a great thing,
  A great thing to me,
When, having drawn across the lawn
  In darkness silently,
A figure flits like one a-wing
  Out from the nearest tree:
O love is, yes, a great thing,
  A great thing to me!

Will these be always great things,
  Great things to me? . . .
Let it befall that One will call,
  'Soul, I have need of thee':
What then? Joy-jaunts, impassioned flings
  Love, and its ecstasy,
Will always have been great things,
  Great things to me!

713   *Midnight on the Great Western*

In the third-class seat sat the journeying boy,
  And the roof-lamp's oily flame
Played down on his listless form and face,
Bewrapt past knowing to what he was going,
  Or whence he came.

In the band of his hat the journeying boy
  Had a ticket stuck; and a string
Around his neck bore the key of his box,
That twinkled gleams of the lamp's sad beams
  Like a living thing.

What past can be yours, O journeying boy
  Towards a world unknown,
Who calmly, as if incurious quite
On all at stake, can undertake
  This plunge alone?

Knows your soul a sphere, O journeying boy
  Our rude realms far above,
Whence with spacious vision you mark and mete
This region of sin that you find you in
  But are not of?

714 *In Time of 'The Breaking of Nations'*

ONLY a man harrowing clods
　In a slow silent walk
With an old horse that stumbles and nods
　Half asleep as they stalk.

Only thin smoke without flame
　From the heaps of couch-grass;
Yet this will go onward the same
　Though Dynasties pass.

Yonder a maid and her wight
　Come whispering by:
War's annals will cloud into night
　Ere their story die.

715 *Afterwards*

WHEN the Present has latched its postern behind my tremulous stay,
　And the May month flaps its glad green leaves like wings,
Delicate-filmed as new-spun silk, will the neighbours say,
　'He was a man who used to notice such things'?

If it be in the dusk when, like an eyelid's soundless blink,
　The dewfall-hawk comes crossing the shades to alight
Upon the wind-warped upland thorn, a gazer may think,
　'To him this must have been a familiar sight.'

If I pass during some nocturnal blackness, mothy and warm,
　When the hedgehog travels furtively over the lawn,
One may say, 'He strove that such innocent creatures should come to
　　no harm,
　But he could do little for them; and now he is gone.'

If, when hearing that I have been stilled at last, they stand at the door,
　Watching the full-starred heavens that winter sees,
Will this thought rise on those who will meet my face no more,
　'He was one who had an eye for such mysteries'?

And will any say when my bell of quittance is heard in the gloom,
  And a crossing breeze cuts a pause in its outrollings,
Till they rise again, as they were a new bell's boom,
  'He hears it not now, but used to notice such things'?

ROBERT BRIDGES

1844–1930

716 *London Snow*

WHEN men were all asleep the snow came flying,
In large white flakes falling on the city brown,
Stealthily and perpetually settling and loosely lying,
  Hushing the latest traffic of the drowsy town;
Deadening, muffling, stifling its murmurs failing;
Lazily and incessantly floating down and down:
  Silently sifting and veiling road, roof and railing;
Hiding difference, making unevenness even,
Into angles and crevices softly drifting and sailing.
  All night it fell, and when·full inches seven
It lay in the depth of its uncompacted lightness,
The clouds blew off from a high and frosty heaven;
  And all woke earlier for the unaccustomed brightness
Of the winter dawning, the strange unheavenly glare:
The eye marvelled—marvelled at the dazzling whiteness;
  The ear hearkened to the stillness of the solemn air;
No sound of wheel rumbling nor of foot falling,
And the busy morning cries came thin and spare.
  Then boys I heard, as they went to school, calling,
They gathered up the crystal manna to freeze
Their tongues with tasting, their hands with snowballing;
  Or rioted in a drift, plunging up to the knees;
Or peering up from under the white-mossed wonder,
'O look at the trees!' they cried, 'O look at the trees!'
  With lessened load a few carts creak and blunder,
Following along the white deserted way,
A country company long dispersed asunder:
  When now already the sun, in pale display
Standing by Paul's high dome, spread forth below
His sparkling beams, and awoke the stir of the day.

For now doors open, and war is waged with the snow;
   And trains of sombre men, past tale of number,
      Tread long brown paths, as toward their toil they go:
    But even for them awhile no cares encumber
   Their minds diverted; the daily word is unspoken,
      The daily thoughts of labour and sorrow slumber
   At the sight of the beauty that greets them, for the charm
      they have broken.

717   *On a Dead Child*

PERFECT little body, without fault or stain on thee,
   With promise of strength and manhood full and fair!
      Though cold and stark and bare,
The bloom and the charm of life doth awhile remain on thee.

Thy mother's treasure wert thou;—alas! no longer
   To visit her heart with wondrous joy; to be
      Thy father's pride;—ah, he
Must gather his faith together, and his strength make stronger.

To me, as I move thee now in the last duty,
   Dost thou with a turn or gesture anon respond;
      Startling my fancy fond
With a chance attitude of the head, a freak of beauty.

Thy hand clasps, as 'twas wont, my finger, and holds it:
   But the grasp is the clasp of Death, heartbreaking and stiff;
      Yet feels to my hand as if
'Twas still thy will, thy pleasure and trust that enfolds it.

So I lay thee there, thy sunken eyelids closing,—
   Go lie thou there in thy coffin, thy last little bed!—
      Propping thy wise, sad head,
Thy firm, pale hands across thy chest disposing.

So quiet! doth the change content thee?—Death, whither hath he
      taken thee?
   To a world, do I think, that rights the disaster of this?
      The vision of which I miss,
Who weep for the body, and wish but to warm thee and awaken thee?

Ah! little at best can all our hopes avail us
　　To lift this sorrow, or cheer us, when in the dark,
　　　　Unwilling, alone we embark,
And the things we have seen and have known and have heard of, fail us.

718

AWAKE, my heart, to be loved, awake, awake!
The darkness silvers away, the morn doth break,
It leaps in the sky: unrisen lustres slake
The o'ertaken moon. Awake, O heart, awake!

She too that loveth awaketh and hopes for thee;
Her eyes already have sped the shades that flee,
Already they watch the path thy feet shall take:
Awake, O heart, to be loved, awake, awake!

And if thou tarry from her,—if this could be,—
She cometh herself, O heart, to be loved, to thee;
For thee would unashamèd herself forsake:
Awake to be loved, my heart, awake, awake!

Awake, the land is scattered with light, and see,
Uncanopied sleep is flying from field and tree:
And blossoming boughs of April in laughter shake;
Awake, O heart, to be loved, awake, awake!

Lo all things wake and tarry and look for thee:
She looketh and saith, 'O sun, now bring him to me.
Come more adored, O adored, for his coming's sake,
And awake my heart to be loved: awake, awake!'

719　　　　*Nightingales*

BEAUTIFUL must be the mountains whence ye come,
　And bright in the fruitful valleys the streams, wherefrom
　　　Ye learn your song:
Where are those starry woods? O might I wander there,
　Among the flowers, which in that heavenly air
　　　Bloom the year long!

774

Nay, barren are those mountains and spent the streams:
Our song is the voice of desire, that haunts our dreams,
      A throe of the heart,
Whose pining visions dim, forbidden hopes profound,
  No dying cadence nor long sigh can sound,
      For all our art.

Alone, aloud in the raptured ear of men
  We pour our dark nocturnal secret; and then,
      As night is withdrawn
From these sweet-springing meads and bursting boughs of May,
  Dream, while the innumerable choir of day
      Welcome the dawn.

720

    MY delight and thy delight
    Walking, like two angels white,
    In the gardens of the night:

    My desire and thy desire
    Twining to a tongue of fire,
    Leaping live, and laughing higher;
    Thro' the everlasting strife
    In the mystery of life.

    Love, from whom the world begun,
    Hath the secret of the sun.

    Love can tell, and love alone,
    Whence the million stars were strewn,
    Why each atom knows its own,
    How, in spite of woe and death,
    Gay is life, and sweet is breath:

    This he taught us, this we knew,
    Happy in his science true,
    Hand in hand as we stood
    Neath the shadows of the wood.
    Heart to heart as we lay
    In the dawning of the day.

721   *Eros*

WHY hast thou nothing in thy face?
Thou idol of the human race,
Thou tyrant of the human heart,
The flower of lovely youth that art;
Yea, and that standest in thy youth
An image of eternal Truth,
With thy exuberant flesh so fair,
That only Pheidias might compare,
Ere from his chaste marmoreal form
Time had decayed the colours warm;
Like to his gods in thy proud dress,
Thy starry sheen of nakedness.

   Surely thy body is thy mind,
For in thy face is nought to find,
Only thy soft unchristened smile,
That shadows neither love nor guile,
But shameless will and power immense,
In secret sensuous innocence.

   O king of joy, what is thy thought?
I dream thou knowest it is nought,
And wouldst in darkness come, but thou
Makest the light where'er thou go.
Ah yet no victim of thy grace,
None who e'er longed for thy embrace,
Hath cared to look upon thy face.

GERARD MANLEY HOPKINS
1844–1889

722   *Heaven-Haven*

                    A nun takes the veil

I HAVE desired to go
     Where springs not fail,
To fields where flies no sharp and sided hail
     And a few lilies blow.

And I have asked to be
Where no storms come,
Where the green swell is in the havens dumb,
And out of the swing of the sea.

723 *The Wreck of the Deutschland*

To the
happy memory of five Franciscan nuns
exiles by the Falck Laws
drowned between midnight and morning of
Dec. 7th, 1875

PART THE FIRST

I

THOU mastering me
God! giver of breath and bread;
World's strand, sway of the sea;
Lord of living and dead;
Thou hast bound bones and veins in me, fastened me flesh,
And after it almost unmade, what with dread,
Thy doing: and dost thou touch me afresh?
Over again I feel thy finger and find thee.

2

I did say yes
O at lightning and lashed rod;
Thou heardst me truer than tongue confess
Thy terror, O Christ, O God;
Thou knowest the walls, altar and hour and night:
The swoon of a heart that the sweep and the hurl of thee trod
Hard down with a horror of height:
And the midriff astrain with leaning of, laced with fire of stress.

3

The frown of his face
Before me, the hurtle of hell
Behind, where, where was a, where was a place?
I whirled out wings that spell
And fled with a fling of the heart to the heart of the Host.
My heart, but you were dovewinged, I can tell,
Carrier-witted, I am bold to boast,
To flash from the flame to the flame then, tower from the grace to the
grace.

777

4

I am soft sift
In an hourglass—at the wall
Fast, but mined with a motion, a drift,
And it crowds and it combs to the fall;
I steady as a water in a well, to a poise, to a pane,
But roped with, always, all the way down from the tall
Fells or flanks of the voel, a vein
Of the gospel proffer, a pressure, a principle, Christ's gift.

5

I kiss my hand
To the stars, lovely-asunder
Starlight, wafting him out of it; and
Glow, glory in thunder;
Kiss my hand to the dappled-with-damson west:
Since, tho' he is under the world's splendour and wonder,
His mystery must be instressed, stressed;
For I greet him the days I meet him, and bless when I understand.

6

Not out of his bliss
Springs the stress felt
Nor first from heaven (and few know this)
Swings the stroke dealt—
Stroke and a stress that stars and storms deliver,
That guilt is hushed by, hearts are flushed by and melt—
But it rides time like riding a river
(And here the faithful waver, the faithless fable and miss).

7

It dates from day
Of his going in Galilee;
Warm-laid grave of a womb-life grey;
Manger, maiden's knee;
The dense and the driven Passion, and frightful sweat:
Thence the discharge of it, there its swelling to be,
Though felt before, though in high flood yet—
What none would have known of it, only the heart, being hard at bay,

8

Is out with it! Oh,
We lash with the best or worst
Word last! How a lush-kept plush-capped sloe
Will, mouthed to flesh-burst,
Gush!—flush the man, the being with it, sour or sweet,
Brim, in a flash, full!—Hither then, last or first,
To hero of Calvary, Christ's feet—
Never ask if meaning it, wanting it, warned of it—men go.

9

Be adored among men,
God, three-numberèd form;
Wring thy rebel, dogged in den,
Man's malice, with wrecking and storm.
Beyond saying sweet, past telling of tongue,
Thou art lightning and love, I found it, a winter and warm;
Father and fondler of heart thou hast wrung:
Hast thy dark descending and most art merciful then.

10

With an anvil-ding
And with fire in him forge thy will
Or rather, rather then, stealing as Spring
Through him, melt him but master him still:
Whether at once, as once at a crash Paul,
Or as Austin, a lingering-out swéet skíll,
Make mercy in all of us, out of us all
Mastery, but be adored, but be adored King.

11

'Some find me a sword; some
The flange and the rail; flame,
Fang, or flood' goes Death on drum,
And storms bugle his fame.
But wé dream we are rooted in earth—Dust!
Flesh falls within sight of us, we, though our flower the same,
Wave with the meadow, forget that there must
The sour scythe cringe, and the blear share come.

12

On Saturday sailed from Bremen,
American-outward-bound,
Take settler and seamen, tell men with women,
Two hundred souls in the round—
O Father, not under thy feathers nor ever as guessing
The goal was a shoal, of a fourth the doom to be drowned;
Yet did the dark side of the bay of thy blessing
Not vault them, the million of rounds of thy mercy not reeve even
them in?

13

Into the snows she sweeps,
Hurling the haven behind,
The Deutschland, on Sunday; and so the sky keeps,
For the infinite air is unkind,
And the sea flint-flake, black-backed in the regular blow,
Sitting Eastnortheast, in cursed quarter, the wind;
Wiry and white-fiery and whirlwind-swivellèd snow
Spins to the widow-making unchilding unfathering deeps.

14

She drove in the dark to leeward,
She struck—not a reef or a rock
But the combs of a smother of sand: night drew her
Dead to the Kentish Knock;
And she beat the bank down with her bows and the ride of her
keel:
The breakers rolled on her beam with ruinous shock;
And canvas and compass, the whorl and the wheel
Idle for ever to waft her or wind her with, these she endured.

15

Hope had grown grey hairs,
Hope had mourning on,
Trenched with tears, carved with cares,
Hope was twelve hours gone;
And frightful a nightfall folded rueful a day
Nor rescue, only rocket and lightship, shone,
And lives at last were washing away:
To the shrouds they took,—they shook in the hurling and horrible airs.

16

One stirred from the rigging to save
The wild woman-kind below,
With a rope's end round the man, handy and brave—
He was pitched to his death at a blow,
For all his dreadnought breast and braids of thew:
They could tell him for hours, dandled the to and fro
Through the cobbled foam-fleece. What could he do
With the burl of the fountains of air, buck and the flood of the wave?

17

They fought with God's cold—
And they could not and fell to the deck
(Crushed them) or water (and drowned them) or rolled
With the sea-romp over the wreck.
Night roared, with the heart-break hearing a heart-broke rabble,
The woman's wailing, the crying of child without check—
Till a lioness arose breasting the babble,
A prophetess towered in the tumult, a virginal tongue told.

18

Ah, touched in your bower of bone,
Are you! turned for an exquisite smart,
Have you! make words break from me here all alone,
Do you!—mother of being in me, heart.
O unteachably after evil, but uttering truth,
Why, tears! is it? tears; such a melting, a madrigal start!
Never-eldering revel and river of youth,
What can it be, this glee? the good you have there of your own?

19

Sister, a sister calling
A master, her master and mine!—
And the inboard seas run swirling and hawling;
The rash smart sloggering brine
Blinds her; but she that weather sees one thing, one;
Has one fetch in her: she rears herself to divine
Ears, and the call of the tall nun
To the men in the tops and the tackle rode over the storm's brawling.

20

She was first of a five and came
Of a coifèd sisterhood.
(O Deutschland, double a desperate name!
O world wide of its good!
But Gertrude, lily, and Luther, are two of a town,
Christ's lily and beast of the waste wood:
From life's dawn it is drawn down,
Abel is Cain's brother and breasts they have sucked the same.)

21

Loathed for a love men knew in them,
Banned by the land of their birth,
Rhine refused them, Thames would ruin them;
Surf, snow, river and earth
Gnashed: but thou art above, thou Orion of light;
Thy unchancelling poising palms were weighing the worth,
Thou martyr-master: in thy sight
Storm flakes were scroll-leaved flowers, lily showers—sweet heaven
was astrew in them.

22

Five! the finding and sake
And cipher of suffering Christ.
Mark, the mark is of man's make
And the word of it Sacrificed.
But he scores it in scarlet himself on his own bespoken,
Before-time-taken, dearest prizèd and priced—
Stigma, signal, cinquefoil token
For lettering of the lamb's fleece, ruddying of the rose-flake.

23

Joy fall to thee, father Francis,
Drawn to the Life that died;
With the gnarls of the nails in thee, niche of the lance, his
Lovescape crucified
And seal of his seraph-arrival! and these thy daughters
And five-livèd and leavèd favour and pride,
Are sisterly sealed in wild waters,
To bathe in his fall-gold mercies, to breathe in his all-fire glances.

24

Away in the loveable west,
On a pastoral forehead of Wales,
I was under a roof here, I was at rest,
And they the prey of the gales;
She to the black-about air, to the breaker, the thickly
Falling flakes, to the throng that catches and quails
Was calling 'O Christ, Christ, come quickly':
The cross to her she calls Christ to her, christens her wild-worst Best.

25

The majesty! what did she mean?
Breathe, arch and original Breath.
Is it love in her of the being as her lover had been?
Breathe, body of lovely Death.
They were else-minded then, altogether, the men
Woke thee with a *We are perishing* in the weather of Gennesareth.
Or is it that she cried for the crown then,
The keener to come at the comfort for feeling the combating keen?

26

For how to the heart's cheering
The down-dugged ground-hugged grey
Hovers off, the jay-blue heavens appearing
Of pied and peeled May!
Blue-beating and hoary-glow height; or night, still higher,
With belled fire and the moth-soft Milky Way,
What by your measure is the heaven of desire,
The treasure never eyesight got, nor was ever guessed what for the
hearing?

27

No, but it was not these.
The jading and jar of the cart,
Time's tasking, it is fathers that asking for ease
Of the sodden-with-its-sorrowing heart,
Not danger, electrical horror; then further it finds
The appealing of the Passion is tenderer in prayer apart:
Other, I gather, in measure her mind's
Burden, in wind's burly and beat of endragonèd seas.

28

But how shall I . . . make me room there:
Reach me a . . . Fancy, come faster—
Strike you the sight of it? look at it loom there,
Thing that she . . . There then! the Master,
Ipse, the only one, Christ, King, Head:
He was to cure the extremity where he had cast her;
Do, deal, lord it with living and dead;
Let him ride, her pride, in his triumph, despatch and have done with
his doom there.

29

Ah! there was a heart right!
There was single eye!
Read the unshapeable shock night
And knew the who and the why;
Wording it how but by him that present and past,
Heaven and earth are word of, worded by?—
The Simon Peter of a soul! to the blast
Tarpeïan-fast, but a blown beacon of light.

30

Jesu, heart's light,
Jesu, maid's son,
What was the feast followed the night
Thou hadst glory of this nun?—
Feast of the one woman without stain.
For so conceivèd, so to conceive thee is done;
But here was heart-throe, birth of a brain,
Word, that heard and kept thee and uttered thee outright.

31

Well, she has thee for the pain, for the
Patience; but pity of the rest of them!
Heart, go and bleed at a bitterer vein for the
Comfortless unconfessed of them—
No not uncomforted: lovely-felicitous Providence
Finger of a tender of, O of a feathery delicacy, the breast of the
Maiden could obey so, be a bell to, ring of it, and
Startle the poor sheep back! is the shipwrack then a harvest, does
tempest carry the grain for thee?

32

I admire thee, master of the tides,
　　Of the Yore-flood, of the year's fall;
The recurb and the recovery of the gulf's sides,
　　The girth of it and the wharf of it and the wall;
Stanching, quenching ocean of a motionable mind;
Ground of being, and granite of it: past all
　　Grasp God, throned behind
Death with a sovereignty that heeds but hides, bodes but abides;

33

With a mercy that outrides
　　The all of water, an ark
For the listener; for the lingerer with a love glides
　　Lower than death and the dark;
A vein for the visiting of the past-prayer, pent in prison,
The-last-breath penitent spirits—the uttermost mark
　　Our passion-plungèd giant risen,
The Christ of the Father compassionate, fetched in the storm of his
　　strides.

34

Now burn, new born to the world,
　　Double-naturèd name,
The heaven-flung, heart-fleshed, maiden-furled
　　Miracle-in-Mary-of-flame,
Mid-numberèd he in three of the thunder-throne!
Not a dooms-day dazzle in his coming nor dark as he came;
　　Kind, but royally reclaiming his own;
A released shower, let flash to the shire, not a lightning of fire hard-
　　hurled.

35

Dame, at our door
　　Drowned, and among our shoals,
Remember us in the roads, the heaven-haven of the reward:
　　Our King back, Oh, upon English souls!
Let him easter in us, be a dayspring to the dimness of us, be a
　　crimson-cresseted east,
More brightening her, rare-dear Britain, as his reign rolls,
　　Pride, rose, prince, hero of us, high-priest,
Our hearts' charity's hearth's fire, our thoughts' chivalry's throng's
　　Lord.

724 *God's Grandeur*

THE world is charged with the grandeur of God.
　It will flame out, like shining from shook foil;
　It gathers to a greatness, like the ooze of oil
Crushed. Why do men then now not reck his rod?
Generations have trod, have trod, have trod;
　And all is seared with trade; bleared, smeared with toil;
　And wears man's smudge and shares man's smell: the soil
Is bare now, nor can foot feel, being shod.

And for all this, nature is never spent;
　There lives the dearest freshness deep down things;
And though the last lights off the black West went
　Oh, morning, at the brown brink eastward, springs—
Because the Holy Ghost over the bent
　World broods with warm breast and with ah! bright wings.

725 *Spring*

NOTHING is so beautiful as Spring—
　When weeds, in wheels, shoot long and lovely and lush;
　Thrush's eggs look little low heavens, and thrush
Through the echoing timber does so rinse and wring
The ear, it strikes like lightnings to hear him sing;
　The glassy peartree leaves and blooms, they brush
　The descending blue; that blue is all in a rush
With richness; the racing lambs too have fair their fling.

What is all this juice and all this joy?
　A strain of the earth's sweet being in the beginning
In Eden garden.—Have, get, before it cloy,

　Before it cloud, Christ, lord, and sour with sinning,
Innocent mind and Mayday in girl and boy,
　Most, O maid's child, thy choice and worthy the winning.

726   *The Windhover*

                    To Christ our Lord

I CAUGHT this morning morning's minion, king-
  dom of daylight's dauphin, dapple-dawn-drawn Falcon, in his
    riding
Of the rolling level underneath him steady air, and striding
High there, how he rung upon the rein of a wimpling wing
In his ecstasy! then off, off forth on swing,
  As a skate's heel sweeps smooth on a bow-bend: the hurl and
    gliding
Rebuffed the big wind. My heart in hiding
Stirred for a bird,—the achieve of, the mastery of the thing!

Brute beauty and valour and act, oh, air, pride, plume, here
  Buckle! AND the fire that breaks from thee then, a billion
Times told lovelier, more dangerous, O my chevalier!

  No wonder of it: shéer plód makes plough down sillion
Shine, and blue-bleak embers, ah my dear,
  Fall, gall themselves, and gash gold-vermilion.

727   *Pied Beauty*

  GLORY be to God for dappled things—
    For skies of couple-colour as a brinded cow;
      For rose-moles all in stipple upon trout that swim;
  Fresh-firecoal chestnut-falls; finches' wings;
    Landscape plotted and pieced—fold, fallow, and plough;
      And áll trádes, their gear and tackle and trim.

  All things counter, original, spare, strange;
    Whatever is fickle, freckled (who knows how?)
      With swift, slow; sweet, sour; adazzle, dim;
  He fathers-forth whose beauty is past change:
                              Praise him.

728   *Felix Randal*

FELIX Randal the farrier, O is he dead then? my duty all ended,
Who have watched his mould of man, big-boned and hardy-handsome
Pining, pining, till time when reason rambled in it and some
Fatal four disorders, fleshed there, all contended?

Sickness broke him. Impatient, he cursed at first, but mended
Being anointed and all; though a heavenlier heart began some
Months earlier, since I had our sweet reprieve and ransom
Tendered to him. Ah well, God rest him all road ever he offended!

This seeing the sick endears them to us, us too it endears.
My tongue had taught thee comfort, touch had quenched thy tears,
Thy tears that touched my heart, child, Felix, poor Felix Randal;

How far from then forethought of, all thy more boisterous years,
When thou at the random grim forge, powerful amidst peers,
Didst fettle for the great grey drayhorse his bright and battering sandal!

729   *Spring and Fall*

                          to a young child

          MÁRGARÉT, áre you gríeving
          Over Goldengrove unleaving?
          Léaves, líke the things of man, you
          With your fresh thoughts care for, can you?
          Áh! ás the heart grows older
          It will come to such sights colder
          By and by, nor spare a sigh
          Though worlds of wanwood leafmeal lie,
          And yet you *will* weep and know why.
          Now no matter, child, the name:
          Sórrow's spríngs áre the same.
          Nor mouth had, no nor mind, expressed
          What heart heard of, ghost guessed:
          It ís the blight man was born for,
          It is Margaret you mourn for.

730   *'No Worst, there is None'*

No worst, there is none. Pitched past pitch of grief,
More pangs will, schooled at forepangs, wilder wring.
Comforter, where, where is your comforting?
Mary, mother of us, where is your relief?
My cries heave, herds-long; huddle in a main, a chief-
woe, world-sorrow; on an age-old anvil wince and sing—
Then lull, then leave off. Fury had shrieked 'No ling-
ering! Let me be fell: force I must be brief'.
O the mind, mind has mountains; cliffs of fall
Frightful, sheer, no-man-fathomed. Hold them cheap
May who ne'er hung there. Nor does long our small
Durance deal with that steep or deep. Here! creep,
Wretch, under a comfort serves in a whirlwind: all
Life death does end and each day dies with sleep.

731   *'I Wake and feel the Fell of Dark'*

I WAKE and feel the fell of dark, not day.
What hours, O what black hoürs we have spent
This night! what sights you, heart, saw; ways you went!
And more must, in yet longer light's delay.

With witness I speak this. But where I say
Hours I mean years, mean life. And my lament
Is cries countless, cries like dead letters sent
To dearest him that lives alas! away.

I am gall, I am heartburn. God's most deep decree
Bitter would have me taste: my taste was me;
Bones built in me, flesh filled, blood brimmed the curse.

Selfyeast of spirit a dull dough sours. I see
The lost are like this, and their scourge to be
As I am mine, their sweating selves; but worse.

732   *'Thou art indeed Just, Lord'*

THOU art indeed just, Lord, if I contend
With thee; but, sir, so what I plead is just.
Why do sinners' ways prosper? and why must
Disappointment all I endeavour end?

Wert thou my enemy, O thou my friend,
How wouldst thou worse, I wonder, than thou dost
Defeat, thwart me? Oh, the sots and thralls of lust
Do in spare hours more thrive than I that spend,

Sir, life upon thy cause. See, banks and brakes
Now, leavèd how thick! lacèd they are again
With fretty chervil, look, and fresh wind shakes

Them; birds build—but not I build; no, but strain,
Time's eunuch, and not breed one work that wakes.
Mine, O thou lord of life, send my roots rain.

ALICE MEYNELL

1847–1922

733   *Renouncement*

I MUST not think of thee; and, tired yet strong,
    I shun the thought that lurks in all delight—
    The thought of thee—and in the blue Heaven's height,
And in the sweetest passage of a song.
O just beyond the fairest thoughts that throng
    This breast, the thought of thee waits hidden yet bright;
    But it must never, never come in sight;
I must stop short of thee the whole day long.
But when sleep comes to close each difficult day,
    When night gives pause to the long watch I keep,
        And all my bonds I needs must loose apart,
Must doff my will as raiment laid away,—
    With the first dream that comes with the first sleep
        I run, I run, I am gathered to thy heart.

734   *Christ in the Universe*

WITH this ambiguous earth
His dealings have been told us. These abide:
The signal to a maid, the human birth,
The lesson, and the young Man crucified.

But not a star of all
The innumerable host of stars has heard
How he administered this terrestrial ball.
Our race have kept their Lord's entrusted Word.

Of his earth-visiting feet
None knows the secret, cherished, perilous
The terrible, shamefast, frightened, whispered, sweet,
Heart-shattering secret of his way with us.

No planet knows that this
Our wayside planet, carrying land and wave,
Love and life multiplied, and pain and bliss,
Bears, as chief treasure, one forsaken grave.

Nor, in our little day,
May his devices with the heavens be guessed,
His pilgrimage to thread the Milky Way,
Or his bestowals there be manifest.

But, in the eternities,
Doubtless we shall compare together, hear
A million alien Gospels, in what guise
He trod the Pleiades, the Lyre, the Bear.

O be prepared, my soul!
To read the inconceivable, to scan
The million forms of God those stars unroll
When, in our turn, we show to them a Man.

WILLIAM ERNEST HENLEY
1849–1903

735

OUT of the night that covers me,
　Black as the Pit from pole to pole,
I thank whatever gods may be
　For my unconquerable soul.

In the fell clutch of circumstance
　I have not winced nor cried aloud.
Under the bludgeonings of chance
　My head is bloody, but unbowed.

Beyond this place of wrath and tears
　Looms but the Horror of the shade,
And yet the menace of the years
　Finds, and shall find, me unafraid.

It matters not how strait the gate,
　How charged with punishments the scroll,
I am the master of my fate:
　I am the captain of my soul

736　　　　　*Margaritae Sorori, I.M.*

A LATE lark twitters from the quiet skies;
And from the west,
Where the sun, his day's work ended,
Lingers as in content
There falls on the old, gray city
An influence luminous and serene,
A shining peace.

The smoke ascends
In a rosy-and-golden haze. The spires
Shine, and are changed. In the valley
Shadows rise. The lark sings on. The sun,
Closing his benediction,

Sinks, and the darkening air
Thrills with a sense of the triumphing night—
Night with her train of stars
And her great gift of sleep.

So be my passing!
My task accomplished and the long day done,
My wages taken, and in my heart
Some late lark singing,
Let me be gathered to the quiet west,
The sundown splendid and serene,
Death.

ROBERT LOUIS STEVENSON

1850–1894

737   *The House Beautiful*

A naked house, a naked moor,
A shivering pool before the door,
A garden bare of flowers and fruit
And poplars at the garden foot:
Such is the place that I live in,
Bleak without and bare within.

Yet shall your ragged moor receive
The incomparable pomp of eve,
And the cold glories of the dawn
Behind your shivering trees be drawn;
And when the wind from place to place
Doth the unmoored cloud-galleons chase,
Your garden gloom and gleam again,
With leaping sun, with glancing rain.
Here shall the wizard moon ascend
The heavens, in the crimson end
Of day's declining splendour; here
The army of the stars appear.
The neighbour hollows dry or wet,
Spring shall with tender flowers beset;
And oft the morning muser see
Larks rising from the broomy lea,

And every fairy wheel and thread
Of cobweb dew-bediamonded.
When daisies go, shall winter time
Silver the simple grass with rime;
Autumnal frosts enchant the pool
And make the cart-ruts beautiful;
And when snow-bright the moor expands,
How shall your children clap their hands!
To make this earth, our hermitage,
A cheerful and a changeful page,
God's bright and intricate device
Of days and seasons doth suffice.

738   *Requiem*

UNDER the wide and starry sky,
Dig the grave and let me lie.
Glad did I live and gladly die,
    And I laid me down with a will.

This be the verse you grave for me:
Here he lies where he longed to be;
Home is the sailor, home from sea,
    And the hunter home from the hill.

739

SING me a song of a lad that is gone,
    Say, could that lad be I?
Merry of soul he sailed on a day
    Over the sea to Skye.

Mull was astern, Rum on the port,
    Eigg on the starboard bow;
Glory of youth glowed in his soul:
    Where is that glory now?

Sing me a song of a lad that is gone,
    Say, could that lad be I?
Merry of soul he sailed on a day
    Over the sea to Skye.

Give me again all that was there,
  Give me the sun that shone!
Give me the eyes, give me the soul,
  Give me the lad that's gone!

Sing me a song of a lad that is gone,
  Say, could that lad be I?
Merry of soul he sailed on a day
  Over the sea to Skye.

Billow and breeze, islands and seas,
  Mountains of rain and sun,
All that was good, all that was fair,
  All that was me is gone.

740   *To S. R. Crockett*

BLOWS the wind today, and the sun and the rain are flying,
  Blows the wind on the moors today and now,
Where about the graves of the martyrs the whaups are crying,
  My heart remembers how!

Grey recumbent tombs of the dead in desert places,
  Standing-stones on the vacant wine-red moor,
Hills of sheep, and the howes of the silent vanished races,
  And winds, austere and pure.

Be it granted me to behold you again in dying,
  Hills of home! and to hear again the call;
Hear about the graves of the martyrs the peewees crying,
  And hear no more at all.

OSCAR WILDE
1856–1900

741   *from* The Ballad of Reading Gaol

HE did not wear his scarlet coat,
  For blood and wine are red,
And blood and wine were on his hands
  When they found him with the dead,
The poor dead woman whom he loved,
  And murdered in her bed.

He walked amongst the Trial Men
  In a suit of shabby grey;
A cricket cap was on his head,
  And his step seemed light and gay;
But I never saw a man who looked
  So wistfully at the day.

I never saw a man who looked
  With such a wistful eye
Upon that little tent of blue
  Which prisoners call the sky,
And at every drifting cloud that went
  With sails of silver by.

I walked, with other souls in pain,
  Within another ring,
And was wondering if the man had done
  A great or little thing,
When a voice behind me whispered low,
  'That fellow's got to swing.'

Dear Christ! the very prison walls
  Suddenly seemed to reel,
And the sky above my head became
  Like a casque of scorching steel;
And, though I was a soul in pain,
  My pain I could not feel.

I only knew what hunted thought
 Quickened his step, and why
He looked upon the garish day
 With such a wistful eye;
The man had killed the thing he loved,
 And so he had to die.

*

Yet each man kills the thing he loves,
 By each let this be heard,
Some do it with a bitter look,
 Some with a flattering word,
The coward does it with a kiss,
 The brave man with a sword!

Some kill their love when they are young,
 And some when they are old;
Some strangle with the hands of Lust,
 Some with the hands of Gold:
The kindest use a knife, because
 The dead so soon grow cold.

Some love too little, some too long,
 Some sell, and others buy;
Some do the deed with many tears,
 And some without a sigh:
For each man kills the thing he loves,
 Yet each man does not die.

He does not die a death of shame
 On a day of dark disgrace,
Nor have a noose about his neck,
 Nor a cloth upon his face,
Nor drop feet foremost through the floor
 Into an empty space.

742   *Theocritus*

A Villanelle

O SINGER of Persephone!
 In the dim meadows desolate
Dost thou remember Sicily?

Still through the ivy flits the bee
  Where Amaryllis lies in state;
O Singer of Persephone!

Simaetha calls on Hecate
  And hears the wild dogs at the gate;
Dost thou remember Sicily?

Still by the light and laughing sea
  Poor Polypheme bemoans his fate;
O Singer of Persephone!

And still in boyish rivalry
  Young Daphnis challenges his mate;
Dost thou remember Sicily?

Slim Lacon keeps a goat for thee,
  For thee the jocund shepherds wait;
O Singer of Persephone!
Dost thou remember Sicily?

JOHN DAVIDSON

1857–1909

743 *London*

ATHWART the sky a lowly sigh
From west to east the sweet wind carried;
The sun stood still on Primrose Hill;
  His light in all the city tarried:
The clouds on viewless columns bloomed
Like smouldering lilies unconsumed.

'Oh sweetheart, see! how shadowy,
  Of some occult magician's rearing,
Or swung in space of heaven's grace
  Dissolving, dimly reappearing,
Afloat upon ethereal tides
St Paul's above the city rides!'

A rumour broke through the thin smoke
　　Enwreathing abbey, tower, and palace,
The parks, the squares, the thoroughfares,
　　The million-peopled lanes and alleys,
An ever-muttering prisoned storm,
The heart of London beating warm.

744　　　　　*Thirty Bob a Week*

I COULDN'T touch a stop and turn a screw,
　　And set the blooming world a-work for me,
Like such as cut their teeth—I hope, like you—
　　On the handle of a skeleton gold key;
I cut mine on a leek, which I eat it every week:
　　I'm a clerk at thirty bob as you can see.

But I don't allow it's luck and all a toss;
　　There's no such thing as being starred and crossed;
It's just the power of some to be a boss,
　　And the bally power of others to be bossed:
I face the music, sir; you bet I ain't a cur;
　　Strike me lucky if I don't believe I'm lost!

For like a mole I journey in the dark,
　　A-travelling along the underground
From my Pillar'd Halls and broad Suburbean Park,
　　To come the daily dull official round;
And home again at night with my pipe all alight,
　　A-scheming how to count ten bob a pound.

And it's often very cold and very wet,
　　And my missis stitches towels for a hunks;
And the Pillar'd Halls is half of it to let—
　　Three rooms about the size of travelling trunks.
And we cough, my wife and I, to dislocate a sigh,
　　When the noisy little kids are in their bunks.

But you never hear her do a growl or whine,
　　For she's made of flint and roses, very odd;
And I've got to cut my meaning rather fine,
　　Or I'd blubber, for I'm made of greens and sod:
So p'r'aps we are in Hell for all that I can tell,
　　And lost and damn'd and served up hot to God.

I ain't blaspheming, Mr Silver-tongue;
　　I'm saying things a bit beyond your art:
Of all the rummy starts you ever sprung,
　　Thirty bob a week's the rummiest start!
With your science and your books and your the'ries about spooks,
　　Did you ever hear of looking in your heart?

I didn't mean your pocket, Mr, no:
　　I mean that having children and a wife,
With thirty bob on which to come and go,
　　Isn't dancing to the tabor and the fife:
When it doesn't make you drink, by Heaven! it makes you think,
　　And notice curious items about life.

I step into my heart and there I meet
　　A god-almighty devil singing small,
Who would like to shout and whistle in the street,
　　And squelch the passers flat against the wall;
If the whole world was a cake he had the power to take,
　　He would take it, ask for more, and eat it all.

And I meet a sort of simpleton beside,
　　The kind that life is always giving beans;
With thirty bob a week to keep a bride
　　He fell in love and married in his teens:
At thirty bob he stuck; but he knows it isn't luck:
　　He knows the seas are deeper than tureens.

And the god-almighty devil and the fool
　　That meet me in the High Street on the strike,
When I walk about my heart a-gathering wool,
　　Are my good and evil angels if you like.
And both of them together in every kind of weather
　　Ride me like a double-seated bike.

That's rough a bit and needs its meaning curled.
　　But I have a high old hot un in my mind—
A most engrugious notion of the world,
　　That leaves your lightning 'rithmetic behind—
I give it at a glance when I say 'There ain't no chance,
　　Nor nothing of the lucky-lottery kind.'

And it's this way that I make it out to be:
  No fathers, mothers, countries, climates—none;
Not Adam was responsible for me,
  Nor society, nor systems, nary one:
A little sleeping seed, I woke—I did, indeed—
  A million years before the blooming sun.

I woke because I thought the time had come;
  Beyond my will there was no other cause;
And everywhere I found myself at home,
  Because I chose to be the thing I was;
And in whatever shape of mollusc or of ape
  I always went according to the laws.

I was the love that chose my mother out;
  I joined two lives and from the union burst;
My weakness and my strength without a doubt
  Are mine alone for ever from the first:
It's just the very same with a difference in the name
  As 'Thy will be done.' You say it if you durst!

They say it daily up and down the land
  As easy as you take a drink, it's true;
But the difficultest go to understand,
  And the difficultest job a man can do,
Is to come it brave and meek with thirty bob a week,
  And feel that that's the proper thing for you.

It's a naked child against a hungry wolf;
  It's playing bowls upon a splitting wreck;
It's walking on a string across a gulf
  With millstones fore-and-aft about your neck;
But the thing is daily done by many and many a one;
  And we fall, face forward, fighting, on the deck.

FRANCIS THOMPSON
1859–1907

745   *In No Strange Land*

O WORLD invisible, we view thee,
O world intangible, we touch thee,
O world unknowable, we know thee,
Inapprehensible, we clutch thee!

Does the fish soar to find the ocean,
The eagle plunge to find the air—
That we ask of the stars in motion
If they have rumour of thee there?

Not where the wheeling systems darken,
And our benumbed conceiving soars!—
The drift of pinions, would we hearken,
Beats at our own clay-shuttered doors.

The angels keep their ancient places;—
Turn but a stone, and start a wing!
'Tis ye, 'tis your estrangèd faces,
That miss the many-splendoured thing.

But (when so sad thou canst not sadder)
Cry;—and upon thy so sore loss
Shall shine the traffic of Jacob's ladder
Pitched betwixt Heaven and Charing Cross.

Yea, in the night, my Soul, my daughter,
Cry,—clinging Heaven by the hems;
And lo, Christ walking on the water,
Not of Gennesareth, but Thames!

ALFRED EDWARD HOUSMAN
1859–1936

746

ON Wenlock Edge the wood's in trouble;
   His forest fleece the Wrekin heaves;
The gale, it plies the saplings double,
   And thick on Severn snow the leaves.

'Twould blow like this through holt and hanger
   When Uricon the city stood:
'Tis the old wind in the old anger,
   But then it threshed another wood.

Then, 'twas before my time, the Roman
   At yonder heaving hill would stare:
The blood that warms an English yeoman,
   The thoughts that hurt him, they were there.

There, like the wind through woods in riot,
   Through him the gale of life blew high;
The tree of man was never quiet:
   Then 'twas the Roman, now 'tis I.

The gale, it plies the saplings double,
   It blows so hard, 'twill soon be gone:
To-day the Roman and his trouble
   Are ashes under Uricon.

747

ON the idle hill of summer,
   Sleepy with the flow of streams,
Far I hear the steady drummer
   Drumming like a noise in dreams.

Far and near and low and louder
   On the roads of earth go by,
Dear to friends and food for powder,
   Soldiers marching, all to die.

East and west on fields forgotten
　　Bleach the bones of comrades slain,
Lovely lads and dead and rotten;
　　None that go return again.

Far the calling bugles hollo,
　　High the screaming fife replies,
Gay the files of scarlet follow:
　　Woman bore me, I will rise.

748

INTO my heart an air that kills
　　From yon far country blows:
What are those blue remembered hills,
　　What spires, what farms are those?

That is the land of lost content,
　　I see it shining plain,
The happy highways where I went
　　And cannot come again.

749

HER strong enchantments failing,
　　Her towers of fear in wreck,
Her limbecks dried of poisons
　　And the knife at her neck,

The Queen of air and darkness
　　Begins to shrill and cry,
'O young man, O my slayer,
　　To-morrow you shall die.'

O Queen of air and darkness,
　　I think 'tis truth you say,
And I shall die to-morrow;
　　But you will die to-day.

750 *Epitaph on an Army of Mercenaries*

THESE, in the day when heaven was falling,
 The hour when earth's foundations fled,
Followed their mercenary calling
 And took their wages and are dead.

Their shoulders held the sky suspended;
 They stood, and earth's foundations stay;
What God abandoned, these defended,
 And saved the sum of things for pay.

751

TELL me not here, it needs not saying,
 What tune the enchantress plays
In aftermaths of soft September
 Or under blanching mays,
For she and I were long acquainted
 And I knew all her ways.

On russet floors, by waters idle,
 The pine lets fall its cone;
The cuckoo shouts all day at nothing
 In leafy dells alone;
And traveller's joy beguiles in autumn
 Hearts that have lost their own.

On acres of the seeded grasses
 The changing burnish heaves;
Or marshalled under moons of harvest
 Stand still all night the sheaves;
Or beeches strip in storms for winter
 And stain the wind with leaves.

Possess, as I possessed a season,
 The countries I resign,
Where over elmy plains the highway
 Would mount the hills and shine,
And full of shade the pillared forest
 Would murmur and be mine.

For nature, heartless, witless nature,
  Will neither care nor know
What stranger's feet may find the meadow
  And trespass there and go,
Nor ask amid the dews of morning
  If they are mine or no.

752

CROSSING alone the nighted ferry
  With the one coin for fee,
Whom, on the wharf of Lethe waiting,
  Count you to find? Not me.

The brisk fond lackey to fetch and carry,
  The true, sick-hearted slave,
Expect him not in the just city
  And free land of the grave.

753 *Parta Quies*

GOOD-NIGHT; ensured release,
Imperishable peace,
    Have these for yours,
While sea abides, and land,
And earth's foundations stand,
    And heaven endures.

When earth's foundations flee,
Nor sky nor land nor sea
    At all is found,
Content you, let them burn:
It is not your concern;
    Sleep on, sleep sound.

ERNEST DOWSON

1867–1900

754 *Non sum qualis eram bonae sub regno Cynarae*

LAST night, ah, yesternight, betwixt her lips and mine
There fell thy shadow, Cynara! thy breath was shed
Upon my soul between the kisses and the wine;
And I was desolate and sick of an old passion,·
    Yea, I was desolate and bowed my head:
I have been faithful to thee, Cynara! in my fashion.

All night upon mine heart I felt her warm heart beat,
Night-long within mine arms in love and sleep she lay;
Surely the kisses of her bought red mouth were sweet;
But I was desolate and sick of an old passion,
    When I awoke and found the dawn was gray: .
I have been faithful to thee, Cynara! in my fashion.

I have forgot much, Cynara! gone with the wind,
Flung roses, roses riotously with the throng,
Dancing, to put thy pale, lost lilies out of mind;
But I was desolate and sick of an old passion,
    Yea, all the time, because the dance was long:
I have been faithful to thee, Cynara! in my fashion.

I cried for madder music and for stronger wine,
But when the feast is finished and the lamps expire,
Then falls thy shadow, Cynara! the night is thine;
And I am desolate and sick of an old passion,
    Yea, hungry for the lips of my desire:
I have been faithful to thee, Cynara! in my fashion.

755 *Vitae summa brevis spem nos vetat incohare longam*

THEY are not long, the weeping and the laughter,
        Love and desire and hate:
I think they have no portion in us after
        We pass the gate.

They are not long, the days of wine and roses:
  Out of a misty dream
Our path emerges for a while, then closes
  Within a dream.

LIONEL JOHNSON

1867–1902

756   *The Dark Angel*

DARK Angel, with thine aching lust
To rid the world of penitence:
Malicious Angel, who still dost
My soul such subtile violence!

Because of thee, no thought, no thing,
Abides for me undesecrate:
Dark Angel, ever on the wing,
Who never reachest me too late!

When music sounds, then changest thou
Its silvery to a sultry fire:
Nor will thine envious heart allow
Delight untortured by desire

Through thee, the gracious Muses turn
To Furies, O mine Enemy!
And all the things of beauty burn
With flames of evil ecstasy.

Because of thee, the land of dreams
Becomes a gathering place of fears:
Until tormented slumber seems
One vehemence of useless tears.

When sunlight glows upon the flowers,
Or ripples down the dancing sea:
Thou, with thy troop of passionate powers,
Beleaguerest, bewilderest, me.

Within the breath of autumn woods,
Within the winter silences:
Thy venomous spirit stirs and broods,
O Master of impieties!

The ardour of red flame is thine,
And thine the steely soul of ice:
Thou poisonest the fair design
Of nature, with unfair device.

Apples of ashes, golden bright;
Waters of bitterness, how sweet!
O banquet of a foul delight,
Prepared by thee, dark Paraclete!

Thou art the whisper in the gloom,
The hinting tone, the haunting laugh:
Thou art the adorner of my tomb,
The minstrel of mine epitaph.

I fight thee, in the Holy Name!
Yet, what thou dost, is what God saith:
Tempter! should I escape thy flame,
Thou wilt have helped my soul from Death:

The second Death, that never dies,
That cannot die, when time is dead:
Live Death, wherein the lost soul cries,
Eternally uncomforted.

Dark Angel, with thine aching lust!
Of two defeats, of two despairs:
Less dread, a change to drifting dust,
Than thine eternity of cares.

Do what thou wilt, thou shalt not so,
Dark Angel! triumph over me:
Lonely, unto the Lone I go;
Divine, to the Divinity.

757   *By the Statue of King Charles*
        At Charing Cross

SOMBRE and rich, the skies;
Great glooms, and starry plains.
Gently the night wind sighs;
Else a vast silence reigns.

The splendid silence clings
Around me: and around
The saddest of all kings
Crowned, and again discrowned.

Comely and calm, he rides
Hard by his own Whitehall:
Only the night wind glides:
No crowds, nor rebels, brawl.

Gone, too, his Court: and yet,
The stars his courtiers are:
Stars in their stations set;
And every wandering star.

Alone he rides, alone,
The fair and fatal king:
Dark night is all his own,
That strange and solemn thing.

Which are more full of fate:
The stars; or those sad eyes?
Which are more still and great:
Those brows; or the dark skies?

Although his whole heart yearn
In passionate tragedy:
Never was face so stern
With sweet austerity.

Vanquished in life, his death
By beauty made amends:
The passing of his breath
Won his defeated ends.

Brief life, and hapless? Nay:
Through death, life grew sublime.
Speak after sentence? Yea:
And to the end of time.

Armoured he rides, his head
Bare to the stars of doom:
He triumphs now, the dead,
Beholding London's gloom.

Our wearier spirit faints,
Vexed in the world's employ:
His soul was of the saints;
And art to him was joy.

King, tried in fires of woe!
Men hunger for thy grace:
And through the night I go,
Loving thy mournful face.

Yet, when the city sleeps;
When all the cries are still:
The stars and heavenly deeps
Work out a perfect will.

RUDYARD KIPLING

1865–1936

758   *Mandalay*

By the old Moulmein Pagoda, lookin' lazy at the sea,
There's a Burma girl a-settin', and I know she thinks o' me;
For the wind is in the palm-trees, and the temple-bells they say:
'Come you back, you British soldier; come you back to Mandalay!'
        Come you back to Mandalay,
        Where the old Flotilla lay:
        Can't you 'ear their paddles chunkin' from Rangoon to
            Mandalay?
        On the road to Mandalay,
        Where the flyin'-fishes play,
        An' the dawn comes up like thunder outer China 'crost the
            Bay!

'Er petticoat was yaller an' 'er little cap was green,
An' 'er name was Supi-yaw-lat—jes' the same as Theebaw's Queen,
An' I seed her first a-smokin' of a whackin' white cheroot,
An' a-wastin' Christian kisses on an 'eathen idol's foot:
   Bloomin' idol made o' mud—
   Wot they called the Great Gawd Budd—
   Plucky lot she cared for idols when I kissed 'er where she
   stud!
   On the road to Mandalay . . .

When the mist was on the rice-fields an' the sun was droppin' slow,
She'd git 'er little banjo an' she'd sing '*Kulla-lo-lo!*'
With 'er arm upon my shoulder an' 'er cheek agin my cheek
We useter watch the steamers an' the *hathis* pilin' teak.
   Elephints a-pilin' teak
   In the sludgy, squdgy creek,
   Where the silence 'ung that 'eavy you was 'arf afraid to speak!
   On the road to Mandalay . . .

But that's all shove be'ind me—long ago an' fur away,
An' there ain't no 'buses runnin' from the Bank to Mandalay;
An' I'm learnin' 'ere in London what the ten-year soldier tells:
'If you've 'eard the East a-callin', you won't never 'eed naught else.'
   No! you won't 'eed nothin' else
   But them spicy garlic smells,
   An' the sunshine an' the palm-trees an' the tinkly temple-
   bells;
   On the road to Mandalay . . .

I am sick o' wastin' leather on these gritty pavin'-stones,
An' the blasted English drizzle wakes the fever in my bones;
Tho' I walks with fifty 'ousemaids outer Chelsea to the Strand,
An' they talks a lot o' lovin', but wot do they understand?
   Beefy face an' grubby 'and—
   Law! wot do they understand?
   I've a neater, sweeter maiden in a cleaner, greener land!
   On the road to Mandalay . . .

Ship me somewheres east of Suez, where the best is like the worst,
Where there aren't no Ten Commandments an' a man can raise a
   thirst;
For the temple-bells are callin', an' it's there that I would be—
By the old Moulmein Pagoda, looking lazy at the sea;

On the road to Mandalay,
Where the old Flotilla lay,
With our sick beneath the awnings when we went to
    Mandalay!
O the road to Mandalay,
Where the flyin'-fishes play,
An' the dawn comes up like thunder outer China 'crost the
    Bay!

759   *Danny Deever*

'WHAT are the bugles blowin' for?' said Files-on-Parade.
'To turn you out, to turn you out,' the Colour-Sergeant said.
'What makes you look so white, so white?' said Files-on-Parade.
'I'm dreadin' what I've got to watch,' the Colour-Sergeant said.
   For they're hangin' Danny Deever, you can hear the Dead March
      play,
   The Regiment's in 'ollow square—they're hangin' him to-day;
   They've taken of his buttons off an' cut his stripes away,
   An' they're hangin' Danny Deever in the mornin'.

'What makes the rear-rank breathe so 'ard?' said Files-on-Parade.
'It's bitter cold, it's bitter cold,' the Colour-Sergeant said.
'What makes that front-rank man fall down?' said Files-on-Parade.
'A touch o' sun, a touch o' sun,' the Colour-Sergeant said.
   They are hangin' Danny Deever, they are marchin' of 'im round,
   They 'ave 'alted Danny Deever by 'is coffin on the ground;
   An' 'e'll swing in 'arf a minute for a sneakin' shootin' hound—
   O they're hangin' Danny Deever in the mornin'!

' 'Is cot was right-'and cot to mine,' said Files-on-Parade.
' 'E's sleepin' out an' far to-night,' the Colour-Sergeant said.
'I've drunk 'is beer a score o' times,' said Files-on-Parade.
' 'E's drinkin' bitter beer alone,' the Colour-Sergeant said.
   They are hangin' Danny Deever, you must mark 'im to 'is place,
   For 'e shot a comrade sleepin'—you must look 'im in the face;
   Nine 'undred of 'is county an' the Regiment's disgrace,
   While they're hangin' Danny Deever in the mornin'.

'What's that so black agin the sun?' said Files-on-Parade.
'It's Danny fightin' 'ard for life,' the Colour-Sergeant said.
'What's that that whimpers over'ead?' said Files-on-Parade.
'It's Danny's soul that's passin' now,' the Colour-Sergeant said.
   For they're done with Danny Deever, you can 'ear the quickstep
     play,
   The Regiment's in column, an' they're marchin' us away;
   Ho! the young recruits are shakin', an' they'll want their beer to-day,
   After hangin' Danny Deever in the mornin'!

760   *'Cities and Thrones and Powers'*

CITIES and Thrones and Powers
   Stand in Time's eye,
Almost as long as flowers,
   Which daily die:
But, as new buds put forth
   To glad new men,
Out of the spent and unconsidered Earth
   The Cities rise again.

This season's Daffodil
   She never hears
What change, what chance, what chill,
   Cut down last year's;
But with bold countenance,
   And knowledge small,
Esteems her seven days' continuance
   To be perpetual.

So Time that is o'erkind
   To all that be,
Ordains us e'en as blind,
   As bold as she:
That in our very death,
   And burial sure,
Shadow to shadow, well persuaded, saith,
   'See how our works endure!'

761

The Way through the Woods

THEY shut the road through the woods
Seventy years ago.
Weather and rain have undone it again,
And now you would never know
There was once a road through the woods
Before they planted the trees.
It is underneath the coppice and heath
And the thin anemones.
Only the keeper sees
That, where the ring-dove broods,
And the badgers roll at ease,
There was once a road through the woods.

Yet, if you enter the woods
Of a summer evening late,
When the night-air cools on the trout-ringed pools
Where the otter whistles his mate,
(They fear not men in the woods,
Because they see so few.)
You will hear the beat of a horse's feet,
And the swish of a skirt in the dew,
Steadily cantering through
The misty solitudes,
As though they perfectly knew
The old lost road through the woods. . . .
But there is no road through the woods.

762

Recessional

June 22, 1897

GOD of our fathers, known of old,
    Lord of our far-flung battle-line,
Beneath whose awful Hand we hold
    Dominion over palm and pine—
Lord God of Hosts, be with us yet,
Lest we forget—lest we forget!

The tumult and the shouting dies;
  The Captains and the Kings depart:
Still stands thine ancient sacrifice,
  An humble and a contrite heart.
Lord God of Hosts, be with us yet,
Lest we forget—lest we forget!

Far-called, our navies melt away;
  On dune and headland sinks the fire:
Lo, all our pomp of yesterday
  Is one with Nineveh and Tyre!
Judge of the Nations, spare us yet,
Lest we forget—lest we forget!

If, drunk with sight of power, we loose
  Wild tongues that have not thee in awe,
Such boastings as the Gentiles use,
  Or lesser breeds without the Law—
Lord God of Hosts, be with us yet,
Lest we forget—lest we forget!

For heathen heart that puts her trust
  In reeking tube and iron shard,
All valiant dust that builds on dust,
  And guarding, calls not thee to guard,
For frantic boast and foolish word—
Thy mercy on thy People, Lord!

WILLIAM BUTLER YEATS

1865–1939

763   *The Lake Isle of Innisfree*

I WILL arise and go now, and go to Innisfree,
And a small cabin build there, of clay and wattles made:
Nine bean-rows will I have there, a hive for the honey-bee,
And live alone in the bee-loud glade.

And I shall have some peace there, for peace comes dropping slow,
Dropping from the veils of the morning to where the cricket sings;
There midnight's all a glimmer, and noon a purple glow,
And evening full of the linnet's wings.

I will arise and go now, for always night and day
I hear lake water lapping with low sounds by the shore;
While I stand on the roadway, or on the pavements grey,
I hear it in the deep heart's core.

764 *Who goes with Fergus?*

WHO will go drive with Fergus now,
And pierce the deep wood's woven shade,
And dance upon the level shore?
Young man, lift up your russet brow,
And lift your tender eyelids, maid,
And brood on hopes and fear no more.

And no more turn aside and brood
Upon love's bitter mystery;
For Fergus rules the brazen cars,
And rules the shadows of the wood,
And the white breast of the dim sea
And all dishevelled wandering stars.

765 *No Second Troy*

WHY should I blame her that she filled my days
With misery, or that she would of late
Have taught to ignorant men most violent ways,
Or hurled the little streets upon the great,
Had they but courage equal to desire?
What could have made her peaceful with a mind
That nobleness made simple as a fire,
With beauty like a tightened bow, a kind
That is not natural in an age like this,
Being high and solitary and most stern?
Why, what could she have done, being what she is?
Was there another Troy for her to burn?

766   *An Irish Airman forsees his Death*

I KNOW that I shall meet my fate
Somewhere among the clouds above;
Those that I fight I do not hate,
Those that I guard I do not love;
My country is Kiltartan Cross,
My countrymen Kiltartan's poor,
No likely end could bring them loss
Or leave them happier than before.
Nor law, nor duty bade me fight,
Nor public men, nor cheering crowds,
A lonely impulse of delight
Drove to this tumult in the clouds;
I balanced all, brought all to mind,
The years to come seemed waste of breath,
A waste of breath the years behind
In balance with this life, this death.

767   *Easter 1916*

I HAVE met them at close of day
Coming with vivid faces
From counter or desk among grey
Eighteenth-century houses.
I have passed with a nod of the head
Or polite meaningless words,
Or have lingered awhile and said
Polite meaningless words,
And thought before I had done
Or a mocking tale or a gibe
To please a companion
Around the fire at the club,
Being certain that they and I
But lived where motley is worn:
All changed, changed utterly:
A terrible beauty is born.

That woman's days were spent
In ignorant good-will,
Her nights in argument
Until her voice grew shrill.
What voice more sweet than hers
When, young and beautiful,
She rode to harriers?
This man had kept a school
And rode our wingèd horse;
This other his helper and friend
Was coming into his force;
He might have won fame in the end,
So sensitive his nature seemed,
So daring and sweet his thought.
This other man I had dreamed
A drunken, vainglorious lout.
He had done most bitter wrong
To some who are near my heart,
Yet I number him in the song;
He, too, has resigned his part
In the casual comedy;
He, too, has been changed in his turn,
Transformed utterly:
A terrible beauty is born.

Hearts with one purpose alone
Through summer and winter seem
Enchanted to a stone
To trouble the living stream.
The horse that comes from the road,
The rider, the birds that range
From cloud to tumbling cloud,
Minute by minute they change;
A shadow of cloud on the stream
Changes minute by minute;
A horse-hoof slides on the brim,
And a horse plashes within it;
The long-legged moor-hens dive,
And hens to moor-cocks call;
Minute by minute they live:
The stone's in the midst of all.

Too long a sacrifice
Can make a stone of the heart.
O when may it suffice?
That is Heaven's part, our part
To murmur name upon name,
As a mother names her child
When sleep at last has come
On limbs that had run wild.
What is it but nightfall?
No, no, not night but death;
Was it needless death after all?
For England may keep faith
For all that is done and said.
We know their dream; enough
To know they dreamed and are dead;
And what if excess of love
Bewildered them till they died?
I write it out in a verse—
MacDonagh and MacBride
And Connolly and Pearse
Now and in time to be,
Wherever green is worn,
Are changed, changed utterly:
A terrible beauty is born.

768   *The Second Coming*

TURNING and turning in the widening gyre
The falcon cannot hear the falconer;
Things fall apart; the centre cannot hold;
Mere anarchy is loosed upon the world,
The blood-dimmed tide is loosed, and everywhere
The ceremony of innocence is drowned;
The best lack all conviction, while the worst
Are full of passionate intensity.

Surely some revelation is at hand;
Surely the Second Coming is at hand.
The Second Coming! Hardly are those words out
When a vast image out of *Spiritus Mundi*
Troubles my sight: somewhere in sands of the desert
A shape with lion body and the head of a man,

A gaze blank and pitiless as the sun,
Is moving its slow thighs, while all about it
Reel shadows of the indignant desert birds.
The darkness drops again; but now I know
That twenty centuries of stony sleep
Were vexed to nightmare by a rocking cradle,
And what rough beast, its hour come round at last,
Slouches towards Bethlehem to be born?

769   *Sailing to Byzantium*

THAT is no country for old men. The young
In one another's arms, birds in the trees
—Those dying generations—at their song,
The salmon-falls, the mackerel-crowded seas,
Fish, flesh, or fowl, commend all summer long
Whatever is begotten, born, and dies.
Caught in that sensual music all neglect
Monuments of unageing intellect.

An agèd man is but a paltry thing,
A tattered coat upon a stick, unless
Soul clap its hands and sing, and louder sing
For every tatter in its mortal dress,
Nor is there singing school but studying
Monuments of its own magnificence;
And therefore I have sailed the seas and come
To the holy city of Byzantium.

O sages standing in God's holy fire
As in the gold mosaic of a wall,
Come from the holy fire, perne in a gyre,
And be the singing-masters of my soul.
Consume my heart away; sick with desire
And fastened to a dying animal
It knows not what it is; and gather me
Into the artifice of eternity.

Once out of nature I shall never take
My bodily form from any natural thing,
But such a form as Grecian goldsmiths make
Of hammered gold and gold enamelling

To keep a drowsy Emperor awake;
Or set upon a golden bough to sing
To lords and ladies of Byzantium
Of what is past, or passing, or to come.

from Meditations in Time of Civil War

(i)

770   *The Road at My Door*

AN affable Irregular,
A heavily-built Falstaffian man,
Comes cracking jokes of civil war
As though to die by gunshot were
The finest play under the sun.

A brown Lieutenant and his men,
Half dressed in national uniform,
Stand at my door, and I complain
Of the foul weather, hail and rain,
A pear-tree broken by the storm.

I count those feathered balls of soot
The moor-hen guides upon the stream,
To silence the envy in my thought;
And turn towards my chamber, caught
In the cold snows of a dream.

(ii)

771   *The Stare's Nest by My Window*

THE bees build in the crevices
Of loosening masonry, and there
The mother birds bring grubs and flies.
My wall is loosening; honey-bees,
Come build in the empty house of the stare.

We are closed in, and the key is turned
On our uncertainty; somewhere
A man is killed, or a house burned,
Yet no clear fact to be discerned:
Come build in the empty house of the stare.

A barricade of stone or of wood;
Some fourteen days of civil war;
Last night they trundled down the road
That dead young soldier in his blood:
Come build in the empty house of the stare.

We had fed the heart on fantasies,
The heart's grown brutal from the fare;
More substance in our enmities
Than in our love; O honey-bees,
Come build in the empty house of the stare.

772   *Two Songs from a Play*

(i)

I saw a staring virgin stand
Where holy Dionysus died,
And tear the heart out of his side,
And lay the heart upon her hand
And bear that beating heart away;
And then did all the Muses sing
Of Magnus Annus at the spring,
As though God's death were but a play.

Another Troy must rise and set,
Another lineage feed the crow,
Another Argo's painted prow
Drive to a flashier bauble yet.
The Roman Empire stood appalled:
It dropped the reins of peace and war
When that fierce virgin and her Star
Out of the fabulous darkness called.

(ii)

In pity for man's darkening thought
He walked that room and issued thence
In Galilean turbulence;
The Babylonian starlight brought
A fabulous, formless darkness in;
Odour of blood when Christ was slain
Made all Platonic tolerance vain
And vain all Doric discipline.

Everything that man esteems
Endures a moment or a day.
Love's pleasure drives his love away,
The painter's brush consumes his dreams;
The herald's cry, the soldier's tread
Exhaust his glory and his might:
Whatever flames upon the night
Man's own resinous heart has fed.

773 *Leda and the Swan*

A SUDDEN blow: the great wings beating still
Above the staggering girl, her thighs caressed
By the dark webs, her nape caught in his bill,
He holds her helpless breast upon his breast.

How can those terrified vague fingers push
The feathered glory from her loosening thighs?
And how can body, laid in that white rush,
But feel the strange heart beating where it lies?

A shudder in the loins engenders there
The broken wall, the burning roof and tower
And Agamemnon dead.
                        Being so caught up,
So mastered by the brute blood of the air,
Did she put on his knowledge with his power
Before the indifferent beak could let her drop?

774 *Among Schoolchildren*

I WALK through the long schoolroom questioning;
A kind old nun in a white hood replies;
The children learn to cipher and to sing,
To study reading-books and histories,
To cut and sew, be neat in everything
In the best modern way—the children's eyes
In momentary wonder stare upon
A sixty-year-old smiling public man.

I dream of a Ledaean body, bent
Above a sinking fire, a tale that she
Told of a harsh reproof, or trivial event
That changed some childish day to tragedy—
Told, and it seemed that our two natures blent
Into a sphere from youthful sympathy,
Or else, to alter Plato's parable,
Into the yolk and white of the one shell.

And thinking of that fit of grief or rage
I look upon one child or t'other there
And wonder if she stood so at that age—
For even daughters of the swan can share
Something of every paddler's heritage—
And had that colour upon cheek or hair,
And thereupon my heart is driven wild:
She stands before me as a living child.

Her present image floats into the mind—
Did Quattrocento finger fashion it
Hollow of cheek as though it drank the wind
And took a mess of shadows for its meat?
And I though never of Ledaean kind
Had pretty plumage once—enough of that,
Better to smile on all that smile, and show
There is a comfortable kind of old scarecrow.

What youthful mother, a shape upon her lap
Honey of generation had betrayed,
And that must sleep, shriek, struggle to escape
As recollection or the drug decide,
Would think her son, did she but see that shape
With sixty or more winters on its head,
A compensation for the pang of his birth,
Or the uncertainty of his setting forth?

Plato thought nature but a spume that plays
Upon a ghostly paradigm of things;
Solider Aristotle played the taws
Upon the bottom of a king of kings;
World-famous golden-thighed Pythagoras
Fingered upon a fiddle-stick or strings
What a star sang and careless Muses heard:
Old clothes upon old sticks to scare a bird.

Both nuns and mothers worship images,
But those the candles light are not as those
That animate a mother's reveries,
But keep a marble or a bronze repose.
And yet they too break hearts—O Presences
That passion, piety or affection knows,
And that all heavenly glory symbolise—
O self-born mockers of man's enterprise;

Labour is blossoming or dancing where
The body is not bruised to pleasure soul,
Nor beauty born out of its own despair,
Nor blear-eyed wisdom out of midnight oil.
O chestnut-tree, great-rooted blossomer,
Are you the leaf, the blossom or the bole?
O body swayed to music, O brightening glance,
How can we know the dancer from the dance?

775   *Byzantium*

THE unpurged images of day recede;
The Emperor's drunken soldiery are abed;
Night resonance recedes, night-walkers' song
After great cathedral gong;
A starlit or a moonlit dome disdains
All that man is,
All mere complexities,
The fury and the mire of human veins.

Before me floats an image, man or shade,
Shade more than man, more image than a shade;
For Hades' bobbin bound in mummy-cloth
May unwind the winding path;
A mouth that has no moisture and no breath
Breathless mouths may summon;
I hail the superhuman;
I call it death-in-life and life-in-death.

Miracle, bird or golden handiwork,
More miracle than bird or handiwork,
Planted on the star-lit golden bough,
Can like the cocks of Hades crow,

Or, by the moon embittered, scorn aloud
In glory of changeless metal
Common bird or petal
And all complexities of mire or blood.

At midnight on the Emperor's pavement flit
Flames that no faggot feeds, nor steel has lit,
Nor storm disturbs, flames begotten of flame,
Where blood-begotten spirits come
And all complexities of fury leave,
Dying into a dance,
An agony of trance,
An agony of flame that cannot singe a sleeve.

Astraddle on the dolphin's mire and blood,
Spirit after spirit! The smithies break the flood,
The golden smithies of the Emperor!
Marbles of the dancing floor
Break bitter furies of complexity,
Those images that yet
Fresh images beget,
That dolphin-torn, that gong-tormented sea.

776   *Lapis Lazuli*

I HAVE heard that hysterical women say
They are sick of the palette and fiddle-bow,
Of poets that are always gay,
For everybody knows or else should know
That if nothing drastic is done
Aeroplane and Zeppelin will come out,
Pitch like King Billy bomb-balls in
Until the town lie beaten flat.

All perform their tragic play,
There struts Hamlet, there is Lear,
That's Ophelia, that Cordelia;
Yet they, should the last scene be there,
The great stage curtain about to drop,
If worthy their prominent part in the play,
Do not break up their lines to weep.
They know that Hamlet and Lear are gay;

Gaiety transfiguring all that dread.
All men have aimed at, found and lost;
Black out; Heaven blazing into the head:
Tragedy wrought to its uttermost.
Though Hamlet rambles and Lear rages,
And all the drop-scenes drop at once
Upon a hundred thousand stages,
It cannot grow by an inch or an ounce.

On their own feet they came, or on shipboard,
Camel-back, horse-back, ass-back, mule-back,
Old civilisations put to the sword.
Then they and their wisdom went to rack:
No handiwork of Callimachus,
Who handled marble as if it were bronze,
Made draperies that seemed to rise
When sea-wind swept the corner, stands:
His long lamp-chimney shaped like the stem
Of a slender palm, stood but a day;
All things fall and are built again,
And those that build them again are gay.

Two Chinamen, behind them a third,
Are carved in lapis lazuli,
Over them flies a long-legged bird,
A symbol of longevity;
The third, doubtless a serving-man,
Carries a musical instrument.

Every discoloration of the stone,
Every accidental crack or dent,
Seems a water-course or an avalanche,
Or lofty slope where it still snows
Though doubtless plum or cherry-branch
Sweetens the little half-way house
Those Chinamen climb towards, and I
Delight to imagine them seated there;
There, on the mountain and the sky,
On all the tragic scene they stare.
One asks for mournful melodies;
Accomplished fingers begin to play.
Their eyes mid many wrinkles, their eyes,
Their ancient, glittering eyes, are gay.

777 *Long-Legged Fly*

THAT civilisation may not sink,
Its great battle lost,
Quiet the dog, tether the pony
To a distant post;
Our master Caesar is in the tent
Where the maps are spread,
His eyes fixed upon nothing,
A hand under his head.
Like a long-legged fly upon the stream
His mind moves upon silence.

That the topless towers be burnt
And men recall that face,
Move most gently if move you must
In this lonely place.
She thinks, part woman, three parts a child,
That nobody looks; her feet
Practise a tinker shuffle
Picked up on a street.
Like a long-legged fly upon the stream
Her mind moves upon silence.

That girls at puberty may find
The first Adam in their thought,
Shut the door of the Pope's chapel,
Keep those children out.
There on that scaffolding reclines
Michael Angelo.
With no more sound than the mice make
His hand moves to and fro.
Like a long-legged fly upon the stream
His mind moves upon silence.

778 *The Circus Animals' Desertion*

I SOUGHT a theme and sought for it in vain,
I sought it daily for six weeks or so.
Maybe at last, being but a broken man,
I must be satisfied with my heart, although
Winter and summer till old age began
My circus animals were all on show,
Those stilted boys, that burnished chariot,
Lion and woman and the Lord knows what.

What can I but enumerate old themes?
First that sea-rider Oisin led by the nose
Through three enchanted islands, allegorical dreams,
Vain gaiety, vain battle, vain repose,
Themes of the embittered heart, or so it seems,
That might adorn old songs or courtly shows;
But what cared I that set him on to ride,
I, starved for the bosom of his faery bride?

And then a counter-truth filled out its play,
The Countess Cathleen was the name I gave it;
She, pity-crazed, had given her soul away,
But masterful Heaven had intervened to save it.
I thought my dear must her own soul destroy,
So did fanaticism and hate enslave it,
And this brought forth a dream and soon enough
This dream itself had all my thought and love.

And when the Fool and Blind Man stole the bread
Cuchulain fought the ungovernable sea;
Heart-mysteries there, and yet when all is said
It was the dream itself enchanted me:
Character isolated by a deed
To engross the present and dominate memory.
Players and painted stage took all my love,
And not those things that they were emblems of.

Those masterful images because complete
Grew in pure mind, but out of what began?
A mound of refuse or the sweepings of a street,
Old kettles, old bottles, and a broken can,
Old iron, old bones, old rags, that raving slut
Who keeps the till. Now that my ladder's gone,
I must lie down where all the ladders start,
In the foul rag-and-bone shop of the heart.

LAURENCE BINYON
1869–1943

779

For the Fallen
(*1917*)

WITH proud thanksgiving, a mother for her children,
England mourns for her dead across the sea.
Flesh of her flesh they were, spirit of her spirit,
Fallen in the cause of the free.

Solemn the drums thrill: Death august and royal
Sings sorrow up into immortal spheres.
There is music in the midst of desolation
And a glory that shines upon our tears.

They went with songs to the battle, they were young,
Straight of limb, true of eye, steady and aglow.
They were staunch to the end against odds uncounted,
They fell with their faces to the foe.

They shall grow not old, as we that are left grow old:
Age shall not weary them, nor the years condemn.
At the going down of the sun and in the morning
We will remember them.

They mingle not with their laughing comrades again;
They sit no more at familiar tables of home;
They have no lot in our labour of the day-time;
They sleep beyond England's foam.

But where our desires are and our hopes profound,
Felt as a well-spring that is hidden from sight,
To the innermost heart of their own land they are known
As the stars are known to the Night;

As the stars that shall be bright when we are dust,
Moving in marches upon the heavenly plain,
As the stars that are starry in the time of our darkness,
To the end, to the end, they remain.

780   *The Burning of the Leaves*

(*1942*)

Now is the time for the burning of the leaves.
They go to the fire; the nostril pricks with smoke
Wandering slowly into a weeping mist.
Brittle and blotched, ragged and rotten sheaves!
A flame seizes the smouldering ruin and bites
On stubborn stalks that crackle as they resist.

The last hollyhock's fallen tower is dust;
All the spices of June are a bitter reek,
All the extravagant riches spent and mean.
All burns! The reddest rose is a ghost;
Sparks whirl up, to expire in the mist: the wild
Fingers of fire are making corruption clean.

Now is the time for stripping the spirit bare,
Time for the burning of days ended and done,
Idle solace of things that have gone before:
Rootless hope and fruitless desire are there;
Let them go to the fire, with never a look behind.
The world that was ours is a world that is ours no more.

They will come again, the leaf and the flower, to arise
From squalor of rottenness into the old splendour,
And magical scents to a wondering memory bring;
The same glory, to shine upon different eyes.
Earth cares for her own ruins, naught for ours.
Nothing is certain, only the certain spring.

HILAIRE BELLOC
1870–1953

781   *On a General Election*

THE accursèd power which stands on Privilege
(And goes with Women, and Champagne and Bridge)
Broke—and Democracy resumed her reign:
(Which goes with Bridge, and Women and Champagne).

782   *The Statesman*

I KNEW a man who used to say,
Not once but twenty times a day,
That in the turmoil and the strife
(His very words) of Public Life
The thing of ultimate effect
Was Character—not Intellect.
He therefore was at strenuous pains
To atrophy his puny brains
And registered success in this
Beyond the dreams of avarice,
Till, when he had at last become
Blind, paralytic, deaf and dumb,
Insensible and cretinous,
He was admitted ONE OF US.
They therefore, (meaning Them by 'They')
His colleagues of the N.C.A.,
The T.U.C., the I.L.P.,
Appointed him triumphantly
To bleed the taxes of a clear
200,000 Francs a year
(Swiss), as the necessary man
For Conferences at Lausanne,
Geneva, Basle, Locarno, Berne:
A salary which he will earn,
Yes—*earn* I say—until he Pops,
Croaks, passes in his checks and Stops:—
When he will be remembered for
A week, a month, or even more.

783

Matilda
Who Told Lies, and was Burned to Death

MATILDA told such Dreadful Lies,
It made one Gasp and Stretch one's Eyes;
Her Aunt, who, from her Earliest Youth,
Had kept a Strict Regard for Truth,
Attempted to Believe Matilda:
The effort very nearly killed her,
And would have done so, had not She
Discovered this Infirmity.
For once, towards the Close of Day,
Matilda, growing tired of play,
And finding she was left alone,
Went tiptoe to the Telephone
And summoned the Immediate Aid
Of London's Noble Fire-Brigade.
Within an hour the Gallant Band
Were pouring in on every hand,
From Putney, Hackney Downs, and Bow
With Courage high and Hearts a-glow
They galloped, roaring through the Town
'Matilda's House is Burning Down!'
Inspired by British Cheers and Loud
Proceeding from the Frenzied Crowd,
They ran their ladders through a score
Of windows on the Ball Room Floor;
And took Peculiar Pains to Souse
The Pictures up and down the House,
Until Matilda's Aunt succeeded
In showing them they were not needed;
And even then she had to pay
To get the Men to go away!

It happened that a few Weeks later
Her Aunt was off to the Theatre
To see that Interesting Play
The Second Mrs Tanqueray.
She had refused to take her Niece
To hear this Entertaining Piece:
A Deprivation Just and Wise
To Punish her for Telling Lies.

That Night a Fire *did* break out—
You should have heard Matilda Shout!
You should have heard her Scream and Bawl,
And throw the window up and call
To People passing in the Street—
(The rapidly increasing Heat
Encouraging her to obtain
Their confidence)—but all in vain!
For every time She shouted 'Fire!'
They only answered 'Little Liar'!
And therefore when her Aunt returned,
Matilda, and the House, were Burned.

WILLIAM HENRY DAVIES

1871–1940

784 *The Kingfisher*

IT was the Rainbow gave thee birth,
  And left thee all her lovely hues;
And, as her mother's name was Tears,
  So runs it in my blood to choose
For haunts the lonely pools, and keep
In company with trees that weep.

Go you and, with such glorious hues,
  Live with proud Peacocks in green parks;
On lawns as smooth as shining glass,
  Let every feather show its marks;
Get thee on boughs and clap thy wings
Before the windows of proud kings.

Nay, lovely Bird, thou art not vain;
  Thou hast no proud, ambitious mind;
I also love a quiet place
  That's green, away from all mankind;
A lonely pool, and let a tree
Sigh with her bosom over me.

785   *Leisure*

WHAT is this life if, full of care,
We have no time to stand and stare.

No time to stand beneath the boughs
And stare as long as sheep or cows.

No time to see, when woods we pass,
Where squirrels hide their nuts in grass.

No time to see, in broad daylight,
Streams full of stars like skies at night.

No time to turn at Beauty's glance,
And watch her feet, how they can dance.

No time to wait till her mouth can
Enrich that smile her eyes began.

A poor life this if, full of care,
We have no time to stand and stare.

786   *The Inquest*

I TOOK my oath I would inquire,
    Without affection, hate, or wrath,
Into the death of Ada Wright—
    So help me God! I took that oath.

When I went out to see the corpse,
    The four months' babe that died so young,
I judged it was seven pounds in weight,
    And little more than one foot long.

One eye, that had a yellow lid,
    Was shut—so was the mouth, that smiled;
The left eye open, shining bright—
    It seemed a knowing little child.

For as I looked at that one eye,
 It seemed to laugh, and say with glee:
'What caused my death you'll never know—
 Perhaps my mother murdered me.'

When I went into court again,
 To hear the mother's evidence—
It was a love-child, she explained.
 And smiled, for our intelligence.

'Now, Gentlemen of the Jury,' said
 The coroner—'this woman's child
By misadventure met its death.'
 'Aye, aye,' said we. The mother smiled.

And I could see that child's one eye
 Which seemed to laugh, and say with glee:
'What caused my death you'll never know—
 Perhaps my mother murdered me.'

787   *The Cat*

    WITHIN that porch, across the way,
     I see two naked eyes this night;
    Two eyes that neither shut nor blink,
     Searching my face with a green light.

    But cats to me are strange, so strange—
     I cannot sleep if one is near;
    And though I'm sure I see those eyes
     I'm not so sure a body's there!

RALPH HODGSON
1871–1962

788   *The Bells of Heaven*

'TWOULD ring the bells of Heaven
The wildest peal for years,
If Parson lost his senses
And people came to theirs,
And he and they together
Knelt down with angry prayers
For tamed and shabby tigers
And dancing dogs and bears,
And wretched, blind pit ponies,
And little hunted hares.

789   *The Hammers*

NOISE of hammers once I heard,
Many hammers, busy hammers,
Beating, shaping, night and day,
Shaping, beating dust and clay
To a palace; saw it reared;
Saw the hammers laid away.

And I listened, and I heard
Hammers beating, night and day,
In the palace newly reared,
Beating it to dust and clay:
Other hammers, muffled hammers,
Silent hammers of decay.

WALTER DE LA MARE
1873–1956

790   *Fare Well*

WHEN I lie where shades of darkness
Shall no more assail mine eyes,
Nor the rain make lamentation
    When the wind sighs;
How will fare the world whose wonder
Was the very proof of me?
Memory fades, must the remembered
    Perishing be?

Oh, when this my dust surrenders
Hand, foot, lip, to dust again,
May these loved and loving faces
    Please other men!
May the rusting harvest hedgerow
Still the Traveller's Joy entwine,
And as happy children gather
    Posies once mine.

Look thy last on all things lovely,
Every hour. Let no night
Seal thy sense in deathly slumber
    Till to delight
Thou have paid thy utmost blessing;
Since that all things thou wouldst praise
Beauty took from those who loved them
    In other days.

791   *All That's Past*

VERY old are the woods;
    And the buds that break
Out of the brier's boughs,
    When March winds wake,
So old with their beauty are—
    Oh, no man knows
Through what wild centuries
    Roves back the rose.

Very old are the brooks;
  And the rills that rise
Where snow sleeps cold beneath
  The azure skies
Sing such a history
  Of come and gone,
Their every drop is as wise
  As Solomon.

Very old are we men;
  Our dreams are tales
Told in dim Eden
  By Eve's nightingales;
We wake and whisper awhile,
  But, the day gone by,
Silence and sleep like fields
  Of amaranth lie.

792   *The Listeners*

'Is there anybody there?' said the Traveller,
  Knocking on the moonlit door;
And his horse in the silence champed the grasses
  Of the forest's ferny floor:
And a bird flew up out of the turret,
  Above the Traveller's head:
And he smote upon the door again a second time;
  'Is there anybody there?' he said.
But no one descended to the Traveller;
  No head from the leaf-fringed sill
Leaned over and looked into his grey eyes,
  Where he stood perplexed and still.
But only a host of phantom listeners
  That dwelt in the lone house then
Stood listening in the quiet of the moonlight
  To that voice from the world of men:
Stood thronging the faint moonbeams on the dark stair,
  That goes down to the empty hall,
Hearkening in an air stirred and shaken
  By the lonely Traveller's call.

And he felt in his heart their strangeness,
   Their stillness answering his cry,
While his horse moved, cropping the dark turf,
   'Neath the starred and leafy sky;
For he suddenly smote on the door, even
   Louder, and lifted his head:—
'Tell them I came, and no one answered,
   That I kept my word,' he said.
Never the least stir made the listeners,
   Though every word he spake
Fell echoing through the shadowiness of the still house
   From the one man left awake:
Ay, they heard his foot upon the stirrup,
   And the sound of iron on stone,
And how the silence surged softly backward,
   When the plunging hoofs were gone.

793   *Napoleon*

'WHAT is the world, O soldiers?
      It is I:
I, this incessant snow,
      This northern sky;
Soldiers, this solitude
      Through which we go
      Is I.'

794   *The Ghost*

'WHO knocks?' 'I, who was beautiful,
   Beyond all dreams to restore,
I, from the roots of the dark thorn am hither.
   And knock on the door.'

'Who speaks?' 'I—once was my speech
   Sweet as the bird's on the air,
When echo lurks by the waters to heed;
   'Tis I speak thee fair.'

'Dark is the hour!' 'Ay, and cold.'
  'Lone is my house.' 'Ah, but mine?'
'Sight, touch, lips, eyes yearned in vain.'
  ʻ 'Long dead these to thine . . .'

Silence. Still faint on the porch
  Brake the flames of the stars.
In gloom groped a hope-wearied hand
  Over keys, bolts, and bars.

A face peered. All the grey night
  In chaos of vacancy shone;
Nought but vast sorrow was there—
  The sweet cheat gone.

795   *The Song of the Mad Prince*

WHO said, 'Peacock Pie'?
  The old King to the sparrow:
Who said, 'Crops are ripe'?
  Rust to the harrow:
Who said, 'Where sleeps she now?
  Where rests she now her head,
Bathed in eve's loveliness'?
  That's what I said.

Who said, 'Ay, mum's the word';
  Sexton to willow:
Who said, 'Green dusk for dreams,
  Moss for a pillow'?
Who said, 'All Time's delight
  Hath she for narrow bed;
Life's troubled bubble broken'?
  That's what I said.

GILBERT KEITH CHESTERTON
1874–1936

796   *The Rolling English Road*

BEFORE the Roman came to Rye or out to Severn strode,
The rolling English drunkard made the rolling English road.
A reeling road, a rolling road, that rambles round the shire,
And after him the parson ran, the sexton and the squire;
A merry road, a mazy road, and such as we did tread
The night we went to Birmingham by way of Beachy Head.

I knew no harm of Bonaparte and plenty of the Squire,
And for to fight the Frenchman I did not much desire;
But I did bash their baggonets because they came arrayed
To straighten out the crooked road an English drunkard made,
Where you and I went down the lane with ale-mugs in our hands,
The night we went to Glastonbury by way of Goodwin Sands.

His sins they were forgiven him; or why do flowers run
Behind him; and the hedges all strengthening in the sun?
The wild thing went from left to right and knew not which was which,
But the wild rose was above him when they found him in the ditch.
God pardon us, nor harden us; we did not see so clear
The night we went to Bannockburn by way of Brighton Pier.

My friends, we will not go again or ape an ancient rage,
Or stretch the folly of our youth to be the shame of age,
But walk with clearer eyes and ears this path that wandereth,
And see undrugged in evening light the decent inn of death;
For there is good news yet to hear and fine things to be seen,
Before we go to Paradise by way of Kensal Green.

797 *Antichrist, or the Reunion of Christendom: an Ode*

'A Bill which has shocked the conscience of every
Christian community in Europe.'—Mr. F. E. Smith,
on the Welsh Disestablishment Bill.

ARE they clinging to their crosses,
    F. E. Smith,
Where the Breton boat-fleet tosses,
    Are they, Smith?
Do they, fasting, trembling, bleeding,
  Wait the news from this our city?
Groaning 'That's the Second Reading!'
  Hissing 'There is still Committee!'
If the voice of Cecil falters,
  If McKenna's point has pith,
Do they tremble for their altars?
    Do they, Smith?

Russian peasants round their pope
    Huddled, Smith,
Hear about it all, I hope,
    Don't they, Smith?
In the mountain hamlets clothing
  Peaks beyond Caucasian pales,
Where Establishment means nothing
  And they never heard of Wales,
Do they read it all in Hansard—
  With a crib to read it with—
'Welsh Tithes: Dr. Clifford Answered.'
    Really, Smith?

In the lands where Christians were,
    F. E. Smith,
In the little lands laid bare,
    Smith, O Smith!
Where the Turkish bands are busy,
  And the Tory name is blessed
Since they hailed the Cross of Dizzy
  On the banners from the West!
Men don't think it half so hard if
  Islam burns their kin and kith,
Since a curate lives in Cardiff
    Saved by Smith.

It would greatly, I must own,
                Soothe me, Smith!
If you left this theme alone,
              Holy Smith!
For your legal cause or civil
      You fight well and get your fee;
For your God or dream or devil
      You will answer, not to me.
Talk about the pews and steeples
      And the Cash that goes therewith!
But the souls of Christian peoples . . .
             Chuck it, Smith!

JOHN MASEFIELD

1878–1967

798   *Cargoes*

QUINQUIREME of Nineveh from distant Ophir
Rowing home to haven in sunny Palestine,
With a cargo of ivory,
And apes and peacocks,
Sandalwood, cedarwood, and sweet white wine.

Stately Spanish galleon coming from the Isthmus,
Dipping through the Tropics by the palm-green shores,
With a cargo of diamonds,
Emeralds, amethysts,
Topazes, and cinnamon, and gold moidores.

Dirty British coaster with a salt-caked smoke stack
Butting through the Channel in the mad March days,
With a cargo of Tyne coal,
Road-rail, pig-lead,
Firewood, iron-ware, and cheap tin trays.

799   *Up on the Downs*

UP on the downs the red-eyed kestrels hover,
Eyeing the grass.
The field-mouse flits like a shadow into cover
As their shadows pass.

Men are burning the gorse on the down's shoulder;
A drift of smoke
Glitters with fire and hangs, and the skies smoulder,
And the lungs choke.

Once the tribe did thus on the downs, on these downs burning
Men in the frame.
Crying to the gods of the downs till their brains were turning
And the gods came.

And to-day on the downs, in the wind, the hawks, the grasses,
In blood and air,
Something passes me and cries as it passes.
On the chalk downland bare.

EDWARD THOMAS
1878–1917

800   *The Owl*

DOWNHILL I came, hungry, and yet not starved;
Cold, yet had heat within me that was proof
Against the North wind; tired, yet so that rest
Had seemed the sweetest thing under a roof.

Then at the inn I had food, fire, and rest,
Knowing how hungry, cold, and tired was I.
All of the night was quite barred out except
An owl's cry, a most melancholy cry

Shaken out long and clear upon the hill,
No merry note, nor cause of merriment,
But one telling me plain what I escaped
And others could not, that night, as in I went.

And salted was my food, and my repose,
Salted and sobered, too, by the bird's voice
Speaking for all who lay under the stars,
Soldiers and poor, unable to rejoice.

801   *In Memoriam (Easter, 1915)*

THE flowers left thick at nightfall in the wood
This Eastertide call into mind the men,
Now far from home, who, with their sweethearts, should
Have gathered them and will do never again.

802   *Adlestrop*

YES. I remember Adlestrop—
The name, because one afternoon
Of heat the express-train drew up there
Unwontedly. It was late June.

The steam hissed. Someone cleared his throat.
No one left and no one came
On the bare platform. What I saw
Was Adlestrop—only the name

And willows, willow-herb, and grass,
And meadowsweet, and haycocks dry,
No whit less still and lonely fair
Than the high cloudlets in the sky.

And for that minute a blackbird sang
Close by, and round him, mistier,
Farther and farther, all the birds
Of Oxfordshire and Gloucestershire.

803   *Lights Out*

I HAVE come to the borders of sleep,
The unfathomable deep
Forest where all must lose
Their way, however straight,
Or winding, soon or late;
They cannot choose.

Many a road and track
That, since the dawn's first crack,
Up to the forest brink,
Deceived the travellers,
Suddenly now blurs,
And in they sink.

Here love ends,
Despair, ambition ends;
All pleasure and all trouble,
Although most sweet or bitter,
Here ends in sleep that is sweeter
Than tasks most noble.

There is not any book
Or face of dearest look
That I would not turn from now
To go into the unknown
I must enter, and leave, alone,
I know not how.

The tall forest towers;
Its cloudy foliage lowers
Ahead, shelf above shelf;
Its silence I hear and obey
That I may lose my way
And myself.

804 *The New House*

Now first, as I shut the door,
  I was alone
In the new house; and the wind
  Began to moan.

Old at once was the house,
  And I was old;
My ears were teased with the dread
  Of what was foretold,

Nights of storm, days of mist, without end;
  Sad days when the sun
Shone in vain: old griefs and griefs
  Not yet begun.

All was foretold me; naught
  Could I foresee;
But I learned how the wind would sound
  After these things should be.

805 *Out in the Dark*

Out in the dark over the snow
The fallow fawns invisible go
With the fallow doe;
And the winds blow
Fast as the stars are slow.

Stealthily the dark haunts round
And, when the lamp goes, without sound
At a swifter bound
Than the swiftest hound,
Arrives, and all else is drowned;

And star and I and wind and deer,
Are in the dark together,—near,
Yet far,—and fear
Drums on my ear
In that sage company drear.

849

How weak and little is the light,
All the universe of sight,
Love and delight,
Before the might,
If you love it not, of night.

JAMES JOYCE

1882–1941

806   *'I hear an army'*

I HEAR an army charging upon the land,
  And the thunder of horses plunging, foam about their knees:
Arrogant, in black armour, behind them stand,
  Disdaining the reins, with fluttering whips, the charioteers.

They cry unto the night their battle-name:
  I moan in sleep when I hear afar their whirling laughter.
They cleave the gloom of dreams, a blinding flame,
  Clanging, clanging upon the heart as upon an anvil.

They come shaking in triumph their long, green hair:
  They come out of the sea and run shouting by the shore.
My heart, have you no wisdom thus to despair?
  My love, my love, my love, why have you left me alone?

JAMES ELROY FLECKER

1884–1915

807   *The Golden Journey to Samarkand*
At the Gate of the Sun, Bagdad, in olden time

The Merchants
(together)

Away, for we are ready to a man!
  Our camels sniff the evening and are glad.
Lead on, O Master of the Caravan:
  Lead on the Merchant-Princes of Bagdad.

JAMES ELROY FLECKER

The Chief Draper

Have we not Indian carpets dark as wine,
  Turbans and sashes, gowns and bows and veils,
And broideries of intricate design,
  And printed hangings in enormous bales?

The Chief Grocer

We have rose-candy, we have spikenard,
  Mastic and terebinth and oil and spice,
And such sweet jams meticulously jarred
  As God's own Prophet eats in Paradise.

The Principal Jews

And we have manuscripts in peacock styles
  By Ali of Damascus; we have swords
Engraved with storks and apes and crocodiles,
  And heavy beaten necklaces, for Lords.

The Master of the Caravan

But you are nothing but a lot of Jews.

The Principal Jews

Sir, even dogs have daylight, and we pay.

The Master of the Caravan

But who are ye in rags and rotten shoes,
  You dirty-bearded, blocking up the way?

The Pilgrims

We are the Pilgrims, master; we shall go
  Always a little further: it may be
Beyond that last blue mountain barred with snow,
  Across that angry or that glimmering sea,

White on a throne or guarded in a cave
  There lives a prophet who can understand
Why men were born: but surely we are brave,
  Who make the Golden Journey to Samarkand.

The Chief Merchant

We gnaw the nail of hurry. Master, away!

One of the Women

O turn your eyes to where your children stand.
Is not Bagdad the beautiful? O stay!

The Merchants
(*in chorus*)

We take the Golden Road to Samarkand.

An Old Man

Have you not girls and garlands in your homes,
    Eunuchs and Syrian boys at your command?
Seek not excess: God hateth him who roams!

The Merchants
(*in chorus*)

We make the Golden Journey to Samarkand.

A Pilgrim with a Beautiful Voice

Sweet to ride forth at evening from the wells
    When shadows pass gigantic on the sand,
And softly through the silence beat the bells
    Along the Golden Road to Samarkand.

A Merchant

We travel not for trafficking alone:
    By hotter winds our fiery hearts are fanned:
For lust of knowing what should not þe known
    We make the Golden Journey to Samarkand.

The Master of the Caravan

Open the gate, O watchman of the night!

The Watchman

Ho, travellers, I open. For what land
Leave you the dim-moon city of delight?

The Merchants
(*with a shout*)

We make the Golden Journey to Samarkand.

(*The Caravan passes through the gate*)

DAVID HERBERT LAWRENCE

The Watchman
(*consoling the women*)
What would ye, ladies? It was ever thus.
Men are unwise and curiously planned.

A Woman
They have their dreams, and do not think of us.

Voices of the Caravan
(*in the distance, singing*)
We make the Golden Journey to Samarkand.

DAVID HERBERT LAWRENCE
1885–1930

808   *Piano*

SOFTLY, in the dusk, a woman is singing to me;
Taking me back down the vista of years, till I see
A child sitting under the piano, in the boom of the tingling strings
And pressing the small, poised feet of a mother who smiles as she sings.

In spite of myself, the insidious mastery of song
Betrays me back, till the heart of me weeps to belong
To the old Sunday evenings at home, with winter outside
And hymns in the cosy parlour, the tinkling piano our guide.

So now it is vain for the singer to burst into clamour
With the great black piano appassionato. The glamour
Of childish days is upon me, my manhood is cast
Down in the flood of remembrance, I weep like a child for the past.

809   *Giorno Dei Morti*

ALONG the avenue of cypresses,
All in their scarlet cloaks and surplices
Of linen, go the chanting choristers,
The priests in gold and black, the villagers. . . .

And all along the path to the cemetery
The round dark heads of men crowd silently,
And black-scarved faces of womenfolk, wistfully
Watch at the banner of death, and the mystery.

And at the foot of a grave a father stands
With sunken head; and forgotten, folded hands;
And at the foot of a grave a mother kneels
With pale shut face, nor either hears nor feels

The coming of the chanting choristers
Between the avenue of cypresses
The silence of the many villagers,
The candle-flames beside the surplices.

810   *Snake*

A SNAKE came to my water-trough
On a hot, hot day, and I in pyjamas for the heat,
To drink there.

In the deep, strange-scented shade of the great dark carob-tree
I came down the steps with my pitcher
And must wait, must stand and wait, for there he was at the trough
   before me.

He reached down from a fissure in the earth-wall in the gloom
And trailed his yellow-brown slackness soft-bellied down, over the
   edge of the stone trough
And rested his throat upon the stone bottom,
And where the water had dripped from the tap, in a small clearness,
He sipped with his straight mouth,
Softly drank through his straight gums, into his slack long body,
Silently.

Someone was before me at my water-trough,
And I, like a second comer, waiting.

He lifted his head from his drinking, as cattle do,
And looked at me vaguely, as drinking cattle do,
And flickered his two-forked tongue from his lips, and mused a
   moment,

And stooped and drank a little more,
Being earth-brown, earth-golden from the burning bowels of the earth
On the day of Sicilian July, with Etna smoking.

The voice of my education said to me
He must be killed,
For in Sicily the black, black snakes are innocent, the gold are
    venomous.

And voices in me said, If you were a man
You would take a stick and break him now, and finish him off.

But must I confess how I liked him,
How glad I was he had come like a guest in quiet, to drink at my
    water-trough
And depart peaceful, pacified, and thankless,
Into the burning bowels of this earth?

Was it cowardice, that I dared not kill him?
Was it perversity, that I longed to talk to him?
Was it humility, to feel so honoured?
I felt so honoured.

And yet those voices:
If you were not afraid, you would kill him!

And truly I was afraid, I was most afraid,
But even so, honoured still more
That he should seek my hospitality
From out the dark door of the secret earth.

He drank enough
And lifted his head, dreamily, as one who has drunken,
And flickered his tongue like a forked night on the air, so black;
Seeming to lick his lips,
And looked around like a god, unseeing, into the air,
And slowly turned his head,
And slowly, very slowly, as if thrice adream,
Proceeded to draw his slow length curving round
And climb again the broken bank of my wall-face.

And as he put his head into that dreadful hole,
And as he slowly drew up, snake-easing his shoulders, and entered
    farther,
A sort of horror, a sort of protest against his withdrawing into that
    horrid black hole,
Deliberately going into the blackness, and slowly drawing himself
    after,
Overcame me now his back was turned.

I looked round, I put down my pitcher,
I picked up a clumsy log
And threw it at the water-trough with a clatter.

I think it did not hit him,
But suddenly that part of him that was left behind convulsed in
    undignified haste,
Writhed like lightning, and was gone
Into the black hole, the earth-lipped fissure in the wall front,
At which, in the intense still noon, I stared with fascination.

And immediately I regretted it.
I thought how paltry, how vulgar, what a mean act!
I despised myself and the voices of my accursed human education.

And I thought of the albatross,
And I wished he would come back, my snake.

For he seemed to me again like a king,
Like a king in exile, uncrowned in the underworld,
Now due to be crowned again.

And so, I missed my chance with one of the lords
Of life.
And I have something to expiate;
A pettiness.

811   *Bavarian Gentians*

NOT every man has gentians in his house
in Soft September, at slow, ad Michaelmas.

Bavarian gentians, big and dark, only dark
darkening the day-time torch-like with the smoking blueness of
    Pluto's gloom,
ribbed and torch-like, with their blaze of darkness spread blue
down flattening into points, flattened under the sweep of white day
torch-flower of the blue-smoking darkness, Pluto's dark-blue daze,
black lamps from the halls of Dis, burning dark blue,
giving off darkness, blue darkness, as Demeter's pale lamps give off
    light,
lead me then, lead me the way.

Reach me a gentian, give me a torch
let me guide myself with the blue, forked torch of this flower
down the darker and darker stairs, where blue is darkened on blueness,
even where Persephone goes, just now, from the frosted September
to the sightless realm where darkness is awake upon the dark
and Persephone herself is but a voice
or a darkness invisible enfolded in the deeper dark
of the arms Plutonic, and pierced with the passion of dense gloom,
among the splendour of torches of darkness, shedding darkness on the
    lost bride and her groom.

EZRA POUND

1885–

812   *The River-Merchant's Wife:
                A Letter* after *Rihaku*

WHILE my hair was still cut straight across my forehead
I played about the front gate, pulling flowers.
You came by on bamboo stilts, playing horse,
You walked about my seat, playing with blue plums.
And we went on living in the village of Chokan:
Two small people, without dislike or suspicion.

At fourteen I married My Lord you.
I never laughed, being bashful.
Lowering my head, I looked at the wall.
Called to, a thousand times, I never looked back.

At fifteen I stopped scowling,
I desired my dust to be mingled with yours
For ever and for ever and for ever.
Why should I climb the look out?

At sixteen you departed,
You went into far Ku-to-yen, by the river of swirling eddies,
And you have been gone five months.
The monkeys make sorrowful noise overhead.

You dragged your feet when you went out.
By the gate now, the moss is grown, the different mosses,
Too deep to clear them away!
The leaves fall early this autumn, in wind.
The paired butterflies are already yellow with August
Over the grass in the West garden;
They hurt me. I grow older.
If you are coming down through the narrows of the river Kiang,
Please let me know beforehand,
And I will come out to meet you
              As far as Cho-fu-Sa.

813   *from* Hugh Selwyn Mauberley

(i)

THE tea-rose tea-gown, etc.
Supplants the mousseline of Cos,
The pianola 'replaces'
Sappho's barbitos.

Christ follows Dionysus,
Phallic and ambrosial
Made way for macerations;
Caliban casts out Ariel.

All things are a flowing,
Sage Heracleitus says;
But a tawdry cheapness
Shall outlast our days.

858

Even the Christian beauty
Defects—after Samothrace;
We see τὸ καλὸν
Decreed in the market place.

Faun's flesh is not to us,
Nor the saint's vision.
We have the Press for wafer;
Franchise for circumcision.

All men, in law, are equals.
Free of Pisistratus,
We choose a knave or an eunuch
To rule over us.

O bright Apollo,
τίν' ἄνδρα, τίν' ἤρωα, τίνα θεὸν,
What god, man, or hero
Shall I place a tin wreath upon!

(ii)

These fought in any case,
and some believing,
                    pro domo, in any case . . .

Some quick to arm,
some for adventure,
some from fear of weakness,
some from fear of censure,
some for love of slaughter, in imagination,
learning later . . .
some in fear, learning love of slaughter;

Died some, pro patria,
                    non 'dulce' non 'et decor' . . .
walked eye-deep in hell
believing in old men's lies, then unbelieving
came home, home to a lie,
home to many deceits,
home to old lies and new infamy;
usury age-old and age-thick
and liars in public places.

τὸ καλὸν] (tŏ kalon) beauty   τίν' ἄνδρα, τίν' ἤρωα, τίνα θεὸν,] tin' andra, tin'
hērōa, tina theon,) what man, what hero, what god,

Daring as never before, wastage as never before.
Young blood and high blood,
fair cheeks, and fine bodies;

fortitude as never before

frankness as never before,
disillusions as never told in the old days,
hysterias, trench confessions,
laughter out of dead bellies.

(iii)

There died a myriad,
And of the best, among them,
For an old bitch gone in the teeth,
For a botched civilization,

Charm, smiling at the good mouth,
Quick eyes gone under earth's lid,

For two gross of broken statues,
For a few thousand battered books.

814   *from* The Pisan Cantos

WHAT thou lovest well remains,
                              the rest is dross
What thou lov'st well shall not be reft from thee
What thou lov'st well is thy true heritage
Whose world, or mine or theirs
                              or is it of none?
First came the seen, then thus the palpable
        Elysium, though it were in the halls of hell,
What thou lovest well is thy true heritage
What thou lov'st well shall not be reft from thee

The ant's a centaur in his dragon world.
Pull down thy vanity, it is not man
Made courage, or made order, or made grace,
  Pull down thy vanity, I say pull down.
Learn of the green world what can be thy place
In scaled invention or true artistry,
Pull down thy vanity,
       Paquin pull down!
The green casque has outdone your elegance.

'Master thyself, then others shall thee beare'
  Pull down thy vanity
Thou art a beaten dog beneath the hail,
A swollen magpie in a fitful sun,
Half black half white
Nor knowst'ou wing from tail
Pull down thy vanity
    How mean thy hates
Fostered in falsity,
     Pull down thy vanity,
Rathe to destroy, niggard in charity,
Pull down thy vanity,
    I say pull down.

But to have done instead of not doing
    this is not vanity
To have, with decency, knocked
That a Blunt should open
    To have gathered from the air a live tradition
or from a fine old eye the unconquered flame
This is not vanity.
  Here error is all in the not done,
all in the diffidence that faltered.

Blunt] Wilfred Scawen Blunt (1840–1922), explorer, politician, and poet,
  opponent of British Imperialism

SIEGFRIED SASSOON
1886–1967

815   *Everyone Sang*

EVERYONE suddenly burst out singing;
And I was filled with such delight
As prisoned birds must find in freedom,
Winging wildly across the white
Orchards and dark-green fields; on—on—and
    out of sight.

Everyone's voice was suddenly lifted;
And beauty came like the setting sun:
My heart was shaken with tears; and horror
Drifted away . . . O, but Everyone
Was a bird; and the song was wordless; the singing
    will never be done.

816   *Attack*

AT dawn the ridge emerges massed and dun
In the wild purple of the glow'ring sun,
Smouldering through spouts of drifting smoke that shroud
The menacing scarred slope; and, one by one,
Tanks creep and topple forward to the wire.
The barrage roars and lifts. Then, clumsily bowed
With bombs and guns and shovels and battle-gear,
Men jostle and climb to meet the bristling fire.
Lines of grey, muttering faces, masked with fear,
They leave their trenches, going over the top,
While time ticks blank and busy on their wrists,
And hope, with furtive eyes and grappling fists,
Flounders in mud. O Jesus, make it stop!

RUPERT BROOKE

1887–1915

817 *The Soldier*

If I should die, think only this of me:
  That there's some corner of a foreign field
That is for ever England. There shall be
  In that rich earth a richer dust concealed;
A dust whom England bore, shaped, made aware,
  Gave, once, her flowers to love, her ways to roam,
A body of England's, breathing English air,
  Washed by the rivers, blest by suns of home.

And think, this heart, all evil shed away,
  A pulse in the eternal mind, no less
    Gives somewhere back the thoughts by England given;
Her sights and sounds; dreams happy as her day;
  And laughter, learnt of friends; and gentleness,
    In hearts at peace, under an English heaven.

818 *Heaven*

Fish (fly-replete, in depth of June,
Dawdling away their wat'ry noon)
Ponder deep wisdom, dark or clear,
Each secret fishy hope or fear.
Fish say, they have their Stream and Pond;
But is there anything Beyond?
This life cannot be All, they swear,
For how unpleasant, if it were!
One may not doubt that, somehow, Good
Shall come of Water and of Mud;
And, sure, the reverent eye must see
A Purpose in Liquidity.
We darkly know, by Faith we cry,
The future is not Wholly Dry.
Mud unto mud!—Death eddies near—
Not here the appointed End, not here!
But somewhere, beyond Space and Time,
Is wetter water, slimier slime!

And there (they trust) there swimmeth One
Who swam ere rivers were begun,
Immense, of fishy form and mind,
Squamous, omnipotent, and kind;
And under that Almighty Fin,
The littlest fish may enter in.
Oh! never fly conceals a hook,
Fish say, in the Eternal Brook,
But more than mundane weeds are there,
And mud, celestially fair;
Fat caterpillars drift around,
And Paradisal grubs are found;
Unfading moths, immortal flies,
And the worm that never dies.
And in that Heaven of all their wish,
There shall be no more land, say fish.

EDWIN MUIR

1887–1959

819   *Ballad of Hector in Hades*

YES, this is where I stood that day,
    Beside this sunny mound.
The walls of Troy are far away,
    And outward comes no sound.

I wait. On all the empty plain
    A burnished stillness lies,
Save for the chariot's tinkling hum,
    And a few distant cries.

His helmet glitters near. The world
    Slowly turns around,
With some new sleight compels my feet
    From the fighting ground.

I run. If I turned back again
    The earth must turn with me,
The mountains planted on the plain,
    The sky clamped to the sea.

The grasses puff a little dust
  Where my footsteps fall.
I cast a shadow as I pass
  The little wayside wall.

The strip of grass on either hand
  Sparkles in the light;
I only see that little space
  To the left and to the right,

And in that space our shadows run,
  His shadow there and mine,
The little flowers, the tiny mounds,
  The grasses frail and fine.

But narrower still and narrower!
  My course is shrunk and small,
Yet vast as in a deadly dream,
  And faint the Trojan wall.
The sun up in the towering sky
  Turns like a spinning ball.

The sky with all its clustered eyes
  Grows still with watching me,
The flowers, the mounds, the flaunting weeds
  Wheel slowly round to see.

Two shadows racing on the grass,
  Silent and so near,
Until his shadow falls on mine.
  And I am rid of fear.

The race is ended. Far away
  I hang and do not care,
While round bright Troy Achilles whirls
  A corpse with streaming hair.

820 *The Combat*

I T was not meant for human eyes,
That combat on the shabby patch
Of clods and trampled turf that lies
Somewhere beneath the sodden skies
For eye of toad or adder to catch.

And having seen it I accuse
The crested animal in his pride,
Arrayed in all the royal hues
Which hide the claws he well can use
To tear the heart out of the side.

Body of leopard, eagle's head
And whetted beak, and lion's mane,
And frost-grey hedge of feathers spread
Behind—he seemed of all things bred.
I shall not see his like again.

As for his enemy, there came in
A soft round beast as brown as clay;
All rent and patched his wretched skin;
A battered bag he might have been,
Some old used thing to throw away.

Yet he awaited face to face
The furious beast and the swift attack.
Soon over and done. That was no place
Or time for chivalry or for grace.
The fury had him on his back.

And two small paws like hands flew out
To right and left as the trees stood by.
One would have said beyond a doubt
This was the very end of the bout,
But that the creature would not die.

For ere the death-stroke he was gone,
Writhed, whirled, huddled into his den,
Safe somehow there. The fight was done,
And he had lost who had all but won.
But oh his deadly fury then.

A while the place lay blank, forlorn,
Drowsing as in relief from pain.
The cricket chirped, the grating thorn
Stirred, and a little sound was born.
The champions took their posts again.

And all began. The stealthy paw
Slashed out and in. Could nothing save
These rags and tatters from the claw?
Nothing. And yet I never saw
A beast so helpless and so brave.

And now, while the trees stand watching, still
The unequal battle rages there.
The killing beast that cannot kill
Swells and swells in his fury till
You'd almost think it was despair.

821   *One Foot in Eden*

ONE foot in Eden still, I stand
And look across the other land.
The world's great day is growing late,
Yet strange these fields that we have planted
So long with crops of love and hate.
Time's handiworks by time are haunted,
And nothing now can separate
The corn and tares compactly grown.
The armorial weed in stillness bound
About the stalk; these are our own.
Evil and good stand thick around
In the fields of charity and sin
Where we shall lead our harvest in.

Yet still from Eden springs the root
As clean as on the starting day.
Time takes the foliage and the fruit
And burns the archetypal leaf
To shapes of terror and of grief
Scattered along the winter way.

But famished field and blackened tree
Bear flowers in Eden never known.
Blossoms of grief and charity
Bloom in these darkened fields alone.
What had Eden ever to say
Of hope and faith and pity and love
Until was buried all its day
And memory found its treasure trove?
Strange blessings never in Paradise
Fall from these beclouded skies.

822   *The Horses*

BARELY a twelvemonth after
The seven days war that put the world to sleep,
Late in the evening the strange horses came.
By then we had made our covenant with silence,
But in the first few days it was so still
We listened to our breathing and were afraid.
On the second day
The radios failed; we turned the knobs; no answer.
On the third day a warship passed us, heading north,
Dead bodies piled on the deck. On the sixth day
A plane plunged over us into the sea. Thereafter
Nothing. The radios dumb;
And still they stand in corners of our kitchens,
And stand, perhaps, turned on, in a million rooms
All over the world. But now if they should speak,
If on a sudden they should speak again,
If on the stroke of noon a voice should speak,
We would not listen, we would not let it bring
That old bad world that swallowed its children quick
At one great gulp. We would not have it again.
Sometimes we think of the nations lying asleep,
Curled blindly in impenetrable sorrow,
And then the thought confounds us with its strangeness.
The tractors lie about our fields; at evening
They look like dank sea-monsters couched and waiting.
We leave them where they are and let them rust:
'They'll moulder away and be like other loam'.
We make our oxen drag our rusty ploughs,
Long laid aside. We have gone back
Far past our fathers' land.

                              And then, that evening
Late in the summer the strange horses came.
We heard a distant tapping on the road,
A deepening drumming; it stopped, went on again
And at the corner changed to hollow thunder.
We saw the heads
Like a wild wave charging and were afraid.
We had sold our horses in our fathers' time
To buy new tractors. Now they were strange to us
As fabulous steeds set on an ancient shield
Or illustrations in a book of knights.
We did not dare go near them. Yet they waited,
Stubborn and shy, as if they had been sent
By an old command to find our whereabouts
And that long-lost archaic companionship.
In the first moment we had never a thought
That they were creatures to be owned and used.
Among them were some half-a-dozen colts
Dropped in some wilderness of the broken world,
Yet new as if they had come from their own Eden.
Since then they have pulled our ploughs and borne our loads,
But that free servitude still can pierce our hearts.
Our life is changed; their coming our beginning.

EDITH SITWELL

1887–1964

823   *The Innocent Spring*

IN the great gardens, after bright spring rain,
We find sweet innocence come once again,
White periwinkles, little pensionnaires
With muslin gowns and shy and candid airs,

That under saint-blue skies, with gold stars sown,
Hide their sweet innocence by spring winds blown,
From zephyr libertines that like Richelieu
And d'Orsay their gold-spangled kisses blew;

And lilies of the valley whose buds blonde and tight
Seem curls of little school-children that light
The priests' procession, when on some saint's day
Along the country paths they make their way;

Forget-me-nots, whose eyes of childish blue,
Gold-starred like heaven, speak of love still true;
And all the flowers that we call 'dear heart',
Who say their prayers like children, then depart

Into the dark. Amid the dew's bright beams
The summer airs, like Weber waltzes, fall
Round the first rose who, flushed with her youth, seems
Like a young Princess dressed for her first ball.

Who knows what beauty ripens from dark mould
After the sad wind and the winter's cold?—
But a small wind sighed, colder than the rose
Blooming in desolation, 'No one knows.'

824   *Neptune—Polka*

    ' "TRA la la la—
         See me dance the polka," '
    Said Mr. Wagg like a bear,
    'With my top hat
    And my whiskers that—
    (Tra la la la) trap the Fair.

    Where the waves seem chiming haycocks
    I dance the polka; there
    Stand Venus' children in their gay frocks,—
    Maroon and marine,—and stare

    To see me fire my pistol
    Through the distance blue as my coat;
    Like Wellington, Byron, the Marquis of Bristol,
    Buzbied great trees float.

    While the wheezing hurdy-gurdy
    Of the marine wind blows me
    To the tune of 'Annie Rooney', sturdy,
    Over the sheafs of the sea;

And bright as a seedsman's packet
With zinnias, candytufts chill,
Is Mrs. Marigold's jacket
As she gapes at the inn door still,

Where at dawn in the box of the sailor,
Blue as the decks of the sea,
Nelson awoke, crowed like the cocks,
Then back to the dust sank he.

And Robinson Crusoe
Rues so
The bright and foxy beer,—
But he finds fresh isles in a negress' smiles,—
The poxy doxy dear,

As they watch me dance the polka,'
Said Mr. Wagg like a bear,
'In my top hat and my whiskers that,—
Tra la la la, trap the Fair.

Tra la la la la—
Tra la la la la—
Tra la la la la la la la la
            La
            La
            La!'

825   *Still Falls the Rain*

(The Raids, 1940. Night and Dawn)

STILL falls the Rain—
Dark as the world of man, black as our loss—
Blind as the nineteen hundred and forty nails
Upon the Cross.

Still falls the Rain
With a sound like the pulse of the heart that is changed to the hammer-
    beat
In the Potters' Field, and the sound of the impious feet

On the Tomb:
                    Still falls the Rain
In the Field of Blood where the small hopes breed and the human
    brain
Nurtures its greed, that worm with the brow of Cain.

Still falls the Rain
At the feet of the Starved Man hung upon the Cross.
Christ that each day, each night, nails there, have mercy on us—
On Dives and on Lazarus:
Under the Rain the sore and the gold are as one.

Still falls the Rain—
Still falls the Blood from the Starved Man's wounded Side
He bears in his Heart all wounds,—those of the light that died,
The last faint spark
In the self-murdered heart, the wounds of the sad uncomprehending
    dark,
The wounds of the baited bear,—
The blind and weeping bear whom the keepers beat
On his helpless flesh . . . the tears of the hunted hare.

Still falls the Rain—
Then—O Ile leape up to my God: who pulles me doune—
See, see where Christ's blood streames in the firmament:
It flows from the Brow we nailed upon the tree
Deep to the dying, to the thirsting heart
That holds the fires of the world,—dark-smirched with pain
As Caesar's laurel crown.

Then sounds the voice of One who like the heart of man
Was once a child who among beasts has lain—
'Still do I love, still shed my innocent light, my Blood, for thee.'

THOMAS STEARNS ELIOT
1888–1965

826   *The Love Song of J. Alfred Prufrock*

LET us go then, you and I,
When the evening is spread out against the sky
Like a patient etherised upon a table;
Let us go, through certain half-deserted streets,
The muttering retreats
Of restless nights in one-night cheap hotels
And sawdust restaurants with oyster-shells:
Streets that follow like a tedious argument
Of insidious intent
To lead you to an overwhelming question . . .
Oh, do not ask, 'What is it?'
Let us go and make our visit.

In the room the women come and go
Talking of Michelangelo.

The yellow fog that rubs its back upon the window-panes,
The yellow smoke that rubs its muzzle on the window-panes
Licked its tongue into the corners of the evening,
Lingered upon the pools that stand in drains,
Let fall upon its back the soot that falls from chimneys,
Slipped by the terrace, made a sudden leap,
And seeing that it was a soft October night,
Curled once about the house, and fell asleep.

And indeed there will be time
For the yellow smoke that slides along the street
Rubbing its back upon the window-panes;
There will be time, there will be time
To prepare a face to meet the faces that you meet;
There will be time to murder and create,
And time for all the works and days of hands
That lift and drop a question on your plate;
Time for you and time for me,
And time yet for a hundred indecisions,
And for a hundred visions and revisions,
Before the taking of a toast and tea.

In the room the women come and go
Talking of Michelangelo.

And indeed there will be time
To wonder, 'Do I dare?' and, 'Do I dare?'
Time to turn back and descend the stair,
With a bald spot in the middle of my hair—
(They will say: 'How his hair is growing thin!')
My morning coat, my collar mounting firmly to the chin,
My necktie rich and modest, but asserted by a simple pin—
(They will say: 'But how his arms and legs are thin!')
Do I dare
Disturb the universe?
In a minute there is time
For decisions and revisions which a minute will reverse.

For I have known them all already, known them all—
Have known the evenings, mornings, afternoons,
I have measured out my life with coffee spoons;
I know the voices dying with a dying fall
Beneath the music from a farther room.
    So how should I presume?

And I have known the eyes already, known them all—
The eyes that fix you in a formulated phrase,
And when I am formulated, sprawling on a pin,
When I am pinned and wriggling on the wall,
Then how should I begin
To spit out all the butt-ends of my days and ways?
    And how should I presume?

And I have known the arms already, known them all—
Arms that are braceleted and white and bare
(But in the lamplight, downed with light brown hair!)
Is it perfume from a dress
That makes me so digress?
Arms that lie along a table, or wrap about a shawl.
    And should I then presume?
    And how should I begin?

        .   .   .   .   .

Shall I say, I have gone at dusk through narrow streets
And watched the smoke that rises from the pipes
Of lonely men in shirt-sleeves, leaning out of windows? . . .

I should have been a pair of ragged claws
Scuttling across the floors of silent seas.

       .   .   .   .   .

And the afternoon, the evening, sleeps so peacefully!
Smoothed by long fingers,
Asleep . . . tired . . . or it malingers,
Stretched on the floor, here beside you and me.
Should I, after tea and cakes and ices,
Have the strength to force the moment to its crisis?
But though I have wept and fasted, wept and prayed,
Though I have seen my head (grown slightly bald) brought in upon a
    platter,
I am no prophet—and here's no great matter;
I have seen the moment of my greatness flicker,
And I have seen the eternal Footman hold my coat, and snicker,
And in short, I was afraid.

And would it have been worth it, after all,
After the cups, the marmalade, the tea,
Among the porcelain, among some talk of you and me,
Would it have been worth while,
To have bitten off the matter with a smile,
To have squeezed the universe into a ball
To roll it towards some overwhelming question,
To say: 'I am Lazarus, come from the dead,
Come back to tell you all, I shall tell you all'—
If one, settling a pillow by her head,
   Should say: 'That is not what I meant at all.
   That is not it, at all.'

And would it have been worth it, after all,
Would it have been worth while,
After the sunsets and the dooryards and the sprinkled streets,
After the novels, after the teacups, after the skirts that trail along the
    floor—
And this, and so much more?—
It is impossible to say just what I mean!
But as if a magic lantern threw the nerves in patterns on a screen:

Would it have been worth while
If one, settling a pillow or throwing off a shawl,
And turning toward the window, should say:
  'That is not it at all,
  That is not what I meant, at all.'

      .   .   .   .   .

No! I am not Prince Hamlet, nor was meant to be;
Am an attendant lord, one that will do
To swell a progress, start a scene or two,
Advise the prince; no doubt, an easy tool,
Deferential, glad to be of use,
Politic, cautious, and meticulous;
Full of high sentence, but a bit obtuse;
At times, indeed, almost ridiculous—
Almost, at times, the Fool.

I grow old . . . I grow old . . .
I shall wear the bottoms of my trousers rolled.

Shall I part my hair behind? Do I dare to eat a peach?
I shall wear white flannel trousers, and walk upon the beach.
I have heard the mermaids singing, each to each.

I do not think that they will sing to me.

I have seen them riding seaward on the waves
Combing the white hair of the waves blown back
When the wind blows the water white and black.

We have lingered in the chambers of the sea
By sea-girls wreathed with seaweed red and brown
Till human voices wake us, and we drown.

827   *Sweeney Among the Nightingales*

    APENECK Sweeney spreads his knees
    Letting his arms hang down to laugh,
    The zebra stripes along his jaw
    Swelling to maculate giraffe.

The circles of the stormy moon
Slide westward toward the River Plate,
Death and the Raven drift above
And Sweeney guards the hornèd gate.

Gloomy Orion and the Dog
Are veiled; and hushed the shrunken seas;
The person in the Spanish cape
Tries to sit on Sweeney's knees

Slips and pulls the table cloth
Overturns a coffee-cup,
Reorganised upon the floor
She yawns and draws a stocking up;

The silent man in mocha brown
Sprawls at the window-sill and gapes;
The waiter brings in oranges
Bananas figs and hothouse grapes;

The silent vertebrate in brown
Contracts and concentrates, withdraws;
Rachel *née* Rabinovitch
Tears at the grapes with murderous paws;

She and the lady in the cape
Are suspect, thought to be in league;
Therefore the man with heavy eyes
Declines the gambit, shows fatigue,

Leaves the room and reappears
Outside the window, leaning in,
Branches of wistaria
Circumscribe a golden grin;

The host with someone indistinct
Converses at the door apart,
The nightingales are singing near
The Convent of the Sacred Heart,

And sang within the bloody wood
When Agamemnon cried aloud,
And let their liquid siftings fall
To stain the stiff dishonoured shroud.

The Waste Land

I. The Burial of the Dead

APRIL is the cruellest month, breeding
Lilacs out of the dead land, mixing
Memory and desire, stirring
Dull roots with spring rain.
Winter kept us warm, covering
Earth in forgetful snow, feeding
A little life with dried tubers.
Summer surprised us, coming over the Starnbergersee
With a shower of rain; we stopped in the colonnade,
And went on in sunlight, into the Hofgarten,
And drank coffee, and talked for an hour.
Bin gar keine Russin, stamm' aus Litauen, echt deutsch.
And when we were children, staying at the arch-duke's,
My cousin's, he took me out on a sled,
And I was frightened. He said, Marie,
Marie, hold on tight. And down we went.
In the mountains, there you feel free.
I read, much of the night, and go south in the winter.

What are the roots that clutch, what branches grow
Out of this stony rubbish? Son of man,
You cannot say, or guess, for you know only
A heap of broken images, where the sun beats,
And the dead tree gives no shelter, the cricket no relief,
And the dry stone no sound of water. Only
There is shadow under this red rock,
(Come in under the shadow of this red rock),
And I will show you something different from either
Your shadow at morning striding behind you
Or your shadow at evening rising to meet you;
I will show you fear in a handful of dust.
                    Frisch weht der Wind
                    Der Heimat zu
                    Mein Irisch Kind,
                    Wo weilest du?
'You gave me hyacinths first a year ago;
'They called me the hyacinth girl.'
—Yet when we came back, late, from the hyacinth garden,

Your arms full, and your hair wet, I could not
Speak, and my eyes failed, I was neither
Living nor dead, and I knew nothing,
Looking into the heart of light, the silence.
Oed' und leer das Meer.

   Madame Sosostris, famous clairvoyante,
Had a bad cold, nevertheless
Is known to be the wisest woman in Europe,
With a wicked pack of cards. Here, said she,
Is your card, the drowned Phoenician Sailor,
(Those are pearls that were his eyes. Look!)
Here is Belladonna, the Lady of the Rocks,
The lady of situations.
Here is the man with three staves, and here the Wheel,
And here is the one-eyed merchant, and this card,
Which is blank, is something he carries on his back,
Which I am forbidden to see. I do not find
The Hanged Man. Fear death by water.
I see crowds of people, walking round in a ring.
Thank you. If you see dear Mrs. Equitone,
Tell her I bring the horoscope myself:
One must be so careful these days.

   Unreal City,
Under the brown fog of a winter dawn,
A crowd flowed over London Bridge, so many,
I had not thought death had undone so many.
Sighs, short and infrequent, were exhaled,
And each man fixed his eyes before his feet.
Flowed up the hill and down King William Street,
To where Saint Mary Woolnoth kept the hours
With a dead sound on the final stroke of nine.
There I saw one I knew, and stopped him, crying: 'Stetson!
'You who were with me in the ships at Mylae!
'That corpse you planted last year in your garden,
'Has it begun to sprout! Will it bloom this year?
'Or has the sudden frost disturbed its bed?
'Oh keep the Dog far hence, that's friend to men,
'Or with his nails he'll dig it up again!
'You! hypocrite lecteur!—mon semblable,—mon frère!'

II. A Game of Chess

The Chair she sat in, like a burnished throne,
Glowed on the marble, where the glass
Held up by standards wrought with fruited vines
From which a golden Cupidon peeped out
(Another hid his eyes behind his wing)
Doubled the flames of sevenbranched candelabra
Reflecting light upon the table as
The glitter of her jewels rose to meet it,
From satin cases poured in rich profusion;
In vials of ivory and coloured glass
Unstoppered, lurked her strange synthetic perfumes,
Unguent, powdered, or liquid—troubled, confused
And drowned the sense in odours; stirred by the air
That freshened from the window, these ascended
In fattening the prolonged candle-flames,
Flung their smoke into the laquearia,
Stirring the pattern on the coffered ceiling.
Huge sea-wood fed with copper
Burned green and orange, framed by the coloured stone,
In which sad light a carvèd dolphin swam.
Above the antique mantel was displayed
As though a window gave upon the sylvan scene
The change of Philomel, by the barbarous king
So rudely forced; yet there the nightingale
Filled all the desert with inviolable voice
And still she cried, and still the world, pursues,
'Jug Jug' to dirty ears.
And other withered stumps of time
Were told upon the walls; staring forms
Leaned out, leaning, hushing the room enclosed.
Footsteps shuffled on the stair.
Under the firelight, under the brush, her hair
Spread out in fiery points
Glowed into words, then would be savagely still.

'My nerves are bad to-night. Yes, bad. Stay with me.
'Speak to me. Why do you never speak. Speak.
'What are you thinking of? What thinking? What?
'I never know what you are thinking. Think.'

I think we are in rats' alley
Where the dead men lost their bones.

'What is that noise?'
                      The wind under the door.
'What is that noise now? What is the wind doing?'
                      Nothing again nothing.
                                            'Do
'You know nothing? Do you see nothing? Do you remember
'Nothing?'

      I remember
Those are pearls that were his eyes.
'Are you alive, or not? Is there nothing in your head?'
                                                    But

O O O O that Shakespeherian Rag—
It's so elegant
So intelligent
'What shall I do now? What shall I do?'
'I shall rush out as I am, and walk the street
'With my hair down, so. What shall we do tomorrow?
'What shall we ever do?'
                      The hot water at ten.
And if it rains, a closed car at four.
And we shall play a game of chess,
Pressing lidless eyes and waiting for a knock upon the door.

    When Lil's husband got demobbed, I said—
I didn't mince my words, I said to her myself,
HURRY UP PLEASE ITS TIME
Now Albert's coming back, make yourself a bit smart.
He'll want to know what you done with that money he gave you
To get yourself some teeth. He did, I was there.
You have them all out, Lil, and get a nice set,
He said, I swear, I can't bear to look at you.
And no more can't I, I said, and think of poor Albert,
He's been in the army four years, he wants a good time,
And if you don't give it him, there's others will, I said.
Oh is there, she said. Something o' that, I said.
Then I'll know who to thank, she said, and give me a straight look.
HURRY UP PLEASE ITS TIME
If you don't like it you can get on with it, I said.
Others can pick and choose if you can't.

But if Albert makes off, it won't be for lack of telling.
You ought to be ashamed, I said, to look so antique.
(And her only thirty-one.)
I can't help it, she said, pulling a long face,
It's them pills I took, to bring it off, she said.
(She's had five already, and nearly died of young George.)
The chemist said it would be all right, but I've never been the same.
You *are* a proper fool, I said.
Well, if Albert won't leave you alone, there it is, I said,
What you get married for if you don't want children?
HURRY UP PLEASE ITS TIME
Well, that Sunday Albert was home, they had a hot gammon,
And they asked me in to dinner, to get the beauty of it hot—
HURRY UP PLEASE ITS TIME
HURRY UP PLEASE ITS TIME
Goonight Bill. Goonight Lou. Goonight May. Goonight.
Ta ta. Goonight. Goonight.
Good night, ladies, good night, sweet ladies, good night, good night.

III. The Fire Sermon

The river's tent is broken: the last fingers of leaf
Clutch and sink into the wet bank. The wind
Crosses the brown land, unheard. The nymphs are departed.
Sweet Thames, run softly, till I end my song.
The river bears no empty bottles, sandwich papers,
Silk handkerchiefs, cardboard boxes, cigarette ends
Or other testimony of summer nights. The nymphs are departed.
And their friends, the loitering heirs of City directors;
Departed, have left no addresses.
By the waters of Leman I sat down and wept . . .
Sweet Thames, run softly till I end my song,
Sweet Thames, run softly, for I speak not loud or long.
But at my back in a cold blast I hear
The rattle of the bones, and chuckle spread from ear to ear.

A rat crept softly through the vegetation
Dragging its slimy belly on the bank
While I was fishing in the dull canal
On a winter evening round behind the gashouse
Musing upon the king my brother's wreck
And on the king my father's death before him.
White bodies naked on the low damp ground

And bones cast in a little low dry garret,
Rattled by the rat's foot only, year to year.
But at my back from time to time I hear
The sound of horns and motors, which shall bring
Sweeney to Mrs. Porter in the spring.
O the moon shone bright on Mrs. Porter
And on her daughter
They wash their feet in soda water
Et O ces voix d'enfants, chantant dans la coupole!

Twit twit twit
Jug jug jug jug jug jug
So rudely forc'd.
Tereu

   Unreal City
Under the brown fog of a winter noon
Mr. Eugenides, the Smyrna merchant
Unshaven, with a pocket full of currants
C.i.f. London: documents at sight,
Asked me in demotic French
To luncheon at the Cannon Street Hotel
Followed by a weekend at the Metropole.

   At the violet hour, when the eyes and back
Turn upward from the desk, when the human engine waits
Like a taxi throbbing waiting,
I Tiresias, though blind, throbbing between two lives,
Old man with wrinkled female breasts, can see
At the violet hour, the evening hour that strives
Homeward, and brings the sailor home from sea,
The typist home at teatime, clears her breakfast, lights
Her stove, and lays out food in tins.
Out of the window perilously spread
Her drying combinations touched by the sun's last rays,
On the divan are piled (at night her bed)
Stockings, slippers, camisoles, and stays.
I Tiresias, old man with wrinkled dugs
Perceived the scene, and foretold the rest—
I too awaited the expected guest.
He, the young man carbuncular, arrives,
A small house agent's clerk, with one bold stare,
One of the low on whom assurance sits

As a silk hat on a Bradford millionaire.
The time is now propitious, as he guesses,
The meal is ended, she is bored and tired,
Endeavours to engage her in caresses
Which still are unreproved, if undesired.
Flushed and decided, he assaults at once;
Exploring hands encounter no defence;
His vanity requires no response,
And makes a welcome of indifference.
(And I Tiresias have foresuffered all
Enacted on this same divan or bed;
I who have sat by Thebes below the wall
And walked among the lowest of the dead.)
Bestows one final patronising kiss,
And gropes his way, finding the stairs unlit . . .

She turns and looks a moment in the glass,
Hardly aware of her departed lover;
Her brain allows one half-formed thought to pass:
'Well now that's done: and I'm glad it's over.'
When lovely woman stoops to folly and
Paces about her room again, alone,
She smoothes her hair with automatic hand,
And puts a record on the gramophone.

'This music crept by me upon the waters'
And along the Strand, up Queen Victoria Street.
O City city, I can sometimes hear
Beside a public bar in Lower Thames Street,
The pleasant whining of a mandoline
And a clatter and a chatter from within
Where fishmen lounge at noon: where the walls
Of Magnus Martyr hold
Inexplicable splendour of Ionian white and gold.

            The river sweats
            Oil and tar
            The barges drift
            With the turning tide
            Red sails
            Wide
            To leeward, swing on the heavy spar.

The barges wash
Drifting logs
Down Greenwich reach
Past the Isle of Dogs.
       Weialala leia
       Wallala leialala

Elizabeth and Leicester
Beating oars
The stern was formed
A gilded shell
Red and gold
The brisk swell
Rippled both shores
Southwest wind
Carried down stream
The peal of bells
White towers
       Weialala leia
       Wallala leialala

'Trams and dusty trees.
Highbury bore me. Richmond and Kew
Undid me. By Richmond I raised my knees
Supine on the floor of a narrow canoe.'

'My feet are at Moorgate, and my heart
Under my feet. After the event
He wept. He promised "a new start."
I made no comment. What should I resent?'

'On Margate Sands.
I can connect
Nothing with nothing.
The broken fingernails of dirty hands.
My people humble people who expect
Nothing.'
      la la

To Carthage then I came

Burning burning burning burning
O Lord Thou pluckest me out
O Lord Thou pluckest

burning

IV. Death By Water

Phlebas the Phoenician, a fortnight dead,
Forgot the cry of gulls, and the deep sea swell
And the profit and loss.
                  A current under sea
Picked his bones in whispers. As he rose and fell
He passed the stages of his age and youth
Entering the whirlpool.
                Gentile or Jew
O you who turn the wheel and look to windward,
Consider Phlebas, who was once handsome and tall as you.

V. What the Thunder said

After the torchlight red on sweaty faces
After the frosty silence in the gardens
After the agony in stony places
The shouting and the crying
Prison and palace and reverberation
Of thunder of spring over distant mountains
He who was living is now dead
We who were living are now dying
With a little patience

Here is no water but only rock
Rock and no water and the sandy road
The road winding above among the mountains
Which are mountains of rock without water
If there were water we should stop and drink
Amongst the rock one cannot stop or think
Sweat is dry and feet are in the sand
If there were only water amongst the rock
Dead mountain mouth of carious teeth that cannot spit
Here one can neither stand nor lie nor sit

There is not even silence in the mountains
But dry sterile thunder without rain
There is not even solitude in the mountains
But red sullen faces sneer and snarl
From doors of mudcracked houses
                              If there were water
    And no rock
    If there were rock
    And also water
    And water
    A spring
    A pool among the rock
    If there were the sound of water only
    Not the cicada
    And dry grass singing
    But sound of water over a rock
    Where the hermit-thrush sings in the pine trees
    Drip drop drip drop drop drop drop
    But there is no water

    Who is the third who walks always beside you?
When I count, there are only you and I together
But when I look ahead up the white road
There is always another one walking beside you
Gliding wrapt in a brown mantle, hooded
I do not know whether a man or a woman
—But who is that on the other side of you?

    What is that sound high in the air
Murmur of maternal lamentation
Who are those hooded hordes swarming
Over endless plains, stumbling in cracked earth
Ringed by the flat horizon only
What is the city over the mountains
Cracks and reforms and bursts in the violet air
Falling towers
Jerusalem Athens Alexandria
Vienna London
Unreal

    A woman drew her long black hair out tight
And fiddled whisper music on those strings
And bats with baby faces in the violet light

Whistled, and beat their wings
And crawled head downward down a blackened wall
And upside down in air were towers
Tolling reminiscent bells, that kept the hours
And voices singing out of empty cisterns and exhausted wells.

    In this decayed hole among the mountains
In the faint moonlight, the grass is singing
Over the tumbled graves, about the chapel
There is the empty chapel, only the wind's home.
It has no windows, and the door swings,
Dry bones can harm no one.
Only a cock stood on the rooftree
Co co rico co co rico
In a flash of lightning. Then a damp gust
Bringing rain

    Ganga was sunken, and the limp leaves
Waited for rain, while the black clouds
Gathered far distant, over Himavant.
The jungle crouched, humped in silence.
Then spoke the thunder
Da
Datta: what have we given?
My friend, blood shaking my heart
The awful daring of a moment's surrender
Which an age of prudence can never retract
By this, and this only, we have existed
Which is not to be found in our obituaries
Or in memories draped by the beneficent spider
Or under seals broken by the lean solicitor
In our empty rooms
Da
Dayadhvam: I have heard the key
Turn in the door once and turn once only
We think of the key, each in his prison
Thinking of the key, each confirms a prison
Only at nightfall, aethereal rumours
Revive for a moment a broken Coriolanus

DA
Damyata : The boat responded
Gaily, to the hand expert with sail and oar
The sea was calm, your heart would have responded
Gaily, when invited, beating obedient
To controlling hands

                                                    I sat upon the shore
Fishing, with the arid plain behind me
Shall I at least set my lands in order?
London Bridge is falling down falling down falling down
Poi s'ascose nel foco che gli affina
Quando fiam uti chelidon—O swallow swallow
Le Prince d'Aquitaine à la tour abolie
These fragments I have shored against my ruins
Why then Ile fit you. Hieronymo's mad againe.
Datta. Dayadhvam. Damyata.
                    Shantih shantih shantih

829   *Eyes that last I saw in tears*

    EYES that last I saw in tears
Through division
Here in death's dream kingdom
The golden vision reappears
I see the eyes but not the tears
This is my affliction.

This is my affliction
Eyes I shall not see again
Eyes of decision
Eyes I shall not see unless
At the door of death's other kingdom
Where, as in this,
The eyes outlast a little while
A little while outlast the tears
And hold us in derision.

830   *Marina*

WHAT seas what shores what grey rocks and what islands
What water lapping the bow
And scent of pine and the woodthrush singing through the fog
What images return
O my daughter.

Those who sharpen the tooth of the dog, meaning
Death
Those who glitter with the glory of the hummingbird, meaning
Death
Those who sit in the sty of contentment, meaning
Death
Those who suffer the ecstasy of the animals, meaning
Death

Are become unsubstantial, reduced by a wind,
A breath of pine, and the woodsong fog
By this grace dissolved in place

What is this face, less clear and clearer
The pulse in the arm, less strong and stronger—
Given or lent? more distant than stars and nearer than the eye

Whispers and small laughter between leaves and hurrying feet
Under sleep, where all the waters meet.

Bowsprit cracked with ice and paint cracked with heat.
I made this, I have forgotten
And remember.
The rigging weak and the canvas rotten
Between one June and another September.
Made this unknowing, half conscious, unknown, my own.
The garboard strake leaks, the seams need caulking.
This form, this face, this life
Living to live in a world of time beyond me; let me
Resign my life for this life, my speech for that unspoken,
The awakened, lips parted, the hope, the new ships.

What seas what shores what granite islands towards my timbers
And woodthrush calling through the fog
My daughter.

831   *Little Gidding*

I

MIDWINTER spring is its own season
Sempiternal though sodden towards sundown,
Suspended in time, between pole and tropic.
When the short day is brightest, with frost and fire,
The brief sun flames the ice, on pond and ditches,
In windless cold that is the heart's heat,
Reflecting in a watery mirror
A glare that is blindness in the early afternoon.
And glow more intense than blaze of branch, or brazier,
Stirs the dumb spirit: no wind, but pentecostal fire
In the dark time of the year. Between melting and freezing
The soul's sap quivers. There is no earth smell
Or smell of living thing. This is the spring time
But not in time's covenant. Now the hedgerow
Is blanched for an hour with transitory blossom
Of snow, a bloom more sudden
Than that of summer, neither budding nor fading,
Not in the scheme of generation.
Where is the summer, the unimaginable
Zero summer?

            If you came this way,
Taking the route you would be likely to take
From the place you would be likely to come from,
If you came this way in may time, you would find the hedges
White again, in May, with voluptuary sweetness.
It would be the same at the end of the journey,
If you came at night like a broken king,
If you came by day not knowing what you came for,
It would be the same, when you leave the rough road
And turn behind the pig-sty to the dull façade
And the tombstone. And what you thought you came for
Is only a shell, a husk of meaning
From which the purpose breaks only when it is fulfilled
If at all. Either you had no purpose
Or the purpose is beyond the end you figured
And is altered in fulfilment. There are other places

Which also are the world's end, some at the sea jaws,
Or over a dark lake, in a desert or a city—
But this is the nearest, in place and time,
Now and in England.

                 If you came this way,
Taking any route, starting from anywhere,
At any time or at any season,
It would always be the same: you would have to put off
Sense and notion. You are not here to verify,
Instruct yourself, or inform curiosity
Or carry report. You are here to kneel
Where prayer has been valid. And prayer is more
Than an order of words, the conscious occupation
Of the praying mind, or the sound of the voice praying.
And what the dead had no speech for, when living,
They can tell you, being dead: the communication
Of the dead is tongued with fire beyond the language of the living.
Here, the intersection of the timeless moment
Is England and nowhere. Never and always.

II

Ash on an old man's sleeve
Is all the ash the burnt roses leave.
Dust in the air suspended
Marks the place where a story ended.
Dust inbreathed was a house—
The wall, the wainscot and the mouse.
The death of hope and despair,
     This is the death of air.

There are flood and drouth
Over the eyes and in the mouth,
Dead water and dead sand
Contending for the upper hand.
The parched eviscerate soil
Gapes at the vanity of toil,
Laughs without mirth.
     This is the death of earth.

Water and fire succeed
The town, the pasture and the weed.
Water and fire deride
The sacrifice that we denied.
Water and fire shall rot
The marred foundations we forgot,
Of sanctuary and choir.
    This is the death of water and fire.

In the uncertain hour before the morning
  Near the ending of interminable night
  At the recurrent end of the unending
After the dark dove with the flickering tongue
  Had passed below the horizon of his homing
  While the dead leaves still rattled on like tin
Over the asphalt where no other sound was
  Between three districts whence the smoke arose
  I met one walking, loitering and hurried
As if blown towards me like the metal leaves
  Before the urban dawn wind unresisting.
  And as I fixed upon the down-turned face
That pointed scrutiny with which we challenge
  The first-met stranger in the waning dusk
  I caught the sudden look of some dead master
Whom I had known, forgotten, half recalled
  Both one and many; in the brown baked features
  The eyes of a familiar compound ghost
Both intimate and unidentifiable.
  So I assumed a double part, and cried
  And heard another's voice cry: 'What! are *you* here?'
Although we were not. I was still the same,
  Knowing myself yet being someone other—
  And he a face still forming; yet the words sufficed
To compel the recognition they preceded.
  And so, compliant to the common wind,
  Too strange to each other for misunderstanding,
In concord at this intersection time
  Of meeting nowhere, no before and after,
  We trod the pavement in a dead patrol.
I said: 'The wonder that I feel is easy,
  Yet ease is cause of wonder. Therefore speak:
  I may not comprehend, may not remember.'

And he: 'I am not eager to rehearse
  My thought and theory which you have forgotten.
  These things have served their purpose: let them be.
So with your own, and pray they be forgiven
  By others, as I pray you to forgive
  Both bad and good. Last season's fruit is eaten
And the fullfed beast shall kick the empty pail.
  For last year's words belong to last year's language
  And next year's words await another voice.
But, as the passage now presents no hindrance
  To the spirit unappeased and peregrine
  Between two worlds become much like each other,
So I find words I never thought to speak
  In streets I never thought I should revisit
  When I left my body on a distant shore.
Since our concern was speech, and speech impelled us
  To purify the dialect of the tribe
  And urge the mind to aftersight and foresight,
Let me disclose the gifts reserved for age
  To set a crown upon your lifetime's effort.
  First, the cold friction of expiring sense
Without enchantment, offering no promise
  But bitter tastelessness of shadow fruit
  As body and soul begin to fall asunder.
Second, the conscious impotence of rage
  At human folly, and the laceration
  Of laughter at what ceases to amuse.
And last, the rending pain of re-enactment
  Of all that you have done, and been; the shame
  Of motives late revealed, and the awareness
Of things ill done and done to others' harm
  Which once you took for exercise of virtue.
  Then fools' approval stings, and honour stains.
From wrong to wrong the exasperated spirit
  Proceeds, unless restored by that refining fire
  Where you must move in measure, like a dancer.'
The day was breaking. In the disfigured street
  He left me, with a kind of valediction,
  And faded on the blowing of the horn.

III

There are three conditions which often look alike
Yet differ completely, flourish in the same hedgerow:
Attachment to self and to things and to persons, detachment
From self and from things and from persons; and, growing
  between them, indifference
Which resembles the others as death resembles life,
Being between two lives—unflowering, between
The live and the dead nettle. This is the use of memory:
For liberation—not less of love but expanding
Of love beyond desire, and so liberation
From the future as well as the past. Thus, love of a country
Begins as attachment to our own field of action
And comes to find that action of little importance
Though never indifferent. History may be servitude,
History may be freedom. See, now they vanish,
The faces and places, with the self which, as it could, loved them,
To become renewed, transfigured, in another pattern.
Sin is Behovely, but
All shall be well, and
All manner of thing shall be well.
If I think, again, of this place,
And of people, not wholly commendable,
Of no immediate kin or kindness,
But some of peculiar genius,
All touched by a common genius,
United in the strife which divided them;
If I think of a king at nightfall,
Of three men, and more, on the scaffold
And a few who died forgotten
In other places, here and abroad,
And of one who died blind and quiet,
Why should we celebrate
These dead men more than the dying?
It is not to ring the bell backward
Nor is it an incantation
To summon the spectre of a Rose.
We cannot revive old factions
We cannot restore old policies
Or follow an antique drum.

These men, and those who opposed them
And those whom they opposed
Accept the constitution of silence
And are folded in a single party.
Whatever we inherit from the fortunate
We have taken from the defeated
What they had to leave us—a symbol:
A symbol perfected in death.
And all shall be well and
All manner of thing shall be well
By the purification of the motive
In the ground of our beseeching.

IV

The dove descending breaks the air
With flame of incandescent terror
Of which the tongues declare
The one discharge from sin and error.
The only hope, or else despair
   Lies in the choice of pyre or pyre—
   To be redeemed from fire by fire.

Who then devised the torment? Love.
Love is the unfamiliar Name
Behind the hands that wove
The intolerable shirt of flame
Which human power cannot remove.
   We only live, only suspire
   Consumed by either fire or fire.

V

What we call the beginning is often the end
And to make an end is to make a beginning.
The end is where we start from. And every phrase
And sentence that is right (where every word is at home,
Taking its place to support the others,
The word neither diffident nor ostentatious,
An easy commerce of the old and the new,
The common word exact without vulgarity,
The formal word precise but not pedantic,
The complete consort dancing together)
Every phrase and every sentence is an end and a beginning,

Every poem an epitaph. And any action
Is a step to the block, to the fire, down the sea's throat
Or to an illegible stone: and that is where we start.
We die with the dying:
See, they depart, and we go with them.
We are born with the dead:
See, they return, and bring us with them.
The moment of the rose and the moment of the yew-tree
Are of equal duration. A people without history
Is not redeemed from time, for history is a pattern
Of timeless moments. So, while the light fails
On a winter's afternoon, in a secluded chapel
History is now and England.

With the drawing of this Love and the voice of this Calling

We shall not cease from exploration
And the end of all our exploring
Will be to arrive where we started
And know the place for the first time.
Through the unknown, remembered gate
When the last of earth left to discover
Is that which was the beginning;
At the source of the longest river
The voice of the hidden waterfall
And the children in the apple-tree
Not known, because not looked for
But heard, half-heard, in the stillness
Between two waves of the sea.
Quick now, here, now, always—
A condition of complete simplicity
(Costing not less than everything)
And all shall be well and
All manner of thing shall be well
When the tongues of flame are in-folded
Into the crowned knot of fire
And the fire and the rose are one.

WALTER JAMES TURNER
1889–1946

832 *Romance*

WHEN I was but thirteen or so
  I went into a golden land,
Chimborazo, Cotopaxi
  Took me by the hand.

My father died, my brother too,
  They passed like fleeting dreams.
I stood where Popocatapetl
  In the sunlight gleams.

I dimly heard the Master's voice
  And boys far-off at play,
Chimborazo, Cotopaxi
  Had stolen me away.

I walked in a great golden dream
  To and fro from 'school—
Shining Popocatapetl
  The dusty streets did rule.

I walked home with a gold dark boy
  And never a word I'd say,
Chimborazo, Cotopaxi
  Had taken my speech away:

I gazed entranced upon his face
  Fairer than any flower—
O shining Popocatapetl
  It was thy magic hour:

The houses, people, traffic seemed
  Thin fading dreams by day,
Chimborazo, Cotopaxi
  They had stolen my soul away!

ISAAC ROSENBERG
1890–1918

833   *August 1914*

WHAT in our lives is burnt
In the fire of this?
The heart's dear granary?
The much we shall miss?

Three lives hath one life—
Iron, honey, gold.
The gold, the honey gone—
Left is the hard and cold.

Iron are our lives
Molten right through our youth.
A burnt space through ripe fields
A fair mouth's broken tooth.

834   *Break of Day in the Trenches*

THE darkness crumbles away—
It is the same old druid Time as ever.
Only a live thing leaps my hand—
A queer sardonic rat—
As I pull the parapet's poppy
To stick behind my ear.
Droll rat, they would shoot you if they knew
Your cosmopolitan sympathies.
Now you have touched this English hand
You will do the same to a German—
Soon, no doubt, if it be your pleasure
To cross the sleeping green between.
It seems you inwardly grin as you pass
Strong eyes, fine limbs, haughty athletes
Less chanced than you for life,
Bonds to the whims of murder,
Sprawled in the bowels of the earth,
The torn fields of France.

What do you see in our eyes
At the shrieking iron and flame
Hurled through still heavens?
What quaver—what heart aghast?
Poppies whose roots are in man's veins
Drop, and are ever dropping;
But mine in my ear is safe,
Just a little white with the dust.

WILFRED OWEN

1893–1918

835   *Anthem for Doomed Youth*

WHAT passing-bells for these who die as cattle?
   Only the monstrous anger of the guns.
Only the stuttering rifles' rapid rattle
   Can patter out their hasty orisons.
No mockeries now for them; no prayers nor bells,
   Nor any voice of mourning save the choirs,—
The shrill, demented choirs of wailing shells;
   And bugles calling for them from sad shires.

What candles may be held to speed them all?
   Not in the hands of boys, but in their eyes
   Shall shine the holy glimmers of good-byes.
The pallor of girls' brows shall be their pall;
   Their flowers the tenderness of patient minds,
   And each slow dusk a drawing-down of blinds.

836   *Strange Meeting*

IT seemed that out of battle I escaped
Down some profound dull tunnel, long since scooped
Through granites which titanic wars had groined.
Yet also there encumbered sleepers groaned,
Too fast in thought or death to be bestirred.
Then, as I probed them, one sprang up, and stared

With piteous recognition in fixed eyes,
Lifting distressful hands as if to bless.
And by his smile I knew that sullen hall,
By his dead smile I knew we stood in Hell.
With a thousand pains that vision's face was grained;
Yet no blood reached there from the upper ground,
And no guns thumped, or down the flues made moan.
'Strange friend,' I said, 'here is no cause to mourn.'
'None,' said the other, 'save the undone years,
The hopelessness. Whatever hope is yours,
Was my life also; I went hunting wild
After the wildest beauty in the world,
Which lies not calm in eyes, or braided hair,
But mocks the steady running of the hour,
And if it grieves, grieves richlier than here.
For by my glee might many men have laughed,
And of my weeping something had been left,
Which must die now. I mean the truth untold,
The pity of war, the pity war distilled.
Now men will go content with what we spoiled.
Or, discontent, boil bloody, and be spilled.
They will be swift with swiftness of the tigress,
None will break ranks, though nations trek from progress.
Courage was mine, and I had mystery,
Wisdom was mine, and I had mastery;
To miss the march of this retreating world
Into vain citadels that are not walled.
Then, when much blood had clogged their chariot-wheels
I would go up and wash them from sweet wells,
Even with truths that lie too deep for taint.
I would have poured my spirit without stint
But not through wounds; not on the cess of war.
Foreheads of men have bled where no wounds were.
I am the enemy you killed, my friend.
I knew you in this dark; for so you frowned
Yesterday through me as you jabbed and killed.
I parried; but my hands were loath and cold.
Let us sleep now . . .'

837 *Miners*

THERE was a whispering in my hearth,
    A sigh of the coal,
Grown wistful of a former earth
    It might recall.

I listened for a tale of leaves
    And smothered ferns;
Frond-forests; and the low, sly lives
    Before the fawns.

My fire might show steam-phantoms simmer
    From Time's old cauldron,
Before the birds made nests in summer,
    Or men had children.

But the coals were murmuring of their mine,
    And moans down there
Of boys that slept wry sleep, and men
    Writhing for air.

And I saw white bones in the cinder-shard.
    Bones without number;
For many hearts with coal are charred
    And few remember.

I thought of some who worked dark pits
    Of war, and died
Digging the rock where Death reputes
    Peace lies indeed.

Comforted years will sit soft-chaired
    In rooms of amber;
The years will stretch their hands, well-cheered
    By our lives' ember.

The centuries will burn rich loads
    With which we groaned,
Whose warmth shall lull their dreaming lids
    While songs are crooned.
But they will not dream of us poor lads
    Lost in the ground.

ROBERT GRAVES
1895–

Full Moon

As I walked out that sultry night,
  I heard the stroke of One.
The moon, attained to her full height,
  Stood beaming like the sun:
She exorcized the ghostly wheat
To mute assent in love's defeat,
  Whose tryst had now begun.

The fields lay sick beneath my tread,
  A tedious owlet cried,
A nightingale above my head
  With this or that replied—
Like man and wife who nightly keep
Inconsequent debate in sleep
  As they dream side by side.

Your phantom wore the moon's cold mask,
  My phantom wore the same;
Forgetful of the feverish task
  In hope of which they came,
Each image held the other's eyes
And watched a grey distraction rise
  To cloud the eager flame—

To cloud the eager flame of love,
  To fog the shining gate;
They held the tyrannous queen above
  Sole mover of their fate,
They glared as marble statues glare
Across the tessellated stair
  Or down the halls of state.

And now warm earth was Arctic sea,
   Each breath came dagger-keen;
Two bergs of glinting ice were we,
   The broad moon sailed between;
There swam the mermaids, tailed and finned,
And love went by upon the wind
   As though it had not been.

839   *Sick Love*

O LOVE, be fed with apples while you may,
And feel the sun and go in royal array,
A smiling innocent on the heavenly causeway,

Though in what listening horror for the cry
That soars in outer blackness dismally,
The dumb blind beast, the paranoiac fury:

Be warm, enjoy the season, lift your head,
Exquisite in the pulse of tainted blood,
That shivering glory not to be despised.

Take your delight in momentariness,
Walk between dark and dark—a shining space
With the grave's narrowness, though not its peace.

840   *Welsh Incident*

'BUT that was nothing to what things came out
From the sea-caves of Criccieth yonder.'
'What were they? Mermaids? dragons? ghosts?'
'Nothing at all of any things like that.'
'What were they, then?'
               'All sorts of queer things,
Things never seen or heard or written about,
Very strange, un-Welsh, utterly peculiar
Things. Oh, solid enough they seemed to touch,
Had anyone dared it. Marvellous creation,
All various shapes and sizes, and no sizes,
All new, each perfectly unlike his neighbour,
Though all came moving slowly out together.'

904

'Describe just one of them.'

                            'I am unable.'

'What were their colours?'

                         'Mostly nameless colours,
Colours you'd like to see; but one was puce
Or perhaps more like crimson, but not purplish.
Some had no colour.'

               'Tell me, had they legs?'
'Not a leg nor foot among them that I saw.'
'But did these things come out in any order?
What o'clock was it? What was the day of the week?
Who else was present? How was the weather?'
'I was coming to that. It was half-past three
On Easter Tuesday last. The sun was shining.
The Harlech Silver Band played *Marchog Jesu*
On thirty-seven shimmering instruments
Collecting for Caernarvon's (Fever) Hospital Fund.
The populations of Pwllheli, Criccieth,
Portmadoc, Borth, Tremadoc, Penrhyndeudraeth,
Were all assembled. Criccieth's mayor addressed them
First in good Welsh and then in fluent English,
Twisting his fingers in his chain of office,
Welcoming the things. They came out on the sand,
Not keeping time to the band, moving seaward
Silently at a snail's pace. But at last
The most odd, indescribable thing of all,
Which hardly one man there could see for wonder,
Did something recognizably a something.'
'Well, what?'

          'It made a noise.'

                    'A frightening noise?'
'No, no.'

      'A musical noise? A noise of scuffling?'
'No, but a very loud, respectable noise—
Like groaning to oneself on Sunday morning
In Chapel, close before the second psalm.'
'What did the mayor do?'

                   'I was coming to that'.

841   *She tells her love while half asleep*

> SHE tells her love while half asleep
>   In the dark hours,
>   With half-words whispered low:
> As Earth stirs in her winter sleep
>   And puts out grass and flowers
>   Despite the snow,
>   Despite the falling snow.

842   *A Slice of Wedding Cake*

> WHY have such scores of lovely, gifted girls
>   Married impossible men?
> Simple self-sacrifice may be ruled out,
>   And missionary endeavour, nine times out of ten.
>
> Repeat 'impossible men': not merely rustic,
>   Foul-tempered or depraved
> (Dramatic foils chosen to show the world
>   How well women behave, and always have behaved).
>
> Impossible men: idle, illiterate,
>   Self-pitying, dirty, sly,
> For whose appearance even in City parks
>   Excuses must be made to casual passers-by.
>
> Has God's supply of tolerable husbands
>   Fallen, in fact, so low?
> Or do I always over-value woman
>   At the expense of man?
>   Do I?
>   It might be so.

EDMUND BLUNDEN

1896–

843   *Forefathers*

HERE they went with smock and crook,
   Toiled in the sun, lolled in the shade,
Here they mudded out the brook
   And here their hatchet cleared the glade:
Harvest supper woke their wit,
Huntsman's moon their wooings lit.

From this church they led their brides,
   From this church themselves were led
Shoulder-high; on these waysides
   Sat to take their beer and bread.
Names are gone—what men they were
These their cottages declare.

Names are vanished, save the few
   In the old brown Bible scrawled;
These were men of pith and thew,
   Whom the city never called;
Scarce could read or hold a quill,
Built the barn, the forge, the mill.

On the green they watched their sons
   Playing till too dark to see,
As their fathers watched them once,
   As my father once watched me;
While the bat and beetle flew
On the warm air webbed with dew.

Unrecorded, unrenowned,
   Men from whom my ways begin,
Here I know you by your ground
   But I know you not within—
There is silence, there survives
Not a moment of your lives.

Like the bee that now is blown
Honey-heavy on my hand,
From his toppling tansy-throne
In the green tempestuous land
I'm in clover now, nor know
Who made honey long ago.

844　　　　　　　*Report on Experience*

I HAVE been young, and now am not too old;
And I have seen the righteous forsaken,
His health, his honour and his quality taken.
　　This is not what we were formerly told.

I have seen a green country, useful to the race,
Knocked silly with guns and mines, its villages vanished,
Even the last rat and last kestrel banished—
　　God bless us all, this was peculiar grace.

I knew Seraphina; Nature gave her hue,
Glance, sympathy, note, like one from Eden.
I saw her smile warp, heard her lyric deaden;
　　She turned to harlotry;—this I took to be new.

Say what you will, our God sees how they run.
These disillusions are his curious proving
That he loves humanity and will go on loving;
　　Over there are faith, life, virtue in the sun.

845　　　　　　　*The Midnight Skaters*

THE hop-poles stand in cones,
　　The icy pond lurks under,
The pole-tops steeple to the thrones
　　Of stars, sound gulfs of wonder;
But not the tallest there, 'tis said,
Could fathom to this pond's black bed.

Then is not death at watch
    Within those secret waters?
What wants he but to catch
    Earth's heedless sons and daughters?
With but a crystal parapet
Between, he has his engines set.

Then on, blood shouts, on, on,
    Twirl, wheel and whip above him,
Dance on this ball-floor thin and wan,
    Use him as though you love him;
Court him, elude him, reel and pass,
And let him hate you through the glass.

STEVIE SMITH

1902–1971

846   *Not Waving But Drowning*

NOBODY heard him, the dead man,
But still he lay moaning:
I was much further out than you thought
And not waving but drowning.

Poor chap, he always loved larking
And now he's dead
It must have been too cold for him his heart gave way,
They said.

Oh, no no no, it was too cold always
(Still the dead one lay moaning)
I was much too far out all my life
And not waving but drowning.

CECIL DAY-LEWIS

1904–1972

847   *A Failure*

THE soil was deep and the field well-sited,
    The seed was sound.
Average luck with the weather, one thought,
    And the crop would abound.

If harrowing were all that is needed for
    Harvest, his field
Had been harrowed enough, God knows, to warrant
    A record yield.

He gazed from a hill in the breezy springtime:
    That field was aflow
With wave upon wave like a sea's green shallows
    Breathing below.

He looked from a gate one summer morning
    When the mists uprolled:
Headland to headland those fortunate acres
    Seemed solid gold.

He stood by the field as the day of harvest
    Dawned. But, oh,
The fruit of a year's work, a lifetime's lore,
    Had ceased to grow.

No wickedest weather could thus have turned,
    As it were overnight,
His field to so wan and weedy a showing:
    Some galloping blight

From earth's metabolism must have sprung
    To ruin all;
Or perhaps his own high hopes had made
    The wizened look tall.

But it's useless to argue the why and wherefore.
    When a crop is so thin,
There's nothing to do but to set the teeth
    And plough it in.

SIR JOHN BETJEMAN

1906–

848   *Death of King George V*

'New King arrives in his capital by air . . .'
Daily Newspaper.

SPIRITS of well-shot woodcock, partridge, snipe
    Flutter and bear him up the Norfolk sky:
In that red house in a red mahogany book-case
    The stamp collection waits with mounts long dry.

The big blue eyes are shut which saw wrong clothing
    And favourite fields and coverts from a horse;
Old men in country houses hear clocks ticking
    Over thick carpets with a deadened force;

Old men who never cheated, never doubted,
    Communicated monthly, sit and stare
At the new suburb stretched beyond the run-way
    Where a young man lands hatless from the air.

849   *Parliament Hill Fields*

RUMBLING under blackened girders, Midland, bound for Crickle-
    wood,
Puffed its sulphur to the sunset where that Land of Laundries stood.
Rumble under, thunder over, train and tram alternate go,
Shake the floor and smudge the ledger, Charrington, Sells, Dale and
    Co.,
Nuts and nuggets in the window, trucks along the lines below.

When the Bon Marché was shuttered, when the feet were hot and
    tired,
Outside Charrington's we waited, by the 'STOP HERE IF REQUIRED',
Launched aboard the shopping basket, sat precipitately down,
Rocked past Zwanziger the baker's, and the terrace blackish brown,
And the curious Anglo-Norman parish church of Kentish Town.

Till the tram went over thirty, sighting terminus again,
Past municipal lawn tennis and the bobble-hanging plane;
Soft the light suburban evening caught our ashlar-speckled spire,
Eighteen-sixty Early English, as the mighty elms retire
Either side of Brookfield Mansions flashing fine French-window fire.

Oh the after-tram-ride quiet, when we heard a mile beyond,
Silver music from the bandstand, barking dogs by Highgate Pond;
Up the hill where stucco houses in Virginia creeper drown—
And my childish wave of pity, seeing children carrying down
Sheaves of drooping dandelions to the courts of Kentish Town.

850 *The Cottage Hospital*

AT the end of a long-walled garden
 in a red provincial town,
A brick path led to a mulberry—
 scanty grass at its feet.
I lay under blackening branches
 where the mulberry leaves hung down
Sheltering ruby fruit globes
 from a Sunday-tea-time heat.
Apple and plum espaliers
 basked upon bricks of brown;
The air was swimming with insects,
 and children played in the street.

Out of this bright intentness
 into the mulberry shade
Musca domestica (housefly)
 swung from the August light
Slap into slithery rigging
 by the waiting spider made
Which spun the lithe elastic
 till the fly was shrouded tight.
Down came the hairy talons
 and horrible poison blade
And none of the garden noticed
 that fizzing, hopeless fight.

Say in what Cottage Hospital
   whose pale green walls resound
With the tap upon polished parquet
   of inflexible nurses' feet
Shall I myself be lying
   when they range the screens around?
And say shall I groan in dying,
   as I twist the sweaty sheet?
Or gasp for breath uncrying,
   as I feel my senses drown'd
While the air is swimming with insects
   and children play in the street?

WILLIAM EMPSON

1906–

851   *To an Old Lady*

RIPENESS is all; her in her cooling planet
Revere; do not presume to think her wasted.
Project her no projectile, plan nor man it;
Gods cool in turn, by the sun long outlasted.

Our earth alone given no name of god
Gives, too, no hold for such a leap to aid her;
Landing, you break some palace and seem odd;
Bees sting their need, the keeper's queen invader.

No, to your telescope; spy out the land;
Watch while her ritual is still to see,
Still stand her temples emptying in the sand
Whose waves o'erthrew their crumbled tracery;

Still stand uncalled-on her soul's appanage;
Much social detail whose successor fades,
Wit used to run a house and to play Bridge,
And tragic fervour, to dismiss her maids.

Years her precession do not throw from gear.
She reads a compass certain of her pole;
Confident, finds no confines on her sphere,
Whose failing crops are in her sole control.

Stars how much further from me fill my night.
Strange that she too should be inaccessible,
Who shares my sun. He curtains her from sight,
And but in darkness is she visible.

852   *Missing Dates*

SLOWLY the poison the whole blood stream fills.
It is not the effort nor the failure tires.
The waste remains, the waste remains and kills.

It is not your system or clear sight that mills
Down small to the consequence a life requires;
Slowly the poison the whole blood stream fills.

They bled an old dog dry yet the exchange rills
Of young dog blood gave but a month's desires.
The waste remains, the waste remains and kills.

It is the Chinese tombs and the slag hills
Usurp the soil, and not the soil retires.
Slowly the poison the whole blood stream fills.

Not to have fire is to be a skin that shrills.
The complete fire is death. From partial fires
The waste remains, the waste remains and kills.

It is the poems you have lost, the ills
From missing dates, at which the heart expires.
Slowly the poison the whole blood stream fills.
The waste remains, the waste remains and kills.

WYSTAN HUGH AUDEN

1907–

853 *O Where are you Going?*

'O WHERE are you going?' said reader to rider,
'That valley is fatal when furnaces burn,
Yonder's the midden whose odours will madden,
That gap is the grave where the tall return.'

'O do you imagine,' said fearer to farer,
'That dusk will delay on your path to the pass,
Your diligent looking discover the lacking
Your footsteps feel from granite to grass?'

'O what was that bird,' said horror to hearer,
'Did you see that shape in the twisted trees?
Behind you swiftly the figure comes softly,
The spot on your skin is a shocking disease.'

'Out of this house'—said rider to reader,
'Yours never will'—said farer to fearer,
'They're looking for you'—said hearer to horror,
As he left them there, as he left them there.

854 *A I walked out one Evening*

As I walked out one evening,
  Walking down Bristol Street,
The crowds upon the pavement
  Were fields of harvest wheat.

And down by the brimming river
  I heard a lover sing
Under an arch of the railway:
  'Love has no ending.

'I'll love you, dear, I'll love you
  Till China and Africa meet,
And the river jumps over the mountain
  And the salmon sing in the street,

915

'I'll love you till the ocean
   Is folded and hung up to dry
And the seven stars go squawking
   Like geese about the sky.

The years shall run like rabbits,
   For in my arms I hold
The Flower of the Ages,
   And the first love of the world.'

But all the clocks in the city
   Began to whirr and chime:
'O let not Time deceive you,
   You cannot conquer Time.

'In the burrows of the Nightmare
   Where Justice naked is,
Time watches from the shadow
   And coughs when you would kiss.

'In headaches and in worry
   Vaguely life leaks away,
And Time will have his fancy
   To-morrow or to-day.

'Into many a green valley
   Drifts the appalling snow;
Time breaks the threaded dances
   And the diver's brilliant bow.

'O plunge your hands in water,
   Plunge them in up to the wrist;
Stare, stare in the basin
   And wonder what you've missed.

'The glacier knocks in the cupboard,
   The desert sighs in the bed,
And the crack in the tea-cup opens
   A lane to the land of the dead.

'Where the beggars raffle the banknotes
   And the Giant is enchanting to Jack,
And the Lily-white Boy is a Roarer,
   And Jill goes down on her back.

'O look, look in the mirror,
  O look in your distress;
Life remains a blessing
  Although you cannot bless.

'O stand, stand at the window
  As the tears scald and start;
You shall love your crooked neighbour
  With your crooked heart.'

It was late, late in the evening,
  The lovers they were gone;
The clocks had ceased their chiming,
  And the deep river ran on.

855   *Lullaby*

      LAY your sleeping head, my love,
      Human on my faithless arm;
      Time and fevers burn away
      Individual beauty from
      Thoughtful children, and the grave
      Proves the child ephemeral:
      But in my arms till break of day
      Let the living creature lie,
      Mortal, guilty, but to me
      The entirely beautiful.

      Soul and body have no bounds:
      To lovers as they lie upon
      Her tolerant enchanted slope
      In their ordinary swoon,
      Grave the vision Venus sends
      Of supernatural sympathy,
      Universal love and hope;
      While an abstract insight wakes
      Among the glaciers and the rocks
      The hermit's carnal ecstasy.

Certainty, fidelity
On the stroke of midnight pass
Like vibrations of a bell
And fashionable madmen raise
Their pedantic boring cry:
Every farthing of the cost,
All the dreaded cards foretell,
Shall be paid, but from this night
Not a whisper, not a thought,
Not a kiss nor look be lost.

Beauty, midnight, vision dies:
Let the winds of dawn that blow
Softly round your dreaming head
Such a day of welcome show
Eye and knocking heart may bless,
Find our mortal world enough;
Noons of dryness find you fed
By the involuntary powers,
Nights of insult let you pass
Watched by every human love.

856   *Musée des Beaux Arts*

ABOUT suffering they were never wrong,
The Old Masters: how well they understood
Its human position; how it takes place
While someone else is eating or opening a window or just walking
    dully along;
How, when the aged are reverently, passionately waiting
For the miraculous birth, there always must be
Children who did not specially want it to happen, skating
On a pond at the edge of the wood:
They never forgot
That even the dreadful martyrdom must run its course
Anyhow in a corner, some untidy spot
Where the dogs go on with their doggy life and the torturer's horse
Scratches its innocent behind on a tree.

In Brueghel's *Icarus*, for instance: how everything turns away
Quite leisurely from the disaster; the ploughman may
Have heard the splash, the forsaken cry,
But for him it was not an important failure; the sun shone
As it had to on the white legs disappearing into the green
Water; and the expensive delicate ship that must have seen
Something amazing, a boy falling out of the sky,
Had somewhere to get to and sailed calmly on.

857   *In Memory of W. B. Yeats*

(d. Jan. 1939)

I

HE disappeared in the dead of winter:
The brooks were frozen, the airports almost deserted,
And snow disfigured the public statues;
The mercury sank in the mouth of the dying day.
What instruments we have agree
The day of his death was a dark cold day.

Far from his illness
The wolves ran on through the evergreen forests,
The peasant river was untempted by the fashionable quays;
By mourning tongues
The death of the poet was kept from his poems.

But for him it was his last afternoon as himself,
An afternoon of nurses and rumours;
The provinces of his body revolted,
The squares of his mind were empty,
Silence invaded the suburbs,
The current of his feeling failed; he became his admirers.

Now he is scattered among a hundred cities
And wholly given over to unfamiliar affections,
To find his happiness in another kind of wood
And be punished under a foreign code of conscience.
The words of a dead man
Are modified in the guts of the living.

But in the importance and noise of to-morrow
When the brokers are roaring like beasts on the floor of the Bourse,
And the poor have the sufferings to which they are fairly accustomed,
And each in the cell of himself is almost convinced of his freedom,
A few thousand will think of this day
As one thinks of a day when one did something slightly unusual.
What instruments we have agree
The day of his death was a dark cold day.

II

You were silly like us; your gift survived it all:
The parish of rich women, physical decay,
Yourself. Mad Ireland hurt you into poetry.
Now Ireland has her madness and her weather still,
For poetry makes nothing happen: it survives
In the valley of its making where executives
Would never want to tamper, flows on south
From ranches of isolation and the busy griefs,
Raw towns that we believe and die in; it survives,
A way of happening, a mouth.

III

Earth, receive an honoured guest:
William Yeats is laid to rest.
Let the Irish vessel lie
Emptied of its poetry.

In the nightmare of the dark
All the dogs of Europe bark,
And the living nations wait,
Each sequestered in its hate;

Intellectual disgrace
Stares from every human face,
And the seas of pity lie
Locked and frozen in each eye.

Follow, poet, follow right
To the bottom of the night,
With your unconstraining voice
Still persuade us to rejoice;

With the farming of a verse
Make a vineyard of the curse,
Sing of human unsuccess
In a rapture of distress;

In the deserts of the heart
Let the healing fountain start,
In the prison of his days
Teach the free man how to praise.

858   *The Shield of Achilles*

SHE looked over his shoulder
    For vines and olive trees,
Marble well-governed cities
    And ships upon untamed seas,
But there on the shining metal
    His hands had put instead
An artificial wilderness
    And a sky like lead.

A plain without a feature, bare and brown,
   No blade of grass, no sign of neighbourhood,
Nothing to eat and nowhere to sit down,
   Yet, congregated on its blankness, stood
   An unintelligible multitude,
A million eyes, a million boots in line,
Without expression, waiting for a sign.

Out of the air a voice without a face
   Proved by statistics that some cause was just
In tones as dry and level as the place:
   No one was cheered and nothing was discussed;
   Column by column in a cloud of dust
They marched away enduring a belief
Whose logic brought them, somewhere else, to grief.

She looked over his shoulder
　For ritual pieties,
White flower-garlanded heifers,
　Libation and sacrifice,
But there on the shining metal
　Where the altar should have been,
She saw by his flickering forge-light
　Quite another scene.

Barbed wire enclosed an arbitrary spot
　Where bored officials lounged (one cracked a joke)
And sentries sweated for the day was hot:
　A crowd of ordinary decent folk
　Watched from without and neither moved nor spoke
As three pale figures were led forth and bound
To three posts driven upright in the ground.

The mass and majesty of this world, all
　That carries weight and always weighs the same
Lay in the hands of others; they were small
　And could not hope for help and no help came:
　What their foes liked to do was done, their shame
Was all the worst could wish; they lost their pride
And died as men before their bodies died.

　　She looked over his shoulder
　　　For athletes at their games,
　　Men and women in a dance
　　　Moving their sweet limbs
　　Quick, quick, to music,
　　　But there on the shining shield
　　His hands had set no dancing-floor
　　　But a weed-choked field.

A ragged urchin, aimless and alone,
　Loitered about that vacancy, a bird
Flew up to safety from his well-aimed stone:
　That girls are raped, that two boys knife a third,
　Were axioms to him, who'd never heard
Of any world where promises were kept,
Or one could weep because another wept.

The thin-lipped armourer,
　Hephaestos hobbled away,
Thetis of the shining breasts
　Cried out in dismay
At what the god had wrought
　To please her son, the strong
Iron-hearted man-slaying Achilles
　Who would not live long.

LOUIS MACNEICE

1907–1963

859　　　　　　　*Snow*

THE room was suddenly rich and the great bay-window was
Spawning snow and pink roses against it
Soundlessly collateral and incompatible:
World is suddener than we fancy it.

World is crazier and more of it than we think,
Incorrigibly plural. I peel and portion
A tangerine and spit the pips and feel
The drunkenness of things being various.

And the fire flames with a bubbling sound for world
Is more spiteful and gay than one supposes—
On the tongue on the eyes on the ears in the palms of one's hands—
There is more than glass between the snow and the huge roses.

860　　　　*The Sunlight on the Garden*

THE sunlight on the garden
Hardens and grows cold,
We cannot cage the minute
Within its nets of gold,
When all is told
We cannot beg for pardon.

Our freedom as free lances
Advances towards its end;
The earth compels, upon it
Sonnets and birds descend;
And soon, my friend,
We shall have no time for dances.

The sky was good for flying
Defying the church bells
And every evil iron
Siren and what it tells:
The earth compels,
We are dying, Egypt, dying

And not expecting pardon,
Hardened in heart anew,
But glad to have sat under
Thunder and rain with you,
And grateful too
For sunlight on the garden.

861 *Bagpipe Music*

I T'S no go the merrygoround, it's no go the rickshaw,
All we want is a limousine and a ticket for the peepshow.
Their knickers are made of crêpe-de-chine, their shoes are made of
    python,
Their halls are lined with tiger rugs and their walls with heads of bison.

John MacDonald found a corpse, put it under the sofa,
Waited till it came to life and hit it with a poker,
Sold its eyes for souvenirs, sold its blood for whisky,
Kept its bones for dumb-bells to use when he was fifty.

It's no go the Yogi-Man, it's no go Blavatsky,
All we want is a bank balance and a bit of skirt in a taxi.

Annie MacDougall went to milk, caught her foot in the heather,
Woke to hear a dance record playing of Old Vienna.
It's no go your maidenheads, it's no go your culture,
All we want is a Dunlop tyre and the devil mend the puncture.

The Laird o'Phelps spent Hogmanay declaring he was sober,
Counted his feet to prove the fact and found he had one foot over.
Mrs. Carmichael had her fifth, looked at the job with repulsion,
Said to the midwife 'Take it away; I'm through with over-production'.

It's no go the gossip column, it's no go the ceilidh,
All we want is a mother's help and a sugar-stick for the baby.

Willie Murray cut his thumb, couldn't count the damage,
Took the hide of an Ayrshire cow and used it for a bandage.
His brother caught three hundred cran when the seas were lavish,
Threw the bleeders back in the sea and went upon the parish.

It's no go the Herring Board, it's no go the Bible,
All we want is a packet of fags when our hands are idle.

It's no go the picture palace, it's no go the stadium,
It's no go the country cot with a pot of pink geraniums,
It's no go the Government grants, it's no go the elections,
Sit on your arse for fifty years and hang your hat on a pension.

It's no go my honey love, it's no go my poppet;
Work your hands from day to day, the winds will blow the profit.
The glass is falling hour by hour, the glass will fall for ever,
But if you break the bloody glass you won't hold up the weather.

862   *Prognosis*

                        Spring 1939

                 GOODBYE, Winter,
                 The days are getting longer,
                 The tea-leaf in the teacup
                 Is herald of a stranger.

                 Will he bring me business
                 Or will he bring me gladness
                 Or will he come for cure
                 Of his own sickness?

                 With a pedlar's burden
                 Walking up the garden
                 Will he come to beg
                 Or will he come to bargain?

Will he come to pester,
To cringe or to bluster,
A promise in his palm
Or a gun in his holster?

Will his name be John
Or will his name be Jonah
Crying to repent
On the Island of Iona?

Will his name be Jason
Looking for a seaman
Or a mad crusader
Without rhyme or reason?

What will be his message—
War or work or marriage?
News as new as dawn
Or an old adage?

Will he give a champion
Answer to my question
Or will his words be dark
And his ways evasion?

Will his name be Love
And all his talk be crazy?
Or will his name be Death
And his message easy?

863   *The British Museum Reading Room*

UNDER the hive-like dome the stooping haunted readers
Go up and down the alleys, tap the cells of knowledge—
    Honey and wax, the accumulation of years—
Some on commission, some for the love of learning,
Some because they have nothing better to do
Or because they hope these walls of books will deaden
    The drumming of the demon in their ears.

Cranks, hacks, poverty-stricken scholars,
In pince-nez, period hats or romantic beards
  And cherishing their hobby or their doom
Some are too much alive and some are asleep
Hanging like bats in a world of inverted values,
Folded up in themselves in a world which is safe and silent:
  This is the British Museum Reading Room.

Out on the steps in the sun the pigeons are courting,
Puffing their ruffs and sweeping their tails or taking
  A sun-bath at their ease
And under the totem poles—the ancient terror—
Between the enormous fluted Ionic columns
There seeps from heavily jowled or hawk-like foreign faces
  The guttural sorrow of the refugees.

864   *Brother Fire*

1943

WHEN our brother Fire was having his dog's day
Jumping the London streets with millions of tin cans
Clanking at his tail, we heard some shadow say
'Give the dog a bone'—and so we gave him ours;
Night after night we watched him slaver and crunch away
The beams of human life, the tops of topless towers.

Which gluttony of his for us was Lenten fare
Who mother-naked, suckled with sparks, were chill
Though cotted in a grille of sizzling air
Striped like a convict—black, yellow and red;
Thus were we weaned to knowledge of the Will
That wills the natural world but wills us dead.

O delicate walker, babbler, dialectician Fire,
O enemy and image of ourselves,
Did we not on those mornings after the All Clear,
When you were looting shops in elemental joy
And singing as you swarmed up city block and spire,
Echo your thought in ours? 'Destroy! Destroy!'

865 *The Truisms*

His father gave him a box of truisms
Shaped like a coffin, then his father died;
The truisms remained on the mantelpiece
As wooden as the playbox they had been packed in
Or that other his father skulked inside.

Then he left home, left the truisms behind him
Still on the mantelpiece, met love, met war,
Sordor, disappointment, defeat, betrayal,
Till through disbeliefs he arrived at a house
He could not remember seeing before,

And he walked straight in; it was where he had come from
And something told him the way to behave.
He raised his hand and blessed his home;
The truisms flew and perched on his shoulders
And a tall tree sprouted from his father's grave.

866 *Thalassa*

Run out the boat, my broken comrades;
Let the old seaweed crack, the surge
Burgeon oblivious of the last
Embarkation of feckless men,
Let every adverse force converge—
Here we must needs embark again.

Run up the sail, my heartsick comrades;
Let each horizon tilt and lurch—
You know the worst: your wills are fickle,
Your values blurred, your hearts impure
And your past life a ruined church—
But let your poison be your cure.

Put out to sea, ignoble comrades,
Whose record shall be noble yet;
Butting through scarps of moving marble
The narwhal dares us to be free;
By a high star our course is set,
Our end is Life. Put out to sea.

KATHLEEN RAINE
1908–

867   *Envoi*

TAKE of me what is not my own,
my love, my beauty, and my poem—
the pain is mine, and mine alone.

See how against the weight in the bone
the hawk hangs perfect in mid-air—
the blood pays dear to raise it there,
the moment, not the bird, divine.

And see the peaceful trees extend
their myriad leaves in leisured dance—
they bear the weight of sky and cloud
upon the fountain of their veins.

In rose with petals soft as air
I bind for you the tides and fire—
the death that lives within the flower,
oh gladly, love, for you I bear!

STEPHEN SPENDER
1909–

868

WHAT I expected was
Thunder, fighting,
Long struggles with men
And climbing.
After continual straining
I should grow strong;
Then the rocks would shake
And I should rest long.

What I had not foreseen
Was the gradual day
Weakening the will
Leaking the brightness away,
The lack of good to touch
The fading of body and soul
Like smoke before wind
Corrupt, unsubstantial.

The wearing of Time,
And the watching of cripples pass
With limbs shaped like questions
In their odd twist,
The pulverous grief
Melting the bones with pity,
The sick falling from earth—
These, I could not foresee.

For I had expected always
Some brightness to hold in trust,
Some final innocence
To save from dust;
That, hanging solid,
Would dangle through all
Like the created poem
Or the dazzling crystal.

869

I THINK continually of those who were truly great.
Who, from the womb, remembered the soul's history
Through corridors of light where the hours are suns
Endless and singing. Whose lovely ambition
Was that their lips, still touched with fire,
Should tell of the Spirit clothed from head to foot in song.
And who hoarded from the Spring branches
The desires falling across their bodies like blossoms.

What is precious is never to forget
The essential delight of the blood drawn from ageless springs
Breaking through rocks in worlds before our earth.
Never to deny its pleasure in the morning simple light
Nor its grave evening demand for love.
Never to allow gradually the traffic to smother
With noise and fog the flowering of the spirit.

Near the snow, near the sun, in the highest fields
See how these names are fêted by the waving grass
And by the streamers of white cloud
And whispers of wind in the listening sky.
The names of those who in their lives fought for life,
Who wore at their hearts the fire's centre.
Born of the sun they travelled a short while towards the sun,
And left the vivid air signed with their honour.

870

MOVING through the silent crowd
Who stand behind dull cigarettes
These men who idle in the road,
I have the sense of falling light.

They lounge at corners of the street
And greet friends with a shrug of shoulder
And turn their empty pockets out,
The cynical gestures of the poor.

Now they've no work, like better men
Who sit at desks and take much pay
They sleep long nights and rise at ten
To watch the hours that drain away.

I'm jealous of the weeping hours
They stare through with such hungry eyes.
I'm haunted by these images,
I'm haunted by their emptiness.

871 *The Room above the Square*

THE light in the window seemed perpetual
Where you stayed in the high room for me;
It flowered above the trees through leaves
Like my certainty.

The light is fallen and you are hidden
In sunbright peninsulas of the sword:
Torn like leaves through Europe is the peace
Which through me flowed.

Now I climb alone to the dark room
Which hangs above the square
Where among stones and roots the other
Peaceful lovers are.

ROY FULLER

1912–

872 *The Statue*

THE noises of the harbour die, the smoke is petrified
Against the thick but vacant, fading light, and shadows slide
From under stone and iron, darkest now. The last birds glide.

Upon this black-boned, white-splashed, far receding vista of grey
Is an equestrian statue, by the ocean, trampling the day,
Its green bronze flaked like petals, catching night before the bay.

Distilled from some sad, endless, sordid period of time,
As from the language of disease might come a consummate rhyme,
It tries to impose its values on the port and on the lime—

The droppings that by chance and from an uncontrollable
And savage life have formed a patina upon the skull;
Abandoned, have blurred a bodied vision once thought spare but full—

On me, as authority recites to boys the names of queens.
Shall I be dazzled by the dynasties, the gules and greens,
The unbelievable art, and not recall their piteous means?

Last night I sailed upon that sea whose starting place is here,
Evaded the contraptions of the enemy, the mere
Dangers of water, saw the statue and the plinth appear.

Last night between the crowded, stifling decks I watched a man,
Smoking a big curved pipe, who contemplated his great wan
And dirty feet while minute after tedious minute ran—

This in the city now, whose floor is permanent and still,
Among the news of history and sense of an obscure will,
Is all the image I can summon up, my thought's rank kill;

As though there dominated this sea's threshold and this night
Not the raised hooves, the thick snake neck, the profile, and the might,
The wrought, eternal bronze, the dead protagonist, the fight,

But that unmoving, pale but living shape that drops no tears,
Ridiculous and haunting, which each epoch reappears,
And is what history is not. O love, O human fears!

873   *Translation*

    Now that the barbarians have got as far as Picra,
    And all the new music is written in the twelve-tone scale,
    And I am anyway approaching my fortieth birthday,
        I will dissemble no longer.

    I will stop expressing my belief in the rosy
    Future of man, and accept the evidence
    Of a couple of wretched wars and innumerable
        Abortive revolutions.

    I will cease to blame the stupidity of the slaves
    Upon their masters and nurture, and will say,
    Plainly, that they are enemies to culture,
        Advancement and cleanliness.

From progressive organisations, from quarterlies
Devoted to daring verse, from membership of
Committees, from letters of various protest
      I shall withdraw forthwith.

When they call me reactionary I shall smile,
Secure in another dimension. When they say
'Cinna has ceased to matter' I shall know
      How well I reflect the times.

The ruling class will think I am on their side
And make friendly overtures, but I shall retire
To the side farther from Picra and write some poems
      About the doom of the whole boiling.

Anyone happy in this age and place
Is daft or corrupt. Better to abdicate
From a material and spiritual terrain
      Fit only for barbarians.

ANNE RIDLER

1912–

874   *Choosing a Name*

MY little son, I have cast you out
    To hang heels upward, wailing over a world
    With walls too wide.
My faith till now, and now my love:
    No walls too wide for that to fill, no depth
    Too great for all you hide.

I love, not knowing what I love,
    I give, though ignorant for whom
    The history and power of a name.
I conjure with it, like a novice
    Summoning unknown spirits: answering me
    You take the word, and tame it.

Even as the gift of life
  You take the famous name you did not choose
  And make it new.
You and the name exchange a power:
  Its history is changed, becoming yours,
  And yours by this: who calls this, calls you.

Strong vessel of peace, and plenty promised,
  Into whose unsounded depths I pour
  This alien power;
Frail vessel, launched with a shawl for sail,
  Whose guiding spirit keeps his needle-quivering
  Poise between trust and terror,

And stares amazed to find himself alive;
  This is the means by which you say *I am*,
  Not to be lost till all is lost,
When at the sight of God you say *I am nothing*,
  And find, forgetting name and speech at last,
  A home not mine, dear outcast.

HENRY REED

1914–

Lessons of the War

Vixi duellis nuper idoneus
Et militavi non sine gloria

(i)

875   *Naming of Parts*

TO-DAY we have naming of parts. Yesterday,
We had daily cleaning. And to-morrow morning,
We shall have what to do after firing. But to-day,
To-day we have naming of parts. Japonica
Glistens like coral in all of the neighbouring gardens,
  And to-day we have naming of parts.

This is the lower sling swivel. And this
Is the upper sling swivel, whose use you will see,
When you are given your slings. And this is the piling swivel,
Which in your case you have not got. The branches
Hold in the gardens their silent, eloquent gestures,
    Which in our case we have not got.

This is the safety-catch, which is always released
With an easy flick of the thumb. And please do not let me
See anyone using his finger. You can do it quite easy
If you have any strength in your thumb. The blossoms
Are fragile and motionless, never letting anyone see
    Any of them using their finger.

And this you can see is the bolt. The purpose of this
Is to open the breech, as you see. We can slide it
Rapidly backwards and forwards: we call this
Easing the spring. And rapidly backwards and forwards
The early bees are assaulting and fumbling the flowers:
    They call it easing the Spring.

They call it easing the Spring: it is perfectly easy
If you have any strength in your thumb: like the bolt,
And the breech, and the cocking-piece, and the point of balance,
Which in our case we have not got; and the almond-blossom
Silent in all of the gardens and the bees going backwards and forwards,
    For to-day we have naming of parts.

(ii)

876   *Judging Distances*

        NOT only how far away, but the way that you say it
        Is very important. Perhaps you may never get
        The knack of judging a distance, but at least you know
        How to report on a landscape: the central sector,
        The right of arc and that, which we had last Tuesday,
            And at least you know

That maps are of time, not place, so far as the army
Happens to be concerned—the reason being,
Is one which need not delay us. Again, you know
There are three kinds of tree, three only, the fir and the poplar,
And those which have bushy tops to; and lastly
    That things only seem to be things.

A barn is not called a barn, to put it more plainly,
Or a field in the distance, where sheep may be safely grazing.
You must never be over-sure. You must say, when reporting:
At five o'clock in the central sector is a dozen
Of what appear to be animals; whatever you do,
    Don't call the bleeders *sheep*.

I am sure that's quite clear; and suppose, for the sake of example,
The one at the end, asleep, endeavours to tell us
What he sees over there to the west, and how far away,
After first having come to attention. There to the west,
On the fields of summer the sun and the shadows bestow
    Vestments of purple and gold.

The still white dwellings are like a mirage in the heat,
And under the swaying elms a man and a woman
Lie gently together. Which is, perhaps, only to say
That there is a row of houses to the left of arc,
And that under some poplars a pair of what appear to be humans
    Appear to be loving.

Well that, for an answer, is what we might rightly call
Moderately satisfactory only, the reason being,
Is that two things have been omitted, and those are important.
The human beings, now: in what direction are they,
And how far away, would you say? And do not forget
    There may be dead ground in between.

There may be dead ground in between; and I may not have got
The knack of judging a distance; I will only venture
A guess that perhaps between me and the apparent lovers,
(Who, incidentally, appear by now to have finished,)
At seven o'clock from the houses, is roughly a distance
    Of about one year and a half.

ALUN LEWIS

1915–1944

877   *All Day it has Rained . . .*

ALL day it has rained, and we on the edge of the moors
Have sprawled in our bell-tents, moody and dull as boors,
Groundsheets and blankets spread on the muddy ground
And from the first grey wakening we have found
No refuge from the skirmishing fine rain
And the wind that made the canvas heave and flap
And the taut wet guy-ropes ravel out and snap.
All day the rain has glided, wave and mist and dream,
Drenching the gorse and heather, a gossamer stream
Too light to stir the acorns that suddenly
Snatched from their cups by the wild south-westerly
Pattered against the tent and our upturned dreaming faces.
And we stretched out, unbuttoning our braces,
Smoking a Woodbine, darning dirty socks,
Reading the Sunday papers—I saw a fox
And mentioned it in the note I scribbled home;—
And we talked of girls, and dropping bombs on Rome,
And thought of the quiet dead and the loud celebrities
Exhorting us to slaughter, and the herded refugees;
—Yet thought softly, morosely of them, and as indifferently
As of ourselves or those whom we
For years have loved, and will again
Tomorrow maybe love; but now it is the rain
Possesses us entirely, the twilight and the rain.

And I can remember nothing dearer or more to my heart
Than the children I watched in the woods on Saturday
Shaking down burning chestnuts for the schoolyard's merry play,
Or the shaggy patient dog who followed me
By Sheet and Steep and up the wooded scree
To the Shoulder o' Mutton where Edward Thomas brooded long
On death and beauty—till a bullet stopped his song.

KEITH DOUGLAS

1920–1944

878   *How to Kill*

UNDER the parabola of a ball,
a child turning into a man,
I looked into the air too long.
The ball fell in my hand, it sang
in the closed fist: *Open Open*
Behold a gift designed to kill.

Now in my dial of glass appears
the soldier who is going to die.
He smiles, and moves about in ways
his mother knows, habits of his.
The wires touch his face: I cry
Now. Death, like a familiar, hears

and look, has made a man of dust
of a man of flesh. This sorcery
I do. Being damned, I am amused
to see the centre of love diffused
and the waves of love travel into vacancy.
How easy it is to make a ghost.

The weightless mosquito touches
her tiny shadow on the stone,
and with how like, how infinite
a lightness, man and shadow meet.
They fuse. A shadow is a man
when the mosquito death approaches.

DYLAN THOMAS

1914–1953

879 *The force that through the green fuse*
drives the flower

THE force that through the green fuse drives the flower
Drives my green age; that blasts the roots of trees
Is my destroyer.
And I am dumb to tell the crooked rose
My youth is bent by the same wintry fever.

The force that drives the water through the rocks
Drives my red blood; that dries the mouthing streams
Turns mine to wax.
And I am dumb to mouth unto my veins
How at the mountain spring the same mouth sucks.

The hand that whirls the water in the pool
Stirs the quicksand; that ropes the blowing wind
Hauls my shroud sail.
And I am dumb to tell the hanging man
How of my clay is made the hangman's lime.

The lips of time leech to the fountain head;
Love drips and gathers, but the fallen blood
Shall calm her sores.
And I am dumb to tell a weather's wind
How time has ticked a heaven round the stars.

And I am dumb to tell the lover's tomb
How at my sheet goes the same crooked worm.

880 *The hand that signed the paper*

THE hand that signed the paper felled a city;
Five sovereign fingers taxed the breath,
Doubled the globe of dead and halved a country;
These five kings did a king to death.

The mighty hand leads to a sloping shoulder,
The finger joints are cramped with chalk;
A goose's quill has put an end to murder
That put an end to talk.

The hand that signed the treaty bred a fever,
And famine grew, and locusts came;
Great is the hand that holds dominion over
Man by a scribbled name.

The five kings count the dead but do not soften
The crusted wound nor stroke the brow;
A hand rules pity as a hand rules heaven;
Hands have no tears to flow.

881   *A Refusal to Mourn the Death, by Fire, of
a Child in London*

NEVER until the mankind making
Bird beast and flower
Fathering and all humbling darkness
Tells with silence the last light breaking
And the still hour
Is come of the sea tumbling in harness

And I must enter again the round
Zion of the water bead
And the synagogue of the ear of corn
Shall I let pray the shadow of a sound
Or sow my salt seed
In the least valley of sackcloth to mourn

The majesty and burning of the child's death.
I shall not murder
The mankind of her going with a grave truth
Nor blaspheme down the stations of the breath
With any further
Elegy of innocence and youth.

Deep with the first dead lies London's daughter,
Robed in the long friends,
The grains beyond age, the dark veins of her mother,
Secret by the unmourning water
Of the riding Thames.
After the first death, there is no other.

882   *Do not go gentle into that good night*

Do not go gentle into that good night,
Old age should burn and rave at close of day;
Rage, rage against the dying of the light.

Though wise men at their end know dark is right,
Because their words had forked no lightning they
Do not go gentle into that good night.

Good men, the last wave by, crying how bright
Their frail deeds might have danced in a green bay,
Rage, rage against the dying of the light.

Wild men who caught and sang the sun in flight,
And learn, too late, they grieved it on its way,
Do not go gentle into that good night.

Grave men, near death, who see with blinding sight
Blind eyes could blaze like meteors and be gay,
Rage, rage against the dying of the light.

And you, my father, there on the sad height,
Curse, bless, me now with your fierce tears, I pray.
Do not go gentle into that good night.
Rage, rage against the dying of the light.

883   *Fern Hill*

NOW as I was young and easy under the apple boughs
About the lilting house and happy as the grass was green,
    The night above the dingle starry,
       Time let me hail and climb
    Golden in the heydays of his eyes,
And honoured among wagons I was prince of the apple towns
And once below a time I lordly had the trees and leaves
       Trail with daisies and barley
    Down the rivers of the windfall light.

And as I was green and carefree, famous among the barns
About the happy yard and singing as the farm was home,
    In the sun that is young once only,
       Time let me play and be
    Golden in the mercy of his means,
And green and golden I was huntsman and herdsman, the calves
Sang to my horn, the foxes on the hills barked clear and cold,
       And the sabbath rang slowly
    In the pebbles of the holy streams.

All the sun long it was running, it was lovely, the hay
Fields high as the house, the tunes from the chimneys, it was air
    And playing, lovely and watery
       And fire green as grass.
    And nightly under the simple stars
As I rode to sleep the owls were bearing the farm away,
All the moon long I heard, blessed among stables, the nightjars
       Flying with the ricks, and the horses
    Flashing into the dark.

And then to awake, and the farm, like a wanderer white
With the dew, come back, the cock on his shoulder: it was all
    Shining, it was Adam and maiden,
       The sky gathered again
    And the sun grew round that very day.
So it must have been after the birth of the simple light
In the first, spinning place, the spellbound horses walking warm
    Out of the whinnying green stable
       On to the fields of praise.

And honoured among foxes and pheasants by the gay house
Under the new made clouds and happy as the heart was long,
    In the sun born over and over,
        I ran my heedless ways,
    My wishes raced through the house high hay
And nothing I cared, at my blue sky trades, that time allows
In all his tuneful turning so few and such morning songs
    Before the children green and golden
        Follow him out of grace,

Nothing I cared, in the lamb white days, that time would take me
Up to the swallow thronged loft by the shadow of my hand,
    In the moon that is always rising,
        Nor that riding to sleep
I should hear him fly with the high fields
And wake to the farm forever fled from the childless land.
Oh as I was young and easy in the mercy of his means,
        Time held me green and dying
    Though I sang in my chains like the sea.

EPILOGUE

LOUIS MACNEICE

884   *A Fanfare for the Makers*

    A CLOUD of witnesses. To whom? To what?
    To the small fire that never leaves the sky.
    To the great fire that boils the daily pot.

    To all the things we are not remembered by,
    Which we remember and bless. To all the things
    That will not even notice when we die,

    Yet lend the passing moment words and wings.

            *

    So Fanfare for the Makers: who compose
    A book of words or deeds who runs may write
    As many do who run, as a family grows

At times like sunflowers turning towards the light,
As sometimes in the blackout and the raids
One joke composed an island in the night,

As sometimes one man's kindliness pervades
A room or house or village, as sometimes
Merely to tighten screws or sharpen blades

Can catch a meaning, as to hear the chimes
At midnight means to share them, as one man
In old age plants an avenue of limes

And before they bloom can smell them, before they span
The road can walk beneath the perfected arch,
The merest greenprint when the lives began

Of those who walk there with him, as in default
Of coffee men grind acorns, as in despite
Of all assaults conscripts counterassault,

As mothers sit up late night after night
Moulding a life, as miners day by day
Descend blind shafts, as a boy may flaunt his kite

In an empty nonchalant sky, as anglers play
Their fish, as workers work and can take pride
In spending sweat before they draw their pay,

As horsemen fashion horses while they ride,
As climbers climb a peak because it is there,
As life can be confirmed even in suicide:

To make is such. Let us make. And set the weather fair.

NOTES AND REFERENCES

TEXTS are based on the author's final version, with a few exceptions noted below. Spelling and punctuation have been modernized, except for poems in the Scottish dialect, and for the poems of Spenser and Chatterton whose spelling is part of their deliberate archaism. In medieval poems, and occasionally after, a dot over the vowel indicates that it has syllabic value. Throughout -èd is used to indicate the uncontracted form of the weak past tense and past participle, and an acute accent indicates that the syllable takes stress.

Titles have throughout been supplied for extracts from poems, for songs from plays and novels, and for the many poems up to the beginning of the seventeenth century which their authors left untitled. Beyond this point, when the practice of giving titles to lyrics had become established, titles have not been supplied to poems their authors thought fit to leave without them. In a few cases titles have been slightly expanded by the provision of dates or explanatory information.

The sources of passages excerpted from poems, and of songs from plays or novels, are given below, as well as line or stanza references where omissions from a poem are substantial. No references are given for poems by authors whose collected poems are easily available, since these can be found by consulting first-line indexes. But references are supplied for authors whose poems have not been collected, or, if they have been, are difficult to obtain.

1–5. ANON. Texts from *The Oxford Book of Medieval English Verse*.

6. WILLIAM LANGLAND, *Piers Plowman*, C Text, II.149–56.

7–10. GEOFFREY CHAUCER: **7.** *Troilus and Criseyde*, V.547–81, 638–44, 1688–1701; **8.** Ibid., 1835–48; **9.** Prologue to *The Legend of Good Women*, F Text, 249–69; **10.** *Cant. Tales*, General Prologue, 118–62.

11–18. ANON. Texts from *The Oxford Book of Medieval English Verse*. **11.** There are two poems with the refrain '*Quia Amore Langueo*', which is taken from the Song of Songs. In the other, beginning 'In a tabernacle of a tower', the Virgin is the speaker.

19. ANON., British Museum MS. Harley 7578.

20. WILLIAM CORNISH, British Museum MS. Additional 31922.

21. ANON., British Museum MS. Royal Appendix 58.

22. WILLIAM DUNBAR. Ten stanzas, in which Dunbar interrupts his *danse macabre* to commemorate dead Scottish poets (mostly unknown to fame), are omitted. The poem gained its traditional title from these stanzas. The refrain, used here as title, is from the Office of the Dead.

24. JOHN SKELTON, *The Book of Philip Sparrow* (*c.* 1545: written *c.* 1505–7), 1–63, 108–46, 386–575. The poem (1,382 lines in all) continues

946

with the speaker, Jane Scrope, apologizing for her lack of poetic skill and with the 'commendations' of Jane.

39. ROBERT WEVER, *Lusty Juventus* (*c.* 1560).

40. THOMAS SACKVILLE, EARL OF DORSET, Induction to *The Mirror for Magistrates* (1563), stanzas 56–68.

41. GEORGE GASCOIGNE, from 'The Adventures of Master F.I.' in *A Hundred Sundry Flowers* (1573).

54. CHIDIOCK TICHBORNE, *Verses of Praise and Joy* (1586). Tichborne wrote these verses in the Tower three days before his execution for complicity in the Babington conspiracy.

55–63. EDMUND SPENSER: **55.** *The Shepherds' Calendar* (1579), 'April', 37–153; **58–63.** *The Faerie Queene* (1590, 1596, and 1609), I.ix.33–44; II.xii.70–5; III.vi.30–42; III.xii.7–18; VI.x.10–16; VII.vii.57–9, VII.viii.1–2.

64. ANTHONY MUNDAY, in *England's Helicon* (1600).

65 and 67. JOHN LYLY, *Campaspe* (1584); texts of the songs were first printed in 1632.

68–70. NICHOLAS BRETON: **68.** *Entertainment at Elvetham* (1591); **69.** *The Arbour of Amorous Devices* (1594); **70.** In *England's Helicon* (1600).

71. THOMAS LODGE, *Rosalynde* (1590).

72–7. GEORGE PEELE: **72.** *The Arraignment of Paris* (1584); **73.** *The Hunting of Cupid* (1591), Drummond MS., Library of the Society of Antiquaries, Edinburgh; **74.** *Polyhymnia* (1590); **75.** *David and Bethsabe* (1599); **77 and 78.** *The Old Wife's Tale* (1595).

78 and 79. ROBERT GREENE, *Menaphon* (1589).

83. ROBERT SOUTHWELL, 'Upon the Image of Death'. Although printed as Southwell's, the mood and style of this poem suggests it was written at an earlier date, probably in the first half of the sixteenth century.

84 and 85. THOMAS NASHE, *Summer's Last Will and Testament* (1600).

86 and 87. CHRISTOPHER MARLOWE, *Hero and Leander* (1598), I.131–76 and II.153–206.

89 and 90. SIR WALTER RALEGH. Both these poems are only doubtfully Ralegh's, though accepted by his latest editor, Agnes Latham. 'The Nymph's Reply', printed as by 'Ignoto' in *England's Helicon* (1600), was attributed to Ralegh by Izaak Walton in *The Compleat Angler* (1653). 'Walsingham', a poem based on an earlier popular ballad, is attributed to Ralegh only in Bodleian MS. Rawlinson 85.

96. FULKE GREVILLE, LORD BROOKE, last chorus from *Mustapha, Certain Learned and Elegant Works* (1609).

97. GEORGE CHAPMAN, *Hero and Leander* (1598), V.432–47.

98. MARK ALEXANDER BOYD. This sonnet was first printed by Q in *The Oxford Book of English Verse* (1900), from a manuscript then in the possession of Miss Boyd of Penkill Castle, a descendant of the poet; the manuscript is now in the National Library of Scotland. 'I suppose this is the most beautiful sonnet in the language, at any rate it has one nomination' (Ezra Pound, *ABC of Reading* (1934)).

99–107. SAMUEL DANIEL: **104.** *Musophilus* (1599), 939–80; **106.** *Tethys' Festival* (1610); **107.** *Hymen's Triumph* (1615).

113. MICHAEL DRAYTON, 'Epistle to Reynolds', 1–40.

115 and **116.** WILLIAM SHAKESPEARE, *Venus and Adonis* (1593), 259–324; *The Rape of Lucrece* (1594), 876–910.

132 and **133.** WILLIAM SHAKESPEARE, 'Sweet Music's Power', *Henry VIII*, and 'A Bridal Song', *The Two Noble Kinsmen*. These may be by John Fletcher.

166. ANON., 'Hierusalem my Happy Home'. The text is from British Museum MS. Additional 15255, a commonplace-book compiled by a Catholic, where the poem has twenty-six stanzas. A shorter version (nineteen stanzas) with some inferior readings, was printed in *The Song of Mary the Mother of Christ* (1601). There exists also a longer version (fifty-five stanzas) which is plainly derivative.

167–75. POEMS FROM SONG-BOOKS. Texts can be found in Fellowes, *English Madrigal Verse* (3rd ed., rev. Sternfeld and Greer, 1967).

176. ANON., 'A Madrigal', in Davison's *Poetical Rhapsody* (1602).

177. ANON., 'Aubade'. This is a better version of the first stanza of a poem in two stanzas set by Dowland in 1612. It appears in the 1669 edition of Donne's *Poems* wrongly prefixed to Donne's poem 'Break of Day', which is in a different metre and is spoken by a woman.

178. HENRY CHETTLE, in *England's Helicon* (1600).

179–81. SIR HENRY WOTTON, *Reliquiae Wottonianae* (1651).

182–4. SIR JOHN DAVIES, *Orchestra* (1596), stanzas 17–19, 39–52; *Nosce Teipsum* (1599), stanzas 38–45 and 225–31. Complete texts of both poems can be found in E. Arber, *English Garner*, v (1882), or A. H. Bullen, *Some Longer Elizabethan Poems* (1903).

185–203. JOHN DONNE: **185.** 'Satire III', 72–110; **187.** 'The Storm', 37–74. Texts from *Satires and Verse-Letters*, ed. Wesley Milgate (1967). Texts of the other poems are from *Elegies and Songs and Sonnets* and *Divine Poems*, ed. Helen Gardner (1965 and 1952). (A conjectural reading in 'The Ecstasy' has been withdrawn.) **203.** 'Hymn'. In the first (posthumous) edition of Donne's poems in 1633 the title was 'Hymn to God the Father'; but in all manuscript copies the title is either 'To Christ' or 'Christo Salvatori'. As the text here follows the manuscripts, whose readings make the established title unsuitable, I have used the non-committal 'Hymn'.

204–19. BEN JONSON: **204.** *Cynthia's Revels* (acted 1600); **205.** *The Silent Woman* (acted 1609); **212.** *The Masque of Queens* (acted 1609); *The Golden Age Restored* (acted 1615). Texts from *Works* (1616). **218.** *The Sad Shepherd*, *Works* (1640); **219.** 'To the Memory of Shakespeare', 17–65, the First Folio (1623).

220. RICHARD BARNFIELD, *Poems in Diverse Humours* (1598).

221–5. JOHN FLETCHER: **221.** *The Faithful Shepherdess* (*c.* 1609); **222.** *The Maid's Tragedy* (*ante* 1611) (possibly by Beaumont); **223.** *The Captain* (*ante* 1612); **224** and **225.** *Valentinian* (*ante* 1614). Beaumont and Fletcher, *Works* (1647 and 1679).

226–8. JOHN WEBSTER: **226.** *The White Devil* (1612); **227.** *The Duchess of Malfi* (1623: acted *c.* 1613); **228.** *The Devil's Law Case* (1623: acted ?1610).

234. SIR JOHN BEAUMONT, *Bosworth Field* (1629).

235. AURELIAN TOWNSHEND, in Henry Lawes, *Airs and Dialogues* (1655).

236. ?FRANCIS BEAUMONT, 'On the Tombs in Westminster Abbey'. First printed as 'A Memento for Mortality' in *A Help to Discourse*, by W. B. and E.P. (1619). Ault suggested that William Basse was the author; but there is no reason to identify W.B. with Basse, and, even if there were, no reason to suppose poems he printed were his own. It appeared, also anonymously, in J. Weever, *Ancient Funeral Monuments* (1631). A shortened version (1–4, 19–30 and a concluding couplet based on 33–4), headed 'On the Tombs in Westminster', was included in Francis Beaumont's *Poems* (1653). The original poem may well be his. It is not unusual to find shortened versions of poems in the seventeenth-century manuscripts which were the source of posthumous collections of an author's works.

241. GILES FLETCHER, *Christ's Victory and Triumph* (1610), IV, stanzas 39–42.

242. JOHN FORD, *The Broken Heart* (1633).

243. SIR FRANCIS KYNASTON, *Leoline and Sydanis* (1642), included in Saintsbury (ed.), *Minor Caroline Poets*, ii.

246. WILLIAM BROWNE, *Inner Temple Masque*, Emmanuel College MS., first printed in *Works* (1772).

278. ANON., 'Preparations', Christ Church, Oxford MS.

279. THOMAS CAREW, lines 25–70 of Carew's Elegy on Donne, printed in *Poems by J.D.* (1633).

284 and **285.** JAMES SHIRLEY, *Poems* (1646) and *Ajax and Ulysses* (1659).

286. WILLIAM STRODE. This stanza was highly popular and much imitated in manuscript. It was first printed in W. Porter, *Madrigals and Airs* (1632).

291–4. SIR WILLIAM DAVENANT, *Works* (1673).

296. SIR EDMUND WALLER, 'Old Age', last two stanzas of 'Of the Last Verses in the Book', *Poems* (1686).

297. SIR RICHARD FANSHAWE, *Il Pastor Fido* (1648).

298–313. JOHN MILTON: **298.** The four stanzas that introduce the Hymn are omitted; **308–11.** *Paradise Lost* (1667), I.76–124; III.1–55; IV.598–656; XII.624–49; **312** and **313.** *Samson Agonistes* (1671), 1268–96, 1745–58.

317. SIDNEY GODOLPHIN, Bodleian MS. Malone 13.

318 and 319. JAMES GRAHAM, MARQUIS OF MONTROSE, in Watson, *Choice Collection* (1711).

320. THOMAS JORDAN, *The Triumphs of London* (1675), last four stanzas omitted. Q's version appears to be a *rifacimento*.

321-5. RICHARD CRASHAW: **322.** 'An Hymn of the Nativity *etc.*' The introductory chorus (sixteen lines) is omitted. The text is from *Steps to the Temple* (1648), a revised and expanded version of the poem in the first edition of 1646. The last two lines of each solo verse are repeated by the chorus. **323.** 'A Hymn to . . . Saint Teresa': text from the revised and expanded version of 1648; **324.** 'The Flaming Heart', 93–108 (conclusion).

326 and 327. SAMUEL BUTLER, *Hudibras*, Part I (1662), 1–14, 187–234 and 451–6, 473–518.

331. ABRAHAM COWLEY, 'On the Death of Mr. William Harvey', first six stanzas of a poem in nineteen stanzas.

343. ANDREW MARVELL, 'Appleton House', stanzas 37–43.

353. JOHN BUNYAN, *The Pilgrim's Progress*, Part 2 (1684).

355-60. BALLADS. Texts are from *The Oxford Book of Ballads*, ed. James Kinsley (1969).

361. ANON., 'A Lyke Wake Dirge', Scott, *Minstrelsy of the Scottish Border* (1802).

362. ANON., 'Loving Mad Tom', British Museum MS. Additional 24665.

363-72. JOHN DRYDEN: **363.** *Annus Mirabilis* (1667), stanzas 293–300; **364.** *Mac Flecknoe* (1682: written 1678), 1–28; **365 and 366.** *Absalom and Achitophel* (1681), 140–99 and 529–68; **367.** *The Medal* (1682), 82–112; **369.** *The Hind and the Panther* (1687), I.62–92; **370.** *The Spanish Friar* (1681).

373. CHARLES SACKVILLE, EARL OF DORSET, *Works* (1749).

374-6. SIR CHARLES SEDLEY, *Miscellaneous Works* (1702).

377. APHRA BEHN, *Poems* (1684).

381. JOHN WILMOT, EARL OF ROCHESTER, 'A Satire against Reason and Mankind', *Poems* (1680), 1–30.

390. JONATHAN SWIFT, 'Verses on the Death of Dr. Swift', Faulkner's Dublin edition (1739), 73–116, 299–374, 459–88 (conclusion).

392 and 393. ISAAC WATTS, *Horae Lyricae* (1709 and 1706).

394-6. JOHN GAY: **394-5.** *The Beggars' Opera* (1728); **396.** *Acis and Galatea* (1732).

397-412. ALEXANDER POPE: **397.** *Pastorals*, *Poet. Misc.* (1709) 'Summer', 59–76; **398.** *An Essay on Criticism* (1711), 215–32; **399 and 400.** *The Rape of the Lock* (1714), I.121–48 and II.1–18, 47–68; **404.** *An Essay on Man* (1733), II.1–18; **405.** *Epistle to Bathurst* (1733), 299–314; **406 and 407.** *Epistle to Dr. Arbuthnot* (1735), 193–214 and 305–33; **408.** *Epistle to a Lady*

(1735), 157–80; **409.** *Epistle to Dr. Arbuthnot* 334–59; **410** and **411.** *Epilogue to the Satires* (1738), I.137–72 and II.197–227; **412.** *The Dunciad* (1743), IV.627–56.

413. HENRY CAREY, *Poems* (1729).

414. ANON. In *The British Musical Miscellany*, i (1734).

415. JOHN BYROM, *Miscellaneous Poems* (1773).

416–18. JAMES THOMSON, *The Seasons* (1746), 'Winter', 722–46; 'Spring', 524–52; 'Autumn', 1080–1100.

420–2. SAMUEL JOHNSON, *The Vanity of Human Wishes* (1749), 135–64, 191–222 and 343–68 (conclusion).

435. WILLIAM COLLINS, 'Ode on the Popular Superstitions of the Highlands', stanzas 9 and 10: written *c.* 1749, first printed in *Trans. Royal Society of Edinburgh* (1788).

436. CHRISTOPHER SMART, *A Song to David* (1763), stanzas 1–3 and 49–86.

438 and **439.** OLIVER GOLDSMITH: **438.** *The Vicar of Wakefield* (1766); **439.** *The Deserted Village* (1760), 1–56.

440. THOMAS OSBERT MORDAUNT. This stanza, from ,'Verses Written during the War 1756–1763', *The Bee*, Edinburgh (1791), was used by Scott as a heading for chapter 33 of *Old Mortality*, ascribed to 'Anon.'. It was for long supposed that Scott was its author.

441. JOHN SCOTT OF AMWELL. *Poetical Works* (1782).

448–52. GEORGE CRABBE: **448.** *The Village* (1783), I.39–84; **449.** *The Parish Register* (1807), III.233–311; **450.** *The Borough* (1810), Letter XXII, 171–204; **451.** 'Sir Eustace Grey', *Poems* (1807), stanzas 22, 35–40; **452.** Crabbe's son, in his Life of his father, in *Works* (1834), quotes these lines as 'found written on a paper in which my dear mother's wedding-ring nearly worn through before she died, was wrapped'.

453–68. WILLIAM BLAKE: **464.** *The Book of Thel* (1789), IV; **467** and **468.** *Milton* (1804–8), Preface and II.34.

469–77. ROBERT BURNS. Texts are from the first printings, and not from critical texts based on manuscripts.

478. SAMUEL ROGERS, *An Ode to Superstition* etc. (1786).

496 and **497.** WILLIAM WORDSWORTH, *The Prelude*, (1805 text, first printed in 1925) I.305–50 and 428–89.

502–7. SIR WALTER SCOTT: **502.** *The Lay of the Last Minstrel* (1805), VI.i and ii; **503.** *Marmion* (1808), V.xii; **504.** *The Lady of the Lake* (1810), I.xxxi; **505.** *Rokeby* (1813), III.xxviii; **506.** *The Heart of Midlothian* (1818), chapter 39; **507.** *The Bride of Lammermuir* (1819), chapter 2.

531. THOMAS LOVE PEACOCK, *The Misfortunes of Elphin* (1829), chapter 11.

534–44. GEORGE GORDON NOEL, LORD BYRON: **536** and **537.** *Childe Harold*, III (1816), xxi–xxviii and IV (1818), cxl–cxli; **538.** *The Prisoner of Chillon* (1816), xi–xiv (conclusion); **540.** *Beppo* (1818), xli–xlviii; **542** and

543. *Don Juan*, I (1819), ccxiii–ccxx and III (1821), after stanza lxxxvi.

545. CHARLES WOLFE, in *Newry Telegraph*, 19 April 1817.

546–58. PERCY BYSSHE SHELLEY: 548. *Prometheus Unbound* (1820), II.v.48–110; 551. 'A Letter to Maria Gisborne', 132–74, 192–291, *Posthumous Poems* (1824); 552. *Adonais* (1821), stanzas 39–44, 52–5 (conclusion); 553. *Hellas* (1822), the last chorus.

559. JOHN CLARE, *The Shepherds' Calendar* (1827).

563. JOHN KEATS, *Endymion* (1818), IV.182–272.

575 and 576. GEORGE DARLEY, *Nepenthe* (1835), I.152–221 and II.432–55.

587–9. THOMAS LOVELL BEDDOES, *Death's Jest Book* (1850).

594. EDWARD FITZGERALD, *The Rubaiyat of Omar Khayyam* (4th ed., 1879) stanzas 12–24.

595–615. ALFRED, LORD TENNYSON: 597. 'The Lotos-Eaters', introductory stanzas (1–46) omitted. 599. These are the first and third stanzas of a poem published as 'Stanzas' in 1837, which finally, with revision, found a place in *Maud* (1855), Part II, 141–4, 151–6; 604–11. *In Memoriam* (1850), ii, vii, xi, xv, lxix, cxv, cxxiii, cxxvi; 612. *Maud*, I.xxii.

636 and 637. EMILY JANE BRONTË. In Emily Brontë's transcription of the 'Gondal Poems' in the British Museum these two poems form part of a long poem headed 'Julian M. and A.G. Rochelle'. Charlotte Brontë published the first three stanzas, with two additional stanzas, which may be her own, under the title of 'The Visionary' in poems added to the 1850 edition of *Wuthering Heights*. Emily had already lifted fifteen stanzas from the manuscript poem and published them as 'The Prisoner: A Fragment', with an additional concluding stanza, in *Poems* by Currer, Ellis, and Acton Bell (1846).

642 and 643. ARTHUR HUGH CLOUGH, *Dipsychus*, IV.130–203 and v.134–85, *Letters and Remains* (1865).

644 and 645. MATTHEW ARNOLD: 644. 'Empedocles on Etna', II.417–68, *Empedocles* etc. (1852); 645. 'Sohrab and Rustum', 857–92 (conclusion), *Poems* (1853).

652 and 653. WILLIAM CORY, *Ionica* (1858).

658. WILLIAM ALLINGHAM, *Poems* (1850).

664. GEORGE MEREDITH, 'Love in the Valley', the revised and extended version (1883) of a poem first published in 1851, stanzas 1–7, 10–11, 23, and 26 (conclusion).

681 and 682. CHARLES LUTWIDGE DODGSON (LEWIS CARROLL), *Through the Looking Glass* (1872), chapters 1 and 8.

683. RICHARD WATSON DIXON, *Historic Odes* (1864).

687 and 688. JAMES THOMSON, *The City of Dreadful Night* (1880), Proem and Part I. 43–84; Part XXI.

741. OSCAR WILDE, *The Ballad of Reading Gaol* (1898), first ten stanzas.

813 and 814. EZRA POUND, *Hugh Selwyn Mauberley* (1920), iii, iv, v, and *Pisan Cantos* (1949), Canto lxxxi (conclusion).

823. EDITH SITWELL, *The Sleeping Beauty* (1924), viii.

EPILOGUE: Louis MacNeice, *Autumn Sequel* (1935), vii, omitting lines 8–105.

INDEX OF AUTHORS

The references are to the numbers of the poems

INDEX OF AUTHORS

INDEX OF FIRST LINES

957

INDEX OF FIRST LINES

INDEX OF FIRST LINES

INDEX OF FIRST LINES

INDEX OF FIRST LINES

INDEX OF FIRST LINES